Dynamical Properties of Solids

Volume 1

Dynamical Properties of Solids

Volume 1

Crystalline Solids, Fundamentals

edited by

G.K. Horton
Rutgers University
New Brunswick, USA

A.A. Maradudin
University of California
Irvine, USA

North-Holland Publishing Company – Amsterdam
American Elsevier Publishing Company, Inc. – New York

Library of Congress Catalog Card Number: 73-81536

North-Holland ISBN: 0 7204 0278 6 (Vol. 1)

North-Holland ISBN: 0 7204 0285 9 (complete series)

American Elsevier ISBN: 0 444 10536 0

Publishers: North-Holland Publishing Company, Amsterdam
North-Holland Publishing Company, Ltd. – London

Sole distributors for the U.S.A. and Canada:

American Elsevier Publishing Company, Inc.

52 Vanderbilt Avenue, New York, N.Y. 10017

Printed in the Netherlands

Preface

In these volumes we have tried to organise a coherent presentation of the dynamics of crystalline and non-crystalline solids that is authoritative, complete and entertaining. The division of the material into three volumes is deliberate, following a suggestion from Eli Burstein. We have tried not to swamp the reader, to be fair to those authors that have been diligent and to leave ourselves with a potential démarche in case we have inadvertantly overlooked a potential contribution. The work on non-crystalline solids will appear in Volume 3.

These volumes seem appropriate at this time since the subject has reached a level of completion and maturity, a plateau of achievement that makes a thorough review both possible and of more than merely transitory value. We suspect that little of the material that we present will be abandoned or drastically modified in the forseeable future – a conviction that is enthusiastically shared by our publishers.

Since the original contributions of Born and von Kármán, our founding fathers, a vast and stylish superstructure has been created. After clarification of the periodic boundary conditions, the application of the sampling techniques by Blackman, the theory developed steadily, though slowly, under the watchful eye of Max Born. After a systematic development following the second world war, the theory received a powerful impetus by the application of many-body theory in both perfect and imperfect crystals. Many of the original authors that decisively shaped the finished product, had the opportunity to present their contribution and point of view in these pages. Since, at the same time, the structure of the theory is essentially complete and the experiments have confirmed and complemented our fundamental ideas, we have a product that is, as we see it, worth the investment. Just to cite one example. Those of us who tried to understand Horner's original 1967 thesis in the Zeitschrift für Physik will envy the readers of the current book, who will not have to suffer the torture some of us had to endure to decipher what was actually accomplished and what was not. We can simply enjoy the final product, honed and refined through many versions at enumerable conferences, review papers and critical discussions. The present version is still not elementary but it has been well thought out.

We would like to thank our friends from North-Holland Publishing Company, Drs. W. H. Wimmers and Dr. P. S. H. Bolman for their cooperation and efficient supervision of the publishing process and, last but not least, for having conceived of the idea in the first place.

Our thanks are also due to Dr. V. V. Goldman who kindly prepared the Subject Index of this volume.

Whether the reader receives value for his money only time will tell. We would be grateful to readers of this first volume for comments and suggestions especially those that will help to improve the subsequent volumes.

June 1974

G.K. Horton
New Brunswick, N.J.
USA

A.A. Maradudin
Irvine, Cal.
USA

Contents

Volume 1

List of Contributors

T.H.K. Barron, Dept. of Theor. Chemistry, University of Bristol, Bristol, UK

H. Bilz, Max-Planck-Institut für Festkörperforschung, Stuttgart, Germany

J.L. Birman, Physics Dept., New York University, Meyer Hall, Washington Square, New York, N.Y. 10012, USA

E.G. Brovman, I.V. Kurchatov Atomic Energy Institute, Moscow, USSR

G. Dolling, Atomic Energy of Canada Limited, Chalk River Nuclear Laboratories, Chalk River, Ontario, Canada

B. Gliss, Max-Planck-Institut für Festkörperforschung, Stuttgart, Germany

W. Götze, Physik-Department der Technischen Universität and Max-Planck-Institut für Physik und Astrophysik, Munich, Germany

W. Hanke, M. Planck-Institut für Festkörperforschung, Stuttgart, Germany

J.R. Hardy, Behlen Laboratory of Physics, The University of Nebraska, Lincoln, Nebraska 68508, USA

H. Horner, Institut für Festkörperforschung 517 Jülich, Germany

Yu.M. Kagan, I.V. Kurchatov Atomic Energy Institute, Moscow, USSR

M.L. Klein, Div. of Chemistry, National Research Council, Ottawa, Canada

A.A. Maradudin, Dept. of Physics, University of California, Irvine, California 92664, USA

K.H. Michel, Institut für Festkörperforschung, 517 Jülich, Germany

L.J. Sham, Dept. of Physics, University of California, San Diego, La Jolla, California 92037, USA

CHAPTER 1

Elements of the Theory of Lattice Dynamics

A.A. MARADUDIN

Dept. of Physics, University of California
Irvine, California 92664
USA

Dynamical Properties of Solids, edited by
G.K. Horton and A.A. Maradudin

Contents

1. The adiabatic approximation

In this chapter the elements of the theory of lattice dynamics will be summarized, in order to make this book self-contained, and as an introduction to the material presented in subsequent chapters. No attempt will be made to provide derivations of all the results presented here, and the reader will often be referred to the literature for these.

The phenomenological theory of lattice dynamics is formulated in terms of the motions of the atomic nuclei making up a crystal, so that only the nuclear momenta and nuclear coordinates appear in the vibrational hamiltonian of the crystal. However, a crystal is a system of nuclei and electrons which interact with each other through Coulomb forces, so that the vibrational hamiltonian, although it contains no explicit reference to the electrons, must incorporate their effects implicitly. It seems appropriate to begin a summary of the elements of the theory of lattice dynamics with a discussion of the formation of the effective hamiltonian for nuclear motion, and consequently of the approximations which underlie the phenomenological theory of lattice dynamics (Born and Huang 1954, section 14 and Appendix VIII).

The hamiltonian for a crystal can be written in the form

$$H = T(\boldsymbol{R}) + U(\boldsymbol{R}) + H_{\mathrm{e}}(\boldsymbol{r}) + H_{\mathrm{ei}}(\boldsymbol{r}, \boldsymbol{R}), \tag{1.1}$$

where $T(\boldsymbol{R})$ is the kinetic energy of the nuclei, $U(\boldsymbol{R})$ is the potential energy of interaction of the nuclei, $H_{\mathrm{e}}(\boldsymbol{r})$ is the electronic hamiltonian, the sum of the kinetic energy of the electrons and their Coulomb energy of interaction, and $H_{\mathrm{ei}}(\boldsymbol{r}, \boldsymbol{R})$ is the hamiltonian describing the interaction of the electrons with the nuclei. We have denoted by $\boldsymbol{R}$ the coordinates of all the nuclei, and by $\boldsymbol{r}$ those of all the electrons.

Because the kinetic energy of the nuclei is generally small owing to their large masses, it is natural to treat $T(\boldsymbol{R})$ as a perturbation on the rest of the hamiltonian, which we denote by $H_0(\boldsymbol{r}, \boldsymbol{R})$:

$$H_0(\boldsymbol{r}, \boldsymbol{R}) = U(\boldsymbol{R}) + H_{\mathrm{e}}(\boldsymbol{r}) + H_{\mathrm{ei}}(\boldsymbol{r}, \boldsymbol{R}). \tag{1.2}$$

The small parameter of the theory is clearly some power of the ratio m/M_0, where m is the electronic mass and M_0 is any one of the nuclear masses or their mean. We denote the expansion parameter by κ,

$$\kappa = (m/M_0)^{\alpha}, \tag{1.3}$$

where the exponent α is to be determined.

To begin the perturbation calculation we assume that the eigenfunctions and corresponding energies of the unperturbed hamiltonian $H_0(\boldsymbol{r}, \boldsymbol{R})$, with the nuclei in arbitrary fixed positions, are known:

$$[H_0(\boldsymbol{r}, \boldsymbol{R}) - E_n(\boldsymbol{R})]\, \Phi_n(\boldsymbol{r}, \boldsymbol{R}) = 0. \tag{1.4}$$

Here n is the electronic quantum number, and we have indicated explicitly that both the eigenfunctions and eigenvalues depend on the nuclear coordinates $\boldsymbol{R}$ as parameters. Our problem is to solve the exact Schrödinger equation

$$[H(\boldsymbol{r}, \boldsymbol{R}) - \mathscr{E}]\, \psi(\boldsymbol{r}, \boldsymbol{R}) = 0. \tag{1.5}$$

We will assume that the functions $\{\Phi_n(\boldsymbol{r}, \boldsymbol{R})\}$ and the corresponding energies $\{E_n(\boldsymbol{R})\}$ are known for the equilibrium configuration $\boldsymbol{R}^0$ of the nuclei, as yet unknown, and will seek the solutions of eq. (1.5) for nuclear configurations which depart only a little from the equilibrium configuration. We express this condition by writing

$$\boldsymbol{R} - \boldsymbol{R}^0 = \kappa \boldsymbol{u} \tag{1.6}$$

and using $\boldsymbol{u}$ for the nuclear coordinates. We will find that the equilibrium configuration $\boldsymbol{R}^0$ is defined in the course of the calculation.

The unperturbed hamiltonian $H_0(\boldsymbol{r}, \boldsymbol{R})$ can be expanded formally in powers of the nuclear displacements

$$H_0(\boldsymbol{r}, \boldsymbol{R}) = H_0(\boldsymbol{r}, \boldsymbol{R}^0 + \kappa\boldsymbol{u}) = H_0^{(0)} + \kappa H_0^{(1)} + \kappa^2 H_0^{(2)} + \cdots, \tag{1.7}$$

where $H_0^{(p)}(\boldsymbol{r}, \boldsymbol{R}_0)$ is an operator with respect to $\boldsymbol{r}$ and a homogeneous function of degree p in $\boldsymbol{u}$. The energy $E_n(\boldsymbol{R})$, and the corresponding wave function $\Phi_n(\boldsymbol{r}, \boldsymbol{R})$, can also be expanded in powers of the nuclear displacements:

$$E_n(\boldsymbol{R}) = E_n(\boldsymbol{R}^0 + \kappa\boldsymbol{u}) = E_n^{(0)} + \kappa E_n^{(1)} + \kappa^2 E_n^{(2)} + \cdots, \tag{1.8}$$

$$\Phi_n(\boldsymbol{r}, \boldsymbol{R}) = \Phi_n(\boldsymbol{r}, \boldsymbol{R}^0 + \kappa\boldsymbol{u}) = \Phi_n^{(0)} + \kappa\Phi_n^{(1)} + \kappa^2\Phi_n^{(2)} + \cdots. \tag{1.9}$$

In terms of the nuclear displacements the nuclear kinetic energy $T(\boldsymbol{R})$ takes the form

$$T(\boldsymbol{R}) = -\kappa^{1/\alpha - 2} \sum_i (M_0/M_i)(\hbar^2/2m)\nabla^2_{\boldsymbol{u}_i} \equiv \kappa^{1/\alpha - 2} H_1^{(1/\alpha - 2)}, \tag{1.10}$$

where i runs over all nuclei, and M_i is the mass of the ith nucleus. If we require that the nuclear kinetic energy be of the same order in κ as the terms in the crystal hamiltonian which are quadratic in the nuclear displacements, so that the harmonic approximation for lattice vibrations be a direct consequence of the present theory, we must have that $1/\alpha - 2 = 2$, or that $\alpha = \frac{1}{4}$. The expansion parameter of the present theory is, therefore,

$$\kappa = (m/M_0)^{1/4}. \tag{1.11}$$

The total hamiltonian H consequently can be expanded as

$$H = H_0^{(0)} + \kappa H_0^{(1)} + \kappa^2 (H_0^{(2)} + H_1^{(2)}) + \kappa^3 H_0^{(3)} + \cdots, \tag{1.12}$$

where it must be kept in mind that $H_1^{(2)}$ operates only on the nuclear coordinates $\boldsymbol{u}$.

We seek a solution of eq. (1.5) in the form

$$\psi(\boldsymbol{r}, \boldsymbol{u}) = \sum_n \chi_n(\boldsymbol{u}) \Phi_n(\boldsymbol{r}, \boldsymbol{u}), \tag{1.13}$$

where $\chi_n(\boldsymbol{u})$ is a function only of the nuclear coordinates and is to be determined. When eq. (1.13) is substituted into eq. (1.5), and use is made of eq. (1.4), we obtain

$$\sum_n [E_n^{(0)} + \kappa E_n^{(1)} + \kappa^2 (H_1^{(2)} + E_n^{(2)}) + \kappa^3 E_n^{(3)} + \cdots] \chi_n(\boldsymbol{u}) \Phi_n(\boldsymbol{r}, \boldsymbol{u}) = \mathscr{E} \sum_n \chi_n(\boldsymbol{u}) \Phi_n(\boldsymbol{r}, \boldsymbol{u}). \tag{1.14}$$

If we now multiply both sides of this equation from the left by $\Phi_m^*(\boldsymbol{r}, \boldsymbol{u})$ and integrate over all electronic coordinates, keeping in mind that the $\{\Phi_n(\boldsymbol{r}, \boldsymbol{u})\}$ as functions of $\boldsymbol{r}$ can be assumed to be orthonormal for all values of $\boldsymbol{u}$, we obtain as the equation for $\chi_m(\boldsymbol{u})$

$$\kappa^2 \sum_n \int \mathrm{d}\boldsymbol{r}\, \Phi_m^*(\boldsymbol{r}, \boldsymbol{u}) H_1^{(2)}(\boldsymbol{u}) \Phi_n(\boldsymbol{r}, \boldsymbol{u}) \chi_n(\boldsymbol{u}) + [E_m^{(0)} + \kappa E_m^{(1)} + \kappa^2 E_m^{(2)} + \kappa^3 E_m^{(3)} + \cdots] \chi_m(\boldsymbol{u}) = \mathscr{E} \chi_m(\boldsymbol{u}). \tag{1.15}$$

We now note that

$$H_1^{(2)}(\boldsymbol{u}) \Phi_n(\boldsymbol{r}, \boldsymbol{u}) \chi_n(\boldsymbol{u}) = -\sum_i (M_0/M_i)(\hbar^2/2m)(\nabla_{\boldsymbol{u}_i}^2 \Phi_n(\boldsymbol{r}, \boldsymbol{u})) \chi_n(\boldsymbol{u}) - \sum_i (M_0/M_i)(\hbar^2/m)(\nabla_{\boldsymbol{u}_i} \Phi_n(\boldsymbol{r}, \boldsymbol{u})) \cdot (\nabla_{\boldsymbol{u}_i} \chi_n(\boldsymbol{u})) + \Phi_n(\boldsymbol{r}, \boldsymbol{u}) H_1^{(2)}(\boldsymbol{u}) \chi_n(\boldsymbol{u}) \tag{1.16}$$

so that

$$\kappa^2 \sum_n \int \mathrm{d}\boldsymbol{r}\, \Phi_m^*(\boldsymbol{r},\boldsymbol{u})\, H_1^{(2)}(\boldsymbol{u})\, \Phi_n(\boldsymbol{r},\boldsymbol{u})\, \chi_n(\boldsymbol{u}) = \kappa^2 H_1^{(2)} \chi_m(\boldsymbol{u})$$
$$- \kappa^2 \sum_n \sum_i (M_0/M_i)\,(\hbar^2/m) \int \Phi_m^*(\boldsymbol{r},\boldsymbol{u})\, \nabla_{\boldsymbol{u}_i} \Phi_n(\boldsymbol{r},\boldsymbol{u})\, \mathrm{d}\boldsymbol{r}) \cdot (\nabla_{\boldsymbol{u}_i} \chi_n(\boldsymbol{u}))$$
$$- \kappa^2 \sum_n \sum_i (M_0/M_i)\,(\hbar^2/2m) \int \Phi_m^*(\boldsymbol{r},\boldsymbol{u})\, \nabla_{\boldsymbol{u}_i}^2 \Phi_n(\boldsymbol{r},\boldsymbol{u})\, \mathrm{d}\boldsymbol{r}\, \chi_n(\boldsymbol{u}). \quad (1.17)$$

It is convenient to separate explicitly the terms with $n=m$ on the right hand side of this equation. They can be written as

$$- \kappa^2 \sum_i (M_0/M_i)\,(\hbar^2/2m)\, \nabla_{\boldsymbol{u}_i} \int [\Phi_m(\boldsymbol{r},\boldsymbol{u})]^2\, \mathrm{d}\boldsymbol{r} \cdot (\nabla_{\boldsymbol{u}_i} \chi_m)$$
$$- \kappa^2 \sum_i (M_0/M_i)\,(\hbar^2/2m) \int \Phi_m(\boldsymbol{r},\boldsymbol{u})\, \nabla_{\boldsymbol{u}_i}^2 \Phi_m(\boldsymbol{r},\boldsymbol{u})\, \mathrm{d}\boldsymbol{r}\, \chi_m, \quad (1.18)$$

if the electronic wave functions $\{\Phi_m(\boldsymbol{r},\boldsymbol{u})\}$ are chosen to be real, which is always possible in the absence of a magnetic field. The first term vanishes because the $\{\Phi_m(\boldsymbol{r},\boldsymbol{u})\}$ have been assumed to be normalized to unity for all $\boldsymbol{u}$.

Making use of this result we can combine eqs. (1.17) and (1.15) to rewrite the equation for $\chi_m(\boldsymbol{u})$ in the following form:

$$[\kappa^2 H_1^{(2)} + E_m(\boldsymbol{u}) + C_m(\boldsymbol{u})]\, \chi_m + \sum_{n\,(\neq m)} C_{mn} \chi_n = \mathscr{E} \chi_m, \quad (1.19)$$

where the operator $C_m(\boldsymbol{u})$ is given by

$$C_m(\boldsymbol{u}) = -\kappa^2 \sum_i (M_0/M_i)\,(\hbar^2/2m) \int \Phi_m(\boldsymbol{r},\boldsymbol{u})\, \nabla_{\boldsymbol{u}_i}^2 \Phi_m(\boldsymbol{r},\boldsymbol{u})\, \mathrm{d}\boldsymbol{r}, \quad (1.20)$$

while

$$C_{mn} = -\kappa^2 \sum_i (M_0/M_i)\,(\hbar^2/m) \int \Phi_m(\boldsymbol{r},\boldsymbol{u})\, \nabla_{\boldsymbol{u}_i} \Phi_n(\boldsymbol{r},\boldsymbol{u})\, \mathrm{d}\boldsymbol{r} \cdot \nabla_{\boldsymbol{u}_i}$$
$$- \kappa^2 \sum_i (M_0/M_i)\,(\hbar^2/2m) \int \Phi_m(\boldsymbol{r},\boldsymbol{u})\, \nabla_{\boldsymbol{u}_i}^2 \Phi_n(\boldsymbol{r},\boldsymbol{u})\, \mathrm{d}\boldsymbol{r}. \quad (1.21)$$

Because $\Phi_n^{(p)}(\boldsymbol{r},\boldsymbol{u})$ is homogeneous of degree p in $\boldsymbol{u}$, we see that the first term on the right hand side of eq. (1.21) begins with terms of $O(\kappa^3)$, while the second term begins with terms which are of $O(\kappa^4)$. The operator $C_m(\boldsymbol{u})$ begins with a constant term of $O(\kappa^4)$.

Before proceeding to a perturbative solution of eq. (1.19) it is instructive to consider some general properties of its solutions. For this it is convenient to rewrite eq. (1.19) in the form

$$O_m \chi_m + \sum_{n\,(\neq m)} C_{mn} \chi_n = \mathscr{E} \chi_m \,, \tag{1.22}$$

and to denote the eigenfunctions and eigenvalues of the operator O_m by χ_{mv} and $\mathscr{E}_{mv}$, respectively,

$$O_m \chi_{mv} = \mathscr{E}_{mv} \chi_{mv} \,, \tag{1.23}$$

where v can be regarded as a vibrational quantum number. We then expand χ_m in terms of the $\{\chi_{mv}\}$ according to

$$\chi_m = \sum_v a_v^{(m)} \chi_{mv} \,, \tag{1.24}$$

whereupon the equation for $a_v^{(m)}$ becomes

$$(\mathscr{E}_{mv} - \mathscr{E})\, a_v^{(m)} + \sum_{n\,(\neq m)} \sum_{v'} \langle mv|\, C_{mn} \,|nv'\rangle \, a_{v'}^{(n)} = 0 \,, \tag{1.25}$$

in an obvious notation. This equation can be rewritten as

$$a_v^{(m)} = -\frac{1}{\mathscr{E}_{mv} - \mathscr{E}} \sum_{n\,(\neq m)} \sum_{v'} \langle mv|\, C_{mn} \,|nv'\rangle \, a_{v'}^{(n)} \,. \tag{1.26}$$

When this expression for $a_v^{(m)}$ is substituted back into eq. (1.25) we obtain an equivalent equation for $a_v^{(m)}$:

$$(\mathscr{E}_{mv} - \mathscr{E})\, a_v^{(m)} - \sum_{n\,(\neq m)} \sum_{v'} \sum_{n'\,(\neq n)} \sum_{v''} \frac{\langle mv|\, C_{mn} \,|nv'\rangle \, \langle nv'|\, C_{nn'} \,|n'v''\rangle}{\mathscr{E}_{nv'} - \mathscr{E}} \, a_{v''}^{(n')} = 0 \,. \tag{1.27}$$

If we retain only the diagonal contribution to the second term, $n'v'' = mv$, and note that as the perturbation represented by the operator C_{mn} is switched off the energy eigenvalue $\mathscr{E}$ tends to $\mathscr{E}_{mv}$, we obtain an equation for $a_v^{(m)}$ (and hence for χ_m) in which the effects of electronic transitions are incorporated to the lowest order of approximation:

$$(\mathscr{E}_{mv} - \mathscr{E})\, a_v^{(m)} + \sum_{n\,(\neq m)} \sum_{v'} \frac{\langle mv|\, C_{mn} \,|nv'\rangle \, \langle nv'|\, C_{nm} \,|mv\rangle}{\mathscr{E}_{mv} - \mathscr{E}_{nv'}} \, a_v^{(m)} = 0 \,, \tag{1.28}$$

from which it follows that

$$\mathscr{E} = \mathscr{E}_{mv} + \sum_{n\,(\neq m)} \sum_{v'} \langle mv|\, C_{mn} \,|nv'\rangle \, \langle nv'|\, C_{nm} \,|mv\rangle / (\mathscr{E}_{mv} - \mathscr{E}_{nv'}) \,. \tag{1.29}$$

Since C_{mn} is at least of $O(\kappa^3)$, the second term on the right hand side of this equation begins with terms of $O(\kappa^6)$. It follows therefore, that the energy levels of the crystal are given correctly to $O(\kappa^5)$ by the eigenvalues $\mathscr{E}_{mv}$ if the terms involving the operators $\{C_{mn}\}$ are omitted from eq. (1.22) or eq. (1.19).

We also note from eqs. (1.19) or (1.22) and eq. (1.13) that when the terms involving the operators $\{C_{mn}\}$ are omitted from the present theory the vibrational wave function $\chi_m(\boldsymbol{u})$ is determined by the properties of only the mth electronic state, and no electronic transitions are induced by the nuclear motion. The wave function for the combined system of electrons in interaction with the nuclei is thus given by

$$\Psi_{mv}(\boldsymbol{r}, \boldsymbol{u}) = \chi_{mv}(\boldsymbol{u})\, \Phi_m(\boldsymbol{r}, \boldsymbol{R}), \tag{1.30}$$

for the state whose energy is $\mathscr{E}_{mv}$.

To what order in κ can the wave function be written correctly in the form (1.30)? A straightforward application of perturbation theory to eq. (1.25) shows that with an error of $O(\kappa^6)$ the element $a_v^{(m)}$ for the state of the crystal whose energy is given by eq. (1.29) is equal to unity, while the remaining elements $a_{v'}^{(n)}$ with $n \neq m$ are given in the lowest approximation by

$$a_{v'}^{(n)} = \langle nv'|\, C_{mn}\, |mv\rangle / (\mathscr{E}_{mv} - \mathscr{E}_{nv'}) . \tag{1.31}$$

Thus, we see that since the operator C_{mn} is of $O(\kappa^3)$, the effect of electronic transitions on the nuclear motion first manifests itself in the contribution to $\chi_m(\boldsymbol{u})$ of $O(\kappa)^3$. We conclude from the preceding results that a wave function for the crystal as a whole of the form given by eq. (1.30) yields a nuclear wave function $\chi_{mv}(\boldsymbol{u})$ exact to $O(\kappa^2)$, and a total energy $\mathscr{E}_{mv}$ exact to $O(\kappa^5)$. This conclusion is consistent with the general result (Löwdin 1964) that knowledge of a perturbed wave function through order κ^s enables the corresponding perturbed energy to be obtained to order κ^{2s+1}.

The wave function (1.30) has a simple interpretation. The first factor describes the nuclear motion, and the second factor shows that during the nuclear motion the electrons move as if the nuclei were fixed in their instantaneous positions. The electrons are said to follow the nuclear motion *adiabatically*, and the approximation to the wave function of the total system of electrons and nuclei given by eq. (1.30) is consequently called the *adiabatic approximation*. In the adiabatic approximation the equation for nuclear motion is given by

$$[\kappa^2 H_1^{(2)} + E_m(\boldsymbol{u}) + C_m(\boldsymbol{u})]\, \chi_{mv}(\boldsymbol{u}) = \mathscr{E}_{mv} \chi_{mv}(\boldsymbol{u}), \tag{1.32}$$

where the effective potential function for nuclear motion is given by the terms in $E_m(\boldsymbol{u})+C_m(\boldsymbol{u})$ through $O(\kappa^5)$, and it must be understood that this equation, and the adiabatic approximation, is no longer correct if the contributions to $\chi_{mv}(\boldsymbol{u})$ of $O(\kappa^3)$ or higher are sought.

We now proceed to solve eq. (1.32) by perturbation theory. We expand $\chi_{mv}(\boldsymbol{u})$ and $\mathscr{E}_{mv}$ according to

$$\chi_{mv}(\boldsymbol{u}) = \chi_{mv}^{(0)} + \kappa\chi_{mv}^{(1)} + \kappa^2\chi_{mv}^{(2)} + \cdots, \tag{1.33a}$$

$$\mathscr{E}_{mv} = \mathscr{E}_{mv}^{(0)} + \kappa\mathscr{E}_{mv}^{(1)} + \kappa^2\mathscr{E}_{mv}^{(2)} + \cdots, \tag{1.33b}$$

and recall the expansions (1.8) and (1.9). In this way we obtain the perturbation equations, through second order,

$$E_m^{(0)}\chi_{mv}^{(0)} = \mathscr{E}_{mv}^{(0)}\chi_{mv}^{(0)}, \tag{1.34a}$$

$$E_m^{(1)}\chi_{mv}^{(0)} + E_m^{(0)}\chi_{mv}^{(1)} = \mathscr{E}_{mv}^{(1)}\chi_{mv}^{(0)} + \mathscr{E}_{mv}^{(0)}\chi_{mv}^{(1)}, \tag{1.34b}$$

$$[H_1^{(2)} + E_m^{(2)}]\,\chi_{mv}^{(0)} + E_m^{(1)}\chi_{mv}^{(1)} + E_m^{(0)}\chi_{mv}^{(2)} = \mathscr{E}_{mv}^{(2)}\chi_{mv}^{(0)} + \mathscr{E}_{mv}^{(1)}\chi_{mv}^{(1)} + \mathscr{E}_{mv}^{(0)}\chi_{mv}^{(2)}. \tag{1.34c}$$

From eq. (1.34a) we see that

$$\mathscr{E}_{mv}^{(0)} = E_m^{(0)}(\boldsymbol{R}^0). \tag{1.35}$$

If we use this result in eq. (1.34b) we obtain the result that

$$E_m^{(1)} = \mathscr{E}_{mv}^{(1)}. \tag{1.36}$$

However, the left hand side of this equation is a homogeneous function of the nuclear displacements $\boldsymbol{u}$ of first degree, while the right hand side is a constant, independent of $\boldsymbol{u}$. Equation (1.36) can only be satisfied, therefore, if $E_m^{(1)}$ vanishes identically:

$$E_m^{(1)} \equiv \sum_i (\partial E_m(\boldsymbol{R})/\partial \boldsymbol{R}_i)_{\boldsymbol{R}^0}\cdot \boldsymbol{u}_i \equiv 0. \tag{1.37}$$

Thus the equilibrium configuration $\boldsymbol{R}^0$, corresponding to the mth electronic state is defined by the condition

$$(\partial E_m(\boldsymbol{R})/\partial \boldsymbol{R}_i)_{\boldsymbol{R}^0} = 0. \tag{1.38}$$

With $\boldsymbol{R}^0$ defined in this way, we have

$$\mathscr{E}_{mv}^{(1)} = 0. \tag{1.39}$$

If we now use eqs. (1.35) and (1.39) in the second order equation, eq. (1.34c), we obtain

$$[H_1^{(2)} + E_m^{(2)} - \mathscr{E}_m^{(2)}]\,\chi_m^{(0)} = 0. \tag{1.40}$$

If we terminate the calculation at this point, eq. (1.40) is the equation determining the nuclear motion. Multiplying this homogeneous equation by κ^2, we see that $\kappa^2 H_1^{(2)}$ is the nuclear kinetic energy, $\kappa^2 E_m^{(2)}$ is the potential energy function for nuclear motion, and $\kappa^2 \mathscr{E}_m^{(2)}$ is the corresponding energy eigenvalue. Because $E_m^{(2)}$ is a homogeneous function of the nuclear displacements of degree two, eq. (1.40) describes harmonic vibrations of the nuclei about their equilibrium positions. The approximation represented by eq. (1.40) is therefore called the *harmonic approximation*. To this approximation, then, the wave function of the crystal can be written as the product

$$\Psi_{mv}(\boldsymbol{r}, \boldsymbol{u}) = \chi_{mv}^{(0)}(\boldsymbol{u})\, \Phi_m^{(0)}(\boldsymbol{r}, \boldsymbol{R}^0), \tag{1.41}$$

since the retention of terms past $\Phi_m^{(0)}(\boldsymbol{r}, \boldsymbol{R}^0)$ in $\Phi_m(\boldsymbol{r}, \boldsymbol{R})$ contributes in higher orders of perturbation theory than those considered thus far. The corresponding energy eigenvalue is the sum of the eigenvalue $E_m^{(0)}(\boldsymbol{R}^0)$ for the electronic motion with the nuclei at their equilibrium positions, and the energy of nuclear vibration in the effective potential $E_m^{(2)}(\boldsymbol{u})$:

$$\mathscr{E}_{mv} = E_m^{(0)}(\boldsymbol{R}^0) + \mathscr{E}_{mv}^{(2)}. \tag{1.42}$$

It is seen, therefore, that the harmonic approximation is a special case of the adiabatic approximation.

The term *adiabatic approximation* is sometimes applied to that approximation in which the effective potential for nuclear motion in the mth electronic state is provided by the electronic energy $E_m(\boldsymbol{u})$. From eq. (1.19) we see that this is the case if the operator $C_m(\boldsymbol{u})$ can be neglected with respect to $E_m(\boldsymbol{u})$. Since $C_m(\boldsymbol{u})$ expanded in powers of the nuclear displacements $\boldsymbol{u}$ begins with a constant term of $O(\kappa^4)$, the electronic energy $E_m(\boldsymbol{u})$ provides the effective potential energy for nuclear motion through terms of $O(\kappa^4)$ and consequently of $O(\boldsymbol{u}^4)$. However, by adding the two lowest order contributions in κ from $C_m(\boldsymbol{u})$, a constant of $O(\kappa^4)$ independent of $\boldsymbol{u}$, and a term of $O(\kappa^5)$ linear in $\boldsymbol{u}$, the approximation is improved, with the electronic motion still remaining adiabatic.

Because the adiabatic approximation is equivalent to the assumption that the electrons, moving much more rapidly than the nuclei due to their lighter masses, see the nuclei as being fixed in position at any given instant, it would seem that the criterion for its validity is that the frequencies of the electronic motions be much greater than the frequencies of the nuclear vibrations. However, it follows from the preceding discussion, in particular from eq. (1.31), that the correct criterion for the validity of the adiabatic approximation, in either of the two senses of this term described above, is that

$$|a_{v'}^{(n)}| = |\langle nv'|\, C_{mn}\,|mv\rangle/(\mathscr{E}_{mv} - \mathscr{E}_{nv'})| \ll 1 \qquad (n \neq m). \tag{1.43}$$

The lowest order (in κ) approximation to the matrix element in the numerator of this expression is found from eq. (1.21) to be

$$\langle nv'|\, C_{mn}^{(3)}\,|mv\rangle = -\sum_i (\hbar^2/M_i) \int \mathrm{d}\boldsymbol{r}\, \Phi_m^{(0)}(\boldsymbol{r})\, \nabla_{\boldsymbol{U}_i} \Phi_n^{(1)}(\boldsymbol{r}, \boldsymbol{U}) \cdot \langle nv'|\, \nabla_{\boldsymbol{U}_i}\,|mv\rangle, \tag{1.44}$$

where we have introduced the physical displacements $\{\boldsymbol{U}\} = \kappa\,\{\boldsymbol{u}\}$. The integral over $\boldsymbol{r}$ in this expression in fact is independent of the nuclear displacements $\{\boldsymbol{U}\}$. Herring (1956) has shown that the criterion (1.43) is equivalent to

$$\left|\frac{\hbar\omega}{\mathscr{E}_{mv} - \mathscr{E}_{nv'}}\,\frac{\bar{U}}{U_1}\right| \ll 1, \tag{1.45}$$

where ω is a typical frequency of the nuclear vibrations, $\bar{U}$ is their root mean square amplitude, and U_1 is the nuclear displacement required to change either of the electronic wave functions $\Phi_m(\boldsymbol{r}, \boldsymbol{U})$ or $\Phi_n(\boldsymbol{r}, \boldsymbol{U})$ toward the other by an appreciable amount, i.e.,

$$\boldsymbol{U}_1 \cdot \int \mathrm{d}\boldsymbol{r}\, \Phi_m(\boldsymbol{r}, \boldsymbol{U})\, \nabla_{\boldsymbol{U}} \Phi_n(\boldsymbol{r}, \boldsymbol{U}) \sim 1. \tag{1.46}$$

Together with eq. (1.46) the estimates

$$(\hbar^2/M)\, |\langle nv'|\, \nabla_{\boldsymbol{u}}\,|mv\rangle| \sim \hbar\omega\,(\hbar/M\omega)^{1/2} \tag{1.47a}$$

and

$$\langle U^2\rangle \sim \hbar/M\omega \tag{1.47b}$$

serve to establish eq. (1.45). When the electronic wave function varies slowly with the nuclear positions, U_1 is large compared with U, and the adiabatic approximation will be better than the simple frequency criterion suggests.

On the face of it, it would appear that while the criterion (1.45) is quite well satisfied in the case of insulators and even in the case of semiconductors, due to the large gaps in their electronic energy spectra, it should not be expected to hold in the case of metals, where the separation between neighboring electronic energy levels can be regarded as arbitrarily small. Nevertheless, as recent investigations have shown (Chester 1961, Brovman and Kagan 1967), despite the breakdown of eq. (1.45), the adiabatic approximation is nevertheless quite accurate for metals (see the discussion by Brovman and Kagan in chapter 4 of this book). Thus, in the rest of this chapter we will assume the validity of the adiabatic approximation in presenting the elements of the theory of lattice dynamics.

2. *Atomic force constants and their properties*

It is convenient to base a discussion of the elements of the theory of lattice dynamics on the assumption of an infinitely extended crystal. The formulation of the theory is greatly simplified by the perfect lattice periodicity and space group symmetry which results from the absence of crystal surfaces.

An arbitrary lattice is a periodic arrangement of points in space, all of whose positions with respect to an origin chosen at one of them are given by the vectors

$$\boldsymbol{x}(l) = l_1\boldsymbol{a}_1 + l_2\boldsymbol{a}_2 + l_3\boldsymbol{a}_3 , \tag{2.1}$$

where l_1, l_2, l_3 are arbitrary integers, which we label collectively by l. The lattice defined by the position vectors (2.1) is said to be *primitive*, or is called a *Bravais lattice*. The three, noncoplanar vectors $\boldsymbol{a}_1$, $\boldsymbol{a}_2$, $\boldsymbol{a}_3$ are called the *primitive translation vectors* of the lattice. The vector $\boldsymbol{x}(l)$ is called a *lattice translation vector*. The parallelepiped bounded by the vectors $\boldsymbol{a}_1$, $\boldsymbol{a}_2$, $\boldsymbol{a}_3$ is called the *primitive unit cell* of the lattice. It will fill all space when it is displaced parallel to itself through all possible lattice translation vectors. This is not the case for any cell of smaller volume.

A crystal is formed when a group of atoms is attached identically to each lattice point of a lattice. This group of atoms is called a *basis*. If there is only one atom in the basis, with no loss of generality we can assume that the positions of the atoms comprising the crystal coincide with the lattice sites given by the lattice translation vectors (2.1). Such crystals are called *primitive* or *Bravais crystals*. If there are r atoms in the basis, where $r>1$, we can assume that all of them are situated in the primitive unit cell associated with each lattice site. The positions of the r atoms in the unit cell, with respect to the origin of the unit cell, are given by the vectors $\boldsymbol{x}(\kappa)$, where the index κ distinguishes the different atoms in the basis, or, equivalently, in the primitive unit cell, and takes the values $1, 2, \cdots, r$. Thus, in general the position vector of the κth atom in the lth primitive unit cell is given by

$$\boldsymbol{x}(l\kappa) = \boldsymbol{x}(l) + \boldsymbol{x}(\kappa). \tag{2.2}$$

Crystals containing more than one atom in a primitive unit cell are called *nonprimitive* crystals.

From eq. (2.2) we see that the difference between the position vectors of *any* two atoms of type κ in a nonprimitive crystal is a lattice translation vector $\boldsymbol{x}(l)$. Therefore, the atoms of type κ, for $\kappa = 1, 2, \cdots, r$, comprise a Bravais lattice by themselves, the same for each κ, whose primitive translation vectors are $\boldsymbol{a}_1$, $\boldsymbol{a}_2$, $\boldsymbol{a}_3$. Consequently, instead of viewing a crystal as a single Bravais lattice each of whose points has a basis of r atoms attached, we can regard it as being made up of r interpenetrating Bravais lattices of the same kind, displaced with respect to each other by the differences of the basis vectors $\boldsymbol{x}(1)-\boldsymbol{x}(2)$, $\boldsymbol{x}(1)-\boldsymbol{x}(3), \cdots, \boldsymbol{x}(1)-\boldsymbol{x}(r)$. Each of the constituent, identical Bravais lattices is called a *sublattice*.

The atomic positions in an infinite crystal defined by the vectors $\{\boldsymbol{x}(l\kappa)\}$ will be referred to generally as the *rest positions* of the atoms. Whether or not the rest positions are also equilibrium positions for the atoms depends on whether or not the equilibrium conditions for an infinite crystal are satisfied. These conditions are (Born and Huang 1954, section 23):

(*i*) every atom is in equilibrium, i.e., there is no net force acting on any atom;
(*ii*) the configuration corresponds to vanishing stresses.

In a finite crystal the fulfillment of the first condition implies the satisfaction of the second, but in an infinite crystal this is not the case. This can be seen if we consider the example of an infinite chain of equal masses connected by identical springs of equal length. If the separation between each pair of consecutive masses is increased by the same amount, each atom will remain in equilibrium, because it remains at a center of inversion symmetry, and the forces acting on it from one side are balanced by those acting on it from the other. However, each spring, and consequently the chain as a whole, is under tension. In this case the equilibrium condition (*ii*) is equivalent to the condition that the tension vanishes. Thus, if we require that an infinite crystal obey the same equilibrium conditions as a finite crystal, we must impose condition (*ii*) in addition to condition (*i*).

An infinite crystal structure for which the two equilibrium conditions are satisfied is called an equilibrium configuration, or a minimum potential energy configuration. In the remainder of this section, to impart a greater generality to the theory than would be the case otherwise, we will assume that the rest positions given by the position vectors $\{\boldsymbol{x}(l\kappa)\}$ are not equilibrium positions, unless they are explicitly labeled as such.

As a result of thermal fluctuations at nonzero temperatures, and of zero-point motion at the absolute zero of temperature, the atoms in the crystal execute vibrations about their rest positions. If we denote by $p_\alpha(l\kappa)$ the α cartesian component of the momentum of the κth atom in the lth primitive unit cell, the total kinetic energy of the crystal can be written as

$$T = \sum_{l\kappa\alpha} p_\alpha^2(l\kappa)/2M_\kappa, \tag{2.3}$$

where M_κ is the mass of the κth kind of atom.

We assume that the potential energy Φ of a crystal is a function of the instantaneous positions of the atoms comprising it. If we denote by $u_\alpha(l\kappa)$ the α cartesian component of the displacement of the κth atom in the lth primitive unit cell from its rest position, given by eq. (2.2), we can formally expand Φ in powers of these components according to

$$\begin{aligned}\Phi = \Phi_0 &+ \sum_{l\kappa\alpha} \Phi_\alpha(l\kappa)\, u_\alpha(l\kappa) \\ &+ \tfrac{1}{2} \sum_{l\kappa\alpha} \sum_{l'\kappa'\beta} \Phi_{\alpha\beta}(l\kappa; l'\kappa')\, u_\alpha(l\kappa)\, u_\beta(l'\kappa') \\ &+ \tfrac{1}{6} \sum_{l\kappa\alpha} \sum_{l'\kappa'\beta} \sum_{l''\kappa''\gamma} \Phi_{\alpha\beta\gamma}(l\kappa; l'\kappa'; l''\kappa'')\, u_\alpha(l\kappa)\, u_\beta(l'\kappa')\, u_\gamma(l''\kappa'') + \cdots . \end{aligned} \tag{2.4}$$

In this expansion Φ_0 is the potential energy of the static lattice (all the atoms at rest at their rest positions), while formally

$$\Phi_\alpha(l\kappa) = \left.\frac{\partial \Phi}{\partial u_\alpha(l\kappa)}\right|_0 \tag{2.5a}$$

$$\Phi_{\alpha\beta}(l\kappa; l'\kappa') = \left.\frac{\partial^2 \Phi}{\partial u_\alpha(l\kappa)\, \partial u_\beta(l'\kappa')}\right|_0 \tag{2.5b}$$

$$\Phi_{\alpha\beta\gamma}(l\kappa; l'\kappa'; l''\kappa'') = \left.\frac{\partial^3 \Phi}{\partial u_\alpha(l\kappa)\, \partial u_\beta(l'\kappa')\, \partial u_\gamma(l''\kappa'')}\right|_0, \quad \text{etc.} \tag{2.5c}$$

where the subscript 0 means that the derivatives are evaluated with all the atoms at the rest positions given by eq. (2.2).

Because a mixed partial derivative is independent of the order in which the differentiations are carried out, it follows from eqs. (2.5) that the coefficients in the expansion (2.4) are completely symmetric in the indices $l\kappa\alpha$, $l'\kappa'\beta$, $l''\kappa''\gamma, \cdots$; for example

$$\Phi_{\alpha\beta}(l\kappa; l'\kappa') = \Phi_{\beta\alpha}(l'\kappa'; l\kappa), \tag{2.6a}$$

$$\begin{aligned}\Phi_{\alpha\beta\gamma}(l\kappa; l'\kappa'; l''\kappa'') &= \Phi_{\gamma\alpha\beta}(l''\kappa''; l\kappa; l'\kappa') = \Phi_{\beta\gamma\alpha}(l'\kappa'; l''\kappa''; l\kappa) \\ &= \Phi_{\gamma\beta\alpha}(l''\kappa''; l'\kappa'; l\kappa) = \Phi_{\beta\alpha\gamma}(l'\kappa'; l\kappa; l''\kappa'') = \Phi_{\alpha\gamma\beta}(l\kappa; l''\kappa''; l'\kappa'). \end{aligned} \tag{2.6b}$$

From its definition, eq. (2.5a), we see that the physical interpretation of the coefficient $\Phi_\alpha(l\kappa)$ is that it is the negative of the force in the α-direction acting on the atom $(l\kappa)$ when it and all the other atoms in the crystal are at their rest positions. Similar interpretations can be given to the higher order coefficients $\Phi_{\alpha\beta\gamma}(l\kappa; l'\kappa'; l''\kappa'')$, $\Phi_{\alpha\beta\gamma\delta}(l\kappa; l'\kappa'; l''\kappa''; l'''\kappa''')$, $\cdots$. Consequently, the coefficients $\Phi_\alpha(l\kappa)$, $\Phi_{\alpha\beta}(l\kappa; l'\kappa')$, $\Phi_{\alpha\beta\gamma}(l\kappa; l'\kappa'; l''\kappa'')$, $\cdots$, are known as *atomic force constants* of the first, second, third, $\cdots$, order, respectively.

From the preceding interpretation of the first order atomic force constant $\Phi_\alpha(l\kappa)$ we see that if the rest positions of the atoms are also equilibrium positions, the first order atomic force constants must vanish identically. However, to impart greater generality to the following discussion we will not assume that the rest configuration is an equilibrium configuration, and will not omit the first order terms in the expansion (2.4) of the potential energy of a crystal in powers of the displacements of the atoms from their rest positions.

There are several problems of physical interest in which it is necessary, or at least convenient, to expand the crystal potential energy in powers of atomic displacements from rest positions which are not equilibrium positions. One is the study of the effects of externally imposed stresses or strains on the dynamical properties of crystals (Ganesan et al. 1970). A second is the temperature dependence of the structure of crystals which are not parameter-free, that is crystals in which the atomic positions are not determined by symmetry alone. In such crystals it is found that with increasing temperature the sublattices comprising the crystal undergo rigid body, relative displacements, even if the crystal is held at constant volume, that is, even if each of the constituent sublattices is not allowed to deform. A convenient way of discussing this problem is based on expanding the crystal potential energy in powers of atomic displacements from rest positions which are not equilibrium positions (Leibfried and Ludwig 1961, section 10b). Finally, in the study of the dynamical properties of crystals bounded by a plane surface it is convenient to expand the potential energy about the equilibrium positions the atoms would have if they were part of an infinite crystal instead of a semi-infinite one. In this case the atoms in the surface layers have unbalanced forces acting on them, and a contribution linear in the atomic displacement is present in the expansion of the crystal potential energy (Dobrzynski and Maradudin 1973).

In all such cases it is convenient and usual to combine the terms linear in the atomic displacements in the expansion of the crystal potential energy with the terms of third and higher order, and to treat them as a perturbation on the contribution to the vibrational hamiltonian obtained from the terms quadratic in the atomic displacements. Thus the vibrational hamiltonian for a crystal can be written as

$$H = H_0 + H_A, \tag{2.7a}$$

where

$$H_0 = \sum_{l\kappa\alpha} \frac{p_\alpha^2(l\kappa)}{2M_\kappa} + \tfrac{1}{2} \sum_{l\kappa\alpha} \sum_{l'\kappa'\beta} \Phi_{\alpha\beta}(l\kappa; l'\kappa')\, u_\alpha(l\kappa)\, u_\beta(l'\kappa'), \tag{2.7b}$$

$$H_A = \sum_{l\kappa\alpha} \Phi_\alpha(l\kappa)\, u_\alpha(l\kappa) + \sum_{n=3}^{\infty} \frac{1}{n!} \sum_{l_1\kappa_1\alpha_1} \cdots \sum_{l_n\kappa_n\alpha_n} \Phi_{\alpha_1\cdots\alpha_n}(l_1\kappa_1; \cdots; l_n\kappa_n)\, u_{\alpha_1}(l_1\kappa_1) \cdots u_{\alpha_n}(l_n\kappa_n). \tag{2.7c}$$

The hamiltonian H_0 is the vibrational hamiltonian in the *harmonic approximation*. The hamiltonian H_A is called the *anharmonic* part of the vibrational hamiltonian.

If a particular, analytic expression is assumed to describe the potential energy of interaction of two or more atoms (e.g., a central-force potential such as the Lennard–Jones or Morse potentials, or a potential from which angle-bending forces are derived), the atomic force constants of all orders are determined uniquely in terms of the parameters entering this expression. In this case little more need be said about the atomic force constants, except to relate them explicitly to the derivatives of the interatomic potential function. This will be done below for the case of two-body, central-force interactions.

More commonly, the atomic force constants are regarded as parameters of the theory, whose values are to be determined from a comparison of the predictions of the theory with experimental data. This comparison is greatly simplified if account is taken of the restrictions placed on the atomic force constants by general invariance conditions every crystal must obey. These conditions are of two types. The first type follow from the invariance and transformation properties of the potential energy of a crystal, and of its derivatives with respect to atomic displacements, when the crystal is subjected to a rigid body translation or rotation. These restrictions are valid for all collections of atoms whose potential energy is a function of their instantaneous positions, whether they are situated at the lattice sites of a crystal or not. The second type of restriction on the atom force constants is a consequence of the structure and symmetry of a particular crystal.

The importance of having such restrictions on the atomic force constants is that they ensure that the potential energy of a crystal be invariant against infinitesimal rigid body translations and rotations of the crystal, as it must be, since it is a scalar quantity; they ensure that a consistent set of atomic force constants is used in the theory of the dynamical properties of a given crystal; and finally, they ensure that there are no more parameters whose values must be obtained from experimental data than are absolutely necessary for a given crystal structure and symmetry.

The conditions imposed on the atomic force constants by the invariance of the potential energy and its derivatives against an infinitesimal rigid body displacement of the crystal are

$$\sum_{l\kappa} \Phi_\alpha(l\kappa) = 0, \tag{2.8a}$$

$$\sum_{l\kappa} \Phi_{\alpha\beta}(l\kappa; l'\kappa') = \sum_{l'\kappa'} \Phi_{\alpha\beta}(l\kappa; l'\kappa') = 0, \tag{2.8b}$$

$$\begin{aligned}\sum_{l\kappa} \Phi_{\alpha\beta\gamma}(l\kappa; l'\kappa'; l''\kappa'') &= \sum_{l'\kappa'} \Phi_{\alpha\beta\gamma}(l\kappa; l'\kappa'; l''\kappa'') \\ &= \sum_{l''\kappa''} \Phi_{\alpha\beta\gamma}(l\kappa; l'\kappa'; l''\kappa'') = 0, \quad \text{etc.}\end{aligned} \tag{2.8c}$$

The restrictions on the atomic force constants due to the invariance and transformation properties of the potential energy and its derivatives against an infinitesimal rigid body rotation of the crystals are (Leibfried and Ludwig 1961, section 2b)

$$\sum_{l\kappa} \Phi_\alpha(l\kappa)\, x_\beta(l\kappa) = \sum_{l\kappa} \Phi_\beta(l\kappa)\, x_\alpha(l\kappa), \tag{2.9a}$$

$$\begin{aligned}&\sum_{l'\kappa'} \Phi_{\alpha\beta}(l\kappa; l'\kappa')\, x_\gamma(l'\kappa') - \delta_{\alpha\beta}\, \Phi_\gamma(l\kappa) \\ &\qquad = \sum_{l'\kappa'} \Phi_{\alpha\gamma}(l\kappa; l'\kappa')\, x_\beta(l'\kappa') - \delta_{\alpha\gamma}\, \Phi_\beta(l\kappa),\end{aligned} \tag{2.9b}$$

$$\begin{aligned}&\sum_{l'\kappa'} \Phi_{\alpha\beta\gamma}(l\kappa; l'\kappa'; l''\kappa'')\, x_\delta(l''\kappa'') - \delta_{\alpha\gamma}\, \Phi_{\delta\beta}(l\kappa; l'\kappa') - \delta_{\beta\gamma}\, \Phi_{\alpha\delta}(l\kappa; l'\kappa') \\ &= \sum_{l'\kappa'} \Phi_{\alpha\beta\delta}(l\kappa; l'\kappa'; l''\kappa'')\, x_\gamma(l''\kappa'') - \delta_{\alpha\delta}\, \Phi_{\gamma\beta}(l\kappa; l'\kappa') - \delta_{\beta\delta}\, \Phi_{\alpha\gamma}(l\kappa; l'\kappa').\end{aligned} \tag{2.9c}$$

To discuss the restrictions placed on the atomic force constants by the symmetry and structure of a particular crystal we must first introduce some notation. The most general symmetry operation which sends a crystal into itself is a proper or improper rigid body rotation of the crystal about some point, often, but not necessarily, a lattice site, plus a rigid body translation of the crystal. We represent such a symmetry operation in the Seitz (1936) notation by $\{\boldsymbol{S}|\boldsymbol{v}(S)+\boldsymbol{x}(m)\}$. This operation transforms the position vector of the rest position of the κth atom in the lth primitive unit cell, $\boldsymbol{x}(l\kappa)$, according to

$$\{\boldsymbol{S} \mid \boldsymbol{v}(S) + \boldsymbol{x}(m)\}\, \boldsymbol{x}(l\kappa) = \boldsymbol{S}\boldsymbol{x}(l\kappa) + \boldsymbol{v}(S) + \boldsymbol{x}(m) = \boldsymbol{x}(LK), \tag{2.10}$$

which is to be interpreted in the active sense (Altmann and Cracknell 1965), i.e., as a rotation of the point $\boldsymbol{x}(l\kappa)$ with respect to a fixed coordinate system, and *not* as a rotation of the coordinate system with respect to a crystal fixed in space. The totality of the operations $\{\boldsymbol{S}|\boldsymbol{v}(S)+\boldsymbol{x}(m)\}$ for a given crystal comprises the *space group* of the crystal. $\boldsymbol{S}$ is a 3×3 real, orthogonal matrix representation of one of the proper or improper rotations of the point group of the space group, $\boldsymbol{v}(S)$ is a vector which is smaller than any of the primitive translation vectors of the crystal, and $\boldsymbol{x}(m)$ is a translation vector of the crystal. Nonzero values of the vector $\boldsymbol{v}(S)$ are associated with the symmetry elements called glide planes and screw axes. Space groups for which $\boldsymbol{v}(S)$ is zero for every rotation $\boldsymbol{S}$ of the point group of the space group are called *symmorphic*; all other space groups are called *nonsymmorphic*. The second equality in eq. (2.10) expresses the fact that because the operation $\{\boldsymbol{S}|\boldsymbol{v}(S)+ +\boldsymbol{x}(m)\}$ sends the crystal into itself, the lattice site $(l\kappa)$ must be sent into another lattice site, occupied by the same kind of atom, which we label by (LK). Here, and where no confusion results from its use, we adopt the convention of labeling by capital letters the site into which a given site, labeled by the corresponding lower case letters, is transformed by the operation $\{\boldsymbol{S}|\boldsymbol{v}(S)+\boldsymbol{x}(m)\}$.

The manner in which the atomic force constants transform when a crystal is subjected to an operation from its space group is given by the relations

$$\Phi_\alpha(LK) = \sum_\lambda S_{\alpha\lambda}\, \Phi_\lambda(l\kappa), \tag{2.11a}$$

$$\Phi_{\alpha\beta}(LK; L'K') = \sum_{\lambda\mu} S_{\alpha\lambda} S_{\beta\mu}\, \Phi_{\lambda\mu}(l\kappa; l'\kappa'), \tag{2.11b}$$

$$\Phi_{\alpha\beta\gamma}(LK; L'K'; L''K'') = \sum_{\lambda\mu\nu} S_{\alpha\lambda} S_{\beta\mu} S_{\gamma\nu}\, \Phi_{\lambda\mu\nu}(l\kappa; l'\kappa'; l''\kappa''), \text{ etc.} \tag{2.11c}$$

If the operations of the space group of the crystal are restricted to those of the subgroup which leaves the site $(l\kappa)$ invariant, i.e., to those of the point group the lattice site $(l\kappa)$, eq. (2.11a) can be used to obtain the independent, nonzero elements of the first order atomic force constant tensor $\Phi_\alpha(l\kappa)$. Similarly, if the operations of the space group are restricted to the subgroup which leaves the sites ($l\kappa$) and ($l'\kappa'$) invariant, or interchanges them, then eqs. (2.11b) and (2.6a) yield the independent, nonzero elements of the second order atomic force constant tensor $\Phi_{\alpha\beta}(l\kappa; l'\kappa')$. In the same way, the independent, nonzero elements of the higher order atomic force constant tensors can be obtained by combining eqs. (2.11) and (2.6).

Important special cases of eqs. (2.11) are obtained when we specialize the space group operation $\{\boldsymbol{S}|\boldsymbol{v}(S)+\boldsymbol{x}(m)\}$ to the operation $\{\boldsymbol{E}|\boldsymbol{x}(m)\}$ describing a rigid body displacement of the crystal through the lattice translation vector $\boldsymbol{x}(m)$. Here $\boldsymbol{E}$ is the 3×3 unit matrix. The effect of this translation is to send the lattice site ($l\kappa$) into the site $(LK)=(l+m\,\kappa)$. Equations (2.11) in this case become

$$\Phi_{\alpha}(l+m\,\kappa) = \Phi_{\alpha}(l\kappa), \tag{2.12a}$$

$$\Phi_{\alpha\beta}(l+m\,\kappa;\, l'+m\,\kappa') = \Phi_{\alpha\beta}(l\kappa;\, l'\kappa'), \tag{2.12b}$$

$$\Phi_{\alpha\beta\gamma}(l+m\,\kappa;\, l'+m\,\kappa';\, l''+m\,\kappa'') = \Phi_{\alpha\beta\gamma}(l\kappa;\, l'\kappa';\, l''\kappa''), \text{ etc.} \tag{2.12c}$$

By setting $m=-l$ in eq. (2.12a) we see that the first order atomic force constant $\Phi_{\alpha}(l\kappa)$ is independent of the cell index l; by setting $m=-l$ and $m=-l'$ in turn in eq. (2.12b) we see that the second order atomic force constant $\Phi_{\alpha\beta}(l\kappa; l'\kappa')$ depends on the cell indices l and l' only through their difference; by setting $m=-l$, $m=-l'$, and $m=-l''$ in turn in eq. (2.12c) we find that the third order atomic force constant $\Phi_{\alpha\beta\gamma}(l\kappa; l'\kappa'; l''\kappa'')$ depends on the cell indices l, l', l'' only through any two of the differences $l'-l$, $l''-l$, $l''-l'$; and so on.

An important special case of interatomic potentials is the so-called central force potential, which describes the interactions of atoms pairwise through a potential function which is a function only of the magnitude of their separation. If the potential function for the interaction of an atom of type κ with an atom of type κ' at a distance r from it is denoted by $\varphi_{\kappa\kappa'}(r)=\varphi_{\kappa'\kappa}(r)$, the potential energy of the crystal can be written as

$$\Phi = \tfrac{1}{2}\sum_{l\kappa}\sum_{l'\kappa'}{}' \varphi_{\kappa\kappa'}(|\boldsymbol{x}(l\kappa;\, l'\kappa') + \boldsymbol{u}(l\kappa;\, l'\kappa')|), \tag{2.13}$$

where we have introduced the notation

$$\boldsymbol{x}(l\kappa;\, l'\kappa') = \boldsymbol{x}(l\kappa) - \boldsymbol{x}(l'\kappa'), \qquad \boldsymbol{u}(l\kappa;\, l'\kappa') = \boldsymbol{u}(l\kappa) - \boldsymbol{u}(l'\kappa'). \tag{2.14a, b}$$

The factor of $\frac{1}{2}$ on the right hand side of eq. (2.13) compensates for the fact that each interaction is counted twice in the sum, and the prime excludes the terms with $(l\kappa)=(l'\kappa')$.

The potential energy expression (2.13) is most naturally expanded in powers of the components of $\boldsymbol{u}(l\kappa; l'\kappa')$:

$$\begin{aligned}\Phi = {} & \tfrac{1}{2}\sum_{l\kappa}\sum_{l'\kappa'}{}' \varphi_{\kappa\kappa'}(|\boldsymbol{x}(l\kappa; l'\kappa')|) \\ & + \tfrac{1}{2}\sum_{l\kappa}\sum_{l'\kappa'}{}'\sum_{\alpha} \varphi_{\alpha}(l\kappa; l'\kappa')\, u_{\alpha}(l\kappa; l'\kappa') \\ & + \tfrac{1}{4}\sum_{l\kappa}\sum_{l'\kappa'}{}'\sum_{\alpha\beta} \varphi_{\alpha\beta}(l\kappa; l'\kappa')\, u_{\alpha}(l\kappa; l'\kappa')\, u_{\beta}(l\kappa; l'\kappa') \\ & + \tfrac{1}{12}\sum_{l\kappa}\sum_{l'\kappa'}{}'\sum_{\alpha\beta\gamma} \varphi_{\alpha\beta\gamma}(l\kappa; l'\kappa')\, u_{\alpha}(l\kappa; l'\kappa')\, u_{\beta}(l\kappa; l'\kappa')\, u_{\gamma}(l\kappa; l'\kappa') + \cdots,\end{aligned} \tag{2.15}$$

where

$$\varphi_{\alpha}(l\kappa; l'\kappa') = \frac{\partial}{\partial x_{\alpha}} \varphi_{\kappa\kappa'}(r)\bigg|_{\boldsymbol{r}=\boldsymbol{x}(l\kappa; l'\kappa')} = \frac{x_{\alpha}}{r} \varphi'_{\kappa\kappa'}(r)\bigg|_{\boldsymbol{r}=\boldsymbol{x}(l\kappa; l'\kappa')}, \tag{2.16a}$$

$$\begin{aligned}\varphi_{\alpha\beta}(l\kappa; l'\kappa') &= \frac{\partial^2}{\partial x_{\alpha}\partial x_{\beta}} \varphi_{\kappa\kappa'}(r)\bigg|_{\boldsymbol{r}=\boldsymbol{x}(l\kappa; l'\kappa')} \\ &= \left\{\frac{x_{\alpha}x_{\beta}}{r^2}\left[\varphi''_{\kappa\kappa'}(r) - \frac{1}{r}\varphi'_{\kappa\kappa'}(r)\right] + \frac{\delta_{\alpha\beta}}{r}\varphi'_{\kappa\kappa'}(r)\right\}\bigg|_{\boldsymbol{r}=\boldsymbol{x}(l\kappa; l'\kappa')},\end{aligned} \tag{2.16b}$$

$$\begin{aligned}\varphi_{\alpha\beta\gamma}(l\kappa; l'\kappa') &= \frac{\partial^3}{\partial x_{\alpha}\partial x_{\beta}\partial x_{\gamma}} \varphi_{\kappa\kappa'}(r)\bigg|_{\boldsymbol{r}=\boldsymbol{x}(l\kappa; l'\kappa')} \\ &= \left\{\frac{x_{\alpha}x_{\beta}x_{\gamma}}{r^3}\left[\varphi'''_{\kappa\kappa'}(r) - \frac{3\varphi''_{\kappa\kappa'}(r)}{r} + \frac{3\varphi'_{\kappa\kappa'}(r)}{r^2}\right]\right. \\ &\quad \left. + \frac{x_{\alpha}\delta_{\beta\gamma} + x_{\beta}\delta_{\gamma\alpha} + x_{\gamma}\delta_{\alpha\beta}}{r^2}\left[\varphi''_{\kappa\kappa'}(r) - \frac{1}{r}\varphi'_{\kappa\kappa'}(r)\right]\right\}\bigg|_{\boldsymbol{r}=\boldsymbol{x}(l\kappa; l'\kappa')},\end{aligned} \tag{2.16c}$$

$$\begin{aligned}\varphi_{\alpha\beta\gamma\delta}(l\kappa; l'\kappa') &= \frac{\partial^4}{\partial x_{\alpha}\partial x_{\beta}\partial x_{\gamma}\partial x_{\delta}} \varphi_{\kappa\kappa'}(r)\bigg|_{\boldsymbol{r}=\boldsymbol{x}(l\kappa; l'\kappa')} \\ = & \left\{\frac{x_{\alpha}x_{\beta}x_{\gamma}x_{\delta}}{r^4}\left[\varphi^{iv}_{\kappa\kappa'}(r) - \frac{6\varphi'''_{\kappa\kappa'}(r)}{r} + \frac{15\varphi''_{\kappa\kappa'}(r)}{r^2} - \frac{15\varphi'_{\kappa\kappa'}(r)}{r^3}\right]\right. \\ & + (x_{\alpha}x_{\beta}\delta_{\gamma\delta} + x_{\alpha}x_{\gamma}\delta_{\beta\delta} + x_{\alpha}x_{\delta}\delta_{\beta\gamma} + x_{\beta}x_{\gamma}\delta_{\alpha\delta} + x_{\beta}x_{\delta}\delta_{\alpha\gamma} + x_{\gamma}x_{\delta}\delta_{\alpha\beta}) \\ \times & \frac{1}{r^3}\left[\varphi'''_{\kappa\kappa'}(r) - \frac{3\varphi''_{\kappa\kappa'}(r)}{r} + \frac{3\varphi'_{\kappa\kappa'}(r)}{r^2}\right] + [\delta_{\alpha\beta}\delta_{\gamma\delta} + \delta_{\alpha\gamma}\delta_{\beta\delta} + \delta_{\alpha\delta}\delta_{\beta\gamma}] \\ & \left.\times \frac{1}{r^2}\left[\varphi''_{\kappa\kappa'}(r) - \frac{1}{r}\varphi'_{\kappa\kappa'}(r)\right]\right\}\bigg|_{\boldsymbol{r}=\boldsymbol{x}(l\kappa; l'\kappa')}.\end{aligned} \tag{2.16d}$$

For many purposes, for example for rewriting the vibrational hamiltonian in terms of normal coordinates, the results given by eqs. (2.14)–(2.16) suffice. However, if it is desired to have expressions for the atomic force constants $\Phi_\alpha(l\kappa)$, $\Phi_{\alpha\beta}(l\kappa; l'\kappa'), \cdots$, in terms of the potential derivatives $\varphi_\alpha(l\kappa; l'\kappa')$, $\varphi_{\alpha\beta}(l\kappa; l'\kappa'), \cdots$, from a comparison of eqs. (2.4) and (2.15) we obtain the following relations for the independent atomic force constants:

$$\Phi_\alpha(l\kappa) = \sum_{l'\kappa'}{}' \varphi_\alpha(l\kappa; l'\kappa'), \tag{2.17a}$$

$$\Phi_{\alpha\beta}(l\kappa; l'\kappa') = -\varphi_{\alpha\beta}(l\kappa; l'\kappa') \quad (l\kappa) \neq (l'\kappa'), \tag{2.18a}$$

$$\Phi_{\alpha\beta}(l\kappa; l\kappa) = \sum_{l'\kappa'}{}' \varphi_{\alpha\beta}(l\kappa; l'\kappa'), \tag{2.18b}$$

$$\Phi_{\alpha\beta\gamma}(l\kappa; l\kappa; l'\kappa') = -\varphi_{\alpha\beta\gamma}(l\kappa; l'\kappa') \quad (l\kappa) \neq (l'\kappa'), \tag{2.19a}$$

$$\Phi_{\alpha\beta\gamma}(l\kappa; l\kappa; l\kappa) = \sum_{l'\kappa'}{}' \varphi_{\alpha\beta\gamma}(l\kappa; l'\kappa'), \tag{2.19b}$$

$$\Phi_{\alpha\beta\gamma\delta}(l\kappa; l\kappa; l\kappa; l'\kappa') = -\varphi_{\alpha\beta\gamma\delta}(l\kappa; l'\kappa') \quad (l\kappa) \neq (l'\kappa'), \tag{2.20a}$$

$$\Phi_{\alpha\beta\gamma\delta}(l\kappa; l\kappa; l'\kappa'; l'\kappa') = \varphi_{\alpha\beta\gamma\delta}(l\kappa; l'\kappa') \quad (l\kappa) \neq (l'\kappa'), \tag{2.20b}$$

$$\Phi_{\alpha\beta\gamma\delta}(l\kappa; l\kappa; l\kappa; l\kappa) = \sum_{l'\kappa'}{}' \varphi_{\alpha\beta\gamma\delta}(l\kappa; l'\kappa'). \tag{2.20c}$$

All of the general invariance conditions which must be satisfied by the atomic force constants are automatically satisfied by the expressions given by eqs. (2.17)–(2.20).

3. *The equations of motion and their solution*

Because the equations of motion of the atoms in a crystal in the harmonic approximation are exactly solvable, and because in many crystals the anharmonic terms in the crystal potential energy are small and can be treated as a perturbation of the harmonic hamiltonian, in this section we study the equations of motion of a crystal in the harmonic approximation.

From the hamiltonian (2.7b) and Hamilton's equations of motion

$$\dot{u}_\alpha(l\kappa) = \partial H_0/\partial p_\alpha(l\kappa) = p_\alpha(l\kappa)/M_\kappa, \tag{3.1a}$$

$$\dot{p}_\alpha(l\kappa) = -\partial H_0/\partial u_\alpha(l\kappa) = -\sum_{l'\kappa'\beta} \Phi_{\alpha\beta}(l\kappa; l'\kappa')\, u_\beta(l'\kappa'), \tag{3.1b}$$

we obtain the equations of motion of a crystal

$$M_\kappa \ddot{u}_\alpha(l\kappa) = -\sum_{l'\kappa'\beta} \Phi_{\alpha\beta}(l\kappa; l'\kappa')\, u_\beta(l'\kappa'). \tag{3.2}$$

We choose as a solution of this set of coupled equations

$$u_\alpha(l\kappa) = M_\kappa^{-1/2} e_\alpha(\kappa)\, \mathrm{e}^{\mathrm{i}\boldsymbol{k}\cdot\boldsymbol{x}(l) - i\omega t}. \tag{3.3}$$

This choice is dictated by the fact that because the atomic force constants $\{\Phi_{\alpha\beta}(l\kappa; l'\kappa')\}$ are invariant against a rigid body translation of the crystal through a lattice translation vector, according to eq. (2.12b), i.e., because the operation of displacement through a lattice translation vector commutes with the atomic force constant matrix, the atomic displacements $u_\alpha(l\kappa)$ must simultaneously be eigenfunctions of the translation operator and of the force constant matrix. The solution (3.3) has the former property, and the coefficient $e_\alpha(\kappa)$ and the frequency ω will be determined by requiring that it possess the latter property as well.

The coefficient function $e_\alpha(\kappa)$ is independent of the cell index l, and satisfies the equation

$$\omega^2 e_\alpha(\kappa) = \sum_{\kappa'\beta} D_{\alpha\beta}(\kappa\kappa' \,|\, \boldsymbol{k})\, e_\beta(\kappa'), \tag{3.4}$$

where

$$D_{\alpha\beta}(\kappa\kappa' \,|\, \boldsymbol{k}) = (M_\kappa M_{\kappa'})^{-1/2} \sum_{l'} \Phi_{\alpha\beta}(l\kappa; l'\kappa')\, \mathrm{e}^{-\mathrm{i}\boldsymbol{k}\cdot[\boldsymbol{x}(l) - \boldsymbol{x}(l')]}. \tag{3.5}$$

Thus the periodicity of the lattice as expressed by eq. (2.12b) enables us to reduce the infinite set of equations of motion (3.2) to the problem of solving a set of $3r$ equations in the $3r$ unknowns, the $e_\alpha(\kappa)$.

The content of eq. (3.4) is that the displacement $u_\alpha(l\kappa)$ given by eq. (3.3) is a solution of the equations of motion (3.2) provided the frequency of the motion ω is not independent of the *wave vector* $\boldsymbol{k}$, but is related to it through the eigenvalue equation (3.4).

The matrix $D_{\alpha\beta}(\kappa\kappa' | \boldsymbol{k})$ defined by eq. (3.5) is called the *dynamical matrix* of the crystal. It is a $3r \times 3r$ hermitian matrix,

$$D_{\alpha\beta}(\kappa\kappa' \,|\, \boldsymbol{k}) = D^*_{\beta\alpha}(\kappa'\kappa \,|\, \boldsymbol{k}) \tag{3.6}$$

and has the further property that

$$D_{\alpha\beta}(\kappa\kappa' \,|\, -\boldsymbol{k}) = D^*_{\alpha\beta}(\kappa\kappa' \,|\, \boldsymbol{k}). \tag{3.7}$$

We see from eq. (3.4) that the allowed values of the square of the frequency ω for a given value of $\boldsymbol{k}$ are the eigenvalues of the dynamical matrix. Because the latter is a $3r \times 3r$ matrix there are $3r$ solutions for ω^2 for each value of $\boldsymbol{k}$, and these will be denoted by $\omega_j^2(\boldsymbol{k})$, where $j = 1, 2, \cdots, 3r$. The $3r$ functions

$\omega_j^2(\boldsymbol{k})$ for each value of $\boldsymbol{k}$ can be regarded as the branches of a multivalued function $\omega^2(\boldsymbol{k})$.

From the hermiticity of the matrix $D_{\alpha\beta}(\kappa\kappa'|\boldsymbol{k})$ it follows that $\omega_j^2(\boldsymbol{k})$ is real. In order that the crystal be stable in the harmonic approximation $\omega_j(\boldsymbol{k})$ must also be real, since from eq. (3.3) it is seen that an imaginary frequency corresponds to atomic motions whose amplitudes erupt exponentially with time either into the past or into the future. Thus, stability requires that $\omega_j^2(\boldsymbol{k})$ not only be real, but that it also be positive. In the remainder of this chapter we will assume that the atomic force constants are such as to ensure this.

For each of the $3r$ values of $\omega_j^2(\boldsymbol{k})$ corresponding to a given value of $\boldsymbol{k}$ there exists a $3r$ component vector $e_\alpha(\kappa)$, whose components are the solutions to the set of equations (3.4). To make explicit the dependence of this vector on the value of $\boldsymbol{k}$ chosen, and its association with the particular branch j, we rewrite it as $e_\alpha(\kappa|\boldsymbol{k}j)$, and rewrite the equation (3.4) determining it as

$$\omega_j^2(\boldsymbol{k})\, e_\alpha(\kappa|\boldsymbol{k}j) = \sum_{\kappa'\beta} D_{\alpha\beta}(\kappa\kappa'|\boldsymbol{k})\, e_\beta(\kappa'|\boldsymbol{k}j). \tag{3.8}$$

If we replace $\boldsymbol{k}$ by $-\boldsymbol{k}$ in eq. (3.8) and take the complex conjugate of the resulting equation, then with the aid of eq. (3.7) we find that $\omega_j^2(-\boldsymbol{k})$ is an eigenvalue of $D_{\alpha\beta}(\kappa\kappa'|\boldsymbol{k})$, and that the corresponding eigenvector is $e_\alpha^*(\kappa|-\boldsymbol{k}j)$. With no loss of generality we can assume that

$$\omega_j(-\boldsymbol{k}) = \omega_j(\boldsymbol{k}), \qquad e_\alpha^*(\kappa|-\boldsymbol{k}j) = e_\alpha(\kappa|\boldsymbol{k}j). \tag{3.9, 10}$$

We do so in what follows.

Because $D_{\alpha\beta}(\kappa\kappa'|\boldsymbol{k})$ is hermitian, and because eq. (3.8) defines $e_\alpha(\kappa|\boldsymbol{k}j)$ only to within an arbitrary multiplicative constant, we can assume that the eigenvectors $e_\alpha(\kappa|\boldsymbol{k}j)$ satisfy the orthonormality and closure conditions

$$\sum_{\kappa\alpha} e_\alpha^*(\kappa|\boldsymbol{k}j)\, e_\alpha(\kappa|\boldsymbol{k}j') = \delta_{jj'}, \qquad \sum_j e_\alpha^*(\kappa|\boldsymbol{k}j)\, e_\beta(\kappa'|\boldsymbol{k}j) = \delta_{\kappa\kappa'}\delta_{\alpha\beta}. \tag{3.11a, b}$$

The conditions (2.8b) on the atomic force constants, which have their origins in the invariance of the force on an atom, and its derivatives, in the rest configuration against an infinitesimal rigid body translation of the crystal, has the consequence that the frequencies of three branches of $\omega(\boldsymbol{k})$ ($j=1, 2, 3$) vanish with vanishing $\boldsymbol{k}$ and the corresponding eigenvectors have the property that $e_\alpha(\kappa|\boldsymbol{0}j)/M_\kappa^{1/2}$ is independent of κ. These three branches are called *acoustic* branches, because in the long wavelength limit they give the frequencies of sound waves propagating through the crystal. The remaining $3r-3$ branches, whose frequencies approach nonzero values as $\boldsymbol{k}$ tends to zero, are called *optical* branches, because it is these branches, in the limit $\boldsymbol{k} \approx 0$, which are observed in infrared absorption and light scattering experiments.

The displacement pattern obtained by substituting into eq. (3.3) a particular eigenvector $e_\alpha(\kappa|\boldsymbol{k}j)$ and the corresponding frequency $\omega_j(\boldsymbol{k})$,

$$u_\alpha(l\kappa) = M_\kappa^{-1/2} e_\alpha(\kappa|\boldsymbol{k}j) \exp[\mathrm{i}\boldsymbol{k}\cdot\boldsymbol{x}(l) - \mathrm{i}\omega_j(\boldsymbol{k})\,t],$$

is called a *normal mode* of the crystal described by the wave vector $\boldsymbol{k}$ and branch index j. It is a solution of eq. (3.3) and is independent of (is uncoupled from) all other normal modes $(\boldsymbol{k}'j') \neq (\boldsymbol{k}j)$.

For certain applications it is convenient to work with the modified dynamical matrix

$$\begin{aligned} C_{\alpha\beta}(\kappa\kappa'|\boldsymbol{k}) &= \mathrm{e}^{-\mathrm{i}\boldsymbol{k}\cdot\boldsymbol{x}(\kappa)}\, D_{\alpha\beta}(\kappa\kappa'|\boldsymbol{k})\, \mathrm{e}^{\mathrm{i}\boldsymbol{k}\cdot\boldsymbol{x}(\kappa')} \\ &= (M_\kappa M_{\kappa'})^{-1/2} \sum_{l'} \Phi_{\alpha\beta}(l\kappa; l'\kappa')\, \mathrm{e}^{-\mathrm{i}\boldsymbol{k}\cdot[\boldsymbol{x}(l\kappa) - \boldsymbol{x}(l'\kappa')]}. \end{aligned} \tag{3.12}$$

The corresponding eigenvectors, which we denote by $\{w_\alpha(\kappa|\boldsymbol{k}j)\}$ are given by

$$w_\alpha(\kappa|\boldsymbol{k}j) = \mathrm{e}^{-\mathrm{i}\boldsymbol{k}\cdot\boldsymbol{x}(\kappa)}\, e_\alpha(\kappa|\boldsymbol{k}j) = w_\alpha^*(\kappa|-\boldsymbol{k}j). \tag{3.13}$$

The equation determining these eigenvectors is

$$\omega_j^2(\boldsymbol{k})\, w_\alpha(\kappa|\boldsymbol{k}j) = \sum_{\kappa'\beta} C_{\alpha\beta}(\kappa\kappa'|\boldsymbol{k})\, w_\beta(\kappa'|\boldsymbol{k}j). \tag{3.14}$$

The eigenvalues $\{\omega_j^2(\boldsymbol{k})\}$ of the matrices $D(\boldsymbol{k})$ and $C(\boldsymbol{k})$ are the same, because these matrices are related by a unitary transformation. From eqs. (3.11) and (3.13) we find that the eigenvectors satisfy the orthonormality and closure conditions.

$$\sum_{\kappa\alpha} w_\alpha^*(\kappa|\boldsymbol{k}j)\, w_\alpha(\kappa|\boldsymbol{k}j') = \delta_{jj'}, \tag{3.15a}$$

$$\sum_{j} w_\alpha^*(\kappa|\boldsymbol{k}j)\, w_\beta(\kappa'|\boldsymbol{k}j) = \delta_{\kappa\kappa'}\delta_{\alpha\beta}. \tag{3.15b}$$

To define completely the problem of determining the dynamical properties of a crystal, we must specify the values the wave vector $\boldsymbol{k}$ is allowed to take. It is clear that they are determined by the boundary conditions imposed on the components of the atomic displacement vectors $\{\boldsymbol{u}(l\kappa)\}$.

Because of the simplicity they impart to the dynamical theory of crystals, the boundary conditions adopted in virtually all lattice dynamical calculations not specifically concerned with surface effects are the *cyclic boundary conditions* of Born and von Karman (1912). These boundary conditions can be introduced in the following way.

We consider an infinitely extended crystal which is subdivided into 'macrocrystals,' each of which contains $L \times L \times L = N$ primitive unit cells. These macrocrystals fill all space without gaps or overlap, and are parallelepipeds whose edges are defined by the vectors $L\boldsymbol{a}_1$, $L\boldsymbol{a}_2$, $L\boldsymbol{a}_3$. Any one of these macrocrystals can be regarded as the physical crystal whose vibrational properties are being studied. The cyclic boundary conditions postulate that the atomic displacements be periodic with the periodicity of the macrocrystals, that is, that

$$\boldsymbol{u}(l_1 l_2 l_3 \kappa) = \boldsymbol{u}(l_1 + n_1 L, l_2 + n_2 L, l_3 + n_3 L \kappa), \tag{3.16}$$

where n_1, n_2, n_3 are any three integers, which can be positive, negative, or zero.

Applied to the components of the displacement vector given by eq. (3.3) the cyclic boundary conditions require that

$$e^{i\boldsymbol{k}\cdot n_1 L\boldsymbol{a}_1} = e^{i\boldsymbol{k}\cdot n_2 L\boldsymbol{a}_2} = e^{i\boldsymbol{k}\cdot n_3 L\boldsymbol{a}_3} = 1. \tag{3.17}$$

The values of the wave vector $\boldsymbol{k}$ allowed by these conditions can be expressed very conveniently in the following way. We define three, noncoplanar vectors $\boldsymbol{b}_1$, $\boldsymbol{b}_2$, $\boldsymbol{b}_3$ by the equations

$$\boldsymbol{a}_i \cdot \boldsymbol{b}_j = 2\pi\delta_{ij}. \tag{3.18}$$

The solutions of these equations can be written

$$\boldsymbol{b}_1 = 2\pi \frac{\boldsymbol{a}_2 \times \boldsymbol{a}_3}{v_a}, \quad \boldsymbol{b}_2 = 2\pi \frac{\boldsymbol{a}_3 \times \boldsymbol{a}_1}{v_a}, \quad \boldsymbol{b}_3 = 2\pi \frac{\boldsymbol{a}_1 \times \boldsymbol{a}_2}{v_a}, \tag{3.19a, b, c}$$

where

$$v_a = |\boldsymbol{a}_1 \cdot \boldsymbol{a}_2 \times \boldsymbol{a}_3| \tag{3.19d}$$

is the volume of a primitive unit cell of the crystal. The points whose positions are given by the vectors

$$\boldsymbol{G}(h) = h_1 \boldsymbol{b}_1 + h_2 \boldsymbol{b}_2 + h_3 \boldsymbol{b}_3, \tag{3.20}$$

where h_1, h_2, h_3 are any three integers, which can be positive, negative, or zero, and to which we refer collectively as h, define a lattice called the *reciprocal lattice* of the direct lattice whose primitive translation vectors are $\boldsymbol{a}_1$, $\boldsymbol{a}_2$, $\boldsymbol{a}_3$. In view of eq. (3.18) the scalar product of a direct lattice vector and a reciprocal lattice vector is

$$\boldsymbol{x}(l)\cdot\boldsymbol{G}(h) = 2\pi\,(l_1h_1 + l_2h_2 + l_3h_3) = 2\pi\,(\text{integer}). \tag{3.21}$$

It follows that an expression for $\boldsymbol{k}$ which satisfies eq. (3.17) is given by

$$\boldsymbol{k} = (1/L)\,\boldsymbol{G}(h) = (h_1/L)\,\boldsymbol{b}_1 + (h_2/L)\,\boldsymbol{b}_2 + (h_3/L)\,\boldsymbol{b}_3\,. \tag{3.22}$$

The values the integers h_1, h_2, h_3 can assume are not unrestricted, however. From eqs. (3.3) and (3.21) we see that if we add to $\boldsymbol{k}$ any translation vector of the reciprocal lattice, the value of $u_\alpha(l\kappa)$ is unaffected. This means that all of the distinct solutions of the equations of motion of a crystal, satisfying cyclic boundary conditions, are obtained if we restrict the values of the wave vector $\boldsymbol{k}$ to lie in one primitive unit cell of the reciprocal lattice:

$$\boldsymbol{k} = (h_1/L)\,\boldsymbol{b}_1 + (h_2/L)\,\boldsymbol{b}_2 + (h_3/L)\,\boldsymbol{b}_3\,,\quad h_1, h_2, h_3 = 1, 2, \cdots, L. \tag{3.23}$$

Thus there are $L^3 = N$ values of $\boldsymbol{k}$ allowed by the cyclic boundary conditions. Since there are $3r$ frequencies $\{\omega_j(\boldsymbol{k})\}$ and eigenvectors $\{e_\alpha(\kappa|\boldsymbol{k}j)\}$ for each value of $\boldsymbol{k}$, this means that there are $3rN$ modes of vibration for the crystal, which exactly equals the total number of degrees of freedom it possesses.

Instead of restricting the allowed values of $\boldsymbol{k}$ to lie inside a primitive unit cell of the reciprocal lattice, it is usually more convenient to restrict them to lie inside the first Brillouin zone of the Bravais lattice for the crystal. This region is obtained by drawing vectors from the origin of the reciprocal lattice to all lattice points, and then constructing the planes which are the perpendicular bisectors of these vectors. The smallest volume containing the origin which is enclosed by these planes is the first Brillouin zone. Its volume is equal to that of a primitive unit cell of the reciprocal lattice, and it is equivalent to the latter in that every allowed value of $\boldsymbol{k}$ in a primitive unit cell of the reciprocal lattice differs from a corresponding point in the first Brillouin zone only by a translation vector of the reciprocal lattice. The usefulness of the first Brillouin zone stems from the fact that it is invariant under the operations of the point group of the crystal (the point group of the space group of the crystal), which is also the point group of the reciprocal lattice. Consequently, if we take a general vector $\boldsymbol{k}$ in this zone, and apply all h operations of the point group of the crystal to it in turn, the h distinct vectors $\boldsymbol{Sk}$ generated in this way all lie inside the first Brillouin zone. This would not be the case if a less symmetric unit cell of the reciprocal lattice were chosen. (A general vector $\boldsymbol{k}$ in the first Brillouin zone is one for which $\boldsymbol{Sk} \neq \boldsymbol{k}$ for all

$h-1$ operations $\boldsymbol{S}\neq\boldsymbol{E}$ of the point group of the crystal.) As a result, one can define a region of the first Brillouin zone, called the irreducible element, whose volume is $1/h$ that of the first Brillouin zone, which has the property that the application of any of the $h-1$ operations $\boldsymbol{S}\neq\boldsymbol{E}$ of the point group of the crystal to any wave vector $\boldsymbol{k}$ inside the irreducible element yields a $\boldsymbol{k}$ vector outside it, but still inside the first Brillouin zone. Since the frequencies $\{\omega_j(\boldsymbol{k})\}$ can be shown to possess the point symmetry of the crystal (Maradudin and Vosko 1968),

$$\omega_j(\boldsymbol{S}\boldsymbol{k}) = \omega_j(\boldsymbol{k}), \tag{3.24}$$

values of $\omega_j(\boldsymbol{k})$ for all $\boldsymbol{k}$ in the first Brillouin zone can be obtained by solving eq. (3.8) for values of $\boldsymbol{k}$ in only the irreducible element of the first zone.

It is often the case that the precise values of the wave vector $\boldsymbol{k}$ allowed by the cyclic boundary conditions are not important. What is important is that they are uniformly and densely distributed throughout the first Brillouin zone, with a density equal to L^3/v, where v is the volume of a primitive unit cell of the reciprocal lattice. This fact allows the replacement of summation over the allowed values of $\boldsymbol{k}$ by integration over the first Brillouin zone, according to

$$\sum_{\boldsymbol{k}} \rightarrow \frac{L^3}{v} \int_{\mathrm{BZ}} \mathrm{d}^3k = \frac{\Omega}{(2\pi)^3} \int_{\mathrm{BZ}} \mathrm{d}^3k, \tag{3.25}$$

where $\Omega = Nv_a$ is the volume of the crystal, and we have used the fact that the volume of a primitive unit cell of the reciprocal lattice is $v = (2\pi)^3/v_a$.

The chief simplification introduced into the theory of lattice dynamics by the adoption of the cyclic boundary conditions on the atomic displacements is that the equations of motion of any atom are the same as for any other equivalent atom. No corrections to the equations of motion for atoms in the surface of a crystal need be made to account for the smaller number of nearest, next nearest, ..., neighbors they possess compared with atoms in the bulk, or for changes in the atomic force constants in the surface layers from their values in the bulk.

The question now arises of whether the imposition of special boundary conditions changes the distribution of the vibration frequencies of a crystal in the limit as N becomes very large. This question was answered in the negative by Ledermann (1944), who showed that provided the atoms in a crystal interact through forces of finite range, the fractional change in the number of normal modes with frequencies in a given frequency interval is of $O(L^{-1})$, in changing from one boundary condition on the atomic displacements to another. This change is negligible in the limit of large L. The use of the cyclic boundary conditions is not justified by Ledermann's result in the case of ionic crystals, in which each ion interacts with all other ions in the crystal by means of the long range Coulomb interaction. However, it has been shown by Hardy (1962) that the use of the cyclic boundary conditions in the presence of Coulomb interactions between ions affects only those optical modes whose wavelengths are comparable with the linear dimensions of the crystal. The number of such modes is of the order of L^2, so that the fractional error introduced into the calculation of the number of modes with frequencies in a given frequency interval is again of the order of L^{-1}, which is negligible when L is large.

By the introduction of the cyclic boundary conditions, our initially infinite crystal has been replaced by a space filling assembly of macrocrystals, each of which contains N primitive unit cells, and can be regarded as the crystal whose dynamical properties are being studied. In this way extensive properties of a crystal can be normalized to a finite volume.

4. Normal coordinate transformations

Because the vibrational hamiltonian in the harmonic approximation, eq. (2.7b), is the sum of two positive definite quadratic forms, one in the components of the momenta and the other in the components of the atomic displacements, it follows from a theorem of matrix algebra (Gantmacher 1959) that it is possible to find a principal axis, or normal coordinate, transformation which simultaneously diagonalizes the kinetic and potential energy terms in this hamiltonian.

Such a principal axis transformation is generated by the following expansions of $u_\alpha(l\kappa)$ and $p_\alpha(l\kappa)$ in terms of plane waves

$$u_\alpha(l\kappa) = (\hbar/2NM_\kappa)^{1/2} \sum_{\boldsymbol{k}j} \omega_j^{-1/2}(\boldsymbol{k})\, e_\alpha(\kappa\,|\,\boldsymbol{k}_j)\, \mathrm{e}^{\mathrm{i}\boldsymbol{k}\cdot\boldsymbol{x}(l)}(b_{\boldsymbol{k}j} + b^+_{-\boldsymbol{k}j}), \tag{4.1a}$$

$$p_\alpha(l\kappa) = \mathrm{i}^{-1}\,(\hbar M_\kappa/2N)^{1/2} \sum_{\boldsymbol{k}j} \omega_j^{1/2}(\boldsymbol{k})\, e_\alpha(\kappa\,|\,\boldsymbol{k}j)\, \mathrm{e}^{\mathrm{i}\boldsymbol{k}\cdot\boldsymbol{x}(l)}(b_{\boldsymbol{k}j} - b^+_{-\boldsymbol{k}j}), \tag{4.1b}$$

where the summation on $\boldsymbol{k}$ is over the values of the wave vector in the first Brillouin zone allowed by the cyclic boundary conditions. From the inverses to these expansions,

$$b_{\boldsymbol{k}j} = (2N\hbar)^{-1/2} \sum_{l\kappa\alpha} e_\alpha^*(\kappa \mid \boldsymbol{k}j)\, \mathrm{e}^{-\mathrm{i}\boldsymbol{k}\cdot\boldsymbol{x}(l)} \times \{[M_\kappa\omega_j(\boldsymbol{k})]^{1/2}\, u_\alpha(l\kappa) + \mathrm{i}\,[M_\kappa\omega_j(\boldsymbol{k})]^{-1/2}\, p_\alpha(l\kappa)\}, \tag{4.2a}$$

$$b_{\boldsymbol{k}j}^+ = (2N\hbar)^{-1/2} \sum_{l\kappa\alpha} e_\alpha(\kappa \mid \boldsymbol{k}j)\, \mathrm{e}^{\mathrm{i}\boldsymbol{k}\cdot\boldsymbol{x}(l)} \times \{[M_\kappa\omega_j(\boldsymbol{k})]^{1/2}\, u_\alpha(l\kappa) - \mathrm{i}\,[M_\kappa\omega_j(\boldsymbol{k})]^{-1/2}\, p_\alpha(l\kappa)\}, \tag{4.2b}$$

and the commutation relations for the $\{u_\alpha(l\kappa)\}$ and the $\{p_\alpha(l\kappa)\}$,

$$\begin{aligned} &[u_\alpha(l\kappa), u_\beta(l'\kappa')] = [p_\alpha(l\kappa), p_\beta(l'\kappa')] = 0, \\ &[u_\alpha(l\kappa), p_\beta(l'\kappa')] = \mathrm{i}\hbar\delta_{ll'}\delta_{\kappa\kappa'}\delta_{\alpha\beta}, \end{aligned} \tag{4.3}$$

we find that the new operators $b_{\boldsymbol{k}j}$ and $b_{\boldsymbol{k}j}^+$ obey the commutation relations

$$[b_{\boldsymbol{k}j}, b_{\boldsymbol{k}'j'}] = [b_{\boldsymbol{k}j}^+, b_{\boldsymbol{k}'j'}^+] = 0, \qquad [b_{\boldsymbol{k}j}, b_{\boldsymbol{k}'j'}^+] = \Delta(\boldsymbol{k}-\boldsymbol{k}')\,\delta_{jj'}. \tag{4.4}$$

In writing these commutation relations we have introduced the function

$$\Delta(\boldsymbol{k}) = (1/N) \sum_l \mathrm{e}^{\mathrm{i}\boldsymbol{k}\cdot\boldsymbol{x}(l)}$$

which equals unity if $\boldsymbol{k}$ is a translation vector of the reciprocal lattice and vanishes otherwise. In the present case, since both $\boldsymbol{k}$ and $\boldsymbol{k}'$ are restricted to lie inside the first Brillouin zone their difference can only be zero in order that $\Delta(\boldsymbol{k}-\boldsymbol{k}')$ should not vanish. From eqs. (4.4) we see that the b operators can be regarded as Bose operators.

The hamiltonian (2.7b) takes a particularly simple form in terms of these new operators

$$H_0 = \sum_{\boldsymbol{k}j} \hbar\omega_j(\boldsymbol{k})\,[b_{\boldsymbol{k}j}^+ b_{\boldsymbol{k}j} + \tfrac{1}{2}]. \tag{4.5}$$

To obtain the eigenstates of the hamiltonian (4.5) we note first that it follows from eqs. (4.4) that the operators $b_{\boldsymbol{k}j}^+ b_{\boldsymbol{k}j}$ commute among themselves. The hamiltonian (4.5) is thus the sum of independent, 'one mode' hamiltonians, $H_{\boldsymbol{k}j} = \hbar\omega_j(\boldsymbol{k})\,[b_{\boldsymbol{k}j}^+ b_{\boldsymbol{k}j} + \frac{1}{2}]$, which can all be diagonalized simultaneously. The way in which one obtains the eigenfunctions and eigenvalues of a harmonic oscillator hamiltonian $h_0 = \hbar\omega\,[b^+ b + \frac{1}{2}]$ are well known (Dirac 1947, chapter VI), and we will merely summarize the results here.

The ground state of h_0, which we denote by $|0\rangle$, is defined by

$$b\,|0\rangle = 0. \tag{4.6a}$$

The corresponding energy is clearly

$$\varepsilon_0 = \tfrac{1}{2}\hbar\omega, \tag{4.6b}$$

and is called the *zero-point energy* of the oscillator. The excited states of h_0 are obtained by operating on the ground state $|0\rangle$ by powers of the operator b^+. The nth excited state is given by

$$|n\rangle = (n!)^{-1/2}(b^+)^n|0\rangle, \tag{4.7a}$$

and obeys the orthonormality condition

$$\langle n|n'\rangle = \delta_{nn'}. \tag{4.7b}$$

The energy of the state $|n\rangle$ is

$$\varepsilon_n = \hbar\omega(n + \tfrac{1}{2}). \tag{4.7c}$$

It differs from the ground state energy by the addition of n quanta of energy $\hbar\omega$ to it. These quanta are called *phonons*. Thus, we can specify any eigenstate of h_0 by giving the number of phonons in that state, that is, by specifying its degree of excitation above the ground state.

The effects of operating on the state $|n\rangle$ with the operators b^+ and b are

$$b^+|n\rangle = (n+1)^{1/2}|n+1\rangle, \qquad b|n\rangle = n^{1/2}|n-1\rangle. \tag{4.8a, b}$$

Thus, the application of the operator b^+ to the state $|n\rangle$ yields a state $|n+1\rangle$ whose energy is higher than that of the state $|n\rangle$ by an amount $\hbar\omega$, independent of n. Conversely, the application of the operator b to the state $|n\rangle$ yields a state $|n-1\rangle$ whose energy is lower than that of $|n\rangle$ by $\hbar\omega$, independent of n. Because the operator b^+ adds a phonon to any state on which it acts, while the operator b removes one phonon from any state on which it acts, these operators are called *phonon creation* and *destruction operators*, respectively.

It follows from eqs. (4.8) that the only nonzero matrix elements of b^+ and b are

$$\langle n+1|b^+|n\rangle = (n+1)^{1/2}, \qquad \langle n-1|b|n\rangle = n^{1/2}. \tag{4.9}$$

It follows from these results that

$$\langle n'|(b^+)^m|n\rangle = \delta_{n',m+n}\left(\frac{(m+n)!}{n!}\right)^{1/2}, \tag{4.10a}$$

$$\langle n'|b^m|n\rangle = \delta_{n',n-m}\left(\frac{n!}{(n-m)!}\right)^{1/2}, \tag{4.10b}$$

so that

$$\langle n'|\,e^{\alpha b^+}\,|n\rangle = \frac{1}{(n'-n)!}\left(\frac{n'!}{n!}\right)^{1/2}\alpha^{n'-n}, \tag{4.11a}$$

$$\langle n'|\,e^{\alpha b}\,|n\rangle = \frac{1}{(n-n')!}\left(\frac{n!}{n'!}\right)^{1/2}a^{n-n'}. \tag{4.11b}$$

Consequently, we obtain the useful results

$$\langle n|\,e^{\alpha b}e^{\beta b^+}\,|n\rangle = \sum_{m=0}^{\infty}\frac{(\alpha\beta)^m}{(m!)^2}\frac{(n+m)!}{n!}, \tag{4.12a}$$

$$\langle n|\,e^{\beta b^+}e^{\alpha b}\,|n\rangle = \sum_{m=0}^{\infty}\frac{(\alpha\beta)^m}{(m!)^2}\frac{n!}{(n-m)!}. \tag{4.12b}$$

The preceding results can now be used to obtain the eigenstates and eigenenergies of the total vibrational hamiltonian H_0. Because H_0 is the sum of independent, sub-hamiltonians of the form of h_0, one for each mode $(\boldsymbol{k}j)$, its eigenstates are the products of the eigenstates of these sub-hamiltonians over all modes, and its energies are the sums of the energies of these sub-hamiltonians over all modes. The ground state $|0\rangle$ of H_0 is defined by

$$b_{\boldsymbol{k}j}\,|0\rangle = 0 \quad \textit{for all} \quad (\boldsymbol{k}j). \tag{4.13}$$

The energy of the ground state is

$$E_0 = \sum_{\boldsymbol{k}j}\tfrac{1}{2}\hbar\omega_j(\boldsymbol{k}). \tag{4.14}$$

This is the zero-point energy of the crystal. The eigenstates of H_0 are generally labeled by the eigenvalues $n_{\boldsymbol{k}j}(=0, 1, 2, \cdots)$ of the operators $b^+_{\boldsymbol{k}j}b_{\boldsymbol{k}j}$, and in normalized form are given by

$$|n_{\boldsymbol{k}_1 j_1}\cdots n_{\boldsymbol{k}_1 j_{3r}}\cdots n_{\boldsymbol{k}_N j_1}\cdots n_{\boldsymbol{k}_N j_{3r}}\rangle = \left(\prod_{\boldsymbol{k}}^{N}\prod_{j}^{3r}(n_{\boldsymbol{k}j})!\right)^{-1/2}\prod_{\boldsymbol{k}}^{N}\prod_{j}^{3r}(b^+_{\boldsymbol{k}j})^{n_{\boldsymbol{k}j}}\,|0\rangle,$$

$$n_{\boldsymbol{k}j} = 0, 1, 2, \cdots. \tag{4.15}$$

If the sum of the exponents on the right-hand side of this equation equals n,

$$\sum_{\boldsymbol{k}}^{N}\sum_{j}^{3r} n_{\boldsymbol{k}j} = n, \tag{4.16}$$

the eigenstate (4.15) is said to be an n-phonon state. The energy of the eigenstate (4.15) is

$$E(\{n_{\boldsymbol{k}j}\}) = \sum_{\boldsymbol{k}}^{N}\sum_{j}^{3r}\hbar\omega_j(\boldsymbol{k})\,[n_{\boldsymbol{k}j}+\tfrac{1}{2}], \quad n_{\boldsymbol{k}j} = 0, 1, 2, \cdots. \tag{4.17}$$

In many applications it leads to less cumbersome expressions to use instead of $b_{\boldsymbol{k}j}$ and $b^{+}_{\boldsymbol{k}j}$ the linear combinations

$$A_{\boldsymbol{k}j} = b_{\boldsymbol{k}j} + b^{+}_{-\boldsymbol{k}j} = A^{+}_{-\boldsymbol{k}j}, \qquad B_{\boldsymbol{k}j} = b_{\boldsymbol{k}j} - b^{+}_{-\boldsymbol{k}j} = -B^{+}_{-\boldsymbol{k}j}, \tag{4.18a, b}$$

called the *phonon field* and *momentum operators*, respectively. The commutation relations obeyed by these operators are

$$[A_{\boldsymbol{k}j}, A_{\boldsymbol{k}'j'}] = [B_{\boldsymbol{k}j}, B_{\boldsymbol{k}'j'}] = 0, \quad [A_{\boldsymbol{k}j}, B_{\boldsymbol{k}'j'}] = -2\Delta(\boldsymbol{k}+\boldsymbol{k}')\,\delta_{jj'}. \tag{4.19a, b}$$

In terms of these operators the normal coordinate transformation (4.1) becomes

$$u_{\alpha}(l\kappa) = (\hbar/2NM_{\kappa})^{1/2} \sum_{\boldsymbol{k}j} \omega_j^{-1/2}(\boldsymbol{k})\, e_{\alpha}(\kappa\,|\,\boldsymbol{k}j)\, \mathrm{e}^{\mathrm{i}\boldsymbol{k}\cdot\boldsymbol{x}(l)}\, A_{\boldsymbol{k}j}, \tag{4.20a}$$

$$p_{\alpha}(l\kappa) = \mathrm{i}^{-1}(\hbar M_{\kappa}/2N)^{1/2} \sum_{\boldsymbol{k}j} \omega_j^{1/2}(\boldsymbol{k})\, e_{\alpha}(\kappa\,|\,\boldsymbol{k}j)\, \mathrm{e}^{\mathrm{i}\boldsymbol{k}\cdot\boldsymbol{x}(l)}\, B_{\boldsymbol{k}j}, \tag{4.20b}$$

from which we see that $A_{\boldsymbol{k}j}$ and $B_{\boldsymbol{k}j}$ are the Fourier coefficients of the atomic displacements and momenta, respectively. In terms of these new operators the hamiltonian (4.5) takes the form

$$H_0 = \sum_{\boldsymbol{k}j} \tfrac{1}{4}\hbar\omega_j(\boldsymbol{k})\,[B^{+}_{\boldsymbol{k}j}B_{\boldsymbol{k}j} + A^{+}_{\boldsymbol{k}j}A_{\boldsymbol{k}j}]. \tag{4.21}$$

If we substitute eq. (4.20a) into eq. (2.7c), we obtain for the anharmonic hamiltonian

$$H_{\mathrm{a}} = \sum_{\boldsymbol{k}j} V(\boldsymbol{k}j)\, A_{\boldsymbol{k}j} + \sum_{n=3}^{\infty} \sum_{\boldsymbol{k}_1 j_1} \cdots \sum_{\boldsymbol{k}_n j_n} V(\boldsymbol{k}_1 j_1; \cdots; \boldsymbol{k}_n j_n)\, A_{\boldsymbol{k}_1 j_1} \cdots A_{\boldsymbol{k}_n j_n}, \tag{4.22a}$$

where

$$\begin{aligned} V(\boldsymbol{k}_1 j_1; \cdots; \boldsymbol{k}_n j_n) &= \frac{(1/n!)\,(\hbar/2N)^{n/2}}{(\omega_{j_1}(\boldsymbol{k}_1)\cdots\omega_{j_n}(\boldsymbol{k}_n))^{1/2}} \sum_{l_1\kappa_1\alpha_1} \cdots \sum_{l_n\kappa_n\alpha_n} \Phi_{\alpha_1\cdots\alpha_n}(l_1\kappa_1; \cdots; l_n\kappa_n) \\ &\quad \times \frac{e_{\alpha_1}(\kappa_1\,|\,\boldsymbol{k}_1 j_1)}{M_{\kappa_1}^{1/2}} \cdots \frac{e_{\alpha_n}(\kappa_n\,|\,\boldsymbol{k}_n j_n)}{M_{\kappa_n}^{1/2}}\, \mathrm{e}^{\mathrm{i}\,[\boldsymbol{k}_1\cdot\boldsymbol{x}(l_1) + \cdots + \boldsymbol{k}_n\cdot\boldsymbol{x}(l_n)]} \\ &= V^{*}(-\boldsymbol{k}_1 j_1; \cdots; -\boldsymbol{k}_n j_n). \end{aligned} \tag{4.22b}$$

In this form it is clear that $V(\boldsymbol{k}_1 j_1; \cdots; \boldsymbol{k}_n j_n)$ is completely symmetric in the indices $(\boldsymbol{k}_1 j_1), \cdots, (\boldsymbol{k}_n j_n)$. If we make use of the property of the atomic force constants that

$$\Phi_{\alpha_1\alpha_2\cdots\alpha_n}(l_1\kappa; l_2\kappa_2; \cdots; l_n\kappa_n) = \Phi_{\alpha_1\alpha_2\cdots\alpha_n}(0\kappa_1; l_2 - l_1\,\kappa_2; \cdots; l_n - l_1\,\kappa_n)$$

which follows from eq. (2.12), we find that eq. (4.22b) can be written equivalently as

$$V(\boldsymbol{k}_1 j_1; \cdots; \boldsymbol{k}_n j_n) = (1/n!)\,(\hbar/2N)^{n/2}\,\frac{N\Delta(\boldsymbol{k}_1 + \cdots + \boldsymbol{k}_n)}{(\omega_{j_1}(\boldsymbol{k}_1) \cdots \omega_{j_n}(\boldsymbol{k}_n))^{1/2}}$$
$$\times \sum_{\kappa_1\alpha_1} \sum_{l_2\kappa_2\alpha_2} \cdots \sum_{l_n\kappa_n\alpha_n} \Phi_{\alpha_1\alpha_2\cdots\alpha_n}(0\kappa_1; l_2\kappa_2; \cdots; l_n\kappa_n)$$
$$\times \frac{e_{\alpha_1}(\kappa_1 | \boldsymbol{k}_1 j_1)}{M_{\kappa_1}^{1/2}} \cdots \frac{e_{\alpha_n}(\kappa_n | \boldsymbol{k}_n j_n)}{M_{\kappa_n}^{1/2}}\, \mathrm{e}^{\mathrm{i}[\boldsymbol{k}_2\cdot\boldsymbol{x}(l_2) + \cdots + \boldsymbol{k}_n\cdot\boldsymbol{x}(l_n)]}. \quad (4.22c)$$

Thus the periodicity of a crystal has the consequence that the Fourier transformed anharmonic force constant $V(\boldsymbol{k}_1 j_1; \cdots; k_n j_n)$ vanishes unless the sum of the wave vectors in its argument equals a translation vector of the reciprocal lattice.

The preceding results allow several useful results to be obtained. The thermodynamic functions of a crystal in the harmonic approximation can be derived directly from the partition function

$$Z = \mathrm{Tr}\, \mathrm{e}^{-\beta H_0}, \quad (4.23)$$

where $\beta = 1/k_B T$, k_B is Boltzmann's constant, and T is the absolute temperature. The trace in eq. (4.23) is most simply evaluated in the representation in which H_0 is diagonal, viz., that provided by eqs. (4.15) and (4.17). In this representation the partition function takes the form

$$Z = \sum_{n_{\boldsymbol{k}_1 j_1}=0}^{\infty} \cdots \sum_{n_{\boldsymbol{k}_N j_{3r}}=0}^{\infty} \exp\Big(-\beta \sum_{\boldsymbol{k}j} \hbar\omega_j(\boldsymbol{k})\,[n_{\boldsymbol{k}j} + \tfrac{1}{2}]\Big)$$
$$= \prod_{\boldsymbol{k}j} \mathrm{e}^{-\frac{1}{2}\beta\hbar\omega_j(\boldsymbol{k})}/(1 - \mathrm{e}^{-\beta\hbar\omega_j(\boldsymbol{k})}). \quad (4.24)$$

The Helmholtz free energy is given by

$$F = -k_B T \ln Z = k_B T \sum_{\boldsymbol{k}j} \ln\{2\sinh(\hbar\omega_j(\boldsymbol{k})/2k_B T)\}. \quad (4.25)$$

The remaining thermodynamic functions are obtained from the Helmholtz free energy by differentiation with respect to temperature. The entropy is

$$S = -\left(\frac{\partial F}{\partial T}\right)_v = k_B \sum_{\boldsymbol{k}j} \left\{\frac{\hbar\omega_j(\boldsymbol{k})}{2k_B T} \coth\frac{\hbar\omega_j(\boldsymbol{k})}{2k_B T} - \ln\left(2\sinh\frac{\hbar\omega_j(\boldsymbol{k})}{2k_B T}\right)\right\}. \quad (4.26)$$

The internal energy is

$$E = F + TS = \sum_{\boldsymbol{k}j} \tfrac{1}{2}\hbar\omega_j(\boldsymbol{k}) \coth(\hbar\omega_j(\boldsymbol{k})/2k_B T), \quad (4.27)$$

while the specific heat at constant volume is

$$C_v = \left(\frac{\partial E}{\partial T}\right)_v = k_B \sum_{\boldsymbol{k}j} \left(\frac{\hbar\omega_j(\boldsymbol{k})}{2k_BT}\right)^2 \frac{1}{\sinh^2(\hbar\omega_j(\boldsymbol{k})/2k_BT)}. \tag{4.28}$$

These results can be extended. The thermodynamic expectation value in the canonical ensemble of any operator O is defined by the equation

$$\langle O \rangle = (\mathrm{Tr}\, \mathrm{e}^{-\beta H} O)/\mathrm{Tr}\, \mathrm{e}^{-\beta H}. \tag{4.29a}$$

In the harmonic approximation this expectation value becomes

$$\langle O \rangle_0 = (\mathrm{Tr}\, \mathrm{e}^{-\beta H_0} O)/\mathrm{Tr}\, \mathrm{e}^{-\beta H_0}. \tag{4.29b}$$

If we note that in the representation in which $b^+_{\boldsymbol{k}j} b_{\boldsymbol{k}j}$ is diagonal, the operator $b^+_{\boldsymbol{k}j} b_{\boldsymbol{k}'j'}$ has no diagonal elements, we are led to the results that

$$\langle b^+_{\boldsymbol{k}j}\, b_{\boldsymbol{k}'j'} \rangle_0 = \Delta(\boldsymbol{k}-\boldsymbol{k}')\, \delta_{jj'} \bar{n}_{\boldsymbol{k}j}, \tag{4.30a}$$

$$\langle b_{\boldsymbol{k}j}\, b^+_{\boldsymbol{k}'j'} \rangle_0 = \Delta(\boldsymbol{k}-\boldsymbol{k}')\, \delta_{jj'} (\bar{n}_{\boldsymbol{k}j} + 1), \tag{4.30b}$$

$$\langle b_{\boldsymbol{k}j}\, b_{\boldsymbol{k}'j'} \rangle_0 = \langle b^+_{\boldsymbol{k}j}\, b^+_{\boldsymbol{k}'j'} \rangle_0 = 0, \tag{4.30c}$$

where $\bar{n}_{\boldsymbol{k}j}$, the mean number of phonons in the vibration mode $(\boldsymbol{k}j)$ at temperature T, is

$$\bar{n}_{\boldsymbol{k}j} = \frac{1}{\mathrm{e}^{\beta\hbar\omega_j(\boldsymbol{k})} - 1}. \tag{4.31}$$

From the commutation relations (4.4) and the hamiltonian (4.5) follow the Heisenberg equations of motion of the operators $b_{\boldsymbol{k}j}$ and $b^+_{\boldsymbol{k}j}$:

$$\mathrm{i}\hbar\, \mathrm{d}b_{\boldsymbol{k}j}/\mathrm{d}t = [b_{\boldsymbol{k}j}, H_0] = \hbar\omega_j(\boldsymbol{k})\, b_{\boldsymbol{k}j}, \tag{4.32a}$$

$$\mathrm{i}\hbar\, \mathrm{d}b^+_{\boldsymbol{k}j}/\mathrm{d}t = [b^+_{\boldsymbol{k}j}, H_0] = -\hbar\omega_j(\boldsymbol{k})\, b^+_{\boldsymbol{k}j}. \tag{4.32b}$$

Integrating these equations, we obtain for the time dependence of these operators

$$b_{\boldsymbol{k}j}(t) = \mathrm{e}^{\mathrm{i}(t/\hbar)H_0}\, b_{\boldsymbol{k}j}(0)\, \mathrm{e}^{-\mathrm{i}(t/\hbar)H_0} = \mathrm{e}^{-\mathrm{i}\omega_j(\boldsymbol{k})t}\, b_{\boldsymbol{k}j}(0), \tag{4.33a}$$

$$b^+_{\boldsymbol{k}j}(t) = \mathrm{e}^{\mathrm{i}(t/\hbar)H_0}\, b^+_{\boldsymbol{k}j}(0)\, \mathrm{e}^{-\mathrm{i}(t/\hbar)H_0} = \mathrm{e}^{\mathrm{i}\omega_j(\boldsymbol{k})t}\, b^+_{\boldsymbol{k}j}(0). \tag{4.33b}$$

Combining the results given by eqs. (4.30) and (4.33) we obtain for the two-time correlation functions $\langle b^+_{\boldsymbol{k}j}(t)\, b_{\boldsymbol{k}'j'}(0)\rangle_0$ and $\langle b_{\boldsymbol{k}j}(t)\, b^+_{\boldsymbol{k}'j'}(0)\rangle_0$ the results

$$\langle b^+_{\boldsymbol{k}j}(t)\, b_{\boldsymbol{k}'j'}(0)\rangle_0 = \Delta(\boldsymbol{k}-\boldsymbol{k}')\,\delta_{jj'}\,\mathrm{e}^{\mathrm{i}\omega_j(\boldsymbol{k})t}\,\bar{n}_{\boldsymbol{k}j}, \tag{4.34a}$$

$$\langle b_{\boldsymbol{k}j}(t)\, b^+_{\boldsymbol{k}'j'}(0)\rangle_0 = \Delta(\boldsymbol{k}-\boldsymbol{k}')\,\delta_{jj'}\,\mathrm{e}^{-\mathrm{i}\omega_j(\boldsymbol{k})t}\left[\bar{n}_{\boldsymbol{k}j}+1\right]. \tag{4.34b}$$

These results yield the following expressions for displacement and momentum correlation functions in the harmonic approximation:

$$\begin{aligned}\langle u_\alpha(l\kappa;t)\,u_\beta(l'\kappa';0)\rangle_0 &= (\hbar/2N)\,(M_\kappa M_{\kappa'})^{-1/2}\\ &\quad\times\sum_{\boldsymbol{k}j}\omega_j^{-1}(\boldsymbol{k})\,e_\alpha(\kappa\,|\,\boldsymbol{k}j)\,e^*_\beta(\kappa'\,|\,\boldsymbol{k}j)\\ &\quad\times\mathrm{e}^{\mathrm{i}\boldsymbol{k}\cdot[\boldsymbol{x}(l)-\boldsymbol{x}(l')]}\left[(\bar{n}_{\boldsymbol{k}j}+1)\,\mathrm{e}^{-\mathrm{i}\omega_j(\boldsymbol{k})t}+\bar{n}_{\boldsymbol{k}j}\,\mathrm{e}^{\mathrm{i}\omega_j(\boldsymbol{k})t}\right],\end{aligned} \tag{4.35a}$$

$$\begin{aligned}\langle p_\alpha(l\kappa;t)\,p_\beta(l'\kappa';0)\rangle_0 &= (\hbar/2N)\,(M_\kappa M_{\kappa'})^{1/2}\\ &\quad\times\sum_{\boldsymbol{k}j}\omega_j(\boldsymbol{k})\,e_\alpha(\kappa\,|\,\boldsymbol{k}j)\,e^*_\beta(\kappa'\,|\,\boldsymbol{k}j)\\ &\quad\times\mathrm{e}^{\mathrm{i}\boldsymbol{k}\cdot[\boldsymbol{x}(l)-\boldsymbol{x}(l')]}\left[(\bar{n}_{\boldsymbol{k}j}+1)\,\mathrm{e}^{-\mathrm{i}\omega_j(\boldsymbol{k})t}+\bar{n}_{\boldsymbol{k}j}\,\mathrm{e}^{\mathrm{i}\omega_j(\boldsymbol{k})t}\right],\end{aligned} \tag{4.35b}$$

$$\begin{aligned}\langle u_\alpha(l\kappa;t)\,p_\beta(l'\kappa';0)\rangle_0 &= \mathrm{i}^{-1}(\hbar/2N)\,(M_{\kappa'}/M_\kappa)^{1/2}\\ &\quad\times\sum_{\boldsymbol{k}j}e_\alpha(\kappa\,|\,\boldsymbol{k}j)\,e^*_\beta(\kappa'\,|\,\boldsymbol{k}j)\\ &\quad\times\mathrm{e}^{\mathrm{i}\boldsymbol{k}\cdot[\boldsymbol{x}(l)-\boldsymbol{x}(l')]}\left[\bar{n}_{\boldsymbol{k}j}\,\mathrm{e}^{\mathrm{i}\omega_j(\boldsymbol{k})t}-(\bar{n}_{\boldsymbol{k}j}+1)\,\mathrm{e}^{-\mathrm{i}\omega_j(\boldsymbol{k})t}\right].\end{aligned} \tag{4.35c}$$

We can now use eqs. (4.12) and (4.35), together with the Baker (1905) and Hausdorff (1906) theorem that

$$\mathrm{e}^{A+B}=\mathrm{e}^A\mathrm{e}^B\mathrm{e}^{-\frac{1}{2}[A,B]}, \tag{4.36}$$

where A and B are two noncommuting operators which commute with their commutator, to obtain the result that

$$\langle\mathrm{e}^{\mathrm{i}\boldsymbol{k}\cdot\boldsymbol{u}(l\kappa)}\rangle_0=\mathrm{e}^{-\frac{1}{2}\langle(\boldsymbol{\kappa}\cdot\boldsymbol{u}(l\kappa))^2\rangle_0}. \tag{4.37}$$

By setting $t=0$ and $(l\kappa)=(l'\kappa')$ in eq. (4.35a), we see that this thermodynamic expectation value is independent of the cell index l. Finally, with the aid of eq. (4.33), we obtain in the same way the exponential correlation function

$$\begin{aligned}\langle\exp[-\mathrm{i}\boldsymbol{\kappa}\cdot\boldsymbol{u}(l\kappa;t)]\,\exp[\mathrm{i}\boldsymbol{\kappa}\cdot\boldsymbol{u}(l'\kappa';0)]\rangle_0&\\ =\exp\left[-\tfrac{1}{2}\langle(\boldsymbol{\kappa}\cdot\boldsymbol{u}(l\kappa))^2\rangle_0-\tfrac{1}{2}\langle(\boldsymbol{\kappa}\cdot\boldsymbol{u}(l'\kappa'))^2\rangle_0\right]&\\ \times\exp\left[\langle\boldsymbol{\kappa}\cdot\boldsymbol{u}(l\kappa;t)\,\boldsymbol{\kappa}\cdot\boldsymbol{u}(l'\kappa';0)\rangle_0\right].&\end{aligned} \tag{4.38}$$

The results of this section provide a convenient starting point for perturbation theoretic calculations of various equilibrium and time-dependent properties of anharmonic crystals, as well as providing the solutions of a variety of lattice dynamical problems in the harmonic approximation.

5. *Frequency spectrum and thermodynamic properties*

For the calculation of an arbitrary additive function of the normal mode frequencies,

$$S = \sum_{\boldsymbol{k}j} f(\omega_j(\boldsymbol{k})), \tag{5.1}$$

it is not necessary to know the individual normal mode frequencies of the crystal. The normal mode frequencies are bounded and, because the number of atoms in a crystal is very large, are very dense. It is therefore more convenient to work with the frequency distribution function, or the frequency spectrum, $g(\omega)$, which is defined in such a way that $g(\omega)\,\mathrm{d}\omega$ is the fraction of normal modes with frequencies in the interval $(\omega, \omega+\mathrm{d}\omega)$ in the limit as $\mathrm{d}\omega \to 0$.

A formal representation of $g(\omega)$ can be obtained in the following way. We introduce a function $N(\omega)$ which gives the number of normal modes with frequencies less than ω. This function can be written in the form

$$N(\omega) = \sum_{\boldsymbol{k}j} \theta(\omega - \omega_j(\boldsymbol{k})), \tag{5.2}$$

where $\theta(x)$ is the Heaviside unit step function

$$\theta(x) = 1 \text{ for } x > 0, \quad \text{and} \quad \theta(x) = 0 \text{ for } x < 0. \tag{5.3}$$

A d-dimensional crystal possesses drN normal modes of vibration. Thus, from its definition we see that $g(\omega)$ is obtained from the relation

$$g(\omega)\,\mathrm{d}\omega = (1/drN)\,[N(\omega + \mathrm{d}\omega) - N(\omega)] \cong N'(\omega)\,\mathrm{d}\omega/drN, \tag{5.4}$$

so that

$$g(\omega) = N'(\omega)/drN = (1/drN) \sum_{\boldsymbol{k}j} \delta(\omega - \omega_j(\boldsymbol{k})), \tag{5.5}$$

where $\delta(x) = \theta'(x)$ is the Dirac delta function, and $\boldsymbol{k}$ is understood to be a d-dimensional wave vector.

Because it is the squares of the normal mode frequencies, and not the frequencies themselves, that are the eigenvalues of the dynamical matrix, for certain theoretical purposes it is sometimes more convenient to work with the distribution function of the squares of the normal mode frequencies $G(\omega^2)$ than with the frequency spectrum $g(\omega)$. The function $G(\omega^2)$ is defined in such a way that $G(\omega^2)\,\mathrm{d}\omega^2$ is the fraction of normal modes the squares of whose frequencies lie in the interval $(\omega^2, \omega^2+\mathrm{d}\omega^2)$, in the limit as $\mathrm{d}\omega^2 \to 0$.

A repetition of the argument which led to eq. (5.5) yields the result that $G(\omega^2)$ is given by

$$G(\omega^2) = (1/drN) \sum_{\mathbf{k}j} \delta(\omega^2 - \omega_j^2(\mathbf{k})). \tag{5.6}$$

From a comparison of eqs. (5.5) and (5.6) we see that the distribution functions are related by

$$g(\omega) = 2\omega G(\omega^2). \tag{5.7}$$

From its definition the frequency spectrum $g(\omega)$ is normalized to unity

$$\int_0^{\omega_L} g(\omega)\,\mathrm{d}\omega = 1, \tag{5.8}$$

where ω_L is the largest normal mode frequency of the crystal.

With the aid of the frequency spectrum the evaluation of any additive function of the normal mode frequencies, eq. (5.1), is reduced to quadratures:

$$S = drN \int_0^{\omega_L} f(\omega)\, g(\omega)\,\mathrm{d}\omega. \tag{5.9}$$

For example, since the vibrational contribution to each of the thermodynamic functions of a crystal is an additive function of the normal mode frequencies, according to eq. (4.25)–(4.28), it can be expressed as an integral over the frequency spectrum in the form given by eq. (5.9).

An important special application of eqs. (5.5) and (5.9) is to the determination of the low temperature behavior of the thermodynamic functions of a crystal. A detailed general analysis (see section 7) shows that in the long wavelength limit the frequencies of the three acoustic branches of an arbitrary crystal are linear functions of the magnitude of the wave vector

$$\omega_j(\mathbf{k}) = c_j(\theta, \varphi)\, k + \mathrm{O}(k^3), \quad j = 1, 2, 3, \tag{5.10}$$

where θ and φ are the polar and azimuthal angles of the wave vector $\boldsymbol{k}$. The coefficient $c_j(\theta, \varphi)$ is the speed of sound for an acoustic wave in the jth branch of the phonon spectrum propagating in the direction (θ, φ). Since the $3r-3$ optical branches of the phonon spectrum possess non-vanishing frequencies, the low frequency end of the frequency spectrum $g(\omega)$ is determined by the dispersion relation (5.10). If we substitute eq. (5.10) into eq. (5.5), with $d=3$, we obtain the result that as $\omega \to 0$

$$g(\omega) = a_2\omega^2 + \mathrm{O}(\omega^4), \tag{5.11a}$$

where

$$a_2 = \{v_a/3r(2\pi)^3\} \sum_{j=1}^{3} \int \sin\theta \, \mathrm{d}\theta \int \mathrm{d}\varphi/c_j^3(\theta, \varphi). \tag{5.11b}$$

In the low-temperature limit the Helmholtz free energy of a crystal can be expanded conveniently as

$$F = E_0 - 3rNk_BT \sum_{n=1}^{\infty} (1/n) \int_0^{\omega_L} g(\omega)\, \mathrm{e}^{-n\hbar\omega/k_BT}\, \mathrm{d}\omega, \tag{5.12}$$

where

$$E_0 = \tfrac{3}{2}rN\hbar \int_0^{\omega_L} \omega g(\omega)\, \mathrm{d}\omega \tag{5.13}$$

is the zero-point energy. For temperatures low enough that $T \ll \hbar\omega_L/k_B$ we see from eq. (5.12) that the presence of the exponential factor in the integrand has the consequence that only frequencies $\omega < \omega_L$ contribute significantly to the integral. Thus little error is made by extending the upper limit of the integral to infinity. When the form of $g(\omega)$ valid at low frequencies, eq. (5.11a), is substituted into eq. (5.12), and integration and summation are carried out, the following result is obtained for the Helmholtz free energy at low temperatures

$$F = E_0 - 3rNa_2 \frac{\pi^4}{45} \frac{(k_BT)^4}{\hbar^3} + \mathrm{O}(T^6). \tag{5.14a}$$

It follows from this result that the internal energy, specific heat, and entropy at low temperatures are given by

$$E = F - T\left(\frac{\partial F}{\partial T}\right)_v = E_0 + 3rNa_2 \frac{\pi^4}{15} \frac{(k_BT)^4}{\hbar^3} + \mathrm{O}(T^6), \tag{5.14b}$$

$$C_v = \left(\frac{\partial E}{\partial T}\right)_v = 3rNk_B a_2 \frac{4\pi^4}{15}\left(\frac{k_B T}{\hbar}\right)^3 + O(T^5), \tag{5.14c}$$

$$S = -\left(\frac{\partial F}{\partial T}\right)_v = 3rNk_B a_2 \frac{4\pi^4}{45}\left(\frac{k_B T}{\hbar}\right)^3 + O(T^5). \tag{5.14d}$$

In his pioneering work Debye (1912) approximated the entire frequency spectrum by its low-frequency limiting behavior, the first term on the right-hand side of eq. (5.11a), cutting it off at a frequency ω_D, which from the normalization condition (5.8) is found to be given in terms of the constant a_2, eq. (5.11b), by $a_2 = 3/\omega_D^3$. While this approximation yields the correct low temperature behavior of the thermodynamic functions, eqs. (5.14), which represented a great advance over the earlier Einstein (1907) theory, it gives rise to incorrect temperature dependences for these functions at higher temperatures.

If it is desired to go beyond limiting expressions of the type of eqs. (5.11) and (5.14), it is necessary to obtain the frequency spectrum $g(\omega)$, or $G(\omega^2)$, over the entire range of frequencies for which it is nonvanishing. The analytic evaluation of the expression (5.6) for $G(\omega^2)$ requires having analytic expressions for the squares of the normal mode frequencies $\omega_j^2(\boldsymbol{k})$ as functions of the components of the wave vector $\boldsymbol{k}$, and that these analytic expressions be simple enough that the integration over the first Brillouin zone in eq. (5.6) can be carried out analytically. Although these requirements can be met for simple models of one- and two-dimensional crystals, they cannot be for realistic models of three-dimensional crystals. Consequently the calculation of the frequency spectrum of a three-dimensional crystal has to be carried out by approximate methods.

Of the several approximate methods which have been devised for this purpose we will discuss only two here: the moment trace method of Montroll (1942, 1943), and recent variants of it; and purely numerical methods stemming from the root sampling method of Blackman (1934a, 1934b, 1936, 1937a, 1937b).

The even moments of the frequency spectrum $g(\omega)$ are defined by

$$\mu_{2n} = \int_0^{\omega_L} \omega^{2n} g(\omega)\, d\omega, \quad n = 0, 1, 2, \cdots. \tag{5.15}$$

Comparing eqs. (5.1) and (5.9) we see that they can be expressed equivalently as

$$\mu_{2n} = (1/drN) \sum_{\boldsymbol{k}j} \omega_j^{2n}(\boldsymbol{k}) = (1/drN) \sum_{\boldsymbol{k}} \mathrm{Tr}\, \boldsymbol{D}^n(\boldsymbol{k}), \tag{5.16a, b}$$

where the second form follows from the invariance of the trace of a matrix against representation, and the fact that the eigenvalues of $\boldsymbol{D}^n(\boldsymbol{k})$ are the $\{\omega_j^{2n}(\boldsymbol{k})\}$. It is just because the moments $\{\mu_{2n}\}$ can be calculated directly from the traces of powers of the dynamical matrix, without the necessity of knowing the frequency spectrum $g(\omega)$ itself, that make them a particularly useful characterization of the frequency spectrum on which to base a calculation of the spectrum. Indeed, Isenberg (1963) has developed computational procedures, utilizing high speed computers, based on this fact which have enabled him to calculate the first 35 even moments of a face centered cubic crystal with nearest neighbor interactions.

Since the frequency spectrum is identically zero for frequencies greater than ω_L, it is natural to consider expanding $g(\omega)$ in a set of orthogonal polynomials in the interval $(0, \omega_L)$, with the coefficients determined from the moments. The orthogonal polynomials defined with respect to a finite interval, and having a constant weight function, are the Legendre polynomials. We therefore write

$$g(\omega) = \sum_{n=0}^{\infty} a_n P_n(\omega/\omega_L), \tag{5.17}$$

where the coefficients $\{a_n\}$ are given by

$$a_n = \tfrac{1}{2}(2n+1) \int_{-1}^{1} g(\omega_L x) P_n(x)\, dx. \tag{5.18}$$

Since $g(\omega)$ can be regarded as an even function of ω in the interval $(-\omega_L, \omega_L)$, only the even coefficients $\{a_{2n}\}$ are nonvanishing. Therefore, in terms of the dimensionless moments

$$u_{2n} = \mu_{2n}/\omega_L^{2n}, \tag{5.19}$$

we obtain the following symbolic expression for a_{2n}

$$\omega_L a_{2n} = (4n+1) P_{2n}(x)\big|_{x^{2n}=u_{2n}}. \tag{5.20}$$

The moment trace method suffers from the drawbacks that very many terms must be retained in the expansion (5.17) to reproduce the spectrum accurately. As we will see below, all frequency spectra possess singular points in the vicinity of which the dependence of $g(\omega)$ on ω is nonanalytic. Such behavior cannot be reproduced by keeping only a finite number of terms in the expansion (5.17), since the result is a polynomial in ω^2, and hence analytic for all finite values of ω. A modification of the moment trace method which correctly incorporates the singularities of the exact spectrum into the approximate spectrum has been developed (Lax and Lebowitz 1954, Rosenstock 1955), but its use requires that all the singularities of the spectrum be known ahead of time, and it lacks the simplicity of the unmodified moment trace method.

Applied to the calculation of an additive function of the normal mode frequencies, eq. (5.9), the moment trace method requires the evaluation of the expression

$$S = drN \sum_{n=0}^{\infty} \omega_{\mathrm{L}} a_{2n} \int_0^1 f(\omega_{\mathrm{L}} x)\, P_{2n}(x)\, \mathrm{d}x\,. \tag{5.21}$$

Thus, as many integrals have to be evaluated, perhaps numerically, as the number of terms retained in the expansion (5.17), and the possibility of loss of accuracy exists due to the rapid oscillations of $P_n(x)$ for large n.

If it is desired to obtain accurate results for additive functions of the normal mode frequencies, and an accurate representation of the frequency spectrum is not required, a variant of the moment trace method, also due to Montroll (1947) can be used to good effect.

Although Montroll developed his method on the basis of the frequency spectrum $g(\omega)$, it is more convenient to work with the distribution function for the squares of the normal mode frequencies, $G(\omega^2)$, and we do so here. In terms of this function eq. (5.9) for an arbitrary additive function of the normal mode frequencies can be rewritten in the form

$$S = drN \int_0^1 \hat{f}(x)\, \hat{G}(x)\, \mathrm{d}x\,, \tag{5.22a}$$

where

$$\hat{f}(x) = f(\omega_{\mathrm{L}} x^{1/2})\,, \tag{5.22b}$$

and

$$\hat{G}(x) = \omega_{\mathrm{L}}^2 G(\omega_{\mathrm{L}}^2 x) \tag{5.22c}$$

is the dimensionless distribution function for the squares of the normal mode frequencies. The problem is to evaluate S knowing nothing about $\hat{G}(x)$ except a finite number of its moments

$$m_n = \int_0^1 x^n \hat{G}(x)\,\mathrm{d}x = \mu_{2n}/\omega_L^{2n} = u_{2n}, \quad n = 0, 1, 2, \cdots. \tag{5.23}$$

In Montroll's method, which is based on the theory of numerical integration (Szegö 1939, Markoff 1896), $\hat{G}(x)$ is approximated by a finite sum of Dirac delta functions

$$\hat{G}(x) = \sum_{i=1}^{n} \lambda_i \delta(x - x_i), \tag{5.24}$$

where the n points x_i and the n weights λ_i are so chosen that the values of all averages of polynomials in x of degree $2n-1$ or less are exact. This is achieved in the following way.

If the set of non-negative powers of x, viz. $1, x, x^2, \cdots, x^n$ is orthogonalized with respect to the function $\hat{G}(x)$, we obtain the set of polynomials $p_0(x)$, $p_1(x), \cdots, p_n(x)$ uniquely determined by the conditions

a) $p_n(x)$ is a polynomial of precise degree n in which the coefficient of x^n is positive;

b) the system $\{p_n(x)\}$ is orthonormal:

$$\int_0^1 p_m(x)\, p_n(x)\, \hat{G}(x)\,\mathrm{d}x = \delta_{mn}, \quad m, n = 0, 1, 2, \cdots. \tag{5.25}$$

Further, for $n \geqslant 1$

$$p_n(x) = (D_{n-1}D_n)^{1/2} \begin{vmatrix} m_0 & m_1 & m_2 & \cdots & m_n \\ m_1 & m_2 & m_3 & \cdots & m_{n+1} \\ \cdots & \cdots & \cdots & \cdots & \cdots \\ m_{n-1} & m_n & m_{n+1} & & m_{2n-1} \\ 1 & x & x^2 & \cdots & x^n \end{vmatrix}, \tag{5.26}$$

$$D_n = \begin{vmatrix} m_0 & m_1 & \cdots & m_n \\ \cdots & \cdots & \cdots & \cdots \\ m_n & m_{n+1} & \cdots & m_{2n} \end{vmatrix}. \tag{5.27}$$

The n points $x_1 < x_2 < x_3 < \cdots < x_n$ in eq. (5.24) are the zeroes of $p_n(x)$. The weights $\{\lambda_i\}$, called Christoffel numbers, are all positive, clearly depend on n, and are given by the following equivalent expressions

$$\lambda_i = \int_0^1 \left(\frac{p_n(x)}{p_n'(x)\,(x - x_i)} \right)^2 \hat{G}(x)\,\mathrm{d}x\,, \tag{5.28a}$$

$$\lambda_i = \frac{k_{n+1}}{k_n} \frac{-1}{p_{n+1}(x_i)\,p_n'(x_i)}, \tag{5.28b}$$

$$\lambda_i^{-1} = \{p_0(x_i)\}^2 + \{p_1(x_i)\}^2 + \cdots + \{p_n(x_i)\}^2\,. \tag{5.28c}$$

Here k_n is the coefficient of x^n in $p_n(x)$, and is given by

$$k_n = (D_{n-1}/D_n)^{1/2}\,. \tag{5.29}$$

When $\hat{f}(x)$ is a continuous function with a continuous derivative of order $2n+1$, the value of the integral in eq. (5.22a) for S is given by (Markoff 1896)

$$\int_0^1 \hat{f}(x)\,\hat{G}(x)\,\mathrm{d}x = \lambda_1 \hat{f}(x_1) + \cdots + \lambda_n \hat{f}(x_n) + \hat{f}^{(2n)}(\xi)/(2n)!\,k_n^2\,, \tag{5.30}$$

where $0 \leqslant \xi \leqslant 1$. Clearly, if $\hat{G}(x)$ is approximated by eq. (5.24) the error is given by the last term on the right-hand side of eq. (5.30), and its magnitude can be determined by finding the value of ξ for which $\hat{f}^{(2n)}(\xi)$ has the largest magnitude.

From eq. (5.30) we see that if $\hat{f}(x)$ is any polynomial of degree $2n-1$ or less, the points $\{x_i\}$ and weights $\{\lambda_i\}$ determined as above are such as to make exact the evaluation of the integral (5.22a) with $\hat{G}(x)$ approximated by eq. (5.24). In particular, the first $2n$ moments $m_n\,(n=0, 1, \cdots, 2n-1)$ of $\hat{G}(x)$ are given exactly by the approximation (5.24).

Montroll's method has been extended and improved by Wheeler and Gordon (1969). The importance of their work, which goes beyond the simplest version of it presented here, is that it provides upper and lower bounds for integrals of the type of (5.22a). These authors assume that the first $M+1$ moments of $\hat{G}(x)$, $m_n\,(n=0, 1, \cdots, M)$, are known, say from the use of eq. (5.16b). If $M+1$ is even $(M+1=2n)$, $\hat{G}(x)$ is approximated by

$$\hat{G}^{\mathrm{e}}(x) = \sum_{i=1}^{n} \lambda_i \delta(x - x_i)\,, \tag{5.31}$$

where the n points x_i and n weights λ_i are determined by the requirement that $\hat{G}^{\mathrm{e}}(x)$ yield the first $2n$ moments of $\hat{G}(x)$ correctly. If $M+1$ is odd

$(M+1=2n+1)$, $\hat{G}(x)$ is approximated by

$$\hat{G}^{\mathrm{o}}(x) = \sum_{i=0}^{n} \lambda_i \delta(x - x_i), \tag{5.32}$$

where the point x_0 is chosen arbitrarily in the interval [0, 1], and the weights and remaining points are determined by the requirement that $\hat{G}^{\mathrm{o}}(x)$ yield the first $2n+1$ moments of $\hat{G}(x)$ correctly. The points x_i and weights λ_i of $\hat{G}^{\mathrm{e}}(x)$ are obtained from the results given by eqs. (5.25)–(5.29); the corresponding quantities for $\hat{G}^{\mathrm{o}}(x)$ are obtained in a similar, but slightly different fashion (Shohat and Tamarkin 1950). The following results can now be established. If $x_0=0$,

$$\int_0^1 \hat{f}(x)\,\hat{G}(x)\,\mathrm{d}x = \int_0^1 \hat{f}(x)\,\hat{G}^{\mathrm{e}}(x)\,\mathrm{d}x + (K^{\mathrm{e}})^2\,\hat{f}^{(2n)}(\xi^{\mathrm{e}})/(2n)! \tag{5.33a}$$

$$= \int_0^1 \hat{f}(x)\,\hat{G}^{\mathrm{o}}(x)\,\mathrm{d}x + (K^{\mathrm{o}})^2\,\hat{f}^{(2n+1)}(\xi^{\mathrm{o}})/(2n+1)!\,, \tag{5.33b}$$

where in each case ξ is some point in the interval [0, 1]. The positive constants $(K^{\mathrm{e}})^2$ and $(K^{\mathrm{o}})^2$ are given by

$$(K^{\mathrm{e}})^2 = \int_0^1 \prod_{i=1}^{n} (x - x_i^{\mathrm{e}})^2\,\hat{G}(x)\,\mathrm{d}x\,, \tag{5.34a}$$

$$(K^{\mathrm{o}})^2 = \int_0^1 (x - x_0) \prod_{i=1}^{n} (x - x_i^{\mathrm{o}})^2\,\hat{G}(x)\,\mathrm{d}x\,, \quad x_0 = 0\,, \tag{5.34b}$$

and become very small as n becomes large.

We see from eqs. (5.33) that if the derivatives $\hat{f}^{(m)}(x)$ are constant in sign in the interval [0, 1], and if successive derivatives have opposite sign, the even and odd approximations to $\hat{G}(x)$ provide a sequence of upper and lower bounds to the integral, since the correction terms are of opposite sign. The functions $\hat{f}(x)$ entering the calculations of the thermodynamic functions of crystals possess both of these properties. Using this method, and extensions of it, and the first 30 moments, Wheeler and Gordon (1969) have calculated the zero point energy of a face-centered cubic crystal with nearest neighbor interactions with an error of about two parts in 10^5. Comparable accuracy was achieved in the evaluation of the temperature dependent parts of the thermodynamic functions for temperatures such that $(k_B T/\hbar\omega_L) \gtrsim 0.02$. The latter restriction is a consequence of the fact that approximations to $\hat{G}(x)$ of the form of (5.31) or (5.32) cannot reproduce the correct power law temperature dependence of these functions at low temperatures, eqs. (5.14), but yield exponential dependence on temperature in this limit, as can be inferred from eq. (5.12).

In contrast with the preceding approaches, which yield the thermodynamic functions of a crystal with great accuracy (subject to the qualification just mentioned), but which produce frequency spectra with poor accuracy, there exist numerical methods for calculating frequency spectra with great precision, from which the thermodynamic functions can be calculated with good accuracy.

The simplest of these methods is an extension of Blackman's root sampling method (Blackman 1934a, b, 1936, 1937a, b). In the latter method the dynamical matrix $\boldsymbol{D}(\boldsymbol{k})$, eq. (3.5), or $\boldsymbol{C}(\boldsymbol{k})$, eq. (3.12), is diagonalized numerically at a large number of uniformly distributed points in the irreducible element of the first Brillouin zone, and from a knowledge of the resulting frequencies an approximation to the frequency spectrum is constructed in the form of a normalized histogram. The accuracy of the result clearly increases with the number of frequencies computed. The problem one faces is that of computing more frequencies, which means diagonalizing the dynamical matrix at more points in the irreducible element of the first Brillouin zone, without at the same time increasing computing time prohibitively. A modification of the root sampling method which accomplishes this has been devised by Gilat and Dolling (1964). These authors diagonalize the dynamical matrix $\boldsymbol{D}(\boldsymbol{k})$ at a comparatively small number M_c of $\boldsymbol{k}$ values, which are spaced regularly on a coarse mesh in the irreducible element of the first Brillouin zone, to obtain the corresponding normal mode frequencies $\{\omega_j(\boldsymbol{k})\}$ and their associated unit eigenvectors $\{e_\alpha(\kappa|\boldsymbol{k}j)\}$. The normal mode frequencies for a fine mesh M_f of $\boldsymbol{k}$ values in the immediate vicinity of each point of the coarse mesh are then obtained from the linear term in a Taylor series expansion of each eigenfrequency about this point. If the points of the coarse mesh are chosen sufficiently close to each other, such a linear approximation suffices for the evaluation of the normal mode frequencies at a large number of points of the fine mesh. The fine mesh surrounding each point of the coarse mesh is arranged to dovetail correctly with the fine meshes about each of the neighboring points of the coarse mesh, so that the irreducible element of the first Brillouin zone is uniformly filled by the fine mesh of wave vectors, whose number equals $M_c M_f$.

If we denote by $\boldsymbol{k}_0+\boldsymbol{k}$ one of the points of the fine mesh surrounding the point $\boldsymbol{k}_0$ of the coarse mesh, the approximation used by Gilat and Dolling can be expressed as

$$\omega_j(\boldsymbol{k}_0+\boldsymbol{k}) = \omega_j(\boldsymbol{k}_0) + \sum_{\mu=1}^{3} k_\mu \frac{\partial}{\partial k_{0\mu}} \omega_j(\boldsymbol{k}_0). \tag{5.35}$$

By differentiating the equation

$$\omega_j^2(\boldsymbol{k}) = \sum_{\kappa\alpha}\sum_{\kappa'\beta} e_\alpha^*(\kappa|\boldsymbol{k}j)\, D_{\alpha\beta}(\kappa\kappa'|\boldsymbol{k})\, e_\beta(\kappa'|\boldsymbol{k}j), \tag{5.36}$$

and using the orthonormality of the eigenvectors, eq. (3.11a), it is straightforward to show that the derivative $\partial\omega_j(\boldsymbol{k}_0)/\partial k_{0\mu}$ entering eq. (5.35) is given by

$$\frac{\partial}{\partial k_{0\mu}} \omega_j(\boldsymbol{k}_0) = \tfrac{1}{2}\omega_j^{-1}(\boldsymbol{k}_0) \sum_{\kappa\alpha}\sum_{\kappa'\beta} e_\alpha^*(\kappa|\boldsymbol{k}_0 j) \frac{\partial}{\partial k_{0\mu}} D_{\alpha\beta}(\kappa\kappa'|\boldsymbol{k}_0)\, e_\beta(\kappa'|\boldsymbol{k}_0 j). \tag{5.37}$$

Since the expressions for the elements of the dynamical matrix can be differentiated analytically, and the values of $\omega_j(\boldsymbol{k}_0)$ and the $\{e_\alpha(\kappa|\boldsymbol{k}_0 j)\}$ are known for all the points of the coarse mesh, eqs. (5.35) and (5.37) provide a simple and convenient way of calculating the normal mode frequencies at the points of the fine mesh.

Gilat and Dolling used this method to calculate the frequency spectrum of sodium. The dynamical matrix was diagonalized for only 440 independent values of $\boldsymbol{k}$, but a total of 34,992,000 frequencies were calculated by their extrapolation method, in about 1/50 the time required to carry out an equivalent calculation by the unmodified root sampling method (Dixon et al. 1963). The resulting spectrum is shown in fig. 1.

A more sophisticated, and faster, version of the extrapolation method for calculating frequency spectra has been proposed by Gilat and his coworkers (Gilat and Raubenheimer 1966, Raubenheimer and Gilat 1967, Kam and Gilat 1968, Gilat and Kam 1969, Gilat and Bohlin 1969, Dalton 1970, Gilat and Dalton 1971). The reader is referred to the original papers for a description of this method.

Because the distribution functions $g(\omega)$ and $G(\omega^2)$ are the sums of contributions from each branch of the phonon spectrum, as is evident from eqs. (5.5) and (5.6), in what follows we confine our attention to the contribution from a given branch, $g_j(\omega)$ or $G_j(\omega^2)$, respectively.

The most striking qualitative feature in frequency spectra calculated either analytically, or numerically with great precision, is the appearance of singu-

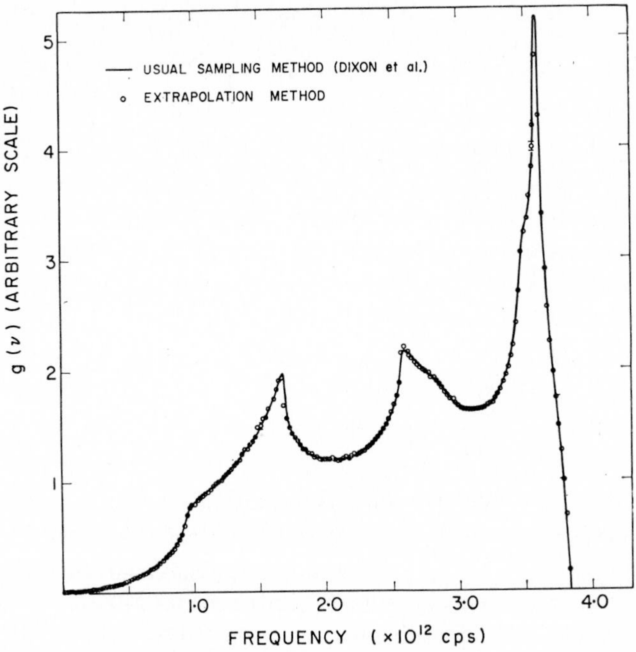

Fig. 1. The frequency spectrum $g(\omega)$ of sodium. The solid line is drawn smoothly through the results of Dixon et al. (1963); these comprise 24576000 frequencies, computed from 180441 independent wave vectors. The circles are obtained by the extrapolation method of Gilat and Dolling (1964), and comprise 34992000 frequencies obtained by diagonalizing the dynamical matrix at 440 independent wave vectors.

larities either in the spectrum itself, or in the derivative of the spectrum. These singularities are a general property of all frequency spectra.

To see their origin it is convenient to rewrite the expression for $G_j(\omega^2)$ which follows from eq. (5.6) with the use of the following representation of the delta-function

$$\delta(x) = (1/2\pi) \int_{-\infty}^{\infty} e^{-ixy}\, dy. \tag{5.38}$$

With an interchange of the orders of summation and integration we obtain for $G(\omega^2)$ the result

$$G_j(\omega^2) = (1/2\pi) \int_{-\infty}^{\infty} e^{-iy\omega^2} f_j(y)\, dy, \tag{5.39}$$

where

$$f_j(y) = (1/drN)\sum_{\boldsymbol{k}} \mathrm{e}^{\mathrm{i}y\omega_j{}^2(\boldsymbol{k})} = \{v_{\mathrm{a}}/dr(2\pi)^d\} \int_{\mathrm{BZ}} \mathrm{e}^{\mathrm{i}y\omega_j{}^2(\boldsymbol{k})}\,\mathrm{d}^3k \qquad (5.40\mathrm{a,\,b})$$

where v_{a} is now the volume of a primitive unit cell in a d-dimensional lattice. It is not difficult to show that the singular behavior of $G_j(\omega^2)$ is completely determined by the large $|y|$ behavior of $f_j(y)$ (Maradudin et al. 1971, section IV.3). According to the method of stationary phase (De Bruijn 1958), the latter is determined by the contributions from the regions of $\boldsymbol{k}$-space about the *critical points* for which $\mathrm{grad}_{\boldsymbol{k}}\,\omega_j^2(\boldsymbol{k})=0$.

Let us assume that about such a critical point $\omega_j^2(\boldsymbol{k})$ has the expansion

$$\omega_j^2(\boldsymbol{k}) = \omega_{\mathrm{c}}^2 + \sum_{\alpha=1}^{d}\sum_{\beta=1}^{d} a_{\alpha\beta}^{(j)} k_\alpha k_\beta + \mathrm{O}(k^2). \qquad (5.41)$$

If the determinant of the matrix $a_{\beta\alpha}^{(j)}$ is nonzero, the critical point at the frequency $\omega_j(\boldsymbol{k})=\omega_{\mathrm{c}}$ is called an *analytic critical point*. Nonanalytic critical points can also occur, but we will not consider them here (see, for example, Phillips 1956). We now make a linear transformation of coordinates from the $\{k_\alpha\}$ to a new set of coordinates $\{\varphi_\alpha\}$ such that

$$\omega_j^2(\boldsymbol{k}) = \omega_{\mathrm{c}}^2 + \sum_{\alpha=1}^{d} \varepsilon_\alpha \varphi_\alpha^2 + \mathrm{O}(\varphi^2), \qquad (5.42)$$

where $\varepsilon_\alpha = \pm 1$ for $\alpha = 1, 2, \cdots, d$. The number of negative ε's in this form is called the *index* of the critical point. The dominant behavior of $f_j(y)$ as $|y| \to \infty$ is obtained by keeping only the quadratic terms in the $\{\varphi_\alpha\}$ on the right hand side of eq. (5.42), and by extending the integration to all of φ-space. In this way we find that

$$f_j(y) \sim \{Av_{\mathrm{a}}/dr(2\pi)^d\}\,\mathrm{e}^{\mathrm{i}y\omega_{\mathrm{c}}{}^2} \prod_{\alpha=1}^{d} \int_{-\infty}^{\infty} \mathrm{e}^{\mathrm{i}y\varepsilon_\alpha\varphi_\alpha{}^2}\,\mathrm{d}\varphi_\alpha, \qquad (5.43)$$

where A is the jacobian of the transformation from the $\{k_\alpha\}$ to the $\{\varphi_\alpha\}$. Thus we obtain finally that

$$f_j(y) \sim \{Av_{\mathrm{a}}/dr(4\pi)^{d/2}\}\,\mathrm{e}^{\mathrm{i}y\omega_{\mathrm{c}}{}^2}\,|y|^{-d/2}\,\mathrm{e}^{\frac{1}{4}\pi\mathrm{i}\,(d-2I)\,\mathrm{sgn}\,y}, \qquad (5.44)$$

where I is the index of the critical point, and $\mathrm{sgn}\,y = +1$ for $y>0$ and -1 for $y<0$.

The form for $f_j(y)$ given by eq. (5.44) implies a specific behavior for $G_j(\omega^2)$ for $\omega^2 \sim \omega_{\mathrm{c}}^2$ by the use of tauberian theorems for Fourier transforms

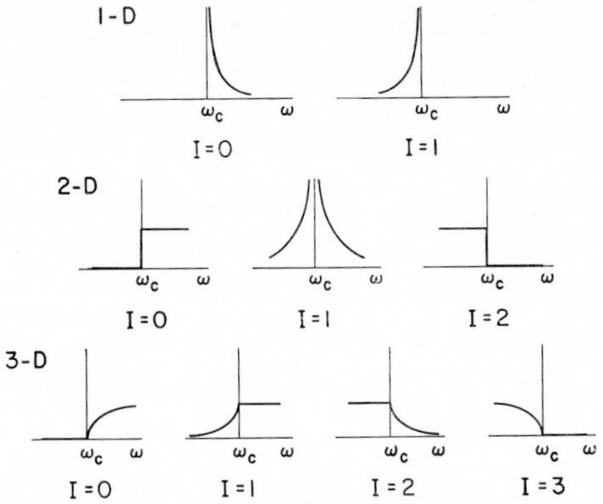

Fig. 2. The nature of the singularities in the distribution function for the squares of the normal mode frequencies, $G(\omega^2)$, as a function of the index of the corresponding analytic critical point, for one-, two-, and three-dimensional crystals.

(Lighthill 1958). The results (see fig. 2) obtained by substituting eq. (5.44) into eq. (5.39) can be summarized as follows (Maradudin and Peretti 1958):

1–D: $I=0$ (minimum) (5.45)

$$G_j(\omega^2) \sim (Av_a/4\pi r)\,|\omega^2-\omega_c^2|^{-1/2}\,[1+\mathrm{sgn}(\omega^2-\omega_c^2)],$$

$I=1$ (maximum)

$$G_j(\omega^2) \sim (Av_a/4\pi r)\,|\omega^2-\omega_c^2|^{-1/2}\,[1-\mathrm{sgn}(\omega^2-\omega_c^2)];$$

2–D: $I=0$ (minimum) (5.46)

$$G_j(\omega^2) \sim (Av_a/16\pi r)\,\mathrm{sgn}(\omega^2-\omega_c^2),$$

$I=1$ (saddlepoint)

$$G_j(\omega^2) \sim -(Av_a/8\pi^2 r)\ln|\omega^2-\omega_c^2|,$$

$I=2$ (maximum)

$$G_j(\omega^2) \sim -(Av_a/16\pi r)\,\mathrm{sgn}(\omega^2-\omega_c^2);$$

3–D: $I=0$ (minimum) (5.47)

$$G_j(\omega^2) \sim (Av_a/24\pi^2 r)\,|\omega^2-\omega_c^2|^{1/2}\,[1+\mathrm{sgn}(\omega^2-\omega_c^2)],$$

$I=1$ (saddlepoint, S_1)

$$G_j(\omega^2) \sim (Av_a/24\pi^2 r)\,|\omega^2-\omega_c^2|^{1/2}\,[-1+\mathrm{sgn}(\omega^2-\omega_c^2)],$$

$I=2$ (saddlepoint, S_2)

$$G_j(\omega^2) \sim -(Av_a/24\pi^2 r)\,|\omega^2-\omega_c^2|^{1/2}\,[1+\mathrm{sgn}(\omega^2-\omega_c^2)],$$

$I=3$ (maximum)

$$G_j(\omega^2) \sim (Av_a/24\pi^2 r)\,|\omega^2-\omega_c^2|^{1/2}\,[1-\mathrm{sgn}(\omega^2-\omega_c^2)].$$

The results expressed by eqs. (5.45)–(5.47) give only the singular part of $G_j(\omega^2)$ for $\omega^2 \sim \omega_c^2$. The total $G_j(\omega^2)$ for $\omega^2 \sim \omega_c^2$ will be the sum of the results given by eqs. (5.45)–(5.47) and an expression which is analytic for $\omega^2 \sim \omega_c^2$.

The method outlined here can also be used to obtain the contribution to $G_j(\omega^2)$ for ω^2 in the vicinity of a nonanalytic critical point.

Thus we see that each type of critical point in the function $\omega_j^2(\boldsymbol{k})$ gives rise to a characteristic singularity in $G_j(\omega^2)$.

The question now arises as to whether the occurrence of critical points is a general result, or is something special for the rather simple crystal models for which it has proved to be possible to obtain analytic expressions for $\omega_j^2(\boldsymbol{k})$. This question was answered by Van Hove (1953), who pointed out that according to a general theorem of Morse (1939) the periodicity of a crystal necessarily implies the existence of critical points in the surfaces of constant frequency in $\boldsymbol{k}$-space, and hence of singularities in the spectrum. Van Hove's statement of Morse's theorem as it applies to analytic critical points is: 'Consider a function f defined on a closed topological manifold satisfying convenient conditions of differentiability and regularity: assume f to be three times continuously differentiable and to have no degenerate critical points. Call the index of a non-degenerate critical point the number of negative† eigenroots of the quadratic form in the Taylor expansion of f near the critical point [the number of negative† terms in the sum (5.42)]. Under these conditions, the number of critical points of index i is at least equal to the Betti number R_i of the manifold for the dimension i.' The Betti, or connectivity, number R_i can be defined as 'the maximum number of closed i-dimensional surfaces on the manifold which cannot be transformed into one another or into a point by continuous deformation on the manifold.'

In applying Morse's theorem to the study of singularities in frequency spectra, we note that the assumption of the cyclic boundary conditions for the atomic displacements in a d-dimensional crystal enables us to regard the function $\omega(\boldsymbol{k})$ as being defined on a d-dimensional torus. If, in addition, we adopt the convention for labeling the different branches of $\omega(\boldsymbol{k})$ that $i<j$ implies that $\omega_i^2(\boldsymbol{k}) \leqslant \omega_j^2(\boldsymbol{k})$, so that two branches can at most touch, but can

† Van Hove's statement of Morse's theorem replaces 'negative' by 'positive.' However, since the Betti numbers R_i for a given manifold are symmetric in i and in $d-i$, where d is the dimensionality of the manifold, as is explicitly demonstrated in eq. (5.48), the content of the statement of the theorem given above is unaffected by this difference. The present choice of the definition of the index is made to conform with that made by Phillips (1956) in extending and generalizing the work of Van Hove.

never cross, each function $\omega_j(\boldsymbol{k})$ satisfies the conditions of the Morse theorem, provided it possesses only analytic critical points.

The Betti numbers for a one-dimensional torus are

$$R_0 = 1, \quad R_1 = 1; \tag{5.48a}$$

for a two-dimensional torus they are

$$R_0 = 1, \quad R_1 = 2, \quad R_2 = 1; \tag{5.58b}$$

and for a three-dimensional torus they are

$$R_0 = 1, \quad R_1 = 3, \quad R_2 = 3, \quad R_3 = 1. \tag{5.48c}$$

These results imply that in one dimension a branch of $\omega(\boldsymbol{k})$ which satisfies the conditions of Morse's theorem will possess at least one minimum and one maximum; in two dimensions it will possess at least one minimum, two saddlepoints, and one maximum; and in three dimensions each branch will possess at least one minimum, three saddlepoints of each kind, and one maximum.

Important contributions to the theory of critical points in surfaces of constant frequency have been made by Rosenstock (1955, 1957), who related the numbers and types of one-dimensional critical points on the bounding curve of a two-dimensional region to the numbers and types of two-dimensional critical points inside the region. In turn, the numbers and types of two-dimensional critical points on the boundary of a region were related to the numbers and types of three-dimensional critical points inside the region. This work, which was largely intuitive in nature, has been extended and made rigorous by Phillips and Rosenstock (1958), and the reader is referred to their paper for the details of the treatment and the results.

The work of Van Hove on the topological basis for the critical points in surfaces of constant frequency in $\boldsymbol{k}$-space has been generalized and extended by Phillips (1956). He has emphasized the usefulness of group theory for finding critical points. Indeed, it is not difficult, starting from eq. (5.37), to formulate a group-theoretic criterion for determining the number of vanishing components of the gradient $\nabla_{\boldsymbol{k}}\omega_j(\boldsymbol{k})$, for a given branch j at a given point $\boldsymbol{k}$ in the first Brillouin zone (see, for example, section 4.7 of the chapter by Birman in this book). Phillips has also presented the topological relations between the numbers of analytical critical points for a branch containing only analytic critical points. In two dimensions if we denote by n_j the number of analytic critical points of index j in the manifold, the following relations hold

$$n_0 \geqslant 1\,; \quad n_1 - n_0 \geqslant 1\,; \quad n_2 - n_1 + n_0 = 0\,. \tag{5.49}$$

In three dimensions the corresponding numbers N_j satisfy

$$\begin{aligned} &N_0 \geqslant 1\,; \quad N_1 - N_0 \geqslant 2\,; \quad N_2 - N_1 + N_0 \geqslant 1\,; \\ &N_3 - N_2 + N_1 - N_0 = 0\,. \end{aligned} \tag{5.50}$$

The inequalities obtained by adding the successive relations in (5.49) and (5.50) are just the Morse relations as stated by Van Hove. Phillips has also shown how the relations (5.49) and (5.50) can be applied in the presence of certain types of nonanalytic critical points, and has determined the nature of the singularities introduced into $G(\omega^2)$ by such singularities.

Despite the great amount of work on the problem by Van Hove, Rosenstock, and Phillips, no general scheme has yet been devised for finding critical points (short of computing surfaces of constant frequency numerically and examining them for critical points) that assures one that *all* critical points have been found. The work just described, however, has greatly simplified this task.

6. *Ionic crystals*

Since we have nowhere specified the range of the interatomic forces in the preceding discussion, it would seem that the results obtained so far apply equally to crystals in which the constituent atoms interact through short range forces and to ionic crystals, in which the ions interact through long range Coulomb forces. In fact, this is only partly true. If the charged ions making up the crystal are treated as rigid, or point, ions, the forces between ions, and consequently their equations of motion, can be derived from a potential function: the Coulomb potential plus the potential describing the short range repulsive interactions. However, ions are not point charges. The electronic charge distribution surrounding each nucleus is of finite extent. It can deform, and be displaced with respect to its nucleus as a consequence of the Pauli exclusion principle as a neighboring ion is brought up to it, and the overlap of the two electronic charge distributions increases. This ionic deformability can increase the dipole moment of the ion above the value obtained by displacing the static charge of the ion from its equilibrium position (Szigeti 1949, 1950), and can even induce dipole moments on atoms which bear no static charge, such as tellurium and graphite (Cochran 1961). The finite extent of the electronic charge distribution about an ion also renders the ion polarizable. It can deform in response to an electric field acting on it in such a way as to acquire a dipole moment in addition to the one it possesses by virtue of its deformability due to overlap and its static charge.

The deformability and polarizability of ions have important consequences for the dynamical properties of ionic crystals. However, because they are essentially electronic in origin, their effects cannot be incorporated into a dynamical theory of crystal lattices by starting from an expansion of the crystal potential energy in powers of the ionic displacements alone: the electronic coordinates have to be taken into account either explicitly, as in the 'shell model' of ionic crystals (Woods et al. 1960), or implicitly, through their consequences, as in the 'deformation dipole' model (Hardy 1962). At the phenomenological level, the results of either approach can be reproduced by supplementing the ionic displacements by the components of the macroscopic electric field in the crystal as independent dynamical variables in writing the equations of motion of a crystal. The components of the macroscopic field are ultimately related to the ionic displacements through the equations of electromagnetic theory, so that the final equations of motion from which the normal mode frequencies are obtained are again expressed in terms of the displacements alone.

However, while such a formulation of the dynamical theory of ionic crystals is only convenient in the context of determining the normal mode frequencies of such crystals (the shell model, for example, shows that it is not necessary), it becomes necessary for the determination of the long wavelength, acoustic mode characteristics of ionic crystal, such as the elastic, piezoelectric, and dielectric constants. The reasons for this are discussed in detail in the following section, and we will not go into them at this point.

To understand in which ways the rigid ion model fails to describe the dynamical properties of ionic crystals correctly, and to point the way to a phenomenological theory which does, we pause here to discuss the dynamical theory of ionic crystals in the rigid ion approximation.

In the rigid ion model of an ionic crystal the forces acting between ions are of two types: (*a*) forces of short range, which arise from the overlap of the electronic charge distributions on neighboring ions, and perhaps from Van der Waals interactions between ions; and (*b*) Coulomb forces, which are long range forces. If we denote the charge on the κth kind of ion by e_κ, then the latter forces are derived from the potential

$$\varphi_{\kappa\kappa'}(r) = e_\kappa e_{\kappa'}/r, \tag{6.1}$$

where r is the distance between a pair of ions.

The elements of the dynamical matrix $C_{\alpha\beta}(\kappa\kappa'|\boldsymbol{k})$ correspondingly separate into a Coulomb and a non-Coulomb part

$$C_{\alpha\beta}(\kappa\kappa'|\boldsymbol{k}) = R_{\alpha\beta}(\kappa\kappa'|\boldsymbol{k}) + T_{\alpha\beta}(\kappa\kappa'|\boldsymbol{k}), \tag{6.2}$$

where

$$R_{\alpha\beta}(\kappa\kappa'|\boldsymbol{k}) = (M_\kappa M_{\kappa'})^{-1/2} \sum_{l'} \Phi^{\mathrm{R}}_{\alpha\beta}(l\kappa; l'\kappa')\, \mathrm{e}^{-i\boldsymbol{k}\cdot[\boldsymbol{x}(l\kappa)-\boldsymbol{x}(l'\kappa')]}, \tag{6.3}$$

$$T_{\alpha\beta}(\kappa\kappa'|\boldsymbol{k}) = (M_\kappa M_{\kappa'})^{-1/2} \sum_{l'} \Phi^{\mathrm{C}}_{\alpha\beta}(l\kappa; l'\kappa')\, \mathrm{e}^{-i\boldsymbol{k}\cdot[\boldsymbol{x}(l\kappa)-\boldsymbol{x}(l'\kappa')]}. \tag{6.4}$$

Here the $\{\Phi^{\mathrm{R}}_{\alpha\beta}(l\kappa; l'\kappa')\}$ are the force constants associated with all the short range forces, while the $\{\Phi^{\mathrm{C}}_{\alpha\beta}(l\kappa; l'\kappa')\}$ are the force constants derived from the Coulomb interaction (6.1). From eq. (2.16b) we find that they are given by

$$\Phi^{\mathrm{C}}_{\alpha\beta}(l\kappa; l'\kappa') = -\, e_\kappa e_{\kappa'} \left\{ \frac{3x_\alpha x_\beta}{r^5} - \frac{\delta_{\alpha\beta}}{r^3} \right\}_{\boldsymbol{r}=\boldsymbol{x}(l\kappa;\, l'\kappa')} \qquad (l\kappa) \neq (l'\kappa'), \tag{6.5a}$$

$$\Phi^{\mathrm{C}}_{\alpha\beta}(l\kappa; l\kappa) = - \sum_{l'\kappa'\,(\neq l\kappa)} \Phi^{\mathrm{C}}_{\alpha\beta}(l\kappa; l'\kappa'). \tag{6.5b}$$

With the aid of Ewald's generalized theta function transformation (Ewald 1917a, b, 1921, 1938), the equations of motion of the crystal, eq. (3.14), which follow from the dynamical matrix (6.2) can be transformed into (Maradudin et al. 1971, section VI.2)

$$\begin{aligned}
\omega_j^2(\boldsymbol{k})\, w_\alpha(\kappa|\boldsymbol{k}j)
&= \sum_{\kappa'\beta} R_{\alpha\beta}(\kappa\kappa'|\boldsymbol{k})\, w_\beta(\kappa'|\boldsymbol{k}j) + \sum_{\kappa''\beta} M_\kappa^{-1} e_\kappa e_{\kappa''}\, Q_{\alpha\beta}(\kappa\kappa''|\boldsymbol{0})\, w_\beta(\kappa|\boldsymbol{k}j) \\
&\quad - \sum_{\kappa'\beta} (M_\kappa M_{\kappa'})^{-1/2}\, e_\kappa e_{\kappa'}\, Q_{\alpha\beta}(\kappa\kappa'|\boldsymbol{k})\, w_\beta(\kappa'|\boldsymbol{k}j) \\
&\quad + \sum_{\kappa'\beta} \frac{e_\kappa}{M_\kappa^{1/2}} \frac{4\pi}{v_{\mathrm{a}}} \frac{k_\alpha k_\beta}{k^2} \frac{e_{\kappa'}}{M_{\kappa'}^{1/2}}\, w_\beta(\kappa'|\boldsymbol{k}j).
\end{aligned} \tag{6.6}$$

The function $Q_{\alpha\beta}(\kappa\kappa'|\boldsymbol{k})$ appearing in this equation is defined by

$$Q_{\alpha\beta}(\kappa\kappa'\,|\,\boldsymbol{k}) = -\,(4\pi/v_{\mathrm{a}})\,(k_\alpha k_\beta/k^2)\,(\mathrm{e}^{-k^2/4P} - 1)$$
$$-\,(4\pi/v_{\mathrm{a}}) \sum_{\boldsymbol{G}\neq 0} \frac{(\boldsymbol{G}+\boldsymbol{k})_\alpha\,(\boldsymbol{G}+\boldsymbol{k})_\beta}{|\boldsymbol{G}+\boldsymbol{k}|^2}\,\mathrm{e}^{-|\boldsymbol{G}+\boldsymbol{k}|^2/4P}\,\mathrm{e}^{\mathrm{i}\boldsymbol{G}\cdot[\boldsymbol{x}(\kappa)-\boldsymbol{x}(\kappa')]}$$
$$+\,P^{3/2} \sum_{l'} H_{\alpha\beta}(\sqrt{P}\,|\boldsymbol{x}(l\kappa) - \boldsymbol{x}(l'\kappa')|)\,\mathrm{e}^{-\mathrm{i}\boldsymbol{k}\cdot[\boldsymbol{x}(l\kappa)-\boldsymbol{x}(l'\kappa')]}, \qquad (6.7)$$

where P is the separation parameter in the Ewald transformation, and the function $H_{\alpha\beta}(x)$ is

$$H_{\alpha\beta}(x) = \frac{\partial^2}{\partial x_\alpha \partial x_\beta}\,\frac{2}{\sqrt{\pi}}\,\frac{1}{x}\int_x^\infty \exp(-s^2)\,\mathrm{d}s \qquad (6.8a)$$

provided $\kappa \neq \kappa'$, and is given by

$$H_{\alpha\beta}(x) = \frac{\partial^2}{\partial x_\alpha \partial x_\beta}\left(-\frac{2}{\sqrt{\pi}}\,\frac{1}{x}\int_0^x \exp(-s^2)\,\mathrm{d}s\right) \qquad (6.8b)$$

in the term with $l' = l$ when $\kappa = \kappa'$. In the latter case the value of $H_{\alpha\beta}(x)$ at $x = 0$ is $(4/3\sqrt{\pi})\,\delta_{\alpha\beta}$.

We now focus our attention on the last term on the right-hand side of eq. (6.6), which is nonanalytic in the components of the wave vector $\boldsymbol{k}$. It is this term which represents the contribution of the macroscopic electric field in the crystal to its equations of motion.

To see this, let us obtain the macroscopic electric field in the crystal set up by a dipolar array defined by situating a dipole at each site $(l\kappa)$ whose moment is given by

$$\boldsymbol{p}(l\kappa) = \boldsymbol{p}(\kappa)\,\mathrm{e}^{\mathrm{i}\boldsymbol{k}\cdot\boldsymbol{x}(l\kappa)}. \qquad (6.9)$$

The wave vector $\boldsymbol{k}$ in this expression is assumed to be so small that $\boldsymbol{p}(l\kappa)$ changes very little in going from one unit cell to another. The polarization density in the crystal, $\boldsymbol{P}(\boldsymbol{x})$, arising from this dipolar array is given by

$$\boldsymbol{P}(\boldsymbol{x}) = \sum_{l\kappa} \boldsymbol{p}(l\kappa)\,\delta(\boldsymbol{x} - \boldsymbol{x}(l\kappa)) = \sum_{\boldsymbol{G}} \hat{\boldsymbol{P}}(\boldsymbol{G})\,\mathrm{e}^{\mathrm{i}(\boldsymbol{k}+\boldsymbol{G})\cdot\boldsymbol{x}}, \qquad (6.10, 11a)$$

where

$$\hat{\boldsymbol{P}}(\boldsymbol{G}) = (1/v_{\mathrm{a}}) \sum_{\kappa} \boldsymbol{p}(\kappa)\,\mathrm{e}^{-\mathrm{i}\boldsymbol{G}\cdot\boldsymbol{x}(\kappa)}. \qquad (6.11b)$$

The macroscopic polarization is given by the term with $\boldsymbol{G}=0$ in eq. (6.11a); the terms with $\boldsymbol{G}\neq 0$ in this equation, which correspond to variations of the polarization throughout the volume of a primitive unit cell of the crystal, describe the so-called local field corrections to the macroscopic polarization. Thus, the macroscopic polarization is given by

$$\boldsymbol{P}(\boldsymbol{x}) = \bar{\boldsymbol{P}}\, e^{i\boldsymbol{k}\cdot\boldsymbol{x}}, \tag{6.12a}$$

with

$$\bar{\boldsymbol{P}} = (1/v_a) \sum_{\kappa} \boldsymbol{p}(\kappa). \tag{6.12b}$$

To obtain the relation between the macroscopic electric field and the polarization in a medium we turn to Maxwell's equations, which we write as

$$\nabla\cdot\boldsymbol{D} = 0, \qquad \nabla\cdot\boldsymbol{H} = 0, \tag{6.13a, b}$$

$$\nabla\times\boldsymbol{E} = -(1/c)\,\dot{\boldsymbol{H}}, \qquad \nabla\times\boldsymbol{H} = (1/c)\,\dot{\boldsymbol{D}}, \tag{6.13c, d}$$

where c is the speed of light, and $\boldsymbol{H}$ and $\boldsymbol{D}$ are the magnetic field and the displacement in the medium. We take the curl of eq. (6.13c) and combine the result with the time derivative of eq. (6.13d) to obtain

$$\nabla\times\nabla\times\boldsymbol{E} = (1/c^2)\,\partial^2\boldsymbol{D}/\partial t^2. \tag{6.14}$$

If we use the fact that $\boldsymbol{D}=\boldsymbol{E}+4\pi\boldsymbol{P}$, the relation between $\boldsymbol{E}$ and $\boldsymbol{P}$ becomes

$$\nabla\times\nabla\times\boldsymbol{E} + (1/c^2)\,\partial^2\boldsymbol{E}/\partial t^2 = -(4\pi/c^2)\,\partial^2\boldsymbol{P}/\partial t^2. \tag{6.15}$$

Writing $\boldsymbol{E}(\boldsymbol{x}, t)$ and $\boldsymbol{P}(\boldsymbol{x}, t)$ in the forms

$$\boldsymbol{E}(\boldsymbol{x}, t) = \bar{\boldsymbol{E}}\, e^{i\boldsymbol{k}\cdot\boldsymbol{x}-i\omega t}, \qquad \boldsymbol{P}(\boldsymbol{x}, t) = \bar{\boldsymbol{P}}\, e^{i\boldsymbol{k}\cdot\boldsymbol{x}-i\omega t}, \tag{6.16a, b}$$

we obtain the relation between the amplitude vectors $\bar{\boldsymbol{E}}$ and $\bar{\boldsymbol{P}}$ from eq. (6.15) in the form

$$\sum_{\beta} [\delta_{\alpha\beta} - \hat{k}_\alpha\hat{k}_\beta - (\omega^2/c^2k^2)\,\delta_{\alpha\beta}]\,\bar{E}_\beta = (4\pi\omega^2/c^2k^2)\,\bar{P}_\alpha, \tag{6.17}$$

where $\hat{\boldsymbol{k}}$ is a unit vector in the direction of $\boldsymbol{k}$. The solution of this equation is

$$\bar{E}_\alpha = -4\pi \sum_{\beta} \hat{k}_\alpha\hat{k}_\beta\bar{P}_\beta + [4\pi/(n^2-1)] \sum_{\beta} (\delta_{\alpha\beta} - \hat{k}_\alpha\hat{k}_\beta)\,\bar{P}_\beta, \tag{6.18}$$

where $n=ck/\omega$ is the index of refraction of the wave under consideration. In the electrostatic approximation, which is the case of interest here, and which is obtained by letting $c \to \infty$, this relation simplifies to

$$\bar{E}_\alpha = -4\pi \sum_\beta \hat{k}_\alpha \hat{k}_\beta \bar{P}_\beta . \tag{6.19}$$

Combining eqs. (6.12b) and (6.19), we find that the amplitude of the macroscopic field set up by the dipolar array (6.9) is

$$\bar{E}_\alpha = -(4\pi/v_\mathrm{a}) \sum_{\kappa'\beta} \hat{k}_\alpha \hat{k}_\beta p_\beta(\kappa') . \tag{6.20}$$

When the ions constituting a crystal are displaced from their equilibrium positions in the normal mode $(\boldsymbol{k}j)$, we have that the time independent displacement is given by

$$u_\alpha(l\kappa) = M_\kappa^{-1/2} w_\alpha(\kappa \,|\, \boldsymbol{k}j)\, \mathrm{e}^{\mathrm{i}\boldsymbol{k}\cdot\boldsymbol{x}(l\kappa)} . \tag{6.21}$$

The dipole moment at the site $(l\kappa)$ induced by this displacement in the rigid ion model is

$$p_\alpha(l\kappa) = e_\kappa u_\alpha(l\kappa) = e_\kappa M_\kappa^{-1/2} w_\alpha(\kappa \,|\, \boldsymbol{k}j)\, \mathrm{e}^{\mathrm{i}\boldsymbol{k}\cdot\boldsymbol{x}(l\kappa)} . \tag{6.22}$$

so that the coefficient $p_\alpha(\kappa)$ in eq. (6.9) is seen to be

$$p_\alpha(\kappa) = e_\kappa M_\kappa^{-1/2} w_\alpha(\kappa \,|\, \boldsymbol{k}j) . \tag{6.23}$$

Substituting this result into eq. (6.20), we find that the contribution of the mode $(\boldsymbol{k}j)$ to the amplitude of the macroscopic field is

$$\bar{E}_\alpha = -(4\pi/v_\mathrm{a}) \sum_{\kappa'\beta} \hat{k}_\alpha \hat{k}_\beta e_{\kappa'} M_{\kappa'}^{-1/2} w_\beta(\kappa' \,|\, \boldsymbol{k}j) . \tag{6.24}$$

Combining eqs. (6.6) and (6.24), we finally obtain

$$\omega_j^2(\boldsymbol{k})\, w_\alpha(\kappa \,|\, \boldsymbol{k}j) = \sum_{\kappa'\beta} \bar{C}_{\alpha\beta}(\kappa\kappa' \,|\, \boldsymbol{k})\, w_\beta(\kappa' \,|\, \boldsymbol{k}j) - e_\kappa\, M_\kappa^{-1/2} \bar{E}_\alpha , \tag{6.25}$$

where we have introduced the notation

$$\begin{aligned} \bar{C}_{\alpha\beta}(\kappa\kappa' \,|\, \boldsymbol{k}) = R_{\alpha\beta}(\kappa\kappa' \,|\, \boldsymbol{k}) &+ \delta_{\kappa\kappa'} M_\kappa^{-1} e_\kappa \sum_{\kappa''} e_{\kappa''} Q_{\alpha\beta}(\kappa\kappa'' \,|\, \boldsymbol{0}) \\ &- (M_\kappa M_{\kappa'})^{-1/2}\, e_\kappa e_{\kappa'}\, Q_{\alpha\beta}(\kappa\kappa' \,|\, \boldsymbol{k}) . \end{aligned} \tag{6.26}$$

Equation (6.25) is in fact the time-independent equation of motion of a crystal driven by a macroscopic electric field.

It is clear from eqs. (6.25) and (6.26) that $\bar{C}_{\alpha\beta}(\kappa\kappa' \,|\, \boldsymbol{k})$ is an effective dynamical matrix. If we represent it in the form

$$\bar{C}_{\alpha\beta}(\kappa\kappa' \,|\, \boldsymbol{k}) = (M_\kappa M_{\kappa'})^{-1/2} \sum_{l'} \bar{\Phi}_{\alpha\beta}(l\kappa;\, l'\kappa')\, \mathrm{e}^{-\mathrm{i}\boldsymbol{k}\cdot[\boldsymbol{x}(l\kappa) - \boldsymbol{x}(l'\kappa')]} , \tag{6.27}$$

the effective atomic force constants $\{\bar{\Phi}_{\alpha\beta}(l\kappa;\, l'\kappa')\}$ defined in this way decrease rapidly with increasing distance between the sites $(l\kappa)$ and $(l'\kappa')$. This conclusion follows from two considerations. On comparing eqs. (6.2), (6.3), (6.26), and (6.27), we see that $\bar{\Phi}_{\alpha\beta}(l\kappa;\, l'\kappa')$ can be written as the sum

$$\bar{\Phi}_{\alpha\beta}(l\kappa;\, l'\kappa') = \Phi^{\mathrm{R}}_{\alpha\beta}(l\kappa;\, l'\kappa') + \Phi^{\mathrm{L}}_{\alpha\beta}(l\kappa;\, l'\kappa'). \tag{6.28}$$

$\Phi^{\mathrm{R}}_{\alpha\beta}(l\kappa;\, l'\kappa')$ is the force constant associated with the short range repulsive interactions between ions, and is usually assumed to be nonzero only if $(l\kappa)$ and $(l'\kappa')$ are no farther apart than nearest neighbors, or in some cases next nearest neighbors. $\Phi^{\mathrm{L}}_{\alpha\beta}(l\kappa;\, l'\kappa')$ is defined implicitly by the equation

$$\delta_{\kappa\kappa'} e_\kappa \sum_{\kappa''} e_{\kappa''} Q_{\alpha\beta}(\kappa\kappa'' \,|\, \mathbf{0}) - e_\kappa e_{\kappa'} Q_{\alpha\beta}(\kappa\kappa' \,|\, \boldsymbol{k}) = \sum_{l'} \Phi^{\mathrm{L}}_{\alpha\beta}(l\kappa;\, l'\kappa')\, \mathrm{e}^{-\mathrm{i}\boldsymbol{k}\cdot[\boldsymbol{x}(l\kappa) - \boldsymbol{x}(l'\kappa')]}. \tag{6.29}$$

It is seen from eq. (6.7) that the left-hand side of this equation can be expanded in a Maclaurin series in the components of the wave vector $\boldsymbol{k}$ in which arbitrarily high powers of these components can occur. It follows from this result and eq. (6.29) that the force constants $\{\Phi^{\mathrm{L}}_{\alpha\beta}(l\kappa;\, l'\kappa')\}$ must decrease with increasing separation between the sites $(l\kappa)$ and $(l'\kappa')$ faster than *any* inverse power of $|\boldsymbol{x}(l\kappa) - \boldsymbol{x}(l'\kappa')|$. Thus both terms on the right hand side of eq. (6.28) are short ranged, and so, therefore is $\bar{\Phi}_{\alpha\beta}(l\kappa;\, l'\kappa')$.

It can be shown that the force constants $\{\Phi^{\mathrm{L}}_{\alpha\beta}(l\kappa;\, l'\kappa')\}$ give the force acting on the ion $(l\kappa)$ due to the contribution to the Lorentz field in the crystal arising from the displacement of the ion $(l'\kappa')$ from its equilibrium position (Maradudin et al. 1971, section VI. 2c). It also follows on setting $\boldsymbol{k}=0$ in eq. (6.29), and summing both sides on κ', that the $\{\Phi^{\mathrm{L}}_{\alpha\beta}(l\kappa;\, l'\kappa')\}$ satisfy the infinitesimal translational invariance condition (2.8b).

We see from the preceding discussion that the macroscopic electric field thus accounts for that portion of the forces on an ion which is not determined by conditions in the immediate vicinity of the ion.

To understand the deficiencies of the rigid ion model, and the ways in which it can be modified to remove these deficiencies, it is instructive to use it to obtain the dielectric tensor of a crystal in the long wavelength limit. This limit suffices for the discussion of all optical properties of crystals which are not spatially dispersive in nature. To simplify the discussion we consider a cubic crystal containing two inequivalent ions in a primitive unit cell, e.g. a crystal possessing the rocksalt, cesium chloride, or zincblende structure. We label the two ions in each primitive unit cell by $\kappa = +, -$.

For such crystals symmetry arguments, together with considerations of infinitesimal translation invariance, show that in the limit as $\boldsymbol{k} \to 0$ the elements of the dynamical matrix $\bar{C}_{\alpha\beta}(\kappa\kappa'|\boldsymbol{k})$ take the form

$$\bar{C}_{\alpha\beta}(\kappa\kappa'|\mathbf{0}) = \delta_{\alpha\beta}\mu(M_\kappa M_{\kappa'})^{-1/2} \operatorname{sgn}\kappa \operatorname{sgn}\kappa' [\omega_0^2 - 4\pi e^2/3\mu v_a], \tag{6.30}$$

where $\operatorname{sgn}\kappa = +1, -1$, if $\kappa = +, -$, respectively, μ is the reduced mass of the two ions in a primitive unit cell, and e is the magnitude of the electronic charge. The first term arises from the short range force constants $\{\Phi^{\mathrm{R}}_{\alpha\beta}(l\kappa; l'\kappa')\}$; the second from the Lorentz field, where we have used the result (Maradudin et al. 1971, p. 212)

$$Q_{\alpha\beta}(\kappa\kappa'|\mathbf{0}) = \delta_{\alpha\beta}\, 4\pi/3v_a, \tag{6.31}$$

and have put

$$e_\kappa = e \operatorname{sgn}\kappa. \tag{6.32}$$

It is convenient to introduce a characteristic frequency ω_{T}^2 by

$$\omega_{\mathrm{T}}^2 = \omega_0^2 - 4\pi e^2/3\mu v_a.$$

The significance of this frequency will be apparent shortly.

If we denote by ω the frequency of the macroscopic electric field in the crystal, and assume solutions for the atomic displacements which have the same time dependence, we obtain from eqs. (6.25), (6.30), and (6.33), the following equation for the displacement amplitudes:

$$\omega^2 w_\alpha(\kappa) = \omega_{\mathrm{T}}^2 \sum_{\kappa'\beta} \delta_{\alpha\beta}\mu(M_\kappa M_{\kappa'})^{-1/2} \operatorname{sgn}\kappa \operatorname{sgn}\kappa'\, w_\beta(\kappa') - M_\kappa^{-1/2} e_\kappa \bar{E}_\alpha. \tag{6.34}$$

The solution of this equation for $w_\alpha(\kappa)$ can be written in the form

$$w_\alpha(\kappa) = \sum_{\kappa'\beta} \sum_{j=1}^{6} \frac{\xi_\alpha(\kappa|j)\,\xi_\beta(\kappa'|j)}{\lambda_j^2 - \omega^2} \frac{e_{\kappa'}}{M_{\kappa'}^{1/2}} \bar{E}_\beta, \tag{6.35}$$

where λ_j^2 is an eigenvalue, and $\xi_\alpha(\kappa|j)$ is the corresponding unit eigenvector, of the equation

$$\omega_{\mathrm{T}}^2 \sum_{\kappa'\beta} \delta_{\alpha\beta}\mu(M_\kappa M_{\kappa'})^{-1/2} \operatorname{sgn}\kappa \operatorname{sgn}\kappa'\, \xi_\beta(\kappa'|j) = \lambda_j^2 \xi_\alpha(\kappa|j), \tag{6.36}$$

where

$$\sum_{\kappa\alpha} \xi_\alpha(\kappa|j)\,\xi_\alpha(\kappa|j') = \delta_{jj'}, \qquad \sum_j \xi_\alpha(\kappa|j)\,\xi_\beta(\kappa'|j) = \delta_{\kappa\kappa'}\delta_{\alpha\beta}. \tag{6.37a, b}$$

The eigenvectors $\{\xi_\alpha(\kappa|j)\}$ can be chosen real with no loss of generality, because they are the eigenvectors of a real, symmetric matrix. It should be noted that the $\{\lambda_j^2\}$ are not necessarily the squares of the frequencies of the $\boldsymbol{k}\approx 0$ modes of the crystal, since they are the eigenvalues of only the short range force contribution to the $\boldsymbol{k}\approx 0$ dynamical matrix (see eq. (6.48) below). Because they enter the expressions for the dielectric susceptibility and dielectric constant of the crystal, the $\{\lambda_j\}$ are often called *dispersion frequencies.*

If we substitute eq. (6.36) into the expression for the amplitude of the macroscopic polarization in the crystal obtained from eqs. (6.12b) and (6.23), we obtain

$$\bar{P}_\alpha = (1/v_a)\sum_\kappa e_\kappa \frac{w_\alpha(\kappa)}{M_\kappa^{1/2}} = (1/v_a)\sum_\beta \sum_{j=1}^{6} \sum_{\kappa\kappa'} \frac{e_\kappa}{M_\kappa^{1/2}} \frac{\xi_\alpha(\kappa|j)\,\xi_\beta(\kappa'|j)}{\lambda_j^2-\omega^2} \frac{e_{\kappa'}}{M_{\kappa'}^{1/2}} \bar{E}_\beta . \tag{6.38}$$

The dielectric susceptibility $\chi_{\alpha\beta}(\omega)$ is obtained directly as

$$\chi_{\alpha\beta}(\omega) = (1/v_a)\sum_{j=1}^{6} \frac{M_\alpha(j)\,M_\beta(j)}{\lambda_j^2-\omega^2}, \tag{6.39}$$

where

$$M_\alpha(j) = \sum_\kappa e_\kappa \xi_\alpha(\kappa|j)/M_\kappa^{1/2} . \tag{6.40}$$

The solutions of eq. (6.36) are of two types. The first type of solution is given by

$$\lambda_j^2 = 0, \qquad \xi_\alpha(\kappa|j) = (M_\kappa/M_c)^{1/2}\, u_\alpha(j), \quad j=1,2,3, \tag{6.41}$$

where $M_c = M_+ + M_-$ is the total mass of a primitive unit cell, and the $\{\boldsymbol{u}(j)\}$ are any three mutually perpendicular unit vectors.

The second type of solution is given by

$$\lambda_j^2 = \omega_T^2, \qquad \xi_\alpha(\kappa|j) = \operatorname{sgn}\kappa\,(\mu/M_\kappa)^{1/2}\, \eta_\alpha(j), \quad j=4,5,6, \tag{6.42}$$

where the $\{\boldsymbol{\eta}(j)\}$ are also any three mutually perpendicular unit vectors.

From the definition (6.40) and eqs. (6.32) and (6.41) we see that the solutions of the first type make no contribution to the susceptibility (6.39), since for these solutions $M_\alpha(j)=0$. Only the solutions of the second type contribute to the susceptibility, which now takes the form

$$\chi_{\alpha\beta}(\omega) = \delta_{\alpha\beta} \frac{e^2}{\mu v_a} \frac{1}{\omega_T^2-\omega^2} . \tag{6.43}$$

From the relations

$$\bar{P}_\alpha = \sum_\beta \chi_{\alpha\beta}(\omega)\,\bar{E}_\beta, \quad \bar{D}_\alpha = \bar{E}_\alpha + 4\pi\bar{P}_\alpha, \quad \bar{D}_\alpha = \sum_\beta \varepsilon_{\alpha\beta}(\omega)\,\bar{E}_\beta, \qquad (6.44\text{a, b, c})$$

relating the amplitudes of the macroscopic electric field, polarization, and displacement in the crystal, we find that the dielectric tensor is given by

$$\varepsilon_{\alpha\beta}(\omega) = \delta_{\alpha\beta}\left(1 + \frac{4\pi e^2}{\mu v_\mathrm{a}}\,\frac{1}{\omega_\mathrm{T}^2 - \omega^2}\right) \equiv \delta_{\alpha\beta}\varepsilon(\omega). \qquad (6.45)$$

We can write $\varepsilon(\omega)$ alternatively as

$$\varepsilon(\omega) = (\omega_\mathrm{L}^2 - \omega^2)/(\omega_\mathrm{T}^2 - \omega^2), \qquad (6.46)$$

where we have introduced the frequency ω_L by

$$\omega_\mathrm{L}^2 = \omega_\mathrm{T}^2 + 4\pi e^2/\mu v_\mathrm{a}. \qquad (6.47)$$

The fact that we have obtained the dielectric susceptibility, and hence the dielectric tensor, by calculating the polarization induced by the macroscopic electric field set up by the ionic motions themselves rather than by some external sources is of no consequence: the susceptibility is defined as the ratio of the polarization in the medium to the macroscopic electric field in the medium, irrespective of the sources of the latter.

The physical significance of the frequencies ω_T and ω_L is readily determined. If we combine eqs. (6.24) and (6.34) we obtain for the equations of motion of the crystal in the long wavelength limit $(j=1, 2, \cdots, 6)$

$$\omega_j^2 w_\alpha(\kappa\,|\,j) = \omega_\mathrm{T}^2 \sum_{\kappa'\beta} \delta_{\alpha\beta}\mu\,(M_\kappa M_{\kappa'})^{-1/2}\,\mathrm{sgn}\,\kappa\;\mathrm{sgn}\,\kappa' w_\beta(\kappa'\,|\,j)$$
$$+ (4\pi/v_\mathrm{a}) \sum_{\kappa'\beta} M_\kappa^{-1/2} e_\kappa\,\hat{k}_\alpha \hat{k}_\beta\, M_{\kappa'}^{-1/2} e_{\kappa'}\, w_\beta(\kappa'\,|\,j). \qquad (6.48)$$

The values of ω obtained from this equation are the frequencies of the crystal in the long wavelength $(\boldsymbol{k}\approx 0)$ limit

The solutions of this equation are of two types. The first type of solution is

$$\omega_j^2 = 0, \qquad w_\alpha(\kappa\,|\,j) = (M_\kappa/M_\mathrm{c})^{1/2}\, u_\alpha(j), \quad j = 1, 2, 3, \qquad (6.49)$$

where the $\{\boldsymbol{u}(j)\}$ are any three mutually perpendicular unit vectors. These solutions are clearly the $\boldsymbol{k}=0$ acoustic modes. The second type of solution is obtained by setting $w_\alpha(\kappa\,|\,j) = \mathrm{sgn}\,\kappa\,(\mu/M_\kappa)^{1/2}\,\eta_\alpha(j)$, $j=4, 5, 6$. The equation satisfied by $\eta_\alpha(j)$ becomes

$$(\omega_j^2 - \omega_\mathrm{T}^2)\,\eta_\alpha(j) = (4\pi e^2/\mu v_\mathrm{a}) \sum_\beta \hat{k}_\alpha \hat{k}_\beta \eta_\beta(j). \tag{6.50}$$

This equation in turn has solutions of two types. If we assume that $\eta_\alpha(j)$ is parallel to $\boldsymbol{k}$, we obtain

$$\omega_4^2 = \omega_\mathrm{T}^2 + 4\pi e^2/\mu v_\mathrm{a} = \omega_\mathrm{L}^2. \tag{6.51}$$

This mode is clearly longitudinal in nature, and is called the longitudinal optical (LO) mode. If we next assume that $\eta_\alpha(j)$ is perpendicular to $\boldsymbol{k}$, and we can choose any two mutually perpendicular unit vectors which are also perpendicular to $\boldsymbol{k}$ for this purpose, we obtain

$$\omega_5^2 = \omega_6^2 = \omega_\mathrm{T}^2. \tag{6.52}$$

These modes are clearly transverse modes, and are called the transverse optical (TO) modes. The difference between the frequencies of the LO and TO modes is due to the fact that, as we can see from eq. (6.24), the LO mode has a macroscopic, longitudinal electric field associated with it, set up by the longitudinal optical ionic vibrations themselves. This field acts back on the ionic vibrations to stiffen the force constant determining the frequency of this mode and to raise its frequency with respect to that of the TO modes, which have no macroscopic field associated with them, in the electrostatic approximation.

A comparison of the expression for the dielectric constant, eqs. (6.45) and (6.46), and for the difference between the frequencies of the LO and TO modes, eq. (6.47), with experimental data reveals the following. The rigid ion model predicts a value of the optical frequency dielectric constant equal to unity,

$$\varepsilon_\infty = 1 \quad \text{(rigid ion model)}. \tag{6.53}$$

(The optical frequency dielectric constant is the value of $\varepsilon(\omega)$ at frequencies large compared with ω_T, but well below the frequency of the lowest electronic transition in the crystal. The latter typically corresponds to energies in the range from 2 to 10 eV.) It is found experimentally that values of ε_∞ for crystals of the type we consider here range between about 1.5 and 16 (see, for example, Burstein 1964). This difference is due to the neglect of the electronic polarizability of the crystal by the rigid ion model. In addition, the rigid ion model predicts a value for the ratio $\omega_\mathrm{L}^2/\omega_\mathrm{T}^2$ which is too large. From eq. (6.46) we find that

$$\omega_L^2/\omega_T^2 = \varepsilon(0) \quad \text{(rigid ion model)}, \tag{6.54}$$

where $\varepsilon(0)$ is the static dielectric constant. If experimental values of ω_L and ω_T are used for calculating the value of the left hand side of eq. (6.54), the values so obtained are smaller than the experimental values of the corresponding static dielectric constants (see, for example, Burstein 1964). The value of the difference

$$\omega_L^2 - \omega_T^2 = 4\pi e^2/\mu v_a \quad \text{(rigid ion model)} \tag{6.55}$$

is also given incorrectly by the rigid ion model. While the latter two discrepancies are due in part to the failure of the rigid ion model to predict the value of ε_∞ correctly, a correct explanation of the observed values of ω_L^2/ω_T^2 and $\omega_L^2-\omega_T^2$ requires that the magnitude of the ionic charge on which the macroscopic electric field acts be greater than that of the electronic charge. The effective charge e_T^*, called the transverse effective charge, which replaces e in the predictions of the rigid ion model is found experimentally to have values ranging from a little larger than e for the alkalihalides, to approximately $2e$ for polar III–V and II–VI semiconductors of the zincblende structure, to as large as $8e$ for lead salts of the rocksalt structure (Burstein et al. 1971b). The fact that a value of e_T^* greater than e is required for a correct determination of the optical mode frequencies of cubic diatomic crystals, while a charge of magnitude e yields values of static properties of alkali–halide crystals such as the cohesive energy and compressibility in good agreement with experiment, is explained by the deformability of the electronic charge distribution of an ion when it is displaced with respect to a second. The deformation of the charge distribution of the moving ion, which is a consequence of the Pauli exclusion principle, can lead to a dipole moment proportional to its displacement being induced on it. Added to the dipole moment resulting from the rigid displacement of the static charge of the ion, which is also proportional to its displacement, this deformation induced dipole moment gives rise to an apparent, or effective charge on the moving ion which is larger than its static value. In highly symmetric deformations of the crystal, however, such as are assumed in the calculations of the equilibrium nearest neighbor separation, the cohesive energy, and the compressibility, in which the site symmetry at an ionic site is not lowered, the deformation of the electron distribution about each ion does not lead to induced dipole moments at the ion sites. Consequently, the static properties of the crystal are well described by the assumption that the net charge on each ion has the nominal value $\pm e$

and not the larger value required for a description of the long wavelength optical vibrations of ionic crystals.

The essential physical phenomena which play a role in determining the vibrational properties of a crystal made up of polarizable and deformable ions can be taken into account phenomenologically by basing the dynamical theory of such crystals on the following expression for their potential energy (Minnick 1970, Burstein et al. 1971a, Maradudin et al. 1971, section VI.7):

$$\Phi = \tfrac{1}{2} \sum_{l\kappa\alpha} \sum_{l'\kappa'\beta} \Phi_{\alpha\beta}(l\kappa; l'\kappa')\, u_\alpha(l\kappa)\, u_\beta(l'\kappa') - \sum_{l\kappa\alpha} \sum_{l'\kappa'\beta} M_{\alpha\beta}(l\kappa; l'\kappa')\, E_\alpha(l\kappa)\, u_\beta(l'\kappa') - \tfrac{1}{2} \sum_{l\kappa\alpha} \sum_{l'\kappa'\beta} P_{\alpha\beta}(l\kappa; l'\kappa')\, E_\alpha(l\kappa)\, E_\beta(l'\kappa'). \quad (6.56)$$

In this expansion the force constants $\{\Phi_{\alpha\beta}(l\kappa; l'\kappa')\}$ describe the effects of all short range forces, including that associated with the Lorentz field, but contain no contribution associated with the macroscopic field. They are the analogues of the force constants $\{\bar{\Phi}_{\alpha\beta}(l\kappa; l'\kappa')\}$ defined by eq. (6.27). The coefficient $M_{\alpha\beta}(l\kappa; l'\kappa')$ is the transverse effective charge tensor, which gives the α-component of the dipole moment induced at the site $(l\kappa)$ when the ion $(l'\kappa')$ is displaced a unit distance in the β-direction. The coefficient $P_{\alpha\beta}(l\kappa; l'\kappa')$ is the electronic polarizability tensor, which gives the α-component of the dipole moment induced at the site $(l\kappa)$ by a unit macroscopic electric field in the β-direction acting on the ion $(l'\kappa')$. The fact that the effective charge tensor and the polarizability tensor, as well as the atomic force constants, are nonlocal is a reflection of the spatial extent of the electronic charge distribution about each ion, whose overlap with the charge distributions on neighboring ions is altered by changes in the internuclear separations and which is distorted by the macroscopic field acting on it, so that a generalized force applied to a given ion can exert an influence on properties associated with a different ion.

Just as the atomic force constants in a non-ionic crystal have certain general properties, which were discussed in section 2, the coefficients entering eq. (6.56) have several useful general properties, which we summarize here.

The coefficients $\Phi_{\alpha\beta}(l\kappa; l'\kappa')$ and $P_{\alpha\beta}(l\kappa; l'\kappa')$ are symmetric in the indices $(l\kappa\alpha)$ and $(l'\kappa'\beta)$:

$$\Phi_{\alpha\beta}(l\kappa; l'\kappa') = \Phi_{\beta\alpha}(l'\kappa'; l\kappa), \quad P_{\alpha\beta}(l\kappa; l'\kappa') = P_{\beta\alpha}(l'\kappa'; l\kappa). \quad (6.57a, b)$$

The invariance of the force on an atom and of the dipole moment of the crystal against a rigid body displacement of the crystal as a whole (infinitesimal translational invariance) yields the conditions

$$\sum_{l\kappa} \Phi_{\alpha\beta}(l\kappa; l'\kappa') = \sum_{l'\kappa'} \Phi_{\alpha\beta}(l\kappa; l'\kappa') = 0, \quad \sum_{l'\kappa'} M_{\alpha\beta}(l\kappa; l'\kappa') = 0. \quad (6.58a, b)$$

The transformation properties of the force on an ion and of the crystal dipole moment under a rigid body rotation of the crystal as a whole (infinitesimal rotational invariance) yield the conditions

$$\sum_{l'\kappa'} \Phi_{\alpha\beta}(l\kappa; l'\kappa')\, x_\gamma(l'\kappa') \quad \text{symmetric in } \beta \text{ and } \gamma, \tag{6.59a}$$

$$\sum_{l\kappa} x_\gamma(l\kappa)\, \Phi_{\alpha\beta}(l\kappa; l'\kappa') \quad \text{symmetric in } \alpha \text{ and } \gamma, \tag{6.59b}$$

$$\sum_{l'\kappa'} M_{\alpha\beta}(l\kappa; l'\kappa')\, x_\gamma(l'\kappa') \quad \text{symmetric in } \beta \text{ and } \gamma. \tag{6.60}$$

Finally, the transformation laws for these coefficients when the crystal is subjected to an operation $\{\boldsymbol{S}|\boldsymbol{v}(S)+\boldsymbol{x}(m)\}$ from its space group are

$$\Phi_{\alpha\beta}(LK; L'K') = \sum_{\mu\nu} S_{\alpha\mu} S_{\beta\nu} \Phi_{\mu\nu}(l\kappa; l'\kappa'), \tag{6.61a}$$

$$M_{\alpha\beta}(LK; L'K') = \sum_{\mu\nu} S_{\alpha\mu} S_{\beta\nu} M_{\mu\nu}(l\kappa; l'\kappa'), \tag{6.61b}$$

$$P_{\alpha\beta}(LK; L'K') = \sum_{\mu\nu} S_{\alpha\mu} S_{\beta\nu} P_{\mu\nu}(l\kappa; l'\kappa'). \tag{6.61c}$$

It follows from these transformation laws that each of the coefficients $\Phi_{\alpha\beta}(l\kappa; l'\kappa')$, $M_{\alpha\beta}(l\kappa; l'\kappa')$, $P_{\alpha\beta}(l\kappa; l'\kappa')$ is a function of the cell indices l and l' only through their difference.

The equations of motion of the crystal are

$$\begin{aligned} M_\kappa \ddot{u}_\alpha(l\kappa) &= -\,\partial\Phi/\partial u_\alpha(l\kappa) \\ &= -\sum_{l'\kappa'\beta} \Phi_{\alpha\beta}(l\kappa; l'\kappa')\, u_\beta(l'\kappa') + \sum_{l'\kappa'\beta} M_{\beta\alpha}(l'\kappa'; l\kappa)\, E_\beta(l'\kappa'). \end{aligned} \tag{6.62}$$

The dipole moment at the site $(l\kappa)$ is given by

$$\begin{aligned} p_\alpha(l\kappa) &= -\,\partial\Phi/\partial E_\alpha(l\kappa) \\ &= \sum_{l'\kappa'\beta} M_{\alpha\beta}(l\kappa; l'\kappa')\, u_\beta(l'\kappa') + \sum_{l'\kappa'\beta} P_{\alpha\beta}(l\kappa; l'\kappa')\, E_\beta(l'\kappa'). \end{aligned} \tag{6.63}$$

We can simplify these equations by taking advantage of the periodicity of the crystal through the substitutions

$$u_\alpha(l\kappa) = M_\kappa^{-1/2} v_\alpha(\kappa)\, e^{i\boldsymbol{k}\cdot\boldsymbol{x}(l\kappa) - i\omega t}, \quad E_\alpha(l\kappa) = E_\alpha\, e^{i\boldsymbol{k}\cdot\boldsymbol{x}(l\kappa) - i\omega t}, \quad (6.64a, b)$$

$$p_\alpha(l\kappa) = p_\alpha(\kappa)\, e^{i\boldsymbol{k}\cdot\boldsymbol{x}(l\kappa) - i\omega t}. \tag{6.64c}$$

Equations (6.62) and (6.63) now become

$$\omega^2 v_\alpha(\kappa) = \sum_{\kappa'\beta} \bar{C}_{\alpha\beta}(\kappa\kappa'\,|\,\boldsymbol{k})\, v_\beta(\kappa') - \frac{1}{\sqrt{M_\kappa}} \sum_{\kappa'\beta} M^*_{\beta\alpha}(\kappa'\kappa\,|\,\boldsymbol{k})\, E_\beta, \tag{6.65}$$

$$p_\alpha(\kappa) = \sum_{\kappa'\beta} M_{\alpha\beta}(\kappa\kappa'\,|\,\boldsymbol{k}) \frac{v_\beta(\kappa')}{\sqrt{M_{\kappa'}}} + \sum_{\kappa'\beta} P_{\alpha\beta}(\kappa\kappa'\,|\,\boldsymbol{k})\, E_\beta, \tag{6.66}$$

where

$$\bar{C}_{\alpha\beta}(\kappa\kappa'\,|\,\boldsymbol{k}) = (M_\kappa M_{\kappa'})^{1/2} \sum_{l'} \Phi_{\alpha\beta}(l\kappa;\, l'\kappa')\, \mathrm{e}^{-\mathrm{i}\boldsymbol{k}\cdot[\boldsymbol{x}(l\kappa)-\boldsymbol{x}(l'\kappa')]}. \tag{6.67a}$$

$$M_{\alpha\beta}(\kappa\kappa'\,|\,\boldsymbol{k}) = \sum_{l'} M_{\alpha\beta}(l\kappa;\, l'\kappa')\, \mathrm{e}^{-\mathrm{i}\boldsymbol{k}\cdot[\boldsymbol{x}(l\kappa)-\boldsymbol{x}(l'\kappa')]},$$

$$P_{\alpha\beta}(\kappa\kappa'\,|\,\boldsymbol{k}) = \sum_{l'} P_{\alpha\beta}(l\kappa;\, l'\kappa')\, \mathrm{e}^{-\mathrm{i}\boldsymbol{k}\cdot(\boldsymbol{x}(l\kappa)-\boldsymbol{x}(l'\kappa'))}. \tag{6.67b, c}$$

The matrices $\bar{C}_{\alpha\beta}(\kappa\kappa'\,|\,\boldsymbol{k})$ and $P_{\alpha\beta}(\kappa\kappa'\,|\,\boldsymbol{k})$ are hermitian.

The amplitude of the macroscopic polarization in the crystal is given by eq. (6.12b), which in the present case takes the form

$$P_\alpha = (1/v_\mathrm{a}) \sum_\kappa p_\alpha(\kappa) = (1/v_\mathrm{a}) \sum_{\kappa'\beta} Z_{\alpha\beta}(\kappa'\,|\,\boldsymbol{k})\, v_\beta(\kappa')/\sqrt{M_{\kappa'}} + \sum_\beta \chi^\infty_{\alpha\beta}(\boldsymbol{k})\, E_\beta, \tag{6.68}$$

where we have introduced the $\boldsymbol{k}$-dependent effective charge tensor for the κth kind of ion

$$Z_{\alpha\beta}(\kappa\,|\,\boldsymbol{k}) = \sum_{\kappa'} M_{\alpha\beta}(\kappa'\kappa\,|\,\boldsymbol{k}), \tag{6.69}$$

and the $\boldsymbol{k}$-dependent optical frequency susceptibility

$$\chi^\infty_{\alpha\beta}(\boldsymbol{k}) = (1/v_\mathrm{a}) \sum_{\kappa\kappa'} P_{\alpha\beta}(\kappa\kappa'\,|\,\boldsymbol{k}). \tag{6.70}$$

We now combine eq. (6.68) with the equation of electrostatics, eq. (6.19), to obtain as the equation relating E_α and $v_\alpha(\kappa)$

$$E_\alpha = -(4\pi/v_\mathrm{a})\,[\hat{k}_\alpha/\varepsilon^\infty_\mathrm{L}(\boldsymbol{k})] \sum_{\kappa'\beta} \left(\sum_\gamma \hat{k}_\gamma Z_{\alpha\beta}(\kappa'\,|\,\boldsymbol{k}) \right) v_\beta(\kappa')/\sqrt{M_{\kappa'}}, \tag{6.71}$$

where

$$\varepsilon^\infty_\mathrm{L}(\boldsymbol{k}) = \sum_{\alpha\beta} \hat{k}_\alpha \varepsilon^\infty_{\alpha\beta}(\boldsymbol{k})\, \hat{k}_\beta, \tag{6.72}$$

and $\varepsilon^\infty_{\alpha\beta}(\boldsymbol{k})$ is the $\boldsymbol{k}$-dependent, optical frequency dielectric tensor of the crystal,

$$\varepsilon^\infty_{\alpha\beta}(\boldsymbol{k}) = \delta_{\alpha\beta} + 4\pi\chi^\infty_{\alpha\beta}(\boldsymbol{k}). \tag{6.73}$$

When eq. (6.71) is substituted into eq. (6.65), and we label the $3r$ solutions of the resulting set of equations by $j=1, 2, \cdots, 3r$, and make explicit their dependence on $\boldsymbol{k}$, we can rewrite these equations as

$$\omega_j^2(\boldsymbol{k})\, v_\alpha(\kappa\,|\,\boldsymbol{k}j) = \sum_{\kappa'\beta} \mathscr{C}_{\alpha\beta}(\kappa\kappa'\,|\,\boldsymbol{k})\, v_\beta(\kappa'\,|\,\boldsymbol{k}j), \tag{6.74}$$

where the modified dynamical matrix $\mathscr{C}_{\alpha\beta}(\kappa\kappa'\,|\,\boldsymbol{k})$ is defined by

$$\mathscr{C}_{\alpha\beta}(\kappa\kappa'\,|\,\boldsymbol{k}) = \bar{C}_{\alpha\beta}(\kappa\kappa'\,|\,\boldsymbol{k}) + \frac{4\pi}{v_a}\frac{1}{\varepsilon_L^\infty(\boldsymbol{k})}\frac{1}{(M_\kappa M_{\kappa'})^{1/2}}\Big(\sum_\mu \hat{k}_\mu Z^*_{\mu\alpha}(\kappa\,|\,\boldsymbol{k})\Big)\Big(\sum_\nu \hat{k}_\nu Z_{\nu\beta}(\kappa'\,|\,\boldsymbol{k})\Big) = \mathscr{C}^*_{\beta\alpha}(\kappa'\kappa\,|\,\boldsymbol{k}). \tag{6.75}$$

The second term on the right-hand side of this equation describes the effects of the macroscopic field in the crystal.

The coefficients $\{\Phi_{\alpha\beta}(l\kappa;\, l'\kappa')\}$, $\{M_{\alpha\beta}(l\kappa;\, l'\kappa')\}$, and $\{P_{\alpha\beta}(l\kappa;\, l'\kappa')\}$ are to be determined from experimental data. For example, for waves propagating along the [100] direction in a crystal of the rocksalt structure, the frequencies of the transverse modes are determined only by the dynamical matrix $\bar{C}_{\alpha\beta}(\kappa\kappa'\,|\,\boldsymbol{k})$, and hence only by the short range force constants $\{\Phi_{\alpha\beta}(l\kappa;\, l'\kappa')\}$; the macroscopic field enters only the calculation of the frequencies of the longitudinal modes (Maradudin et al. 1971, p. 280). From experimental data for the frequencies of the transverse modes propagating in this direction, as well as from the elastic constants, considerable information concerning the $\{\Phi_{\alpha\beta}(l\kappa;\, l'\kappa')\}$ can be obtained. The experimental values of the transverse effective charge and the piezoelectric constants (in piezoelectric crystals) yield information about the coefficients $\{M_{\alpha\beta}(l\kappa;\, l'\kappa')\}$. Finally, experimental values for the optical frequency dielectric constant, the optical gyrotropic tensor (in optically active crystals), and higher order spatially dispersive optical properties of the crystal (Pastrnak and Vedam 1971, Yu and Cardona 1971) enable values of the coefficients $\{P_{\alpha\beta}(l\kappa;\, l'\kappa')\}$ to be obtained.

Several consequences of the preceding phenomenological approach to the dynamical theory of ionic crystals, or, more generally, of crystals made up of deformable and polarizable ions, have been discussed by Maradudin et al. (1971, section VI.7), and by Burstein et al. (1971a), while others are worked out in the next section.

In the long wavelength limit, for cubic crystals containing two inequivalent ions in a primitive unit cell, considerations of symmetry and infinitesimal translational invariance yield the results that

$$\bar{C}_{\alpha\beta}(\kappa\kappa'\,|\,\mathbf{0}) = \delta_{\alpha\beta}\mu\,(M_\kappa M_{\kappa'})^{-1/2}\ \mathrm{sgn}\,\kappa\ \mathrm{sgn}\,\kappa'\ \omega_{\mathrm{T}}^2, \tag{6.76a}$$

$$Z_{\alpha\beta}(\kappa\,|\,\mathbf{0}) = \delta_{\alpha\beta}\ \mathrm{sgn}\,\kappa e_{\mathrm{T}}^*, \tag{6.76b}$$

$$\varepsilon_{\mathrm{L}}^{\infty}(\mathbf{0}) = \varepsilon_\infty, \tag{6.76c}$$

$$\chi_{\alpha\beta}^{\infty}(\mathbf{0}) = \delta_{\alpha\beta}\chi_\infty = \delta_{\alpha\beta}(\varepsilon_\infty - 1)/4\pi. \tag{6.76d}$$

The arguments which were used to obtain eqs. (6.45) and (6.46) now lead to the following expression for the dielectric tensor

$$\varepsilon_{\alpha\beta}(\omega) = \delta_{\alpha\beta}\left\{\varepsilon_\infty + \frac{4\pi\,(e_{\mathrm{T}}^*)^2}{\mu v_{\mathrm{a}}}\,\frac{1}{\omega_{\mathrm{T}}^2 - \omega^2}\right\} = \delta_{\alpha\beta}\varepsilon(\omega), \tag{6.77}$$

or equivalently,

$$\varepsilon(\omega) = \varepsilon_\infty\,(\omega_{\mathrm{L}}^2 - \omega^2)/(\omega_{\mathrm{T}}^2 - \omega^2), \tag{6.78}$$

where

$$\omega_{\mathrm{L}}^2 = \omega_{\mathrm{T}}^2 + 4\pi\,(e_{\mathrm{T}}^*)^2/\varepsilon_\infty \mu v_{\mathrm{a}} \equiv \omega_{\mathrm{T}}^2 + \omega_{\mathrm{p}}^2, \tag{6.79}$$

where ω_{p} is the so-called ion plasma frequency. From eq. (6.78) we see that the ratio of ω_{L}^2 to ω_{T}^2 is now given by

$$\omega_{\mathrm{L}}^2/\omega_{\mathrm{T}}^2 = \varepsilon(0)/\varepsilon_\infty. \tag{6.80}$$

This relation, known as the Lyddane–Sachs–Teller relation (Lyddane et al. 1941), is very well satisfied experimentally, as is eq. (6.79).

In this way theory and experiment can be reconciled in the study of the dynamical properties of ionic crystals.

The discussion in this section so far has been based on the electrostatic approximation, in which it is assumed that the Coulomb force acts instantaneously between the ions. In fact, it propagates with the speed of light. The retardation of the Coulomb interaction can be neglected provided that the time needed to traverse the distance between two lattice sites in the crystal with the speed of light is negligible compared with the period of the vibrations with which we are concerned. If ω is the frequency of an optical vibration mode in the infrared region this condition is satisfied for values of the wave vector $k \gg \omega/c$. However, for values of $k < \omega/c$ the retardation of the Coulomb interaction can no longer be neglected. We conclude this section with a brief discussion of one of the consequences of taking retardation into account in the dynamical theory of ionic crystals. For simplicity we again confine our attention to cubic crystals with two inequivalent ions in a primitive unit cell.

Just as the long wavelength longitudinal optical modes of an ionic crystal in the electrostatic approximation give rise to a longitudinal macroscopic electric field, which acts back on the ions to raise the frequency of the LO mode above that of the TO modes, when the retardation of the Coulomb interaction is taken into account it is found that the long wavelength transverse optical modes give rise to a transverse electromagnetic field. This field acts back on the transverse modes which are its source to alter their frequencies from what they are in its absence. At the same time, the dispersion relation for the transverse electromagnetic field propagating through the crystal is altered by its coupling to the polarization field set up by the transverse modes. The normal modes of this linearly coupled system of electromagnetic waves and mechanical vibrations are called *polaritons* (Huang 1951a, b, Fano 1956, Hopfield 1958). We now turn to obtain the dispersion relation for the polaritons.

Since retardation effects are important only for very small values of the wave vector, we can treat the dynamical properties of the crystal in the limit $\boldsymbol{k}=0$. Then we combine eqs. (6.17) and (6.44) to obtain the equation describing the propagation of an electromagnetic wave through a crystal

$$\sum_{\beta} [\delta_{\alpha\beta} - \hat{k}_\alpha \hat{k}_\beta - (\omega^2/c^2k^2)\, \varepsilon_{\alpha\beta}(\omega)]\, \bar{E}_\beta = 0 . \tag{6.81}$$

For a dielectric tensor of the form of eq. (6.77), we find that for longitudinal fields, for which $\bar{\boldsymbol{E}} \parallel \boldsymbol{k}$, eq. (6.81) reduces to

$$\varepsilon(\omega)\, \bar{E}_\alpha = 0 , \tag{6.82}$$

while for transverse fields, for which $\bar{\boldsymbol{E}} \perp \boldsymbol{k}$, we obtain

$$[1 - (\omega^2/c^2k^2)\, \varepsilon(\omega)]\, \bar{E}_\alpha = 0 \quad \text{(twice)}. \tag{6.83}$$

From eq. (6.78) we see that eq. (6.82) yields the result that

$$\omega = \omega_{\mathrm{L}} , \tag{6.84}$$

so that the frequency of longitudinal waves is not affected by retardation effects. In contrast, eq. (6.83) becomes

$$c^2k^2 = \omega^2 \varepsilon(\omega) = \varepsilon_\infty \omega^2 (\omega_{\mathrm{L}}^2 - \omega^2)/(\omega_{\mathrm{T}}^2 - \omega^2). \tag{6.85}$$

The solutions of eq. (6.85) can be written

$$\omega_{\pm}^2(k) = \tfrac{1}{2}\{\omega_L^2 + (c^2k^2/\varepsilon_\infty) \pm [(\omega_L^2 + c^2k^2/\varepsilon_\infty)^2 - 4\omega_T^2c^2k^2/\varepsilon_\infty]^{1/2}\}. \tag{6.86}$$

The two branches of this dispersion relation are the two branches of the polariton dispersion curve. Only experimentally determinable quantities appear in eq. (6.86).

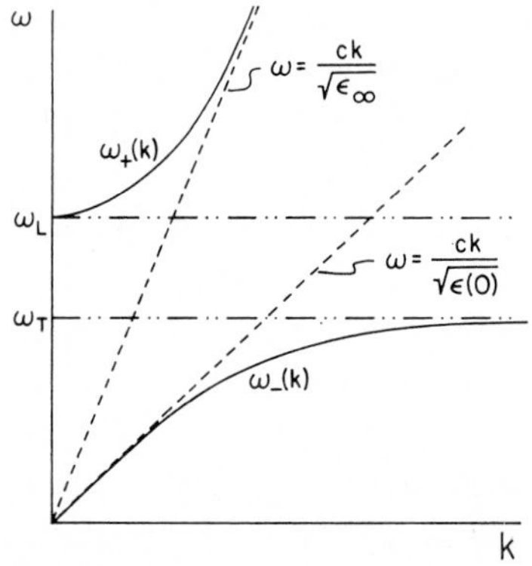

Fig. 3. A schematic representation of the polariton dispersion curves for a cubic ionic crystal with two inequivalent ions in a primitive unit cell.

The functions $\omega_{\pm}(k)$ are plotted in fig. 3. We see that as $k \to 0$, $\omega_-(k) \to ck/\sqrt{\varepsilon(0)}$, which is the dispersion relation for an electromagnetic wave propagating through a medium whose dielectric constant is the static dielectric constant $\varepsilon(0)$. As $k \to \infty$, $\omega_-(k) \to \omega_T$, which is the dispersion relation for purely mechanical transverse optical modes in the absence of retardation. The upper branch $\omega_+(k)$ corresponds to purely mechanical vibrations with the frequency ω_L as $k \to 0$, and describes the propagation of an electromagnetic wave through a medium whose dielectric constant has the optical frequency value ε_∞, in the limit as $k \to \infty$. In the region $k \approx \omega_T/c\sqrt{\varepsilon(0)}$ the modes whose frequencies are given by eq. (6.86) have no such simple, purely electromagnetic or purely mechanical, nature. They consist of admixtures of electromagnetic and mechanical vibrations. In agreement with the qualitative remarks made earlier we see that it is only for $k < \omega_T/c$ that the effects of retardation are significant.

In recent years polaritons in a variety of crystals have been studied experimentally by the techniques of inelastic light scattering [for discussions of these experiments see the review articles by Burstein and Mills (1969), and Scott (1971)].

7. Elastic, piezoelectric, and dielectric constants

So far in this chapter we have considered the theory of lattice dynamics from an atomistic, or microscopic, point of view. If this theory is applied to the study of the long-wavelength acoustic modes of an arbitrary crystal, in which the atomic displacements vary slowly from atom to atom as a consequence of infinitesimal translational invariance according to the discussion following eq. (3.11), we are dealing with the propagation of sound waves, which is ordinarily described by the macroscopic equations of motion of an elastic medium. If the crystal is ionic, its normal mode frequencies are determined by the atomic force constants $\Phi_{\alpha\beta}(l\kappa; l'\kappa')$, the effective charge tensors $M_{\alpha\beta}(l\kappa; l'\kappa')$, and the polarizability tensors $P_{\alpha\beta}(l\kappa; l'\kappa')$. Such crystals, in general, have to be regarded as piezoelectric, so that the frequencies of sound waves in an elastic dielectric are determined by the macroscopic elastic, piezoelectric, and dielectric constants of the solid. Thus, a comparison of the predictions of the microscopic and macroscopic theories for the frequencies of sound waves yields expressions for the macroscopic crystal tensors in terms of the atomic force constants and the effective charge and polarizability tensors. We conclude this chapter with the derivation of these relations. Such relations are useful to have because, as has been pointed out in the last section, in the general theory of lattice dynamics the atomic force constants, effective charge tensors, and polarizabilities are parameters of the theory, whose values are determined from comparisons of the predictions of the theory with experimental results. Although determinations of phonon dispersion curves by neutron spectroscopy provide more detailed information concerning phonon frequencies in crystals than can possibly be obtained from macroscopic considerations, the satisfaction of the relations to be obtained in this section ensures that a given lattice dynamical model at the very least predicts the correct speeds of sound for a crystal, and is otherwise compatible with the requirements of macroscopic theory.

Although for the sake of greater generality the discussion is presented here in the context of the theory of ionic crystals, the results obtained can be applied to nonionic crystals, e.g. metals, by setting to zero the tensors $M_{\alpha\beta}(l\kappa; l'\kappa')$ and $P_{\alpha\beta}(l\kappa; l'\kappa')$.

The starting point for our discussion are the equations of motion of an arbitrary ionic crystal, eqs. (6.74), which we write in the form

$$\omega_j^2(\boldsymbol{k})\, v_\alpha(\kappa|\boldsymbol{k}j) = \sum_{\kappa'\beta} \bar{C}_{\alpha\beta}(\kappa\kappa'|\boldsymbol{k})\, v_\beta(\kappa'|\boldsymbol{k}j) - M_\kappa^{-1/2} \sum_\beta Z^*_{\beta\alpha}(\kappa|\boldsymbol{k})\, E_\beta \tag{7.1a}$$

and

$$E_\alpha = -(4\pi/v_a)\frac{\hat{k}_\alpha}{\varepsilon_L^\infty(\boldsymbol{k})}\sum_{\kappa'\beta}\left(\sum_\gamma \hat{k}_\gamma Z_{\gamma\beta}(\kappa'|\boldsymbol{k})\right)v_\beta(\kappa'|\boldsymbol{k}j)/\sqrt{M_{\kappa'}}. \tag{7.1b}$$

In the case of a general crystal which has optical modes whose frequencies do not vanish as $\boldsymbol{k}\to 0$, it is necessary to carry out a perturbation calculation about the zero frequency solutions of eqs. (7.1). This is the method of long waves of Born (1923). We thus expand all quantities appearing in eq. (7.1) in powers of $\boldsymbol{k}$, up to second order:

$$\omega_j(\boldsymbol{k}) = \omega_j^{(1)}(\boldsymbol{k}) + \tfrac{1}{2}\omega_j^{(2)}(\boldsymbol{k}) + \cdots, \tag{7.2a}$$

$$v_\alpha(\kappa|\boldsymbol{k}j) = v_\alpha^{(0)}(\kappa|\boldsymbol{k}j) + \mathrm{i}v_\alpha^{(1)}(\kappa|\boldsymbol{k}j) + \tfrac{1}{2}v_\alpha^{(2)}(\kappa|\boldsymbol{k}j) + \cdots, \tag{7.2b}$$

$$E_\alpha = E_\alpha^{(0)} + \mathrm{i}E_\alpha^{(1)} + \tfrac{1}{2}E_\alpha^{(2)} + \cdots, \tag{7.2c}$$

$$\bar{C}_{\alpha\beta}(\kappa\kappa'|\boldsymbol{k}) = \bar{C}_{\alpha\beta}^{(0)}(\kappa\kappa') + \mathrm{i}\sum_\gamma \bar{C}_{\alpha\beta\gamma}^{(1)}(\kappa\kappa')\,k_\gamma + \tfrac{1}{2}\sum_{\gamma\lambda}\bar{C}_{\alpha\beta\gamma\lambda}^{(2)}(\kappa\kappa')\,k_\gamma k_\lambda + \cdots, \tag{7.2d}$$

$$Z_{\alpha\beta}(\kappa|\boldsymbol{k}) = Z_{\alpha\beta}^{(0)}(\kappa) + \mathrm{i}\sum_\gamma Z_{\alpha\beta\gamma}^{(1)}(\kappa)\,k_\gamma + \tfrac{1}{2}\sum_{\gamma\lambda}Z_{\alpha\beta\gamma\lambda}^{(2)}(\kappa)\,k_\gamma k_\lambda + \cdots, \tag{7.2e}$$

$$\chi_{\alpha\beta}^\infty(\boldsymbol{k}) = \chi_{\alpha\beta}^\infty + \mathrm{i}\sum_\gamma \chi_{\alpha\beta\gamma}^{(1)}k_\gamma + \tfrac{1}{2}\sum_{\gamma\lambda}\chi_{\alpha\beta\gamma\lambda}^{(2)}k_\gamma k_\lambda + \cdots, \tag{7.2f}$$

$$\varepsilon_L^\infty(\boldsymbol{k}) = \varepsilon_L^\infty + \tfrac{1}{2}\sum_{\gamma\lambda}\varepsilon_{L\gamma\lambda}^\infty k_\gamma k_\lambda + \cdots. \tag{7.2g}$$

The coefficient functions entering these expansions which will be required below are given by

$$\bar{C}_{\alpha\beta}^{(0)}(\kappa\kappa') = (M_\kappa M_{\kappa'})^{-1/2}\sum_{l'}\Phi_{\alpha\beta}(l\kappa;l'\kappa'), \tag{7.3a}$$

$$\bar{C}_{\alpha\beta\gamma}^{(1)}(\kappa\kappa') = -(M_\kappa M_{\kappa'})^{-1/2}\sum_{l'}\Phi_{\alpha\beta}(l\kappa;l'\kappa')\,x_\gamma(l\kappa;l'\kappa'), \tag{7.3b}$$

$$\bar{C}_{\alpha\beta\gamma\lambda}^{(2)}(\kappa\kappa') = -(M_\kappa M_{\kappa'})^{-1/2}\sum_{l'}\Phi_{\alpha\beta}(l\kappa;l'\kappa')\,x_\gamma(l\kappa;l'\kappa')\,x_\lambda(l\kappa;l'\kappa'), \tag{7.3c}$$

$$Z_{\alpha\beta}^{(0)}(\kappa) = \sum_{l'\kappa'}M_{\alpha\beta}(l\kappa';l'\kappa), \tag{7.4a}$$

$$Z_{\alpha\beta\gamma}^{(1)}(\kappa) = -\sum_{l'\kappa'}M_{\alpha\beta}(l\kappa';l'\kappa)\,x_\gamma(l\kappa';l'\kappa). \tag{7.4b}$$

$$\chi_{\alpha\beta}^\infty = (1/v_a)\sum_{l'\kappa\kappa'}P_{\alpha\beta}(l\kappa;l'\kappa'), \tag{7.5}$$

$$\varepsilon_L^\infty = 1 + 4\pi\sum_{\alpha\beta}\hat{k}_\alpha\,\chi_{\alpha\beta}^\infty\,\hat{k}_\beta, \tag{7.6}$$

$$E_\alpha^{(0)} = -(4\pi/v_a)(\hat{k}_\alpha/\varepsilon_L^\infty)\sum_{\kappa'\beta}\left(\sum_\gamma \hat{k}_\gamma Z_{\gamma\beta}^{(0)}(\kappa')\right)v_\beta^{(0)}(\kappa'|\boldsymbol{k}j)/\sqrt{M_{\kappa'}}. \tag{7.7}$$

Substituting eqs. (7.2) into eq. (7.1a), we obtain the perturbation equations

$$\sum_{\kappa'\beta} \bar{C}^{(0)}_{\alpha\beta}(\kappa\kappa')\, v^{(0)}_{\beta}(\kappa'|\boldsymbol{k}j) - M_{\kappa}^{-1/2} \sum_{\beta} Z^{(0)}_{\beta\alpha}(\kappa)\, E^{(0)}_{\beta} = 0, \tag{7.8a}$$

$$\sum_{\kappa'\beta} \bar{C}^{(0)}_{\alpha\beta}(\kappa\kappa')\, v^{(1)}_{\beta}(\kappa'|\boldsymbol{k}j) - M_{\kappa}^{-1/2} \sum_{\beta} Z^{(0)}_{\beta\alpha}(\kappa)\, E^{(1)}_{\beta}$$
$$= - \sum_{\kappa'\beta\gamma} \bar{C}^{(1)}_{\alpha\beta\gamma}(\kappa\kappa')\, k_{\gamma} v^{(0)}_{\beta}(\kappa'|\boldsymbol{k}j) - M_{\kappa}^{-1/2} \sum_{\beta\gamma} Z^{(1)}_{\beta\alpha\gamma}(\kappa)\, k_{\gamma} E^{(0)}_{\beta}, \tag{7.8b}$$

$$\sum_{\kappa'\beta} \bar{C}^{(0)}_{\alpha\beta}(\kappa\kappa')\, v^{(2)}_{\beta}(\kappa'|\boldsymbol{k}j) - M_{\kappa}^{-1/2} \sum_{\beta} Z^{(0)}_{\beta\alpha}(\kappa)\, E^{(2)}_{\beta}$$
$$= 2[\omega^{(1)}_{j}(\boldsymbol{k})]^2\, v^{(0)}_{\alpha}(\kappa|\boldsymbol{k}j) + 2 \sum_{\kappa'\beta\gamma} \bar{C}^{(1)}_{\alpha\beta\gamma}(\kappa\kappa')\, k_{\gamma} v^{(1)}_{\beta}(\kappa'|\boldsymbol{k}j)$$
$$- \sum_{\kappa'\beta\gamma\lambda} \bar{C}^{(2)}_{\alpha\beta\gamma\lambda}(\kappa\kappa')\, k_{\gamma} k_{\lambda} v^{(0)}_{\beta}(\kappa'|\boldsymbol{k}j) + 2M_{\kappa}^{-1/2} \sum_{\beta\gamma} Z^{(1)}_{\beta\alpha\gamma}(\kappa)\, k_{\gamma} E^{(1)}_{\beta}$$
$$+ M_{\kappa}^{-1/2} \sum_{\beta\gamma\lambda} Z^{(2)}_{\beta\alpha\gamma\lambda}(\kappa)\, k_{\gamma} k_{\lambda} E^{(0)}_{\beta}. \tag{7.8c}$$

The solution of the zero order equation is

$$v^{(0)}_{\alpha}(\kappa|\boldsymbol{k}j) = \sqrt{M_{\kappa}}\, u_{\alpha}(j), \tag{7.9}$$

where $\boldsymbol{u}(j)$ ($j=1, 2, 3$) are three mutually perpendicular vectors, but are otherwise unspecified at this point. That this is indeed a zero order solution follows from the fact that the coefficients $\bar{C}^{(0)}_{\alpha\beta}(\kappa\kappa')$ obey the conditions

$$\sum_{\kappa'} \sqrt{M_{\kappa'}}\, \bar{C}^{(0)}_{\alpha\beta}(\kappa\kappa') = 0 \tag{7.10}$$

as a consequence of infinitesimal translational invariance, and because the zero order electric field vanishes,

$$E^{(0)}_{\alpha} = - (4\pi/v_{\mathrm{a}})\,(\hat{k}_{\alpha}/\varepsilon^{\infty}_{\mathrm{L}}) \sum_{\kappa'\beta} \Big(\sum_{\gamma} \hat{k}_{\gamma} Z^{(0)}_{\gamma\beta}(\kappa') \Big)\, u_{\beta}(j) = 0, \tag{7.11}$$

since the effective charge tensor $Z^{(0)}_{\alpha\beta}(\kappa)$ obeys the conditions

$$\sum_{\kappa} Z^{(0)}_{\alpha\beta}(\kappa) = 0, \tag{7.12}$$

which are also consequences of infinitesimal translational invariance.

The solvability condition for the first order equation, viz., that the inhomogeneous term be orthogonal to the solutions of the corresponding homogeneous equation, can be shown to be satisfied, with the aid of the relation (Maradudin et al. 1971, section 2.1c)

$$\sum_{\kappa\kappa'} (M_{\kappa} M_{\kappa'})^{1/2}\, \bar{C}^{(1)}_{\alpha\beta\gamma}(\kappa\kappa') = 0. \tag{7.13}$$

The solution for $v_\alpha^{(1)}(\kappa|\boldsymbol{k}j)$ is given by

$$v_\alpha^{(1)}(\kappa|\boldsymbol{k}j) = \sum_{\beta\kappa'} \bar{\Gamma}_{\alpha\beta}(\kappa\kappa') \times \left\{\sum_\gamma M_{\kappa'}^{-1/2} Z_{\gamma\beta}^{(0)}(\kappa') E_\gamma^{(1)} - \sum_{\kappa''\gamma\delta} \bar{C}_{\beta\gamma\delta}^{(1)}(\kappa'\kappa'') k_\delta M_{\kappa''}^{1/2} u_\gamma(j)\right\}. \quad (7.14)$$

The matrix $\bar{\Gamma}_{\alpha\beta}(\kappa\kappa')$ is an effective inverse to the (singular) matrix $\bar{C}_{\alpha\beta}^{(0)}(\kappa\kappa')$ (Maradudin et al. 1971, section 2.1c)

$$\bar{\Gamma}_{\alpha\beta}(\kappa\kappa') = \sum_{j=4}^{3r} \xi_\alpha(\kappa|j)\, \xi_\beta(\kappa'|j)/\lambda_j^2, \quad (7.15)$$

where $\xi_\alpha(\kappa|j)$ and λ_j^2 are the eigenvectors and eigenvalues of $\bar{C}_{\alpha\beta}^{(0)}(\kappa\kappa')$:

$$\sum_{\kappa'\beta} \bar{C}_{\alpha\beta}^{(0)}(\kappa\kappa')\, \xi_\beta(\kappa'|j) = \lambda_j^2 \xi_\alpha(\kappa|j), \quad j = 1, 2, \cdots, 3r. \quad (7.16)$$

The displacement $v_\alpha^{(1)}(\kappa|\boldsymbol{k}j)$ can be shown to be the rigid body displacement of the sublattice κ as a result of the combined force exerted on it by the macroscopic electric field in the crystal [the first term on the right hand side of eq. (7.14)] and by a homogeneous strain in the crystal accompanying a long wavelength acoustic wave [the second term on the right hand side of eq. (7.14)]. Such a rigid body displacement of a sublattice is sometimes referred to as an *inner displacement*.

With the result (7.14) the solvability condition for the second order equation can be written in the form

$$\rho[\omega_j^{(1)}(\boldsymbol{k})]^2 u_\alpha(j) = \sum_\beta \sum_{\gamma\lambda} \{[\alpha\beta, \gamma\lambda] + (\alpha\gamma, \beta\lambda)\} k_\gamma k_\lambda u_\beta(j) - \sum_\beta \left\{\sum_\gamma [\beta, \alpha\gamma] k_\gamma\right\} E_\beta^{(1)}, \quad (7.17)$$

where $\varrho = \sum_\kappa M_\kappa / v_\mathrm{a}$ is the mass density of the crystal, and

$$[\alpha\beta, \gamma\lambda] = (1/2v_\mathrm{a}) \sum_{\kappa\kappa'} (M_\kappa M_{\kappa'})^{1/2} \bar{C}_{\alpha\beta\gamma\lambda}^{(2)}(\kappa\kappa'), \quad (7.18a)$$

$$(\alpha\gamma, \beta\lambda) = -(1/v_\mathrm{a}) \sum_{\kappa\kappa'} \sum_{\mu\nu} (M_\kappa M_{\kappa'})^{-1/2} \bar{\Gamma}_{\mu\nu}(\kappa\kappa') \times \left\{\sum_{\kappa''} (M_\kappa M_{\kappa''})^{1/2} \bar{C}_{\mu\alpha\gamma}^{(1)}(\kappa\kappa'')\right\} \left\{\sum_{\kappa'''} (M_{\kappa'} M_{\kappa'''})^{1/2} \bar{C}_{\nu\beta\lambda}^{(1)}(\kappa'\kappa''')\right\}, \quad (7.18b)$$

$$[\beta, \alpha\gamma] = (1/v_\mathrm{a}) \sum_\kappa Z_{\beta\alpha\gamma}^{(1)}(\kappa) + (1/v_\mathrm{a}) \sum_{\kappa\kappa'\kappa''} \sum_{\mu\nu} (M_\kappa M_{\kappa'})^{1/2} \bar{C}_{\alpha\mu\gamma}^{(1)}(\kappa\kappa') \times (M_{\kappa'} M_{\kappa''})^{-1/2} \bar{\Gamma}_{\mu\nu}(\kappa'\kappa'') Z_{\beta\nu}^{(0)}(\kappa''). \quad (7.18c)$$

In writing eq. (7.18b) we have used the fact that $\bar{C}^{(1)}_{\alpha\beta\gamma}(\kappa\kappa')$ is antisymmetric in the interchange of $(\kappa\alpha)$ and $(\kappa'\beta)$. The brackets satisfy the symmetry relations

$$[\alpha\beta, \gamma\lambda] = [\alpha\beta, \lambda\gamma] = [\beta\alpha, \gamma\lambda], \tag{7.19a}$$

$$(\alpha\beta, \gamma\lambda) = (\alpha\beta, \lambda\gamma) = (\beta\alpha, \gamma\lambda) = (\gamma\lambda, \alpha\beta), \tag{7.19b}$$

$$[\beta, \alpha\gamma] = [\beta, \gamma\alpha]. \tag{7.19c}$$

The relation (7.19c) is a consequence of the fact that $\sum_\kappa (M_\kappa M_{\kappa'})^{1/2}\, \bar{C}^{(1)}_{\alpha\beta\gamma}(\kappa\kappa')$ is symmetric in α and γ, in view of eqs. (7.3b), (2.12b), and (2.9b).

The equations of motion of an elastic dielectric can be written in the form (Cady 1964)

$$\rho\ddot{u}_\alpha = \sum_{\beta\gamma\lambda} C_{\alpha\gamma\beta\lambda} \frac{\partial^2 u_\beta}{\partial x_\gamma \partial x_\lambda} - \sum_{\beta\gamma} e_{\beta\alpha\gamma} \frac{\partial E_\beta}{\partial x_\gamma}, \tag{7.20}$$

where ϱ is the mass density, and the tensors $C_{\alpha\gamma\beta\lambda}$ and $e_{\beta\alpha\gamma}$ are the elastic moduli and piezoelectric constants, respectively. These possess the following symmetry properties

$$C_{\alpha\gamma\beta\lambda} = C_{\gamma\alpha\beta\lambda} = C_{\alpha\gamma\lambda\beta} = C_{\beta\lambda\alpha\gamma}, \qquad e_{\beta\alpha\gamma} = e_{\beta\gamma\alpha}. \tag{7.21a, b}$$

If we assume that an elastic wave

$$u_\alpha(\boldsymbol{x}, t) = \bar{u}_\alpha\, \mathrm{e}^{\mathrm{i}\boldsymbol{k}\cdot\boldsymbol{x} - \mathrm{i}\omega t} \tag{7.22}$$

gives rise to a macroscopic electric field

$$E_\alpha(\boldsymbol{x}, t) = \bar{E}_\alpha\, \mathrm{e}^{\mathrm{i}\boldsymbol{k}\cdot\boldsymbol{x} - \mathrm{i}\omega t}, \tag{7.23}$$

then from eq. (7.20) we obtain as the relation between the amplitudes $\bar{u}_\alpha$ and $\bar{E}_\alpha$

$$\rho\omega^2\bar{u}_\alpha = \sum_{\beta\gamma\lambda} C_{\alpha\gamma\beta\lambda} k_\gamma k_\lambda \bar{u}_\beta + \sum_\beta \left(\sum_\gamma e_{\beta\alpha\gamma} k_\gamma\right) \mathrm{i}\bar{E}_\beta. \tag{7.24}$$

On the other hand, the atomic displacements and the macroscopic electric field in an acoustic lattice vibration are given by

$$\begin{aligned} u_\alpha(l\kappa; t) &= M_\kappa^{-1/2} v_\alpha(\kappa|\boldsymbol{k}j)\, \mathrm{e}^{\mathrm{i}\boldsymbol{k}\cdot\boldsymbol{x}(l\kappa) - \mathrm{i}\omega_j(\boldsymbol{k})t} \\ &= M_\kappa^{-1/2} [v_\alpha^{(0)}(\kappa|\boldsymbol{k}j) + \mathrm{i}v_\alpha^{(1)}(\kappa|\boldsymbol{k}j) + \cdots]\, \mathrm{e}^{\mathrm{i}\boldsymbol{k}\cdot\boldsymbol{x}(l\kappa) - \mathrm{i}\omega_j(\boldsymbol{k})t}, \end{aligned} \tag{7.25}$$

$$E_\alpha(\boldsymbol{x}, t) = [E_\alpha^{(0)} + \mathrm{i}E_\alpha^{(1)} + \cdots]\, \mathrm{e}^{\mathrm{i}\boldsymbol{k}\cdot\boldsymbol{x}(l\kappa) - \mathrm{i}\omega_j(\boldsymbol{k})t}. \tag{7.26}$$

In the method of long waves the quantities of the macroscopic theory are to be compared with the lowest order nonvanishing terms in the expansions of the corresponding quantities in the lattice theory. Since we have seen that the amplitude $E_\alpha^{(0)}$ of the lattice theory vanishes, we must identify $\bar{E}_\alpha$ with $\mathrm{i}E_\alpha^{(1)}$ in eqs. (7.17). Similarly, we must identify $\bar{u}_\alpha$ with $v_\alpha^{(0)}(\kappa|\boldsymbol{k}j)/M_\alpha^{1/2}$. Equations (7.17) and (7.24) then become identical if

$$\sum_{\gamma\lambda} C_{\alpha\gamma\beta\lambda} k_\gamma k_\lambda = \sum_{\gamma\lambda} \{[\alpha\beta, \gamma\lambda] + (\alpha\gamma, \beta\lambda)\} k_\gamma k_\lambda , \tag{7.27a}$$

$$\sum_{\gamma} e_{\beta\alpha\gamma} k_\gamma = \sum_{\gamma} [\beta, \alpha\gamma] k_\gamma . \tag{7.27b}$$

The solutions of these equations are (Maradudin et al. 1971, section 2.1c)

$$C_{\alpha\gamma\beta\lambda} = [\alpha\beta, \gamma\lambda] + [\gamma\beta, \alpha\lambda] - [\alpha\gamma, \beta\lambda] + (\alpha\gamma, \beta\lambda), \tag{7.28}$$

$$e_{\beta\alpha\gamma} = [\beta, \alpha\gamma], \tag{7.29}$$

where the first solution holds subject to the conditions [the Huang (1950) conditions] that

$$[\alpha\beta, \gamma\lambda] = [\gamma\lambda, \alpha\beta] . \tag{7.30}$$

It has been shown by Huang (1950) that when the conditions (7.30) are satisfied the strain energy of the crystal is invariant against rigid body rotations, and the five anisotropic stresses, $T_{xx}-T_{yy}$, $T_{yy}-T_{zz}$, T_{xy}, T_{yz}, T_{zx} vanish. The treatment presented here does not yield an explicit expression for the pressure $p=-\frac{1}{3}(T_{xx}+T_{yy}+T_{zz})$, since it cannot be expressed in terms of the derivatives of the total crystal potential energy with respect to the atomic displacements. Consequently, the second equilibrium condition for a crystal, viz., that the equilibrium configuration correspond to vanishing stresses, cannot be incorporated into the general theory of lattice dynamics, in which only the derivatives of the crystal potential energy appear. The hydrostatic pressure has to be implicitly understood to vanish in the applications of the results of the general theory. A specific lattice model, e.g. one in which the atoms interact through central forces, is required before an expression for the pressure can be obtained.

With the aid of the relations (2.10) and (2.11b) it can be shown that the Huang relations (7.30) are automatically satisfied for cubic crystals, and hence yield no additional conditions on the atomic force constants for such crystals (Leibfried and Ludwig 1960). It can also be shown that the Huang conditions can be obtained directly from eq. (2.9b), which is a consequence of the transformation property of the force on an atom under a rigid body rotation of the crystal (Leibfried and Ludwig 1960, Hedin 1960).

The elastic wave (7.22) also has associated with it a macroscopic polarization

$$P_\alpha(\boldsymbol{x}, t) = \bar{P}_\alpha \, \mathrm{e}^{\mathrm{i}\boldsymbol{k}\cdot\boldsymbol{x} - \mathrm{i}\omega t}. \tag{7.31}$$

According to the macroscopic theory the polarization is associated with the displacement field and macroscopic electric field by (Cady 1964)

$$P_\alpha = \sum_{\beta\gamma} e_{\alpha\beta\gamma} \, \partial u_\beta / \partial x_\gamma + \sum_\beta \chi_{\alpha\beta} E_\beta, \tag{7.32}$$

where $\chi_{\alpha\beta}$ is the dielectric susceptibility tensor. Substituting eqs. (7.22), (7.23) and (7.31) into eq. (7.32) we obtain the relation

$$\bar{P}_\alpha = \mathrm{i} \sum_{\beta\gamma} e_{\alpha\beta\gamma} k_\gamma \bar{u}_\beta + \sum_\beta \chi_{\alpha\beta} \bar{E}_\beta. \tag{7.33}$$

According to the lattice theory, eq. (6.12b), the amplitude of the polarization wave associated with a lattice wave $M_\kappa^{-1/2} v_\alpha(\kappa | \boldsymbol{k}j) \exp[\mathrm{i}\boldsymbol{k}\cdot\boldsymbol{x} - \mathrm{i}\omega_j(\boldsymbol{k})\, t]$ can be written as

$$\begin{aligned}
P_\alpha &= (1/v_\mathrm{a}) \sum_\kappa p_\alpha(\kappa) = P_\alpha^{(0)} + \mathrm{i}P_\alpha^{(1)} + \cdots \\
&= (1/v_\mathrm{a}) \sum_{\kappa'\beta} Z_{\alpha\beta}(\kappa' | \boldsymbol{k})\, M_{\kappa'}^{-1/2} v_\beta(\kappa' | \boldsymbol{k}j) + (1/v_\mathrm{a}) \sum_\beta \chi_{\alpha\beta}(\boldsymbol{k})\, E_\beta \\
&= (1/v_\mathrm{a}) \sum_{\kappa'\beta} \Big[Z_{\alpha\beta}^{(0)}(\kappa') + \mathrm{i} \sum_\gamma Z_{\alpha\beta\gamma}^{(1)}(\kappa')\, k_\gamma + \cdots \Big] \\
&\qquad \times [v_\beta^{(0)}(\kappa' | \boldsymbol{k}j) + \mathrm{i} v_\beta^{(1)}(\kappa' | \boldsymbol{k}j) + \cdots] / \sqrt{M_{\kappa'}} \\
&\quad + (1/v_\mathrm{a}) \sum_\beta \Big[\chi_{\alpha\beta}^{(0)} + \mathrm{i} \sum_\gamma \chi_{\alpha\beta\gamma}^{(1)} k_\gamma + \cdots \Big] [E_\beta^{(0)} + \mathrm{i} E_\beta^{(1)} + \cdots].
\end{aligned} \tag{7.34}$$

Since the zero order term vanishes, due to infinitesimal translational invariance, it follows that $\bar{P}_\alpha$ must be compared with the first order lattice result $\mathrm{i}P_\alpha^{(1)}$

$$\begin{aligned}
\mathrm{i}P_\alpha^{(1)} &= (\mathrm{i}/v_\mathrm{a}) \sum_{\kappa'\beta} Z_{\alpha\beta}^{(0)}(\kappa')\, v_\beta^{(1)}(\kappa' | \boldsymbol{k}j) / \sqrt{M_{\kappa'}} \\
&\quad + (\mathrm{i}/v_\mathrm{a}) \sum_{\kappa'\beta\gamma} Z_{\alpha\beta\gamma}^{(1)}(\kappa')\, k_\gamma\, v_\beta^{(0)}(\kappa' | \boldsymbol{k}j) / \sqrt{M_{\kappa'}} + (\mathrm{i}/v_\mathrm{a}) \sum_\beta \chi_{\alpha\beta}^{(0)} E_\beta^{(1)}.
\end{aligned} \tag{7.35}$$

When eq. (7.14) is substituted into eq. (7.35), and the result compared with eq. (7.33), we find that

$$e_{\alpha\beta\gamma} = (1/v_a) \sum_{\kappa} Z^{(1)}_{\alpha\beta\gamma}(\kappa) - (1/v_a) \sum_{\kappa\kappa'\kappa''} \sum_{\mu\nu} Z^{(0)}_{\alpha\mu}(\kappa)\,(M_\kappa M_{\kappa'})^{-1/2}\,\bar{\Gamma}_{\mu\nu}(\kappa\kappa')\,(M_{\kappa'} M_{\kappa''})^{1/2}\,\bar{C}^{(1)}_{\nu\beta\gamma}(\kappa'\kappa''), \tag{7.36}$$

$$\chi_{\alpha\beta} = (1/v_a)\,\chi^{(0)}_{\alpha\beta} + (1/v_a) \sum_{\kappa\kappa'} \sum_{\mu\nu} Z^{(0)}_{\alpha\mu}(\kappa)\,(M_\kappa M_{\kappa'})^{-1/2}\,\bar{\Gamma}_{\mu\nu}(\kappa\kappa') Z^{(0)}_{\beta\nu}(\kappa'). \tag{7.37}$$

The equivalence of the two results for the piezoelectric tensor given by eqs. (7.18c) and (7.36) is readily established if it is taken into account that $\bar{\Gamma}_{\mu\nu}(\kappa\kappa')$ is symmetric in $(\kappa\mu)$ and $(\kappa'\nu)$, while $\bar{C}^{(1)}_{\alpha\beta\gamma}(\kappa\kappa')$ is antisymmetric in $(\kappa\alpha)$ and $(\kappa'\beta)$.

The dielectric tensor of the crystal, $\varepsilon_{\alpha\beta}$, is given in terms of the dielectric susceptibility $\chi_{\alpha\beta}$ by $\varepsilon_{\alpha\beta} = \delta_{\alpha\beta} + 4\pi\chi_{\alpha\beta}$. From eqs. (7.15) and (7.37) it follows that the dielectric tensor can be written in the form

$$\varepsilon_{\alpha\beta} = \delta_{\alpha\beta} + (4\pi/v_a)\,\chi^{(0)}_{\alpha\beta} + (4\pi/v_a) \sum_{j=4}^{3r} M_\alpha(j)\, M_\beta(j)/\lambda_j^2, \tag{7.38a}$$

where

$$M_\alpha(j) = \sum_{\kappa\mu} Z^{(0)}_{\alpha\mu}(\kappa)\,\xi_\mu(\kappa|j)/\sqrt{M_\kappa}. \tag{7.38b}$$

If we compare this result with eq. (6.39) we see that the dielectric tensor given by eq. (7.38) is the static dielectric tensor.

If every ion is at a center of inversion symmetry, then the application of eqs. (2.10) and (2.11b) to eq. (7.3b) yields the result that the coefficients $\bar{C}^{(1)}_{\alpha\beta,\gamma}(\kappa\kappa')$ vanish identically. The round brackets $(\alpha\gamma, \beta\lambda)$ consequently also vanish in this case. We will also see below that the crystal cannot be piezoelectric. If, in addition, the atoms interact pairwise with central forces, then from eqs. (7.3c), (7.18a), (2.16b), and (2.18a) we find that the square bracket $[\alpha\beta, \gamma\lambda]$ is given by

$$[\alpha\beta, \gamma\lambda] = (1/2v_a) \sum_{\kappa} \sum_{l'\kappa'} \left\{ x_\alpha x_\beta x_\gamma x_\lambda \left[\frac{1}{r^2}\,\varphi''_{\kappa\kappa'}(r) - \frac{1}{r^3}\,\varphi'_{\kappa\kappa'}(r) \right] + \delta_{\alpha\beta} x_\gamma x_\lambda \frac{1}{r}\,\varphi'_{\kappa\kappa}(r) \right\}_{r = x(l\kappa;\, l'\kappa')}. \tag{7.39}$$

Thus, if the sums

$$T_{\gamma\lambda} = (1/2v_a) \sum_{\kappa} \sum_{l'\kappa'} \left\{ x_\gamma x_\lambda \frac{1}{r}\,\varphi'_{\kappa\kappa}(r) \right\}_{r = x(l\kappa;\, l'\kappa')} \tag{7.40}$$

vanish, we see from eq. (7.40) that $[\alpha\beta, \gamma\lambda]$ is completely symmetric in all four indices

$$[\alpha\beta, \gamma\lambda] = (1/2v_a) \sum_{\kappa} \sum_{l'\kappa'} \left\{ x_\alpha x_\beta x_\gamma x_\lambda \left[\frac{1}{r^2} \varphi''_{\kappa\kappa'}(r) - \frac{1}{r^3} \varphi'_{\kappa\kappa'}(r) \right] \right\}_{\boldsymbol{r}=\boldsymbol{x}(l\kappa;\, l'\kappa')} . \tag{7.41}$$

Since $T_{\gamma\lambda}$ can be shown to be the $\gamma\lambda$ element of the stress tensor for the crystal (Born and Huang 1954, section 29), its vanishing is seen to be the condition that the crystal be stress-free. Thus, in a crystal in which (*a*) every atom is at a center of inversion; (*b*) the atoms interact pairwise through central forces; and (*c*) the crystal is stress-free, the elastic constant $C_{\alpha\gamma\beta\lambda}$ is just equal to the corresponding square bracket,

$$\begin{aligned} C_{\alpha\gamma\beta\lambda} &= [\alpha\beta, \gamma\lambda] \\ &= (1/2v_a) \sum_{\kappa} \sum_{l'\kappa'} \left\{ x_\alpha x_\beta x_\gamma x_\lambda \left[\frac{1}{r^2} \varphi''_{\kappa\kappa'}(r) - \frac{1}{r^3} \varphi'_{\kappa\kappa'}(r) \right] \right\}_{\boldsymbol{r}=\boldsymbol{x}(l\kappa;\, l'\kappa')} , \end{aligned} \tag{7.42}$$

and consequently is symmetric in all four indices. The additional relations among the elastic constants, over and above those given by eq. (7.21a), which follow from the complete symmetry of $C_{\alpha\gamma\beta\lambda}$ in all four indices, are known as the *Cauchy relations*. They can be summarized by the relation

$$C_{\alpha\gamma\beta\lambda} = C_{\alpha\beta\gamma\lambda} . \tag{7.43}$$

The piezoelectric tensor $e_{\beta\alpha\gamma}$ vanishes for all crystals possessing a center of inversion. A detailed study shows that of the 32 crystal classes only 20 permit the phenomenon of piezoelectricity, viz., C_1, C_s, C_2, C_{2v}, D_2, C_4, S_4, C_{4v}, S_{4v}, D_4, C_3, C_{3v}, D_3, C_{3h}, C_6, D_{3h}, C_{6v}, D_6, T, T_d. From eqs. (7.18c) or (7.36) it is seen that the piezoelectric tensor is made up of two contributions, the first having its origin in the nonlocality of the effective charge tensor, $M_{\alpha\beta}(l\kappa;\, l'\kappa')$, which gives rise to a strain dependence of the transverse effective charge $Z_{\alpha\beta}(\kappa|\boldsymbol{k})$, the second having its origin in the displacement of the $\boldsymbol{k}=0$ effective charges accompanying the inner displacements of the sublattices in response to a homogeneous deformation of the crystal. The former contribution is absent in a rigid-ion model of an ionic crystal.

The analysis of the present section shows why it is necessary to separate the contribution of the macroscopic electric field explicitly in the treatment of the long wavelength acoustic modes in the dynamical theory of ionic crystals for which each ion is not at a center of inversion, notwithstanding the fact that the macroscopic field is established by the ionic motions themselves.

Mathematically, this is due to the fact that if the atomic force constants $\{\Phi_{\alpha\beta}(l\kappa; l'\kappa')\}$ entering the perturbation calculations of this section had contained the full contribution of the Coulomb interaction, and not just that part corresponding to the Lorentz field, the zero order coefficient $\bar{C}^{(0)}_{\alpha\beta}(\kappa\kappa')$ would have diverged. Physically, this divergence is due to the fact that in such crystals a long wavelength acoustic wave gives rise to rigid body displacements of the sublattices with respect to each other. These inner displacements in turn produce a uniform dielectric polarization. In a finite crystal this polarization creates surface charges, which establish a macroscopic electric field which exerts forces on the ions. This electric field, and consequently the forces acting on the ions, depends on the shape of the crystal. Consequently these forces have no unique limiting values for an infinitely extended crystal of arbitrary shape, such as we have assumed in our work. However, if every ion is at a center of inversion no inner displacements accompany long wavelength homogeneous deformations of the sublattices, and the above mentioned difficulties do not arise.

Thus, in an arbitrary ionic crystal the force acting on an ion is due not only to its interactions with other ions through forces whose range is microscopic, but, because the total force depends on the shape of the crystal, has a contribution from ions at a macroscopic distance as well. This latter force is taken into account by the explicit introduction of the macroscopic field, which is ultimately determined by the atomic displacements through the equations of the electromagnetic theory. Thus, in general the elastic properties of ionic crystals cannot be treated independently of their electrical properties, a fact long recognized in the macroscopic theory.

Acknowledgement

The research was supported in part by the Air Force Office of Scientific Research, Office of Aerospace Research, USAF, under Grant No. AFOSR 71-2018.

References

Altmann, S.L. and Cracknell, A.P. (1965), Rev. Mod. Phys. **37**, 19.
Baker, H.F. (1905), Proc. London Math. Soc. **3**, 24.
Blackman, M. (1934a), Proc. Roy. Soc. (London) **A148**, 365.
Blackman, M. (1934b), Proc. Roy. Soc. (London) **A148**, 384.
Blackman, M. (1936), Phil. Trans. Roy. Soc. (London) **A236**, 103.
Blackman, M. (1937a), Proc. Camb. Phil. Soc. **33**, 94.

BLACKMAN, M. (1937b), Proc. Roy. Soc. (London) **A159**, 416.
BORN, M. (1923), *Atomtheorie des festen Zustandes*, second edition (Teubner, Leipzig), pp. 578–87.
BORN, M. and K. HUANG (1954), *Dynamical theory of crystal lattices* (Oxford University Press, Oxford).
BORN, M. and TH. VON KARMAN (1912), Phys. Z. **13**, 297.
BROVMAN, E.G. and YU.M. KAGAN (1967), Soviet Physics–JETP **25**, 365.
BURSTEIN, E. (1964), in *Phonons and phonon interactions*, ed. by T.A. Bak (W.A. Benjamin, Inc., New York), p. 276.
BURSTEIN, E. and D.L. MILLS (1969), Comments on Solid State Physics **2**, 111.
BURSTEIN, E., A.A. MARADUDIN, and R. MINNICK (1971a), Ind. J. of Pure and Appl. Phys. **9**, 883.
BURSTEIN, E., A. PINCZUK and R.F. WALLIS (1971b), J. Phys. Chem. Solids Supplement 1 **32**, 251.
CADY, W.G. (1964), *Piezoelectricity* (Dover, New York), **1**, 183.
CHESTER, G.V. (1961), Advan. Phys. **10**, 357.
COCHRAN, W. (1961), Nature **191**, 60.
DALTON, N.W. (1970), Solid State Commun. **8**, 1047.
DE BRUIJN, N. (1958), *Asymptotic methods in analysis* (North-Holland, Amsterdam).
DEBYE, P. (1912), Ann. Phys. **39**, 789.
DIRAC, P.A.M. (1947), *The principles of quantum mechanics* (Oxford University Press, Oxford), Chap. VI.
DIXON, A.E., A.D.B. WOODS, and B.N. BROCKHOUSE (1963), Proc. Phys. Soc. London **81**, 973.
DOBRZYNSKI, L. and A.A. MARADUDIN (1973), Phys. Rev. **B7**, 1207.
EINSTEIN, A. (1907), Ann. Phys. **22**, 180.
EWALD, P.P. (1917a), Ann. Phys. (Leipzig) **54**, 519.
EWALD, P.P. (1917b), Ann. Phys. (Leipzig) **54**, 557.
EWALD, P.P. (1921), Ann. Phys. (Leipzig) **64**, 253.
EWALD, P.P. (1938), Nachr. Ges. Wiss. Göttingen, Jahresber. Geschäftsführ. Math.-Phys. Kl. Fachgruppen **1**, 55.
FANO, U. (1956), Phys. Rev. **103**, 1202.
GANESAN, S., A.A. MARADUDIN and J. OITMAA (1970), Annals of Physics (N.Y.) **56**, 556.
GANTMACHER, F.R. (1959), *Applications of the theory of matrices* (Wiley-Interscience, New York), p. 53.
GILAT, G. and L. BOHLIN (1969), Solid State Commun. **7**, 1727.
GILAT, G. and N.W. DALTON (1971), Solid State Commun. **9**, 961.
GILAT, G. and G. DOLLING (1964), Phys. Letters **8**, 304.
GILAT, G. and Z. KAM (1969), Phys. Rev. Letters **22**, 715.
GILAT, G. and L.J. RAUBENHEIMER (1966), Phys. Rev. **144**, 390.
HARDY, J.R. (1962), Phil. Mag. **7**, 315.
HAUSDORFF, F. (1906), Ber. Verhandl. Sächs. Akad. Wiss., Leipzig, Math.-Phys. Kl. **58**, 19.
HEDIN, L. (1960), Ark. Fys. **18**, 369.
HERRING, C. (1956), in *Photoconductivity conference*, ed. by R.G. Breckenridge, B.R. Russell and E.E. Hahn (John Wiley and Sons, Inc., New York) p. 81.
HOPFIELD, J.J. (1958), Phys. Rev. **112**, 1555.
HUANG, K. (1950), Proc. Roy. Soc. (London) **A203**, 178.

HUANG, K. (1951a), Nature **167**, 779.

HUANG, K. (1951b), Proc. Roy. Soc. (London) **A208**, 352.

ISENBERG, C. (1963), Phys. Rev. **132**, 2427.

KAM, Z. and G. GILAT (1968), Phys. Rev. **175**, 1156.

LAX, M. and J. LEBOWITZ (1954), Phys. Rev. **96**, 594.

LEDERMANN, W. (1944), Proc. Roy. Soc. (London) **A182**, 362.

LEIBFRIED, G. and W. LUDWIG (1960), Z. Physik **160**, 80.

LEIBFRIED, G. and W. LUDWIG (1961), in *Solid state physics*, ed. by F. Seitz and D. Turnbull (Academic Press, Inc., New York), **12**, 275.

LIGHTHILL, M.J. (1958), *Fourier analysis and generalized functions* (Cambridge University Press, London and New York).

LÖWDIN, P.O. (1964), J. Molec. Spectr. **13**, 326.

LYDDANE, R.M., R.G. SACHS and E. TELLER (1941), Phys. Rev. **59**, 673.

MARADUDIN, A.A., E.W. MONTROLL, G.H. WEISS, and I.P. IPATOVA (1971), *Theory of lattice dynamics in the harmonic approximation* (Academic Press, Inc., New York).

MARADUDIN, A.A. and J. PERETTI (1958), Compt. Rend. **247**, 2310.

MARADUDIN, A.A. and S.H. VOSKO (1968), Rev. Mod. Phys. **40**, 1.

MARKOFF, A.A. (1896), *Differenzenrechnung* (Leipzig).

MINNICK, R. (1970), Ph.D. Thesis, Univ. of California, Irvine (unpublished).

MONTROLL, E.W. (1942), J. Chem. Phys. **10**, 218.

MONTROLL, E.W. (1943), J. Chem. Phys. **11**, 481.

MONTROLL, E.W. (1947), Quart. Appl. Math. **V**, 223.

MORSE, M. (1939), *Functional topology and abstract variational theory*, Fascicule 92 (Gauthier-Villars, Paris).

PASTRNAK, J. and K. VEDAM (1971), Phys. Rev. **B3**, 2567.

PHILLIPS, J.C. (1956), Phys. Rev. **104**, 1263.

PHILLIPS, J.C. and H.B. ROSENSTOCK (1958), J. Phys. Chem. Solids **5**, 288.

RAUBENHEIMER, L.J. and G. GILAT (1967), Phys. Rev. **157**, 586.

ROSENSTOCK, H.B. (1955), Phys. Rev. **97**, 290.

ROSENSTOCK, H.B. (1957), J. Phys. Chem. Solids **2**, 44.

SCOTT, J.F. (1971), Am. J. Phys. **39**, 1360.

SEITZ, F. (1936), Ann. Math. **37**, 17.

SHOHAT, J.A. and J.D. TAMARKIN (1950), *The problem of moments* (American Mathematical Society, Providence, R.I.).

SZEGÖ, G. (1939), *Orthogonal polynomials* (American Mathematical Society, New York), Chap. III.

SZIGETI, B. (1949), Trans. Faraday Soc. **45**, 155.

SZIGETI, B. (1950), Proc. Roy. Soc. (London) **A204**, 51.

VAN HOVE, L. (1953), Phys. Rev. **89**, 1189.

WHEELER, J.C. and R.G. GORDON (1969), J. Chem. Phys. **51**, 5566.

WOODS, A.D.B., W. COCHRAN and B.N. BROCKHOUSE (1960), Phys. Rev. **119**, 980.

YU., P.Y. and M. CARDONA (1971), Solid State Commun. **9**, 1421.

CHAPTER 2

A Quick Trip Through Group Theory and Lattice Dynamics

Joseph L. BIRMAN*

Physics Dept., New York University
Meyer Hall, Washington Square
New York, N.Y. 10012
USA

* *Address after September 1974: Physics Department, City College of the City University of New York, 138 St, and Convent Ave., New York, N.Y. 10031, USA*

Dynamical Properties of Solids, edited by G. K. Horton and A. A. Maradudin

Contents

1. Introduction and plan

In this chapter a résumé will be given of the theory and practice of the application of group theory in the lattice dynamic problem. Since group theory methods seem destined to play a continuing important role in many aspects of the lattice dynamics of solids, it appears desirable to make these methods as accessible as possible to as wide an audience as possible. Even so, the limitations of space preclude the possibility of giving any more than an abbreviated discussion of methodology, and a selected few applications chosen for pedagogical purposes. Many topics touched on only briefly here are discussed at much greater length in various review articles including a recent treatment by the present author (Birman 1974) which contains a large number of references to other work.

This chapter is divided into seven sections. In section 2 a review of basic symmetry notation for space groups is given; including definition of the effect of transformations on configuration space position vectors, and on functions of position vectors. In section 3 a review is given of the application of group theory to a quantum-mechanical hamiltonian: this section develops ideas used later as well as providing a bridge between the generally familiar quantum applications of group theory and the applications in the classical case. Section 4 gives the major content of the methodology of application of group theory in the lattice dynamic problem: a number of proofs are given in detail. In section 5 the quantum-mechanical lattice dynamic problem is analysed from the group theory viewpoint and the symmetry of the multiphonon (harmonic) lattice eigenfunction is explicitly obtained by a method first used in the analogous molecular case by Tisza (1933). Owing to its importance we give some detail of the proofs here. In section 6 the representation theory of space groups is reviewed: sufficient detail and proofs are given so that the representations can be constructed, and selection rules and Clebsch–Gordan coefficients obtained, following the procedures developed.

The final section, 7, is intended to sum up all of the previous work, by giving in some detail a worked example: the lattice dynamics at point $\boldsymbol{X}_3$ in diamond structure (space group O_h^7–Fd3m), and related physical properties such as optical absorption, critical points, and selection rules. This illustrative material is worked through in order to show how an actual calculation can be carried out for any space group. It is hoped this will encourage the novice to overcome his hesitation, and, by working the example through along the lines indicated, develop expertise.

One entire area omitted from consideration here is the application of group theory in the many-body treatment of the lattice dynamic properties of solids. It can be anticipated that there will be developments in this area in the future, although at present only a few aspects have been explored.

Another related area which has not been included in this chapter is the applications of group theory (and symmetry arguments in general) to the theory of phase transitions in solids: in particular those transitions which are displacive second-order phase transitions driven by a 'soft' lattice mode. The group theory methods developed in this chapter have been applied to discussion of such transitions, and applications along these lines may also be expected to grow in the future (Birman 1973a).

In writing this chapter we have in mind the reader who has a general knowledge of group theory as applied to various simple problems: the level of familiarity presupposed is that of the work by Landau and Lifschitz (1958), chapter 12. The reader is also presumed to have a general knowledge of lattice dynamics at the level of the standard works in this field: Born and Huang (1954), Maradudin et al. (1971).

2. *Crystal space group symmetry operators*

In this section we shall assemble some results useful in the analyses to be given below (International Tables 1952).

2.1. Transformation of space

A physical symmetry transformation in a crystal is a linear inhomogeneous transformation which we shall understand in the active sense as a mapping of point $\boldsymbol{r}$ onto a point $\boldsymbol{r}'$, with respect to fixed coordinate axes:

$$\boldsymbol{r}' = R\boldsymbol{r} \quad \text{or} \quad \boldsymbol{r} \overset{R}{\Rightarrow} \boldsymbol{r}'. \tag{2.1}$$

We write the general symmetry transformation in the crystal more explicitly as

$$\boldsymbol{r}' = \{\boldsymbol{\phi} \,|\, \boldsymbol{t}(\boldsymbol{\phi})\}\cdot\boldsymbol{r} \equiv \boldsymbol{\phi}\cdot\boldsymbol{r} + \boldsymbol{t}(\boldsymbol{\phi}) \tag{2.2, 3}$$

$$= \boldsymbol{\phi}\cdot\boldsymbol{r} + \boldsymbol{\tau}(\boldsymbol{\phi}) + \boldsymbol{R}_{\mathrm{L}}. \tag{2.4}$$

In these expressions ϕ is a linear operator corresponding to rotation, so $\phi \cdot r$ is the vector r rotated about the origin. The operator ϕ can be represented as a real unitary, or orthogonal 3×3 matrix $\phi^{-1} = \tilde{\phi}$ (if cartesian coordinates are employed), or more generally as a self-adjoint dyadic operator if a general rectilinear non-orthogonal basis is used. The translation vector R_{L} is a lattice vector with

$$R_{\mathrm{L}} = l_j a_j \quad \text{(sum convention)}, \tag{2.5}$$

where l_j are integers, and the a_j the non-coplanar triad which span the lattice. Depending on the crystal space group, there may or may not be a fractional translation $\tau(\phi)$ associated with the rotation ϕ. In case of the non-symmorphic space groups for which for at least one ϕ, $\tau(\phi)$ is necessarily non-zero, we assume some canonical choice is made, specifying the precise $\tau(\phi)$ to be associated to a ϕ.

The space group $\mathscr{G}$ of the crystal is the set

$$\mathscr{G} = \{\varepsilon|0\}, \{\phi_2|\tau(\phi_2)\}, \cdots, \{\varepsilon|R_{\mathrm{L}}\}, \cdots \{\phi_{\mathrm{p}}|t(\phi_{\mathrm{p}})\} \tag{2.6}$$

consisting of all admissible symmetry operations. The translation group $\mathscr{T}$ is the set of all pure lattice translations

$$\mathscr{T} = \{\varepsilon|\mathbf{0}\}, \cdots, \{\varepsilon|R_{\mathrm{L}}\}, \cdots. \tag{2.7}$$

The point group of the space group is the factor group

$$\mathscr{P} \equiv \mathscr{G}|\mathscr{T} \tag{2.8}$$

consisting of cosets

$$\mathscr{T}, \{\phi_2|\tau(\phi_2)\}\mathscr{T}, \cdots, \{\phi_{\mathrm{p}}|\tau(\phi_{\mathrm{p}})\}\mathscr{T} \tag{2.9}$$

and is isomorphic to the crystal point group

$$\mathscr{P} = \varepsilon, \phi_2, \cdots, \phi_{\mathrm{p}}, \tag{2.10}$$

where (2.10) consists of pure rotations above. There is some arbitrariness in the choice of coset representatives in (2.9) but we assume some set of $\{\phi_\sigma|\tau(\phi_\sigma)\}$ has been properly chosen a priori in accordance with international convention, and once so chosen they are regarded as fixed.

The multiplication law of symmetry elements follows directly from (2.2). Consider for example the product of two coset representatives, each with a fractional translational:

$$\{\phi_1|\tau(\phi_1)\}\cdot\{\phi_2|\tau(\phi_2)\} = \{\phi_1\cdot\phi_2|\phi_1\cdot\tau(\phi_2) + \tau(\phi_1)\}. \tag{2.11}$$

Now the translation part of the latter expression is in general *not* the "canonical" (fractional) translation associated with the rotation $(\phi_1 \cdot \phi_2)$ in the coset decomposition (2.9). Consequently we can rewrite (2.11)

$$\{\varepsilon | \boldsymbol{R}_{12}\} \cdot \{\phi_{12} | \tau(\phi_{12})\}, \tag{2.12}$$

where

$$\phi_{12} \equiv \phi_1 \cdot \phi_2, \qquad \tau(\phi_{12}) \equiv \tau(\phi_1 \cdot \phi_2), \tag{2.13a, b}$$

$$\boldsymbol{R}_{12} = \phi_1 \cdot \tau(\phi_2) + \tau(\phi_1) - \tau(\phi_{12}) \tag{2.13c}$$

and $\boldsymbol{R}_{12}$ is in general a pure lattice translation vector.

The multiplication law then can be read as: the product of two coset representatives in the decomposition (2.9) is a coset representative modulo an element from $\mathscr{T}$, the group of pure lattice translations.

The inverse element is then given as

$$\{\phi | \tau(\phi)\}^{-1} = \{\phi^{-1} | -\phi^{-1} \cdot \tau(\phi)\}. \tag{2.14}$$

We shall not demonstrate that the associativity law holds but it is a straightforward if tedious exercise.

The set of all symmetry operations of the type $\{\phi | t(\phi)\}$ forms a mathematical group: the space group of the crystal which we designate $\mathscr{G}$. It is important to recognize the similarity and difference between the laws of multiplication of corresponding elements in $\mathscr{G}$, and $\mathscr{P}$. Thus, the correspondence is: between coset representative in $\mathscr{G}$, and pure rotation in $\mathscr{P}$:

$$\{\phi_1 | \tau(\phi_1)\} \leftrightarrow \phi_1, \tag{2.15}$$

so that the multiplication is

$$\{\phi_1 | \tau(\phi_1)\} \cdot \{\phi_2 | \tau(\phi_2)\} = \{\varepsilon | \boldsymbol{R}_{12}\} \cdot \{\phi_{12} | \tau(\phi_{12})\} \tag{2.16}$$

corresponding to

$$\phi_1 \cdot \phi_2 = \phi_{12}. \tag{2.17}$$

2.2 Transformation of functions

We require the definition of the corresponding functional operator. If $f(\boldsymbol{r})$ is any scalar function then (Wigner 1959)

$$P_{\{\phi | \tau(\phi)\}} f(\{\phi | \tau(\phi)\} \cdot \boldsymbol{r}) = f(\boldsymbol{r}) \tag{2.18}$$

or

$$P_{\{\phi | \tau(\phi)\}} f(\boldsymbol{r}) = f(\{\phi | \tau(\phi)\}^{-1} \cdot \boldsymbol{r}) = f(\phi^{-1} \cdot \boldsymbol{r} - \phi^{-1} \cdot \tau(\phi)). \tag{2.19}$$

In evaluating the field point we use the rule for the effect of a general transformation (2.4).

Let $F(r)$ be some nth rank cartesian tensor function of the field point r. Then the corresponding expression for the transformation of this function is symbolically

$$P_{\{\phi \mid \tau(\phi)\}}F(r) = \sum_{\cdots} ((\phi)^n F)(\{\phi \mid \tau(\phi)\}^{-1} \cdot r). \tag{2.20}$$

That is, the components of F are also transformed into linear combinations of components. For a first rank tensor (vector) function F with three components F_α,

$$P_{\{\phi \mid \tau(\phi)\}}F_\gamma(r) = \sum_{\alpha=1}^{3} \phi_{\alpha\gamma}F_\alpha(\{\phi \mid \tau(\phi)\}^{-1} \cdot r). \tag{2.21}$$

In lattice dynamics we have to do most often with scalar, vector, and second rank tensor functions; but tensors of higher rank can also arise in study of higher order coupling (force) coefficients, and in other parts of the theory.

3. *Basic group theory*

In the present section we review the familiar applications of group theory using the simplest possible notation, unencumbered by indices except the most necessary (Wigner 1959).

3.1. Representations and degeneracy in quantum mechanics

It is simplest to consider a quantum-mechanical system, characterized by a scalar hamiltonian operator $H(r)$. In general H is an operator which operates upon the space–time function $\psi(r, t)$ and satisfies (taking $\hbar = 1$)

$$H(r)\psi(r, t) = \mathrm{i}\,\partial\psi(r, t)/\partial t. \tag{3.1}$$

If the hamiltonian is a real scalar operator then it is invariant under complex conjugation. Denoting by K the operator of complex conjugation we have

$$KHK^{-1} \equiv H^* = H. \tag{3.2}$$

The first identity follows by definition, the second equality by assumption that H is real. It follows that (3.1) can be transformed by K to give

$$KHK^{-1}K\psi = K(\mathrm{i}\,\partial\psi/\partial t) = -\mathrm{i}\,\partial K\psi/\partial t. \tag{3.3}$$

Recall that

$$K\psi = \psi^* \quad \text{and} \quad K^2 = 1 \tag{3.4}$$

So then (3.3) becomes

$$H\psi^* = -\,\mathrm{i}\,\partial\psi^*/\partial t \tag{3.5}$$

or

$$H\psi^* = \mathrm{i}\,\partial\psi^*/\partial(-t). \tag{3.6}$$

Consequently

$$H\psi^*(\boldsymbol{r}, -t) = \mathrm{i}\,\partial\psi^*(\boldsymbol{r}, -t)/\partial(-t). \tag{3.7}$$

It follows then that $\psi^*(\boldsymbol{r}, -t)$ obeys the same equation as $\psi(\boldsymbol{r}, t)$.

In a stationary state

$$\psi(\boldsymbol{r}, t) = \psi(\boldsymbol{r})\exp(-\mathrm{i}Et), \qquad \psi^*(\boldsymbol{r}, -t) = \psi^*(\boldsymbol{r})\exp(-\mathrm{i}Et) \tag{3.8, 9}$$

and

$$H\psi(\boldsymbol{r}) = E\psi(\boldsymbol{r}), \quad HK\psi(\boldsymbol{r}) = H\psi^*(\boldsymbol{r}) = E\psi^*(\boldsymbol{r}) = EK\psi(\boldsymbol{r}). \tag{3.10a, b}$$

Consequently

$$\psi(\boldsymbol{r}) \quad \text{and} \quad K\psi(\boldsymbol{r}) = \psi^*(\boldsymbol{r}) \tag{3.11}$$

are degenerate members of the linear vector space of eigenvalue E. The argument just given [esp. eq. (3.4b)] applies in case the hamiltonian is a scalar (spin zero), or in general has integer spin. Clearly K is the operator of time reversal in a theory with spinless, scalar hamiltonian.

Now turn to spatial symmetry. Let R be a physical symmetry transformation which transforms field point $\boldsymbol{r}$ to an equivalent point $\boldsymbol{r}'$:

$$\boldsymbol{r}' = R\boldsymbol{r}. \tag{3.12}$$

Then we introduce the corresponding operator P_R such that

$$P_R H(\boldsymbol{r})\, P_R^{-1} \equiv H(R^{-1}\boldsymbol{r}) \tag{3.13}$$

and

$$P_R\psi(\boldsymbol{r}) = \psi(R^{-1}\boldsymbol{r}). \tag{3.14}$$

If points $\boldsymbol{r}$ and $\boldsymbol{r}'$ are equivalent then P_R is a symmetry transformation on H and

$$H(R^{-1}\boldsymbol{r}) = H(\boldsymbol{r}). \tag{3.15}$$

Consequently transforming (3.10a) gives

$$P_R H P_R^{-1} P_R \psi = E P_R \psi \tag{3.16a}$$

or

$$H P_R \psi = E P_R \psi \, . \tag{3.16b}$$

Thus

$$\psi \quad \text{and} \quad P_R \psi \tag{3.17}$$

are degenerate members of the linear vector space of eigenvalue E.

The set of unitary operators

$$\mathcal{G} \sim P_E, \cdots, P_R, \cdots, P_Z \tag{3.18}$$

with P_E the identity operator

$$P_E \psi = \psi \, , \tag{3.19}$$

forms a collection isomorphic to the group of physical transformations. When this set is augmented by K, to include symmetry under time reversal we obtain the full space–time operator group of the hamiltonian

$$\mathsf{G} = \mathcal{G} + K\mathcal{G} \tag{3.20}$$

which consists of the set of all unitary operators plus the set of all unitary operators

$$K\mathcal{G} = KP_E, \cdots, KP_R, \cdots, KP_Z \, . \tag{3.21a}$$

It is important to realize that the key group in any dynamical problem is the full space–time operator group G or $\mathcal{G}$ if time-reversal symmetry is ignored. The symmetry group of physical transformations (set of R) underlies the operator group, of course, but is not the major object of analysis.

The set of wave functions obtained from a given wave function ψ, which belongs to energy E, by applying all operators in $\mathcal{G}$ are a closed set. We can write them as

$$\{\psi \equiv P_E \psi, \cdots, \psi_R \equiv P_R \psi, \cdots, \psi_Z \equiv P_Z \psi\} \, . \tag{3.21b}$$

Among this set there are l_j linearly independent functions which we identify as

$$\{\psi_1^{(j)}, \psi_2^{(j)}, \cdots, \psi_\mu^{(j)}, \cdots, \psi_{l_j}^{(j)}\} \equiv \Sigma^{(j)} \, . \tag{3.22}$$

Then the set (3.22) is a basis for the irreducible representation $D^{(j)}$ of the group $\mathscr{G}$. Explicitly

$$P_R\psi^j_\mu = \sum_{\nu=1}^{l_j} D^{(j)}(R)_{\nu\mu}\,\psi^j_\nu. \tag{3.23}$$

It is also usual to affix the index j to the eigenenergy so

$$H\psi^j_\nu = E^j\psi^j_\nu, \qquad \nu = 1, \cdots, l_j. \tag{3.24}$$

The level E^j is then l_j-fold degenerate, and the states ψ^j_ν, $\nu=1,\cdots, l_j$ belong to the species, or irreducible representation $D^{(j)}$. If necessary we use the symbol $\Sigma^{(j)}$ to represent the linear vector space spanned by the set (3.22).

When the time reversal operation is included, the set

$$S^{(j)} \equiv \Sigma^{(j)} + K\Sigma^{(j)} \tag{3.25}$$

spans a vector space $S^{(j)}$ which is a basis for the corepresentation $D^{(\mathrm{co})(j)}$. The corepresentation $D^{(\mathrm{co})(j)}$ is also known as a physically irreducible representation. Depending upon the structure of the irreducible representation the corepresentation may be of dimension l_j or $2l_j$. Then, including the time reversal, each energy E of a quantum-mechanical problem corresponds to a physically irreducible representation, or corepresentation.

Tests for irreducibility for representations and for corepresentations are based on the Schur-lemma. Let P_R be a unitary operator; if the only matrix M which commutes with *all* matrices $D^{(j)}(R)$ is a constant, then $D^{(j)}$ is irreducible. That is

$$MD^{(j)}(R) = D^{(j)}(R)\,M \tag{3.26}$$

implies

$$M = mD^{(j)}(E), \quad \text{with } m \text{ a number}. \tag{3.27}$$

Let $P_R \equiv u_R$ be a unitary operator, and $KP_R \equiv a_R$ be an anti-unitary operator and let M be hermitian. If $D^{(\mathrm{co})(j)}$ is an irreducible corepresentation, the only M with the property

$$MD^{(\mathrm{co})(j)}(u_R) = D^{(\mathrm{co})(j)}(u_R)\,M, \qquad MD^{(\mathrm{co})(j)}(a_R) = D^{(\mathrm{co})(j)}(a_R)\,M^* \tag{3.28, 29}$$

(for all u_R, a_R in G) is a constant.

The test for irreducibility of corepresentations is consistent with that for representations if we restrict ourselves to the unitary elements u_R.

The preceding discussion can be summarized in the 'lemma of necessary degeneracy'. This epitomizes the aspect of the application of group theory having to do with the classification of the eigenstates of a quantum-mechanical system. Given a quantum-mechanical system whose hamiltonian H admits the space–time symmetry group G. Then each eigenstate spans one physically irreducible representation of the group G. These concise statements give the generality of classification of eigenstates. It remains to put flesh on the bare bones of these statements, and this will be done in the detailed discussion following.

3.2. Transition processes and selection rules

When the states of a quantum-mechanical system have been classified according to the irreducible (co)representations of $(G)\mathcal{G}$ a major part of the work is done. Next in importance is the analysis of transition processes from a state ψ^j_α in the manifold $\{\psi^j\}$ to a state ψ^l_γ in the manifold $\{\psi^l\}$ under the application of a perturbation operator O^k_β which belongs in the manifold $\{\boldsymbol{O}^k\}$. The relevant matrix element is

$$(\psi^j_\alpha, O^k_\beta \psi^l_\gamma) \equiv \int \mathrm{d}^3\boldsymbol{r}\, \psi^j_\alpha(\boldsymbol{r})^* \, O^k_\beta \, \psi^l_\gamma(\boldsymbol{r}). \tag{3.30}$$

Group theory permits us to determine whether this matrix element vanishes. A related question concerns the number of linearly independent matrix elements from among the total number of $(l_j l_k l_l)$ of eq. (3.30) when $\alpha = 1, \cdots, l_j$, $\beta = 1, \cdots, l_k$, $\gamma = 1, \cdots, l_l$. The analysis of the matrix elements produces selection rules which are the closest approximations to directly observable consequences of group theory.

From a theoretical point of view, the central quantities for analysis of selection rules and the related questions are the vector coupling or Clebsch–Gordan coefficients of the groups G or $\mathcal{G}$. Most work has been concentrated upon the determination of these coefficients in the absence of time reversal, although specific results including time reversal can also be obtained with some additional effort. A definition of the Clebsch–Gordan coefficients is given by writing the proper linear combination of product functions from each of the two spaces $\Sigma^{(j)}$ and $\Sigma^{(l)}$ which transforms as the basis for the νth row of representation $D^{(k)}$. In general we may write:

$$\psi^{(k),\gamma}_\nu = \sum_{\lambda,\mu} \begin{pmatrix} jl & k,\gamma \\ \lambda\mu & \nu \end{pmatrix} \psi^j_\lambda \psi^l_\mu, \qquad \gamma = 1, \cdots, c_m. \tag{3.31}$$

This expression defines the general Clebsch–Gordan coefficient. In the case that $c_m > 1$, there are more than one (in fact c_m) linear combinations of products $\psi^j_\lambda \psi^l_\mu$ which transform as ψ^k_ν; it is then necessary to distinguish each of these linearly independent combinations of the same symmetry by an additional index, taken here as γ. In this case *any* linear combination of the

$$\psi_\nu^{(k)1}, \cdots, \psi_\nu^{(k)\gamma}, \cdots, \psi_\nu^{(k)c_m} \tag{3.32}$$

will still have the correct transformation properties, so some convention is required to determine a set of coefficients $\left(\begin{smallmatrix} jl \\ \lambda\mu \end{smallmatrix} \middle| \begin{smallmatrix} k, \gamma \\ \nu \end{smallmatrix}\right)$.

When $c_m = 1$ there is unique combination of products $\psi^j_\lambda \psi^l_\mu$ which produce a ψ^k_ν. One can determine this unique linear combination for example by using the projection operator

$$P^k_{\nu\tau} \equiv (l_k/g) \sum_R D^{(k)}(R)^*_{\nu\tau} \, P_R, \tag{3.33}$$

where l_k is the dimension of the representation $D^{(k)}$, g is the order of $\mathcal{G}$ and the sum is over all elements P_R in $\mathcal{G}$. It is easy to verify that for any admissible function ψ, the function

$$P^k_{\nu\tau}\psi \equiv \psi^k_\nu \tag{3.34}$$

transforms as a basis function for the νth row of irreducible representation $D^{(k)}$; e.g. consistently with (3.23). This follows from the algebraic property of the elements $P^k_{\nu\tau}$ and in particular

$$P_S P^k_{\nu\tau} = \sum_\alpha D^{(k)}(S)_{\alpha\nu} \, P^k_{\alpha\tau}, \tag{3.35}$$

or if ψ^k_ν is defined by (3.34) we have

$$P_S \psi^k_\nu = \sum_\alpha D^{(k)}(S)_{\alpha\nu} \, \psi^k_\alpha \tag{3.36}$$

which demonstrates the consistency of the definitions. In this case, $c_m = 1$, and an expression for the Clebsch–Gordan coefficient can be directly found, by applying the operator (3.33) to a typical product. We have

$$P^k_{\nu\tau} \psi^j_\lambda \psi^l_\mu = \sum_{\alpha,\beta} \{(l_k/g) (\sum_R D^{(k)}(R)^*_{\nu\tau} \, D^{(j)}(R)_{\alpha\lambda} \, D^{(l)}(R)_{\beta\mu})\} \, \psi^j_\alpha \psi^l_\beta \tag{3.37}$$

from which we can find the Clebsch–Gordan coefficients directly. Since (3.37) may give unnormalized functions ψ^k_ν, the '$\psi^j_{\bar\lambda}\psi^l_{\bar\mu}$ component' is obtained by taking the scalar product of $\psi^j_{\bar{\lambda}}\psi^l_{\bar{\mu}}$ with (3.37):

$$(\psi^j_{\bar{\lambda}}\psi^l_{\bar{\mu}}, P^k_{\nu\tau}\psi^j_{\lambda}\psi^l_{\mu}) = (l_k/g)\sum_R D^{(k)}(R)^*_{\nu\tau}\, D^{(j)}(R)_{\bar{\lambda}\lambda}\, D^{(l)}(R)_{\bar{\mu}\mu}\,. \tag{3.38}$$

The Clebsch–Gordan coefficient can be considered as a matrix element of a unitary matrix which produces the transformation from the set of normalized product functions [on the right hand side of (3.31)] to the set ψ^k_ν. In order to ensure unitarity it is necessary to divide (3.31) by the proper normalizing factor to obtain the Clebsch–Gordan coefficient. Then

$$\begin{pmatrix} j & l & \big| & k \\ \bar{\lambda} & \bar{\mu} & \big| & \nu \end{pmatrix} = N/D^{1/2}, \tag{3.39}$$

where

$$N \equiv (\psi^j_{\bar{\lambda}}\psi^l_{\bar{\mu}}, P^k_{\nu\tau}\psi^j_{\lambda}\psi^l_{\mu}), \qquad D \equiv (\psi^j_{\lambda}\psi^l_{\mu}, P^k_{\nu\nu}\psi^j_{\lambda}\psi^l_{\mu}). \tag{3.40, 41}$$

This corresponds to a choice of phase such that the element of the inverse Clebsch–Gordan matrix

$$\begin{pmatrix} k & \big| & j & l \\ \nu & \big| & \lambda & \mu \end{pmatrix} \tag{3.42}$$

is real and positive. This expression gives the solution; it is of course assumed that for the selected (fixed) $\lambda\mu$, the left hand side of (3.37) is non-zero.*

When $c_m > 1$ no such simple form can be given, although a systematic method for determining the coefficients is also available, for this case.

In order to determine whether or not a particular matrix element such as (3.30) vanishes, it is required to examine the appropriate Clebsch–Gordan coefficient. Thus if the representation by which the set

$$\{\psi^{j*}_1, \ldots \psi^{j*}_\alpha, \ldots \psi^{j*}_{l_j}\} \tag{3.43}$$

transforms is denoted D^{j*} *and* if for the representations involved, $c_m = 1$, the appropriate Clebsch–Gordan coefficient is

$$\begin{pmatrix} j^* & l & \big| & k \\ \alpha & \gamma & \big| & \beta \end{pmatrix}. \tag{3.44}$$

If this coefficient vanishes then the matrix element is zero, and there is the corresponding selection rule: the transition from state ψ^l_γ to state ψ^{j*}_α under the action of the perturbing operator O^k_β is strictly forbidden. Selection rules for $c_m = 1$ are then immediate consequences of the Clebsch–Gordan coeffi-

* It may be that D equals 1, in which case (3.37) gives the Clebsch–Gordan coefficients directly, and the matrix is unitary a priori.

cients and these coefficients can be determined for any group $\mathscr{G}$ by systematic procedure. As might be expected, the situation for $c_m > 1$, and when the time reversal symmetry is included is more complicated, but can be in principle solved also (Koster 1958).

Often in finding selection rules one does not require the complete information contained in the Clebsch–Gordan coefficients, but rather that in the Clebsch–Gordan Series. These quantities answer the question of whether from the product $\psi^j_\lambda \psi^l_\mu$ one can construct a function ψ^k_ν irrespective of row. These 'reduction coefficients' then give the number of times a given irreducible representation $D^{(k)}$ appears in the reduction of the direct product: $D^{(j)} \otimes D^{(l)}$ and are

$$D^{(j)} \otimes D^{(l)} = \sum_{\oplus} (jl \,|\, k)\, D^{(k)}. \tag{3.45}$$

Evidently, if $(jl \,|\, k) = 0$ then, referring back to the matrix element (3.30), we can assert that the transition from any of the states of the manifold $D^{(j)}$ to any state of the manifold $D^{(l)}$ is forbidden under action of the perturbation $D^{(k)}$.

The work of this section can be summarized simply. For a quantum-mechanical system whose equation of motion is governed by the hamiltonian H, the relevant symmetry group is the space–time group G of operator transformations which leave H invariant. The group G contains both unitary and anti-unitary operators. The states of the system can be classified into species according to the irreducible corepresentations of G, or irreducible representations of the unitary subgroup $\mathscr{G}$, if time reversal is excluded from consideration. To determine selection rules requires the prior determination of the Clebsch–Gordan, or vector coupling, coefficients, or if less information suffices, the reduction coefficients.

Everything in this section was couched in the familiar frame of reference of the quantum-mechanical problem. But in lattice dynamics we have to do at first with the classical problem of the normal modes of vibration of an assembly of ions interacting via Hooke's law forces. This classical problem admits generalization to the inclusion of anharmonicity. A final step in the generalization is to quantum-mechanical lattice dynamics. The group theory work is of assistance in every stage of this program.

4. *Classical harmonic lattice dynamics and symmetry*

In this section it will be demonstrated that the normal coordinates of the classical harmonic lattice dynamic theory are bases for irreducible (co)representations of G or $\mathscr{G}$, if time reversal is included or excluded, respectively. In order to demonstrate this result one proceeds just as in the more familiar quantum-mechanical situation, described in the previous section.

4.1. Eigenvectors of the dynamical matrix

Let $\mu_\alpha(l\kappa)$ be the αth cartesian component of the real displacement of the particle initially at the position $(l\kappa)$, which is the κth basis position in the lth cell. The equation of motion for the displacement of this particle, in harmonic approximation is

$$M_\kappa \frac{\partial^2 \mu_\alpha(l\kappa)}{\partial t^2} + \sum_{l'\kappa'\beta} \Phi_{\alpha\beta}(l\kappa \,|\, l'\kappa')\, \mu_\beta(l'\kappa') = 0\,, \tag{4.1}$$

where M_κ is the mass of the particle and $\Phi_{\alpha\beta}$ the real force constant matrix. Recall that owing to translational invariance, $\Phi_{\alpha\beta}$ depends only on the *difference* $(l-l')$.

Introduce the Fourier transform mass-weighted displacements by assuming a particular form for the solution:

$$\mu_\alpha(l\kappa) = (M_\kappa)^{-1/2}\, \eta_\alpha(\kappa \,|\, \boldsymbol{k} j_\mu) \exp(i\boldsymbol{k}\cdot\boldsymbol{R}_{\mathrm{L}})\,.$$

Then the equation of motion of $\boldsymbol{\eta}(\,|\,\boldsymbol{k}j_\mu)$ is

$$\partial^2 \eta_\alpha(\kappa \,|\, \boldsymbol{k}j_\mu)/\partial t^2 + \sum_{\kappa'\beta} D_{\alpha\beta}(\boldsymbol{k} \,|\, \kappa\kappa')\, \eta_\beta(\kappa' \,|\, \boldsymbol{k}j_\mu) = 0\,, \tag{4.2}$$

where the dynamical matrix at wave vector $\boldsymbol{k}$ is:

$$D_{\alpha\beta}(\boldsymbol{k} \,|\, \kappa\kappa') \equiv \sum_{\lambda} (\Phi_{\alpha\beta}(\boldsymbol{\lambda} \,|\, \kappa\kappa') \exp(-\,i\boldsymbol{k}\cdot\boldsymbol{R}_\lambda))\,(M_\kappa M_{\kappa'})^{-1/2}\,. \tag{4.3}$$

In this equation the branch index j and degeneracy index μ are affixed to the Fourier transformed displacements in anticipation of the later results and $\boldsymbol{R}_\lambda = \boldsymbol{R}_{\mathrm{L}} - \boldsymbol{R}_{\mathrm{L}'}$.

The complete set of linearly independent solutions of (4.2) for the fixed wave vector $\boldsymbol{k}$ are the $3s$ vectors which we denote as

$$\varepsilon_\alpha(\kappa \,|\, \boldsymbol{k}j_\mu)\,. \tag{4.4}$$

A particular solution has $\boldsymbol{k}$ and j_μ fixed. Each such solution has $3s$ non-vanishing components with $\alpha = 1, \cdots, 3$; $\kappa = 1, \cdots, s$. The degeneracy index μ labels the distinct solutions, for $\boldsymbol{k}$ and j (branch index) fixed, if the branch is multidimensional at that $\boldsymbol{k}$. One could abbreviate (4.4) for clarity by suppressing the indices (α and κ) which refer to cartesian components and by writing the set of $3s$ vectors as:

$$\{\varepsilon(|\boldsymbol{k}1), \cdots, \varepsilon(|\boldsymbol{k}j_1), \cdots, \varepsilon(|\boldsymbol{k}j_{l_j}), \cdots, \varepsilon(|\boldsymbol{k}3s)\}. \tag{4.5}$$

Because this set is complete, any solution of the dynamical equation at wave vector $\boldsymbol{k}$ can be written as a linear combination of the members of the above set.

To continue, the time dependence is separated by writing

$$\varepsilon(|\boldsymbol{k}j_\mu) = \boldsymbol{e}(|\boldsymbol{k}j_\mu) \exp[-\mathrm{i}\omega(\boldsymbol{k}|j)\, t], \tag{4.6}$$

where $\omega(\boldsymbol{k}|j)$ is the eigenfrequency and is independent of μ, and $\boldsymbol{e}(|\boldsymbol{k}j_\mu)$ is an eigenvector satisfying

$$\omega^2(\boldsymbol{k}|j)\, e_\alpha(\kappa|\boldsymbol{k}j_\mu) = \sum_{\kappa'\beta} D_{\alpha\beta}(\boldsymbol{k}|\kappa\kappa')\, e_\beta(\kappa'|\boldsymbol{k}j_\mu). \tag{4.7}$$

Again note that the vector $\boldsymbol{e}(|\boldsymbol{k}j_\mu)$ for fixed $\boldsymbol{k}$ and j_μ has $3s$ components $e_\alpha(\kappa|\boldsymbol{k}j_\mu)$ because $\alpha = 1, 2, 3$, $\kappa = 1, \cdots, s$. A complete set of eigenvectors of (4.7) for fixed $\boldsymbol{k}$ is

$$\{\boldsymbol{e}(|\boldsymbol{k}\,1), \cdots, \boldsymbol{e}(|\boldsymbol{k}\,j_\mu), \cdots, \boldsymbol{e}(|\boldsymbol{k}\,3s)\} \equiv \Sigma^{(\boldsymbol{k})}. \tag{4.8}$$

Now apply a general spatial transformation operator to eq. (4.7). First rewrite it using the vector notation

$$[\boldsymbol{D}(\boldsymbol{k})]\cdot\boldsymbol{e}(|\boldsymbol{k}j_\mu) = \omega^2(\boldsymbol{k}|j)\, \boldsymbol{e}(|\boldsymbol{k}j_\mu). \tag{4.9}$$

In this equation the components of $[\boldsymbol{D}(\boldsymbol{k})]$ are $D_{\alpha\beta}(\boldsymbol{k}|\kappa\kappa')$. Then in transforming equation (4.9) the $[\boldsymbol{D}(\boldsymbol{k})]$ should be considered as an operator (recall the treatment of the hamiltonian in section 2). We find

$$P_{\{\phi\,|\,\tau(\phi)\}}[\boldsymbol{D}(\boldsymbol{k})]\, P^{-1}_{\{\phi\,|\,\tau(\phi)\}} \cdot P_{\{\phi\,|\,\tau(\phi)\}}\boldsymbol{e}(|\boldsymbol{k}j_\mu) = \omega^2(\boldsymbol{k}|j)\, P_{\{\phi\,|\,\tau(\phi)\}}\boldsymbol{e}(|\boldsymbol{k}j_\mu). \tag{4.10}$$

By straightforward application of the transformation operator we find

$$P_{\{\phi\,|\,\tau(\phi)\}}[\boldsymbol{D}(\boldsymbol{k})]\, P^{-1}_{\{\phi\,|\,\tau(\phi)\}} = [\boldsymbol{D}(\phi\cdot\boldsymbol{k})]. \tag{4.11}$$

We have had to use the invariance of the force matrix of the crystal to a symmetry operation. We define a force matrix tensor analogously to the dynamical matrix tensor, from eq. (4.1) and call it $[\boldsymbol{\Phi}]$. Then this $[\boldsymbol{\Phi}]$ has components $\Phi_{\alpha\beta}(ll'|\kappa\kappa')$. Under transformation we have

$$P_{\{\phi\,|\,\tau(\phi)\}}[\boldsymbol{\Phi}]\, P^{-1}_{\{\phi\,|\,\tau(\phi)\}} = [\boldsymbol{\Phi}] \tag{4.12}$$

which expresses the invariance of $[\boldsymbol{\Phi}]$.

The result (4.11) can now be immediately used. Thus the transformed equation (4.10) becomes

$$[\boldsymbol{D}(\boldsymbol{\phi}\cdot\boldsymbol{k})]\cdot P_{\{\phi\,|\,\tau(\phi)\}}\, \boldsymbol{e}(\,|\,\boldsymbol{k}j_\mu) = \omega^2(\boldsymbol{k}\,|\,j)\, P_{\{\phi\,|\,\tau(\phi)\}}\, \boldsymbol{e}(\,|\,\boldsymbol{k}j_\mu). \tag{4.13}$$

Then, as this is the dynamical equation at wave-vector $\boldsymbol{\phi}\cdot\boldsymbol{k}$ we must have

$$\omega^2(\boldsymbol{\phi}\cdot\boldsymbol{k}\,|\,\bar{j}) = \omega^2(\boldsymbol{k}\,|\,j), \tag{4.14}$$

that is: $\omega^2(\boldsymbol{k}\,|\,j)$ must equal one of the eigenvalues at $\boldsymbol{\phi}\cdot\boldsymbol{k}$. Secondly $P_{\{\phi\,|\,\tau(\phi)\}}\boldsymbol{e}(\,|\,\boldsymbol{k}j_\mu)$ must be an eigenvector at $\boldsymbol{\phi}\cdot\boldsymbol{k}$, or in general, a linear combination of the basic complete set of eigenvectors at $\boldsymbol{\phi}\cdot\boldsymbol{k}$

$$\{\boldsymbol{e}(\,|\,\boldsymbol{\phi}\cdot\boldsymbol{k}\;1), \cdots, \boldsymbol{e}(\,|\,\boldsymbol{\phi}\cdot\boldsymbol{k}\;3s)\}. \tag{4.15}$$

By direct transformation of the eigenvector we can also find

$$P_{\{\phi\,|\,\tau(\phi)\}} e_\alpha(\kappa\,|\,\boldsymbol{k}j_\mu) = \sum_\beta \phi_{\alpha\beta} e_\beta(\{\boldsymbol{\phi}\,|\,\boldsymbol{\tau}(\boldsymbol{\phi})\}^{-1}\cdot\boldsymbol{r}_\kappa\,|\,\boldsymbol{\phi}\cdot\boldsymbol{k}j_\mu). \tag{4.16}$$

At the moment this result is less useful although we reserve it for the future. It does explicitly demonstrate that $\boldsymbol{e}(\,|\,\boldsymbol{k}j_\mu)$ transforms like a vector field function of (lattice site) position: recall (2.21).

All the results just given apply for any symmetry operator. An interesting situation occurs when the operator is such that

$$\boldsymbol{\phi}\cdot\boldsymbol{k} = \boldsymbol{k} + \boldsymbol{B}_{\mathrm{H}} = \boldsymbol{k}(\mathrm{mod}\,\boldsymbol{B}_{\mathrm{H}}), \tag{4.17}$$

where $\boldsymbol{B}_{\mathrm{H}} = 2\pi h_i \boldsymbol{b}_i$ (sum convention) is 2π times a reciprocal lattice vector, with h_i integer. Then consider the set of all operators such that the rotational part satisfies (4.17). This set forms the unitary space group of the wave vector $\boldsymbol{k}$. Denote it as $\mathscr{G}(\boldsymbol{k})$ so that for any operator $P_{\{\phi_l\,|\,\tau(\phi_l)\}}$ in $\mathscr{G}(\boldsymbol{k})$ the rotational part satisfies (4.17).

Then we may make an important observation, which is crucial to the following analysis. The object

$$P_{\{\phi_l\,|\,\tau(\phi_l)\}}\boldsymbol{e}(\,|\,\boldsymbol{k}j_\mu) \tag{4.18}$$

which is obtained from eq. (4.9) by transformation with the operator $P_{\{\phi_l\,|\,\tau(\phi_l)\}}$, is an eigenvector of (4.9) or, a linear combination of the complete set of $3s$ eigenvectors denoted $\Sigma^{(\boldsymbol{k})}$ in eq. (4.8). Consequently the set or space $\Sigma^{(\boldsymbol{k})}$ is closed under transformation by all operators in $\mathscr{G}(\boldsymbol{k})$. The closure of this space, plus its completeness, implies the assertion that the space $\Sigma^{(\boldsymbol{k})}$ is a basis for a representation of $\mathscr{G}(\boldsymbol{k})$. But $\mathscr{G}(\boldsymbol{k})$ is a finite group. Hence, by a well-known theorem due to Maschke the representation based on $\Sigma^{(\boldsymbol{k})}$ is either irreducible, or decomposable. We may then choose as basis vectors in $\Sigma^{(\boldsymbol{k})}$ the correct linear combinations so that the eigenvectors in (4.8) are bases for irreducible representations of $\mathscr{G}(\boldsymbol{k})$.‡ Then

$$P_{\{\phi_l \mid \tau(\phi_l)\}} \boldsymbol{e}(\,|\,\boldsymbol{k}j_\mu) = \sum_{\nu=1}^{l_j} D^{(\boldsymbol{k})(j)}(\{\phi_l \mid \tau(\phi_l)\})_{\nu\mu}\, \boldsymbol{e}(\,|\,\boldsymbol{k}j_\nu). \tag{4.19}$$

Here $D^{(\boldsymbol{k})(j)}$ is the *allowable* irreducible representation of $\mathscr{G}(\boldsymbol{k})$; it is fully characterized by wave-vector $\boldsymbol{k}$, and by the branch index j. This equation gives the transformation properties of *entire* eigenvectors: thus $\boldsymbol{e}(\,|\,\boldsymbol{k}j_\mu)$ transforms as the μth row of $D^{(\boldsymbol{k})(j)}$.

It follows by the 'lemma of necessary degeneracy' that the subset of eigenvectors

$$\Sigma^{(\boldsymbol{k})(j)} \equiv \{\boldsymbol{e}(\,|\,\boldsymbol{k}j), \cdots, \boldsymbol{e}(\,|\,\boldsymbol{k}j_{l_j})\} \tag{4.20}$$

are degenerate and all correspond to squared eigenvalue $\omega^2(\boldsymbol{k}\,|\,j)$. The subset $\Sigma^{(\boldsymbol{k})(j)}$ is evidently a basis for $D^{(\boldsymbol{k})(j)}$.

Conversely given one eigenvector, say $\boldsymbol{e}(\,|\boldsymbol{k}j_\nu)$, of a degenerate set, the remaining partners belonging to the same representation $D^{(\boldsymbol{k})(j)}$ can be obtained by application of the projection operator such as:

$$P_{\mu\nu}^{(\boldsymbol{k})(j)} \equiv (l_j/g) \sum_{R \in \mathscr{G}(\boldsymbol{k})} D^{(\boldsymbol{k})(j)}(R)_{\mu\nu}^{*}\, P_R, \tag{4.21}$$

where R is in $\mathscr{G}(\boldsymbol{k})$, and the sum is extended over all such elements. Then

$$\boldsymbol{e}(\,|\,\boldsymbol{k}j_\mu) = P_{\mu\nu}^{(\boldsymbol{k})(j)} \boldsymbol{e}(\,|\,\boldsymbol{k}j_\nu) \tag{4.22}$$

is an eigenvector transforming as basis for row μ of $D^{(\boldsymbol{k})(j)}$. Use of this projection operator is not convenient owing to the required sum over all space group elements in $\mathscr{G}(\boldsymbol{k})$, but an operator which is fully equivalent is obtained by summing over those cosets R which are in the factor group of the wave vector

$$\mathscr{P}(\boldsymbol{k}) = \mathscr{G}(\boldsymbol{k})/\mathscr{T}(\boldsymbol{k}) \tag{4.23}$$

where $\mathscr{T}(\boldsymbol{k})$ is the translation group such that the mapping

$$\mathscr{T}(\boldsymbol{k}) \to D^{(\boldsymbol{k})(j)}(\{\varepsilon \mid 0\}). \tag{4.24}$$

‡ A more complete discussion of the space group theory including complete definitions of all quantities is given in section 6 of this chapter.

It should be emphasized that one of the major applications of group theory in lattice dynamics is epitomized by these results: one can obtain the properly symmetrized eigenvectors by use of an algebraic technique. Again a compli-, cation may arise if, for fixed $\boldsymbol{k}$ a given $D^{(\boldsymbol{k})(j)}$ occurs more than once. Then just as for the analogous problem of the Clebsch–Gordan coefficients with multiplicity $c_m > 1$, any linear combination of eigenvectors which transform according to the same row is an acceptable basis:

$$\boldsymbol{e}(\,|\,\boldsymbol{k}j_\mu)^\gamma = \sum_{\alpha=1}^{c_m} \lambda_{\alpha\gamma}\boldsymbol{e}(\,|\,\boldsymbol{k}j_\mu)^\alpha . \tag{4.25}$$

In (4.25) the constants $\lambda_{\alpha\gamma}$ must still be determined; the superscripts γ and α merely enumerate multiplicity.

Summarizing then: the space or representation module $\Sigma^{(\boldsymbol{k})}$ can be re-arranged, by taking suitable linear combinations, as follows:

$$\Sigma^{(\boldsymbol{k})} = \{\boldsymbol{e}(\,|\,\boldsymbol{k}1), \cdots, \boldsymbol{e}(\,|\,\boldsymbol{k}j_1)^{\alpha=1}, \cdots, \boldsymbol{e}(\,|\,\boldsymbol{k}j_{l_j})^{\alpha=1}, \cdots, \\ \boldsymbol{e}(\,|\,\boldsymbol{k}j_1)^{\alpha=c_m}, \cdots, \boldsymbol{e}(\,|\,\boldsymbol{k}j_{l_j})^{\alpha=c_m}, \cdots, \boldsymbol{e}(\,|\,\boldsymbol{k}3s)\} . \tag{4.26}$$

It will be shown that this disjoint decomposition, in the sense of taking new linear combinations, corresponds to a maximum partitioning of the dynamical matrix, and hence a maximum factorization of the dynamical secular equation. The orthonormality rules for the eigenvectors are

$$\sum_\kappa \sum_\alpha e_\alpha^*(\kappa\,|\,\boldsymbol{k}j_\nu)\, e_\alpha(\kappa\,|\,\boldsymbol{k}j'_{\nu'}) = \delta_{jj'}\delta_{\nu\nu'} \tag{4.27}$$

and

$$\sum_{j\nu} e_\beta^*(\kappa'\,|\,\boldsymbol{k}j_\nu)\, e_\alpha(\kappa\,|\,\boldsymbol{k}j_\nu) = \delta_{\alpha\beta}\delta_{\kappa\kappa'} . \tag{4.28}$$

4.2. Normal coordinates

Complex normal coordinates can now be defined from the expression for the time dependent cartesian displacements by

$$\mu_\alpha(l\kappa) = (M_\kappa N)^{-1/2} \sum_j \sum_\mu \sum_{\boldsymbol{k}} \exp(-\,\mathrm{i}\boldsymbol{k}\cdot\boldsymbol{R}_\mathrm{L})\, e_\alpha^*(\kappa\,|\,\boldsymbol{k}j_\mu)\, Q(\boldsymbol{k}j_\mu\,|\,t) . \tag{4.29}$$

The quantities $Q(\boldsymbol{k}j_\mu\,|\,t)$ are the time dependent complex normal coordinates. The inverse of (4.29) is

$$Q(\boldsymbol{k}j_\mu\,|\,t) = N^{-1/2} \sum_l \sum_\kappa \sum_\alpha \exp(\mathrm{i}\boldsymbol{k}\cdot\boldsymbol{R}_\mathrm{L})\, e_\alpha(\kappa\,|\,\boldsymbol{k}j_\mu)\, \mu_\alpha(l\kappa)\, M_\kappa^{1/2} . \tag{4.30}$$

Using the expression for $\mu_\alpha(l\kappa)$ in the equation of motion of the complex cartesian displacements we obtain the equation of motion of the complex normal coordinates

$$\partial^2 Q(\boldsymbol{k}j_\mu|t)/\partial t^2 + \omega^2(\boldsymbol{k}|j)\,Q(\boldsymbol{k}j_\mu|t) = 0\,, \quad \mu = 1, \cdots, l_j\,. \tag{4.31}$$

The same equation can be derived from the classical hamiltonian function expressed in terms of the complex normal coordinates

$$\mathscr{H} = \tfrac{1}{2}\sum_{\boldsymbol{k}}\sum_{j}\sum_{\mu}\{\dot{Q}(\boldsymbol{k}j_\mu|t)^*\,\dot{Q}(\boldsymbol{k}j_\mu|t) + \omega^2(\boldsymbol{k}|j)\,Q(\boldsymbol{k}j_\mu|t)^*\,Q(\boldsymbol{k}j_\mu|t)\}\,. \tag{4.32}$$

The solution of the equation of motion is

$$Q(\boldsymbol{k}j_\mu|t) = Q(\boldsymbol{k}j_\mu)\exp[\pm\,\mathrm{i}\omega(\boldsymbol{k}|j)\,t]\,. \tag{4.33}$$

When this is substituted into (4.31) we obtain

$$\mu_\alpha(l\kappa) = (M_\kappa N)^{-1/2}\sum_{j}\sum_{\mu}\sum_{\boldsymbol{k}}\exp(-\,\mathrm{i}\boldsymbol{k}\cdot\boldsymbol{R}_{\mathrm{L}}) \times e_\alpha(\kappa|\boldsymbol{k}j_\mu)\,Q(\boldsymbol{k}j_\mu)\exp[\pm\,\mathrm{i}\omega(\boldsymbol{k}|j)\,t]\,. \tag{4.34}$$

The complex amplitude $Q(\boldsymbol{k}j_\mu)$ is the coefficient in the expansion of the time dependent physical cartesian displacements in terms of the complete basis set of functions which are the solutions of the equations of motion.

To determine the transformation properties of the normal coordinates under application of a unitary transformation operator we proceed directly from (4.30), and also use (4.19). We restrict ourselves to the case where the symmetry operator is contained in $\mathscr{G}(\boldsymbol{k})$. Then

$$\begin{aligned} P_{\{\phi_l|\tau(\phi_l)\}}Q(\boldsymbol{k}j_\mu|t) &= N^{-1/2}\sum_{l}\sum_{\kappa}\sum_{\alpha}\exp(\mathrm{i}\boldsymbol{k}\cdot\boldsymbol{R}_{\mathrm{L}})\,P_{\{\phi_l|\tau(\phi_l)\}}e_\alpha(\kappa|\boldsymbol{k}j_\mu)\,\mu_\alpha(l\kappa)\,M_\kappa^{1/2} \\ &= N^{-1/2}\sum_{l}\sum_{\kappa}\sum_{\alpha}\exp(\mathrm{i}\boldsymbol{k}\cdot\boldsymbol{R}_{\mathrm{L}})\sum_{\nu}D^{(\boldsymbol{k})(j)}(\{\phi_l|\tau(\phi_l)\})_{\nu\mu} \\ &\qquad\times e_\alpha(\kappa|\boldsymbol{k}j_\nu)\,\mu_\alpha(l\kappa)\,M_\kappa^{1/2} \\ &= \sum_{\nu}D^{(\boldsymbol{k})(j)}(\{\phi_l|\tau(\phi_l)\})_{\nu\mu}\,Q(\boldsymbol{k}j_\nu|t)\,. \end{aligned} \tag{4.35}$$

It follows that $Q(\boldsymbol{k}j_\mu|t)$ is a basis function for the μth row of the irreducible representation $D^{(\boldsymbol{k})(j)}$.

It should be remarked that the definition of the complex normal coordinate which we used differs from that usually given. Had we adopted the usual convention (Maradudin et al. 1971, p. 47, eq. 2.3.1) it would have followed that the normal coordinates transformed as the adjoint representation, or $D^{(\boldsymbol{k})(j)*}$. But there is no physical consequence of one or another choice, and for purposes of simplicity we can adhere to the definition (4.29) in the present chapter.

When there is no possibility of confusion we can partially suppress the indices $\boldsymbol{k}$ and j in Q and write for (4.35)

$$P_{R_k} Q_\mu = \sum_\nu D^{(\boldsymbol{k})(j)}(R_{\boldsymbol{k}})_{\nu\mu}\, Q_\nu \quad \text{if} \quad R_{\boldsymbol{k}} \in \mathcal{G}(\boldsymbol{k}), \tag{4.36}$$

where we abbreviate $R_{\boldsymbol{k}} \equiv \{\phi_l | \tau(\phi_l)\}$ as an element in $\mathcal{G}(\boldsymbol{k})$. It is important to note that this transformation rule follows from the rule for transformation of the eigenvectors and is a result of the completeness of the set.

One may also examine the transformation of the normal coordinate $Q(\boldsymbol{k}j_\mu | t)$ by subjecting the terms on the right-hand side of (4.29) to transformation following the rule (4.19). This produces a rule equivalent to (4.35).

It follows that the set of normal coordinates at fixed $\boldsymbol{k}$:

$$\{Q(\boldsymbol{k}1 | t), \cdots, Q(\boldsymbol{k}j_1 | t), \cdots, Q(\boldsymbol{k}j_{l_j} | t), \cdots, Q(\boldsymbol{k}\, 3s | t)\} \equiv \Sigma^{(\boldsymbol{k})} \tag{4.37}$$

is a complete set which produces the fully reduced or decomposed representation

$$D^{(\boldsymbol{k})(1)} \oplus \cdots \oplus D^{(\boldsymbol{k})(j)} \oplus \cdots. \tag{4.38}$$

The subspaces

$$\Sigma^{(\boldsymbol{k})(j)} \equiv \{Q(\boldsymbol{k}j_1 | t), \cdots, Q(\boldsymbol{k}j_{l_j} | t)\} \tag{4.39}$$

each span an irreducible representation $D^{(\boldsymbol{k})(j)}$, and are consequently closed under transformation by an element in $\mathcal{G}(\boldsymbol{k})$:

$$P_{R_k} \Sigma^{(\boldsymbol{k})(j)} = \Sigma^{(\boldsymbol{k})(j)} D^{(\boldsymbol{k})(j)}. \tag{4.40}$$

Finally one can similarly establish a rule for the transformation of a normal coordinate under a general unitary symmetry transformation operator, not necessarily a member of the appropriate $\mathcal{G}(\boldsymbol{k})$. This is

$$P_{\{\phi_p | t(\phi_p)\}} Q(\boldsymbol{k}_\tau j_\nu) = \sum_{\sigma=1}^{s} \sum_{\mu=1}^{l_m} D^{(*\boldsymbol{k})(j)}(\{\phi_p | t(\phi_p)\})_{\sigma\mu,\, \tau\nu}\, Q(\boldsymbol{k}_\sigma j_\mu). \tag{4.41}$$

In this expression $\boldsymbol{k}_\tau$ and $\boldsymbol{k}_\sigma$ are members of $*\boldsymbol{k}$, j_ν and j_μ label νth and μth rows of the allowable irreducible full space group representation $D^{(*\boldsymbol{k})(j)}$.

4.3. Time reversal

We now resume the discussion of lattice dynamics in order to include time reversal. Apply the operator K of complex conjugation to eqs. (4.2) and (4.4) to obtain:

$$K(\partial^2/\partial t^2)\, K^{-1} \cdot K\varepsilon_\alpha(\kappa \,|\, \boldsymbol{k} j_\mu) + \sum_{\kappa'\beta} KD_{\alpha\beta}(\boldsymbol{k} \,|\, \kappa\kappa')\, K^{-1} \cdot K\varepsilon_\beta(\kappa' \,|\, \boldsymbol{k} j_\mu) = 0 \,. \tag{4.42}$$

But

$$K(\partial^2/\partial t^2)\, K^{-1} = \partial^2/\partial t^2 \tag{4.43}$$

since $\partial^2/\partial t^2$ is a real operator, and

$$KD_{\alpha\beta}(\boldsymbol{k} \,|\, \kappa\kappa')\, K^{-1} \equiv D_{\alpha\beta}(\boldsymbol{k} \,|\, \kappa\kappa')^* = D_{\alpha\beta}(-\,\boldsymbol{k} \,|\, \kappa\kappa'), \tag{4.44}$$

where the last equation follows from (4.3) and the reality of the force matrix $\Phi_{\alpha\beta}$. Consequently

$$(\partial^2/\partial t^2)\, K\varepsilon_\alpha(\kappa \,|\, \boldsymbol{k} j_\mu) + \sum_{\kappa'\beta} D_{\alpha\beta}(-\,\boldsymbol{k} \,|\, \kappa\kappa')\, K\varepsilon_\beta(\kappa' \,|\, \boldsymbol{k} j_\mu) = 0 \,. \tag{4.45}$$

But then $K\varepsilon_\alpha(\kappa | \boldsymbol{k} j_\mu)$ satisfies a dynamical equation with dynamical matrix at wave vector $-\boldsymbol{k}$. It follows that

$$K\varepsilon_\alpha(\kappa \,|\, \boldsymbol{k} j_\mu) \equiv \varepsilon_\alpha^*(\kappa \,|\, \boldsymbol{k} j_\mu) = \varepsilon_\alpha(\kappa \,|\, -\,\boldsymbol{k} \bar{j}_\mu), \tag{4.46}$$

where $\varepsilon_\alpha(\kappa | -\boldsymbol{k} \bar{j}_\mu)$ is a solution at $-\boldsymbol{k}$, and $\bar{j}_\mu$ is the allowable irreducible representation at $-\boldsymbol{k}$ into which j_μ is transformed. It is worth remarking at this point that it is necessary to determine $\bar{j}_\mu$. The groups $\mathscr{G}(\boldsymbol{k})$ and $\mathscr{G}(-\boldsymbol{k})$ are strictly isomorphic so that they possess identical irreducible representations. But one cannot assume that under complex conjugation a basis function for row μ of irreducible representation j at $\boldsymbol{k}$ goes into the function for the same row of the same irreducible representation at $-\boldsymbol{k}$ (Frei 1966, Birman 1974, section 94).

It is useful to examine the effect of the time reversal operator from a slightly different perspective than used heretofore. That is taking the form (4.6) we have

$$K\varepsilon(\,|\, \boldsymbol{k} j_\mu) = \boldsymbol{e}^*(\,|\, \boldsymbol{k} j_\mu) \exp[+\,\mathrm{i}\omega(\boldsymbol{k} \,|\, j)\, t]$$

or

$$Ke(\,|\, \boldsymbol{k} j_\mu) = \boldsymbol{e}(\,|\, -\,k\bar{j}_\mu) \exp[+\,\mathrm{i}\omega(\boldsymbol{k} \,|\, \bar{j})\, t] \,. \tag{4.47}$$

Substituting back into the time dependent equation we find that $e_\alpha^*(\kappa|\boldsymbol{k}j_\mu)$ is an eigenvector satisfying the equation

$$\omega^2(\boldsymbol{k}|j)\, e_\alpha^*(\kappa|\boldsymbol{k}j_\mu) = \sum_{\kappa'\beta} D_{\alpha\beta}(-\boldsymbol{k}|\kappa\kappa')\, e_\beta^*(\kappa'|\boldsymbol{k}j_\mu) \tag{4.48}$$

and so

$$\omega^2(-\boldsymbol{k}|\bar{j})\, e_\alpha(\kappa|-\boldsymbol{k}\bar{j}_\mu) = \sum_{\alpha'\beta} D_{\alpha\beta}(-\boldsymbol{k}|\kappa\kappa')\, e_\beta(\kappa'|-\boldsymbol{k}j_\mu)\,. \tag{4.49}$$

It follows that

$$\omega^2(\boldsymbol{k}|j) = \omega^2(-\boldsymbol{k}|\bar{j}) \tag{4.50}$$

and that*

$$\boldsymbol{e}^*(|\boldsymbol{k}j_\mu) = \boldsymbol{e}(|-\boldsymbol{k}\bar{j}_\mu)\,. \tag{4.51}$$

To continue, consider the representation module, or set of functions $S^{(\boldsymbol{k})}$ constructed from the basic set of symmetrized eigenvectors $\Sigma^{(\boldsymbol{k})}$ of (4.8) by:

$$S^{(\boldsymbol{k})} \equiv \Sigma^{(\boldsymbol{k})} \oplus P_{\{\bar{\varphi}_l|\tau(\bar{\varphi}_l)\}} K\Sigma^{(\boldsymbol{k})}\,. \tag{4.52}$$

The operation $P_{\{\bar{\varphi}_l|\tau(\bar{\varphi}_l)\}}$ is defined as a member of the space group $\mathscr{G}$ with the property

$$\bar{\varphi}_l\cdot\boldsymbol{k} = -\boldsymbol{k} + \boldsymbol{B}_{\mathrm{H}}, \tag{4.53}$$

so that the rotational part transforms wave vector $\boldsymbol{k}$ into a wave-vector equivalent to $-\boldsymbol{k}$. It is evident that $S^{(\boldsymbol{k})}$ is the most general invariant and complete set of eigenvector solutions of the dynamical equation, at wave-vector $\boldsymbol{k}$. Looked at from an equivalent viewpoint, the module $S^{(\boldsymbol{k})}$ is left invariant by the space–time symmetry group $G(\boldsymbol{k})$ where:

$$G(\boldsymbol{k}) = \mathscr{G}(\boldsymbol{k}) + P_{\{\bar{\varphi}_l|\tau(\bar{\varphi}_l)\}} K\mathscr{G}(\boldsymbol{k})\,. \tag{4.54}$$

The space–time group $G(\boldsymbol{k})$, consists of a familiar unitary normal subgroup $\mathscr{G}(\boldsymbol{k})$, composed of purely unitary operators plus a coset

$$P_{\{\bar{\varphi}_l|\tau(\bar{\varphi}_l)\}} K\mathscr{G}(\boldsymbol{k}) \tag{4.55}$$

composed of purely anti-unitary operators.

* A unimodular phase factor may occur on the right side of (4.51) multiplying the eigenvector $\boldsymbol{e}(|-\boldsymbol{k}\bar{j}_\mu)$. Here we take it as $+1$. A fuller discussion is given in Birman (1974).

Since $S^{(k)}$ is closed under $G(k)$, it is a basis for a corepresentation $D^{(\text{co}\,k)}$. By an obvious extension of Maschke's theorem, a corepresentation of the finite group $G(k)$, is decomposable. Consequently the representation module $S^{(k)}$ can be decomposed into irreducible components:

$$S^{(k)} = S^{(\text{co}\,k)\,(1)} \oplus \cdots \oplus S^{(\text{co}\,k)\,(j)} \oplus \cdots \tag{4.56}$$

corresponding to the decomposition of the corepresentation

$$D^{(\text{co}\,k)} = D^{(\text{co}\,k)\,(1)} \oplus \cdots \oplus D^{(\text{co}\,k)\,(j)} \oplus \cdots. \tag{4.57}$$

As a basis in the module $S^{(k)}$ we can choose the subspace

$$\begin{aligned} S^{(\text{co}\,k)\,(j)} \equiv \{&Q(kj_1\,|\,t), \cdots, Q(kj_{l_j}\,|\,t), \\ &P_{\{\bar{\phi}_l\,|\,\tau(\bar{\phi}_l)\}} K Q(kj_1\,|\,t), \cdots, P_{\{\bar{\phi}_l\,|\,\tau(\bar{\phi}_l)\}} K Q(kj_{l_j}\,|\,t)\}. \end{aligned} \tag{4.58}$$

According to the 'lemma of necessary degeneracy', each such subspace corresponds to a distinct eigenvalue; the degeneracy being the dimension of $S^{(\text{co}\,k)\,(j)}$; either l_j or $2l_j$. The transformation properties of the normal coordinates which span $S^{(\text{co}\,k)\,(j)}$ are fully specified by $D^{(\text{co}\,k)\,(j)}$.

Although the general basis of corepresentation theory is by now well established, relatively few explicit cases have been worked out in detail. Consequently in the interest of conciseness the remainder of our presentation in this chapter will be framed in terms of the ordinary representation theory. But, the results given above can be applied as required to construct corepresentations from the representations, and to test whether corepresentations (or physically irreducible representations, as they are also known) do or do not produce added degeneracy, and selection rules (Birman 1974, Litvin and Zak 1968).

4.4. Representations generated by eigenvectors

To complete the discussion of the transformation of the eigenvectors of the dynamical problem, return to equation (4.16). For a transformation operator whose rotational part is an operator in $\mathscr{G}(k)$, we can write

$$P_{\{\phi_l\,|\,\tau(\phi_l)\}} e_\alpha(\kappa\,|\,kj_\mu) = \sum_\beta \sum_{\kappa''} D^{(k)\,(e)}(\{\phi_l\,|\,\tau_l\})_{\alpha\kappa,\,\beta\kappa''}\, e_\beta(\kappa''\,|\,kj_\mu), \tag{4.59}$$

where the representation matrix $D^{(k)\,(e)}$ is

$$D^{(k)\,(e)}(\{\phi_l\,|\,\tau(\phi_l)\})_{\alpha\kappa,\,\beta\kappa''} = (\phi_l)_{\alpha\beta}\, D^{(k)}(\{\varepsilon\,|\,-R_N(\kappa_l, \kappa'')\})\, \delta_{\kappa_l,\,\kappa''} \tag{4.60}$$

and κ and κ'' both label the positions of basis atoms in the unit cell, and are related by

$$\boldsymbol{r}_\kappa \to \{\phi_l | \tau(\phi_l)\}^{-1} \cdot \boldsymbol{r}_\kappa \equiv \boldsymbol{r}_{\kappa''} + R_N(\kappa, \kappa''). \tag{4.61}$$

In this expression $\boldsymbol{R}_N$ is a lattice vector

$$\boldsymbol{R}_N \equiv \phi_l^{-1} \cdot \boldsymbol{r}_k - \phi_l \cdot \tau(\phi_l) - \boldsymbol{r}_{\kappa''} \tag{4.62}$$

and $\boldsymbol{r}_{\kappa''}$ is the canonical label of the basis atom. Of course $\boldsymbol{r}_\kappa$ and $\boldsymbol{r}_{\kappa''}$ may or may not be identical, and R_N may or may not be zero. Also

$$\begin{aligned} \delta_{\kappa_l, \kappa''} &= 1, \quad \text{if} \quad \kappa, \kappa'' \text{ are related by (4.61),} \\ &= 0, \quad \text{otherwise.} \end{aligned} \tag{4.63}$$

It should be noted that the transformation given above is a transformation of the components of a single eigenvector. The matrix $D^{(k)(e)}$ is a matrix which is a direct product of a matrix $D^{(r)}$, specifying the transformation of an ordinary polar vector, times $D^{(\mathrm{perm})}$, which is a permutation matrix specifying the permutation of basis atoms, so that

$$D^{(k)\,(e)}_{\alpha\kappa,\,\beta\kappa''} = D^{(r)}_{\alpha\beta}\, D^{(\mathrm{perm})}_{\kappa\,\kappa''}. \tag{4.64}$$

For calculational purposes it is the trace of this matrix which is needed in order to determine the symmetry of the modes which actually arise at $\boldsymbol{k}$. This is

$$\operatorname{tr} D^{(k)\,(e)}(\{\phi_l | \tau(\phi_l)\}) = \sum_{\kappa''} \pm (1 + 2\cos\phi_l)\, D^{(k)}(\{\varepsilon | -\boldsymbol{R}_N(\kappa_l, \kappa'')\})\, \delta_{\kappa_l, \kappa''}. \tag{4.65}$$

In comparing the two results which have just been obtained observe that in (4.19) the transformation of eigenvectors was based upon the transformation of a particular row of an irreducible representation into a linear combination of other rows, while in (4.59) use was made of the transformation law for a vector field. Under transformation the components of the vector field are simultaneously rotated and displaced. One may view the relationship simply by forming a $3s \times 3s$ matrix whose columns are the eigenvectors $\boldsymbol{e}(|kj_\mu)$, with j_μ fixed in each column. Then the transformation (4.19) relates the different columns, j_μ and j_ν for a fixed row, while the transformation (4.59) relates different rows for fixed column index.

The matrix $D^{(k)(e)}$ has a useful property which enables the factorization of the dynamical matrix. To see this, we begin with the transform of the dynamical equation (4.9). For the present purposes we assume the transformation operator is contained in $\mathscr{G}(\boldsymbol{k})$ and so we use (4.7), (4.9), and (4.59). Then let us abbreviate the space group operator in $\mathscr{G}(\boldsymbol{k})$, calling it R_l so we have

$$\begin{aligned}\sum_{\beta\kappa'} D(\boldsymbol{k}\,|\,\kappa\kappa')_{\alpha\beta}\, P_{R_l} e_\beta(\kappa'\,|\,\boldsymbol{k}j_\mu)\\
&= \sum_{\beta\kappa}\sum_{\gamma\kappa''} D(\boldsymbol{k}\,|\,\kappa\kappa')_{\alpha\beta}\, D^{(\boldsymbol{k})\,(e)}(R_l)_{\beta\kappa',\,\gamma\kappa''}\, e_\gamma(\kappa''\,|\,\boldsymbol{k}j_\mu)\\
&= \sum_{\bar\beta\bar\kappa'} D^{(\boldsymbol{k})\,(e)}(R_l)_{\alpha\kappa,\,\bar\beta\bar\kappa'}\, e_{\bar\beta}(\bar\kappa'\,|\,\boldsymbol{k}j_\mu)\,\omega^2(\boldsymbol{k}\,|\,j_\mu)\\
&= \sum_{\bar\beta\bar\kappa'}\sum_{\bar\gamma\bar\kappa'} D^{(\boldsymbol{k})\,(e)}(R_l)_{\alpha\kappa,\,\bar\beta\bar\kappa'}\, D(\boldsymbol{k}\,|\,\bar\kappa\bar\kappa'')_{\bar\beta\bar\gamma}\, e_{\bar\gamma}(\bar\kappa''\,|\,\boldsymbol{k}j_\mu).\end{aligned} \tag{4.66}$$

Now the dynamical matrix is hermitian so

$$D(\boldsymbol{k}\,|\,\kappa\kappa')_{\alpha\beta} = D(\boldsymbol{k}\,|\,\kappa'\kappa)^*_{\beta\alpha}. \tag{4.67}$$

When this expression is substituted into (4.66) and the coefficient of the same component $e_\gamma(\kappa''\,|\,\boldsymbol{k}j_\mu)$ is equated from each side of this equation we find that the matrix equation

$$D^{(\boldsymbol{k})\,(e)}(R_l)\, D(\boldsymbol{k}) = D(\boldsymbol{k})\, D^{(\boldsymbol{k})\,(e)}(R_l) \tag{4.68}$$

is satisfied. Here $D(\boldsymbol{k})$ is the familiar dynamical matrix. This equation is true for all R_l in $\mathscr{G}(\boldsymbol{k})$. Since a non-constant matrix, viz $D(\boldsymbol{k})$ commutes with all matrices $D^{(\boldsymbol{k})\,(e)}(R_l)$ Schur's lemma can be employed. Evidently the set of matrices

$$D^{(\boldsymbol{k})\,(e)}(R_l) \tag{4.69}$$

is a representation of $\mathscr{G}(\boldsymbol{k})$. Hence $D^{(\boldsymbol{k})\,(e)}$ must be reducible into a direct sum of irreducible representations $D^{(\boldsymbol{k})\,(j)}$ of $\mathscr{G}(\boldsymbol{k})$.

Two approaches are open to us. First we shall bring the dynamical matrix to diagonal form, under the assumption that we know the eigenvectors. Form the $3s \times 3s$ dimensional matrix $\boldsymbol{E}(\boldsymbol{k})$ by taking as its columns the eigenvectors $\boldsymbol{e}(\,|\,\boldsymbol{k}j_\mu)$. Thus

$$\boldsymbol{E}(\boldsymbol{k}) = \begin{pmatrix} e_x(1\,|\,\boldsymbol{k}\;1) & \cdots & e_x(1\,|\,\boldsymbol{k}\;3s)\\ \vdots & & \vdots\\ e_z(s\,|\,\boldsymbol{k}\;1) & \cdots & e_z(s\,|\,\boldsymbol{k}\;3s)\end{pmatrix}. \tag{4.70}$$

The rows of $\boldsymbol{E}(\boldsymbol{k})$ are labelled by indices $\alpha\kappa$, the columns by index j_μ:

$$(\boldsymbol{E}(\boldsymbol{k}))_{\alpha\kappa,\,j_\mu} \equiv e_\alpha(\kappa\,|\,\boldsymbol{k}j_\mu). \tag{4.71}$$

The matrix $\boldsymbol{E}(\boldsymbol{k})$ is unitary and brings $[\boldsymbol{D}(\boldsymbol{k})]$ to diagonal form:

$$\boldsymbol{E}(\boldsymbol{k})^{-1}[\boldsymbol{D}(\boldsymbol{k})]\,\boldsymbol{E}(\boldsymbol{k}) = \Delta(\boldsymbol{k}), \tag{4.72}$$

where

$$\Delta(\boldsymbol{k}) = \begin{pmatrix} \omega^2(\boldsymbol{k}|1)\,\boldsymbol{I}_{l_1} & \cdots & 0 & & 0 \\ 0 & \ddots & 0 & & 0 \\ & & \omega^2(\boldsymbol{k}|j)\,\boldsymbol{I}_{l_j} & & 0 \\ & & & \ddots & \\ 0 & \cdots & 0 & & \omega^2(\boldsymbol{k}|3s)\,\boldsymbol{I}_l \end{pmatrix}, \tag{4.73}$$

where $\boldsymbol{I}_l$ is the unit matrix of dimension l, etc.
Each eigenvalue appears as often as the degree of its degeneracy: $\omega^2(\boldsymbol{k}|j)$ appears l_j times–except in case of accidental degeneracy which we do not consider. To complete this discussion we transform eq. (4.68) using $\boldsymbol{E}(\boldsymbol{k})$ to obtain:

$$\boldsymbol{E}(\boldsymbol{k})^{-1}\,D^{(\boldsymbol{k})(e)}\boldsymbol{E}(\boldsymbol{k})\,\Delta(\boldsymbol{k}) \tag{4.74}$$

$$= \Delta(\boldsymbol{k})\,\boldsymbol{E}(\boldsymbol{k})^{-1}\,D^{(\boldsymbol{k})(e)}\boldsymbol{E}(\boldsymbol{k}), \tag{4.75}$$

or if we define the barred matrix as the transform

$$\bar{D}^{(\boldsymbol{k})(e)} \equiv \boldsymbol{E}(\boldsymbol{k})^{-1}\,D^{(\boldsymbol{k})(e)}\boldsymbol{E}(\boldsymbol{k}) \tag{4.76}$$

then, restoring the element $\boldsymbol{R}_l$ as argument:

$$\bar{D}^{(\boldsymbol{k})(e)}(R_l)\,\Delta(\boldsymbol{k}) = \Delta(\boldsymbol{k})\,\bar{D}^{(\boldsymbol{k})(e)}(R_l). \tag{4.77}$$

This equation holds for all R_l in $\mathcal{G}(\boldsymbol{k})$. But, because $\Delta(\boldsymbol{k})$ is a direct sum of constant matrices [compare (4.73)]

$$\Delta(\boldsymbol{k}) = \omega^2(\boldsymbol{k}|1)\,\boldsymbol{I}_{l_1} \oplus \cdots \oplus \omega^2(\boldsymbol{k}|j)\,\boldsymbol{I}_{l_j} \oplus \cdots. \tag{4.78}$$

From Schur's lemma we can immediately conclude that $\bar{D}^{(\boldsymbol{k})(e)}(R_l)$ partitions correspondingly into a direct sum

$$\bar{D}^{(\boldsymbol{k})(e)}(R_l) = D^{(\boldsymbol{k})(1)} \oplus \cdots \oplus D^{(\boldsymbol{k})(j)} \oplus \cdots. \tag{4.79}$$

This is true for each of the matrices (i.e. for all R_l). In case each species (irreducible representation) occurs only once we can put together eqs. (4.76) and (4.79). Then taking the $j_\mu j'_{\nu'}$ matrix element of (4.76) we find

$$\begin{aligned} \bar{D}^{(\boldsymbol{k})(e)}(R_l)_{j_\mu j'_{\nu'}} &= \sum_{\beta\kappa'}\sum_{\alpha\kappa} e^*_\beta(\kappa'|\boldsymbol{k}j_\mu)\,D^{(\boldsymbol{k})(e)}(R_l)_{\alpha\kappa,\beta\kappa'}\,e_\alpha(\kappa|\boldsymbol{k}j'_{\mu'}) \\ &= D^{(\boldsymbol{k})(j)}(R_l)_{\mu\nu}\,\delta_{jj'}. \end{aligned} \tag{4.80}$$

The difficulty in practice with this approach is that it presupposes a knowledge of the eigenvectors, which we do not usually possess.

The sole instance for which we may find eigenvectors without the necessity of solving the dynamical equations is if each irreducible representation which appears on the right hand side of (4.79) appears only once. In that case we can find the eigenvectors directly. We first construct the complete set of projection operators $P_{\mu\nu}^{(\boldsymbol{k})\,(j)}$ for each of the irreducible representations which appears in the decomposition (4.79). The complete $3s$-dimensional linear vector space upon which these operators will act is spanned by the $3s$ unit cartesian displacements

$$\Sigma^{(\Delta)} \equiv \{\Delta_\alpha(\kappa)\}, \quad \alpha = 1, 2, 3, \quad \kappa = 1, \cdots, s. \tag{4.81}$$

corresponding to unit displacement in x-, y- or z-direction for each basis atom. Then

$$e(|\,\boldsymbol{k}j_\mu) = P_{\mu\nu}^{(\boldsymbol{k})\,(j)}\,\Sigma^{(\Delta)}. \tag{4.82}$$

In order to apply this operator properly, we recall the effect of a space group transformation operator upon a vector field as in eq. (2.21). Then

$$P_{\{\phi\,|\,\boldsymbol{t}(\phi)\}}\Delta_\alpha(\kappa) = \sum_\beta \phi_{\alpha\beta}\Delta_\beta(\{\phi\,|\,\boldsymbol{t}(\phi)\}^{-1}\cdot\boldsymbol{r}_\kappa). \tag{4.83}$$

Thus the unit displacement is rotated and shifted. The proper superposition of these rotated and translated unit cartesian displacements is the symmetrized eigenvector.

4.5. Eigenvectors generated by representations

The second procedure is the inverse. If the matrix U which reduces $D^{(\boldsymbol{k})\,(e)}$ can be found

$$D^{(\boldsymbol{k})\,(e)}U = U\bar{D}^{(\boldsymbol{k})\,(e)}, \tag{4.84}$$

then

$$U = E(\boldsymbol{k}). \tag{4.85}$$

In this way the eigenvectors can be found by reading off the rows or columns of U. To find U one can proceed stepwise. The first step is to write out $\bar{D}^{(\boldsymbol{k})\,(e)}$

in fully reduced form:

$$\bar{D}^{(\boldsymbol{k})\,(e)} = \begin{pmatrix} D^{(\boldsymbol{k})\,(j)} & & 0 & \cdots \\ & \ddots & & \\ 0 & & D^{(\boldsymbol{k})\,(j)} & \\ & & & \ddots \end{pmatrix}. \tag{4.86}$$

The particular irreducible $D^{(\boldsymbol{k})\,(j)}$ which arise can be determined from the trace of $D^{(\boldsymbol{k})\,(e)}$

$$\operatorname{tr} D^{(\boldsymbol{k})\,(e)}_{j_{\mu'}j'_{\nu'}} = \sum_j (\boldsymbol{k}\, e\,|\, j)\, \chi^{(\boldsymbol{k})\,(j)}. \tag{4.87}$$

The trace is simply found from (4.65). A significant complication arises if $(\boldsymbol{k}e\,|\,j) > 1$. For bookkeeping purposes we shall affix an additional index γ to deal with the cases of multiplicity thus

$$D^{(\boldsymbol{k})\,(j),\,\gamma}, \quad \gamma = 1, \cdots, c_m. \tag{4.88}$$

We can assume the block matrices in $\bar{D}^{(\boldsymbol{k})\,(e)}$ are all given in some canonical form. Then for the matrix element of $\bar{D}^{(\boldsymbol{k})\,(e)}$ we have following eq. (4.76)

$$\bar{D}^{(\boldsymbol{k})\,(e)}{}_{j_{\mu'}j'_{\nu'}} = D^{(\boldsymbol{k})\,(j),\,\gamma}_{\mu\nu}\, \delta_{jj'}. \tag{4.89}$$

we used j, j' to index the species of allowable irreducible representation, and μ and ν are row and column indices. As usual the coupling matrix U bears asymmetric indices. Taking the matrix element of (4.84) we find for the element $(\beta\kappa', j'_{\nu'})$

$$\sum_{\alpha\kappa} D^{(\boldsymbol{k})\,(e)}_{\beta\kappa',\,\alpha\kappa}\, U_{\alpha\kappa,\,\nu'}{}^{\boldsymbol{k}j'\gamma'} = \sum_{\gamma,\,j,\,\mu} U_{\beta\kappa',\,\mu}{}^{\boldsymbol{k}j\gamma}\, \bar{D}^{(\boldsymbol{k})\,(e)}_{j_\mu,\,j'_{\nu'}}. \tag{4.90}$$

Thus for U:

$$U_{\alpha\kappa,\,\nu'}{}^{\boldsymbol{k}j'\gamma'} \equiv e_\alpha(\kappa\,|\,\boldsymbol{k}j'_{\nu'}, \gamma'). \tag{4.91}$$

In many cases U can be found by stepwise reduction of $D^{(\boldsymbol{k})\,(e)}$, taking advantage of the property of $D^{(\boldsymbol{k})\,(e)}$ as a direct product matrix, as illustrated in eq. (4.64). The principle of this method is to reduce each "factor" into irreducible components.

Recall now the definition of the Clebsch–Gordan coefficients (3.31) which is equivalent to the definition by

$$D^{(j)\otimes(j')}C = C\bar{D}^{(j\otimes j')}, \tag{4.92}$$

where, as before, the barred matrix is in fully reduced form:

$$\bar{D}^{(j\otimes j')}_{\bar{j}\bar{\mu},\,\bar{j}'\bar{\nu}} = D^{(\bar{j})\,\gamma}_{\bar{\mu}\bar{\nu}}\,\delta_{\bar{j}\bar{j}'}\,. \tag{4.93}$$

Then

$$\sum_{\bar{\gamma}\nu\nu'} D^{(j\times j')}_{\mu\mu'\nu\nu'} C_{\nu\nu',\,\bar{\mu}}^{\;\bar{j},\,\bar{\gamma}} = \sum_{\bar{\gamma}'\bar{j}'\bar{\mu}'} C_{\mu\mu',\,\bar{\mu}'}^{\;\bar{j}'\bar{\gamma}'}\,\bar{D}^{(j\otimes j')}_{\bar{j}'\bar{\mu}',\,\bar{j}\bar{\mu}}\,. \tag{4.94}$$

The connection between this equation and (3.31) is

$$C^{jj',\,\bar{j}\gamma}_{\nu\nu',\,\bar{\mu}} \equiv \left(\begin{array}{cc|c} j & j' & \bar{j}\,\gamma \\ \nu & \nu & \bar{\nu} \end{array}\right). \tag{4.95}$$

These coupling coefficients can be assumed known for the irreducible representations of interest.

Now let us write V for the matrix which reduces $D^{(r)}$:

$$D^{(r)}V = V\bar{D}^{(r)} \tag{4.96}$$

with

$$(\bar{D}^{(r)})_{j\alpha,\,j'\beta} = D^{(j)\,\gamma}_{\alpha\beta}\,\delta_{jj'}\,, \tag{4.97}$$

and S for the matrix which reduces $D^{(\mathrm{perm})}$:

$$D^{(\mathrm{perm})}S = S\bar{D}^{(\mathrm{perm})} \tag{4.98}$$

with

$$\bar{D}^{(\mathrm{perm})}_{\bar{j}\bar{\alpha}\bar{j}'\bar{\beta}} = D^{(\bar{j})}_{\bar{\alpha}\bar{\beta}}\,\delta_{\bar{j}\bar{j}'}\,. \tag{4.99}$$

Then taking appropriate matrix elements we write

$$\sum_{\beta} D^{(r)}_{\alpha\beta} V_{\beta,\,\mu}^{\;j} = \sum_{j'\mu'} V_{\alpha,\,\mu'}^{\;j'} D^{(j')}_{\mu'\mu}\,, \tag{4.100}$$

$$\sum_{\kappa'} D^{(\mathrm{perm})}_{\kappa\kappa'} S_{\kappa',\,\bar{\mu}}^{\;\bar{j}} = \sum_{\bar{j}'\bar{\mu}'} S_{\kappa,\,\bar{\mu}'}^{\;\bar{j}'} D^{(\bar{j}')}_{\bar{\mu}'\bar{\mu}}\,. \tag{4.101}$$

Multiply these equations to find:

$$\sum_{\beta}\sum_{\kappa'} D^{(r)}_{\alpha\beta} D^{(\mathrm{perm})}_{\kappa\kappa'} V_{\beta,\,\mu}^{\;j} S_{\kappa',\,\bar{\mu}}^{\;\bar{j}} = \sum_{j'\mu'}\sum_{\bar{j}'\bar{\mu}'} V_{\alpha,\,\mu'}^{\;j'} S_{\bar{\kappa},\,\bar{\mu}'}^{\;\bar{j}'} D^{(j')}_{\mu'\mu} D^{(\bar{j}')}_{\bar{\mu}',\,\bar{\mu}}\,. \tag{4.102}$$

Now multiply both sides of (4.102) by $C^{j'\bar{j}',\,l}_{\mu\bar{\mu},\,\tau}$ and sum μ, $\bar{\mu}$, then use (4.94) to find

$$\sum_{\beta}\sum_{\kappa'}\sum_{\mu}\sum_{\bar{\mu}} D^{(k)\,(l)}_{\alpha\kappa,\,\beta\kappa'} V_{\beta,\,\mu}^{\;j}\, S_{\kappa'\bar{\mu}}^{\;\bar{j}}\, C^{j'\bar{j}',\,l}_{\mu\bar{\mu},\,\tau} = \sum_{j'\mu'}\sum_{\bar{j}'\bar{\mu}'}\sum_{l'\sigma} V^{j'}_{\alpha\mu'}\, S_{\kappa,\,\bar{\mu}'}^{\;\bar{j}'}\, C^{j'\bar{j}',\,l'}_{\mu'\bar{\mu}',\,\sigma}\, D^{(l')}_{\sigma\tau}\,. \tag{4.103}$$

This is in the required form. We then read off the matrix U

$$U_{\beta x',\,\tau}^{\;\;\;\;l} = \sum_{\mu\bar{\mu}} V_{\beta,\,\mu}^{\;\;j}\, S_{\kappa'\bar{\mu}}^{\;\;\bar{j}} C_{\mu\bar{\mu},\,\tau}^{j'\bar{j}',\,l}\,. \tag{4.104}$$

Although this seems to be a very complicated expression it may often be rather simple in practice. The elements of V and S can often be read directly into matrix form owing to the simplicity of $D^{(r)}$ and $D^{(\mathrm{perm})}$ and the a priori knowledge of the irreducible components they contain, obtained by reducing the trace. The elements of C are of course available by hypothesis, since they are the assumed known Clebsch–Gordan coefficients.

The method just given derives from work of Huang (1962); it has been also discussed by Wesson (1970) and Klein (1969). Extension to non-symmorphic groups via incorporation of ray-representation and also the corepresentation method have not yet been given, to our knowledge.

4.6. Connectivity of representations

Before concluding this section an important matter needs to be discussed: the connectivity of representations in the reciprocal space. Going back to the equation which defines the dynamical matrix (4.3) observe that $[\boldsymbol{D}(\boldsymbol{k})]$ is periodic in reciprocal space:

$$[\boldsymbol{D}(\boldsymbol{k}+\boldsymbol{B}_{\mathrm{H}})] = [\boldsymbol{D}(\boldsymbol{k})]\,. \tag{4.105}$$

In view of this the eigenvalue-eigenvector equation has the property

$$\begin{aligned}[\boldsymbol{D}(\boldsymbol{k}+\boldsymbol{B}_{\mathrm{H}})]\cdot \boldsymbol{e}(\,|\,\boldsymbol{k}+\boldsymbol{B}_{\mathrm{H}},\, j_{\mu}) &= [\boldsymbol{D}(\boldsymbol{k})]\cdot \boldsymbol{e}(\,|\,\boldsymbol{k}+\boldsymbol{B}_{\mathrm{H}},\, j_{\mu})\\ &= \omega^2(\boldsymbol{k}+\boldsymbol{B}_{\mathrm{H}}\,|\,j)\, \boldsymbol{e}(\,|\,\boldsymbol{k}+\boldsymbol{B}_{\mathrm{H}},\, j_{\mu})\,.\end{aligned} \tag{4.106}$$

Now, comparing this equation with the dynamical equation for the eigenvalue–eigenvector at wave vector $\boldsymbol{k}$, namely eq. (4.9), we observe that the same operator $[\boldsymbol{D}(\boldsymbol{k})]$ appears. Recall that the set of eigenvectors of $[\boldsymbol{D}(\boldsymbol{k})]$ is complete. Consequently consider the two sets of eigenvalues

$$\{\omega^2(\boldsymbol{k}\,|\,1), \cdots, \omega^2(\boldsymbol{k}\,|\,j), \cdots, \omega^2(\boldsymbol{k}\,|\,3s)\} \tag{4.107}$$

and

$$\{\omega^2(\boldsymbol{k}+\boldsymbol{B}_{\mathrm{H}}\,|\,1), \cdots, \omega^2(\boldsymbol{k}+\boldsymbol{B}_{\mathrm{H}}\,|\,\bar{j}), \cdots\} \tag{4.108}$$

and the two sets of eigenvectors

$$\{\boldsymbol{e}(\,|\,\boldsymbol{k}\;1), \cdots, \boldsymbol{e}(\,|\,\boldsymbol{k}\;j_{\mu}), \cdots, \boldsymbol{e}(\,|\,\boldsymbol{k}\;3s)\} \tag{4.109}$$

and

$$\{e(|k+B_H 1), \cdots, e(|k+B_H \bar{j}_{\bar{\mu}}), \cdots\}. \tag{4.110}$$

We conclude that the eigenvalues must be pairwise equal:

$$\omega^2(k+B_H|\bar{j}) = \omega^2(k|j), \tag{4.111}$$

and each eigenvector

$$e(|k+B_H \bar{j}_{\bar{\mu}}) \tag{4.112}$$

must be linearly dependent upon the set

$$\{e(|kj_\mu)\}, \quad \mu = 1, \cdots, l_j. \tag{4.113}$$

To determine the correspondence between $\bar{j}_{\bar{\mu}}$ and j_μ one can examine the transformation of eigenvectors directly under application of the operators in $\mathscr{G}(k)$. It is sometimes more efficient to find the relationship between $\bar{j}_{\bar{\mu}}$ and j_μ by examining the matrices $D^{(k)(j)}$, of the allowable irreducible representation of $\mathscr{G}(k)$. As $k \to k + B_H$

$$D^{(k)(j)} \to D^{(k+B_H)(\bar{j})} \tag{4.114}$$

the relationship $j \to \bar{j}$ can then be established by inspection of the character tables. Alternatively one can examine the connectivity of representations by selecting a wave vector

$$\bar{k}_\delta \equiv \tfrac{1}{2}B_H - \delta, \tag{4.115}$$

where $\bar{k}_\delta$ is close to a zone boundary point. Then one can examine

$$D^{(\bar{k}_\delta)(j)} \tag{4.116}$$

as δ goes through zero, to negative values since, for δ negative $\bar{k}_\delta$ is a vector on the prolongation of $\bar{k}_\delta$, beyond the first Brillouin zone and hence equivalent to $(-\frac{1}{2}B_H + \delta)$, which is in the first Brillouin zone. This approach has been used in establishing the relation between $\bar{j}$ and j in diamond structure.

In case $D^{(k)(j)}$ is one-dimensional,

$$e(|k+B_H \bar{j}_{\bar{\mu}}) = e^{i\phi} e(|kj_\mu), \tag{4.117}$$

the phase factor $e^{i\phi}$ can be given by

$$\exp(iB_H \cdot \tau) \tag{4.118}$$

for a crystal with screw axis or glide plane, where τ is the appropriate fractional. The phase factor $e^{i\phi}$ cannot in general be set equal to one.

4.7. Determination of critical points

In eq. (4.9) the eigenvalue equation

$$[D(k)]\cdot e(|kj_\mu) = \omega^2(k|j)\, e(|kj_\mu) \tag{4.119}$$

was presented. For fixed j_μ the values of $\omega^2(k|j)$ define an energy surface as k assumes all permitted values in the first Brillouin zone. In the case of degeneracy at wave vector k the different energy surfaces associated with the l_j distinct values of μ touch. On a given energy surface the fraction of squared frequencies with values in the interval $(\omega^2, \omega^2 + d\omega^2)$ is

$$G_j(\omega^2)\, d\omega^2 = d\omega^2 \oint dS/|\nabla_k \omega^2(k|j)|\,, \tag{4.120}$$

where the integral is taken over a surface in k space corresponding to the interval $(\omega^2, \omega^2 + d\omega^2)$. At points k_0 in k space where

$$\nabla_k \omega^2(k|j)|_{k_0} = 0\,, \tag{4.121}$$

the function $G_j(\omega^2)\, d\omega^2$ is no longer analytic: for example, the density of frequencies may have slope discontinuities. It is of some interest to locate the critical points k_0 which satisfy (4.121) on a particular branch, or surface.

Consider the dynamical matrix, the squared eigenfrequency, and the set of degenerate eigenvectors to be functions of the variable k. We assume a power series expansion in a region around k_0:

$$[D(k)] = [D(k_0)] + \xi\cdot\nabla_k [D(k)]_{k_0} + \cdots\,, \tag{4.122}$$

$$\omega^2(k|j) = \omega^2(k_0|j) + \xi\cdot\nabla_k \omega^2(k|j)|_{k_0} + \cdots\,, \tag{4.123}$$

$$\text{with} \quad \xi \equiv k - k_0\,. \tag{4.124}$$

For the eigenvector assume that the perturbed eigenvector at k is a linear combination of the degenerate unperturbed eigenvectors at k_0:

$$e(|kj) = \sum_\mu A_{\mu j} e(|k_0 j_\mu)\,. \tag{4.125}$$

Substitute eqs. (4.123)–(4.125) into (4.122) to find

$$\sum_\mu A_{\mu j}\, \xi\cdot\nabla_k [D(k)]_{k_0}\cdot e(|k_0 j_\mu) = \xi\cdot\nabla\omega^2(k|j)_0 \sum_\mu A_{\mu j} e(|k_0 j_\mu)\,. \tag{4.126}$$

Next take the scalar product of (4.126) with $e(|k_0 j_\nu)$ and use the orthogonality

(4.28) to obtain

$$\sum_{\mu} A_{\mu j}\{e(|k_0 j_\nu)^* \cdot (\xi \cdot \nabla_k [D(k)]_{k_0}) \cdot e(|k_0 j'_\mu) - \xi \cdot \nabla_k \omega^2(k|j)\,\delta_{\mu\nu}\} = 0. \tag{4.127}$$

The condition for a solution of this system is that the determinant shall vanish

$$\|D^{(1)}_{\nu\mu} - (\omega^{(1)})^2\,\delta_{\mu\nu}\| = 0, \tag{4.128}$$

where

$$D^{(1)}_{\nu\mu} \equiv e(|k_0 j_\nu)^* \cdot (\xi \cdot \nabla_k [D(k)]) \cdot e(|k_0 j_\mu), \tag{4.129}$$

$$(\omega^{(1)})^2 \equiv \xi \cdot \nabla_k \omega^2(k|j). \tag{4.130}$$

In general $D^{(1)}_{\nu\mu} \neq 0$ and there will be l_j roots $(\omega^{(1)})^2 \neq 0$; some may coincide.

However, a sufficient condition for all $(\omega^{(1)})^2 = 0$ is if $D^{(1)}_{\mu\nu} = 0$. Then all matrix elements of the operator $\xi \cdot \nabla_k [D(k)]$ are identically zero in the degenerate manifold of eigenvectors $\{e(|k_0 j_\mu)\}$, $\mu = 1, \ldots, l_j$). In this case there will be no linear term in the expansion of $\omega^2(k|j)$ about k_0, and k_0 will be a critical point.

To determine whether $D^{(1)}_{\nu\mu}$ must vanish, consider the value of the scalar product of transformed quantities:

$$D^{(1)'}_{\nu\mu} = P_{R_l} e(|k_0 j_\nu)^* \cdot P_{R_l}(\xi \cdot \nabla_k [D(k)])\, P^{-1}_{R_l} \cdot P_{R_l} e(|k j_\mu) \tag{4.131}$$

which must equal $D^{(1)}_{\nu\mu}$ owing to the unitary property of the operator P_{R_l}. Recall that P_{R_l} is an element in $\mathscr{G}(k_0)$. The transformation of the eigenvectors under the P_{R_l} was given in (4.19). The gradient of the dynamical matrix can be shown to transform as a first-rank tensor (vector) operator, or [refer to (2.21)]:

$$P_{R_l}(\xi \cdot \nabla_k)_\gamma [D(k)] = \sum_{\alpha} (\phi_l)_{\alpha\gamma} (\xi \cdot \nabla_k)_\alpha [D(k)]. \tag{4.132}$$

Consequently the total scalar product transforms as

$$D^{(k_0)(j)*} \otimes D^{(k_0)(\mathbf{v})} \otimes D^{(k_0)(j)}, \tag{4.133}$$

where $D^{(k)(\mathbf{v})}$ is the representation by which a polar vector transforms under the operators in $\mathscr{G}(k_0)$. Then if the triple product (4.133) does *not* contain $D^{(k_0)(1)}$, the identity representation, $D^{(1)}_{\nu\mu} = 0$. In this case k_0 is a critical point. Observe that the three components of the vector $\xi = k - k_0$ provide different bases in $\mathscr{G}(k_0)$ and that each component can be separately tested. In certain directions $\nabla\omega^2(k|j)$ may vanish, while in others it can be non-zero.

4.8. Summary

We close this section with a brief summary: the major results of symmetry on the classical, harmonic, lattice dynamics problem are that

a) the eigenvectors $\boldsymbol{e}(|\boldsymbol{k}j_\mu)$ can be chosen to be bases for irreducible representations of the unitary symmetry group $\mathscr{G}(\boldsymbol{k})$ in the absence of consideration of time reversal, or bases for corepresentations of $G(k)$ if time reversal is included;

b) then also the normal coordinates $Q(\boldsymbol{k}j_\mu)$ can be chosen to be symmetrized so that the basic hamiltonian in harmonic approximation is the form (4.32);

c) functions of the normal coordinates can then be constructed by finding properly symmetrized sums of products, according to the overall symmetry of the function to be constructed: e.g. the energy, dipole moment operator, polarizibility tensor operator, etc.;

d) the secular, dynamical equation can be factorized to the maximum extent if symmetrized coordinates are used as bases.

5. *Quantum lattice dynamics and symmetry*

In this section some discussion will be given regarding the elements of the construction of a quantum theory of lattice dynamics. Of particular note is the manner by which the symmetry of the normal coordinates is carried over to quantum theory. This permits the classification of the eigenstates according to transformation with respect to the symmetry operators of the quantum mechanical hamiltonian. A second important aspect is the analyses of matrix elements for transition processes between different states under the action of a perturbation operator, and hence the prediction of selection rules.

5.1. Eigenstates of the quantum hamiltonian

The first task is to quantize the theory in such a fashion that symmetry related consequences can be drawn. It is necessary to construct a hamiltonian in terms of the appropriate canonically conjugate variables. The lagrangian function of the system, in terms of complex normal coordinates, corresponding to the hamiltonian given in eq. (4.32) is

$$\mathscr{L} = \tfrac{1}{2} \sum_{\boldsymbol{k}} \sum_{j} \sum_{\mu} \{\dot{Q}(\boldsymbol{k}j_\mu|t)^* \dot{Q}(\boldsymbol{k}j_\mu|t) - \omega^2(\boldsymbol{k}|j)\, Q(\boldsymbol{k}j_\mu|t)^* Q(\boldsymbol{k}j_\mu|t)\}. \tag{5.1}$$

From this we determine the momentum canonically conjugate to $Q(\boldsymbol{k}j_\mu|t)$ as

$$\Pi(\boldsymbol{k}j_\mu|t) = \partial\mathscr{L}/\partial\dot{Q}(\boldsymbol{k}j_\mu|t). \tag{5.2}$$

At this point it should be recalled that the complete set $\{Q(\boldsymbol{k}j_\mu|t)\}$ for all $\boldsymbol{k}, j_\mu$, is not independent of the set $\{Q(\boldsymbol{k}j_\mu|t)^*\}$, since

$$Q(\boldsymbol{k}j_\mu|t)^* = Q(-\boldsymbol{k}\bar{j}_{\bar{\mu}}|t). \tag{5.3}$$

This relation which follows from the time reversal invariance or reality of the displacement $\mu_\alpha(l\kappa)$ as explained in subsections 4.2–4.3 is also necessary in order that the total number of independent normal coordinates ($3sN$) shall be equal to the total number of components of displacement. Consequently, in the sum over all $\boldsymbol{k}$ in $\mathscr{L}$, a given complex normal coordinate appears twice, once as $Q(\boldsymbol{k}j_\mu|t)$, and a second time as $Q(-\boldsymbol{k}\bar{j}_{\bar{\mu}}|t)^*$. Consequently we have

$$\Pi(\boldsymbol{k}j_\mu|t) = \dot{Q}(\boldsymbol{k}j_\mu|t)^*. \tag{5.4}$$

Likewise the momentum conjugate to $Q(\boldsymbol{k}j_\mu|t)^*$ is

$$\Pi^*(\boldsymbol{k}j_\mu|t) = \dot{Q}(\boldsymbol{k}j_\mu|t). \tag{5.5}$$

While a quantum theory could be developed in terms of the complex normal coordinates and their canonical momenta, even passing to the Schrödinger representation via the usual prescription, it is clear that a complication does arise, owing to the necessity to deal with the reality condition (5.3). In other words we are not at liberty to use the complex normal coordinates $Q(\boldsymbol{k}j|t)$ and $Q(\boldsymbol{k}j|t)^*$ as independent variables owing to (5.3). It may also be recalled that for a scalar hamiltonian which is bilinear in complex (field) coordinates a gauge transformation of the first kind

$$Q(\boldsymbol{k}j_\mu|t) \to \mathrm{e}^{\mathrm{i}\alpha}Q(\boldsymbol{k}j_\mu|t) \tag{5.6}$$

exists as an added symmetry of the lagrangian, and the hamiltonian, and consequently a conserved current. Evidently the dependence indicated in (5.3) breaks this symmetry.

In order to avoid problems of this kind, connected with the use of complex normal coordinates namely the $Q(\boldsymbol{k}j_\mu|t)$ and the $Q(\boldsymbol{k}j_\mu|t)^*$, which are not independent, it is usual to introduce real normal coordinates of the first or second kind at this point in the analysis. However, as we shall now remark, this usual procedure is not without its own problems. Recall that the complex $Q(\boldsymbol{k}j_\mu|t)$ are bases for the irreducible representations $D^{(\boldsymbol{k})(j)}$ of $\mathscr{G}(\boldsymbol{k})$:

$$P_{R_{\boldsymbol{k}}}Q_\mu = \sum_\nu D^{(\boldsymbol{k})(j)}(R_{\boldsymbol{k}})_{\nu\mu}\,Q_\nu. \tag{5.7}$$

The normal coordinates of the first kind are conventionally defined as

$$q_1(\boldsymbol{k}j_\mu|t) = (\tfrac{1}{2}\sqrt{2})\,[Q(\boldsymbol{k}j_\mu|t) + Q(\boldsymbol{k}j_\mu|t)^*], \tag{5.8}$$

$$q_2(\boldsymbol{k}j_\mu|t) = (-\tfrac{1}{2}\mathrm{i}\sqrt{2})\,[Q(\boldsymbol{k}j_\mu|t) - Q(\boldsymbol{k}j_\mu|t)^*], \tag{5.9}$$

and

$$q_1(\boldsymbol{k}j_\mu|t) = q_1(-\boldsymbol{k}j_\mu|t), \quad q_2(\boldsymbol{k}j_\mu|t) = -q_2(-\boldsymbol{k}j_\mu|t) \tag{5.10, 11}$$

with restriction that only half of the $\boldsymbol{k}$-vectors in the Brillouin zone shall be used, in order to be certain that the proper total number of degrees of freedom are obtained. Now to determine the transformation properties of $q_{1,2}$ we apply the operator P_{R_k} and then, also using (4.46) we have, with minor change in notation to bring out essential features

$$P_{R_k} q_{1,\mu} = \sum_\nu (\bar{\Delta}^{(\boldsymbol{k})(j)}_{\nu\mu} q_{1\nu} + \mathrm{i}\bar{\bar{\Delta}}^{(\boldsymbol{k})(j)}_{\nu\mu} q_{2\nu}) \tag{5.12}$$

and

$$P_{R_k} q_{2,\mu} = \sum_\nu (-\mathrm{i}\bar{\bar{\Delta}}^{(\boldsymbol{k})(j)}_{\nu\mu} q_{1\nu} + \bar{\Delta}^{(\boldsymbol{k})(j)}_{\nu\mu} q_{2\nu}), \tag{5.13}$$

where

$$\bar{\Delta}^{(\boldsymbol{k})(j)}_{\nu\mu} \equiv \tfrac{1}{2}(D^{(\boldsymbol{k})(j)}_{\nu\mu} + D^{(\boldsymbol{k})(j)*}_{\nu\mu}) \tag{5.14}$$

and

$$\bar{\bar{\Delta}}^{(\boldsymbol{k})(j)}_{\nu\mu} \equiv \tfrac{1}{2}(D^{(\boldsymbol{k})(j)}_{\nu\mu} - D^{(\boldsymbol{k})(j)*}_{\nu\mu}). \tag{5.15}$$

In obtaining (5.14) and (5.15) use was made of the inverse of (5.8) and (5.9); the argument (element) R_k was suppressed in the matrices. It is clear from (5.12), (5.13) that the real normal coordinates of the first kind do not in general generate a useful representation of the unitary group of spatial transformation operators P_R. If there is any doubt on this score, one can evaluate

$$P_{S_k} \cdot P_{R_k} q_{j,\mu} \quad j = 1, 2. \tag{5.16}$$

It is then immediate that the real ($q_{1\mu}$) or imaginary ($q_{2\mu}$) parts of the complex normal coordinates $Q(\boldsymbol{k}j_\mu|t)$ are not a suitable basis for the symmetry analysis. Of course, if the representation $D^{(\boldsymbol{k})(j)}$ is purely real then $\bar{\bar{\Delta}}$ is 0, the null matrix, and in that special case

$$\bar{\Delta}^{(\boldsymbol{k})(j)} = D^{(\boldsymbol{k})(j)}, \quad \text{if} \quad D^{(\boldsymbol{k})(j)} \text{ is real,} \tag{5.17}$$

and then the real or imaginary parts, $q_{1\mu}$ and $q_{2\mu}$ respectively, are bases for a representation of the unitary group.

Now turn to the real normal coordinates of the second kind, defined conventionally by the canonical transformation

$$q(kj_\mu) = \tfrac{1}{2}[Q(kj_\mu|t) + Q(-kj_\mu|t)] + (\mathrm{i}/2\omega(kj))[\dot{Q}(kj_\mu|t) - \dot{Q}(-kj_\mu|t)], \quad (5.18)$$

with inverse

$$Q(kj_\mu|t) = \tfrac{1}{2}[q(kj_\mu|t) + q(-kj_\mu|t)] + (\mathrm{i}/2\omega(kj))[\dot{q}(kj_\mu|t) - \dot{q}(kj_\mu|t)]. \quad (5.19)$$

The transformation of these normal coordinates under application of the transformation operator P_{R_k} is given by

$$P_{R_k}q_\mu = \tfrac{1}{2}\{\sum_\nu D^{(k)(j)}_{\nu\mu}q_\nu + \sum_\nu D^{(k)(j)}_{\nu\mu}q^*_\nu + (\mathrm{i}/\omega(kj))(\sum_\nu D^{(k)(j)}_{\nu\mu}\dot{q}_\nu - \sum_\nu D^{(k)(j)*}_{\nu\mu}\dot{q}^*_\nu)\}. \quad (5.20)$$

Again, it is clear that the conventional normal coordinates of the second kind do not transform in general in any simple fashion under transformation by the unitary operators P_{R_k} in $\mathcal{G}(\boldsymbol{k})$ and hence are unsuitable as bases of a representation.

Again observe that in case the representation $D^{(k)(j)}$ is real, the transformation rule simplifies to

$$P_R q_\mu = \tfrac{1}{2}\sum_\nu D^{(k)(j)}_{\nu\mu}(q_\nu + q^*_\nu) + (\mathrm{i}/2\omega(kj))\sum_\nu D^{(k)(j)}_{\nu\mu}(\dot{q}_\nu - \dot{q}^*_\nu). \quad (5.21)$$

In eqs. (5.20)–(5.21) the abbreviation was used of omitting subscripts except the most necessary.

The conclusion to be drawn from the analysis just given is that the conventional procedure for choosing real normal coordinates is inconsistent with maintaining proper symmetrization. If the complex normal coordinates $Q(kj_\mu|t) \equiv Q_\mu$ are chosen as bases for irreducible representations, or corepresentations the sets of real normal coordinates $q_{1\mu}$, $q_{2\mu}$ or q_μ are not appropriate, except if the representation $D^{(k)(j)}$ is real.

It follows from the discussion just given that if the representation $D^{(k)(j)}$ is real, then real normal coordinates $Q(kj_\mu|t)$ can be chosen, and the familiar canonical quantization procedure employed, as for the well-known case of harmonic oscillators. In what follows in this section we shall restrict ourselves to this particular case of real normal coordinates. At the time of writing the more general case, including representations which are complex does not seem to have been discussed.

For real coordinates take $Q^* = Q$ so that the classical hamiltonian becomes quadratic in the real normal coordinates and not merely a hermitian bilinear form. The conventional operator substitution

$$\dot{Q}(\boldsymbol{k}j_\mu \,|\, t) \equiv P(\boldsymbol{k}j_\mu \,|\, t) = (\hbar/\mathrm{i})\, \partial/\partial Q(\boldsymbol{k}j_\mu) \tag{5.22}$$

then produces the Schrödinger equation for the nuclear lattice motion:

$$\tfrac{1}{2}\sum_{\boldsymbol{k}}\sum_{j}\sum_{\mu}\{-\hbar^2(\partial^2/\partial Q^2(\boldsymbol{k}j_\mu)) + \omega^2(\boldsymbol{k}\,|\,j)\, Q^2(\boldsymbol{k}j_\mu) - (\hbar/\mathrm{i})(\partial/\partial t)\}\, \Psi(\{Q\}) = 0\,. \tag{5.23}$$

The total time dependence can be separated by writing

$$\Psi(\{Q\}) = \chi(\{Q\}) \exp(-\mathrm{i}Et/\hbar), \tag{5.24}$$

where $\chi(\{Q\})$ is the time independent eigenfunction which satisfies the equation

$$\tfrac{1}{2}\sum_{\boldsymbol{k}}\sum_{j}\sum_{\mu}\{-\hbar^2(\partial^2/\partial Q^2(\boldsymbol{k}j_\mu)) + \omega^2(\boldsymbol{k}\,|\,j)\, Q^2(\boldsymbol{k}j_\mu) - E\}\, \chi(\{Q\}) = 0\,. \tag{5.25}$$

Since the equation is evidently separable, the wave function can be written as a product of factors χ_a

$$\chi(\{Q\}) = \prod_{a=1}^{3sN} \chi_a(\{Q(\boldsymbol{k}j_\mu)\})\,. \tag{5.26}$$

Each factor χ_a depends only on a single normal coordinate and satisfies the harmonic oscillator equation in that coordinate:

$$\tfrac{1}{2}\{-\hbar^2\partial^2/\partial Q^2(\boldsymbol{k}j_\mu) + \omega^2(\boldsymbol{k}\,|\,j)\, Q^2(\boldsymbol{k}j_\mu) - \varepsilon_a(n_{a,\boldsymbol{k},j})\}\, \chi_a(Q(\boldsymbol{k}j_\mu)) = 0\,, \tag{5.27}$$

where

$$\varepsilon_a(n) = (n + \tfrac{1}{2})\, \hbar\omega(\boldsymbol{k}\,|\,j)\,. \tag{5.28}$$

The total energy is

$$E = \sum_a \varepsilon_a\,. \tag{5.29}$$

Each individual oscillator eigenfunction can be written as a product of three factors: a normalizing constant, an exponential, and an Hermite polynomial. Dropping all subscripts for clarity we may write

$$\chi_a(Q) = C \exp(-\tfrac{1}{2}\gamma Q^2)\, H_n(\gamma Q)\,. \tag{5.30}$$

Then the total harmonic eigenfunction can be written as a product as shown in eq. (5.26).

At this point it should be noted that the eigenfunction given above, in eq. (5.26) is not yet complete, owing to the necessity for symmetrization. That is, degenerate normal modes belonging to the same irreducible representation are to be considered identical Bose particles, and the corresponding wave function must be symmetric under interchange. This symmetrization will be discussed below.

5.2. Symmetry of the harmonic eigenstates

In order to obtain the symmetry property of the eigenstates, it is necessary to write them out in full notational complexity:

$$\chi(\{Q\}) = \bar{C} \exp\left(-\frac{1}{2} \sum_{\boldsymbol{k}, j, \mu} \gamma_{\boldsymbol{k}, j} Q(\boldsymbol{k}j_{\mu})^2 \right) \prod_{\boldsymbol{k}, j, \mu} H_{n_{\boldsymbol{k}, j, \mu}}(\gamma_{\boldsymbol{k}, j} Q(\boldsymbol{k}j_{\mu})). \quad (5.31)$$

An eigenstate of the harmonic hamiltonian is fully specified when the set of quantum numbers $\{n_{\boldsymbol{k}, j_{\mu}}\}$ is specified. This set prescribes the occupancy of each of the oscillator states. So, if a prescribed ordering of the states is given, the ordered set of integers completely defines the state.

Let us subject the eigenfunction $\chi(\{Q\})$ to a transformation by unitary operator P_R^{-1}. Then, every normal coordinate is transformed by P_R:

$$\chi(\{Q\}) \Rightarrow P_R^{-1} \chi(\{Q\}) = \chi(\{P_R Q\}) \quad (5.32)$$

Now in the transformed eigenfunction we must use the property (4.41) that each $Q(\boldsymbol{k}j_{\mu})$ is a basis of an irreducible representation $D^{(\boldsymbol{k})(j)}$ of $\mathscr{G}(\boldsymbol{k})$. Observe that in the exponential there appears a sum of squares of the normal coordinates. It is well known that such a sum of squares is an absolute invariant, and this is anyhow easily proven:

$$\sum_{\boldsymbol{k}j\mu} \gamma_{\boldsymbol{k}j} (P_R Q(\boldsymbol{k}j_{\mu}))^2 = \sum_{\boldsymbol{k}j\mu} \gamma_{\boldsymbol{k}j} Q^2(\boldsymbol{k}j_{\mu}). \quad (5.33)$$

Consequently the entire transformation property of the eigenfunction $\chi(\{Q\})$ is connected with the transformation of the product of Hermite polynomials under the P_R.

To be explicit we restrict ourselves to the case of the product of factors referring to a *single irreducible representation* $D^{(\boldsymbol{k})(j)}$ i.e. consider the functions depending on the partners:

$$Q(\boldsymbol{k}j_{\mu}), \quad \mu = 1, \cdots, l_j. \quad (5.34)$$

This is

$$\prod_{\mu} H_{n_{k,j,\mu}}(\gamma_{k,j} Q(kj_\mu)). \tag{5.35}$$

We require the transformation of the entire polymonial H_n, but observe that the Hermite polynomial H_n is a sum of monomials, of which the term of highest power is of nth degree. The term of highest degree in (5.35) is then of form

$$Q(kj_1)^{n_{k,j(1)}} Q(kj_2)^{n_{k,j(2)}} \times \cdots \times Q(kj_{l_j})^{n_{k,l(j)}}. \tag{5.36}$$

Now recall that the transformation operator† P_{R_k} produces a linear, homogeneous, transformation of the $Q(kj_\mu)$. Consequently a term of dth degree is transformed into a term (or sum of terms) of the same degree. In particular the term above of highest degree:

$$n_{k,j_1} + n_{k,j_2} + \cdots + n_{k,j_{l(j)}} \equiv n_{k,j} \tag{5.37}$$

is sent into a term of the same degree. Clearly $n_{k,j}$ represents the total number of quanta present, belonging to any one of the different rows μ of the irreducible representation $D^{(k)(j)}$. These quanta correspond to the same energy $\omega(k|j)$, i.e. are degenerate.

At this point it is necessary to interject the observation that as written (5.31) is not complete owing to the necessity to symmetrize the total wave-function in order to take account of the statistics. For a set of degenerate bosons the many-body eigenstate needs to be symmetric under interchange of identical objects. This applies to the set of oscillators whose normal coordinates are given in (5.34): the members of this degenerate set can be regarded as the identical (interchangeable) objects. Consequently the symmetrization should be with regard to the set of normal coordinates (5.34) and all equivalent sets into which the members of (5.34) are sent by application of any symmetry element in $\mathscr{G}$. Thus the equivalent sets are

$$\{Q(k_\sigma j_\mu)\}, \quad \mu = 1, \cdots, l_j, \quad \sigma = 1, \ldots, s, \tag{5.38}$$

where each set (fixed σ) has l_j members, and each σ specifies a wave vector in the star $^*k$, with

$$k_\sigma \equiv \phi_\sigma \cdot k \neq k + B_{\mathrm{H}}. \tag{5.39}$$

In particular then, working in the subspace of normal coordinates with wave vector k, belonging to $D^{(k)(j)}$, it is necessary to symmetrize (5.35) with

† Recal that R_k was defined in the line below (4.36).

respect to interchange of the equivalent members of (5.34). This replaces (5.35) by the symmetrized product

$$\mathscr{S}\prod_{\mu} H_{n_{\boldsymbol{k}},\,j(\mu)}\big(\gamma_{\boldsymbol{k},\,j_\mu} Q(\boldsymbol{k}, j_\mu)\big). \tag{5.40}$$

Then, the leading term (of highest degree) in (5.39) is the set (5.36) symmetrized on the equivalent $Q(\boldsymbol{k}j_\mu)$. To simplify the notation we write the leading term

$$\mathscr{S} Q_1^{n_1} Q_2^{n_2} \cdots Q_{l_j}^{n_{l(j)}}, \tag{5.41}$$

which stands for the symmetrized set of monomials of fixed total degree

$$n_j \equiv n_1 + \cdots + n_{l_j}. \tag{5.42}$$

Consider now one such monomial of the set:

$$Q_1^{n_1} Q_2^{n_2} \cdots Q_{l_j}^{n_{l(j)}} \tag{5.43}$$

with

$$n_j \equiv n_1 + \cdots + n_{l_j}. \tag{5.44}$$

By what was just said, the space of functions with n_j fixed is complete. To determine the representation of $\mathscr{G}(k)$ spanned by this space, and hence the representation spanned by (5.41), a simplification due to Tisza (1933) is helpful. Let us select *one* element P_S in $\mathscr{G}(\boldsymbol{k})$, and for *this* element we bring the representation $D^{(\boldsymbol{k})(j)}$ to diagonal form:

$$D^{(\boldsymbol{k})(j)}_{\mu\nu} = d^j_\mu \delta_{\mu\nu} \tag{5.45}$$

In other words we work in a basis in which each Q_μ is merely multiplied by a number d^j_μ when transformed by P_S:

$$P_S Q_\mu = d^j_\mu Q_\mu. \tag{5.46}$$

Clearly, the trace of the representation spanned by the set of monomials (5.39) is invariant under the transformation from the original complex normal coordinates to the equivalent set which transforms as (5.42). Then under linear transformation by P_S, (5.39) is transformed into: the factor

$$(d^j_1)^{n_1}(d^j_2)^{n_2} \cdots (d^j_{l_j})^{n_{l(j)}} \tag{5.47}$$

times the monomial (5.43).

Coming back to the symmetrized set, observe that *each* term is multiplied by a factor of type (5.47). The character of the representation spanned by the *set* of monomials is then

$$[\chi(S)]_{(n_j)} = \sum (d_1^j)^{n_1} (d_2^j)^{n_2} \cdots (d_{l_j}^j)^{n_{l(j)}} \tag{5.48}$$

with the sum over all partitions of the fixed integer n_j into l_j groups. Since the basis of the representation is the symmetrized set of monomials, it is clear that the representation itself is a symmetrized power. The symbol on the left-hand side gives this identification as the symmetrized n_jth Kronecker power.

A further advance can be made using the same simplified basis to obtain explicit results. From (5.46) we obtain, for the character of powers of the element P_S:

$$\chi(S) = \sum_{\mu=1}^{l_j} d_\mu^j, \qquad \chi(S^p) = \sum_{\mu=1}^{l_j} (d_\mu^j)^p. \tag{5.49, 50}$$

Since the sums (5.49) and (5.50) can be computed it remains to express (5.48) in terms of these sums. As a first step write the character (5.48) in terms of the 'elementary symmetric functions' in the variables $d_{\mu'}^j$, of degree n_j:

$$[\chi(S)]_{(n_j)} = \sum (d_\mu^j)^{n_j} + \sum (d_\mu^j)^{n_\mu} (d_{\mu'}^j)^{n_{\mu'}} + \cdots + \sum (d_\mu^j)^{n_\mu} (d_{\mu'}^j)^{n_{\mu'}} \cdots (d_{\mu'''}^j)^{n_{\mu'''}}. \tag{5.51}$$

The sums indicated are sums in which the indices are permuted through all permitted values, subject to the restriction that the degree of each function is fixed at n_j, so in each case:

$$n_\mu + n_{\mu'} = n_j; \; \cdots; \; n_\mu + n_{\mu'} + \cdots + n_{\mu'''} = n_j. \tag{5.52}$$

The elementary symmetric functions are symmetric polymonials indicated in (5.51) as individual terms. These are evidently a complete set for the decomposition of $[\chi(S)]_{(n)}$.

It is straightforward, although complicated to express $[\chi(S)]_{(n)}$ in terms of the sets (5.51), and then the latter, via (5.49) and (5.50) in terms of the elementary powers. The result is

$$[\chi(S)]_{(n_j)} = \sum \frac{\chi(S^{q_1})^{r_1} \cdots \chi(S^{q_\nu})^{r_\nu}}{r_1!\, q_1^{r_1} \cdots r_\nu!\, q_\nu^{r_\nu}} \tag{5.53}$$

with the sum over all possible partitions of the fixed number n_j such that

$$n_j = r_1 q_1 + \cdots + r_\nu q_\nu \tag{5.54}$$

with r_j and q_j integers.

The character $[\chi(S)]_{(n_j)}$ can then be reduced into irreducible components $D^{(\boldsymbol{k})(j)}$. In this fashion we obtain the transformation of the part of the eigenfunction belonging to the symmetrized subspace (5.40).

The total symmetrized lattice eigenfunction (replacing (5.31) must be written

$$\chi_{\text{sym}}(\{Q\}) \equiv \mathscr{S}\chi(\{Q\}), \tag{5.55}$$

where the symmetrization operator $\mathscr{S}$ acts on all labels of partners within an irreducible representation (these are the equivalent bosons of the theory). Replacing the missing indices, the character of the (reducible) representation by which (5.40) transforms is then the product of factors like (5.53) or

$$\chi^{(\text{vib})}(S) = \prod_{\boldsymbol{k}j} [\chi^{(\boldsymbol{k})(j)}(S)]_{(n_{\boldsymbol{k},j})}, \tag{5.56}$$

where S is some symmetry operator. Note the index μ no longer appears, owing to the symmetrization and to the fact that we are taking the trace.

5.3. Selection rules for transitions

The rate of transitions from a state $|\text{i}\rangle$ to a state $|\text{f}\rangle$ caused by a perturbation H' is

$$\omega_{\text{i}\to\text{f}} = (2\pi/\hbar) \sum_{\text{f}} |\langle\text{f}|\, H'\, |\text{i}\rangle|^2\, \delta(E_\text{f} - E_\text{i}). \tag{5.57}$$

In general, selection rules arise from the analysis of the matrix element, taking into account the symmetry of initial and final states and of the perturbation hamiltonian H'. To be specific we take the initial state

$$|\text{i}\rangle \equiv \psi_\alpha^{(\text{i})} \tag{5.58}$$

to be one member of a manifold corresponding to irreducible representation $D^{(\text{i})}$; the final state can be taken to be a member of the manifold $D^{(\text{f})}$:

$$|\text{f}\rangle \equiv \psi_\beta^{(\text{f})}. \tag{5.59}$$

The perturbation operator H' can be decomposed into sets of irreducible (tensor) operators

$$H' = \{H^{(j)}\} + \{H^{(n)}\} + \{H^{(l)}\} + \cdots, \tag{5.60}$$

where e.g. the set $\{H^{(j)}\}$ transforms as a basis for irreducible representation $D^{(j)}$. In all cases above, the group under which the transformation occurs is the same.

The integral, or scalar product, $\langle \mathrm{f}|H'|\mathrm{i}\rangle$ can be decomposed into integrals involving only one irreducible tensor operator at a time such as

$$\langle \mathrm{f}|\, H^{(j)}\,|\mathrm{i}\rangle \equiv \int \psi_\beta^{(\mathrm{f})*} H_\mu^{(j)} \psi_\alpha^{(\mathrm{i})}\, \mathrm{d}\tau\,. \tag{5.61}$$

Since this object is a number, its value must equal

$$\int P_R^{-1} \psi_\beta^{(\mathrm{f})*} P_R H_\mu^{(j)} P_R^{-1} P_R \psi_\alpha^{(\mathrm{i})}\, \mathrm{d}\tau\,, \tag{5.62}$$

where P_R is a unitary operator, and $\mathrm{d}\tau$ an invariant volume element. But, (5.61) transforms according to

$$D^{(\mathrm{f})*} \otimes D^{(j)} \otimes D^{(\mathrm{i})}\,. \tag{5.63}$$

If the triple product (5.63) contains the identity, or trivial representation $D^{(1)}$, then (5.62) equals (5.61) and the matrix element is non-zero. If, by a selection rule we mean a vanishing of the matrix element, then if $D^{(1)}$ is *not* in the product, the matrix element vanishes.

An equivalent formulation makes use of the Clebsch–Gordan coefficients, defined in (3.31). For finite groups one invariant function transforming like $D^{(1)}$ can be constructed as a bilinear from the bases of each irreducible representation. It is

$$\sum_{\mu=1}^{l_j} \psi_\mu^{(j)*} \psi_\mu^{(j)}\,. \tag{5.64}$$

Then if the integral (5.61) is to be non-zero, it is necessary that from the bilinear product of: bases for $D^{(\mathrm{f})*}$ times bases for $D^{(\mathrm{i})}$, it should be possible to construct bases for $D^{(j)}$, in order to produce the match indicated in (5.64). Then if the Clebsch–Gordan coefficient

$$\begin{pmatrix} \mathrm{i} & \mathrm{f}^* & \big| & j \\ \alpha & \beta & \big| & \mu \end{pmatrix} \neq 0\,, \tag{5.65}$$

we can produce a function transforming as the μth row, jth irreducible representation:

$$\phi_\mu^j = \sum_{\alpha,\,\beta} \begin{pmatrix} \mathrm{i} & \mathrm{f}^* & \big| & j \\ \alpha & \beta & \big| & \mu \end{pmatrix} \psi_\beta^{(\mathrm{f})*} \psi_\alpha^{(\mathrm{i})}\,. \tag{5.66}$$

In this case the object corresponding to (5.62) will be

$$\sum_\mu \sum_{\alpha\beta} \begin{pmatrix} \mathrm{i} & \mathrm{f}^* & \big| & j \\ \alpha & \beta & \big| & \mu \end{pmatrix} (\psi_\beta^{\mathrm{f}},\, H_\mu^j \psi_\alpha^{\mathrm{i}})\,. \tag{5.67}$$

It is in general non-zero. Another, equivalent statement of this result, is that the quantity

$$\sum_{\alpha,\beta} \begin{pmatrix} \mathrm{i} & \mathrm{f}^* & j \\ \alpha & \beta & \mu \end{pmatrix} (\psi_\beta^{\mathrm{f}}, H_\mu^{(j)} \psi_\alpha^{(\mathrm{i})}) \tag{5.68}$$

is independent of μ: i.e. has the same value for all rows.

These statements can be put into a closer rapport with the so-called Wigner–Eckart theorem that the scalar product

$$(\psi_\beta^{(\mathrm{f})}, \phi_\beta^{(\mathrm{f})}) \tag{5.69}$$

is independent of β. To produce a function $\phi_\beta^{(\mathrm{f})}$, we construct the bilinear expression

$$\phi_\beta^{(\mathrm{f})} = \sum_{\alpha\mu} \begin{pmatrix} j & \mathrm{i} & \mathrm{f} \\ \mu & \alpha & \beta \end{pmatrix} H_\mu^j \psi_\alpha^{\mathrm{i}} \tag{5.70}$$

which either vanishes, or has the correct transformation properties. If it is non-zero then

$$\sum_{\alpha\mu} \begin{pmatrix} j & \mathrm{i} & \mathrm{f} \\ \mu & \alpha & \beta \end{pmatrix} (\psi_\beta^{\mathrm{f}}, H_\mu^j \psi_\alpha^{\mathrm{i}}) \tag{5.71}$$

will be non-zero in general, and independent of β. In these cases we focus attention on the related question of whether $D^{(j)} \otimes D^{(\mathrm{i})}$ contains $D^{(\mathrm{f})}$. If $D^{(\mathrm{f})}$ is contained more than once, i.e. if in

$$D^{(j)} \otimes D^{(\mathrm{i})} = \sum_{\mathrm{f}} (j\mathrm{i}|\mathrm{f})\, D^{(\mathrm{f})}, \tag{5.72}$$

we have

$$(j\mathrm{i}|\mathrm{f}) > 1, \tag{5.73}$$

then $(j\mathrm{i}|\mathrm{f})$ distinct bases of symmetry like $\phi_\beta^{(\mathrm{f})}$ can be constructed. In this case, there are $(j\mathrm{i}|\mathrm{f})$ distinct, independent, non-zero matrix elements.

To apply this analysis to a specific transition process involving lattice vibrations use (5.56) to find the character system for the representation generated by initial and final states $|\mathrm{i}\rangle$ and $|\mathrm{f}\rangle$ respectively. The character system is then reduced to irreducible components, which are treated one at a time. The transition operator H' is decomposed as in (5.60). Finally use of the relevant Clebsch–Gordan coefficients permits evaluation of the independent set of matrix elements.

All this work is a direct consequence of the symmetry analysis of the harmonic lattice eigenfunction, and of the transition operator H'.

6. *Space group theory*

In this section we give a précis of the representation theory of space groups, and the theory of the Clebsch–Gordan, or vector coupling coefficients of space groups.

6.1. Space group representations as ray representations

In order to obtain an irreducible représentation of a group of transformation operators it is necessary to construct a minimal linear vector space, closed under the group operators. The coset decomposition of the space group $\mathscr{G}$, into the translation subgroup $\mathscr{T}$ plus the left cosets with respect to $\mathscr{T}$, as given in eq. (2.9) provides us with the essential clue. As a first step we reduce $\mathscr{T}$.

Because $\mathscr{T}$ is an abelian group – in fact the product of three abelian groups (one for each primitive direction in the crystal) – the reduction of $\mathscr{T}$ is simple. The space which reduces $\mathscr{T}$ is spanned by Bloch functions

$$\psi^{(\boldsymbol{k})}(\boldsymbol{r}) = \exp(\mathrm{i}\boldsymbol{k}\cdot\boldsymbol{r})\, u_n(\boldsymbol{k}, \boldsymbol{r}). \tag{6.1}$$

The index n on u represents any additional quantum numbers. Consider the space

$$\Sigma^{(\boldsymbol{k})} \equiv \{\psi_1^{(\boldsymbol{k})}, \cdots, \psi_{l_j}^{(\boldsymbol{k})}\} \tag{6.2}$$

consisting of l_j linearly independent functions, each one of which is a Bloch function of wave vector $\boldsymbol{k}$. Evidently $\Sigma^{(\boldsymbol{k})}$ is closed under $\mathscr{T}$ and spans a representation which is reducible as the direct sum of $D^{(\boldsymbol{k})}$ (l_j times). Here

$$D^{(\boldsymbol{k})}(\{\varepsilon\,|\,\boldsymbol{R}_\mathrm{L}\}) = \exp(-\,\mathrm{i}\boldsymbol{k}\cdot\boldsymbol{R}_\mathrm{L}), \tag{6.3}$$

with $\boldsymbol{R}_\mathrm{L}$ a lattice vector, and $\boldsymbol{k}$ a vector of the first Brillouin zone. Let

$$R_\alpha \equiv \{\phi_\alpha\,|\,\tau(\phi_\alpha)\} \tag{6.4}$$

then the function

$$P_{R_\alpha}\psi^{(\boldsymbol{k})} \equiv \psi^{(\boldsymbol{k}_\alpha)} \tag{6.5}$$

is a Bloch function at wave vector

$$\boldsymbol{k}_\alpha \equiv \boldsymbol{\phi}_\alpha \cdot \boldsymbol{k}. \tag{6.6}$$

Recall that two wave vectors $\boldsymbol{k}$ and $\boldsymbol{k}'$ are equivalent if

$$\boldsymbol{k} - \boldsymbol{k}' = \boldsymbol{B}_\mathrm{H}, \tag{6.7}$$

where $\boldsymbol{B}_\mathrm{H}$ is a lattice vector in 'Fourier space' (with the factor 2π included). The proof of the assertion is an immediate consequence of the product rule

$$\{\varepsilon \,|\, \boldsymbol{R}_\mathrm{L}\} \cdot \{\boldsymbol{\phi}_\alpha \,|\, \boldsymbol{\tau}_\alpha\} = \{\boldsymbol{\phi}_\alpha \,|\, \boldsymbol{\tau}_\alpha\}\, \{\varepsilon \,|\, \boldsymbol{\phi}_\alpha^{-1} \cdot \boldsymbol{R}_\mathrm{L}\} \tag{6.8}$$

Consequently, the set of operators consisting of

$$\mathscr{T} + \{\boldsymbol{\phi}_{l_2} \,|\, \boldsymbol{\tau}_2\}\, \mathscr{T} + \cdots + \{\boldsymbol{\phi}_{l_k} \,|\, \boldsymbol{\tau}_k\}\, \mathscr{T} \equiv \mathscr{G}(\boldsymbol{k}), \tag{6.9}$$

where

$$\boldsymbol{\phi}_{l_\mu} \cdot \boldsymbol{k} = \boldsymbol{k} + \boldsymbol{B}_\mathrm{H} \tag{6.10}$$

defines a space group $\mathscr{G}(\boldsymbol{k})$, the space group of $\boldsymbol{k}$. The representations space $\Sigma^{(\boldsymbol{k})}$ remains closed or invariant under $\mathscr{G}(\boldsymbol{k})$. Without loss of generality assume that the representation of $\mathscr{G}(\boldsymbol{k})$ based on the space $\Sigma^{(\boldsymbol{k})}$ is irreducible, and we call it $D^{(\boldsymbol{k})(j)}$. Then also affix the label to the space (6.2) and to the functions which span it:

$$\Sigma^{(\boldsymbol{k})(j)} = \{\psi_1^{(\boldsymbol{k})(j)}, \cdots, \psi_{l_j}^{(\boldsymbol{k})(j)}\}. \tag{6.11}$$

The space $\Sigma^{(\boldsymbol{k})(j)}$ has two important properties: 1) $D^{(\boldsymbol{k})(j)}$ is irreducible; 2) the representation of $\mathscr{T}$ based on $\Sigma^{(\boldsymbol{k})(j)}$ is:

$$\{\varepsilon \,|\, \boldsymbol{R}_\mathrm{L}\} \rightarrow \exp(-\,\mathrm{i}\boldsymbol{k} \cdot \boldsymbol{R}_\mathrm{L})\, D^{(\boldsymbol{k})(j)}(\{\varepsilon \,|\, \boldsymbol{0}\}) \tag{6.12}$$

i.e. every translation is represented by phase factor $\exp(-\mathrm{i}\boldsymbol{k} \cdot \boldsymbol{R}_\mathrm{L})$ times the matrix representing the identity.

Consider the matrix representatives in $D^{(\boldsymbol{k})(j)}$ of the product of coset representatives in $\mathscr{G}(\boldsymbol{k})$:

$$\{\boldsymbol{\phi}_{l_\alpha} \,|\, \boldsymbol{\tau}_{l_\alpha}\} \cdot \{\boldsymbol{\phi}_{l_\beta} \,|\, \boldsymbol{\tau}_{l_\beta}\} = \{\varepsilon \,|\, \boldsymbol{R}_{\mathrm{L}_{\alpha\beta}}\} \cdot \{\boldsymbol{\phi}_{l_{\alpha\beta}} \,|\, \boldsymbol{\tau}_{l_{\alpha\beta}}\}. \tag{6.13}$$

In equation (6.13) each coset representative is one of the specified ones in the decomposition (6.9), the pure translation is

$$\boldsymbol{R}_{\mathrm{L}_{\alpha\beta}} \equiv \boldsymbol{\phi}_{l_\alpha} \cdot \boldsymbol{\tau}_{l_\beta} + \boldsymbol{\tau}_{l_\alpha} - \boldsymbol{\tau}_{l_{\alpha\beta}}. \tag{6.14}$$

For brevity write equation (6.13) as

$$R_\alpha \cdot R_\beta = T_{\alpha\beta} \cdot R_{\alpha\beta}, \tag{6.15}$$

where R is a coset representative, and T a translation. In $D^{(\boldsymbol{k})(j)}$ this equation is

$$D^{(\boldsymbol{k})(j)}(R_\alpha)\, D^{(\boldsymbol{k})(j)}(R_\beta) = D^{(\boldsymbol{k})(j)}(T_{\alpha\beta})\, D^{(\boldsymbol{k})(j)}(R_{\alpha\beta}), \tag{6.16}$$

where

$$D^{(\boldsymbol{k})(j)}(T_{\alpha\beta}) = \exp(-\,\mathrm{i}\boldsymbol{k}\cdot \boldsymbol{R}_{\mathrm{L}_{\alpha\beta}})\, D^{(\boldsymbol{k})(j)}(\{\varepsilon\,|\,0\}). \tag{6.17}$$

Consider now the point group $\mathscr{P}(\boldsymbol{k}) \equiv \mathscr{G}(\boldsymbol{k})/\mathscr{T}$ isomorphic to the set of rotations

$$\mathscr{P}(\boldsymbol{k}) = \varepsilon,\, \phi_{l_2}, \cdots, \phi_\alpha, \cdots, \phi_\beta, \cdots, \phi_{l_k}. \tag{6.18}$$

Let $D^{(j)}$ be an irreducible representation of $\mathscr{P}(\boldsymbol{k})$, then in $D^{(j)}$

$$D^{(j)}(\phi_\alpha)\cdot D^{(j)}(\phi_\beta) = D^{(j)}(\phi_{\alpha\beta}). \tag{6.19}$$

Comparing (6.19) and (6.16) notice that $D^{(\boldsymbol{k})(j)}$ of $\mathscr{G}(\boldsymbol{k})$ is a "representation up to a factor" or a ray representation of $\mathscr{P}(\boldsymbol{k})$. The factor system is a set of unimodular complex numbers

$$\lambda^{(\boldsymbol{k})}(\alpha, \beta) \equiv \exp(-\,\mathrm{i}\boldsymbol{k}\cdot \boldsymbol{R}_{\mathrm{L}_{\alpha\beta}}). \tag{6.20}$$

Then the ray representation method consists in finding a set of irreducible matrices (representation up to a factor) $D^{(j)}(\phi)$ one for each element in the point group $\mathscr{P}(\boldsymbol{k})$, which obey the rule

$$D^{(j)}(\phi_\alpha)\, D^{(j)}(\phi_\beta) = \lambda^{(\boldsymbol{k})}(\alpha, \beta)\, D^{(j)}(\phi_{\alpha\beta}), \tag{6.21}$$

with $\lambda^{(\boldsymbol{k})}$ given by (6.20). The factor system defined by (6.20) is consistent with the mathematical requirement of associativity of products, etc. The ray representation matrices for all point groups, using this factor system have been tabulated (Hurley 1966), and can then be directly taken over for the space group coset representatives by the correspondence

$$D^{(\boldsymbol{k})(j)}(R_\alpha) \leftrightarrow D^{(j)}(\phi_\alpha), \tag{6.22}$$

it being understood that the $D^{(j)}$ are ray representation matrices with factor system (6.20).

Instead of using the ray representation matrices $D^{(j)}(\phi_\alpha)$ a 'p-equivalent' set is often more convenient. It is defined by

$$\hat{D}^{(j)}(\phi_\alpha) = \exp(\mathrm{i}\boldsymbol{k}\cdot\boldsymbol{\tau}_\alpha)\, D^{(j)}(\phi_\alpha), \tag{6.23}$$

where $\boldsymbol{\tau}_\alpha$ is the fractional associated with $\{\phi_\alpha|\tau_\alpha\}$. Consequently the ray representation matrices multiply according to the rule

$$\hat{D}^{(j)}(\phi_\alpha)\, \hat{D}^{(j)}(\phi_\beta) = \hat{\lambda}^{(\boldsymbol{k})}(\alpha, \beta)\, \hat{D}^{(j)}(\phi_{\alpha\beta}), \tag{6.24}$$

with the factor set

$$\hat{\lambda}(\alpha, \beta) = \exp[-\mathrm{i}(\phi_\alpha^{-1}\cdot\boldsymbol{k} - \boldsymbol{k})\cdot\boldsymbol{\tau}_\beta]. \tag{6.25}$$

This factor set has been used by Kovalev (1965). Evidently, if one is given the ray representation matrices $\hat{D}^{(j)}$ the association to space group coset representatives is now

$$D^{(\boldsymbol{k})(j)}(R_\alpha) \rightarrow \exp(-\mathrm{i}\boldsymbol{k}\cdot\boldsymbol{\tau}_\alpha)\, \hat{D}^{(j)}(\phi_\alpha). \tag{6.26}$$

Once one has all matrices for the coset representatives in $\mathscr{G}(\boldsymbol{k})$ the matrix for any element can be obtained by multiplying by the diagonal matrix which corresponds to the added pure translation.

6.2. Induction of full space group irreducible representations

It is always necessary to understand the structure of the full space group irreducible representation, $D^{(*\boldsymbol{k})(j)}$ which is obtained by induction from the acceptable $D^{(\boldsymbol{k})(j)}$. Decompose the space group $\mathscr{G}$ into cosets with respect to the group $\mathscr{G}(\boldsymbol{k})$:

$$\mathscr{G} = \mathscr{G}(\boldsymbol{k}) + \cdots + \{\phi_\sigma|\tau_\sigma\}\,\mathscr{G}(\boldsymbol{k}) + \cdots + \{\phi_s|\tau_s\}\,\mathscr{G}(\boldsymbol{k}). \tag{6.27}$$

From (6.5) it follows that the operators in every coset save $\mathscr{G}(\boldsymbol{k})$, send a Bloch function $\psi^{(\boldsymbol{k})(j)}$ into a Bloch function with inequivalent wave vector: $\psi^{(\boldsymbol{k}_\sigma)(j)}$. There are s such inequivalent wave vectors corresponding to wave vector $\boldsymbol{k}$, they span the star of $\boldsymbol{k}$

$$^*\boldsymbol{k} = \{\boldsymbol{k}_1, \cdots, \boldsymbol{k}_\sigma, \cdots, \boldsymbol{k}_s\}. \tag{6.28}$$

Reserve the indices (σ, τ) to refer only to coset representatives *not* in $\mathscr{G}(\boldsymbol{k})$.

The vector space $\Sigma^{(\boldsymbol{k})(j)}$ is sent into the distinct space $\Sigma^{(\boldsymbol{k}_\sigma)(j)}$ by the operator $P_{\{\phi_\sigma|\tau_\sigma\}}$. Consequently under the collection of operators in $\mathscr{G}$ an invariant space is the union of the s-spaces

$$\sum^{(*\boldsymbol{k})\,(j)} = \{\sum^{(\boldsymbol{k})\,(j)} \oplus \cdots \oplus \sum^{(\boldsymbol{k}_\sigma)\,(j)} \oplus \cdots \oplus \sum^{(\boldsymbol{k}_s)\,(j)}\}. \tag{6.29}$$

The full irreducible representation $D^{(*\boldsymbol{k})\,(j)}$ is a direct sum of block matrices, corresponding to the space (6.29). To specify completely the structure of $D^{(*\boldsymbol{k})\,(j)}$ it is necessary to give the block matrix in the (σ, τ) block. Assume that

$$P_{\{\boldsymbol{\phi}_\sigma \mid \boldsymbol{\tau}_\sigma\}} \psi_\mu^{(\boldsymbol{k})\,(j)} = \psi_\mu^{(\boldsymbol{k}_\sigma)\,(j)}, \tag{6.30}$$

so that the μth basis function of $D^{(\boldsymbol{k})\,(j)}$ is transformed into the μth basis function of $D^{(\boldsymbol{k}_\sigma)\,(j)}$, by the unitary operator.

Corresponding to the ordering of subspaces in (6.29) we can immediately write down the *block* matrices in $D^{(*\boldsymbol{k})\,(j)}$. They are

$$D^{(*\boldsymbol{k})\,(j)}(X)_{11} = \dot{D}^{(\boldsymbol{k})\,(j)}(X), \tag{6.31}$$

where

$$\begin{aligned} \dot{D}^{(\boldsymbol{k})\,(j)}(X) &= D^{(\boldsymbol{k})\,(j)}(X) \quad \text{if } X \text{ is in } \mathscr{G}(\boldsymbol{k}), \\ &= \boldsymbol{0} \ \text{ otherwise}. \end{aligned} \tag{6.32}$$

and $\boldsymbol{0}$ is the $l_j \times l_j$ null matrix. Also

$$D^{(*\boldsymbol{k})\,(j)}(R_\sigma)_{\sigma 1} = D^{(\boldsymbol{k})\,(j)}(\{\varepsilon \mid \boldsymbol{0}\}), \tag{6.33}$$

$$D^{(*\boldsymbol{k})\,(j)}(R_\sigma^{-1})_{1\sigma} = D^{(\boldsymbol{k})\,(j)}(\{\varepsilon \mid \boldsymbol{0}\}), \tag{6.34}$$

where

$$R_\sigma \equiv \{\boldsymbol{\phi}_\sigma \mid \boldsymbol{\tau}_\sigma\}, \tag{6.35}$$

and index σ, τ always refer to a coset not in $\mathscr{G}(k)$. All other block matrices in the first column or row are zero, besides those in (6.31)–(6.33).

Now, let R_p be an arbitrary coset representative. Let R_σ and R_τ be among the set of coset representatives in (6.9). Let the product

$$R_p \cdot R_\tau \quad \text{be in coset } R_\sigma \mathscr{G}(\boldsymbol{k}) \tag{6.36}$$

so that

$$R_\sigma^{-1} R_p R_\tau \quad \text{is in } \mathscr{G}(\boldsymbol{k}). \tag{6.37}$$

Then for the σ, τ-block matrix element in $D^{(*\boldsymbol{k})\,(j)}$ we obtain

$$D^{(*\boldsymbol{k})\,(j)}(R_p)_{\sigma\tau} = \dot{D}^{(\boldsymbol{k})\,(j)}(R_\sigma^{-1} R_p R_\tau). \tag{6.38}$$

This is the general solution to the construction of full irreducible representations from the known $D^{(\boldsymbol{k})(j)}$. The process of construction is called *induction* from $D^{(\boldsymbol{k})(j)}$ of $\mathscr{G}(k)$. Proofs of irreducibility and completeness are straightforward and are given elsewhere (Birman 1974).

The transformation of Bloch functions which corresponds to the induced representation can be easily given. Let R_p be the general element in $\mathscr{G}$, and

$$\psi_{\mu}^{(\boldsymbol{k}_\tau)(j)} = P_{R_\tau}\psi_{\mu}^{(\boldsymbol{k})(j)}, \tag{6.39}$$

where $\boldsymbol{k}$ is the canonical wave vector of $^*\boldsymbol{k}$. Then

$$P_{R_p}\psi_{\mu}^{(\boldsymbol{k}_\tau)(j)} = \sum_{\bar{\mu}} \dot{D}^{(\boldsymbol{k})(j)}(R_\sigma^{-1}R_pR_\tau)_{\bar{\mu}\mu}\,\psi_{\bar{\mu}}^{(\boldsymbol{k}_\sigma)(j)}. \tag{6.40}$$

In obtaining the matrix $\dot{D}^{(\boldsymbol{k})(j)}$ we are free to use either of the ray representation methods previously given. Recall, however, that R_σ, R_p, and R_τ are all coset representatives so that we write

$$R_\sigma^{-1}R_pR_\tau = \{\varepsilon\,|\,\boldsymbol{R}_{\bar{\sigma}p\tau}\}\,\{\phi_\sigma^{-1}\phi_p\phi_\tau\,|\,\boldsymbol{\tau}_{\bar{\sigma}p\tau}\}, \tag{6.41}$$

where the pure lattice translation $R_{\bar{\sigma}p\tau}$ is given as

$$\boldsymbol{R}_{\bar{\sigma}p\tau} \equiv \phi_\sigma^{-1}\phi_p\boldsymbol{\tau}_\tau + \phi_\sigma^{-1}\boldsymbol{\tau}_p - \phi_\sigma^{-1}\boldsymbol{\tau}_\sigma - \boldsymbol{\tau}_{\bar{\sigma}p\tau} \tag{6.42}$$

and $\boldsymbol{\tau}_{\bar{\sigma}p\tau}$ is the canonical fractional which is associated with $\phi_\sigma^{-1}\phi_p\phi_\tau$ in the coset decomposition of $\mathscr{G}$. Then using the first convention for the ray representations

$$\dot{D}^{(\boldsymbol{k})(j)}(R_\sigma^{-1}R_pR_\tau) = \exp(-\mathrm{i}\boldsymbol{k}\cdot\boldsymbol{R}_{\bar{\sigma}p\tau})\,D^{(j)}(\phi_\sigma^{-1}\phi_p\phi_\tau). \tag{6.43}$$

When this expression is substituted in (6.40) we obtain the complete transformation formula.

6.3. Projection operators

In order to obtain a basis function $\psi_{\mu}^{(\boldsymbol{k})(j)}$ for the μth row of allowable irreducible representation $D^{(\boldsymbol{k})(j)}$ of $\mathscr{G}(\boldsymbol{k})$ it is helpful to use a projection operator technique. Let $\psi^{(\boldsymbol{k})}$ be a Bloch function at wave-vector $\boldsymbol{k}$: it may be a plane wave function, or a tight binding function, or some other representation. Then the projection operator is

$$P_{\mu\mu}^{(\boldsymbol{k})(j)} = (l_j/l_k)\sum_{\alpha=1}^{l_k} D^{(\boldsymbol{k})(j)}(R_\alpha)_{\mu\mu}^{*}\,P_{R_\alpha}, \tag{6.44}$$

where l_j is the dimension of irreducible representations $D^{(\mathbf{k})(j)}$, l_k the number of distinct coset representatives in (6.9), R_α is a coset representative $R_\alpha \equiv \{\phi_{l_\alpha} | \tau_\alpha\}$, and the sum is over all coset representatives ($\alpha = 1, \cdots, l_k$). Thus

$$\psi_\mu^{(\mathbf{k})(j)} = P_{\mu\mu}^{(\mathbf{k})(j)} \psi^{(\mathbf{k})} . \tag{6.45}$$

This operator must be applied to a Bloch function to satisfy the translation requirements. The off-diagonal operator $P_{\mu\nu}^{(\mathbf{k})(j)}$ is also useful. The matrix elements $D_{\mu\nu}^{(\mathbf{k})(j)}$ can be taken from the ray-representation matrices. Either choice of factor system is acceptable, so the matrices $D^{(j)}$ or $\hat{D}^{(j)}$ can be used.

The projection operators have the usual valuable property

$$P_{\mu\nu}^{(\mathbf{k})(j)} P_{\sigma\tau}^{(\mathbf{k})(j')} = \delta_{jj'} \delta_{\nu\sigma} P_{\mu\tau}^{(\mathbf{k})(j)} . \tag{6.46}$$

The scalar product

$$(\psi_\mu^{(\mathbf{k})(j)}, \psi_\mu^{(\mathbf{k})(j)}) \tag{6.47}$$

can be written

$$(\psi^{(\mathbf{k})}, P_{\mu\mu}^{(\mathbf{k})(j)} \psi^{(\mathbf{k})}) \equiv N^2 , \tag{6.48}$$

since $\psi^{(\mathbf{k})}$ can be decomposed as

$$\psi^{(\mathbf{k})} = \sum_{j\mu'} \psi_{\mu'}^{(\mathbf{k})(j)} \tag{6.49}$$

and the only contribution to N will then be when indices $j'\mu'$ match $j\mu$. Then

$$\psi_\mu^{(\mathbf{k})(j)} = N^{-1} P_{\mu\mu}^{(\mathbf{k})(j)} \psi^{(\mathbf{k})} . \tag{6.50}$$

The wave function (6.50) is normalized; recall also that N is independent of μ.

6.4. Clebsch–Gordan coefficients

We shall only deal here with the situation where there is no multiplicity, so that in (3.31) $\gamma = 1$; that is in taking the product $D^{(l)} \otimes D^{(j)}$ a representation $D^{(\mathbf{k})}$ appears once, or not at all. Consequently there is only one function $\psi_\nu^{(\mathbf{k})}$ transforming as the νth row of $D^{(\mathbf{k})}$ which can be constructed from a linear combination of products $\psi_\lambda^j \psi_\mu^l$. Recall that any statement involving the exact form of a representation is only meaningful modulus a unitary similarity transformation of the representations to an equivalent form. We shall proceed as in the discussion leading to eq. (3.39).

To be specific, we desire to find the Clebsch–Gordan coefficient for coupling functions $\psi_{\mu}^{(\boldsymbol{k}_\tau)(j)}$ and $\psi_{\mu'}^{(\boldsymbol{k}'_{\tau'})(j')}$ to form functions $\psi_{\mu''}^{(\boldsymbol{k}'')(j'')}$. We assume that the *resultant* wave vector $\boldsymbol{k}''$ is the canonical wave vector $(\boldsymbol{k}''_1)$ of its star. Then

$$\boldsymbol{k}_\tau + \boldsymbol{k}'_{\tau'} = \boldsymbol{k}''(\text{mod}\,\boldsymbol{B}_{\text{H}}), \tag{6.51}$$

where $\boldsymbol{k}_\tau$ and $\boldsymbol{k}'_{\tau'}$ are in general *not* the canonical wave vectors of their stars. We have then, the definition of each of the factors (Bloch functions) in terms of its canonical member [just as in (6.5)]:

$$\psi_{\mu}^{(\boldsymbol{k}_\tau)(j)} = P_{R_\tau}\psi_{\mu}^{(\boldsymbol{k})(j)}, \qquad \psi_{\mu'}^{(\boldsymbol{k}'_{\tau'})(j')} = P_{R_{\tau'}}\psi_{\mu'}^{(\boldsymbol{k}')(j')}. \tag{6.52a, b}$$

Construct the projection operator

$$P_{\mu''\nu''}^{(\boldsymbol{k}'')(j'')} = (l_{j''}/l_{\boldsymbol{k}''})\sum_{\alpha''} D^{(\boldsymbol{k}'')(j'')}(R_{\alpha''})^*_{\mu''\nu''}P_{R_{\alpha''}}, \tag{6.53}$$

where $P_{R_{\alpha''}}$ is a coset representative in $\mathscr{G}(k'')$, and the sum is over all such α''. Then applying this operator to the product functions we obtain:

$$\begin{aligned} P_{\mu''\nu''}^{(\boldsymbol{k}'')(j'')}\psi_{\mu}^{(\boldsymbol{k}_\tau)(j)}\psi_{\mu'}^{(\boldsymbol{k}'_{\tau'})(j')} &= (l_{j''}/l_{\boldsymbol{k}''})\sum_{\alpha''}\sum_{\bar{\mu}}\sum_{\bar{\mu}'} D^{(\boldsymbol{k}'')(j'')}(R_{\alpha''})^*_{\mu''\nu''} \\ &\times \dot{D}^{(\boldsymbol{k})(j)}(R_\sigma^{-1}R_{\alpha''}R_\tau)_{\bar{\mu}\mu}\,\dot{D}^{(\boldsymbol{k}')(j')}(R_{\sigma'}^{-1}R_{\alpha''}R_{\tau'})_{\bar{\mu}'\mu'}\,\psi_{\bar{\mu}}^{(\boldsymbol{k}_\sigma)(j)}\psi_{\mu'}^{(\boldsymbol{k}'_{\sigma'})(j')}. \end{aligned} \tag{6.54}$$

Clearly the dotted matrices are zero unless the element which is the argument is in the appropriate group $\mathscr{G}(\boldsymbol{k})$ or $\mathscr{G}(\boldsymbol{k}')$ respectively. And, we use the conventions

$$\boldsymbol{\phi}_{\alpha''}\cdot\boldsymbol{k}_\tau = \boldsymbol{k}_\sigma(\text{mod}\,\boldsymbol{B}_{\text{H}}), \qquad \boldsymbol{\phi}_{\alpha''}\cdot\boldsymbol{k}_{\tau'} = \boldsymbol{k}_{\sigma'}(\text{mod}\,\boldsymbol{B}'_{\text{H}}). \tag{6.55a, b}$$

Then, the Clebsch–Gordan coefficient is obtained from (3.39) and (3.40) as:

$$\left(\begin{matrix}\boldsymbol{k}_\tau j & \boldsymbol{k}'_{\tau'}j' \\ \bar{\mu} & \bar{\mu}'\end{matrix}\middle|\begin{matrix}\boldsymbol{k}'' \\ \mu''\end{matrix}\right) = N/D^{1/2}, \tag{6.56}$$

with

$$\begin{aligned} N = (l_{j''}/l_{\boldsymbol{k}''})\sum_{\alpha''} D^{(\boldsymbol{k}'')(j'')}(R_{\alpha''})^*_{\mu''\nu''} \\ \times \dot{D}^{(\boldsymbol{k})(j)}(R_\sigma^{-1}R_{\alpha''}R_\tau)_{\bar{\mu}\mu}\,\dot{D}^{(\boldsymbol{k}')(j')}(R_{\sigma'}^{-1}R_{\alpha''}R_{\tau'})_{\bar{\mu}'\mu'}, \end{aligned} \tag{6.57}$$

and

$$\begin{aligned} D \equiv (l_{j''}/l_{\boldsymbol{k}''})\sum_{\alpha''} D^{(\boldsymbol{k}'')(j'')}(R_{\alpha''})^*_{\nu''\nu''} \\ \times \dot{D}^{(\boldsymbol{k})(j)}(R_\tau^{-1}R_{\alpha''}R_\tau)_{\mu\mu}\,\dot{D}^{(\boldsymbol{k}')(j')}(R_{\tau'}^{-1}R_{\alpha''}R_{\tau'})_{\mu'\mu'}. \end{aligned} \tag{6.58}$$

In applying these formulae one can use the ray matrices to obtain the value of the dotted matrices as illustrated above. One needs to find a triplet $(\mu'' \mu \mu')$ such that the left hand side of (6.56) is non-zero and likewise one requires a non-zero value of D, to be achieved by selection of a suitable set of subscripts $(\nu'' \mu \mu')$. In these formulae $(\tau, \tau', \boldsymbol{k}''$ and $\mu = 1, \cdots, l_{j''})$ are assumed fixed.

6.5. Clebsch–Gordan series: reduction coefficient

It remains to determine the redundancy index γ. This is the number of distinct linear combinations of product wave-functions of identical type. It is also the reduction coefficient, or element, which arises in the Clebsch–Gordan series

$$D^{(*\boldsymbol{k})(j)} \otimes D^{(*\boldsymbol{k}')(j')} = \sum (*\boldsymbol{k}j \; *\boldsymbol{k}'j' \,|\, *\boldsymbol{k}''j'')\, D^{(*\boldsymbol{k}'')(j'')} \tag{6.59}$$

for the reduction of the direct product of two irreducible representations. Clearly, the numerical value of γ is exactly that coefficient.

One way to determine this coefficient is to use the well-known reduction formulae involving the full-group characters:

$$\begin{aligned}(*\boldsymbol{k}j \; *\boldsymbol{k}'j' \,|\, *\boldsymbol{k}''j'') \\ = (1/hN) \sum_{g} \sum_{\mathrm{L}} \chi^{(*\boldsymbol{k})(j)}(R_{g\mathrm{L}})\, \chi^{(*\boldsymbol{k}')(j')}(R_{g\mathrm{L}})\, \chi^{(*\boldsymbol{k}'')(j'')}(R_{g\mathrm{L}})^{*},\end{aligned} \tag{6.60}$$

where

$$R_{g\mathrm{L}} \equiv \{\boldsymbol{\phi}_g \,|\, \boldsymbol{\tau}_g + \boldsymbol{R}_{\mathrm{L}}\} \tag{6.61}$$

is a general space group operator, with $\boldsymbol{R}_{\mathrm{L}}$ a lattice translation, h is the order of the factor group (2.8) and N the order of the translation group $\mathscr{T}$. From (6.43) we obtain for the character which enters in (6.60)

$$\chi^{(*\boldsymbol{k})(j)}(R_{g\mathrm{L}}) = \sum_{\sigma} \dot{\chi}^{(\boldsymbol{k})(j)}(R_{\sigma}^{-1} R_{g\mathrm{L}} R_{\sigma}), \tag{6.62}$$

where R_{σ} is one of the fixed coset representatives in the decomposition of $\mathscr{G}$ with respect to $\mathscr{G}(\boldsymbol{k})$. The dotted character is

$$\begin{aligned}\dot{\chi}^{(\boldsymbol{k})(j)}(X) &= \chi^{(\boldsymbol{k})(j)}(X), \quad \text{if } X \text{ is in } \mathscr{G}(\boldsymbol{k}), \\ &= 0, \qquad\qquad\qquad \text{otherwise}.\end{aligned} \tag{6.63}$$

A typical term in (6.60) is the product

$$\dot{\chi}^{(\boldsymbol{k})(j)}(R_{\sigma}^{-1} R_g R_{\sigma})\, \dot{\chi}^{(\boldsymbol{k}')(j')}(R_{\sigma'}^{-1} R_g R_{\sigma'})\, \dot{\chi}^{(\boldsymbol{k}'')(j'')}(R_{\sigma''}^{-1} R_g R_{\sigma''})^{*}. \tag{6.64}$$

A little consideration shows that this term, summed over $\boldsymbol{R}_{\mathrm{L}}$ vanishes unless

$$\boldsymbol{k}''_{\sigma''} = \boldsymbol{k}'_{\sigma'} + \boldsymbol{k}_{\sigma} (\mathrm{mod}\, \boldsymbol{B}_{\mathrm{H}}). \tag{6.65}$$

Thus the only non-zero contributions to the reduction coefficient are those for which momentum conservation is satisfied. Further, the 'dots' restrict the arguments (elements) so that non-zero contributions only arise from elements $R_g \equiv \{\phi_g | \tau_g\}$ which have property

$$R_g \text{ is in } \mathscr{G}(\boldsymbol{k}''_{\sigma''}),\ \mathscr{G}(\boldsymbol{k}'_{\sigma'}) \text{ and } \mathscr{G}(\boldsymbol{k}_{\sigma}) \tag{6.66}$$

simultaneously.

Now let us *fix* a final wave vector $\boldsymbol{k}''$ and irreducible representation j'', and let $\boldsymbol{k}''$ be the canonical wave vector of its star. Let σ and σ' be such that

$$\boldsymbol{k}'' = \boldsymbol{k}_{\sigma} + \boldsymbol{k}_{\sigma'} (\mathrm{mod}\, \boldsymbol{B}'_{\mathrm{H}}), \tag{6.67}$$

and let $n_{\boldsymbol{k}''\boldsymbol{k}_{\sigma}}$ be the number of elements in common to the three groups $\mathscr{G}(\boldsymbol{k}'')$, $\mathscr{G}(\boldsymbol{k}_{\sigma})$ and $\mathscr{G}(\boldsymbol{k}'_{\sigma'})$ i.e. the order of the intersection group. Then we can define a subgroup reduction coefficient which gives the multiplicity of the fixed $\boldsymbol{k}''j''$ from all possible pairs of factors

$$(\{\boldsymbol{k}_{\sigma} + \boldsymbol{k}'_{\sigma'}\}\, jj' \,|\, \boldsymbol{k}''j''). \tag{6.68}$$

To determine this coefficient we select from the products on the right-hand side of (6.64) all those terms referring to the fixed final wave vector. This can be written

$$(1/g_{k''}) \sum_{g} \sum_{\sigma} \sum_{\sigma'} \dot{\chi}^{(\boldsymbol{k})(j)}(R_{\sigma}^{-1} R_g R_{\sigma})\, \dot{\chi}^{(\boldsymbol{k}')(j')}(R_{\sigma'}^{-1} R_g R_{\sigma'}) \times \dot{\chi}^{(\boldsymbol{k}'')(j'')}(R_g)^* \,\Delta(\boldsymbol{k}_{\sigma} + \boldsymbol{k}_{\sigma'} - \boldsymbol{k}''), \tag{6.69}$$

where

$$\Delta(\boldsymbol{k}) = 1, \quad \text{if} \quad \boldsymbol{k} = 0\, (\mathrm{mod}\, \boldsymbol{B}_{\mathrm{H}}), \qquad = 0, \quad \text{otherwise}. \tag{6.70}$$

The sum on g is now over all coset representatives R_g in $\mathscr{G}(\boldsymbol{k}'')$; and evidently we select the term with $\sigma''=1$, corresponding to fixed wave vector $\boldsymbol{k}''$. This expression can be still further manipulated formally, using the expression for the character of an element in terms of the ray representation characters. An illustration will be given below, and it will be seen that actual calculations are straightforward despite an apparent formal complexity.

7. *Illustration: point X_3 in diamond*

In this section we shall illustrate many of the important results previously given. Application to the lattice dynamics of non-symmorphic diamond space group O_h^7–Fd3m will be given. In particular an examination of the lattice dynamics at the zone edge point X_3 illustrates many of the interesting points, and permits discussion and analysis of physical processes involving the phonons with symmetry $^*X(j)$.

7.1. Symmetry operators

The diamond space group is based on two interpenetrating face-centered-cubic lattices. In table 1 we give the symmetry elements of the diamond space group. Note that half the coset representatives are associated with the fractional translation τ_1.

7.2. The wave vector X_3 and $\mathscr{G}(X_3)$

The wave vector we select for study is

$$X_3 = (0, 0, 2\pi)(1/a) = \tfrac{1}{2}(B_2 + B_3). \tag{7.1}$$

From table 1 we obtain the space group $\mathscr{G}(X_3)$, by selecting all operators in $\mathscr{G}$ which leave X_3 invariant mod B_H. Note that the space group $\mathscr{G}(X_3)$ is itself a non-symmorphic group: half the coset representatives are associated with τ_1. The space group $\mathscr{G}(X_3)$ consists of the translation group $\mathscr{T}$ combined with each of the coset representatives:

$$\{\phi|0\}: \{\varepsilon|0\}, \{\delta_{2z}|0\}, \{\delta_{2x}|0\}, \{\delta_{2y}|0\}, \\ \{\sigma_{4z}|0\}, \{\sigma_{4z}|0\}^{-1}, \{\rho_{xy}|0\}, \{\rho_{x\bar{y}}|0\} \tag{7.2}$$

and the product of each with $\{i|\tau_1\}$:

$$\{i\phi|\tau_1\}. \tag{7.3}$$

7.3. Ray representations of $\mathscr{G}(X_3)$

The factor group $\mathscr{G}(X_3)/\mathscr{T} = \mathscr{P}(X_3)$ is isomorphic to the point group D_{4h}. As an abstract group, the dihedral crystal point group D_{4h} can be described in terms of three generators A, B, C and certain relations. Thus if we make

TABLE 1

Rotational symmetry operations for diamond.

Type $\{\phi\|0\}$		Type $\{\phi\|\tau_1\}$	
ε	xyz	$\boldsymbol{i}$	$\bar{x}\bar{y}\bar{z}$
$\boldsymbol{\delta}_{2x}$	$x\bar{y}\bar{z}$	$\boldsymbol{\rho}_x$	$\bar{x}yz$
$\boldsymbol{\delta}_{2y}$	$\bar{x}y\bar{z}$	$\boldsymbol{\rho}_y$	$x\bar{y}z$
$\boldsymbol{\delta}_{2z}$	$\bar{x}\bar{y}z$	$\boldsymbol{\rho}_z$	$xy\bar{z}$
$\boldsymbol{\sigma}_{4x}$	$\bar{x}z\bar{y}$	$\boldsymbol{\delta}_{4x}$	$x\bar{z}y$
$(\boldsymbol{\sigma}_{4x})^{-1}$	$\bar{x}\bar{z}y$	$(\boldsymbol{\delta}_{4x})^{-1}$	$xz\bar{y}$
$\boldsymbol{\sigma}_{4y}$	$\bar{z}\bar{y}x$	$(\boldsymbol{\delta}_{4y})$	$zy\bar{x}$
$(\boldsymbol{\sigma}_{4y})^{-1}$	$z\bar{y}\bar{x}$	$(\boldsymbol{\delta}_{4y})^{-1}$	$\bar{z}yx$
$\boldsymbol{\sigma}_{4z}$	$y\bar{x}\bar{z}$	$\boldsymbol{\delta}_{4z}$	$\bar{y}xz$
$(\boldsymbol{\sigma}_{4z})^{-1}$	$\bar{y}x\bar{z}$	$(\boldsymbol{\delta}_{4z})^{-1}$	$y\bar{x}z$
$\boldsymbol{\rho}_{xy}$	$\bar{y}\bar{x}z$	$\boldsymbol{\delta}_{2xy}$	$yx\bar{z}$
$\boldsymbol{\rho}_{x\bar{y}}$	yxz	$\boldsymbol{\delta}_{2x\bar{y}}$	$\bar{y}\bar{x}\bar{z}$
$\boldsymbol{\rho}_{xz}$	$\bar{z}y\bar{x}$	$\boldsymbol{\delta}_{2xz}$	$z\bar{y}x$
$\boldsymbol{\rho}_{x\bar{z}}$	zyx	$\boldsymbol{\delta}_{2x\bar{z}}$	$\bar{z}\bar{y}\bar{x}$
$\boldsymbol{\rho}_{yz}$	$x\bar{z}\bar{y}$	$\boldsymbol{\delta}_{2yz}$	$\bar{x}zy$
$\boldsymbol{\rho}_{y\bar{z}}$	xzy	$\boldsymbol{\delta}_{2y\bar{z}}$	$\bar{x}\bar{z}\bar{y}$
$\boldsymbol{\delta}_{3xyz}$	yzx	$\boldsymbol{\sigma}_{6xyz}$	$\bar{y}\bar{z}\bar{x}$
$(\boldsymbol{\delta}_{3xyz})^{-1}$	zxy	$(\boldsymbol{\sigma}_{6xyz})^{-1}$	$\bar{z}\bar{x}\bar{y}$
$\boldsymbol{\delta}_{3\bar{x}\bar{y}z}$	$\bar{z}x\bar{y}$	$\boldsymbol{\sigma}_{6\bar{x}\bar{y}z}$	$z\bar{x}y$
$(\boldsymbol{\delta}_{3\bar{x}\bar{y}z})^{-1}$	$y\bar{z}\bar{x}$	$(\boldsymbol{\sigma}_{6\bar{x}\bar{y}z})^{-1}$	$\bar{y}zx$
$\boldsymbol{\delta}_{3\bar{x}y\bar{z}}$	$z\bar{x}\bar{y}$	$\boldsymbol{\sigma}_{6\bar{x}y\bar{z}}$	$\bar{z}xy$
$(\boldsymbol{\delta}_{3\bar{x}y\bar{z}})^{-1}$	$\bar{y}\bar{z}x$	$(\boldsymbol{\sigma}_{6\bar{x}y\bar{z}})^{-1}$	$yz\bar{x}$
$\boldsymbol{\delta}_{3x\bar{y}\bar{z}}$	$\bar{z}\bar{x}y$	$\boldsymbol{\sigma}_{6x\bar{y}\bar{z}}$	$zx\bar{y}$
$(\boldsymbol{\delta}_{3x\bar{y}\bar{z}})^{-1}$	$\bar{y}z\bar{x}$	$(\boldsymbol{\sigma}_{6x\bar{y}\bar{z}})^{-1}$	$y\bar{z}x$

Translation vectors:

$$\boldsymbol{t}_1 = (\tfrac{1}{2},\ \tfrac{1}{2},\ 0)\ a$$
$$\boldsymbol{t}_2 = (\tfrac{1}{2},\ 0,\ \tfrac{1}{2})\ a$$
$$\boldsymbol{t}_3 = (0,\ \tfrac{1}{2},\ \tfrac{1}{2})\ a$$
$$\boldsymbol{\tau}_1 \equiv (\tfrac{1}{4},\ \tfrac{1}{4},\ \tfrac{1}{4})\ a$$

Reciprocal set:

$$\boldsymbol{B}_1 \equiv (\ 1,\ \ 1,\ -1)\ (2\pi/a)$$
$$\boldsymbol{B}_2 = (\ 1,\ -1,\ \ 1)\ (2\pi/a)$$
$$\boldsymbol{B}_3 = (-1,\ \ 1,\ \ 1)\ (2\pi/a)$$

Crystal space lattice vector: $\boldsymbol{R}_{\mathrm{L}} = l_1\boldsymbol{t}_1 + l_2\boldsymbol{t}_2 + l_3\boldsymbol{t}_3$ (l_j integer)

Fourier space lattice vector: $\boldsymbol{B}_{\mathrm{H}} = h_1\boldsymbol{B}_1 + h_2\boldsymbol{B}_2 + h_3\boldsymbol{B}_3$ (h_j integer)

$$\boldsymbol{B}_i \cdot \boldsymbol{t}_j = 2\pi\delta_{ij}$$

the association:

$$A \sim \delta_{4z}, \quad B \sim \rho_y, \quad C \sim \rho_z \tag{7.4}$$

then the group is prescribed by

$$A^4 = B^2 = C^2 = E, \quad BA = A^3B, \quad CA = AC, \quad CB = BC. \tag{7.5}$$

The group is of order 16. However, as is seen in table 1, all the above listed rotations in (7.4) are combined with the fractional $\boldsymbol{\tau}_1$ in $\mathscr{G}(\boldsymbol{X}_3)$.

Recalling the discussion in section (6.1) it is necessary to determine the factor set λ, in order to determine acceptable irreducible ray representations of D_{4h}. Since the group can be specified by generators and relations we write down the factor set for $\boldsymbol{k}=\boldsymbol{X}_3$ corresponding to the generators listed in eq. (7.4). These are

$$\lambda(A^3, B) = \lambda(A, A) = \lambda(B, A) = \lambda(B, B) = \lambda(B, C) = \lambda(A, C) = -1 \tag{7.6}$$

and

$$\lambda(C, C) = \lambda(C, B) = \lambda(C, A) = +1. \tag{7.7}$$

The remaining factors can be easily obtained. Notice the effect of this factor set upon the defining relations in the ray representation $D^{(j)}$ of D_{4h}:

$$\begin{aligned} &D^{(j)}(A)\cdot D^{(j)}(A) = -D^{(j)}(A^2), \quad D^{(j)}(A^3)\cdot D^{(j)}(B) = -D^{(j)}(BA),\\ &D^{(j)}(B)\cdot D^{(j)}(B) = -D^{(j)}(E), \quad D^{(j)}(B)\cdot D^{(j)}(C) = -D^{(j)}(C)\cdot D^{(j)}(B),\\ &D^{(j)}(C)\cdot D^{(j)}(A) = -D^{(j)}(A)\cdot D^{(j)}(C). \end{aligned} \tag{7.8a–e}$$

The other relations are unchanged in $D^{(j)}$.

To determine a set of irreducible $D^{(j)}$ with the factor set as in eq. (7.8) is straightforward. The method is given elsewhere (Birman 1974) but in essence goes back to Schur. One constructs a covering group $^*\mathscr{P}$, corresponding to $\mathscr{P}$, such that $^*\mathscr{P}$ is the extension of $\mathscr{P}$ by an abelian group $\mathscr{A}$. Thus the irreducible ray representations of $\mathscr{P}$ are irreducible vector representations of $^*\mathscr{P}$, and can be easily identified. The program of finding all such extensions for the dihedral group was carried out by Schur.

A recent tabulation of the irreducible ray representations has been given by Kovalev (1965) and we find it convenient to take over his matrices. However, to utilize the Kovalev tables, it is necessary to make some change of factor set as illustrated in eq. (6.26). Observe that for wave vector $\boldsymbol{X}_3$ the phase factor is

$$\exp(-\mathrm{i}\boldsymbol{X}_3\cdot\boldsymbol{\tau}_1) = -\mathrm{i}. \tag{7.9}$$

Consequently the rule (6.26) becomes

$$D^{(\boldsymbol{k})(j)}(\{\phi_{X_3}|\tau_1\}) = -\mathrm{i}\hat{D}^{(j)}(\phi_{X_3}), \tag{7.10}$$

where $\hat{D}^{(j)}(\phi_{X_3})$ is a Kovalev matrix. Note that the factor $-\mathrm{i}$ multiplies *only* those matrices for coset representatives with fractional. A further relabelling is required owing to the fact that Kovalev's labelling of the irreducible representations is *not* the conventional one, as introduced by Herring (1942). The identification we use is as follows from table 159 of Kovalev's book: the Kovalev matrices are labelled $\hat{\tau}^{(j)}(h_\alpha)$ where $j=1, 2, 3, 4$ and h_α is a space group operator. Then for space group elements the correspondence is

$$\{\delta_{4_z}|\tau\} \to h_{14} \to A, \quad \{\rho_y|\tau\} \to h_{27} = B, \quad \{\rho_z|\tau\} \to h_{28} \to C. \tag{7.11–13}$$

For irreducible representations

$$D^{(X_3)(1)} \to \hat{\tau}^{(3)}, \quad D^{(X_3)(2)} \to \hat{\tau}^{(4)}, \quad D^{(X_3)(3)} \to \hat{\tau}^{(2)}, \quad D^{(X_3)(4)} \to \hat{\tau}^{(1)}. \tag{7.14a, b, c, d}$$

Recall that we use the symbol $D^{(\boldsymbol{k})(j)}$ and that $\boldsymbol{k}=\boldsymbol{X}_3$ corresponds to the particular labelling of the arms of $^*\boldsymbol{X}$ which we take as canonical. Then, in table 2 we give an enumeration of the matrices $D^{(\boldsymbol{k})(j)}$ for the generators in each of the allowable irreducible representations. These matrices multiply

TABLE 2

Matrices for irreducible representations at $\boldsymbol{X}_3$.

	$\{\delta_{4_z}\|\tau\}$	$\{\rho_y\|\tau\}$	$\{\rho_z\|\tau\}$
$D^{(X_3)(1)}$	$\begin{pmatrix}-\mathrm{i} & 0\\ 0 & \mathrm{i}\end{pmatrix}$	$\begin{pmatrix}-\mathrm{i} & 0\\ 0 & \mathrm{i}\end{pmatrix}$	$\begin{pmatrix}0 & -\mathrm{i}\\ \mathrm{i} & 0\end{pmatrix}$
$D^{(X_3)(2)}$	$\begin{pmatrix}-\mathrm{i} & 0\\ 0 & \mathrm{i}\end{pmatrix}$	$\begin{pmatrix}\mathrm{i} & 0\\ 0 & -\mathrm{i}\end{pmatrix}$	$\begin{pmatrix}0 & \mathrm{i}\\ -\mathrm{i} & 0\end{pmatrix}$
$D^{(X_3)(3)}$	$\begin{pmatrix}-1 & 0\\ 0 & 1\end{pmatrix}$	$\begin{pmatrix}0 & \mathrm{i}\\ \mathrm{i} & 0\end{pmatrix}$	$\begin{pmatrix}0 & \mathrm{i}\\ -\mathrm{i} & 0\end{pmatrix}$
$D^{(X_3)(4)}$	$\begin{pmatrix}-1 & 0\\ 0 & 1\end{pmatrix}$	$\begin{pmatrix}0 & -\mathrm{i}\\ -\mathrm{i} & 0\end{pmatrix}$	$\begin{pmatrix}0 & \mathrm{i}\\ -\mathrm{i} & 0\end{pmatrix}$

according to the correct rule for $D^{(k)(j)}$, so that given the matrices $D^{(k)(j)}(R_\alpha)$, $D^{(k)(j)}(R_\beta)$ for two such elements (e.g. two of the generators) the matrix for the product is

$$D^{(k)(j)}(R_{\alpha\beta}) = \lambda^{(k)}(\alpha, \beta)\, D^{(k)(j)}(R_\alpha)\, D^{(k)(j)}(R_\beta). \tag{7.15}$$

In this way the matrices for the entire representation can be obtained from those of the generators.

7.4. Phonon symmetry in diamond at X_3

We can now use the results of the previous sections to analyse the symmetry of phonons at X_3 in diamond. Recall the discussion of section 4 in which the projection operator technique was described. In application it is most convenient to proceed in two steps: first form a Bloch sum: i.e. a function symmetrized under the translation group $\mathscr{T}$; then apply a projection operator to obtain the function symmetrized according to allowable irreducible representation of $\mathscr{G}(X_3)$.

The basic set is the cartesian displacements. Owing to the two interpenetrating f.c.c. lattices there are 2 basis atoms: one centered at the origin 0, the other at τ. Correspondingly the 6 displacements $\Delta_\alpha(0)$, and $\Delta_\alpha(\tau)$, $\alpha = 1, 2, 3$ span a vector space for cell 0. From these we can define 6 Bloch sums

$$\psi_\alpha^{(k)}(0) = P^{(k)}\Delta_\alpha(0), \quad \alpha = 1, 2, 3; \tag{7.16a}$$

$$\psi_\alpha^{(k)}(\tau) = P^{(k)}\Delta_\alpha(\tau), \quad \alpha = 1, 2, 3, \tag{7.16b}$$

where $P^{(k)}$ is the projector which produces a Bloch function at wave vector $\boldsymbol{k}$:

$$P^{(k)} = N^{-1} \sum_{\mathrm{L}} D^{(k)}(\{\varepsilon|\boldsymbol{R}_\mathrm{L}\})^* \, P_{\{\varepsilon|-\boldsymbol{R}_\mathrm{L}\}}. \tag{7.17}$$

It is important to realize that the Bloch sums (7.16) are phased linear combinations of the cartesian components of displacements at each site. Under translation (i.e. application of translation operator $P_{\{\varepsilon|\boldsymbol{R}_\mathrm{M}\}}$) the Bloch sum is multiplied by the phase $\exp(\mathrm{i}\boldsymbol{k}\cdot\boldsymbol{R}_\mathrm{M})$.

To obtain the properly symmetrized function the projection operator $P_{\mu\nu}^{(k)(j)}$ is applied

$$P_{\mu\nu}^{(k)(j)} \cdot \psi_\nu^{(k)}(\kappa) = \psi_\mu^{(k)(j)}, \tag{7.18}$$

where κ labels the basis atom and $\kappa = 0$, or τ; then this produces a function belonging to the μth row of $D^{(\boldsymbol{k})(j)}$. Here

$$P^{(\boldsymbol{k})(j)}_{\mu\nu} = (l_j/g_k) \sum_{\alpha} D^{(\boldsymbol{k})(j)}(R_\alpha)^*_{\mu\nu}\, P_{R_\alpha}, \tag{7.19}$$

where g_k is the order of $\mathscr{P}(\boldsymbol{k})$ and R_α is an element (coset representative) in $\mathscr{P}(\boldsymbol{k})$. Again it is useful to observe the effect of a space group operator on a Bloch function $\psi^{(\boldsymbol{k})}_\alpha(\kappa)$ following our definition (2.21):

$$P_{\{\boldsymbol{\phi}_\lambda \mid \boldsymbol{\tau}_\lambda\}}\psi^{(\boldsymbol{k})}_\alpha(\kappa) = \sum_{\beta} \phi_{\alpha\beta}\psi^{(\boldsymbol{k})}_\beta(\boldsymbol{\phi}_\lambda^{-1}\cdot\boldsymbol{\kappa} - \boldsymbol{\phi}_\lambda^{-1}\cdot\boldsymbol{\tau}_\lambda). \tag{7.20}$$

Now note that all Bloch sums are to be related to the basic 6 given in (7.16). Hence if $\kappa = \boldsymbol{\tau}$ and the space group operator is such that $\boldsymbol{\tau}_\lambda = \boldsymbol{\tau}$ (i.e. for all coset representatives with fractional) then $\psi^{(\boldsymbol{k})}_\alpha(\boldsymbol{\tau})$ is sent into a linear combination of the $\psi^{(\boldsymbol{k})}_\beta(0)$. But, e.g. if $\kappa = 0$ and $\boldsymbol{\tau}_\lambda = \boldsymbol{\tau}$ then $\psi^{(\boldsymbol{k})}_\alpha(0)$ is sent into a linear combination of the $\psi^{(\boldsymbol{k})}_\beta(-\boldsymbol{\phi}_\lambda^{-1}\cdot\boldsymbol{\tau})$. In general $-\boldsymbol{\phi}_\lambda^{-1}\cdot\boldsymbol{\tau} = \boldsymbol{\tau} + \boldsymbol{R}_{\mathrm{M}}$, where $\boldsymbol{R}_{\mathrm{M}}$ is a non-zero lattice vector. Hence in that case attention must be paid to the phase which is introduced under translation: $\exp(\mathrm{i}\boldsymbol{X}_3\cdot\boldsymbol{R}_{\mathrm{M}}) = \pm 1$, this depends on the specific operation under consideration.

As a specific example, if we consider the transformation of the Bloch function $\psi_x(0)$ under the generator $\{\boldsymbol{\delta}_{4z} \mid \boldsymbol{\tau}\}$ we find

$$P_{\{\delta_{4z} \mid \boldsymbol{\tau}\}}\psi_x(0) = \psi_y(\boldsymbol{\tau}). \tag{7.21}$$

The reader may find it useful to verify this result, which involves cancellations of signs, etc.

From the matrices given in table 2 all matrices can be constructed and then all projection operators; and the symmetrized functions based on the symmetrized Bloch basis. The results, for the partners in the representations $D^{(\boldsymbol{x}_3)(j)}$ which appear are:

$$(j=1):\ \boldsymbol{e}(\boldsymbol{x}_3 \mid 1_1) = \psi_z(0) + \mathrm{i}\psi_z(\boldsymbol{\tau}),\quad \boldsymbol{e}(\boldsymbol{x}_3 \mid 1_2) = -\psi_z(0) + \mathrm{i}\psi_z(\boldsymbol{\tau}); \tag{7.22}$$

$$(j=3):\ \boldsymbol{e}(\boldsymbol{x}_3 \mid 3_1) = \psi_y(0) + \psi_x(\boldsymbol{\tau}),\quad \boldsymbol{e}(\boldsymbol{x}_3 \mid 3_2) = \mathrm{i}(\psi_x(0) + \psi_y(\boldsymbol{\tau})); \tag{7.23}$$

$$(j=4):\ \boldsymbol{e}(\boldsymbol{x}_3 \mid 4_1) = \psi_x(0) - \psi_y(\boldsymbol{\tau}),\quad \boldsymbol{e}(\boldsymbol{x}_3 \mid 4_2) = -\mathrm{i}(\psi_y(0) - \psi_x(\boldsymbol{\tau})); \tag{7.24}$$

This agrees with the well-known result that the mode symmetries which appear for phonons are (1)⊕(3)⊕(4), a result which can also be obtained in a more conventional way using the character tables only. Note that for this case the propagation or $\boldsymbol{k}$-vector is in the 'z' crystal direction and the two longitudinal modes are partners for representation (1), while the transverse modes are in (3) and (4).

7.5. Critical points at X_3

As shown in subsection 4.7, a sufficient condition for

$$\nabla_{k_\alpha}\omega(\boldsymbol{k}_0|j) = 0 \tag{7.25}$$

is if

$$D^{(\boldsymbol{k}_0)(j)*} \otimes D^{(\boldsymbol{k}_0)(\nabla_\alpha)} \otimes D^{(\boldsymbol{k}_0)(j)} \tag{7.26}$$

does not contain the identity representation. This would then produce a vanishing αth component of the gradient on branch j at $\boldsymbol{k}_0$, and hence one variety of critical point. In applying this test only the operators R_l in the intersection group $\mathscr{G}(\boldsymbol{k}_0) \cap \mathscr{G}(\nabla_\alpha)$ are considered. These are operations which simultaneously leave $\boldsymbol{k}_0$ and ∇_α invariant. The operations R_l which transform $\boldsymbol{k}_0$ into a vector equivalent to $\boldsymbol{k}_0$ (mod $\boldsymbol{B}_\mathrm{H}$) are dealt with a little later (vide infra). The most straightforward way to proceed is to determine $D^{(\boldsymbol{k}_0)(\nabla_\alpha)}$, this is the representation by which ∇_α transforms. Evidently ∇_α is an object at wave vector $\boldsymbol{\Gamma}$ so that the product

$$D^{(\boldsymbol{k}_0)(\nabla_\alpha)} \otimes D^{(\boldsymbol{k}_0)(j)}$$

can be reduced into a sum of irreducible representations at $\boldsymbol{k}_0$. It follows in the usual way that $D^{(\boldsymbol{k}_0)(j)*} \otimes D^{(\boldsymbol{k}_0)(\bar{j})}$ will only contain the identity if $j=\bar{j}$.

To find critical points at X_3 a natural cartesian system is the crystal xyz-system. It is necessary then to determine the representation appropriate to ∇_x, ∇_y, ∇_z (since ∇_{k_α} transform similarly) under the operations in the point group $\mathrm{D_{4h}}$. A précis of the relevant parts of character tables is given in table 3. This character table was obtained from the full matrices for all ele-

TABLE 3

Critical points at X_3 in diamond.

R_l \ $X_3(j)$	$j=1$	$j=2$	$j=3$	$j=4$	∇_z	(∇_y, ∇_x)
$\{\varepsilon\|\boldsymbol{0}\}=h_1$	2	2	2	2	1	2
$\{\delta_{2z}\|\boldsymbol{0}\}=h_4$	2	2	−2	−2	1	−2
$\{\delta_{2x\bar{y}}\|\boldsymbol{\tau}\}=h_{13}$	0	0	−2	2	−1	0
$\{\delta_{2xy}\|\boldsymbol{\tau}\}=h_{16}$	0	0	2	−2	−1	0
$\{\rho_{x\bar{y}}\|\boldsymbol{0}\}=h_{37}$	2	−2	0	0	1	0
$\{\rho_{xy}\|\boldsymbol{0}\}=h_{40}$	2	−2	0	0	1	0

ments in $\mathscr{G}(X_3)$, using the partial information already given to generate all needed matrices: the characters of all other coset representatives vanish.

First consider the situation for the modes $X_3(1)$ which are the longitudinal modes. From the table

$$\nabla_z \otimes X_3(1) = X_3(1), \tag{7.27}$$

so that

$$X_3(1) \otimes \nabla_z \otimes X_3(1) \sim \Gamma(1+), \tag{7.28}$$

where $\Gamma(1+)$ is the identity representation. Hence the slope of the longitudinal phonon branch $X_3(1)$ is non-zero in the longitudinal direction. Using the eigenvectors of (7.22–4) as basis we can go further. Thus assume that the eigenvectors $e(X_3|1_\mu)$ are preserved as we move away from X_3 in the direction ∇_z toward $\Gamma = 000$. Then, the slopes on the two branches can be shown to be negatives of each other. To prove this consider the slope on the branch corresponding to eigenvector $e(X_3|1_1)$ which is in first-order perturbation theory the scalar product:

$$\nabla_z \omega(X_3|1_1) \sim e(X_3|1_1)^* \cdot (\xi \cdot \nabla_z D(X_3))\, e(X_3|1_1). \tag{7.29}$$

Now transform this scalar product by the operator $h_{15} = \{i|\tau\}$ which sends

$$\nabla_z \to -\nabla_z; \quad e(X_3|1_1) \to e(X_3|1_2) = -e(X_3|1_1)^*, \tag{7.30}$$

then after transformation

$$\begin{aligned} \nabla_z \omega(X_3|1_1) &\sim e(X_3|1_2)^* \cdot (\xi \cdot \nabla_{-z} D(X_3))\, e(X_3|1_2) \\ &= -\, e(X_3|1_2)^* (\xi \cdot \nabla_z D(X_3))\, e(X_3|1_2) \\ &= -\, \nabla_z \omega(X_3|1_2). \end{aligned} \tag{7.31}$$

Thus the longitudinal slope on branch $X_3(1)$ is non-zero, and in fact the slopes on the two branches into which $X_3(1)$ splits are equal and opposite as the branches come together to form the doubly degenerate longitudinal mode $X_3(1)$. Hence the longitudinal slope is discontinuous at X_3.

Now consider the transverse slopes. We have

$$(\nabla_x, \nabla_y) \otimes X_3(1) = X_3(3) \oplus X_3(4), \tag{7.32}$$

so that

$$X_3(1) \otimes (\nabla_x, \nabla_y) \otimes X_3(1) \not\approx \Gamma(1+), \tag{7.33}$$

the slope vanishes on this branch in the two transverse directions.

The conclusion of this analysis, which was evidently carried out entirely group theoretically is that the longitudinal $X_3\,(1)$ branch has a singular critical point at the X_3 point: the slope vanishes in two transverse directions, and is discontinuous in the longitudinal direction.

Using the information in table 3 one finds also that the two remaining pairs of degenerate branches corresponding to modes $X_3\,(3)$ and $X_3\,(4)$ have both got vanishing gradients in all three directions so they are ordinary analytic critical points.

7.6. Factorization of the dynamical matrix at X_3

Following the general discussion in subsections 4.4, and 4.5 we shall illustrate how a complete factorization of the dynamical matrix at X_3 in diamond can be achieved. One of the key results to be used is eq. (4.68) which is

$$D^{(\boldsymbol{k})\,(e)}(R_l)\,D(\boldsymbol{k})^* = D(\boldsymbol{k})^*\,D^{(\boldsymbol{k})\,(e)}(R_l), \tag{7.34}$$

where $D^{(\boldsymbol{k})\,(e)}(R_l)$ is the matrix representative associated with operation R_l in $\mathscr{G}(X_3)$ based on the eigenvectors, and $D(\boldsymbol{k})=D(X_3)$ is the dynamical matrix at X_3. The use of this equation can be illustrated by assuming the most general form for $D(X_3)$ then determining the restrictions which are consequences of eq. (7.34) as R_l runs through all elements in $\mathscr{P}(X_3)$.

The most general $D(X_3)$ in diamond is a 6×6 hermitian matrix:

$$D_{\alpha\beta}(X_3\,|\,\mathbf{0},\,\boldsymbol{\tau}) = D_{\beta\alpha}(X_3\,|\,\boldsymbol{\tau},\,\mathbf{0})^*\,. \tag{7.35}$$

To use (7.34) we construct the three matrices $D^{(\boldsymbol{k})\,(e)}(R_l)$ for $R_l=h_{14},\,h_{27},\,h_{28}$ which are the three generators of $\mathscr{G}(X_3)$. In table 4 the information needed to construct the full matrix for each R_l is given. Recall that $D^{(\boldsymbol{k})\,(e)}(R_l)$ has matrix elements $D^{(\boldsymbol{k})\,(e)}(R_l)_{\alpha\kappa;\,\beta\kappa'}$. Here $(\alpha\kappa)$ and $(\beta\kappa')$ stand for one of the six Bloch sums defined in eq. (7.16). In the table each row represents one fixed element R_l. The column head in the table is $(\alpha\kappa)$. Then the entry in the row

TABLE 4

Matrices $D^{(\boldsymbol{k})\,(e)}(R_l)$.

R_l	$\beta\kappa'$ \ $\alpha\kappa$	$\psi_1(0)$	$\psi_2(0)$	$\psi_3(0)$	$\psi_1(\tau)$	$\psi_2(\tau)$	$\psi_3(\tau)$
$\{\delta_{4z}\|\tau\}=h_{14}$		$\psi_2(\tau)$	$-\psi_1(\tau)$	$-\psi_3(\tau)$	$-\psi_2(0)$	$\psi_1(0)$	$\psi_3(0)$
$\{\rho_y\|\tau\}=h_{27}$		$-\psi_1(\tau)$	$\psi_2(\tau)$	$-\psi_2(\tau)$	$\psi_1(0)$	$-\psi_2(0)$	$\psi_3(0)$
$\{\rho_z\|\tau\}=h_{28}$		$\psi_1(\tau)$	$\psi_2(\tau)$	$-\psi_3(\tau)$	$\psi_1(0)$	$\psi_2(0)$	$-\psi_3(0)$

in the table is the only non-zero entry $(\beta\kappa')$ in the row $(\alpha\kappa)$ of the matrix. In this fashion we find the following non-zero elements of the dynamical matrix:

$$D_{xx}(X_3\,|\,0, 0) = D_{yy}(X_3\,|\,0, 0) = D_{xx}(X_3\,|\,\tau, \tau) = D_{yy}(X_3\,|\,\tau, \tau), \tag{7.36}$$

$$D_{zz}(X_3\,|\,0, 0) = D_{zz}(X_3\,|\,\tau, \tau), \tag{7.37}$$

and

$$D_{xy}(X_3\,|\,\mathbf{0}, \tau) = D_{yx}(X_3\,|\,\mathbf{0}, \tau) = D_{xy}(X_3\,|\,\tau, \mathbf{0}) = D_{yx}(X_3\,|\,\tau, \mathbf{0}). \tag{7.38}$$

All other elements of $[\boldsymbol{D}(\boldsymbol{X}_3)]$ are zero.

The second step follows eq. (4.72). From the previous sub-section the eigenvectors have been determined, and therefore the matrix $\boldsymbol{E}(\boldsymbol{k})$. Recall that this follows because each symmetry species $D^{(\boldsymbol{k})(j)}$ appears only once in the denumeration of phonons at $\boldsymbol{X}_3$, so the eigenvectors are completely determined by symmetry. Then

$$\boldsymbol{E}(\boldsymbol{X}_3)^{-1}\,[\boldsymbol{D}(\boldsymbol{X}_3)]\,\boldsymbol{E}(\boldsymbol{X}_3) = \boldsymbol{\Delta}(\boldsymbol{X}_3) \tag{7.39}$$

the eigenvalues can be immediately read off. We find each eigenvalue is double and

$$\omega^2(X_3\,|\,1) = 2D_{zz}(X_3\,|\,\tau, \tau), \tag{7.40}$$

$$\omega^2(X_3\,|\,3) = 2\,[D_{xx}(X_3\,|\,\mathbf{0}, \mathbf{0}) + D_{xy}(X_3\,|\,\mathbf{0}, \tau)], \tag{7.41}$$

$$\omega^2(X_3\,|\,4) = 2\,[D_{xx}(X_3\,|\,\mathbf{0}, \mathbf{0}) - D_{xy}(X_3\,|\,\mathbf{0}, \tau)]. \tag{7.42}$$

This represents the complete solution of the dynamical problem at wavevector $\boldsymbol{X}_3$ in diamond structure. Evidently group theory has permitted a complete solution.

Contact can now be made with other treatments. For example on a near-neighbor-only model with two force constants α and β we identify

$$2\alpha/M = D_{xx}(X_3\,|\,0, 0) = D_{zz}(X_3\,|\,\mathbf{0}, \mathbf{0}), \tag{7.43}$$

$$-\,2\beta/M = D_{xy}(X_3\,|\,\mathbf{0}, \tau), \tag{7.44}$$

so

$$M\omega^2(X_3\,|\,1) = 4\alpha, \qquad \text{LO + LA}; \tag{7.45}$$

$$M\omega^2(X_3\,|\,3) = 4(\alpha - \beta), \qquad \text{TA}; \tag{7.46}$$

$$M\omega^2(X_3\,|\,4) = 4(\alpha + \beta), \qquad \text{TO}. \tag{7.47}$$

If α and $\beta > 0$ and $\beta > \frac{1}{2}\alpha$ the order of the states at $\boldsymbol{X}_3$ in Ge and Si is obtained; the situation in diamond is different (Herman 1959).

7.7 Connectivity of representations at X_3

The changes of labelling of representations appropriate to phonons in the direction $(0, 0, \kappa) = \Delta_3$ near X_3 provides an important illustration of the connectivity, discussed in subsection 4.6. In table 5 the relevant parts of the character table for allowable irreducible representations of $\mathcal{G}(X_3)$ and of $\mathcal{G}(\Delta_3)$ are given: these parts are adequate to the determinations we shall make.

TABLE 5

Character table for connectivity at X_3 [$\omega \equiv \exp(-\frac{1}{4}i\kappa a)$].

	$X_3(j)$				$\Delta_3(j)$				
R_e	$j=1$	2	3	4	$j=1$	2	2′	1′	5
$\{\varepsilon\|0\}$	2	2	2	2	1	1	1	1	2
$\{\delta_{2z}\|0\}$	2	3	-2	-2	1	1	1	1	-2
$\{\delta_{4z}\|\tau\}$	0	0	0	0	ω	$-\omega$	$-\omega$	ω	0
$\{\delta_{4z}^{-1}\|\tau\}$	0	0	0	0	ω	$-\omega$	$-\omega$	ω	0
$\{\rho_x\|\tau\}$	0	0	0	0	ω	ω	$-\omega$	$-\omega$	0
$\{\rho_y\|\tau\}$	0	0	0	0	ω	ω	$-\omega$	$-\omega$	0
$\{\rho_{x\bar{y}}\|0\}$	2	-2	0	0	1	-1	1	-1	0
$\{\rho_{xy}\|0\}$	2	-2	0	0	1	-1	1	-1	0

Observe that in the direction Δ_3 the only symmetry elements in $\mathcal{G}(\Delta_3)$ are those which leave Δ_3 strictly invariant: the remaining elements in $\mathcal{G}(X_3)$ send Δ_3 into its negative. Thus $\mathcal{G}(\Delta_3)$ is a subgroup of index 2 of $\mathcal{G}(X_3)$. The group $\mathcal{P}(\Delta_3)$ is isomorphic to the point group C_{4v}. Consequently we can first consider the representation subduced on $\mathcal{P}(\Delta_3)$ by the allowable irreducible representations of $\mathcal{P}(X_3)$. By direct inspection of the character table 5 we find

$$X_3(1) \to \Delta_3(1) \oplus \Delta_3(2'), \quad X_3(2) \to \Delta_3(2) \oplus \Delta_3(1'), \tag{7.48, 49}$$

$$X_3(3) \to \Delta_3(5), \quad X_3(4) \to \Delta_3(5). \tag{7.50, 51}$$

Thus the LO–LA branch $X_3(1)$ splits as we leave X_3 in the direction Δ_3, while the TO and TA branches remain degenerate. If it were useful the eigenvectors for representations $\Delta_3(1)$ and $\Delta_3(2')$ could be uniquely determined, since they occur only once; for $\Delta_3(5)$ there is ambiguity owing to the evident multiplicity.

Consider now the situation when the wave-vector $\boldsymbol{\Delta}_3 \to \boldsymbol{X}_3$, then increases, and is prolonged beyond $\boldsymbol{X}_3$ in the same direction. Clearly, since $\boldsymbol{X}_3$ is equivalent to $-\boldsymbol{X}_3$ we can trace the situation by having the wave vector re-enter the diametrically opposite face. Now

$$-\boldsymbol{\Delta}_3 = \boldsymbol{\Delta}_3 - (\boldsymbol{B}_2 + \boldsymbol{B}_3), \tag{7.52}$$

where

$$\boldsymbol{B}_2 + \boldsymbol{B}_3 = (0, 0, 4\pi/a). \tag{7.53}$$

Thus

$$(0, 0, -\kappa) = (0, 0, \kappa) - (0, 0, 4\pi/a). \tag{7.54}$$

However, when

$$\kappa \to -\kappa = \kappa - 4\pi/a, \tag{7.55}$$

then

$$\omega \to -\omega = \omega^*. \tag{7.56}$$

Consulting table 5 this implies certain changes in the one dimensional representations epitomized by

$$(1) \to (2'), \quad (2) \to (1'). \tag{7.57a, b}$$

There are several equivalent ways of interpreting this result. A continuous cycle of the representations can be defined (Herring 1942) such that one has starting from $\boldsymbol{\Gamma}$

$$\begin{aligned} &\boldsymbol{\Gamma}(15-) \to \boldsymbol{\Delta}_3(1) \to \boldsymbol{X}_3(1) \to -\boldsymbol{\Delta}_3(2') \\ &\qquad \to \boldsymbol{\Gamma}(25+) \to \boldsymbol{\Delta}_3(2') \to \boldsymbol{X}_3(1) \to \boldsymbol{\Gamma}(15-). \end{aligned} \tag{7.58}$$

A completed (closed) cycle requires two traverses of the first Brillouin zone. The same result is obtained if the pair (2), (1′) is considered.

Alternatively, consider the prolongation of the vector as defining a state in the second Brillouin zone. Then, the interpretation which is appropriate follows from the relation given in eq. (4.111):

$$\omega(\boldsymbol{\Delta}_3 + (\boldsymbol{B}_2 + \boldsymbol{B}_3) \,|\, 1) = \omega(\boldsymbol{\Delta}_3 \,|\, 2'). \tag{7.59}$$

This can be interpreted as: the frequency of mode of species (branch) $j=1$ in the second zone equals the frequency of mode $j=2'$ in the first zone. The second interpretation has been of recent importance in properly assigning selection rules for intervalley scattering by phonons in silicon (Rode 1972, Streitwolf 1970, Lax and Birman 1972).

7.8. Induced full group representations $^*X(j)$

The allowable full group irreducible representations corresponding to wave vector X_3 can be obtained by the induction procedure given in subsection 6.2. In terms of the space group $\mathcal{G}(X_3)$ the space group is decomposed as

$$\mathcal{G} = \mathcal{G}(X_3) + \{\delta_{3xyz}|0\}\,\mathcal{G}(X_3) + \{\delta_{3xyz}^{-1}|0\}\,\mathcal{G}(X_3). \tag{7.60}$$

Then the complete character table for irreducible representations $^*X(j)$ can be obtained from the formula (6.62), (6.63) in terms of the dotted characters. In the present case the coset representatives $\{\phi_\sigma|0\}$ are given above so that it merely remains to work out the conjugates which are the arguments of the dotted characters. Conventional multiplication tables are available giving the products of rotational elements (Kovalev 1965) so we shall not give any details, but merely remark that attention must be paid to the phases which may be introduced in the transformation.

TABLE 6

Abbreviated character table for $\Gamma(j)$ and $^*X(j)$.

	$\{\varepsilon\|0\}$	$\{\delta_{2x}\|0\}$	$\{\rho_{x\bar{y}}\|0\}$	$\{\sigma_{4z}\|0\}$	$\{\delta_{3xyz}\|0\}$	$\{i\|\tau\}$	$\{\rho_x\|\tau\}$	$\{\delta_{2xy}\|\tau\}$	$\{\delta_{4z}\|\tau\}$	$\{\sigma_{6xyz}\|\tau\}$
$\Gamma(1\pm)$	1	1	±1	±1	1	±1	±1	1	1	±1
$\Gamma(2\pm)$	1	1	∓1	∓1	1	±1	±1	-1	-1	±1
$\Gamma(12\pm)$	2	2	0	0	-1	±2	±2	0	0	±1
$\Gamma(15\pm)$	3	-1	∓1	±1	0	±3	∓1	-1	1	0
$\Gamma(25\pm)$	3	-1	±1	∓1	0	±3	∓1	1	-1	0
$^*X(1)$	6	2	2	0	0	0	0	0	0	0
$^*X(2)$	6	2	-2	0	0	0	0	0	0	0
$^*X(3)$	6	-2	0	0	0	0	0	-2	0	0
$^*X(4)$	6	-2	0	0	0	0	0	2	0	0

In table 6 results are given for the full group characters of certain elements in $\mathcal{G}$ in the irreducible representations $^*X(j)$ and $\Gamma(j)$. The reader can verify these results to consolidate his understanding. Some more details which may be helpful are given in Birman (1974).

7.9. Some selection rules

The contents of table 6 can be used in a variety of ways. One important use is to obtain a part of the Clebsch–Gordan series for products such as

$$^*\boldsymbol{X}(j) \otimes {}^*\boldsymbol{X}(j'). \tag{7.61}$$

Since the basis for the direct product representation is the product space, as discussed in subsection 6.4, we immediately realize that in the reduction of the direct product above there will appear representations (inter alia) at $\boldsymbol{\Gamma}$. A basis for these is the products diagonal in wave vector like

$$\psi^{(\mathbf{X}_\alpha)\,(j)}\psi^{(\mathbf{X}_\alpha)\,(j')}, \quad \alpha = 1, 2, 3, \tag{7.62}$$

since

$$2\boldsymbol{X}_\alpha = \boldsymbol{\Gamma}. \tag{7.63}$$

There will also appear representations at $^*\boldsymbol{X}$, since

$$\boldsymbol{X}_\alpha + \boldsymbol{X}_\beta = \boldsymbol{X}_\gamma + \boldsymbol{B}_{\mathrm{H}} \quad (\alpha \neq \beta \neq \gamma). \tag{7.64}$$

An example of a reduction which is an easy consequence of the character table (table 6) is

$$\begin{aligned} {}^*\boldsymbol{X}(3) \otimes {}^*\boldsymbol{X}(4) = {} & \boldsymbol{\Gamma}(2+) \oplus \boldsymbol{\Gamma}(2-) \oplus \boldsymbol{\Gamma}(12+) \oplus \boldsymbol{\Gamma}(12-) \oplus \boldsymbol{\Gamma}(15+) \\ & \oplus \boldsymbol{\Gamma}(15-) \oplus {}^*\boldsymbol{X}(1) \oplus {}^*\boldsymbol{X}(2) \oplus {}^*\boldsymbol{X}(3) \oplus {}^*\boldsymbol{X}(4). \end{aligned} \tag{7.65}$$

All products of type (7.61) as well as

$$\boldsymbol{\Gamma}(j) \otimes {}^*\boldsymbol{X}(j') \tag{7.66}$$

can be found from the entries in table 6. A complete tabulation is available (Birman 1962, 1974).

7.10. Optical two-phonon processes at $^*X$

We can now examine important optical processes related to the phonons of symmetry $^*\boldsymbol{X}(j)$. To be specific we examine certain of the optically permitted phonon processes.

The first crucial point is to analyze the symmetry of the ingredients of the process. Following the discussion in subsection 5.3 we require the symmetry of the initial and final states and of the perturbation operator H' of eq. (5.60). A more detailed justification from first principles of the results to be cited below is available in the literature so we shall be brief.

For an optical infrared (dipole allowed) transition, the perturbation hamiltonian H' which represents the coupling of induced electric moment to the electric field of the electromagnetic wave, can be taken to be an object with 3 components

$$\{H'\} \sim \boldsymbol{M}(\boldsymbol{R}, \boldsymbol{k}), \tag{7.67}$$

where $\boldsymbol{R}$ represents the set of ion coordinates, $\boldsymbol{k}$ is the photon wave vector and $\boldsymbol{M}$ a three component object. Examination of the microscopic derivation of (7.67) shows that $\boldsymbol{M}$ transforms as a polar vector (tensor of the first rank) field as given in eq. (2.21). Then

$$H' \sim D^{(\boldsymbol{v})(\boldsymbol{k})}, \tag{7.68}$$

that is the perturbation transforms as a polar vector does under the operations of the group. Depending on the group, $D^{(\boldsymbol{v})(\boldsymbol{k})}$ may be already an irreducible tensor field, or may be decomposed into a sum of such, as discussed in subsection 5.3.

For a Raman scattering process by phonons the perturbation hamiltonian which represents a charge deformation or polarizability induced coupling can be taken to be an object which transforms as a symmetric second rank tensor operator which depends on $\boldsymbol{R}$ and on incident and scattered photon wave vectors $\boldsymbol{k}_1$ and $\boldsymbol{k}_2$ respectively. Then

$$H'' \sim D_{\text{sym}}^{(\boldsymbol{vv})(\boldsymbol{k}_1\boldsymbol{k}_2)}. \tag{7.69}$$

In the microscopic theory these results for H' and H'' are seen to be only approximate: here they are adequate for our purposes.

In diamond, taking all photon wave vectors as zero

$$H' \sim \boldsymbol{\Gamma}(15-), \qquad H'' \sim \boldsymbol{\Gamma}(1+) \oplus \boldsymbol{\Gamma}(12+) \oplus \boldsymbol{\Gamma}(25+). \tag{7.70, 71}$$

We are neglecting all spatial dispersion or wavelength-dependent effects, and assuming all photons away from resonance.

Now we consider the symmetry of initial and final states. As long as we work in the harmonic approximation the results of subsection 5.2 apply. Initial and final state eigenfunctions will be of type shown in eq. (5.31) and the symmetry of the state is then given in the discussion terminating at eq. (5.56).

As a specific case consider the possibility of optical transitions from the ground state of the lattice with all $n_j = 0$ and symmetry $\boldsymbol{\Gamma}(1+)$ to the excited state with two phonons present:

$$^*\boldsymbol{X}(3) \otimes {}^*\boldsymbol{X}(4) = \text{TA} \oplus \text{TO}. \tag{7.72}$$

In this excited state there will be two phonons, one of them in the manifold $^*\boldsymbol{X}(3)$, another in $^*\boldsymbol{X}(4)$. It is important to realize the impossibility of establishing *which* state in each manifold is occupied owing to the degeneracy of all states in the manifold. The excited state, with two phonons present, transforms as the product $^*\boldsymbol{X}(3)\otimes{}^*\boldsymbol{X}(4)$ which we have just reduced in eq. (7.65).

In the notation of eq. (5.57) we have for the symmetry of initial lattice state

$$|\mathrm{i}\rangle \sim \boldsymbol{\Gamma}(1+) \tag{7.73}$$

and final state

$$|\mathrm{f}\rangle \sim {}^*\boldsymbol{X}(3) \otimes {}^*\boldsymbol{X}(4). \tag{7.74}$$

For the infrared absorption the perturbation is H' of eq. (7.43), while for Raman scattering it is H'' of (7.43). The reduction of the direct product in the final state was carried out in eq. (7.65).

The matrix elements

$$\langle \mathrm{f}|\,\boldsymbol{\Gamma}(15-)\,|\mathrm{i}\rangle \neq 0, \tag{7.75a}$$

and

$$\langle \mathrm{f}|\,\boldsymbol{\Gamma}(12+)\,|\mathrm{i}\rangle \neq 0. \tag{7.75b}$$

Thus it is clear that the transition from vibrational ground state to this

$$\mathrm{TA} + \mathrm{TO} = {}^*\boldsymbol{X}(3) \otimes {}^*\boldsymbol{X}(4) \tag{7.76}$$

is allowed in infrared absorption. It is also allowed in Raman scattering in the polarization of incident and scattered photon which corresponds to $\boldsymbol{\Gamma}(12+)$.

It should be pointed out that the same selection rule as in eq. (7.75) applies to a process in which we have $|\mathrm{i}\rangle={}^*\boldsymbol{X}(3)$ and $|\mathrm{f}\rangle={}^*\boldsymbol{X}(4)$ i.e. in which a TA phonon at $^*\boldsymbol{X}$ is destroyed and a TO created. Evidently the earlier two phonon addition process corresponds to photon energy

$$\omega({}^*\boldsymbol{X}\,|\,3) + \omega({}^*\boldsymbol{X}\,|\,4), \tag{7.77}$$

while the latter is a two phonon difference process requiring photon energy

$$\omega({}^*\boldsymbol{X}\,|\,4) - \omega({}^*\boldsymbol{X}\,|\,3). \tag{7.78}$$

All the other multiphonon processes involving states $\boldsymbol{\Gamma}(j)$ and $^*\boldsymbol{X}(j')$ can be treated in this fashion using table 6. Again remark that many other illustrations are given in the references especially in Birman (1974) and, also Berenson (1974).

Acknowledgement

I wish to thank Prof. R. Fox for permitting me to adapt a title used by him. I also thank Ms. R. Berenson for her assistance.

This work was supported in part by the Army Research Office, Durham, and the National Science Foundation.

References

Berenson, R. (1974), *Theory and applications of crystal Clebsch–Gordan coefficients* (Ph. D. Thesis, New York University, Phys. Dept.). This thesis contains many coefficients for diamond, replacing the work of Novosadov et al. (1969, 1970) which seems to contain errors.

Birman, J.L. (1962), Phys. Rev. **127**, 1093.

Birman, J.L. (1973), *Symmetry changes in continuous phase transitions in crystals, Group Theor. Methods in Phys.* Netherlands Colloq. 1973. Proc. ed. by T. Janssen and A. Janner, and references therein.

Birman, J.L. (1974), *Space group theory and infra-red and Raman optical processes in crystals*, Handbuch d. Physik, Vol. 25/2b.

Born, M. and Huang, K. (1954), *Dynamical theory of crystal lattices*, Oxford University Press.

Cornwall, J.F. (1970), Phys. Stat. Sol. **37**, 225.

Frei, V. (1966), Czech. J. of Physics **16**, 207.

Herman, F.J. (1959), J. Phys. Chem. Solids **8**, 405.

Herring, C. (1942), J. Franklin Inst. **233**, 525.

Huang, K. (1962), Z. für Physik **171**, 213.

Hurley, A.C. (1966), Phil. Trans. Roy. Soc. (London) **260**, 1.

International tables for X-ray crystallography, Vol. 1. Published for the Intern. Union of Crystall. by Kynoch Press, Birmingham England (1952). Ed. by N.F.M. Henry, Kathleen Lonsdale.

Klein, B. (1969), *Theory of phonon spectra in V_3Si*, Ph.D. Thesis, Physics Dep., New York Univ.

Koster, G.F. (1958), Phys. Rev. **109**, 227.

Kovalev, O.V. (1965), *Irreducible representations of space groups* (Engl. Transl. Gordon and Breach Publ., N.Y.

Landau, L.D. and Lifshitz, I.M. (1958), *Quantum mechanics, non-relativistic theory.* (Addison Wesley Publ.).

Lax, M. and Birman, J.L. (1972), Phys. Stat. Solidi. **(b)49**, K153.

Litvin, D.B. and Zak, J. (1968), J. Math. Phys. **9**, 212.

Maradudin, A.A., Montroll, E., Weiss, G. and Ipatova, I.P. (1971), *Theory of lattice dynamics in the harmonic approximation*, Sec. Ed., Academic Press, N.Y.

Maradudin, A.A. and Vosko, S.H. (1968), Rev. Mod. Phys. **40**, 1.

Novosadov, B.K., Saulevich, L.K., Sviridov, D.T. and Smirnov, Y.F. (1969), Soviet Physics, Doklady **14**, 50.

NOVOSADOV, B.K., SAULEVICH, L.K., SVIRIDOV, D.T., and SMIRNOV, Y.F. (1970), Soviet Physics Crystall. **15**, 351 and 355.

RODE, D. (1972), Phys Stat. Solidi **(b)53**, 245.

STREITWOLF, H. (1970), Phys. Stat. Solidi K47, 37.

TISZA, L. (1933), Z. für Physik **82**, 48.

WESSON, R. (1970), *Ultrasonic dispersion in* $SrTiO_3$. Ph.D. Thesis, Physics Dep. New York Univ.

WIGNER, E.P. (1959), *Group theory and its application to the quantum mechanics of atomic spectra*, Academic Press, N.Y.

CHAPTER 3

Phenomenological Models in Lattice Dynamics

J.R. HARDY

Behlen Laboratory of Physics,
The University of Nebraska,
Lincoln, Nebraska 68508
USA

Dynamical Properties of Solids, edited by
G. K. Horton and A. A. Maradudin

Contents

1. Introduction

The solid state theorist, no matter what his field of specialization, is repeatedly faced with the need to construct a theoretical model which will be adequate to describe the physics of the system which he is studying. Lattice dynamics is no exception to this rule. Ideally one should attempt a full-scale solution of the Schrödinger equation. However this is impractical. Thus, when we are faced with the problem of calculating phonon frequencies and phonon dispersion curves for a real crystal, we are confronted with the necessity of constructing a simplified model which will enable us to proceed with our calculations and thus to predict what the results of experimental measurements should be. Conversely, the experimental results are a check on the degree to which our initial model adequately describes the dynamics of this particular crystal.

The object of this chapter will be to present and discuss the models that have been developed to date with particular emphasis on the dynamics of ionic crystals; we shall also describe more briefly some of the work that has been done on the lattice dynamics of metals and of covalently-bonded crystals. However, the number of models that have been developed to date is very large and growing rapidly. Thus it is impossible to discuss all of them in great detail.

The main reason for concentrating the discussion in this chapter on the subject of ionic, and to a lesser extent on covalently bonded materials, is that it is for these materials that phenomenological models have been most extensively used. The interpretation of the dynamics of metals has made very little use of phenomenological models and has been carried out in terms of pseudopotential theory and one can reasonably argue that this type of approach is at a more fundamental level and makes little use of phenomenology.

We shall begin our discussion by outlining the basic theory of lattice dynamics, we shall then proceed to review briefly the more important phenomenological models, and of these models we shall select certain examples for more specific and extended discussion. Finally, we will provide a brief discussion of the manner in which future progress is likely to take place and will review certain possible extensions of the current model calculations which may be of future interest.

2. *General theory*

According to the adiabatic approximation, which we shall not discuss further in this chapter, it can be shown (Born and Huang 1954) that there exists a potential function governing the motion of the atomic nuclei and, as the name implies, the electrons in the solid follow the nuclear motion instantaneously or adiabatically. This particular approximation is good for large band gap materials and it appears to be perfectly adequate for semiconducting materials, such as silicon or germanium and can indeed be used with caution in the case of metals.

Given the existence of such a potential function U then one can express it as a power series in the nuclear displacements ξ alone. Thus:

$$U = U_0 + \sum_{l,k,\alpha} \left(\frac{\partial U}{\partial \xi_\alpha \binom{l}{k}} \right)_0 \xi_\alpha \binom{l}{k} + \tfrac{1}{2} \sum_{ll',kk',\alpha\beta} \xi_\alpha \binom{l}{k} \left(\frac{\partial^2 U}{\partial \xi_\alpha \binom{l}{k} \partial \xi_\beta \binom{l'}{k'}} \right)_0 \xi_\beta \binom{l'}{k'}, \quad (1)$$

where $l(l')$ are cell indices, $k(k')$ refer to the constituent sublattices and $\alpha(\beta)$ are the cartesian coordinates.

For our purposes the zero-order term is a constant and, if we expand U about the equilibrium configuration of the lattice, [implied by the subscript 0], the first-order term is identically zero. Thus the lowest order non-vanishing term is the second-order term. If we truncate the series at this point, we have the so-called harmonic approximation to the lattice dynamics of the perfect crystal. The essential feature of this approximation is that, as we shall see, it makes possible the decomposition of any arbitrary motion of the atoms or ions in the lattice into plane wave normal modes which oscillate independently of one another. The existence of such independent normal modes is a general property of mechanical systems which are executing small oscillations and in which the restoring forces acting on the constituent particles are of a generalized hookeian nature.

Given the potential energy as specified in eq. (1) above, we can at once proceed to write down the equations of a motion of a particular atom of mass m_k as follows:

$$m_k \frac{\partial^2 \xi_\alpha\binom{l}{k}}{\partial t^2} = - \sum_{l', k', \beta} \left(\frac{\partial^2 U}{\partial \xi_\alpha\binom{l}{k}\, \partial \xi_\beta\binom{l'}{k'}} \right)_0 \xi_\beta \binom{l'}{k'}. \tag{2}$$

When we proceed to solve these equations, we can do so by the following substitution:

$$\xi_\alpha \binom{l}{k} = (N m_k)^{-1/2}\, Q\binom{\boldsymbol{q}}{j}\, e_\alpha(k, j) \exp\left\{ \mathrm{i}\left[\boldsymbol{q}\cdot \boldsymbol{r}\binom{l}{k} - \omega\binom{\boldsymbol{q}}{j} t \right] \right\}, \tag{3}$$

where $\boldsymbol{q}$ is the wave vector, $\boldsymbol{r}\binom{l}{k}$ the perfect lattice coordinate of ion $\binom{l}{k}$, and N the number of cells; i.e. we assume that the displacements have a plane wave character with a polarization whose direction is to be determined by the details of the interatomic forces. Since the lattice is translationally invariant, the solution of the foregoing equation depends only on the difference between cell indices l and l'. Thus a solution for one ion is in fact a solution for all ions of the given sublattice in the whole crystal. The solubility condition becomes:

$$\omega^2 \binom{\boldsymbol{q}}{j} e_\alpha(kj) = \sum_{k', \beta} (m_k m_{k'})^{-1/2} \left(\frac{\partial^2 U}{\partial \xi_\alpha\binom{l}{k}\, \partial \xi_\beta\binom{l'}{k'}} \right)_0 \times \exp\left\{ -\mathrm{i}\boldsymbol{q}\cdot\left[\boldsymbol{r}\binom{l}{k} - \boldsymbol{r}\binom{l'}{k'} \right] \right\} e_\beta(k'j) \tag{4}$$

which equation defines eigenfrequencies $\omega\binom{q}{j}$ and eigenvectors $e_\alpha(kj)$. The latter satisfy the orthogonality requirement that $\sum_{k\alpha} e_\alpha^*(kj)\, e_\alpha(kj') = \delta_{jj'}$. With the aid of this result it may be shown that the hamiltonian for the whole system, again within the harmonic approximation, can be written in the following form:

$$H = \tfrac{1}{2} \left\{ \sum_{\boldsymbol{q}, j} \left[\dot{Q}^*\binom{\boldsymbol{q}}{j} \dot{Q}\binom{\boldsymbol{q}}{j} + \omega^2\binom{\boldsymbol{q}}{j} Q^*\binom{\boldsymbol{q}}{j} Q\binom{\boldsymbol{q}}{j} \right] \right\}.$$

To do this we substitute from eq. (3) into the direct space hamiltonian

$$H = \tfrac{1}{2} \left\{ \sum_{ll', kk', \alpha\beta} \left[m_k \dot{\xi}_\alpha \binom{l}{k}^2 + \xi_\beta \binom{l}{k} \left(\frac{\partial^2 U}{\partial \xi_\alpha\binom{l}{k}\, \partial \xi_\beta\binom{l'}{k'}} \right)_0 \xi_\beta \binom{l}{k'} \right] \right\}$$

and use the orthogonality of the eigenvectors together with the fact that $\sum_l \exp[\mathrm{i}(\boldsymbol{q}+\boldsymbol{q}')\cdot \boldsymbol{r}\binom{l}{k}] = \delta_{-\boldsymbol{q}\boldsymbol{q}'}$.

These then are the formal essentials of the subject and it is obvious that any theory of the dynamics of a perfect lattice, and indeed also of any imperfect lattice, is going to require an explicit knowledge of the transformed potential function:

$$(m_k m_{k'})^{-1/2}\left(\frac{\partial^2 U}{\partial\xi_\alpha\binom{l}{k}\,\partial\xi_\beta\binom{l'}{k'}}\right)_0 \exp\left\{i\boldsymbol{q}\cdot\left[\boldsymbol{r}\binom{l'}{k'}-\boldsymbol{r}\binom{l}{k}\right]\right\},$$

otherwise known as the dynamical matrix. It is with this particular aspect of the problem that the present chapter is concerned. Ideally we want to compute this quantity from first principles by a direct quantum-mechanical calculation. While it is true that considerable progress in this direction has been made in the case of metals (Harrison 1965), in the case of insulators there are still considerable difficulties to be overcome.

It will be observed that if we have a lattice which contains one atom per primitive cell, then the dynamical matrix can be written down as the Fourier transform of sets of interatomic forces which extend as far as one wishes. And this has led to the assumption that these force constants, often referred to as the Born–Von Kármán force constants (Born and Von Kármán 1912, 1913) can be uniquely determined if all the normal mode frequencies are measured. Such a measurement is somewhat hypothetical, since the measurements that are made by the technique of inelastic neutron scattering, discussed elsewhere in this volume, are generally restricted to the determination of phonon frequencies for a restricted number of high symmetry directions. However, even if these experiments were to be performed, Leigh et al. (1971) have recently shown that it is not possible to proceed in this manner; since there exists an infinity of sets of force constants that will give a specific set of eigenfrequencies. This is even more obviously so in the case of lattices which have a basis (i.e. more than one atom in the primitive cell) where the polarization vectors of the two or more constituents are manifestly dependent on the nature of the interatomic forces. Thus, interpretation of results in terms of Born–Von Kármán force constants is of somewhat restricted value.

In the past it has been assumed that if one can obtain a satisfactory set of force constants which fits the dispersion curves, i.e. the plots of frequency vs. wave vector along the symmetry directions, then these can be used to calculate the phonon frequencies throughout the first Brillouin zone. However, in view of the foregoing conclusions, this would appear to be suspect. However, Leigh et al. [1971] point out that if it were possible to make measurements of a number of eigenvectors, for modes not propagating along any direction of high symmetry, then it would be possible to discriminate between the various possible sets of model force constants. They illustrate their first conclusion by reference to Herman's original calculations on germanium (Herman 1959). However, this is possibly a little unfair to Herman in the sense that he was never really in the position of claiming that he had determined a unique set of force constants. The crux of his work was a demonstration of the fact that interatomic force constants acting between atoms as far apart as fifth neighbors were essential if one were ever going to fit the measured dispersion curves for germanium.

Attempts have been made to compute the appropriate potential function for a variety of metals using pseudo-potential theory. This is based on the assumption that it is possible to simulate the effects of the lattice on the behaviour of the electron gas by that of a weak effective potential or pseudo-potential, whose effects can be treated by perturbation theory. In this way, results have been obtained for a number of simple metals but it would be overstating the case to say that this type of approach is on a very firm footing. Indeed in many respects it is still, in spite of its appearance, phenomenological in the sense that the ionic pseudo-potential usually contains one or more adjustable parameters which are adjusted to fit the observed phonon or normal mode frequencies.‡ However, our concern in this chapter will be with the work that has been done on calculating phonon dispersion curves for a number of crystals; in particular ionic crystals, using semi-classical models whose validity can, to a certain degree, be justified quantum-mechanically, but at the same time they contain a good deal of physical intuition.

The main point about the earliest of these semi-classical models is that they were developed at the same time as accurate phonon dispersion curves were first being measured by the Chalk River group of Professor Brockhouse and they have achieved a surprising degree of success. The philosophy that we choose to adopt in this chapter is to recognize that any of the models that have been developed is bound to be an approximation to the true situation; none of them is developed by a true a priori quantum mechanical calculation. However, at present, it would seem that they still have a very important role to play. The reason for this is that, although it is now in principle possible to do a priori quantum-mechanical calculations, in practice it seems that such calculations are prohibitively difficult. One must always bear in mind that one should beware of what one might describe as the 'super-computer complex' which Wigner and Seitz (1955) refer to in their comments on the

‡ At this point it should be observed that the terms phonon and normal mode are apt to be used interchangeably. However, the phonons are strictly the quantized excitations of the normal modes.

possibility of making exact calculations of the ground state energies of metallic crystals. If one had such a super computer, then it should be possible to feed in nothing more than the ionic masses, the interionic spacings and the number of electrons per ion and then to compute the exact eigenfrequencies for any given wave vector. However, the question then arises as to just what one has done and this is not a question that can be answered with any degree of physical insight. What has taken place, has taken place in the hardware of the computer and one has no clear insight into what the important physical features of the calculation are. Thus, in this sense, the model calculations, their shortcomings being admitted, are very definitely more useful in understanding the nature of the interatomic or interionic interaction in solids, and in elucidating such things as what are the dominant terms, what must be included and what can be neglected. We make this point here to attempt to set the various model calculations that have been made into perspective.

3. *General review of model calculations*

These can be classed in two categories. The first category are those calculations made by workers who have had at their disposal actual measured phonon dispersion curves. The other category are those calculations made by other workers who have attempted to predict what the dispersion curves should be. Moreover some prediction of the eigenvectors is necessary in the case of diatomic crystals (e.g. the alkali halides) since it is important to be able to ascertain, when using the 'constant $\boldsymbol{Q}$ method', where to scan for the various phonon peaks for a given symmetry direction. Having located these peaks by virtue of using the initial model, one can proceed to refine that model to obtain a good fit to the measured phonon frequencies. However, there is a limit to this process which is set by the requirement that the parameters in the model have some physical meaning and, it is also essential that they do not predict a totally erroneous value for some other physical property that is not measured by inelastic neutron scattering. Thus it is our feeling that one should do the best one can with a model whose parameters have a definite physical meaning and then recognize that there are discrepancies and attempt to ascertain their origin with the object of improving the model in a physically meaningful way. To make this recipe specific, one could say that one should look for a model which fits the measured static and optical dielectric constants, the elastic constants and the infra-red dispersion frequency (or frequencies in the case of a polyatomic material) and one could also include the single phonon Raman frequencies. All these are data which can be established without reference to inelastic neutron scattering. Thus one has a way of fitting the model parameters. It is undesirable to proceed further with a fitting procedure designed to reproduce the observed dispersion curves although the temptation to do so is very considerable. There are two problems involved in this approach, the first is that there are certain parameters which one includes to obtain a fit to the foregoing data, such as the interaction between second neighbor like ions, that one cannot partition between the two types of ion in the crystal on the basis of elastic constant measurements alone. The second problem is that the simplest models are based on central pairwise potentials and one cannot from these obtain any violation of the Cauchy relations although experimentally one observes that these relations are violated to a greater or lesser degree. For cubic crystals the general relations reduce to a statement that the elastic constants C_{12} and C_{44} are equal. For less symmetric crystals it is possible to obtain a violation of the Cauchy relations if the structure is not such that all ions are centers of inversion symmetry; since one then obtains an internal strain contribution to the elastic constants which is in itself sufficient to cause violation of the Cauchy relations. However, even for the centrosymmetric materials one knows from experimental measurements that there are definite violations of the relation $C_{12}=C_{44}$ which are not explicable in terms of any central pairwise model potential. One can obtain such a violation if one removes the requirement that the lattice is in static equilibrium. However, while there is good theoretical justification for doing this in the case of metals, the situation in the case of semiconductors and insulators is still obscure. Certainly in the case of the 'ideal' insulator where the ions or atoms are self-contained, well-defined entities, there is no obvious reason for inserting into the total potential energy of the lattice a volume dependent term although this has been done. There are, however, other ways of obtaining models that violate the Cauchy relations and the most simple is to recognize that the interionic potential functions may contain contributions which are intrinsically of a 'many body character'.

At this point one is brought face to face with the fact that the expansion given in eq. (1) is done in terms of displacements measured with respect to some absolute frame of reference. This is, of course, unphysical but fortunately, so long as one restricts oneself to pairwise potentials, there is no difference in the results obtained by this approach and by the alternative approach of using an expansion in terms of relative displacements. This is evident from the following equation:

$$\sum_{ll',kk',\alpha\beta} \left[\xi_\alpha\binom{l}{k} - \xi_\alpha\binom{l'}{k'}\right]\left[\xi_\beta\binom{l}{k} - \xi_\beta\binom{l'}{k'}\right]$$
$$\times\left(\frac{\partial^2\phi\left(\left|r\binom{l}{k} - r\binom{l'}{k'}\right|\right)}{\partial\left[\xi_\alpha\binom{l}{k} - \xi_\alpha\binom{l'}{k'}\right]\partial\left[\xi_\beta\binom{l}{k} - \xi_\beta\binom{l'}{k'}\right]}\right)_0$$
$$= \sum_{ll',kk'}\left(\frac{\partial^2\phi\left(\left|r\binom{l}{k} - r\binom{l'}{k'}\right|\right)}{\partial\xi_\alpha\binom{l}{k}\,\partial\xi_\beta\binom{l'}{k'}}\right)_0 \xi_\alpha\binom{l}{k}\xi_\beta\binom{l'}{k'} = 2\left(\frac{\partial^2 U}{\partial\xi_\alpha\binom{l}{k}\,\partial\xi_\beta\binom{l'}{k'}}\right)_0,$$

where $U=\frac{1}{2}\sum_{ll',kk'}\phi\left(\left|r\binom{l}{k}-r\binom{l'}{k'}\right|\right)$ and one can see that differentiation with respect to absolute displacements has the same effect as differentiation with respect to relative displacements. If however, one includes different terms in the potential function that have intrinsic many body character, then the situation changes, since differentiation with respect of the relative displacements of two ions or atoms in one bond can be combined with differentiation with respect to the displacements of ions or atoms in the second bond; and one still has terms that are quadratic in bond length changes. This makes it possible to obtain a violation of the Cauchy relation.

Our objective is to describe the various phenomenological models that have been used to the present and to attempt to assess relative merits. We shall concentrate our attention on ionic crystals and on semiconducting materials such as silicon and germanium, since these are the materials for which most work has been done. If we go back to the origins of the various models that have been used for ionic crystals we are led back to work carried out in the mid 1930's by Lyddane and Herzfeld (1938). These authors demonstrated that if one includes ionic polarization in the equations of motion for the atoms, then one is forced to the conclusion that use of the point dipole approximation to describe the multipole field associated with a displaced ion can lead to the prediction that the lattice is unstable. They found this to be the case for sodium chloride, which was the material which they studied. The origin of this instability is not hard to find since one can see that it has its origins in the dipole–dipole coupling which tends to destabilize the lattice when it is distorted by a plane wave. For a plane wave of infinite wavelength this interaction causes the Lorentz local field. The problem of the long-wave vibrations was re-examined by Szigeti in two papers (Szigeti 1949, 1950) where he was able to demonstrate that it was necessary to assume that the 'dynamical charge' of the ions in cubic crystals was considerably less than unity. In the case of the alkali halides this leads to an apparent inconsistency with the results of the Born–Mayer theory (Tosi 1964) which accounts very well for their cohesive energy. This theory assumes that the ions are spherical charge distributions of net charge plus or minus e where e is |the electronic charge| held apart by a short range repulsion originating from quantum mechanical effects which come into play when the ions overlap. However, for long-wavelength optical vibrations, if one assumes that the point dipole approximation is valid, this implies that the effective field acting on an ion is equal to the macroscopic field plus $4\pi/3$ times the crystal polarization. One is then forced to the conclusion that the dynamical charge, or effective charge, of the ions is typically on the order of 75% of the electronic charge.

To circumvent this difficulty, Szigeti suggested that there was another mechanism for polarizing the ions than that provided by the microscopic electric field. He suggested that the short range repulsive interactions between close neighbors had associated with them deformations of the ionic charge clouds from their basically spherical character. This theory was taken up by Huang (1951) who reformulated Szigeti's work to provide a general description of the long wavelength optical vibrations of a diatomic ionic crystal. Such vibrations can be regarded as an antiphase motion of the two sublattices in which the center of mass of each unit cell remains fixed. However, it is necessary that this antiphase motion be modulated by a plane wave in order to avoid surface effects which have the property of rendering the normal modes of the system dependent on the geometry of the specimen as a whole. It should be said that this effect is real and there is some evidence for it in the case of small crystals.

On the other hand, if one is dealing with a crystal of normal dimensions, one cannot then, for very long wavelength vibrations, use the electrostatic approximation to describe the interionic forces, i.e. one must allow for retardation of the electromagnetic field. This is a subject which we do not propose to discuss here although it has been discussed very thoroughly by Huang and led him to the concept of what are now known as polaritons. These are normal modes of a mixed character involving both the lattice motion and oscillations of the electromagnetic field.

This deviation of the effective ionic charges from unity led to a number of attempts to explain it in the late 1950's, the most well-known being that due to Dick and Overhauser (1958) who postulated that the ions should be regarded as 'cores' to which a massless 'shells', representing the outer valence electrons, are bound by isotropic springs. It should also be mentioned that in their original paper they were concerned with the importance of taking into account the distortion that arises due to ionic overlap. This arises from the fact that the wave functions for the free ions cease to be orthogonal when the ions are in close juxtaposition and this results in the need to orthogonalize them in order that the Pauli principle be satisfied. This orthogonalization procedure in turn results in a distortion of the ionic charge clouds. However, this distortion is of a rather diffuse character and in the subsequent development of the shell model (Woods et al. 1960, Cochran 1959a, b), it was neglected or, more precisely, was lumped in with the point dipole type of distortion which arises from the relative motion of the cores and shells.

Thus we have seen the essential features of the shell model as it has been widely used. Subsequently it has been extended first by Schröder (1966), Nüsslein and Schröder (1967), who developed the breathing shell model and independently by Basu and Sengupta (1968), Verma and Singh (1969), and Singh and Verma (1969, 1970), who incorporated into the shell model the many body forces originally suggested by Lundquist (1952, 1955, 1957).

The alternative approach is the so-called deformation dipole model (Hardy 1959, 1962, Karo and Hardy 1960, 1963) which is a generalization of the ideas of Szigeti and Huang to the problem of dealing with the ionic deformation polarization for normal modes of finite wavelength.

The deformation dipole model, allows for the existence of two possible types of polarization corresponding to the two different polarization mechanisms itemized previously: i.e. electric field induced polarization and overlap deformation polarization; and one assumes that these two are independent. This is distinct from the shell model where there is only one type of polarization which is manifested by a relative displacement of the core and the shell no matter whether this be brought about by the application of an external electric field or by the influence of short-range forces. The conceptual advantage of the shell model is that it automatically implies that the distortion of the charge cloud about a given ion produced by a lattice wave is equivalent to a point dipole at the undisplaced position of the ion. To obtain higher multipoles, one would have to consider terms that were non-linear in the core-shell displacement. However, it is evident that this picture must be an oversimplified representation of reality. In the case of the deformation dipole model it is in principle possible to remove this limitation by abandoning the assumption that the dipoles produced by overlap deformation are located at the center of the negative ion. (In general this seems to be the most useful assumption.)

As regards the extensions of the shell model, Nüsslein and Schröder (1967) have done so by introducing the idea that, in addition to its displacement as a rigid sphere, the shell can also "breathe" i.e. its radius can be changed. This has the advantage that it enables them to explain the fact that the measured [111] longitudinal optic dispersion curves for sodium iodide (NaI) are almost flat, which is in marked contrast with the predictions of both the simple shell model and the deformation dipole model.

The fullest presentation of the ideas of Nüsslein and Schröder has been given in a paper by Sangster et al. (1970) where they describe in detail the derivation of the appropriate equations. In addition Cochran (1971) has recently reviewed the field and gives a fairly extensive treatment of the shell model and its modifications. The last of these is due to Singh and Verma (1969, 1970) following on their earlier work (Verma and Singh 1969) who have incorporated into the shell model their extension of the results of an earlier quantum-mechanical calculation by Lundquist (1952, 1955, 1957) which was in turn based on an extension to the study of crystal dynamics of the ideas first developed by Löwdin (1948) to account for the cohesive energies of ionic crystals and also to explain the violation of the Cauchy relation in terms of what have come to be referred to as many-body forces. This too leads to significantly better agreement with the experimental dispersion curves. However, it is questionable whether the use of these many-body terms really brings one any closer to an a priori quantum-mechanical calculation since the parameters involved are selected as much as anything to give the best overall agreement with the measured dispersion curves and thus these are still model calculations. However, this approach, together with the breathing shell model, is certainly an improvement over extending the simple shell model by some least squares fitting procedure which involves the use of an excessively large number of disposable parameters.

This then is an outline of the various models that have been used for the computation of lattice dynamical normal mode frequencies for the alkali halides and also for a number of other crystals such as the IV–IV, III–V and fluorite structure materials. We shall now proceed to examine the models in more detail.

4. *Detailed description of certain models*

The various types of model are best introduced by considering the equations of motion for long-wave optical vibrations in the manner employed by Huang (1951). For a diatomic cubic crystal we have:

$$\ddot{\boldsymbol{w}} = b_{11}\boldsymbol{w} + b_{12}\boldsymbol{E}, \qquad \boldsymbol{P} = b_{21}\boldsymbol{w} + b_{22}\boldsymbol{E}, \tag{5, 6}$$

where

$$\boldsymbol{w} = (\mu/V_{\mathrm{a}})^{1/2}\,(\boldsymbol{u}_1 - \boldsymbol{u}_2)$$

is the coordinate of the center of mass of the unit cell, μ the reduced mass of the ions, V_a is the unit cell volume and $\boldsymbol{u}_1$ and $\boldsymbol{u}_2$ are the sublattice displacements. The fields $\boldsymbol{E}$ and $\boldsymbol{P}$ are the macroscopic electric field and the macroscopic polarization, respectively. The various coefficients in these equations are defined as follows:

$$b_{11} = -\,\omega_0^2,\ b_{12} = b_{21} = (1/2\sqrt{\pi})\,(\varepsilon_0 - \varepsilon_\infty)^{1/2}\,\omega_0,\ b_{22} = (\varepsilon_\infty - 1)/4\pi,$$

where ε_0 and ε_∞ are the static and high frequency dielectric constants respectively and ω_0 is the infra-red dispersion frequency. If we work out the response of the crystal to an external applied field of frequency ω, we obtain the following equations:

$$-\,\omega^2 \boldsymbol{w} = b_{11}\boldsymbol{w} + b_{12}\boldsymbol{E}, \qquad \boldsymbol{P} = b_{21}\boldsymbol{w} + b_{22}\boldsymbol{E}.$$

Eliminating $\boldsymbol{w}$ from these two equations gives:

$$\boldsymbol{P} = [\,(b_{22} + b_{12}^2/(-\,b_{11} - \omega^2)]\,\boldsymbol{E} \tag{7}$$

whence the dielectric constant $\varepsilon(\omega)$ is given by:

$$\varepsilon(\omega) = 1 + 4\pi b_{22} + 4\pi b_{12}^2/(-\,b_{11} - \omega^2),$$

These then are the macroscopic equations; it remains to give the various coefficients microscopic interpretation.

To do this we consider the situation when the lattice is subject to a plane wave displacement whose wavelength is long compared with the interionic spacing but short compared with the size of the specimen. Then, if we restrict ourselves to isotropic crystals, having ionic charges $\pm Ze$ we have

$$\boldsymbol{P} = (1/V_a)\,[Ze\,(\boldsymbol{u}_1 - \boldsymbol{u}_2) + (\alpha_1 + \alpha_2)\,\boldsymbol{E}_{\text{eff}}], \tag{8}$$

where $\boldsymbol{E}_{\text{eff}}$ is the effective field given by:

$$\boldsymbol{E}_{\text{eff}} = \boldsymbol{E} + (4\pi/3)\,\boldsymbol{P}. \tag{9}$$

Thus, substituting from eq. (9) into eq. (8) we obtain:

$$\boldsymbol{P} = \frac{1}{1 - \frac{4}{3}\pi\,(\alpha_1 + \alpha_2)/V_a}\left[\frac{Ze\,(\boldsymbol{u}_1 - \boldsymbol{u}_2)}{V_a} + \frac{\alpha_1 + \alpha_2}{V_a}\,\boldsymbol{E}\right].$$

Written in terms of $\boldsymbol{w}$ this assumes the form:

$$\boldsymbol{P} = \frac{1}{1 - \frac{4}{3}\pi\,(\alpha_1 + \alpha_2)/V_a}\left[\frac{Ze}{(\mu V_a)^{1/2}}\,\boldsymbol{w} + \frac{\alpha_1 + \alpha_2}{V_a}\,\boldsymbol{E}\right]. \tag{10}$$

Whence we find that

$$b_{12} = \frac{Ze}{(\mu V_a)^{1/2}\,[1 - \frac{4}{3}\pi(\alpha_1 + \alpha_2)/V_a]} \quad \text{and} \quad b_{22} = \frac{\alpha_1 + \alpha_2}{V_a[1 - \frac{4}{3}\pi(\alpha_1 + \alpha_2)/V_a]}$$

if we compare eqs. (10) and (6). If we now use the macroscopic definition of b_{22} we obtain the Clausius–Mossotti relation:

$$\tfrac{4}{3}\pi(\alpha_1 + \alpha_2)/V_a = (\varepsilon_\infty - 1)/(\varepsilon_\infty + 2).$$

To express the remaining coefficient b_{11} in terms of microscopic variables we must consider the derivation of the first of the two macroscopic equations. In terms of microscopic theory this has the form:

$$-\omega^2\mu(\boldsymbol{u}_1 - \boldsymbol{u}_2) = -g(\boldsymbol{u}_1 - \boldsymbol{u}_2) + Ze\,\boldsymbol{E}_{\text{eff}}, \quad \text{or}$$
$$\omega^2\boldsymbol{w} = (g/\mu)\,\boldsymbol{w} - Ze(\mu V_a)^{-1/2}\boldsymbol{E}_{\text{eff}},$$

where g is an isotropic tensor for 'diagonally cubic' materials (e.g. sodium chloride or zinc blende structures) and represents the short-range nearest neighbor restoring force constant which acts between the two sublattices and is associated with the ionic overlap.

Thus, again using the fact that $\boldsymbol{E}_{\text{eff}} = \boldsymbol{E} + (4\pi/3)\,\boldsymbol{P}$, and then substituting for $\boldsymbol{P}$ from eq. (10) we obtain:

$$-\omega^2\boldsymbol{w} = \left(-\frac{g}{\mu} + \frac{4\pi}{3}\frac{(Ze)^2}{\mu V_a[1 - \frac{4}{3}\pi(\alpha_+ + \alpha_-)/V_a]}\right)\boldsymbol{w} + \frac{Ze}{(\mu V_a)^{1/2}\,[1 - \frac{4}{3}\pi(\alpha_+ + \alpha_-)/V_a]}\boldsymbol{E}. \tag{11}$$

Hence, comparing eqs. (11) and (5), we obtain:

$$b_{11} = \frac{-g}{\mu} + \frac{4\pi}{3}\frac{(Ze)^2}{\mu V_\alpha[1 - \frac{4}{3}\pi(\alpha_+ + \alpha_-)/V_a]}.$$

If the short range potential $\phi(r)$ extends only as far as first neighbors, then it can be shown that the restoring force constant g is given by

$$g = \tfrac{1}{3}n[\phi''(r_0) + (2/r_0)\,\phi'(r_0)], \tag{12}$$

where n is the coordination number and the primes denote derivatives with respect to the nearest neighbor separation r evaluated at $r = r_0$. (As specified earlier, this result holds only for diagonally cubic structures; in general g is a second rank tensor.) However, if we consider the compressibility of the crystal β, this is defined by

$$1/\beta = V_a (d^2u/dV^2)_0$$

(the suffix 0 implying that the derivative is evaluated at the static equilibrium lattice spacing r_0 and u is the energy per unit cell). Now

$$u(r) = -\alpha_m (e^2/r) + n\,\phi(r),$$

where α_m is the Madelung constant, thus the equilibrium condition becomes:

$$(du/dr)_{r=r_0} = \alpha_m e^2/r_0^2 + n\,\phi'(r_0) = 0. \tag{13}$$

Also

$$\frac{1}{\beta} = V_a \left(\frac{d^2u}{dV^2}\right)_0 = \left[\tfrac{1}{3} r_0 \frac{d}{dr}\left(\frac{r}{3V}\frac{du}{dr}\right)\right]_0$$
$$= (r_0^2/9V_a)(d^2u/dr^2)_0 = (r_0^2/9V_a)\left[-2\alpha_m e^2/r_0^3 + n\phi''(r_0)\right].$$

Using the equilibrium equation (13) we obtain finally that

$$1/\beta = (nr_0^2/9V_a)\left[\phi''(r_0) + 2\phi'(r_0)/r_0\right]. \tag{14}$$

Thus using eqs. (12) and (14):

$$1/\beta = (r_0^2/3V_a)\, g\,.$$

If we now rewrite the equation for b_{11} $(= -\omega_0^2)$ somewhat differently we have

$$-\omega_0^2 = -(g/\mu) + \tfrac{4}{3}\pi\, b_{12}^2 \left[1 - \tfrac{4}{3}\pi(\alpha_1 + \alpha_2)/V_a\right]$$
$$= -(g/\mu) + \tfrac{1}{3}(\varepsilon_0 - \varepsilon_\infty)\,\omega_0^2\left[1 - \tfrac{4}{3}\pi(\alpha_1 + \alpha_2)/V_a\right],$$
$$\therefore g/\mu = \omega_0^2\left\{\tfrac{1}{3}(\varepsilon_0 - \varepsilon_\infty)\left[1 - \tfrac{4}{3}\pi(\alpha_1 + \alpha_2)/V_a\right] + 1\right\}.$$

Whence, using the Clausius–Mossotti relation, we have:

$$\frac{g}{\mu} = \omega_0^2\left(\frac{\varepsilon_0 - \varepsilon_\infty}{\varepsilon_\infty + 2} + 1\right), \qquad \therefore \frac{g}{\mu} = \left(\frac{\varepsilon_0 + 2}{\varepsilon_\infty + 2}\right)\omega_0^2,$$

thus

$$\frac{1}{\beta} = \frac{\mu r_0^2}{3V_a}\left(\frac{\varepsilon_0 + 2}{\varepsilon_\infty + 2}\right). \tag{15}$$

This relation was first derived by Szigeti (1949, 1950) and, as we have seen, it is only valid for short-range central interactions which extend only as far as nearest neighbors (i.e. nearest *unlike* neighbors). If this is not the case, then it is possible for this relation to be violated. Testing this relation is not quite as simple as it may appear at first sight since the relation is derived on the assumption that the lattice is perfectly harmonic, which is not the case, since there are significant anharmonic contributions to the measured elastic constants as derived by ultrasonic techniques. However, at least for the simplest calculations it has been the practice to ignore this difference and to use

TABLE 1

Comparison of the compressibilities calculated from the first Szigeti relation with observed values and values of the dynamic effective charges for the alkali halides (Lowndes and Martin 1969).

Compound	β_{calc}/β_{obs}	$b_{12\ obs}/b_{12\ calc}$
LiF	0.90	0.80
LiCl	1.17	0.77
NaF	0.94	0.82
NaCl	1.00	0.76
NaBr	1.06	0.73
NaI	1.15	0.71
KF	0.97	0.88
KCl	0.98	0.79
KBr	0.99	0.75
KI	0.91	0.72
RbCl	1.04	0.81
RbBr	1.01	0.78
RbI	1.00	0.74
CsCl	1.08*	0.85
CsBr	1.00**	0.82
CsI	0.97**	0.77

*β from Aleksandov and Ryzhova (1961);
**β from Reinitz (1961).

the measured elastic constants as they are, since it is only fairly recently that the precision of such measurements has been improved to the point where different workers have obtained consistent results for the same crystal. In table 1 values of the ratio β_{calc}/β_{obs} are shown for a number of alkali halides. It can be seen that for many of these crystals this ratio is close to unity, deviating most in the case when the ions are of very different size which is evidently the situation where one expects second neighbor overlap effects to be important. In this table we have taken the values given by Lowndes and Martin (1969) which refer to the low temperature limit where anharmonic effects should be least.

However if we reconsider the macroscopic and microscopic expressions for the coefficient $b_{12}(=b_{21})$ which serves to define the 'dynamic effective charge' we have:

$$b_{12}(\text{obs}) = (1/2\sqrt{\pi})\,(\varepsilon_0 - \varepsilon_\infty)^{1/2}\,\omega_0, \tag{15}$$

where all quantities on the right-hand side are measured (again close to 0 K), and

$$b_{12}(\text{calc}) = \frac{Ze}{(\mu V_a)^{1/2}\,[1 - \frac{4}{3}\pi(\alpha_1 + \alpha_2)/V_a]} = \frac{Ze(\varepsilon_\infty + 2)}{3(\mu V_a)^{1/2}}. \tag{16}$$

Thus

$$\frac{b_{12}(\text{obs})}{b_{12}(\text{calc})} = \frac{\omega_0}{Ze}\left(\frac{\varepsilon_0 - \varepsilon_\infty}{4\pi}\right)^{1/2}\left(\frac{3}{\varepsilon_\infty + 2}\right)(\mu V_a)^{1/2}$$

(this is the second Szigeti (1950) relation) and we show the values of this ratio for the same set of crystals in table 1. The derivation of the Szigeti relation between the compressibility and the dielectric data does not involve any assumption with regard to the magnitude of b_{12} since this quantity is eliminated from the equations.

By examining the data in table 1, we find that consistency can only be obtained by assuming values of Z that are typically on the order of 25% less than unity. This type of effective charge is usually referred to as the Szigeti (1950) effective charge and as stated previously it is in strong disagreement with the ionic charge that is consistent with the cohesive energies of the alkali halides, since, in this case it is found that $Z=1$ gives excellent agreement with the measured values.

The resolution of this paradox is the foundation of the more sophisticated phenomenological models that have been used of recent years to study the dynamics of alkali halide crystals. The original suggestion by Szigeti, which has been incorporated into the deformation dipole model, is to assume that the charge clouds around the ions in the crystal are distorted from true spherical symmetry and in the perfect lattice have a component of cubic symmetry. The actual magnitude of this distortion can be very small. However, if its rate of variation is assumed, as is plausible, to follow that of the overlap repulsion, then, since the latter has the form $V(r)=A\exp(-r/\rho)$, where the exponent ρ is typically of the order of 10% of the equilibrium lattice constant, it is possible to explain the deviation of the Szigeti effective charge from unity while retaining the assumption that the ions have, to a good approximation, spherical charge distributions in the perfect lattice. The effect of the small cubic component is then assumed to be absorbed into the short-range forces.

We now have to examine Szigeti's arguments in detail and understand their relation to those of the shell model and the deformation dipole model. Szigeti's original picture involved the assumption that the charge cloud about a given ion was slightly distorted by overlap with the charge distributions of

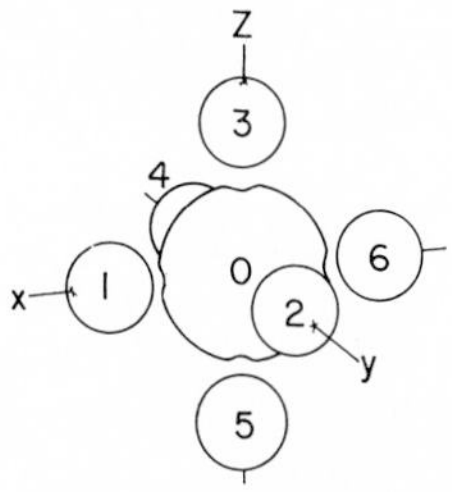

Fig. 1. Illustration of the configuration of the six positive ions about the central negative ion showing the numerical labeling scheme. The central ion 0 corresponds to $\binom{l}{k}$.

its neighboring ions; in particular by overlap with the charge clouds of its first neighbors. Thus we have the situation represented pictorially in fig. 1 where we presuppose that charge is extruded from the region of high overlap. Energetically the work needed to create these dipoles forms part of the overlap repulsive potential. If we assume that the dipole moment in each bond remains directed along that bond when the ions are displaced, then to first order in the displacements the dipole induced on ion $\binom{l}{k}$ is:

$$\mu_{\rm d}\binom{l}{k}_{\alpha} = \gamma_k\left[\xi_\alpha\binom{2}{k'} + \xi_\alpha\binom{3}{k'} + \xi_\alpha\binom{4}{k'} + \xi_\alpha\binom{5}{k'} - 4\xi_\alpha\binom{l}{k}\right] + \gamma'_k\left[\xi_\alpha\binom{1}{k'} + \xi_\alpha\binom{6}{k'} - 2\xi_\alpha\binom{l}{k}\right],$$

when $\alpha = x$, $\gamma_k = \mu_k(r_0)/r_0$, $\gamma'_k = \mathrm{d}\mu_k(r)/\mathrm{d}r|_{r=r_0}$ and similar equations for $\alpha = y, z$.

This expression is specific to the rocksalt structure: for other structures the expression is more complicated.

In a uniform antiphase motion of the two sub-lattices the resultant dipole moment is

$$[2(\gamma'_2 - \gamma'_1) + 4(\gamma_2 - \gamma_1)](\boldsymbol{u}_1 - \boldsymbol{u}_2) = h(\boldsymbol{u}_1 - \boldsymbol{u}_2).$$

It then follows that the dipole moment associated with this motion is

$$(Ze + h)\,(\boldsymbol{u}_1 - \boldsymbol{u}_2).$$

The effect of this modification is to change the microscopic expression for b_{12} into

$$b_{12} = \frac{Ze + h}{(\mu V_{\mathrm{a}})^{1/2}\,[1 - \frac{4}{3}\pi\,(\alpha_1 + \alpha_2)/V_{\mathrm{a}}]}. \tag{17}$$

Thus we can determine the parameter h from eqs. (15), (16), and (17) whence

$$Ze + h = (\mu V_{\mathrm{a}})^{1/2}\,\omega_0 \left(\frac{\varepsilon_0 - \varepsilon_\infty}{4\pi}\right)^{1/2} \frac{3}{\varepsilon_\infty + 2}.$$

However this does not fix the parameters $\gamma_1\gamma_2$, $\gamma_1'\gamma_2'$ separately. Thus far it seems that the best method of fixing these is to set $\gamma_1 = \gamma_1' = 0$ and to assume the $\gamma_2 \propto \exp(-r/\rho)$, where ρ is the Born–Mayer screening radius.

Generalizing the foregoing arguments to the case of arbitrary displacements we find that the potential function for the deformation dipole model can now be written in matrix form as:

$$Y = \tfrac{1}{2}\tilde{\xi}\,(R - H)\,\xi - \tfrac{1}{2}\boldsymbol{\mu}' UH\xi - \tfrac{1}{2}\tilde{\xi}HU\boldsymbol{\mu}' - \tfrac{1}{2}\tilde{\boldsymbol{\mu}}' UHU\boldsymbol{\mu}' + \tfrac{1}{2}\tilde{\boldsymbol{\mu}}\alpha^{-1}\boldsymbol{\mu}, \tag{18}$$

where

$$\boldsymbol{\mu}' = \boldsymbol{\mu} + \tilde{S}^*\xi.$$

In these equations ξ and $\boldsymbol{\mu}$ are the column matrices of displacements and dipole moments; R and $-H$ are the matrices of force constants referring to the overlap repulsion and the dipole–dipole Coulomb interaction respectively. $\tilde{S}^*\xi$ is the deformation dipole moment.

The matrices α and U are defined as follows:

$$\alpha_{\kappa\lambda} = \alpha_\lambda \delta_{\kappa\lambda}, \qquad U_{\kappa\lambda} = e_\lambda^{-1}\delta_{\kappa\lambda},$$

where the α's are the crystal polarizabilities of the ions and e_λ is the monopole charge. Note that we are using single suffixes which run over the whole range of l, k and α [c.f. eq. (1)].

It will be noticed that the self energy term in eq. (18) only refers to the polarization dipoles; as stated previously the self energy of the deformation dipoles is included in the repulsive interaction.

For the shell model the corresponding potential function is

$$X = \tfrac{1}{2}\tilde{\xi}\,(R - H)\,\tilde{\xi} + \tfrac{1}{2}\tilde{\xi}T\boldsymbol{\mu} + \tfrac{1}{2}\boldsymbol{\mu}\tilde{T}^*\xi - \tfrac{1}{2}\tilde{\boldsymbol{\mu}}UH\xi - \tfrac{1}{2}\tilde{\xi}HU\boldsymbol{\mu} - \tfrac{1}{2}\tilde{\boldsymbol{\mu}}UHU\boldsymbol{\mu} + \tfrac{1}{2}\tilde{\boldsymbol{\mu}}A\boldsymbol{\mu}, \tag{19}$$

where $\boldsymbol{\mu}$ is the *total* dipole moment. The significance of the various terms is almost the same as before, but the matrices $\tilde{T}$ and T^* are new and refer to the short-range dipole–displacement coupling, while the matrix A is modified to allow for the possibility of non-diagonal terms which will cause interference between the polarizations of neighboring ions. For alkali halides these terms are probably small as they would lead to non additive polarizabilities which is contrary to observation (Tessman et al. 1953). It can be seen that the self energies of the total dipoles are included explicitly in the last term. Finally it should be noted that for a general shell model the structures of the matrices R, T, etc. are more complex.

We now have both potential functions cast in a similar form and we can obtain the equations of motion by taking the derivatives of Y and X with respect to ξ and $\boldsymbol{\mu}$ and setting the first equal to $-m\ddot{\xi}$ where $m_{\kappa\lambda} = m_\kappa \delta_{\kappa\lambda}$, and the second equal to zero. (This last condition is implicit in the adiabatic approximation.) Thus we have, assuming $\xi \propto \exp\{\mathrm{i}[\boldsymbol{q}\cdot\boldsymbol{r}(^l_\kappa) - \omega t]\}$.

Deformation dipole model

$$\begin{aligned} m\omega^2\xi &= [R - (\mathbf{1} + SU)H(\mathbf{1} + U\tilde{S}^*)]\,\xi - (\mathbf{1} + SU)HU\boldsymbol{\mu}, \\ 0 &= (\alpha^{-1} - UHU)\,\boldsymbol{\mu} - UH(\mathbf{1} + U\tilde{S}^*)\,\xi. \end{aligned}$$

Eliminating $\boldsymbol{\mu}$ we obtain, after a little manipulation

$$m\omega^2\xi = [R - (\mathbf{1} + SU)HUC^{-1}U^{-1}(\mathbf{1} + U\tilde{S}^*)], \tag{20}$$

where $C = \mathbf{1} - \alpha UHU$.

Shell model

$$\begin{aligned} m\omega^2\xi &= (R - H)\,\xi + (T - HU)\,\boldsymbol{\mu}, \\ 0 &= (\tilde{T}^* - UH)\,\xi + (A - UHU)\,\boldsymbol{\mu}. \end{aligned}$$

Again eliminating $\boldsymbol{\mu}$ we obtain

$$\begin{aligned} m\omega^2\xi &= R - TA^{-1}\tilde{T}^* \\ &\quad - (\mathbf{1} - TA^{-1}U)HU(\mathbf{1} - A^{-1}UHU)^{-1}\,U^{-1}(\mathbf{1} - UA^{-1}\tilde{T}^*). \end{aligned} \tag{21}$$

In both cases it is to be understood that the matrices are the Fourier transforms of those appearing in eqs. (18) and (19). Apart from the second term on the right-hand side of eq. (21), the two equations (20) and (21) are identical in form but the underlying assumptions are very different.

One should note that since the matrix A is not necessarily diagonal one can have 'interference' or non-Coulomb coupling between the dipole moments of different ions. The matrix $TA^{-1}\tilde{T}^*$ reflects a modification of the short-range repulsion which now depends implicitly on the state of polarization of the ions. This modification is also present for neutral atoms (Cochran 1959a).

The elements of various other matrices that occur in these equations are either related directly to various macroscopic parameters, e.g. compressibility, lattice constant, dielectric constants, etc., or can be derived from these by making certain reasonable assumptions.

The H matrix is the matrix of dipole–dipole coupling constants first studied by Kellermann (1940) who showed how to reduce these into two rapidly converging sums; one over the lattice points in direct space and one over points of the reciprocal lattice. These results are now standard and will not be reproduced here.

At this point it seems important to ask the nature of the assumptions which can be regarded as 'reasonable'. Both models contain parameters that are potentially variable to fit data other than the long-wavelength phonon frequencies, dielectric data, etc. However, one's first inclination is to try for simplicity and to attempt to predict the measured phonon dispersion curves using only the dielectric data, the elastic constants and the infra-red dispersion frequency.

In the simplest version of the shell model the short-range forces were restricted to act only between nearest neighbor shells, the monopole charge Z was taken as 1, and the positive ion was assumed to be non-polarizable. This left three parameters to be fitted and these were adjusted to reproduce the observed values of ε_∞, ε_0 and the elastic constant C_{11}.

The deformation dipole model of comparable simplicity allows one to fit the T.K.S. polarizabilities (Tessman et al. 1953) (and thus ε_∞), ε_0 and the compressibility (or C_{11}).

If the compound being studied satisfies the first Szigeti relation then the infra-red dispersion frequency ω_0 will also be correctly reproduced.

In order to illustrate the type of agreement between theory and experiment which can be achieved by model calculations which do not use as input data the measured phonon frequencies, we show in figs. 2 and 3 dispersion curves calculated for KCl and CsCl. These have been calculated using the deformation dipole model with short-range forces acting only between nearest neighbors and, in each case, the second derivative of this potential has been chosen to reproduce the observed $\boldsymbol{q}=0$ transverse optic frequency. The ionic polarizabilities are those given by Jaswal and Sharma (1973). In both cases the ions

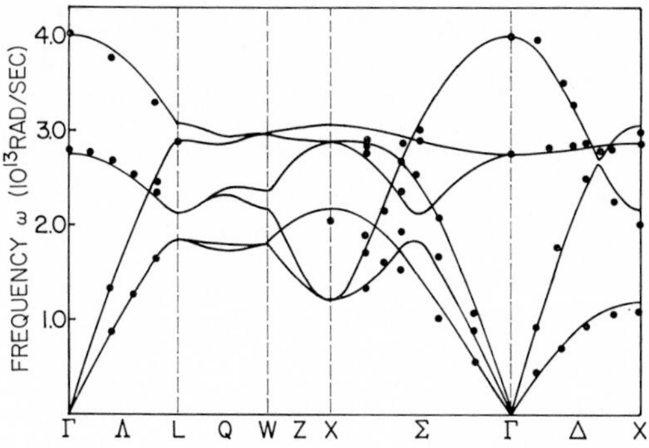

Fig. 2. Comparison of calculated deformation dipole model phonon dispersion curves for KCl at 80 K (full line) with experimental data Copley et al. (1969) (dots). The symmetry axes and points are labeled according to the notation of Bouckaerdt et al. (1936).

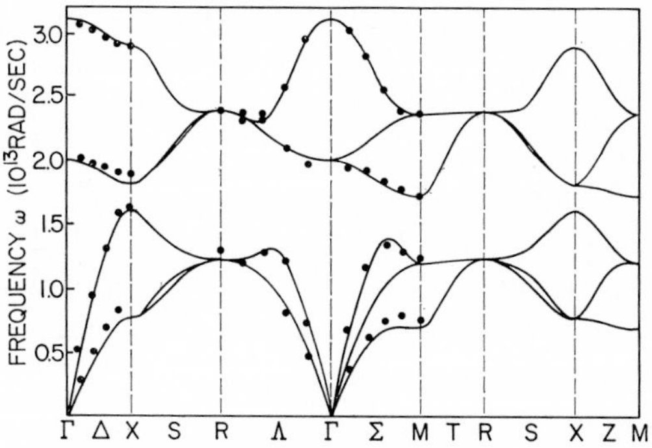

Fig. 3. Comparison of calculated deformation dipole model phonon dispersion curves for CsCl at 80 K (full line) with experimental data Ahmad et al. (1972) (dots). The symmetry axes and points are labeled according to the notation of Bouckaerdt et al. (1936).

are assumed to carry the full monopole charge ($Z=1$). Better agreement between theory and experiment can be obtained by reducing Z; specifically if Z is set equal to 0.97 for CsCl nearly perfect agreement is obtained.

It is interesting to observe that for KCl, the agreement between the theoretical and experimental dispersion curves along the [111] direction is very close, the main discrepancies being confined to the X point.

These results suggest that no one model is equally good for all the alkali halides. If a given model in its simplest form is good for NaI or LiF the same model may be much less satisfactory for RbF or CsCl. In the first two cases the positive ions are light and of low polarizability, whereas for the second two cases the reverse is true.

These then are the simplest models and have the advantage that the model parameters have clear physical meanings. Moreover we have additional experimental parameters: two elastic constants and ω_0 which are not necessarily reproduced by either model. One can fit all these data by introducing second neighbor forces and non-central or angle bending forces into either model. However there is no unique way of partitioning such forces between the two types of second neighbors without reference to the neutron scattering data.

At this point one has to recognize that the number of parameters for either model is bound to proliferate rapidly during any subsequent refinements. Specifically the structure of the T, R, and A matrices for the shell model is such that one can introduce different core–core, core–shell and shell–shell short-range forces. The physical significance of the resultant parameters is dubious. Similarly one can extend the deformation dipole model. For example one could allow for deformation of the positive ion, second neighbor deformation dipoles etc. The number of parameters does not increase as rapidly and their physical significance is somewhat clearer.

None the less it would seem reasonable to argue that when either model is pushed to the point where all parameters are allowed to float in order to obtain the best fit to the measured dispersion curves then it becomes simply an interpolation procedure and all, or most, of the physical content is lost.

The principal shortcoming of both deformation dipole and shell models is their failure to fit the frequencies of longitudinal optic modes propagating along $\langle 111 \rangle$ directions. However, this discrepancy is not universal and is only marked for those materials where the negative ion is much heavier and more polarizable than the positive ion. In the extreme limit, when the wave vector of these modes lies on the zone surface, the heavier ions are at rest and the lighter ions alone move. Since these ions are unpolarizable (or nearly so) the resultant frequencies are the same as those obtained for a rigid ion model (Kellermann 1940). This conclusion also applies to the results of deformation dipole calculations. There is thus no "softening" of the mode by forces between field induced dipoles.

The breathing shell model and the inclusion of many body forces by charge transfer both represent means of providing an additional softening mechanism. In the case of the breathing shell model this is provided by the radial deformation of the shells, which is usually only significant for the negative ions. This is so because the radial force constant is assumed to be the same as that which resists core–shell displacements and thus fixes the ionic polarizability. Thus for the $\boldsymbol{q}=0$ optic modes the breathing degree of freedom has no effect, but for the same branches at $\boldsymbol{q}=[\frac{1}{2}\frac{1}{2}\frac{1}{2}]$ this is no longer so and compression of the shell gives "softening" of the effective short-range force constants for the longitudinal optic branch.

The work of Verma and Singh is based on an extension of ideas developed by Lundquist from Löwdin's original work on calculating the cohesive energies of alkali halides quantum-mechanically.

This work leads to the conclusion that the lattice energies contain terms which depend explicitly on the coordinates of three ions. The physical interpretation of these terms is of considerable interest. For the ionic crystals one can interpret them as arising from the 'exchange charges' introduced by Dick and Overhauser. These arise from the non-orthogonality of the wave functions of electrons on neighboring ions. When one orthogonalizes them, the effect on the charge density is to produce an electron deficiency in the overlap region which is compensated by a uniform enhancement of the charge densities of both neighbors.

However in Lundquist's work it appeared best to locate the charge deficiency on the positive ion site. Thus one has an effective enhancement of the monopole charges of both types of ion. This enhancement is a function of the overlap and thus of the nearest neighbor separation. Consequently, when the lattice is distorted by a set of plane wave displacements there is an associated change in the monopole charge of a given ion which is first order in these displacements. Thus the monopole field at any other ion site is correspondingly modified. This effect thus leads to the presence of three-body terms in the potential function.

For long-wavelength optical vibrations, as Lundquist pointed out, this charge transfer goes some way towards explaining the deviation of the Szigeti charge from unity, however it also affects the elastic constants and causes the Cauchy relation to be violated. The associated softening of the longitudinal optical modes at $\boldsymbol{q}=[\frac{1}{2}\frac{1}{2}\frac{1}{2}]$ is presumably associated with an effect similar to that obtained when one allows for short-range deformation of the positive ions but requires that the induced dipoles be directed *towards* the ion centers. However this analogy is not exact.

Recently this type of model has been extended to the treatment of covalent materials (Feldkamp 1972). Only for these it is assumed that the charge transfer *increases* as the ions are brought closer together.

Finally one should mention two other models. The first is due to Vetelino and Mitra (1969) which is a modification of Kellermann's rigid ion model in which the ionic charge, together with first and second neighbour Born–Von

Kármán force constants, are adjusted to fit the long-wavelength optical mode frequencies and the three elastic constants. This produces reasonable dispersion curves, but cannot be regarded as more than an interpolation procedure. However, it does have the virtue of simplicity and it makes no use of the measured phonon frequencies for $\boldsymbol{q} \neq 0$.

Finally there is the deformable bond model of Nusimovici (1969), Kunc et al. (1971) which has been applied to the II–VI compounds (e.g. ZnS). This is basically the same as the deformation dipole model. However a different form is used for the $\gamma_k \gamma_k'$ parameters; in fact it appears that γ_k is set equal to zero. Also the monopole charges are determined by an estimate of the ionicity of the bonding which correlates reasonably well with Pauling's ionicity scale (Pauling 1960).

5. *Conclusions and overview*

Thus we have now completed our review of the various phenomenological models that are currently in use. We have only given a detailed mathematical treatment of two of them in the hope of avoiding the possible confusion that can be generated by too much mathematical discussion. It is thus now appropriate to provide a general overview of the viability of these various models. One can say at the outset that the number of models has proliferated to the extent that one would like to see the development of an a priori quantum-mechanical calculation which retains the conceptual simplicity of the model calculations but it would appear that we have not yet reached this stage. Once again we stress that the availability of experimentally measured dispersion curves leads naturally to various groups being constrained to fit their model parameters to these dispersion curves. This is predicated on the assumption that one is merely interested in getting the best possible fit to the measured dispersion curves. However, one should not assume that such a model is necessarily good for all points in the Brillouin zone. Specifically, recent tunneling experiments on lead and other materials Rowell and Dynes (1971) have indicated that frequency spectra calculated from force constants fitted to high symmetry phonons can be seriously in error.

In this final section of the chapter, having previously described the various models that are available 'for use', we wish to raise what seem to us to be certain fundamental questions which should be answered before further progress can be made in understanding the lattice dynamics of insulating crystals.

At the moment we are not specifically concerned with metals although some of these points that we shall raise with regard to insulating crystals have recently appeared to be of importance in understanding the behaviour of such materials as transition metal carbides (Weber et al. 1972) and intermetallic compounds (Sham 1971). In the first place we have to ask just how much longer it is possible to continue to use the various types of point dipole approximations that are inherent in the shell model and its various extensions and the deformation dipole model. This naturally leads us to the consideration of much wider issues. One of the original remarkable results of the shell model was the prediction of the dispersion curves of germanium (Cochran 1959a). Now one is bound to adopt the view that materials such as germanium, or for that matter, any of the III–V, II–VI and IV–IV compounds cannot be treated by this type of dipolar approximation, since one knows that, in many respects, these materials are closer to being metals than they are to being the type of insulator typified by the alkali halides. Specifically, the valence electrons in these materials are very largely delocalized. The crucial difference between these materials and true metals is that they do possess an absolute band gap even though it is very small in a number of cases (e.g. for InSb). And one is thus led to hypothesize that these materials at least should be treated by some extension and refinement of the methods used to treat the lattice dynamics of metals. The crucial difficulty is presented by the fact that, owing to the finite band gap, the diagonal parts of the dielectric matrices for these materials go to a finite limit as the wave vector $\boldsymbol{q}$ is decreased to zero, and any attempt to use a diagonal dielectric constant matrix $\varepsilon(\boldsymbol{q})$ is doomed to failure because the acoustic mode frequencies calculated in this manner will not vanish in the limit of zero wave vector. This is most simply illustrated by considering the oversimplified model of "jellium" in which the ions are regarded as point charges of magnitude Z embedded in the electronic background. In this case the limiting longitudinal acoustic mode frequency has the form $\Omega_{\mathrm{p}}/\varepsilon^{1/2}(0)$ where Ω_{p} is the bare ion plasma frequency. This model is very much oversimplified but it highlights the basic difficulty; if $\varepsilon(0)$ is finite then this frequency will be finite. However, the formal resolution of this difficulty is apparently contained in the review by Sham and Ziman (1963) where they point out that for a real crystal the dielectric constant is not a scalar but is in fact a matrix which has the following form:

$$\varepsilon(\boldsymbol{G}+\boldsymbol{q},\boldsymbol{G}'+\boldsymbol{q}) = \delta_{\boldsymbol{G}\boldsymbol{G}'} - \frac{4\pi e^2}{V[\boldsymbol{G}+\boldsymbol{q}]^2}\sum_{\boldsymbol{k}\boldsymbol{k}'}\frac{n_{\boldsymbol{k}}-n_{\boldsymbol{k}'}}{E_{\boldsymbol{k}}-E_{\boldsymbol{k}'}}\langle\Psi_{\boldsymbol{k}}|e^{-i(\boldsymbol{G}+\boldsymbol{q})\cdot\boldsymbol{r}}|\Psi_{\boldsymbol{k}'}\rangle\langle\Psi_{\boldsymbol{k}'}|e^{i(\boldsymbol{G}'+\boldsymbol{q})\cdot\boldsymbol{r}}|\Psi_{\boldsymbol{k}}\rangle .$$

The inverse of this matrix is such that it has the property of connecting off-diagonal parts of the Fourier transformed bare ion potential function; specifically it connects elements whose Fourier components correspond to the phonon wave vector plus a reciprocal lattice vector with those components having the periodicity of the phonon wave vector alone. It has been proved formally by a number of workers e.g. Pick et al. (1970) that there does exist a so-called acoustic sum-rule which involves these off-diagonal components of the dielectric matrix and is such as to ensure that the acoustic phonon frequencies do indeed vanish in the limit of zero wave vector. However, this result, together with the demonstration that frequencies of these modes at small but finite $\boldsymbol{q}$ are linear functions of the wave vector $\boldsymbol{q}$ is about the sum of what has been demonstrated formally. This problem will be discussed in much greater detail in chapter 5 of this book. However, one can see that this type of a priori calculation is very far, at least to the author's knowledge, from providing one with a means of computing the phonon dispersion curves for any given material. Moreover, as we indicated earlier, there is something aesthetically unpleasing about it even if it were possible, namely that, in the last resort, it commits one to a giant computer program for the computation of phonon frequencies which lacks any means of giving us a true physical insight into the details of the calculation. It may well be that we shall ultimately have to accept such calculations; however, it is difficult at present to see how the dielectric matrix is to be computed reliably, together with the unscreened effective potential or pseudo-potential that describes the electron–ion interactions, at this stage of our understanding of many body theory. Thus we still feel that some intuitive considerations must be an essential part of any theory that is developed in the immediate future. This has been the view of Martin (1969) who has circumvented the difficulty of the incomplete screening of the ionic monopole charges by introducing effective 'bond charges'. These bond charges are chosen to ensure that the 'pile-up' of electron charge at the centers of the bonds about a given site is just sufficient to neutralize unscreened excess charge at that site. How far this takes us is a matter of some debate at present; it certainly deals with the problem of non-vanishing acoustic mode frequencies but does so in a manner that is open to some question in the sense that one has no obvious guarantee that the model will be adequate to describe the behaviour of the system for modes of arbitrary wave lengths.

A potentially useful hybrid model is that recently developed by Sinha (1968, 1969) and Sinha et al. (1971) in which the electron charge distribution is regarded as being composed of a uniform background with extended dipolar components suitably located at intermediate points along the bond between a given pair of atoms. It is evident that Martin's model represents one extreme case of Sinha's more general approach.

In this context it seems that the deformation dipole model has consequences that have not yet been fully explored. The principle assumptions inherent in this model are:

a) that there is a dipole moment induced in each bond about a given atom associated exclusively with the overlap repulsion;

b) that this dipole moment is not in any way coupled to the electric field induced dipole moment;

c) that this dipole moment may be regarded as a point dipole at the ion center (this is manifestly dubious), and

d) that the local field equation (generalized to arbitrary wave vectors) provides an appropriate description of the dipole–dipole interactions in the crystal when it is distorted by a lattice wave of arbitrary wave vector.

This last assumption follows from the point dipole approximation for both polarization and deformation dipoles and it appears to us unlikely that it can be sustained if this assumption is relaxed for either type of dipole. Moreover, there is a related assumption which stems from the determination of the polarizabilities of the ions either by the procedure of Tessman et al. (1953) or by the more recent procedure suggested by Pirenne and Kartheuser (1964) and used by Jaswal and Sharma (1973). (The second approach is in all probability more reliable, since it is based on minimizing the *relative* mean square deviation of the total polarizability for all the salts considered rather than its absolute value.) The polarizabilities so determined are assumed to be totally independent of wave vector. This last assumption is also true of the simple shell model as applied to alkali halides where the positive ion is assumed to be non-polarizable. It is however not implicit in the shell model as applied to germanium and silicon where, as Cochran points out (Cochran 1959a) there is a definite long-range mechanical force between polarized ions and a corresponding dependence of the ionic polarizability on the wave vector. However, there is good reason for believing, as discussed earlier, that anything which is based on a point dipole model cannot be sustained for small band gap materials except by somewhat artificial assumptions with regard to the ionic polarization.

Let us now examine the assumptions inherent in the deformation dipole model and explore the possibility of relaxing some of them in a manner that may well enhance the applicability of this model to materials other than alkali halides and also to improve the results it produces when applied to alkali halides.

When this model was initially developed (Hardy 1959, 1962) it was of considerable surprise to the author that the agreement between theory and experiment was so close. The reason for this, which we would like to stress, since this point tends to be overlooked, is that the incorporation of the field induced polarization by itself has a *catastrophic* effect on the computed phonon dispersion curves as compared with those predicted by the rigid ion model (Kellermann 1940). Indeed for many of the alkali halides, the lattice is barely stable (Lyddane and Herzfeld 1938) and for those having highly polarizable anions, in general lattice instability is predicted. This was demonstrated by Woods et al. (1960) and also by Karo and Hardy (1963). One can thus see that incorporation of this type of polarization alone produces calculated phonon frequencies that are in gross disagreement with experiment and it is remarkable that the incorporation of short-range polarization, either using the shell model or the deformation dipole model removes this discrepancy in the outer parts of the Brillouin zone as well as allowing one to achieve perfect agreement between theory and experiment at the center of the zone where the optic mode frequencies are fitted. Thus it is important to realize that for both models there is a delicate balance between two effects each of which is very large and neither of which is a relatively minor correction to the results of Kellermann's calculations. However, the results of the deformation dipole calculations still leave something to be desired.

Thus one is led to ask how it is possible to improve the deformation dipole model in order to obtain better agreement between theory and experiment. Once again the philosophy is to obtain a good fit to the measured dispersion curves without using input parameters that are determined from the dispersion curves themselves. We have already itemized the shortcomings of the deformation dipole model, the most obvious of which is the treatment of the deformation dipoles as point dipoles at the negative ion centers.

At present, it seems unlikely that one is going to be able to do much better than represent the effect of the deformation by point dipoles; however, their location is certainly something which can be improved upon. Thus we are left with the possibility of locating the deformation dipoles at some point other than the negative ion center which is a highly desirable modification. The other possible modification is to remove the Lorentz local field assumption. This last objective is certainly most desirable in the case of small band gap materials. The ideal situation would be, of course, to have a theory which would treat the lattice dynamics of ionic and covalent crystals with equal facility. In principle, the dielectric matrix of Sham and Ziman, when incorporated into the lattice dynamical formalism, offers an approach which is of universal validity. However in practice, for the present, one is almost certainly going to be compelled to use different phenomenological models for different classes of material. As regards the deformation dipole model, it seems reasonable to retain the local field assumption as far as the polarization induced dipoles are concerned but to consider the deformation dipoles separately. This has not been done as yet and it is an undertaking of some complexity. The virtue of such an approach is that it should be possible by using dipoles whose location and strength are disposable parameters to fit both the violation of the Cauchy relation for any given material and the effective charge. This is important because from Dick and Overhauser's early work, subsequently extended by Dick (1965), it was apparent that it was not possible to do this by using overlap deformation alone and it may well have been this fact that led them to introduce the idea of core–shell polarization.

The basic point regarding the use of dipoles that have a variable location along the nearest neighbor bonds, is that, at one extreme, it is possible, by placing the dipoles actually on one or other ion site to obtain a deviation of the effective charge from unity without any violation of the Cauchy relation; while moving them away from the ion centers will lead to a violation of the Cauchy relation which, hopefully, one can adjust to agree with the observed violation. It should, however, be stressed that if one is going to use this procedure, the appropriate elastic constants should be 'athermal' and not the elastic constants as measured. To obtain these athermal elastic constants one has to follow the prescription given by Leibfried and Ludwig (1961): namely one measures the elastic constants ultrasonically over a wide range of temperatures starting from close to absolute zero, plots them as a function of temperature, and then extrapolates linearly to absolute zero from the straight portion of these curves and thus obtains the athermal values. As regards the elastic constant C_{44}, this is no great matter since its temperature variation is usually quite small.

Thus, in this new model one will have a series of dipoles induced by overlap deformation each located at some point between a given pair of first neighbors and it will be necessary to compute their interactions. As regards computing the dipole–dipole interaction one cannot see any great difficulty with modern computers. The main problem would be with regard to the interactions between dipoles on the same ion and the interaction between the deformation and polarization dipoles on a particular ion. In the case of the latter effect, it would probably be best at this stage to neglect it, since we cannot see any very reliable way of computing it. How good such a model would be can, of course, only be tested by using it for computation; and that is something for the future.

Such a model would not, of course, be particularly useful for studying the dynamics of covalently bonded materials. For these at present it would seem that Martin's calculations (Martin 1969) or those of Sinha et al. (1971) are still the best. However, one cannot but feel that improvements or refinements in the actual use of Sinha's model would be probably the best ultimate solution to the problem, as he himself points out.

In conclusion one can say that the dynamics of metals is reasonably well understood using pseudo-potential theory. Certainly the use of such an approach is a great advance on the use of Born–Von Kármán force constants to fit the measured dispersion curves. However, in the case of more complex metals there remains the question of how one includes the effect of closed or semi-closed shells corresponding to the d bands and recent work by Weber et al. (1972) and Sham (1971) has indicated that in this area there is still much to be done.

The approach of Weber et al. (1972) is phenomenological in that they use an interesting extension of the breathing shell model where the shells represent the tightly bound d electrons, while the cores, as before, represent the nuclei plus the inner shells of electrons and the remainder of the electrons are treated as free. Thus we have a model for which there is no splitting of the longitudinal optical and transverse optical branches at $\boldsymbol{q}=0$, since the long-range electrostatic field is screened by the free electrons. However, for large $\boldsymbol{q}$ values this screening becomes ineffective and, if the lattice has some degree of ionicity the longitudinal optical–transverse optical splitting becomes large for large values of $\boldsymbol{q}$.

This approach has some quantum mechanical justification since Pick (1971) and Hanke (1971) have been able to show how it is possible to separate the contributions to the dielectric constant into a free electron component and a component arising from excitations of the tightly bound electrons. This result provides reasonable justification for the phenomenological approach and is similar to Sinha et al.'s results (Sinha et al. 1971).

Similar considerations appear to have been used by Sham (1971), however his work is carried through using the microscopic theory and has enabled him to demonstrate that elastic instability of Nb_3Sn can be driven by a soft zone center optic mode which does not itself have zero frequency.

As regards the dynamics of alkali halide crystals, one is left with the impression that current phenomenological models provide a very close description of their behaviour but again one would like to see these calculations placed on a firmer a priori footing. Similarly one can say the same with regard to studies of the dynamics of covalent materials.

One final comment is appropriate and this concerns the desirability of using neutron scattering data to obtain information about phonon eigenvectors (dynamical structure analysis). In view of earlier comments (Leigh et al. 1971) it would seem to be important to do so since this information provides an additional and more stringent test of the theoretical predictions.

References

AHMAD, A.A.Z., SMITH, H.G., WAKABAYASHI N., and WILKINSON, M.K. (1972), Phys. Rev. **B6**, 3956.

ALEKSANDOV, K.S. and RYZHOVA, T.V. (1961), Soviet Phys. Crystall. **6**, 228.

BASU, A.N. and SENGUPTA, S. (1968), Phys. Stat. Sol. **29**, 367.

BORN, M. and VON KÁRMÁN, T. (1912), Physik. Z. **13**, 297.

BORN, M. and VON KÁRMAN, T. (1913), Physik Z. **14**, 15.

BORN, M. and HUANG, K. (1954), *Dynamical theory of crystal lattices*, 1st ed. (Oxford University Press) IV, §14.

BOUCKAERDT, L.P., SMOLUCHOWSKI, R. and WIGNER, E. (1936), Phys. Rev. **50**, 58.

COCHRAN, W. (1971), *Lattice dynamics of ionic and covalent crystals*, C.R.C. Critical Reviews in Solid State Science **2**, 1.

COCHRAN, W. (1959a), Proc. Roy. Soc. **A253**, 260.

COCHRAN, W. (1959b), Phil. Mag. **4**, 1082.

COPLEY, J.R.D., MACPHERSON, R.W., and TIMUSK, T. (1969), Phys. Rev. **182**, 965.

DICK, B.G. and OVERHAUSER, A.W. (1958), Phys. Rev. **112**, 90.

DICK, B.G. (1965), *Lattice dynamics* (Pergamon Press, Oxford), p. 159.

FELDKAMP, L.A. (1972), J. Phys. Chem. Solids **33**, 711.

HANKE, W. (1971), *Phonons*, Proc. Int. Conf. on Phonons (Flammarion Press, Paris), p. 294.

HARDY, J.R. (1959), Phil. Mag. **4**, 1278.

HARDY, J.R. (1962), Phil. Mag. **7**, 315.

HARRISON, W.A. (1965), *Pseudo potentials in the theory of metals* (W.A. Benjamin, New York).

HERMAN, F. (1959), J. Phys. Chem. Solids **8**, 405.

HUANG, K. (1951), Proc. Roy. Soc. (London) **A208**, 352.

JASWAL, S.S. and SHARMA, T.P. (1973), J. Phys. Chem. Solids **34**, 509.

KARO, A.M. and HARDY, J.R. (1960), Phil. Mag. **5**, 859.

KARO, A.M. and HARDY, J.R. (1963), Phys. Rev. **129**, 2024.

KELLERMANN, E.W. (1940), Phil. Trans. Roy. Soc. (London) **A238**, 513.

KUNC, K., BALKANSKI, M. and NUSIMOVICI, M.A. (1971), *Phonons*, Proc. Int. Conf. on Phonons (Flammarion Press, Paris), p. 109.

LEIBFRIED, G. and LUDWIG, W. (1961), Solid State Physics (Academic Press, New York) **12**, 276.

LEIGH, R.S., SZIGETI, B. and TEWARY, V.K. (1971), Proc. Roy. Soc. (London) **A320**, 505.

LORENTZ, H.A. (1909), *Theory of Electrons* (Teubner), pp. 137–150.
LÖWDIN, P.O. (1948), *A theoretical investigation into some properties of ionic crystals* (Thesis) (Almquist and Wiksells).
LOWNDES, R.P. and MARTIN, D.H. (1969), Proc. Roy. Soc. (London) **A308**, 473.
LUNDQUIST, S.O. (1952), Ark. Fysik **6**, 25.
LUNDQUIST, S.O. (1955), Ark. Fysik **9**, 435.
LUNDQUIST, S.O. (1957), Ark. Fysik **12**, 263.
LYDDANE, R.H. and HERZFELD, K.F. (1938), Phys. Rev. **54**, 846.
MARTIN, R.M. (1969), Phys. Rev. **186**, 871.
NUSIMOVICI, M. (1969), Ann. Phys. (France) **4**, 97.
NÜSSLEIN, V. and SCHRÖDER, U. (1967), Phys. Stat. Sol. **21**, 309.
PAULING, L. (1960), *The nature of the chemical bond*, 3rd ed. (Cornell Univ. Press); see also 1939 edition.
PICK, R.M., COHEN, M.H., and MARTIN, R.M. (1970), Phys. Rev. **B1**, 910.
PICK, R.M. (1971), *Phonons*, Proc. Int. Conf. on Phonons (Flammarion Press, Paris), p. 20.
PIRENNE, J. and KARTHEUSER, E. (1964), Physica **30**, 2005.
REINITZ, K. (1961), Phys. Rev. **123**, 1615.
ROWELL, J.M. and DYNES, R.C. (1971), *Phonons*, Proc. Int. Conf. on Phonons (Flammarion Press, Paris), p. 150.
SANGSTER, M.J.L., PECKHAM, G. and SAUNDERSON, D.H. (1970), J. Phys. C (Solid State Phys.) **3**, 1026.
SCHRÖDER, U. (1966), Solid State Comm. **4**, 347.
SHAM, L.J. and ZIMAN, J.M. (1963), Solid State Physics (Academic Press, New York) **15**, 221.
SHAM, L.J. (1971), Phys. Rev. Letters **27**, 1725.
SHARMA, T.P. and JASWAL, S.S. (1973), J. Phys. Chem. Solids.
SINGH, R.K. and VERMA, M.P. (1969), Phys. Stat. Sol. **36**, 335.
SINGH, R.K. and VERMA, M.P. (1970), Phys. Stat. Sol. **38**, 851.
SINHA, S.K. (1968), Phys. Rev. **169**, 477.
SINHA, S.K. (1969), Phys. Rev. **177**, 1256.
SINHA, S.K., GUPTA, R.P. and PRICE, D.L. (1971), Phys. Rev. Letters **26**, 1324.
SZIGETI, B. (1949), Trans. Faraday Soc. **45**, 155.
SZIGETI, B. (1950), Proc. Roy. Soc. **A206**, 51.
TESSMAN, J.R., KAHN, A.H., and SCHOCKLEY, W. (1953), Phys. Rev. **92**, 890.
TOSI, M.P. (1964), Solid State Physics (Academic Press, New York) **16**, 1.
VERMA, M.P. and SINGH, R.K. (1969), Phys. Stat. Sol. **33**, 769.
VETELINO, J.F. and MITRA, S.S. (1969), Phys. Rev. **178**, 1349.
WEBER, W., BILZ, H. and SCHRÖDER, U. (1972), Phys. Rev. Letters **28**, 600.
WIGNER, E.P. and SEITZ, F. (1955), Solid State Physics, (Academic Press, New York) **1**, 97.
WOODS, A.D.B., COCHRAN, W. and BROCKHOUSE, B.N. (1960), Phys. Rev. **119**, 980.

CHAPTER 4

Phonons in Non-Transition Metals

E. G. BROVMAN and Yu. M. KAGAN

I. V. Kurchatov Atomic Energy Institute, Moscow, U.S.S.R.

Dynamical Properties of Solids, edited by G. K. Horton and A. A. Maradudin

Contents

1. Introduction

In recent years significant progress has been achieved in the development of our understanding of the dynamical properties of a metal. The theory of these properties, which only recently possessed a phenomenological character, to a significant degree has become a microscopic theory. It permits one to carry out practically exhaustive qualitative and quantitative analyses for non-transition metals, based only on elementary interactions of a clearly physical nature.

This progress is connected in the first place with the general development of the electron theory of metals, which occurred in the 1960's. For the problem of the formation of the phonon spectrum it is precisely the best understood, in fact the basic, ideas concerning the electron–ion system in non-transition metals which turn out to be the most significant (see, for example, Harrison 1966, Heine and Weaire 1970). These can be formulated briefly in the following way.

1. In metals all valence electrons collectivize, forming a single subsystem of quasi-free electrons. The ions which remain possess comparatively small dimensions, each occupying roughly 10% of the volume per atom in the crystal. Consequently, the ions to all intents and purposes do not overlap, so that the direct interaction between ions has a Coulombic character.

A calculation of the weak overlap or Van der Waals forces between ions in such metals, seemingly would exceed the limit accuracy of the theory as its current state of development.

2. The strong oscillations of the wave function of an electron in the interior of an ion core lead to a sharp decrease in the effective electron–ion interaction at small distances, and, consequently, in the scattering amplitude of an electron by an ion for large momentum transfers. The success of the nearly free electron model for the description of electrons in the vicinity of the Fermi surface is directly related to the fact that in a regular metal it is the scattering of electrons with the transfer of a large momentum, equal to a reciprocal lattice vector $\boldsymbol{K}$, that is the most important.

3. In the analysis of the properties of a metal the details of the behavior of the wave function of a conduction electron in the interior of an ion core more often than not does not play the principal role. In connection with this there arises the natural idea of introducing instead of the true interaction with an ion some effective single particle potential (nonlocal in general), which is weaker than the true potential inside the ion, but which preserves the scattering properties of the true ion. The resulting pseudopotential, or model potential, is usually obtained from first principles or on the basis of limited experimental information (see Harrison 1966, Cohen and Heine 1970, the many references contained in these reviews, as well as subsection 3.2 of this chapter).

Thus, in the absence of overlap between ion cores a metal represents a degenerate plasma whose electron density is determined by the valence, and with a specific effective electron–ion interaction vertex. This interaction introduces the small parameter of the theory, which is the ratio $V_{\boldsymbol{K}}/\mathscr{E}_{\mathrm{F}}$, where the $V_{\boldsymbol{K}}$ are the Fourier components of the effective potential evaluated at the reciprocal lattice vectors (in the language of a local potential).

From what is said it is easy to conclude that phonons in a metal represent the low-frequency collective excitations of the electron–ion plasma, the ground state of which is the periodic arrangement of the ions. In connection with this any consistent dynamical theory of a metal in principle is constructed from the very beginning as a many body theory, and inevitably bears the imprint of those difficulties characteristic of a many body theory at intermediate densities (see, for example, Pines and Nozieres 1966).

At the same time, up to now the theory of metals developed in the main as a single particle theory, and it is just in this way that it achieved its greatest quantitative successes. This is connected with the fact that the dispersive properties of the electronic spectrum at the Fermi surface, the energy versus wave vector relation $E_{\boldsymbol{k}}$, which in principle can be described from the single particle point of view, are most sensitive to the character of the electron–ion interaction, while it is often sufficient to take the electron–electron interaction into account only in the form of a static screening of the potential of an isolated ion.

If, further, it is desired to obtain the energy of the electron gas in a metal as a sum of single particle energies, calculated in the second order of perturbation theory, then in that energy appears a contribution effectively containing a pairwise indirect interaction between ions through the conduction electrons (see, for example, Harrison 1966, Heine and Weaire 1970). Separated explicitly, this interaction, together with the direct Coulomb interaction, constitutes the full pair interaction between ions, which can already be utilized for finding the vibrational spectrum within the framework of the traditional Born–von Karman scheme (see, for example, Born and Huang 1954, Maradudin et al. 1971). The alternative approach in which the indirect interaction between two ions is determined directly with a self-consistent calculation of the screening (see, for example, the review by Cochran 1965), or in which the energy of the electron gas is found in the Hartree–Fock approximation to second order in the electron–ion interaction, in fact lead to the very same result. The only differences between them can consist only in differing degrees of accuracy in the calculation of the screening.

The overwhelming number of investigations analyzing phonon spectra in specific metals have been carried out in just this approximation. (For references to this work see section 3 of this chapter, as well as the review of Heine and Weaire 1970.) Among these a special place is occupied by the work of Toya (1958) and of Vosko et al. (1965). The work of Toya, in general, represents the first attempt to obtain the phonon spectrum of a metal on the basis of a microscopic investigation. The work of Vosko et al. was the first serious attempt to analyze the entire problem as a whole, and it remains to this day one of the best works in this field. (Although somewhat differing methods were used in these two papers, at the final stage the physical approximations made turn out to be equivalent.)

Inasmuch as the approach in many respects remained a single-particle one, then, as in the case of the electronic spectrum, the basic interest of the majority of the work turned out to be connected with the definition of the effective electron–ion interaction – an atomic rather than a solid state characteristic of a metal. In the course of this there often arose the illusion of the correctness of this very simplified approximation, and all inaccuracies in the results were assumed to be due to the limitation of our knowledge about the correct electron–ion interaction and the dielectric function of a homogeneous electron gas.

In fact, the true picture of the many-body interactions in a metal turns out to be much more complex. In addition to the pairwise interaction, there exists a non-pairwise interaction, which is the indirect interaction, through the conduction electrons, of three and more ions. This interaction plays the principal role, particularly in the dynamics of vibrations (see below), predetermining, in particular, the appearance of a covalent type of force in a metal. A consistent investigation of it presents significant formal difficulties, for there arises the necessity of calculating simultaneously with the change of the electronic spectrum the influence of the reconstruction of the electronic wave function in a crystal on the character of the screening of the ions and the energy of the Coulomb interaction of the electron gas.

In recent years there have appeared papers (Sham 1969, Pick et al. 1970), in which some general microscopic approach to the analysis of the dynamics of a crystal is studied, which expresses the force constants, or the elements of the dynamical matrix, through the full inverse dielectric susceptibility matrix, pertaining to all electrons of the substance. (The first formulation of the dynamical problem in terms of the inverse dielectric matrix in the Hartree approximation with application to a metal was given in the work of Sham 1965). In such a general form the representation obtained is rigorous for any substance and therefore can be used, for example, to obtain limiting relations of a general type. Unfortunately, it is very difficult to use it constructively for the analysis of the dynamics of a metal, if it is desired to take into account many-ion effects in a controlled approximation. As a result, the approximation used by Sham (1965) for the calculation of phonons in Na, turns out to be completely equivalent to the approximation of pairwise interactions. The attempt at a partial calculation of the many-ion interaction in a metal within the framework of such an approach was in fact undertaken only by Maradudin and Koppel (Koppel and Maradudin 1967, Koppel 1968).

In the work of the present authors (Brovman and Kagan 1967, 1969, Kagan and Brovman 1968) a many-particle theory of metals was developed, which allows the consistent calculation of the non-pairwise interionic interaction through the conduction electrons together with the pairwise interaction. These investigations are based on the use from the very beginning of an electron plasma hamiltonian with the introduction into the electron–ion interaction vertex of an effective, model potential, and finding the energy of the electronic ground state as a functional of the static configuration of the ions. This energy is obtained in the form of a series in powers of the electron–ion interaction, while the electron–electron interaction in each term of this series is treated exactly. From a physical point of view the expansion obtained describes in an explicit way successively the two-ion, three-ion, etc. indirect interaction; from the formal point of view it reduces to a series in powers of the small parameter $V_{\boldsymbol{K}}/\mathscr{E}_{\mathrm{F}}$. Knowing the energy of the ground state and taking into account the correctness of the adiabatic approximation, it is not difficult to determine the dynamical matrix for the vibrational problem, as well as other characteristics of a metal which are integrals over the electronic spectrum such as, for example, the equation of state, the compressibility, the elastic constants, etc.

We use this approach here in order to analyze in a unified manner all general problems of the dynamical theory of metals (the nature and role of covalency, the problem of the compressibility, singularities in the phonon spectrum, dynamical stability, etc.). On the other hand we utilize it for finding the phonon spectrum and basic static characteristics of non-transition metals in order to demonstrate that the present state of the theory allows one, with reasonable quantitative accuracy, to describe a whole host of quantities within the framework of one and the same set of approximations, and using information only about the electron–ion interaction. It seems to us that it is in just such generality that the basic problem of a quantitative physical theory lies. Correspondingly, the presentation divides into two main sections. In the first (section 2) general problems of the dynamical theory of metals are discussed. The second (section 3) is devoted to the analysis of the dynamical and static properties of specific metals.

2. *General theoretical considerations*

2.1. The adiabatic approximation in a metal

As is well known, the adiabatic approximation of Born and Oppenheimer plays a cardinal role in the dynamical theory of lattices (Born and Huang 1954). At first glance it appears as if the basic criterion of adiabaticity – the absence in the electronic spectrum of excitations with energies of the scale of the nuclear vibrational frequencies ω – is violated in a metal. Indeed, in the vicinity of the Fermi surface electronic transitions are possible with arbitrarily small excitation energies, and in any case for electrons with energies within ω of the Fermi energy the adiabatic approximation is surely not correct. However, at the same time the excitation energy is of the order of $\mathscr{E}_F$, for the majority of the collectivized electrons and therefore they must follow the vibrating nuclei adiabatically. The last circumstance in fact makes possible the use of the adiabatic approximation in the determination of properties which are integrals over the electronic spectrum. This problem was analyzed in detail by Chester (1961) and by the authors (Brovman and Kagan 1967). In the latter work the principal attention was devoted to the question of the magnitude of the renormalization of the adiabatic phonons due to the electron–phonon interaction for arbitrary phonon momenta. Clearly, it is just this problem which is the determining one for estimates of the accuracy of the adiabatic approximation in obtaining the phonon spectrum of a metal.

For the solution of this problem at the first stage we can employ the traditional procedure of separating the electronic and ionic degrees of freedom. If the hamiltonian of the system has the form

$$H = H_e(\boldsymbol{r}) + H_i(\boldsymbol{R}) + H_{ei}(\boldsymbol{r}, \boldsymbol{R}), \tag{1}$$

then separating of the Schrödinger equation for the electrons for fixed positions of the ions

$$[H_e(\boldsymbol{r}) + H_{ei}(\boldsymbol{r}, \boldsymbol{R})]\, \psi_m(\boldsymbol{r}, \boldsymbol{R}) = E_m(\boldsymbol{R})\, \psi_m(\boldsymbol{r}, \boldsymbol{R}), \tag{2}$$

we pass directly to the system of equations describing the vibrational problem

$$[H_i(\boldsymbol{R}) + E_n(\boldsymbol{R})]\, \Phi_n(\boldsymbol{R}) + \sum_m (A_{nm} + B_{nm})\, \Phi_m(\boldsymbol{R}) = E\Phi_n(\boldsymbol{R}), \tag{3}$$

where

$$A_{nm} = -(1/M) \sum_j (\nabla_{\boldsymbol{R}_j})_{nm}\, \nabla_{\boldsymbol{R}_j}, \qquad B_{nm} = -(1/M) \sum_j (\nabla^2_{\boldsymbol{R}_j})_{nm} \tag{4}$$

($\boldsymbol{R}_j$ is the coordinate of the jth ion; the remaining notation is standard).

If the off-diagonal terms of A_{nm} and B_{nm} are neglected, then eq. (3) represents an equation determining the adiabatic vibrational spectrum, while the off-diagonal terms describe the non-adiabatic interaction of the vibrational and electronic systems.

The next step consists of finding the non-adiabatic parts of the total energy, ΔE. For this one can go over to the second quantization representation in terms of the electron states of the periodic lattice and the adiabatic phonons, and make use of the relation, which follows directly from eq. (2)

$$(\nabla_{\boldsymbol{R}_j})_{nm} = -[\nabla_{\boldsymbol{R}_j} H_{ei}(\boldsymbol{r}, \boldsymbol{R})]_{nm} / [E_n(\boldsymbol{R}) - E_m(\boldsymbol{R})]. \tag{5}$$

If ΔE is found, then for the renormalization of the phonons $\delta\omega_{\boldsymbol{q}\lambda}$ and electrons $\delta E_{\boldsymbol{k}}$ due to the electron–phonon interaction the procedure of varying the energy of the system with respect to the corresponding occupation numbers can be used, analogous to the method used in Landau's theory of the Fermi liquid (Landau 1956). According to this method

$$\delta\omega_{\boldsymbol{q}\lambda} = \delta(\Delta E)/\delta N_{\boldsymbol{q}\lambda}, \qquad \delta E_{\boldsymbol{k}} = \delta(\Delta E)/\delta n_{\boldsymbol{k}} \tag{6}$$

($\boldsymbol{q}$, λ are the phonon wave vector and branch index, respectively; $\boldsymbol{k}$ is the wave vector of the electron).

Such a program was carried out (Brovman and Kagan 1967), in which the energy ΔE was obtained by perturbation theory to second order in A and first order in B. Referring to this work for the details, we present here only the final result for the renormalization of the phonons,

$$\delta\omega_{q\lambda} = \sum_{k} |M_{k,q\lambda}|^2 (n_k - n_{k+q})/(E_k - E_{k+q} - \omega_{q\lambda} + \mathrm{i}\delta) \\ - \sum_{k} |M_{k,q\lambda}|^2 (n_k - n_{k+q})/(E_k - E_{k+q}), \quad (7)$$

where $M_{k,q\lambda}$ is the standard Bloch matrix element of the electron–phonon interaction, while n_k are the electron occupation numbers. The sense of this expression is easily understood. The second term in it describes the adiabatic contribution of the electrons to the frequency of phonon excitation, and by itself can be of the order of $\omega_{q\lambda}$. However, the purely non-adiabatic renormalization turns out to be very small. For the overwhelming part of phase space eq. (7) yields

$$\Delta\omega_{q\lambda} = \mathrm{Re}\,\delta\omega_{q\lambda} \sim \omega_{q\lambda}\ \omega_0/\mathscr{E}_\mathrm{F})^2, \quad (8)$$

where ω_0 is a characteristic phonon frequency. The phonon damping function $\Gamma_{q\lambda}$ is determined only by the first term in eq. (7), and a result is insensitive to the adiabatic procedure, and the estimate for $\Gamma_{q\lambda}$ is the standard one

$$\Gamma_{q\lambda} \sim \mathrm{Im}\,\delta\omega_{q\lambda} \sim \omega_{q\lambda}(\omega_0/\mathscr{E}_\mathrm{F}). \quad (9)$$

In a narrow range of momenta, where $|q-2k_\mathrm{F}|/k_\mathrm{F} \sim \omega_0/\mathscr{E}_\mathrm{F}$, a stronger shift in phonon frequencies than that given by eq. (8) occurs,

$$\Delta\omega_{q\lambda} \sim \omega_{q\lambda}(\omega_0/\mathscr{E}_\mathrm{F}). \quad (8^1)$$

For the renormalization of the electronic spectrum the variational procedure (6) leads to the expression (retaining only the dominant term)

$$\Delta E_k = \sum_{q\lambda} |M_{k,q\lambda}|^2\, \omega_{q\lambda}(1 - 2n_{k+q})/[(E_k - E_{k+q})^2 - \omega_{q\lambda}^2]. \quad (10)$$

A simple analysis shows that far from the Fermi surface

$$\Delta E_k \sim \omega_0(\omega_0/\mathscr{E}_\mathrm{F}),$$

at the same time that in the narrow 'crust' $|\mathscr{E}_k - \mathscr{E}_\mathrm{F}| \sim \omega_0$ the renormalization of the electronic velocities turns out to be significant and does not contain the parameter $(\omega_0/\mathscr{E}_\mathrm{F})$. The last result was first obtained by Migdal (1958).

The estimates presented above permit the formulation of general conclusions about the use of the adiabatic approximation in a metal and the role of the electron–phonon interaction.

1. The phonon spectrum of a metal is determined with great accuracy within the framework of the purely adiabatic approximation. Taking into

account the influence of the electron–phonon interaction on the dispersion law leads to a very small renormalization.

2. Macroscopic quantities, determined from a microscopic approach within the framework of the adiabatic approximation, are obtained with a relative error no larger than $(\omega_0/\mathscr{E}_F)$.

3. For the determination of properties connected with the electrons on the Fermi surface of a metal to zero order in the parameter $\omega_0/\mathscr{E}_F$, it is essential after obtaining the adiabatic phonon spectrum and the electronic spectrum in the static lattice to carry out a renormalization of the electrons near the Fermi surface due to the electron–phonon interaction.

4. The renormalization of the phonons in general does not impose any constraints on the electron–phonon coupling constant, stemming from the requirements of the stability of the lattice. The converse assertion, which arises as a result of the use of the Fröhlich hamiltonian (see, Tyablikov and Tolmachev 1958, Joshi and Rajagopal 1968), is incorrect, and is connected with the fact that the electron–ion interaction, roughly speaking, is taken into account twice – once during the determination of the 'dressed' phonons, giving rise to normal longitudinal sound velocities, and a second time in the calculation of the renormalization in the form of the first term of eq. (7). We note that this result is very important for the problem of superconductivity.

The validity of the adiabatic approximation significantly simplifies the application of field theoretic methods (see, for example, Abrikosov et al. 1963) to the analysis of the dynamics of a metal. It is clear from the preceding that the problem of obtaining the phonon spectrum in this case in fact reduces to the determination of the energy of interaction of the electron gas with the static field of fixed ions, for which diagrammatic techniques can be utilized directly.

Within the framework of field theoretic methods a different approach is possible, based on finding the renormalization of 'dressed' phonons due to the electron–phonon interaction (Migdal 1958). In this approach a significant role is played by the result, obtained by Migdal, that with an accuracy given by the same adiabatic parameter $\omega_0/\mathscr{E}_F$ the vertex part of the electron–phonon interaction reduces to a simple vertex. However, it is significant that the electron–ion system of a metal cannot be reduced self-consistently to a system of 'bare' electrons and phonons with a definite interaction between them (the Fröhlich hamiltonian), which would be the analogue of the situation found in quantum electrodynamics. This is connected with the fact that the introduction of any 'dressed' phonons in a metal already automatically presupposes the participation of the electrons in their formation. Therefore, the use of the Fröhlich hamiltonian has a distinctly model character. This model, however, turns out to be adequate for discussions of the influence of the electron–phonon interaction on electrons close to the Fermi surface, i.e., for example, for the description of the kinetics of electrons, their mass renormalization, and electronic lifetimes (Migdal 1958), for obtaining the gap equations in the theory of superconductivity (see, for example, Eliashberg 1963, Schrieffer 1964, etc.).

We note, in a purely prescriptive way, that in these problems when adiabatic phonons are utilized all phonon lines must be left unrenormalized. [When this is done, a result is obtained for the mass operator in particular which, in fact, coincides with eq. (12).] A full analysis of the role of the non-adiabatic interaction of the electrons and phonons falls outside the scope of the present paper, and must form the subject of a special review.

We note that it is also possible to investigate consistently the problem in the language of field theory if for the 'bare' Bose excitations are chosen the plasma-like vibrations of the ions in a stationary, neutralizing, electronic background, and simultaneously the electron–electron and the electron–phonon interactions are taken into account through a vertex which is defined by a 'bare' electron–ion potential. In the 'jellium' model such a problem was analyzed, for example, in Schrieffer's book (Schrieffer 1964). A consistent investigation, which takes into account the discrete structure of the metal, in principle must yield a phonon spectrum which coincides with the spectrum of adiabatic phonons, obtained within the framework of the results described above.

In what follows the discussion will be based on the first approach, i.e., on the determination of the energy of interacting electrons as a function of the positions of the ions. This approach, for the purposes of the present review, possesses a significant advantage, for it allows us to obtain in a unified way the properties of the static metal lattice on the one hand, and the phonons in it on the other, while at the same time it is the most transparent from the point of view of analyzing the physical nature of the interactions responsible for the formation of these quantities.

2.2. The electronic energy

As follows from the preceding subsection, for the determination of the electronic contribution to the vibrational spectrum it is essential to find the energy of the electronic system in the field of fixed ions, $E(\boldsymbol{R}_1, \cdots, \boldsymbol{R}_n)$, which in the equation for the adiabatic phonons (3) plays the role of the potential energy. It is sufficient to consider this problem at $T=0$, since at fixed specific volume the corrections to the energy due to a finite temperature are proportional to $(T/\mathscr{E}_{\mathrm{F}})^2$.

Therefore, we are concerned with the determination of the ground state energy of the hamiltonian entering eq. (2). In the second quantization representation with respect to plane waves

$$\hat{H} = \sum_{\boldsymbol{k}} \mathscr{E}_{\boldsymbol{k}} a_{\boldsymbol{k}}^{+} a_{\boldsymbol{k}} + \tfrac{1}{2} \sum_{\boldsymbol{k}\boldsymbol{k}'\boldsymbol{q}} (4\pi e^2/q^2\Omega)\, a_{\boldsymbol{k}-\boldsymbol{q}}^{+} a_{\boldsymbol{k}'+\boldsymbol{q}}^{+} a_{\boldsymbol{k}'} a_{\boldsymbol{k}} + \sum_{\boldsymbol{k}\boldsymbol{q}} U_{\boldsymbol{k},\boldsymbol{k}+\boldsymbol{q}} a_{\boldsymbol{k}}^{+} a_{\boldsymbol{k}+\boldsymbol{q}},$$
$$\mathscr{E}_{\boldsymbol{k}} = k^2/2m. \tag{11}$$

The interaction of an electron with the system of ions is defined here in the following way:

$$U_{\boldsymbol{k},\boldsymbol{k}+\boldsymbol{q}} = V_{\boldsymbol{k},\boldsymbol{k}+\boldsymbol{q}}\, N^{-1} \sum_{m} \exp(\mathrm{i}\boldsymbol{q}\cdot\boldsymbol{R}_m), \tag{12}$$

where N is the total number of ions. (For simplicity, we restrict ourselves here to mono-atomic metals.)

For the vertex of the interaction of an electron with an individual ion $V_{\boldsymbol{k},\boldsymbol{k}+\boldsymbol{q}}$ we will make use of the idea of a weak pseudopotential, which effectively takes into account the reduction of the interaction inside the ion core (see section 1) and correctly gives the value of the scattering amplitude for the scattering of an electron by an isolated ion. In the general case this model potential is non-local, but when it can be approximated by a local potential its matrix element will depend only on the difference of the wave vectors,

$$V_{\boldsymbol{k},\boldsymbol{k}+\boldsymbol{q}} \rightarrow V_{\boldsymbol{q}}. \tag{13}$$

For the purpose of simplification we will first obtain the basic results for a local pseudopotential, and then will carry out a special analysis of those changes which have to be taken into account with the introduction of non-locality (see subsection 2.10).

We will seek the ground state energy of the electronic system in the form of an expansion in powers of the electron–ion interaction. It is not difficult to write down the general form of such an expansion

$$E_{\mathrm{e}} = E^{(0)} + E^{(1)} + E^{(2)} + E^{(3)} + \cdots, \tag{14}$$

$$E^{(n)} = \Omega \sum_{\boldsymbol{q}_1 \cdots \boldsymbol{q}_n} \Gamma^{(n)}(\boldsymbol{q}_1, \cdots, \boldsymbol{q}_n)\, U_{\boldsymbol{q}_1} \cdots U_{\boldsymbol{q}_n}\, \Delta(\boldsymbol{q}_1 + \cdots + \boldsymbol{q}_n). \tag{15}$$

Here, the delta symbol $\Delta(\boldsymbol{q})$ expresses the conservation of momentum, which is a consequence of the homogeneity of the unperturbed system (the quantization is carried out in a basis of plane waves). The multi-pole functions $\Gamma^{(n)}$ introduced in this fashion are universal characteristics. They clearly depend only on the electron–electron interaction and are independent of the positions of the ions and of the properties of a specific ion. It follows from eq. (15) that without loss of generality the multi-pole functions can be regarded as completely symmetric in all their arguments.

To obtain eqs. (14) and (15) in an explicit form diagrammatic techniques can be employed (see, for example, Abrikosov et al. 1963), regarding as the perturbation in the S matrix the operator

$$H_{\text{int}} = H_{\text{ee}} + H_{\text{ei}},$$

where H_{ee} and H_{ei} are the second and third terms on the right hand side of eq. (11), respectively. In this calculation the ground state energy can be associated with the set of all 'connected' vacuum diagrams. Each term in eq. (14) corresponds to the set of all diagrams of a definite order in H_{ei} and of arbitrary order in H_{ee} (see below for terms with $n \geqslant 4$).

The electron–ion interaction in these diagrams plays the role of a static, external field, in view of the adiabatic nature of the problem. To each term of a given order in H_{ei} corresponds a diagram with the same number of wavy lines describing the interaction with the external field (see fig. 1). If these

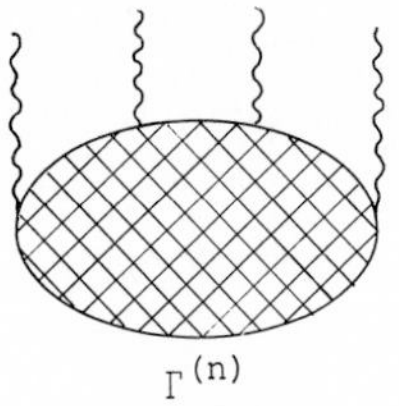

$\Gamma^{(n)}$

Fig. 1

interaction lines are regarded as free, with fixed values of the momenta, then we are led to polarization-type diagrams, which are convenient in that by using standard diagrammatic techniques (cf. Abrikosov et al. 1963), the coefficient in any diagram is found to be independent of its order in the perturbation expansion. The totality of all such diagrams with n external field lines $\Gamma_{\text{d}}^{(n)}(\boldsymbol{q}_1, \cdots, \boldsymbol{q}_n)$, symmetrized in the momenta $\boldsymbol{q}_i$, is connected to the multi-pole function appearing in eq. (15) by the simple relation (see, the discussion by Brovman and Kagan 1969)

$$\Gamma^{(n)}(\boldsymbol{q}_1, \cdots, \boldsymbol{q}_n) = (1/n)\, \Gamma_{\text{d}}^{(n)}(\boldsymbol{q}_1, \cdots, \boldsymbol{q}_n).$$

In the study of any many-body problem in a metal it is convenient to take into account the condition of electrical neutrality in an explicit way in the starting hamiltonian (1). In the Fourier representation (this can be done even before the transformation to second quantization), electrical neutrality leads to the vanishing of the $\boldsymbol{q}=0$ component of the Coulomb interaction in all three terms of eq. (1). These components must be absent, consequently, from the hamiltonian (1), while the 'bare' ion–ion interaction in what follows must be considered together with a compensating, uniform background of negative charge. At the same time, however, it is necessary to take into account that, because an ion is not a point charge, it is always the case that for small values of $\boldsymbol{q}$

$$V_{\boldsymbol{q}\to 0} = -(4\pi Z e^2/q\Omega_0) + b/\Omega_0\,, \tag{16}$$

where Ze is the ionic charge, while Ω_0 is the volume per ion. Therefore, in the presence of the mutual cancellation of all Coulomb interactions at $\boldsymbol{q}=0$, the electron–ion potential retains a volume averaged non-Coulomb part. Corresponding to this, in the hamiltonian (11) it is necessary to retain the $\boldsymbol{q}=0$ component

$$V_{\boldsymbol{q}=0} = b/\Omega_0\,. \tag{17}$$

The resulting effective, uniform potential plays a very significant role in the determination of various properties of a metal (see below), and is absent only in the case of metallic hydrogen (cf. Brovman et al. 1971b).

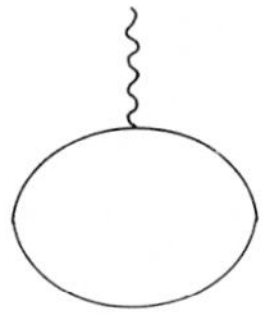

$\Gamma^{(1)}$

Fig. 2

We pass now to a systematic investigation of the individual multi-pole functions $\Gamma^{(n)}$. The multi-pole function $\Gamma^{(1)}$ is described by a single diagram (fig. 2), where the heavy line denotes the full electron Green's function G, and it is not difficult to see that all possible complications of the diagram due to the electron–electron interactions are automatically included in it. Therefore (the notation is standard – see Abrikosov et al. 1963)

$$\Gamma^{(1)}(\mathbf{0}) = -\,[2\mathrm{i}/(2\pi)^4] \int \mathrm{d}^4 p\, G(p) = n_0\,, \tag{18}$$

where n_0 is the density of the electron gas. Combining this result with eqs. (5) and (7), we obtain

$$E^{(1)} = NbZ/\Omega_0, \tag{19}$$

(we have taken into account that $n_0 = Z/\Omega_0$). Together with the energy of the uniform electron gas $E^{(0)}$ this term gives rise to the structureless part of the total energy, which is important for volume-dependent properties of a metal, but which plays no role in the formation of the vibrational spectrum.

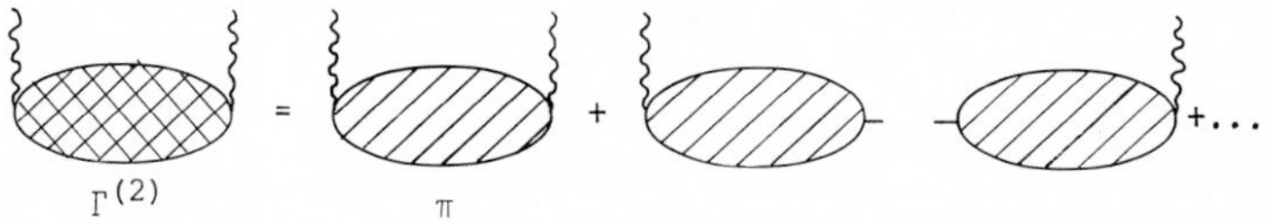

Fig. 3

For $\Gamma^{(2)}$ we have the graphical equation depicted in fig. 3, where the dotted line denotes the electron–electron interaction, while $\pi(\boldsymbol{q})$ denotes the irreducible (proper) block with respect to these lines, and represents in fact a static polarization operator. The summation is carried out directly, with the result that

$$\Gamma^{(2)}(\boldsymbol{q}, -\boldsymbol{q}) = -\tfrac{1}{2}\pi(\boldsymbol{q})/\mathscr{E}(\boldsymbol{q}), \tag{20}$$

where

$$\mathscr{E}(\boldsymbol{q}) = 1 + (4\pi e^2/q^2)\,\pi(\boldsymbol{q}) \tag{21}$$

is the static dielectric function of a homogeneous electron gas.

Let us now investigate the multi-pole function $\Gamma^{(n)}$ for an arbitrary value of n. It is significant that diagrams of the type described above (fig. 1) permit the carrying out of a partial summation, corresponding to the replacement of each external field line by a 'heavy' line with the aid of the graphical relation in fig. 4. This leads to the expression

$$\Gamma^{(n)}(\boldsymbol{q}_1, \cdots, \boldsymbol{q}_n) = \Lambda^{(n)}(\boldsymbol{q}_1, \cdots, \boldsymbol{q}_n)/\mathscr{E}(\boldsymbol{q}_1)\cdots\mathscr{E}(\boldsymbol{q}_n), \quad n > 2, \tag{22}$$

where $\Lambda^{(n)}$ is the sum of all diagrams with n external field lines not containing blocks (polarization parts), which could be related to 'heavy' external lines. Further simplification of $\Lambda^{(n)}$ now depends on making some particular approximation (see below).

The terms beginning with $n=4$ require a special investigation, since the usual techniques of perturbation theory for obtaining the ground state are inapplicable to them (Brovman and Kagan 1973). More precisely, the total energy determined by their use no longer corresponds to the state of the system with lowest energy. This is due to the fact that beginning with $n=4$ it is essential in obtaining the ground state to take into account from the outset the deformation of the shape of the Fermi surface, while in perturbation theory we continue to assume a spherical filling up of momentum space,

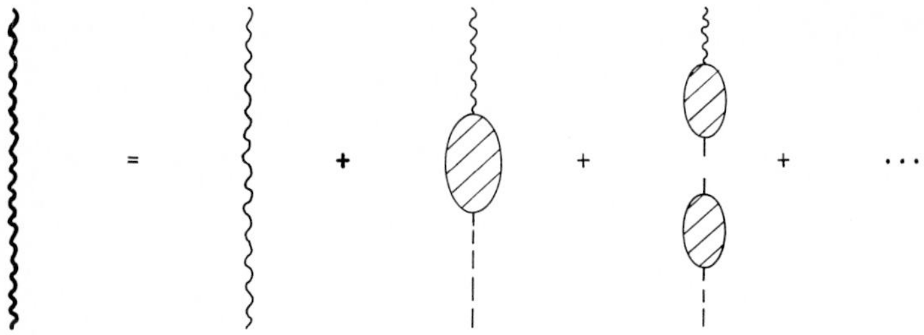

Fig. 4

characteristic of the ground state of the unperturbed system. In other words, a change in the symmetry of the ground state occurs, specific to a crystal, and in order to take it into account it is necessary to modify standard perturbation theory to ensure the additional variation with respect to the shape of the Fermi surface. Alternatively, one can utilize thermodynamic perturbation theory (Abrikosov et al. 1963), in which the lowest energy states are taken into account automatically, following which the limit $T \to 0$ is taken.

In an actual calculation the procedure consists of finding the thermodynamic potential Ω through the summation of diagrams possessing a completely analogous structure but defined now for temperature Green's functions, and a subsequent transition from Ω (as a function of the chemical potential μ) to the energy of the system E (as a function of the number of particles). In this calculation the expansion for Ω as well as for E will have the form given by eqs. (14) and (15). It is also natural that the procedure of partial summation of diagrams leading to eq. (22) remains valid for the coefficients in the series for Ω. In the transition to E, the multi-pole function $\Lambda_{\Omega}^{(n)}$ which arises, generally speaking, is renormalized and becomes equal to (Brovman and Kagan 1973):

$$\Lambda^{(n)}(\mathbf{q}_1, \cdots, \mathbf{q}_n) = \Lambda_{\Omega}^{(n)}(\mathbf{q}_1, \cdots, \mathbf{q}_n) + \Lambda_{\mu}^{(n)}(\mathbf{q}_1, \cdots, \mathbf{q}_n). \tag{23}$$

Here $\Lambda_{\mu}^{(n)}(\mathbf{q}_1, \cdots, \mathbf{q}_n)$ is a multi-pole function arising due to the renormalization of the chemical potential, and differing from zero for $n \geqslant 4$, and only for a strictly defined set of momenta $\boldsymbol{q}_i$. Thus for $n=4$, the only component different from zero is

$$\Lambda_{\mu}^{(4)}(\boldsymbol{q}_1, -\boldsymbol{q}_1, \boldsymbol{q}_2, -\boldsymbol{q}_2) = \frac{1}{24}\left(\frac{\partial\mu}{\partial n_0}\right)\left(\frac{\partial\pi(\boldsymbol{q}_1)}{\partial\mu}\right)\left(\frac{\partial\pi(\boldsymbol{q}_2)}{\partial\mu}\right). \tag{24}$$

For this set of external momenta (when the sum over certain consecutive $\boldsymbol{q}_i$ vanishes) in the thermodynamic perturbation theory for $\Lambda_{\Omega}^{(n)}$ a specific, 'anomalous' contribution appears in the passage to the limit $T \to 0$, together with the usual contribution corresponding to the diagrammatic expansion of the energy ($T=0$). We note that 'anomalous' contributions first appeared in the problem of a Fermi gas with nonspherical interactions (Kohn and Luttinger 1960). For a general set of external momenta, not satisfying any special conditions, both the 'anomalous' contributions as well as the term $\Lambda_{\mu}^{(n)}$ are absent, and the multi-pole function $\Lambda^{(n)}$ can be determined by standard perturbation theory.

It is now possible to obtain the structure-dependent part of the electronic energy. We note in this connection that on taking into account eq. (12) the coordinates of n ions in the nth term of the series appear so that $E^{(2)}$ contains the coordinates of pairs of ions, that is, it corresponds to an effective pairwise interaction, while $E^{(n)}$ contains the coordinates of n ions and corresponds to nonpairwise, indirect interactions among n ions through the conduction electrons.

The expressions obtained above are valid, naturally, for any arbitrary fixed configuration of the ions. In finding the static part of the pair energy in a nonperiodic system (e.g., a liquid metal) an average over all possible configurations must be carried out, while in a periodic crystal a drastic simplification due to interferences occurs, connected with the transformation to summation only over the reciprocal lattice vectors $\boldsymbol{K}$. Indeed, using eq. (12) it is not difficult to obtain

$$E^{(2)} = -\tfrac{1}{2}\Omega \sum_{\boldsymbol{K}\neq 0} \frac{\pi(\boldsymbol{K})}{\mathscr{E}(\boldsymbol{K})} |V_{(\boldsymbol{K})}|^2 \, |S(\boldsymbol{K})|^2 , \tag{25}$$

$$E^{(n)} = \Omega \sum_{\boldsymbol{K}_1\cdots\boldsymbol{K}_n\neq 0} \frac{\Lambda^{(n)}(\boldsymbol{K}_1,\cdots,\boldsymbol{K}_n)}{\mathscr{E}(\boldsymbol{K}_1)\cdots\mathscr{E}(\boldsymbol{K}_n)} V_{\boldsymbol{K}_1}\cdots V_{\boldsymbol{K}_n} S_{\boldsymbol{K}_1}\cdots S_{\boldsymbol{K}_n} \times \Delta(\boldsymbol{K}_1+\cdots+\boldsymbol{K}_n), \quad n>2. \tag{26}$$

The result presented here is for the general case, and correspondingly the structure factor

$$S(\boldsymbol{q}) = (1/v)\sum_s \exp(\mathrm{i}\boldsymbol{q}\cdot\boldsymbol{\rho}_s) \tag{27}$$

arises from eq. (12). The summation in this expression is over all ν ions in a primitive unit cell, whose coordinates with respect to the origin of the unit cell are $\boldsymbol{\rho}_s$. From the form of eq. (26) it is easy to understand now that the expansion of the electronic energy of a static lattice, commencing with $n=2$, in fact represents a series in powers of the small parameter $V_{\boldsymbol{k}}/\mathscr{E}_{\mathrm{F}}$.

In concluding the present section we note that the perturbation theory employed is approximate in fact, since the coherent reconstruction of the electronic spectrum near the Brillouin zone boundaries is taken into account only approximately within its framework. However, as well known analysis shows (Williams and Weaire 1970), the determination of properties which are given by integrals over the electronic spectrum is carried out with great accuracy by this method. This result is apparently sufficiently general to be applicable to 'good' non-transition metals.

2.3. The dynamical matrix

We now turn to the determination of the phonon spectrum of a metal. For this purpose we take into account that, in accordance with the adiabatic approximation, the role of the potential energy in the vibrational problem for a metal is played by the quantity [see eq. (3)]

$$U(\boldsymbol{R}) = U_{\mathrm{i}}(\boldsymbol{R}) + E_{\mathrm{e}}(\boldsymbol{R}), \tag{28}$$

where $U_{\mathrm{i}}(\boldsymbol{R})$ is the potential energy of the ionic lattice (immersed in a compensating uniform negative background), while $E_{\mathrm{e}}(\boldsymbol{R})$ is the ground state energy of the electronic system, obtained as a function of the ionic positions. We first find the equilibrium positions of the nuclei corresponding to the potential (28). They are given by the condition that the potential energy be stationary, and for the sth ion in the mth primitive unit cell this condition leads to the requirement

$$(\partial U/\partial \boldsymbol{R}_{ms})_0 = 0. \tag{29}$$

The contribution of the indirect interionic interaction to this condition is obtained directly from eq. (15)

$$\left(\frac{\partial E^{(n)}}{\partial \boldsymbol{R}_{ms}}\right)_0 = -\frac{n\Omega}{N\nu}\sum_{\boldsymbol{K}_1\cdots\boldsymbol{K}_n} \boldsymbol{K}_n \Gamma^{(n)}(\boldsymbol{K}_1,\cdots,\boldsymbol{K}_n)\, V_{\boldsymbol{K}_1}\cdots V_{\boldsymbol{K}_n}$$
$$\times \operatorname{Im}[S(\boldsymbol{K}_1)\cdots S(\boldsymbol{K}_{n-1})\exp(\mathrm{i}\boldsymbol{K}_n\cdot\boldsymbol{\rho}_s)]\,\Delta(\boldsymbol{K}_1+\cdots+\boldsymbol{K}_n). \tag{30}$$

(N is the number of primitive unit cells.) In this expression we have used the result that $V_{-K}=V_K$, and the symmetry of the multi-pole function in its arguments. The condition obtained is independent of the cell index m, as must be the case. In the case of a mono-atomic, Bravais lattice the right hand side of eq. (30) vanishes identically. For a lattice with two atoms in a primitive unit cell eq. (30) vanishes identically only if a displacement of the second atom changes the space group of the lattice. (This is not the case, for example, for structures of the type of bismuth for displacements along the trigonal axis.) In the general case it is only the total force acting on an ion that vanishes. In this case eq. (29) in fact becomes an equation for finding the equilibrium positions $\boldsymbol{\rho}_s$ for the atoms in a primitive unit cell.

For the study of the vibrational problem in the harmonic approximation it is essential now to obtain the force matrix (see, for example, Born and Huang 1954, Maradudin et al. 1971), defined with respect to the equilibrium positions (29)

$$(\boldsymbol{A})^{\alpha\beta}_{ms;m's'} = (\partial^2 U/\partial \boldsymbol{R}^{\alpha}_{ms}\,\partial \boldsymbol{R}^{\beta}_{m's'})_0 \tag{31}$$

(here and in what follows the upper indices label the cartesian axes). The contribution to eq. (31) from the ionic lattice with purely Coulomb interactions (U_{i}) has the standard form. The indirect interaction, corresponding to E_{e}, in accordance with eqs. (14)–(15) can again be represented in the form of an expansion in powers of the electron–ion potential. This series, as can easily be understood, begins with $n=2$, and its general term can be written in the following form

$$\begin{aligned}(\boldsymbol{A}^{(n)})^{\alpha\beta}_{ms;m's'} &= \frac{-\,n(n-1)}{v^2}\frac{\Omega}{N^2}\sum_{\boldsymbol{q}_1\boldsymbol{q}_2}\sum_{\boldsymbol{K}_3\cdots\boldsymbol{K}_n}\Gamma^{(n)}(\boldsymbol{q}_1,\boldsymbol{q}_2,\boldsymbol{K}_3\cdots\boldsymbol{K}_n)\,q_1^{\alpha}q_2^{\beta}\\ &\times V_{\boldsymbol{q}_1}V_{\boldsymbol{q}_2}V_{\boldsymbol{K}_3}\cdots V_{\boldsymbol{K}_n}\exp\left(\mathrm{i}\boldsymbol{q}_1\cdot(\boldsymbol{R}^{(0)}_m-\boldsymbol{R}^{(0)}_{m'})+\mathrm{i}\boldsymbol{q}_1\cdot\boldsymbol{\rho}_s+\mathrm{i}\boldsymbol{q}_2\cdot\boldsymbol{\rho}_{s'}\right)S(\boldsymbol{K}_3)\cdots S(\boldsymbol{K}_n)\\ &\times \Delta(\boldsymbol{q}_1+\boldsymbol{q}_2+\boldsymbol{K}_3+\cdots+\boldsymbol{K}_n)\quad (ms\neq m's').\end{aligned} \tag{32}$$

At the same time for the matrix with $(ms)=(m's')$ the following relation is automatically obtained,

$$(\boldsymbol{A}^{(n)})^{\alpha\beta}_{ms;ms} = -\sum_{m's'(\neq ms)}(\boldsymbol{A}^{(n)})^{\alpha\beta}_{ms;m's'}\,, \tag{33}$$

This relation is valid for each n, and in fact is a consequence of translational symmetry, which has been incorporated into eq. (14) through the exact conservation of momentum in each term (15) [we use the notation $\boldsymbol{R}_{ms}^{(0)} = \boldsymbol{R}_m^{(0)} + \boldsymbol{\rho}_s$ for the equilibrium position of the ion (ms)]. For the first term of the series (32) we obtain the following expression

$$(\boldsymbol{A}^{(2)})_{ms;m's'}^{\alpha\beta} = -(\Omega/N^2 v^2) \sum_{\boldsymbol{q}} q^\alpha q^\beta |V_{\boldsymbol{q}}|^2 \, [\pi(\boldsymbol{q})/\mathscr{E}(\boldsymbol{q})] \times \exp\left(\mathrm{i}\boldsymbol{q} \cdot (\boldsymbol{R}_{ms}^{(0)} - \boldsymbol{R}_{m's'}^{(0)})\right). \quad (34)$$

The elements of this matrix are functions only of the distance between ions and correspond to axial symmetry, which reflects the central nature of the indirect interaction between two ions in $E^{(2)}$. The ionic contribution to the force matrix clearly possesses the very same symmetry. Therefore, if the remaining terms of the series are omitted, the general force matrix in a metal will also possess axial symmetry.

However, the succeeding terms in eq. (32) lead to a force matrix of a more general form, restricted only by the requirements of the space group of the crystal (Maradudin and Vosko 1968), which in the general theory would correspond to the presence of covalent forces. This is formally related to the fact that for $n > 2$ the expression (32) depends not only on the positions of a pair of ions, but also on the structure of the crystal through the summation over the translation vectors of the reciprocal lattice (the latter is absent only for $n = 2$), while physically the appearance of such terms is dependent on the existence of a non-pairwise indirect interaction between ions. This matter is examined in greater detail in subsection 2.9.

Knowing the force matrix and utilizing standard procedures, it is easy to obtain the dynamical matrix, whose diagonalization yields the phonon spectrum:

$$D_{ss'}^{\alpha\beta}(\boldsymbol{q})\, e_{s'}^{\beta}(\boldsymbol{q}) = \omega^2 e_s^{\alpha}(\boldsymbol{q}), \quad (35)$$

$$D_{ss'}^{\alpha\beta}(\boldsymbol{q}) = (1/M) \sum_{m'} (\boldsymbol{A})_{ms;m's'}^{\alpha\beta} \exp\left(-\mathrm{i}\boldsymbol{q} \cdot (\boldsymbol{R}_{m's'}^{(0)} - \boldsymbol{R}_{ms}^{(0)})\right). \quad (36)$$

Taking account of infinitesimal translational invariance, it is convenient to introduce ahead of time the following definition for each contribution to the dynamical matrix

$$D_{ss'}^{\alpha\beta}(\boldsymbol{q}) = \bar{D}_{ss'}^{\alpha\beta}(\boldsymbol{q}) - \delta_{ss'} \sum_{s''(\neq s')} \bar{D}_{ss''}^{\alpha\beta}(\boldsymbol{0}).$$

Then we can write

$$D_{ss'}^{\alpha\beta}(\boldsymbol{q}) = D_{\mathrm{i}ss'}^{\alpha\beta}(\boldsymbol{q}) + D_{\mathrm{e}ss'}^{\alpha\beta}(\boldsymbol{q}) = D_{\mathrm{i}ss'}^{\alpha\beta}(\boldsymbol{q}) + \sum_{n \geqslant 2} D_{(n)ss'}^{\alpha}(\boldsymbol{q}). \quad (37)$$

For the ionic contribution to the dynamical matrix we have

$$\bar{D}^{\alpha\beta}_{\mathrm{i}ss'}(\boldsymbol{q}) = (\Omega_0/Mv) \sum_{\boldsymbol{K}} (\boldsymbol{q}+\boldsymbol{K})^\alpha (\boldsymbol{q}+\boldsymbol{K})^\beta (4\pi Z^2 e^2/|q+K|^2\, \Omega_0^2) \times \exp[\mathrm{i}\boldsymbol{K}\cdot(\boldsymbol{\rho}_s - \boldsymbol{\rho}_{s'})], \quad (38)$$

while the electronic contribution is given by

$$\bar{D}^{\alpha\beta}_{(n)ss'}(\boldsymbol{q}) = \Omega_0 \frac{n(n-1)}{Mv} \sum_{\boldsymbol{K}_1\cdots\boldsymbol{K}_n} (\boldsymbol{q}+\boldsymbol{K}_1)^\alpha (\boldsymbol{q}+\boldsymbol{K}_2)^\beta \times \Gamma^{(n)}(\boldsymbol{q}+\boldsymbol{K}_1, -\boldsymbol{q}-\boldsymbol{K}_2, \boldsymbol{K}_3, \cdots, \boldsymbol{K}_n)\, V_{\boldsymbol{q}+\boldsymbol{K}_1} V_{-(\boldsymbol{q}+\boldsymbol{K}_2)} V_{\boldsymbol{K}_3} \cdots V_{\boldsymbol{K}_n} \times \exp[\mathrm{i}(\boldsymbol{K}_1\cdot\boldsymbol{\rho}_s - \boldsymbol{K}_2\cdot\boldsymbol{\rho}_{s'})]\, S(\boldsymbol{K}_3)\cdots S(\boldsymbol{K}_n)\, \Delta(\boldsymbol{K}_1 - \boldsymbol{K}_2 + \boldsymbol{K}_3 + \cdots + \boldsymbol{K}_n). \quad (39)$$

In the important special case $n=2$ the dynamical matrix reduces to the following simple form

$$\bar{D}^{\alpha\beta}_{(2)ss'}(\boldsymbol{q}) = \frac{\Omega_0}{Mv} \sum_{\boldsymbol{K}} (\boldsymbol{q}+\boldsymbol{K})^\alpha (\boldsymbol{q}+\boldsymbol{K})^\beta |V_{\boldsymbol{q}+\boldsymbol{K}}|^2 \frac{\pi(\boldsymbol{q}+\boldsymbol{K})}{\mathscr{E}(\boldsymbol{q}+\boldsymbol{K})} \times \exp[\mathrm{i}\boldsymbol{K}\cdot(\boldsymbol{\rho}_s - \boldsymbol{\rho}_{s'})].$$

Let us analyze the expression obtained. It is most significant that the nature of the expansion of D_e in powers of the electron–ion interaction differs in principle from the corresponding series for the static electronic energy E_e. Indeed, each term of the former expansion contains two factors $V_{\boldsymbol{q}}$, for arbitrary values of $\boldsymbol{q}$, in the general case, at the same time that in the terms of the series for the energy only the Fourier coefficients with $\boldsymbol{q}=\boldsymbol{K}\neq 0$ appear. However, the assertion about the presence of the small parameter $V_{\boldsymbol{K}}/\mathscr{E}_\mathrm{F}$, which corresponds to pseudopotential theory is in no way equivalent to the assertion of the smallness of the potential in general. On the contrary, it is easy to understand that for small momentum transfers the electron–ion interaction is by no means small, and that

$$\mathscr{E}_\mathrm{F}^{-1} V_{\boldsymbol{q}}/\mathscr{E}(\boldsymbol{q}) \underset{\boldsymbol{q}\to 0}{\approx} 1 \quad (40)$$

[we have explicitly introduced here the dielectric function $\mathscr{E}(\boldsymbol{q})$, having in mind that according to eq. (22) the expansion proceeds in powers of just this ratio].

Therefore, the determination of the static energy and of phonons with the same accuracy requires retaining different numbers of terms in the two series. Thus, to obtain the energy through terms of the order of $(V_{\boldsymbol{K}}/\mathscr{E}_\mathrm{F})^2$ it is sufficient to retain only the term with $n=2$ in eq. (25), while in the series for D_e generally speaking it is necessary to take into account the terms with $n=3$ and $n=4$ [for $n=5$ the corresponding terms in the dynamical matrix have a degree of smallness of at least $(V_{\boldsymbol{K}}/\mathscr{E}_F)^3$].

The preceding result has a very general nature. The presence of a small parameter allows all quantities in a metal which are integrals over the electronic spectrum to be expressed in the form of a series in powers of $V_{\boldsymbol{K}}/\mathscr{E}_F$, but the higher the order of the derivative of the energy with respect to the ionic coordinates which enters the problem, the greater the number of terms of the series that must be taken into account (this fact must be taken into account, for example, in the study of anharmonicity).

Keeping in mind this circumstance, we now obtain the dynamical matrix, retaining terms no smaller than $(V_{\boldsymbol{K}}/\mathscr{E}_F)^2$. For small values of $\boldsymbol{q}$ the situation is clear, and together with the term $D_{(2)}$ we must retain in the term $n=3$ the contributions with $\boldsymbol{K}_1$ or $\boldsymbol{K}_2$ equal to zero while in the term with $n=4$ we must retain the contribution with $\boldsymbol{K}_1=\boldsymbol{K}_2=0$. Thus, we find that

$$\begin{aligned} D^{\alpha\beta}_{ss'}(\boldsymbol{q}) = (\Omega_0/Mv)\sum_{\boldsymbol{K}} \{ & (\boldsymbol{q}+\boldsymbol{K})^\alpha (\boldsymbol{q}+\boldsymbol{K})^\beta \exp[\mathrm{i}\boldsymbol{K}\cdot(\boldsymbol{\rho}_s-\boldsymbol{\rho}_{s'})]\,[\varphi(\boldsymbol{q}+\boldsymbol{K})/\Omega_0] \\ & + [q^\alpha(\boldsymbol{q}+\boldsymbol{K})^\beta \exp(-\mathrm{i}\boldsymbol{K}\cdot\boldsymbol{\rho}_{s'})\,S(\boldsymbol{K}) + q^\beta(\boldsymbol{q}+\boldsymbol{K})^\alpha \exp(\mathrm{i}\boldsymbol{K}\cdot\boldsymbol{\rho}_s)\,S^*(\boldsymbol{K})] \\ & \times V_{\boldsymbol{K}} V_{-(\boldsymbol{q}+\boldsymbol{K})} V_{\boldsymbol{q}} \Gamma^{(3)}(\boldsymbol{q}, -\boldsymbol{q}-\boldsymbol{K}, \boldsymbol{K}) \\ & + 12 q_\alpha q_\beta |V_{\boldsymbol{q}}|^2 |V_{\boldsymbol{K}}|^2 |S(\boldsymbol{K})|^2 \Gamma^{(4)}(\boldsymbol{q}, -\boldsymbol{q}, \boldsymbol{K}, -\boldsymbol{K})\}, \end{aligned} \tag{41}$$

where we have introduced the function

$$\varphi(\boldsymbol{q}) = 4\pi Z^2 e^2/q^2\Omega_0 - \Omega_0 |V_{\boldsymbol{q}}|^2 \pi(\boldsymbol{q})/\mathscr{E}(\boldsymbol{q}). \tag{42}$$

In the expression given by eq. (41) the first term represents the dynamical matrix D_p, corresponding to purely pairwise interactions – the direct Coulomb, and the indirect, arising from $E^{(2)}$. [If terms of $O((V_{\boldsymbol{K}}/\mathscr{E}_F)^3)$ are retained, additional contributions to the pair interaction are contained in $E^{(3)}$ (see subsection 2.9).] The remaining terms in eq. (41) correspond to non-pairwise interactions, and, generally speaking are of the same order of magnitude as those corresponding to pairwise interactions.

For larger values of $\boldsymbol{q}$, comparable with phonon wave vectors at the boundary of the first Brillouin zone, each succeeding term in the expansion of D_e [see eq. (37)] contains one more power of the small parameter, beginning in fact with $n=3$. Therefore, there is reason to hope for the rapid convergence of the series, and the possibility of separating off the pairwise term for large $\boldsymbol{q}$. However, there is a circumstance which makes the determination of $D_{(3)}$ for all values of $\boldsymbol{q}$ in the first Brillouin zone very essential. This is that in a majority of cases, particularly in the case of polyvalent metals, a strong cancellation occurs between the direct and indirect pairwise interaction contributions to D_{p} (Kagan and Brovman 1968), and the contribution $D_{(3)}$ must be compared not with $D_{(2)}$ but with D_{p}. Thus, the evaluation of at least $D_{(3)}$ for all values of $\boldsymbol{q}$ in the first Brillouin zone is necessary not only in principle (from the standpoint of symmetry), but also from a quantitative standpoint. This circumstance is discussed in detail in section 3 of this chapter. We note that the approximation expressed by eq. (41) is valid only for small $\boldsymbol{q}$. For large values of $\boldsymbol{q}$ the remaining terms in eq. (38) become as large as the contribution from non-pairwise forces to eq. (41), and therefore eq. (41) does not satisfy the periodicity condition in reciprocal space $D(\boldsymbol{q}=\boldsymbol{K})=D(\boldsymbol{q})$. For this reason the general expression (39) should be used for large $\boldsymbol{q}$.

In concluding this subsection we pause briefly to discuss another possible method of determining the vibrational dynamical matrix, which is based on the use of the dielectric formalism for periodic structures. The corresponding results can be obtained most simply if, proceeding from the validity of the adiabatic approximation, the hamiltonian (11) is used, in which the electron–ion interaction term is expanded in powers of the displacements of the ions from their equilibrium positions. Next, the problem can be posed of obtaining the change in the energy of the electronic system due to a displacement wave with a definite wave vector $\boldsymbol{q}$. In the harmonic approximation it is necessary to obtain the energy only to second order in the displacements. The problem turns out to be formally completely equivalent to that of obtaining the exact dielectric susceptibility of the electronic system (see Baym 1961, Pines and Nozieres 1966).

We introduce as basis functions $|n\rangle$ the exact wave functions of the total hamiltonian of the periodic, static lattice, taking into account the electron–electron interaction. In this basis the response of the system to a displacement wave is obtained directly, and for the electronic part of the dynamical matrix in a mono-atomic crystal the following expression is obtained (Sham 1969, Pick et al. 1970, Pethick 1970):

$$\bar{D}_{\mathrm{e}}^{\alpha\beta}(\boldsymbol{q}) = (1/M\Omega_0) \sum_{\boldsymbol{K},\boldsymbol{K}'} (\boldsymbol{q}+\boldsymbol{K})^{\alpha} (\boldsymbol{q}+\boldsymbol{K}')^{\beta} \times V_{\boldsymbol{q}+\boldsymbol{K}} V_{-\boldsymbol{q}-\boldsymbol{K}'} \chi(\boldsymbol{q}+\boldsymbol{K}, -\boldsymbol{q}-\boldsymbol{K}'). \quad (43)$$

In this expression

$$\chi(\boldsymbol{q},\boldsymbol{q}') = \sum_n \langle 0| \rho_{\boldsymbol{q}}^{+} |n\rangle \langle n| \rho_{-\boldsymbol{q}'} |0\rangle / (E_0 - E_n) \quad (44)$$

is the static density–density response function (cf. Pines and Nozieres 1966), and $\rho_{\boldsymbol{q}}$ is the Fourier coefficient of the electron number density operator.

In the RPA approximation an analogous expression was first obtained by Sham (1965). In principle, the result (43) possesses great generality. In particular, it is applicable to transition metals and dielectrics when an appropriate separation of the electronic and ionic subsystems is made. However, this expression is simple only at first glance, and its use in its exact original form is practically impossible.

If the exact many-body wave function $|0\rangle$ is represented in the form of a perturbation series in powers of the electron–ion interaction in a periodic lattice, then it is easy to trace through that eq. (44) will be described by the totality of many-tailed diagrams, depicted in fig. 1, where the two external field lines carry the momenta $\boldsymbol{q}$ and $\boldsymbol{q}'$, while the remainder carry momenta equal to reciprocal lattice vectors. The latter will be summed over together with the corresponding factors of $V_{\boldsymbol{K}}$. The coefficient of every diagram with n tails turns out to be $n-1$.

Comparing this result with eq. (39), we see immediately that the vibrational dynamical matrix obtained from eq. (43) coincides exactly with the result derived earlier in this section (Brovman and Kagan 1967).

Thus, if the electron–ion interaction is treated by perturbation theory, then eq. (43) does not lead to any new result (see also Pethick 1970). However, in its original form it is more general, for it also contains in principle the coherent reconstruction of the electronic spectrum near the boundaries of the Brillouin zone, where, strictly speaking, an expansion in powers of the electron–ion interaction is invalid.

As we have already mentioned in subsection 2.2, there exists yet another field-theoretic method of determining the vibration spectrum, based on the renormalization of correctly chosen 'bare' particles, and the use of a simple vertex for the electron–phonon interaction. The problem in this case reduces to the solution of a system of Dyson equations. It can be shown that if the possibility of multiple scattering from a static lattice is correctly taken into account, then the result in its final form coincides with eq. (38).

2.4. Long-wavelength phonons in a metal

We begin a more detailed investigation with an analysis of sound in a metal, restricting ourselves at this stage for simplicity to the case of one atom in a primitive unit cell and an accuracy of the order of $(V_{\boldsymbol{K}}/\mathscr{E}_{\mathrm{F}})^2$. For this we pass to the long wavelength limit and expand eq. (41) in a series of powers of q. The expansion of the pairwise interaction contribution to the dynamical matrix, D_p [the first term on the right hand side of eq. (41)], is easily carried out, if it is taken into account that eq. (42) leads to the expression

$$\varphi(\boldsymbol{q} \to 0) = Z^2/\pi(0)\,\Omega_0 + 2bZ/\Omega_0 = \varphi(0). \tag{45}$$

Thus we obtain

$$D_p^{\alpha\beta}(\boldsymbol{q}) = M^{-1} q^\alpha q^\beta \varphi(0) + M^{-1} \sum_{\boldsymbol{K} \neq 0} \Big\{ q_\alpha q_\beta \varphi(\boldsymbol{K}) + (q^\alpha K^\beta + q^\beta K^\alpha)\, q^\gamma \frac{\partial \varphi(\boldsymbol{K})}{\partial K^\gamma} + \tfrac{1}{2} q^\gamma q^\delta K^\alpha K^\beta \frac{\partial^2 \varphi(\boldsymbol{K})}{\partial K^\gamma\, \partial K^\delta} \Big\}. \tag{46}$$

The three-particle contribution to the dynamical matrix is also obtained directly from eq. (41). It is convenient to introduce the irreducible multi-pole functions immediately, according to eq. (22), whereupon we obtain

$$\begin{aligned} D_{(3)}^{\alpha\beta}(\boldsymbol{q}) = -\frac{6}{M}\frac{Z}{\pi(0)} \sum_{\boldsymbol{K} \neq 0} \Big\{ & 2q^\alpha q^\beta \left(\frac{V_{\boldsymbol{K}}}{\mathscr{E}(\boldsymbol{K})}\right)^2 \Lambda^{(3)}(\boldsymbol{0}, \boldsymbol{K}, -\boldsymbol{K}) \\ & + (q^\alpha K^\beta + q^\beta K^\alpha)\, q^\gamma \Big[\left(\frac{V_{\boldsymbol{K}}}{\mathscr{E}(\boldsymbol{K})}\right) \frac{\partial}{\partial K^\gamma} \left(\frac{V_{\boldsymbol{K}}}{\mathscr{E}(\boldsymbol{K})}\right) \Lambda^{(3)}(\boldsymbol{0}, \boldsymbol{K}, -\boldsymbol{K}) \\ & + \left(\frac{V_{\boldsymbol{K}}}{\mathscr{E}(\boldsymbol{K})}\right)^2 \left(\frac{\partial}{\partial q^\gamma} \Lambda^{(3)}(\boldsymbol{q}, -\boldsymbol{q} - \boldsymbol{K}, \boldsymbol{K})\right)_{q \to 0} \Big] \Big\}. \end{aligned} \tag{47}$$

In an analogous fashion we obtain for the four-particle contribution

$$D_{(4)}^{\alpha\beta}(\boldsymbol{q}) = (12/M\Omega_0)\,(Z/\pi(0))^2\, q^\alpha q^\beta \sum_{\boldsymbol{K} \neq 0} (V_{\boldsymbol{K}}/\mathscr{E}(\boldsymbol{K}))^2\, \Lambda^{(4)}(\boldsymbol{0}, \boldsymbol{0}, \boldsymbol{K}, -\boldsymbol{K}). \tag{48}$$

In the derivation of eqs. (47) and (48) we have used the fact that according to eqs. (16) and (21)

$$\left(\frac{V_{\boldsymbol{q}}}{\mathscr{E}(\boldsymbol{q})}\right)_{\boldsymbol{q} \to 0} \to -\frac{Z}{\pi(0)\,\Omega_0}, \qquad \left(\frac{\partial}{\partial q} \frac{V_{\boldsymbol{q}}}{\mathscr{E}(\boldsymbol{q})}\right)_{\boldsymbol{q} \to 0} \to 0.$$

As can be seen from the expressions obtained, for a complete determination of the velocities of sound or of the elastic moduli it is essential to obtain the explicit form of the multi-pole functions $\Lambda^{(3)}$ and $\Lambda^{(4)}$, for the particular case that one or two of their arguments are zero. It turns out that this problem can be solved in a general form, and a number of exact relations of the type of Ward identities can be established for the multi-pole function valid for an arbitrary normal Fermi liquid (Brovman and Kagan 1969, Pethick 1970). The diagrammatic derivation of these relations is based on the technique of 'skeleton' diagrams (Luttinger and Ward 1960), and the differentiation of 'heavy' electron Green's functions with respect to the chemical potential, which is equivalent to the introduction of an additional vertex with an in-flowing zero momentum. The details of this derivation can be found in the paper of Brovman and Kagan (1969). In it the following system of identities is established

$$\mathscr{E}(0)\,\Gamma^{(n+1)}(\boldsymbol{q}_1,\cdots,\boldsymbol{q}_n,\boldsymbol{0})=\frac{-1}{n+1}\frac{\mathrm{d}\Gamma^{(n)}(\boldsymbol{q}_1,\cdots,\boldsymbol{q}_n)}{\mathrm{d}\mu}. \tag{49}$$

Here the divergence of $\mathscr{E}(\boldsymbol{q})$ as $\boldsymbol{q}\to 0$ is compensated by a corresponding divisor in $\Gamma^{(n+1)}$. Therefore, for $n>2$ it is convenient to rewrite eq. (49), introducing the irreducible multi-pole functions (22)

$$\frac{\Lambda^{(n+1)}(\boldsymbol{q}_1,\cdots,\boldsymbol{q}_n,\boldsymbol{0})}{\mathscr{E}(\boldsymbol{q}_1)\cdots\mathscr{E}(\boldsymbol{q}_n)}=\frac{-1}{n+1}\frac{\mathrm{d}\Gamma^{(n)}(\boldsymbol{q}_1,\cdots,\boldsymbol{q}_n)}{\mathrm{d}\mu}. \tag{50}$$

For the particular cases essential for our purposes we find, taking into account eq. (20),

$$\frac{\Lambda^{(3)}(\boldsymbol{0},\boldsymbol{K},-\boldsymbol{K})}{[\mathscr{E}(\boldsymbol{K})]^2}=\frac{1}{6}\frac{\mathrm{d}}{\mathrm{d}\mu}\left(\frac{\pi(\boldsymbol{K})}{\mathscr{E}(\boldsymbol{K})}\right). \tag{51}$$

In obtaining the quantities $\Lambda^{(4)}(0,0,\boldsymbol{K},-\boldsymbol{K})$ it should be kept in mind that we are interested in a definite limit, namely $\Lambda^{(4)}_{\boldsymbol{q}\to 0}(\boldsymbol{q},-\boldsymbol{q},\boldsymbol{K},-\boldsymbol{K})$. At the same time, as it is easy to understand, certain diagrams drop out of this expression due to electrical neutrality, so that carrying out the repeated differentiation of eq. (49) with respect to μ, it is not necessary to differentiate $\mathscr{E}(0)$. As a result we obtain

$$\frac{\Lambda^{(4)}(0,0,\boldsymbol{K},-\boldsymbol{K})}{[\mathscr{E}(\boldsymbol{K})]^2}=-\frac{1}{24}\frac{\mathrm{d}^2}{\mathrm{d}\mu^2}\left(\frac{\pi(\boldsymbol{K})}{\mathscr{E}(\boldsymbol{K})}\right). \tag{52}$$

With the aid of eq. (49) yet one more important relation can be established. Let us investigate the case $n=2$. Then in accordance with eqs. (18) and (20) we obtain

$$\pi(0)=\mathrm{d}n_0/\mathrm{d}\mu\,. \tag{53}$$

This result, which in the theory of the Fermi liquid is usually obtained by a different method (Pines and Nozieres 1966), is seen to be a simple special case of eq. (49). It enables us to transform the differentiations with respect to the chemical potential in eqs. (51) and (52) into differentiations with respect to the electron number density

$$\frac{\Lambda^{(3)}(\mathbf{0}, \boldsymbol{K}, -\boldsymbol{K})}{[\mathscr{E}(\boldsymbol{K})]^2} = \frac{\pi(0)}{6} \frac{\mathrm{d}}{\mathrm{d}n_0}\left(\frac{\pi(\boldsymbol{K})}{\mathscr{E}(\boldsymbol{K})}\right). \tag{54}$$

With the aid of eq. (53) we can also transform eq. (52). At the same time, it should be noted that in the preceding expressions by $\Lambda^{(n)}$ in fact is meant $\Lambda_{\Omega}^{(n)}$ [see eq. (23)], because for $n \leqslant 3$, $\Lambda_{\Omega}^{(n)}$ and $\Lambda^{(n)}$ coincide. For the determination of the full four-pole function the contribution $\Lambda_{\mu}^{(4)}$, eq. (24), must be added to the expression given by eq. (52). Setting $\boldsymbol{q}_1 = 0$ in it, after simple transformations we obtain finally:

$$\frac{\Lambda^{(4)}(\mathbf{0}, \mathbf{0}, \boldsymbol{K}, -\boldsymbol{K})}{[\mathscr{E}(\boldsymbol{K})]^2} = -\frac{\pi^2(0)}{24} \frac{\mathrm{d}^2}{\mathrm{d}n_0^2}\left(\frac{\pi(\boldsymbol{K})}{\mathscr{E}(\boldsymbol{K})}\right). \tag{55}$$

Finally, one more identity can be obtained for the differentiation of the irreducible multi-pole functions (Brovman and Kagan 1969)

$$\left[\frac{\partial}{\partial q^{\alpha}} \Lambda^{(3)}(\boldsymbol{q}, -\boldsymbol{q} - \boldsymbol{K}, \boldsymbol{K})\right]_{\boldsymbol{q} \to 0} = \frac{1}{2} \frac{\partial}{\partial K^{\alpha}} \Lambda^{(3)}(\mathbf{0}, \boldsymbol{K}, -\boldsymbol{K}). \tag{56}$$

Thus, the expressions (54)–(56) show that the dynamical matrix for small $\boldsymbol{q}$, and consequently all sound velocities, depend on the properties of the electronic liquid only through the polarizability $\pi(\boldsymbol{q})$ and its derivatives.

The analysis of the velocities of sound is conveniently carried out in terms of the dynamical elastic moduli. For this purpose we introduce the notation of Born and Huang (1954)

$$D^{\alpha\beta}(\boldsymbol{q}) = (\Omega_0/M)\,[\alpha\beta, \gamma\delta]\, q^{\gamma} q^{\delta}, \tag{57}$$

and utilize the general expression for the elastic moduli of a primitive crystal

$$C_{\alpha\beta\gamma\delta} = [\alpha\gamma, \beta\delta] + [\gamma\beta, \alpha\delta] - [\gamma\delta, \alpha\beta]. \tag{58}$$

Comparison of eq. (57) with eqs. (46), (47), (48) gives rise to the possibility of obtaining the values of the moduli $C_{\alpha\beta\gamma\delta}$ for an arbitrary crystal. For simplicity we restrict ourselves here to the case of cubic symmetry. Then, for the elastic modulus $C_{11} = C_{xxxx}$, corresponding to the velocity of longitudinal sound for $\boldsymbol{q}$ along the edge of the unit cube, we obtain, using the above identities,

$$C_{11} = \frac{n_0^2}{\pi(0)} + \frac{2bn_0}{\Omega_0} + \frac{1}{\Omega_0}\sum_{\boldsymbol{K}\neq 0}\left[\varphi(\boldsymbol{K}) + 2K_x\frac{\partial\varphi(\boldsymbol{K})}{\partial K_x} + \tfrac{1}{2}K_x^2\frac{\partial^2\varphi(\boldsymbol{K})}{\partial K_x^2}\right]$$
$$- n_0\sum_{\boldsymbol{K}\neq 0}\left[2|V_{\boldsymbol{K}}|^2\frac{\partial}{\partial n_0}\left(\frac{\pi(\boldsymbol{K})}{\mathscr{E}(\boldsymbol{K})}\right) + \tfrac{1}{3}K^\alpha\frac{\partial}{\partial K^\alpha}\left\{|V_{\boldsymbol{K}}|^2\frac{\partial}{\partial n_0}\left(\frac{\pi(\boldsymbol{K})}{\mathscr{E}(\boldsymbol{K})}\right)\right\}\right.$$
$$\left. + \tfrac{1}{2}n_0|V_{\boldsymbol{K}}|^2\frac{\partial^2}{\partial n_0^2}\left(\frac{\pi(\boldsymbol{K})}{\mathscr{E}(\boldsymbol{K})}\right)\right]. \tag{59}$$

Taking into account that neither the direct ion–ion interaction nor the 'bare' electron–ion interaction depends on the electron number density, eq. (59) can be rewritten in the following convenient form, in terms of the pairwise interaction function $\varphi(\boldsymbol{q})$ defined by eq. (42),

$$C_{11} = \frac{\varphi(\mathbf{0})}{\Omega_0} + \frac{1}{\Omega_0}\sum_{\boldsymbol{K}\neq 0}\left[\varphi(\boldsymbol{K}) + 2K_x\frac{\partial\varphi(\boldsymbol{K})}{\partial K_x} + \tfrac{1}{2}K_x^2\frac{\partial^2\varphi(\boldsymbol{K})}{\partial K_x^2}\right]$$
$$+ \frac{1}{\Omega_0}\sum_{\boldsymbol{K}\neq 0}\left[2n_0\frac{\partial\varphi(\boldsymbol{K})}{\partial n_0} + \tfrac{1}{3}n_0K^\alpha\frac{\partial^2\varphi(\boldsymbol{K})}{\partial K^\alpha\,\partial n_0} + \tfrac{1}{2}n_0^2\frac{\partial^2\varphi(\boldsymbol{K})}{\partial n_0^2}\right]. \tag{60}$$

The expressions given by eqs. (59) and (60) determine the square of the velocity of longitudinal sound in a metal with an accuracy through terms of $O((V_{\boldsymbol{K}}/\mathscr{E}_F)^2)$. Their analysis is very instructive from the physical standpoint. The first two terms on the right hand side of eq. (59) [the first term on the right hand side of eq. (60)] describe the contribution from a uniform continuous medium and coincide with the well-known result of Bardeen and Pines (1955). The first term corresponds to a plasma with point ions, and if the value of $\pi(0)$ obtained from the self-consistent field method or in the random phase approximation is used $(\pi(0)=\frac{3}{2}n_0/\mathscr{E}_F)$, then it gives the expression for the speed of longitudinal sound first obtained by Bohm and Staver (1950). However, the second term on the right hand side of eq. (59), which is associated with the departure of the ions from point charges, plays a very significant role in the formation of longitudinal sound in a metal, and as a rule exceeds the first term in magnitude.

The non-uniformity of the medium is reflected in the presence of the third and fourth terms on the right hand side of eq. (59), which contain the contributions from the direct interactions between the ions of the discrete lattice [the first term in $\varphi(K)$ and its derivatives], and also from the indirect ionic interaction through the conduction electrons. In this regard it is significant that the contribution of many-body forces to the structure dependent part of the velocity of longitudinal sound [the last term in eqs. (59) and (60)] does not contain the small parameter $(V_{\boldsymbol{K}}/\mathscr{E}_{\mathrm{F}})$, and turns out to be of the same order of magnitude as the contribution from the indirect pairwise interaction. In particular, it follows from this that any representation which rests only on the pair part of the dynamical matrix $\boldsymbol{D}_{\mathrm{p}}$, clearly describes the long-wavelength region of the phonon spectrum incorrectly.

Comparing eq. (57) with eqs. (46)–(48), and making use of eq. (42), it is not difficult to obtain the shear moduli also, corresponding to transversely polarized sound. With the same accuracy, through terms of $\mathrm{O}((V_{\boldsymbol{K}}/\mathscr{E}_{\mathrm{F}})^2)$ it is found that

$$C_{44} = (1/2\Omega_0) \sum_{\boldsymbol{K}\neq 0} (K^x)^2 \frac{\partial^2 \varphi(\boldsymbol{K})}{\partial (K^y)^2}, \tag{61}$$

$$C' = \tfrac{1}{2}(C_{11} - C_{12}) = \frac{1}{4\Omega_0} \sum_{\boldsymbol{K}\neq 0} \left\{ (K^y)^2 \frac{\partial^2 \varphi(\boldsymbol{K})}{\partial (K^x)^2} + (K^x)^2 \frac{\partial^2 \varphi(\boldsymbol{K})}{\partial (K^y)^2} - 2K^x K^y \frac{\partial^2 \varphi(\boldsymbol{K})}{\partial K^x\, \partial K^y} \right\}. \tag{62}$$

It follows from these expressions that in the approximation in which only terms through $\mathrm{O}((V_{\boldsymbol{K}}/\mathscr{E}_{\mathrm{F}})^2)$ are kept, the shear moduli are determined solely by the pairwise interactions and do not contain contributions from the many-body interactions. The latter contributions, as in the energy of the static lattice, begin with the terms of $\mathrm{O}((V_{\boldsymbol{K}}/\mathscr{E}_{\mathrm{F}})^3)$. However, it should be noted that the role of these terms can become very significant from the quantitative standpoint. This is due to the fact that the transverse velocity of sound, as opposed to the longitudinal, eqs. (59) and (60), does not contain terms corresponding to a uniform medium ($\boldsymbol{K}=0$). Therefore, if the electronic and ionic contributions to eqs. (61) and (62) are comparable in magnitude, then a calculation of the terms of third order in $(V_{\boldsymbol{K}}/\mathscr{E}_{\mathrm{F}})$ will give an important first correction to the total magnitude of the elastic moduli. This circumstance becomes particularly important when the velocity of transverse sound turns out to be small. Well-known cases, for example, are tin (Brovman and Kagan 1967) or zinc (Kagan and Brovman 1968), for which the ionic lattice is generally unstable with respect to certain transverse vibrations, and is made stable only due to the electronic contribution. In such situations the many body terms may even play the determining role (for a more detailed discussion see section 3 of this chapter).

In the opposite case, when the electronic contribution to eqs. (61) and (62) is small in comparison with the ionic due to a particularly small value of the parameter $V_{\boldsymbol{K}}/\mathscr{E}_{\mathrm{F}}$ as, for example, in metallic sodium, transverse sound will be almost completely determined by the ionic lattice.

In metals with several ions in a primitive unit cell optical vibration modes occur, in addition to the acoustic modes, which can also be analyzed in the long-wavelength limit. We consider, as an example, a metal with two identical atoms in a primitive unit cell, and assume the symmetry of the lattice to be so high that the matrix (36) for $\boldsymbol{q}=0$ becomes diagonal with respect to a set of cartesian axes. In this case there exist three independent optical modes, polarized along each of the cartesian axes. Using eq. (41), with an accuracy through terms of $\mathrm{O}((V_{\boldsymbol{K}}/\mathscr{E}_{\mathrm{F}})^2)$, we find for the limiting frequencies

$$\omega_\alpha^2(\boldsymbol{q}=0) = -(2/M) \sum_{\boldsymbol{K}\neq 0} (K^\alpha)^2\, \varphi(\boldsymbol{K}) \cos(\boldsymbol{K}\cdot\boldsymbol{\rho}), \quad \alpha = x, y, z. \tag{63}$$

In structure this expression is close to those in eqs. (61) and (62) for the shear moduli. A contribution from the homogeneous electron gas ($\boldsymbol{K}=0$) is also absent here, and the many-body forces contribute only to the terms of $\mathrm{O}((V_{\boldsymbol{K}}/\mathscr{E}_{\mathrm{F}})^3)$ and higher.

In connection with the result given by eq. (63), all of the considerations discussed previously still apply. In particular, for polyvalent metals it is often the case that there is a strong mutual compensation of the electronic and ionic contributions to eq. (63), in the presence of which the role of the many-body interactions becomes very significant (Brovman and Kagan 1967, Brovman et al. 1971).

2.5. The problem of the compressibility

One of the interesting problems in the theory of metals is the question of the relation between the dynamical compressibility, i.e., that obtained from the velocities of sound, and the static compressibility, defined in terms of the energy by

$$1/\kappa \equiv B = \Omega(\partial^2 E/\partial\Omega^2)_N. \tag{64}$$

(B is the bulk modulus). If we analyze the commonly used expressions for the energy and the dynamical matrix, obtained from only the pairwise ionic interactions, i.e., from the terms with $n=2$ in eqs. (14) and (37), it turns out that we obtain expressions for the compressibility which do not coincide. At first glance, from the formal point of view this may seem natural for a system in which a significant role is played by the electron liquid, for the static compressibility is determined by all the terms in eq. (14), while the dynamical compressibility is obtained only from the parts of these terms with $n \geqslant 2$. In addition, the dynamical problem in a metal is studied at a constant electron number density, while in the static case terms enter explicitly which correspond to changes in the density and, consequently, in the dielectric function, for example.

However, as was shown by a detailed analysis (Brovman and Kagan 1969, Brovman et al. 1969a, Pethick 1970), even though all of the problems just mentioned do indeed exist, by consistently incorporating the many ion interaction in the investigation it is possible to demonstrate the equality of the static and dynamical compressibilities.

For a discussion of this problem, we first determine the static compressibility (64), restricting the investigation for simplicity to lattices with one atom in a primitive unit cell (the generalization to an arbitrary lattice presents no difficulties in principle). For this purpose we use the expression for the total static energy

$$E = E_{\mathrm{i}} + E_{\mathrm{e}}, \tag{65}$$

where E_{e} has been defined in subsection 2.2, while for E_{i} we have

$$\begin{aligned} E_{\mathrm{i}} &= \tfrac{1}{2} \sum_{m \neq m'} \sum_{\boldsymbol{q} \neq 0} \frac{4\pi Z^2 e^2}{q^2 \Omega} \exp\left[\mathrm{i}\boldsymbol{q}\cdot(\boldsymbol{R}_m - \boldsymbol{R}_{m'})\right] \\ &= \tfrac{1}{2} N \sum_{\boldsymbol{K} \neq 0} \frac{4\pi Z^2 e^2}{K^2 \Omega_0} - \tfrac{1}{2} \sum_{\boldsymbol{q} \neq 0} \frac{4\pi Z^2 e^2}{q^2 \Omega_0}. \end{aligned} \tag{66}$$

The contribution to the bulk modulus $B^{(0)}$ from the energy of a uniform, interacting electron gas $E^{(0)}$ can be obtained, if we take into account that

$$(\kappa^{(0)})^{-1} = n_0^2 \, \mathrm{d}\mu/\mathrm{d}n_0,$$

and use the expression (53)

$$B^{(0)} = n_0^2/\pi(\mathbf{0}). \tag{67}$$

The contribution from $E^{(1)}$ is found directly from eq. (19),

$$B^{(1)} = 2bZ/\Omega_0. \tag{68}$$

In determining the compressibility associated with the structure dependent terms in eq. (65), it is essential to keep in mind that the energy, in addition to its explicit dependence on volume, possesses an implicit dependence as well, through the reciprocal lattice vectors and through the dependence of the polarization operator $\pi(\boldsymbol{q})$ on the density of the electron gas n_0. Accordingly, we have that (Brovman et al. 1969a)

$$\frac{\partial}{\partial\Omega}=\left(\frac{\partial}{\partial\Omega}\right)_{\boldsymbol{K},n_0}-\frac{K^\alpha}{3\Omega}\left(\frac{\partial}{\partial K^\alpha}\right)_{\Omega,n_0}-\frac{n_0}{\Omega}\left(\frac{\partial}{\partial n_0}\right)_{\Omega,\boldsymbol{K}} \tag{69}$$

(all differentiations are carried out for constant N). The form in which we have written the second term on the right hand side of eq. (69) assumes that a primitive unit cell does not change its shape when its volume is changed. In a cubic crystal subjected to an external, hydrostatic pressure, this assumption is automatically satisfied. For simplicity of exposition we restrict ourselves in the following to just this case.

We now calculate the contribution to the compressibility associated with E_i, eq. (66), and $E^{(2)}$, eq. (25). We first 'fix' the electron density and find that part of the compressibility which is given by the first two terms in eq. (69). In doing this we keep in mind that the second term in eq. (66) does not depend on the volume in general (Ω appears in the transformation from summation to integration over $\boldsymbol{q}$, but $\Omega/\Omega_0=N$), while the first depends on Ω, both explicitly and through $\boldsymbol{K}$, In addition, we take into account that by definition

$$V_{\boldsymbol{q}}\sim 1/\Omega_0 .$$

Then a direct calculation yields

$$B_\mathrm{p}^{(2)}=B_\mathrm{i}+B_1^{(2)}=\frac{1}{\Omega_0}\sum_{\boldsymbol{K}\neq 0}\left[\varphi(\boldsymbol{K})+\tfrac{5}{9}K^\alpha\frac{\partial\varphi(\boldsymbol{K})}{\partial K^\alpha}+\tfrac{1}{18}K^\alpha K^\beta\frac{\partial^2\varphi(\boldsymbol{K})}{\partial K^\alpha\,\partial K^\beta}\right], \tag{70}$$

where $\varphi(\boldsymbol{K})$ is defined by eq. (42). It is not difficult to see that the contribution from $E^{(2)}$ associated with the change in the electron density n_0 has the following form

$$B_\mathrm{np}^{(2)}=-\sum_{\boldsymbol{K}\neq 0}\left\{\tfrac{1}{2}n_0^2|V_{\boldsymbol{K}}|^2\frac{\partial^2}{\partial n_0^2}\left(\frac{\pi(\boldsymbol{K})}{\mathscr{E}(\boldsymbol{K})}\right)+2n_0|V_{\boldsymbol{K}}|^2\frac{\partial}{\partial n_0}\left(\frac{\pi(\boldsymbol{K})}{\mathscr{E}(\boldsymbol{K})}\right)\right.$$
$$\left.+\tfrac{1}{3}n_0K^\alpha\frac{\partial}{\partial K^\alpha}\left[|V_{\boldsymbol{K}}|^2\frac{\partial}{\partial n_0}\left(\frac{\pi(\boldsymbol{K})}{\mathscr{E}(\boldsymbol{K})}\right)\right]\right\}. \tag{71}$$

Introducing as in subsection 2.4 the pair interaction $\varphi(\boldsymbol{q})$, and collecting all of the contributions to the static compressibility, we obtain finally

$$\begin{aligned}B&=B^{(0)}+B^{(1)}+B_\mathrm{p}^{(2)}+B_\mathrm{np}^{(2)}\\&=\frac{\varphi(0)}{\Omega}+\frac{1}{\Omega_0}\sum_{\boldsymbol{K}\neq 0}\left[\varphi(\boldsymbol{K})+\tfrac{5}{9}K^\alpha\frac{\partial\varphi(\boldsymbol{K})}{\partial K^\alpha}+\tfrac{1}{18}K^\alpha K^\beta\frac{\partial^2\varphi(\boldsymbol{K})}{\partial K^\alpha\,\partial K^\beta}\right]\\&\quad+\frac{1}{\Omega_0}\sum_{\boldsymbol{K}\neq 0}\left[2n_0\frac{\partial\varphi(\boldsymbol{K})}{\partial n_0}+\tfrac{1}{3}n_0K^\alpha\frac{\partial^2\varphi(\boldsymbol{K})}{\partial K^\alpha\,\partial n_0}+\tfrac{1}{2}n_0^2\frac{\partial^2\varphi(\boldsymbol{K})}{\partial n_0^2}\right].\end{aligned} \tag{72}$$

Taking into account the next term in the expansion of the electronic energy would have led to a contribution to the compressibility of the order of $(V_{\boldsymbol{K}}/\mathscr{E}_{\mathrm{F}})^3$, so that eq. (72) determines the static compressibility through terms of $\mathrm{O}\left((V_{\boldsymbol{K}}/\mathscr{E}_{\mathrm{F}})^2\right)$. We now compare eq. (72) with the expression for the dynamical compressibility

$$k^{-1} = B = \tfrac{1}{3}(C_{11} + 2C_{12}) = C_{11} - \tfrac{4}{3}C', \tag{73}$$

which will be obtained with the same accuracy, if we use the results of the preceding section, eqs, (60) and (62), obtained from the investigation of long-wavelength phonons in the dynamical problem. In connection with this, for the transformation of the pairwise interaction terms it is convenient to go over to the derivatives of $\varphi(\boldsymbol{K})$ with respect to the magnitude of $\boldsymbol{K}$–φ' and φ'':

$$\frac{\partial \varphi(\boldsymbol{K})}{\partial K^\alpha} = \varphi' \frac{K^\alpha}{|\boldsymbol{K}|}, \qquad \frac{\partial^2 \varphi(\boldsymbol{K})}{\partial K^\alpha\, \partial K^\beta} = \frac{K^\alpha K^\beta}{|\boldsymbol{K}|^2}\left[\varphi'' - \frac{\varphi'}{|\boldsymbol{K}|}\right] + \varphi' \frac{\delta_{\alpha\beta}}{|\boldsymbol{K}|}.$$

A direct comparison of all contributions to the static and dynamical compressibilities shows that both expressions coincide exactly.

An analogous proof can be constructed to any order in $(V_{\boldsymbol{K}}/\mathscr{E}_{\mathrm{F}})$. In this regard it is essential to remember that, as follows from the preceding section, it is necessary to retain two more terms in the expansion for the dynamical matrix in each case than in the corresponding expansion for the energy.

The result obtained possesses a rather nontrivial nature, for in the static approach it was found necessary to take into account the terms $E^{(0)}$, $E^{(1)}$, and $E^{(2)}$ in the expansion (14), while in the dynamical approach the completely different terms $E^{(2)}$, $E^{(3)}$, and $E^{(4)}$ had to be taken into account. Therefore, it is expedient to consider the situation in somewhat greater detail. The term $E^{(2)}$ in the expansion of the energy (14), if we consider a fixed electron density, in conjunction with E_{i} describes the effective pairwise interaction between ions, and it is natural that the equivalent contribution B_{p} to the dynamical compressibility, eq. (70), is obtained from the part of the dynamical matrix due to pairwise interactions [the second term of eq. (46)]. However, when the volume is changed not only the distance between ions but also their interaction changes, due to the change of the electron density. An unusual non-pairwise interaction between ions thus arises in a metal, even though it is obtained from $E^{(2)}$ in the static problem. This non-pairwise interaction leads to the appearance of the term $B_{\mathrm{np}}^{(2)}$, eq. (71). It is characteristic that the equivalent contribution in the dynamical problem is already explicitly connected with the many-ion terms of third and fourth orders in the electron–ion interaction. In connection with this it should be underlined that when the many-ion interactions are not taken into account, the equality of the static and dynamical compressibilities in general cannot be obtained in this fashion. The quantitative difference between them can be rather significant, particularly in polyvalent metals, although even in the alkali metals it reaches 30%. (Numerical examples will be presented below in subsection 3.3.)

The part of the compressibility corresponding to the uniform medium $B^{(0)} = B^{(1)}$ is also obtained from D_{p} in the dynamical problem [the first term of eq. (46), which is independent of $\boldsymbol{K}$], whereupon the equality of the corresponding contributions to the compressibility is achieved only by taking the relation (53) into account. Inasmuch as this relation is valid only in the exact theory of the interacting electron gas, in which all orders of perturbation theory are taken into account, in approximate theories $\Omega(\partial^2 E^{(0)}/\partial\Omega^2)$ does not coincide with eq. (67) in general (this equation is strongly violated in the random phase approximation, for example).

The energy of an electron gas, as is well known, possesses the property of stationarity (Luttinger and Ward 1960), and therefore is usually determined with greater accuracy than such a property as the polarizability $\pi(\boldsymbol{q})$. Therefore, particularly in the analysis of the phonon spectrum of metals, to obtain self-consistent results it is expedient to use representations for $\pi(\boldsymbol{q})$ which satisfy eq. (67) (Geldart and Vosko 1966, Kagan and Brovman 1968; subsection 3.2 of this chapter).

2.6. The nature of the breakdown of the Cauchy relations in metals

As is well known (Born and Huang 1954), if the interaction between atoms in a crystal possesses a pairwise (central) nature, then in the absence of an external pressure the elastic moduli must satisfy the so-called ‘Cauchy relations’

$$C_{\alpha\beta\gamma\delta} = C_{\alpha\gamma\beta\delta}\,.$$

In the case of cubic crystals they reduce to the single relation

$$C_{12} = C_{44}\,. \tag{74}$$

However, it is experimentally established that the Cauchy relations are not obeyed in any metal. In the absence of overlap of the ion cores one possible explanation of this is connected with the role of the many-ion interaction investigated above, which leads directly to noncentral forces. However, there clearly exist metals in which the many-body forces are small, but for which the Cauchy relations break down completely. Na and K can serve as examples, where the measured phonon spectrum (Woods et al. 1962, Cowley et al. 1966) is very well described in the approximation of purely central force interactions between ions. The explanation of this must be sought in the fact that in the establishment of the equilibrium of the lattice the electron liquid introduces a contribution which leads to not only a pairwise interaction between ions. A qualitative understanding of this circumstance apparently can be found in the work of a number of authors; however, a full analysis of the problem was given only recently (Brovman et al. 1969).

From the expressions (59)–(62) obtained above, with an accuracy through terms of $\mathrm{O}\left((V_{\boldsymbol{K}}/\mathscr{E}_{\mathrm{F}})^2\right)$, one can write directly for crystals of cubic symmetry that

$$C_{12} - C_{44} = \frac{n_0^2}{\pi(0)} + \frac{2bn_0}{\Omega_0} + \frac{1}{\Omega_0}\sum_{\boldsymbol{K}\neq 0}\left\{\varphi(\boldsymbol{K}) + \tfrac{1}{3}K^\alpha \frac{\partial\varphi(\boldsymbol{K})}{\partial K^\alpha}\right\} - \sum_{\boldsymbol{K}\neq 0}\left\{2n_0|V_{\boldsymbol{K}}|^2 \frac{\partial}{\partial n_0}\left(\frac{\pi(\boldsymbol{K})}{\mathscr{E}(\boldsymbol{K})}\right) + \tfrac{1}{3}K^\alpha \frac{\partial}{\partial K^\alpha}\left[|V_{\boldsymbol{K}}|^2 \frac{\partial}{\partial n_0}\left(\frac{\pi(\boldsymbol{K})}{\mathscr{E}(\boldsymbol{K})}\right)\right] + \tfrac{1}{2}n_0^2 \frac{\partial^2}{\partial n_0^2}\left(\frac{\pi(\boldsymbol{K})}{\mathscr{E}(\boldsymbol{K})}\right)\right\}. \tag{75}$$

Now, in order to introduce the condition of equilibrium, we find a general expression for the pressure $P = -(\partial E/\partial\Omega)$. In accordance with eqs. (65) and (14) we obtain

$$P = P_{\mathrm{i}} + \sum_{n=0}^{\infty} P^{(n)}. \tag{76}$$

It is convenient to express the pressure produced by a uniform interacting electron gas

$$P^{(0)} = -\,\partial E^{(0)}/\partial\Omega$$

in terms of the polarization operator. For this it is necessary to integrate the reciprocal of the compressibility (67) with respect to density

$$P^{(0)} = \tfrac{1}{2}\frac{n_0^2}{\pi(0)} - \tfrac{1}{2}\int_0^{n_0} \mathrm{d}n_0 n_0^2 \frac{\partial}{\partial n_0}\left(\frac{1}{\pi(0)}\right). \tag{77}$$

For $P^{(1)}$ we have from eq. (2.9)

$$P^{(1)} = bZ/\Omega_0^2. \tag{78}$$

The remaining terms of the series (76) can be obtained from the energy by a direct application of the operator (69). Restricting ourselves to the previous accuracy of terms through $O((V_{\boldsymbol{K}}/\mathscr{E}_{\mathrm{F}})^2)$, and correspondingly omitting in eq. (76) the terms with $n \geqslant 3$, we finally obtain after a series of transformations

$$P = \tfrac{1}{2}\frac{n_0^2}{\pi(0)} + \frac{bn_0}{\Omega_0} + \frac{1}{2\Omega_0}\sum_{\boldsymbol{K}\neq 0}\left\{\varphi(\boldsymbol{K}) + \tfrac{1}{3}K^{\alpha}\frac{\partial\varphi(\boldsymbol{K})}{\partial K^{\alpha}}\right\}$$
$$-\tfrac{1}{2}\int_0^{n_0} \mathrm{d}n_0 n_0^2 \frac{\partial}{\partial n_0}\left(\frac{1}{\pi(0)}\right) - \tfrac{1}{2}n_0\sum_{\boldsymbol{K}\neq 0}|V_{\boldsymbol{K}}|^2\frac{\partial}{\partial n_0}\left(\frac{\pi(\boldsymbol{K})}{\mathscr{E}(\boldsymbol{K})}\right). \tag{79}$$

Now, if in eqs. (75) and (79) we neglect the terms which contain derivatives with respect to the electron density, then $C_{12} - C_{44} = 2P$, and the equilibrium condition $P=0$ leads directly to $C_{12} = C_{44}$, i.e., to the satisfaction of the Cauchy relations. The presence of derivatives with respect to density precisely reflects the fact that the picture of interactions in a metal cannot be described adequately in the language of pairwise forces.

Taking into account the equilibrium condition, and retaining all terms, we find that

$$C_{12} - C_{44} = \int_0^{n_0}\mathrm{d}n_0 n_0^2\frac{\partial}{\partial n_0}\left(\frac{1}{\pi(0)}\right) - \sum_{\boldsymbol{K}\neq 0}\left\{n_0|V_{\boldsymbol{K}}|^2\frac{\partial}{\partial n_0}\left(\frac{\pi(\boldsymbol{K})}{\mathscr{E}(\boldsymbol{K})}\right)\right.$$
$$\left. - \tfrac{1}{3}K^{\alpha}\frac{\partial}{\partial K^{\alpha}}\left[|V_{\boldsymbol{K}}|^2\frac{\partial}{\partial n_0}\left(\frac{\pi(\boldsymbol{K})}{\mathscr{E}(\boldsymbol{K})}\right)\right] + \tfrac{1}{2}n_0^2\frac{\partial^2}{\partial n_0^2}\left(\frac{\pi(\boldsymbol{K})}{\mathscr{E}(\boldsymbol{K})}\right)\right\}. \tag{80}$$

The last term can also be rewritten in terms of derivatives of $\varphi(\boldsymbol{K})$. This expression clearly demonstrates the presence of two reasons for the breakdown of the Cauchy relations in a metal. The first is related to the non-pairwise nature of the indirect interionic interaction, and to it corresponds the second term on the right hand side of eq. (80) (see the discussion in the preceding section). The second reason has its origin in the peculiar role which the electron liquid plays in the establishment of the equilibrium condition for a metal, and in fact is connected with the circumstance that the Cauchy relations are not satisfied for a uniform electron gas. To it corresponds the first term on the right hand side of eq. (80), which can also be rewritten in the form

$$\int_0^{n_0}\mathrm{d}n_0 n_0^2\frac{\partial}{\partial n_0}\left(\frac{1}{\pi(\mathbf{0})}\right) = -2P^{(0)} + 1/\kappa^{(0)}. \tag{81}$$

It is interesting that this contribution does not reduce to simply twice the pressure of the electron liquid, as was sometimes asserted in earlier work.

The expression (81) depends only on the properties of the electron liquid, and can be found for specific metals, if use is made of the energy $E^{(0)}$, for example in the interpolative form of Nozieres and Pines. This estimate shows that both of the reasons for the breakdown of the Cauchy relations mentioned above give contributions of the same order in the alkali metals. Numerical examples will be presented below, in the section 3 of this chapter (see table 12). For a given structure the relations (76) or (79), which can be rewritten in the form

$$P = P(\Omega_0),$$

are in fact equations of state of the metal at $T=0$. In this connection the equilibrium condition in the absence of an external pressure,

$$P(\Omega_0) = 0,$$

leads to an important relation between the parameters in a model definition of an effective electron–ion interaction (see section 3).

We note that an analysis of the equation of state shows that in non-transition metals a very essential role in the equilibrium condition is played by the non-Coulomb part of the averaged electron–ion interaction, i.e., the term (78) (its analogue for the condition of dynamical stability is the term (68) in the compressibility). For $b=0$ at normal densities the pressure and compressibility generally become negative which, in particular, allows us to understand why the metallic phase of hydrogen crystallizes at significantly large densities, in contrast with the alkali metals.

2.7. The electron multi-pole functions. The singularities of the ring diagrams

As is clear from the preceding sections, in the many electron theory of metals an essential role is played by the electron multi-pole functions $\Gamma^{(n)}$ – which are polarization diagrams with an arbitrary number of external field lines (see fig. 1). For the analysis of specific problems it is essential to have an explicit, analytic representation for them. However, in a number of cases (singularities in the phonon dispersion law, the asymptotic behavior of the interionic interaction, etc.) it is only the 'singular' part of these multi-pole functions, i.e., the nature and location of the singularities of the multi-pole functions as functions of the external momenta, which are of the greatest interest. We will begin with a general analysis of just this problem.

In work by the authors (Brovman and Kagan 1972) a method was developed which allows one to find the singularities of the multi-pole functions without an explicit analytic evaluation of the diagrams. This method is analogous to the method of Landau (Landau 1959) for determining the singularities of diagrams in quantum field theory. The basic feature which significantly distinguishes the case of electron multi-pole functions is the presence of a background of Fermi particles and the Fermi surface in momentum space, as well as the three-dimensionality of the problem, which leads to singularities of a specific form.

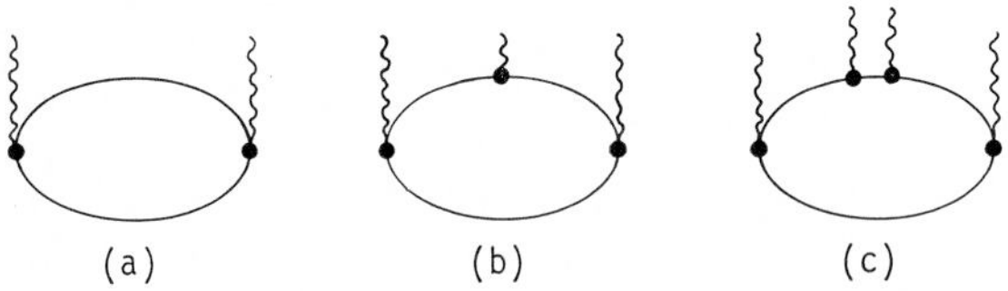

Fig. 5

We will investigate in detail the ring diagrams, i.e., diagrams which contain no electron–electron interaction lines (fig. 5a-c). As will become clear in what follows, it is just these diagrams which determine the leading singularities of a multi-pole function, i.e., the set of all diagrams with a fixed number of external field lines.

For ring diagrams with static external ends, which are the only ones discussed in the preceding sections due to the adiabaticity of the problem, the characteristic singularity is the presence of one and the same frequency ω in all electron propagators. As a result it is convenient to use the following representation for the Green's function of a free electron, corresponding to a line in the diagrams

$$G_0(\boldsymbol{p}, \omega) = \frac{1}{\omega - \mathscr{E}_0(\boldsymbol{p}) + \mathrm{i}\delta \operatorname{sgn}(\omega - \mu)}, \tag{82}$$

where $\mathscr{E}_0(\boldsymbol{p}) = p^2/2m$, while μ is the chemical potential. In the limit as $\delta \to 0$ this expression coincides with the usual one (Abrikosov et al. 1963); however, for our purposes it has the advantage that the imaginary term in the denominator of eq. (82) is the same for all Green's functions in the ring. To the ring diagram with n external field lines (see fig. 5c) corresponds the following expression [we omit the coefficients, whose retention would yield the expression for $\Gamma^{(0)}(\boldsymbol{q}_1, \cdots, \boldsymbol{q}_n)$]

$$J^{(n)}(\boldsymbol{q}_1, \cdots, \boldsymbol{q}_n) = \frac{2}{\mathrm{i}} \int \frac{\mathrm{d}\boldsymbol{p}\, \mathrm{d}\omega}{(2\pi)^4}$$

$$\times \frac{1}{[\omega - \mathscr{E}_0(\boldsymbol{p}_1) + \mathrm{i}\delta \operatorname{sgn}(\omega - \mu)] \cdots [\omega - \mathscr{E}_0(\boldsymbol{p}_n) + \mathrm{i}\delta \operatorname{sgn}(\omega - \mu)]}. \tag{83}$$

Here all $\boldsymbol{p}_i$ are linearly related to $\boldsymbol{p}$ and the $\boldsymbol{q}_i$. Making use of the well-known Feynman parametrization we can rewrite eq. (83) in the form

$$J^{(n)}(\boldsymbol{q}_1, \cdots, \boldsymbol{q}_n) = (n-1)! \frac{2}{\mathrm{i}} \int \frac{\mathrm{d}\boldsymbol{p}\, \mathrm{d}\omega}{(2\pi)^4} \int_0^1 \cdots \int_0^1 \frac{\mathrm{d}\alpha_1 \cdots \mathrm{d}\alpha_n}{[f]^n} \delta\left(\sum_{i=1}^n \alpha_i - 1\right), \tag{84}$$

$$f = \omega - \sum_{i=1}^n \alpha_i \mathscr{E}_0(\boldsymbol{p}_i) + \mathrm{i}\delta \operatorname{sgn}(\omega - \mu). \tag{85}$$

In writing eq. (85) we have made explicit use of the condition

$$\sum_{i=1}^n \alpha_i = 1. \tag{86}$$

According to 'Hadamard's principle' the singularities of a multiple integral of the type of (84) arise only for that set of real parameters $q_i^{(0)}$ for which f vanishes, and for which 1) the zero is a zero of second order in each integration variable simultaneously ('pinch' singularity), or 2) each integration variable coincides with the fixed boundaries of the integration contour ('border' singularity). We will analyze the expressions (84) and (85) from this point of view.

It follows directly from the form of eq. (85) that any singularity with respect to ω can only be of the second type. In the integration over ω the entire integration contour can be displaced with the exception of the point $\omega = \mu$ which remains fixed. From this we obtain the first condition

$$\omega = \mu. \tag{87}$$

On the other hand, with respect to the variable $\boldsymbol{p}$ any singularities can be only of the first type. The condition $\partial f / \partial \boldsymbol{p} = 0$ in this case leads to the relation

$$\sum_{i=1}^n \alpha_i \boldsymbol{p}_i = 0. \tag{88}$$

The singularities with respect to the variables α_i can be either of the first type or of the second type. In the first case, eliminating α_n from eq. (84) with the aid of eq. (86), from the condition $\partial f/\partial\alpha_i=0$ we obtain

$$\mathscr{E}_0(\boldsymbol{p}_i)=\mathscr{E}_0(\boldsymbol{p}_n).$$

Taking into account the alternative possibility of the appearance of a boundary singularity with respect to any of the variables α_i, and also the condition $f=0$, we obtain finally

$$\mathscr{E}_0(\boldsymbol{p}_i)=\mu \quad \text{or} \quad \alpha_i=0, \quad i=1,2,\cdots,n. \tag{89}$$

In this way the necessary condition for the appearance of a singularity of the function $J^{(n)}(\boldsymbol{q}_1,\cdots,\boldsymbol{q}_n)$ defined by eq. (83) is the satisfaction of the relations (88) and (89). In the case $\alpha_i=0$ the propagator corresponding to a given electron line generally drops out of the problem, and the singularity will be due to a singularity of a diagram of lower order (of a 'reduced' diagram), obtained by the contraction of the given electron line into a point.

We now determine the nature of the singularities that arise. For this we carry out explicitly the integration on ω in eq. (84), and then on $\boldsymbol{p}$. A direct calculation yields

$$J^{(n)}(\boldsymbol{q}_1,\cdots,\boldsymbol{q}_n)=\frac{m(-1)^{n-1}}{\pi^2}\frac{\partial^{n-2}}{\partial\mu^{n-2}}\int_0^1 \mathrm{d}\alpha_1\int_0^{1-\alpha_1}\mathrm{d}\alpha_2\cdots\int_0^{1-\sum_j^{n-2}\alpha_j}\mathrm{d}\alpha_{n-1}$$
$$\times\left(2m\mu+\sum_{i,j}^{n-1}\boldsymbol{\kappa}_i\cdot\boldsymbol{\kappa}_j\alpha_i\alpha_j-\sum_i^{n-1}\alpha_i\boldsymbol{\kappa}_i^2\right)^{1/2}. \tag{90}$$

Here

$$\boldsymbol{\kappa}_s=\boldsymbol{q}_1+\cdots+\boldsymbol{q}_s. \tag{91}$$

In eq. (90) it is assumed that the integration extends only over that region in which the expression under the square root sign is positive. In addition, we have taken into account that $\boldsymbol{\kappa}_n=0$, and explicitly evaluated the integral on α_n.

The quadratic form under the square root in eq. (90) is positive definite, for it is constructed on the basis of coefficients which constitute a Gram determinant. For fixed values of the external momenta $\boldsymbol{q}_i$ the expression under the square root has a minimum at the point $\{\alpha_i^{(0)}\}$ defined as the solution of the system of equations

$$\sum_{j=1}^{n-1}\boldsymbol{\kappa}_i\cdot\boldsymbol{\kappa}_j\bar{\alpha}_j=\tfrac{1}{2}\boldsymbol{\kappa}_i^2. \tag{92}$$

At this point the expression under the square root becomes (k_F is the Fermi momentum)

$$\Delta = k_F^2 - \kappa^2, \quad \kappa^2 = \left(\sum_{i=1}^{n-1} \bar{\alpha}_i \boldsymbol{\kappa}_i\right)^2. \tag{93}$$

We note that the conditions for the existence of singularity, eqs. (88) and (89), lead, naturally, to the same system of equations (92), so that at the singular point itself

$$\Delta = 0. \tag{94}$$

At the same time the singularity occurs only for those values of the external momenta $\boldsymbol{q}_i^{(0)}$ (or $\boldsymbol{\kappa}_i^{(0)}$) for which the solution of the system of equations (92), to which eq. (93) corresponds, lies in the domain of integration of eq. (90).

Expanding the expression under the square root in eq. (90) in powers of Δ in the neighborhood of $\{\alpha_i^{(0)}\}$ and carrying out the integration for the singular part of $J^{(n)}$, we find after a series of transformations (Brovman and Kagan 1972)

$$J^{(n)} \sim (-1)^{(2n+s-1)/2} \frac{\partial^{(n-2)}(\Delta^{(s+1)/2} \ln|\Delta|)}{\partial \Delta^{(n-2)}}$$
$$\sim (-1)^{(2n+s-1)/2} \Delta^{(s-2n+5)/2} \ln|\Delta| \quad (s \text{ odd}), \tag{95}$$

where Δ may have either sign here;

$$J^{(n)} \sim (-1)^{(2n+s+2)/2} \frac{\partial^{(n-2)}}{\partial \Delta^{(n-2)}} \Delta^{(s+1)/2}$$
$$\sim (-1)^{(2n+s+2)/2} (\Delta)^{(s-2n+5)/2}, \quad \Delta > 0 \quad (s \text{ even}). \tag{96}$$

For $\Delta < 0$ the diagram possesses no singularities. Here s is the rank of the square matrix made up from the $\boldsymbol{\kappa}_i$:

$$\|\boldsymbol{\kappa}_i \cdot \boldsymbol{\kappa}_j\|. \tag{97}$$

The expressions (95) and (96) determine the behavior of $J^{(n)}$ in the vicinity of the leading singularity of a ring diagram with n tails. Such a diagram in fact will contain additional, weaker 'boundary' singularities which correspond in eq. (89) to the vanishing of one or several α_1. The behavior of $J^{(n)}$ in the vicinity of a boundary singularity which corresponds to k parameters $\alpha_i = 0$ will also be described by eqs. (95) and (96) with the replacement

$$n \to n' = n - k, \quad s \to s',$$

where s' is the rank of the square matrix of n'th order, resulting from crossing out in the original matrix $\|\boldsymbol{\kappa}_i \cdot \boldsymbol{\kappa}_j\|$ the k rows and columns whose indices correspond to the vanishing α_i.

The expressions (95) and (96) together with eqs. (87)–(89) [or (92)–(94)] completely solve the problem of the nature and location of the singularities of the ring diagrams with static external field tails for a system of Fermi particles. Together with this result it seems that these singularities remain the dominant singularities for the total multi-pole function with n external field tails as well. Indeed, the most notable result here is that fact that it is essential for the occurrence of singularities that all virtual particles lie on the Fermi surface [see eq. (89)]. This is a reflection of the role of the sharp boundary in momentum space which is characteristic for the Fermi distribution. As is well known, this sharp boundary is preserved when the interaction between electrons is taken into account (see Migdal 1958, Abrikosov et al. 1963). On the other hand, in more complicated diagrams two-electron propagators and simultaneously an additional four-dimensional integration are associated with each interaction line. As a result, one may think that taking into account diagrams with electron interactions will lead neither to the appearance of stronger singularities nor to the smearing out of the singularities found above.

We now investigate the singularities of particular multipole functions. In the case of the two-pole function (fig. 5a) the solution of eq. (92) gives $\bar{\alpha}_1 = \frac{1}{2}$. Then, taking into account that $s=1$ and $\boldsymbol{\kappa}_1 = \boldsymbol{q}_1$, from eqs. (94) and (95) we find for the singular part

$$J^{(2)}(\boldsymbol{q}_1, -\boldsymbol{q}_1) \sim (k_F^2 - \tfrac{1}{4}q_1^2)\ln(k_F^2 - \tfrac{1}{4}q_1^2). \tag{98}$$

We are thus led to the well-known singularity, characteristic of the ordinary polarization loop (Lindhard 1954).

For the three-pole function (fig. 5c) the rank of the matrix (97) is $s=2$, and the solution of the system of equations (92) yields

$$\bar{\alpha}_1 = \tfrac{1}{2}\kappa_2^2 \frac{\boldsymbol{\kappa}_1^2 - \boldsymbol{\kappa}_1 \cdot \boldsymbol{\kappa}_2}{\kappa_1^2\kappa_2^2 - (\boldsymbol{\kappa}_1 \cdot \boldsymbol{\kappa}_2)^2}, \qquad \bar{\alpha}_2 = \tfrac{1}{2}\kappa_1^2 \frac{\boldsymbol{\kappa}_2^2 - \boldsymbol{\kappa}_1 \cdot \boldsymbol{\kappa}_2}{\kappa_1^2\kappa_2^2 - (\boldsymbol{\kappa}_1 \cdot \boldsymbol{\kappa}_2)^2}.$$

The sum of these quantities must be less than unity. From this the restriction

$$\angle(\kappa_1, \kappa_2) < \tfrac{1}{2}\pi$$

follows immediately. Taking into account eq. (91) ($\boldsymbol{\kappa}_1 = \boldsymbol{q}_1$, $\boldsymbol{\kappa}_2 = -\boldsymbol{q}_3$) and the arbitrariness in the labeling of the external momenta, one may conclude from this condition that a singularity occurs only when the vectors $\boldsymbol{q}_1, \boldsymbol{q}_2, \boldsymbol{q}_3$ form an acute-angled triangle.

Utilizing the values of the $\bar{\alpha}_i$ just obtained, we find that

$$\kappa^2 = \tfrac{1}{4}\frac{(\boldsymbol{\kappa}_1 - \boldsymbol{\kappa}_2)^2}{1 - (\boldsymbol{\kappa}_1 \cdot \boldsymbol{\kappa}_2)^2/\kappa_1^2\kappa_2^2} = \tfrac{1}{4}\frac{q_2^2}{\sin^2 \angle(\boldsymbol{q}_1, \boldsymbol{q}_3)} \equiv q_{\mathrm{R}}^2,$$

where q_{R} is the radius of the circumscribed circle for the triangle formed from the vectors $\boldsymbol{q}_1, \boldsymbol{q}_2, \boldsymbol{q}_3$. Then for the singular part of the three-pole function we obtain from eq. (96)

$$J^{(3)}(\boldsymbol{q}_1, \boldsymbol{q}_2, \boldsymbol{q}_3) \sim \sqrt{k_{\mathrm{F}}^2 - q_{\mathrm{R}}^2}, \quad q_{\mathrm{R}} < k_{\mathrm{F}}. \tag{99}$$

($J^{(3)}$ is an analytic function for $q_{\mathrm{R}} > k_{\mathrm{F}}$.) In the degenerate case, when the vectors $\boldsymbol{q}_1$ and $\boldsymbol{q}_2$ are parallel, the rank of the matrix (97) is reduced to $s=1$, and we are led to the stronger singularity

$$J^{(3)}(\boldsymbol{q}_1, -\boldsymbol{q}_1, \boldsymbol{0}) \sim \ln|k_{\mathrm{F}}^2 - \tfrac{1}{4}q_1^2|. \tag{100}$$

In the case of the four-pole function we obtain from eq. (95) for the leading singularity ($s=3$)

$$J^{(4)}(\boldsymbol{q}_1, \boldsymbol{q}_2, \boldsymbol{q}_3, \boldsymbol{q}_4) \sim \ln|k_{\mathrm{F}}^2 - \kappa_{\mathrm{R}}^2|, \tag{101}$$

where the quantity $\boldsymbol{\kappa}_{\mathrm{R}}^2$ is obtained from eqs. (92) and (93), and corresponds to the radius of the sphere circumscribed about the tetrahedron with sides $\boldsymbol{q}_1, \boldsymbol{q}_2, \boldsymbol{q}_3, \boldsymbol{q}_4, \boldsymbol{q}_1+\boldsymbol{q}_2, \boldsymbol{q}_1+\boldsymbol{q}_3$. If all vectors lie in the same plane, then the rank of the matrix is reduced to $s=2$, and in this case from eq. (96) we find that

$$J^{(4)}(\boldsymbol{q}_1, \boldsymbol{q}_2, \boldsymbol{q}_3, \boldsymbol{q}_4) \sim 1/\sqrt{k_{\mathrm{F}}^2 - \kappa^2}, \quad \kappa < k_{\mathrm{F}}. \tag{102}$$

An interesting problem arises for multi-pole functions of higher order, which is related to the three-dimensionality of space, i.e., to the fact that $s \leqslant 3$ always, while the number of external tails grows. We will not analyze this case here, referring to the paper cited above for the details (Brovman and Kagan 1972).

All of the singularities investigated above are clearly manifested in the phonon dispersion curves of a metal. This matter will be discussed in greater detail in the following subsection.

The representation (84) also turns out to be useful for the direct evaluation of the ring diagrams. It was shown in subsection 2.2 that for multi-pole functions with $n>2$ a partial summation can be carried out, corresponding to the screening of all external field lines. As a consequence the problem is reduced to finding the irreducible multi-pole function $\Lambda^{(n)}(\boldsymbol{q}_1, \cdots, \boldsymbol{q}_n)$ in eq. (22). Apparently, the approximation of $\Lambda^{(n)}$ by a ring diagram in this case is a reasonable one. Physically, this approximation corresponds to taking into account the multiple scattering of an electron by screened ions without exchange with the electrons of the perturbed background. An analogous interpretation can be given in the language of the 'self-consistent' field (Solt 1969). We emphasize by the way that such an approximation preserves all the dominant singularities of the multi-pole function.

We note that in this sense the two-pole function ($\Gamma^{(2)}$), or the polarization operator in terms of which it is uniquely expressed, is sharply distinct in this hierarchy of multi-pole functions. In the first place, $\pi(\boldsymbol{q})$ enters the definition of all $\Gamma^{(n)}$ through $\mathscr{E}(\boldsymbol{q})$; in the second place, the accuracy of the leading term in the indirect interaction, arising from $E^{(2)}$, is to a significant degree related to the accuracy of its determination; finally, its determination in the self-consistent field approximation (or the RPA) suffers from that inadequacy that it itself does not satisfy any fundamental conditions, such as eq. (53), for example. Therefore in what follows we will pause for a detailed analysis of $\pi(\boldsymbol{q})$, going beyond the limits of the RPA, i.e., beyond the limits of the single-particle approximation.

We now evaluate explicitly the contribution of the ring diagram with three tails, for which we use the expression (90), and carry out the integration over α_2. Let us assume at first that the $\boldsymbol{q}_i$ are such that $\boldsymbol{q}_{\mathrm{R}} < k_{\mathrm{F}}$ and, consequently, in particular that $\boldsymbol{q}_i < 2k_{\mathrm{F}}$. Then there is no restriction on the range of integration with respect to α_1, and (collecting coefficients) we obtain

$$J^{(3)}(\boldsymbol{q}_1, \boldsymbol{q}_2, \boldsymbol{q}_3) = \frac{m^2}{\pi^2 q_3} \int_0^1 \mathrm{d}\alpha_1$$

$$\times \ln \frac{2q_3 [k_{\mathrm{F}}^2 - q_1^2 \alpha_1 (1-\alpha_1)]^{1/2} + \alpha_1 (q_2^2 - q_1^2 - q_3^2) + q_3^2}{2q_3 [k_{\mathrm{F}}^2 - q_2^2 \alpha_1 (1-\alpha_1)]^{1/2} + \alpha_1 (q_2^2 - q_1^2 + q_3^2) - q_3^2},$$

The remaining integration with respect to α_1 presents no difficulties in principle. We obtain as the result

$$J^{(3)}(\boldsymbol{q}_1, \boldsymbol{q}_2, \boldsymbol{q}_3) = \frac{2m^2}{\pi^2} \frac{q_{\mathrm{R}}^2}{q_1 q_2 q_3}$$

$$\times \left[\sum_m \cos\theta_m \ln\left(\frac{2k_{\mathrm{F}} + q_m}{2k_{\mathrm{F}} - q_m}\right) - 2(1-x^2)^{1/2} \tan^{-1} A \right],$$

where

$$A = \frac{q_1 q_2 q_3}{(2k_F)^3 \left[1 - \frac{1}{2}(q_1^2 + q_2^2 + q_3^2)/(2k_F)^2\right]}$$
$$= \frac{\sin\theta_1 \sin\theta_2 \sin\theta_3}{x^3 - x(1 + \cos\theta_1 \cos\theta_2 \cos\theta_3)}, \quad x = k_F/q_R .$$

We have introduced the notation $\cos\theta_k = -\boldsymbol{q}_l\, \boldsymbol{q}_m/|\boldsymbol{q}_l|\, |\boldsymbol{q}_m|$. The branch $0 \leqslant \tan^{-1} x \leqslant \pi$ is assumed for the arctangent.

In order to obtain an expression for $J^{(3)}$ valid over the entire range of variation of the external parameters, we will formally investigate the expression (90), dropping the restriction on the sign of the expression under the square root, regarded as a function of a complex variable. This function will be defined, in particular, even for those real values of x which in some region of variation of x correspond to a negative value of the expression under the square root. We wil make use of the relation, valid everywhere on the real axis

$$\theta(\psi(x))/\sqrt{\psi(x)} = \mathrm{Re}\left(1/\sqrt{\psi(x)}\right),$$

(θ is the usual Heaviside unit step function). Then for the determination of $J^{(3)}$ for all values of the parameters it is sufficient to carry out an analytic continuation of the expression obtained into the region of smaller real values of x. As the result of this procedure the following final expression is obtained (restoring all coefficients and returning to $\Lambda^{(3)}$).

$$\Lambda_0^{(3)}(\boldsymbol{q}_1, \boldsymbol{q}_2, \boldsymbol{q}_3) = \frac{2m^2}{3\pi\hbar^4} \frac{q_R^2}{q_1 q_2 q_3} \left(\sum_m \cos\theta_m \ln \left|\frac{2k_F + q_m}{2k_F - q_m}\right| - \Delta \times \begin{cases} \ln|(1 - \Delta A)/(1 + \Delta A)|, & \text{for } k_F/q_R < 1 \\ 2\tan^{-1} \Delta A, & \text{for } k_F/q_R > 1 \end{cases} \right), \tag{103}$$

where $\Delta = |x^2 - 1|^{1/2}$. It is easy to determine that this expression contains only singularities of the type of eqs. (99) and (100), as was predicted by the general analysis. The complete multi-pole function $\Gamma^{(3)}(\boldsymbol{q}_1, \boldsymbol{q}_2, \boldsymbol{q}_3)$ which enters the expressions for the energy and the dynamical matrix, is equal to

$$\Gamma^{(3)}(\boldsymbol{q}_1, \boldsymbol{q}_2, \boldsymbol{q}_3) = \Lambda_0^{(3)}(\boldsymbol{q}_1, \boldsymbol{q}_2, \boldsymbol{q}_3)/\mathscr{E}(\boldsymbol{q}_1)\, \mathscr{E}(\boldsymbol{q}_2)\, \mathscr{E}(\boldsymbol{q}_3). \tag{104}$$

This expression was used by us in specific calculations (see, for example, Brovman et al. 1971a, 1971b, 1972).

We note that one is led to a result of the type of eq. (103) by a direct calculation of the one electron energy to third order in the electron–ion interaction. This was first done in the work of Lloyd and Sholl (1968).

In the general case the four-pole diagram $\Gamma^{(4)}(\boldsymbol{q}_1, \boldsymbol{q}_2, \boldsymbol{q}_3, \boldsymbol{q}_4)$ depends on six independent variables and is described by a cumbersome expression (Brovman and Kagan 1973). However, there exists an important special case $\Gamma^{(4)}(\boldsymbol{q}_1, -\boldsymbol{q}_1, \boldsymbol{q}_2, -\boldsymbol{q}_2)$, which makes a large contribution to the static energy of the lattice (for example, $\Gamma^{(4)}(\boldsymbol{K}, -\boldsymbol{K}, \boldsymbol{K}, -\boldsymbol{K})$ for the 'strongest' site $V_{\boldsymbol{K}}$), as well as to the long-wavelength phonons [see eq. (41)], and at the same time is given by a compact, analytic expression.

The symmetrized four-pole function can be represented in the following form:

$$\Lambda^{(4)}_{\Omega}(\boldsymbol{q}_1, -\boldsymbol{q}_1, \boldsymbol{q}_2, -\boldsymbol{q}_2) = \tfrac{1}{12}[J^{(4)}_{\mathrm{A}}(\boldsymbol{q}_1, \boldsymbol{q}_2, -\boldsymbol{q}_1, -\boldsymbol{q}_2) + J^{(4)}_{\mathrm{B}}(\boldsymbol{q}_1, -\boldsymbol{q}_1, -\boldsymbol{q}_2, \boldsymbol{q}_2) + J^{(4)}_{\mathrm{B}}(\boldsymbol{q}_1, -\boldsymbol{q}_1, \boldsymbol{q}_2, -\boldsymbol{q}_2)].$$

Here $J^{(4)}_{\mathrm{A}}$ and $J^{(4)}_{\mathrm{B}}$ correspond to the following diagrams

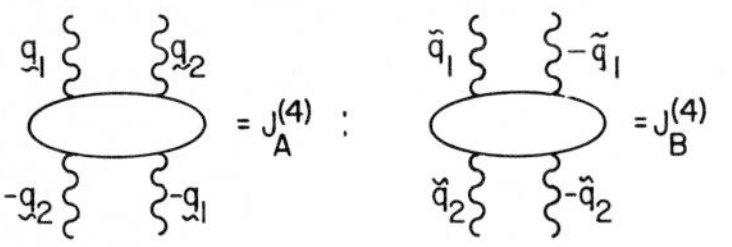

The diagram $J^{(4)}_{\mathrm{B}}$ is a typical example of a diagram containing an 'anomalous contribution' (see subsection 2.2). It is easily calculated

$$J^{(4)}_{\mathrm{Ba}} = -2\int \frac{\mathrm{d}^3 p}{(2\pi)^3}\,\delta(\mathscr{E}_{\boldsymbol{p}} - \mu)\,\frac{1}{(\mathscr{E}_{\boldsymbol{p}} - \mathscr{E}_{\boldsymbol{p}+\boldsymbol{q}_1})(\mathscr{E}_{\boldsymbol{p}} - \mathscr{E}_{\boldsymbol{p}-\boldsymbol{q}_2})}. \tag{105}$$

The integration can be carried out directly, and we obtain (Brovman and Kagan 1973)

$$\Lambda^{(4)}_{\Omega\mathrm{a}}(\boldsymbol{q}_1, -\boldsymbol{q}_1, \boldsymbol{q}_2, -\boldsymbol{q}_2) = -\frac{1}{12}\frac{m^3}{\pi^2}\frac{1}{q_1 q_2 q_3^+ \Delta^+}\ln\left|\frac{A_3^+ + 2k_{\mathrm{F}} q_3^+ \Delta^+}{A_3^+ - 2k_{\mathrm{F}} q_3^+ \Delta^+}\right| - \frac{1}{12}\frac{m^3}{\pi^2}\frac{1}{q_1 q_2 q_3^- \Delta^-}\ln\left|\frac{A_3^- + 2k_{\mathrm{F}} q_3^- \Delta^-}{A_3^- - 2k_{\mathrm{F}} q_3^- \Delta^-}\right|$$

(for $k_{\mathrm{F}}/q_{\mathrm{R}}^-$, $k_{\mathrm{F}}/q_{\mathrm{R}}^+ < 1$). Here, $\boldsymbol{q}_3^\pm = -(\boldsymbol{q}_1 \pm \boldsymbol{q}_2)$, and the index $\pm$ appears in a corresponding fashion in Δ, q_{R}, and A_3,

$$A_3^\pm = q_1 q_2 \pm 4k_{\mathrm{F}}^2(\boldsymbol{q}_1 \cdot \boldsymbol{q}_2 / q_1 q_2).$$

In fact, it is not essential to calculate the 'anomalous' and 'normal' contributions separately. The reason is that the representation of the multipole functions with the aid of Green's functions, eq. (82), in fact is equivalent to taking the limit $T \to 0$ in the finite temperature perturbation theory, and therefore expression (90) automatically contains the sum of a 'normal' and an 'anomalous' contribution. Calculations can be made in a manner analogous to the way this was done for the three-pole function. The functions $J_{\mathrm{A}}^{(4)}$ and $J_{\mathrm{B}}^{(4)}$ separately lead to unwieldy expressions; however, the symmetrized multi-pole function $\Lambda_{\Omega}^{(4)}$ simplified greatly:

$$\Lambda_{\Omega}^{(4)}(\boldsymbol{q}_1, -\boldsymbol{q}_1, \boldsymbol{q}_2, -\boldsymbol{q}_2) =$$
$$-\frac{m^3}{6\pi^2}\frac{(4k_{\mathrm{F}}^2 - q_3^{+2})}{q_1 q_2 q_3^{+}(\boldsymbol{q}_1\cdot\boldsymbol{q}_2)}\frac{1}{\Delta^{+}} \times \begin{Bmatrix} -\frac{1}{2}\ln\left|\dfrac{1-\Delta^{+}A^{+}}{1+\Delta^{+}A^{+}}\right| & \text{for } k_{\mathrm{F}}/q_{\mathrm{R}}^{+} < 1 \\ \tan^{-1}\Delta^{+}A^{+} & \text{for } k_{\mathrm{F}}/q_{\mathrm{R}}^{+} > 1 \end{Bmatrix}$$
$$+\frac{m^3}{6\pi^2}\frac{(4k_{\mathrm{F}}^2 - q_3^{-2})}{q_1 q_2 q_3^{-}(\boldsymbol{q}_1\cdot\boldsymbol{q}_2)}\frac{1}{\Delta^{-}} \times \begin{Bmatrix} -\frac{1}{2}\ln\left|\dfrac{1-\Delta^{-}A^{-}}{1+\Delta^{-}A^{-}}\right| & \text{for } k_{\mathrm{F}}/q_{\mathrm{R}}^{-} < 1 \\ \tan^{-1}\Delta^{-}A^{-} & \text{for } k_{\mathrm{F}}/q_{\mathrm{R}}^{-} > 1 \end{Bmatrix}. \quad (106)$$

Finally, the contribution $\Lambda_{\mu}^{(4)}$ follows directly from eq. (24) for the loop diagram, and is given by

$$\Lambda_{\mu}^{(4)}(\boldsymbol{q}_1, -\boldsymbol{q}_1, \boldsymbol{q}_2, -\boldsymbol{q}_2) = \frac{1}{24}\frac{m^3}{\pi^2 k_{\mathrm{F}} q_1 q_2}\ln\left|\frac{2k_{\mathrm{F}}+q_1}{2k_{\mathrm{F}}-q_1}\right|\ln\left|\frac{2k_{\mathrm{F}}+q_2}{2k_{\mathrm{F}}-q_2}\right|. \quad (107)$$

The final expression for the four-pole function $\Lambda_0^{(4)}$ (23) is given by the sum of eqs. (106) and (107).

We now return to a more detailed discussion of the polarization operator $\pi(\boldsymbol{q})$. From eq. (90) we readily find the well-known expression for the simple polarization loop

$$\pi_0(\boldsymbol{q}) = \frac{3}{2}\frac{n_0}{\mathscr{E}_{\mathrm{F}}}\left\{\frac{1}{2} + \frac{1}{4}\frac{1-(q/2k_{\mathrm{F}})^2}{q/2k_{\mathrm{F}}}\ln\left|\frac{1+q/2k_{\mathrm{F}}}{1-q/2k_{\mathrm{F}}}\right|\right\}.$$

The approximation which is based on the replacement of $\pi(\boldsymbol{q})$ by $\pi_0(\boldsymbol{q})$ turns out to be valid in the high-density limit, $r_s \ll 1$ (see, for example, Pines and Nozieres 1966), while a more accurate description is required at metallic densities. Unfortunately, at such densities there is no small parameter in the electron gas, which fact has thus far prevented the development of a regular technique, controllable in its accuracy, adequate for this problem.

However, notwithstanding the difficulties, the last few years have seen progress in the analysis of this problem, which is based on the use of certain self-consistent schemes or on attempts to select and sum entire classes of diagrams. All of these efforts lead to an expression for the polarization operator which, in the static case, can be represented in the form

$$\pi(\boldsymbol{q}) = \frac{\pi_0(\boldsymbol{q})}{1-(4\pi e^2/q^2)\,G(\boldsymbol{q})\,\pi_0(\boldsymbol{q})}. \quad (108)$$

They differ only in the function $G(\boldsymbol{q})$, which plays the role of an effective electron-electron interaction.

The first attempt to go beyond the RPA was made by Hubbard (1957), who attempted to sum approximately the simplest class of exchange diagrams. As a result he was led to an expression of the type of eq. (108) with

$$G_{\mathrm{H}}(q) = \tfrac{1}{2}q^2/(q^2 + k_{\mathrm{F}}^2). \tag{109}$$

However, in this form $\pi(\boldsymbol{q})$ does not satisfy the identity (67). Subsequently several modifications of eq. (109) were proposed. The form most frequently used was that introduced by Geldart and Vosko (1966)

$$G_{\mathrm{HGV}}(q) = \tfrac{1}{2}q^2/(q^2 + \xi k_{\mathrm{F}}^2), \tag{110}$$

where the parameter ξ is determined from the condition that eq. (108) obey the identity (53). Because, as we have already noted in subsection 2.5, the compressibility κ is obtained from the energy with rather high accuracy, $\pi(0)$ together with $\mathscr{E}(\boldsymbol{q})$ for small q is obtained from this expression with completely reasonable accuracy. In the region of metallic densities the basic role in the compressibility is played by the exchange term (see, for example, Pines and Nozieres 1966), and

$$\xi = \frac{2}{1 + 0.0155\pi/k_{\mathrm{F}}a_{\mathrm{B}}} \approx 2. \tag{111}$$

(where a_{B} is the Bohr radius). Even earlier (Hohenberg and Kohn 1964, Kohn and Sham 1965) a systematic formulation of the one electron problem, generalizing the Fermi-Thomas method for weakly inhomogeneous systems, led to the expression

$$G_{\mathrm{HKS}}(q) = \gamma q^2 \tag{112}$$

in the region of small q (Hedin and Lundquist 1971), where the coefficient γ in fact has the same value as is obtained from eqs. (110) and (111) for $q \to 0$.

A further step was taken in a recent series of papers (Geldart and Taylor 1970a, 1970b, 1971), in which an attempt was made to select the most significant class of diagrams for the static polarization operator. At every stage of this calculation a mutual cancellation of definite sets of diagrams was observed, which is particularly evident in the Coulomb case. Particular attention was paid to the necessity of satisfying the identity (53). The authors came to the very significant result that in the representation (108) the function $G_{\mathrm{GT}}(q)/q^2$ decreases with increasing q much more slowly than in eq. (110), remaining practically unchanged out to $q \sim 2k_{\mathrm{F}}$.

A completely different approach, but one yielding similar results for the same region of q, was developed in papers by the Argonne group (Singwi et al. 1968, 1970). In these papers an approximate attempt was made to include in a self-consistent way the corrections to the local field with the aim of taking account of correlations between electrons at small distances, for which purpose the pair correlation function was used. The result once again can be represented in the form (108) with the function $G_{SSTL}(q)$ given in numerical form. A two-parameter interpolation formula for these numerical values was proposed in the latter work (Singwi et al. 1970).

An approach based on the method of decoupling the equations of motion of Green's functions was proposed by Toigo and Woodruff (1970, 1971). In principle this approach to the problem under study can turn out to be very useful. The authors came to the conclusion that $G_{TW}(\boldsymbol{q})$ is a universal function of $(q/2k_F)$ and gave a representation for it in numerical form. It is interesting that in this approach the function $G_{TW}(q)/q^2$ also falls off weakly with increasing q. Investigations of $\mathscr{E}(q)$ were also carried out in several other papers (Kleinman 1967, 1968, Langreth 1969, Shaw 1970).

We note that in the dynamical matrix and for the description of static properties we are first of all interested in the behavior of the static polarization operator for $q \leqslant 2k_F$. The sharp decrease of $\pi_0(q)$ for $q > 2k_F$ produces an insignificant error in the determination of $G(q)$ in this range of q. However, for $q \leqslant 2k_F$ all recent investigations give results for the behavior of $G(q)$ which are more or less in agreement, and it may be thought that it reproduces the true behavior in this range with reasonable accuracy. This is also confirmed by a detailed analysis of the shapes of the dispersion curves for simple metals (see subsection 3.13).

The different functions $G(q)/q^2$ are reproduced in fig. 6. It is seen that for $q \lesssim 2k_F$ Hubbard's approximation, which does not satisfy the identity (53), differs sharply from the rest. The behaviour of $G_{HGV}(q)$ for intermediate values of q also appears to be inaccurate, displaying a relatively rapid decrease of this function. At the same time the resemblance of the behaviors of $G_{TW}(q)$ and $G_{GT}(q)$ appears quite notable to us.

In this section, in studying multi-pole functions of high order ($n > 2$), we took account of the electron–electron interaction only through the screening of the electron–ion interaction lines. In principle it is possible to take into account another significant class of diagrams by replacing the simple vertices in ring diagrams by the full vertex part T. This approximation corresponds to the investigation of the multiple scattering of an electron by screened ions, but now taking into account exchange and correlation of this electron with

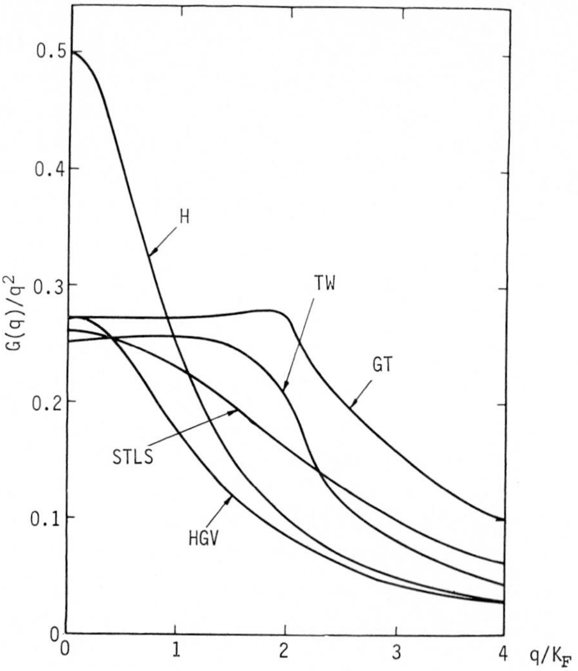

Fig. 6. The 'effective interaction' function $G(q)/q^2$ in different approximations.

the perturbed screened ion. In this approximation, for example, we obtain for the three-pole function

$$\Lambda^{(3)}(\boldsymbol{q}_1, \boldsymbol{q}_2, \boldsymbol{q}_3) = -2\mathrm{i} \int \frac{\mathrm{d}^4 p}{(2\pi)^4} T(p, q_1) T(p + q_1, q_2) \times T(p - q_3, q_3) G(p) G(p + q_1) G(p - q_3). \quad (113)$$

In this language we obtain the following *exact* expression for the polarization operator

$$\pi(\boldsymbol{q}) = 2 \int \frac{\mathrm{d}^4 p}{(2\pi)^4} T(p, q) G(p) G(p + q). \quad (114)$$

If we make the approximation of a local interaction for T, i.e., if we regard the vertex part as depending only on the momentum transfer $\boldsymbol{q}_i$, and replace G in eq. (113) by G_0, then we obtain for $\Lambda^{(3)}$

$$\Lambda^{(3)}(\boldsymbol{q}_1, \boldsymbol{q}_2, \boldsymbol{q}_3) = T(\boldsymbol{q}_1) T(\boldsymbol{q}_2) T(\boldsymbol{q}_3) \Lambda_0^{(3)}(\boldsymbol{q}_1, \boldsymbol{q}_2, \boldsymbol{q}_3). \quad (115)$$

In this approximation, comparing the right hand side of eq. (114) with eq. (108), we obtain

$$T(\boldsymbol{q}) = \frac{1}{1 - (4\pi e^2/q^2)\, G(\boldsymbol{q})\, \pi_0(\boldsymbol{q})}. \tag{116}$$

Maintaining this approximation and performing the same transition as in eq. (114), then on taking account of eqs. (22), (108), and (116), we obtain for the basic multi-pole functions

$$\Gamma^{(n)}(\boldsymbol{q}_1, \cdots, \boldsymbol{q}_n) = \Lambda_0^{(n)}(\boldsymbol{q}_1, \cdots, \boldsymbol{q}_n)/\tilde{\mathscr{E}}(\boldsymbol{q}_1) \cdots \tilde{\mathscr{E}}(\boldsymbol{q}_n), \tag{117}$$

where

$$\tilde{\mathscr{E}}(\boldsymbol{q}) = 1 + (4\pi e^2/q^2)\,[1 - G(\boldsymbol{q})]\, \pi_0(\boldsymbol{q}).$$

2.8. On anomalies in phonon dispersion curves

As was shown in the preceding section the presence of a sharp Fermi surface in the distribution of electrons in momentum space leads to the appearance of a whole 'hierarchy' of singularities in the electron multi-pole functions (95) and (96).

It is a significant fact that singularities of this type can be observed experimentally in a direct way with the aid of measurements of phonon dispersion curves. Indeed, in the study of phonons throughout all momentum space a continuous variation of $\boldsymbol{q}$ will necessarily lead to the satisfaction of the critical conditions (88) and (89) for the multi-pole functions, entering the dynamical matrix (39). The simplest of the singularities investigated above is the singularity in the two-pole function, corresponding to the polarization operator of a homogeneous electron gas. The first assertion that this singularity should manifest itself in the phonon spectrum was made by Kohn (1959). Subsequently Kohn anomalies were observed several times in neutron scattering experiments (Brockhouse et al. 1961, 1962, Stedman et al. 1967, etc.)

It follows from the form of the dynamical matrix that a singularity for a phonon with wave vector $\boldsymbol{q}$ occurs when the condition

$$|\boldsymbol{q} + \boldsymbol{K}| = 2k_{\mathrm{F}} \tag{118}$$

is satisfied. If the Fermi surface close to the Brillouin zone boundary is strongly reconstructed, then in addition to the singularities predicted by eq. (118), whose positions may be somewhat displaced in principle singularities can occur at some other values of $\boldsymbol{q}$. This is easily understood on the basis of the analysis presented in subsection 2.7. Indeed, on taking explicit account of the anisotropy of the electron dispersion law entering Green's functions the condition (88) is replaced by

$$\sum_i \alpha_i \, \partial\mathscr{E}(\boldsymbol{p}_i)/\partial \boldsymbol{p}_i = \sum_i \alpha_i \boldsymbol{v}_i(\boldsymbol{p}_i) = 0 . \tag{119}$$

Here $\boldsymbol{v}_i(\boldsymbol{p})$ is the electron group velocity. (The remaining conditions remain unchanged.) From the condition that the α_i be positive it follows directly in the case of the two-pole function that a singularity occurs for vectors $\boldsymbol{q}+\boldsymbol{K}$ which connect two points on the Fermi surface at which the group velocities of the electrons are strictly oppositely directed. In the case of a spherical Fermi surface the condition (119) coincides with (118), while for a Fermi surface which departs markedly from sphericity additional singularities can occur. In such a case the nature of the singularity can be sharply strengthened. For example, for pieces of the Fermi surfaces possessing a cylindrical form the singularity in the derivative of the dispersion curve becomes of the inverse square root type, while for planar sections of the Fermi surface the most singular part becomes logarithmic (Afanas'ev and Kagan 1963). It is interesting that the 'plane' situation occurs for electrons in a strong magnetic field (Blank and Kaner 1966).

The singularities which correspond to more complicated diagrams ($\Gamma^{(n)}$), are associated with the direct interaction between three and more ions, and the corresponding multi-pole functions enter the dynamical matrix with certain momenta equal to reciprocal lattice vectors. We will investigate in some detail the singularity corresponding to the three-pole function. In this case, as is seen from eq. (39), one of the momenta, say $\boldsymbol{q}_3$, must be set equal to a reciprocal lattice vector $\boldsymbol{K}_3$. From the conditions obtained above it is clear, therefore, that 'triangle' singularities can be associated only with vectors $|\boldsymbol{K}|<2k_{\mathrm{F}}$. Consequently, in monovalent metals such singularities, as well as more complicated ones, are generally absent and they occur only in polyvalent metals, and only for the reciprocal lattice vectors of smallest magnitude. In this case the condition $q_{\mathrm{R}}=k_{\mathrm{F}}$ must be satisfied for a triangle with sides $\boldsymbol{q}+\boldsymbol{K}_1$, $\boldsymbol{q}-\boldsymbol{K}_1-\boldsymbol{K}_3$, $\boldsymbol{K}_3$.

In fig. 7 is presented a geometric construction demonstrating the location and nature of the singularities in a metal with fcc structure and $r_s\sim 2$ (characteristic of Pb). The Kohn anomalies, corresponding to the reduced 'three-tail' diagrams, are indicated as well. These are related to q_2 as well as to q. A definite reciprocal lattice vector has been chosen, corresponding to the site III, and several phonon propagation directions $\boldsymbol{q}$ (labeled by numbers) are investigated. Singularities occur when the end of the vector $\boldsymbol{q}$, denoted

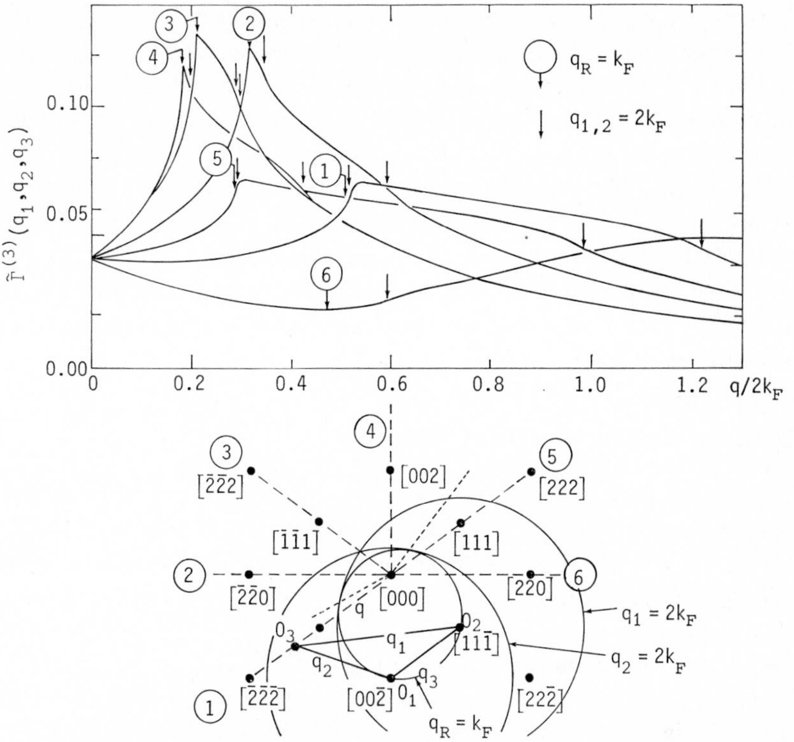

Fig. 7. The geometry of the distribution of singularities of the three-pole function and of Kohn singularities, as well as the behavior of the function $\Gamma^{(3)}(q_1q_2q_3)$.

by O_3, intersects the circumference of a circle of radius k_F constructed on the vector III. From the diagram it can be seen clearly how the singularity, which is well defined for acute triangles (2, 3, 4), is smoothed out and disappears for obtuse triangles, for example (6). This circumstance can be used for the experimental differentiation of triangle singularities from Kohn anomalies.

It is essential to note that the results obtained in subsection 2.7 correspond to the use of perturbation theory on the electron–ion interaction, and are inapplicable for electrons close to Brillouin zone boundaries. Inasmuch as one of the vectors of the three-pole function must be a reciprocal lattice vector, the expression (98) is valid outside a narrow region about the singularity. Inside this region the behavior of the three-pole function will have a more complicated nature, depending on the specific form of the Fermi surface and the electronic wave functions, and the singularity will be somewhat smeared out. This is a general result for the manifestation of singularities of multipole functions in phonon dispersion curves. The only exception to this result is the singularity of the two-pole function, which is not smeared out. However, as is seen from fig. 7, the anomalous nature of the three-pole function shows up in a significantly larger region. Therefore, notwithstanding the smearing out, it can manifest itself to a sufficiently strong degree. It should be noted that although multi-pole functions of higher order possess stronger singularities (also smeared out, in principle), the appearance each time of an additional factor of $V_{\mathbf{K}}/\mathscr{E}_{\mathrm{F}}$ with the increase of n apparently makes the observation of the singularities of multi-pole functions with $n>3$ difficult. In section 3 of this chapter a quantitative analysis of the singularities is carried out for the case of aluminum.

2.9. Interionic forces in a metal. Covalency

The entire preceding analysis of static and dynamical characteristics of a metal was carried out in momentum space. However, an alternative description in coordinate space is also possible, in principle. Indeed, due to the validity of the adiabatic approximation, the energy of the electronic system in the field of the ions plays the role of the potential in the problem of ionic motion (see subsection 2.1). This potential [see eq. (15)] can be regarded as an effective interionic interaction, and in this way we are led to the concept of forces binding the atoms in a metal.

As has already been indicated, this concept is not essential for the problems under consideration. Nevertheless, it turns out to be useful for the discussion of a number of physical problems which are traditionally studied in direct space, for example, the problem of covalency. The traditional theory of the dynamics of crystals was also formulated in this language (Born and Huang 1954). In particular, the existence of a pairwise, centrally symmetric interaction between ions was thought to be characteristic of metals, and reflects an additivity of the interatomic forces.

However, the theory developed above shows that significantly more complicated interionic interactions exist in a metal. Indeed, pairwise, central forces arise naturally from the direct ion–ion interaction, and from the indirect interaction

$$\varphi_2^{(2)}(\mathbf{R}_1-\mathbf{R}_2)=(2!\Omega/N^2)\sum_{\mathbf{q}\neq 0}\Gamma^{(2)}(\mathbf{q},-\mathbf{q})\,|V_{\mathbf{q}}|^2\exp\{\mathrm{i}\mathbf{q}\cdot(\mathbf{R}_1-\mathbf{R}_2)\}\tag{120}$$

However, in addition to these, there also exist interactions connecting triplets and larger numbers of ions. Thus, from the term $E^{(3)}$ we find ($\boldsymbol{R}_1 \neq \boldsymbol{R}_2 \neq \boldsymbol{R}_3$)

$$\varphi_3^{(3)}(\boldsymbol{R}_1 - \boldsymbol{R}_3, \boldsymbol{R}_2 - \boldsymbol{R}_3) = (3!\Omega/N^3) \sum_{\boldsymbol{q}_1\boldsymbol{q}_2} \Gamma^{(3)}(\boldsymbol{q}_1, \boldsymbol{q}_2, -\boldsymbol{q}_1 - \boldsymbol{q}_2) \times V_{\boldsymbol{q}_1} V_{\boldsymbol{q}_2} V_{-\boldsymbol{q}_1-\boldsymbol{q}_2} \exp\{\mathrm{i}\boldsymbol{q}_1 \cdot (\boldsymbol{R}_1 - \boldsymbol{R}_3) + \mathrm{i}\boldsymbol{q}_2 \cdot (\boldsymbol{R}_2 - \boldsymbol{R}_3)\}. \quad (121)$$

The presence of such a term immediately indicates the nonadditivity of inter-ionic interactions and the occurrence of special non-pairwise forces of covalent type in a metal.

The expansion (15) indicates yet one more interesting circumstance. The term of nth order contains contributions not only from interactions of n ions but also from interactions of a smaller number of 'different' ions, since it takes into account the possibility of multiple scattering from one and the same individual ion. Thus, for example, $E^{(3)}$ contains an indirect pairwise interaction as well, as a result of the double scattering from one ion and a single scattering from a second:

$$\varphi_2^{(3)}(\boldsymbol{R}_1 - \boldsymbol{R}_2) = (3 \cdot 2!\Omega/N^3) \sum_{\boldsymbol{q}_1, \boldsymbol{q}_2 \neq 0} \exp\{\mathrm{i}\boldsymbol{q}_1 \cdot (\boldsymbol{R}_1 - \boldsymbol{R}_2)\} \times \Gamma^{(3)}(\boldsymbol{q}_1, \boldsymbol{q}_2, -\boldsymbol{q}_1 - \boldsymbol{q}_2) V_{\boldsymbol{q}_1} V_{\boldsymbol{q}_2} V_{-\boldsymbol{q}_1-\boldsymbol{q}_2}. \quad (122)$$

In addition, there is also a homogeneous term arising from the triple scattering from one and the same ion:

$$\varphi_1^{(3)} = (\Omega/N^3) \sum_{\boldsymbol{q}_1, \boldsymbol{q}_2 \neq 0} \Gamma^{(3)}(\boldsymbol{q}_1, \boldsymbol{q}_2, -\boldsymbol{q}_1 - \boldsymbol{q}_2) V_{\boldsymbol{q}_1} V_{\boldsymbol{q}_2} V_{-\boldsymbol{q}_1-\boldsymbol{q}_2}. \quad (123)$$

Such a term is clearly contained in $E^{(2)}$ as well,

$$\varphi_1^{(2)} = (\Omega/N) \sum_{\boldsymbol{q}} \Gamma^{(2)}(\boldsymbol{q}, -\boldsymbol{q}) |V_{\boldsymbol{q}}|^2. \quad (124)$$

It is clear that in the general case the electronic energy can be represented in the form of a series

$$E_\mathrm{e} = \varphi_0 + \sum_n \varphi_1(\boldsymbol{R}_n) + \frac{1}{2!} \sum_{n \neq m} \varphi_2(\boldsymbol{R}_n - \boldsymbol{R}_m) + \frac{1}{3!} \sum_{n \neq m \neq l} \varphi_3(\boldsymbol{R}_n - \boldsymbol{R}_m, \boldsymbol{R}_n - \boldsymbol{R}_l) + \cdots. \quad (125)$$

According to the preceding discussion, each term of this expansion, describing the simultaneous indirect interaction between k different ions, can be represented in turn in the form of a series

$$\varphi_\kappa(\{\boldsymbol{R}_i\}) = \sum_{p \geqslant k} \varphi_k^{(p)}(\{\boldsymbol{R}_i\}). \quad (126)$$

If the expressions obtained are analyzed, then we come up against the following interesting result. The series (125) and (126) are expansions in powers of the electron–ion interaction, but by no means in powers of the small parameter $V_{\boldsymbol{K}}/\mathscr{E}_{\mathrm{F}}$ as, for example, in eq. (24). From every term of a definite order in $V_{\boldsymbol{K}}/\mathscr{E}_{\mathrm{F}}$, for example from $E^{(3)}$, several terms (121)–(123) arise, containing $V_{\boldsymbol{q}}$ in the range of intermediate momenta where the potential, generally speaking, is not weak [see eq. (40)]. If the role of small $\boldsymbol{q}$ values in eqs. (122 and 123) is significant, as is the case for a number of polyvalent metals, then the convergence of the series (126) turns out to be slow. In particular, the pairwise interaction, which in accordance with customary practice is obtained only from $E^{(2)}$, is significantly changed in fact, and this can be important for a number of problems in which the coordinate representation is employed, for example in the description of a vacancy. It would therefore be desirable to construct techniques for the summation of the series (126), and to express the result, for example, in terms of the exact scattering amplitude for the scattering of an electron by a single ion. However, owing to the presence of the electron–electron interaction, strictly speaking this is not possible in principle for characteristic electron densities in metals. At the same time, if this were done, the convergence of the expansion (125) apparently would be more rapid.

We note that this is not required for our problem, because in a metal crystal in equilibrium a mutual compensation of the electronic scattering occurs due to interference, corresponding to the terms $\varphi_k^{(p)}$ for a fixed value of p. As a result there remain only contributions from the scattering of electrons with momentum transfers equal to reciprocal lattice vectors. It is because of just this that the total interionic interaction in a metal is expressed in a series of powers of the small parameter $V_{\boldsymbol{K}}/\mathscr{E}_{\mathrm{F}}$, even though the interactions in clusters of several ions in the electronic fluid do not contain this parameter explicitly, and the series (126) is represented by a more slowly convergent expansion. As a result of this the separation of the pairwise and non-pairwise interactions from the terms of a particular order in $V_{\boldsymbol{K}}/\mathscr{E}_{\mathrm{F}}$ in eq. (15) in calculations turns out to be significantly less effective than the determination of their mutual contribution. Thus, for example, the corrections to the pairwise interaction from $E^{(3)}$, eq. (122), and the three particle interaction (121) from the same term, turn out to be quantities of the same order of magnitude, and as a rule larger than $E^{(3)}$ itself, as a direct analysis shows (for specific numbers see subsection 3.13).

In this fashion the cooperative nature of the interactions in a metal lead to the appearance of non-pairwise forces of a complicated nature, which represent the forces binding 'clusters' of three, four, etc., ions. If the regions of phase space near the Brillouin zone boundaries turn out to be important for any reason, we must make use of an expression of the type of (43) for the description of the contribution of this region to the interaction, not carrying out an expansion in powers of the electron-ion potential. In the course of this yet one more addition to (125) arises, not possessing a 'cluster-like' nature, but referring in a coherent manner to the entire crystal as a whole. In particular, such non-pairwise terms must be significant for the cohesion and dynamics of semiconductors, which lack a free Fermi surface, and also in those metals where a large number of gaps lie on the Fermi surface (e.g. in Be). It apparently plays no noticeable role for the majority of metallic crystals (nor for liquid metals).

We now turn to a discussion of the asymptotic behavior of the forces obtained. The total pairwise indirect interaction between ions is described by the term φ_2 in eq. (125). The first term of the expansion (126) for φ_2 represents the usual expression, used for the description of the interaction between two ions in the electronic liquid (see, for example, Harrison 1966), which leads to an axially symmetric force constant matrix of the form of eq. (34). As is well known, due to the nonanalyticity of the polarization operator at $q-2k_{\mathrm{F}}$ [see eq. (97)], the function $\varphi_2^{(2)}$ given by eq. (120) possesses a non-exponential asymptotic behavior [Friedel (1958) oscillations]

$$\varphi_2^{(2)} \sim \frac{\cos 2k_{\mathrm{F}} |\boldsymbol{R}_1 - \boldsymbol{R}_2|}{k_{\mathrm{F}}^3 |R_1 - R_2|^3} . \tag{127}$$

It is not difficult to understand that the succeeding terms in φ_2 at any rate decrease no more slowly than eq. (127). This can be seen from the fact that although, for example, $\Gamma^{(3)}$ has a stronger degree of nonanalyticity than $\Gamma^{(2)}$ [see eq. (98)], nevertheless $\varphi^{(3)}$ given by eq. (122) contains an additional integration over $\boldsymbol{q}$. An analogous situation occurs for all the remaining contributions to the pairwise interaction. Thus, the dominant asymptotic behavior of the pairwise interaction has the form of eq. (127), while the coefficient of this term will be given in the form of an expansion in powers of the pseudopotential.

The long-range nature of this interaction is responsible for the slow decrease of the elements of the force constant matrix with an increase in the number of the coordination sphere, which was first observed in the now classic experiments measuring the phonon spectrum of lead (Brockhouse 1962), where the indirect interaction plays a very big role (see section 3).

We note that taking account the nonsphericity of a real Fermi surface can alter the asymptotic behavior of the pairwise forces in certain cases. Thus, in the case of a strictly cylindrical form for the Fermi surface, due to the stronger singularity in the polarization operator (Afanas'ev and Kagan 1963) in place of the factor $1/r^3$ in eq. (127) a factor of $1/r^2$ appears, while in the case of a plane surface even a factor of $1/r$ can appear.

The set of terms φ_k with $k \geqslant 3$ describes the non-pairwise indirect interaction for a fixed electron density. Comparing again the nature of the leading singularity of the multi-pole function of nth order [see eq. (100)] and the general expression (22) with the number of integrations over $\boldsymbol{q}$, one is led to the conclusion that the non-pairwise interaction decreases asymptotically no more slowly with increasing distance between any pair of ions than eq. (127).

We note in conclusion that the non-pairwise interaction, which depends on the mutual distribution in space of several ions, and which leads to the appearance of forces of covalent type, is sensitive to the structure of the crystal. Therefore it differs in principle from the pairwise forces, and cannot be initiated by them for any special choice of the electron-ion interaction, even of a nonlocal form. The role of the non-pairwise forces in the dynamics of polyvalent metals can be very significant, and in a number of cases determining, for example, in the problem of the dynamical stability of complex metals (Brovman and Kagan 1967, Kagan and Brovman 1968). All features of this interaction are already displayed in principle by the leading term, eq. (121), and it contributes to the term with $n=3$ in the dynamical matrix, eq. (39). Therefore, it appears to us that in the analysis of the phonon spectra of polyvalent metals it is of principal importance to take into account this term at the very least in the dynamical matrix.

2.10. The many-body problem with consideration of the non-locality of the electron–ion interaction

Up to now our investigations have been based on the assumption of a local electron–ion interaction, which correspond to making the replacement (13) in the starting hamiltonian (11). From the standpoint of principle, the non-local nature of the potential does not introduce any new physical aspects into the problem, and all qualitative results remain unchanged. However, taking the nonlocal nature of the potential into account leads to certain formal complications within the framework of a many-body theory. This is connected with the fact that in this case the factorization into factors referring separately to ionic and to electronic properties, which greatly simplifies the problem, is absent, since the electron–ion interaction vertex, which now depends on the initial momentum, is present in an integrand (fig. 8).

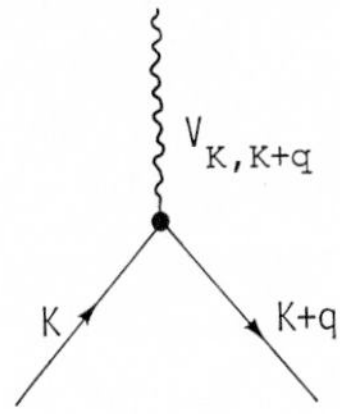

Fig. 8

We will discuss specially only the question of obtaining the ground state energy, having in mind that the transition to the dynamical matrix and to other quantities remains exactly the same as in the case of a local potential. If we do not make the replacement, eq. (13), then the diagram for $E^{(1)}$ (fig. 2) clearly gives

$$E^{(1)} = \sum_{k<k_F} V_{\boldsymbol{k},\boldsymbol{k}} n_{\boldsymbol{k}} \tag{128}$$

in place of eq. (19). In an analogous fashion we can use the same diagrammatic techniques as before (fig. 3) in order to obtain the energy $E^{(2)}$ However, characteristic blocks now appear, which are irreducible in the electron-electron interaction (figs. 9a and b), but which now cannot be expressed in

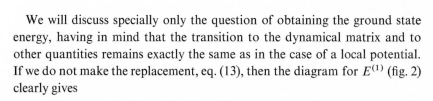

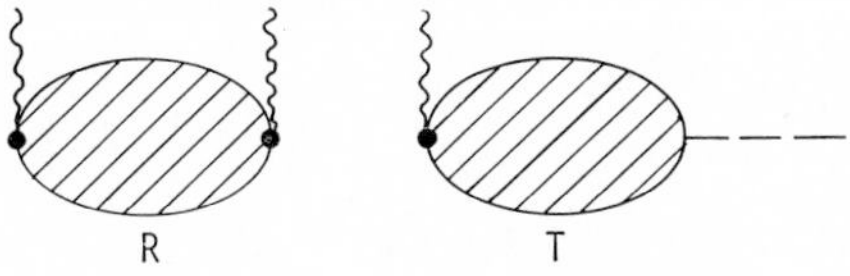

Fig. 9

terms of the irreducible polarization block $\pi(\boldsymbol{q})$. Carrying out the summation over all polarization blocks, threaded on the lines of the electron-electron interaction, we obtain

$$E^{(2)} = \tfrac{1}{2} \sum_{\boldsymbol{q}} |(1/N) \sum_{n} \exp(\mathrm{i}\boldsymbol{q}\cdot\boldsymbol{R}_n)|^2 \{R(\boldsymbol{q}) - [4\pi e^2/q^2 \mathscr{E}(\boldsymbol{q})] \, |T(q)|^2\}. \tag{129}$$

In the local case $R(\boldsymbol{q}) = V_{-\boldsymbol{q}} T(\boldsymbol{q}) = |V_{\boldsymbol{q}}|^2 \pi(\boldsymbol{q})$, and the expression given by eq. (129) reduces to the usual one, eq. (20). The simplest approximation, corresponding to the RPA (for the non-local case), consists of neglecting the electron–electron interaction in $R(\boldsymbol{q})$ and $T(\boldsymbol{q})$

$$R(\boldsymbol{q}) = \int \frac{\mathrm{d}^3k}{(2\pi)^3} \frac{n_{\boldsymbol{k}} - n_{\boldsymbol{k}-\boldsymbol{q}}}{\mathscr{E}_{\boldsymbol{k}} - \mathscr{E}_{\boldsymbol{k}-\boldsymbol{q}}} |V_{\boldsymbol{k},\boldsymbol{k}+\boldsymbol{q}}|^2, \quad T(\boldsymbol{q}) = \int \frac{\mathrm{d}^3k}{(2\pi)^3} \frac{n_{\boldsymbol{k}} - n_{\boldsymbol{k}-\boldsymbol{q}}}{\mathscr{E}_{\boldsymbol{k}} - \mathscr{E}_{\boldsymbol{k}-\boldsymbol{q}}} V_{\boldsymbol{k},\boldsymbol{k}+\boldsymbol{q}}. \tag{130}$$

Substituting these expressions into eq. (129), we are led to an expression for $E^{(2)}$ which coincides with the expression ordinarily used in practice in the presence of a nonlocal potential (Animalu 1965).

It is of interest to separate out in an explicit form the screening of a non-local potential. In graphical form the corresponding expression has a form which coincides with that given by fig. 4 when the more complicated vertex (fig. 8) is taken into account. In analytic form this corresponds to

$$\tilde{V}_{\boldsymbol{k},\boldsymbol{k}+\boldsymbol{q}} = V_{\boldsymbol{k},\boldsymbol{k}+\boldsymbol{q}} + V_{\mathrm{sq}}(\boldsymbol{q}), \quad V_{\mathrm{sq}}(\boldsymbol{q}) = -\,T(\boldsymbol{q})\, 4\pi e^2/q^2\mathscr{E}(\boldsymbol{q}). \tag{131, 132}$$

Thus screening potential $V_{\mathrm{sq}}(\boldsymbol{q})$ is always local. If the starting potential is also local, then we come to the natural expression

$$\tilde{V}_{\boldsymbol{k},\boldsymbol{k}+\boldsymbol{q}} \to V_{\boldsymbol{q}}/\mathscr{E}(\boldsymbol{q}), \tag{133}$$

which was used by us in separating out the irreducible blocks, eq. (20). Now, on substituting into eq. (129) the screening potential $V_{\mathrm{sq}}(\boldsymbol{q})$ instead of one of the $T(\boldsymbol{q})$, we obtain another general representation of $E^{(2)}$. In the approximation represented by eq. (130) it corresponds to the following widely used form

$$E^{(2)} = \tfrac{1}{2} \sum_{\boldsymbol{q}} \left|(1/N) \sum_{n} \exp(\mathrm{i}\boldsymbol{q}\cdot\boldsymbol{R}_n)\right|^2 \int \frac{\mathrm{d}^3k}{(2\pi)^3} \frac{n_{\boldsymbol{k}} - n_{\boldsymbol{k}+\boldsymbol{q}}}{\mathscr{E}_{\boldsymbol{k}} - \mathscr{E}_{\boldsymbol{k}+\boldsymbol{q}}} V_{\boldsymbol{k},\boldsymbol{k}+\boldsymbol{q}} \tilde{V}_{\boldsymbol{k}+\boldsymbol{q},\boldsymbol{k}}. \tag{134}$$

We now examine an arbitrary term $E^{(n)}$ with $n>2$. This term will be determined by a block with n external field tails (see fig. 1), in which all vertices again depend on the electron momentum before and after scattering and therefore must be included in the general integration of each diagram. It is interesting that in this case a partial summation can be carried out, which leads to the replacement of every external field line by a 'heavy' line (see fig. 4), which in the present case is equivalent to the replacement $V_{\boldsymbol{k},\boldsymbol{k}+\boldsymbol{q}} \to \tilde{V}_{\boldsymbol{k},\boldsymbol{k}+\boldsymbol{q}}$.

We present here in an explicit form the expression for $E^{(3)}$ [analogous to eq. (134)] corresponding to taking into account only ring diagrams, i.e., to the absence of electron–electron interaction lines inside the ring (see the discussion in subsection 2.7):

$$E^{(3)} = \tfrac{1}{3} \sum_{q_1 q_2 q_3} N^{-3} \sum_{n_1 n_2 n_3} \exp\{\mathrm{i}\boldsymbol{q}_1 \cdot \boldsymbol{R}_{n_1} + \mathrm{i}\boldsymbol{q}_2 \cdot \boldsymbol{R}_{n_2} + \mathrm{i}\boldsymbol{q}_3 \cdot \boldsymbol{R}_{n_3}\} \times Q^{(3)}(\boldsymbol{q}_1, \boldsymbol{q}_2, \boldsymbol{q}_3)\, \Delta(\boldsymbol{q}_1 + \boldsymbol{q}_2 + \boldsymbol{q}_3), \quad (135a)$$

$$Q^{(3)}(\boldsymbol{q}_1, \boldsymbol{q}_2, \boldsymbol{q}_3) = \frac{2}{\mathrm{i}} \int \frac{\mathrm{d}^3 p\, \mathrm{d}\omega}{(2\pi)^4} \tilde{V}_{\boldsymbol{p}, \boldsymbol{p}+\boldsymbol{q}_1} \tilde{V}_{\boldsymbol{p}+\boldsymbol{q}_1, \boldsymbol{p}+\boldsymbol{q}_1+\boldsymbol{q}_2} \tilde{V}_{\boldsymbol{p}+\boldsymbol{q}_1+\boldsymbol{q}_2, \boldsymbol{p}} \times G^{(0)}(\boldsymbol{p}, \omega)\, G^{(0)}(\boldsymbol{p}+\boldsymbol{q}_1, \omega)\, G^{(0)}(\boldsymbol{p}+\boldsymbol{q}_1+\boldsymbol{q}_2, \omega), \quad (135b)$$

where the electron Green's function is defined according to eq. (82). We note that the integration over ω in this expression is carried out in as elementary a fashion as before.

In the case of a local potential the relation (133) is valid and we have

$$Q^{(3)}(\boldsymbol{q}_1, \boldsymbol{q}_2, \boldsymbol{q}_3) = \frac{V(\boldsymbol{q}_1)}{\mathscr{E}(\boldsymbol{q}_1)} \frac{V(\boldsymbol{q}_2)}{\mathscr{E}(\boldsymbol{q}_2)} \frac{V(\boldsymbol{q}_3)}{\mathscr{E}(\boldsymbol{q}_3)} \Lambda_0^{(3)}(\boldsymbol{q}_1, \boldsymbol{q}_2, \boldsymbol{q}_3),$$

where $\Lambda^{(3)}$ is the three-pole function obtained in subsection 2.7. The expression for $E^{(n)}$ for arbitrary n has an analogous structure.

From the form of the expressions presented above, and from an analysis of the general starting equations it can be shown that all general results are completely preserved in the case of a non-local potential. This refers, in particular, to the relation between the dynamic and static compressibilities, to the location and nature of the singularities in the phonon spectrum, to the nonpairwise nature of the indirect interionic interaction, etc. (In connection with this, taking into account the nonlocal nature of the potential does not by itself change the picture of the interactions between ions in a metal, and consequently in no way represents an alternative to taking into account the many-particle forces, as is sometimes asserted.)

Therefore, the fact that it provides a correct description of the qualitative picture together with analytic simplicity makes the approximation of a local effective electron–ion interaction attractive every time that the physical side of the results is of primary significance.

3. *Analysis of phonon spectra of metals*

3.1. The role of electrons in forming the phonon spectrum and equilibrium structure of a metal

In the first section of this chapter results concerning a many-particle theory of non-transition metals were presented. The most interesting aspects of such a theory are connected with the indirect interaction between ions through the conduction electrons, which is fully characteristic only of metals possessing a free Fermi surface. At the same time the qualitative singularities of such an interaction obviously must be most clearly apparent in the analysis of differential properties of a metal, although from a quantitative point of view the role of the electrons is occasionally determining as well for all properties which can be expressed as integrals over the electron spectrum.

However, if one does not go into a detailed comparison of the phonon dispersion law in a metal and a dielectric, then at first glance no striking differences are observed. It is not suprising, therefore, that in the first stage of neutron spectroscopic investigations the analysis of the results was carried out in terms of the standard Born–von Kármán model with uncorrelated, phenomenological atomic force constants for interactions between atoms on different coordination spheres. Inasmuch as it turned out that the adiabatic approximation is valid for a metal (see subsection 2.2), such an analysis is correct in principle. However, it soon became clear that for an adequate description of the phonon spectrum of a metal it is essential to take into account interactions between distant neighbors. This result was a direct reflection of the long-range nature of the indirect interionic interaction in a metal, which has been examined in detail in subsection 2.9. It was first observed in lead (Brockhouse 1962), where it proved necessary to take into account interactions between 17th neighbors, in order to obtain good agreement with experiment. An even clearer indication of the long-range nature of the interaction was provided in the case of metallic tin, where moderate agreement with experiment required taking into account six coordination spheres and 14 atomic force constants (Brovman and Kagan 1966), a bit better agreement required 12 coordination spheres and 26 atomic force constants (Price 1967), while decent agreement for only one direction in the Brillouin zone required 20 constants (Rowe 1967).

It is clear that an analysis in such terms, requiring an enormous number of independent constants, becomes senseless. At the same time, in a microscopic theory the long-range interaction, which arises on taking into account the indirect interaction in a natural fashion, leads to a 'correlation' among the atomic force constants for different coordination spheres, and the number of independent force constants in fact turns out to be very small (Brovman and Kagan 1967).

An even clearer role of the conduction electrons is apparent in the study of the fine structure in phonon dispersion curves connected with Kohn singularities (see subsection 2.8). The location of these singularities is related in general to the geometry of the Fermi surface, and the topology of the latter is clearly manifested in the phonon spectra of metals. Kohn singularities were first observed by Brockhouse et al. (1961) in lead, and subsequently were observed in many polyvalent metals.

Recently, when a big step was taken in the precise measurement of dispersion curves (Stedman et al. 1966, 1967, Weymouth and Stedman 1970), it became possible to observe singularities connected with the non-pairwise interionic interaction through the conduction electrons as well (see subsection 3.1).

We will return to these experiments later. Now we note only that the more accurately the phonon spectrum of a metal is measured, the finer are the aspects of the indirect interaction that are observed. We will present below a qualitative analysis of the role of the conduction electrons in the establishment of a stable structure of a metal and its phonon spectrum.

3.1.1. The formation of the equilibrium static lattice

The microscopic theory developed in subsections 2.2–2.4 possesses the property that it allows one to describe the vibrational spectrum as well as the equilibrium structure of a metal, to the same degree of accuracy and with the aid of the same quantities. Therefore, before going on to an investigation of phonons, it is natural to examine the role of electrons in the formation of the static lattice itself.

The problem posed in turn breaks up into two – the explanation of the characteristic density of the metal produced, and the study of its crystallographic structure and, as will be clear in what follows, these two problems are of significantly different degrees of difficulty, and in a known sense can be solved in two stages.

In fig. 10 is presented the dependence of the total energy and its separate contributions on the volume of a unit cell of Na for a model potential which shall be examined in subsection 3.3, and which yields a value of Ω_0 which equals the experimental value. It is interesting that the role of the structure-dependent terms $E^{(2)}$ and $E^{(3)}$ in Na turns out to be very small, while the ionic energy E_i, whose role is significant, in fact depends weakly on structure. Therefore the determining role for crystallization at one or another density is played by the competition between the two basic terms – the ionic energy $E_i \sim -\Omega_0^{-1/3}$ and the energy $E^{(1)} \sim \Omega_0^{-1}$ [see eq. (19)], determining the value of Ω_0. At the stationary point $\partial E/\partial\Omega = -P = 0$. It is seen from this that the non-Coulomb part b of the amplitude for the forward scattering of an electron by an ion, eq. (16), has a decisive significance here. We note that an exception is metallic hydrogen, for which $b=0$, and whose equilibrium density is determined by a competition between E_i and $E^{(0)}$ (see, for example, Brovman et al. 1971, 1972a).

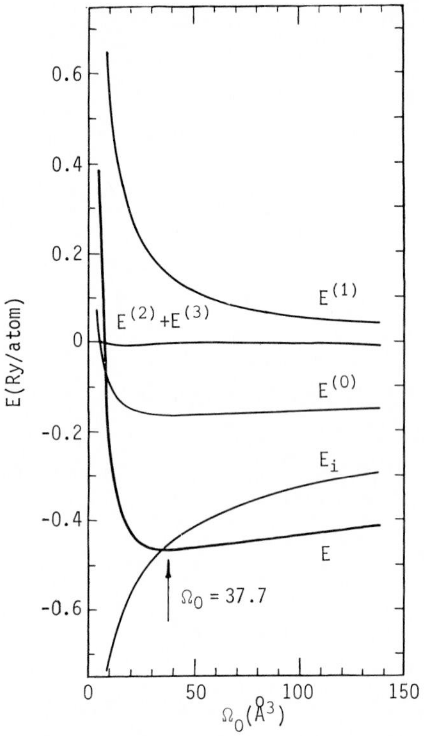

Fig. 10. The dependence of the total energy of Na and of the individual contributions to it on the volume of a primitive unit cell Ω_0.

However, the problem of cohesion, i.e., of the energetic advantage of such a metallic phase in comparison with free atoms or a phase of a different origin (for example, molecular), must be solved separately in each case (i.e., we can make assertions only about the existence of a local, but not of an absolute, minimum). The considerations which have been advanced show that at least for an approximate estimate of the pressure P and compressibility B it is sufficient to use the two basic contributions E_i and $E^{(0)}$ (the 'zero-order model', Brovman et al. 1970), which leads to a universal equation of state $P/B(0)$ (the argument '0' denotes the equilibrium point) (Brovman et al. 1970). This result is indeed in good agreement with experiment for alkali metals (Bernardes and Svensson 1963), for which the 'zero-order' model is the most adequate.

The problem of explaining the realization of one or another structure is significantly more delicate, inasmuch as here the large volume dependent terms drop out of consideration and it is essential to study the small structure-dependent terms.

We examine first the problem of explaining the 'anisotropy' of uniaxial metals, i.e. the manner in which the theory presented explains the different values of (c/a) for metals. We note first of all that now the competition is between the ionic energy E_i and the electronic energy $E^{(2)}+E^{(3)}+\cdots$. In this case the ionic energy has its least value for the close-packed structures. With regard to the most important of the electronic contributions ($E^{(2)}$), it displays a tendency to make structures anisotropic, as was first noted by Heine and Weaire (1966, 1970). This is not difficult to understand. Only the values of the potential at reciprocal lattice vectors contribute to the electronic energy of a static lattice [see eq. (25)]. It is clear from eq. (25) that if the anisotropy be increased, i.e., if some of the lattice sites of the reciprocal lattice are shifted to regions of smaller $\boldsymbol{q}$ values, where $V(\boldsymbol{q})$ is stronger, then we always have an energetically more favorable situation. However, very large distortions are known to be disadvantageous due to the sharp increase in the electrostatic energy (arising from the decrease in the separation between charges); therefore the real situation for intermediate distortions depends on the scale of the potential $V(\boldsymbol{q})$.

These considerations are illustrated in fig. 11 for the example of Mg (Brovman et al. 1970). It is seen that in Mg the electronic energy has a tendency toward anisotropy, but the value of c/a departs only slightly from the value corresponding to the minimum of the ionic energy.

An analogous situation apparently exists in metallic tin (β-Sn). In fig. 12 the Madelung constant α_M for this structure is plotted as a function of c/a. It has a minimum for $c/a=0.545$, close to the experimentally observed value (at $T=0$ $c/a=0.553$), so that the electronic contribution also shifts the minimum which already exists for the ionic lattice only slightly. (We note that the Ge lattice with $c/a=\sqrt{2}$ corresponds to a maximum on this curve.)

However, a situation is possible in principle in which a strong electron-ion interaction dominates, and leads to anisotropic structures.

As a striking example we investigate the metallic phase of hydrogen (Brovman et al. 1971, 1972a), where the electron–ion coupling constant is very large due to the absence of an ion core. In fig. 13 the total energy is

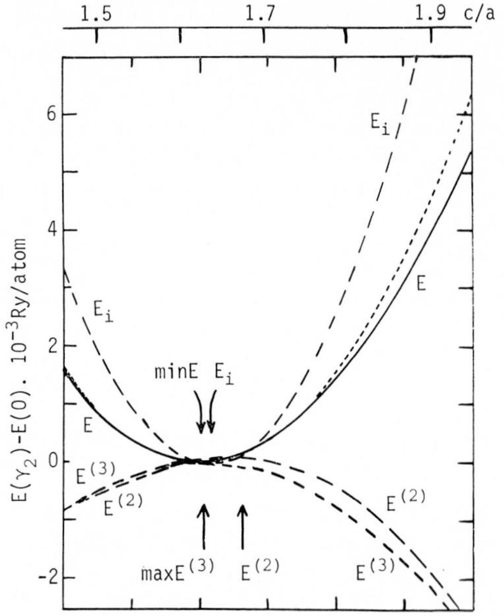

Fig. 11. The dependence of the total energy of Mg and of the individual contributions to it on (c/a).

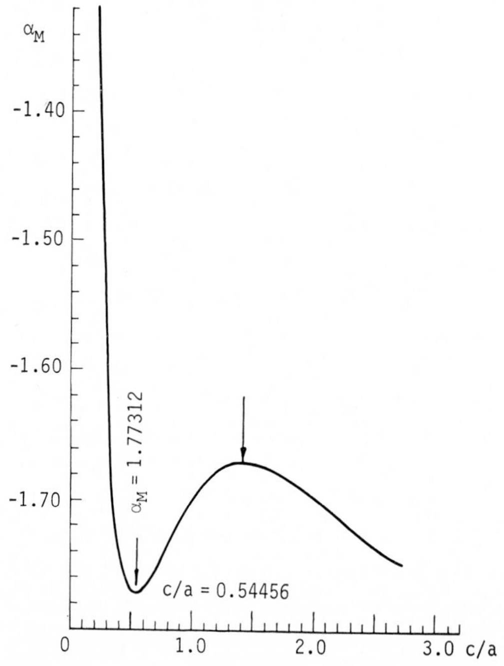

Fig. 12. The Madelung constant for the ionic energy of the β-Sn structure as a function of (c/a). The diamond structure corresponds to $c/a = \sqrt{2}$.

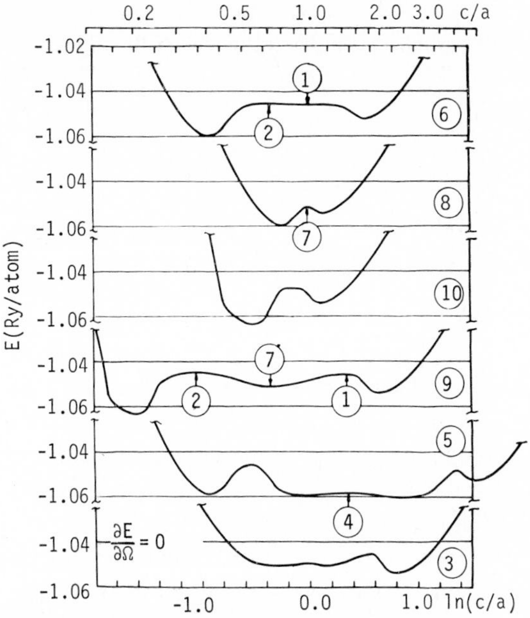

Fig. 13. The total energy of uniaxial lattices of metallic hydrogen. The following structures are indicated: 1. face centered cubic (fcc); 2. body centered cubic (bcc); 3. hexagonal close packed (hcp); 4. diamond; 5. white tin (β-Sn); 6. face centered tetragonal (fct); 7. simple cubic (sc); 8. simple tetragonal (st); 9. trigonal (rhombohedral) (rh); 10. simple hexagonal.

plotted as a function of c/a for a series of uniaxial structures (cubic structures are represented by isolated points). Anisotropy is evident everywhere, i.e. the dominance of the electronic contribution and a departure from close-packed structures, whereupon in all cases 'double-humped' curves arise and the distortion is severe. It is possible that a similar situation is realized in Zn and Cd, for which large deviations of c/a from the ideal value are observed. (The same considerations have been discussed previously for Zn and Cd in a qualitative manner by Heine and Weaire, 1970.)

Finally, in the case of Mg we study a comparison of the energies for different possible modifications. In Table 1 the energy and several elastic moduli for different modifications are presented for one and the same model potential (subsection 3.3), whereupon in each case a volume exists corresponding to a minimum energy.

It is seen, first of all, that 'close-packed' lattices possess an energy significantly lower than that of "porous" structures (β-Sn with an ideal c/a ratio,

TABLE 1
(Energy in Ry/atom; elastic moduli in 10^{11} dyne/cm^2).

Type of structure	Ω_0	E	B	$\frac{1}{2}(C_{11}-C_{12})$	B_{22}
bcc	23.228	−1.76828	3.137	−0.551	–
fcc	23.173	−1.76942	3.241	−2.376	–
hcp	22.912	−1.77055	3.382	1.915	3.005
β-Sn	26.551	−1.75127	2.491	–	3.854
Ge	39.574	−1.71465	1.555	–	−0.678

and particularly Ge). At the same time the energy difference between 'close-packed' phases is quite small, $\Delta E \sim 10^{-3}$ Ry ~ 150 K. It turns out that the hcp lattice indeed has the minimum energy, and in addition the remainder turn out to be unstable with respect to some shear moduli (at the same time that the bulk moduli B are practically the same).

Thus, the considerations and examples presented in this section show that the microscopic theory, which takes the electrons explicitly into account, allows a qualitative understanding of a series of basic regularities in the construction of static crystalline lattices.

3.1.2. The formation of the phonon spectrum. The screening of the vibrations of the ionic lattice by the electrons

We turn now to an analysis of the general regularities in the effects of the electrons on the formation of the phonon spectrum of metals. The determining factor in this is the following circumstance.

The study of spectral properties discloses a unique possibility for a comparison of theoretical ideas with experiment, since we are speaking here about the determination of the phonon spectrum throughout all phase space. Correspondingly, the results will be sensitive to the behavior of the electron-ion as well as of the electron–electron interactions for a continuous interval of momenta, in contrast with static properties, which are determined by the values of the corresponding quantities at the discrete lattice sites of the reciprocal lattice.

The role of the electrons is most clearly apparent if we compare the vibration spectrum of the ionic lattice of a metal with the observed experimental spectrum. In fig. 14 the dispersion curves for the ionic lattice of Na and the experimental points (Woods et al. 1962) are plotted. The longitudinal branches, naturally, undergo the most significant reconstruction: on taking

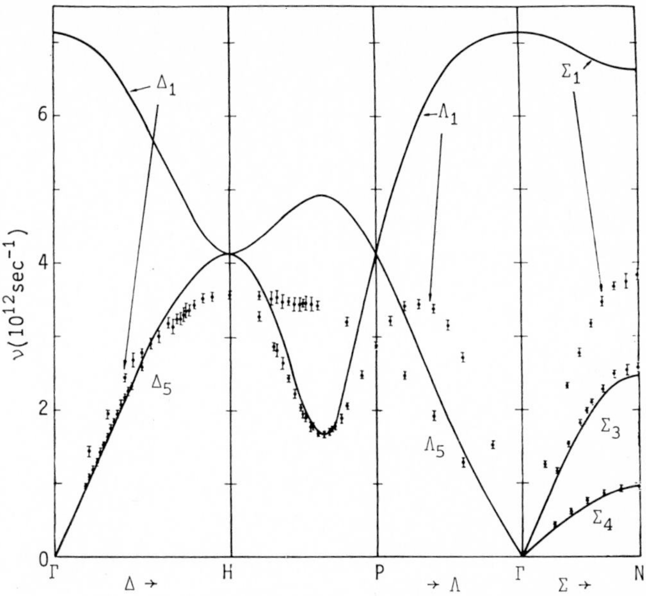

Fig. 14. Vibration frequencies of the ionic lattice and experimental phonon frequencies in Na.

into account the response of the electrons they are transformed from optical, ion plasma vibrations into acoustic vibrations. (For small momenta this problem is discussed in detail in subsection 2.4.) More unexpected is the result that the ionic lattice determines the characteristic magnitude of the frequencies, while certain transverse branches are generally very well described by this approximation [an analogous picture obtains in the case of the shear moduli (see below)].

A strongly differing situation is observed in metallic Al (see fig. 15). The experimental results presented are taken from the work of Stedman and Nilsson (1966). Here the characteristic frequencies of the ionic lattice at the zone boundary are already twice as large as the corresponding experimental values. An even more significant compensation occurs for phonons in Pb. To illustrate the situation, the values of the quantities $(\omega_i/\omega_0)^2$ and $(\omega_{exp}/\omega_0)^2$ are presented in table 2. Here ω_0 is the ion plasma frequency, which is a natural scale characteristic of the spectrum, while ω_i^2 and ω_{exp}^2 are taken at the Brillouin zone boundary in the [001] direction.

The table demonstrates the enormous growth of the electronic contribution in the series Na, Al, Pb (see the analogous discussion by Vosko et al.

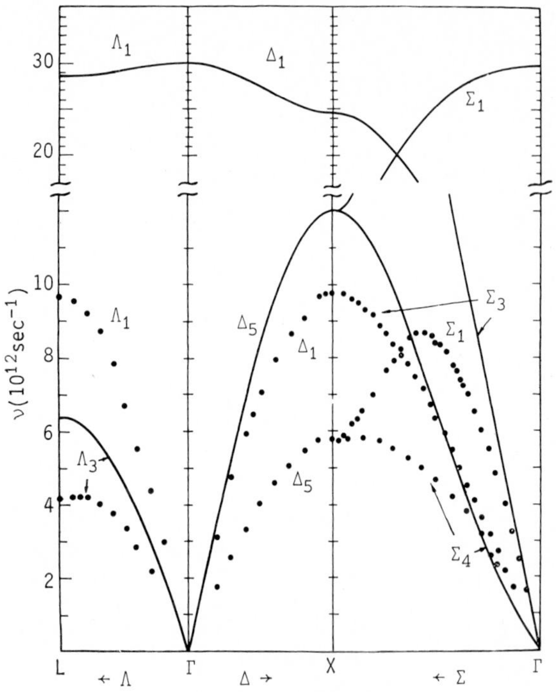

Fig. 15. Vibration frequencies of the ionic lattice and experimental phonon frequencies in Al.

TABLE 2

(Squared frequencies in units of the plasma frequency).

	Na	Al		Pb	
	L, T(H_{15})	L(X_1)	T(X_5)	L(X_1)	T(X_5)
$(\omega_i/\omega_0)^2$	0.333	0.678	0.161	0.678	0.161
$(\omega_{exp}/\omega_0)^2$	0.248	0.105	0.037	0.031	0.007

1965). Thus, an analysis of experimental results without the introduction of any concrete theoretical framework already permits one to make the deduction that the role of the electrons changes very strongly from metal to metal.

We now show that the microscopic theory provides a perfectly natural explanation of the indicated regularity. For simplicity we will investigate the electronic contribution only to the second order in the pseudopotential (for Na and Al, as is shown in the succeeding sections, the role of the third order terms is indeed small; however in the case of Pb it apparently is extremely significant). We introduce for convenience the following definition

$$\psi(\boldsymbol{q}) = \frac{|V_{\boldsymbol{q}}|^2 \pi(\boldsymbol{q}) q^2}{\mathscr{E}(\boldsymbol{q})} \frac{\Omega_0}{4\pi Z^2 e^2}. \tag{136}$$

Then the electronic contribution to the dynamical matrix of a mono-atomic metal assumes the following form

$$D_{(2)}^{\alpha\beta}(\boldsymbol{q}) = -\omega_0^2 \left[\sum_{\boldsymbol{K}} \frac{(\boldsymbol{q}+\boldsymbol{K})^\alpha (\boldsymbol{q}+\boldsymbol{K})^\beta}{|\boldsymbol{q}+\boldsymbol{K}|^2} \psi(\boldsymbol{q}+\boldsymbol{K}) - \frac{K^\alpha K^\beta}{K^2} \psi(\boldsymbol{K}) \right], \tag{137}$$

in agreement with eq. (38). For all three metals, for all symmetry directions of q depicted in figs. 14 and 15 the dynamical matrix factorizes, and all branches of the vibration spectrum become purely longitudinal and purely transverse.

It is not difficult to see from an investigation of the corresponding angles that the term with $\boldsymbol{K}=0$ does not contribute to the transverse branches of the vibration spectrum, and we obtain

$$\omega_\ell^2 = \omega_{\ell \mathrm{i}}^2 - \omega_0^2 \times \left\{ \psi(\boldsymbol{q}) + \sum_{\boldsymbol{K}\neq 0} [\psi(\boldsymbol{q}+\boldsymbol{K}) \cos^2(\angle\, \boldsymbol{e}_\ell, \boldsymbol{q}+\boldsymbol{K}) - \psi(\boldsymbol{K}) \cos^2(\angle\, \boldsymbol{e}_\ell, \boldsymbol{K})] \right\}, \tag{138}$$

$$\omega_{\mathrm{t}}^2 = \omega_{\mathrm{ti}}^2 - \omega_0^2 \times \left\{ \sum_{\boldsymbol{K}\neq 0} [\psi(\boldsymbol{q}+\boldsymbol{K}) \cos^2(\angle\, \boldsymbol{e}_{\mathrm{t}}, \boldsymbol{q}+\boldsymbol{K}) - \psi(\boldsymbol{K}) \cos^2(\angle\, \boldsymbol{e}_{\mathrm{t}}, \boldsymbol{K})] \right\}. \tag{139}$$

Thus the transverse branches are screened only with the aid of 'Umklapp' processes and do not possess a contribution from the 'uniform medium' [this circumstance was already discussed in connection with the problem of the shear moduli (see subsection 2.4)]. From the expressions (138) and (139) it is clear that the nature of the behavior of the function $\psi(\boldsymbol{q})$ and the disposition of the reciprocal lattice vectors for a given, concrete metal acquires an essential significance.

In fig. 16 the function $\psi(\boldsymbol{q})$ is presented for Na, Al and Pb, and the positions of the reciprocal lattice points are indicated, where for uniformity the calculations of Animalu (1966), based on the Heine-Abarenkov model, are used. (For convenience part of the figure is repeated in enlarged form.)

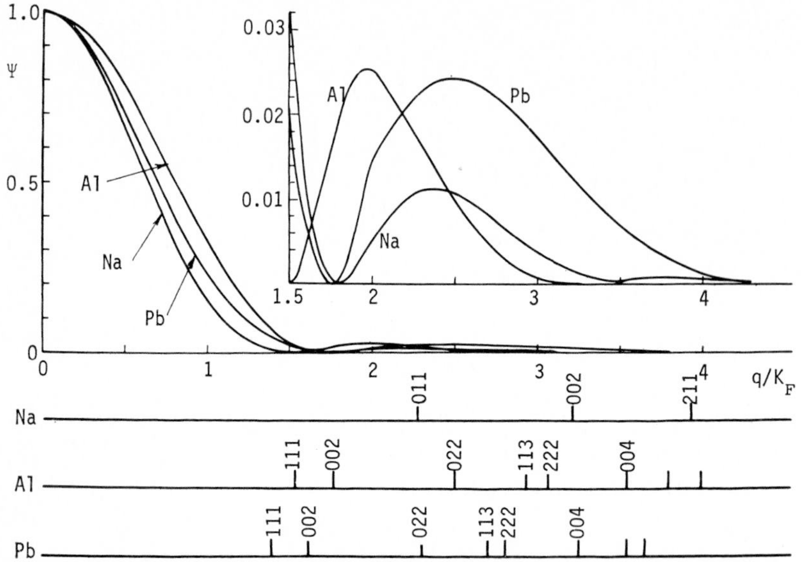

Fig. 16. The energy characteristic $\psi(\boldsymbol{q})$ for Na, Al, Pb and the locations of the lattice sites of the corresponding reciprocal lattices.

It is now clear that for Na the determining factor is just the disposition of the reciprocal lattice points, the nearest of which is far to the right of q_0, the first zero of $V(\boldsymbol{q})$. This, clearly, corresponds to the fact that in monovalent Na the Fermi surface is totally contained within the first Brillouin zone, i.e., $2k_F < K_{min}$, while q_0 is usually somewhat smaller than $2k_F$. As a result, terms with $\boldsymbol{K} \neq 0$ in eqs. (138) and (139) play a very small role, and therefore the transverse branches in Na are almost completely determined by the ionic lattice (particularly for small $\boldsymbol{q}$). With regard to the longitudinal branches, the basic electronic contribution here is the term with $\boldsymbol{K}=0$ in eq. (138). As is easily understood, the electronic contribution to the longitudinal phonons at the zone boundary is determined mainly by the magnitude of $\psi(\boldsymbol{q})$ for q equal to half the distance to the corresponding lattice site, and therefore the electrons weakly screen the ionic lattice in Na. In connection with this it is clear, in complete accordance with fig. 14, that the values of the frequencies with $\boldsymbol{q}$ along the [011] direction must undergo the largest shifts.

The nearest sites of the reciprocal lattices for Al and Pb are significantly closer to the origin than in Na which, of course, is connected with the fact that these are polyvalent metals. As a result, first of all, the terms with $\boldsymbol{K} \neq 0$ begin to play a significant role, and, secondly, the term corresponding to the "uniform medium" at the Brillouin zone boundary becomes very large. All of this explains the significant strengthening of the role of the electrons, whereupon from fig. (16) it is clear that the behavior of $V(\boldsymbol{q})$ and the disposition of the reciprocal lattice sites indicate that the maximum strength of the electronic contribution should indeed occur in Pb.

Even more interesting opportunities for a comparison of theory with experiment is provided by an analysis of diatomic metals, which possess optical vibration branches. We will specially investigate the limiting optical frequencies at $\boldsymbol{q}=0$, denoting them by $\omega_c^2(\mathbf{0})$ and $\omega_a^2(\mathbf{0})$, in correspondence with the directions of polarization of these vibrations (in uniaxial crystals

TABLE 3

(Squared frequencies in units of the plasma frequency).

	Be		Mg		Zn		Sn	
	(Z)	(X, Y)	(Z)	(X, Y)	(Z)	(X, Y)	(Z)	(X, Y)
$(\omega_i/\omega_0)^2$	0.890	0.055	0.906	0.047	0.953	0.024	0.001	0.499
$(\omega_{exp}/\omega_0)^2$	0.166	0.074	0.175	0.046	0.121	0.026	0.007	0.066

two frequencies $\omega_a^2(\mathbf{0})$ are degenerate). In table 3 data for these frequencies for Be, Mg, Zn and Sn are presented in the same notation as in the case of table 2. It is seen that each element possesses a low frequency, the electronic contribution to which is small, and a high frequency, to which it is significant. For an explanation of this result (Brovman and Kagan 1967, Brovman et al. 1968) we make use of eq. (63), which we rewrite taking into account the definition (136), as

$$\omega_s^2(\mathbf{0}) = \omega_{si}^2(\mathbf{0}) - \omega_0^2 \sum_{\boldsymbol{K}\neq 0} \psi(\boldsymbol{K}) \cos(\boldsymbol{K}\cdot\boldsymbol{\rho}) \cos^2(\angle\, \boldsymbol{e}_s, \boldsymbol{K}), \qquad s = a, c. \tag{140}$$

Here $\boldsymbol{\rho}$ is the basis vector of the second atom, and $\boldsymbol{e}_s$ is the polarization of the vibration branch.

With the aid of fig. 17, on which is reproduced the function $\psi(\boldsymbol{q})$ for the corresponding elements, the data presented in table 3 can be explained. Indeed, the factor cos $(\angle\, \boldsymbol{e}, \boldsymbol{K})$ makes the role of individual sites of the reciprocal lattice completely different for frequencies with different polarizations. In hexagonal metals the 'strongest' site, which is the [001] site, contributes only to the screening of $\omega_c^2(\mathbf{0})$, while in tin the [110] site, in contrast strongly

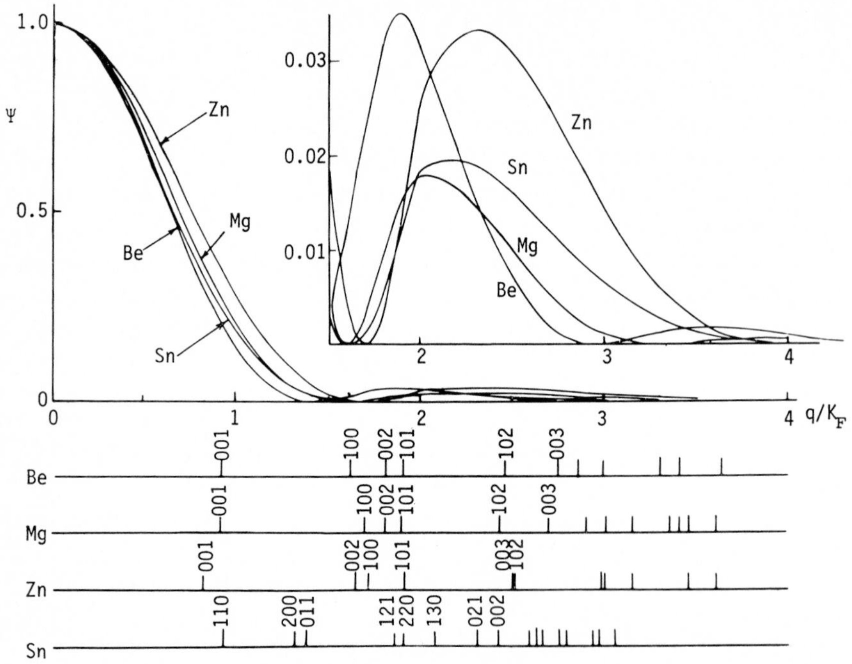

Fig. 17. The energy characteristic $\psi(q)$ for Be, Mg, Zn, Sn and the locations of the lattice sites of the corresponding reciprocal lattices.

screens just the frequency $\omega_a^2(\mathbf{0})$. Other frequencies are weakly screened. In addition, from fig. 17 it is clearly seen that the intensity of screening associated with the site [001] grows in the series Be, Mg, Zn, which correlates with the results figuring in table 3. Thus, the specific behavior of the optical frequencies also finds a natural explanation in the microscopic theory. We note in passing that the considerations which have been presented clarify not only how the electronic screening changes from metal to metal, but indicates also how in the presence of an isotropic interaction ($V|\boldsymbol{q}|$) a sharply anisotropic nature of the vibration spectrum arises as a result only of the distribution of reciprocal lattice sites.

Stabilization of the phonon spectrum. We now investigate the role of the electrons in the dynamical stabilization of the lattice of a metal. As we have noted already, in symmetrical lattices the sum of all the forces acting on a given atom at its equilibrium position vanishes, i.e., the given configuration is a stationary point, while in other lattices, for example in bismuth, this occurs only when certain conditions are satisfied. However, the situation can correspond not only to a minimum, but also to a maximum, or to a saddle point. As a consequence the lattice turns out to be dynamically unstable, and imaginary vibration frequencies appear. It is natural to distinguish between long-wavelength, elastic instability, i.e., instability with respect to a definite strain, and short-wavelength instability, corresponding to phonons with finite momenta.

In the papers of Brovman and Kagan (Brovman and Kagan 1967, Kagan and Brovman 1968) it was first shown for the examples of Sn and Zn that the ionic lattice of real metals may display dynamic instability. The corresponding results are presented in figs. 18 and 19. It is seen that the instability possesses a complex character, displaying a short-wavelength instability as well as a long-wavelength one. Thus, the ionic lattices of Sn and Zn, although stable against changes in (c/a) (see fig. 13), turn out to be unstable against more complicated deformations.

The indirect interaction through the electrons stabilizes the lattice, as is clear from the very existence of these metals in the corresponding crystalline

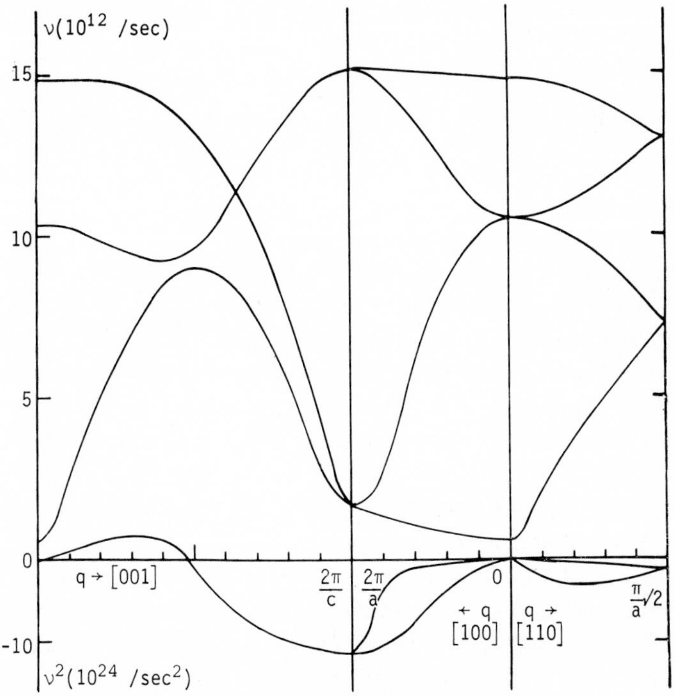

Fig. 18. Vibration frequencies of the ionic lattice for β-Sn.

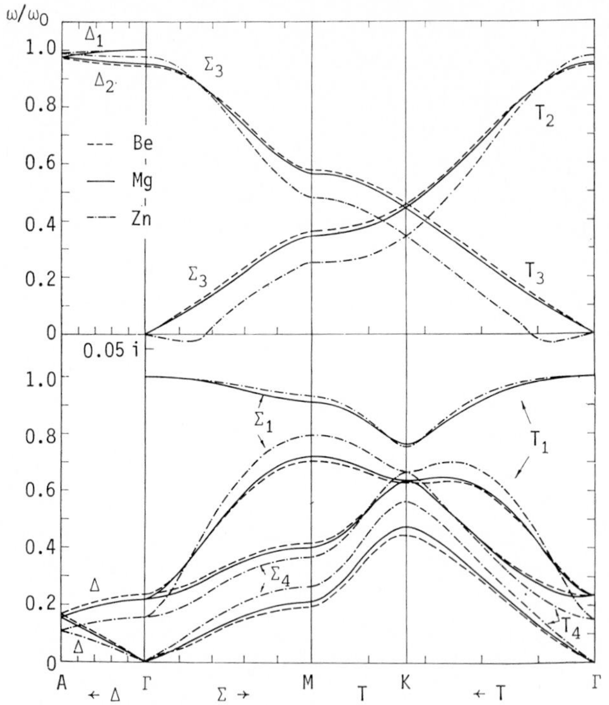

Fig. 19. Vibration frequencies of the ionic lattice for hexagonal metals (Be, Mg, Zn).

phases. In connection with this, as we have already noted in subsection 2.4, in the general case the role of the terms in the expansion of the energy beginning with $n \geqslant 3$ becomes significant. The quantitative analysis available up to the present time for β-Sn (Brovman and Kagan 1967), and for Zn (Brovman et al. 1968) shows that on using a potential of the Abarenkov–Heine type the dynamical instability remains in both metals on taking into account only $D_{(2)}$. In connection with this the general question arises: Is the existence of intrinsically non-pairwise interionic forces fundamental for the stability of similar metals, or can such stabilization be achieved by means of pairwise forces alone? This question is all the more interesting because, as was shown in subsection 2.9, the terms of higher order in the potential also contain a contribution to the pairwise interaction. A rigorous answer to this question is lacking. A correct separation of the non-pairwise interaction (see below), together with a sharpening of our knowledge of the electron–ion potential, might clarify the situation to a significant degree, at least for specific metals. However, it appears to us that in metals of the type of metallic tin many-ion forces of covalent type certainly must play an important role in the dynamical stability of the lattice.

We note that the electronic contribution can not only stabilize the lattice, but in the presence of a strong electron–ion potential it can 'over-screen' the direct ion–ion interaction. Thus for metallic hydrogen (at $p=0$) all cubic lattices which of course were stable on taking only the ion–ion interaction into account become unstable (Brovman et al. 1971). In this case, therefore, only strongly anisotropic structures are stable. At high pressures, however, the role of the direct ion–ion interaction becomes dominant, and accordingly cubic lattices of metallic hydrogen become stable (Brovman et al. 1972a).

Singularities of the phonon spectrum. Reflection of the Fermi surface in dispersion curves. Perhaps the most striking manifestation of the role of electrons in the formation of the phonon spectrum is the direct reflection of the topology of the Fermi surface in the dispersion curves. In contrast with non-metals, where $\omega_\alpha(\boldsymbol{q})$ is an analytic function of $\boldsymbol{q}$, at any rate away from points of degeneracy, this function is non-analytic in a metal. The singularities in the phonon dispersion law, as was investigated in detail in subsections 2.7 and 2.8, appear because of the existence of a sharp Fermi boundary in momentum space, and their positions are uniquely connected with the geometry of the Fermi surface. The value of the vector $\boldsymbol{q}$ which corresponds to the singularity arising from pairwise forces, is determined by the relation (118), or in the more general case is found from eq. (119). The position of the leading singularity in the spectrum due to many-ion scattering and determined by the singularities of the three-pole function, is found from the relation (96), etc. From the expression for the dynamical matrix (39), it is easy to conclude that the term $D_{(2)}$, containing the singularity, in the first case is proportional to $|V(q=2k_\mathrm{F})|^2$ at the singular point, while the term $D_{(3)}$ containing the singularity of the three-pole function, in addition to two $V_{\boldsymbol{q}}$ for large $\boldsymbol{q}_i$, has an additional factor of $V_{\boldsymbol{q}_i}$. The singularities of multi-pole functions of higher order will be connected with higher terms in the expansion of D_e, but each succeeding term will introduce each time an additional factor of $V_{\boldsymbol{K}}/\mathscr{E}_\mathrm{F}$. It is clear that the larger the quantities $V(q=2k_\mathrm{F})/\mathscr{E}_\mathrm{F}$, $V_{\boldsymbol{K}}/\mathscr{E}_\mathrm{F}$ or, in other words, the more pronounced the effect of compensation for short wavelength phonons (see the beginning of this section), the more apparent will be the nonanalytic behavior of the dispersion law. From table 2 one can conclude at once that it is very difficult to expose the singularities, and consequently the geometry of the Fermi surface, in the case of the alkali metals, and significantly easier in the case of polyvalent metals, particular of the third and fourth groups.

The singularities in the phonon spectrum correspond to the group velocity of the electrons $\boldsymbol{v}_\alpha(\boldsymbol{q})=\partial\omega_\alpha(\boldsymbol{q})/\partial\boldsymbol{q}$ becoming infinite [see, for example, eqs. (95) and (97)]. Therefore they should be manifested most strikingly in curves showing the dependence of the group velocity on $\boldsymbol{q}$. In figs. 20 and 21 are presented theoretical curves of $\boldsymbol{v}_\alpha(\boldsymbol{q})$ along the three symmetry directions for the cases of Na and Al obtained, taking into account $D_{(2)}$ and $D_{(3)}$. (The parameters of the corresponding model potentials are presented in the last section.) It is seen how strikingly the curves differ from each other: the almost complete absence of fine structure in the first case and the extraordinarily sharply pronounced fine structure in the second. (In the case of Na the singularities of the three-pole and higher order multi-pole functions are absent in general, since $K_{\min}>2k_F$.) This is particularly notable for the reason that from just looking at the dispersion curves of the two metals (see figs. 25 and 27) it is difficult to guess how much different information they contain. In particular, the reason becomes clear why it is so easy to describe the spectrum of Na within the framework of a phenomenological model with short range forces, in contrast with metals such as Al, Pb, and Sn.

The form of the curves in fig. 21 is very distinctive. The regions of smooth variation of $\boldsymbol{v}_\alpha(\boldsymbol{q})$ are separated by many singularities, either of the Kohn type, or belonging to the three-pole functions. [In this case only Kohn singularities of the 'diametral' type were included, i.e., singularities associated with the basic sphere of quasi-free electrons together with the condition

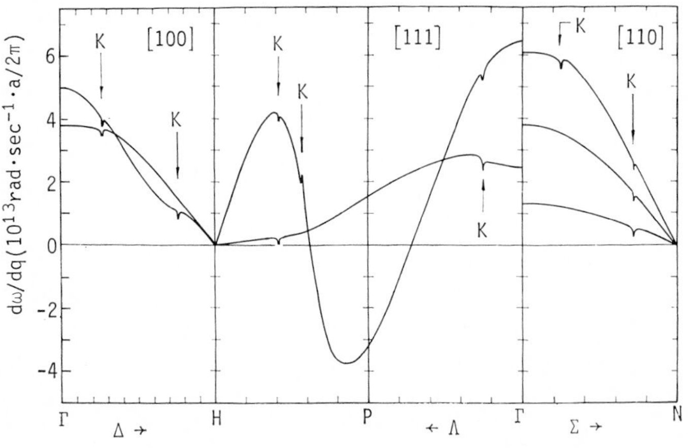

Fig. 20. Group velocity $d\omega/d\boldsymbol{q}$ for phonons in Na.

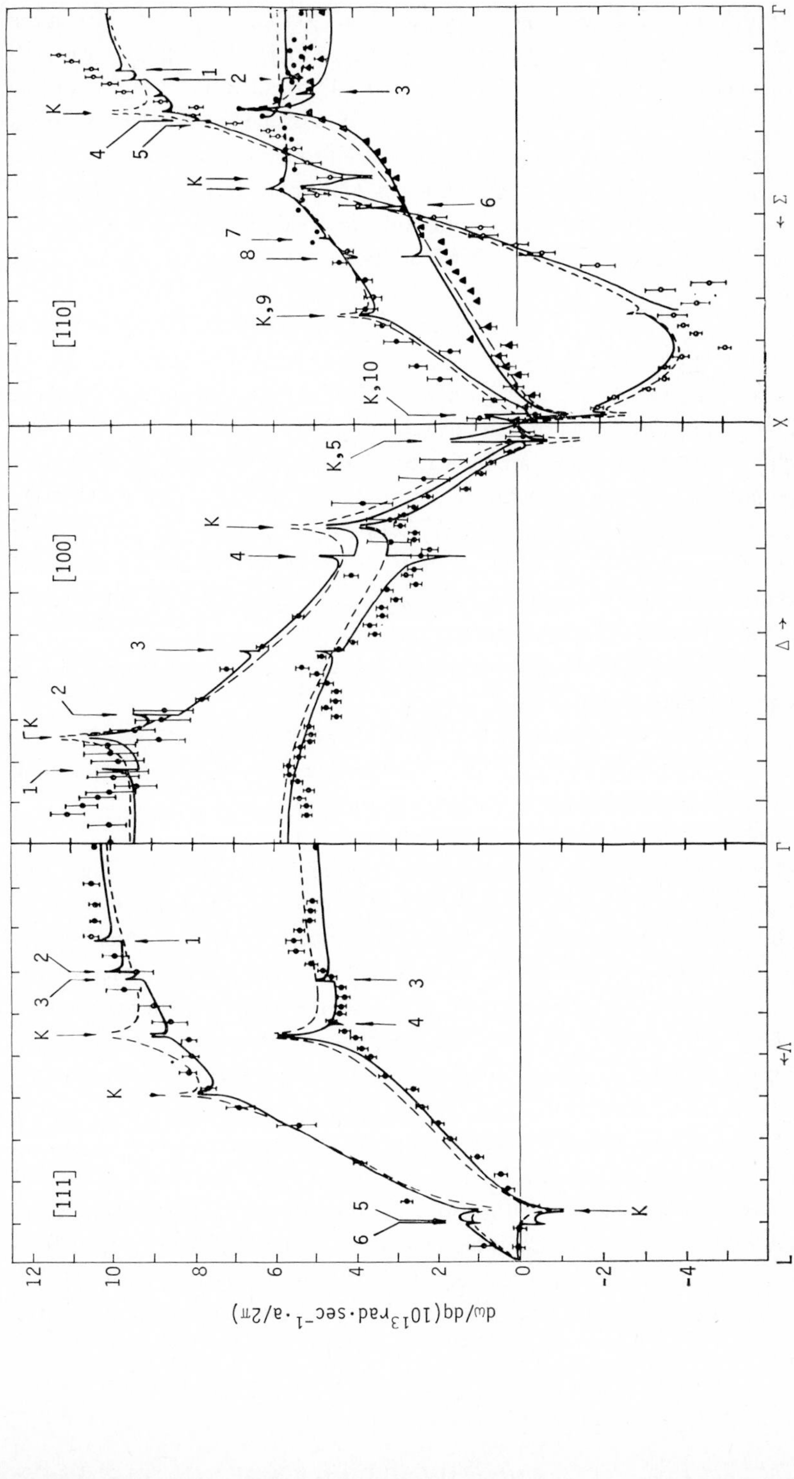

Fig. 21. Group velocity $d\omega/d\boldsymbol{q}$ for phonons in Al.

(118).] We have already noted (see subsection 2.8) that the singularities in the phonon spectrum associated with the many-ion interaction are not true mathematical singularities and must be partially washed out. Because of this the behavior of the curves near the singularities of the three-pole function is depicted conditionally. It is interesting that although each singularity due to the nonpairwise interaction contains an additional factor of $V_{\boldsymbol{K}}/\mathscr{E}_{\mathrm{F}}$, due to its strong nature and the noticeable interval over which it extends a noticeable reconstruction of whole portions of the curves of $\boldsymbol{v}_\alpha(\boldsymbol{q})$ occurs.

In tables 4–6 the calculated positions of the singularities of the three-pole function are presented for all three principal symmetry directions in Al. At the same time the corresponding reciprocal lattice vectors $\boldsymbol{K}_1$ and $\boldsymbol{K}_3$, and the full set of equivalent sets of pairs of vectors which lead to one and the same singularity in the spectrum, are indicated. Three cases where a singularity of a three-pole function merges with a Kohn singularity are indicated by asterisks. The geometrical coefficient $(\boldsymbol{q}+\boldsymbol{K}_1)^\alpha \times (\boldsymbol{q}+\boldsymbol{K}_2)^\beta$, figuring in $D_{(3)}(\boldsymbol{q})$, on taking the equivalent sets into account leads to definite values of the ratio of the corresponding contributions of $D_{(3)}$ to the transverse and longitudinal branches at the singular point. It is interesting that in a number of cases a singularity is absent from the transverse branches at the same time that it is always present in a longitudinal branch.

In fig. 21 are also presented the results of exceptionally precise measurements by Weymouth and Stedman (1970), which allowed them to determine the phonon group velocity in Al as a function of $\boldsymbol{q}$. (It should be noted that the first measurements of the phonon spectrum of a metal of such high quality were also carried out on Al (Stedman and Nilsson 1966).) The work was devoted to a special search for Kohn anomalies. In addition to those singularities of the two-pole function which appear in the theoretical curve, the authors found a whole series of anomalies associated with the reconstruction of the electronic spectrum in the vicinity of the Brillouin zone boundaries, whose positions are dictated by the positions of the points on the Fermi surface at which the group velocities of the electrons are antiparallel [see eq. (119)].

At least two singularities were discovered in this work which cannot be identified as Kohn singularities. They occur at $q=0.43$ along the [100] and at $q=0.33$ along the [110] direction (in units of $2\pi/a$). Comparing these values with the entries in the tables, we see that singularity no. 3 in table 4 and no. 3 in table 5 are close in position of those observed experimentally. The agreement becomes closer if we take into account that $2k_{\mathrm{F}}$ changes in the experiment from 2.23 to 2.27 while the tables are constructed on the basis of the fixed value $2k_F = 2.255$.

Thus in this experiment, apparently, singularities arising from the three-particle interaction have been observed for the first time. We note the generally reasonable agreement between the theoretical curves and the experimental results, which at the level of the derivative of the phonon dispersion curve has a decidely nontrivial nature, and which in principle could be achieved only within the framework of a microscopic investigation.

The exposure of non-pairwise forces. One of the most interesting manifestations of the indirect interaction through the conduction electrons is the appearance of non-pairwise forces between ions. In this section we have already discussed the role of these forces in the analysis of the dynamical stability of complex metals. The direct observation of the existence of these forces is the experimental discovery of the singularities associated with the three-pole function and higher order singularities in phonon dispersion curves discussed above. We pause here over yet one more experimental manifestation of the role of the non-pairwise forces – their role in the removal of degeneracies in the phonon spectrum.

As has already been noted, the pairwise interaction leads to an axial symmetry of the force constant matrix for each pair of ions. As a consequence of this the dynamical matrix in the general case can possess a higher symmetry than is dictated by the space group symmetry of the lattice. This circumstance can lead to an additional symmetry in the phonon spectrum at particular points in the Brillouin zone, which, however, is removed in the presence of the non-pairwise forces. Therefore, the removal of the degeneracy itself gives evidence of the existence of non-pairwise forces, and its scale makes it possible to estimate their quantitative characteristics.

A striking example of such a situation is the behavior of the phonon dispersion law in a hexagonal metal at the symmetry point K (Brovman et al. 1968) (see, for example, fig. 26). A group-theoretic analysis shows that at this point the values of the four phonon frequencies for polarizations in the basal plane are given by the expressions

$$\left.\begin{aligned} \omega_1^2 &= \operatorname{Re} D_{11}^{xx} + \operatorname{Im} D_{11}^{xy} \\ \omega_2^2 &= \operatorname{Re} D_{11}^{xx} - \operatorname{Im} D_{11}^{xy} + 2 \operatorname{Re} D_{12}^{xx} \end{aligned}\right\} \quad K_1$$

$$\left.\begin{aligned} \omega_3^2 &= \operatorname{Re} D_{11}^{xx} + \operatorname{Im} D_{11}^{xy} \\ \omega_4^2 &= \operatorname{Re} D_{11}^{xx} - \operatorname{Im} D_{11}^{xy} - 2 \operatorname{Re} D_{12}^{xx} \end{aligned}\right\} \quad K_4$$

TABLE 4

([100] direction, q in units of $2\pi/a$, $2k_F = 2.255$).

N	q	K_1	K_2	K_3	Number of equivalent contributions	$\Delta\omega_T^2/\Delta\omega_L^2$
1	0.1790	1 −1 −1	2 0 0	1 1 1	8	0
2	0.3103	1 −1 −1	1 −1 1	0 0 2	8	0
3	0.4593	0 0 −2	1 1 −1	1 1 1	16	1.49
4	0.6878	−1 −1 −1	1 −1 −1	2 0 0	8	−1.90
5*	0.9584	−2 0 0	−2 0 2	0 0 2	8	0

TABLE 6

([111] direction, q in units of $2\pi/a$, $2k_F = 2.255$).

N	q	K_1	K_2	K_3	Number of equivalent contributions	$\Delta\omega_T^2/\Delta\omega_L^2$
1	0.2067	2 0 0	1 1 1	−1 1 1	6	0
2	0.2731	1 1 −1	1 1 1	0 0 2	6	0
3	0.2844	1 −1 1	0 0 2	−1 1 1	12	0.54
4	0.3756	1 −1 −1	2 0 0	1 1 1	6	−4.31
5	0.7791	0 −2 −2	1 −1 −1	1 1 1	6	−4.31
6	0.7859	1 −1 −1	1 −1 1	0 0 2	12	2.34

TABLE 5

([110] direction, q in units of $2\pi/a$, $2k_F = 2.255$).

N	q	K_1			K_2			K_3			Number of equivalent contributions	$\Delta\omega_{Tz}^2/\Delta\omega_L^2$	$\Delta\omega_{Tz}^2/\Delta\omega_L^2$
1	0.2033	1	1	−1	0	2	0	−1	1	1	8	0	0
2	0.2341	1	1	−1	1	1	1	0	0	2	2	0	−0.37
3	0.2857	1	−1	−1	2	0	0	1	1	1	8	4.11	0
4	0.3747	0	0	2	1	1	3	1	1	1	4	0	8.94
5	0.3806	1	−1	−1	1	1	−1	0	2	0	8	0	1.46
6	0.6777	−2	−2	0	−2	0	0	0	2	0	4	0	0
7	0.7851	1	−1	1	0	0	2	−1	1	1	8	0	3.24
8	0.8467	1	−1	−1	1	−1	1	0	0	2	4	2.78	−1.39
9*	1.0416	0	0	0	0	0	2	0	0	2	4	0	0
10*	1.3845	−2	−2	0	−3	−1	1	−1	1	1	8	0	0

If the non-pairwise interaction is absent, then it is easy to show that $\mathrm{Im}\, D_{11}^{xy}=0$. In this case the picture of the splitting of the frequencies is the following: there exist two degenerate frequencies $\omega_1^2=\omega_3^2$ and two others, ω_2^2 and ω_4^2, on opposite sides and separated from them rigorously by the same distance $2\,\mathrm{Re}\, D_{12}^{xx}$. Such a picture, in particular, is always observed in the results of calculations which take only $E^{(2)}$ into account (see for example, fig. 29). In the presence of non-pairwise forces the situation changes in a cardinal fashion. Now the degenerate level $\omega_1^2=\omega_3^2$ is displaced with respect to the center $\frac{1}{2}(\omega_2^2+\omega_4^2)$ by the amount $2\mathrm{Im}\, D_{11}^{xy}$. The experimental data available at the present time (see, for example, fig. 26) convincingly testify on behalf of the presence of non-pairwise forces, and allow one in principle to estimate their magnitude in hexagonal metals.

3.2. The electron-ion and electron-electron interactions. The direct and inverse problems

In the quantitative description of the phonon spectrum of a metal we first of all come up against the problem of the choice of the effective electron-ion interaction entering all the general expressions. In fact, in the absence of the overlap between ions, all of the concrete information differentiating one metal from another, and predetermining the features of the structure and the spectral properties of a particular metal, is concealed in this quantity. We note that the problem of obtaining the vertex of the electron–ion interaction for a given metal is more a problem of atomic physics than of the physics of metals, and in essence is 'external' to the whole circle of problems connected with the determination of purely metallic properties, which is particularly clearly manifested when model potentials are used.

The determination of the vertex of the electron–ion interaction V in principle can be carried out within the framework of the direct or inverse problem. In the first case V_q is found from 'first principles' without involving experimental information. In the second, the effective potential is parametrized, and the corresponding parameters are obtained from certain experimental data. It is natural that the first approach is the more attractive, for it makes the theory of metals a microscopic one, starting from the atomic level. However, and this is also completely natural, the accuracy of first principles calculations is very limited, and the second approach, which separates the problem of determining V from the microscopic theory of the metal itself, undoubtedly remains the preferable one up to the present time.

In a calculation from first principles the potential of a free ion in the one electron approximation, obtained from atomic calculations is used, and the corresponding wave functions of the inner electrons. For obtaining the matrix element of the electron–ion interaction either the OPW method or the related initial formulation of the pseudopotential method (Phillips and Kleinman 1959, Harrison 1966) is used most frequently. Calculations of this type were used in obtaining the phonon spectra of alkali metals (Vosko et al. 1965, Geldart et al. 1970), of hexagonal metals of the second group (Roy and Venkataraman 1967, Sahni and Venkataraman 1969, Koppel and Maradudin 1967, King and Cutler 1970, 1971, and others), and in Al and Pb (Harrison 1966, Vosko et al. 1965).

Even a superficial analysis of these results shows that the calculations turn out to be successful in fact only in those cases when the contribution of the indirect interaction through the electrons is not very significant, as is the case for the alkali metals. If this contribution is large, then, as a rule, the calculations agree poorly with the experimental results. Analyzing the results presented in table 2, it is easy to understand that if due to inaccuracies in the determination of $V(\boldsymbol{q})$ we make an error in $\psi(\boldsymbol{q})$ [eq. (136)] of only 5% in a significant interval of $\boldsymbol{q}$, then for Na we will make an error of 1.5% in the final results. However, in the case of Pb an analogous error will lead to an error of the order of 100%, and can even lead to the occurrence of imaginary frequencies. The latter is indeed observed in the calculations of a number of authors (Harrison 1966, Schmuck and Quitner 1968, Yamamoto 1970). It is clear that at the present time a theory proceeding strictly from first principles cannot yield the accuracy for $\psi(\boldsymbol{q})$ required in this case.

Most natural for the theory of metals is the use of experimental information about properties of an isolated ion. In this case the true electron-ion potential is replaced by a model potential which gives approximately the same scattering of electrons as the true potential, or, what is the same thing, the correct value for the wave function outside the ion. At the same time the behavior of the wave function inside the ion core can differ greatly from the true behavior, which is of no significance for the determination of metallic properties. The ideology of the pseudopotential is used here, obviously, in the most pronounced form (see, for example, Harrison 1966, Cohen and Heine 1970). The direct determination of the parameters of the pseudopotential could be carried out by measuring the amplitude for the scattering of an electron by a single ion. Heine and Abarenkov (1964) (see also Abarenkov and Heine 1965, Animalu and Heine 1965, Animalu 1966) proposed finding the parameters of the pseudopotential from a comparison with experimental values of the energy levels of a free ion, choosing the following form for the potential

$$V(r)=\begin{cases}-e^2\sum_l A_l(E)\hat{P}_l, & r<R_{\mathrm{M}}\\ -Ze^2/r, & r>R_{\mathrm{M}}.\end{cases} \tag{141}$$

The value of $A_l(E)$ is different for each partial wave l and, generally speaking, depends on the energy of the electron ($\hat{P}_l$ is a projection operator, which extracts the l component from the wave function). R_{M} is some effective radius of the ion. Inasmuch as the quantities A_l are determined from experimental data, the potential automatically incorporates, in an averaged form, the effective decrease of the interaction inside the ion, which is a most important effect in the scattering of slow electrons (for a more detailed discussion see Cohen and Heine 1970).

Subsequently some 'optimized' modification of the Heine–Abarenkov potential was proposed (Shaw 1968).

In several papers a special study was made of the problem of introducing the essential corrections to such a potential in the transition from an isolated ion to a metal (Shaw 1969a, 1969b, Ballentine and Gupta 1971, and others). We note that in the majority of cases the introduction of such corrections is not done in a completely consistent fashion, having in mind particularly the presence of higher order terms than the second in the expansion of the energy in powers of the effective potential. Potentials of the type described were used in a whole series of papers: in the analysis of the phonon spectrum in alkali metals and aluminum (Animalu et al. 1966, Coulthard 1970), in hexagonal metals (Brovman et al. 1968, Gilat et al. 1969, Shaw and Pynn 1969), and in lead (Schmuck and Quitner 1968, Coulthard 1970).

Without doubt, the use of experimental information concerning an isolated ion significantly improved the general agreement between calculated and experimental values for polyvalent metals. However, further analysis showed that in many cases the accuracy of potentials of the type of (141) is still insufficient, particularly if an analysis of the dynamic and static properties of a metal is simultaneously to be made with one and the same potential. The point is that, as a rule, the pseudopotential obtained, as is also the case for a potential determined from first principles, does not ensure the satisfaction of the fundamental conditions

$$\left(\frac{\partial E}{\partial \Omega}\right)_0=-P=0, \qquad \left(\frac{\partial E}{\partial (c/a)}\right)_0=0. \tag{142, 143}$$

The first of these indicates that the total energy of a metal must have a minimum for that volume of the primitive unit cell which is observed experimentally. Its violation leads to the lattice, in fact, being studied under pressure, which can noticeably affect its properties, particularly the compressibility and the longitudinal vibration branches.

The condition (143) refers to uniaxial crystals. Its violation is equivalent to the presence of anisotropic stresses, which in principle destroy the true symmetry of the lattice (the Voigt symmetry of the elastic moduli, the Born–Huang conditions).

Another source of errors, again possessed by calculations from first principles as well, is the significant inaccuracy in the determination of the Fourier components of the electron–ion interaction for large momenta. This fact has little effect on calculations of the Fermi surface, for which the only significant values of the potential are those corresponding to a few nearest neighbor lattice sites of the reciprocal lattice, but is very important for the determination of the phonon spectrum and static characteristics of a metal.

All of this is in accord with the fact that the accuracy of 'a priori' potentials being insufficient for a description of the fine properties of the structure and dynamics of metals, has predetermined a wide use of model potentials in direct or in momentum space, whose parameters are obtained within the framework of the inverse problem with the aid of definite experimental characteristics of a metal. In this connection, the form of the model potential itself, naturally, must reflect the fact of the effective reduction of the interaction inside the ion. The flexibility in the choice of the precise form of the potential which arises must allow the satisfaction of the conditions (142) and (143), and simultaneously must sharpen the behavior of the tail of the potential for large $\boldsymbol{q}$, as well as in the region $q<2k_{\mathrm{F}}$, which is not verifiable on the basis of measurements of the Fermi surface. (Striking examples of the latter are the hexagonal metals and Sn, for which the behavior of the function $\psi(\boldsymbol{q})$ in the vicinity of the [001] and [110] reciprocal lattice points, respectively, plays an extraordinarily significant role in the determination of their phonon spectra (see subsection 3.1), at the same time that the structure factor $S(\boldsymbol{K})$ for these sites vanishes, and they have no effect on the structure of the Fermi surface.) The simplest, and most widely used, forms in $\boldsymbol{q}$ space are the two-parameter model potential of Harrison (Harrison 1966),

$$V(q) = -\frac{4\pi Ze^2}{q^2\Omega_0} + \frac{\beta/\Omega_0}{[1+(qr_c)^2]^2}, \tag{144}$$

and the potential

$$V(q) = -\frac{4\pi Ze^2}{q^2\Omega_0}\left[(1+u)\cos qr_0 - u\,\frac{\sin qr_0}{qr_0}\right], \tag{145}$$

which is a local form of the Heine–Abarenkov potential. A special case of eq. (145) is the potential with $u=0$ ('complete cancellation') which was proposed and widely used by Ashcroft (1966, 1967, 1968).

Sometimes a potential of the Bardeen (1936) form is also used, rewritten as a two-parameter model potential (Sham and Ziman 1963),

$$V(q) = -\left(\frac{4\pi Ze^2}{q^2\Omega_0} + U\right)\frac{3(\sin qr_0 - qr_0\cos qr_0)}{(qr_0)^3}. \tag{146}$$

In using a two-parameter potential one of the parameters must be obtained from the condition (142). This was first done in the work of Ashcroft and Langreth (1966) (see also, Brovman et al. 1970 and below).

In noncubic metals both conditions must be satisfied simultaneously. A two-parameter form for the potential, clearly, is not sufficiently flexible in this case to describe correctly, the behavior of the tail of the potential, for example. It is necessary, therefore, to go over to a three-parameter or four-parameter potential. An example of such a modification of the potential (145) can be found in the analysis of the static and dynamic properties of magnesium (Brovman et al. 1971), where for the determination of the parameters both of the conditions (142) and (143) were used. A different form of a four parameter potential, representing a generalization of the expression (144), was used in the work of Schneider and Stoll (1966). The necessity of reproducing the tail of the potential for large q makes it reasonable to use for the determination of the other parameters the experimental value of a quantity such as the transverse elastic modulus or, in a number of cases, simply the value of the potential at a reciprocal lattice point, which is known from measurements of the Fermi surface. On the other hand, when the behavior of $\psi(\boldsymbol{q})$ for intermediate values of q smaller than $2k_\mathrm{F}$ becomes very important, in the case of crystals with two atoms in a primitive unit cell one can use the limiting value of the optical frequency for the verification of this region.

An analysis of the results shows that utilizing only equilibrium parameters of the unit cell and one or two long-wavelength characteristics of the crystal for the determination of the model potential, it is possible to obtain entirely reasonable agreement between experimental and theoretical results for the whole range of dynamic and static properties of a metal in many cases (see the following subsection). The number of investigations carried out with the aid of model potentials is very large. As examples one can cite the calculations of the phonon spectrum and elastic moduli of alkali metals (Sham 1965, Schneider and Stoll 1966, Ashcroft 1968, Wallace 1968, 1969, Suzuki et al. 1968, Brovman et al. 1970, Price et al. 1970, Fehlner 1971), of hexagonal metals (Brovman et al. 1968, Schneider and Stoll 1968, Floyd and Kleinman 1970, Brovman et al. 1971), aluminum (Harrison 1966, Schneider and Stoll 1966, Wallace 1969, 1970, Schmuck 1971, Benckert 1971, Suzuki 1971), lead (Harrison 1966, Gupta and Tripathi 1971, Krasko and Gurski 1971, Suzuki 1971,), and metallic tin (Brovman and Kagan 1967, Brovman and Solt 1970).

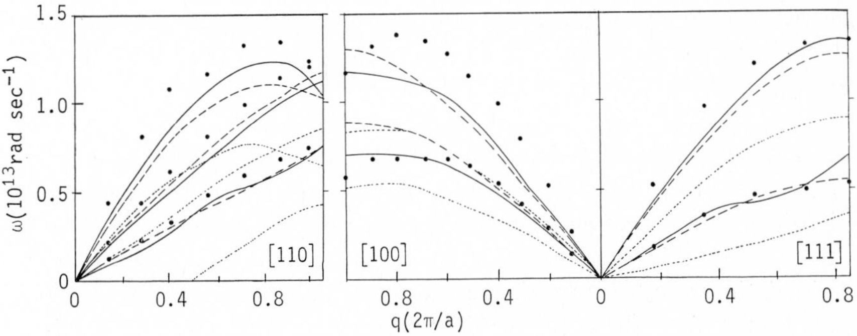

Fig. 22. Phonon dispersion curves for lead. ——— Gupta and Tripathi (1970); ---- Coulthard (from Gupta and Tripathi 1970); .... Schmuck and Quitner (1968).

The use of a model potential with parameters determined within the framework of the inverse problem, is particularly effective when the role of the indirect interaction is large. In fig. 22 dispersion curves for lead, obtained by various authors in approximations equivalent to taking only $E^{(2)}$ into account are presented. The use of the Heine–Abarenkov potential lead to a strongly unstable spectrum (Schmuck and Quitner 1968). In the framework of the inverse problem (Coulthard 1970, Gupta and Tripathi 1971) it is possible to obtain a stable spectrum and values of characteristic frequencies which are close to experimental values (Stedman et al. 1967). We note that Coulthard used the form of the Abarenkov–Heine potential (141), but the parameters A_0, A_1, A_2 were obtained from the inverse problem.

A certain extreme form of the inverse problem consists of reconstructing the entire function $\psi(\boldsymbol{q})$ appearing in $D_{(2)}$ from the results of measurements of the phonon spectrum of lead. The function thus obtained, as it turned out, enabled the vibrational spectrum of Pb to be reproduced with an error of less than 1% (Bortolani and Ottaviani 1969). The behavior of the function $\psi(\boldsymbol{q})$ itself obtained in this work differs strongly from the usual one, obtained, for example, from the data of Animalu (1965), in the position of the first zero,

q_0. This, apparently, is indirect evidence that terms with higher powers of $V(\boldsymbol{q})$ play a significant role in lead. The possibility of finding a function $\psi(\boldsymbol{q})$ which reproduces the phonon spectrum so well might be evidence of the dominant role of the pairwise interionic interaction and, by the same token, of the existence of only multiple scattering from one and the same ion (see subsection 2.9). The final answer to this question can be given, apparently, by measurements of the dispersion curves for lead for arbitrary directions and an analysis of the possibility of describing them with the aid of the same function $\psi(\boldsymbol{q})$.

So far the discussion in this section has been based primarily on the assumption of a local effective potential. It is natural that a local form is very convenient from the point of view of the general theory (see section 2), physical analysis, and modeling the potential. However, the vertex of the electron–ion interaction is non-local in the general case (see subsection 2.10). On the one hand this is connected with the exchange of the conduction electrons with the inner electrons even in the true potential, but to a greater extent with the passage from the true potential to a weak, effective one (see Harrison 1966, Cohen and Heine 1970). At the same time, an analysis of experimental data gives evidence that for a whole host of metals the representation of the electron–ion interaction in the form of a local potential turns out to be entirely reasonable for an adequate description not only of properties of the electronic spectrum, for example in Al (Ashcroft 1963), Na (Lee 1966), Mg (Kimball et al. 1967), but especially of properties which are integrals over the electronic spectrum as well.

At the same time the so called 'band structure characteristic' the non-local analogue of $\psi(\boldsymbol{q})$, can change greatly in going from a local to a non-local description (Shaw 1970, Yamamoto 1970). This is tied in part, apparently, to the fundamental non-uniqueness in the choice of a pseudopotential (Harrison 1966, Cohen and Heine 1970), which leads to the possibility of choosing the 'maximally local' form for it, and in part to the weak sensitivity of individual physical quantities to nonlocality. This problem has been little studied as a whole, although it is known that in certain cases nonlocality definitely plays an essential role, for example in lithium, where p-states are absent from the ion core states (Bortolani and Pizzichini 1969), or in zinc and cadmium (Stark and Falicov 1967), where d-shell electrons play a significant role.

In order to demonstrate the typical scale of the changes when one goes over to a nonlocal potential, in fig. 23 are presented phonon dispersion curves for Al (Coulthard 1970) calculated on the basis of the general Heine–

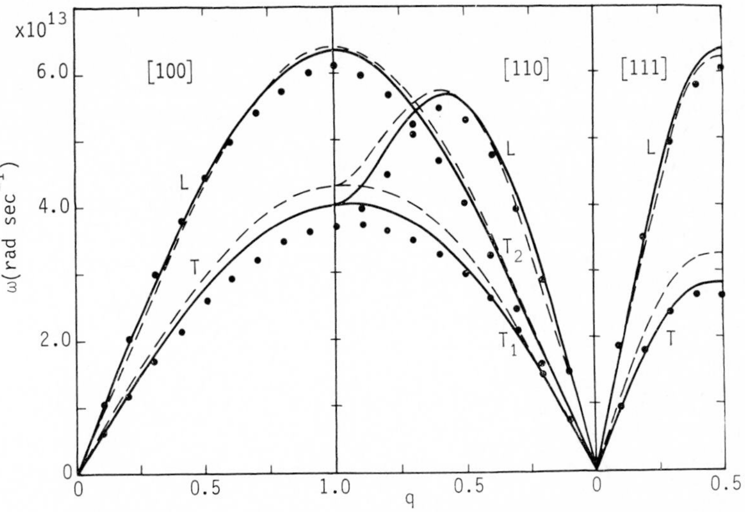

Fig. 23. Phonon dispersion curves for Al. Solid line — calculated with a non local potential due to Shaw; dotted line --- calculated with a local version of the Heine–Abarenkov potential.

Abarenkov potential (12.1), and by the use of an effective local form of it, in which the momenta of an electron before and after scattering are taken to lie on the Fermi surface (Animalu 1965, 1966). It is seen that the changes are of the order of 5–10%, turns out to be significantly smaller than the large difference in the initial band structure characteristic itself (Shaw 1970).

For a quantitative analysis of the phonon spectrum, in addition to the electron-ion potential it is essential to know the electronic 'multi-pole' functions (see section 2). It is very significant, at any rate for a local electron–ion potential, that these multi-pole functions depend only on the electron density and, therefore, are universal characteristics of the interacting electron gas. Unfortunately, the experimental determination of the multi-pole functions and a comparison with theoretical results (see subsection 2.7) cannot be carried out independently. Indeed, the measurement of the phonon spectrum of a metal represents the only real method at the present time for the study of the properties of a degenerate electron gas, which thus always exists in the field of a crystal lattice. Therefore, the sensitivity of the phonon spectrum to the value of the polarization operator can be analyzed most clearly in the case of alkali metals, where the smallness of the parameter $V_{\boldsymbol{K}}/\mathscr{E}_{\mathrm{F}}$ has the consequence that the terms of third and higher order in the expansion of the ground state energy can be deliberately neglected. As a consequence the

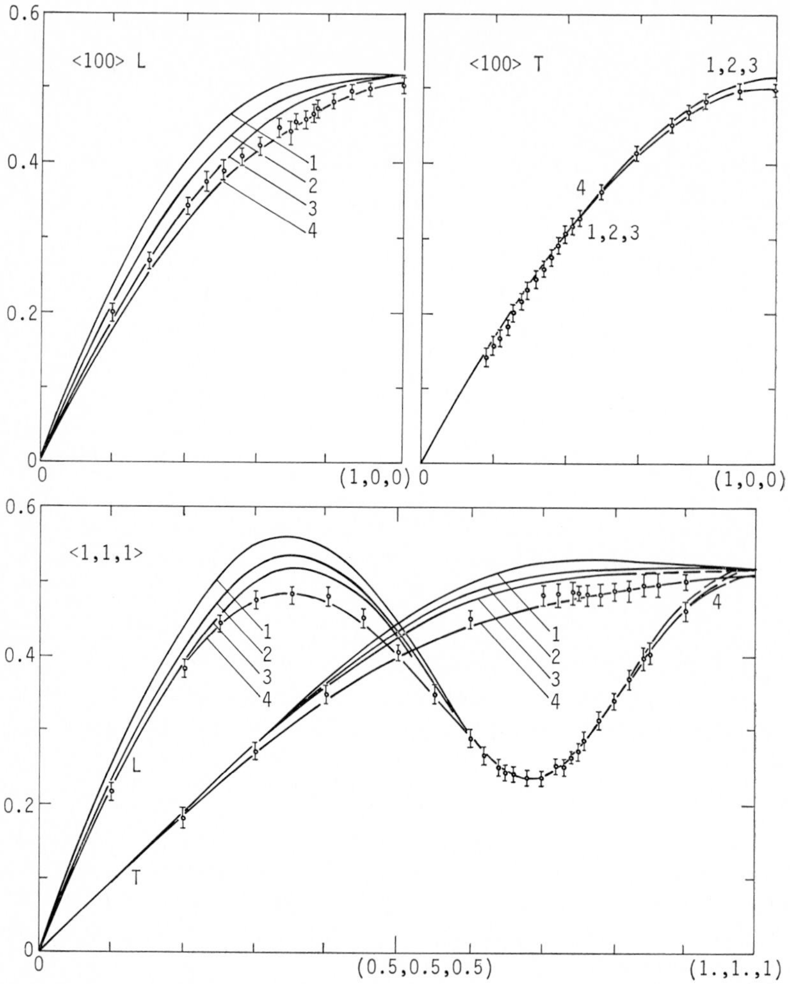

Fig. 24. Phonon dispersion curves for Na for different choices of the dielectric function.

dynamical matrix will depend only on the two-pole function. In fig. 24 phonon dispersion curves of Na are presented, obtained on the basis of different choices for the function $G(q)$ (see subsection 2.7) in the expression for the polarization operator $\pi(q)$ (Geldart et al. 1970). The electron–ion interaction was described with the aid of the empirical potential of Prokofiev (1929), which reproduces the energy level scheme of Na with great accuracy. It is seen that there are noticeable differences between the dispersion curves. The use of the RPA gives a significant departure from the experimental results, while the best agreement is found for the variant GT. It is significant that not only the magnitudes of the frequencies are improved for the longitudinal branches, but the forms of the dispersion curves themselves as well.

The influence of the choice of $G(q)$ on the phonon spectrum was also studied by other authors (Prakash and Joshi 1969, 1970, Price et al. 1970, Coulthard 1970, Floyd and Kleinman 1970, Shaw and Pynn 1969). The results of these investigations demonstrate anew the marked sensitivity of the dispersion curves to the form of $G(q)$, particularly in polyvalent metals. The analysis of all the results taken as a whole, as well as our analysis of the influence of the form of $G(q)$ on the form of the dispersion curves in different metals, leads to the conclusion that the functions $G_{\mathrm{GT}}(q)$ and $G_{\mathrm{TW}}(q)$ yield values of the polarization operator in the region of metallic densities significantly closer to the true value than do the functions $G_{\mathrm{H}}(q)$ or $G_{\mathrm{HGV}}(q)$.

Thus, the investigation of the phonon dispersion law in a metal allows conclusions to be made about the polarization properties of the electron gas. Of course their accuracy is limited at the present time, in view of the uncertainty in the value of the electron–ion interaction vertex. However, the universal nature of the polarization operator allows us to count on obtaining unified information about it on the basis of analyses of different metals.

With regard to the multi-pole functions of higher orders, their comparison with experiment at the present time can be carried out only indirectly through a general comparison of final theoretical and experimental results.

3.3. A unified analysis of the static and dynamic properties of metals. The role of non-pairwise forces

The basic problem of the present subsection is the discussion of the possibility of a quantitative description of a large number of different properties of a metal lattice simultaneously, properties which are integrals over the electronic spectrum, within the framework of a unified approach. It appears to us that just such a possibility, to the extent that it exists, is the most important for checking the microscopic theory.

Everywhere in this section we consider especially the quantitative and qualitative role of terms of higher than second order in the pseudopotential ('non-pairwise forces') in view of the fact that this question has been very little studied until recently. We can cite only calculations for phonons in Na (Fehlner 1971), carried out in the 'two Umklapp' approximation, and the unpublished calculations of Johnson for phonons in Al, referred to in the review by Sandström (1970). Therefore the material in this subsection is based wholly on our own calculations (Brovman and Kagan 1967, Brovman et al. 1970a, 1971a, 1972, 1973), in which for the analysis of static and dynamic characteristics, terms of up to, and including, third order were taken into account. The investigation is carried out for the examples of sodium (a monovalent metal), magnesium (divalent), and aluminum (trivalent), and for qualitative discussions white tin (a quadrivalent metal) is used.

This selection is related to a significant extent to the fact that, as has already been mentioned, from an analysis of the results of measurements of the Fermi surface in these metals it was possible to conclude that nonlocality plays a very small role in the effective electron–ion interaction (Ashcroft 1963, Lee 1966, Kimball et al. 1967).

In order to focus mainly on the elucidation of several metallic properties, and not on the properties of isolated ions, we worked within the framework of the inverse problem, and utilized a local potential, taking the representation (145) as our basis. In accordance with common practice the expression was multiplied by $\exp\{-\xi(q/2k_F)^2\}$ to cut down the oscillations in the tail of $V(q)$ (Animalu and Heine 1965). In the case of magnesium, where a more flexible potential is essential, due to the presence of two atoms in a primitive unit cell, the quantity ξ was also taken to be a variable parameter. In addition, in the calculations of properties of the undeformed magnesium lattice an additional contribution β_2 was incorporated into the potential at $\boldsymbol{q}=0$, allowing an additional variation of the non-Coulomb contribution b to the forward scattering of an electron by an ion [the quantity β_1 is determined from the parameters of the potential (145)]

$$b = 4\pi Z e^2 \beta, \qquad \beta = \beta_1 + \beta_2, \qquad \beta_1 = \tfrac{1}{6} r_0^2 [3 + 2uq_0 r_0].$$

In this fashion we have two-parameter potentials for sodium and aluminum, while for magnesium we have a four-parameter potential. For the description of $\pi(q)$ in sodium and aluminum we used the form $G_{TW}(q)$ for $G(q)$ (for comparison, the form $G_{HGV}(q)$ was also used); in the case of magnesium, for which the calculations were carried out earlier, only the form $G_{HGV}(q)$ was used.

The potential parameters were obtained within the framework of the inverse problem, and in each case one of the parameters was obtained from the equilibrium condition (142). The second parameter in the case of Na and Al was determined from the best fit to the phonon spectrum. In the case of magnesium the second equilibrium condition (143) was used as well, and in order to fix the potential in the important region $q<2k_F$ the pure shear modulus B_{22} and the $\boldsymbol{q}=0$ limiting optical frequency $[\omega_c(\mathbf{0})]$ were also used (see below).

From the solution of the inverse problem the following values of the parameters were obtained: for sodium $q_0/2k_F=1.0$, $r_0=1.255$ Å, $\xi=0.03$; for magnesium $q_0/2k_F=0.76$, $r_0=0.550$ Å, $\xi=0.205$, $\beta_2/a_B^2=0.1054$; for aluminum $q_0/2k_F=0.754$, $r_0=0.642$ Å, $\xi=0.15$. (The parameter ξ was not optimized in the cases of Na and Al.)

The elastic moduli were determined by the method of homogeneous deformation, in the context of which strains were chosen which have a simple physical sense and are convenient for arbitrary crystals. The corresponding derivatives with respect to these strains (B_i, B_{ik}) are simply related to the usual elastic moduli C_i, C_{ik} (Brovman et al. 1971a). The basic results of the calculations for Na, Mg, and Al, carried out on the basis of a unified potential, obtained above within the framework of the inverse problem, are collected in tables 7–9 and in figs. 25–27. Presented are the energy, the elastic moduli of the first and second order, as well as the phonon dispersion curves along symmetry directions in the first Brillouin zone. In the row labeled 'experiment' the data on the elastic moduli of Na (Ho and Ruoff 1968), Mg (Slutsky and Garland 1957), and Al (Kamm and Alers 1964), extrapolated to $T=0$, are presented, while the experimental points on the dispersion curves were obtained from neutron experiments for Na (Woods et al. 1962), Mg (Pindor and Pynn 1969) and Al (Stedman and Nilsson 1966). The lattice constants used were: $a=4.225$ Å for Na (Barrett 1956), $a=2.1945$ Å, $c/a=$ $=1.6231$ for Mg (Pearson 1958); $a=4.03183$ Å for Al (Figgins et al. 1956).

TABLE 7

(Energy in Ry/atom; elastic moduli in 10^{11} dyne/cm²).

Na	E	P	B	B_{33}	B_{44}
$E^{(0)}$	−0.1627	0.042	0.260	–	–
$E^{(1)}$	0.1516	0.876	1.753	–	–
$E^{(2)}$	−0.0026	−0.043	−0.125	−0.011	0.037
$E^{(3)}$	+0.0001	0.003	+0.008	−0.002	−0.007
E_i	−0.4558	−0.878	−1.171	0.072	0.537
E	−0.4689	0.000	0.724	0.059	0.567
Exper.	−0.4593 ±0.0015	0	0.763 ±0.014	0.073 ±0.002	0.622 ±0.015

$B_{11}=B=\frac{1}{3}(C_{11}+2C_{12})$, $B_{33}=\frac{1}{2}(C_{11}-C_{12})$, $B_{44}=C_{44}$.

TABLE 8

(Energy in Ry/atom; elastic moduli in 10^{11} dyne/cm^2).

Mg	E	$B_1 = P$	$B_{11} = B$	B_2	B_{22}	B_{12}	B_{44}	$B_{88} = \frac{1}{4}\rho a^2 \omega_a^2$	$B_{99} = \frac{1}{4}\rho c^2 \omega_c^2$	$B_{33} = B_{66}$	B_{68}	$B_{33} - (B_{68})^2/B_{88}$
E_i	−2.1524	−6.82	−9.10	−0.0438	5.66	0.015	1.70	2.65	134.5	2.98	2.26	–
$E^{(0)}$	−0.2304	1.62	3.56	0	0	0	0	0	0	0	0	–
$E^{(1)}$	0.6705	6.38	12.76	0	0	0	0	0	0	0	0	–
$E^{(2)}$	−0.0906	−1.94	−5.79	0.0407	−1.19	−0.057	0.90	1.06	−97.7	0.19	−0.93	–
$E^{(3)}$	−0.0323	0.77	1.95	0.0031	−1.46	0.007	0.79	−0.93	−10.9	−1.04	−0.55	–
E	−1.7705	0.00	3.38	0.0000	3.01	−0.035	1.81	2.78	26.0	2.13	0.78	1.91
Exper.	−1.7787 ±0.0060	0.00	3.69	0.0000	3.01	−0.028	1.84	2.57	26.0	–	–	1.88

$B_{11} = B = {}^1\!/_9(2C_{11} + 2C_{12} + C_{33} + 4C_{13})$, $B_{22} = {}^1\!/_9(2C_{11} + 2C_{12} + 4C_{33} - 8C_{13})$, $B_{12} = {}^1\!/_9(2C_{13} + 2C_{33} - 2C_{11} - 2C_{12})$,
$B_{33} - (B_{68})^2/B_{88} = \frac{1}{2}(C_{11} - C_{12})$, $B_{44} = C_{44}$.

TABLE 9

(Energy in Ry/atom; elastic moduli in 10^{11}dyne/cm^2).

Al	E	P	B	B_{33}	B_{44}
$E^{(0)}$	-0.0537	7.478	14.706	–	–
$E^{(1)}$	1.3230	17.600	35.200	–	–
$E^{(2)}$	-0.0882	$-$ 1.734	-13.127	1.284	-11.042
$E^{(3)}$	0.0160	0.671	$+$ 1.549	-0.624	$-$ 0.216
E_i	-5.4158	-24.015	-32.021	1.662	14.902
E	-4.2187	0.000	6.307	2.322	3.644
Exper.	-4.1423	0	7.945	2.612	3.170

It must be noted, first of all, that the entire set of data presented is in good agreement on the whole with experiment. The total energy agrees rather well with the experimental values, composed of the cohesive energy and the ionization energy. The latter is the sum of successive ionization potentials, three in the case of aluminum, for example. The pressure in all cases, in view of the way in which the potential was determined, is equal to zero for the lattice constants given above. It is interesting that the $T=0$ equation of state obtained, $P=P(\Omega)$, for fixed values of the potentials gave very good agreement with experiment for a wide range of pressures (Brovman et al. 1969b, 1970, 1971a).

As an example, the equation of state for Mg is presented in fig. 28 (Brovman et al. 1971). We note the significant point that for a noncubic metal it is necessary to determine a new value of c/a for each new value of Ω_0, according to the condition (143). Experimental results due to Drickamer (1965) are also included in this figure. The reasonable values obtained for the elastic moduli is very remarkable. The fact of the matter is that often a theory which describes the phonon spectrum quite well turns out to be completely unsuitable for obtaining the elastic moduli, and vice versa. This was known in the case of aluminum, for example (Wallace 1969, 1970).

Of course one of the reasons for difficulties is always an insufficiently flexible form of the model potential. Even for the case of Na, using the same model potential (145) it is possible to improve significantly the description of the elastic moduli, if it is not desired to describe the short-wavelength phonons well. As an example, in table 10, are presented results of calculations of the elastic moduli of Na, if the second parameter in the potential is ob-

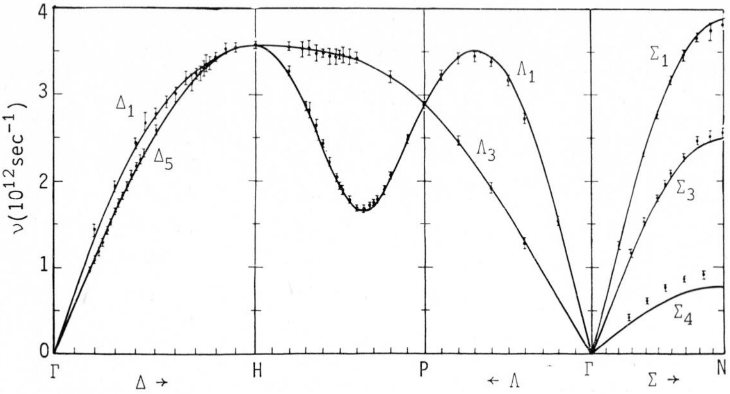

Fig. 25. Phonon dispersion curves in Na.

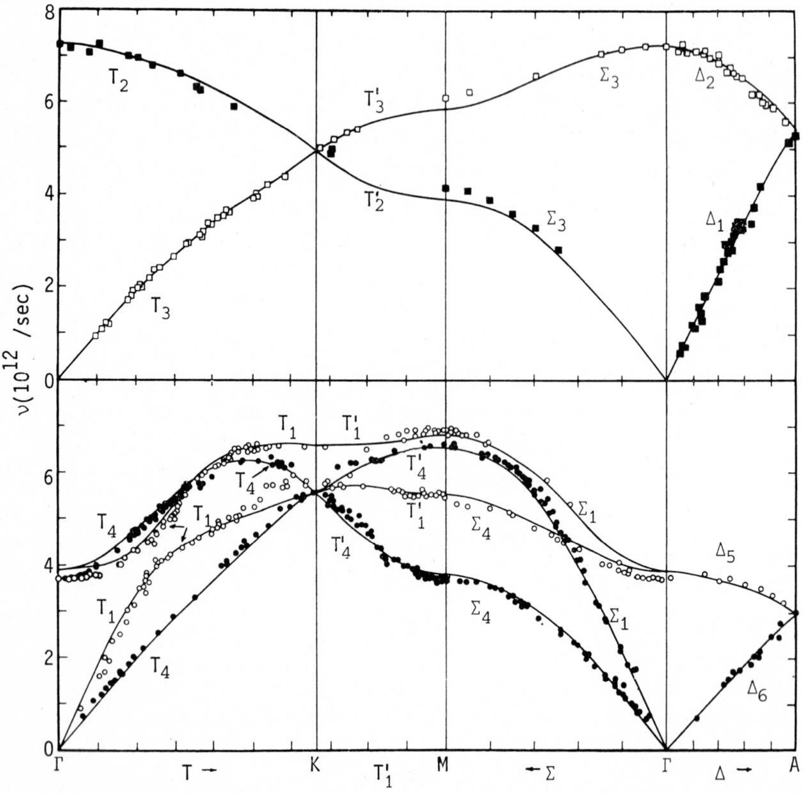

Fig. 26. Phonon dispersion curves in Mg.

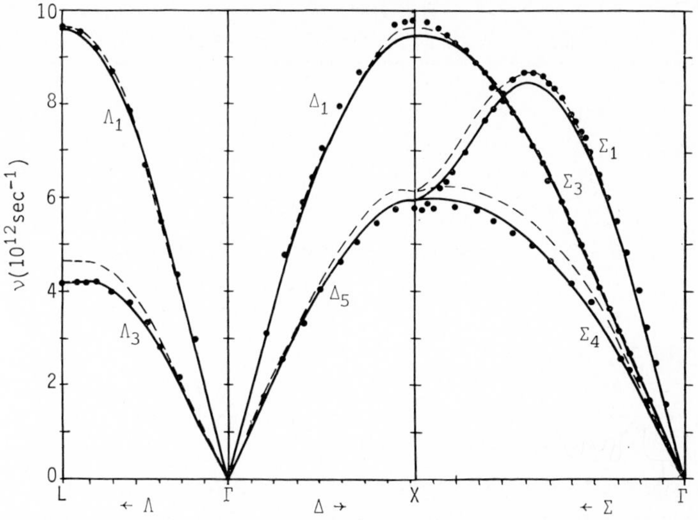

Fig. 27. Phonon dispersion curves in Al. (Dotted line --- without $D_{(3)}$.)

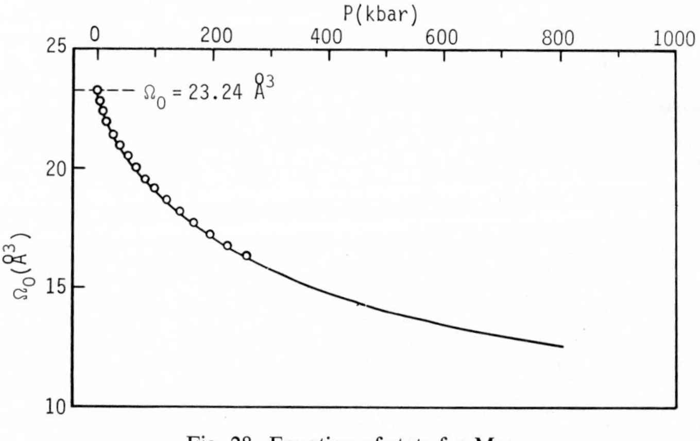

Fig. 28. Equation of state for Mg.

tained from the condition of the best description of the moduli ($q_0/2k_F=0.9$, $r_0/a_B=1.06$, $\xi=0.03$). Another reason can be the influence of terms of higher than third order in the expansion in powers of the potential, as well as the deformation of the Fermi surface in the vicinity of the Brillouin zone boundaries, particularly in the presence of so strong a cancellation between the electronic and ionic contributions as is the case for several of the moduli in Mg and Al.

TABLE 10

(Energy in Ry/atom; elastic moduli in 10^{11} dyne/cm^2).

Na*	E	P	B	B_{33}	B_{44}
$E^{(0)}$	−0.1627	0.042	0.260	–	–
$E^{(1)}$	0.1648	0.953	1.905	–	–
$E^{(2)}$	−0.0124	−0.137	−0.268	0.009	0.132
$E^{(3)}$	0.0021	0.020	0.027	−0.009	−0.037
E_i	0.4558	−0.878	−1.171	0.072	0.537
E	−0.4640	0.000	0.753	0.072	0.632
Exper.	−0.4593 ±0.0015	0	0.763 ±0.014	0.073 ±0.002	0.622 ±0.015

The phonon dispersion curves depicted in figs. 25–27 demonstrate the very good agreement with experiment. (The upper figure for Mg describes the vibrations polarized along the c axis.) We remind the reader in this regard that for all three metals only one of the potential parameters was obtained from experimental phonon data. We note further that the choice of the function $G_{TW}(q)$ in the expression (108) for $\pi(q)$ turned out to be essential for a correct description of the forms of the dispersion curves in Na and Al, at the same time that, for example, the agreement with experiment turned out to be worse when the function G_{HGV} was used.

We turn now to a quantitative discussion of the role of the third order terms in the pseudopotential, and accordingly to a discussion of the non-pairwise nature of the interaction between ions in the metals studied. It may be hoped that due to the good agreement of the final results with experiment the following analysis will yield a reasonable estimate of these contributions. We will discuss, first of all, the long wavelength aspect of the problem. As was shown in subsection 2.5, due to the different nature of the expansions in powers of the pseudopotential in the static and dynamic problems, in the long wavelength limit for phonons it is essential always to take into account terms of higher order than for the static lattice (by two orders). Only in this way do the compressibilities obtained from both approaches coincide. It is of interest to give a quantitative estimate of the importance of these additional terms, connected with the specific non-pairwise nature of the interactions in a metal. In table 11 we present data for the compressibility obtained from the static approach, including terms of second order in the potential (E_{2st}), and terms of third order (E_{3st}), as

TABLE 11
(Moduli in 10^{11} dyne/cm²).

	Na*	Al	Al(W)
E_{2st}	0.726	4.758	1.576
E_{2dyn}	1.023	6.367	5.464
E_{3st}	0.753	6.307	7.159
E_{3dyn}	0.944	6.943	6.660

well as from the dynamic approach, including $D_{(2)}$ (E_{2dyn}) and $D_{(3)}$ (E_{3dyn}).

It is seen that the difference everywhere is very significant, and in the 'usual' approximation the dynamic approach yields a value which is not less than 50% too high, while in certain cases the error can become catastrophic, for example for the moduli of Wallace (1969, 1970), values of which calculated by us are given in the last column of table 11. In a higher approximation the difference between E_{3st} and E_{3dyn} decreases.

TABLE 12
(Moduli in 10^{11} dyne/cm²).

	$(C_{12}-C_{44})/C_{44}$	$C_{12}-C_{44}$	$(C_{12}-C_{44})_0$	$(C_{12}-C_{44})_{\mathbf{K}\neq 0}$
Na*	14.5%	0.073	0.176	−0.103
Al	32%	1.176	0.250	0.926

Another interesting estimate of the extent to which the interionic forces are non-pairwise can be obtained by investigating the breakdown of the Cauchy relations in the cubic metals Na and Al (see subsection 2.6). In table 12 data corresponding to the results obtained in subsection 2.6 are presented. It is seen that the breakdown of the Cauchy relations arising from the presence of the electron liquid itself [$(C_{12}-C_{44})_0$] [see eq. (81)] is of the same order of magnitude as the effect of the non-pairwise nature of the interionic interaction [$(C_{12}-C_{44})_{\mathbf{K}\neq 0}$]. The latter term plays a significantly large role in Al, which is connected with the general increase in the effect of the Umklapp processes.

In tables 7–10 complete information regarding the contributions of the terms of third order in the pseudopotential ($V_{\mathbf{K}}/\mathscr{E}_{\mathrm{F}}$) to the properties of the static lattice (obtained using the method of homogeneous deformation) is presented. It is seen that their role increases in going from the energy to the pressure and the moduli, and that for several of the elastic moduli the contributions from $E^{(3)}$ are already of the same magnitude as the final answer itself. The third order terms are relatively weak in Na, for the obvious reason that $V_{\mathbf{K}}/\mathscr{E}_{\mathrm{F}}$ is small. But even in Na they can be important in specific cases. For example, it is known (see table 7) that the modulus B_{33} is very well described by the ionic lattice; while the inclusion of $E^{(2)}$ only worsens the agreement significantly, so that its departure from the experimental value can be as large as 20% (Coulthard 1970) or even 50% (Pick 1967). An analogous situation is observed in table 7 as well, where the role of $E^{(3)}$ is small However, the potential which yields the best description of the moduli corresponds to the case that the contributions from $E^{(2)}$ and $E^{(3)}$ to B_{33} are of the same order, and then the agreement with experiment is restored (see table 10). On the whole, it can be said that due to the significant cancellation occurring between the terms E_{i} and $E^{(2)}$, the contribution of $E^{(3)}$ to the elastic moduli turns out to be very significant.

We investigate now the magnitude of the third order contribution $D_{(3)}$ to the total dynamical matrix. For this purpose we present in tables 13–15 the contributions of the ionic lattice $D_{(i)}$, of the terms through second order in the pseudopotential $D_{\mathrm{i}}+D_{(2)}$, and of the terms through third order, $D_{\mathrm{i}}+D_{(2)}+D_{(3)}$, to the squares of the characteristic phonon frequencies at the boundaries of the Brillouin zone (it is the squares of the frequencies that are additive). It is seen that the contributions arising from $D_{(3)}$ are comparatively small for Na and Al, but in certain cases give up to 7–20% of the total (for example, in the case of the low lying transverse branch L_3 in Al). In Mg their role on the whole is significantly larger and, due to the significant cancellation between D_{i} and $D_{(2)}$, can contribute ~40% of the total for certain branches.

TABLE 13

(Squared frequencies for Na, given in units of the plasma frequency).

$(\omega/\omega_0)^2$	H_{15}	N_1	N_4	N_3
D_{i}	0.3333	0.8624	0.0173	0.1203
$D_{\mathrm{i}}+D_{(2)}$	0.2530	0.3015	0.0125	0.1243
$D_{\mathrm{i}}+D_{(2)}+D_{(3)}$	0.2485	0.2955	0.0120	0.1227

TABLE 14

(Squared frequencies for Mg, given in units of the plasma frequency).

	Γ		A		M					
$(\omega/\omega_0)^2$	Γ_3^+	Γ_5^+	A_1	A_3	M_4^-	M_3^+	M_1^+	M_2^-	M_3^-	M_4^+
D_i	0.9061	0.0469	0.9536	0.0232	0.3140	0.1188	0.8368	0.5237	0.1622	0.0443
$D_i + D_{(2)}$	0.2386	0.0641	0.1356	0.0375	0.1679	0.0704	0.2131	0.2056	0.1378	0.0642
$D_i + D_{(2)} + D_{(3)}$	0.1686	0.0480	0.0920	0.0268	0.1085	0.0477	0.1466	0.1344	0.0958	0.0462
D_p	0.1063	0.0538	0.0646	0.0323	0.0846	0.0350	0.0907	0.1011	0.0864	0.0541

TABLE 15

(Squared frequencies for Al, given in units of the plasma frequency).

$(\omega/\omega_0)^2$	L_1	L_3	X_1	X_5
D_i	0.909	0.046	0.678	0.161
$D_i + D_{(2)}$	0.103	0.024	0.102	0.042
$D_i + D_{(2)} + D_{(3)}$	0.102	0.020	0.100	0.039

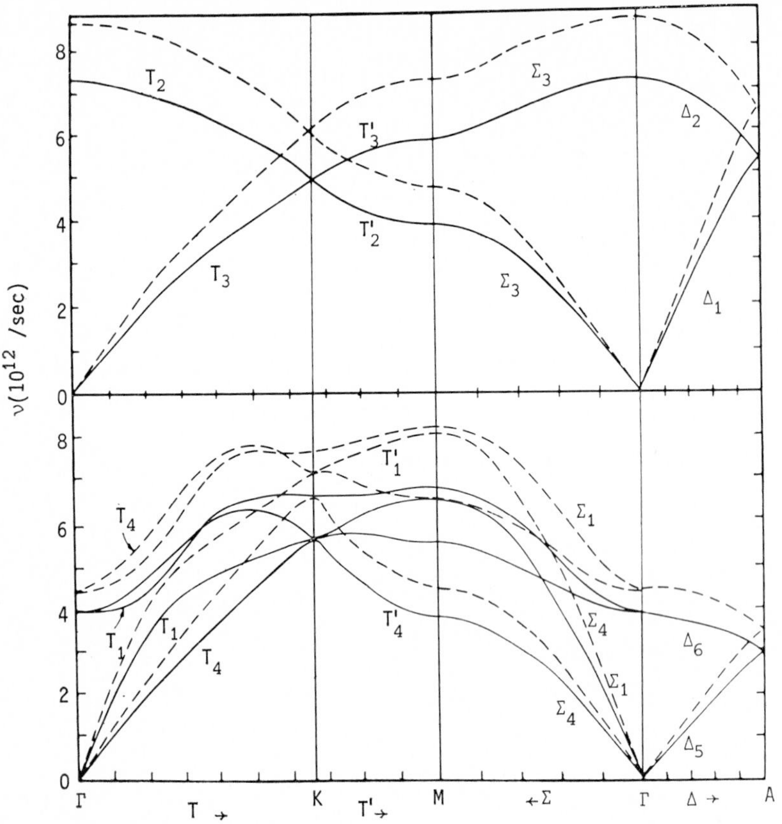

Fig. 29. Phonon dispersion curves for Mg. (Dotted line --- without $D_{(3)}$.)

In fig. 29 this contribution can be seen for all of the dispersion curves in Mg (the solid line gives the results computed on the basis of $D_{\mathrm{i}}+D_{(2)}+D_{(3)}$, the dotted line gives the results computed on the basis of $D_{\mathrm{i}}+D_{(2)}$ only). It is interesting to observe how the splitting of the frequencies at the point 'K', which is symmetric on the basis of $D_{\mathrm{i}}+D_{(2)}$, becomes asymmetric on the inclusion of $D_{(3)}$, which is a direct manifestation of the existence of non-pairwise forces (see subsection 3.1). The experimental results clearly show the asymmetry of this splitting. The analogous curve (without $D_{(3)}$) in Al is given by the dotted line in fig. 27.

On the last line of table 14 for Mg are also given the frequencies corresponding to the "pairwise" approximation, i.e., including in addition to the contribution from $D_{(2)}$ the pairwise interaction term from $D_{(3)}$ (see subsection 2.9). Comparing these values with the total result (obtained from

$D_{\mathrm{i}} + D_{(2)} + D_{(3)}$) we see that the scale of the non-pairwise contribution turns out to be very large. However, the poor convergence of the series giving the pairwise forces should be kept in mind (subsection 2.9), and the corresponding figures have only a qualitative significance.

A very striking example of the influence of many-particle forces on the dynamics of a metal lattice is provided by quadrivalent tin (β-Sn). It crystallizes in a strongly anisotropic tetragonal lattice with two atoms in a primitive unit cell. The origin of the large value of c/a is clear from fig. 12, and is connected with the dominating contribution to the dependence of E on c/a from the ionic lattice. However, the ionic lattice of tin, as is seen from fig. 18, turns out to be unstable with respect to other kinds of deformations (Brovman and Kagan 1967), and the determining role in stabilizing it is played, consequently, by the conduction electrons. The term $D_{(2)}$ proves to be insufficiently strong for this purpose, so that one can expect that an essential role is played by the non-pairwise forces. A direct calculation of $D_{(3)}$ confirms this expectation. In fig. 30 are presented the phonon dispersion curves along the [001] direction, for which the transverse acoustic branch of the ionic lattice is unstable. The potential (145) was used in these calculations with the following choice of parameters: $q_0/2k_{\mathrm{F}} = 0.83$, $r_0 = 0.9125$ Å, $\xi = 0.03$,

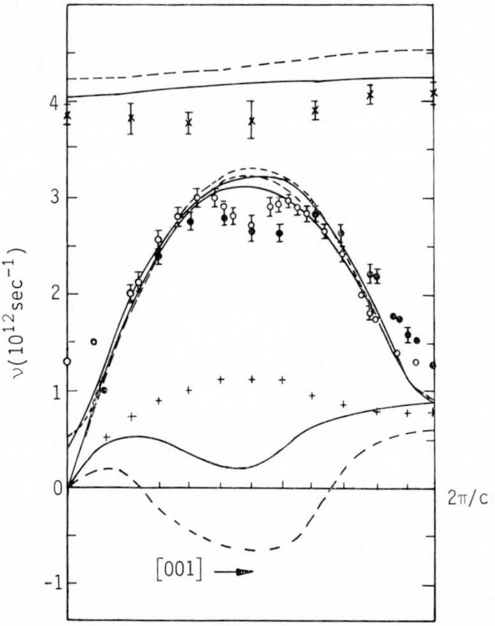

Fig. 30. An example of phonon dispersion curves for β-Sn.

and $G_{TW}(q)$ was used for the function $G(q)$ in the polarization operator $\pi(q)$. This potential reproduces well the characteristic frequencies of the majority of the vibration branches. It is seen from these results that the low-lying branch remains unstable in the approximation of retaining only D_i and $D_{(2)}$, but becomes stable on the inclusion of $D_{(3)}$. This branch as a whole turns out to be extremely sensitive to the contribution $D_{(3)}$, for a specific reason connected with the diatomic nature of the lattice and its anisotropy. The terms of higher order play a determining role in the formation of the frequency $\omega_{x,y}^2(\mathbf{0})$ as well, which for any reasonable choice of the potential in the approximation of retaining only D_i and $D_{(2)}$ always lies significantly below the experimental value. The inclusion of $D_{(3)}$ can give the required magnitude of this frequency (Brovman and Solt 1970). The situation here in some sense is reminiscent of the role of covalency in the formation of a gap in dielectrics, where the second approximation cannot give a correct description in a number of cases (Heine and Jones 1969).

On the whole, with regard to the dynamics of tin it can be said that if the high-frequency region of the vibration spectrum can be described adequately within the framework of that simple approach, the low-lying vibrations require a more complicated analysis, and that it is possible that even the succeeding terms of the expansion are required for their determination.

In the work referred to above (Brovman and Kagan 1967) a phenomenological approach to the description of the many-ion indirect interaction was proposed, which consists of approximating it by a non-pairwise interaction in direct space between an ion and its neighbors in the nearest coordination

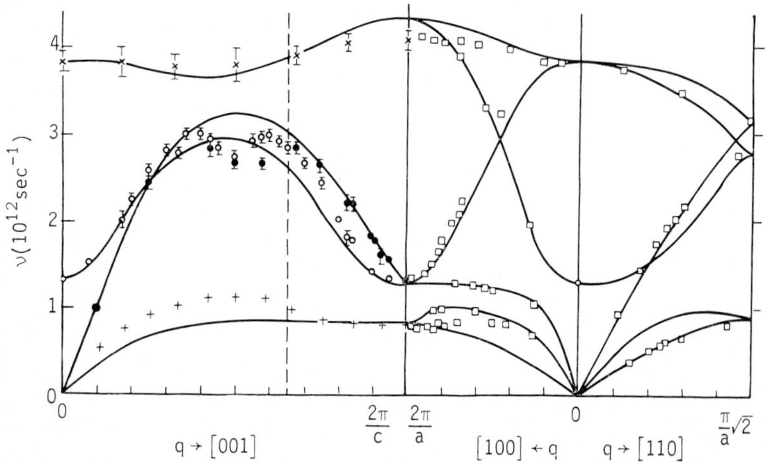

Fig. 31. Phonon dispersion curves for β-Sn.

sphere. Three parameters, describing this interaction completely, were obtained within the framework of the inverse problem together with the two parameters of the model potential. The results of the calculations, and the experimental data, are presented in fig. 31. Bearing in mind the very complicated nature of the spectrum, the agreement between theory and experiment must be regarded as completely reasonable.

Thus, the results of calculations for a number of metals presented in this section clearly demonstrate that fact that the scheme adopted for the description of a non-transition metal, even on the basis of an exceedingly simple method for determining the electron–ion interaction, leads to a completely adequate quantitative description of a large number of properties characterizing a metal.

References

ABARENKOV, I.V. and Heine V. (1965), Phil Mag. **12**, 529.

ABRIKOSOV, A.A., GORKOV, L.P., DZYALOSHINSKI, I.E. (1963), *Methods of quantum field theory in statistical physics* (Prentice Hall, Englewood Cliffs, N.J.).

AFANAS'EV, A.M. and KAGAN, YU.M. (1963), Soviet Physics–JETP, **16**, 1030.

ANIMALU, A.O.E. and Heine V. (1965), Phil. Mag. **12**, 1249.

ANIMALU, A.O.E. 1965), Phil. Mag. **11**, 379.

ANIMALU, A.O.E. (1966), Proc. Roy. Soc. **A294**, 376.

ANIMALU, A.O.E., BONSIGNORI, F. and BORTOLANI, V. (1966), Nuovo Cimento **44B**, 159.

ASHCROFT, N.W. (1963), Phil. Mag. **8**, 2055.

ASHCROFT, N.W. (1966), Phys. Lett. **23**, 48.

ASHCROFT, N.W. (1968), J. Phys. C **1**, 232.

ASHCROFT, N.W. and LANGRETH, D.E. (1966), Phys. Rev. **155**, 682.

BALLENTINE, L.E. and GUPTA, O.P. (1971), Canad. J. Phys. **49**, 1549.

BARDEEN, J. (1937), Phys. Rev. **52**, 688.

BARDEEN, J. and PINES, D. (1955), Phys. Rev. **99**, 1140.

BARRETT, C.S. (1965), Acta Cryst. **9**, 671.

BAYM, G. (1961), Ann. Phys. **14**, 1.

BENCKERT, S. (1971), Phys. Stat. Sol. **43**, 681.

BERNARDES, N. and SVENSSON, C.A. (1963), *Solids under Pressure*, ed. PAUL, W., (Warshauer, New York).

BLANK, A.Ya. and KANER, E.A. (1966), Soviet Physics–JETP **23**, 673.

BOM, D. and STAVER, T. (1950), Phys. Rev. **84**, 836.

BORN, M. and HUANG, K. (1954), *Dynamical theory of crystal lattices* (Oxford Univ. Press, London and New York).

BORTOLANI, V. and OTTAVIANI, P. (1969), Nuovo Cim. **62B**, 379.

BORTOLANI, V. and PIZZICHINI, G. (1969), Phys. Rev. Lett. **22**, 840.

BROCKHOUSE, B.N., RAO, K.R. and WOODS, A.D.B. (1961) Phys. Rev. Lett. **7**, 93.

BROCKHOUSE, B.N., ARASE, T., CAGLIOTI, C., RAO, K.R. and WOODS, A.D.B. (1962), Phys. Rev. **128**, 1099.

BROVMAN, E.G. and KAGAN, YU. (1966), Soviet Physic–Solid State **8**, 1120.

BROVMAN, E.G. and KAGAN, YU. (1967), Soviet Physics–JETP **25**, 365.
BROVMAN, E.G. and KAGAN, YU. (1969), Zh. Exp. Teor. Fys. **57**, 1329 [(1970) Soviet Physics–JETP **30**, 721].
BROVMAN, E.G. and KAGAN, YU. (1972), Zh. Exp. Teor. Fys. **63**, 1937.
BROVMAN, E.G. and KAGAN, YU. (1973), Zh. Exp. Teor. Fys. (to appear).
BROVMAN, E.G., KAGAN, YU. and HOLAS, A. (1968), *Neutron inelastic scattering*, Vol. 1 (IAEA, Vienna) p. 165.
BROVMAN, E.G., KAGAN, Yu. and HOLAS, A. (1969a), Zh. Exp. Teor. Fys. **57**, 1635 [Soviet Physics–JETP **30**, 883 (1970)].
BROVMAN, E.G., KAGAN, YU. and HOLAS, A. (1969b), JETP Letters **10**, 30.
BROVMAN, E.G., KAGAN, YU. and HOLAS, A. (1969c), The Second Solid State Theory Conference (Moscow) Thesis, **I-20**, 14.
BROVMAN, E.G., KAGAN, YU. and HOLAS, A. (1970), Sov. Phys.-Sol. St. **12**, 786.
BROVMAN, E.G., KAGAN, YU. and HOLAS, A. (1971a), Zh. Exp. Teor. Fys. **61**, 737.
BROVMAN, E.G., KAGAN, YU. and HOLAS, A. (1971b), Zh. Exp. Teor. Fys. **61**, 2429.
BROVMAN, E.G., KAGAN, YU. and HOLAS, A. (1972a), Zh. Exp. Teor. Fys. **62**, 1492.
BROVMAN, E.G., SOLT, G. (1970), Solid State Commun. **8**, 903.
BROVMAN, E.G., HOLAS, A., PUSHKAREV, V.V. (1973), Zh. Exp. Teor. Fys. (in press).
COCHRAN, W. (1965), *Neutron inelastic scattering*, Vol. 1 (IAEA Vienna) p. 3.
COHEN, M.L. and HEINE, V. (1970), Solid State Phys., Vol. 24, ed. by H. Ehrenreich, F. Seitz and D. Turnbull (Academic Press, New York) p. 37.
Coulthard, M. (1970), J. Phys. C **3**, 820.
Cousins, C.S.G. (1970), J. Phys. C **3**, 1677.
COWLEY, R.A., WOODS, A.D.B. and DOLLING, G. (1966), Phys. Rev. **150**, 487.
CHESTER, G.V. (1961), Adv. Phys. **10**, 357.
DRICKAMER, H.G. (1965), Solid State Physics Vol. 17, ed. by F. Seitz and D. Turnbull (Academic Press, New York), p. 1.
ELIASHBERG, G.M. (1973), Soviet Physics–JETP **16**, 780.
ENGLESBERG, S. and SCHRIEFFER, J.R. (1963), Phys. Rev. **131**, 993.
FEHLNER, W.R. (1971), Ph.D. Thesis, U. of Illinois (unpublished).
FIGGINS, B.F., JONES, G.O. and RILEY, D.P. (1956), Phil. Mag. **1**, 747.
FLOYD, E.R., KLEINMAN, L. (1970), Phys. Rev. B **2**, 3947.
FRIEDEL, J. (1958), Nuovo Cimento (Suppl.) **7**, 287.
FUCHS, K. (1936), Proc. Roy, Soc. London **A157**, 444.
GELDART, D.J.W. and VOSKO, S.H. (1966), Canad. J. Phys. **44**, 2137.
GELDART, D.J.W. and TAYLOR, R. (1970a), Canad. J. Phys. **48**, 155.
GELDART, D.J.W. and TAYLOR, R. (1970b), Canad. J. Phys. **48**, 167.
GELDART, D.J.W. and TAYLOR, R. (1971), Solid St. Commun. **9**, 7.
GELDART, D.J.W., TAYLOR, R. and VARSHNI, Y.P. (1970), Canad. J. Phys. **48**, 183.
GILAT, G., RIZZI, G. and CUBBIOTTI, G. (1969), Phys. Rev. **185**, 971.
GUPTA, H.C., TRIPATHI, B.B. (1971), Phys. Stat. Sol. B **45**, 537.
HARRISON, W. (1966), *Pseudopotentials in the theory of metals* (Benjamin, New York).
HEDIN, L. and LUNDQUIST, B.I. (1971), J. Phys. C **4**, 2064.
HEINE, V. (1970), Solid State Physics Vol. 24, ed. by H. Ehrenreich, F. Seitz and D. Turnbull (Academic Press, New York), p. 1.
HEINE, V. and ABARENKOV, I.V. (1964), Phil. Mag. **9**, 451.
HEINE, V. and JONES, R.O. (1969), J. Phys. C **2**, 719.

HEINE, V. and WEAIRE, D. (1966), Phys. Rev. **152**, 603.

HEINE, V. and WEAIRE, D. (1970), Solid State Physics Vol. 24, ed. by H. Ehrenreich, F. Seitz and D. Turnbull (Academic Press, New York) p. 249.

HO, P.S. and RUOFF, A.L. (1968), J. Phys. Chem. Sol. **29**, 2101.

HOHENBERG, P. and KOHN, W. (1964), Phys. Rev. **136B**, 864.

HUBBARD, J. (1957), Proc. Roy. Soc. **A243**, 336.

JOSHI, S.K. and RAJAGOPAL, A.K. (1968), Solid State Physics Vol. 22, ed. by F. Seitz, D. Turnbull and H. Ehrenreich (Academic Press, New York) p. 259.

JOHNSON, R. (1970), Kongl. Dansk. Vid. Selsk. Mat. Phys. **37**, 9.

KAGAN, YU.M. and BROVMAN, E.G. (1968), *Neutron inelastic scattering* (IAEA, Vienna), **1**, 3.

KAMM, G.N. and ALERS, G. (1964), J. Appl. Phys. **35**, 327.

KIMBALL, J.C., STARK, R.W. and MUELLER, F. M. (1967), Phys. Rev. 1**62**, 600.

KING, W.F. and CUTLER, P.H. (1970), Phys. Rev. **B2**, 1733.

KING, W.F. and CUTLER, P.H. (1971), Phys. Rev. **B3**, 2485.

KLEINMAN, L. (1967), Phys. Rev. **160**, 585.

KLEINMAN, L. (1968), Phys. Rev. **173**, 383.

KOPPEL, J.U., MARADUDIN, A.A. (1967), Phys. Lett. **24A**, 224.

KOPPEL, J.U. (1968), Ph.D. Thesis, U. of California, San Diego (unpublished).

KOHN, W. (1959), Phys. Rev. Lett. **2**, 393.

KOHN, W. and LUTTINGER, J.M. (1960), Phys. Rev. **118**, 41.

KOHN, W. and SHAM, L.J. (1965), Phys. Rev. **140A**, 1133.

KRASKO, G.L. and GURSKI, Z.A. (1971), Soviet Phys. Sol. St. **13**, 2463.

LANDAU, L. (1956), Soviet Physics–JETP **3**, 920.

LANDAU, L. (1959), Nuclear Phys. **13**, 181.

LANGRETH, D. (1969), Phys. Rev. **181**, 753.

LEE, M.J.G. (1966), Proc. Roy. Soc. A **295**, 440.

LLOYD, P. and SHOLL, C.A. (1968), J. Phys. C **1**, 1620.

LUTTINGER, J.M. and WARD, J.C. (1960), Phys. Rev. **118**, 1417.

LINDHART, J. (1954), Kgl. Danske Videnskab, Selskab, Mat-fys. Medd. **28**, 8.

MIGDAL, A.B. (1957), Soviet Physics-JETP **5**, 333.

MIGDAL, A.B. (1958), Soviet Physics–JETP **7**, 996.

MARADUDIN, A.A., MONTROLL, E.Q., WEISS, G.H. and IPATOVA, I.P. (1971) *Theory of lattice dynamics in the harmonic approximation* (Academic Press, New York).

MARADUDIN, A.A. and VOSKO, S. H. (1968), Rev. Mod. Phys. **40**, 1.

PEARSON, H.B. (1958), *Handbook of lattice spacings and structure of metals and alloys* (Pergamon Press, New York).

PETHICK, C.J. (1970), Phys. Rev. **B2**, 1789.

PHILLIPS, J.C. and KLEINMAN, L. (1959), Phys. Rev. **116**, 287.

PICK, R.M. (1967), J. Phys. (France) **28**, 539.

PICK, R.M., COHEN, M.H. and MARTIN, R.M. (1970), Phys. Rev. **B1**, 910.

PINES, D. and NOZIERES, P. (1966), *The theory of quantum liquids* (Benjamin, New York).

PINDOR, A., PYNN, R. (1969), J. Phys. C **2**, 1037.

PRAKASH, S., JOSHI, S.K. (1969), Phys. Rev. **187**, 808.

PRAKASH, S., JOSHI, S.I. (1970), Phys. Rev. **B1**, 1468.

PRANGE, R.E., SACHS, A. (1967), Phys. Rev. **158**, 672.

PRICE, D.L. (1967), Proc. Roy. Soc. **300**, 25.

PRICE, D.L., SINGWI, K.S. and TOSI, M.P. (1970), Phys. Rev. **2**, 2983.

PROKOFIEV, V. (1929), Z. Phys. **58**, 255.
ROY, A.P. and VENKATARAMAN, G. (1967), Phys. Rev. **156**, 769.
ROWE, J.M. (1967), Phys. Rev. **163**, 547.
SANDSTRÖM, R. (1970), Preprint S-10044 Stockholm (unpublished).
SCHRIEFFER, J.E. (1964), *Theory of superconductivity* (W.A. Benjamin, Inc., New York).
SAHNI, V.C. and VENKATARAMAN, G. (1969), Phys. Rev. **185**, 1062.
SCHMUCK, PH. and QUITNER, G. (1968), Phys. Lett. **28A**, 228.
SCHMUCK, PH. (1971), Z. Phys. **248**, 111.
SCHMUNK, R.E. (1966), Phys. Rev. **149**, 450.
SCHNEIDER, T. and STOLL, E. (1966), Phys. Kond. Mat. **5**, 331.
SCHNEIDER, T. and STOLL, E. (1968), *Neutron inelastic scattering* (IAEA, Vienna), **1**, 101.
SHAM, L.J. and ZIMAN, J.M. (1963), Solid State Phys. Vol. 15, ed. by F. Seitz and D. Turnbull (Academic Press, New York) p. 221.
SHAM, L.J. (1965), Proc. Roy. Soc. A **283**, 33.
SHAM, L.J. (1969), Phys. Rev. **188**, 1431.
SHAW, R.W. (1968), Phys. Rev. **174**, 769.
SHAW, R.W. (1969a), J. Phys. C **2**, 2350.
SHAW, R.W. (1969b), J. Phys. C **2**, 2335 (1969).
SHAW, R.W. (1970), J. Phys. C **3**, 1140.
SHAW, R.W. and HARRISON, W.A. (1967), Phys. Rev. **163**, 604.
SHAW, R.W. and PYNN, R. (1969), J. Phys. C **2**, 2071.
SHAW, R.W. and SMITH, N.V. (1969), Phys. Rev. **178**, 985.
SINGWI, K.S., TOSI, M.P., LAND, R.H. and SJOLANDER, A. (1968), Phys. Rev. **176**, 589.
SINGWI, K.S., SJOLANDER, A., TOSI, M.P. and LAND, R.H. (1970), Phys. Rev. **B1**, 1044.
SLUTSKY, I.J. and GARLAND, G.W. (1957), Phys. Rev. **107**, 972.
SOLT, G. (1969), Acta Phys. Hung. **26**, 261.
STARK, R.W. and FALICOV, L.M. (1967), Phys. Rev. Lett. **19**, 795.
STEDMAN, R. and NILSSON, G. (1966), Phys. Rev. **145**, 492.
STEDMAN, R., ALMQUIST, L., NILSSON, G. and RAUNIO, G. (1967), Phys. Rev. **162**, 545.
SUZUKI, T., GRANATO, A.V. and THOMAS, J.F. (1968), Phys. Rev. **175**, 766.
SUZUKI, T. (1971), Phys. Rev. **B3**, 4007.
TOYA, T. (1958), J. Res. Inst. Catal. Hokkaido Univ. **6**, 161, 183.
TOIGO, F. and WOODRUFF, T. O. (1970), Phys. Rev. **B2**, 3958.
TOIGO, F. and WOODRUFF, T.O. (1971), Phys. Rev. **4**, 4312.
TYABLIKOV, S.V., TOLMACHEV, V.V. (1958), Soviet Physics–JETP **7**, 867.
VOSKO, S.H. (1964), Phys. Lett. **13**, 97.
VOSKO, S.H., Taylor, R., KEECH, G.H. (1965), Canad. J. Phys. **43**, 1187.
WALLACE, D.C. (1968), Phys. Rev. **176**, 832.
WALLACE, D.C. (1969a), Phys. Rev. **182**, 778.
WALLACE, D.C. (1969b), Phys. Rev. **187**, 991.
WALLACE, D.C. (1970), Phys. Rev. **1B**, 3963.
WEYMOUTH, J.W. and STEDMAN, R. (1970), Phys. Rev. **B2**, 4743.
WILLIAMS, A.R. and WEAIRE, D. (1970), J. Phys. C. **3**, 386.
WOODS, A.D.B., BROCKHOUSE, B.N., MARCH, R.H., STEWART, A.T. and BOWERS, R. (1962), Phys. Rev. **128**, 1112.
YAMAMOTO, T. (1970), J. Phys. Soc. Jap. **28**, 938.

CHAPTER 5

Theory of Lattice Dynamics of Covalent Crystals

L.J. SHAM

Dept. of Physics, University of California
San Diego, La Jolla, California 92037
USA

Dynamical Properties of Solids, edited by
G. K. Horton and A. A. Maradudin

Contents

1. Introduction

In this chapter, we wish to examine the theory of lattice dynamics in covalent crystals by concentrating on one fundamental aspect, namely the electron dynamics in a lattice wave which contributes to the effective force between the ions, which in turn determines the frequency dispersion of the lattice vibration. We shall work unashamedly in the harmonic approximation, leaving the niceties of the anharmonic correction to Barron's chapter (chapter 7) in this book.

Let us concede at the outset that we do not yet have a first-principles calculation of the phonon spectrum in covalent crystals, on a par with some of the calculations which have been done for the simple metals (see chapter 4 by Kagan). The reason is obvious. The nearly free electron approximation works well for the simple metals but misses out on important effects in covalent crystals. However, the important works of Martin (1969) and of Sinha et al. (1971) on the lattice dynamics of covalent crystals put us at the stage where, I venture to predict, a first-principles calculation is imminent. Thus, it is important for us to know the story so far.

Section 2 is devoted to the microscopic theory of lattice dynamics, as developed independently by Pick et al. (1970) and by this author (Sham 1969b). We show formally what we need in the knowledge of the electron dynamics for lattice vibrations is contained in the electron density response. We introduce this and other concepts in many-electron physics and derive some approximations for the density response by simple, expedient and physical methods rather than by the systematic standard many-body theory. To be sure, to go beyond these approximations we must appeal to the many-body theory, but let us test what we have got for the covalent crystals first. In §2, we also examine the long-wavelength limit where the quirks of the covalent crystal are most evident and obtain several exact relations, i.e. sum rules. These are good pointers for departing from the nearly free electron approximation to seek more appropriate ones for the covalent crystal.

Phenomenological models have, of course, been used to account for the measured phonon spectra in covalent crystals. Fairly long-range interaction in homopolar crystals deduced from the Born–Von Kármán force constant model (Herman 1959) has been accounted for by the shell model, which has since been widely used in the analysis of the covalent crystals. In §3, a formal justification of the shell model shows a rather large amount of arbitrariness possible in defining the parameters. A survey is made of all shell model calculations for the covalent crystals. The physical picture of the covalent bonds being described by shells centered at the ions is not an appealing one.

The valence force field model, taken from the theory of molecular vibrations, does attempt to let the covalent bond play a central role. Especially encouraging is the fact that the values of parameters survive quite well transplantation from molecules to molecules and from molecules to solids. In §3, we describe this and related models. An intriguing model is the recent one proposed by Vasil'ev et al. (1971) which allows the component orbitals in a bond to bend relative to each other and which produces good fit with experiment with as few as four parameters.

Finally, in §4, we describe the works of Martin and of Sinha et al. which bring us to the frontier. We describe two possible routes for the take-off of first-principles calculations. The empirical pseudo-potential method is one where the computational problem appears to be under control. The other is formally a representation in Wannier functions and in practice will probably be a tight-binding approximation. Hopefully, both of these methods will be used fairly soon. They will complement each other.

2. *Microscopic formulation of lattice dynamics*

In this section, we shall describe the formal theory of lattice vibrations in terms of the interactions of the electrons and ions which make up the solid. Although, at first sight, the inclusion of the electrons appears to be a formidable many-body problem, we shall show that a few simple concepts are all that are necessary to describe the effects of the electrons. We shall examine the long-wavelength behavior of the phonon and describe several exact results, such as the so-called acoustic sum rules and the Lyddane–Sachs–Teller relation (Lyddane et al. 1941). A brief discussion is given on the validity of the adiabatic approximation.

2.1. The dynamical matrix

Ideally, we may regard the solid as made up of nuclei which oscillate about some regular equilibrium positions and of electrons which move around accordingly. In actual practice, we separate the electrons into two groups: core electrons which move rigidly with the nuclei and valence electrons whose motion has to be determined by the Schrödinger equation. We regard an ion as a single entity. The ion–ion interaction is taken to be Coulombic. The electron–ion potential is Coulombic outside the core region but may deviate from being Coulombic inside. We shall include in the electron–ion potential the effect of repulsion due to the fact that the valence electron wave function must be orthogonal to the core electron wave function, and thus, regard the valence electron–ion interaction potential as a pseudo-potential. For more details on the subject of pseudo-potentials, see the recent review articles by Heine (1970), and Cohen and Heine (1970). The Coulombic interaction between electrons will also be taken into account.

We confine our treatment to the harmonic approximation. It is straightforward to extend the general theory to include anharmonic terms. We shall use the adiabatic approximation (Born and Oppenheimer 1927) and relegate comments on its validity to §2.4.

Let the lattice vector be $\boldsymbol{x}_l$ and the equilibrium ion position be $\boldsymbol{x}_{l\kappa}=\boldsymbol{x}_l+\boldsymbol{x}_\kappa$. Let the charge of the $(l\kappa)$ ion be $Z_\kappa e$, e being the charge of a proton and the mass be M_κ. Let the small displacement from equilibrium be $\boldsymbol{u}_{l\kappa}$.

The force constants $\Phi_{\alpha\alpha'}(l\kappa, l'\kappa')$, where α, α' denote the cartesian axes, are defined as the coefficients of the total effective ion potential energy to second order in the displacements. We could construct the effective potential energy to include the effects of electrons and derive an expression for the force constant (see, for example, Sham 1969a). The following method is equivalent to this.

When $(l\kappa)$ and $(l'\kappa')$ do not denote the same ion, the force on the $(l\kappa)$ ion in the α-direction due to the displacement $u_{l'\kappa'\alpha'}$ of the $(l'\kappa')$ ion is

$$-\Phi_{\alpha\alpha'}(l\kappa, l'\kappa')\, u_{l'\kappa'\alpha'}. \tag{2.1}$$

The force consists of two parts. One is the direct ion–ion interaction, giving

$$-Z_\kappa Z_{\kappa'}\left[\partial^2 v(\boldsymbol{x}_{l\kappa}-\boldsymbol{x}_{l'\kappa'})/\partial x_{l\kappa\alpha}\partial x_{l'\kappa'\alpha'}\right] u_{l'\kappa'\alpha'}, \tag{2.2}$$

where $v(r)=e^2/r$ is the Coulomb potential. The other part is due to the mediation of the electrons

$$-\int \mathrm{d}\boldsymbol{r}\left[\partial v(\boldsymbol{r}-\boldsymbol{x}_{l\kappa};\kappa)/\partial x_{l\kappa\alpha}\right]\delta n_{l'\kappa'\alpha'}(\boldsymbol{r}), \tag{2.3}$$

where $v(\boldsymbol{r}-\boldsymbol{x}_{l\kappa};\kappa)$ is the electron–ion pseudo-potential and $\delta n_{l'\kappa'\alpha'}(\boldsymbol{r})$ is the change in the electron density due to the ionic displacement $u_{l'\kappa'\alpha'}$. The ionic displacement causes a change $[\partial v(\boldsymbol{r}-\boldsymbol{x}_{l'\kappa'};\kappa')/\partial \boldsymbol{x}_{l'\kappa'\alpha'}]\, u_{l'\kappa'\alpha'}$ in the electron–ion potential which in turn creates a change in electron density linear in the small change of potential. Thus,

$$\delta n_{l'\kappa'\alpha'}(\boldsymbol{r}) = \int \mathrm{d}\boldsymbol{r}' \chi(\boldsymbol{r}, \boldsymbol{r}')\, [\partial v(\boldsymbol{r}' - \boldsymbol{x}_{l'\kappa'}; \kappa')/\partial x_{l'\kappa'\alpha'}]\, u_{l'\kappa'\alpha'}, \tag{2.4}$$

where $\chi(\boldsymbol{r}, \boldsymbol{r}')$ is known as the static electron density response function, which we shall study more closely later. The use of the adiabatic approximation here consists in regarding the change of the electron–ion potential as a static change. Therefore, the force constant, when $(l\kappa) \neq (l'\kappa')$, is given by

$$\Phi_{\alpha\alpha'}(l\kappa, l'\kappa') = V_{\alpha\alpha'}(\boldsymbol{x}_{l\kappa}\kappa; \boldsymbol{x}_{l'\kappa'}\kappa'), \tag{2.5}$$

where

$$V_{\alpha\alpha'}(\boldsymbol{x}\kappa; \boldsymbol{x}\kappa') = \partial^2 V(\boldsymbol{x}\kappa; \boldsymbol{x}'\kappa')/\partial x_\alpha \partial x'_{\alpha'}, \tag{2.6}$$

and $V(\boldsymbol{x}\kappa;\boldsymbol{x}'\kappa')$ is the total effective ion–ion interaction including the contribution via the electrons, given by

$$V(\boldsymbol{x}\kappa;\boldsymbol{x}'\kappa') = Z_\kappa Z_{\kappa'} v(\boldsymbol{x} - \boldsymbol{x}') + \int \mathrm{d}\boldsymbol{r} \int \mathrm{d}\boldsymbol{r}' v(\boldsymbol{x} - \boldsymbol{r}; \kappa)\chi(\boldsymbol{r}, \boldsymbol{r}')\, v(\boldsymbol{r}' - \boldsymbol{x}'; \kappa'). \tag{2.7}$$

The force constant $\Phi_{\alpha\alpha'}(l\kappa, l\kappa)$ is the force per unit displacement on the ion $(l\kappa)$ in the α-direction due to all other ions when the $(l\kappa)$ ion alone is moved in the α'-direction. Thus, from above,

$$\Phi_{\alpha\alpha'}(l\kappa, l\kappa) = -\sum_{l'\kappa'} V_{\alpha\alpha'}(\boldsymbol{x}_{l\kappa}\kappa; \boldsymbol{x}_{l'\kappa'}\kappa'). \tag{2.8}$$

It is understood that, in the summation, $(l'\kappa')$ does not equal $(l\kappa)$. We obviously have the condition of infinitesimal translation invariance,

$$\sum_{l\kappa} \Phi_{\alpha\alpha'}(l\kappa, l'\kappa') = 0. \tag{2.9}$$

In this way, from quite simple considerations, we have obtained the expressions (2.5) and (2.8) for the force constants in terms of the interactions of the particles and the electron density response, which includes all the many-electron effects of relevance to the interatomic force. Whether this electron response is adequately portrayed becomes an important criterion for a phenomenological model or a first-principles calculation.

The normal modes of lattice vibration with wave vector $\boldsymbol{q}$ are determined by the dynamical matrix

$$\Phi_{\alpha\alpha'}(\boldsymbol{q}, \kappa\kappa') = (M_\kappa M_{\kappa'})^{-1/2} \sum_l \exp(-\mathrm{i}\boldsymbol{q}\cdot\boldsymbol{x}_l)\, \Phi_{\alpha\alpha'}(l\kappa, 0\kappa'). \tag{2.10}$$

For a derivation of this, see chapter 1 by Maradudin or Born and Huang (1954). In terms of the double Fourier transforms of the effective ion interaction, the dynamical matrix is (Sham 1969a, b, Pick et al. 1970)

$$\Phi_{\alpha\alpha'}(\boldsymbol{q}, \kappa\kappa') = (M_\kappa M_{\kappa'})^{-1/2}\, \Omega_0^{-1} \times \sum_{\boldsymbol{G}, \boldsymbol{G}'} \left[V_{\alpha\alpha'}(\boldsymbol{q}+\boldsymbol{G}\ \kappa; \boldsymbol{q}+\boldsymbol{G}'\ \kappa') - \delta_{\kappa\kappa'} \sum_{\kappa''} V_{\alpha\alpha'}(\boldsymbol{G}\ \kappa; \boldsymbol{G}'\ \kappa'')\right], \tag{2.11}$$

where

$$V_{\alpha\alpha'}(\boldsymbol{q}+\boldsymbol{G}\,\kappa; \boldsymbol{q}+\boldsymbol{G}'\,\kappa') = \exp[\mathrm{i}(\boldsymbol{q}+\boldsymbol{G})\cdot\boldsymbol{x}_\kappa]\,(\boldsymbol{q}+\boldsymbol{G})_\alpha \times V(\boldsymbol{q}+\boldsymbol{G}\,\kappa; \boldsymbol{q}+\boldsymbol{G}'\,\kappa')\,(\boldsymbol{q}+\boldsymbol{G}')_{\alpha'} \exp[-\mathrm{i}(\boldsymbol{q}+\boldsymbol{G}')\cdot\boldsymbol{x}_{\kappa'}]. \tag{2.12}$$

$\boldsymbol{G}$ and $\boldsymbol{G}'$ are the reciprocal lattice vectors and Ω_0 is the volume of the unit cell. The effective ion interaction is, from eq. (2.7),

$$V(\boldsymbol{q}+\boldsymbol{G}\,\kappa; \boldsymbol{q}+\boldsymbol{G}'\,\kappa') = Z_\kappa Z_{\kappa'} v(\boldsymbol{q}+\boldsymbol{G})\,\delta_{\boldsymbol{G},\boldsymbol{G}'} + v(\boldsymbol{q}+\boldsymbol{G};\kappa)\,\chi(\boldsymbol{q}+\boldsymbol{G}, \boldsymbol{q}+\boldsymbol{G}')\,v(\boldsymbol{q}+\boldsymbol{G}';\kappa'). \tag{2.13}$$

We have used the same symbols for the Fourier transforms of the quantities. The Fourier transform of the Coulomb potential is given by

$$v(q) = 4\pi e^2/q^2, \quad \text{if } q \neq 0, \qquad = 0, \quad \text{if } q = 0. \tag{2.14}$$

By defining the average of the interaction as zero, we take care of the neutrality of the whole system of ions and electrons.

2.2. The electron density response

The electron density response function plays such a central role in the microscopic theory of lattice dynamics that we shall study in some depth its properties in this subsection. First of all, we work out a formal expression for it in order to clarify the nature of this quantity.

By definition (2.4), when the crystal is perturbed by a small electric potential $\delta v(\boldsymbol{r})$, the change in the electron density distribution is

$$\delta n(\boldsymbol{r}) = \int \mathrm{d}\boldsymbol{r}'\, \chi(\boldsymbol{r}, \boldsymbol{r}')\, \delta v(\boldsymbol{r}). \tag{2.15}$$

Now the perturbation to the many-electron hamiltonian is $\int \mathrm{d}\boldsymbol{r}'\, n(\boldsymbol{r})\, \delta v(\boldsymbol{r})$ where $n(\boldsymbol{r})$ is the quantum-mechanical electron density operator. By the first order perturbation theory, we can calculate the change in the ground state wave function of our many-electron system and hence obtain a change in density, of the form (2.15), giving

$$\chi(\boldsymbol{r}, \boldsymbol{r}') = \sum_j \left[n_{0j}(\boldsymbol{r})\, n_{j0}(\boldsymbol{r}') + n_{0j}(\boldsymbol{r}')\, n_{j0}(\boldsymbol{r})\right]/(E_0 - E_j\ , \tag{2.16}$$

in terms of the matrix elements between the unperturbed many-electron ground state and the unperturbed excited states j with energies E_0 and E_j respectively.

If the applied electric potential is time varying, the perturbation theory will give a more general expression for the time dependent response function (Kubo 1956), from which we may obtain Kramers–Kronig relations and the fluctuation-dissipation theorem (see, for example, Pines and Noziéres 1966).

The response function is given in terms of the electronic states of the unperturbed crystal and, hence, the translational symmetry of the crystal ensures that

$$\chi(\boldsymbol{r} + \boldsymbol{x}_l, \boldsymbol{r}' + \boldsymbol{x}_l) = \chi(\boldsymbol{r}, \boldsymbol{r}'). \tag{2.17}$$

The Fourier transform $\chi(\boldsymbol{q}, \boldsymbol{q}')$ is non-zero only if $\boldsymbol{q}$ and $\boldsymbol{q}'$ differ by a reciprocal lattice vector, a property which we have already used in obtaining eq. (2.11).

The total electric potential induced by the applied potential $\delta v(\boldsymbol{r})$ is

$$\delta\varphi(\boldsymbol{r}) = \delta v(\boldsymbol{r}) + \int \mathrm{d}\boldsymbol{r}_1 \int \mathrm{d}\boldsymbol{r}_2\, v(\boldsymbol{r} - \boldsymbol{r}_1)\, \chi(\boldsymbol{r}_1, \boldsymbol{r}_2)\, \delta v(\boldsymbol{r}_2). \tag{2.18}$$

Thus, we can define a dielectric function $\varepsilon(\boldsymbol{r}, \boldsymbol{r}')$ by

$$\delta\varphi(\boldsymbol{r}) = \int \mathrm{d}\boldsymbol{r}'\, \varepsilon^{-1}(\boldsymbol{r}, \boldsymbol{r}')\, \delta v(\boldsymbol{r}'), \tag{2.19}$$

giving,

$$\varepsilon^{-1}(\boldsymbol{r}, \boldsymbol{r}') = \delta(\boldsymbol{r} - \boldsymbol{r}') + \int \mathrm{d}\boldsymbol{r}''\, v(\boldsymbol{r} - \boldsymbol{r}'')\, \chi(\boldsymbol{r}'', \boldsymbol{r}'). \tag{2.20}$$

Also, we define a polarizability function $\tilde{\chi}(\boldsymbol{r}, \boldsymbol{r}')$ by

$$\delta n(\boldsymbol{r}) = \int \mathrm{d}\boldsymbol{r}'\, \tilde{\chi}(\boldsymbol{r}, \boldsymbol{r}')\, \delta\varphi(\boldsymbol{r}'). \tag{2.21}$$

It is a measure of the induced electron density in terms of the total electric potential. It is also known as the proper (or irreducible) polarization part.

From the above equations, we obtain the relations familiar in electrostatics,

$$\chi = \tilde{\chi}\varepsilon^{-1}, \quad \varepsilon^{-1} = \delta + v\tilde{\chi}\varepsilon^{-1}, \quad \varepsilon = \delta - v\tilde{\chi}. \tag{2.22a, b, c}$$

We have used a shorthand notation where all the coordinates and integrations over them are understood.

The expression (2.16) for the density response function is not a particularly convenient one for an actual calculation of the quantity. The most systematic way of calculating the density response is by the use of field theory, thus calculating a perturbation series in powers of the electron–electron interaction. We refer to the book by Abrikosov et al. (1963) for details of the field theoretical techniques and, instead, give here simpler derivations for a couple of most commonly used approximations.

In the Hartree approximation, each electron is regarded as moving independently in the electrostatic field due to the lattice and all other electrons. In the same spirit, the change of the electron density due to the total electric potential $\delta\varphi(\boldsymbol{r})$ may be calculated by treating the electrons as independent of each other, thus yielding an approximation for the polarizability,

$$\begin{aligned}\tilde{\chi}_0(\boldsymbol{q}+\boldsymbol{G}, \boldsymbol{q}+\boldsymbol{G}') = \Omega^{-1} \sum_{\nu\nu'\boldsymbol{k}} \frac{f_{\nu'\boldsymbol{k}+\boldsymbol{q}} - f_{\nu\boldsymbol{k}}}{\mathscr{E}_{\nu'\boldsymbol{k}+\boldsymbol{q}} - \mathscr{E}_{\nu\boldsymbol{k}}} \\ \times \langle \nu\boldsymbol{k}|\, \mathrm{e}^{-\mathrm{i}(\boldsymbol{q}+\boldsymbol{G})\cdot\boldsymbol{r}}\, |\nu'\boldsymbol{k}+\boldsymbol{q}\rangle \langle \nu'\boldsymbol{k}+\boldsymbol{q}|\, \mathrm{e}^{\mathrm{i}(\boldsymbol{q}+\boldsymbol{G}')\cdot\boldsymbol{r}}\, |\nu\boldsymbol{k}\rangle .\end{aligned} \tag{2.23}$$

$|\nu\boldsymbol{k}\rangle$ denotes the single-particle Bloch state with wave vector $\boldsymbol{k}$, band index ν, energy $\mathscr{E}_{\nu\boldsymbol{k}}$ and occupation number $f_{\nu\boldsymbol{k}}$. This approximation is also known as the random phase approximation and may be derived either by the equation of motion method (Ehrenreich and Cohen 1959) or by a self-consistent Hartree approximation (see, for example, Sham and Ziman 1963).

The polarizability function, eq. (2.23), in the Hartree approximation, consists just of the polarization of an electron–hole pair (see fig. 1a). From eqs. (2.22), the density response is given by

$$\begin{aligned}\chi(\boldsymbol{q}+\boldsymbol{G}, \boldsymbol{q}+\boldsymbol{G}') = \tilde{\chi}_0(\boldsymbol{q}+\boldsymbol{G}, \boldsymbol{q}+\boldsymbol{G}') \\ + \sum_{\boldsymbol{G}''} \tilde{\chi}_0(\boldsymbol{q}+\boldsymbol{G}, \boldsymbol{q}+\boldsymbol{G}'')\, v(\boldsymbol{q}+\boldsymbol{G}'')\, \chi(\boldsymbol{q}+\boldsymbol{G}'', \boldsymbol{q}+\boldsymbol{G}').\end{aligned} \tag{2.24}$$

The density response includes not only the elementary electron–hole polarization due directly to the excitation of the applied field but also the polarization due to induced field coming from the polarization of all other electron–

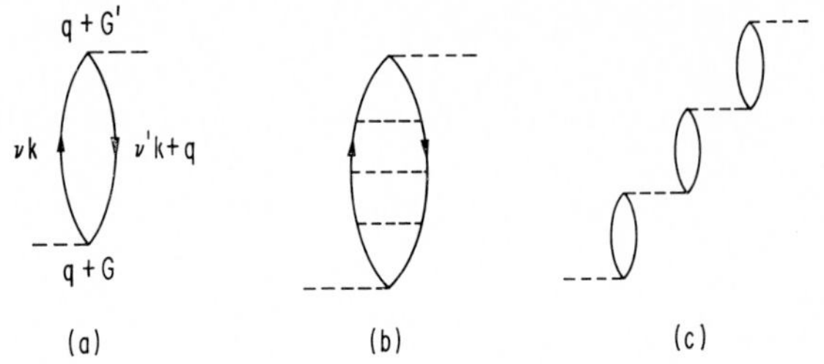

Fig. 1. (a) Electron–hole polarization. (b) Exchange processes in the polarizability function. (c) Density response in the Hartree approximation. Solid lines represent electrons and holes and dashed lines represent Coulomb interaction.

hole pairs. (A typical term is represented by fig. 1c). The solution of this equation is not trivial if crystalline effects are taken into account, and will be discussed in some details later.

The density response in the Hartree approximation is at least qualitatively correct but it may not be an adequate approximation because it leaves out the exchange and correlation effects. Exchange can be included by a self-consistent Hartree–Fock calculation (Peng 1941, Sham and Ziman 1963). The change in the total potential seen by an electron is the sum of the change in external potential and the change in the Hartree–Fock term due to the changes in electronic wave functions which in turn depend on the change in the total potential. Thus, we have an integral equation as in the Hartree case, except that the kernel now has a rather unmanageable structure.

One way to approximate the exchange effects is due to Hubbard (1958). The density response involves the electron–hole polarization induced by the electric potential due to another electron–hole pair. For each direct Coulomb interaction, there is an exchange counterpart. Hubbard approximated each exchange term by a factor times the direct Coulomb term because of the similarity of two types of terms. Thus, the density response is given by

$$\chi(\boldsymbol{q}+\boldsymbol{G}, \boldsymbol{q}+\boldsymbol{G}') = \tilde{\chi}_0(\boldsymbol{q}+\boldsymbol{G}, \boldsymbol{q}+\boldsymbol{G}') + \sum_{\boldsymbol{G}''} \tilde{\chi}_0(\boldsymbol{q}+\boldsymbol{G}, \boldsymbol{q}+\boldsymbol{G}'')\, v(\boldsymbol{q}+\boldsymbol{G}'')\, \{1-f(\boldsymbol{q}+\boldsymbol{G}'')\}\, \chi(\boldsymbol{q}+\boldsymbol{G}'', \boldsymbol{q}+\boldsymbol{G}'). \tag{2.25}$$

The difference from the Hartree approximation, eq. (2.24), is just a factor $-f$ which accounts approximately for the exchange processes; f is chosen to be

$$f(\boldsymbol{q}+\boldsymbol{G}) = (\boldsymbol{q}+\boldsymbol{G})^2/2\{(\boldsymbol{q}+\boldsymbol{G})^2 + q_s^2\}, \tag{2.26}$$

where q_s is some constant; $f(\boldsymbol{q}+\boldsymbol{G})$ tends to $\frac{1}{2}$ for large momentum transfer.

This accounts for the fact that at short distances, two electrons with parallel spins cannot approach each other.

Let us formally solve eq. (2.25) by considering the quantities as infinite matrices. Then,

$$\chi = \tilde{\chi}_0 \Lambda , \tag{2.27}$$

where Λ denotes the vertex correction in the Hubbard approximation, given by

$$\Lambda^{-1} = 1 - (1 - f)\, v\tilde{\chi}_0 . \tag{2.28}$$

From eq. (2.22b), the dielectric function becomes

$$\varepsilon = 1 - v\tilde{\chi}_0 (1 + f v\tilde{\chi}_0)^{-1} . \tag{2.29}$$

In general, the vertex correction, being a measure of the change of the potential seen by an electron, depends on the electronic state. Only in the Hubbard approximation, does it become independent of the particular electronic state and assume the form of eq. (2.28). Sham and Ziman (1963) have called Λ^{-1} a new kind of dielectric function. To avoid confusion, we shall use the field theoretic term, the vertex correction.

From eqs. (2.22c) and (2.29), the polarizability function is given by

$$\tilde{\chi} = \tilde{\chi}_0 (1 + f v\tilde{\chi}_0)^{-1} . \tag{2.30}$$

In the Hartree–Fock approximation, the exchange contribution to the polarizability is the polarization of a pair of electron and hole which repeatedly interact with each other via the Coulomb interaction, as shown in fig. 1b. In the Hubbard approximation, this series of processes becomes a geometrical series which is summed to give eq. (2.30).

Since the use of Hubbard's approximation by Sham (1965) in the calculation of sodium phonon spectrum, it has become widely used. Although there is still belief in its validity (Cohen and Heine 1970), it has also been criticized (see, for example, Langreth 1969, Woo and Jha 1971). There are also other approximations, such as Price et al. (1970). However, all calculations so far are for one plane wave approximation of the electron wave functions.

For insulators, there is at least one instance where Hubbard's approximation is not adequate. The exchange processes of the electron–hole pair depicted in fig. 1b are effectively long-range attraction between the electron–hole pair, which can lead to the formation of an exciton. A rigorous derivation along these lines has been given by Sham and Rice (1966). In this case, Hubbard's approximation tends to overestimate the attraction responsible for the exciton binding. Its use by Kübler (1971) has led to very different conclusions on the exciton contribution to the dielectric constant from the more accurate treatment by Sham and Ramakrishnan (1971). For covalent crystals, the contribution of the exciton to the dielectric constant is unimportant (Elliot 1957, Sham and Ramakrishnan 1971). Hubbard's approximation still seems to be quite adequate for the polarization of electron–hole pair which does not bind into an exciton (Sinha et al. 1971, and Sinha, private communication).

2.3. The long-wavelength behavior

Because of the long-range nature of the Coulomb interaction between the particles, the study of the properties of a long-wavelength phonon requires a careful examination of the wave vector $\boldsymbol{q}$ tending to zero limit. The dynamical matrix involves the interaction $v(\boldsymbol{q}+\boldsymbol{G})$ for all reciprocal lattice vectors $\boldsymbol{G}$. For $\boldsymbol{G}=0$, the long-range part of the interaction $v(q)$ diverges as $q \to 0$ by eq. (2.14). So, we define the short-range part as

$$\begin{aligned} \hat{v}(\boldsymbol{q}+\boldsymbol{G}) &= v(\boldsymbol{q}+\boldsymbol{G}), \text{ if } G \neq 0, \\ &= 0, \qquad\qquad\quad \text{if } G = 0. \end{aligned} \tag{2.31}$$

A similar definition is applied to the pseudo-potential $v(\boldsymbol{q}+\boldsymbol{G};\kappa)$. We proceed to separate out in the dynamical matrix the long-range part, i.e. containing factors $v(q)$, and the short-range part. It then becomes simple to take the long-wavelength limit.

Let $\hat{\chi}(\boldsymbol{q}+\boldsymbol{G}, \boldsymbol{q}+\boldsymbol{G}')$ be given by the matrix equation

$$\hat{\chi} = \tilde{\chi} + \tilde{\chi}\hat{v}\hat{\chi}. \tag{2.32}$$

$\hat{\chi}$ is the sum of all polarization processes not involving the long-range part of the Coulomb interaction $v(q)$ (Ambegaokar and Kohn 1960). We may term it the susceptibility. We introduce a new dielectric function $\varepsilon(\boldsymbol{q})$ given by

$$\varepsilon(\boldsymbol{q}) = 1 - v(q)\,\hat{\chi}(\boldsymbol{q}, \boldsymbol{q}). \tag{2.33}$$

Hence,

$$\varepsilon^{-1}(\boldsymbol{q}, \boldsymbol{q}) = 1/\varepsilon(q). \tag{2.34}$$

Now, the effective ion–ion interaction, given by eq. (2.13), can be written as follows:

$$
\begin{aligned}
V(\boldsymbol{q}\kappa;\boldsymbol{q}\kappa') &= v(q) + v(\boldsymbol{q};\kappa)\,\{\hat{\chi}(\boldsymbol{q},\boldsymbol{q})/\varepsilon(\boldsymbol{q})\}\,v(\boldsymbol{q};\kappa'),\\
V(\boldsymbol{q}\kappa;\boldsymbol{q}+\boldsymbol{G}'\kappa') &= v(\boldsymbol{q};\kappa)\,\hat{\chi}(\boldsymbol{q},\boldsymbol{q}+\boldsymbol{G}')\,v(\boldsymbol{q}+\boldsymbol{G}';\kappa')/\varepsilon(\boldsymbol{q}),\\
V(\boldsymbol{q}+\boldsymbol{G}\kappa;\boldsymbol{q}\kappa') &= v(\boldsymbol{q}+\boldsymbol{G};\kappa)\,\hat{\chi}(\boldsymbol{q}+\boldsymbol{G},q)\,v(\boldsymbol{q};\kappa')/\varepsilon(\boldsymbol{q}),\\
V(\boldsymbol{q}+\boldsymbol{G}\kappa;\boldsymbol{q}+\boldsymbol{G}'\kappa') &= \hat{V}(\boldsymbol{q}+\boldsymbol{G}\kappa;\boldsymbol{q}+\boldsymbol{G}'\kappa') + v(\boldsymbol{q}+\boldsymbol{G};\kappa)\\
&\quad\times\hat{\chi}(\boldsymbol{q}+\boldsymbol{G},\boldsymbol{q})\,\{v(\boldsymbol{q})/\varepsilon(\boldsymbol{q})\}\,\hat{\chi}(\boldsymbol{q},\boldsymbol{q}+\boldsymbol{G}')\,v(\boldsymbol{q}+\boldsymbol{G}';\kappa'). \qquad (2.35)
\end{aligned}
$$

The short-range part of the effective interaction $\hat{V}$ is obtained from the total effective interaction V in eq. (2.13) by putting $v(q)$ to zero but keeping $v(\boldsymbol{q}+\boldsymbol{G})$ for $G\neq 0$. Thus, we have formulas for the effective ion interaction which show explicitly the dependence on the long-range part of the Coulomb interaction $v(q)$.

We can do the same for the dynamical matrix by substituting eq. (2.35) into eq. (2.11), obtaining,

$$
\begin{aligned}
\Phi_{\alpha\alpha'}(\boldsymbol{q};\kappa\kappa') = (M_\kappa M_{\kappa'})^{-1/2}\,\Omega_0^{-1}\big[&\exp\{\mathrm{i}\boldsymbol{q}\cdot(\boldsymbol{x}_\kappa-\boldsymbol{x}_{\kappa'})\}\\
&\times q_\alpha q_{\alpha'}\{Z_\kappa Z_{\kappa'}v(\boldsymbol{q}) - v(\boldsymbol{q};\kappa)\,v(\boldsymbol{q};\kappa')/v(\boldsymbol{q})\}\\
&+\exp\{\mathrm{i}\boldsymbol{q}\cdot(\boldsymbol{x}_\kappa-\boldsymbol{x}_{\kappa'})\}\,Z_\alpha^+(\boldsymbol{q};\kappa)\,Z_{\alpha'}(\boldsymbol{q};\kappa')\,v(\boldsymbol{q})/\varepsilon(\boldsymbol{q})\\
&+\{T_{\alpha\alpha'}(\boldsymbol{q};\kappa\kappa') - \delta_{\kappa\kappa'}\sum_{\kappa''}T_{\alpha\alpha'}(0;\kappa\kappa'')\}\big]. \qquad (2.36)
\end{aligned}
$$

where

$$
\begin{aligned}
Z_\alpha(\boldsymbol{q},\kappa) = -\,\mathrm{i}\big[&q_\alpha v(\boldsymbol{q};\kappa)/v(\boldsymbol{q})\\
&+\sum_{\boldsymbol{G}}\hat{\chi}(\boldsymbol{q},\boldsymbol{q}+\boldsymbol{G})\,\hat{v}(\boldsymbol{q}+\boldsymbol{G};\kappa)\,(q_\alpha+G_\alpha)\exp(-\,\mathrm{i}\boldsymbol{G}\cdot\boldsymbol{x}_\kappa)\big], \qquad (2.37)
\end{aligned}
$$

and

$$
T_{\alpha\alpha'}(\boldsymbol{q};\kappa\kappa') = \sum_{\boldsymbol{G},\boldsymbol{G}'}\hat{V}_{\alpha\alpha'}(\boldsymbol{q}+\boldsymbol{G}\,\kappa;\boldsymbol{q}+\boldsymbol{G}'\,\kappa'). \qquad (2.38)
$$

$Z_\alpha(\boldsymbol{q},\kappa)$ may be regarded as the effective charge of the κ sublattice per unit displacement in the α-direction in a lattice wave of wave vector $\boldsymbol{q}$. The second term in the dynamical matrix is interpreted as the interaction of the sublattices via the long-range Coulomb interaction $v(q)$ in the dielectric medium with the dielectric function $\varepsilon(\boldsymbol{q})$. The first term comes from the deviation of the pseudo-potential from the Coulomb potential. It is very important in a compressional wave. The third term contains the short-range interactions.

By means of eq. (2.36), it is a simple matter to examine the $q\to 0$ limit of the dynamical matrix. Up till now, everything we have done is equally applicable to conducting and insulating crystals, but their long-wavelength behaviors are different. We shall, from now on, confine ourselves to a study of the insulators following the treatment of Sham (1969b) and Pick et al. (1970). Keating (1968) treated the long-wavelength limit incorrectly and subsequently published a correction (Keating 1969) after the work of Pick et al. We refer to Sham (1972) for the case of the conducting crystal.

In an insulator at zero temperature, for small q the polarizability has the following leading terms:

$$\tilde{\chi}(\boldsymbol{q}, \boldsymbol{q}) = q_\alpha \tilde{\chi}^{(2)}_{\alpha\alpha'} q_{\alpha'} + \mathrm{O}(q^4), \tag{2.39a}$$

$$\tilde{\chi}(\boldsymbol{q}, \boldsymbol{q}+\boldsymbol{G}) = q_\alpha \tilde{\chi}^{(1)}_\alpha (0, \boldsymbol{G}) + \mathrm{O}(q^2), \tag{2.39b}$$

$$\tilde{\chi}(\boldsymbol{q}+\boldsymbol{G}, \boldsymbol{q}) = q_\alpha \tilde{\chi}^{(1)}_\alpha (\boldsymbol{G}, 0) + \mathrm{O}(q^2), \tag{2.39c}$$

$$\tilde{\chi}(\boldsymbol{q}+\boldsymbol{G}, \boldsymbol{q}+\boldsymbol{G}') = \tilde{\chi}(\boldsymbol{G}, \boldsymbol{G}') + \mathrm{O}(q), \tag{2.39d}$$

summation over the Greek indices being understood. These equations are easily verified in the Hartree approximation given by eq. (2.23) since the energy difference between conduction and valence band states is finite and their wave functions are orthogonal. They can be proved to all orders in the electron–electron interaction (Kohn 1958, Sham 1966). Consequently, the susceptibility $\hat{\chi}$, as defined by eq. (2.32), has exactly the same limiting behavior because, unlike the density response χ, it does not involve singular factors of $v(q)$.

From eq. (2.33), we have

$$\lim_{q \to 0} \varepsilon(\boldsymbol{q}) = 1 - 4\pi e^2 \hat{q}_\alpha \hat{\chi}^{(2)}_{\alpha\alpha'} \hat{q}_{\alpha'} = \varepsilon(\hat{\boldsymbol{q}}), \tag{2.40}$$

where $\hat{\boldsymbol{q}}$ denotes the unit vector in $\boldsymbol{q}$-direction. From eq. (2.34) we see that this is just the macroscopic dielectric constant, including all internal field effects through the summation over Bragg diffractions in eq. (2.32) (Adler 1962, Wiser 1963).

By eq. (2.37), the leading term in a small q-expansion of the effective charge is given by

$$Z_\alpha(\boldsymbol{q}, \kappa) = \mathrm{i} Z_{\alpha\beta}(\kappa)\, q_\beta + \mathrm{O}(q^2), \tag{2.41}$$

with

$$Z_{\alpha\beta}(\kappa) = Z_\kappa \delta_{\alpha\beta} - \sum_{\boldsymbol{G}} \hat{\chi}^{(1)}_\beta (0, \boldsymbol{G})\, \hat{v}(\boldsymbol{G}; \kappa)\, G_\alpha \exp(-\mathrm{i}\boldsymbol{G}\cdot\boldsymbol{x}_\kappa), \tag{2.42}$$

since the leading term of $v(\boldsymbol{q}; \kappa)$ is $-Z_\kappa v(q)$. Fourier transforming back to configuration space gives

$$Z_{\alpha\beta}(\kappa) = Z_\kappa \delta_{\alpha\beta} - N^{-1} \int \mathrm{d}\boldsymbol{r} \int \mathrm{d}\boldsymbol{r}'\, r_\alpha \chi(\boldsymbol{r}, \boldsymbol{r}') \sum_l \partial v(\boldsymbol{r}' - \boldsymbol{x}_{l\kappa}; \kappa)/\partial x_{l\kappa\beta}, \tag{2.43}$$

N being the number of unit cells in the crystal. For a more careful discussion of the derivation of this equation, see Sham (1969b).

If the sublattice of κ ions is moved rigidly through a small distance, by eq. (2.4),

$$\int \mathrm{d}\boldsymbol{r}'\, \chi(\boldsymbol{r}, \boldsymbol{r}') \sum_l \partial v(\boldsymbol{r}' - \boldsymbol{x}_{l\kappa}; \kappa)/\partial x_{l\kappa\beta}$$

is the change in electron density per unit displacement in the β-direction. The integral in eq. (2.43) is, therefore, the dipole moment of the displaced electronic charge per unit displacement of the κ sublattice. $Z_{\alpha\beta}(\kappa)$ is, thus, the effective charge tensor associated with the κ sublattice when it moves bodily relative to the rest of the lattice. If the whole lattice is moved through a small distance slowly, then the dipole moment per unit displacement due to the displaced electrons must be compensated by the ionic charges. We have

$$\sum_\kappa Z_{\alpha\beta}(\kappa) = 0. \tag{2.44}$$

In the case of elemental covalent crystals, such as the group IV elements, all sublattices are identical, and we have, for all κ

$$Z_{\alpha\beta}(\kappa) = 0. \tag{2.44a}$$

The sum rule (2.44) can also be proved without the use of eq. (2.43) (Sham 1969b).

By eqs. (2.40) and (2.41), the leading terms of the dynamical matrix from eq. (2.36) for small q are given by

$$\begin{aligned}\Phi_{\alpha\alpha'}(\boldsymbol{q}; \kappa\kappa') = (M_\kappa M_{\kappa'})^{-1/2}\, \Omega_0^{-1} [Z^*_{\alpha\beta}(\kappa)\, Z_{\alpha'\beta'}(\kappa')\, 4\pi e^2\, \hat{q}_\beta \hat{q}_{\beta'}/\varepsilon(\hat{q}) \\ + T_{\alpha\alpha'}(0; \kappa\kappa') - \delta_{\kappa\kappa'} \sum_{\kappa''} T_{\alpha\alpha'}(0; \kappa\kappa'')].\end{aligned} \tag{2.45}$$

Because of the neutrality sum rule of the effective charges, eq. (2.44), we have, from eq. (2.45), for small q, the leading terms obeying,

$$\sum_{\kappa'} \Phi_{\alpha\alpha'}(\boldsymbol{q}; \kappa\kappa') = 0. \tag{2.46}$$

This shows that the frequencies of the acoustic modes tend to zero as $q \to 0$ as expected. In the phenomenological approach which gives the correct form

(2.45) of the dynamical matrix, the sum rule (2.44) becomes a necessary condition (Cochran and Cowley 1962).

By dividing $Z_\alpha(\boldsymbol{q}, \kappa)$ given in eq. (2.37) by $\varepsilon(\boldsymbol{q})$ of eq. (2.33), the neutrality sum rule (2.44) can be written in an alternative form,

$$\lim_{q \to 0} q_\alpha \sum_{\kappa \boldsymbol{G}} \varepsilon^{-1}(\boldsymbol{q}, \boldsymbol{q}+\boldsymbol{G})(q_\beta + G_\beta)\, v(\boldsymbol{q}+\boldsymbol{G}; \kappa) \exp(-\mathrm{i}\boldsymbol{G}\cdot\boldsymbol{x}_\kappa) = 0. \tag{2.47}$$

This condition on the inverse dielectric function also leads to vanishing frequencies for long wavelength acoustic phonons and is, therefore, called the acoustic sum rule (Pick et al. 1970).

From either the acoustic sum rule (2.47) or the neutrality sum rule (2.44) with the effective charge given by eq. (2.42), we note a restriction on the screening properties of the electrons in an insulating crystal. This is very important for any calculation of the phonon spectrum. For example, unlike the case of a simple metal, one cannot use a diagonal dielectric function or density response, because these conditions cannot then be satisfied.

A calculation of the electromagnetic response of the crystal (Sham 1969b, Pick et al. 1970) yields the following expression for the macroscopic dielectric tensor as a function of frequency, in the infrared range,

$$\varepsilon_{\alpha\beta}(\omega) = \delta_{\alpha\beta} - 4\pi\left[e^2 \hat{\chi}^{(2)}_{\alpha\beta} + \sum_j M_\alpha(j)\, M^+_\beta(j)/(\omega^2 - \omega_j^2)\right]. \tag{2.48}$$

j ranges over the zero wave-vector optical modes. ω_j is the phonon frequency given by the $\boldsymbol{q}=0$ dynamical matrix, i.e. without the effective charge term in eq. (2.45). The electric dipole moment $M_\alpha(j)$ is given by

$$M_\alpha(j) = \Omega_0^{-1/2} e \sum_\kappa Z_{\alpha\beta}(\kappa)\, M_\kappa^{-1/2} e_\alpha(\kappa|0j), \tag{2.49}$$

where $e_\alpha(\kappa|0j)$ is the polarization vector of the zero wave-vector optical mode. We see that the effective charge $Z_{\alpha\beta}(\kappa)$ which is deduced from the microscopic theory does indeed play the role of the Born effective charge (Born and Huang 1954) in the macroscopic electrical response.

From here it is a simple step to deduce the Lyddane–Sachs–Teller relation (Lyddane et al. 1941) extended to apply to general crystals (Cochran and Cowley 1962). Let us consider the special class of diatomic crystals with tetrahedral symmetry (Born and Huang 1954, Appendix VI) which virtually covers all the crystals we are interested in. Then, by symmetry (Sham 1969b),

$$T_{\alpha\alpha'}(0; \kappa\kappa') = \delta_{\alpha\alpha'}\left[4\pi Z_\kappa Z_{\kappa'} e^2/3\Omega_0 - s\right], \tag{2.50}$$

for $\kappa \neq \kappa'$. The first term comes from the bare ion interaction and s is the electronic contribution. The $\kappa = \kappa'$ element does not enter the dynamical matrix. The effective charge and electronic susceptibility are given by

$$Z_{\alpha\beta}(\kappa) = \delta_{\alpha\beta} z_\kappa , \tag{2.51}$$

and

$$\hat{\chi}^{(2)}_{\alpha\beta} = \delta_{\alpha\beta} \chi . \tag{2.52}$$

The transverse optical mode frequency is given by

$$\omega_0^2 = (4\pi e^2 Z_1 Z_2 / 3\Omega_0 - s)/M , \tag{2.53}$$

where M is the reduced mass of the two ions in the unit cell. The dielectric constant is

$$\varepsilon(\omega) = \varepsilon_\infty + 4\pi e^2 z_1^2 / \Omega_0 M (\omega_0^2 - \omega^2) , \tag{2.54}$$

where the high frequency dielectric constant is

$$\varepsilon_\infty = 1 - 4\pi e^2 \chi . \tag{2.55}$$

The long-wavelength longitudinal optical mode, is from, eq. (2.45), given by

$$\omega_l = (\varepsilon_0 / \varepsilon_\infty)^{1/2} \omega_0 . \tag{2.56}$$

Thus, we have here a microscopic proof of the Lyddane–Sachs–Teller relation. Indeed, it is rather satisfying that we have shown, at least formally, how to relate various macroscopic quantities such as the dielectric constant, dipole moment, effective charge, to microscopic properties. This effort clarifies the definitions of the macroscopic quantities. We are now ready to consider evaluation of the formulas involving the microscopic properties, in particular, the electron density response.

2.4. The adiabatic approximation

We give here a brief discussion of the Born–Oppenheimer approximation from a modern viewpoint and refer the reader to Born and Huang (1954) and Chester (1961) for a discussion of the classic expansion in powers of the electron to ion mass ratio, $(m/M)^{1/4}$.

As a matter of fact, it is possible to formulate the theory in §2.1 without the use of the adiabatic approximation by the method of Green's functions (Baym 1961, Gliss and Bilz 1968). A simple treatment is given by Sham

(1969a). The generalization needed is simply that the electron density response function must be calculated at the frequency ω of the perturbation, i.e. the phonon wave. The extension of the dynamical matrix to the finite frequency case is the phonon self-energy. The phonon frequency is determined by the secular equation involving the real part of the phonon self-energy which implicitly depends on the phonon frequency. Keating (1968) has given a very involved derivation and used unnecessarily the one-particle approximation for the electron occupation number in the phonon self-energy.

The adiabatic approximation then consists in (a) neglecting the phonon contributions to the electron density response and (b) approximating the dynamic response by a static one. For insulators, the existence of a finite energy gap and the small mass ratio, m/M, ensure the validity of the approximations. For metals, they can also be proved valid (Migdal 1958), notwithstanding many statements in the literature to the contrary. The in-between case of zero-gap semiconductors has been examined by Sherrington (1971). The adiabatic approximation appears to break down only for extremely long wavelengths.

3. *Phenomenological models*

Many phenomenological models with adjustable parameters have been used to fit the phonon spectra of covalent crystals (group IV semiconductors) and partly ionic crystals (such as III–V compounds). In this section, we examine the shell model and several valence bond models, not caring so much for the success of a particular fit to experiment (After all, any half-way sensible model with a sufficiently large number of parameters can provide a perfect fit.) as for its physical reasonableness. In other words, we are most interested in how well each of these models describes the electron response in a lattice vibration. We refer to chapter 3 by Hardy for details of the workings of the phenomenological models.

3.1. The shell model

The valence electrons are regarded as shells centered at the ions. A lattice wave will move the shells relative to the ions. The displacements of shells and ions are governed by the force constants which connect them. This model has been widely used to interpret phonon spectra in solids. For reviews, see, for example, Cochran (1963), Dick (1964), and Cochran and Cowley (1967).

Mathematically, the shell model is equivalent to the dipole model of Tolpygo (1950). The dynamical variables are the ion displacements $\boldsymbol{u}$ and the dipole moments $\boldsymbol{p}$ (or the shell displacements). To defoliage the undergrowth of indices, we apply the vector notation with the vector components running over the indices $l\kappa\alpha$. In the harmonic approximation, the effective ion potential energy (i.e. including contributions from the valence electrons) is a quadratic in the dynamical variables.

$$U = \tfrac{1}{2}\boldsymbol{u}\cdot R\cdot\boldsymbol{u} + \tfrac{1}{2}\boldsymbol{p}\cdot S\cdot\boldsymbol{p} + \boldsymbol{u}\cdot T\cdot\boldsymbol{p}\,. \tag{3.1}$$

Each matrix of force constants, R, S or T, is composed of two parts, a long-range Coulomb interaction and a short-range part. The equation of motion for the ions is

$$\omega^2 M\cdot\boldsymbol{u} = R\cdot\boldsymbol{u} + T\cdot\boldsymbol{p}\,, \tag{3.2}$$

where M is the diagonal mass matrix, and that for the dipoles (or shells) is

$$0 = T^{+}\cdot\boldsymbol{u} + S\cdot\boldsymbol{p}\,, \tag{3.3}$$

where the mass of the shell is neglected (the adiabatic approximation). Eliminating $\boldsymbol{p}$, we have the secular equation for the phonon in the usual form,

$$\omega^2 M\cdot\boldsymbol{u} = (R + T\cdot S^{-1}\cdot T^{+})\cdot\boldsymbol{u}\,. \tag{3.4}$$

A quantum-mechanical justification of the dipole model was given by Mashkevich (1960) and by Tolpygo (1961), and extended by Cowley (1962) to include all multipoles. We give here a justification of the shell model based on a multipole expansion of the electron density response (Sham 1969a). Sinha (1969) has given a justification which is somewhat similar in its approach.

We simply need to derive the form of the effective ion potential energy given by eq. (3.1) from first-principles. In the adiabatic approximation the effective ion potential energy is the sum of the bare ion energy and the total electron energy. Hohenberg and Kohn (1964) have shown that the total ground state energy of the interacting electron system can be written in the form

$$E(\boldsymbol{R}) = \int \mathrm{d}\boldsymbol{r}\, n(\boldsymbol{r})\, W(\boldsymbol{r}, \boldsymbol{R}) + \tfrac{1}{2}\int \mathrm{d}\boldsymbol{r} \int \mathrm{d}\boldsymbol{r}'\, v(\boldsymbol{r}-\boldsymbol{r}')\, n(\boldsymbol{r})\, n(\boldsymbol{r}') + G[n]\,. \tag{3.5}$$

The first term is just the potential energy of the electrons due to the lattice potential, when the ions are in their instantaneous positions $\boldsymbol{R}_{l\kappa}$ (the adiabatic approximation), given by

$$W(\boldsymbol{r}, \boldsymbol{R}) = \sum_{l\kappa} v(\boldsymbol{r}-\boldsymbol{R}_{l\kappa};\, \kappa). \tag{3.6}$$

The second term is the electrostatic interaction energy of the electron density distribution. $G[n]$ includes the rest, namely, the electron kinetic energy, exchange and correlation energy. $G[n]$ is completely determined by the electron density distribution $n(\boldsymbol{r})$. These authors have also proved the variational theorem that the energy is minimum with respect to variation in $n(\boldsymbol{r})$ given a fixed lattice potential. This can be used to determine the density distribution (Kohn and Sham 1965).

The electron energy of second order in the ionic displacements is

$$E^{(2)} = \int \mathrm{d}\boldsymbol{r}\, n^{(0)}(\boldsymbol{r})\, W^{(2)}(\boldsymbol{r}) + \int \mathrm{d}\boldsymbol{r}\, n^{(1)}(\boldsymbol{r})\, W^{(1)}(\boldsymbol{r})$$
$$+ \tfrac{1}{2} \int \mathrm{d}\boldsymbol{r} \int \mathrm{d}\boldsymbol{r}' \,\{v(\boldsymbol{r}-\boldsymbol{r}') + K(\boldsymbol{r}, \boldsymbol{r}')\}\, n^{(1)}(\boldsymbol{r})\, n^{(1)}(\boldsymbol{r}). \tag{3.7}$$

where $W^{(j)}(\boldsymbol{r})$ is of jth order in $\boldsymbol{u}$. The terms involving $n^{(2)}(\boldsymbol{r})$ are absent by virtue of the variational theorem. $K(\boldsymbol{r}, \boldsymbol{r}')$ is the second functional derivative of $G[n]$ with respect to $n(\boldsymbol{r})$. It is minus the inverse of the polarizability $\tilde{\chi}(\boldsymbol{r}, \boldsymbol{r}')$, as can be seen by differentiating $E^{(2)}$ with respect to $n^{(1)}(\boldsymbol{r})$, giving

$$W^{(1)}(\boldsymbol{r}) + \int \mathrm{d}\boldsymbol{r}'\, v(\boldsymbol{r}-\boldsymbol{r}')\, n^{(1)}(\boldsymbol{r}') = -\int \mathrm{d}\boldsymbol{r}'\, K(\boldsymbol{r}, \boldsymbol{r}')\, n^{(1)}(\boldsymbol{r}'). \tag{3.8}$$

The left-hand side is the total self-consistent potential. By comparing eq. (3.8) with eq. (2.21), we obtain

$$\int \mathrm{d}\boldsymbol{r}'\, K(\boldsymbol{r}, \boldsymbol{r}')\, \tilde{\chi}(\boldsymbol{r}', \boldsymbol{r}'') = -\delta(\boldsymbol{r}-\boldsymbol{r}''). \tag{3.9}$$

The first term in the expression (3.7) for $E^{(2)}$ can be lumped with the bare ion potential energy to give the term $\frac{1}{2}\boldsymbol{u}\cdot\mathsf{R}\cdot\boldsymbol{u}$ in eq. (3.1).

If the valence electrons are fairly well localized in the neighborhood of the ion sites, we can attribute the first order change of the electron density to the ion sites,

$$n^{(1)}(\boldsymbol{r}) = \sum_{l\kappa} \sigma^{(1)}(\boldsymbol{r}, l\kappa), \tag{3.10}$$

where $\sigma^{(1)}(\boldsymbol{r}, l\kappa)$ is localized in the neighborhood of $\boldsymbol{x}_{l\kappa}$. Now expand $\sigma^{(1)}(\boldsymbol{r}, l\kappa)$

in terms of a complete set of functions $\varphi_j(\boldsymbol{r})$,

$$\sigma^{(1)}(\boldsymbol{r}, l\kappa) = \sum_j p_{l\kappa j}\varphi_j(\boldsymbol{r} - \boldsymbol{x}_{l\kappa}). \tag{3.11}$$

Substituting eqs. (3.10) and (3.11) into eq. (3.7), we are able to put the potential energy term $\int \mathrm{d}\boldsymbol{r}\, n^{(1)}\, W^{(1)}$ into the form $\boldsymbol{u}\cdot T\cdot\boldsymbol{p}$ and the interaction energy term involving $n^{(1)}$ twice into the form $\frac{1}{2}\boldsymbol{p}\cdot S\cdot\boldsymbol{p}$. Thus, we have derived the shell model in its most general form from first principles. Because $K(\boldsymbol{r}, \boldsymbol{r}')$ is short-ranged (Sham and Kohn 1966), S has a long-range part from $v(\boldsymbol{r}-\boldsymbol{r}')$ and a short-range part from $K(\boldsymbol{r}, \boldsymbol{r}')$. In terms of a set of functions $\psi_j(\boldsymbol{r})$ conjugate to $\varphi_j(\boldsymbol{r})$, i.e.

$$\int \mathrm{d}\boldsymbol{r}\, \psi_j(\boldsymbol{r})\, \varphi_i(\boldsymbol{r}) = \delta_{ji}, \tag{3.12}$$

the coefficients $p_{l\kappa j}$ in eq. (3.11) are

$$p_{l\kappa j} = \int \mathrm{d}\boldsymbol{r}\, \psi_j(\boldsymbol{r})\, \sigma^{(1)}(\boldsymbol{r}, l\kappa). \tag{3.13}$$

$p_{l\kappa j}$ are some kind of moments of the change of electron density in the neighborhood of the $(l\kappa)$ ion.

To obtain a multipole expansion, we need to take $\psi_j(\boldsymbol{r})$ to be the set of functions $1, r_\alpha, r_\alpha r_\beta, \cdots$. Then $\varphi_j(\boldsymbol{r})$ are $\delta(\boldsymbol{r})$, $\partial\delta(\boldsymbol{r})/\partial r_\alpha$, $\partial^2\delta(\boldsymbol{r})/\partial r_\alpha \partial r_\beta, \cdots$. These define the off-diagonal elements of S and T. The diagonal elements represent self-interaction energy of the charges within the same atom, for which there is no multipole expansion. If we choose only three functions of $\varphi_j(\boldsymbol{r})$ with p-type symmetry, we obtain the dipole model. If we take an s-like function, we get the breathing mode (Schröder 1966).

The earliest use of the phenomenological model for the lattice vibrations in diamond (Smith 1948), and germanium and silicon (Hsieh 1954) is the nearest neighbor force constant model. The agreement with the measured phonon spectra is very poor. Herman (1959) showed that to obtain a good fit with the measured spectrum in germanium, the force constants had to extend to the fifth nearest neighbors, involving fifteen independent parameters (see also Pope 1964). This led Cochran (1959) to apply the shell model to explain the phonon spectrum in germanium. The long-range interaction is provided by the induced dipole interaction and the short-range interaction is restricted to the nearest neighbors. Because the elastic constants of germanium satisfy a relation due to Born, Cochran introduced simplifying assumptions reducing the number of independent parameters from seven to five.

A reasonable overall fit was obtained to the room temperature measurements of Brockhouse and Iyengar (1958). (Recent measurements at 80 K by Nilsson and Nelin (1971) gave generally lower frequencies.) This was the first shell model calculation of the phonon spectrum, although earlier Mashkevich and Tolpygo (1957) had introduced an equivalent dipole model for the study of elastic and dielectric properties of the covalent crystals.

Dolling (1963) has made a careful analysis for silicon and germanium using several shell models with progressive complexities. In silicon, since the elastic constants do not closely satisfy the Born relation as in germanium, the restrictions on the first nearest neighbor constants used by Cochran have to be removed. A nearly perfect fit with experiment is possible by extending the non-Coulombic part of the interaction to the second nearest neighbors, using in all eleven parameters. Demidenko et al. (1961, 1962) have reached the same conclusion for germanium.

In fact, the eleven-parameter shell model with the short-range part extending to the second nearest neighbors have been used with more or less success to fit all the group IV semiconductors and quite a few of the III–V compounds. The list includes diamond (Kucher and Nechiporuk 1966) Dolling and Cowley 1966, Warren et al. 1967), GaAs (Waugh and Dolling 1963, Korol and Tolpygo 1971), GaP (Yarnell et al. 1968), InSb and α-Sn (Price et al. 1971).

Kress (1972) has included the breathing mode in his modified shell model. Only six parameters are used and fitted to macroscopic data and the infrared absorption. The agreement of the calculated phonon spectra of silicon, germanium and grey tin with experiment rivals that of the conventional eleven parameter shell model.

Price et al. (1971) have found that although the shell model gives a good fit of the phonon spectra in α-Sn and InSb, the values of the parameters cannot be interpreted as being reasonable approximations of the properties in the dipole model. In the derivation of the shell model above, we have made use of a very general expansion of the change of the electronic density distribution. Thus, it is not surprising that a successful fit of the shell model does not necessarily give reasonable values of the dipole moments of the change in electronic density. However, the shell model does invoke the working hypothesis that the rearrangement of the electron distribution in a lattice wave can be adequately described by a reasonably small number of functions well localized on the ions. Physically, this does not seem to describe the electrons in a crystal with strong directed valence bonds. X-ray diffraction studies (Renninger 1955, Göttlicher and Wölfel 1959, Brill 1959) and the calculation by Walter and Cohen (1971) show that a substantial portion of the electronic charge is distributed in the space between the nearest neighbor atoms.

3.2. The bond models

In this section, we shall describe several models for which the point of view is taken that, in the covalent crystals of the group IV elements, the valence bonds play an important role in cohesion and must, therefore, be involved in lattice vibrations.

In the theory of molecular vibrations in hydrocarbons, the potential energy is written in terms of bond stretching and change of angle between bonds (Herzberg 1945, Wilson et al. 1955). This method of valence force field was applied to lattice dynamics in diamond by Musgrave and Pople (1962). It is well known that the diamond structure consists of two interpenetrating f.c.c. lattices such that each carbon atom has four nearest neighbors tetrahedrally situated. The second order potential energy is a quadratic in terms of the 'valence coordinates', (*i*) bond stretching, i.e. the change in the distance between nearest neighbor carbon atoms, and (*ii*) the change of the bond angle, the angle between two bonds subtended at an atom. It is then straight-forward to find the force constants in terms of the valence force field since there are geometrical relations between the valence coordinates and the displacements of the ions.

Musgrave and Pople included in the second order potential energy only quadratic terms due to changes of the bond distances and the bond angles with apices on a common atom. Thus, they obtained five parameters. This model gives the six force constants extending to second neighbors. The values of the parameters derived from the vibrations of the neopentane molecules gave poor agreement with measured Raman frequency and elastic constants.

McMurry et al. (1967) applied the valence force field method to calculate the phonon spectrum in diamond. They introduced a sixth parameter, coming from a quadratic term in the potential energy due to the changes in two bond angles which have a common bond. Now the Born–Von Kármán force constants include first, second and fifth neighbors. Schachtschneider and Snyder (1963) obtained a set of valence force field parameters from an analysis of a large number of hydrocarbons. When these values were used by McMurry et al. to calculate the phonon spectrum in diamond, a reasonable agreement with experiment was obtained. Relatively small adjustments of the six parameters yielded an almost perfect fit, fully comparable with the eleven parameter shell model fit of Dolling and Cowley (1966) and Warren et al. (1967).

The six parameter valence force field model was used to fit the phonon spectrum in silicon by Singh and Dayal (1970) and by Solbrig (1971), with moderate success. It is not as good as the eleven parameter shell model of Dolling (1963). However, by introducing three more parameters coming from quadratic terms in the potential energy involving the changes of bond angles with apices on next nearest neighbor atoms, Solbrig obtained a very good fit for silicon, though still not as good as Dolling's. The three extra parameters bring into play third and fourth neighbor Born–Von Kármán force constants. This indicates that in silicon long-range interaction between atoms is more important than in diamond. This is supported by the fact that the second neighbor Born–Von Kármán force constant model gives a pretty good fit for diamond (Warren 1965) but not silicon or germanium (Brockhouse and Iyengar 1958).

The advantage of the valence force field model over the shell model in the case of diamond is apparent. For silicon and germanium, where longer range interaction is required, the valence force field model gets quite complex. It is not clear then that the potential energy is adequately described by a function of bond lengths and angles only. Another defect is that we do not know how to calculate the dielectric properties in this model.

The indication of the existence of bond charges at mid-points between nearest neighbor atoms by the x-ray studies of Göttlicher and Wölfel (1959) and of Brill (1959) has led Warren (1965) to introduce the bond charge model. The bond is idealized as a point charge with its magnitude Z as an adjustable parameter and with its position always constrained at the mid-point between two neighboring atoms. The Coulomb interaction between the bond charges and the ions is calculated by the usual method. The short-range interaction is given by Born–Von Kármán force constants extended to second nearest neighbors. A good fit to the phonon spectrum in diamond requires Z^2 to be negative, an unphysical result. However, Martin (1969) pointed out that Warren had left out the Coulomb force constant connecting the bond charge to itself. This force constant measures the force on the bond charge due to all other charges when it is moved relative to the rest of the crystal, rather like eq. (2.8).

Martin (1968) used the bond charge model in a different way. The effective potential energy of a diatomic molecule (Borkman and Parr 1968) has a $1/r$ term which is the Coulomb energy due to the ions and the bond charge and a $1/r^2$ term due to the kinetic energy of the bond charge, r being the distance between the two atoms. Martin used this form of the potential energy for the covalent crystal, treating the bond charge as a parameter and fixing the constant in $1/r^2$ term by the equilibrium condition. A reasonable fit was obtained for diamond but not silicon and germanium which are homologous to each other but not to diamond. Martin (1969) has improved upon this model in a very fundamental way which will be described in the next section.

Vasil'ev et al. (1971) proposed a different model which takes into account the covalent bond. In each atom, the sp^3 valence electron wave functions are hybridized (Pauling 1931, 1960, Coulson 1961) into four directional orbitals. The overlap of two such orbitals from neighboring atoms forms the covalent bond. Vasil'ev et al. postulated that, in a lattice vibration, the relative directions of the hybridized orbitals from the same atom remain unchanged. The bond, therefore, gets bent. This provides a long-range interaction. Two parameters are used to specify bond bending. Two more are used for the central force constants up to the second neighbors. It is remarkable that this four parameter model gives excellent fit for diamond, silicon and germanium. One cannot help feeling that this model gives a good description of the electron response in the lattice vibration of a covalent crystal.

4. *Towards a first-principles calculation of the phonon frequencies*

From the phenomenological models described in the last section, we turn to a consideration of more fundamental constructions of the electron response in a lattice wave which gives an important contribution to the phonon frequency. The problem has essentially two parts. (1) We have to calculate the polarizability $\tilde{\chi}$ from a knowledge of the band structure of the covalent crystal. This, in principle, can be done at least in the Hartree approximation and with some exchange corrections (see §2.2). (2) From the polarizability $\tilde{\chi}$, we have to obtain the density response χ by solving an integral equation. This means summing the induced fields due to all induced dipoles, etc., i.e. solving the internal field problem. In the multipole expansion, the solution has been given by Adler (1962) and Wiser (1963). We need a more general solution than that.

In this section, we describe a couple of possible ways of obtaining the density response from the polarizability. Once that problem is breached, we are well on our way to the construction of the dynamical matrix and the calculation of the dispersion curve. We also describe a couple of semi-phenomenological models recently introduced which do get into the heart of the problem of the electron response.

4.1. The pseudo-potential method

The numerical computation of a finite matrix of $\tilde{\chi}(\boldsymbol{q}+\boldsymbol{G}, \boldsymbol{q}+\boldsymbol{G}')$ by the formulas in §2.2 and of $\chi(\boldsymbol{q}+\boldsymbol{G}, \boldsymbol{q}+\boldsymbol{G}')$ by a matrix inversion is somewhat complicated. Such an attempt to calculate the phonon spectrum in diamond, starting with a linear combination of orthogonalized plane waves for the electron Bloch states has been made by Young and Maradudin (1967).

A simpler way is to start with the electron energies and wave functions obtained by the empirical pseudo-potential method. (For a review, see Cohen and Heine 1970.) A number of plane waves and self-consistent pseudo-potential form factors are used to reproduce the knowledge of the band structure gained from experiment. Eqs. (2.23) and (2.24) can then be used to evaluate the matrix $\tilde{\chi}$ and the matrix χ. Then, χ is combined with the bare pseudo-potential $v(\boldsymbol{q}+\boldsymbol{G}; \kappa)$ to obtain the dynamical matrix. The awkward feature of this scheme is that the bare pseudo-potential $v(\boldsymbol{q}+\boldsymbol{G}; \kappa)$ is constructed from a different source than the experiments which give the self-consistent pseudo-potential for the band structure. However, Walter and Cohen (1970) have shown that the two pseudo-potentials are quite consistent by the theory of Phillips (1968a).

Nara (1965a, b), and Walter and Cohen (1970) have calculated the diagonal elements $\tilde{\chi}(\boldsymbol{q}+\boldsymbol{G}, \boldsymbol{q}+\boldsymbol{G})$ for Si, Ge, GaAs and ZnSe. It will take little further effort to obtain the complete matrix. Swanson and Maradudin (1970) have used the pseudo-potential method to calculate the Raman tensor in the homopolar semiconductors, which is the first derivative of the electron polarizability with respect to the ionic displacement. Thus, we are at a stage where, before too long, such a first-principles calculation of the phonon frequencies will be made.

4.2. Electron response in the Wannier representation

Sinha (1969), and Hayashi and Shimizu (1969) pointed out for the insulators and metals respectively that if the bands involved in the polarization, given by eq. (2.23), are well approximated by the tight-binding approximation, then the Hartree (or RPA) polarizability is of the separable form. In other words, $\tilde{\chi}(\boldsymbol{q}+\boldsymbol{G}, \boldsymbol{q}+\boldsymbol{G}')$ is a sum of a small number of products of functions of $\boldsymbol{q}+\boldsymbol{G}$, functions of $\boldsymbol{q}+\boldsymbol{G}'$ and functions of $\boldsymbol{q}$ only. Then, eq. (2.24) is reduced to a matrix equation with a small dimension rather than one running over a large number of reciprocal lattice vectors. We examine here more generally the existence of the separable form by expressing the polarizability in terms of Wannier (1937) functions rather than Bloch waves.

Consider the extension of eq. (2.23), the dynamic polarizability at frequency ω in the Hartree approximation (Ehrenreich and Cohen 1959),

$$\tilde{\chi}(\boldsymbol{q}+\boldsymbol{G}, \boldsymbol{q}+\boldsymbol{G}'; \omega) = \Omega^{-1} \sum_{\nu\nu'\boldsymbol{k}} \frac{f_{\nu'\,\boldsymbol{k}+\boldsymbol{q}} - f_{\nu\,\boldsymbol{k}}}{\mathscr{E}_{\nu'\,\boldsymbol{k}+\boldsymbol{q}} - \mathscr{E}_{\nu\,\boldsymbol{k}} - \omega}$$

$$\times \langle \nu\boldsymbol{k}|\, \rho(\boldsymbol{q}+\boldsymbol{G})\, |\nu'\boldsymbol{k}+\boldsymbol{q}\rangle \langle \nu'\boldsymbol{k}+\boldsymbol{q}|\, \rho^{+}(\boldsymbol{q}+\boldsymbol{G}')\, |\nu\boldsymbol{k}\rangle, \quad (4.1)$$

where we have introduced the one-electron density operator

$$\rho(\boldsymbol{q}+\boldsymbol{G}) = \exp\{-\mathrm{i}(\boldsymbol{q}+\boldsymbol{G})\cdot\boldsymbol{r}\}. \quad (4.2)$$

$|\nu\boldsymbol{k}\rangle$ and $\mathscr{E}_{\nu\boldsymbol{k}}$ are the eigenfunctions and eigenenergy of the one-electron hamiltonian

$$H = -(1/2m)\,\nabla^2 + V(\boldsymbol{r}), \quad (4.3)$$

where we have put $\hbar = 1$ and $V(\boldsymbol{r})$ is the self-consistent perfect lattice potential.

The polarizability can be expressed in terms of the current operator,

$$\boldsymbol{j}(\boldsymbol{q}) = (\boldsymbol{p}\,\mathrm{e}^{-\mathrm{i}\boldsymbol{q}\cdot\boldsymbol{r}} + \mathrm{e}^{-\mathrm{i}\boldsymbol{q}\cdot\boldsymbol{r}}\,\boldsymbol{p})/2m, \quad (4.4)$$

where $\boldsymbol{p}$ is the electron momentum operator. By the relation

$$[\rho(\boldsymbol{q}), H] = \boldsymbol{q}\cdot\boldsymbol{j}(\boldsymbol{q}), \quad (4.5)$$

we can write,

$$\tilde{\chi}(\boldsymbol{q}+\boldsymbol{G}, \boldsymbol{q}+\boldsymbol{G}'; \omega) = \Omega^{-1} \sum_{\nu\nu'\boldsymbol{k}} \frac{f_{\nu'\,\boldsymbol{k}+\boldsymbol{q}} - f_{\nu\,\boldsymbol{k}}}{(\mathscr{E}_{\nu'\,\boldsymbol{k}+\boldsymbol{q}} - \mathscr{E}_{\nu\,\boldsymbol{k}} - \omega)\,(\mathscr{E}_{\nu'\,\boldsymbol{k}+\boldsymbol{q}} - \mathscr{E}_{\nu\,\boldsymbol{k}})^2}$$

$$\times \langle \nu\,\boldsymbol{k}|\, (\boldsymbol{q}+\boldsymbol{G})\cdot\boldsymbol{j}(\boldsymbol{q}+\boldsymbol{G})\, |\nu'\,\boldsymbol{k}+\boldsymbol{q}\rangle \langle \nu'\,\boldsymbol{k}+\boldsymbol{q}|\, (\boldsymbol{q}+\boldsymbol{G}')\cdot\boldsymbol{j}(-\boldsymbol{q}-\boldsymbol{G}')\, |\nu\,\boldsymbol{k}\rangle. \quad (4.6)$$

Indeed, we can introduce an extension of the oscillator strength,

$$f_{\alpha\alpha'}(\boldsymbol{q}+\boldsymbol{G}, \boldsymbol{q}+\boldsymbol{G}'; \nu\,\boldsymbol{k}, \nu'\,\boldsymbol{k}+\boldsymbol{q}) = \langle \nu\,\boldsymbol{k}|\, j_\alpha(\boldsymbol{q}+\boldsymbol{G})\, |\nu'\,\boldsymbol{k}+\boldsymbol{q}\rangle$$

$$\times \langle \nu'\,\boldsymbol{k}+\boldsymbol{q}|\, j_{\alpha'}(-\boldsymbol{q}-\boldsymbol{G}')\, |\nu\,\boldsymbol{k}\rangle \frac{2mf_{\nu\,\boldsymbol{k}}(1 - f_{\nu'\,\boldsymbol{k}+\boldsymbol{q}})}{\mathscr{E}_{\nu'\,\boldsymbol{k}+\boldsymbol{q}} - \mathscr{E}_{\nu\,\boldsymbol{k}}},$$

and write

$$\tilde{\chi}(\boldsymbol{q}+\boldsymbol{G}, \boldsymbol{q}+\boldsymbol{G}'; \omega) = (m\Omega)^{-1} \sum_{\nu\nu'\boldsymbol{k}} (q_\alpha + G_\alpha)$$

$$\times f_{\alpha\beta}(\boldsymbol{q}+\boldsymbol{G}, \boldsymbol{q}+\boldsymbol{G}'; \nu\,\boldsymbol{k}, \nu'\,\boldsymbol{k}+\boldsymbol{q})\,(q_\beta + G'_\beta)/\{\omega^2 - (\mathscr{E}_{\nu'\,\boldsymbol{k}+\boldsymbol{q}} - \mathscr{E}_{\nu\,\boldsymbol{k}})^2\}. \quad (4.8)$$

By the relation,

$$[[\rho(\boldsymbol{q}), H], \rho(-\boldsymbol{q}')] = \boldsymbol{q}\cdot\boldsymbol{q}'\rho(\boldsymbol{q}-\boldsymbol{q}')/m, \tag{4.9}$$

we obtain the f-sum rule,

$$\sum_{\nu\nu'\boldsymbol{k}} (q_\alpha + G_\alpha) f_{\alpha\beta}(\boldsymbol{q}+\boldsymbol{G}, \boldsymbol{q}+\boldsymbol{G}'; \nu\,\boldsymbol{k}, \nu'\,\boldsymbol{k}+\boldsymbol{q})(q_\beta + G'_\beta)$$
$$= (\boldsymbol{q}+\boldsymbol{G})\cdot(\boldsymbol{q}+\boldsymbol{G}')\sum_{\nu\,\boldsymbol{k}} f_{\nu\boldsymbol{k}}\langle\nu\,\boldsymbol{k}|\exp\{-\mathrm{i}(\boldsymbol{G}-\boldsymbol{G}')\cdot\boldsymbol{r}\}|\nu\,\boldsymbol{k}\rangle. \tag{4.10}$$

In particular, the diagonal element ($\boldsymbol{G}=\boldsymbol{G}'$) is related to the total electron density.

All the results we have derived above in the one-electron approximation can be extended to apply exactly in many-electron systems (Pines and Noziéres 1966). For the sake of simplicity, consider first a crystal with one atom per unit cell in which all relevant electron bands are separated from each other (non-degenerate). Then, the Bloch wave can be expanded in terms of a set of Wannier functions $\varphi_\nu(\boldsymbol{r})$ which fall off exponentially at infinity (Des Cloizeaux 1964),

$$\psi_{\nu\boldsymbol{k}}(\boldsymbol{r}) = N^{-1/2}\sum_l \exp(\mathrm{i}\boldsymbol{k}\cdot\boldsymbol{x}_l)\,\varphi_\nu(\boldsymbol{r}-\boldsymbol{x}_l). \tag{4.11}$$

The polarizability, given in terms of the matrix element of the density in eq. (4.1), can be written as

$$\tilde{\chi}(\boldsymbol{q}+\boldsymbol{G}, \boldsymbol{q}+\boldsymbol{G}'; \omega) = \sum_{l\nu l'\nu'} \theta_{\nu\nu'}(\boldsymbol{q}\omega; \boldsymbol{x}_l - \boldsymbol{x}_{l'})$$
$$\times F_{\nu\nu'}(\boldsymbol{q}+\boldsymbol{G}; \boldsymbol{x}_l)\, F^*_{\nu\nu'}(\boldsymbol{q}+\boldsymbol{G}'; \boldsymbol{x}_{l'}), \tag{4.12}$$

in terms of a new polarizability function

$$\theta_{\nu\nu'}(\boldsymbol{q}\omega; \boldsymbol{x}_l - \boldsymbol{x}_{l'}) = \Omega^{-1}\sum_{\boldsymbol{k}} \exp\{\mathrm{i}\boldsymbol{k}\cdot(\boldsymbol{x}_l - \boldsymbol{x}_{l'})\}$$
$$\times (f_{\nu'\,\boldsymbol{k}+\boldsymbol{q}} - f_{\nu\,\boldsymbol{k}})/(\mathscr{E}_{\nu'\,\boldsymbol{k}+\boldsymbol{q}} - \mathscr{E}_{\nu\,\boldsymbol{k}} - \omega) \tag{4.13}$$

and the form factors of the density,

$$F_{\nu\nu'}(\boldsymbol{q}+\boldsymbol{G}; \boldsymbol{x}_l) = \int \mathrm{d}\boldsymbol{r}\,\varphi^*_\nu(\boldsymbol{r}+\boldsymbol{x}_l)\exp\{-\mathrm{i}(\boldsymbol{q}+\boldsymbol{G})\cdot\boldsymbol{r}\}\,\varphi_{\nu'}(\boldsymbol{r}). \tag{4.14}$$

Exactly the same form as eq. (4.12) can be obtained by starting from the expression (4.7) in terms of the current operator, except that

$$\theta_{\nu\nu'}(q\omega; \boldsymbol{x}_l - \boldsymbol{x}_{l'}) = \Omega^{-1}\sum_{\boldsymbol{k}} \exp\{\mathrm{i}\boldsymbol{k}\cdot(\boldsymbol{x}_l - \boldsymbol{x}_{l'})\}$$
$$\times \frac{2f_{\nu\,\boldsymbol{k}}(1 - f_{\nu'\,\boldsymbol{k}+\boldsymbol{q}})}{\{\omega^2 - (\mathscr{E}_{\nu'\,\boldsymbol{k}+\boldsymbol{q}} - \mathscr{E}_{\nu\,\boldsymbol{k}})^2\}(\mathscr{E}_{\nu'\,\boldsymbol{k}+\boldsymbol{q}} - \mathscr{E}_{\nu\,\boldsymbol{k}})}, \tag{4.15}$$

and

$$F_{\nu\nu'}(\boldsymbol{q}+\boldsymbol{G};\boldsymbol{x}_l)=\int \mathrm{d}\boldsymbol{r}\,\varphi_\nu^*(\boldsymbol{r}+\boldsymbol{x}_l)\,(\boldsymbol{q}+\boldsymbol{G})\cdot\boldsymbol{j}(\boldsymbol{q}+\boldsymbol{G})\,\varphi_{\nu'}(\boldsymbol{r}). \tag{4.16}$$

The current form has the advantage that the short wave-vector properties, (2.39), are more evident but the density form is simpler to interpret physically, as we shall see presently. Let Λ stand for the whole set of indices l, l', ν and ν'. Then, eq. (4.12) is of the form

$$\tilde{\chi}(\boldsymbol{q}+\boldsymbol{G},\boldsymbol{q}+\boldsymbol{G}';\omega)=\sum_\Lambda F_\Lambda(\boldsymbol{q}+\boldsymbol{G})\,\theta_\Lambda(\boldsymbol{q}\omega)\,F_\Lambda^*(\boldsymbol{q}+\boldsymbol{G}'). \tag{4.17}$$

The inversion of the dielectric function reduces to the calculation of the screening matrix

$$\mathsf{E}=(\mathbf{1}-\mathsf{X})^{-1}. \tag{4.18}$$

where X is the matrix with elements given by

$$X_{\Lambda\Lambda'}(\boldsymbol{q}\omega)=\sum_{\boldsymbol{G}} F_\Lambda^*(\boldsymbol{q}+\boldsymbol{G})\,v(\boldsymbol{q}+\boldsymbol{G})\,F_{\Lambda'}(\boldsymbol{q}+\boldsymbol{G})\,\theta_{\Lambda'}(\boldsymbol{q}\omega). \tag{4.19}$$

The inverse dielectric function and the density response are respectively,

$$\begin{aligned}\varepsilon^{-1}(\boldsymbol{q}+\boldsymbol{G},\boldsymbol{q}+\boldsymbol{G}';\omega)&=\delta_{\boldsymbol{G},\boldsymbol{G}'}\\&\quad+v(\boldsymbol{q}+\boldsymbol{G})\sum_{\Lambda\Lambda'}F_\Lambda(\boldsymbol{q}+\boldsymbol{G})\,\theta_\Lambda(\boldsymbol{q}\omega)\,E_{\Lambda\Lambda'}(\boldsymbol{q}\omega)\,F_{\Lambda'}^*(\boldsymbol{q}+\boldsymbol{G}'),\end{aligned} \tag{4.20}$$

and

$$\chi(\boldsymbol{q}+\boldsymbol{G},\boldsymbol{q}+\boldsymbol{G}';\omega)=\sum_{\Lambda\Lambda'}F_\Lambda(\boldsymbol{q}+\boldsymbol{G})\,\theta_\Lambda(\boldsymbol{q}\omega)\,E_{\Lambda\Lambda'}(\boldsymbol{q}\omega)\,F_{\Lambda'}^*(\boldsymbol{q}+\boldsymbol{G}'). \tag{4.21}$$

Needless to say, this scheme is practical only if the Wannier functions are fairly well localized and if only a manageable number of electronic bands are needed. Consider the idealized case of just one completely occupied valence band and one empty conduction band which are, further, well approximated by the extremely tight-binding limit. The form factors can all be neglected save the one with $\boldsymbol{x}_l=0$. Then, X is a scalar. A phonon wave excites an electron density wave described by the form factor $F_\Lambda(\boldsymbol{q}+\boldsymbol{G})$ given by eq. (4.14) with a probability $\theta_\Lambda(\boldsymbol{q}\omega)$. X represents the interaction energy between the electron density waves as can be seen from eq. (4.19) or the Fourier transform of the sum over the reciprocal lattice vectors to a lattice sum. This manner of electron screening does give the inverse dielectric function the form of a

Lorentz field correction. We could further make a multipole expansion of the interaction term X.

It is a matter of multiplying $v(\boldsymbol{q}+\boldsymbol{G})$ by a suitable factor if we wish to include the exchange correction in the Hubbard approximation, as described in §2.2. Now, in the tight-binding approximation, the most important exchange effect is the exclusion of two electrons with the same spin from occupying the same orbital on the same site. Thus, an alternative way of including the exchange is simply to remove such a contribution from $X_{\Lambda\Lambda'}$. This has worked well for the d-bands in the intermetallic compounds of β-tungsten structure (Sham 1971) but has not been tried on insulators.

Extension of the preceding results to apply to a crystal with more than one atom per unit cell but still with non-degenerate bands requires just the introduction of a structure factor into the form factor in eq. (4.14) or (4.16). Extension to the case of electronic bands which have some points of degeneracy – the case for the covalent semiconductors – calls for a more careful formulation.

Consider a number of electronic bands which have some contact with each other but are isolated from the other bands. Then it is possible to construct the Wannier functions related to the Bloch waves in these bands with exponential decay at infinity (Des Cloizeaux 1963, 1964). The number of Wannier functions $\varphi_\lambda(\boldsymbol{r})$ associated with a unit cell is equal to the number of the connected bands. The usual relation, eq. (4.11) gives what Des Cloizeaux called the quasi-Bloch waves,

$$\xi_{\lambda\boldsymbol{k}}(\boldsymbol{r}) = N^{-1/2} \sum_{l} \exp(\mathrm{i}\boldsymbol{k}\cdot\boldsymbol{x}_l)\, \varphi_\lambda(\boldsymbol{r}-\boldsymbol{x}_l), \tag{4.22}$$

They are not energy eigenstates. The Bloch waves are obtained by a unitary transformation,

$$\psi_{\nu\boldsymbol{k}}(\boldsymbol{r}) = \sum_{\lambda} c_{\nu\lambda}(\boldsymbol{k})\, \xi_{\lambda\boldsymbol{k}}(\boldsymbol{r}). \tag{4.23}$$

In terms of these Wannier functions, the polarizability has the following form

$$\tilde{\chi}(\boldsymbol{q}+\boldsymbol{G}, \boldsymbol{q}+\boldsymbol{G}'; \omega) = \sum_{\Lambda\Lambda'} F_\Lambda(\boldsymbol{q}+\boldsymbol{G})\, \theta_{\Lambda\Lambda'}(\boldsymbol{q}\omega)\, F^*_{\Lambda'}(\boldsymbol{q}+\boldsymbol{G}'), \tag{4.24}$$

Λ now stands for the indices l, λ_1, λ_2, such that

$$F_\Lambda(\boldsymbol{q}+\boldsymbol{G}) = \int \mathrm{d}\boldsymbol{r}\, \varphi^*_{\lambda_1}(\boldsymbol{r}+\boldsymbol{x}_l)\, \rho(\boldsymbol{q}+\boldsymbol{G})\, \varphi_{\lambda_2}(\boldsymbol{r}), \tag{4.25}$$

and

$$\theta_{\Lambda\Lambda'}(\boldsymbol{q}\omega) = \Omega^{-1} \sum_{\nu\nu'\boldsymbol{k}} \exp\{\mathrm{i}\boldsymbol{k}\cdot(\boldsymbol{x}_l - \boldsymbol{x}_{l'})\}\, c^*_{\nu\lambda_1}(\boldsymbol{k})\, c_{\nu'\lambda_2}(\boldsymbol{k}+\boldsymbol{q})$$

$$\times\, c_{\nu\lambda'_1}(\boldsymbol{k})\, c^*_{\nu'\lambda'_2}(\boldsymbol{k}+\boldsymbol{q})\, \frac{f_{\nu'\,\boldsymbol{k}+\boldsymbol{q}} - f_{\nu\,\boldsymbol{k}}}{\mathscr{E}_{\nu'\,\boldsymbol{k}+\boldsymbol{q}} - \mathscr{E}_{\nu\,\boldsymbol{k}} - \omega}. \tag{4.26}$$

Alternatively, we can express them in terms of the current operator, similar to eqs. (4.15) and (4.16). The density response is now given by

$$\chi(\boldsymbol{q}+\boldsymbol{G}, \boldsymbol{q}+\boldsymbol{G}'; \omega) = \sum_{\Lambda\Lambda'} F_\Lambda(\boldsymbol{q}+\boldsymbol{G})\, S_{\Lambda\Lambda'}(\boldsymbol{q}\omega)\, F^*_{\Lambda'}(\boldsymbol{q}+\boldsymbol{G}'), \tag{4.27}$$

where

$$\mathsf{S} = \boldsymbol{\theta}(\mathbf{1} - \mathsf{Y}\boldsymbol{\theta})^{-1}, \tag{4.28}$$

and

$$Y_{\Lambda\Lambda'}(\boldsymbol{q}\omega) = \sum_{\boldsymbol{G}} F^*_\Lambda(\boldsymbol{q}+\boldsymbol{G})\, v(\boldsymbol{q}+\boldsymbol{G})\, F_{\Lambda'}(\boldsymbol{q}+\boldsymbol{G}). \tag{4.29}$$

Formally, eqs. (4.21), etc. are just special cases of these above with the diagonal matrix θ.

From eqs. (2.11)–(2.13), we have the dynamical matrix made up of two parts, (1) a part due to point ion Coulomb interaction only, which can be evaluated by the usual Ewald's method (Born and Huang 1954), and (2) a part due to the mediation of the electrons, of the form

$$(M_\kappa M_{\kappa'})^{-1/2}\, \Omega_0^{-1} [\exp\{\mathrm{i}\boldsymbol{q}\cdot(\boldsymbol{x}_\kappa - \boldsymbol{x}_{\kappa'})\}\, T_{\alpha\alpha'}(\boldsymbol{q}; \kappa\kappa') - \delta_{\kappa\kappa'} \sum_{\kappa''} T_{\alpha\alpha'}(0; \kappa\kappa'')], \tag{4.30}$$

where

$$T_{\alpha\alpha'}(\boldsymbol{q}; \kappa\kappa') = \sum_{\Lambda\Lambda'} \zeta_{\alpha\Lambda}(\boldsymbol{q}, \kappa)\, S_{\Lambda\Lambda'}(\boldsymbol{q})\, \zeta^+_{\alpha'\Lambda'}(\boldsymbol{q}, \kappa'), \tag{4.31}$$

with

$$\zeta_{\alpha\Lambda}(\boldsymbol{q}, \kappa) = \mathrm{i} \sum_{\boldsymbol{G}} \exp(\mathrm{i}\boldsymbol{G}\cdot\boldsymbol{x}_\kappa)\, (q_\alpha + G_\alpha)\, v(\boldsymbol{q}+\boldsymbol{G}; \kappa)\, F^*_\Lambda(\boldsymbol{q}+\boldsymbol{G}). \tag{4.32}$$

The last quantity measures the interaction of the displaced ions with the induced electron density wave. Thus, we conclude the formal description of a method of determining phonon spectrum by means of Wannier functions.

Although there have been many applications using Wannier function expansion as a formalism (e.g. Blount 1962) and there are quite a few discussions of the general properties of the Wannier functions (e.g. Des Cloizeaux

1963, 1964), there is a lack of practical construction of Wannier functions (see, for example, Ferreira and Parada 1970). Kohn (1972) has begun a series of investigations on the construction of the Wannier functions. However, a slightly different approach whereby the method just described can still be used is the tight-binding approximation. We describe a construction due to Hall (1952, 1958) (see also Coulson et al. 1962, Rédei 1962) which apply to the covalent crystals.

The s and three p atomic wave functions in the valence shell have approximately the same radial part. It is, therefore, possible to make four hybridized wave functions (Pauling 1931), given by

$$\chi_{\boldsymbol{n}}(\boldsymbol{r}) = \tfrac{1}{2}R(r)\left[1 + 3^{1/2}\boldsymbol{n}\cdot\boldsymbol{r}/r\right], \tag{4.33}$$

where $R(r)$ is the radial wave function and $\boldsymbol{n}$ represents the four vectors $(1, 1, 1)$, $(1, -1, 1)$, $(-1, 1, -1)$, $(-1, -1, 1)$. The hybridized functions are localized in these four tetrahedral directions. We take the two atoms in the unit cell of a diamond lattice to be at the origin and $b(1, 1, 1)$ where $4b$ is the lattice constant. In the space between two neighboring atoms, the hybridized orbitals from the two atoms in the direction of the line joining the two atoms have considerable overlap. We can make the bonding and antibonding orbitals,

$$\varphi_{\boldsymbol{n}\pm}(\boldsymbol{r}) = (1/\sqrt{2})\left[\chi_{\boldsymbol{n}}(\boldsymbol{r}) \pm \chi_{-\boldsymbol{n}}(\boldsymbol{r} - b\boldsymbol{n})\right]. \tag{4.34}$$

These form the starting point of constructing the Bloch waves belonging to the four highest valence bands and four lowest conduction bands by means of eqs. (4.22) and (4.23) and determining the band structure by the tight-binding method.

Slater and Koster (1954) pointed out that this method by Hall is no different from the usual tight-binding approximation calculating the overlaps of the atomic orbitals, since the bonding and antibonding orbitals ultimately are expressed in terms of the atomic orbitals. Nevertheless, for our purpose, it may be more convenient to use the bonding and antibonding orbitals. For example, in evaluating the form factors $F_{\Lambda}(\boldsymbol{q}+\boldsymbol{G})$ by eq. (4.25), we can easily decide which overlaps of bond orbitals are more important. Hall's method also has the advantage of presenting a clear physical picture of the bond charge distribution.

The method, which we have just described, of using the bond orbitals in eqs. (4.25)–(4.32) has a very appealing, though crude physical picture. In the perfect crystal configuration, the electron system is in its ground state and the two electrons contributed by two neighboring atoms reside in the bonding orbital with opposite spins. When the ions are displaced from their equilibrium positions, the electrons in the bond may be excited to the antibonding state, creating a density wave with form factor $F_A(\boldsymbol{q}+\boldsymbol{G})$. The polarizability, given by eq. (4.26), vaguely resembles the atomic polarizability. The screening due to the electrons is determined by the polarizability and the interaction energy of the electron density waves. The electronic contribution to the force constant is finally calculated in terms of the interaction energy of the ion with the electron density waves screened by the interaction of the electron density waves among themselves.

The method has not yet been tested. It is hoped that in the near future a first-principles calculation along these lines will be carried out. This will complement nicely the empirical pseudo-potential approach described in the last subsection.

4.3. The bond charge model

For simple metals, the electronic properties can be calculated by perturbation theory in terms of the pseudo-potential linearly screened by a diagonal dielectric function (Cohen and Phillips 1961, Harrison 1966). Phillips (1968a) showed how in a covalent crystal the incomplete screening of the ion by a diagonal dielectric function can be compensated by bond charges situated mid-way between neighboring ions. The idealized point bond charge model can be used to explain the difference between the linearly screened atomic pseudo-potential and the empirical pseudo-potential obtained from optical data. Phillips (1968a) also gave a detailed description of how to use the bond charge model to calculate the phonon spectrum, but did not actually carry out an evaluation. Martin (1969) has applied Phillips' (1968a) idea in a simpler way to a calculation of the phonon spectrum of silicon. We shall describe Martin's work in more detail. This work is quite different in detail from the simple bond charge models of Warren (1965) and Martin (1968) mentioned in §3.2.

The overall band structure of silicon is nearly free-electron like. Martin (1969) first calculated the phonon spectrum of silicon using a diagonal homogeneous electron gas response. The resultant optical modes and the longitudinal acoustic modes actually are fairly close to the measured values. All the transverse acoustic modes are unstable. Since the diagonal screening gives central forces with a range of less than second neighbors, we know from the work of Born (1914) that the diamond lattice is unstable against shear.

Wohlfarth (1952) has calculated the elastic constants by using a homogeneous gas response and obtained a negative $c_{11}-c_{12}$ shear constant.

The presence of the bond charges not on the ionic sites give effective non-central forces to the ions and provide stability for the diamond lattice. The bond charges are used to provide the off-diagonal screening. In a homopolar crystal, the effective charge on each sublattice vanishes by eq. (2.44a). By eq. (2.42), this means that the effective charge provided by the off-diagonal screening exactly compensates the bare ion charge. Thus, if a bond charge is attributed to the mid-point between every pair of nearest neighbor ions, the bond charge is $-2e$. From eq. (2.36), we see that the interaction of the bond charges and the ionic charges is screened by the dielectric function $\varepsilon(\boldsymbol{q})$ which in the long-wavelength limit is just the macroscopic dielectric constant.

Martin separated the dynamical matrix sum, eq. (2.11), into diagonal and non-diagonal parts. The diagonal part consists of the Ewald sum of bare ion interaction and the electronic contribution involving $\varepsilon^{-1}(\boldsymbol{q}+\boldsymbol{G}, \boldsymbol{q}+\boldsymbol{G})$ which is approximated by $1/\varepsilon(\boldsymbol{q}+\boldsymbol{G}, \boldsymbol{q}+\boldsymbol{G})$. The diagonal element $\varepsilon(\boldsymbol{q}+\boldsymbol{G}, \boldsymbol{q}+\boldsymbol{G})$ is calculated in a two-band model by Penn (1962) and Srinivasan (1969). However, the calculation gives a positive curvature of $\varepsilon(\boldsymbol{q}, \boldsymbol{q})$ at small wave-vectors. This gives a negative elastic constant c_{11}. Martin fit the curvature (negative) to give the experimental elastic constant. Subsequently, the calculation by Walter and Cohen (1970) in fact shows a negative curvature.

Martin used the model pseudo-potential of the Heine–Abarenkov type (Heine and Abarenkov 1964). The non-diagonal part is approximated by the Coulomb interaction of the bond charges and the ionic charges screened by the macroscopic dielectric constant, with the bond charge always remaining in the mid-point between the two atoms which contribute to the bond.

Martin's model can also be put in the separable form given by (4.30)–(4.32) with the form factor given by the point bond charge and the interaction involving the bond charges being Coulombic screened by the macroscopic dielectric constant, except the interaction between the bond charge and its parent ions or its sibling bond charges which is simulated in such a way that the bond charge always stays half-way between the two ions.

The calculated phonon spectrum by Martin has fairly good overall agreement with experiment. The Raman frequency is too high and the transverse acoustic branch near the [100] zone boundary is not as flat as experiment. The latter may be improved by spreading out the bond charge distribution. Although the agreement is not as good as some of the shell models of Dolling (1963), this calculation is important in that it is a serious attempt to account for the electron screening in a lattice wave without any adjustable parameter.

The fitting of the curve of $\varepsilon(\boldsymbol{q}, \boldsymbol{q})$ is not necessary now that Walter and Cohen's calculation is available.

Gillis (1971) has extended this method for partly ionic and partly covalent crystals and examined the role of covalency in crystals with the sodium chloride structure, in particular MgO.

4.4. The generalized shell model

Sinha et al. (1971) proposed an Ansatz for the polarizability of the form

$$\begin{aligned}\tilde{\chi}(\boldsymbol{q}+\boldsymbol{G}, \boldsymbol{q}+\boldsymbol{G}') &= \chi_0(\boldsymbol{q}+\boldsymbol{G})\,\delta_{\boldsymbol{G},\boldsymbol{G}'} \\ &+ \sum_{s\alpha s'\alpha'} [\exp\{-\mathrm{i}(\boldsymbol{q}+\boldsymbol{G})\cdot\boldsymbol{x}_s\}\, f_s(\boldsymbol{q}+\boldsymbol{G})\,(q_\alpha + G_\alpha)] \\ &\times \theta^{ss'}_{\alpha\alpha'}(\boldsymbol{q})\,[(q_{\alpha'} + G_{\alpha'})\, f^*_{s'}(\boldsymbol{q}+\boldsymbol{G}')\exp\{\mathrm{i}(\boldsymbol{q}+\boldsymbol{G}')\cdot\boldsymbol{x}_{s'}\}]\,. \qquad (4.35)\end{aligned}$$

A diagonal term is separated out as $\chi_0(\boldsymbol{q}+\boldsymbol{G})$. The rest of the contribution is non-diagonal and written in the separable form as a plausible extension of the tight-binding limit observed by Sinha (1969). $\boldsymbol{x}_s$ forms a set of suitably chosen sites in the unit cell which preserve the original crystal symmetry. The form factor $f_s(\boldsymbol{q})$ is normalized at unity for $\boldsymbol{q}=0$.

The Ansatz is very similar to the form (4.24) of the polarizability derived in terms of the Wannier functions, which may be regarded as a sort of formal justification of the Ansatz. However, the functional form of $(q_\alpha+G_\alpha)\,\theta^{ss'}_{\alpha\alpha'}(\boldsymbol{q}) \times (q_\alpha+G'_{\alpha'})$ in the Ansatz is not quite correct. We see from §4.2 that, whether in terms of the density or current operator, the vector product of $\boldsymbol{q}+\boldsymbol{G}$ should be with a form factor which is a vector function of $\boldsymbol{q}+\boldsymbol{G}$, leaving the matrix $\boldsymbol{\theta}$ in the form independent of the cartesian directions α and α' in general.

From eq. (4.35), the solution of the density response and the inverse dielectric function is similar to the procedure outlined in §4.2. The effect of the extra diagonal term $\chi_0(\boldsymbol{q}+\boldsymbol{G})$ is easily taken care of by introducing a dielectric function

$$\varepsilon_0(\boldsymbol{q}+\boldsymbol{G}) = 1 - v(\boldsymbol{q}+\boldsymbol{G})\,\chi_0(\boldsymbol{q}+\boldsymbol{G})\,, \qquad (4.36)$$

which screens (i.e. divides) the Coulomb interaction term $Y_{\Lambda\Lambda'}(\boldsymbol{q})$ in eq. (4.29) and the form factors in the density response expression, eq. (4.27).

Sinha et al. examined the long-wavelength limit obtaining expressions for the macroscopic dielectric constant and the neutrality sum rule. Let us assume, for simplicity,

$$\theta^{ss'}_{\alpha\alpha'}(\boldsymbol{q}) = -\,a\delta_{\alpha\alpha'}\,, \qquad (4.36)$$

where a is a constant independent of the wave-vector. The macroscopic dielectric constant is given by eq. (2.40). We first have to evaluate the susceptibility function $\hat{\chi}(\boldsymbol{q}, \boldsymbol{q})$ defined by eq. (2.32). This is obtained by using the modified form of eq. (4.28) leaving out the long-range Coulomb part $v(\boldsymbol{q})$. Hence, the dielectric constant is given by

$$\varepsilon = 1 - 4\pi e^2 \chi_0^{(2)} + 4\pi e^2 n^2 a/(1 + aK). \tag{4.37}$$

$\chi_0^{(2)}$ is the second derivative at $q=0$ of the diagonal part $\chi_0(q)$; n is the number of sites over which s ranges, and

$$K = \sum_{\boldsymbol{G}\neq 0} \tfrac{1}{3} G^2 \left|\sum_s f_s(\boldsymbol{G}) \exp(-\mathrm{i}\boldsymbol{G}\cdot\boldsymbol{x}_s)\right|^2 v(\boldsymbol{G})/\varepsilon_0(\boldsymbol{G}). \tag{4.38}$$

The neutrality sum rule, eq. (2.44), is evaluated by working out $\hat{\chi}(\boldsymbol{q}, \boldsymbol{q}+\boldsymbol{G})$ in the same procedure as just described, giving,

$$a = -(J + K)^{-1}, \tag{4.39}$$

where

$$J = Z^{-1} \sum_{\boldsymbol{G}} \tfrac{1}{3} G^2 \left(n \sum_s \mathrm{e}^{-\mathrm{i}\boldsymbol{G}\cdot\boldsymbol{x}_s} f_s(\boldsymbol{G})/\varepsilon_0(\boldsymbol{G})\right) \left(\tfrac{1}{2} \sum_\kappa \mathrm{e}^{\mathrm{i}\boldsymbol{G}\cdot\boldsymbol{x}_\kappa} v(\boldsymbol{G};\kappa)\right). \tag{4.40}$$

In the expression for J, we have taken the lattice to be that of diamond with the ionic charge $Z=4e$.

Actually, the assumption of the simple form, eq. (4.36) is unnecessary to obtain eqs. (4.37)–(4.40). For a cubic crystal, as $q \to 0$,

$$\theta_{\alpha\alpha'}^{ss'}(\boldsymbol{q}) \to \theta^{ss'} \delta_{\alpha\alpha'}. \tag{4.41}$$

Then, by symmetry arguments‡, expressions (4.37)–(4.40) are still valid, provided a is defined by

$$a = -n^{-1} \sum_s \theta^{ss'} = -n^{-2} \sum_{ss'} \theta^{ss'}. \tag{4.42}$$

The Ansatz, (4.35), still leaves a large degree of freedom of choice. Sinha et al. chose $\chi_0(\boldsymbol{q}+\boldsymbol{G})$ to include the whole of the diagonal part. If the sites s are chosen at the centers of the covalent bonds, it becomes the bond charge model, relaxing, however, the point charge restriction. If the sites s are chosen at the ionic sites, Sinha et al. called this the generalized shell model because the form factor replacing the multipole expansion of the shell structure describes a density distribution around the ion.

‡ I am grateful to S.K. Sinha for a clarification of this point.

Sinha et al. chose the generalized shell model to calculate the phonon spectrum of silicon. The form factor $f_s(\boldsymbol{q}+\boldsymbol{G})$ is chosen to be that of a uniform distribution inside a sphere of radius r_G centered at the ionic site. The pseudopotential is of the Heine–Abarenkov (1964) form. The diagonal part $\chi_0(\boldsymbol{q}+\boldsymbol{G})$ is taken from Walter and Cohen (1970). The constant a in eq. (4.36) is determined by the sum rule. The radius r_G is adjusted to fit the measured phonon spectrum. Hubbard's approximation of exchange is used to modify $v(\boldsymbol{q}+\boldsymbol{G})$.

The over-all agreement with experiment is quite good for this one-parameter model. The inclusion of the exchange effect à la Hubbard is quite important (Sinha, private communication). It is a pity that Sinha et al. had not also calculated a phonon spectrum by choosing the sites s at the bond sites. The importance of the calculation of Sinha et al. is not in the success of the generalized shell model but in proposing quite a realistic form of the screening function and showing how the calculation can be carried through without further model construction.

List of symbols

c_{ij}	= elastic constant,
$c_{\nu\lambda}(\boldsymbol{k})$	= elements of the unitary transformation from quasi-Bloch waves to Bloch waves,
E_j	= energy of jth state of the many-electron system,
$E_{\Lambda\Lambda'}(\boldsymbol{q}\omega)$	= inverse dielectric matrix in the Wannier representation,
$\mathscr{E}_{\nu\boldsymbol{k}}$	= energy of an electron in the Bloch state $\nu\boldsymbol{k}$,
e	= charge of a proton,
$e_\alpha(\kappa\|0j)$	= polarization vector of the phonon mode $(0j)$,
$F_\Lambda(\boldsymbol{q}+\boldsymbol{G})$	= form factor of the electron density wave,
$f(\boldsymbol{q}+\boldsymbol{G})$	= exchange correction factor in the Hubbard approximation,
$f_{\nu\boldsymbol{k}}$	= occupation number of electronic state $\nu\boldsymbol{k}$,
$\boldsymbol{G}$	= reciprocal lattice vector,
H	= one-electron hamiltonian,
$\boldsymbol{j}(\boldsymbol{q})$	= electron current density operator,
$\boldsymbol{k}$	= electron wave-vector,
l	= index of a lattice vector,
M_κ	= mass of the κ ion,
$M_\alpha(j)$	= dipole moment associated with phonon mode (0j),

m	=	mass of the electron,
N	=	total number of unit cells in the crystal,
$\delta n_{l\kappa\alpha}(\boldsymbol{r})$	=	change of electron density when the $(l\kappa)$ ion is displaced,
$\boldsymbol{p}$	=	dipole moment variable in the shell model,
$\boldsymbol{q}$	=	phonon wave-vector,
$\boldsymbol{r}$	=	electron position vector,
$S_{\Lambda\Lambda'}(\boldsymbol{q}\omega)$	=	electron density response in the Wannier representation
$T_{\alpha\alpha'}(\boldsymbol{q};\kappa\kappa')$	=	part of the dynamical matrix,
$u_{l\kappa\alpha}$	=	displacement of $(l\kappa)$ ion in the α-direction,
$V(\boldsymbol{x}\kappa;\boldsymbol{x}'\kappa')$	=	effective ion–ion interaction,
$V(\boldsymbol{q}+\boldsymbol{G}\kappa;\boldsymbol{q}+\boldsymbol{G}'\kappa')$	=	double Fourier transform of the above quantity,
$\hat{V}(\boldsymbol{q}+\boldsymbol{G}\kappa;\boldsymbol{q}+\boldsymbol{G}'\kappa')$	=	short-range part of the effective ion–ion interaction,
$v(\boldsymbol{r})$	=	Coulomb interaction,
$v(\boldsymbol{q}+\boldsymbol{G})$	=	Fourier transform of the Coulomb interaction,
$\hat{v}(\boldsymbol{q}+\boldsymbol{G})$	=	short-range part of the Coulomb interaction,
$v(\boldsymbol{r}-\boldsymbol{x}_\kappa;\kappa)$	=	electron–ion pseudo-potential,
$v(\boldsymbol{q}+\boldsymbol{G};\kappa)$	=	Fourier transform of above,
$W(\boldsymbol{r},\boldsymbol{R})$	=	total ionic potential,
$X_{\Lambda\Lambda'}(\boldsymbol{q}\omega)$	=	screening matrix in the Wannier representation,
$\boldsymbol{x}_\kappa$	=	position vector of the κ ion in the unit cell at the origin,
$\boldsymbol{x}_l$	=	lattice vector,
$\boldsymbol{x}_{l\kappa}$	=	position vector of the κth ion in the lth unit cell,
$Y_{\Lambda\Lambda'}(\boldsymbol{q}\omega)$	=	interaction energy of the electron density waves,
$Z_\alpha(\boldsymbol{q},\kappa)$	=	effective charge of the sublattice in a phonon wave,
$Z_{\alpha\beta}(\kappa)$	=	effective charge tensor of the κ sublattice when it is rigidly displaced,
Z_κ	=	bare ionic charge,
α	=	cartesian direction,
$\varepsilon(\boldsymbol{r},\boldsymbol{r}')$	=	dielectric function,
$\varepsilon(\boldsymbol{q}+\boldsymbol{G},\boldsymbol{q}+\boldsymbol{G}')$	=	double Fourier transform of above,
$\varepsilon^{-1}(\boldsymbol{r},\boldsymbol{r}')$	=	inverse dielectric function,
$\varepsilon(\boldsymbol{q})$	=	macroscopic dielectric function,
$\varepsilon(\hat{q})$	=	macroscopic dielectric constant in the zero wave-vector limit,
$\varepsilon_{\alpha\beta}(\omega)$	=	infrared dielectric tensor,
$\theta_{\Lambda\Lambda'}(\boldsymbol{q}\omega)$	=	polarizability in the Wannier representation,

κ = index of an ion in the unit cell,
Λ = vertex correction,
Λ = index covering $(ll'\nu\nu')$ or $(l\lambda\lambda')$,
λ = index of a Wannier function for a set of degenrate bands,
ν = band index,
$\xi_{\lambda \boldsymbol{k}}(\boldsymbol{r})$ = quasi-Bloch wave,
$\rho(\boldsymbol{q}+\boldsymbol{G})$ = electron density operator,
$\Phi_{\alpha\alpha'}(l\kappa, l'\kappa')$ = force constant,
$\Phi_{\alpha\alpha'}(\boldsymbol{q}; \kappa\kappa')$ = dynamical matrix,
$\varphi_{\lambda}(\boldsymbol{r})$ = Wannier function for a set of degenerate bands,
$\varphi_{\nu}(\boldsymbol{r})$ = Wannier function for a non-degenerate band,
$\delta\varphi(\boldsymbol{r})$ = total self-consistent potential,
$\chi(\boldsymbol{r}, \boldsymbol{r}')$ = electron density response,
$\chi(\boldsymbol{q}+\boldsymbol{G}, \boldsymbol{q}+\boldsymbol{G}')$ = double Fourier transform of above,
$\tilde{\chi}$ = polarizability function,
$\tilde{\chi}_0$ = polarizability function in the Hartree approximation,
$\hat{\chi}$ = susceptibility function,
$\psi_{\nu \boldsymbol{k}}(\boldsymbol{r})$ = Bloch wave,
Ω = volume of the whole crystal,
Ω_0 = volume of the unit cell,
ω = phonon frequency,
ω_j = frequency of phonon mode j with zero wave-vector.

Acknowledgement

Work supported in part by the National Science Foundation, Grant No. 28997.

References

ABRIKOSOV, A.A., GORKOV, L.P. and DZYALOSHINSKI, I.E. (1963), *Method of quantum field theory in statistical physics* (Prentice Hall, New Jersey).
ADLER, S.L. (1962), Phys. Rev. **126**, 413.
AMBEGAOKAR, V. and KOHN, W. (1960), Phys. Rev. **117**, 423.
BAYM, G. (1961), Ann. Phys. (N.Y.) **14**, 1.
BLOUNT, E.I. (1962), Solid State Physics **13**, 306.
BORKMAN, R.F. and PARR, R.G. (1968), J. Chem. Phys. **48**, 1116.
BORN, M. (1914), Ann. Physik **44**, 605.
BORN, M. and HUANG, K. (1954), *Dynamical theory of crystal lattices* (Oxford University Press).

BORN, M. and OPPENHEIMER, R. (1927), Ann. Physik **84**, 457.
BRILL, R. (1959), Z. Elektrochem. **63**, 1088.
BROCKHOUSE, B.N. and IYENGAR, P.K. (1958), Phys. Rev. **111**, 747.
CHESTER, G.V. (1961), Adv. in Phys. **10**, 357.
COCHRAN, W. (1959), Proc. Roy. Soc. (London) A **253**, 260. ‘
COCHRAN, W. (1963), Rept. Prog. in Phys. **26**, 1.
COCHRAN, W. and COWLEY, R.A. (1962), J. Phys. Chem. Solids **23**, 447.
COCHRAN, W. and COWLEY, R.A. (1967), H. d. Physik **XXV 2a**, 59.
COHEN, M.H. and PHILLIPS, J.C. (1961), Phys. Rev. **124**, 1818.
COHEN, M.L. and HEINE, V. (1970), Solid State Physics **24**, 38.
COULSON, C.A. (1961), *Valence*, 2nd ed. (Oxford University Press).
COULSON, C.A., REDEI, L.B. and STOCKER, D. (1962), Proc. Roy. Soc. (London) A **270**, 357.
COWLEY, R.A. (1962), Proc. Roy. Soc. (London) A **268**, 109.
DEMIDENKO, Z.A., KUCHER, T.J. and TOLPYGO, K.B. (1961), Fiz. Tver. Tela **3**, 2482 [English Transl. Sov. Phys. Solid State **3**, 1803].
DEMIDENKO, Z.A., KUCHER, T.J. and TOLPYGO, K.B. (1962), Fiz. Tver. Tela. **4**, 104 [English Transl. Sov. Phys. Solid State **4**, 73].
DES CLOIZEAUX, J. (1963), Phys. Rev. **129**, 554.
DES CLOIZEAUX, J. (1964), Phys. Rev. **135**A, 685 and 698.
DICK, B.G. (1964), *Lattice dynamics*, ed. by R.F. Wallis, (Pergamon Press, Oxford) p. 159.
DOLLING, G. (1963), *Inelastic scattering of neutrons in solids and liquids*, (IAEA, Vienna), **2**, 37.
DOLLING, G. and COWLEY, R.A. (1966), Proc. Phys. Soc. (London) **88**, 463.
EHRENREICH, H. and COHEN, M.H. (1959), Phys. Rev. **115**, 786.
ELLIOT, R.J. (1957), Phys. Rev. **108**, 1384.
FERREIRA, L.G. and PARADA, N.J. (1970), Phys. Rev. B**2**, 1614.
GILLIS, N.S. (1971), Phys. Rev. B**3**, 1482.
GLISS, B. and BILZ, H. (1968), Phys. Rev. Letters **21**, 884.
GÖTTLICHER, S. and WÖLFEL, E. (1959), Z. Elektrochem **63**, 891.
HALL, G.G. (1952), Phil. Mag. **43**, 338.
HALL, G.G. (1958), Phil. Mag. **3**, 429.
HARRISON, W.A. (1966), *Pseudo-potentials in the theory of metals* (W.A. Benjamin, New York).
HAYASHI, E. and SHIMIZU, M. (1969), J. Phys. Soc. Japan **26**, 1396.
HEINE, V. (1970), Solid State Physics **24**, 1.
HEINE, V. and ABARENKOV, I. (1964), Phil. Mag. **9**, 451.
HERMAN, F. (1959), J. Phys. Chem. Solids, **8**, 405.
HERZBERG, G. (1945), *Infrared and Raman spectra* (Van Nostrand, New York).
HOHENBERG, P. and KOHN, W. (1964), Phys. Rev. **136** B, 864.
HSIEH, Y.C. (1954), J. Phys. Chem. Solids **22**, 306.
HUBBARD, J. (1958), Proc. Roy. Soc. (London) A **243**, 336.
KEATING, P.N. (1968), Phys. Rev. **175**, 1171.
KEATING, P.N. (1969), Phys. Rev. **187**, 1190.
KOHN, W. (1958), Phys. Rev. **110**, 857.
KOHN, W. (1972), Phys. Rev. **B7**, 4388.
KOHN, W. and SHAM, L.J. (1965), Phys. Rev. **140**, A1133.
KOROL, E.N. and TOLPYGO, K.B. (1971), Phys. Stat. Sol. **45**, 71.

KRESS, W. (1972), Phys. Stat. Sol. (b) **49**, 235.
KÜBLER, J. (1971), *The physics of semimetals and narrow-gap semiconductors*, ed. by D.L. Carter and R.T. Bate (Pergamon Press, Oxford), p. 209.
KUBO, R. (1956), Can. J. Phys. **34**, 1274.
KUCHER, T.I. and NECHIPORUK, V.V. (1966), Fiz. Tverd. Tela. **8**, 317 [English Transl. Sov. Phys. Solid State **8**, 261].
LANGRETH, D. (1969), Phys. Rev. **181**, 753.
LYDDANE, R.H., SACHS, R.G. and TELLER, E. (1941), Phys. Rev. **59**, 673.
MARTIN, R.M. (1968), Chem. Phys. Letters **2**, 268.
MARTIN, R.M. (1969), Phys. Rev. **186**, 871.
MASHKEVICH, V.S. (1960), Fiz. Tverd. Tela. **2**, 2629 [English Transl. Sov. Phys. Solid State **2**, 2345 (1961)].
MASHKEVICH, V.S. and TOLPYGO, K.B. (1957), JETP **32**, 520 [English Transl. Sov. Phys. JETP **5**, 435].
MCMURRY, H.L., SOLBRIG, A.W. JR., BOYTER, J.K. and NOBLE, C. (1967), J. Phys. Chem. Solids **28**, 2359.
MIGDAL, A.B. (1958), JETP **34**, 1438 [English Transl. Sov. Phys. JETP **7**, 996].
MUSGRAVE, M.J.P. and POPLE, J.A. (1962), Proc. Roy. Soc. (London) A**268**, 474.
NARA, H. (1965a), J. Phys. Soc. Japan **20**, 778.
NARA, H. (1965b), Science Rept. Tohoku University, **48**, 123.
NILSSON, G. and NELIN, G. (1971), Phys. Rev. B**3**, 364.
PAULING, L. (1931), J. Amer. Chem. Soc. **53**, 1367.
PAULING, L. (1960), *The nature of the chemical bond* (Cornell University Press, Ithaca).
PENG, H.W. (1941), Proc. Roy. Soc. (London) A**178**, 449.
PENN, D.R. (1962), Phys. Rev. **128**, 2093.
PHILLIPS, J.C. (1968a), Phys. Rev. **166**, 832.
PHILLIPS, J.C. (1968b), Phys. Rev. **168**, 917.
PICK, R.M., COHEN, M.H. and MARTIN, R.M. (1970), Phys. Rev. B**1**, 910.
PINES, D. and NOZIÉRES, P. (1966), *The theory of quantum liquids* (W.A. Benjamin, New York), **1**.
POPE, N.K. (1964), *Lattice dynamics*, ed. by R.F. Wallis (Pergamon Press, Oxford), p. 147.
PRICE, D.L., SINGWI, K.S. and TOSI, M.P. (1970), Phys. Rev. B**2**, 2983.
PRICE, D.L., ROWE, J.M. and NICKLOW, R.M. (1971), Phys. Rev. B**3**, 1268.
REDEI, L.B. (1962), Proc. Roy. Soc. (London) A **270**, 383.
RENNINGER, M. (1955), Acta Cryst. **8**, 606.
SCHACHTSCHNEIDER, J.H. and SNYDER, R.G. (1963), Spectrochim. Acta **19**, 117.
SCHRÖDER, U. (1966), Solid State Comm. **4**, 347.
SHAM, L.J. (1965), Proc. Roy. Soc. (London) A **283**, 33.
SHAM, L.J. (1966), Phys. Rev. **150**, 720.
SHAM, L.J. (1969a), Modern Solid State Physics, *Phonons and their interactions*, ed. by R.H. Enns and R.R. Haering (Gordon and Breach, London), **2**, 189.
SHAM, L.J. (1969b), Phys. Rev. **188**, 1431.
SHAM, L.J. (1971), Phys. Rev. Letters **27**, 1725.
SHAM, L.J. (1972), Phys. Rev. **B6**, 3581.
SHAM, L.J. and KOHN, W. (1966), Phys. Rev. **145**, 561.
SHAM, L.J. and RAMAKRISHNAN, T.V. (1971), *The physics of semimetals and narrow-gap semiconductors*, ed. by D.L. Carter and R.T. Bate (Pergamon Press, Oxford), p. 219.

SHAM, L.J. and RICE, T.M. (1966), Phys. Rev. **144**, 708.
SHAM, L.J. and ZIMAN, J.M. (1963), Solid State Physics **15**, 223.
SHERRINGTON, D. (1971), J. Phys. **C4**, 2771.
SINGH, B.D. and DAYAL, B. (1970), Phys. Stat. Sol. **38**, 141.
SINHA, S.K. (1969), Phys. Rev. **177**, 1256.
SINHA, S.K., GUPTA, R.P. and PRICE, D.L. (1971), Phys. Rev. Letters **26**, 1324.
SLATER, J.C. and KOSTER, G.F. (1954), Phys. Rev. **94**, 1498.
SMITH, H.M.J. (1948), Phil. Trans. Roy. Soc. (London) A **241**, 105.
SOLBRIG, A.W. (1971), J. Phys. Chem. Solids **32**, 1761.
SRINIVASAN, G. (1969), Phys. Rev. **178**, 1244.
SWANSON, L.R. and MARADUDIN, A.A. (1970), Solid State Comm. **8**, 859.
TOLPYGO, K.B. (1950), JETP **20**, 497.
TOLPYGO, K.B. (1961), Fiz. Tverd. Tela **3**, 943 [English Transl. Sov. Phys. Solid State **3**, 685].
VASIL'EV, L.N., LOGACHEV, YU.A., MOIZHES, B.YA and YURÉV, M.S. (1971), Fiz. Tver. Tela. **13**, 450 [English Transl. Sov. Phys. Solid State **13**, 363].
WALTER, J.P. and COHEN, M.L. (1970), Phys. Rev. B**2**, 1821.
WALTER, J.P. and COHEN, M.L. (1971), Phys. Rev. Letters **26**, 17.
WANNIER, G. (1937), Phys. Rev. **52**, 191.
WARREN, J.L. (1965), *Symp. on Inelastic scattering of neutrons by condensed systems* (Brookhaven Nat. Lab.), p. 88.
WARREN, J.L., YARNELL, J.L., DOLLING, G. and COWLEY, R.A. (1967), Phys. Rev. **158**, 805.
WAUGH, J.L.T. and DOLLING, G. (1963), Phys. Rev. **132**, 2410.
WILSON, E.B. JR., DECIUS, J.C. and CROSS, P.C. (1955), *Molecular vibrations* (McGraw-Hill, New York).
WISER, N. (1963), Phys. Rev. **129**, 62.
WOHLFARTH, E.P. (1952), Phil. Mag. **43**, 474.
WOO, J.W.F. and JHA, S.S. (1971), Phys. Rev. B**3**, 87.
YARNELL, J.L., WARREN, J.L., WENZEL, R.G. and DEAN, P.J. (1968), *Neutron inelastic scattering* (IAEA Vienna) **1**, 301.
YOUNG, J.A. and MARADUDIN, A.A. (1967), Bull. Am. Phys. Soc. **12**, 690.

CHAPTER 6

Theory of Phonons in Ionic Crystals

H. BILZ, B. GLISS and W. HANKE*

Max-Planck-Institut für Festkörperforschung, Stuttgart, Germany

* *Present address: Dept. of Physics, University of California San Diego, California 92037, USA.*

Dynamical Properties of Solids, edited by G. K. Horton and A. A. Maradudin

Contents

Introduction

Phonons are excitations in a crystal caused by correlations between the displacements of the different ions. The natural mathematical equivalent for these correlations are two-particle Green functions and, therefore, the first section begins with a representation of the interionic force constants in terms of those functions. Here, the adiabatic and harmonic approximation is always used as the background for the investigation of ionic crystals with large energy gaps and strong interionic forces. A short discussion of anharmonic effects is given in subsection 4.4 but they do not seem to effect the principal validity of the harmonic approximation in ionic crystals.

The discussion in section 1 continues with the random-phase approximation which leads in a natural way to the introduction of a dielectric function describing the screening of the Coulomb interaction between the ions by the electronic charge density.

The dielectric function method is a useful tool to exhibit the general properties of the screening mechanism and to establish some important sumrules. Since these properties are discussed in detail in Sham's article in this volume, (chapter 5) we focus attention on the question of a unified approach to the lattice dynamics of all (adiabatic non-quantum) crystals (section 2). It is shown that the dielectric function can be factorized by using a Wannier-type representation of the electronic charge density. Thus, one obtains a generalized screened dipole model which applies to metals as well as to insulators.

The practical application of the dielectric function method is still restricted to various approximations and the method does not provide a convenient basis for the fact that in ionic crystals the main part of the electronic charge density is carried along when the ions are displaced from their equilibrium positions. Therefore in section 3 other approximations are discussed, in particular the overlap method which uses a non-orthogonal set for localized wave functions. In this method a rigid overlap part can be separated from a polarization part thus leading to a description very similar to that used in phonon models.

Another rather drastic approximation is the closure approximation (subsection 3.2) which allows for a convenient representation of the dielectric function and seems to be a promising tool for further investigations.

The last section of this article deals with the interrelations of the phonon models for ionic crystals (refer to Hardy's article, chapter 3 of this volume) and the microscopic theory in its different representations. At the present time, it seems that the overlap method is most helpful in understanding the qualitative features of phonons in ionic crystals. However, the dielectric function method which encounters some basic problems, such as the non-trivial definition of the static charge in the rigid ion model, may finally become more important due to its close relation to electronic band structure, and to the ease it provides for applying general relations and sum rules.

1. *Adiabatic harmonic force constants in microscopic theory*

In order to establish a common basis for the discussions that follow in subsequent sections, we shall give a brief account of the microscopic expressions for the adiabatic, harmonic force constants. They can be derived in various equivalent ways (e.g. by using linear response theory). We rely on the use of causal Green functions hoping that this method helps to clarify some of the approximations leading to the usual Hartree dielectric function expressions.

In harmonic, adiabatic theory the force constants $\varphi_{\text{tot}}(\boldsymbol{l}, \boldsymbol{l}')$ determining the interaction of two lattice particles with equilibrium positions $\boldsymbol{X}(\boldsymbol{l})$, $\boldsymbol{X}(\boldsymbol{l}')$ and instantaneous displacements $\boldsymbol{u}(\boldsymbol{l})$, $\boldsymbol{u}(\boldsymbol{l}')$ contain a contribution from the direct interaction between the lattice particles $(\phi_{\text{c}}(\boldsymbol{l}, \boldsymbol{l}'))$ and another one $(\phi(\boldsymbol{l}, \boldsymbol{l}'))$ that stems from the instantaneous readjustment of the electron subsystem to the displacements $\boldsymbol{u}(\boldsymbol{l})$ and $\boldsymbol{u}(\boldsymbol{l}')$. In principle, $\phi_{\text{c}}(\boldsymbol{l}, \boldsymbol{l}')$ governs the harmonic Coulomb interaction between two charged nuclei while $\phi(\boldsymbol{l}, \boldsymbol{l}')$ includes contributions from all electrons in the crystal. The large binding energy of some of the electrons, however, localizes their wave-functions in the neighborhood of the nuclei so that they are mostly exposed to the strong field of particular nuclei and a change in the potential caused by the displacement of the other nuclei may be ignored. Therefore, the total electronic system is split into a set of 'valence electrons' which appear explicitly in the theory and a set of non-interacting core electrons that enter through a modification of $\phi_{\text{c}}(\boldsymbol{l}, \boldsymbol{l}')$ and of the potential the valence electrons experience during their interaction with an atom core.† The large binding energies of the core electrons usually suffice to concentrate their wave functions in a region that is small compared to interatomic distances. It is therefore common practice to assume the cores to be non-overlapping so that $\phi_c(\boldsymbol{l}, \boldsymbol{l}')$ is modified by changing the respective charges $Z(\boldsymbol{l})$. The electron lattice potential

$$U(\boldsymbol{r}, \boldsymbol{r}') = \delta(\boldsymbol{r} - \boldsymbol{r}') \sum_{\boldsymbol{l}} - Z(\boldsymbol{l}) \, |\boldsymbol{r} - \boldsymbol{X}(\boldsymbol{l}) - \boldsymbol{u}(\boldsymbol{l})|^{-1}$$

becomes a separable pseudopotential

$$U(\boldsymbol{r}, \boldsymbol{r}') = \sum_{\boldsymbol{l}} V(\boldsymbol{r}, \boldsymbol{r}'; \boldsymbol{l}).$$

If the core states can be chosen as well localized when compared to valence electron wave functions, non-local effects in the electron–core pseudopotential influence only a small portion of the valence electron wavefunction and one may neglect them for a determination of the valence electron energy.‡ Then, $\mathrm{U}(\boldsymbol{r}, \boldsymbol{r}')$ again becomes a local potential

$$U(\boldsymbol{r}, \boldsymbol{r}') = \delta(\boldsymbol{r} - \boldsymbol{r}') \sum_{\boldsymbol{l}} V(\boldsymbol{r}; \boldsymbol{l}). \tag{1.1}$$

Assuming core and valence states to be suitably determined, $\phi(\boldsymbol{l}, \boldsymbol{l}')$ is given by

$$\phi_{\alpha\beta}(\boldsymbol{l}, \boldsymbol{l}') = \frac{\partial}{\partial u_\alpha(\boldsymbol{l})} \frac{\partial}{\partial u_\beta(\boldsymbol{l}')} \langle 0| \, H \, |0\rangle ,$$

where $|0\rangle$ is the electronic ground state and H is the hamiltonian for the valence electrons only

$$H = (\hbar^2/2m) \, \Delta + \sum_{\boldsymbol{l}} V(\boldsymbol{r}; \boldsymbol{l}) + |\boldsymbol{r} - \boldsymbol{r}'|^{-1} .$$

The Hellmann–Feynman theorem yields

$$\phi_{\alpha\beta}(\boldsymbol{l}, \boldsymbol{l}') = \frac{\partial}{\partial u_\alpha(\boldsymbol{l})} \left\langle 0 \left| \frac{\partial V(\boldsymbol{r}; \boldsymbol{l}')}{\partial u_\beta(\boldsymbol{l}')} \right| 0 \right\rangle$$

because $U(\boldsymbol{r}, \boldsymbol{r}')$ is local and separable.

The ground-state average may now be rewritten in terms of the causal one-electron Green's function

$$G(\boldsymbol{r}, t; \boldsymbol{r}', t') = -\,\mathrm{i} \langle \tau(\psi(\boldsymbol{r}, t) \, \psi^+(\boldsymbol{r}', t')) \rangle .$$

† For a discussion of the formal aspects of this splitting, see Adams (1962).

‡ Further comments may be found in the book by Phillips (1969).

τ denotes time ordering, ψ and ψ^+ are appropriate Heisenberg field operators, and $\langle\rangle$ is the ground-state average. (The properties of G are explained in the book by Abrikosov et al. 1963). This gives

$$\phi_{\alpha\beta}(\boldsymbol{l}, \boldsymbol{l}') = -\,\mathrm{i} \lim_{\substack{\varepsilon\to 0\\ \varepsilon>0}} \int \mathrm{d}\boldsymbol{r} \Big\{ \delta(\boldsymbol{l}, \boldsymbol{l}')\, G(\boldsymbol{r}, t; \boldsymbol{r}, t+\varepsilon) \times \frac{\partial^2 V(\boldsymbol{r}; \boldsymbol{l}')}{\partial u_\alpha(\boldsymbol{l})\, \partial u_\beta(\boldsymbol{l}')} + \frac{\partial G(\boldsymbol{r}, t; \boldsymbol{r}, t+\varepsilon)}{\partial u_\alpha(\boldsymbol{l})} \frac{\partial V(\boldsymbol{r}; \boldsymbol{l}')}{\partial u_\beta(\boldsymbol{l}')} \Big\}. \tag{1.2}$$

Thus, because of the local approximation to U [cf. eq. (1.1)], ϕ involves only the diagonal elements of $G(\boldsymbol{r}, t; \boldsymbol{r}', t')$ and its first derivative, i.e. the electron density and its change under a lattice displacement. Since $G(\boldsymbol{r}, t; \boldsymbol{r}', t')$ is determined by an equation of motion involving H, it depends on the lattice configuration through its functional dependence on $V(\boldsymbol{r}; \boldsymbol{l})$. Using the chain rule and standard techniques (see for example, Kadanoff and Baym 1962), one can show that

$$\begin{aligned}\frac{\partial G(\boldsymbol{r}, t; \boldsymbol{r}', t')}{\partial \boldsymbol{u}(\boldsymbol{l})} &= \int \mathrm{d}\boldsymbol{r}_1 \frac{\delta G(\boldsymbol{r}, t; \boldsymbol{r}', t')}{\delta \boldsymbol{u}(\boldsymbol{r}_1)} \frac{\partial V(\boldsymbol{r}_1; \boldsymbol{l})}{\partial \boldsymbol{u}(\boldsymbol{l})}\\ &= -\lim_{\substack{\varepsilon\to 0\\ \varepsilon>0}} \int \mathrm{d}\boldsymbol{r}_1\, \mathrm{d}t_1 \{G_2(\boldsymbol{r}, t; \boldsymbol{r}_1, t_1; \boldsymbol{r}', t'; \boldsymbol{r}_1, t_1+\varepsilon)\\ &\quad - G(\boldsymbol{r}, t; \boldsymbol{r}', t')\, G(\boldsymbol{r}_1, t_1; \boldsymbol{r}_1, t_1+\varepsilon)\} \frac{\partial V(\boldsymbol{r}_1; \boldsymbol{l})}{\partial \boldsymbol{u}(\boldsymbol{l})},\end{aligned} \tag{1.3}$$

where

$$\begin{aligned}&G_2(\boldsymbol{r}_1, t_1; \boldsymbol{r}_2, t_2; \boldsymbol{r}_3, t_3; \boldsymbol{r}_4, t_4)\\ &\quad = (-\mathrm{i})^2 \langle \tau(\psi(\boldsymbol{r}_1, t_1)\, \psi(\boldsymbol{r}_2, t_2)\, \psi^+(\boldsymbol{r}_4, t_4)\, \psi^+(\boldsymbol{r}_3, t_3))\rangle\end{aligned}$$

is the two-particle Green's function. When inserting eq. (1.3) into eq. (1.2), the connection of the present method to the one based on the density–density correlation function becomes obvious. One defines a time-dependent density fluctuation operator by

$$\tilde{\rho}(\boldsymbol{r}, t) = \psi^+(\boldsymbol{r}, t)\, \psi(\boldsymbol{r}, t) - \langle \psi^+(\boldsymbol{r}, t)\, \psi(\boldsymbol{r}, t)\rangle$$

and gets

$$\phi_{\alpha\beta}(\boldsymbol{l}, \boldsymbol{l}') = \int \mathrm{d}\boldsymbol{r}\, \mathrm{d}\boldsymbol{r}'\, \mathrm{d}t'\, \mathrm{i}^{-1} \langle \tau[\tilde{\rho}(\boldsymbol{r}, t)\, \tilde{\rho}(\boldsymbol{r}', t')]\rangle \times \frac{\partial V(\boldsymbol{r}; \boldsymbol{l})}{\partial u_\alpha(\boldsymbol{l})} \frac{\partial V(\boldsymbol{r}'; \boldsymbol{l}')}{\partial u_\beta(\boldsymbol{l}')} + \left\langle \frac{\partial^2 V(\boldsymbol{r}; \boldsymbol{l})}{\partial u_\alpha(\boldsymbol{l})\, \partial u_\beta(\boldsymbol{l}')} \right\rangle.$$

We note in passing that our formulation is easily generalized to non-local electron–core potentials.

The usual Hartree dielectric function result follows from eq. (1.2) and eq. (1.3) by approximating G_2. Using the exact expression

$$G_2(1,2,3,4) = G(1,3)\,G(2,4) - G(1,4)\,G(2,3) + \mathrm{i}\int \mathrm{d}1' \cdots \mathrm{d}4'\, G(1,1')\,G(2,2') \times \Gamma(1',2',3',4')\,G(3',3)\,G(4',4),\; 1 = (\boldsymbol{r}, t), \text{ etc.} \tag{1.4}$$

and determining the vertex part Γ from an integral equation $\Gamma = \Gamma_0 + (-\mathrm{i}) \times \Gamma_0 G G \Gamma$ that relies on the approximate kernel (random phase approximation)

$$\Gamma_0(1,2,3,4) = \delta(1-3)\,\delta(2-4)\,|\boldsymbol{r}_1 - \boldsymbol{r}_2|^{-1}\,\delta(t_1 - t_2), \tag{1.5}$$

we get

$$\phi_{\alpha\beta}(\boldsymbol{l},\boldsymbol{l}') = \lim_{\substack{\varepsilon\to 0\\ \varepsilon>0}} (-\mathrm{i}) \int \mathrm{d}\boldsymbol{r}\,\mathrm{d}t'\, \frac{\partial V(\boldsymbol{r};\boldsymbol{l})}{\partial u_\alpha(\boldsymbol{l})} \frac{\partial V(\boldsymbol{r}';\boldsymbol{l}')}{\partial u_\beta(\boldsymbol{l}')} \times \Big\{ G(1,1'^{+})\,G(1',1^{+}) + (-\mathrm{i}) \int \mathrm{d}1'' \cdots \mathrm{d}4''\, G(1,1'')\,G(1',2'') \times \Gamma(1'',2'',3'',4'')\,G(3'',1^{+})\,G(4'',1'^{+}) \Big\} + \left\langle 0 \left| \frac{\partial^2 V(\boldsymbol{r};\boldsymbol{l}')}{\partial u_\alpha(\boldsymbol{l})\,\partial u_\beta(\boldsymbol{l}')} \right| 0 \right\rangle,$$

where $1^{+} = (\boldsymbol{r}, t+\varepsilon)$ and $1'^{+} = (\boldsymbol{r}', t'+\varepsilon')$. Introducing the Fourier transform of G with respect to time variables and defining a time independent Hartree propagator by

$$P(\boldsymbol{r},\boldsymbol{r}') = -\mathrm{i} \lim_{\substack{\varepsilon\to 0\\ \varepsilon>0}} \int \mathrm{d}t'\, G(\boldsymbol{r},t;\boldsymbol{r}',t')\,G(\boldsymbol{r}',t';\boldsymbol{r},t+\varepsilon) = \frac{1}{2\pi\mathrm{i}} \lim_{\substack{\varepsilon\to 0\\ \varepsilon>0}} \int \mathrm{d}\omega\, \mathrm{e}^{\mathrm{i}\omega\varepsilon} G(\boldsymbol{r},\boldsymbol{r}',\omega)\,G(\boldsymbol{r}',\boldsymbol{r},\omega) \tag{1.6}$$

one obtains

$$\phi_{\alpha\beta}(\boldsymbol{l},\boldsymbol{l}') = \int \mathrm{d}\boldsymbol{r}\,\mathrm{d}\boldsymbol{r}'\, \frac{\partial U(\boldsymbol{r})}{\partial u_\alpha(\boldsymbol{l})} \times \Big\{ P(\boldsymbol{r},\boldsymbol{r}') + \int \mathrm{d}\boldsymbol{r}_1\,\mathrm{d}\boldsymbol{r}_2\, P(\boldsymbol{r},\boldsymbol{r}_1)\,v(\boldsymbol{r}_1,\boldsymbol{r}_2)\,P(\boldsymbol{r}_2,\boldsymbol{r}') + \cdots \Big\} \frac{\partial U(\boldsymbol{r}')}{\partial u_\beta(\boldsymbol{l}')} + \left\langle 0 \left| \frac{\partial^2 V(\boldsymbol{r};\boldsymbol{l}')}{\partial u_\alpha(\boldsymbol{l})\,\partial u_\beta(\boldsymbol{l}')} \right| 0 \right\rangle, \tag{1.7}$$

where $v(\boldsymbol{r}_1, \boldsymbol{r}_2) = |\boldsymbol{r}_1 - \boldsymbol{r}_2|^{-1}$ and the higher order terms originate from subsequent, iterative approximations to Γ. Noting that

$$\Delta v(\boldsymbol{r}_1, \boldsymbol{r}_2) = -4\pi\delta(\boldsymbol{r}_1 - \boldsymbol{r}_2)$$

we can replace $\partial V/\partial u_\alpha(\boldsymbol{l})$ in eq. (1.7) by

$$-(1/4\pi)\int \mathrm{d}\boldsymbol{r}_3\,[\partial V(\boldsymbol{r}_3;\boldsymbol{l})/\partial u_\alpha(\boldsymbol{l})]\,\Delta v(\boldsymbol{r}_3, \boldsymbol{r})$$

and sum the geometric series. This gives

$$\phi_{\alpha\beta}(\boldsymbol{l}, \boldsymbol{l}') = \left\langle 0 \frac{\partial^2 V(\boldsymbol{r};\boldsymbol{l}')}{\partial u_\alpha(\boldsymbol{l})\,\partial u_\beta(\boldsymbol{l}')} 0 \right\rangle - \frac{1}{4\pi}\int \mathrm{d}\boldsymbol{r}\,\mathrm{d}\boldsymbol{r}'\,\frac{\partial V(\boldsymbol{r};\boldsymbol{l})}{\partial u_\alpha(\boldsymbol{l})}\{(1 - vP)^{-1} - 1\}_{\boldsymbol{r},\boldsymbol{r}'}\frac{\partial V(\boldsymbol{r}';\boldsymbol{l}')}{\partial u_\beta(\boldsymbol{l}')},$$

where v stands for the Coulomb interaction and 1 for a δ-function in $\boldsymbol{r}$ and $\boldsymbol{r}'$. Comparing this result to the electrostatic definition of the dielectric function relating the density response to a change in the electron–ion potential

$$\int \mathrm{d}\boldsymbol{r}'\,v(\boldsymbol{r}, \boldsymbol{r}')\frac{\partial\rho(\boldsymbol{r}')}{\partial \boldsymbol{u}(\boldsymbol{l}')} = -\int \mathrm{d}\boldsymbol{r}'\,[1 - \varepsilon^{-1}]_{\boldsymbol{r},\boldsymbol{r}'}\frac{\partial V(\boldsymbol{r}';\boldsymbol{l}')}{\partial \boldsymbol{u}(\boldsymbol{l}')},$$

$$\frac{\partial\rho(\boldsymbol{r})}{\partial u_\alpha(\boldsymbol{l})} = \frac{1}{4\pi}\Delta\int \mathrm{d}\boldsymbol{r}'\,[1 - \varepsilon^{-1}]_{\boldsymbol{r},\boldsymbol{r}'}\frac{\partial V(\boldsymbol{r}';\boldsymbol{l}')}{\partial u_\alpha(\boldsymbol{l}')}, \tag{1.8}$$

we get

$$\phi_{\alpha\beta}(\boldsymbol{l}, \boldsymbol{l}') = \left\langle \frac{\partial^2 V(\boldsymbol{r};\boldsymbol{l}')}{\partial u_\alpha(\boldsymbol{l})\,\partial u_\beta(\boldsymbol{l}')} \right\rangle + \frac{1}{4\pi}\int \mathrm{d}\boldsymbol{r}\,\mathrm{d}\boldsymbol{r}'\,\frac{\partial V(\boldsymbol{r};\boldsymbol{l})}{\partial u_\alpha(\boldsymbol{l})}[1 - \varepsilon]^{-1}_{\boldsymbol{r},\boldsymbol{r}'}\frac{\partial V(\boldsymbol{r}';\boldsymbol{l}')}{\partial u_\beta(\boldsymbol{l}')}, \tag{1.9}$$

$$\varepsilon(\boldsymbol{r}, \boldsymbol{r}') = \delta(\boldsymbol{r} - \boldsymbol{r}') - \int \mathrm{d}\boldsymbol{r}_1\,v(\boldsymbol{r} - \boldsymbol{r}_1)\,P(\boldsymbol{r}_1, \boldsymbol{r}').$$

Eq. (1.9) is the usual starting point for the dielectric function approach. We note that it is based on the assumption that the most important diagrams contributing to the harmonic adiabatic force constants are those of long-range Coulomb type; these diagrams always involve products

$$\int \mathrm{d}\boldsymbol{r}_1\,v(\boldsymbol{r}, \boldsymbol{r}_1)\,P(\boldsymbol{r}_1, \boldsymbol{r}'),$$

where P may be generalized towards a general two-point propagator that may contain terms of more complicated structure than the simple Hartree product of eq. (1.6). Such a generalization might improve the description of short-range force constants by taking the short-range exchange and correlation effects into account. Following Pick et al. (1969), one can show for a Coulomb-type potential between electrons and nuclei that the δ-function term of (1.9) cancels against $\phi_c(\boldsymbol{l}, \boldsymbol{l}')$ and that the first term in this equation may be eliminated by exploiting the translational symmetry of the total system. Thus, the total harmonic, adiabatic force constant matrix $\phi_{tot}(\boldsymbol{l}, \boldsymbol{l}')$ may be expressed by the bare charges $[Z(\boldsymbol{l})$ and $Z(\boldsymbol{l}')]$, the derivative of the Coulomb potential, and the inverse dielectric function. For the local pseudopotentials assumed here, eq. (1.9) preserves at least its structure.

So far, the Hartree inverse dielectric function has been defined in terms of the one-electron Green's function $G(\boldsymbol{r}, \boldsymbol{r}', \omega)$ that still contains all exchange and correlation effects for the equilibrium configuration. In order to further simplify the result, one approximates $G(\boldsymbol{r}, \boldsymbol{r}', \omega)$ by a sum over single particle states and energies, i.e.

$$G(\boldsymbol{r}, \boldsymbol{r}', \omega) = \sum_i \psi_i(\boldsymbol{r})\, \psi_i^*(\boldsymbol{r}') \\ \{[1 - f_i]\,(\omega - E_i + \mathrm{i}\delta)^{-1} + f_i\,(\omega - E_i - \mathrm{i}\delta)^{-1}\}.$$

Here, f_i denotes the occupation number of state i with energy E_i and δ is an infinitesimal positive quantity. Carrying out the frequency integral one finally gets

$$\varepsilon(\boldsymbol{r}, \boldsymbol{r}') = \delta(\boldsymbol{r} - \boldsymbol{r}') \\ - \sum_{i,i'} \frac{f_i - f_{i'}}{E_i - E_{i'}} \int \mathrm{d}\boldsymbol{r}_1\, |\boldsymbol{r} - \boldsymbol{r}_1|^{-1}\, \psi_i(\boldsymbol{r}_1)\, \psi_i^*(\boldsymbol{r}')\, \psi_{i'}(\boldsymbol{r}')\, \psi_{i'}^*(\boldsymbol{r}_1), \qquad (1.10)$$

where i and i' refer to the single particle states. Eqs. (1.9) and (1.10) serve as starting points for a Wannier function treatment of the problem in the next section.

2. *A unified approach to lattice dynamics*

Superficially, calculations of dispersion curves for metallic, covalent, and ionic crystals are based on several computational schemes which seem to lack a common concept. In this section we establish a unified formalism that provides a link between the theories of lattice dynamics for all these substances.

It is based on the microscopic expression for the static Hartree dielectric function $\varepsilon(\boldsymbol{q}+\boldsymbol{G}, \boldsymbol{q}+\boldsymbol{G}')$, i.e. the Fourier transform of $\varepsilon(\boldsymbol{r}, \boldsymbol{r}')$ of eq. (1.10), (RPA),† and avoids some of the difficulties that occur when an inversion of $\varepsilon(\boldsymbol{q}+\boldsymbol{G}, \boldsymbol{q}+\boldsymbol{G}')$ in reciprocal space is attempted. Since Sham (chapter 5 of this volume) and Pick (1971) have independently derived equivalent results, we only outline the procedure; for more details the reader is referred to the original papers (Hanke 1971, Hanke and Bilz 1972).

The dielectric matrix in the Hartree approximation is given by

$$\varepsilon(\boldsymbol{q}+\boldsymbol{G}, \boldsymbol{q}+\boldsymbol{G}') = \delta_{\boldsymbol{G}\boldsymbol{G}'} - v(\boldsymbol{q}+\boldsymbol{G}) \sum_{n, n', \boldsymbol{k}} \frac{f(n, \boldsymbol{k}) - f(n', \boldsymbol{q}+\boldsymbol{k})}{E(n, \boldsymbol{k}) - E(n', \boldsymbol{q}+\boldsymbol{k})} \times \langle n, \boldsymbol{k}| \exp[-\mathrm{i}(\boldsymbol{q}+\boldsymbol{G})\boldsymbol{r}] |n', \boldsymbol{q}+\boldsymbol{k}\rangle \times \langle n', \boldsymbol{q}+\boldsymbol{k}| \exp[\mathrm{i}(\boldsymbol{q}+\boldsymbol{G}')\boldsymbol{r}] |n, \boldsymbol{k}\rangle . \tag{2.1}$$

In this expression the single particle states are numbered by wave vector $\boldsymbol{k}$, and band index n. The Fourier transform of the electron–electron interaction includes local corrections for exchange and correlation effects. We now change representations and express $\varepsilon(\boldsymbol{q}+\boldsymbol{G}, \boldsymbol{q}+\boldsymbol{G}')$ in terms of generalized Wannier states $|n\,\boldsymbol{l}\rangle (\varphi_n(\boldsymbol{r}-\boldsymbol{R}(\boldsymbol{l})) = \langle \boldsymbol{r}\,|nl\rangle$.△ We get

$$\varepsilon(\boldsymbol{q}+\boldsymbol{G}, \boldsymbol{q}+\boldsymbol{G}') = \delta_{\boldsymbol{G}\boldsymbol{G}'} - v(\boldsymbol{q}+\boldsymbol{G}) \sum_{ss'} A_s(\boldsymbol{q}+\boldsymbol{G}) N_{ss'}(\boldsymbol{q}) A^*_{s'}(\boldsymbol{q}+\boldsymbol{G}'), \tag{2.2}$$

where

$$A_s(\boldsymbol{q}+\boldsymbol{G}) = \int \mathrm{d}\boldsymbol{r}\, \varphi_n(\boldsymbol{r}) \exp[-\mathrm{i}(\boldsymbol{q}+\boldsymbol{G})\boldsymbol{r}]\, \varphi_{n'}(\boldsymbol{r}+\boldsymbol{X}(\boldsymbol{l}))$$

and

$$N_{ss'}(\boldsymbol{q}) = \sum_{\boldsymbol{k}} \frac{f(n, \boldsymbol{k}) - f(n', \boldsymbol{q}+\boldsymbol{k})}{E(n, \boldsymbol{k}) - E(n', \boldsymbol{q}+\boldsymbol{k})} \exp\{-\mathrm{i}(\boldsymbol{q}+\boldsymbol{k})[\boldsymbol{X}(\boldsymbol{l}) - \boldsymbol{X}(\boldsymbol{l}')]\} .$$

Here, the index s stands for the lattice vector $\boldsymbol{l}$ and for the pair of band indices (n, n').

We now split the dielectric function of eq. (2.1) into two parts

$$\varepsilon(\boldsymbol{q}+\boldsymbol{G}, \boldsymbol{q}+\boldsymbol{G}') = \varepsilon_0(\boldsymbol{q}+\boldsymbol{G})\, \delta_{\boldsymbol{G}\boldsymbol{G}'} - v(\boldsymbol{q}+\boldsymbol{G})\, \chi(\boldsymbol{q}+\boldsymbol{G}, \boldsymbol{q}+\boldsymbol{G}'),$$

† Random Phase Approximation.

△ For simplicity we only treat the case of one particle per unit cell.

where the choice of ε_0 depends on the substance that is investigated. For systems of nearly uniform electronic densities (metal) we may choose

$$\varepsilon_0(\boldsymbol{q}) = 1 - v(\boldsymbol{q}) \sum_{\boldsymbol{k}} \frac{f(n, \boldsymbol{k}) - f(n, \boldsymbol{q}+\boldsymbol{k})}{E(n, \boldsymbol{k}) - E(n, \boldsymbol{q}+\boldsymbol{k})} \times \langle n, \boldsymbol{k}| \mathrm{e}^{i\boldsymbol{q}\boldsymbol{r}} |n, \boldsymbol{q}+\boldsymbol{k}\rangle \langle n, \boldsymbol{q}+\boldsymbol{k}| \mathrm{e}^{+i\boldsymbol{q}\boldsymbol{r}} |n, \boldsymbol{k}\rangle, \tag{2.3}$$

i.e., ε_0 contains the free-electron part of the intraband transitions in the conduction band n. (For some of the problems involved in an application of dielectric function theory to insulators, see next section).

Assuming (2.3) to hold and treating interband transitions in the Wannier representation, we get:

$$\varepsilon(\boldsymbol{q}+\boldsymbol{G}, \boldsymbol{q}+\boldsymbol{G}') = \varepsilon_0(\boldsymbol{q}+\boldsymbol{G})\, \delta_{\boldsymbol{G}\boldsymbol{G}'} - v(\boldsymbol{q}+\boldsymbol{G}) \sum_{ss'} A_s(\boldsymbol{q}+\boldsymbol{G})\, N_{ss'}(\boldsymbol{q})\, A^*_{s'}(\boldsymbol{q}+\boldsymbol{G}'). \tag{2.4}$$

The splitting picks out the smooth part of the conduction band wave function and treats it separately, because its inclusion in the factorization procedure of eq. (2.2) would enhance the number of lattice vectors $(\boldsymbol{X}(\boldsymbol{l}), \boldsymbol{X}(\boldsymbol{l}'))$ that are needed in the summation over s and s'. Then the dimension of the matrix N would be large and an explicit solution of the inversion problem would be difficult.

Eq. (2.4) enables us to calculate the inverse dielectric matrix

$$\varepsilon^{-1}(\boldsymbol{q}+\boldsymbol{G}, \boldsymbol{q}+\boldsymbol{G}') = \left\{ \delta_{\boldsymbol{G}\boldsymbol{G}'} - \frac{v(\boldsymbol{q}+\boldsymbol{G})}{\varepsilon_0(\boldsymbol{q}+\boldsymbol{G})} \sum_{ss'} A_s(\boldsymbol{q}+\boldsymbol{G}) \times [V(\boldsymbol{q}) + N^{-1}(\boldsymbol{q})]^{-1}_{ss'} A^*_{s'}(\boldsymbol{q}+\boldsymbol{G}') \right\} \frac{1}{\varepsilon_0(\boldsymbol{q}+\boldsymbol{G}')}, \tag{2.5}$$

where the matrix V is defined by

$$V_{ss'}(\boldsymbol{q}) = -\sum_{\boldsymbol{G}} A_s(\boldsymbol{q}+\boldsymbol{G}) \frac{v(\boldsymbol{q}+\boldsymbol{G})}{\varepsilon_0(\boldsymbol{q}+\boldsymbol{G})} A^*_{s'}(\boldsymbol{q}+\boldsymbol{G}).$$

One can show that by employing a localized description even for crystals of a complicated band structure (transition metals) the problem of inversion of the dielectric matrix can be reduced to the inversion of a small-dimensional matrix $(V+N^{-1})^{-1}$ *if* a suitable subspace of energy band functions is formed from crossing, touching, or hybridizing bands and if the Wannier functions are thought to represent local states for all electrons in the subspace (Des Cloizeaux 1963, 1964, and Bross 1971).

In order to interpret our results, we now consider the response of the electron system to a weak, external perturbation. (Our discussion is similar to that given by Sinha et al. 1971).

We make use of the following definition (Sinha 1968, Hanke and Bilz 1972).

$$A_s(\boldsymbol{q}+\boldsymbol{G}) = \sum_\alpha (\boldsymbol{q}+\boldsymbol{G})_\alpha \, f_s^\alpha(\boldsymbol{q}+\boldsymbol{G}) \,. \tag{2.6}$$

(α denotes the α component of a three-dimensional vector).

In the RPA, the density response to a weak external perturbation $\delta V(\boldsymbol{q})$ is given by [cf. eq. (1.9)]

$$\delta\rho(\boldsymbol{q}) = -\frac{1}{v(\boldsymbol{q})} \sum_{\boldsymbol{G}} (1-\varepsilon)^{-1}_{\boldsymbol{q},\boldsymbol{q}+\boldsymbol{G}} \, \delta V(\boldsymbol{q}+\boldsymbol{G}) \,.$$

Using eqs. (2.5) and (2.6) we get

$$\delta\rho(\boldsymbol{q}) = -\frac{1}{v(\boldsymbol{q})}\left(1-\frac{1}{\varepsilon_0(\boldsymbol{q})}\right)\delta V(\boldsymbol{q}) + \mathrm{i}\sum_\alpha q_\alpha p_\alpha(\boldsymbol{q}) \,, \tag{2.7}$$

where

$$p_\alpha(\boldsymbol{q}) = -\sum_{s,s'} \frac{f_s(\boldsymbol{q})}{\varepsilon_0(\boldsymbol{q})} S_{ss'}(q) \sum_{\beta \boldsymbol{G}'} (\boldsymbol{q}+\boldsymbol{G})_\beta \frac{f_{s'}^\beta(\boldsymbol{q}+\boldsymbol{G})^*}{\varepsilon_0(\boldsymbol{q}+\boldsymbol{G})} \delta V(\boldsymbol{q}+\boldsymbol{G}) \,,$$

$$S_{ss'}(\boldsymbol{q}) = [V(\boldsymbol{q}) + N^{-1}(\boldsymbol{q})]^{-1}_{ss'} \,. \tag{2.8}$$

The first term in eq. (2.7) can be interpreted as the Hartree electron response for a system of uniform charge density that is determined by a scalar dielectric function. The second term corresponds to the electron density associated with dipole distributions. This term has been given in an approximate ad-hoc fashion by Sinha et al. (1971).

The dipole distribution $\boldsymbol{p}(\boldsymbol{q})$ as defined in eq. (2.8) arises from an interaction of the external potential $V(\boldsymbol{q})$ with the screened dipole distribution $\boldsymbol{f}_s(\boldsymbol{q})/\varepsilon_0(\boldsymbol{q})$. The resulting modified charge distribution then yields, by means of a polarization tensor $\boldsymbol{S}$ of the whole medium, a modification of the dipole distribution $\boldsymbol{f}_s(\boldsymbol{q})/\varepsilon_0(\boldsymbol{q})$. We note that this interpretation parallels that of the shell model familiar from the lattice dynamics of insulators. The interrelation between the microscopic theory and the shell model will become even more apparent if we consider the dynamical matrix. For Coulomb type electron–core potentials, the adiabatic, harmonic force constants and their Fourier transform, the dynamical matrix, depend on the inverse dielectric function and the static charges, only (compare the discussion of section 1 for the implications of introducing a pseudopotential). Following Keating (1968), Sham (1969), and Pick et al. (1969) one gets

$$D_{\alpha\beta}(\boldsymbol{q}) = \bar{D}_{\alpha\beta}(\boldsymbol{q}) - \bar{D}_{\alpha\beta}(0), \tag{2.9a}$$

where

$$\bar{D}_{\alpha\beta}(\boldsymbol{q}) = \frac{4\pi Z^2 e^2}{\Omega_0} \sum_{\boldsymbol{G}\boldsymbol{G}'} \frac{(\boldsymbol{q}+\boldsymbol{G})_\alpha (\boldsymbol{q}+\boldsymbol{G}')_\beta}{|\boldsymbol{q}+\boldsymbol{G}|^2} \varepsilon^{-1}(\boldsymbol{q}+\boldsymbol{G}, \boldsymbol{q}+\boldsymbol{G}'),$$

and Z is the charge of the nucleus situated in a cell of volume Ω_0. After solving the inversion problem we are in the position to derive, by means of eqs. (2.5), (2.6) and (2.8), an explicit expression for the dynamical matrix:

$$\bar{D}_{\alpha\beta}(\boldsymbol{q}) = \frac{4\pi Z^2 e^2}{\Omega_0} \sum_{\boldsymbol{G}} \frac{(\boldsymbol{q}+\boldsymbol{G})_\alpha (\boldsymbol{q}+\boldsymbol{G})_\beta}{|\boldsymbol{q}+\boldsymbol{G}|^2} \left[1 + \left(\frac{1}{\varepsilon_0(\boldsymbol{q}+\boldsymbol{G})} - 1\right)\right] + \frac{Z^2}{\Omega_0} \sum_{ss'} W_\alpha(s)\, S_{ss'}(\boldsymbol{q})\, W^*_\beta(s'), \tag{2.9b}$$

where

$$W_{\alpha s}(\boldsymbol{q}) = \sum_{\beta\boldsymbol{G}} (\boldsymbol{q}+\boldsymbol{G})_\alpha (\boldsymbol{q}+\boldsymbol{G})_\beta\, f_s^\beta(\boldsymbol{q}+\boldsymbol{G}) \frac{v(\boldsymbol{q}+\boldsymbol{G})}{\varepsilon_0(\boldsymbol{q}+\boldsymbol{G})}.$$

This may be put into the more concise form:

$$\bar{D}_{\alpha\beta}(\boldsymbol{q}) = C_{\alpha\beta}(\boldsymbol{q}) + E_{\alpha\beta}(\boldsymbol{q}) + \sum_{ss'} W_{\alpha s}(\boldsymbol{q})\, S_{ss'} W^*_{\beta s'}(\boldsymbol{q}) \tag{2.9c}$$

Here, $\boldsymbol{C}$ is the Coulomb matrix and corresponds to the electrostatic coupling coefficient between the nuclei, and $\boldsymbol{E}$ is the expression used for the dynamical matrix of simple metals where the free-electron dielectric function has been replaced by $\varepsilon_0(\boldsymbol{q})$. The last term in eq. (2.9) is due to dipole distributions which are not necessarily centered on the atom sites $\boldsymbol{X}(\boldsymbol{l})$.

In the case of a simple metal one usually approximates the dielectric matrix by a diagonal matrix $\varepsilon_0(\boldsymbol{q}+\boldsymbol{G})$ and neglects the $N_{ss}'(\boldsymbol{q})$ term of eq. (2.2). This leads to the well-known Lindhard-type screening.

Formula (2.9) contains also the other extreme, namely that of an ideal insulator. Here $\varepsilon_0(\boldsymbol{q})=1$, which leads to vanishing $\boldsymbol{E}$ and to dipolar models. For noble and transition metals and for covalent solids, both the $\varepsilon_0(\boldsymbol{q})$ and $N_{ss}'(\boldsymbol{q})$ terms are necessary to approximate $\varepsilon(\boldsymbol{q}+\boldsymbol{G}, \boldsymbol{q}+\boldsymbol{G}')$; hence we get a 'screened dipole model' (Hanke 1971).

Expression (2.9) for the dynamical matrix enables us to examine the validity of the various methods and models used to describe lattice vibrations in all solids and to study their explicit relationship to each other. Furthermore, a practical scheme for calculating lattice dynamical properties in terms of microscopic quantities has been established. It should be noted that the structure of formula (2.9) is preserved if we assume, instead of the bare Coulomb potential of the nucleus, a local pseudopotential of an ion. In this case only the electrons which are not included in the formation of the ions take part in the dynamical screening process.

We now investigate the simplifications that result for a 'screened dipole model' if the dipole contributions are centered on the atom sites.

It was found that a sufficient condition for having the dipole distributions centered around $\boldsymbol{X}(\boldsymbol{l})$ is given by the following relation (Hanke 1971)

$$\sum_{ss'} f_s^{\alpha}(\boldsymbol{q}+\boldsymbol{G})\, N_{ss'}(\boldsymbol{q})\, f_{s'}^{\beta}(\boldsymbol{q}+\boldsymbol{G}')^* = \tilde{f}^{\alpha}(\boldsymbol{q}+\boldsymbol{G})\, N(\boldsymbol{q})\, \tilde{f}^{\beta}(\boldsymbol{q}+\boldsymbol{G}')^*, \tag{2.10}$$

where $\tilde{f}$ and $\tilde{N}$ are suitably chosen effective quantities. From this relation we get for the dipole contribution to the dynamical matrix

$$\sum_{ss'} \boldsymbol{W}_s(\boldsymbol{q})\, S_{ss'}\, \boldsymbol{W}_{s'}^{\dagger}(\boldsymbol{q}) = \tilde{\boldsymbol{W}}\tilde{S}\tilde{\boldsymbol{W}}^{\dagger}. \tag{2.11}$$

We now insert for $\delta V(\boldsymbol{q})$ [cf. eq. (2.8)] the potential of the displaced cores:

$$\delta V(\boldsymbol{q}) = -\mathrm{i}\sum_{\alpha} q_{\alpha}\, e_{\alpha}(\boldsymbol{q})\, U(\boldsymbol{q}).$$

[We have assumed that the bare nuclear potential is replaced by a local pseudopotential $U(\boldsymbol{q})$.] $\boldsymbol{e}(\boldsymbol{q})$ denotes the polarization vector of the phonon with wave-vector $\boldsymbol{q}$; then we obtain from eq. (2.8).

$$\varepsilon_0(\boldsymbol{q})\,\tilde{S}\,\tilde{\boldsymbol{W}} + \tilde{\boldsymbol{W}}^{\dagger}\boldsymbol{e} = 0, \tag{2.12}$$

with

$$W_{\alpha}(\boldsymbol{q}) = P_{\alpha}(\boldsymbol{q})/\tilde{f}^{\alpha}(\boldsymbol{q}).$$

Eqs. (2.9), (2.11) and (2.12) correspond to the shell model equations, but are in fact representatives of a general 'screened dipole model' which is valid not only for insulators and homopolar crystals but also for metals. These equations have already been given in similar form by Sinha et al. (1971). In Sinha's paper, however, the factorization of the susceptibility $\chi(\boldsymbol{q}+\boldsymbol{G}, \boldsymbol{q}+\boldsymbol{G}')$ which corresponds to the factorization Ansatz in eq. (2.10) is a guess, while we have brought out its physical basis.

In order to discuss its meaning we assume the functions $\varphi_n(\boldsymbol{r})$ to be well localized, so that in the sum over lattice vectors $\boldsymbol{X}(\boldsymbol{l})$ and $\boldsymbol{X}(\boldsymbol{l}')$ of eq. (2.2) only the term where $\boldsymbol{l}=\boldsymbol{l}'=\boldsymbol{0}$ survives. Moreover, we use an effective two-band model for the band structure of the crystal and (in the case of a metal) assume that conduction-band contributions to the dielectric function enter only through the scalar function $\varepsilon_0(\boldsymbol{q})$. The factorization according to eq. (2.10) is then trivially fulfilled. (For two flat bands in an ionic crystal a similar discussion has been given by Sinha 1969, for metals see Eschrig, 1973).

A microscopic shell model which was based essentially on these approximations has been applied to the lattice dynamics of the transition metals Ni (Hanke and Bilz 1972) and Pd (Hanke 1973b) with fair success.[△] Furthermore, it has been shown that a phenomenological shell-model treatment of phonons in some noble and transition metals yields excellent agreement with experiment (Hanke and Bilz 1971). We therefore believe that even in these crystals the complicated band structure does not enter into the phonon calculations in detail and, therefore, an average having the form of eq. (2.10) is plausible.

3. Alternative methods for the calculation of the force constant matrix

While the Dielectric Function Method (DFM) provides an adequate approach to the computation of phonon dispersion curves in metallic substances, it meets some practical difficulties when applied to insulators. In this section we shall illustrate some of these difficulties by commenting on alternative methods for determining $\phi(\boldsymbol{l}, \boldsymbol{l}')$. A different approach to the problem is based on a parametrization of the configuration dependence of the electronic ground state. Suppose we employ the single particle approximation and assume the configuration dependence of the ground-state wave functions to be known. Then, the electronic ground-state energy can be expressed as a sum of integrals between Hartree–Fock functions, and $\phi(\boldsymbol{l}, \boldsymbol{l}')$ can be obtained by direct differentiation of $\langle 0|H|0\rangle$.

[△] The nondiagonal elements in the dipole-dipole interaction i.e. those elements containing $\tilde{\jmath}^{\alpha}(\boldsymbol{q}+\boldsymbol{G})\tilde{\jmath}^{\beta}(\boldsymbol{q}+\boldsymbol{G}')^*$ for $\boldsymbol{G}\neq\boldsymbol{G}'$, contribute about 20% to the longitudinal branches for these elements, even if the d-electron matrix S_{ss}, is computed in our completely local approximation. This demonstrates the importance of local field corrections in transition metals.

3.1. The overlap method

The overlap method of Landshoff, Löwdin and Lundqvist (Landshoff 1936, Löwdin 1950 and Lundqvist 1952, 1957) achieves the parametrization of the configuration dependence by expressing the Hartree–Fock functions in terms of non-orthogonal functions centered around the instantaneous positions of the nuclei. For the equilibrium positions, the relation between these functions and the Bloch states is given by

$$\psi_{k\alpha}(\boldsymbol{r}) = \mathrm{O}_{\boldsymbol{k}}\left\{\sum_{l'\alpha'} \varphi_{\alpha'}(\boldsymbol{r} - \boldsymbol{X}(\boldsymbol{l}'))\, \Delta_{\alpha'\alpha}^{-1/2}(\boldsymbol{l}', \boldsymbol{l})\right\}. \tag{3.1}$$

Here, $O_{\boldsymbol{k}}$ projects on the $\boldsymbol{k}$th irreducible representation of the translation group and $\Delta_{\alpha\alpha'}(\boldsymbol{l}, \boldsymbol{l}')$ contains the overlap integral

$$\mathrm{O}_{\boldsymbol{k}} f(\boldsymbol{r}) = (1/\sqrt{N}) \sum_{\boldsymbol{l}} \exp[\mathrm{i}\boldsymbol{k}\boldsymbol{X}(\boldsymbol{l})]\, f(\boldsymbol{r} - \boldsymbol{X}(\boldsymbol{l})),$$

$$\Delta_{\alpha\beta}(\boldsymbol{l}, \boldsymbol{l}') = \int \mathrm{d}\boldsymbol{r}\, \varphi_{\alpha}^{*}(\boldsymbol{r} - \boldsymbol{X}(\boldsymbol{l}))\, \varphi_{\beta}(\boldsymbol{r} - \boldsymbol{X}(\boldsymbol{l}'))$$

$$= \delta_{\alpha\beta}\delta(\boldsymbol{l}, \boldsymbol{l}') + S_{\alpha\beta}(\boldsymbol{l}, \boldsymbol{l}'). \tag{3.2}$$

It is assumed that for arbitrary displacements of the nuclei the functional form of φ remains unchanged. Then the computational problem reduces to calculating multicenter integrals and to inverting the non-orthogonality matrix Δ. For small overlap $(|S_{\alpha\beta}(\boldsymbol{l}, \boldsymbol{l}')| \ll 1)$ the latter problem can be solved by expanding $\Delta^{-1/2}$ in powers of $\boldsymbol{S}$ and by truncating the series after quadratic terms (linear terms vanish).

This approximate version of the overlap method has been successful in predicting the cohesive energies and the elastic constants of alcali halide crystals (in particular the deviation from the Cauchy relations: Löwdin 1950, Lundqvist 1952, Abarenkov and Antonova 1970).

Superficially, the overlap method seems inferior to the DFM because it is based on a (plausible) guess of the configuration dependence of $|0\rangle$. As was shown above, however, a practical application of the DFM involves various approximations; eventually it leads to the calculation of perturbation sums of the type

$$\sum_{ii'} \frac{f_i - f_{i'}}{E_i - E_{i'}}\, \psi_i(\boldsymbol{r})\, \psi_i^{*}(\boldsymbol{r}')\, \psi_{i'}(\boldsymbol{r}')\, \psi_{i'}^{*}(\boldsymbol{r})$$

which are usually treated in a 'few band approximation'. (A computational application of the few band DFM to insulators was partly successful (Gliss 1968, Gliss and Bilz 1968).

A physical reason for the difficulties encountered by a few band DFM in tightly bound systems was given by Sinha (1968). He points out that most of the charge cloud surrounding a nucleus tends to follow its motion during a displacement rigidly and that only a small part of the charge is deformed. The overlap approximation overstates the amount of charge that moves rigidly, i.e. it allows for no deformation. The few band DFM, on the other hand, may be unable to account for the predominance of the rigid motion in insulators, because the rigidly displaced wavefunctions do not appear in the expansion set for the perturbed wavefunctions.

Attempts to overcome these difficulties were made by Sinha on the basis of the APW-method (Sinha 1968, 1969). Later Sinha et al. (1973a) succeeded in recasting their division of charge (into a rigid and a deformable part) in the form of a canonical transformation. They introduce elementary cells $V_0(\boldsymbol{l})$ (which are subunits of the unit cell) centered around the nuclei. The current operator $\boldsymbol{J}(\boldsymbol{r})$ associated with the displacement of the cell-charge generates a canonical transformation e^S by

$$S = \sum_{l} O_l; \qquad O_l = u_l \operatorname{Im}\{\boldsymbol{J}(\boldsymbol{r})\}, \text{ for } \boldsymbol{r} \text{ inside } V_0(\boldsymbol{l}),$$
$$O_l = 0, \qquad \text{for } \boldsymbol{r} \text{ outside } V_0(\boldsymbol{l}).$$

By applying e^S to the wavefunctions they succeed in eliminating the influence of the rigidly displaced charge within the harmonic approximation and obtain a weak residual interaction potential for the coupling of the deformable charge to the motion of the nuclei. We note that their method does not suffer from a division of the electron states into core- and valence-electron states (however, the choice of the cells $V_0(\boldsymbol{l})$ is arbitrary) and that the transformation holds beyond the adiabatic approximation.

A simple approach to the problem was made by Gliss et al. (1971). Here the rigidly displaced non-orthogonal wavefunctions are included in the expansion set. A similar ground state was used by Kühner (Kühner 1969) in an attempt to link the equations of motion of the 'breathing shell model' to microscopic expressions. The deformation of the charge cloud is taken into account by allowing an admixture of excited states of the system to the displaced ground state

$$|\boldsymbol{u}\rangle = \sum_{jt} (b_j^+ + c_j^t a_t^+)\, a_j |0\rangle,$$

where b_j^+ creates a properly orthogonalized displaced ground-state function, the c_j^t are admixture coefficients for excited states (numbered by t), and a_j annihilates the jth undisplaced ground state wave function. The 'rigid overlap approximation' results when all c_j are set equal to zero. It is equivalent to the Löwdin method if the basis functions are chosen to be free ion wave functions*, but, in principle, the basis functions could be determined by any appropriate computational scheme; e.g., one may assume them to be solutions of the Adams–Gilbert equations (Adams 1962, Gilbert 1964). As in Sinha's method, the deformation part is governed by a pseudopotential so that one may hope for an improved convergence of the perturbation sums.

It is worthwhile to note that the idea of decomposing the charge density into a rigid and a deformable part complies with recent model calculations for the silver halides (Fischer et al. 1972) and is also suggested by the Hohenberg–Kohn–Sham formulation of the many-electron problem (Hohenberg and Kohn 1964, Kohn and Sham 1965). The apparent success of the auxiliary neutral atom approximation based on it in metals (Dagens 1972) may explain the applicability of models based upon such a decomposition to metallic substances (Hanke and Bilz 1972).

3.2. The closure approximation

We pointed out in the preceding subsection that any approximation to $\phi(l, l')$ must account for the displacement and the deformation of the electronic wave function during a displacement of the ions. Both effects are contained in the DFM if all diagrams are computed by summing over all excited states. It is this summation which (for inhomogeneous systems where the single-particle states are not plane waves) provides a big obstacle even to an approximate numerical calculation of ϕ. A similar problem appears in the calculation of atomic polarizabilities. There, it is sometimes solved approximately by neglecting the quantum number dependence of the energy denominator and using closure (for an assessment of the method see Dalgarno 1962). We here propose to follow the same arguments and use the mean energy denominator as an adjustable parameter, so that all excited states are taken into account in an average way. From the atomic case it is evident that such a procedure may yield reasonable results for the polarizability. We shall now show that it also describes the mean displacement of charge.

* For a report on the contribution of the Löwdin term to the effective charges see the paper by Zeyher (1971).

Let us consider the example given by Sinha (1969) (a displaced atom in free space). If $\varphi(\boldsymbol{r})$ is the ground-state wave function before displacement, then $\varphi(\boldsymbol{r}-\boldsymbol{u})$ is the displaced wave function. The center of gravity of the displaced charge is then at

$$\begin{aligned}\langle \boldsymbol{r} \rangle &= \int \mathrm{d}\boldsymbol{r}\, \varphi^*(\boldsymbol{r}-\boldsymbol{u})\, \boldsymbol{r}\, \varphi(\boldsymbol{r}-\boldsymbol{u}) \\ &= \int \mathrm{d}\boldsymbol{r}\, \varphi^*(\boldsymbol{r}-\boldsymbol{u})\,(\boldsymbol{r}-\boldsymbol{u})\, \varphi(\boldsymbol{r}-\boldsymbol{u}) + \boldsymbol{u} = \boldsymbol{u}\end{aligned}$$

if it was at $\mathbf{0}$ for the undisplaced case. In closure approximation $\langle \boldsymbol{r} \rangle$ is given to first order in $\boldsymbol{u}$ by

$$\begin{aligned}\langle \boldsymbol{r} \rangle &= \langle \boldsymbol{r} \rangle_0 - \left\{ \sum_{\lambda} \langle 0 |\, \boldsymbol{r}\, | \lambda \rangle\, (E_\lambda - E_0)^{-1} \left\langle \lambda \left| \frac{\partial V}{\partial \boldsymbol{r}} \right| 0 \right\rangle (-\boldsymbol{u}) + \text{c.c.} \right\} \\ &= -\frac{1}{\Delta E} \left\{ \langle 0 |\, \boldsymbol{r} \left(\frac{\partial V}{\partial \boldsymbol{r}} \cdot (-\boldsymbol{u}) \right) | 0 \rangle + \text{c.c.} \right\}\end{aligned}$$

since $\langle \boldsymbol{r} \rangle_0 = \langle 0 | \boldsymbol{r} | 0 \rangle$ equals zero.

For spherically symmetric systems this can be rewritten as

$$\langle \boldsymbol{r} \rangle = \tfrac{8}{3} \pi \frac{1}{\Delta E} \int \mathrm{d}r r^3 \rho(r) \frac{\mathrm{d}V}{\mathrm{d}r}\, \boldsymbol{u}\,.$$

For a hydrogen-like atom of nuclear charge Z we get

$$\langle \boldsymbol{r} \rangle = -\tfrac{2}{3} \frac{\boldsymbol{u}}{\Delta E} \langle 0 |\, V\, | 0 \rangle = \tfrac{2}{3} Z^2 e^2 \frac{1}{a} \frac{\boldsymbol{u}}{\Delta E},$$

where $a = 4\pi\hbar^2/me^2$ is Bohr's radius. Since

$$\Delta E = -\tfrac{1}{2} Z^2 e^2 \frac{1}{a} \left(\frac{1}{\tilde{n}^2} - 1 \right),$$

where $\tilde{n}$ is an effective principal quantum number for the hydrogen spectrum, an infinite value of $\tilde{n}$ would lead to optimum agreement of the resulting $\langle \boldsymbol{r} \rangle$ with that of the exact theory

$$\langle \boldsymbol{r} \rangle = \tfrac{2}{3} Z^2 e^2 \frac{1}{a} \frac{2a}{Z^2 e^2}\, \boldsymbol{u} = \tfrac{4}{3} \boldsymbol{u}\,.$$

This is in agreement with Dalgarno's comment that for ΔE equaling the ionization energy of the atom, a reasonable value for the polarizability is obtained.

We arrive at a corresponding approximation for the Hartree dielectric function by introducing a mean energy denominator into eq. (1.10). ε may then be expressed in terms of the ground-state density matrix ρ

$$\varepsilon_{\mathrm{CN}}(\boldsymbol{r}, \boldsymbol{r}') = \delta(\boldsymbol{r}-\boldsymbol{r}') + \frac{2}{\Delta E}\int \mathrm{d}\boldsymbol{r}'' v(\boldsymbol{r}, \boldsymbol{r}'')\{\delta(\boldsymbol{r}'-\boldsymbol{r}'') - \rho(\boldsymbol{r}', \boldsymbol{r}'')\}\,\rho(\boldsymbol{r}'', \boldsymbol{r}'), \tag{3.3}$$

where

$$\rho(\boldsymbol{r}, \boldsymbol{r}') = \sum_{\mathrm{g}} \psi_{\mathrm{g}}(\boldsymbol{r})\,\psi^*_{\mathrm{g}}(\boldsymbol{r}')$$

is the approximate ground-state density matrix.

Analyzing ρ in terms of localized functions and assuming a single non-degenerate filled band (ground state of an insulator), we may finally express $\varepsilon_{\mathrm{CN}}$ in terms of a non-orthogonal expansion set and invert it up to a given order in the overlap. According to eqs. (3.1) and (3.2) Δ^{-1} may be written as

$$\Delta^{-1}_{\alpha\beta}(\boldsymbol{l}, \boldsymbol{l}') = \delta_{\alpha\beta}\delta_{\boldsymbol{l}\boldsymbol{l}'} - \sum_{\substack{\sigma\tau \\ \boldsymbol{l}''\boldsymbol{l}'''}} S^{1/2}_{\alpha\sigma}(\boldsymbol{l}, \boldsymbol{l}'')\,\Delta^{-1}_{\sigma\tau}(\boldsymbol{l}'', \boldsymbol{l}''')\,S^{1/2}_{\tau\beta}(\boldsymbol{l}''', \boldsymbol{l}'). \tag{3.4}$$

Omitting the subscript that enumerates different basis functions on the same site one gets from the well-known expression

$$\rho(\boldsymbol{r}, \boldsymbol{r}') = \sum_{\boldsymbol{l}\boldsymbol{l}'} \varphi(\boldsymbol{r}-\boldsymbol{l})\,\Delta^{-1}(\boldsymbol{l}, \boldsymbol{l}')\,\varphi^*(\boldsymbol{r}'-\boldsymbol{l}')$$

and from eqs. (3.3) and (3.4) for the terms of zero order in the overlap

$$\varepsilon_0(\boldsymbol{r}, \boldsymbol{r}') = \delta(\boldsymbol{r}-\boldsymbol{r}') + \frac{2}{\Delta E}\int \mathrm{d}\boldsymbol{r}'' v(\boldsymbol{r}, \boldsymbol{r}'')\{\delta(\boldsymbol{r}'-\boldsymbol{r}'') - \rho_0(\boldsymbol{r}', \boldsymbol{r}'')\}\,\rho_0(\boldsymbol{r}'', \boldsymbol{r}') \tag{3.4a}$$

Here, $\rho_0(\boldsymbol{r}, \boldsymbol{r}')$ is defined as

$$\rho_0(\boldsymbol{r}, \boldsymbol{r}') = \sum_{\boldsymbol{l}} \varphi(\boldsymbol{r}-\boldsymbol{l})\,\varphi^*(\boldsymbol{r}'-\boldsymbol{l}).$$

If we now include the second term of eq. (3.4), we obtain the remaining terms of an expansion of ε in the overlap. The lowest order off-diagonal term in S is:

$$\rho_2(\boldsymbol{r}, \boldsymbol{r}') = \sum_{\boldsymbol{l}\boldsymbol{l}'} \varphi(\boldsymbol{r}-\boldsymbol{l})\,S(\boldsymbol{l}, \boldsymbol{l}')\,\varphi^*(\boldsymbol{r}'-\boldsymbol{l}').$$

It is of second order in the overlap, since $\boldsymbol{S}(\boldsymbol{l}, \boldsymbol{l})$ vanishes identically [see eq. (3.2) for its definition]. Therefore, we get the following result for including terms of second order in the overlap:

$$\varepsilon_{\mathrm{CN}}(\boldsymbol{r}, \boldsymbol{r}') = \varepsilon_0(\boldsymbol{r}, \boldsymbol{r}') - \frac{2}{\Delta E}\int \mathrm{d}\boldsymbol{r}'' v(\boldsymbol{r}, \boldsymbol{r}'')$$
$$\times \{[\delta(\boldsymbol{r}'' - \boldsymbol{r}') - \rho_0(\boldsymbol{r}'', \boldsymbol{r}')]\, \rho_2(\boldsymbol{r}', \boldsymbol{r}'') - \rho_2(\boldsymbol{r}'', \boldsymbol{r}')\, \rho_0(\boldsymbol{r}', \boldsymbol{r}'')\}$$
$$+ \frac{2}{\Delta E}\int \mathrm{d}\boldsymbol{r}'' v(\boldsymbol{r}, \boldsymbol{r}'') \sum_{ll'} S(\boldsymbol{l}, \boldsymbol{l}')\, \tilde{\rho}(\boldsymbol{r}'' - \boldsymbol{l}')\, S(\boldsymbol{l}', \boldsymbol{l})\, \tilde{\rho}(\boldsymbol{r}' - \boldsymbol{l}), \quad (3.5)$$

where

$$\tilde{\rho}(\boldsymbol{r} - \boldsymbol{l}) = \varphi(\boldsymbol{r} - \boldsymbol{l})\, \varphi^*(\boldsymbol{r} - \boldsymbol{l}).$$

We abbreviate all second order terms by $\sum_2(\boldsymbol{r}, \boldsymbol{r}')$ and obtain

$$\varepsilon_{\mathrm{CN}}(\boldsymbol{r}, \boldsymbol{r}') = \varepsilon_0(\boldsymbol{r}, \boldsymbol{r}') + \frac{2}{\Delta E}\int \mathrm{d}\boldsymbol{r}_1\, v(\boldsymbol{r}, \boldsymbol{r}_1) \sum\nolimits_2(\boldsymbol{r}_1, \boldsymbol{r}'). \quad (3.6)$$

Inverting eq. (3.6) and dropping all terms of higher order than second, we get

$$\varepsilon_{\mathrm{CN}}^{-1}(\boldsymbol{r}, \boldsymbol{r}') = \int \mathrm{d}\boldsymbol{r}_1\, \varepsilon_0^{-1}(\boldsymbol{r}, \boldsymbol{r}_1)$$
$$\times \left\{\delta(\boldsymbol{r}_1 - \boldsymbol{r}') - \frac{2}{\Delta E}\int \mathrm{d}\boldsymbol{r}_2\, \mathrm{d}\boldsymbol{r}_3\, v(\boldsymbol{r}_1, \boldsymbol{r}_2) \sum\nolimits_2(\boldsymbol{r}_2, \boldsymbol{r}_3)\, \varepsilon_0^{-1}(\boldsymbol{r}_3, \boldsymbol{r}')\right\}. \quad (3.7)$$

Eq. (3.7) has a form that is similar to that of eq. (2.5) expressing the inverse dielectric function in terms of a diagonal and non-diagonal part. The unified theory of section 2, however, still contains infinite perturbation sums and – in principle – the inverse of an infinite matrix, while our simplified expression allows for a systematic expansion in terms of ground-state wave functions and overlap charges.

The ε_0 of this section has the well-defined meaning of including all zero overlap effects. It thus corresponds to the dielectric function one would obtain for an ensemble of non-overlapping atoms if the atomic polarizabilities were treated in the closure approximation. Therefore, one may expect $\varepsilon_{\mathrm{CN}}^{-1}$ to provide an approximation to the real ε^{-1} which – for tightly bound systems – may be superior to that of a few band dielectric function.

In conclusion we remark that analogous simplifications result, if closure is envoked for more elaborate response functions. If, instead of (1.6) the configuration dependence of exchange diagrams were included in the theory, the integral equation for Γ would involve the antisymmetrized four point function

$$\Gamma_0(1,2,3,4) = v(\boldsymbol{r}_1,\boldsymbol{r}_2)\,\delta(t_1-t_2) \times \{\delta(1-3)\,\delta(2-4) - \tfrac{1}{2}\delta(1-4)\,\delta(2-3)\}.$$

The resulting integral equation would involve a four-point Hartree–Fock propagator

$$P(\boldsymbol{r}_1,\boldsymbol{r}_2,\boldsymbol{r}_3,\boldsymbol{r}_4) = \frac{1}{2\pi\mathrm{i}} \lim_{\substack{\varepsilon\to 0\\ \varepsilon>0}} \int \mathrm{d}\omega\, \mathrm{e}^{\mathrm{i}\omega\varepsilon}\, G(\boldsymbol{r}_1,\boldsymbol{r}_4,\omega)\, G(\boldsymbol{r}_3,\boldsymbol{r}_2,\omega)$$

which could again be approximated by using closure. The equation for Γ is then much more difficult to solve, however, since Γ is now a four point function and the inverse of Γ_0 is no longer obtained by having the laplacian operate on $|\boldsymbol{r}-\boldsymbol{r}'|^{-1}$.

While from arguments of Löwdin's theory an inclusion of the configuration dependence of exchange terms seems plausible, the importance of correlation terms for determining phonon force constants in insulators is still unclear.

4. *Interrelations of microscopic theory and model treatments*

In the foregoing sections we have mainly developed the principles of the microscopic theory of phonons in the adiabatic harmonic approximation and have then discussed some important approximations which restrict the numerical effort for actual calculations to a manageable size. While calculations along these lines have shown some promising results during the last few years (refer to Sinha 1973, e.g.), the use of models is still an indispensable tool in the majority of cases, where dispersion curves of crystals have to be described with the help of a set of parameters fitted to experimental data.

The different models are investigated in detail by Hardy in chapter 3 of this volume. Here, we shall focus attention to some general features of the model treatments which illuminate certain aspects of the microscopic theory.

In section 2 a generalized 'screened dipole model' was briefly discussed which was derived from a description of the dielectric function in terms of localized electronic wave functions (Wannier functions). In particular, a sufficient condition was given [eq. (2.10)] for having the dipoles centered around the ion lattice sites. The resulting representation of the dynamical matrix obtained is very analogous to a 'shell' or 'deformation dipole' model (see Hardy's chapter in this volume). This interrelation between the dipole models and the microscopic theory originates from the basic work of Tolpygo (1950). (For a recent review, see Cochran 1971.).

The rigorous treatment within the RPA (see chapter 5 of this volume, Pick 1971, Hanke 1971) is based essentially on an explicitly local description of the screening of the ionic pseudo-potential by the electronic charge density.

This local approach reflects the physical situation in ionic crystals where 'ions' with rather well-defined radii are a useful concept which naturally leads to the rigid-ion model as a first approximation; it must then be corrected by considering the deformation of the electronic charge density around the ions. The heart of the matter is the separation of the charge distribution into a 'rigid' part which follows the ionic motion without deformation (and defines a static charge Z) and a 'deformation' part due to the dynamical screening of the interionic forces by the polarized electrons (defining a dynamical 'Szigeti' charge Z_S). We have discussed this problem in connection with the overlap approach, subsection 3.1, but shall come back to it here in connection with the model treatments.

4.1. Summary of phonon models

The crystal hamiltonian, in the adiabatic harmonic approximation, may be written as a bilinear form in terms of electronic and ionic displacements, $\boldsymbol{w}(\lambda)$ and $\boldsymbol{u}(\lambda)$, respectively

$$H = T + V = T_i + V_i + V_e + V_{ei}\,. \tag{4.1}$$

Here, the ionic kinetic energy is T_i and the ionic part of the lattice potential is given by

$$V_i = \tfrac{1}{2} \sum_{\lambda, \lambda'} \boldsymbol{u}(\lambda)\, \phi_{ii}(\lambda, \lambda')\, \boldsymbol{u}(\lambda') = \tfrac{1}{2}\boldsymbol{u}\phi\boldsymbol{u}\,. \tag{4.2}$$

Where $\lambda = (l, \kappa)$ denotes the κth particle in the lth cell. In this approximation the electronic part of the lattice potential, V_e and V_{ei}, is given by

$$V_e = \tfrac{1}{2} \sum_{\lambda, \lambda'} \boldsymbol{w}^{\dagger}(\lambda)\, \phi_{ee}(\lambda, \lambda')\, \boldsymbol{w}(\lambda') \equiv \tfrac{1}{2}\boldsymbol{w}^{\dagger}\phi_{ee}\boldsymbol{w}\,, \tag{4.3}$$

$$V_{ei} = \tfrac{1}{2} \sum_{\lambda, \lambda'} [\boldsymbol{w}^{\dagger}(\lambda)\, \phi_{ei}(\lambda, \lambda')\, \boldsymbol{u}(\lambda') + \text{c.c.}] \equiv \tfrac{1}{2}[\boldsymbol{w}^{\dagger}\phi_{ei}\boldsymbol{u} + \text{c.c.}]\,. \tag{4.4}$$

The expansion coefficients, ϕ_{ii}, etc., describe long-range Coulomb-like as well as short-range interactions, the latter ones due to overlap (exchange and correlation) effects.

In order to make the local description of the lattice potential as explicit as possible we divide, in addition, the contributions of the different ions into symmetry degrees of freedom; Γ is compatible with the site symmetry of the ions under consideration and reflects the symmetry of the interaction of the ion with its neighbors. For example:

$$\boldsymbol{w}^{\dagger}(\lambda)\,\phi_{\text{ei}}(\lambda,\lambda')\,\boldsymbol{w}(\lambda') = \sum_{\Gamma,\Gamma'} \boldsymbol{w}_{\Gamma}^{\dagger}(\lambda)\,\phi_{\text{ei}}^{\Gamma\Gamma'}(\lambda,\lambda')\,\boldsymbol{w}_{\Gamma'}(\lambda'). \tag{4.5}$$

The $\boldsymbol{w}_{\Gamma}(\lambda)$ are generalized symmetry coordinates which obviously describe the local distortion of the electronic charge densities at the ion λ.

For convenience, we distinguish between distortions with long-range interactions (multipole 'polarizabilities') and those of short-range character ('deformabilities'). The deformation dipole model and the shell model, for example, both contain a dipolar polarizability of Γ_{15}^{-} symmetry while the shell model assumes, in addition, a Γ_{15}^{-} deformability. Since the ion cores can be considered as practically rigid in this treatment, no internal degrees of freedom for the cores must be introduced.

Prior to a discussion of the different types of charge distortions let us solve for the dynamical problem. The equations of motion are

$$-M_{\kappa}\ddot{\boldsymbol{u}}(\lambda) = \frac{\partial V}{\partial \boldsymbol{u}^{\dagger}(\lambda)} = \sum_{\lambda'}\Big[\phi_{\text{ii}}(\lambda,\lambda')\,\boldsymbol{u}(\lambda') + \sum_{\Gamma'}\phi_{\text{ei}}^{\Gamma'}(\lambda,\lambda')\,\boldsymbol{w}_{\Gamma'}(\lambda')\Big], \tag{4.6}$$

$$0 = \frac{\partial V}{\partial \boldsymbol{w}_{\Gamma}^{\dagger}(\lambda)} = \sum_{\lambda'}\Big[\phi_{\text{ei}}^{\Gamma\dagger}(\lambda,\lambda')\,\boldsymbol{u}(\lambda') + \sum_{\Gamma'}\phi_{\text{ee}}^{\Gamma\Gamma'}(\lambda,\lambda')\,\boldsymbol{w}_{\Gamma'}(\lambda')\Big], \tag{4.7}$$

where eq. (4.7) means that the generalized adiabatic forces on the electrons have to vanish.

With the help of the usual Fourier transformation (see chapter 1 by Maradudin, this volume), we obtain

$$\boldsymbol{M}\omega^2\boldsymbol{U}\begin{pmatrix}\boldsymbol{q}\\ j\end{pmatrix} = \boldsymbol{D}_{\text{ii}}(\boldsymbol{q})\,\boldsymbol{U}\begin{pmatrix}\boldsymbol{q}\\ j\end{pmatrix} + \boldsymbol{D}_{\text{ei}}^{\Gamma}(\boldsymbol{q})\,\boldsymbol{W}_{\Gamma}\begin{pmatrix}\boldsymbol{q}\\ j\end{pmatrix}, \tag{4.8}$$

$$0 = \boldsymbol{D}_{\text{ei}}^{\Gamma\dagger}(\boldsymbol{q})\,\boldsymbol{U}\begin{pmatrix}\boldsymbol{q}\\ j\end{pmatrix} + \boldsymbol{D}_{\text{ee}}^{\Gamma\Gamma'\dagger}\,\boldsymbol{W}_{\Gamma'}\begin{pmatrix}\boldsymbol{q}\\ j\end{pmatrix}. \tag{4.9}$$

Here the $\boldsymbol{D}$'s are the transformed ϕ's, $\boldsymbol{M}$ is the mass matrix (M_k) and a summation convention with respect to the different Γ's is used. $\boldsymbol{U}$ and $\boldsymbol{W}$ denote the eigenvectors of the ionic and the electronic (adiabatic) normal vibrations, respectively.

Elimination of the electronic degrees of freedom leads to

$$\boldsymbol{M}\omega^2 \boldsymbol{U}\begin{pmatrix}\boldsymbol{q}\\ j\end{pmatrix} = \boldsymbol{D}(\boldsymbol{q})\,\boldsymbol{U}\begin{pmatrix}\boldsymbol{q}\\ j\end{pmatrix}, \tag{4.10}$$

with the dynamical matrix

$$\boldsymbol{D}(\boldsymbol{q}) = \boldsymbol{D}_{\text{ii}}(\boldsymbol{q}) - \boldsymbol{D}_{\text{ei}}^{\Gamma}(\boldsymbol{q})\,[\boldsymbol{D}_{\text{ee}}^{\Gamma\Gamma'}(\boldsymbol{q})]^{-1}\,\boldsymbol{D}_{\text{ei}}^{\Gamma'\dagger}(\boldsymbol{q}). \tag{4.11}$$

The first part gives the direct (rigid) interactions between the ions while the second part describes their indirect interactions via the adiabatically distorted electrons.

The principal advantage of such a treatment as compared with a more formal one where the force constants between the complete (i.e. deformable) ions are defined immediately in terms of ionic displacements is well known. The explicit treatment of the electronic degrees of freedom leads usually to force constants ϕ_{ii}, ϕ_{ei} and ϕ_{ee} much more restricted in space than the 'formal' force constants are, aside from the genuine long-range Coulomb forces which have to be treated in a standard Kellermann procedure. As a result, the number of disposable parameters can often be reduced drastically.

Furthermore, these models allow for an explicit description of the dielectric properties and suggest non-linear extensions for the treatment of infra-red absorption, Raman scattering, etc. In these cases, also the electronic eigenvectors $\boldsymbol{W}_\Gamma$ become important. They have no direct meaning in the harmonic approximation but are open to classes of unitary transformations leaving the eigenfrequencies ω_j unchanged (Leigh et al. 1971). The analysis of experimental data related to non-linear electron–ion, etc., coupling provides therefore a useful possibility to find out whether a phonon model is merely a lucky simulation of dispersion curves or whether it is of more general validity (subsection 4.3).

The different $\boldsymbol{D}$ matrices contain a short-range and a long-range Coulomb part,

$$\boldsymbol{D}_{\text{ii}}(\boldsymbol{q}) = \boldsymbol{D}_{\text{ii}}^{\text{SR}}(\boldsymbol{q}) + \boldsymbol{D}_{\text{ii}}^{\text{C}}(\boldsymbol{q}), \quad \text{etc.} \tag{4.12}$$

The different elements of the dynamical matrix will be discussed in detail in subsection 4.3. Here, we note that at the present time, it seems that the dipole approximation is sufficient for the description of *long-range* forces, if treated in the extended scheme that contains the electronic degrees of freedom. One reason is that quadrupolar corrections due to the (rigid) overlap of charges seem to be small (see Zeyher 1971 for the case of alkali halides). Another reason is that the models discussed above are by themselves able to describe 'formal' multipole forces. For example, in the diamond structure the interatomic forces between the ions do not have a dipolar part but start with quadrupole interactions due to the high symmetry of the lattice and to charge neutrality (Lax 1965, Ginter and Mycielski 1971). On the other hand, the shell model represents these quadrupolar forces by configurations of dipolar electron–ion forces which eventually, after eliminating the electrons lead to effective ion–ion forces of quadrupolar symmetry.

In order to understand the generalized deformable shell model presented in the foregoing section in more detail, we exemplify some of the important features for the case of diatomic ionic cubic crystals, especially for the alkali halides. The reader who is interested in a survey of dispersion curves in ionic crystals is referred to Hardy's article in this volume (chapter 3) and to Cochran's recent review (Cochran 1971).

The problems we shall discuss briefly in the following subsections are:
a) the static and dynamic charges of the ions and the effective field;
b) the polarizabilities of ions in crystals and
c) the ionic deformabilities.
These properties are naturally interrelated one with another.

4.2. The problem of the static charge and the rigid ion model

We consider the situation in NaBr as a specific example. We have chosen this crystal for our discussion since it has some convenient properties. Firstly, the large mass difference between Na^+ and Br^- leads to a clear separation of acoustic and optic branches. Secondly, the electronic polarizability α^+ of the positive ion, i.e. Na^+, can be neglected as compared with $\alpha^- = \alpha(Br^-)$.

The dispersion curves of this crystal have been investigated in detail by Reid et al. (1972) and are shown in fig. 1.

In the simplest microscopic approximation, one starts from the closed-shell configurations Na^+ and Br^- of the free ions. This gives a fairly good description of the equilibrium cohesive energy which may be described by a nearest-neighbor Born–Mayer potential. This is the conceptual basis of

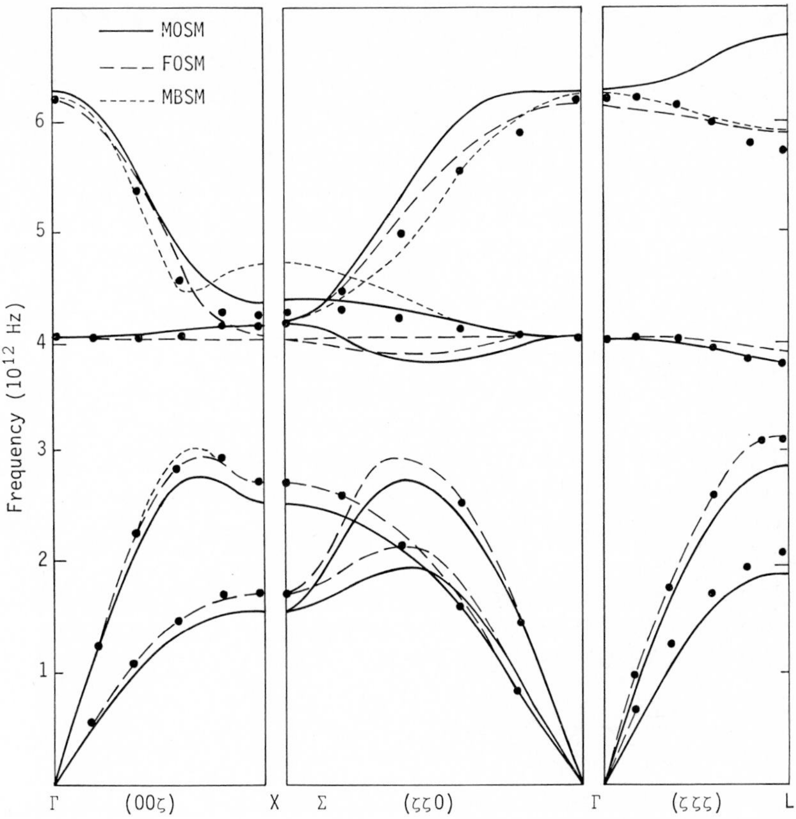

Fig. 1. Lattice dispersion curves of NaBr. OSM = Overlap – SM, BSM = Breathing SM, M... = Macroscopic..., F... = Fitted... (see text). (After Reid et al. 1970).

the rigid ion model, first discussed by Kellermann (1940). The model has only the static charge $|Z| = 1$ and one or two nearest neighbor force constants as parameters. Its simplicity may be a tempting reason to overlook the difficulties in deriving the model from a microscopic basis.

Let us first discuss the overlap method (subsection 3.1). Here, the static charge Z is not derived by some self-consistent procedure but comes from the assumption (which is very successful in calculations of ionic molecules) that the most important Heitler–London configuration in the ground-state energy is the ionic closed-shell configuration with $|Z| = 1$. Given that plausible ad-hoc assumption as a starting point the method is succesful in calculating elastic constants including the deviation from the Cauchy relation.

Even in its simplest version, where only ground-state free-ion wave functions are used ('rigid overlap approximation') the method leads to a correction of the static charge Z, which was first calculated by Lundqvist (1957) at long wavelengths and later on extended by Zeyher (1971) to all wavelengths. A similar extension was investigated by Verma and Singh (1969) who used, however, some invalid approximations (Zeyher 1971). In the rigid-ion and also in the shell model the rigid overlap screening of the static charge can approximately taken into account by lowering the static charge to values $Z \approx 0.9$ for NaCl and even lower values for NaBr and NaI depending on the asymmetry of the overlap charge distributions between the ions (Zeyher 1971). Marston and Dick (1967) have tried to take into account the overlap corrections in their exchange charge model but stopped its further development when their first results were found to be not really satisfactory.

If we now discuss the rigid ion model in the framework of the dielectric function method (DFM, section 2), we must first decide about the appropriate starting point for the calculation. In a first approximation we may treat only the outer six p-electrons of a halogen ion as taking part in the screening assuming the other more tightly bound electrons completely fixed to the nuclei. We obtain then, in a convenient short-hand notation for the dynamical matrix‡ [refer to eq. (2.9a)]:

$$\bar{\boldsymbol{D}}(\boldsymbol{q}) = \frac{4\pi e^2}{\Omega_0} \boldsymbol{Z}^2 \sum_{\boldsymbol{Q},\boldsymbol{Q}'} \frac{\boldsymbol{K}}{K} \boldsymbol{\varepsilon}^{-1}(\boldsymbol{K}, \boldsymbol{K}') \frac{\boldsymbol{K}'}{K'} \exp[\mathrm{i}(\boldsymbol{Q}\boldsymbol{r}_\kappa - \boldsymbol{Q}'\boldsymbol{r}_{\kappa'})], \tag{4.13}$$

where $\boldsymbol{K} = \boldsymbol{q} + \boldsymbol{Q}$ denotes an unrestricted wave vector and $\boldsymbol{\varepsilon}^{-1}(\boldsymbol{K}, \boldsymbol{K}')$ is the dielectric matrix in $\boldsymbol{K}$ space. The diagonal charge tensor has the form

$$\boldsymbol{Z} = \begin{pmatrix} Z_\kappa & \\ & Z_{\kappa'} \end{pmatrix} = \begin{pmatrix} +5 & \\ & +1 \end{pmatrix}$$

and demonstrates the analogy of the treatment to that used in metallic systems where the long-range *repulsive* Coulomb forces between the ions are balanced by *attractive* electron–ion forces contained in the dielectric matrix $\boldsymbol{\varepsilon}$. At a first glance, it is not easy to see how this approach is related to the usual description of the long-range ion–ion forces in ionic crystals as predominantly *attractive* forces between the positive and negative ions being in dynamical equilibriums with the short-range *repulsive* forces.

‡ For shortness, we do not introduce pseudopotentials for the core part of the bare charges. This does not affect the correctness of the following conclusions.

To understand the situation in more detail let us discuss a simple model approach where we assume that around each halogen ion (l, κ) we find the six p-electrons ('belonging' to this ion), distributed in a spherical symmetric charge distribution $\rho_\kappa(r)$ that is concentrated between the radii r_i and r_a (fig. 2). Inside that charge distribution, i.e. for $r_\kappa \lesssim r_\mathrm{i}$, the Coulomb potential

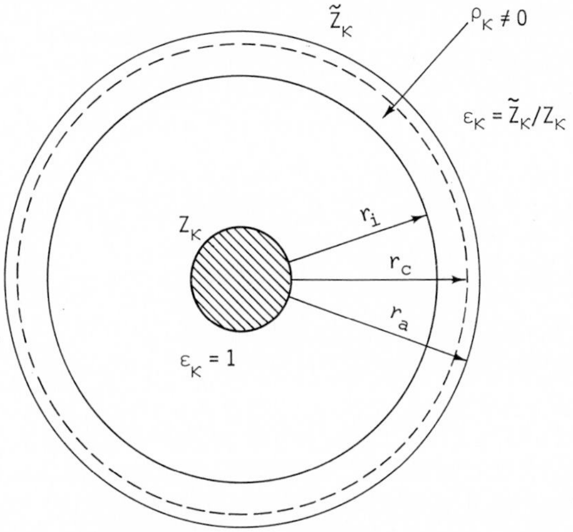

Fig. 2. Schematic charge distribution of a halogen ion. Z_κ = bare charge $(= +5)$; $\tilde{Z}_\kappa$ = static (rigid ion) charge (≈ -1). Potential: $V_\kappa(r) = Z_\kappa/\varepsilon_\kappa(r)\, r \equiv \tilde{Z}_\kappa(r)/r \to \tilde{Z}_\kappa/r$ if $r > r_\mathrm{a}$. Critical radius r_c: $V_\kappa(r_\mathrm{c}) = 0$, $\varepsilon_\kappa(r_\mathrm{c}) = \infty$.

is $Z_\kappa e/r_\kappa = 5e/r_\kappa$, while outside of $\rho_\kappa(r)$, say for $r_\kappa \gtrsim r_\mathrm{a}$, $\tilde{Z}_\kappa e/r_\kappa = -1e/r_\kappa$; that means the static charge $\tilde{Z}_\kappa e$ is then equal to the usual ionic charge. The continuous transition from 'inside' to 'outside' can be described by a potential

$$V_\kappa(r_\kappa) = \frac{Z_\kappa e}{\varepsilon_\kappa(r_\kappa)\, r_\kappa} \equiv \frac{\tilde{Z}_\kappa(r_\kappa)\, e}{r_\kappa}, \tag{4.14}$$

with

$$\varepsilon_\kappa \approx +1, \quad \text{for} \quad r_\kappa \leqslant r_\mathrm{i},$$
$$\varepsilon_\kappa \approx -5, \quad \text{for} \quad r_\kappa \gtrsim r_\mathrm{a}.$$

The local dielectric function has obviously a pole for some critical value r_c, where the potential V_κ is screened to zero. For values of $r_\kappa > r_\mathrm{c}$, the dielectric function has a negative sign and becomes asymptotically

$$\varepsilon_\kappa(r_\kappa \to \infty) \to -5.$$

For a positive ion (l, κ'), $Z_{\kappa'} = \tilde{Z}_{\kappa'} = +1$, in the point ion approximation, $\varepsilon_{\kappa'}(r_{\kappa'}) \equiv +1$.

If we now consider two well separated ions, the interaction potential is given by

$$V_{\kappa\kappa'}(r_{\kappa\kappa'}) = \frac{Z_\kappa Z_{\kappa'} e^2}{\varepsilon_{\kappa\kappa'}(r_{\kappa\kappa'})\, r_{\kappa\kappa'}} \approx \frac{\tilde{Z}_\kappa(r_\kappa > r_\mathrm{a})\, \tilde{Z}_{\kappa'}(r_{\kappa'} > r_\mathrm{a})\, \mathrm{e}^2}{r_{\kappa\kappa'}}, \tag{4.15}$$

with

$$\varepsilon_{\kappa\kappa'}(r_{\kappa\kappa'}) \approx \varepsilon_\kappa(r_\kappa > r_\mathrm{a})\, \varepsilon_{\kappa'}(r_{\kappa'} > r_\mathrm{a}). \tag{4.16}$$

Here, overlap effects have been excluded. For example, for two halogen ions with $Z_{\kappa'} = +5$ and $\tilde{Z}_\kappa = -1$, as in NaBr,

$$\varepsilon_{\kappa'\kappa'} \approx (-5)(-5) = 25, \tag{4.17}$$

while for the interaction between a Na^+ ion and a Br^- ion, with $Z_\kappa = \tilde{Z}_\kappa = +1$,

$$\varepsilon_{\kappa\kappa'} \approx Z_\kappa Z_{\kappa'} / \tilde{Z}_\kappa \tilde{Z}_{\kappa'} = -5. \tag{4.18}$$

In the latter case, the repulsive ion–ion interaction between the bare ions is transformed into an attractive one between the 'rigid' ions with the help of the attractive forces between the ions and the electrons trapped near the halogen ion. Then, the system would not be stable against a continuous decrease of the distance $r_{\kappa\kappa'}$ if we would not consider the repulsive effect due to the overlap between electrons in the cores of neighboring rigid ions. Usually, one takes care of this short-range forces by introducing a pseudopotential, e.g. a Born–Mayer potential, but a proper treatment using the dielectric function would be preferable. We shall not follow this problem here.

We note, that the transformation as described by eq. (4.15) or (4.18) ensures charge neutrality of the system:

$$\tilde{Z}_\kappa + \tilde{Z}_{\kappa'} = 0. \tag{4.19}$$

The foregoing discussion contains all the elements which we need to understand the situation in a crystal. As can be seen from eqs. (4.14)–(4.18) the rigid-ion approximation can be derived in the dielectric function method by factorizing $\boldsymbol{\varepsilon}$ into two off-diagonal matrices analogous to eq. (4.16), neglecting overlap and polarization effects

$$\boldsymbol{\varepsilon}^{-1}(\boldsymbol{K}, \boldsymbol{K}') \approx \boldsymbol{\varepsilon}_\mathrm{ri}^{-1}(\boldsymbol{q}, \boldsymbol{K})\, \boldsymbol{\varepsilon}_\mathrm{ri}^{-1}(\boldsymbol{K}', \boldsymbol{q}). \tag{4.20}$$

$\varepsilon_{\rm ri}$ characterizes the charge renormalization since it leads in eq. (4.13) to

$$\begin{aligned}\bar{D}(\boldsymbol{q}) &= (4\pi e^2/\Omega_0) \sum_{\boldsymbol{Q},\boldsymbol{Q}'} (\boldsymbol{K}/K)\, \boldsymbol{Z}\, \varepsilon_{\rm ri}^{-1}(\boldsymbol{q}, \boldsymbol{K}) \\ &\qquad \times \varepsilon_{\rm ri}^{-1}(\boldsymbol{K}', \boldsymbol{q})\, \boldsymbol{Z}\, (\boldsymbol{K}/K') \exp[\mathrm{i}(\boldsymbol{Q}\boldsymbol{r}_\kappa - \boldsymbol{Q}'\boldsymbol{r}_{\kappa'})] \\ &\equiv (4\pi e^2/\Omega_0) \sum_{\boldsymbol{Q},\boldsymbol{Q}'} (\boldsymbol{K}/K)\, \tilde{\boldsymbol{Z}}(\boldsymbol{K}) \\ &\qquad \times \tilde{\boldsymbol{Z}}(\boldsymbol{K}')\, (\boldsymbol{K}'/K) \exp[\mathrm{i}(\boldsymbol{Q}\boldsymbol{r}_\kappa - \boldsymbol{Q}'\boldsymbol{r}_{\kappa'})]. \end{aligned} \tag{4.21}$$

The factorization, eq. (4.20), is a consequence of that in the ordinary space, since

$$\begin{aligned}\varepsilon^{-1}(\boldsymbol{K}, \boldsymbol{K}') &= \frac{1}{V^2} \int \varepsilon^{-1}(\boldsymbol{r}, \boldsymbol{r}') \exp[\mathrm{i}(-\boldsymbol{K}\boldsymbol{r} + \boldsymbol{K}'\boldsymbol{r}')]\, \mathrm{d}^3\boldsymbol{r}\, \mathrm{d}^3\boldsymbol{r}' \\ &\approx \frac{1}{V} \int \mathrm{d}^3\boldsymbol{r}\, \varepsilon_\kappa^{-1}(\boldsymbol{r})\, \mathrm{e}^{-\mathrm{i}\boldsymbol{K}\boldsymbol{r}} \times \frac{1}{V} \int \mathrm{d}^3\boldsymbol{r}'\, \varepsilon_{\kappa'}^{-1}(\boldsymbol{r}')\, \mathrm{e}^{\mathrm{i}\boldsymbol{K}'\boldsymbol{r}'} \\ &\approx \frac{\tilde{Z}_\kappa}{Z_\kappa} \frac{1}{V} \int \mathrm{d}^3\boldsymbol{r}\, \mathrm{e}^{-\mathrm{i}\boldsymbol{K}\boldsymbol{r}} \times \frac{\tilde{Z}_{\kappa'}}{Z_{\kappa'}} \frac{1}{V} \int \mathrm{d}^3\boldsymbol{r}'\, \mathrm{e}^{-\mathrm{i}\boldsymbol{K}'\boldsymbol{r}'}. \end{aligned} \tag{4.22}$$

For small q, i.e. $\boldsymbol{K} \to \boldsymbol{Q}$, and with $\sum_{\boldsymbol{Q}} e^{\mathrm{i}\boldsymbol{Q}(\boldsymbol{l}-\boldsymbol{l}')} = \delta_{\boldsymbol{l}\boldsymbol{l}'}$, $(1/V)\int \mathrm{d}^3 r e^{\mathrm{i}\boldsymbol{K}\boldsymbol{r}} = \sum_{\boldsymbol{Q}} \delta_{\boldsymbol{K},-\boldsymbol{Q}}$, we obtain from eq. (4.22)

$$D(\boldsymbol{q}) \approx \frac{4\pi e^2}{\Omega_0} \tilde{\boldsymbol{Z}} \frac{\boldsymbol{q}}{q} \otimes \frac{\boldsymbol{q}}{q} \tilde{\boldsymbol{Z}}, \tag{4.23}$$

with the rigid-ion charge matrix $\tilde{\boldsymbol{Z}}$ which reads for a crystal like NaBr

$$\boldsymbol{Z} = \begin{pmatrix} \tilde{Z}_\kappa & \\ & \tilde{Z}_\kappa \end{pmatrix} = \begin{pmatrix} -1 & \\ & +1 \end{pmatrix}.$$

Eq. (4.19) becomes now the acoustic sum rule (see, for example, Sham's article, chapter 5 of this volume), which ensures the proper behavior of the longitudinal acoustic frequencies when going to $\boldsymbol{q} \to 0$.

The derivation of the (Coulomb part of the) rigid ion model given here is basically correct as long as overlap and polarization effects are sufficiently small. The formal use of the dielectric function method should, however, not mask the fact that $\boldsymbol{\varepsilon}^{-1}$ is a singular matrix for certain high $\boldsymbol{K}$ values due to the fact that the single ε_κ functions become singular near the halogen ions for small values of r_κ.

Correspondingly, the ionic potential is very strong in order to exhibit the localization of the electronic charge and the 'drag' effect on this charge when the halogen ion is displaced. Therefore, the dielectric function method, while still correct in its general formal aspects cannot be specified as has been done in eq. (2.7) where the dielectric function was used to describe the density response to a *weak* external perturbation.

We note that the rigid-ion approximation turns out to be, as one would expect, the complete opposite to the case of a simple metal. While in the latter case a divergent *diagonal* dielectric function $\varepsilon^{-1}(\boldsymbol{q}, \boldsymbol{q})$ describes completely the screening of the ion–ion interaction at long wavelengths (see, e.g. chapter 4 by Kagan, this volume), in ionic insulators the *off-diagonal* part of the dielectric function, $\varepsilon^{-1}(\boldsymbol{q}, \boldsymbol{q}+\boldsymbol{Q})$ is responsible for the screening of the bare charge into a 'rigid-ion' charge and, as a consequence, for the validity of the acoustic sum rule. The 'rigid-ion' transformation provides a diagonalization of the main (singular) part of the dielectric function via a charge renormalization and leaves the effect of the electronic polarization as a smaller correction. We come with that to the problem of general 'effective' charges which will be discussed in the next subsection.

At this point, we would like to remark that the closure approximation, as defined for the non-overlapping part of the charge densities in eq. (3.4a) leads essentially to the same result. Here, the advantage is that no restrictions with respect to a singular part have to be considered. The localization of the electronic charge density near the ionic position site automatically leads to a factorization of ε and, consequently, to a renormalization of the bare charge into a rigid-ion charge. The closure approximation demonstrates, therefore, again its usefulness in numerical applications.

4.3. Dynamical charges and dipolar models

The interaction of the static ionic charges is modified by the polarization of the electronic charge density during a lattice vibration. This leads to q-dependent dynamical charges which are related to the crystal's polarizability. Now, we discuss the different descriptions of these charges in the dipolar models, the dielectric function method and the overlap treatment.

We specify the dynamical matrix of a dipolar model, eq. (4.11), to the case of a diatomic cubic crystal such as NaBr and restrict the short-range deformabilities of symmetry Γ to those induced by nearest-neighbor longitudinal displacements of the nearly rigid positive ions (Na^+) against the deformable negative ions (Br^-) at rest. We obtain three different deformabilities of spherical (Γ_1^+), dipolar (Γ_{15}^-) and quadrupolar (Γ_{12}^+) symmetry, respectively, which are visualized in fig. 3 (Bilz 1972).

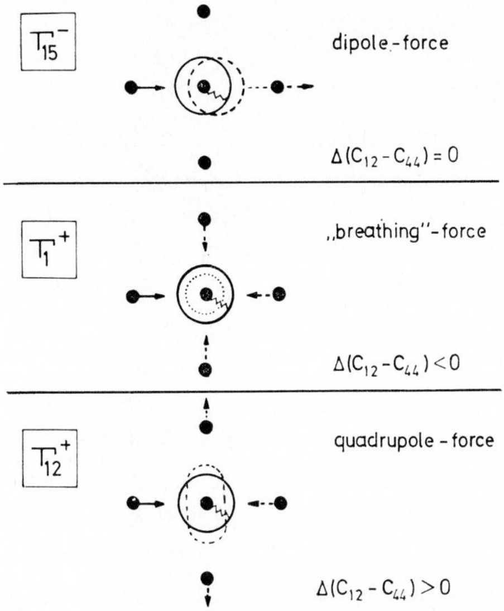

Fig. 3. Local symmetries of the displacement induced ion–electron–ion forces in a cubic crystal (Bilz 1972).

If we first restrict the discussion to dipolar forces we obtain the so-called simple shell model with the dynamical matrix $\bar{\boldsymbol{D}}^{\mathrm{SM}}$ (refer to Cochran 1971, and to chapter 3 of this volume)

$$\begin{aligned}\bar{\boldsymbol{D}}^{\mathrm{SM}}(\boldsymbol{q}) &= \boldsymbol{R} + \boldsymbol{ZCZ} - (\boldsymbol{T} + \boldsymbol{ZCY})(\boldsymbol{S} + \boldsymbol{YCY})^{-1}(\boldsymbol{T}^{\dagger} + \boldsymbol{YCZ}) \\ &= \boldsymbol{R}'(\boldsymbol{q}) + \boldsymbol{Z}'(\boldsymbol{q})\,\boldsymbol{C}'(\boldsymbol{q})\,\boldsymbol{Z}'(\boldsymbol{q}),\end{aligned} \tag{4.24}$$

with

$$\boldsymbol{R}' = \boldsymbol{R} - \boldsymbol{TS}^{-1}\boldsymbol{T}^{\dagger},$$

an effective short-range matrix,

$$\boldsymbol{Z}' = \boldsymbol{Z} - \boldsymbol{TS}^{-1}\boldsymbol{Y},$$

an effective (Szigeti) charge matrix, and

$$\boldsymbol{C}' = (\boldsymbol{CI} + \boldsymbol{CYS}^{-1}\boldsymbol{Y})^{-1}\,\boldsymbol{C},$$

an effective Coulomb interaction ($\boldsymbol{I}$ is the unit matrix). In the notation of subsection 4.1 the symbols of eq. (4.24) mean [refer to eqs. (4.11) and (4.12)]

$$\boldsymbol{R} \equiv \boldsymbol{D}_{\mathrm{ii}}^{\mathrm{SR}}, \qquad \boldsymbol{T} \equiv (\boldsymbol{D}_{\mathrm{ei}}^{15-})^{\mathrm{SR}}, \qquad \boldsymbol{S} \equiv (\boldsymbol{D}_{\mathrm{ee}}^{15-})^{\mathrm{SR}},$$
$$\boldsymbol{ZCZ} \equiv \boldsymbol{D}_{\mathrm{ii}}^{\mathrm{C}}, \qquad \boldsymbol{YCY} \equiv \boldsymbol{D}_{\mathrm{ee}}^{\mathrm{C}}.$$

The crystal polarizability is given by

$$\alpha_\infty = e^2 \boldsymbol{Y}\boldsymbol{S}^{-1}\boldsymbol{Y}. \tag{4.25}$$

The transition to the rigid ion case is most easily carried out by keeping the electronic shell charges Y_κ finite but assuming $\boldsymbol{S} \to \infty$. Since the essential part of $\boldsymbol{S}$ is the local electron-shell–ion-core coupling K_κ this means that the polarizable electrons in the 'shell' with charge Y_κ become completely tightly bound electrons.

The rigid-ion model with one or two nearest neighbor force constants in the matrix $\boldsymbol{R}$ and the static charge $|Z|=1$ manages to describe the acoustic branches at lower q-values and the transverse optic branches quite well (refer to fig. 1). Therefore, the main effect of the dipolar models is to improve the agreement between the measured and the calculated longitudinal optic modes. One must add at least two parameters (Y and K of the negative ion) for the description of the long-range and the short-range induced dipolar forces. Usually six or more parameters are used in order to obtain dispersion curves which fit the experimental data within a few percent (refer to chapter 3 of this volume). Then the situation becomes ambiguous since often fits of comparable quality are obtained by using different models. For example, second-nearest neighbor forces can partially replace ionic deformabilities, etc. One needs therefore additional arguments for the decision whether or not a workable model may also be considered to be a sensible model.

The following criteria (among others) may be helpful in this respect:

a) a model should work not only for one or two specific crystals but for a whole family of similar crystals, such as the alkali halides;

b) the model parameters should exhibit at least some qualitative resemblance to the microscopic theory of phonons;

c) non-linear extensions of the model are useful tests for the (shell or core) eigenvectors given by the model. Such extensions are calculations of Raman spectra (refer to subsection 4.4), phonon sidebands, etc;

d) the model should allow for a distinction between genuine harmonic parameters and those parameters which are used to compensate for anharmonic (thermal expansion or self-energy) effects. As a consequence temperature dependences of dispersion curves have to be analysed;

e) among different models fulfilling the foregoing criteria equally well, those with fewer parameters may be preferable.

One might summarize the above cited five criteria into the single one that a phonon model should be consistent with the complete (available) knowledge about the other physical properties of a crystal.

In the case of alkali halides, essentially two different approaches have been used. The first one starts from a fit of the model parameters to macroscopic data, i.e. the three elastic constants, the two optic frequencies and the ratio $\varepsilon_0/\varepsilon_\infty$ of the dielectric constants. This restricts the number of independent parameters to six. The model then tries to predict the dispersion curves for all other q-values. Among these 'macroscopic' models the most successful was the 'breathing' or deformable shell model (BSM) introduced by Schroeder (1966). This model considers a short-range deformability of Γ_1^+ symmetry of the halogen ions (refer to fig. 3) which leads to a second deformability matrix in $\boldsymbol{R}'$, eq. (4.20):

$$\boldsymbol{R}'^{\mathrm{BSM}} = \boldsymbol{R}' - \boldsymbol{T}_{1+}\boldsymbol{S}_{1+}^{-1}\boldsymbol{T}_{1+}^{+}\,, \tag{4.26}$$

where the matrices $\boldsymbol{T}_{1+}$ and $\boldsymbol{S}_{1+}$ are similar to $\boldsymbol{T}$ and $\boldsymbol{S}$ but having $\boldsymbol{T}_1^+$ symmetry.

The main effect of this additional radial symmetric deformability is the following: a simple shell model with 6 parameters fitted to the macroscopic parameters predicts the dispersion curves in the main symmetry directions within 5–10% except for the longitudinal optic branch near the L-point where the discrepancy amounts to about 20% in NaBr and NaI (refer to fig. 1). A breathing deformability allows for a substantial improvement of the fit, in particular for this mode but to a certain extent for other modes, too (fig. 1).

The remarkable success of the deformable shell model in predicting and describing dispersion curves of alkali halides with sodium–chloride and cesium–chloride structure (Mahler and Engelhardt 1971) has led to several attempts to find a microscopic basis for a Γ_1^+ deformability in the electronic structure of alkali halides (Zeyher 1971, Kuehner et al. 1970, see also Chochran 1971). While the dipolar polarizability of these crystals can be derived to a good approximation from the polarizability of the free halogen and alkali ions (Tessmann et al. 1953) the derivation of the Γ_1^+ (and the Γ_{12}^+) deformabilities in a quantitative way is more difficult.

There exist strong indications of the possibility that the breathing deformability as used for the dispersion curves of alkali halides is merely a compensation for anharmonic effects (Bilz et al. 1974a). The main reason for this may be the fact that the macroscopic elastic constants are usually determined as adiabatic or isothermal constants (collision-dominated regime) while the bulk of phonons in a crystal like NaBr at $T \approx 100\,\mathrm{K}$ have frequencies in the collision-free regime. The extrapolated elastic constants from this regime (zero sound) differ remarkably from the former (first sound) elastic constants. For example, the extrapolated value of c_{11} exceeds the isothermal value in NaBr and NaI by about 10% (Reid et al. 1970). This causes a serious inconsistency of the macroscopic models with the majority of phonon frequencies as measured by neutron spectroscopy and weakens the argument of an independent calculation of measured data.

It may therefore be preferable to use another approach where the model parameters are fitted to the experimental frequencies in a least-square procedure. The result of such a fit for NaBr is shown again in fig. 1 (Reid et al. 1970). Here, the same model has been used as for the macroscopic fit. Now, the discrepancies of this former calculation are nearly removed without using a shell-deformability. The same result is obtained for NaI, KBr, etc. (Bilz et al. 1974b). The remaining small discrepancies in particular in the longitudinal optic branches are not significant since in this frequency regime the one-phonon states are strongly broadened by two-phonon combination states. A careful analysis of the line shape of measured phonon intensities is required in order to determine the proper harmonic phonon frequencies (refer to Cowley and Cowley 1965, 1966).

From this analysis one might conclude that the breathing deformability is merely a useful compensation routine to overcome the inconsistency of macroscopic models with the phonon frequencies in the collision free regime. Therefore, it is not surprising that no evidence can be found for an intra-ionic non-linearity of the breathing type in the Raman spectra of alkali halides (refer to subsection 4.4).

In this situation, it would be very useful if measurements of phonon dispersion curves could be repeated at very low temperatures and if temperature dependencies for selected phonons could be measured, in particular for longitudinal optic modes. The six parameter shell model used for the calculation of the dispersion curves of NaBr in fig. 1 contains one unusual feature. To clarify this point the model parameters are sketched in fig. 4. Usually, a simple shell model uses two nearest-neighbor force constants, two parameters (Y_- and K_-) for the polarizable halogen ion and two second-nearest neighbor force constants between the halogen ions (refer to chapter 3 of this volume). This model seems to be a very physical approach to the interionic forces in alkali halides such as NaBr and NaI. In fact, this model does not work in the longitudinal optic branch near the L point even not in a least-square fit since at the L-point the negative ions are at rest in this mode. Therefore, no use is made of the last four parameters and the model is equivalent to the rigid-ion model at the L-point.

The weak point in this model is probably the overestimation of second-nearest neighbor interactions. We can see this by looking at the situation in the light of the overlap method (subsection 3.1). As discussed in the foregoing section the rigid-overlap approximation causes in the simplest approximation a renormalization of the static charge $|Z|=1$ to a lower value ≈ 0.9.

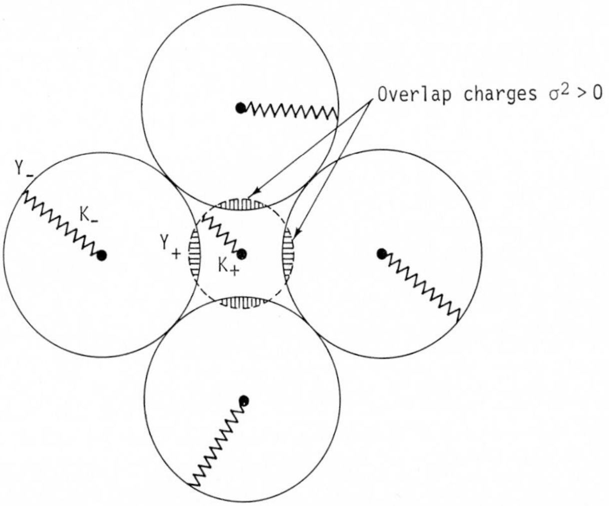

Fig. 4. Overlap-shell model. σ^2 = overlap charge; Y_+ = pseudo-shell charge; K_+ = pseudo-shell core coupling (Bilz et al. 1974a).

If we now include the polarization, we have to consider two effects. The first is the polarizability of the halogen ions (Br^-, I^-) which is taken into account in the shell model. The second effect is the overlap polarization which requires the consideration of excited states in the overlap charge density. A calculation of this effect would give a further contribution to the dynamical charge and would require a rather lengthy treatment similar to that of the q-dependent rigid overlap charge in the work of Zeyher (1971). We might therefore look for a simple model description of this effect, analogous to the modification of the static charge mentioned above.

We take advantage of the fact that the ionic radii are very different for the positive and the negative ions in NaBr, NaI and many other alkali halides. Then, the center of gravity of the overlap charges is rather close to the lattice sites of the positive ions. Therefore we may expect that in a multipole expansion of the overlap polarization the leading term is given by induced dipole moments at the positive ion lattice sites. That means, in a shell model, that we attribute a 'shell' to the positive ions with a positive shell charge Y_+ corresponding to the positive sign of the overlap charge (refer to Zeyher 1971). A similar argument was first given by Cowley et al. (1963).

The short-range dipolar distortions of the overlap charge are described by the shell–core coupling K_+. The parameters Y_+ and G_+ replace the second nearest-neighbor constants of the usual simple shell model.

The surprising success of this overlap-shell model in NaBr (Reid et al. 1970) NaI, KBr, and CaO (Bilz et al. 1974a) indicates that the foregoing discussion may be not far from being correct. On the other hand, the model may represent an ultimate limit of the point charge model. One cannot expect that in crystals with strongly overlapping charge densities and comparable sizes of the different ions our description of the situation in terms of pseudo-polarizabilities of the positive ions will manage to give satisfactory results. In these cases a separate treatment of the overlap charge analogous to a 'bond charge' might be necessary and indeed lead to an interpolation scheme between ionic and covalent crystals (refer to chapter 5 of this volume). Another possibility is the introduction of form factors for the charge distribution (Sinha 1969, Kuehner et al. 1972) which take care of the spatial extension of the electronic charge density. In this context it is interesting to note that the overlap-shell model as discussed above tends to overestimate the value of the dielectric constant ε_∞ by 10–20% if the value of the local field ($\boldsymbol{E}_{\mathrm{loc}}$) correction is taken in the point ion model where

$$\boldsymbol{E}_{\mathrm{loc}} = \boldsymbol{E}_{\mathrm{mac}} + \tfrac{4}{3}\pi\gamma\boldsymbol{P}, \tag{4.27}$$

with $\boldsymbol{E}_{\mathrm{mac}}$, the macroscopic field, and $\gamma=1$. The effect of overlapping charges leads to a decrease of the local field correction, i.e. to a parallel decrease of γ (Adler 1962, Wiser 1963):

$$\varepsilon_\infty \approx 1 + 4\pi \frac{\alpha_+ + \alpha_-}{1 - \frac{4}{3}\pi\gamma(\alpha_+ + \alpha_-)}. \tag{4.28}$$

This decrease is consistent with the above mentioned tendency of the overlap-shell model. The consequences of this discussion for the dynamical effective charge Z', eq. (4.24), are obvious and we do not go into details here. As a summary, we note that the overlap treatment allows again for some important qualitative arguments which illuminate the physical back-ground of the dipolar models in ionic crystals.

Since the local charge deformations of dipolar symmetry Γ_{15}^- (shell model) and of spherical symmetry Γ_1^+ (breathing shell model) have turned out to be useful degrees of freedom, one might ask whether or not there exists evidence for deformations with quadrupolar symmetry Γ_{12}^{+}. Wagner and his co-workers (Kühner and Wagner 1972, Bluthardt et al. 1973) have discussed the influence of these deformations on the lattice vibrations of several alkali halides and found, at least in KBr, a small but probably significant correction, in particular in the calculated U-center sidebands of this crystal. The effect is more pronounced in the silver halides, ACl and AgBr, where virtual excitations of the d-electrons of the Ag^{+} ion seem to lead to a strong decrease of the transverse optic branch, in particular near the L-point $[\boldsymbol{q}=\pi/2a(111)]$ (Fischer et al. 1972). In fig. 5 the dispersion curves of AgCl are compared with those of RbCl where the positive ion is missing the filled d-shell. We note, that, in addition to the Γ_{12}^{+} deformability, the Ag^{+}-ion exhibits a 'covalency' effect in such a way that it supports a coherent rotation (Γ_{15}^{+} symmetry) of its four nearest Cl^{-}-neighbors in a (100) plane. On the other hand, the overlap-shell model discussed above does not improve the description of the dispersion curves in AgCl (Bilz et al. 1974a). This is not surprising, since the accumulation of electronic charge density between the ions is important in the silver halides and destroys the applicability of a point-ion model.

Summarizing we can say that the idea of local ionic deformabilities and polarizabilities in combination with short-range overlap forces is a very successful concept in the lattice dynamics of ionic crystals.

The situation is more difficult in the dielectric function method. The strength of this method is to give general theorems such as the acoustical sum rule which we have discussed in the rigid ion approximation in the foregoing section.

In the dielectric function method, the effective ionic charge in the limit $\boldsymbol{q}\to 0$, can be defined (Sham 1969, Pick et al. 1969)

$$Z_{\kappa}^{\text{eff}} = \lim_{\boldsymbol{q}\to 0}\left[\frac{\Omega_0}{4\pi e^2}\sum_{\boldsymbol{Q}}\frac{\varepsilon^{-1}(\boldsymbol{q},\boldsymbol{q}+\boldsymbol{Q})}{\varepsilon^{-1}(\boldsymbol{q},\boldsymbol{q})}\,\boldsymbol{q}(\boldsymbol{q}+\boldsymbol{Q})\,V_{\kappa}(|\boldsymbol{q}+\boldsymbol{Q}|)\exp[-i\boldsymbol{Q}\boldsymbol{r}_{\kappa}]\right]. \tag{4.29}$$

In a cubic crystal,

$$\lim_{\boldsymbol{q}\to 0}[\varepsilon^{-1}(\boldsymbol{q},\boldsymbol{q})]^{-1} = \varepsilon_{\infty}\,. \tag{4.30}$$

With the bare potential

$$V_{\kappa}(|\boldsymbol{q}+\boldsymbol{Q}|) = \frac{4\pi e^2}{\Omega_0}\frac{Z_{\kappa}}{|\boldsymbol{q}+\boldsymbol{Q}|^2}, \tag{4.31}$$

The dynamical matrix (4.13) becomes

$$\bar{\boldsymbol{D}}(\boldsymbol{q}) = \frac{4\pi e^2}{\Omega_0} \boldsymbol{Z}^{\text{eff}*} \frac{\boldsymbol{q}}{q} [\varepsilon^{-1}(\boldsymbol{q},\boldsymbol{q})]^{-1} \frac{\boldsymbol{q}}{q} \boldsymbol{Z}^{\text{eff}}, \tag{4.32}$$

with

$$\begin{aligned} Z_\kappa^{\text{eff}} &= \lim_{\boldsymbol{q}\to 0} \varepsilon_\infty Z_\kappa \sum_{\boldsymbol{Q}} \varepsilon^{-1}(\boldsymbol{q},\boldsymbol{q}+\boldsymbol{Q}) \frac{\boldsymbol{q}(\boldsymbol{q}+\boldsymbol{Q})}{(\boldsymbol{q}+\boldsymbol{Q})^2} \exp[\mathrm{i}\boldsymbol{Q}\boldsymbol{r}_\kappa], \\ &= Z_\kappa - \lim_{\boldsymbol{q}\to 0} \varepsilon_\infty Z_\kappa {\sum_{\boldsymbol{Q}}}' \varepsilon^{-1}(\boldsymbol{q},\boldsymbol{q}+\boldsymbol{Q}) \frac{\boldsymbol{q}(\boldsymbol{q}+\boldsymbol{Q})}{(\boldsymbol{q}+\boldsymbol{Q})^2} \exp[\mathrm{i}\boldsymbol{Q}\boldsymbol{r}_\kappa]. \end{aligned} \tag{4.33}$$

The second term defines a screening charge Z_κ^{sc},

$$Z_\kappa^{\text{eff}} = Z_\kappa - Z_\kappa^{\text{sc}},$$

where the prime means that the sum is missing the term $\boldsymbol{Q}=0$.

Eq. (4.33) is completely equivalent to eq. (4.24). (Note that we have not considered the short-range overlap corrections in this discussion). The effective charges interact via a screened Coulomb-interaction. The only difference is that the effective charge Z^{eff} defined here deviates from the Szigeti charge Z' of eq. (4.13) by a factor (Cochran 1971)

$$Z_{\text{T}}^{\text{eff}} = \varepsilon_\infty Z_{\text{L}}^{\text{eff}} = \tfrac{1}{3}(\varepsilon_\infty + 2) Z', \tag{4.34}$$

where T and L denote transverse and longitudinal optic modes, respectively.

The acoustic sum rule [refer to eq. (4.19)] requires

$$Z_\kappa^{\text{eff}} + Z_{\kappa'}^{\text{eff}} = Z_\kappa + Z_{\kappa'} - (Z_\kappa^{\text{sc}} + Z_{\kappa'}^{\text{sc}}) = 0.$$

Since the sum of the bare charges Z_κ is equal to the total charge of the screening electrons, it is certainly unequal to zero. Therefore the screening charges Z_κ^{sc} (i.e. at least one of them) cannot disappear which means, as stated before, that off-diagonal elements in the dielectric matrix are essential in an insulator to ensure the validity of the sum rule.

It is interesting to look again at the rigid-ion limit, e.g. in NaBr. In this case, $\varepsilon_\infty = 1$, and with $\tilde{Z}_\kappa = Z_\kappa$ or $Z_\kappa^{\text{sc}} = 0$ for the positive Na^+ ion,

$$\tilde{Z}_\kappa + \tilde{Z}_{\kappa'} = Z_\kappa + Z_{\kappa'} - Z_{\kappa'}^{\text{sc}} = 0.$$

Since the rigid-ion limit defines a consistent and very good first approximation we may try to separate this charge renormalisation from the rest of the problem by dividing the dielectric function into two parts:

$$\varepsilon^{-1}(\boldsymbol{q},\boldsymbol{q}+\boldsymbol{Q}) = \varepsilon_\infty^{-1}\varepsilon_{\text{ri}}^{-1}(\boldsymbol{q},\boldsymbol{q}+\boldsymbol{Q}) + \varepsilon_{\text{pol}}^{-1}(\boldsymbol{q},\boldsymbol{q}+\boldsymbol{Q}). \tag{4.35}$$

Eq. (4.33) reads then

$$Z_\kappa^{\text{eff}} = \tilde{Z}_\kappa - Z_\kappa^{\text{P}} \tag{4.36}$$

with the rigid-ion charge $\tilde{Z}_\kappa$ and the 'polarization' charge

$$Z_\kappa^{\text{P}} = \lim_{q \to 0} \varepsilon_\infty Z_\kappa \sum_{Q}{}' \varepsilon_{\text{pol}}^{-1}(q, q + Q). \tag{4.37}$$

Since the rigid-ion charges $\tilde{Z}_\kappa$ fulfill by themselves the acoustic sum rule the remaining off-diagonal part $\varepsilon_{\text{pol}}^{-1}$ of the dielectric matrix may become small and might be calculated in a perturbation scheme. The 'best choice' of the rigid-ion charge is subject to overlap corrections as has been discussed above. A treatment of the dynamical matrix along the lines discussed here might be more promising than the attempt to start immediately from the bare ionic charges.

The microscopic theory of phonons in insulators has been discussed recently in detail by Sinha et al. (1973a, b). While very similar in the general spirit their discussion focusses on a 'factorization Ansatz' which is practically equivalent to our treatment in section 2. Here, we have avoided a procedure which relies upon a specific representation of the dielectric function in order to exhibit clearly the particular features of phonons in strongly ionic crystals. For further details of the interrelation between the model theories and the dielectric function method the reader is referred to the reviews by Cochran (1971), Sinha (1973) and by Sham (chapter 5 of this volume).

4.4. Non-linear effects and anharmonicities

The adiabatic theory which has been used in the foregoing sections seems to be a well-justified framework for ionic crystals. If the polarizability becomes strong, non-adiabatic effects may become more important. So far, only the case of a covalent crystal, namely α-Sn was investigated by Sherrington (1971) where non-adiabatic effects can be expected in a small regime in the acoustic branches.

The importance of anharmonic effects is less clear. We have mentioned in the foregoing section the possibility that the spherical deformability of the halogen ions in alkali halides as used in the shell models seems to compensate for the anharmonic disagreement between zero-sound and first-sound elastic constants. This is supported by the fact that the temperature dependence of the fitted 'breathing' parameter of the chlorine ion in AgCl is one order of magnitude higher than that of all other force constants (K. Fischer, private communication).

Generally, we have to ask whether or not the pseudo-harmonic theory (Cowley 1963) is appropriate for the description of phonons if the temperature is not too high. The concept of this theory is to replace the proper renormalization of all phonon frequencies by a continuous re-adjustment of the model parameters when the temperature is changed accordingly. There are, unfortunately, not many measurements of the temperature dependence of phonons and, in particular, very few at low temperatures.

The longitudinal optic modes deserve particular attention, in this context. For example, in the alkali halides the density maximum of the two-phonon decay modes of phonons coincides often with longitudinal modes between the Γ ($\triangleq$(0,00)) and the L ($\triangleq$(111)) point (Bilz et al. 1974a). This Fermi-resonance leads to a strong broadening of the longitudinal modes which is well-known since the beginning of the neutron-scattering era (Woods et al. 1960). On the other hand, the effect on the frequency shift of phonons seems to be less dramatic than one might expect from a calculation of the spectral function (Cowley and Cowley 1966). The reason for this may be found in the circumstance that a consideration of the finite lifetime of *all* phonons in the decay channels leads to a washing out of specific features in the phonon self energy (K. Fischer, private communication). Nevertheless, there resist uncertainties of about 5% or more about the one-phonon frequencies in the longitudinal optic regime. Low-temperature measurements would be helpful for claryfying the situation because a 'freezing-out' of those parameters would appear which are not genuine harmonic force constants but merely simulation parameters of anharmonic origin.

At least of equal importance is the investigation of non-linear extensions of the harmonic theory. They fall into two categories. The first contains all anharmonic (i.e. phonon–phonon) interactions. For these, the infra-red absorption is a typical phenomenon. The detailed analysis of infra-red spectra in terms of anharmonic self-energies (life-time and line-width of infrared active modes) in ionic crystals shows that Coulomb anharmonicity as well as short-range nearest-neighbor (Born–Mayer) anharmonicity provide a rather satisfactory description of anharmonic effects (see Bilz et al. 1974b). The same is true for the interpretation of thermal expansion etc. in terms of mode Grüneisen parameters (see, for example, the analysis of rubidium halides by Kress 1974 and Jex 1974). Since the electronic polarizability plays only a minor role in these effects we rely more or less still upon the rigid-ion model.

In order to test the model concepts which are essentially related to the electron–ion interaction, such as the deformabilities of ions, we have to look into effects which result from non-linear extensions of this interaction.

A typical effect of this type is the electronic phonon Raman effect. It can be considered as a weakly perturbed Rayleigh scattering where a very small part of the electronic polarization energy ($\sim 10^{-7}$) is scattered into phonon modes via non linear electron–phonon coupling. The question is to what extent this non-linear interaction can be determined by a straightforward extension of the harmonic electron–ion coupling as known from the (model and microscopic) theory of phonons.

Starting from the harmonic theory we may distinguish between completely local electron–ion interactions, i.e. 'intra'-ionic forces (for example the shell–core spring at a halogen-ion lattice site), and such interactions where two or more ions are involved, i.e. 'inter'-ionic forces (Cowley 1964). The former forces have no analogy to the rigid-ion forces and are therefore of special interest. Bruce (1972), Bruce and Cowley (1972) have tried to show that the second-order Raman spectra of alkali halides may be explained to a large extent by introducing two intra-ionic fourth-order forces: a quartic 'dipolar' and a quartic 'breathing' deformability at the halogen ions. This result has been questioned by Krauzmann (1973), and a subsequent analysis (Haberkorn) has shown that in this case inter-ionic forces are very probably the predominant ones. Instead, it was demonstrated (Haberkorn et al. 1973) that the intra-ionic quartic dipolar deformability of the oxygen ion governs the second order Raman spectra of the earth alkaline oxides (Rieder et al. 1973). The reason for the strong Raman scattering efficiency of the oxygen ion can be found in the fact that the polarizability of the oxygen ion is strongly dependent on the lattice constant (Tessmann et al. 1953) and might tend to become infinite if the lattice constant is larger than a certain critical value, i.e. the O^{-2} ion is not stable as a free ion. There are interesting consequences for the Raman scattering of all oxides, in particular the perovskites, such as $SrTiO_3$, quartz, Al_2O_3, etc.

In fig. 6 we show the result of a calculation of the Raman spectra of MgO where only one parameter, namely the quartic 'shell–core' coupling of the oxygen has been used (Haberkorn et al. 1973). The success of this calculation shows that the dipolar models, in particular the shell model, lead naturally to non-linear extensions which are consistent with the experimental observation.

One might ask why only the non-linear dipolar deformability of ions exemplifies itself in the Raman spectra but not the volume (breathing) and the quadrupolar deformabilities. In fact, the situation is different if we consider the *first* order impurity induced Raman spectra in alkali halides. Here it might be that the deformability of the impurity ion dominates the spectra, i.e. volume Γ_1^+ scattering for Cl^-, Br^-, I^- and quadrupolar Γ_{12}^+ scattering for Ag^+ (Kaiser and Möller 1972). Here, the coupling is only of

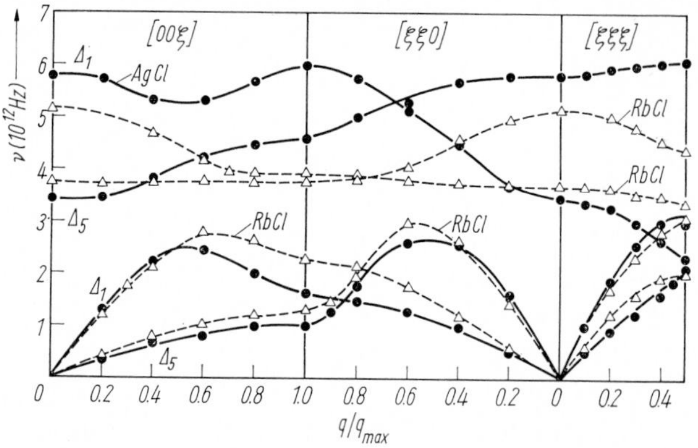

Fig. 5. Comparison of dispersion curves in AgCl and RbCl (Fischer et al. 1972).

cubic order, and we may understand the fact that the second order spectra of alkali halides (see Krauzmann 1969) and silver halides (Von der Osten 1973) do not exhibit these deformabilities because probably inter-ionic quartic couplings mask the contributions of the iterated cubic (and therefore effectively quartic) intra-ionic terms.

5. *Summary*

The microscopic and the model theory of phonons was discussed in the harmonic-adiabatic framework with emphasis on the diatomic cubic crystals. It was tried to show that the rigid-ion model is a consistent first approximation but that the consideration of the electron–ion interaction leads to interesting modifications which can be expressed in terms of ionic deformabilities, overlap effects and effective charges. The overlap method which uses a Heitler–London scheme with overlapping wave functions gives an appealing and 'natural' approach to the calculation of the interionic force constants. The dielectric function method, on the other hand, has difficulties to describe the 'condensation' of electrons in the neighborhood of the ions since it originates conceptually from a description of metals where the electrons are nearly free. Eventually, a proper treatment of the off-diagonal elements of the dielectric matrix leads to interesting general rules, such as the acoustic sum rule and a clear recipe how to treat the electronic polarisation or the related effective charges.

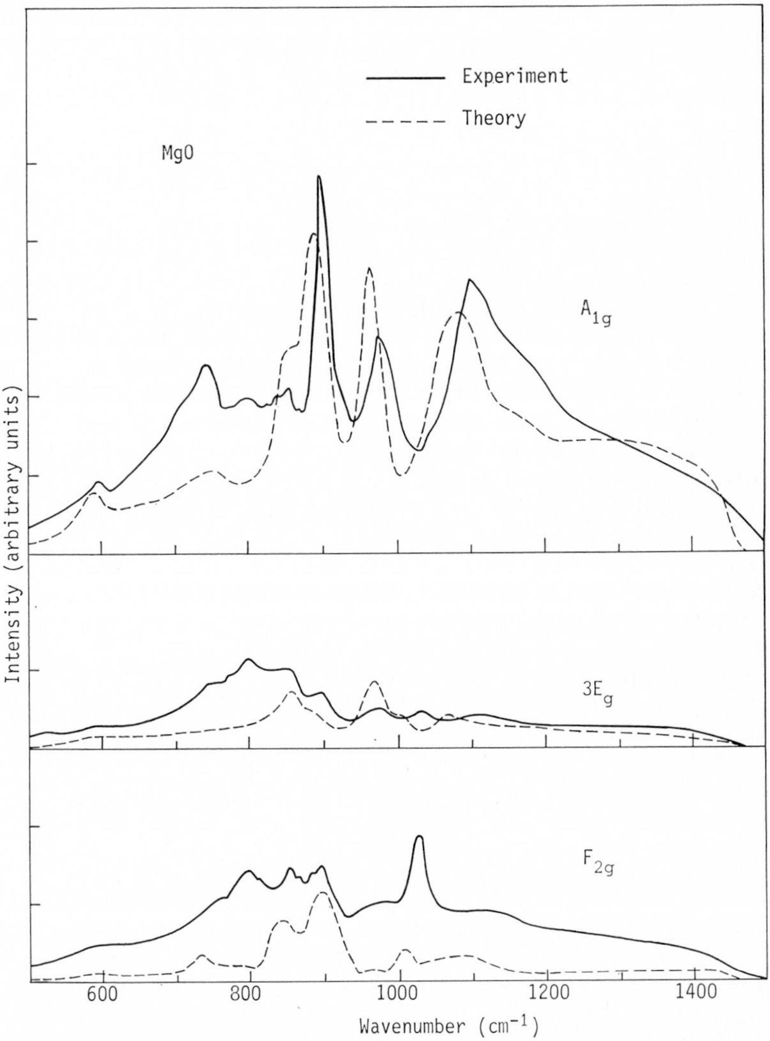

Fig. 6. Second order Raman spectra of MgO. Solid line: experimental data, dashed line: theory (Haberkorn et al. 1973).

Acknowledgements

The authors are indebted to Professors S. K. Sinha and R. Pick and to the members of the theoretical group of the Max-Planck-Institut für Festkörperforschung, in particular to Dr. R. Zeyher, for discussions. A critical reading of the manuscript by Drs. M. Buchanan and T. P. Martin is gratefully acknowledged.

References

ABARENKOV, I. V. and I. M. ANTONOVA (1970), Phys. Stat. Sol. **38**, 783.

ABRIKOSOV, A.A., L.P. GORKOV and I.E. DZYALOSHINSKI (1963), *Methods of quantum field theory in statistical physics* (Prentice Hall, London).

ADAMS, W.H. (1962), J. Chem. Phys. **37**, 2009.

ADLER, S. (1962), Phys. Rev. **126**, 413.

BILZ, H. (1972), Phonons Dispersion Relations, in: *Computational solid state physics*, ed. F. Herman, N. W. Dalton and T. R. Kochter (Plenum Press, New York).

BILZ, H., M. BUCHANAN, K. FISCHER and R. HABERKORN (1974a), (to be published).

BILZ, H., D. STRAUCH and R. K. WEHNER (1974b), *Handbuch der Physik*, **25** 2b.

BLUTHARDT, W., W. SCHNEIDER and M. WAGNER (1973), Phys. Stat. Sol. (6) 56, 453.

BROSS, H. (1971), Z. Physik **243**, 311.

BRUCE, A.D., and R.A. COWLEY (1972), J. Phys. C **5**, 595.

BRUCE, A.D. (1972), J. Phys. C **5**, 2909.

BUCHANAN, M., R. HABERKORN and H. BILZ (1974), J. Phys. C. **7**, 439.

DES CLOIZEAUX, J. (1963), Phys. Rev. **129**, 554.

DES CLOIZEAUX, J. (1964), Phys. Rev. **135**, 698.

COCHRAN, W. (1971), Critical Reviews in Solid State Sciences **2**, 1.

COWLEY, R.A. (1962), Proc. Roy. Soc. *A***268**, 109 and 121.

COWLEY, R. A. (1963), Advan. Phys. **12**, 421.

COWLEY, R. A. (1964), Proc. Phys. Soc. **84**, 281.

COWLEY, E.R. and R.A. COWLEY (1965), Proc. Roy. Soc. A, **287**, 259.

COWLEY, R. A., W. COCHRAN, B. N. BROCKHOUSE and A. D. B. WOODS (1963), Phys. Rev. **131**, 1030.

COWLEY, E.R. and R.A. COWLEY (1966), Proc. Roy. Soc. A, **292**, 209.

DAGENS, L. (1972), J. Phys. C. **5**, 2333.

DALGARNO, A. (1962), Advances in Physics **11**, 281.

ESCHRIG, H. (1973), Phys. Stat. Sol. (b) **56**, 197.

FISCHER, K., H. BILZ, R. HABERKORN and W. WEBER (1972), Phys. Stat. Sol. **54**, 285.

GILBERT, T.L. (1964), *Molecular orbitals in chemistry, physics, and biology*, ed. P.O. Löwdin (Academic Press).

GINTER, J. and J. MYCIELSKI (1971), J. Phys. C **4**, 1540.

GINTER, J. (1972), J. Phys. C **6**, 819.

GLISS, B. (1968), Thesis, University of Frankfurt.

GLISS B., and H. BILZ (1968), Phys. Rev. Letters, **21**, 884.

GLISS, B., R. ZEYHER and H. BILZ (1971), Phys. Stat. Sol. **44**, 747.

HABERKORN, R., M. BUCHANAN and H. BILZ (1973), Solid State Commun. **12**, 681.
HANKE, W. (1971), in: *Phonons* M.A. Nusimovici ed. (Flammarion Sciences, Paris).
HANKE, W. (1973a), Phys. Rev. B**8**, 4585.
HANKE, W. (1973b), Phys. Rev. B**8**, 4591.
HANKE, W. and H. BILZ (1971), Z. f. Naturf. **26**, 585.
HANKE, W. and H. BILZ (1972), Phonons in Metals, in: *Neutron inelastic scattering* (Int. Atomic Energy Agency, Viennal.
HOHENBERG, P. C. and W. KOHN (1964), Phys. Rev. **136B**, 364.
JEX, H. (1974), Phys. Stat. Sol. (b), (to be published).
KADANOFF, L. P., and G. BAYM (1962), *Quantum statistical mechanics* (Benjamin, New York).
KEATING, P. N. (1968), Phys. Rev. **175**, 1171.
KELLERMANN, E.W. (1940), Phil. Trans. Roy. Joc. **A 238**, 513.
KOHN, W., and L.J. Sham (1965), Phys. Rev. **140**, 1163.
KRAUZMAN, M. (1969), Thesis, University of Paris.
KRAUZMAN, M. (1973), Solid State Commun. **12**, 157.
KRESS, W. (1974), Phys. Stat. Sol. (b) 62, no 2.
KUEHNER, D.H. (1969), Z. Phys. **230**, 108.
KUEHNER, D.H., H.V. LAUER and W.E. BRON (1972), Phys. Rev. **B5**, 4112.
KUEHNER, D.H., and M. WAGNER (1970), Phys. Stat. Sol. (b) **40**, 517.
KUNC, K. (1973), Thesis, University of Paris.
LANDHOFF, R. (1936), Z. f. Phys. **102**, 201.
LAX, M. (1965), in: *Lattice dynamics*, ed: R.F. Wallis (Oxford, Pergamon Press).
LEIGH, R.S., B. SZIGETI and V. TEWARY (1971), Proc. Roy. Soc. **A320**, 505.
LÖWDIN, P.O. (1950), Z. Chem. Phys. **18**, 365.
LUCOVSKY, G., R.M. MARTIN and E. BURSTEIN (1971), Phys. Rev. **B4**, 1367.
LUNDQVIST, S. (1952), Ark. för Fysik **6**, 325.
LUNDQVIST, S. (1957), Ark. för Fysik **12**, 8 and 263.
MAHLER, G. and P. ENGELHARDT (1971), Phys. Stat. Sol. (b) **45**, 543.
MARSTON, R.L. and B.G. DICK (1967), Solid State Comm. **5**, 731.
MÖLLER, W. and R. KAISER (1972), Phys. Stat. Sol. (b) **50**, 155.
PHILLIPS, J.C., (1960), *Covalent bonding in crystals, molecules, and polymers* (Chicago University Press).
PICK, R., M.H. COHEN and R.M. MARTIN (1969), Phys. Rev. **B1**, 910.
PICK, R. (1971), in: *Phonons*, ed. M.A. Nusimovici (Flammarion Sciences, Paris).
REID, J.S., T.S. SMITH and W.J.L. BUYERS (1970), Phys. Rev. **B1**, 1833.
RIEDER, K.H., B.A. WEINSTEIN, MANUEL CARDONA and H. BILZ (1973), Phys. Rev. **B8**, 4780.
SCHROEDER, U. (1966), Solid State Comm. **4**, 347.
SCHROEDER, U. and V. NÜSSLEIN (1967), Phys. Stat. Sol. **21**, 309.
SHAM, L.J. (1969), Phys. Rev. **188**, 1431.
SHERRINGTON, D. W. (1971), J. Phys. C (Solid State Phys.) **4**, 2771.
SHERRINGTON, D., and W. KOHN (1968), Phys. Rev. Lett. **21**, 153.
SINHA, S.K. (1968), Phys. Rev. **169**, 477.
SINHA, S.K. (1969), Phys. Rev. **117**, 1256.
SINHA, S.K. (1973), Critical Reviews in Solid State Sciences, **4**, 273.

Sinha, S.K., R.P. Gupta and D.L. Pryce (1971), Phys. Rev. Lett. **26**, 1324.
Sinha, S.K., R.P. Gupta and D.L. Pryce (1973a), Phys. Rev. B., (to be publ.)
Sinha, S.K., R.P. Gupta and D.L. Pryce (1973b), Phys. Rev. B., (to be publ.).
Tessman, J.R., A.H. Kahn and W. Shocklay (1953), Phys. Rev. **92**, 890.
Tolpygo, K.B. (1950), JETP (USSR) **20**, 497.
Verma, M.P., and R.K. Singh (1969a), Phys. Stat. Sol. **33**, 769.
Verma, M.P., and R.K. Singh (1969b), Phys. Stat. Sol. **36**, 335.
Verma, M.P., and R.K. Singh (1970), Phys. Stat. Sol. **38**, 851.
Von der Osten, W. (1973), Phys. Rev. B, (to be published).
Wiser, N. (1963), Phys. Rev. **129**, 62.
Woods, A. D. B., W. Cochran and B. N. Brockhouse (1960), Phys. Rev. **119**, 980.
Zeyher, R. (1971), Phys. Stat. Sol. (b) **48**, 711.

CHAPTER 7

Perturbation theory of anharmonic crystals

T.H.K. BARRON

Dept. of Theoretical Chemistry
University of Bristol
Bristol
UK

M.L. KLEIN

Div. of Chemistry
National Research Council
Ottawa
Canada

Dynamical Properties of Solids, edited by
G. K. Horton and A. A. Maradudin

Contents

1. Introduction

The purpose of this chapter is to describe the methods of many-body perturbation theory as they are applied to anharmonic crystals. Although these methods are usually first met in other contexts, the treatment here is self-contained; it may indeed serve as an introduction to many-body theory for those whose chief interest is in lattice vibrations. The main emphasis is on thermodynamic and elastic properties, although we also discuss briefly the thermodynamic Green functions used in calculating dielectric properties and the interaction with radiation.

In a real solid, the lattice vibrations are not harmonic and cannot rigorously be resolved into independent normal modes. One approach is then to use perturbation theory, taking a harmonic hamiltonian for the unperturbed system. The anharmonic perturbation leads to coupling between the modes of the unperturbed system, and hence to a typical 'many-body' problem. Historically, many of the standard techniques for such problems were developed in application to quantum electrodynamics, and only later extended to deal with systems of interacting electrons and phonons in solids – notably by van Hove (collected reprints in Van Hove et al. 1961) and by a number of Russian workers (Zubarev 1960; Alekseev 1961; Tyablikov and Bonch-Bruevich 1962; Abrikosov et al. 1963). The extensive application of perturbation theory to anharmonic crystals by Leibfried and Ludwig (1961) made little use of such techniques; but later, following work by Maradudin and others (e.g., Maradudin and Fein 1962), Cowley (1963) employed them to give a unified theory of many different vibrational properties, with extensive applications to alkali halides (Cowley and Cowley 1965, 1966). Despite important later developments, notably the equation of motion and functional derivative techniques,‡ we feel that a more elegant exposition has yet to appear.

Cowley's work referred back to papers concerned not only with lattice

‡ See, e.g., Thompson (1963), Pathak (1965), Wehner (1966), Mavroyannis and Pathak (1969), Shukla and Muller (1971); and also the more general review of Ludwig (1967).

vibrations but also with electrons in solids, which in turn referred back to papers in quantum field theory. In presenting a more self-contained account we here follow the example of the important monograph of Choquard (1967), although unlike Choquard we are not primarily concerned with self-consistent theories nor specifically with central force models. Self-consistent theories and applications to specific models are, however, discussed in the review by Glyde and Klein (1971).

Several of the fundamental concepts are most simply introduced in classical statistical mechanics, as described in section 2. The quantum theory is then discussed in section 3, the extension of the theory to thermal expansion and elastic constants in section 4, and interaction with radiation in section 5. The basic texts for harmonic lattice theory, viz. Born and Huang (1954) and Maradudin, Montroll and Weiss (1963), will be referred to by the initials BH and MMW respectively.

2. *Helmholtz energy: classical theory*

2.1. The moment and cumulant expansions

Consider a crystal with $3\mathscr{N}$ position coordinates x_i and conjugate momenta p_i, with the hamiltonian split for a perturbation treatment:

$$H(x_1, \cdots, p_{3\mathscr{N}}) = H_0(x_1, \cdots, p_{3\mathscr{N}}) + H_1(x_1, \cdots, p_{3\mathscr{N}}). \tag{2.1}$$

The canonical partition function

$$Z = h^{-3\mathscr{N}} \int dx_1 \cdots \int dp_{3\mathscr{N}} \exp\{-\beta(H_0 + H_1)\} \tag{2.2}$$

can then be expressed as the product of the unperturbed partition function Z_0 and a perturbation factor Z_1:

$$Z = h^{-3\mathscr{N}} \int dx_1 \cdots \int dp_{3\mathscr{N}} \exp(-\beta H_0) \exp(-\beta H_1) \tag{2.3}$$

$$= Z_0 \frac{\int dx_1 \cdots \int dp_{3\mathscr{N}} \exp(-\beta H_0) \exp(-\beta H_1)}{\int dx_1 \cdots \int dp_{3\mathscr{N}} \exp(-\beta H_0)}, \tag{2.4}$$

where $\beta = (kT)^{-1}$. The factor Z_1 is seen to be the mean of $\exp(-\beta H_1)$ when averaged over the unperturbed canonical ensemble:

$$Z_1 = \langle \exp(-\beta H_1) \rangle_0 . \tag{2.5}$$

The perturbation series for Z_1 is obtained by expanding the exponential

$$Z_1 = 1 + \sum_{n=1}^{\infty} \frac{(-\beta)^n}{n!} \langle H_1^n \rangle_0 , \tag{2.6}$$

where $\langle H_1^n \rangle_0$ is called the nth *moment* of H_1 for the unperturbed ensemble and the expansion for Z_1 is called the *moment expansion.* The perturbation series for the Helmholtz energy is then obtained by expanding the logarithmic function in

$$A_1 = -kT \ln Z_1 = -\beta^{-1} \ln \left(1 + \sum_{n=1}^{\infty} \frac{(-\beta)^n}{n!} \langle H_1^n \rangle_0 \right). \tag{2.7}$$

Such expansions are well known in statistics, and have widespread applications in physics (Kubo 1962). The coefficient of $(-\beta)^n/n!$ in the expansion of $\ln \langle \exp(-\beta H_1) \rangle_0$ is called the nth *cumulant*, and is written $\langle H_1^n \rangle_{0,c}$; thus

$$A_1 = -\beta^{-1} \sum_{n=1}^{\infty} \frac{(-1)^n}{n!} \beta^n \langle H_1^n \rangle_{0,c} , \tag{2.8}$$

where the series is called the cumulant expansion. The problem of calculating the perturbation series for the Helmholtz energy is thus seen to be that of calculating the cumulants $\langle H_1^n \rangle_{0,c}$.

Three further remarks are conveniently made at this point: (*i*) If there are no terms in H_0 mixing momentum and position coordinates, and if also the perturbation H_1 involves only position coordinates, then the integrals over the momenta in eq. (2.4) cancel, giving

$$Z_1 = \frac{\int \mathrm{d}x_1 \cdots \int \mathrm{d}x_{3\mathcal{N}} \exp(-\beta V_0) \exp(-\beta H_1)}{\int \mathrm{d}x_1 \cdots \int \mathrm{d}x_{3\mathcal{N}} \exp(-\beta V_0)} , \tag{2.9}$$

where V_0 is the unperturbed potential energy.

(*ii*) Despite the similarity of notation, the moments $\langle H_1^n \rangle_0$ and the cumulants $\langle H_1^n \rangle_{0,c}$ are in general quite distinct: expanding eq. (2.7) and comparing with eq. (2.8) gives

$$\begin{aligned} &\langle H_1 \rangle_{0,c} = \langle H_1 \rangle_0 , \qquad \langle H_1^2 \rangle_{0,c} = \langle H_1^2 \rangle_0 - \{\langle H_1 \rangle_0\}^2 , \\ &\langle H_1^3 \rangle_{0,c} = \langle H_1^3 \rangle_0 - 3 \langle H_1^2 \rangle_0 \langle H_1 \rangle_0 + 2 \langle H_1 \rangle_0^3 , \text{ etc.} \end{aligned} \tag{2.10}$$

(*iii*) The step between eqs. (2.2) and (2.3) is valid only because in classical mechanics H_0 and H_1 commute. A more elaborate procedure is required in the corresponding quantum treatment (see section 3).

2.2. Use of normal coordinates

We take the harmonic hamiltonian for the unperturbed system H_0. For most purposes it is convenient to use the complex normal coordinates $Q\binom{\boldsymbol{q}}{j} \equiv Q(\boldsymbol{q}j)$, where $\boldsymbol{q}$ is the wave vector (equivalent to $2\pi\boldsymbol{y}$ of BH and $2\pi\boldsymbol{k}$ of MMW) and j is the polarisation index. The harmonic hamiltonian then becomes [eq. (2.39) of MMW]

$$H_0 = \tfrac{1}{2} \sum_{\boldsymbol{q},j} \left\{ \dot{Q}^* \begin{pmatrix} \boldsymbol{q} \\ j \end{pmatrix} \dot{Q} \begin{pmatrix} \boldsymbol{q} \\ j \end{pmatrix} + \omega^2 \begin{pmatrix} \boldsymbol{q} \\ j \end{pmatrix} Q^* \begin{pmatrix} \boldsymbol{q} \\ j \end{pmatrix} Q \begin{pmatrix} \boldsymbol{q} \\ j \end{pmatrix} \right\}, \tag{2.11}$$

where the $\omega(\boldsymbol{q}, j)$ are angular frequencies of the normal modes and the summations are taken over all j and over all $\boldsymbol{q}$ within the first Brillouin zone. The anharmonic terms in H can be written in the form [eq. (39.2) and (39.8) of BH]

$$H_{\mathrm{A}} = \sum_{s=3}^{\infty} \frac{1}{s!} \frac{1}{N^{\frac{1}{2}s-1}} \sum_{\substack{\boldsymbol{q}_1 \cdots \boldsymbol{q}_s \\ j_1 \cdots j_s}} \Delta(\boldsymbol{q}_1 + \cdots + \boldsymbol{q}_s) \Phi \begin{pmatrix} \boldsymbol{q}_1 \cdots \boldsymbol{q}_s \\ j_1 \cdots j_s \end{pmatrix} Q \begin{pmatrix} \boldsymbol{q}_1 \\ j_1 \end{pmatrix} \cdots Q \begin{pmatrix} \boldsymbol{q}_s \\ j_s \end{pmatrix}, \tag{2.12}$$

where $\Delta(\boldsymbol{q})$ is unity when $\boldsymbol{q}/2\pi$ is a reciprocal lattice vector and zero otherwise, and N is the number of primitive cells in the lattice. The reality of the atomic displacements is ensured by the restriction

$$Q^*(\boldsymbol{q}j) = Q(-\boldsymbol{q}j). \tag{2.13}$$

In classical statistical mechanics, however, the most elementary theory uses real independent coordinates, such as the standing wave coordinates $q_1(\boldsymbol{q}j)$ and $q_2(\boldsymbol{q}j)$ defined by

$$Q(\boldsymbol{q}j) = \{q_1(\boldsymbol{q}j) + \mathrm{i}q_2(\boldsymbol{q}j)\}/\sqrt{2}. \tag{2.14}$$

A complete set of independent coordinates is obtained by taking the wave-vector $\boldsymbol{q}$ only over a half-zone lying on one side of an arbitrary plane through the origin (UMW, p. 33). The harmonic energy then becomes

$$\tfrac{1}{2} \sum_{\boldsymbol{q}'>0} \sum_{j} \left[\dot{q}_1^2 \begin{pmatrix} \boldsymbol{q}' \\ j \end{pmatrix} + \dot{q}_2^2 \begin{pmatrix} \boldsymbol{q}' \\ j \end{pmatrix} + \omega^2 \begin{pmatrix} \boldsymbol{q}' \\ j \end{pmatrix} \left\{ q_1^2 \begin{pmatrix} \boldsymbol{q}' \\ j \end{pmatrix} + q_2^2 \begin{pmatrix} \boldsymbol{q}' \\ j \end{pmatrix} \right\} \right], \tag{2.15}$$

where $\boldsymbol{q}'>0$ conventionally denotes restriction to the half-zone. The momenta conjugate to the $q_\lambda(\boldsymbol{q}'j)$ are

$$p_\lambda(\boldsymbol{q}'j) = \dot{q}_\lambda(\boldsymbol{q}'j). \tag{2.16}$$

When the $q_\lambda(\boldsymbol{q}j)$ are substituted for the $3\mathcal{N}$ position coordinates, the differential $\exp(-\beta V_0)\,\mathrm{d}x_1\,\mathrm{d}x_2 \cdots \mathrm{d}x_{3\mathcal{N}}$ in eq. (2.9) becomes

$$\prod_{\boldsymbol{q}'>0}\prod_{j} \exp\left[-\tfrac{1}{2}\beta\omega^2\begin{pmatrix}\boldsymbol{q}'\\ j\end{pmatrix}\left\{q_1^2\begin{pmatrix}\boldsymbol{q}'\\ j\end{pmatrix}+q_2^2\begin{pmatrix}\boldsymbol{q}'\\ j\end{pmatrix}\right\}\right]\mathrm{d}q_1\begin{pmatrix}\boldsymbol{q}'\\ j\end{pmatrix}\mathrm{d}q_2\begin{pmatrix}\boldsymbol{q}'\\ j\end{pmatrix}. \quad (2.17)$$

The form of this suggests transformation to polar coordinates in the $q_1 q_2$ planes, or equivalently to coordinates $J(\boldsymbol{q}'j)$ and $\psi(\boldsymbol{q}'j)$ defined by (Choquard 1967, p. 20)

$$Q(\boldsymbol{q}j) = J^{1/2}(\boldsymbol{q}j)\exp\{\mathrm{i}\psi(\boldsymbol{q}j)\}, \quad (2.18)$$

so that

$$J(\boldsymbol{q}j) = J(-\boldsymbol{q}j), \qquad \psi(\boldsymbol{q}j) = -\psi(-\boldsymbol{q}j). \quad (2.19)$$

The differential then takes the simpler form

$$\prod_{\boldsymbol{q}'>0}\prod_{j}\exp\left\{-\beta\omega^2\begin{pmatrix}\boldsymbol{q}'\\ j\end{pmatrix}J\begin{pmatrix}\boldsymbol{q}'\\ j\end{pmatrix}\right\}\mathrm{d}J\begin{pmatrix}\boldsymbol{q}'\\ j\end{pmatrix}\mathrm{d}\psi\begin{pmatrix}\boldsymbol{q}'\\ j\end{pmatrix}. \quad (2.20)$$

Before using this differential to derive the perturbation expansion, we illustrate the method by deriving the harmonic partition function Z_0. The integrals over the $\mathrm{d}p(\boldsymbol{q}'j)$, $\mathrm{d}J(\boldsymbol{q}'j)$ and $\mathrm{d}\psi(\boldsymbol{q}'j)$ are all separable. Integrating over the momenta gives a factor

$$h^{-3\mathcal{N}}\left\{\int_{-\infty}^{\infty} \mathrm{e}^{-\frac{1}{2}\beta p^2}\,\mathrm{d}p\right\}^{3\mathcal{N}} = (2\pi/\beta h^2)^{3\mathcal{N}/2}. \quad (2.21)$$

Integrating over the $J(\boldsymbol{q}'j)$ and $\psi(\boldsymbol{q}'j)$ gives the remaining factor

$$\prod_{\boldsymbol{q}'>0}\prod_{j}\int_0^\infty \mathrm{d}J(\boldsymbol{q}'j)\int_0^{2\pi}\mathrm{d}\psi(\boldsymbol{q}'j)\exp\{-\beta\omega^2(\boldsymbol{q}'j)\,J(\boldsymbol{q}'j)\}$$

$$= \prod_{\boldsymbol{q}'>0}\prod_{j}\{2\pi/\beta\omega^2(\boldsymbol{q}'j)\} \quad (2.22)$$

$$= \prod_{\boldsymbol{q}}\prod_{j}\{2\pi/\beta\}^{1/2}/\omega(\boldsymbol{q}j). \quad (2.23)$$

Taking the product with the factor derived in eq. (2.21) then gives the familiar result for a harmonic crystal:

$$Z_0 = \prod_{\boldsymbol{q}}\prod_{j}\{\beta\hbar\omega(\boldsymbol{q}j)\}^{-1}. \quad (2.24)$$

The same coordinates are also convenient for calculating thermal averages: if M is any function of the normal coordinates, then

$$\langle M\rangle_0 = \frac{\prod_{q'>0}\prod_j \int_0^\infty \mathrm{d}J(q'j) \int_0^{2\pi} \mathrm{d}\psi(q'j)\, M \exp\{-\beta^2\omega^2(q'j)\, J(q'j)\}}{\prod_{q'>0}\prod_j \int_0^\infty \mathrm{d}J(q'j) \int_0^\infty \mathrm{d}\psi(q'j) \exp\{-\beta^2\omega^2(q'j)\, J(q'j)\}}. \tag{2.25}$$

In particular, we find

$$\langle Q(qj)\, Q(-qj)\rangle_0 = \langle J(qj)\rangle_0 = \{\beta\omega^2(qj)\}^{-1}, \tag{2.26}$$

$$\langle \{Q(qj)\, Q(-qj)\}^\nu\rangle_0 = \langle\{J(qj)\}^\nu\rangle_0 = \nu!\,\{\beta\omega^2(qj)\}^{-\nu}. \tag{2.27}$$

2.3. Method of calculating the perturbation expansion

After these preliminaries, we can now suggest what needs to be done to calculate the perturbation expansion for the Helmholtz energy: derive the moments $\langle H_A^n\rangle$, using the expansion (2.12) for H_A, and substitute these in eq. (2.8). At first sight the complexity of such a programme appears prohibitive, except for the very lowest order terms; it involves multiple summations over the indices s in H_A^n, averages of arbitrary products of normal coordinates, multiple summation over the indices qj and derivation of the cumulant expansion from the moment expansion. However, we shall see that the procedure can be simplified in a number of ways, summarised as follows:

(*i*) Thermal averages of the type $\langle Q(q_1 j_1)\, Q(q_2 j_2) \cdots Q(q_r j_r)\rangle_0$ are zero unless the indices $q_i j_i$ occur in opposite pairs qj, $-qj$.
(*ii*) A 'pairing theorem' establishes a method of treating each such pair of coordinates as independent when the average is taken over the unperturbed distribution.
(*iii*) The moment expansion can then be expressed as the sum of terms represented by diagrams, in which lines represent pairings of coordinates and vertices represent coefficients in the expansion (2.12).
(*iv*) The cumulant expansion can then be expressed as the sum of terms represented by a restricted class of the diagrams appearing in the moment expansion.

We end this section by proving (*i*), which is essentially a consequence of phase averaging. We first shorten the notation by replacing the pair of indices qj by a single index λ, with the conventions that $-\lambda$ denotes $-qj$ and that $\lambda > 0$ denotes the same as $q > 0$. The normal coordinates can then be written as $Q(\varepsilon\lambda')$, where $\varepsilon = \pm 1$ and $\lambda' > 0$.

With this notation, consider the use of eq. (2.25) to evaluate

$$\langle Q(\varepsilon_1\lambda_1')\,Q(\varepsilon_2\lambda_2')\cdots Q(\varepsilon_r\lambda_r')\rangle_0 . \tag{2.28}$$

Integration over all the variables $J(\lambda')$ and $\psi(\lambda')$ is separable, and integration over any one variable $\psi(\lambda')$ gives a factor

$$(1/2\pi)\int_0^{2\pi} \mathrm{d}\psi(\lambda')\exp\left[\mathrm{i}\left\{\sum_{k=1}^{r}\delta_{\lambda_k'\lambda'}\,\varepsilon_k\right\}\psi(\lambda')\right]. \tag{2.29}$$

This vanishes unless $\sum_{k=1}^{r}\delta_{\lambda'_k\lambda'}\varepsilon_k=0$, i.e. unless λ' and $-\lambda'$ occur an equal number of times in the sequence $\lambda_1', \lambda_2', \cdots, \lambda_r'$; thus ($i$) is proved. It also follows from the separability of the variables that when the expression (2.28) does not vanish it reduces to a product of the form

$$\langle\{Q(\lambda^{(1)})\,Q(-\lambda^{(1)})\}^{n_1}\rangle_0\,\langle\{Q(\lambda^{(2)})\,Q(-\lambda^{(2)})\}^{n_2}\rangle_0 \cdots\langle\{Q(\lambda^{(p)})\,Q(-\lambda^{(p)})\}^{n_p}\rangle_0, \tag{2.30}$$

where the $\lambda^{(k)}$ are all distinct, and n_k is the number of times $\lambda^{(k)}$ and $\lambda^{(-k)}$ occur in the sequence $\lambda_1, \lambda_2, \cdots, \lambda_v$.

2.4. The pairing theorem

There are

$$(2\nu-1)(2\nu-3)\cdots 3\cdot 1 = (2\nu)!/2^{\nu}(\nu!) \tag{2.31}$$

ways of pairing the indices in the thermal average

$$X_{2\nu} = \langle Q(\lambda_1)\,Q(\lambda_2)\cdots Q(\lambda_{2\nu})\rangle_0 \equiv \left\langle \prod_{i=1}^{2\nu} Q(\lambda_i)\right\rangle_0 . \tag{2.32}$$

The pairing theorem states that $X_{2\nu}$ can be expressed as a sum of contributions due to each of these pairing schemes:

$$X_{2\nu} = \langle Q(\lambda_1)\,Q(\lambda_2)\rangle_0\,\langle Q(\lambda_3)\,Q(\lambda_4)\rangle_0\cdots\langle Q(\lambda_{2\nu-1})\,Q(\lambda_{2\nu})\rangle_0 + \text{similar contributions from all other pairing schemes.} \tag{2.33}$$

For example,

$$X_4 = \langle Q(\lambda_1)\,Q(\lambda_2)\rangle_0\,\langle Q(\lambda_3)\,Q(\lambda_4)\rangle_0 + \langle Q(\lambda_1)\,Q(\lambda_3)\rangle_0\,\langle Q(\lambda_2)\,Q(\lambda_4)\rangle_0 + \langle Q(\lambda_1)\,Q(\lambda_4)\rangle_0\,\langle Q(\lambda_2)\,Q(\lambda_3)\rangle_0 . \tag{2.34}$$

To prove the theorem, we show first that

$$X_{2\nu} = \sum_{k=2}^{2\nu} \langle Q(\lambda_1)\, Q(\lambda_k)\rangle_0 \left\langle \prod_{i\neq 1,\, k} Q(\lambda_i)\right\rangle_0 . \tag{2.35}$$

This is trivial if the λ_i cannot be arranged in opposite pairs, since then both sides of the equation vanish. If the λ_i can be arranged in opposite pairs, then $X_{2\nu}$ can be reduced to an expression of the form (2.30) with $\lambda^{(1)}=\lambda_1$. Since $\langle Q(\lambda_1)\, Q(\lambda_k)\rangle_0$ vanishes unless $\lambda_k=-\lambda_1$, and since $-\lambda^{(1)}$ occurs n_1 times in the sequence $\lambda_2, \lambda_3, \cdots, \lambda_{2\nu}$, there are n_1 nonvanishing terms on the right-hand side of eq. (2.35), each with the same value

$$\begin{aligned}&\langle Q(\lambda^{(1)})\, Q(-\lambda^{(1)})\rangle_0 \langle\{Q(\lambda^{(1)})\, Q(-\lambda^{(1)})\}^{n_1-1}\rangle_0 \\ &\quad\times \langle\{Q(\lambda^{(2)})\, Q(-\lambda^{(2)})\}^{n_2}\rangle_0 \cdots \langle\{Q(\lambda^{(p)})\, Q(-\lambda^{(p)})\}^{n_p}\rangle_0;\end{aligned} \tag{2.36}$$

this, by eq. (2.26) and (2.27), equals $X_{2\nu}/n_1$. Hence (2.35) is valid for all sets of indices $\lambda_1, \lambda_2, \cdots, \lambda_{2\nu}$.

The pairing theorem follows immediately by iteration, using the corresponding equation for $X_{2(\nu-1)}$ to break down the averages $\langle\prod_{i\neq 1,k} Q(\lambda_i)\rangle_0$, and so on until the only averages remaining are of products of pairs $\langle Q(\lambda_i) \times Q(\lambda_j)\rangle_0$.

Evaluation of these averages is given by eqs. (2.26) and (2.29):

$$\langle Q(\lambda_i)\, Q(\lambda_j)\rangle_0 = \delta_{\lambda_i - \lambda_j}/\beta\omega(\lambda_i)\, \omega(\lambda_j). \tag{2.37}$$

2.5. The use of diagrams

Diagrams can be used to represent terms occurring in the moment expansion, each diagram representing the contribution of a particular pairing scheme or group of equivalent pairing schemes.

The expansion (2.12) for H_{A} can be written in the shorter form

$$H_{\mathrm{A}} = \sum_{s=3}^{\infty} \sum_{\lambda_1\cdots\lambda_s} W(\lambda_1 \cdots \lambda_s)\, Q(\lambda_1) \cdots Q(\lambda_s), \tag{2.38}$$

where the coefficient

$$W(\lambda_1 \cdots \lambda_s) = \frac{1}{s!}\, \frac{1}{N^{(s-2)/2}}\, \Delta(\boldsymbol{q}_1 + \cdots + \boldsymbol{q}_s)\, \Phi\begin{pmatrix}\boldsymbol{q}_1 \cdots \boldsymbol{q}_s \\ j_1 \cdots j_s\end{pmatrix} \tag{2.38a}$$

vanishes unless $(\boldsymbol{q}_1 + \cdots + \boldsymbol{q}_s)$ is a reciprocal lattice vector. With this notation, consider for example the lowest order contribution to the second term in the moment expansion,

$$\frac{(-\beta)^2}{2!} \sum_{\lambda_1 \cdots \lambda_6} W(\lambda_1\lambda_2\lambda_3)\, W(\lambda_4\lambda_5\lambda_6)\, \langle Q(\lambda_1) \cdots Q(\lambda_6)\rangle_0 . \tag{2.39}$$

The coefficients $W(\lambda_1\lambda_2\lambda_3)$ and $W(\lambda_4\lambda_5\lambda_6)$ are symmetric with respect to interchanges of indices, but their product is not; e.g.

$$W(\lambda_1\lambda_2\lambda_3)\, W(\lambda_4\lambda_5\lambda_6) \neq W(\lambda_4\lambda_2\lambda_3)\, W(\lambda_1\lambda_5\lambda_6) . \tag{2.40}$$

The fifteen possible pairing schemes thus fall into two groups, depending upon whether all the pairings are between indices in different coefficients or whether there is only one such pairing:

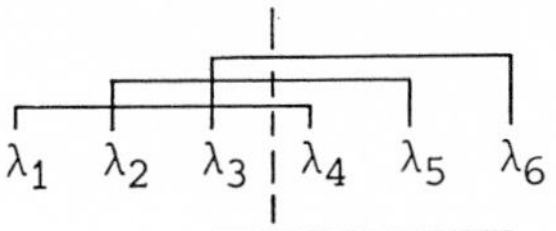

+ 5 equivalent schemes, (2.41a)

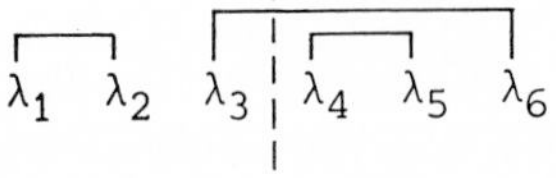

+ 8 equivalent schemes. (2.41b)

By eqs. (2.33) and (2.37), the corresponding terms in the moment expansion are

$$\frac{(-\beta)^2}{2!} \frac{6}{\beta^3} \sum_{\lambda_1\lambda_2\lambda_3} \frac{W(\lambda_1\lambda_2\lambda_3)\, W(-\lambda_1 - \lambda_2 - \lambda_3)}{\omega^2(\lambda_1)\, \omega^2(\lambda_2)\, \omega^2(\lambda_3)} , \tag{2.42a}$$

$$\frac{(-\beta)^2}{2!} \frac{9}{\beta^3} \sum_{\lambda_1\lambda_2\lambda_3} \frac{W(\lambda_1 - \lambda_1\lambda_3)\, W(\lambda_2 - \lambda_2 - \lambda_3)}{\omega^2(\lambda_1)\, \omega^2(\lambda_2)\, \omega^2(\lambda_3)} . \tag{2.42b}$$

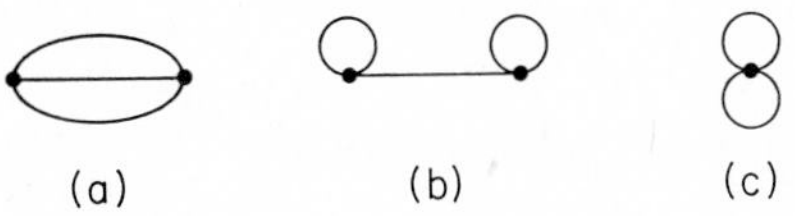

Fig. 1. Some diagrams occurring in the moment and cumulant expansions.

These detailed expressions are concisely represented by the diagrams in figs. 1a and 1b. Each triple vertex represents a third order coefficient $W(\lambda_i\lambda_j\lambda_k)$ and the lines represent pairings which contribute factors $(\beta\omega^2)^{-1}$. To get the term represented by the diagram we sum over all independent phonons λ and multiply both by the number of pairing schemes consistent with the diagram and by the factor $(-\beta)^n/n!$, where n is the number of vertices. Thus fig. 1c represents the lowest order non-vanishing contribution to the first term in the moment expansion, for which there are three equivalent pairing schemes [see eq. (2.34)], giving

$$(-\beta)\frac{3}{\beta^2}\sum_{\lambda_1\lambda_2} W(\lambda_1 - \lambda_1\lambda_2 - \lambda_2)/\omega^2(\lambda_1)\,\omega^2(\lambda_2). \tag{2.43}$$

Consider next figs. 2a, 2b and 2c, which differ from each other in the ordering of the vertices but are topologically identical. We could regard these as three distinct diagrams, making separate equal contributions to $\{(-\beta)^3/3!\}\langle H_A^3\rangle_0$, corresponding to the coefficient 3 occurring in the term $3H_3^2H_4$ in the expansion of $(H_3+H_4+H_5+\cdots)^3$. These contributions would then be obtained from the diagrams in the same way as already described

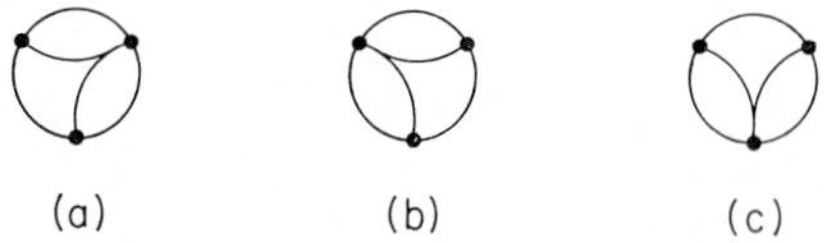

Fig. 2. Equivalent diagrams representing a contribution to $\langle H_A{}^3\rangle_0$.

for the diagrams of fig. 1. It is however more convenient to regard diagrams 2a, 2b and 2c as equivalent, including only one of them when we enumerate the diagrams contributing to the moment expansion but multiplying its contribution by an additional factor, namely, the number of distinct figures that can be obtained by permuting the vertices. For diagrams with all n vertices topologically distinct this factor is $n!$, which then cancels the denominator in $(-\beta)^n/n!$ to give a combined factor $(-\beta)^n$. More generally we can introduce a 'symmetry number' S, defined as the number of permutations of the vertices of a diagram that result in an identical figure, e.g., $S=2$ for fig. 1a, $S=1$ for fig. 4c, $S=4!$ for fig. 4h. The combined factor is then $(-\beta)^n/S$.

To sum up, there is a one-to-one correspondence between terms in the moment expansion and topologically distinct diagrams in which all lines terminate in a vertex at each end and all vertices are of third or higher order. To obtain a term from a diagram, ascribe labels λ_i, $-\lambda_i$ to each phonon pair, introduce factors $\{\beta\omega^2(\lambda_i)\}^{-1}$ for each phonon line and factors $W(\lambda', \lambda'', \cdots)$ for each vertex, and sum over all independent phonons λ_i; then multiply by the number of pairing schemes allowed by the diagram, and also by the factor $(-\beta)^n/S$, where n is the number of vertices and S is the symmetry number. [Note: This procedure applies only to contributions to the moment expansion. For calculating contributions to the Helmholtz energy, the factor $(-\beta)^n/S$ is replaced by $(-\beta)^{n-1}/S$, as shown in the next section.]

2.6. Connected diagrams and the cumulant expansion

The diagrams of figs. 1 and 2 are all said to be *connected*, in contrast to *disconnected* diagrams which consist of separate components – e.g. the diagram of fig. 3, which occurs in the fifth order term in the moment expansion.

Fig. 3. A disconnected diagram contributing to $\langle H_A{}^5 \rangle_0$.

In a disconnected diagram the pairing schemes within the separate components are independent of each other, and the summations over the λ_i factorize; so also do the number of equivalent pairing schemes and the factor $(-\beta)^n$. Thus the only factor for the disconnected diagram that is not a product of the corresponding factors for the components is S^{-1}. If therefore we write the contribution of a diagram to the moment expansion as F/S, and consider a composite diagram consisting of p different types of connected component, with ν_i components of type i, then

$$F = \prod_{i=1}^{p} F_i^{\nu_i}. \tag{2.44}$$

It remains to consider S. There are two ways in which we can permute the vertices so as to get an identical figure: (i) by permuting similar components with each other, which can be done in $\prod_{i=1}^{p} \nu_i!$ ways; (ii) by permuting vertices within each component, which can be done in $\prod_{i=1}^{p} S_i^{\nu_i}$ ways. Thus

$$S = \prod_{i=1}^{p} \nu_i!\, S_i^{\nu_i}. \tag{2.45}$$

The contribution of the disconnected diagram to the moment expansion can therefore be written as

$$F/S = \prod_{i=1}^{p} (1/\nu_i!)\,(F_i/S_i)^{\nu_i}, \tag{2.46}$$

which can be identified as one of the terms occurring in the expansion of

$$[1/(\nu_1 + \nu_2 + \cdots + \nu_p)!] \left(\sum_{i=1}^{p} F_i/S_i \right)^{\nu_1+\nu_2+\cdots\nu_p} \tag{2.47}$$

and hence as one of the terms occurring in the expansion of exp $\{\sum_c (F_c/S_c)\}$, the summation being now taken over all connected diagrams. There is a one-to-one correspondence between terms in the exponential and terms in the moment expansion, which is thus given by

$$Z_A = 1 + \sum_{\substack{\text{all} \\ \text{diagrams}}} F/S = \exp\left(\sum_{c} F_c/S_c \right). \tag{2.48}$$

The cumulant expansion thus takes the simple form $\sum_c F_c/S_c$, and the anharmonic correction to the Helmholtz energy is

$$A_A = (-\beta)^{-1} \sum_{c} F_c/S_c . \tag{2.49}$$

The subscript c in eq. (2.8) was said to denote that $\langle H_1^n \rangle_{0,c}$ was a *cumulant* average, but we see now that it could equally well be taken to mean that only *connected* diagrams contribute. To distinguish between these two concepts, we shall in future use the subscript 'conn' to denote that only connected diagrams be taken. Because of the factor β^{-1} in eq. (2.49), the term in A_A corresponding to a given connected diagram contains a factor $(-\beta)^{n-1}/S$ instead of $(-\beta)^n/S$. Otherwise, it is calculated in the same way as its contribution to the moment expansion. The contributions of connected diagrams are all proportional to N, giving the correct dependence of the Helmholtz energy on the size of the crystal.

2.7. Effect of the factors $\Delta(\boldsymbol{q}_1 + \cdots + \boldsymbol{q}_s)$

Summation over the λ_i involves an integration over reciprocal space for each independent $\boldsymbol{q}_i$. The number of independent $\boldsymbol{q}_i$ is reduced by the factors $\Delta(\boldsymbol{q}_1 + \cdots + \boldsymbol{q}_s)$ provided by each vertex. If there are p phonon lines and n vertices, the number of integrations needed is $p-n+1$.

If by cutting a single phonon line we can divide a connected diagram into two parts, as in fig. 1b, the factors $\Delta(\sum_i \boldsymbol{q}_i)$ at each vertex cause the contribution to A_A to be zero unless $\boldsymbol{q}=0$ for all such lines. For a Bravais lattice, $\boldsymbol{q}=0$ gives pure translations which cannot affect the energy; the coefficients W at each end of the line vanish, and the diagram does not contribute. More generally, such diagrams can be omitted for any lattice in which the positions of atoms within the unit cell are determined by symmetry (see subsection 4.5).

2.8. Grouping of terms in the perturbation expansion

Since there are an infinite number of connected diagrams, we need a criterion for grouping terms in successive orders of approximation. If the amplitude of vibrations is sufficiently small, we can assign orders of magnitude to successive terms in the expansion (2.12) for H_A, regarding the cubic term as being of the first order in the anharmonicity, the quartic term as of the second order, and so on. Each vertex of order s in a connected diagram then contributes $s-2$ to the order of magnitude of its contribution to A_A,

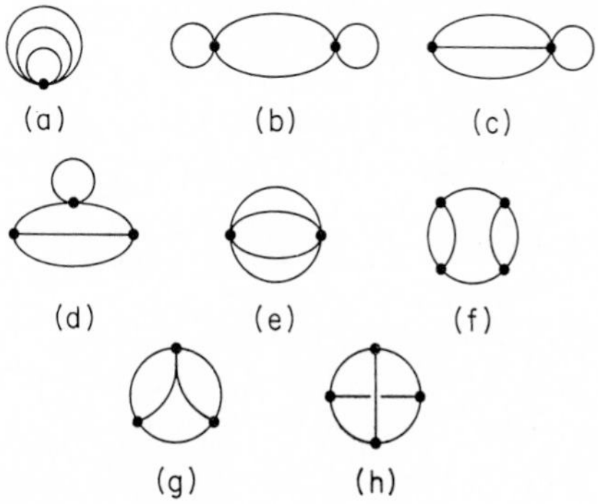

Fig. 4. Diagrams contributing to the T^3 term in the Helmholtz energy.

giving an order $2(p-n)$ for the entire diagram. All diagrams of the same order therefore require the same number of integrations over reciprocal space, $p-n+1$, and have the same temperature dependence (T^{p-n+1}). The lowest order terms are of the second order, and are derived from the diagrams of fig. 1. Explicit expressions are obtained by multiplying the expressions (2.42a), (2.42b) and (2.43) by $(-\beta)^{-1}$, giving terms in T^2 for the Helmholtz energy and consequently terms in T for the entropy and heat capacity at constant volume. The next lowest terms are of the fourth order, and give terms in T^3 for the Helmholtz energy. Some of the diagrams contributing to this order of approximation are shown in fig. 4, namely those without any $\boldsymbol{q}=0$ lines; there are also seven diagrams with $\boldsymbol{q}=0$ lines.

The complexity of the calculation increases rapidly with the order of approximation – both because of the increased number of diagrams, and because of the additional integrals over reciprocal space. Calculations are therefore seldom carried beyond the first approximation represented by figs. 1a and 1c. For simple models it is possible to go to the next order of perturbation theory (Shukla and Cowley 1971). When this approach breaks down, in principle it can be replaced by one of three other methods: (*i*) self-consistent phonon theory, equivalent to summing some of the perturbation terms to infinite order (see Götze and Michel ch. 9, and Horner ch. 8); (*ii*) Monte-Carlo techniques (Wood 1968); (*iii*) molecular dynamics (Alder 1959, Rahman 1964).

3. *Helmholtz energy: quantum theory*

3.1. Moment and cumulant expansions

In quantum statistical mechanics, the canonical partition function is given by

$$Z = \mathrm{tr}\,\{\mathrm{e}^{-\beta H}\} \equiv \sum_i \langle i|\,\mathrm{e}^{-\beta H}\,|i\rangle, \tag{3.1}$$

where H is the hamiltonian operator and the quantum states $|i\rangle$ comprise any complete orthonormal set for the system. If the $|i\rangle$ are chosen as the true energy states, this takes the form $Z=\sum_i \exp(-\beta E_i)$, but here we choose the $|i\rangle$ as the unperturbed energy states of the hamiltonian H_0. Thermal averages are given by

$$\langle M\rangle = Z^{-1}\,\mathrm{tr}\,\{\mathrm{e}^{-\beta H}\,M\} \tag{3.2}$$

and averages over the unperturbed system by

$$\langle M\rangle_0 = Z_0^{-1}\,\mathrm{tr}\,\{\mathrm{e}^{-\beta H_0}\,M\}. \tag{3.3}$$

To obtain the expansion for Z, we define an operator $S(\beta)$ by

$$\mathrm{e}^{-\beta(H_0+H_1)} = \mathrm{e}^{-\beta H_0}\,S(\beta), \tag{3.4}$$

so that, by eqs. (3.1) and (3.3),

$$Z = Z_0\,\langle S(\beta)\rangle_0\,. \tag{3.5}$$

The analogue of eq. (2.5) is thus

$$Z_1 = \langle S(\beta)\rangle_0\,, \tag{3.6}$$

and we shall again call the expansion of Z_1 in powers of H_1 the moment expansion, although it no longer takes the simple form of $\langle e^{-\beta H_1}\rangle_0$ unless H_1 and H_0 commute. To obtain the expansion, we first differentiate eq. (3.4) with respect to β:

$$\begin{aligned} e^{-\beta H_0}[S'(\beta) - H_0 S(\beta)] &= -(H_0 + H_1)\, e^{-\beta(H_0+H_1)} \\ &= -(H_0 + H_1)\, e^{-\beta H_0} S(\beta). \end{aligned}$$

Hence $S'(\beta) = -e^{\beta H_0} H_1 e^{-\beta H_0} S(\beta)$ and, since $S(0)=1$, this can be solved by iteration to give

$$S(\beta) = 1 + \sum_{n=1}^{\infty} (-1)^n \int_0^{\beta} d\tau_1 \int_0^{\tau_1} d\tau_2 \cdots \int_0^{\tau_{n-1}} d\tau_n \tilde{H}_1(\tau_1)\, \tilde{H}_1(\tau_2) \cdots \tilde{H}_1(\tau_n), \tag{3.7}$$

where the tilde above an operator denotes

$$\tilde{H}_1(\tau) = e^{\tau H_0} H_1 e^{-\tau H_0}. \tag{3.8}$$

The awkward restriction of the range of integration to $\beta > \tau_1 > \tau_2 > \cdots > \tau_n$ can be removed by introducing the Dyson τ ordering policeman T_τ, which reorders products of functions of the τ_i so that the values of τ increase from right to left; e.g.,

$$\begin{aligned} T_\tau f(\tau_1)\, g(\tau_2) &= f(\tau_1)\, g(\tau_2) \quad \text{when} \quad \tau_1 > \tau_2, \\ &= g(\tau_2)\, f(\tau_1) \quad \text{when} \quad \tau_1 < \tau_2. \end{aligned} \tag{3.9}$$

The moment expansion (3.7) then becomes

$$\begin{aligned} Z_1 = \langle S(\beta)\rangle_0 = 1 &+ \sum_{n=1}^{\infty} [(-1)^n/n!] \\ &\times \int_0^{\beta} d\tau_1 \cdots \int_0^{\beta} d\tau_n \langle T_\tau \tilde{H}_1(\tau_1) \cdots \tilde{H}_n(\tau_n)\rangle_0, \end{aligned} \tag{3.10}$$

which is sometimes written in the compact form

$$Z_1 = \left\langle T_\tau \exp\left[\int_0^{\beta} d\tau \tilde{H}_1(\tau)\right]\right\rangle_0. \tag{3.10a}$$

The correction to the unperturbed Helmholtz energy is given as before by $-\beta^{-1} \ln Z_1$.

Eq. (3.7), (3.8) and (3.10) are identical to equations obtained for the time-dependence of a many-body system, except that t is replaced by $-i\hbar\tau$. This formal equivalence of inverse temperature to imaginary time will be discussed in Section 5.

3.2. Use of normal coordinates

We rescale the normal coordinates $Q(\lambda)$ by writing (Glyde and Klein 1971, p. 185)

$$Q(\lambda) = \{\hbar/2\omega(\lambda)\}\, A(\lambda). \tag{3.11}$$

It is sometimes convenient to write the indices λ as subscripts, e.g.,

$$Q_\lambda = \{\hbar/2\omega_\lambda\}\, A_\lambda, \tag{3.11a}$$

and we shall from now on follow the example of Cowley (1963) and use these notations interchangeably. The A_λ can be expressed as the sum of creation and destruction operators for travelling waves [MMW, eqs. (2.3.32)]:

$$A_\lambda = a^*_{-\lambda} + a_\lambda, \tag{3.12}$$

where a^*_λ and a_λ are defined by

$$a_\lambda |n_\lambda\rangle = n_\lambda^{1/2} |n_\lambda - 1\rangle, \qquad a^*_\lambda |n_\lambda\rangle = (n_\lambda + 1)^{1/2} |n_\lambda + 1\rangle, \tag{3.13}$$

with $|n_\lambda\rangle$ denoting the normalised n_λth quantum state of the travelling wave λ. The harmonic hamiltonian then becomes

$$H = \tfrac{1}{2} \sum_\lambda (a_\lambda a^*_\lambda + a^*_\lambda a_\lambda)\, \hbar\omega_\lambda. \tag{3.14}$$

The $A(\lambda)$ are related to the atomic displacements $\boldsymbol{u}(l\kappa)$ by the linear transformation

$$u_\alpha(l\kappa) = \sum_{\boldsymbol{q}j} T_\alpha(l\kappa, \boldsymbol{q}j)\, A(\boldsymbol{q}j), \tag{3.15}$$

where

$$T_\alpha(l\kappa, \boldsymbol{q}j) = \{\hbar/2NM_\kappa\omega_\lambda\}^{1/2}\, e^{i\boldsymbol{q}\cdot\boldsymbol{r}(l)}\, e_\alpha(\kappa, \boldsymbol{q}j), \tag{3.16}$$

and the $\boldsymbol{e}(\kappa, \boldsymbol{q}j)$ are normalised polarisation vectors [MMW, eqs. (2.1.27 and (2.1.29a)]. The anharmonic part of the hamiltonian is thus

$$H_\mathrm{A} = \sum_{s=3}^{\infty} \sum_{\lambda_1 \cdots \lambda_s} V(\lambda_1 \cdots \lambda_s)\, A(\lambda_1) \cdots A(\lambda_s), \tag{3.17}$$

where the coefficients are related to the displacement force-constants by

$$V(\lambda_1 \cdots \lambda_s) = \frac{1}{s!} \sum_{l_1\kappa_1\alpha_1} \cdots \sum_{l_s\kappa_s\alpha_s} T_{\alpha_1}(l_1\kappa_1, \lambda_1) \cdots T_{\alpha_s}(l_s\kappa_s, \lambda_s)\, \Phi_{\alpha_1\cdots\alpha_s}\begin{pmatrix} l_1 \cdots l_s \\ \kappa_1 \cdots \kappa_s \end{pmatrix} \tag{3.18}$$

and to the coefficients of eq. (2.38) by

$$V(\lambda_1 \cdots \lambda_s) = (\hbar/2)^s\, W(\lambda_1 \cdots \lambda_s)/\{\omega(\lambda_1) \cdots \omega(\lambda_s)\}. \tag{3.19}$$

From eq. (3.18) it follows also that

$$V(\lambda_1 \cdots \lambda_s) = \{V(-\lambda_1 \cdots -\lambda_s)\}^*. \tag{3.19a}$$

Eigenstates of H_0 are labelled by quantum numbers for each travelling wave, n_λ, called phonon occupation numbers; the state $|n_1\, n_2 \cdots n_\lambda \cdots\rangle$ has the energy $\sum_\lambda (n_\lambda + \frac{1}{2})\, \hbar\omega_\lambda$. Eq. (3.3) then gives thermal averages of the form

$$\langle M \rangle_0 = (1/Z_0) \sum_{n_1 n_2 \cdots} \exp\Big(-\beta \sum_\lambda (n_\lambda + \tfrac{1}{2})\, \hbar\omega_\lambda\Big) \times \langle \cdots n_\lambda \cdots n_1\, |M|\, n_1 \cdots n_\lambda \cdots \rangle. \tag{3.20}$$

If M is a product of creation and annihilation operators, the matrix element is zero unless for each mode a_λ and a_λ^* occur an equal number of times.

We end this section by quoting commutation relations and other useful properties of a_λ and a_λ^*. The number operator n_λ is given by

$$n_\lambda = a_\lambda^* a_\lambda, \qquad n_\lambda + 1 = a_\lambda a_\lambda^*, \tag{3.21}$$

so that $[a_\lambda, a_\lambda^*] = 1$. All other pairs commute, whence

$$[a_\lambda, a_{\lambda'}^*] = \delta_{\lambda\lambda'}, \qquad [a_\lambda, a_{\lambda'}] = [a_\lambda^*, a_{\lambda'}^*] = 0. \tag{3.22}$$

Commutation with the harmonic hamiltonian is given by

$$[a_\lambda, H_0] = a_\lambda, \qquad [a_\lambda^*, H_0] = -\, a_\lambda^*, \tag{3.23}$$

and interchange with the Boltzmann operator $\mathrm{e}^{-\beta H_0}$ by

$$a_\lambda\, e^{-\beta H_0} = \mathrm{e}^{-\beta\hbar\omega_\lambda}\, \mathrm{e}^{-\beta H_0}\, a_\lambda, \qquad a_\lambda^*\, \mathrm{e}^{-\beta H_0} = \mathrm{e}^{\beta\hbar\omega_\lambda}\, \mathrm{e}^{-\beta H_0}\, a_\lambda^*. \tag{3.24}$$

Thermal averages in constant use are

$$\bar{n}_\lambda \equiv \langle n_\lambda \rangle_0 = \frac{1}{\mathrm{e}^{\beta\hbar\omega_\lambda} - 1}, \qquad \bar{n}_\lambda + 1 = \frac{1}{1 - \mathrm{e}^{-\beta\hbar\omega_\lambda}} = \frac{\mathrm{e}^{\beta\hbar\omega_\lambda}}{\mathrm{e}^{\beta\hbar\omega_\lambda} - 1}. \tag{3.25}$$

3.3. Thermal averages in the perturbation expansion

From eqs. (3.8) and (3.17), the operators $\tilde{H}_1(\tau)$ to be substituted in eq. (3.7) are of the form

$$H_A(\tau) = \sum_{s=3}^{\infty} \sum_{\lambda_1 \cdots \lambda_s} V(\lambda_1 \cdots \lambda_s) \tilde{A}_{\lambda_1}(\tau) \cdots \tilde{A}_{\lambda_s}(\tau), \tag{3.26}$$

where

$$\tilde{A}_\lambda(\tau) = e^{\tau H_0}(a_\lambda + a_{-\lambda})^* e^{-\tau H_0} = - e^{-\tau\hbar\omega_\lambda} a_\lambda + e^{\tau\hbar\omega_\lambda} a^*_{-\lambda} \tag{3.27}$$

by eqs. (3.24). Eq. (3.10) thus involves thermal averages of the form

$$X_{2\nu} = \langle T_\tau \tilde{A}_{\lambda_1}(\tau_1) \cdots \tilde{A}_{\lambda_{2\nu}}(\tau_{2\nu})\rangle_0; \tag{3.28}$$

since a_λ and a^*_λ must occur an equal number of times if $X_{2\nu}$ is to be non zero, it follows from eq. (3.27) that the A_λ must occur in pairs $\lambda, -\lambda$. The simplest of this type involves only two normal coordinates; by eqs. (3.27) and (3.21),

$$\langle \tilde{A}_\lambda(\tau_1) \tilde{A}_{-\lambda}(\tau_2)\rangle_0 = \bar{n}_\lambda e^{(\tau_1-\tau_2)\hbar\omega_\lambda} + (\bar{n}_\lambda + 1) e^{-(\tau_1-\tau_2)\hbar\omega_\lambda}. \tag{3.29}$$

More generally we write

$$\langle T_\tau \tilde{A}_\lambda(\tau_1) \tilde{A}_{\lambda'}(\tau_2)\rangle_0 = \delta_{\lambda-\lambda'} g(\lambda, \tau_1 - \tau_2), \tag{3.30}$$

where $g(\lambda, \tau_1 - \tau_2)$ is called the harmonic phonon propagator, defined in the range $-\beta < \tau < \beta$ by

$$g(\lambda, \tau) = \langle T_\tau \tilde{A}_\lambda(\tau) \tilde{A}_{-\lambda}(0)\rangle_0 = \bar{n}_\lambda e^{|\tau|\hbar\omega_\lambda} + (\bar{n}_\lambda + 1) e^{-|\tau|\hbar\omega_\lambda}. \tag{3.31}$$

3.4. The pairing theorem

As for the classical crystal, a pairing theorem can be proved:

$$\begin{aligned} X_{2\nu} = {} & \langle T_\tau \tilde{A}_{\lambda_1}(\tau_1) \tilde{A}_{\lambda_2}(\tau_2)\rangle_0 \langle T_\tau \tilde{A}_{\lambda_3}(\tau_3) \tilde{A}_{\lambda_4}(\tau_4)\rangle_0 \\ & \cdots \langle T_\tau \tilde{A}_{\lambda_{2\nu-1}}(\tau_{2\nu-1}) \tilde{A}_{\lambda_{2\nu}}(\tau_{2\nu})\rangle_0 \\ & + \text{similar contributions from all pairing schemes.} \end{aligned} \tag{3.32}$$

This can be regarded as an application of Wick's theorem, which is fundamental in many-body perturbation theory (Abrikosov et al. 1963); in its present context it is most easily proved by a method due to Gaudin (Choquard 1967, pp. 197–199), in which it follows by iteration from the analogue of eq. (2.35):

$$X_{2\nu} = \sum_{k=2}^{2\nu} \langle T_\tau \tilde{A}_{\lambda_1}(\tau_1)\, \tilde{A}_{\lambda_k}(\tau_k)\rangle_0 \left\langle \prod_{i\neq 1,k} T_\tau \tilde{A}_{\lambda_i}(\tau_i)\right\rangle_0 . \tag{3.33}$$

The proof of eq. (3.33) is a little more intricate than that of (2.35). Without loss of generality, we can take the τ_i as already ordered, so that $\tau_1 > \tau_2 \cdots > \tau_{2\nu}$. By eqs. (3.27) and (3.22),

$$[\tilde{a}_{\lambda_1}(\tau_1), \tilde{A}_{\lambda_k}(\tau_k)] = \exp[-\hbar\omega_{\lambda_1}(\tau_1 - \tau_k)]\, \delta_{\lambda_1 - \lambda_k}; \tag{3.34}$$

the commutator is thus a *c-number*, i.e., a constant that will itself commute with any other operator and can be removed as a factor from any average. Hence

$$\begin{aligned}
&\langle \tilde{a}_{\lambda_1}(\tau_1)\, \tilde{A}_{\lambda_2}(\tau_2) \cdots \tilde{A}_{\lambda_{2\nu}}(\tau_{2\nu})\rangle_0 \\
&\quad = [\tilde{a}_{\lambda_1}(\tau_1), \tilde{A}_{\lambda_2}(\tau_2)]\, \langle \tilde{A}_{\lambda_3}(\tau_3) \cdots \tilde{A}_{\lambda_{2\nu}}(\tau_{2\nu})\rangle_0 \\
&\qquad\qquad + \langle \tilde{A}_{\lambda_2}(\tau_2)\, \tilde{a}_{\lambda_1}(\tau_1)\, \tilde{A}_{\lambda_3}(\tau_3) \cdots \tilde{A}_{\lambda_{2\nu}}(\tau_{2\nu})\rangle_0 \\
&\quad = \sum_k [\tilde{a}_{\lambda_1}(\tau_1), \tilde{A}_{\lambda_k}(\tau_k)] \left\langle \prod_{i\neq 1,k} T_\tau \tilde{A}_{\lambda_i}(\tau_i)\right\rangle_0 \\
&\qquad\qquad + \langle \tilde{A}_{\lambda_2}(\tau_2)\, \tilde{A}_{\lambda_3}(\tau_3) \cdots \tilde{A}_{\lambda_{2\nu}}(\tau_{2\nu})\, \tilde{a}_{\lambda_1}(\tau_1)\rangle_0 ,
\end{aligned} \tag{3.35}$$

where $\tilde{a}_{\lambda_1}(\tau_1)$ has been moved step by step to the right. By eq. (3.3), the cyclic property of the trace and eq. (3.24), the final term is

$$\begin{aligned}
&Z_0^{-1} \operatorname{tr}\{e^{-\beta H_0}\, \tilde{A}_{\lambda_2}(\tau_2) \cdots \tilde{A}_{\lambda_{2\nu}}(\tau_{2\nu})\, \tilde{a}_{\lambda_1}(\tau_1)\} \\
&\qquad = \operatorname{tr}\{\tilde{a}_{\lambda_1}(\tau_1)\, e^{-\beta H_0}\, \tilde{A}_{\lambda_2}(\tau_2) \cdots \tilde{A}_{\lambda_{2\nu}}(\tau_{2\nu})\} \\
&\qquad = \exp(-\beta\hbar\omega_{\lambda_1}) \langle \tilde{a}_{\lambda_1}(\tau_1)\, \tilde{A}_{\lambda_2}(\tau_2) \cdots \tilde{A}_{\lambda_{2\nu}}(\tau_{2\nu})\rangle_0 ,
\end{aligned} \tag{3.36}$$

so that eq. (3.35) becomes

$$\langle \tilde{a}_{\lambda_1}(\tau_1)\, \tilde{A}_{\lambda_2}(\tau_2) \cdots \tilde{A}_{\lambda_{2\nu}}(\tau_{2\nu})\rangle_0$$

$$= \frac{1}{1 - \exp(-\beta\hbar\omega_{\lambda_1})} \sum_k [\tilde{a}_{\lambda_1}(\tau_1), \tilde{A}_{\lambda_k}(\tau_k)] \left\langle \prod_{i\neq 1,k} T_\tau \tilde{A}_{\lambda_i}(\tau_i)\right\rangle_0 \tag{3.37}$$

$$= \sum_k \delta_{\lambda_1 - \lambda_k} (\bar{n}_{\lambda_1} + 1) \exp[-\hbar\omega_{\lambda_1}(\tau_1 - \tau_k)] \left\langle \prod_{i\neq 1,k} T_\tau \tilde{A}_{\lambda_i}(\tau_i)\right\rangle_0 \tag{3.38}$$

by eqs. (3.25) and (3.34). Similarly it can be shown that

$$\begin{aligned}
&\langle \tilde{a}^*_{-\lambda_1}(\tau_1)\, \tilde{A}_{\lambda_2}(\tau_2) \cdots \tilde{A}_{\lambda_{2\nu}}(\tau_{2\nu})\rangle_0 \\
&\qquad = \sum_k \delta_{\lambda_1 - \lambda_k} \bar{n}_{\lambda_1} \exp[\hbar\omega_{\lambda_1}(\tau_1 - \tau_k)] \left\langle \prod_{i\neq 1,k} T_\tau \tilde{A}_{\lambda_i}(\tau_i)\right\rangle_0 .
\end{aligned} \tag{3.39}$$

Addition of eqs. (3.38) and (3.39) gives eq. (3.33), and hence establishes the pairing theorem (3.32).

3.5. Use of diagrams

Diagrams are used to represent pairing schemes precisely as for the classical theory. Only connected diagrams contribute to the expansion for the Helmholtz energy, which can therefore be written in abbreviated form as

$$A_{\text{anh}} = -\beta^{-1}\langle S(\beta) - 1\rangle_{0,\,\text{conn}}. \tag{3.40}$$

The terms corresponding to each diagram differ from the classical terms mainly in that each phonon line λ ending in vertices i and j contributes a factor $g(\lambda, |\tau_i - \tau_j|)$, as defined in eq. (3.31); the product of all these factors is then integrated over all the τ_i in the range $0 < \tau_i < \beta$. The remaining factors are the same as for the classical evaluation, except that $W(\lambda_1 \cdots \lambda_s)$ is replaced by $V(\lambda_1 \cdots \lambda_s)$ and the factor β is omitted because it has already been included in the integration.

The integration may either be carried out directly, or transformed into a summation of products of Fourier transforms. We illustrate and compare these techniques by applying them to the diagrams of figs. 1a and 1c. The rules for evaluating diagrams are summarised in the Appendix.

3.6. Direct integration

The diagram of fig. 1c contributes to the Helmholtz energy

$$A_4 \equiv (-\beta)^{-1}\, 3(-1) \sum_{\lambda_1\lambda_2} V(\lambda_1 - \lambda_1\lambda_2 - \lambda_2) \int_0^\beta g(\lambda_1, 0)\, g(\lambda_2, 0)\, \mathrm{d}\tau \tag{3.41}$$

$$= 3 \sum_{\lambda_1\lambda_2} V(\lambda_1 - \lambda_1\lambda_2 - \lambda_2)\, \{2\bar{n}(\lambda_1) + 1\}\, \{2\bar{n}(\lambda_2) + 1\}, \tag{3.42}$$

by eq. (3.31). The diagram of fig. 1a contributes

$$A_3 = (-\beta)^{-1}\, \tfrac{6}{2}(-1)^2 \sum_{\lambda_1\lambda_2\lambda_3} V(\lambda_1\lambda_2\lambda_3)\, V(-\lambda_1 - \lambda_2 - \lambda_3)$$

$$\times 2 \int_0^\beta \mathrm{d}\tau_1 \int_0^{\tau_1} \mathrm{d}\tau_2\, g(\lambda_1, \tau_1 - \tau_2)\, g(\lambda_2, \tau_1 - \tau_2)\, g(\lambda_3, \tau_1 - \tau_2). \tag{3.43}$$

The integrand can be expanded with the aid of eq. (3.31) to give

$$\begin{aligned}
&\{\bar{n}(\lambda_1)+1\}\{\bar{n}(\lambda_2)+1\}\{\bar{n}(\lambda_3)+1\} \\
&\quad \times \exp[-(\tau_1-\tau_2)\hbar\{\omega(\lambda_1)+\omega(\lambda_2)+\omega(\lambda_3)\}] \\
&\quad + \bar{n}(\lambda_1)\bar{n}(\lambda_2)\bar{n}(\lambda_3)\exp[(\tau_1-\tau_2)\hbar\{\omega(\lambda_1)+\omega(\lambda_2)+\omega(\lambda_3)\}] \\
&\quad + \bar{n}(\lambda_1)\{\bar{n}(\lambda_2)+1\}\{\bar{n}(\lambda_3)+1\} \\
&\quad \times \exp[-(\tau_1-\tau_2)\hbar\{\omega(\lambda_2)+\omega(\lambda_3)-\omega(\lambda_1)\}] + 2\,\text{cyclic terms} \\
&\quad + \{\bar{n}(\lambda_1)+1\}\bar{n}(\lambda_2)\bar{n}(\lambda_3) \\
&\quad \times \exp[(\tau_1-\tau_2)\hbar\{\omega(\lambda_2)+\omega(\lambda_3)-\omega(\lambda_1)\}] + 2\,\text{cyclic terms}\,. \qquad (3.44)
\end{aligned}$$

The resulting integrals are all of the form

$$\int_0^\beta d\tau_1 \int_0^{\tau_1} d\tau_1 \exp[\hbar\Omega(\tau_1-\tau_2)] = \frac{1}{\hbar\Omega}\left\{\frac{\exp(\beta\hbar\Omega)-1}{\hbar\Omega} - \beta\right\}. \qquad (3.45)$$

For each bracket of the expression (3.44) the terms of the type $\{\exp(\beta\hbar\Omega)-$ $-1\}/(\hbar\Omega)^2$ cancel when eqs. (3.25) are used to put

$$\exp(\beta\hbar\omega_\lambda) = (\bar{n}_\lambda+1)/\bar{n}_\lambda\,, \qquad \exp(-\beta\hbar\omega_\lambda) = \bar{n}_\lambda/(\bar{n}_\lambda+1)\,. \qquad (3.46)$$

The remaining terms then give

$$\begin{aligned}
A_3 = &-\frac{6}{\hbar}\sum_{\lambda_1\lambda_2\lambda_3} |V(\lambda_1\lambda_2\lambda_3)|^2 \\
&\times \left\{\frac{[\bar{n}(\lambda_1)+1][\bar{n}(\lambda_2)+1][\bar{n}(\lambda_3)+1] - \bar{n}(\lambda_1)\bar{n}(\lambda_2)\bar{n}(\lambda_3)}{\omega(\lambda_1)+\omega(\lambda_2)+\omega(\lambda_3)}\right. \\
&\left. + 3\,\frac{\bar{n}(\lambda_1)[\bar{n}(\lambda_2)+1][\bar{n}(\lambda_3)+1] - [\bar{n}(\lambda_1)+1]\bar{n}(\lambda_2)\bar{n}(\lambda_3)}{\omega(\lambda_2)+\omega(\lambda_3)-\omega(\lambda_1)}\right\}, \qquad (3.47)
\end{aligned}$$

since the symmetry of $V(\lambda_1\lambda_2\lambda_3)$ ensures the equality of the three cyclic terms.

3.7. The Fourier transforms

The phonon propagator $g(\lambda, \tau)$ defined by eq. (3.31) is periodic in τ:

$$g(\lambda, \tau+\beta) = g(\lambda, \tau)\,, \qquad -\beta < \tau < 0\,. \qquad (3.48)$$

Its Fourier expansion is then

$$g(\lambda, \tau) = \sum_{n=-\infty}^{\infty} g(\lambda, i\omega_n)\exp(i\hbar\omega_n\tau)\,, \qquad (3.49)$$

where

$$\omega_n = 2\pi n/\beta\hbar, \tag{3.50}$$

and the Fourier transform is given by*

$$g(\lambda, \mathrm{i}\omega_n) = \frac{1}{\beta\hbar}\left\{\frac{1}{\omega_\lambda - \mathrm{i}\omega_n} + \frac{1}{\omega_\lambda + \mathrm{i}\omega_n}\right\} = \frac{2\omega_\lambda}{\beta\hbar(\omega_\lambda^2 + \omega_n^2)}. \tag{3.51}$$

Eq. (3.49) can be used to replace each propagator $g(\lambda, \tau_i - \tau_j)$ by $\sum_{n=-\infty}^{\infty} g(\lambda, \mathrm{i}\omega_n) \exp\{\mathrm{i}\hbar\omega_n(\tau_i - \tau_j)\}$, where if i and j are different vertices we shall always take the subscript i as referring to the vertex on the left. For each vertex i there is then an integral of the form

$$\int_0^\beta \mathrm{d}\tau_i \exp\{\mathrm{i}\hbar\tau_i([\omega_{n'}^{(\mathrm{r})} + \omega_{n''}^{(\mathrm{r})} + \cdots] - [\omega_{n'}^{(\ell)} + \omega_{n''}^{(\ell)} + \cdots])\}$$
$$= \beta\delta([\omega_{n'}^{(\mathrm{r})} + \cdots], [\omega_{n''}^{(\ell)} + \cdots]), \tag{3.52}$$

where the $\omega_n^{(\mathrm{r})}$ and $\omega_n^{(l)}$ come from phonon lines respectively to the right and to the left of vertex i; since $\hbar\omega_n$ is an energy, the Kronecker delta is said to give energy conservation at each vertex for phonons arriving on the left and leaving from the right. The Fourier transform thus replaces integration over the τ_i by summation over the 'phonon energies' ω_{n_j}. For the Helmholtz energy this does not appear to be any simpler, but the Fourier transforms are so widely used for related properties that the rules for evaluating diagrams are usually stated in terms of the Fourier transforms (e.g. Cowley 1963, p. 428). These rules are summarised in the Appendix.

Summation over the ω_n is usually done by contour integration. The method is to use a function with an infinite set of poles, one for each value of n, all with the same residue – e.g. $f(z) = \{\exp(\beta\hbar z) - 1\}^{-1}$, which has poles on the imaginary axis at $z = \mathrm{i}2\pi n/\beta\hbar = \mathrm{i}\omega_n$, all with residues $(\beta\hbar)^{-1}$. To find a sum of the form $\sum_n \phi(\mathrm{i}\omega_n)$, we integrate the product $f(z)\,\phi(z)$ round the square with centre at the origin and sides of length $D_N = \omega_N + \omega_{N+1}$. Provided that $\phi(z) \to 0$ faster than $|z|^{-1}$, the contour integral tends to zero as $N \to \infty$ and the sum of the residues of $f(z)\,\phi(z)$ is therefore zero. If the poles of $\phi(z)$ are at $z = a_p \neq \mathrm{i}\omega_n$, then

$$\sum_n \phi(\mathrm{i}\omega_n) = -\beta\hbar \sum_p R_p, \tag{3.53}$$

where R_p is the residue of $f(z)\,\phi(z)$ at $z = a_p$.

* The notation $g(\lambda, \mathrm{i}\omega_n)$ anticipates the needs of section 5, which exploits the formal equivalence of inverse temperature to imaginary time.

We shall sketch the method for the diagram of fig. 1a, which after elimination of the delta function gives a double summation:

$$S = \sum_n \sum_m \frac{2\omega(\lambda_1)}{\omega^2(\lambda_1) + \omega_n^2} \frac{2\omega(\lambda_2)}{\omega^2(\lambda_2) + \omega_m^2} \frac{2\omega(\lambda_3)}{\omega^2(\lambda_3) + [\omega_n + \omega_m]^2}. \tag{3.54}$$

Resolution into partial fractions gives eight terms, of which we take one as example:

$$S = \sum_n \sum_m [\{\omega(\lambda_1) - \mathrm{i}\omega_n\} \{\omega(\lambda_2) - \mathrm{i}\omega_m\} \{\omega(\lambda_3) + [\mathrm{i}\omega_n + \mathrm{i}\omega_m]\}]^{-1}. \tag{3.55}$$

For the summation over n we take

$$\phi(z) = [\{\omega(\lambda_1) - z\} \{\omega(\lambda_2) - \mathrm{i}\omega_m\} \{\omega(\lambda_3) + \mathrm{i}\omega_m + z\}]^{-1}. \tag{3.56}$$

At the poles of $\phi(z)$ the values of $f(z)$ are

$$f(\omega(\lambda_1)) = \{\exp[\beta\hbar\omega(\lambda_1)] - 1\}^{-1} = \bar{n}(\lambda_1), \tag{3.57}$$

$$f(-\omega(\lambda_3) - \mathrm{i}\omega_m) = \{\exp[-\beta\hbar\omega(\lambda_3)] - 1\}^{-1} = -(\bar{n}(\lambda_3) + 1),$$

since $\exp(\mathrm{i}\beta\hbar\omega_m) = 1$ for all integral m. Hence, by eq. (3.53),

$$\sum_n \phi(\mathrm{i}\omega_n) = \frac{\beta\hbar\{\bar{n}(\lambda_1) + \bar{n}(\lambda_3) + 1\}}{[\omega(\lambda_2) - \mathrm{i}\omega_m][\omega(\lambda_1) + \omega(\lambda_3) + \mathrm{i}\omega_m]}. \tag{3.58}$$

The same method can be used now to sum over m, giving for the double summation

$$S = \frac{(\beta\hbar)^2 [\{\bar{n}(\lambda_1) + 1\} \{\bar{n}(\lambda_2) + 1\} \{\bar{n}(\lambda_3) + 1\} - \bar{n}(\lambda_1)\bar{n}(\lambda_2)\bar{n}(\lambda_3)]}{\omega(\lambda_1) + \omega(\lambda_2) + \omega(\lambda_3)}. \tag{3.59}$$

The other partial fractions are summed similarly, leading eventually to the result contained in equ. (3.47). Alternatively, the same method can be applied without preliminary resolution into partial fractions, but the individual steps are then more complicated.

4. *Stress tensor and elastic constants; thermal expansion*

4.1. Thermodynamic definitions

Of the many different ways of defining elastic constants (see, e.g., Thurston 1964, Leibfried and Ludwig 1961, Barron and Munn 1970, Wallace 1970) the simplest thermodynamically is to define them as derivatives of an appropriate energy function with respect to the Lagrange finite strain parameters $\eta_{\alpha\beta}$. Thus isothermal elastic stiffnesses are defined by

$$A/\mathring{V} = \mathring{A}/\mathring{V} + \sum_{\alpha\beta} C^{\mathrm{T}}_{\alpha\beta}\eta_{\alpha\beta} + (1/2!) \sum_{\alpha\beta\gamma\delta} C^{\mathrm{T}}_{\alpha\beta\gamma\delta}\eta_{\alpha\beta}\eta_{\gamma\delta} + \cdots, \tag{4.1}$$

where the superscript $\circ$ refers to the reference state of strain.

For lattice model calculations, however, it is convenient to follow Huang (1950) and use the homogeneous linear strain-rotation parameters $u_{\alpha\beta}$, defined by

$$X_\alpha(l) = \sum_\beta (\delta_{\alpha\beta} + u_{\alpha\beta})\, \mathring{X}_\beta(l); \tag{4.2}$$

in terms of these the Lagrange parameters are given by

$$\eta_{\alpha\beta} = \tfrac{1}{2}\big(u_{\alpha\beta} + u_{\beta\alpha} + \sum_\gamma u_{\gamma\alpha}u_{\gamma\beta}\big). \tag{4.3}$$

The Taylor series for $A/\mathring{V}$ then becomes

$$A/\mathring{V} = \mathring{A}/\mathring{V} + \sum_{\alpha\beta} B^{\mathrm{T}}_{\alpha\beta}u_{\alpha\beta} + (1/2!) \sum_{\alpha\beta\gamma\delta} B^{\mathrm{T}}_{\alpha\beta\gamma\delta}u_{\alpha\beta}u_{\gamma\delta} + \cdots, \tag{4.4}$$

where we use the symbols $B^{\mathrm{T}}_{\alpha\beta}$, etc., instead of Huang's original $S^{\mathrm{T}}_{\alpha\beta}$, etc., to avoid confusion with the usual notation for elastic compliances.

The first order coefficients of eqs. (4.1) and (4.4) can both be identified with the stress tensor $\sigma_{\alpha\beta}$,

$$\sigma_{\alpha\beta} = C^{\mathrm{T}}_{\alpha\beta} = B^{\mathrm{T}}_{\alpha\beta}, \tag{4.5}$$

while higher order coefficients can be related to each other; e.g.

$$C^{\mathrm{T}}_{\alpha\beta\gamma\delta} = B^{\mathrm{T}}_{\alpha\beta\gamma\delta} - \delta_{\alpha\gamma}\sigma_{\beta\delta}. \tag{4.6}$$

The coefficients of thermal expansion are given by

$$\alpha_{\alpha\beta} \equiv (\partial\eta_{\alpha\beta}/\partial T)_\sigma = -\sum_{\gamma\delta} S^{\mathrm{T}}_{\alpha\beta\gamma\delta}(\partial\sigma_{\gamma\delta}/\partial T)_u, \tag{4.7}$$

where the elastic compliances $S^{\mathrm{T}}_{\alpha\beta\gamma\delta}$ can be obtained from the inverse of the elastic stiffness matrix. The second-order adiabatic elastic stiffnesses are given by

$$C^{\mathrm{S}}_{\alpha\beta\gamma\delta} = C^{\mathrm{T}}_{\alpha\beta\gamma\delta} + (VT/C_\eta)(\partial\sigma_{\alpha\beta}/\partial T)_u(\partial\sigma_{\gamma\delta}/\partial T)_u, \tag{4.8}$$

where C_η is the heat capacity at constant strain.

Similar but more complicated relationships exist for higher order stiffnesses. We can therefore derive all the thermo-elastic properties from the coefficients of eq. (4.4).

4.2. Static lattice contributions

If each atom in the lattice is a centre of symmetry, the position of each atom in static equilibrium is a known function of strain:

$$X_\alpha(l\kappa) = \sum_\beta (\delta_{\alpha\beta} + u_{\alpha\beta})\, \mathring{X}_\beta(l\kappa). \tag{4.9}$$

It is then straightforward to derive the static lattice energy Φ_0 as a function of strain, and so obtain the stress tensor and the elastic constants. If there are some atoms which are not centres of symmetry, we need to allow for the relative motions of atoms within the unit cell when calculating the second and higher order coefficients. One way of doing this is to treat the parameters describing the relative positions of the atoms as additional thermodynamic variables (Barron et al. 1971).

The procedure described in the last paragraph is called the 'method of homogeneous deformation'. It yields elastic stiffnesses to all orders, and will be used throughout the present section. The second-order elastic constants can also be obtained by the 'method of long waves' (BH, chapter V), in which the velocity of acoustic modes is obtained in the limit as $\boldsymbol{q} \to 0$. The generalisation of this method to anharmonic vibrating crystals, using linear response theory, involves some subtleties (see, e.g., Cowley 1963).

4.3. The quasi-harmonic approximation

For any state of strain, the potential energy can be expanded in terms of the atomic displacements from static equilibrium, giving a Helmholtz energy of the form

$$\Phi_0 + \beta^{-1} \sum_\lambda \{\tfrac{1}{2}\beta\hbar\omega_\lambda + \ln\{1 - \exp(-\beta\hbar\omega_\lambda)\} + A_{\text{anh}}, \tag{4.10}$$

where the ω_λ are the harmonic frequencies for the given state of strain. The quasi-harmonic approximation is to neglect A_{anh}, although the anharmonic strain-dependence of the frequencies ω_λ is retained.* Differentiation with respect to strain gives for the vibrational terms

$$\mathring{V}\sigma_{\alpha\beta}(\text{vib}) = \sum_\lambda [\hbar\{\bar{n}(\lambda) + \tfrac{1}{2}\}\, \omega_{\alpha\beta}(\lambda)], \tag{4.11}$$

* Cowley (1963) and some other authors use the term quasi-harmonic in a different sense. We here follow the usage of Leibfried and Ludwig (1961), and Ludwig (1967) – see Cowley (1963), p. 434.

$$\mathring{V} B^{\mathrm{T}}_{\alpha\beta\gamma\delta}(\mathrm{vib}) = -\sum_{\lambda} [\beta\hbar^2 \bar{n}(\lambda)\{\bar{n}(\lambda)+1\}\,\omega_{\alpha\beta}(\lambda)\,\omega_{\gamma\delta}(\lambda) + \hbar\{\bar{n}(\lambda)+\tfrac{1}{2}\}\,\omega_{\alpha\beta\gamma\delta}(\lambda)], \quad (4.12)$$

where

$$\omega_{\alpha\beta}(\lambda) = \left(\frac{\partial\omega(\lambda)}{\partial u_{\alpha\beta}}\right)_{u'}, \qquad \omega_{\alpha\beta\gamma\delta}(\lambda) = \left(\frac{\partial^2\omega(\lambda)}{\partial u_{\alpha\beta}\partial u_{\gamma\delta}}\right)_{u'}. \quad (4.13)$$

Since the squares of the frequencies are obtained as eigenvalues of the dynamical matrix, it is convenient to rewrite these equations in terms of derivatives of the $\omega^2(\lambda)$. If we also introduce the dimensionless Grüneisen parameters, defined by

$$\gamma_{\alpha\beta}(\lambda) = -\left(\frac{\partial \ln\omega(\lambda)}{\partial u_{\alpha\beta}}\right)_{u'} = -\frac{1}{2}\left(\frac{\partial \ln\omega^2(\lambda)}{\partial u_{\alpha\beta}}\right)_{u'}, \quad (4.14)$$

then eqs. (4.11) and (4.12) become

$$\mathring{V}\sigma_{\alpha\beta}(\mathrm{vib}) = -\sum_{\lambda}\gamma_{\alpha\beta}(\lambda)\{\bar{n}(\lambda)+\tfrac{1}{2}\}\,\hbar\omega_{\lambda}, \quad (4.15)$$

$$\mathring{V}B_{\alpha\beta\gamma\delta}(\mathrm{vib}) = -\sum_{\lambda}\gamma_{\alpha\beta}(\lambda)\,\gamma_{\sigma\tau}(\lambda)\,[\beta\hbar^2\omega^2(\lambda)\,\bar{n}(\lambda)\{\bar{n}(\lambda)+1\} + \hbar\omega(\lambda)\{\bar{n}(\lambda)+\tfrac{1}{2}\}] - \sum_{\lambda}\{\hbar/2\omega(\lambda)\}\{\bar{n}(\lambda)+\tfrac{1}{2}\}\{\partial^2\omega^2(\lambda)/\partial u_{\alpha\beta}\partial u_{\gamma\delta}\}_{u'}. \quad (4.16)$$

The thermal expansion is given by eq. (4.7), with

$$\mathring{V}(\partial\sigma_{\alpha\beta}/\partial T)_u = -k\sum_{\lambda}\gamma_{\alpha\beta}(\lambda)\{\beta\hbar\omega(\lambda)\}^2\,\bar{n}(\lambda)\{\bar{n}(\lambda)+1\} \quad (4.17)$$

$$= -k\sum_{\lambda}\gamma_{\alpha\beta}(\lambda)\,c(\lambda), \quad (4.18)$$

where $c(\lambda)$ is the contribution of mode λ to C_η.

The quasi-harmonic approximation is widely used; it is conceptually simple, and gives correctly the lowest order anharmonic effects in the elastic constants and thermal expansion. It could be extended by taking successive terms of A_{anh} in eq. (4.10), but this would be cumbersome because the propagators as well as the vertices would depend on strain. It is easier to reformulate the theory consistently on the basis of perturbation theory.

4.4. Strain dependence of the Helmholtz energy

We describe the positions of atoms in the strained crystal by giving their displacements from their reference position in the unstrained crystal:

$$u_\alpha(l\kappa) = \sum_{\beta}(\delta_{\alpha\beta}+u_{\alpha\beta})\,\mathring{X}_\beta(l\kappa) + \sum_{\lambda} T_\alpha(l\kappa,\lambda)\,A(\lambda), \quad (4.19)$$

where the first term gives the macroscopic strain and the second term gives displacements of atoms within the unit cell (to which the cyclic boundary condition is still applied). The $A(\lambda)$ are normal coordinates of the unstrained lattice; the co-ordinates of the strained lattice, as used in the quasi-harmonic theory, are linear combinations of the form

$$\sum_j b(\boldsymbol{q}j)\, A(\boldsymbol{q}j). \tag{4.20}$$

Substituting for $u(l\kappa)$ in the hamiltonian gives

$$H = H_0 + H_{\text{int}}, \tag{4.21}$$

where H_0 is as before the harmonic hamiltonian of the unstrained crystal and H_{int} is the double power series of the form

$$\begin{aligned} H_{\text{int}} = &\Big(\sum_{\lambda_1\lambda_2\lambda_3} V(\lambda_1\lambda_2\lambda_3)\, A(\lambda_1)\, A(\lambda_2)\, A(\lambda_3) + \cdots\Big) \\ &+ \sum_{\alpha\beta} u_{\alpha\beta}\Big(V_{\alpha\beta} + \sum_{\lambda_1} V_{\alpha\beta}(\lambda_1)\, A(\lambda_1) \\ &\qquad + \sum_{\lambda_1\lambda_2} V_{\alpha\beta}(\lambda_1\lambda_2)\, A(\lambda_1)\, A(\lambda_2) + \cdots\Big) \\ &+ \tfrac{1}{2}\sum_{\alpha\beta\gamma\delta} u_{\alpha\beta}u_{\gamma\delta}\Big(V_{\alpha\beta\gamma\delta} + \sum_{\lambda_1} V_{\alpha\beta\gamma\delta}(\lambda_1)\, A(\lambda_1) \\ &\qquad + \sum_{\lambda_1\lambda_2} V_{\alpha\beta\gamma\delta}(\lambda_1\lambda_2)\, A(\lambda_1)\, A(\lambda_2) + \cdots\Big) + \cdots. \end{aligned} \tag{4.22}$$

The derivation of the coefficients $V_{\alpha\beta}$, etc., from the force-constants of the lattice is straightforward, e.g.:

$$\begin{aligned} V_{\alpha\beta}(\lambda_1\lambda_2) = \frac{1}{2!} \sum_{\substack{ll'l'' \\ \kappa\kappa'\kappa''}} \sum_{\mu\nu} \Phi_{\alpha\mu\nu}\begin{pmatrix} l & l' & l'' \\ \kappa & \kappa' & \kappa'' \end{pmatrix} \\ \times X_\beta(l\kappa)\, T_\mu(l'\kappa', \lambda_1)\, T_\nu(l''\kappa'', \lambda_2). \end{aligned} \tag{4.23}$$

The cumulant expansion for the Helmholtz energy can now be derived as in Section 3, but with H_{int} taking the place of H_{anh}. In addition to the

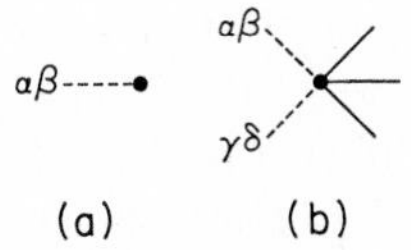

Fig. 5. Typical strain vertices.

vertices $V(\lambda_1\lambda_2\lambda_3)$, etc., we also have vertices involving the strain coefficients, such as $u_{\alpha\beta}V_{\alpha\beta}$ and $\frac{1}{2}u_{\alpha\beta}u_{\gamma\delta}V_{\alpha\beta\gamma\delta}(\lambda_1\lambda_2\lambda_3)$. We draw such vertices as in fig. 5, where wave number and energy conservation still applies to the phonon lines.

To obtain the Huang elastic constants $B^{\mathrm{T}}_{\alpha\beta}$, $B^{\mathrm{T}}_{\alpha\beta\gamma\delta}$, etc., we differentiate $A/\mathring{V}$ with respect to the $u_{\alpha\beta}$ and evaluate at $u_{\alpha\beta}=0$. Let us write eq. (4.22) in the abbreviated form

$$H_{\mathrm{int}} = \mathring{H}_{\mathrm{anh}} + H_{\mathrm{s}}\,, \tag{4.24}$$

where

$$H_{\mathrm{s}} = \sum_{\alpha\beta} u_{\alpha\beta}H_{\alpha\beta} + \tfrac{1}{2}\sum_{\alpha\beta\gamma\delta} u_{\alpha\beta}u_{\gamma\delta}H_{\alpha\beta\gamma\delta} + \cdots. \tag{4.25}$$

The moment expansion can then be shown to be

$$S(\beta) = \left\langle T_\tau\left(1 - \int_0^\beta \mathrm{d}\tau'\, \tilde{H}_{\mathrm{s}}(\tau') + \frac{1}{2!}\int_0^\beta \mathrm{d}\tau' \int_0^\beta \mathrm{d}\tau''\, \tilde{H}_{\mathrm{s}}(\tau')\,\tilde{H}_{\mathrm{s}}(\tau'') - \cdots\right)\mathring{S}(\beta)\right\rangle_0, \tag{4.26}$$

where $\mathring{S}(\beta)$ is given by the right-hand side of eq. (3.7) and T_τ orders τ', τ'', $\cdots$ along with $\tau_1, \tau_2, \cdots$. Picking out the coefficients of powers of the $u_{\alpha\beta}$ then gives for the stress tensor and elastic constants

$$\mathring{V}\sigma_{\alpha\beta} = \beta^{-1}\int_0^\beta \mathrm{d}\tau' \langle T_\tau \tilde{H}_{\alpha\beta}(\tau')\,\mathring{S}(\beta)\rangle_{0,\,\mathrm{conn}}\,, \tag{4.27}$$

$$\mathring{V}B^{\mathrm{T}}_{\alpha\beta\gamma\delta} = \beta^{-1}\int_0^\beta \mathrm{d}\tau' \langle T_\tau \tilde{H}_{\alpha\beta\gamma\delta}(\tau)\,\mathring{S}(B)\rangle_{0,\,\mathrm{conn}} - \beta^{-1}\int_0^\beta \mathrm{d}\tau' \int_0^\beta \mathrm{d}\tau'' \langle T_\tau \tilde{H}_{\alpha\beta}(\tau')\,H_{\gamma\delta}(\tau'')\,\mathring{S}(\beta)\rangle_{0,\,\mathrm{conn}}\,, \tag{4.28}$$

etc. Diagrams are drawn as for the Helmholtz energy, but containing one strain line (dashed) for $\mathring{V}\sigma_{\alpha\beta}$, two for $\mathring{V}B^{\mathrm{T}}_{\alpha\beta\gamma\delta}$, etc. Their evaluation is similar, except that the symmetry number S refers only to re-ordering of the vertices $V(\lambda_1\lambda_2\lambda_3)$, $V(\lambda_1\lambda_2\lambda_3\lambda_4)$, etc., of the unstrained lattice.

To group the terms according to their order of magnitude as anharmonic effects, we sum over all vertices in a diagram where each vertex contributes an order equal to the number of lines meeting at the vertex in excess of two; e.g., the vertex in fig. 5b contributes an order of three. With the exception of the diagram consisting solely of the vertex (a), which has order zero, the order of a diagram is given by $2(p-v)+s$, where p and v have the same meanings as in subsection 2.8 and s is the number of strain lines.

4.5. Internal strain

By internal strain we mean changes in the relative average positions of atoms within the primitive cell. Such changes are described by non-zero values of $\langle A(0j)\rangle$ for one or more optical modes with $\boldsymbol{q}=0$. Internal strain occurs only when the positions of the lattice sites are not wholly determined by symmetry. By eq. (3.2),

$$\langle A(0j)\rangle = \frac{\operatorname{tr}[\exp(-\beta H)\, A(0j)]}{\operatorname{tr}[\exp(-\beta H)]} = \frac{\langle S(\beta)\, A(0j)\rangle_0}{\langle S(\beta)\rangle_0}. \tag{4.29}$$

The numerator, as well as the denominator, can be evaluated by the diagrammatic technique, the factor $A(0j)$ giving an "external" phonon line with one end free. When such diagrams are disconnected, only one of the components contains the external line. Arguments like those of subsection 2.6 shew that the effect of the disconnected components is to contribute a factor $\langle S(\beta)\rangle_0$, thus cancelling the denominator and giving

$$\langle A(0j)\rangle = \langle S(\beta)\, A(0j)\rangle_{0,\,\mathrm{conn}}\,. \tag{4.30}$$

If the perturbation contains only terms of third and higher order, the lowest order term is given by fig. 6a:

$$\begin{aligned}\langle A(0j)\rangle &= g(0j, \mathrm{i}\omega_n = 0) \sum_{\lambda} V\begin{pmatrix}0\\ j\end{pmatrix}\!\!\begin{array}{|c}\lambda\; -\lambda\end{array}\Big) \sum_{m} g(\lambda, \mathrm{i}\omega_m) \\ &= 2\{\beta\hbar\omega(0j)\}^{-1} \sum_{\lambda} V\begin{pmatrix}0\\ j\end{pmatrix}\!\!\begin{array}{|c}\lambda\; -\lambda\end{array}\Big) \{2\bar{n}_\lambda + 1\}.\end{aligned} \tag{4.31}$$

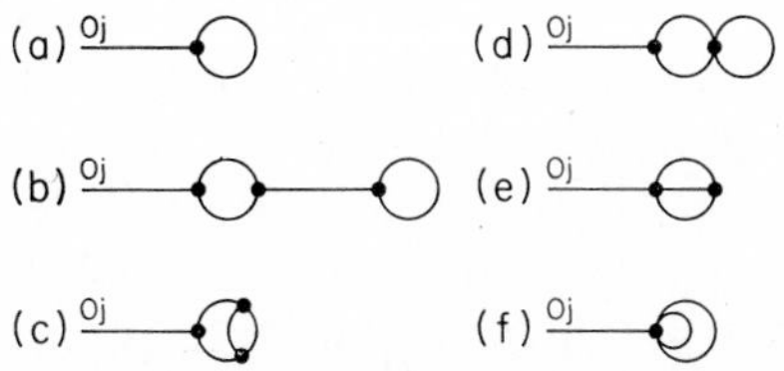

Fig. 6. Diagrams contributing to $\langle A(0j)\rangle$.

Here $V(\lambda_1\lambda_2\lambda_3)\propto 1/\sqrt{N}$, and the sum over λ is proportional to N, giving $\langle A(0j)\rangle \propto \sqrt{N}$, consistent with atomic displacements independent of N. Eq. (4.31) can be identified with the lowest order result of the quasi-harmonic theory. Figs. 6b–f give the terms of next lowest order.

We can now prove a result already quoted in subsection 2.7. If each lattice site is fixed by symmetry, then $\langle A(0j)\rangle$ must vanish for all orders of approximation. In particular, the summation in eq. (4.31) must vanish, and hence so does the contribution of any diagram such as fig. 1b which contains the feature —○ . From the next order of approximation, it follows that the sum of figs. 6c–f vanishes, and hence, by a slightly more intricate argument, that the sum of contributions of all diagrams containing these features vanishes. By taking successive orders of approximation it is proved that for such lattices the sum of contributions of diagrams containing $\boldsymbol{q}=0$ lines is zero.

4.6. The stress tensor

Diagrams contributing to the stress tensor contain only one strain line. These are of two types – those that arise only from the expansion of $H_{\alpha\beta}$ in phonon coordinates and those that contain additional vertices from $S(\beta)$. Fig. 7 gives typical examples.

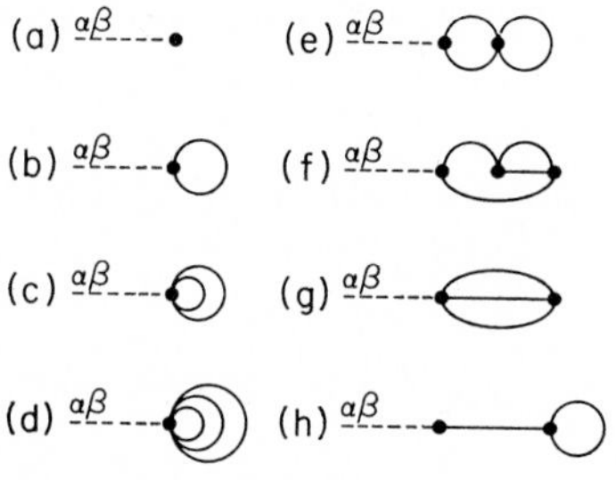

Fig. 7. Diagrams contributing to $\mathring{V}\sigma_{\alpha\beta}$.

Diagram (a) contains solely the bare $V_{\alpha\beta}$ vertex, and is the static lattice contribution $V_{\alpha\beta}$. Diagram (b) contributes

$$\beta^{-1}\sum_{\lambda} V_{\alpha\beta}(\lambda-\lambda)\int_0^{\beta} g(\lambda, 0)\,\mathrm{d}\tau = \sum_{\lambda} V_{\alpha\beta}(\lambda-\lambda)\,\{2\bar{n}(\lambda)+1\}. \qquad (4.32)$$

For a lattice in which each atom is a centre of symmetry this is the only first order term, and can be identified with the quasiharmonic term in eq. (4.15), with

$$\gamma_{\alpha\beta}(\lambda) = -2V_{\alpha\beta}(\lambda, -\lambda)/\hbar\omega(\lambda). \tag{4.33}$$

For other lattices we have also the first order diagram (h), which contributes

$$3\beta^{-1} \sum_{\lambda_1\lambda_2} V_{\alpha\beta}(\lambda_1)\, V(-\lambda_1\lambda_2-\lambda_2) \int_0^\beta \mathrm{d}\tau' \int_0^\beta \mathrm{d}\tau_1\, g(\lambda_1, \tau'-\tau_1)\, g(\lambda_2, 0)$$
$$= 12 \sum_{j=4}^{3n} \left\{\hbar\omega\begin{pmatrix}0\\j\end{pmatrix}\right\}^{-1} V_{\alpha\beta}\begin{pmatrix}0\\j\end{pmatrix} \sum_{q'j'} V\begin{pmatrix}0 & q & -q\\ j & j' & j'\end{pmatrix} \{\bar{n}(q'j') + \tfrac{1}{2}\},$$

since $V_{\alpha\beta}(q_1 j_1)$ vanishes except when $q_1 = 0$. Then

$$\gamma_{\alpha\beta}(\lambda) = -\frac{2V_{\alpha\beta}(\lambda-\lambda)}{\hbar\omega(\lambda)} - 12 \sum_{j=4}^{3n} \frac{V_{\alpha\beta}\binom{0}{j}\, V\left(\binom{0}{j}\middle|\, \lambda - \lambda\right)}{\hbar\omega\binom{0}{j}\, \hbar\omega(\lambda)}, \tag{4.35}$$

where the second term is caused by adjustment in the internal coordinates of the unit cell (cf. Barron et al. 1971, for the corresponding quasi-harmonic theory).

Diagrams (c), (e), (f) and (g) comprise the third order diagrams required for lattices in which each atom is a centre of symmetry. They are the lowest order terms not taken into account by the quasi-harmonic theory. In evaluating these terms it should be noted that (f) has symmetry number $S = 2$.

The temperature derivative

$$[\partial\bar{n}(\lambda)/\partial T]_{\omega(\lambda)} = T^{-1}\beta\hbar\omega(\lambda)\,\bar{n}(\lambda)\,\{\bar{n}(\lambda)+1\} \tag{4.36}$$

can be used to derive contributions to $\mathring{V}(\partial\sigma_{\alpha\beta}/\partial T)_u$.

4.7. Isothermal elastic constants

Diagrams contributing to the second order elastic constants $\mathring{V} B_{\alpha\beta\gamma\delta}$ contain two strain lines, which may belong either to the same vertex or to different vertices [see eq. (4.28)].

The terms of zero order are given by figs. 8a and b. Fig. 8a gives $V_{\alpha\beta\gamma\delta}$. Fig. 8b allows for internal relaxation of lattice sites which are not centres of symmetry, giving

$$-\beta^{-1}\sum_j V_{\alpha\beta}\binom{0}{j} V_{\gamma\delta}\binom{0}{j}\int_0^\beta \mathrm{d}\tau' \int_0^\beta \mathrm{d}\tau''\, g(\lambda, \tau' - \tau'')$$
$$= -2\sum_j V_{\alpha\beta}\binom{0}{j} V_{\gamma\delta}\binom{0}{j}\Big/\hbar\omega\binom{0}{j}; \quad (4.37)$$

this can be shown to be equivalent to the term given by the method of homogeneous deformation [cf. eq. (2.45) of Barron et al. (1971), with the $A\binom{0}{j}$ chosen as internal strains].

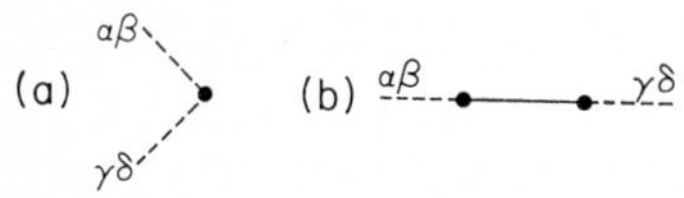

Fig. 8. Static lattice contributions to $\mathring{V}B^{\mathrm{T}}{}_{\alpha\beta\gamma\delta}$.

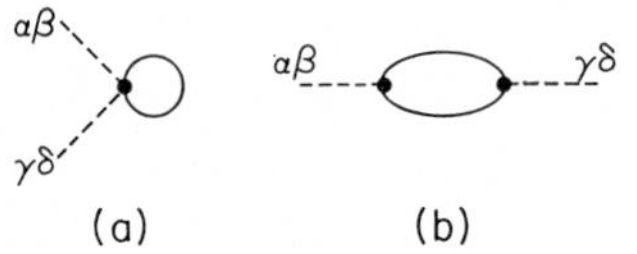

Fig. 9. Quasi-harmonic contributions to $\mathring{V}B^{\mathrm{T}}{}_{\alpha\beta\gamma\delta}$.

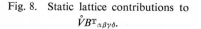

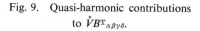

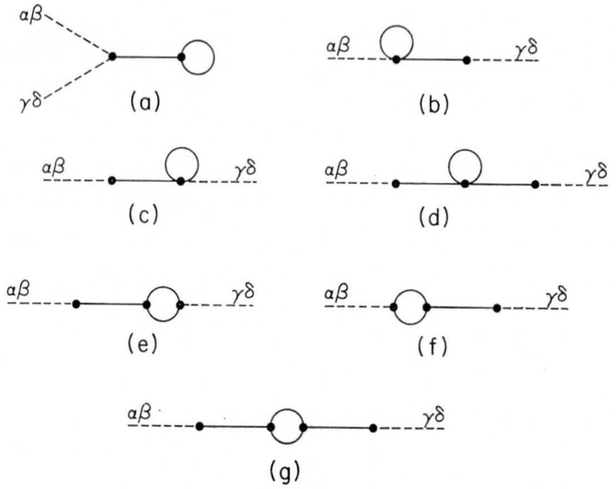

Fig. 10. Additional quasi-harmonic contributions to $\mathring{V}B^{\mathrm{T}}{}_{\alpha\beta\gamma\delta}$ when not all lattice sites are centres of symmetry.

Inclusion of second order terms is equivalent to the quasi-harmonic approximation. If each atom is a centre of symmetry, the only contributing diagrams are those of figs. 9a and b. Fig. 9a gives

$$\sum_\lambda V_{\alpha\beta\gamma\delta}(\lambda - \lambda)\,\{2\bar{n}(\lambda) + 1\}. \quad (4.38)$$

Fig. 9b as evaluated by the Fourier transforms gives

$$-2\beta \sum_{\boldsymbol{q}} \sum_{j_1, j_2} V_{\alpha\beta}\begin{pmatrix} \boldsymbol{q} & -\boldsymbol{q} \\ j_1 & j_2 \end{pmatrix} V_{\gamma\delta}\begin{pmatrix} -\boldsymbol{q} & \boldsymbol{q} \\ j_1 & j_2 \end{pmatrix} \sum_n g(\boldsymbol{q}j_1, \mathrm{i}\omega_n)\, g(\boldsymbol{q}j_2, -\mathrm{i}\omega_n). \tag{4.39}$$

For $\omega(\boldsymbol{q}j_1) \equiv \omega_1 \neq \omega_2 \equiv \omega(\boldsymbol{q}j_2)$,

$$\sum_n g(\boldsymbol{q}j_1, \mathrm{i}\omega_n)\, g(\boldsymbol{q}j_2, \mathrm{i}\omega_n) = \frac{2}{\beta\hbar}\left\{\frac{\omega_2(2\bar{n}_1+1)}{\omega_2^2-\omega_1^2} + \frac{\omega_1(2\bar{n}_2+1)}{\omega_1^2-\omega_2^2}\right\}, \tag{4.40}$$

where $\bar{n}_1 = n(\boldsymbol{q}j_1)$, etc. When $\omega_1 = \omega_2$, this takes the limiting form

$$\sum_n g(\lambda, \mathrm{i}\omega_n)\, g(\lambda, -\mathrm{i}\omega_n) = \frac{1}{\beta\hbar}\left\{\frac{2\bar{n}_\lambda+1}{\omega_\lambda} + 2\beta\hbar\bar{n}_\lambda[\bar{n}_\lambda+1]\right\}. \tag{4.41}$$

When $j_1 = j_2$ the frequencies are necessarily identical, and the corresponding terms in expression (4.39) give the first term in eq. (4.16); the terms with $j_1 \neq j_2$, together with expression (4.38), give the second term in eq. (4.16). If there are some lattice sites which are not centres of symmetry, there are additional contributions from the diagrams in figs. 10a–g. In figs. 10d–g we again have phonon lines which necessarily have the same $\boldsymbol{q}$, and so require separate treatment of terms with equal and unequal values of j.

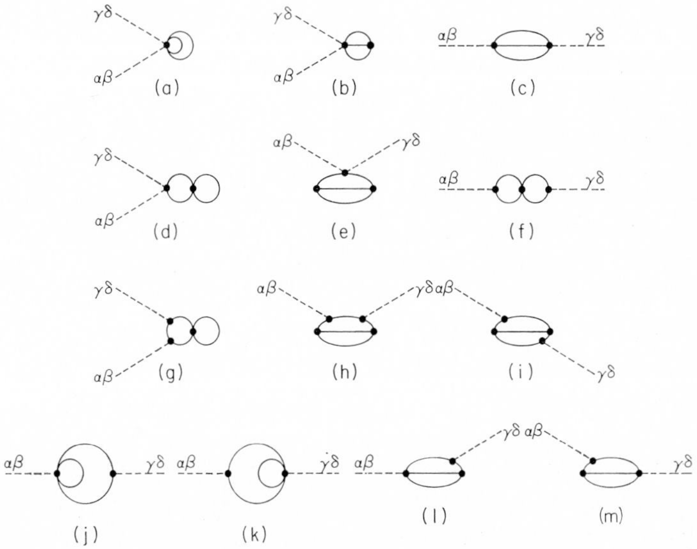

Fig. 11. Fourth order contributions to $\mathring{V}B\mathrm{T}_{\alpha\beta\gamma\delta}$.

In the fourth order we shall consider only diagrams with no $\boldsymbol{q}=0$ lines. These are obtained by adding strain lines to diagrams 1a and 1c, and are of three types: (*i*) the strain lines enter at already existing vertices (figs. 11a–c), so that the strain is modifying the anharmonic force constants; (*ii*) the strain lines enter only at new vertices (figs. 11d–i), so that the strain is modifying the basis modes; (*iii*) one strain line enters at an existing vertex and the other at a new vertex (figs. 10j–m), so that the strain is modifying both the anharmonic force constants and the basis modes.

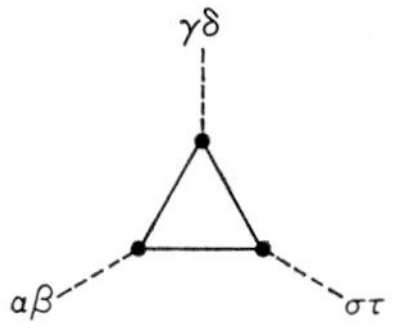

Fig. 12. A diagram contributing to $\mathring{V}B^{\mathrm{T}}{}_{\alpha\beta\gamma\delta\sigma\tau}$.

Higher order elastic constants are given by diagrams containing three or more strain lines, such as fig. 12. Such diagrams give the Huang stiffnesses $B_{\alpha\beta\gamma\delta\sigma\tau}$, etc., which can be converted thermodynamically to the finite strain stiffnesses $C_{\alpha\beta\gamma\delta\sigma\tau}$, etc.

5. *Green functions, correlation functions, and the dielectric and scattering properties of crystals*

5.1. Introduction

Both the linear response of the crystal to external fields and its scattering properties in the first Born approximation are determined by time correlation functions for the equilibrium state (see, e.g., Kubo 1957, 1966, Van Hove 1954) of the form

$$\langle A(t)\,B(0)\rangle = \int_{-\infty}^{\infty} \mathrm{d}\omega\, \mathrm{e}^{-\mathrm{i}\omega t}\, \rho(AB, \omega), \tag{5.1}$$

The Fourier transform $\rho(AB, \omega)$ is called the *spectral density function*; when there is no danger of ambiguity, we shall write it simply as $\rho(\omega)$. A widely used method of evaluating $\rho(\omega)$ and the related experimental properties is to employ *thermodynamic Green functions*, of which the harmonic phonon propagator $g(\lambda, \tau) = \langle T_\tau A_\lambda(\tau)\, A_{-\lambda}(0)\rangle_0$ is a simple example. More generally we define a *temperature Green function* by

$$G(AB, \tau) = \langle T_\tau A(\tau)\, B(0)\rangle, \tag{5.2}$$

where now A and B are arbitrary operators and both the τ-dependence and the thermal averaging are governed by the full hamiltonian H rather than by H_0:

$$A(\tau) = \mathrm{e}^{\tau H} A\, \mathrm{e}^{-\tau H}, \qquad \langle X\rangle = Z^{-1}\, \mathrm{tr}\,(\mathrm{e}^{-\beta H} X). \tag{5.3}$$

Provided that A and B can be expressed as sums of products of the A_λ, $G(AB, \tau)$ and its Fourier transform $G(AB, \mathrm{i}\omega_n)$ can be calculated by the same diagrammatic technique we have already used for the Helmholtz energy (subsection 5.3).

Although $G(AB, \mathrm{i}\omega_n)$ is initially defined only for the discrete imaginary frequencies $\mathrm{i}\omega_n$, it can be analytically continued as a continuous function of complex frequency. The behaviour of this function in the neighbourhood of the real axis determines the Fourier transforms both of the time correlation function $\langle A(t)\, B(0)\rangle$ relevant to scattering theory and of the retarded Green function relevant to response theory (subsection 5.2).

5.2. The temperature Green function and its relation to experimental properties

5.2.1. Fourier transform of the temperature Green function

$G(AB, \tau)$ has the same periodic property (3.48) as $g(\lambda, \tau)$:

$$G(AB, \tau + \beta) = G(AB, \tau), \qquad -\beta < \tau < 0. \tag{5.4}$$

This follows from the cyclic property of the trace, since, for $\tau < 0$,

$$\begin{aligned}\langle B(0)\, A(\tau)\rangle &= Z^{-1}\, \mathrm{tr}\,(\mathrm{e}^{-\beta H} B\, \mathrm{e}^{\tau H} A\, \mathrm{e}^{-\tau H}) = Z^{-1}\, \mathrm{tr}\,(\mathrm{e}^{\tau H} A\, \mathrm{e}^{-(\tau+\beta) H} B) \\ &= Z^{-1}\, \mathrm{tr}\,(\mathrm{e}^{-\beta H}\, \mathrm{e}^{(\tau+\beta) H} A\, \mathrm{e}^{-(\tau+\beta) H} B) = \langle A(\tau+\beta)\, B(0)\rangle .\end{aligned} \tag{5.5}$$

The Fourier transform is then

$$G(AB, \mathrm{i}\omega_n) = \beta^{-1} \int_0^\beta \mathrm{d}\tau\, \mathrm{e}^{\mathrm{i}\hbar\tau\omega_n} \langle A(\tau)\, B(0)\rangle, \tag{5.6}$$

with $\omega_n = 2\pi n/\beta\hbar$.

5.2.2. The time correlation function and its spectral representation

According to the Heisenberg representation of quantum mechanics, the time correlation function between two operators is

$$\langle A(t)\,B(0)\rangle = \langle \mathrm{e}^{\mathrm{i}Ht/\hbar} A\, \mathrm{e}^{-\mathrm{i}Ht/\hbar} B\rangle . \tag{5.7}$$

Using this to define a function of a complex variable t, we find that for $t=-\mathrm{i}\hbar\tau$ the function can be identified with the average $\langle A(\tau)\,B(0)\rangle$ occurring in eq. (5.2). Putting $t=-\mathrm{i}\hbar\tau$ in eq. (5.1) gives

$$\langle A(\tau)\,B(0)\rangle = \int_{-\infty}^{\infty} \mathrm{d}\omega\, \mathrm{e}^{-\hbar\omega\tau} \rho(\omega), \tag{5.8}$$

and hence, by eq. (5.6), the spectral representation of G is

$$G(AB, \mathrm{i}\omega_n) = \beta^{-1} \int_{-\infty}^{\infty} \mathrm{d}\omega\, \rho(\omega) \int_0^{\beta} \mathrm{d}\tau\, \mathrm{e}^{\hbar\tau(\mathrm{i}\omega_n-\omega)} \tag{5.9}$$

$$= (\beta\hbar)^{-1} \int_{-\infty}^{\infty} \mathrm{d}\omega\, \rho(\omega)\,(1-\mathrm{e}^{-\beta\hbar\omega})/(\omega-\mathrm{i}\omega_n), \tag{5.10}$$

since $\exp(\mathrm{i}\beta\hbar\omega_n)=1$ for all n.

This result has been obtained by taking a function of a real variable t and continuing it analytically over the complex plane. We now treat $G(AB, \mathrm{i}\omega_n)$ in a similar way, and use eq. (5.10) to define a function of a continuous complex variable w:

$$G(AB, w) = (\beta\hbar)^{-1} \int \mathrm{d}\omega\, \rho(\omega)\,(1-\mathrm{e}^{-\beta\hbar\omega})/(\omega - w). \tag{5.11}$$

This function is analytic except on the real axis. Near the real axis $w=\Omega\pm\mathrm{i}\varepsilon$, where Ω is real and ε is small; as the real axis is approached $(\varepsilon\to+0)$

$$\frac{1}{\omega-\Omega\mp\mathrm{i}\varepsilon} \to \left(\frac{1}{\omega-\Omega}\right)_{\mathrm{P}} \pm \mathrm{i}\pi\delta(\omega-\Omega), \tag{5.12}$$

where the subscript P denotes that in an integral over ω we take the principal value (Jeffreys and Jeffreys 1950, §12.02; Abrikosov et al. 1963, §7.1). Hence

$$\lim_{\varepsilon\to+0} G(AB, \Omega\pm\mathrm{i}\varepsilon) = (\beta h)^{-1} \times \left(\mathrm{P}\int_{-\infty}^{\infty} \mathrm{d}\omega\, \rho(\omega)\frac{1-\mathrm{e}^{-\beta\hbar\omega}}{\omega-\Omega} \pm \mathrm{i}\pi\rho(\Omega)\,(1-\mathrm{e}^{-\beta\hbar\Omega})\right). \tag{5.13}$$

The spectral density $\rho(\omega)$ can therefore be obtained if we have an analytic form for $G(AB, \omega)$;

$$\rho(\Omega) = -(\mathrm{i}\beta\hbar/2\pi) \lim_{\varepsilon \to +0} \{G(AB, \Omega + \mathrm{i}\varepsilon) - G(AB, \Omega - \mathrm{i}\varepsilon)\}/(1 - \mathrm{e}^{-\beta\hbar\Omega}). \tag{5.14}$$

5.2.3. *Linear response to an external perturbation: the retarded Green function*

Consider a system with hamiltonian H interacting with a field $E(t)$ in such a way that the total hamiltonian is

$$\mathscr{H} = H + H_E, \qquad H_E = -BE, \tag{5.15}$$

where B is a dynamical variable of the system (e.g., if E is a component of the electric field, B is the corresponding component of the electric dipole). The response of the system can be studied by measuring the time variation of a dynamical variable A, which may or may not be the same as B. To the first order in E we can then write the general linear relation

$$\langle A \rangle_{\mathscr{H}} = \langle A \rangle + \lambda \int_{-\infty}^{\infty} \mathrm{d}t'\, G_r(AB, t - t')\, E(t'), \tag{5.16}$$

where λ is a suitably chosen constant and $G_r(AB, t-t')$ determines the mean response of A at time t due to the field $E(t')$ acting during the time interval $t', t'+\mathrm{d}t'$. By the principle of causality $G_r(t-t')=0$ unless t is later than t', and $G_r(t-t')$ is therefore called the *retarded Green function.* Different choices of λ cause trivial differences of notation; here we follow Zubarev (1960) and take $\lambda = -\hbar^{-1}$.

To get an explicit expression for G_r we compare eq. (5.16) with the general result (as derived, e.g., by Cowley 1963, §5) for the linear response of an observable A to a perturbation $H_E(t)$:

$$\langle A \rangle_{\mathscr{H}} = \langle A \rangle + (\mathrm{i}\hbar)^{-1} \int_{-\infty}^{t} \langle [A(t), H_E(t')] \rangle\, \mathrm{d}t'. \tag{5.17}$$

Hence (with $\lambda = -\hbar^{-1}$)

$$G_r(AB, t) = -\mathrm{i}\theta(t) \langle [A(t), B(0)] \rangle, \tag{5.18}$$

where the step function $\theta(t)$ is unity for $t>0$ and zero for $t<0$.

The frequency dependence of the response is obtained by taking $E(t) = E_0 \exp(\mathrm{i}\Omega t + \varepsilon t)$. As $\varepsilon \to 0$ the factor $\exp(\varepsilon t)$ indicates that the amplitude has been increased slowly from the remote past, so that there are no transients.

The response is then given by the Fourier transform $G_r(AB, \Omega)$ of $G_r(AB, t)$:

$$\langle A \rangle_{\mathscr{H}} - \langle A \rangle = -2\pi h^{-1} G_r(AB, \Omega) E_0 \,\mathrm{e}^{-\mathrm{i}\Omega t}. \tag{5.19}$$

The coefficient of the field thus plays the role of a complex susceptibility.

2.5.4. Relation of $G_r(AB, \Omega)$ to $\rho(\omega)$ and $G(AB, w)$
By a derivation similar to that of eq. (5.4), we have

$$\langle B(0)\, A(t) \rangle = \langle A(t - \mathrm{i}\hbar\beta)\, B(0) \rangle = \int_{-\infty}^{\infty} \mathrm{d}\omega\, \rho(\omega)\, \mathrm{e}^{-\beta\hbar\omega}\, \mathrm{e}^{-\mathrm{i}\omega t} \tag{5.21}$$

by eq. (5.8). Combining eqs. (5.8), (5.18) and (5.21) gives

$$G_r(AB, t) = -\mathrm{i}\theta(t) \int_{-\infty}^{\infty} \mathrm{d}\omega\, \rho(\omega)\, (1 - \mathrm{e}^{-\beta\hbar\omega})\, \mathrm{e}^{-\mathrm{i}\omega t}. \tag{5.22}$$

To get the Fourier transform, it is convenient to express $\theta(t)$ as an integral of an exponential function of time, which can be done by contour integration (Zubarev 1960, §3.2):

$$\theta(t) = -(\mathrm{i}/2\pi) \lim_{\varepsilon \to +0} \int_{-\infty}^{\infty} \frac{\mathrm{e}^{\mathrm{i}xt}}{x - \mathrm{i}\varepsilon}\, \mathrm{d}x. \tag{5.23}$$

Then, rearranging the order of integration, we find

$$\begin{aligned} G_r(AB, \Omega) &= -(1/2\pi) \lim_{\varepsilon \to +0} \int_{-\infty}^{\infty} \mathrm{d}\omega\, \rho(\omega)\, (1 - \mathrm{e}^{-\beta\hbar\omega}) \\ &\qquad \times \int_{-\infty}^{\infty} \frac{\mathrm{d}x}{x - \mathrm{i}\varepsilon} (1/2\pi) \int_{-\infty}^{\infty} \mathrm{d}t\, \mathrm{e}^{\mathrm{i}t(\Omega - \omega + x)} \\ &= -(1/2\pi) \lim_{\varepsilon \to +0} \int_{-\infty}^{\infty} \mathrm{d}\omega\, \rho(\omega)\, (1 - \mathrm{e}^{-\beta\hbar\omega}) \\ &\qquad \times \int_{-\infty}^{\infty} \frac{\mathrm{d}x}{x - \mathrm{i}\varepsilon}\, \delta(x - \omega + \Omega) \\ &= -(1/2\pi) \lim_{\varepsilon \to +0} \int_{-\infty}^{\infty} \mathrm{d}\omega\, \rho(\omega) \frac{1 - \mathrm{e}^{-\beta\hbar\omega}}{\omega - (\Omega + \mathrm{i}\varepsilon)} \qquad (5.24) \\ &= -(\beta\hbar/2\pi) \lim_{\varepsilon \to +0} G(AB, \Omega + \mathrm{i}\varepsilon) \qquad (5.25) \end{aligned}$$

by eq. (5.11). In this way $G_r(AB, \Omega)$ can be obtained from an analytic expression for the temperature Green function.

Provided that $\rho(\omega)$ is real we can easily express G_r as a sum of real and imaginary parts: by eqs. (5.12) and (5.24),

$$G_r(AB, \Omega) = -(1/2\pi)\,\mathrm{P}\int \mathrm{d}\omega\,\rho(\omega)\frac{1-\mathrm{e}^{-\beta\hbar\omega}}{\omega-\Omega} - \tfrac{1}{2}\mathrm{i}\rho(\Omega)(1-\mathrm{e}^{-\beta\hbar\Omega}). \tag{5.26}$$

In particular,

$$2\,\mathrm{Im}\,G_r(AB, \Omega) = -\rho(\Omega)(1-\mathrm{e}^{-\beta\hbar\Omega}), \tag{5.27}$$

which is the basis for the common statement that the imaginary part of G_r determines the scattering properties of crystals. However, we shall take (5.14) rather than (5.27) as the fundamental equation for calculating scattering properties.

5.2.5. *A note on other Green functions*

The temperature Green function $G(AB, w)$ has a discontinuity along the real axis. Approaching the real axis from below gives the *advanced Green function* $G_a(AB, \Omega)$, so that eq. (5.14) could be rewritten in terms of the difference between G_r and G_a (Zubarev 1960, §3.3).

The *causal Green function* is defined by

$$G_c(AB, t) = \langle T_t A(t)\, B(0)\rangle, \tag{5.28}$$

where T_t is the ordering operator in real time. Despite its apparent similarity, G_c is quite distinct from the temperature Green function of eq. (5.2), and its Fourier transform cannot be analytically continued over the complex frequency plane.

5.2.6. *The harmonic phonon propagator*

The simplest example of the related functions we have been discussing is provided by the phonon propagator for harmonic lattices:

$$G_0(A_\lambda A^*_{\lambda'}, \mathrm{i}\omega_n) = \delta_{\lambda\lambda'}\,g(\lambda, \mathrm{i}\omega_n). \tag{5.29}$$

By eq. (3.51) the analytic continuation is

$$G_0(\lambda\lambda', w) = (\beta\hbar)^{-1}\{(\omega_\lambda + w)^{-1} + (\omega_\lambda - w)^{-1}\} = 2\omega_\lambda/\beta\hbar(\omega_\lambda^2 - w^2). \tag{5.30}$$

By eq. (5.12), (5.14) and (3.25) the spectral density is

$$\rho(\omega) = \bar{n}_\lambda\delta(\omega+\omega_\lambda) + (\bar{n}_\lambda + 1)\,\delta(\omega-\omega_\lambda), \tag{5.31}$$

and by eq. (5.25) the retarded Green function is

$$G_{r,0}(\lambda\lambda', \Omega) = -(1/2\pi)\,\delta_{\lambda\lambda'}\{[2\omega_\lambda/(\omega_\lambda^2 - \Omega^2)]_P + i\pi[\delta(\omega_\lambda - \Omega) - \delta(\omega_\lambda + \Omega)]\}. \quad (5.32)$$

The real term gives the familiar response of a classical harmonic oscillator to a periodic force, and the signs of the delta functions indicate a component of the response lagging by a phase difference $\frac{1}{2}\pi$, corresponding to perfectly sharp absorption resonance. We shall see later that for an anharmonic crystal the resonance is both shifted and broadened.

5.3. Perturbation theory of the Green functions

5.3.1. Generalisation of the operator $S(\beta)$

Eq. (3.7) can be written in the condensed form

$$S(\beta) = T_\tau \exp\left(-\int_0^\beta d\tau'\, \tilde{H}(\tau')\right), \quad (5.33)$$

where T_τ orders products in the expansion of the exponential. More generally we can define an operator

$$S(\tau_2, \tau_1) = T_\tau \exp\left(-\int_{\tau_1}^{\tau_2} d\tau'\, \tilde{H}(\tau')\right), \qquad \tau_2 > \tau_1. \quad (5.34)$$

This behaves like any other exponential provided that the ordering of the operators is preserved. Thus

$$S(\tau_3, \tau_2)\, S(\tau_2, \tau_1) = S(\tau_3, \tau_1), \qquad \tau_3 > \tau_2 > \tau_1, \quad (5.35)$$

and in particular

$$S(\tau_2, \tau_1)\, S(\tau_1) = S(\tau_2, 0) = S(\tau_2). \quad (5.36)$$

If an inverse operator is defined by

$$S(\tau)\, S^{-1}(\tau) = S^{-1}(\tau)\, S(\tau) = 1, \quad (5.37)$$

then multiplying eq. (5.36) on the right by $S^{-1}(\tau_1)$ gives

$$S(\tau_2, \tau_1) = S(\tau_2)\, S^{-1}(\tau_1). \quad (5.38)$$

The operators can also be used to relate $A(\tau)$ and $\tilde{A}(\tau)$:

$$A(\tau) = S^{-1}(\tau)\, e^{H_0\tau} A\, e^{-H_0\tau} S(\tau) = S^{-1}(\tau)\, \tilde{A}(\tau)\, S(\tau). \quad (5.39)$$

5.3.2. The temperature Green function

For $\tau>0$, by eqs. (5.2), (3.2), (3.4) and (5.39),

$$G(AB,\tau)=Z^{-1}\operatorname{tr}[\mathrm{e}^{-\beta H_0}S(\beta)\,S^{-1}(\tau)\,\tilde{A}(\tau)\,S(\tau)\,B(0)]. \tag{5.40}$$

By eqs. (5.38) and (3.5) this becomes

$$\begin{aligned}G(AB,\tau)&=\operatorname{tr}[\mathrm{e}^{-\beta H_0}S(\beta,\tau)\,\tilde{A}(\tau)\,S(\tau)\,\tilde{B}(0)]/Z_0\langle S(\beta)\rangle_0\\&=\langle T_\tau\tilde{A}(\tau)\,\tilde{B}(0)\,S(\beta)\rangle_0/\langle S(\beta)\rangle_0,\end{aligned} \tag{5.41}$$

where T_τ orders the operators in the expansion of $S(\beta)$ simultaneously with $\tilde{A}(\tau)$ and $\tilde{B}(0)$. If the operators A and B can be expressed as sums of products of the A_λ, the average in the numerator has to be taken over a linear combination of ordered products of operators $\tilde{A}_\lambda(\tau_i)$. It can therefore be evaluated by the diagrammatic techniques used in section 3 for $\langle S(\beta)\rangle_0$, but with additional vertices derived from terms in $\tilde{A}(\tau)$ and $\tilde{B}(0)$ on the left and right respectively. The denominator $\langle S(\beta)\rangle_0$ cancels the effect of all diagrams with components connected neither to A nor B, giving finally

$$G(AB,\tau)=\langle T_\tau\tilde{A}(\tau)\,B(0)\,S(\beta)\rangle_{0,\,\text{conn to }AB}, \tag{5.42}$$

where 'conn to AB' denotes diagrams such that all parts are connected to at least one vertex derived from A or B. The diagrams in which A and B are not connected to each other correspond to independent averaging of $A(\tau)$ and $B(0)$, giving a contribution independent of τ:

$$\langle A(\tau)\rangle\,\langle B(0)\rangle=\langle A\rangle\,\langle B\rangle.$$

In many applications this contribution vanishes.

Evaluation is usually carried out for the Fourier transform $G(AB,\mathrm{i}\omega_n)$, which includes integration over τ as well as over the τ_i in $S(\beta)$. The resultant energy conservation requires that lines leaving A and arriving at B have frequencies summing to ω_n. The rules for evaluating diagrams are summarised in the appendix.

When A and B are exponentials of sums of products of the A_λ, cumulant averages can be used in eq. (5.41). This is useful when discussing scattering theory (see subsection 5.5).

5.4. The phonon propagator

5.4.1. The self-energy matrix

When both A and B in eq. (5.42) are single phonon coordinates, we get the *phonon propagator*

$$G(\lambda\lambda',\tau)=\langle T_\tau\tilde{A}_\lambda(\tau)\,\tilde{A}_{-\lambda'}(0)\,S(\beta)\rangle_{0,\,\text{conn to }A_\lambda A_{-\lambda}}. \tag{5.43}$$

The Fourier transform can be written

$$G(\lambda\lambda', \mathrm{i}\omega_n) = G(\boldsymbol{q}jj', \mathrm{i}\omega_n)\, \Delta(\boldsymbol{q} - \boldsymbol{q}'), \tag{5.44}$$

where the conservation of wave-vector results from translational symmetry.

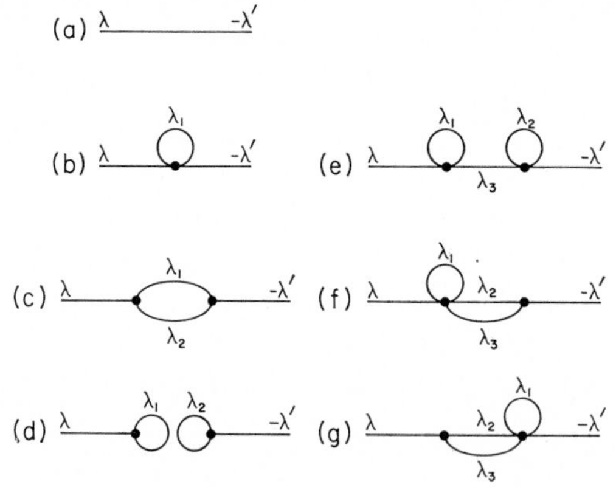

Fig. 13. Diagrams contributing to the phonon propagator $G(\lambda\lambda', \mathrm{i}\omega_n)$.

Some of the simpler diagrams contributing to the propagator are shown in fig. 13: (a) is the harmonic term, and (b), (c), (d) are the lowest order anharmonic terms. We consider only lattices in which each atom is a centre of inversion symmetry; the term (d) then vanishes, and the contributing diagrams are of two distinct types – *proper diagrams*, which cannot be split into two parts by cutting an internal phonon line [e.g. (b) and (c)], and improper diagrams, which can be so split [e.g. (e)]. Each proper diagram P beyond (a) contributes to $G(\boldsymbol{q}jj', \mathrm{i}\omega_n)$ a term of the form

$$g(\boldsymbol{q}j, \mathrm{i}\omega_n)\, \Sigma_{(\mathrm{P})}(\boldsymbol{q}jj', \mathrm{i}\omega_n)\, g(\boldsymbol{q}j', \mathrm{i}\omega_n). \tag{5.45}$$

For example, diagrams 13(b) and (c) have respectively

$$\Sigma_{(\mathrm{b})}(\boldsymbol{q}jj', \mathrm{i}\omega_n) = -12\beta \sum_{\boldsymbol{q}j_1} V\begin{pmatrix} \boldsymbol{q} & -\boldsymbol{q} & \boldsymbol{q}_1 & -\boldsymbol{q}_1 \\ j & j' & j_1 & j_1 \end{pmatrix} \sum_m g(\boldsymbol{q}j_1, \mathrm{i}\omega_m), \tag{5.46}$$

and, in more condensed notation,

$$\Sigma_{(\mathrm{c})}(\mathrm{i}\omega_n) = 18\beta^2 \sum_{\lambda_1\lambda_2} V(\lambda - \lambda_1 - \lambda_2)\, V(-\lambda'\lambda_1\lambda_2) \times \sum_m g(\lambda_1, \mathrm{i}\omega_m)\, g(\lambda_2, \mathrm{i}\omega_n - \mathrm{i}\omega_m), \tag{5.47}$$

where the factors 12 and 18 arise from the number of pairing schemes (Maradudin and Fein 1962, pp. 2598–9). The total contribution of all proper diagrams gives the approximation

$$G(\boldsymbol{q}jj', \mathrm{i}\omega_n) \simeq g(\boldsymbol{q}j, \mathrm{i}\omega_n)\,\delta_{jj'} + g(\boldsymbol{q}j, \mathrm{i}\omega_n)\,\Sigma(\boldsymbol{q}jj', \mathrm{i}\omega_n)\,g(\boldsymbol{q}j', \mathrm{i}\omega_n), \quad (5.48)$$

where

$$\Sigma(\boldsymbol{q}jj', \mathrm{i}\omega_n) = \sum_{\mathrm{P}} \Sigma_{(\mathrm{P})}(\boldsymbol{q}jj', \mathrm{i}\omega_n) \quad (5.49)$$

is called the *self-energy matrix*. In condensed matrix notation eq. (5.48) may be written

$$\mathsf{G}(\boldsymbol{q}) \simeq \mathsf{G}_0(\boldsymbol{q}) + \mathsf{G}_0(\boldsymbol{q})\,\Sigma(\boldsymbol{q})\,\mathsf{G}_0(\boldsymbol{q}). \quad (5.50)$$

This is represented diagrammatically in fig. 14a, where the representation of Σ is called the 'self-energy bubble'. The complete expansion for G is given by fig. 14b, and the Dyson equation of fig. 14c follows immediately. Rearranging the Dyson equation gives G in terms of Σ and G_0

$$\mathsf{G} = (\mathsf{I} - \mathsf{G}_0\,\Sigma)^{-1}\,\mathsf{G}_0, \quad (5.51)$$

where I is the unit matrix. In general Σ is not diagonal, and for an exact calculation a matrix inversion would be needed unless the modes j all belonged to different symmetry species.

From eq. (3.51) it can be shown that for any diagram the sum over the intermediate energies ω_m leads to a real function of ω_n. From eq. (3.19a) it can be shown that the contribution to $\Sigma(\lambda\lambda', \mathrm{i}\omega_n)$ has for its complex conjugate the contribution of the mirror image diagram to $\Sigma(\lambda'\lambda, \mathrm{i}\omega_n)$; an example of mirror images is given by diagrams (f) and (g) of fig. 13. It

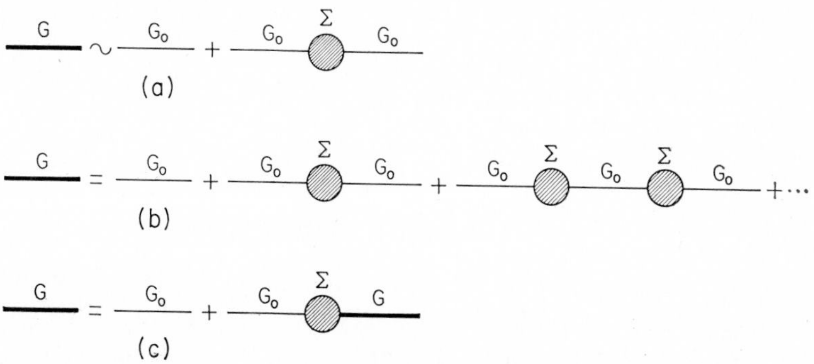

Fig. 14. Derivation of the Dyson equation for the phonon propagator.

follows that the total self-energy matrix $\Sigma(\boldsymbol{q}jj', \mathrm{i}\omega_n)$ is hermitian and can be diagonalised for any given ω_n^2 by choosing a new set of basis coordinates. However, in general it is not possible to diagonalise Σ simultaneously for all values of ω_n, and thus non-diagonal elements remain which mix modes of different j. In many applications of the theory the effect of the non-diagonal elements is small, and in calculating the diagonal elements of G they are usually neglected. Eq. (5.51) then gives

$$G(\boldsymbol{q}jj, \mathrm{i}\omega_n) \equiv G(\lambda, \mathrm{i}\omega_n) \simeq \{G_0^{-1}(\lambda, \mathrm{i}\omega_n) - \Sigma(\lambda, \mathrm{i}\omega_n)\}^{-1}$$
$$\simeq \frac{2\omega_\lambda/\beta\hbar}{-(\mathrm{i}\omega_n)^2 + \omega_\lambda^2 - (2\omega_\lambda/\beta\hbar)\,\Sigma(\lambda, \mathrm{i}\omega_n)}. \tag{5.53}$$

The reason why Σ is called the self-energy can now be seen: to the first order its diagonal part has the effect of altering the frequencies ω_λ and hence the effective phonon energy. A power series expansion for the effect of non-diagonal terms is given in eq. (4.23) of Maradudin and Fein (1962).

In actual calculations only a few low order terms in the self energy are included. However, the resulting expression (5.53) is then equivalent to summing certain classes of diagrams for G to infinite order.

5.4.2. *The self-energy – shifts and widths*

Because $\Sigma(\boldsymbol{q}jj', \mathrm{i}\omega_n)$ is a hermitian function of ω_n^2, its analytic continuation is of the form $S(w) + \mathrm{i}\,A(w)$, where S and A are real symmetric and antisymmetric matrices respectively. It follows that near the real axis

$$\Sigma(\lambda\lambda', \Omega \pm \mathrm{i}\varepsilon) \xrightarrow[\varepsilon \to +0]{} -\beta\hbar\{\boldsymbol{\Delta}(\lambda\lambda', \Omega) \mp \mathrm{i}\boldsymbol{\Gamma}(\lambda\lambda', \Omega)\}, \tag{5.54}$$

where $\boldsymbol{\Delta}$ and $\boldsymbol{\Gamma}$ are themselves hermitian matrices with real diagonal elements. By eqs. (5.53) and (5.25) the retarded Green function has diagonal elements

$$G_\mathrm{r}(\lambda, \Omega) \simeq -\frac{1}{2\pi}\frac{2\omega_\lambda}{-\Omega^2 + \omega_\lambda^2 + 2\omega_\lambda\Delta_\lambda(\Omega) - 2\mathrm{i}\omega_\lambda\Gamma_\lambda(\Omega)}, \tag{5.55}$$

with spectral densities

$$\rho_\lambda(\Omega) \simeq \frac{1}{2\pi}\frac{8\omega_\lambda^2\Gamma_\lambda(\Omega)\,(1 - \exp[-\beta\hbar\Omega])^{-1}}{\{-\Omega^2 + \omega_\lambda^2 + 2\omega_\lambda\Delta_\lambda(\Omega)\}^2 + 4\omega_\lambda^2\Gamma_\lambda^2(\Omega)}. \tag{5.56}$$

Comparison of eq. (5.55) with the response of a damped harmonic oscillator (e.g. Slater and Frank 1933, §22) indicates that, provided Δ_λ and Γ_λ vary slowly with Ω, to the first order Δ_λ shifts the resonance from ω_λ to $\omega_\lambda + \Delta_\lambda(\omega_\lambda)$ and Γ_λ broadens it with lorentzian half-width $\Gamma_\lambda(\omega_\lambda)$.

The lowest order of approximation takes diagrams 13(b) and (c) only. By eq. (5.46) the contributions of (b) are independent of frequency Ω:

$$\Delta_{(b)}(\lambda, \Omega) = 12\hbar^{-1}(2\bar{n}_\lambda + 1)\sum_{\lambda_1} V(\lambda - \lambda\lambda_1 - \lambda_1), \qquad \Gamma_{(b)}(\lambda, \Omega) = 0. \tag{5.57}$$

By methods used already to derive eq. (3.58), the summation over m in eq. (5.47) gives

$$\frac{\bar{n}_1 + \bar{n}_2 + 1}{\omega_1 + \omega_2 + \mathrm{i}\omega_n} + \frac{\bar{n}_1 + \bar{n}_2 + 1}{\omega_1 + \omega_2 - \mathrm{i}\omega_n} + \frac{\bar{n}_2 - \bar{n}_1}{\omega_1 - \omega_2 + \mathrm{i}\omega_n} + \frac{\bar{n}_1 - \bar{n}_2}{\omega_2 - \omega_1 + \mathrm{i}\omega_n}, \tag{5.58}$$

leading to

$$\Delta_{(c)} = -18\hbar^{-2}\sum_{\lambda_1\lambda_2}|V(\lambda\lambda_1\lambda_2)|^2 \times \left[\frac{\bar{n}_1 + \bar{n}_2 + 1}{(\omega_1 + \omega_2 + \Omega)_\mathrm{P}} + \cdots + \frac{\bar{n}_1 - \bar{n}_2}{(\omega_2 - \omega_1 + \Omega)_\mathrm{P}}\right], \tag{5.59}$$

$$\Gamma_{(c)} = 18\pi\hbar^{-1}\sum_{\lambda_1\lambda_2}|V(\lambda\lambda_1\lambda_2)|^2 \times [(\bar{n}_1 + \bar{n}_2 + 1)\{-\delta(\omega_1 + \omega_2 + \Omega) + \delta(\omega_1 + \omega_2 - \Omega)\} + (\bar{n}_1 - \bar{n}_2)\{\delta(\omega_2 - \omega_1 - \Omega) - \delta(\omega_2 - \omega_1 + \Omega)\}]. \tag{5.60}$$

In calculations approximate representations are needed for the principle

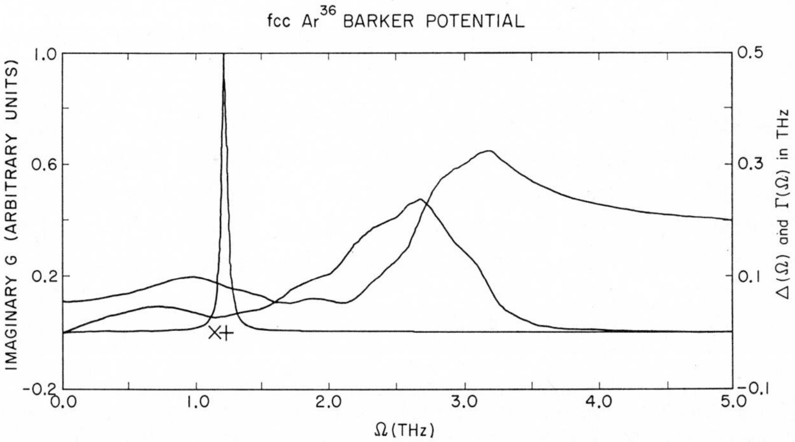

Fig. 15. The sharply peaked curve is the imaginary part of the Green function [eq. (5.55)] for the T phonon (0.7, 0, 0) in ^{36}Ar at 40 K and $a = 5.35$ Å. Also shown are $\Delta(\Omega)$ [eq. (5.57) plus (5.59)] and $\Gamma(\Omega)$ [eq. (5.60)], which are readily identified since $\Delta(0) \neq 0$ and $\Gamma(0) = 0$. The quasi-harmonic frequency ω is indicated by $\times$ and $+$ indicates $\omega + \Delta(\omega)$.

parts and the delta functions. For example, Maradudin and Fein (1962) took

$$\delta(x) \simeq \frac{1}{\pi}\frac{\varepsilon}{x^2+\varepsilon^2}, \qquad \frac{1}{x_{\mathrm{P}}} \simeq \frac{x}{x^2+\varepsilon^2}, \tag{5.61}$$

with small but finite ε.

Results for a particular example are shown in fig. 15. The pronounced structure in both Δ and Γ indicates how the properties of the apparent modes in an anharmonic crystal depend on the frequency of the probe.

5.4.3. Self energy insertions

Three of the higher order diagrams contributing to the phonon propagator are shown in fig. 16. These particular diagrams have internal lines which contain the simple self energy parts of figs. 15b and 15c: fig. 16a has $\Sigma_{(b)}$ inserted into fig. 13b; 16b has $\Sigma_{(c)}$ inserted into 13b; 16c has $\Sigma_{(b)}$ and $\Sigma_{(c)}$

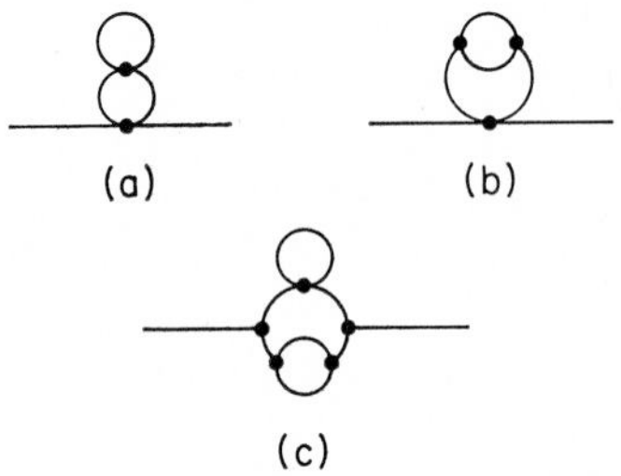

Fig. 16. Formation of higher order diagrams by self energy insertions.

inserted into different inner lines of 13c. The effect of all such insertions can be summed by replacing the 'bare' internal propagator $g(\lambda, \mathrm{i}\omega_m)$ by the 'dressed' propagator $G(\lambda\lambda', \mathrm{i}\omega_m)$, which we shall represent by a thick line. For example, the contributions of figs. 16a and b are both included with that of fig. 13b by using a self-energy term written formally as

$$-12\beta \sum_{\boldsymbol{q}_1 j_1} \sum_{j'} \sum_{m} V\begin{pmatrix} \boldsymbol{q} & -\boldsymbol{q} & \boldsymbol{q}_1 & -\boldsymbol{q}_1 \\ j & j' & j_1 & j_1' \end{pmatrix} G(\boldsymbol{q}_1 j_1 j_1', i\omega_m). \tag{5.62}$$

We then need to consider only those diagrams with no self-energy insertions. However, this leads to an equation for the propagator rather than to an explicit expression, and the sum over m is no longer straightforward.

Self-energy insertions can also be put into diagrams for the Helmholtz energy, but because there are no ingoing and outgoing lines the same higher order diagram may then be obtained in different ways – e.g., fig. 4d can be derived both from fig. 1a and from fig. 1c. Using the dressed propagator in all diagrams lacking self energy insertions would therefore be equivalent to counting such higher order diagrams more than once, and is invalid. To the lowest order of approximation, however, the correct entropy is obtained by substituting $\omega_\lambda + \Delta_\lambda$ in place of ω_λ in the harmonic expression for the entropy (Barron 1965).

5.5. Scattering of neutrons

5.5.1. The differential scattering cross-section

According to the first Born approximation, the differential scattering cross-section for momentum transfer $\hbar \boldsymbol{Q}$ and energy transfer $\hbar\Omega$ can be written as (see, e.g., Cowley 1963, pp. 465–6):

$$\left|\frac{\boldsymbol{k}'}{\boldsymbol{k}_0}\right| \sum_{\substack{ll'\\ \kappa\kappa'}} W_\kappa(\boldsymbol{Q})\, W_{\kappa'}(\boldsymbol{Q}) \exp\left[-i\boldsymbol{Q}\cdot\left\{\boldsymbol{X}\begin{pmatrix} l\\ \kappa\end{pmatrix} - \boldsymbol{X}\begin{pmatrix} l'\\ \kappa'\end{pmatrix}\right\}\right] B_{l\kappa,\, l'\kappa'}(\boldsymbol{Q}, \Omega), \tag{5.63}$$

where $\boldsymbol{k}_0$ and $\boldsymbol{k}'$ are the wave-vectors of the incident and scattered radiation, $\boldsymbol{Q} = \boldsymbol{k}_0 - \boldsymbol{k}'$, $W_\kappa(\boldsymbol{Q})$ and $W_{\kappa'}(\boldsymbol{Q})$ are form factors for the specific type of radiation, and

$$B_{l\kappa,\, l'\kappa'}(\boldsymbol{Q}, \Omega) = (1/2\pi) \int_{-\infty}^{\infty} \mathrm{d}t\, \mathrm{e}^{\mathrm{i}\Omega t} \langle \mathrm{e}^{-\mathrm{i}\boldsymbol{Q}\cdot\boldsymbol{u}(l\kappa,\, t)} \mathrm{e}^{\mathrm{i}\boldsymbol{Q}\cdot\boldsymbol{u}(l'\kappa',\, 0)} \rangle . \tag{5.64}$$

By subsection 5.2, $B_{l\kappa,\, l'\kappa'}$ can be identified as the spectral density corresponding to the temperature Green function

$$G(\tau) = \langle T_\tau \exp[-\mathrm{i}\boldsymbol{Q}\cdot\{\boldsymbol{u}(l\kappa, \tau) - \boldsymbol{u}(l'\kappa', 0)\}]\rangle \tag{5.65}$$

$$= \frac{\langle T_\tau \exp[-\mathrm{i}\boldsymbol{Q}\cdot\boldsymbol{u}(l\kappa, \tau) + \mathrm{i}\boldsymbol{Q}\cdot\boldsymbol{u}(l'\kappa', 0) - \int_0^\beta \mathrm{d}\tau_1 \tilde{H}_1(\tau_1)]\rangle_0}{\langle T_\tau \exp[-\int_0^\beta \mathrm{d}\tau_1 \tilde{H}_1(\tau_1)]\rangle_0} . \tag{5.66}$$

If we use cumulant averages (see sections 2 and 3) to evaluate $\ln G(\tau)$, the diagrams derived solely from $\tilde{H}_1$ cancel, giving

$$\ln G(\tau)$$

$$= \left\langle T_\tau \exp\left[-\mathrm{i}\boldsymbol{Q}\cdot\boldsymbol{u}(l\kappa, \tau) + \mathrm{i}\boldsymbol{Q}\cdot\boldsymbol{u}(l'\kappa', 0) - \int_0^\beta \mathrm{d}\tau_1 \tilde{H}_1(\tau_1)\right]\right\rangle_{0,\, \mathrm{conn}(\boldsymbol{uu}')} , \tag{5.67}$$

where 'conn$(\boldsymbol{uu}')$' denotes that we take only those connected diagrams which contain phonons derived from $\boldsymbol{u}(l\kappa)$ or $\boldsymbol{u}(l'\kappa')$ or both.

Such diagrams fall into three classes, as displayed schematically in fig. 17: (a) those connected only to $\boldsymbol{u}(l\kappa)$; (b) those connected only to $\boldsymbol{u}(l'\kappa')$; (c) those connected to both. Classes (a) and (b) do not involve correlations

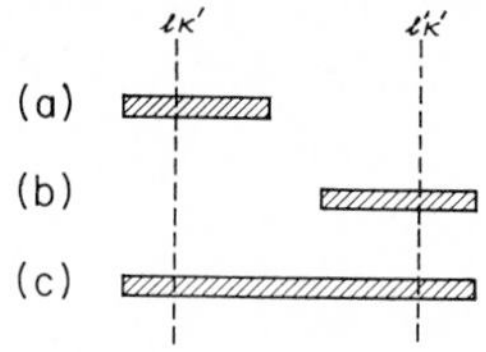

Fig. 17. Schematic representation of three types of connected diagram contributing to ln $G(\tau)$.

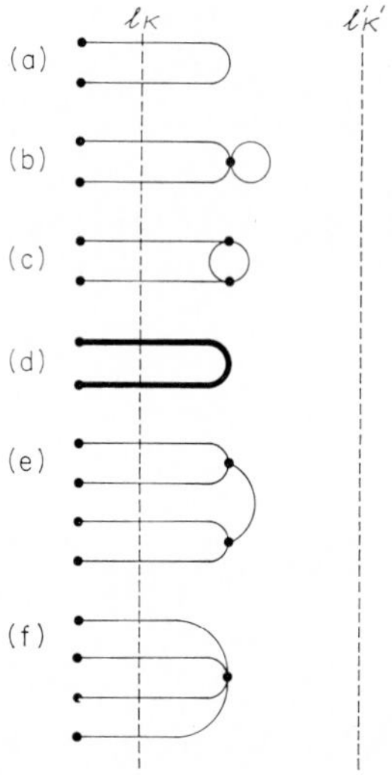

Fig. 18. Contributions to the Debye–Waller exponent $Y(\kappa)$.

between different atoms and different values of τ, and give rise to 'Debye–Waller' factors $\exp\{-Y(\kappa)\}$ and $\exp\{-Y(\kappa')\}$ in $G(\tau)$ which are independent of τ. Class (c) gives rise to the inelastic scattering.

5.5.2. *The Debye–Waller factors*

For a harmonic crystal the only diagram contributing to $Y(\kappa)$ is that of fig. 18(a). For this diagram the symmetry number $S=2$, and by eqs. (3.15),

(3.16) and (5.67) we find

$$Y(\kappa) = (\hbar/4NM_\kappa) \sum_\lambda \{\boldsymbol{Q}\cdot\boldsymbol{e}(\lambda)\}^2 (2\bar{n}_\lambda + 1)/\omega_\lambda . \tag{5.68}$$

Anharmonic terms are given by diagrams with internal vertices derived from $S(\beta)$. Some of these, such as figs. 18b and c, can be treated as self-energy insertions in the harmonic diagram (a) and are thus included in the corresponding diagram (d) with a dressed phonon. Others, such as (e) and (f), must be considered explicitly (see Maradudin and Flinn 1963, Cowley 1963).

5.5.3. *Inelastic scattering*

According to eq. (5.67), inelastic scattering arises from a factor in the Green function of the form

$$G'(\tau) = \exp f(\tau). \tag{5.69}$$

where $f(\tau)$ is given by connected diagrams of the type shown in fig. 17c. A difficulty arises here, because our standard methods of diagram evaluation give the Fourier transforms of contributions to $f(\tau)$; to obtain the Fourier transform of $G'(\tau)$ we have to expand the exponential. If

$$f(\tau) = \sum_{m_1} f_{m_1} \exp(\mathrm{i}\hbar\omega_m\tau), \tag{5.70}$$

then

$$\begin{aligned} G'(\mathrm{i}\omega_n) &= (1/\beta)\int_0^\beta \mathrm{d}\tau \exp(-\mathrm{i}\hbar\omega_n\tau)\,[1 + f(\tau) + (1/2!)\,f^2(\tau) + \cdots] \\ &= \delta_{0,n} + f_n + (1/2!)\sum_{m_1} f_{m_1} f_{n-m_1} \\ &\qquad + (1/3!)\sum_{m_1 m_2} f_{m_1} f_{m_2} f_{n-m_1-m_2} + \cdots . \end{aligned} \tag{5.71}$$

The analytic continuation of the first term is indeterminate, but reference to eqs. (5.63) to (5.65) reveals that it corresponds to the elastic scattering, the remaining terms giving the inelastic scattering. Since the expansion of the exponential is effectively 'undoing' the work of the cumulant averaging, the remaining terms in eq. (5.71) can be regarded as equivalent to summation over disconnected as well as connected diagrams [excluding of course disconnected components from $S(\beta)$]. The disconnected diagrams still have the correct dependence on N, because of the factor $N^{-1/2}$ in each external vertex. The theory can indeed be developed without using cumulant averaging at all (Cowley 1963), but the derivation of the Debye–Waller factor is then more cumbersome.

The only harmonic contribution to f_n is given by fig. 19a:

$$f_n(\text{har}) = \sum_{\alpha\beta} Q_\alpha Q_\beta \sum_\lambda T_\alpha(l\kappa, \lambda)\, T_\beta(l'\kappa', -\lambda)\, g(\lambda, \mathrm{i}\omega_n), \tag{5.72}$$

where the $T_\alpha(l\kappa, \lambda)$ are as defined in eq. (3.16). The harmonic one-phonon cross section is derived from the first inelastic term of eq. (5.71), with a spectral density for each mode proportional to that of eq. (5.31), indicating

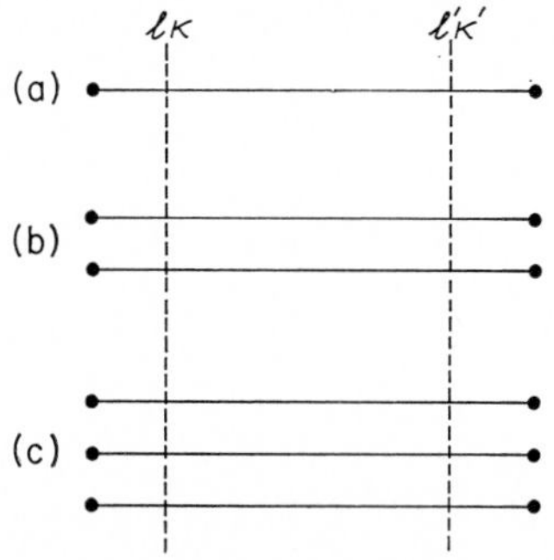

Fig. 19. Harmonic contributions to the inelastic scattering. Only diagram (a) contributes to ln $G(\tau)$.

both absorption and emission of single phonons. The harmonic two-phonon scattering is derived from the second inelastic term of eq. (5.71), which becomes

$$\tfrac{1}{2} Q_\alpha Q_\beta Q_\gamma Q_\delta \sum_{\lambda_1\lambda_2} T_\alpha(l\kappa, \lambda_1)\, T_\beta(l'\kappa', -\lambda_1)\, T_\gamma(l\kappa, \lambda_2)\, T_\delta(l'\kappa', -\lambda_2)$$
$$\times \sum_m g(\lambda_1, \mathrm{i}\omega_m)\, g(\lambda_2, \mathrm{i}\omega_n - \mathrm{i}\omega_m). \tag{5.73}$$

The summation over m is the same as that required for diagram 13(c), and is given in eq. (A4) of the Appendix. The spectral density then follows from eq. (5.14), and the final expression for the two-phonon harmonic scattering cross-section is (Cowley 1963, §8):

$$\left|\frac{\boldsymbol{k}'}{\boldsymbol{k}_0}\right| \frac{\hbar^2 N}{16\pi} \sum_{\lambda_1\lambda_2} \Delta(\boldsymbol{Q} - \boldsymbol{q}_1 - \boldsymbol{q}_2) \frac{H(\lambda_1\lambda_2, \Omega)}{\omega_1\omega_2}$$
$$\times \sum_{\kappa\kappa'} \frac{\{\boldsymbol{Q}\cdot\boldsymbol{e}(\kappa, \lambda_1)\}\{\boldsymbol{Q}\cdot\boldsymbol{e}(\kappa', \lambda_2)\}\{\boldsymbol{Q}\cdot\boldsymbol{e}(\kappa, \lambda_2)\}\{\boldsymbol{Q}\cdot\boldsymbol{e}(\kappa', \lambda_2)\}}{M_\kappa M_{\kappa'}}$$
$$\times \exp\{-Y(\kappa) - Y(\kappa')\}\, W_\kappa W_{\kappa'} \exp\{-\mathrm{i}(\boldsymbol{Q} - \boldsymbol{q}_1 - \boldsymbol{q}_2)\cdot\boldsymbol{R}_{\kappa\kappa'}\}, \tag{5.74}$$

where $\boldsymbol{R}_{\kappa\kappa'}$ is a vector between two lattice points in the same unit cell and

$$\begin{aligned} &H(\lambda_1\lambda_2, \Omega) \\ &= 2\pi\{(\bar{n}_1+1)(\bar{n}_2+1)\,\delta(\Omega-\omega_1-\omega_2)+\bar{n}_1\bar{n}_2\,\delta(\Omega+\omega_1+\omega_2) \\ &\quad +\bar{n}_1(\bar{n}_2+1)\,\delta(\Omega+\omega_1-\omega_2)+(\bar{n}_1+1)\,\bar{n}_2\,\delta(\Omega-\omega_1+\omega_2)\}. \qquad (5.75) \end{aligned}$$

Anharmonic contributions to f_n are of two kinds: those, like figs. 20a–c, which can be regarded as formed by self-energy insertions in fig. 19c and those, like figs. 20d–g, which cannot. The largest anharmonic effects are usually due to self-energy terms, and are accounted for by dressing the phonon

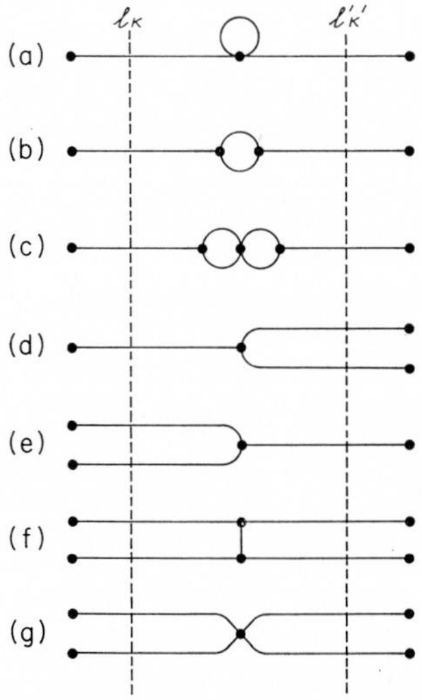

Fig. 20. Anharmonic contributions to ln $G(\tau)$.

in fig. 19a. The one-phonon scattering is then derived from a spectral density proportional to the right-hand side of eq. (5.56), so that the phonon peaks are both shifted and broadened. The total scattering includes not only the effect of higher terms in eq. (5.71) but also the effect of further contributions to f_n. For example, diagrams 20(d) and (e) add asymmetrical contributions to the one-phonon peaks (Thompson 1963).

In the same way that the solution to the Dyson equation determines the one-phonon scattering, the solution to its two phonon analogue (called the Bethe–Salpeter equation) determines the two-phonon scattering. There appears to be only preliminary discussion of this in the phonon literature (Maradudin 1971, Werthamer 1972).

5.6. Infra-red absorption

We treat the electromagnetic radiation classically, and use the linear response theory of subsection 5.2.3 with

$$H_E = -\boldsymbol{M}\cdot\boldsymbol{E} = -\sum_{\alpha=1}^{3} M_\alpha E_\alpha\,, \tag{5.76}$$

where $\boldsymbol{M}$ is the electric dipole moment of the crystal and $\boldsymbol{E}$ is the electric field vector of the radiation. The complex electric susceptibility tensor $\chi_{\alpha\beta}(\Omega)$ is defined by

$$\langle M_\alpha\rangle_{\mathscr{H}} - \langle M_\alpha\rangle = \sum_\beta V\chi_{\alpha\beta}(\Omega)\,E_\beta\,, \tag{5.77}$$

where $\boldsymbol{E}=\boldsymbol{E}_0\exp(-\mathrm{i}\Omega t)$. Hence by eqs. (5.19) and (5.25),

$$\chi_{\alpha\beta}(\Omega) = \beta V^{-1}\lim_{\varepsilon\to+0} G(M_\alpha M_\beta, \Omega + \mathrm{i}\varepsilon)\,. \tag{5.78}$$

The infra-red absorption is given by the imaginary part of $\chi_{\alpha\beta}$.

For a crystal with no permanent dipole moment the expansion of M_α in terms of the $A(\lambda)$ is [BH, eq. (39.11)]

$$M_\alpha = \sum_j M_\alpha\begin{pmatrix}0\\ j\end{pmatrix} A\begin{pmatrix}0\\ j\end{pmatrix} + \sum_{\boldsymbol{q}jj'} M_\alpha\begin{pmatrix}\boldsymbol{q} & -\boldsymbol{q}\\ j & j'\end{pmatrix} A\begin{pmatrix}\boldsymbol{q}\\ j\end{pmatrix} A\begin{pmatrix}-\boldsymbol{q}\\ j'\end{pmatrix} + \cdots \tag{5.79}$$

where the coefficients are related to those of BH by factors of $\{N\hbar/2\omega(0j)\}^{1/2}$ and $\{\hbar^2/4\omega(\boldsymbol{q}j)\,\omega(\boldsymbol{q}j')\}$ respectively. The lowest order approximation is thus given by

$$G(M_\alpha M_\beta, \mathrm{i}\omega_n) \simeq \sum_{jj'} M_\alpha(0j)\,M_\beta(0j')\,G(0jj', \mathrm{i}\omega_n)\,. \tag{5.80}$$

The response is thus determined to a first approximation by the phonon propagator discussed in the previous section, with corrections arising from the higher order terms in the expansion (5.79).

In diagrammatic representation the external vertices represent the coefficients $M_\alpha(\lambda)$, $M_\alpha(\lambda\lambda')$, etc. As usual we use thick lines for the dressed

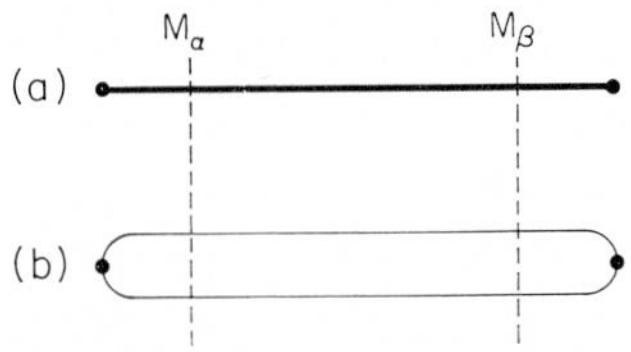

Fig. 21. Contributions to the dielectric susceptibility $\chi_{\alpha\beta}(\Omega)$.

phonons and thin lines for the bare phonons. Fig. 21a represents the simple one-phonon absorption process of eq. (5.80); fig. 21b represents the two-phonon absorption, for which bare phonons are used to facilitate the sum over ω_m [see eq. (A4)]. Further details, concerning both the higher order diagrams and the derivation of dielectric properties from the Green function, can be found in Cowley (1963) and in Cowley and Cowley (1965).

5.7. Raman scattering

Raman scattering arises because the electronic polarisability tensor is a function of the phonon coordinates [BH, eq. (39.12)]:

$$P_{\alpha\beta} = P^0_{\alpha\beta} + \sum_j P_{\alpha\beta}\begin{pmatrix}0\\j\end{pmatrix} A\begin{pmatrix}0\\j\end{pmatrix} + \sum_{\boldsymbol{q}jj'} P_{\alpha\beta}\begin{pmatrix}\boldsymbol{q} & -\boldsymbol{q}\\ j & j'\end{pmatrix} A\begin{pmatrix}\boldsymbol{q}\\j\end{pmatrix} A\begin{pmatrix}-\boldsymbol{q}\\j'\end{pmatrix} + \cdots . \tag{5.81}$$

The electric field $\boldsymbol{E}$ of the incident light induces an oscillating dipole moment whose amplitude depends on the phonon coordinates:

$$M_\alpha/V = \sum_\beta P_{\alpha\beta}E_\beta . \tag{5.82}$$

The intensity of Raman scattering per unit solid angle has an intensity (BH, p. 368)

$$I = (\omega_0^4/2\pi c^3) \sum_{\alpha\beta\gamma\delta} n_\alpha n_\beta \boldsymbol{I}_{\alpha\beta\gamma\delta} E_\gamma E_\delta , \tag{5.83}$$

where ω_0 is the frequency of the incident light and $\boldsymbol{n}$ is a unit vector giving the polarisation of the electric vector of the scattered light. For a given initial vibrational state $|\mathrm{i}\rangle$, the tensor $\boldsymbol{I}$ is given by

$$\boldsymbol{I}^{(\mathrm{i})}_{\alpha\beta\gamma\delta} = \sum_{\mathrm{f}} \langle\mathrm{i}|\, P_{\alpha\gamma}\, |\mathrm{f}\rangle \langle\mathrm{f}|\, P_{\beta\delta}\, |\mathrm{i}\rangle\, \delta(\Omega + [\varepsilon_\mathrm{i} + \varepsilon_\mathrm{f}]/\hbar) , \tag{5.84}$$

where Ω is the change in frequency of the light. The ensemble average over initial states then gives

$$\boldsymbol{I}_{\alpha\beta\gamma\delta} = (2\pi)^{-1} \int_{-\infty}^{\infty} \mathrm{e}^{\mathrm{i}\Omega t} \langle P_{\alpha\gamma}(t)\, P_{\beta\delta}(0)\rangle\, \mathrm{d}t , \tag{5.85}$$

which is a spectral density function of the type discussed in subsection 5.1:

$$\boldsymbol{I}_{\alpha\beta\gamma\delta} = \rho(P_{\alpha\gamma}P_{\beta\delta}, \Omega) . \tag{5.86}$$

Thus diagrammatic perturbation theory is immediately applicable, with external vertices representing coefficients in the expansion (5.81). Further details can be found in Cowley (1964).

Appendix Notes on the diagrammatic technique

A1. Nature of the diagrams; definition of the term 'topologically distinct'

Diagrams are used to indicate different types of pairing schemes. A diagram is thus defined by its vertices and the links between them, and in mathematical language would be termed a graph (Ore 1963). For the Helmholtz energy (sections 2 and 3) there is only one type of vertex; for the elastic stiffnesses (section 4) and other properties (section 5) there are external vertices (or external lines) which are of a different type from the internal vertices and may also differ from each other.

Two graphs are said to be isomorphic if there is a 1–1 correspondence between similar vertices such that each graph gives the same system of links between vertices. In the phonon literature, the term *topologically distinct* is often used to denote two diagrams which are not isomorphic graphs.*

A2. Notations for connected diagrams

The notations used in this chapter are as follows:

Subscript 'conn' denotes that diagrams must be connected.

Subscript 'conn to AB' denotes that while diagrams may have components disconnected from each other, each component must contain at least one term derived from A or B (see subsection 5.3).

Subscript 'conn (AB)' denotes that diagrams must both be connected and also contain at least one term derived from A or B (see subsection 5.5).

A3. Rules for evaluating diagrams

We give here rules for the quantum crystal, using the Fourier transforms of the propagators. Classical methods are discussed in section 2, and direct integration over τ in section 3.

(*i*) Draw all relevant topologically distinct diagrams, and ascribe directions to the phonon lines.

(*ii*) Each phonon line contributes a factor $g(\boldsymbol{q}j, \mathrm{i}\omega_m)$.

(*iii*) Energy $\sum \omega_m$ is conserved at each vertex (see section 3.7).

(*iv*) Wave number $\sum \boldsymbol{q}$ is conserved at each vertex (modulo reciprocal lattice vector divided by 2π).

* We thank Professor C. Kent for discussion on this point.

(*v*) Sum over all independent internal ω_m.

(*vi*) Each vertex contributes its appropriate coefficient, with indices $\boldsymbol{q}j$ for directed phonon lines departing from the vertex and $-\boldsymbol{q}j$ for lines arriving at the vertex.

(*vii*) Sum over all independent internal $\boldsymbol{q}j$.

(*viii*) Multiply by the number of pairing schemes.

(*ix*) Divide by the symmetry number (see subsection 2.5).

(*x*) For diagrams giving the Helmholtz energy or its strain derivatives, multiply by $(-\beta)^{n-1}$, where n is the number of vertices.

(*xi*) For other diagrams, multiply by $(-\beta)^n$.

A4. Summations

Summations over the ω_m that occur in the evaluation of perturbation theory diagrams by the 'Fourier transform method' are usually carried out by contour integration, as described in subsection 3.7. We list below some of the summations that are often required. Additional useful results can be extracted from the papers of Cowley (1963) and Shukla and Cowley (1971).

$$\sum_m g(\lambda, \mathrm{i}\omega_m) = 2\bar{n}(\lambda) + 1\,, \tag{A1}$$

$$\sum_m g(\lambda_1, \mathrm{i}\omega_m)\, g(\lambda_2, -\mathrm{i}\omega_m) = \frac{2\{\omega_1(2\bar{n}_2 + 1) - \omega_2(2\bar{n}_1 + 1)\}}{\beta\hbar(\omega_1^2 - \omega_2^2)}\,, \tag{A2}$$

$$\text{where } \omega_1 \equiv \omega(\lambda_1),\ \bar{n}_1 \equiv \bar{n}(\lambda_1), \text{ etc}.$$

$$\sum_m g(\lambda_1, \mathrm{i}\omega_m)\, g(\lambda_2, \mathrm{i}\omega_m)\, g(\lambda_3, \mathrm{i}\omega_m) = \frac{4\omega_2\omega_3(2\bar{n}_1 + 1)}{(\beta\hbar)^2(\omega_1^2 - \omega_2^2)(\omega_1^2 - \omega_3^2)} + \{\text{two other terms from cyclic permutation of } 1, 2, 3\}\,, \tag{A3}$$

$$\sum_m g(\lambda_1, \mathrm{i}\omega_m)\, g(\lambda_2, \mathrm{i}\omega_l - \mathrm{i}\omega_m) = (\beta\hbar)^{-1}\left[\frac{\bar{n}_1 - \bar{n}_2}{\omega_1 - \omega_2 + \mathrm{i}\omega_l} + \frac{\bar{n}_1 - \bar{n}_2}{\omega_1 - \omega_2 + \mathrm{i}\omega_l} - \frac{\bar{n}_1 + \bar{n}_2 + 1}{\omega_1 + \omega_2 + \mathrm{i}\omega_l} - \frac{\bar{n}_1 + \bar{n}_2 + 1}{\omega_1 + \omega_2 - \mathrm{i}\omega_l}\right], \tag{A4}$$

$$\sum_m \sum_n g(\lambda_1, i\omega_m)\, g(\lambda_2, i\omega_n)\, g(\lambda_3, -i\omega_m - i\omega_n)$$
$$= \frac{(\bar{n}_1 + 1)(\bar{n}_2 + 1)(\bar{n}_3 + 1) - (\bar{n}_1 \bar{n}_2 \bar{n}_3)}{\beta\hbar(\omega_1 + \omega_2 + \omega_3)}$$
$$+ \left[\frac{(\bar{n}_2 + 1)(\bar{n}_3 + 1)\,\bar{n}_1 - \bar{n}_2 \bar{n}_3 (\bar{n}_1 + 1)}{\beta\hbar(\omega_2 + \omega_3 + \omega_1)} \right.$$
$$\left. + \{\text{two other terms from cyclic permutation of } 1, 2, 3\} \right]. \quad \text{(A5)}$$

The sum (A1) arises explicitly whenever a simple bubble occurs in a diagram (e.g., figs. 6a and 13b). (A2) arises in fig. 9b, (A.3) in fig. 12, (A.4) in fig. 13c and (A.5) in fig. 1a.

When there is equality between two or more phonon frequencies ω_1, ω_2, etc., as in eq. (4.41), these expressions may become indeterminate. We can then either take the limit of the expressions as equality is approached, or repeat the contour integration taking care to handle multiple poles properly.

References

ABRIKOSOV, A. A., L. P. GORKOV, and I. E. DZYALOSHINSKI (1963), *Methods of Quantum field theory in statistical physics* (Englewood Cliffs, N. J.: Prentice–Hall).

ALDER, B. J. and T. E. WAINWRIGHT (1959), J. Chem. Phys. **31**, 459–466.

ALEKSEEV, A. I. (1961), Soviet Phys. Uspekhi **4**, 23–50.

BARRON, T. H. K. (1965), Proc. Int. Conf. Lattice Dynamics (Copenhagen 1963), J. Phys. Chem. Solids Suppl. 1, 247–254.

BARRON, T. H. K. and R. W. MUNN (1970), Pure and Appl. Chem. **22**, 527–532.

BARRON, T. H. K., T. G. GIBBONS and R. W. MUNN (1971), J. Phys. C: Sol. St. Phys. **4**, 2805–2821.

BORN, M. and K. HUANG (1954), *Dynamical theory of crystal lattices* (Oxford: Clarendon Press).

CHOQUARD, P. F. (1967), *The anharmonic crystal* (New York: Benjamin).

COWLEY, E. R. and R. A. COWLEY (1965), Proc. Roy. Soc. A**287**, 259–280.

COWLEY, E. R. and R. A. COWLEY (1966), Proc. Roy. Soc. **A292**, 209–223.

COWLEY, R. A. (1963), Adv. Phys. **12**, 421–480.

COWLEY, R. A. (1964), Proc. Phys. Soc. **84**, 281–296.

COWLEY, R. A. (1968), Rep. Prog. Phys. **31**, 123–166.

GLYDE, H. R., and M. L. KLEIN (1971), Critical Reviews in Solid State Sciences **2**, 181–254.

GÖTZE, W. and K. H. MICHEL (1968), Z. f. Phys. **217**, 170–187.

HORNER, H. (1967), Z. f. Phys. **205**, 72–89.

HUANG, K. (1950), Proc. Roy. Soc. **A203**, 178–194.

JEFFREYS, H., and B. S. JEFFREYS (1950), *Methods of mathematical physics* (2nd edn.), (Cambridge: University Press).

KUBO, R. (1957), J. Phys. Soc. (Japan) **12**, 570–586.

KUBO, R. (1962), J. Phys. Soc. (Japan) **17**, 1100–1120.
KUBO, R. (1966), Reports on Progress in Physics **29**, 255–284.
LEIBFRIED, G. and W. LUDWIG (1961), Solid State Physics **12**, 275–444.
LUDWIG, W. (1967), *Recent developments in lattice theory* (Springer Tracts in Modern Physics, Vol. 43), (Berlin: Springer-Verlag).
MARADUDIN, A. A. (1971), *Phonons* (Ed. M. A. Nusimovici), p427, (Paris: Flammarion).
MARADUDIN, A. A. and A. E. FEIN (1962), Phys. Rev. **128**, 2589–2608.
MARADUDIN, A. A. and P. A. FLINN (1963), Phys. Rev. **129**, 2529–2545.
MARADUDIN, A. A., E. W. MONTROLL and G. H. WEISS (1963), *Theory of lattice dynamics in the harmonic approximation* (Solid State Physics, Suppl. 3) (New York: Academic Press).
MAVROYANNIS, C. and N. K. PATHAK (1969), Phys. Rev. **182**, 872–884.
ORE, O. (1963), *Graphs and their uses* (New York: Random House).
PATHAK, K. N. (1965), Phys. Rev. **139**, A1569–A1580.
RAHMAN, A. (1964), Phys. Rev. **136**, A405–A411.
SHUKLA, R. C. and E. R. COWLEY (1971a), Phys. Rev. **B3**, 4055–4065.
SHUKLA, R. C. and E. R. MULLER (1971b), Physica Status Solidi **43**, 413–422.
SLATER, J. C. and N. H. FRANK (1933), *Introduction to theoretical physics*, (New York: McGraw-Hill).
THOMPSON, B. V. (1963), Phys. Rev. **131**, 1420–1427.
THURSTON, R. N. (1964), Phys. Acoust. **1A**, 1–110.
TYABLIKOV, S. V. and V. L. BONCH–BRUEVICH (1962), Adv. Phys. **11**, 317–48.
VAN HOVE, L. (1954), Phys. Rev. **95**, 249–262.
VAN HOVE, L., N. H. HUGENHOLTZ and L. P. HOWLAND (1961), *Problems in quantum theory of many particle systems* (New York: Benjamin).
WALLACE, D. C. (1970), Solid State Physics **25**, 301–404.
WEHNER, R. (1966), Phys. Stat. Solidi **15**, 725–738.
WEHNER, R. (1967), Phys. Stat. Solidi **22**, 527–535.
WERTHAMER, N. R. (1972), Phys. Rev. **B5**, 285–290.
WOOD, W. W. (1968), *Physics of simple liquids* (Ed. H. N. V. Temperley, J. S. Rowlinson, and G. S. Rushbrooke), Chap. 5, (New York: Wiley).
ZUBAREV, D. N. (1960), Soviet Phys. Uspekhi **3**, 320–345.

CHAPTER 8

Strongly Anharmonic Crystals with Hard Core Interaction

H. HORNER

Institut für Festkörperforschung der Kernforschungsanlage
517 Jülich, Germany

Dynamical Properties of Solids, edited by
G. K. Horton and A. A. Maradudin

Contents

1. Introduction

Sixty years ago the theory of lattice vibrations originated from the fundamental papers of Debye (1912), and of Born and Von Kármán (1912). The basic assumption is that the oscillations of the atoms in a crystal due to zero point motions or thermal energy are small enough such that an expansion of the potential energy is sufficient. This leads to the conventional anharmonic perturbation theory as discussed for instance by Leibfried and Ludwig (1961). At low enough temperatures this is well justified for most crystals. As the temperature is increased, however, the amplitudes of the lattice vibrations also increase until some critical value is reached at which the crystal melts. The existence of such a critical value is just what is meant by the melting formula of Lindemann (1910). At least at this point the harmonic approximation or a low order anharmonic perturbation theory will fail. It was shown by Klein and Horton (1968) that pronounced deviations from the behaviour predicted by low order anharmonic theory appear for instance already at one half of the melting temperature in the heavier rare gas crystals.

An extreme situation exists for the so called quantum crystals, He, H_2 and to some degree Ne, where already zero point motions are strong enough to create large anharmonic effects. In helium at not too high pressures the harmonic approximation even fails to give real phonon frequencies.

Strong anharmonic effects which can not be treated in low order perturbation theory also exist near structural phase transitions including ferroelectric transitions.

Librational motions in the ordered phases of some molecular crystals are another example of lattice vibrations which become more and more anharmonic if the temperature is raised until a more or less free rotation of the molecules sets in.

Finally we like to mention some kinds of impurities like Li in KCl, or hydrogen bonded ferroelectrics like KDP which again can be considered as extremely anharmonic systems.

For none of these cases harmonic theory or low order perturbation expansion will be appropriate and more powerful approximation schemes have been developed to treat strongly anharmonic crystals. Among those the renormalized harmonic approximation plays a basic role. It goes back to Born (1951) and Hooton (1955) and was reformulated by Boccara and Samara (1965) from a variational treatment in the context of ferroelectrics. Koehler (1966) used an expansion of the potential in Hermite polynomials and applied the theory to quantum crystals. Many-body perturbation theory was used by Choquard (1967) and Green's functions by Horner (1967) to rederive the renormalized harmonic theory and to calculate the form of residual anharmonic corrections. The same corrections were derived by Werthamer (1969) using a variational approach. Götze and Michel (1969) obtained transport equations generalizing the renormalized harmonic approximation and Götze (1967) investigated exact results for an arbitrary anharmonic crystal in the long wavelength and in the low temperature limit using diagrammatic techniques. Choquard (1967), and Plakida and Siklos (1969) observed an instability in the frame work of the renormalized harmonic theory which might be of interest with respect to phase transitions.

There is still an increasing number of other papers giving slightly different derivations or pointing out special aspects, some of which will be mentioned later.

A great deal of work has been devoted to the lattice dynamics of rare gas solids mainly because the interaction among the atoms is sufficiently well known. They also have simple crystal structures and an increasing number of experimental results makes them almost ideal model substances. The most interesting among those is probably solid helium due to its large zero point motions.

The problem here is not only strong anharmonicities but also the need for short range correlations due to the hard core character of the interatomic potential. Their importance was recognized first by Nosanow (1966) and since a great deal of work has been done in this field, some of which again will be mentioned later. Most of this work is based on an Einstein approach to the solid and on a Jastrow wave function concentrating mainly on the motion of single particles. Brenig (1963), and Fredkin and Werthamer (1965) have shown that phonons appear in this single particle picture as collective excitations. However, expressions derived for instance for the damping of the collective excitations by Kerr and Sjölander (1970) are so much more involved that, at least in the moment, the anharmonic phonon picture appears superior.

Short range correlations can also be treated within the Einstein approach introducing a Brueckner t-matrix. Most of the present literature on this method in the context of quantum crystals has been cited and compared by

Brandow (1971). It should, in principle, also be possible to calculate collective excitations from the t-matrix, this would, however, again result in extremely complicated expressions. The 'single particle' and the 'anharmonic phonon' picture have been compared by Werthamer (1969).

In most of the work done in the phonon picture again Jastrow factors were introduced and phonon frequencies were calculated in a more or less uncritical fashion. Koehler (1968), and Koehler and Werthamer (1971) have pointed out that the frequencies obtained for instance from a variational calculation should not be identified with the 'physical' phonons. To obtain those they construct approximate wave functions for the low lying states using arguments similar to those used by Feynman (1954) and Feenberg (1969) for the phonon–roton spectrum in liquid helium. The method has been generalized by Gillessen and Biem (1971) for damping processes but it is still restricted to zero temperature. A different approach which is applicable at any temperature was derived by Horner (1971b, 1972) from general properties of the pair correlation function and from consistency arguments.

Although a great deal of work has been done on the heavier rare gas solids in the renormalized harmonic approximation including residual anharmonicities, short range correlations were generally ignored. It might, however, well be that the effect of higher order residual anharmonicities is suppressed if such correlations are included, as discussed by Horner (1971a).

The field of structural phase transitions, especially ferroelectric transitions has been investigated somewhat less using the methods for strongly anharmonic crystals. Qualitatively the results agree with the molecular field approach for other phase transitions. In ferroelectrics complications arise from the long range electrostatic interaction and in general the potential among the lattice particles is not known.

2. *Many-body formulation*

In this chapter we establish some mathematical tools necessary to carry out a thorough investigation of the problem of strongly anharmonic crystals including hard core interactions. The Green's function technique used further on is standard in many-body theory and is described in the book of Kadanoff and Baym (1962). Since an anharmonic crystal corresponds formally to a condensed system, where the displacement field plays the role of the condensate, some of the methods developed by De Dominicis and Martin (1964) will be used.

Although most of the results derived later can be obtained by less sophisticated methods, this formulation allows a rather condensed and elegant treatment. Furthermore we can often see quite easily what type of corrections can exist and how generalizations can be obtained. This will certainly be of value even if it leads in most cases to forms which are intractable at present.

2.1. Green's functions

Subject of our investigation will be an idealized crystal in the sense that individual particles can be distinguished and that there is a one-to-one correspondence between lattice sites and particles. We will further assume that the mean square fluctuations of a particle around its lattice site are finite–they need, however, not be small. This latter restriction could even be relaxed somewhat. Nevertheless this is an idealization of a crystal since it excludes for instance particle diffusion or exchange processes which would be responsible for the magnetic properties of ^{3}He. We further assume that the interaction among the lattice particles can be described by a potential. We will, however, allow for non-primitive lattices and more than one kind of particles.

The particles are described by their position operators

$$\boldsymbol{x}(l\kappa) = \boldsymbol{X}(l\kappa) + \boldsymbol{u}(l\kappa) \tag{2.1}$$

and by the momentum operators $\boldsymbol{p}(l\kappa)$. These operators obey the usual commutator relations

$$\begin{aligned} [p_\alpha(l\kappa), x_\beta(l'\kappa')] &= -\mathrm{i}\, \delta_{ll'}\delta_{\kappa\kappa'}\delta_{\alpha\beta}, \\ [p_\alpha(l\kappa), p_\beta(l'\kappa')] &= [x_\alpha(l\kappa), x_\beta(l'\kappa')] = 0, \end{aligned} \tag{2.2}$$

where units are used such that $\hbar = k_\mathrm{B} = 1$. The lattice vectors are

$$\boldsymbol{X}(l\kappa) = \boldsymbol{X}(l) + \boldsymbol{X}(\kappa) = l_1\boldsymbol{a}_1 + l_2\boldsymbol{a}_2 + l_3\boldsymbol{a}_3 + \boldsymbol{X}(\kappa), \tag{2.3}$$

where l labels the cell and κ the particle within the cell for non-primitive lattices. The $\boldsymbol{a}_i$ are the primitive lattice vectors. The $\boldsymbol{u}$ are displacement operators.

Assuming a local interaction the hamiltonian of the crystal is

$$H = \sum_{l\kappa} \boldsymbol{p}^2(l\kappa)/2m(\kappa) + \phi(\{\boldsymbol{x}\}), \tag{2.4}$$

where $m(\kappa)$ is the mass of the particle sort κ. We will assume pair interaction, although a generalization to many-body forces would be easy,

$$\phi(\{\boldsymbol{x}\}) = \tfrac{1}{2} \sum_{l\kappa} \sum_{l'\kappa'}{}' V(\kappa\kappa'; |\boldsymbol{x}(l\kappa) - \boldsymbol{x}(l'\kappa')|), \tag{2.5}$$

where the prime indicates $\{l'\kappa'\} \neq \{l\kappa\}$. $V(\kappa\kappa'; r)$ is the potential between particles of sort κ and κ'.

We consider a crystal under the influence of some external force giving rise to an additional contribution to the hamiltonian of the form

$$H' = \sum_{l\kappa} \boldsymbol{f}(l\kappa) \cdot \boldsymbol{x}(l\kappa), \tag{2.6}$$

where $\boldsymbol{f}(l\kappa)$ is the force on particle $l\kappa$. In the simplest case it might be realized by an external pressure.

The partition function of the crystal under the forces $\boldsymbol{f}(l\kappa)$ is

$$Z = \operatorname{tr} \exp[-\beta \{H + \sum_{l\kappa} \boldsymbol{f}(l\kappa) \cdot \boldsymbol{x}(l\kappa)\}], \tag{2.7}$$

where $\beta = 1/T$ is the inverse temperature. The free enthalpy is

$$\mathscr{G} = -(1/\beta) \ln Z. \tag{2.8}$$

From those definitions we see easily that the lattice vectors are

$$\langle \boldsymbol{x}(l\kappa) \rangle = \boldsymbol{X}(l\kappa) = \partial \mathscr{G} / \partial \boldsymbol{f}(l\kappa). \tag{2.9}$$

This is just a more general form of the well known thermodynamic relation $V = \partial \mathscr{G} / \partial P$.

We will now allow for time dependent forces including forces quadratic in the position operators. Although there is no physical realization to this latter kind it will be convenient as a mathematical tool. We define a functional of these forces

$$\mathscr{G} = -(1/\beta) \ln \operatorname{tr} T \exp \left[-\mathrm{i} \int_0^{-\mathrm{i}\beta} \mathrm{d}\tau \left\{ H(\tau) + \sum_{l\kappa} \boldsymbol{f}^{(1)}(l\kappa\tau) \cdot \boldsymbol{x}(l\kappa\tau) \right.\right.$$
$$\left.\left. + \tfrac{1}{2} \int_0^{-\mathrm{i}\beta} \mathrm{d}\tau' \sum_{l\kappa} \sum_{l'\kappa'} \boldsymbol{x}(l\kappa\tau) \cdot \boldsymbol{f}^{(2)}(l\kappa\tau, l'\kappa'\tau') \cdot \boldsymbol{x}(l'\kappa'\tau') \right\} \right] \tag{2.10}$$

which in equilibrium, this is in the limit $\boldsymbol{f}^{(1)}(l\kappa t) \to \boldsymbol{f}(l\kappa)$ and $\boldsymbol{f}^{(2)}(l\kappa t, l'\kappa' t') \to 0$, turns into the free enthalpy, eq. (2.8). The operators in eq. (2.10) are Schrödinger operators and the time variable serves only for the time ordering operator T which rearranges the operators such that the operators appear from left to right with decreasing $\mathrm{i}\tau$. The forces are the analytic continuations in the complex t-plane with the boundary condition $\boldsymbol{f}^{(1)}(-\mathrm{i}\beta)=\boldsymbol{f}^{(1)}(0)$ and correspondingly for $\boldsymbol{f}^{(2)}$. Obviously $\boldsymbol{f}^{(2)}$ is a tensor. It is convenient to introduce a short notation

$$A(\bar{1})\,B(\bar{1}) = \int_0^{-\mathrm{i}\beta} \mathrm{d}\tau \sum_{l\kappa\alpha} A_\alpha(l\kappa\tau)\,B_\alpha(l\kappa\tau). \tag{2.11}$$

In this notation

$$\mathscr{G} = -(1/\beta)\ln \operatorname{tr} T \exp\left[-\mathrm{i}\left\{\int_0^{-\mathrm{i}\beta} \mathrm{d}\tau\, H(\tau) + f(\bar{1})\,x(\bar{1}) + \tfrac{1}{2}x(\bar{1})\,f(\bar{1}\bar{2})\,x(\bar{2})\right\}\right]. \tag{2.12}$$

Here and in the following we drop the superscripts on $f^{(1)}(1)$ and $f^{(2)}(12)$ unless they are necessary to avoid confusion.

In analogy to eq. (2.9) we define the one-point Green's function

$$d^{(1)}(1) = \langle x(1)\rangle_f = -\mathrm{i}\beta\,\delta\mathscr{G}/\delta f(1)|_{f^{(2)}} \tag{2.13}$$

which similar to the functional $\mathscr{G}$, turns into the lattice vector $\boldsymbol{X}(l\kappa)$ in the limit $f^{(1)}(1)\to\boldsymbol{f}(l\kappa)$ and $f^{(2)}(12)\to 0$. The expectation value in eq. (2.13) is a generalization analogous to eq. (2.10).

The higher order derivatives of $\mathscr{G}$ define higher order Green's functions. The second derivative

$$d^{(2)}(12) = \langle T\,x(1)\,x(2)\rangle_f - \langle x(1)\rangle_f\,\langle x(2)\rangle_f = \mathrm{i}\,\delta d^{(1)}(1)/\delta f^{(1)}(2)|_{f^{(2)}} \tag{2.14}$$

has the fluctuations in the positions of the particles as its equilibrium limit and the general definition of the ν-point function is

$$d^{(\nu)}(1\cdots\nu) = \mathrm{i}\,\delta d^{(\nu-1)}(1\cdots\nu-1)/\delta f^{(1)}(\nu)|_{f^{(2)}}. \tag{2.15}$$

Differentiating with respect to $f^{(2)}$ we obtain again the Green's functions, for instance

$$d^{(2)}(12) + d^{(1)}(1)\,d^{(1)}(2) = -2\mathrm{i}\beta\,\delta\mathscr{G}/\delta f^{(2)}(12)|_{f^{(1)}}. \tag{2.16}$$

To derive the equations of motion for the Green's functions we write the one-point function more explicitly

$$\boldsymbol{d}(l\kappa t) = \mathrm{tr}\left[\left\{T\exp\left(-\mathrm{i}\int_t^{-\mathrm{i}\beta} \mathrm{d}\tau \left[H(\tau) + \sum \boldsymbol{f}^{(1)}(\tau)\,\boldsymbol{x}(\tau)\right.\right.\right.\right.$$

$$\left.\left.\left. + \tfrac{1}{2}\int_t^{-\mathrm{i}\beta} \mathrm{d}\tau' \sum \boldsymbol{x}(\tau)\cdot\boldsymbol{f}^{(2)}(\tau\tau')\,\boldsymbol{x}(\tau')\right]\right)\right\}$$

$$\times \left\{T\,\boldsymbol{x}(l\kappa t)\exp\left(-\mathrm{i}\int_t^{-\mathrm{i}\beta}\mathrm{d}\tau\int_0^t \mathrm{d}\tau' \sum \boldsymbol{x}(\tau)\boldsymbol{f}^{(2)}(\tau\tau')\,\boldsymbol{x}(\tau')\right)\right\}$$

$$\left.\times \left\{T\exp\left(-\mathrm{i}\int_0^t \mathrm{d}\tau \left[H(\tau) + \cdots + \tfrac{1}{2}\int_0^t \mathrm{d}\tau' \cdots\right]\right)\right\}\right], \tag{2.17}$$

where the time ordering operators now act only within the curly brackets. Differentiating eq. (2.17) with respect to time we obtain contributions only from the boundaries of the integrals

$$\partial\boldsymbol{d}(l\kappa t)/\partial t = -\mathrm{i}\left\langle T\left[\boldsymbol{x}(l\kappa t), \left\{H(t) + \boldsymbol{f}^{(1)}(t)\cdot\boldsymbol{x}(t) \right.\right.\right.$$

$$\left.\left.\left. + \int_0^{-\mathrm{i}\beta} \mathrm{d}\tau\,\boldsymbol{x}(t)\cdot\boldsymbol{f}^{(2)}(t\tau)\cdot\boldsymbol{x}(\tau)\right\}\right]\right\rangle_f$$

$$= m^{-1}(\kappa)\,\langle\boldsymbol{p}(l\kappa t)\rangle_f\,. \tag{2.18}$$

Differentiating again

$$-\,m(\kappa)\,\partial^2\boldsymbol{d}(l\kappa t)/\partial t^2 = \mathscr{K}(l\kappa t) + \boldsymbol{f}(l\kappa t) + \int_0^{-\mathrm{i}\beta}\mathrm{d}\tau \sum_{l'\kappa'} \boldsymbol{f}(l\kappa t, l'\kappa'\tau)\cdot\boldsymbol{d}(l'\kappa'\tau), \tag{2.19}$$

where

$$\mathscr{K}(l\kappa t) = \mathrm{i}\,\langle[\boldsymbol{p}(l\kappa t), \phi(\{\boldsymbol{x}(t)\})]\rangle_f$$

$$= \sum_{l'\kappa'}{}' \,\langle\boldsymbol{\nabla}V(\kappa\kappa'; |\boldsymbol{x}(l\kappa t) - \boldsymbol{x}(l'\kappa' t)|)\rangle_f\,. \tag{2.20}$$

Eq. (2.19) is just Newton's law averaged. The right-hand side contains the external forces and the average force $\mathscr{K}(l\kappa t)$ on particle $l\kappa$ exerted from all the other particles.

Differentiating eq. (2.19) with respect to $f^{(1)}$ at constant $f^{(2)}$ we obtain the equation of motion of the two-point function.

$$-m(\kappa_1)\,\partial^2 d(12)/\partial t_1^2 = \mathrm{i}\delta(12) + f(1\bar{1})\,d(\bar{1}2) + \mathscr{M}(1\bar{1})\,d(\bar{1}2), \qquad (2.21)$$

with $\delta(11') = \delta_{ll'}\delta_{\kappa\kappa'}\delta_{\alpha\alpha'}\delta(t-t')$ and

$$\mathscr{M}(1\bar{1})\,d(\bar{1}2) = \delta\mathscr{K}(1)/\delta f(2)\big|_{f^{(2)}}. \qquad (2.22)$$

The internal force $\mathscr{K}$ will of course primarily depend on the positions of the other particles and the obvious interpretation of eq. (2.22) is that $\mathscr{M}(1\bar{1})$ means the change in the internal force on particle 1 if particle $\bar{1}$ is moved. $d(\bar{1}2)$ describes just the movement of particle $\bar{1}$ if the force on particle 2 is changed.

Formally we can use eq. (2.19)

$$f(1) = -m(\kappa_1)\,\partial d(1)/\partial t_1^2 - f(1\bar{1})\,d(\bar{1}) - \mathscr{K}(1) \qquad (2.23)$$

to determine $f^{(1)}$ as a functional of $d^{(1)}$ and $f^{(2)}$ and consider $\mathscr{K}(1)$ as a functional of the same variables, then

$$\mathscr{M}(12) = \delta\mathscr{K}(1)/\delta d(2)\big|_{f^{(2)}} \qquad (2.24)$$

in accordance with our physical picture.

The problem is so far reduced to that of calculating $\mathscr{K}$ and its derivatives. We introduce the pair correlation function

$$\begin{aligned} g_f(l\kappa\, l'\kappa';\, \boldsymbol{r}t) &= \langle \delta(\boldsymbol{r} - \boldsymbol{x}(l\kappa t) + \boldsymbol{x}(l'\kappa' t))\rangle_f \\ &= (2\pi)^{-3}\int \mathrm{d}^3k\, \mathrm{e}^{\mathrm{i}\boldsymbol{k}\cdot\boldsymbol{r}}\,\langle \mathrm{e}^{-\mathrm{i}\boldsymbol{k}\cdot\{\boldsymbol{x}(l\kappa t) - \boldsymbol{x}(l'\kappa' t)\}}\rangle_f \end{aligned} \qquad (2.25)$$

giving the probability to find the particles $l\kappa$ and $l'\kappa'$ separated by the vector $\boldsymbol{r}$ at time t. The subscript f reminds on the presence of the time dependent external forces. With this definition

$$\mathscr{K}(l\kappa t) = \sum_{l'\kappa'}{}' \int \mathrm{d}^3r\, g_f(l\kappa\, l'\kappa';\, \boldsymbol{r}t)\,\boldsymbol{\nabla} V(\kappa\kappa';\, r). \qquad (2.26)$$

The pair correlation function again can be expressed by Green's functions. Replacing $\boldsymbol{f}(l\kappa\tau)$ by $\boldsymbol{f}(l\kappa\tau) + \boldsymbol{k}\delta(t-\tau)$ and $\boldsymbol{f}(l'\kappa'\tau)$ by $\boldsymbol{f}(l'\kappa'\tau) - \boldsymbol{k}\delta(t-\tau)$ in eq. (2.12) and observing the definitions (2.13)–(2.15) we find

$$\begin{aligned} &g_f(l\kappa\, l'\kappa';\, \boldsymbol{r}t) \\ &= (2\pi)^{-3}\int \mathrm{d}^3k\, \mathrm{e}^{\mathrm{i}\boldsymbol{k}\cdot\boldsymbol{r}} \exp\Big[\sum_\nu [(-\mathrm{i})^\nu/\nu!]\, d^{(\nu)}(\bar{1}\cdots\bar{\nu}) \prod_{i=1}^{\nu} (\boldsymbol{k}\cdot\hat{\boldsymbol{\delta}}(\bar{\imath}))\Big], \end{aligned} \qquad (2.27)$$

where $\hat{\delta}_\alpha(i)=\delta_{\alpha\alpha_i}\delta(t-t_i)\{\delta_{ll_i}\delta_{\kappa\kappa_i}-\delta_{l'l_i}\delta_{\kappa'\kappa_i}\}$. Unfortunately g_f contains all ν-point functions and, as we will see, a truncation of the sum after the first few terms will not be sufficient for hard core interactions. Our task therefore has to be to find appropriate approximative forms for g.

At least the equilibrium form of $g(r)$ can be measured by X-ray or neutron scattering. In a lattice containing just one kind of particles for instance the relation to the static structure factor is

$$S(\boldsymbol{k})=(1/N)\int \mathrm{d}^3r\,\mathrm{e}^{\mathrm{i}\boldsymbol{k}\cdot\boldsymbol{r}}\sum_{l\kappa}\sum_{l'\kappa'} g(l\kappa\, l'\kappa';\boldsymbol{r}). \tag{2.28}$$

2.2. The phonon propagator

A quantity of prime interest is the phonon propagator defined in eq. (2.14). It contains various information about the static and dynamical properties of the crystal, for instance the mean square displacements of the lattice particles or the phonon frequencies and life times. Before we proceed with the formal development of our theory we investigate the structure of the phonon propagator in equilibrium and establish some sum rules.

In equilibrium, that is in the absence of external time-dependent forces, $d(l\kappa t, l\kappa' t')$ depends on $t-t'$ and $l-l'$ only and is periodic in time with the period $-\mathrm{i}\beta$ and has the lattice periodicity. This allows to use a Fourier representation with the Fourier transform

$$d_{\alpha\beta}(\kappa\kappa';\boldsymbol{k}z_\nu)$$
$$=-\mathrm{i}[m(\kappa)\,m(\kappa')]^{1/2}\sum_l\int_0^{-\mathrm{i}\beta}\mathrm{d}\tau\,\exp[-\mathrm{i}\boldsymbol{k}\cdot\boldsymbol{X}(l)+\mathrm{i}z_\nu\tau]\,d_{\alpha\beta}(l\kappa\tau, l'\kappa'\tau'), \tag{2.29}$$

with $z_\nu=2\pi\nu/(-\mathrm{i}\beta)$ and l' and τ' being arbitrary, for instance $l'=0$ and $\tau'=0$. The quasi-momentum vectors are

$$\boldsymbol{k}=(h_1/N_1)\,\boldsymbol{b}_1+(h_2/N_2)\,\boldsymbol{b}_2+(h_3/N_3)\,\boldsymbol{b}_3\,,$$

where h_i are integers, $\boldsymbol{b}_1$ the primitive lattice vectors of the reciprocal lattice and N_i the number of cells in the direction of $\boldsymbol{a}_i$ assuming periodic boundary conditions. The relationship between the primitive vectors of the real and the reciprocal lattice is $\boldsymbol{a}_i\cdot\boldsymbol{b}_j=2\pi\delta_{ij}$.

The Fourier coefficients, eq. (2.29) are defined only at the points z_ν along the imaginary axis of the complex z-plane. An analytic continuation can be found which has, as the only singularity, a branch cut along the real axis. We can therefore find a spectral representation

$$d_{\alpha\beta}(\kappa\kappa'; \boldsymbol{k}z) = (1/2\pi) \int \mathrm{d}\omega\, a_{\alpha\beta}(\kappa\kappa'; \boldsymbol{k}\omega)/(z-\omega). \tag{2.30}$$

Transforming back eq. (2.29), a sum over the z_ν appears. This sum can be converted into a contour integral

$$-(1/\mathrm{i}\beta)\sum_\nu \mathrm{e}^{-\mathrm{i}z_\nu t} \to (1/2\pi)\oint \mathrm{d}z\, \mathrm{e}^{-\mathrm{i}zt} \begin{cases} n(z), & -\beta < \mathrm{i}t < 0, \\ 1+n(z), & \beta > \mathrm{i}t > 0, \end{cases} \tag{2.31}$$

where the contour surrounds the poles of $n(z) = 1/\{\exp(\beta z) - 1\}$ at the z_ν counter-clockwise. To express the time dependent two-point function by the spectral function defined in eq. (2.30) we introduce the displacement–displacement correlation function and find, inserting eq. (2.30)

$$\begin{aligned} d^{>}(11') &= \langle x(1)\, x(1')\rangle - \langle x(1)\rangle \langle x(1')\rangle = \{m(\kappa)\, m(\kappa')\}^{-1/2} \\ &\times (1/N) \sum_{\boldsymbol{k}} \mathrm{e}^{\mathrm{i}\boldsymbol{k}\cdot\{\boldsymbol{X}(l)-\boldsymbol{X}(l')\}} (1/2\pi) \int \mathrm{d}\omega\, \mathrm{e}^{-\mathrm{i}\omega(t-t')}\, a_{\alpha\alpha'}(\kappa\kappa'; \boldsymbol{k}\omega)\, \{1+n(\omega)\}, \end{aligned} \tag{2.32}$$

where N is the total number of cells of the crystal and the sum over $\boldsymbol{k}$ is restricted to the first Brillouin zone. This function is an analytic function for complex times $0 > \mathrm{Im}\, t' > -\beta$. Equation (2.32) establishes the connection between the Green's functions for imaginary times and the real time functions which are of immediate physical interest. Furthermore

$$d(11') = \begin{cases} d^{>}(11'), & \beta > \mathrm{i}t > \mathrm{i}t' > 0 \\ d^{>}(1'1), & 0 < \mathrm{i}t < \mathrm{i}t' < \beta. \end{cases} \tag{2.33}$$

Corresponding relations hold for the phonon self energy $\mathscr{M}(12)$. Analogous to eq. (2.29)

$$\mathscr{M}_{\alpha\beta}(\kappa\kappa'; \boldsymbol{k}z_\nu) = \{m(\kappa)\, m(\kappa')\}^{-1/2} \sum_l \int_0^{-\mathrm{i}\beta} \mathrm{d}\tau\, \mathrm{e}^{-\mathrm{i}\boldsymbol{k}\cdot\boldsymbol{X}(l) + \mathrm{i}z_\nu t}\, \mathscr{M}_{\alpha\beta}(l\kappa\tau, l'\kappa'\tau'). \tag{2.34}$$

The analytic continuation of $\mathscr{M}$ now also contains a constant term $\mathscr{M}^0$

$$\mathscr{M}_{\alpha\beta}(\kappa\kappa'; \boldsymbol{k}z) = \mathscr{M}^0_{\alpha\beta}(\kappa\kappa'; k) + (1/2\pi) \int \mathrm{d}\omega\, \Gamma_{\alpha\beta}(\kappa\kappa'; \boldsymbol{k}\omega)/(z-\omega) \tag{2.35}$$

which results from the instantaneous part of $\mathscr{M}(tt')$ being proportional to $\delta(t-t')$.

The Fourier transform of the equation of motion (2.21) in the absence of $f^{(2)}$ is a simple matrix equation

$$d_{\alpha\beta}^{-1}(\kappa\kappa'; \boldsymbol{k}z) = z^2 \delta_{\alpha\beta}\delta_{\kappa\kappa'} - \mathscr{M}_{\alpha\beta}(\kappa\kappa'; \boldsymbol{k}z) \tag{2.36}$$

for $3\nu \times 3\nu$ matrices where ν is the number of atoms in the unit cell. The zeros of the right-hand side determine the phonon frequencies and life times, and the corresponding eigenvectors are the polarization vectors.

An examination of the phonon propagator for large z yields sum rules for the spectral function which are often useful as a test on any approximation. Expanding eqs. (2.36) and (2.35) and on the other hand eq. (2.30) in powers of $1/z$ we obtain

$$\begin{aligned} \boldsymbol{d}(\boldsymbol{k}z) &= \frac{1}{z^2\mathbf{1} - \mathscr{M}(\boldsymbol{k}z)} = \frac{1}{z^2}\mathbf{1} + \frac{1}{z^4}\mathscr{M}^0(\boldsymbol{k}) + \cdots \\ &= \sum_{n=0}^{\infty} z^{-n-1}(1/2\pi)\int \mathrm{d}\omega\, \omega^n \boldsymbol{a}(\boldsymbol{k}\omega). \end{aligned} \tag{2.37}$$

where $\boldsymbol{d}$, $\mathscr{M}$ and $\boldsymbol{a}$ are $3\nu \times 3\nu$ matrices and $\mathbf{1}$ a unit matrix.

The first nonvanishing moments are

$$(1/2\pi)\int \mathrm{d}\omega\, \omega a_{\alpha\beta}(\kappa\kappa'; \boldsymbol{k}\omega) = \delta_{\kappa\kappa'}\delta_{\alpha\beta} \tag{2.38}$$

which is in analogy to the f-sum rule for the dynamic structure function, and the third moment

$$(1/2\pi)\int \mathrm{d}\omega\, \omega^3 a_{\alpha\beta}(\kappa\kappa'; \boldsymbol{k}\omega) = \mathscr{M}_{\alpha\beta}^0(\kappa\kappa'; k). \tag{2.39}$$

The moments of the spectral function can, on the other hand, be related to the expectation values of equal time commutators. From eq. (2.32) and the symmetry $a_{\alpha\beta}(\kappa\kappa'; \boldsymbol{k}\omega) = -a_{\beta\alpha}(\kappa'\kappa; -\boldsymbol{k} - \omega)$ following from eqs. (2.29) and (2.30) we obtain

$$\begin{aligned} (1/2\pi)\int \mathrm{d}\omega\, \omega^n a_{\alpha\beta}(\kappa\kappa'; \boldsymbol{k}\omega) &= \{m(\kappa)\, m(\kappa')\}^{1/2} \\ &\times \sum_l \mathrm{e}^{-\mathrm{i}\boldsymbol{k}\cdot\boldsymbol{X}(l)} (\mathrm{i}\partial/\partial t)^n \langle [x_\alpha(l\kappa t), x_\beta(l'\kappa' 0)]\rangle\big|_{t=0}, \end{aligned} \tag{2.40}$$

where, as already in eq. (2.32), the operators are now Heisenberg operators. For the first moment eq. (2.38) is recovered and the third moment yields an expression for the instantaneous part of the phonon self energy

$$\mathcal{M}^{0}_{\alpha\beta}(\kappa\kappa';\boldsymbol{k}) = -\mathrm{i}\{m(\kappa)\,m(\kappa')\}^{1/2}\sum_{l}\mathrm{e}^{-\mathrm{i}\boldsymbol{k}\cdot\boldsymbol{X}(l)}\langle[\dot{x}_{\alpha}(l\kappa 0),\ \ddot{x}_{\beta}(0\kappa' 0)]\rangle$$

$$= \{m(\kappa)\,m(\kappa')\}^{-1/2}\sum_{l}\{1-\mathrm{e}^{\mathrm{i}\boldsymbol{k}\cdot\boldsymbol{X}(l)}\}\int \mathrm{d}^{3}r\, g(l\kappa\, 0\kappa';\boldsymbol{r})\,\nabla_{\alpha}\nabla_{\beta}V(\kappa\kappa';r). \tag{2.41}$$

This form and its relation to the third moment sum rule has been discussed by Meissner (1968). This expression resembles very much the harmonic approximation except that the second derivative of the potential is not taken at the equilibrium positions but rather averaged over the pair distribution function.

Comparison of this expression with eqs. (2.24)–(2.27) yields

$$\mathcal{M}^{0}(12) = \delta\mathcal{K}(1)\,\delta d^{(1)}(2)|_{d^{(2)},d^{(3)},\ldots}. \tag{2.42}$$

This means $\mathcal{M}^{0}$ is obtained from the full result if the only change in the pair correlation function due to the change of the mean position of any particle is a rigid displacement of $g(\boldsymbol{r})$.

2.3. Renormalization and free energy

As we have seen the pair correlation function and with it $\mathcal{K}$ and $\mathcal{M}$ depend primarily on the n-point functions which themselves depend on the external forces. For this and for other reasons it is opportune to introduce at least the one- and two-point functions as the independent variables. This is done by a generalized Legendre transformation analogous to ordinary thermodynamics. We introduce the free energy functional

$$\mathcal{F} = \mathcal{G} - \frac{1}{-\mathrm{i}\beta}\,d(\bar{1})\,f(\bar{1}) - \frac{1}{-2\mathrm{i}\beta}\{d(\bar{1}\bar{2}) + d(\bar{1})\,d(\bar{2})\}\,f(\bar{1}\bar{2}) \tag{2.43}$$

which is now considered as a functional of $d^{(1)}$ and $d^{(2)}$. The first derivatives with respect to its natural variables are

$$\begin{aligned} -\mathrm{i}\beta\,\delta\mathcal{F}/\delta d^{(1)}(1)|_{d^{(2)}} &= -f(1) - f(1\bar{1})\,d(\bar{1}),\\ -2\mathrm{i}\beta\,\delta\mathcal{F}/\delta d^{(2)}(12)|_{d^{(2)}} &= -f(12). \end{aligned} \tag{2.44}$$

$f^{(1)}$ and $f^{(2)}$ are now the dependent variables and have eventually to be determined such that their equilibrium values $f^{(1)}(t) = f^{(1)}$ and $f^{(2)} \equiv 0$ are reached.

Introducing

$$\Delta(11') = -m(\kappa)\frac{\partial^2}{\partial t^2}\,\delta_{ll'}\delta_{\kappa\kappa'}\delta_{\alpha\alpha'}\,\delta(t-t') \tag{2.45}$$

and using eqs. (2.21) and (2.23) the derivatives become

$$\begin{aligned} -\,\mathrm{i}\beta\,\delta\mathscr{F}/\delta d(1)\big|_{d^{(2)}} &= \mathscr{K}(1) - \Delta(1\bar{1})\,d(\bar{1}),\\ -\,2\mathrm{i}\beta\,\delta\mathscr{F}/\delta d(12)\big|_{d^{(1)}} &= \mathscr{M}(12) - \Delta(12) + \mathrm{i}(d^{(2)})^{-1}(12). \end{aligned} \tag{2.46}$$

Since Δ does not depend on $d^{(1)}$ or $d^{(2)}$ there must be a functional Ψ such that

$$\mathscr{F} = \Psi + (1/2\mathrm{i}\beta)\,\Delta(\bar{1}\bar{2})\,\{d(\bar{1}\bar{2}) + d(\bar{1})\,d(\bar{2})\} - (1/2\beta)(\ln d^{(2)})(\bar{1}\bar{1}) \tag{2.47}$$

and

$$\mathscr{K}(1) = -\,\mathrm{i}\beta\,\delta\Psi/\delta d(1)\big|_{d^{(2)}}, \quad \mathscr{M}(12) = -\,2\mathrm{i}\beta\,\delta\Psi/\delta d(12)\big|_{d^{(1)}}. \tag{2.48, 49}$$

The last term in eq. (2.47) is the 'trace' of $(\ln d^{(2)})\,(12)$ where a function of $d^{(2)}$ is defined analogous to the function of a matrix.

We have now a second definition for the phonon self energy. The original definition, eq. (2.24) can be rewritten using the identity $\delta d^{(2)} = -d^{(2)} \times \delta\,(d^{(2)})^{-1} d^{(2)}$

$$\mathscr{M}(12) = \frac{\delta\mathscr{K}(1)}{\delta d(2)}\bigg|_{d^{(2)}} - \frac{\delta\mathscr{K}(1)}{\delta d(\bar{1}\bar{2})}\bigg|_{d^{(1)}} d(\bar{1}\bar{3})\,d(\bar{2}\bar{4})\,Q(\bar{3}\bar{4}2), \tag{2.50}$$

where

$$\begin{aligned} Q(123) &= \frac{\delta\,(d^{(2)})^{-1}\,(12)}{\delta d(3)}\bigg|_{f^{(2)}}\\ &= \mathrm{i}\,\frac{\delta\mathscr{M}(12)}{\delta d(3)}\bigg|_{d^{(2)}} - \mathrm{i}\,\frac{\delta\mathscr{M}(12)}{\delta d(\bar{1}\bar{2})}\bigg|_{d^{(1)}} d(\bar{1}\bar{3})\,d(\bar{2}\bar{4})\,Q(\bar{3}\bar{4}3). \end{aligned} \tag{2.51}$$

The existence of this latter relation for the self energy of the two-point function is characteristic for a condensed many-body system and would be absent in normal systems.

Approximations are usually found by choosing an appropriate form of Ψ. Besides the exact Ψ, however, no approximate form is known which gives the same $\mathscr{M}$ from eq. (2.51) and from eqs. (2.50) and (2.51). Consistency can therefore be achieved only in an approximate way, say up to some order in some expansion parameter. The existence of two equations allows, however, to improve in a systematic fashion the particular approximation choosen initially.

3. *Anharmonic expansions*

Starting from the general structure derived in the previous chapter we will now discuss several forms of an expansion in terms of anharmonic contributions. We will have to examine how different terms in this expansion have to be grouped together and what can be said about an expansion parameter and the convergency. Although conventional anharmonic theory is not the subject of this paper we will start with it partially to get familiar with the methods derived, but also to see its limitations and generalizations.

Some of the expressions for the first anharmonic corrections of the free energy or the phonon self energy will be spelled out in more detail than necessary because equivalent expressions will appear later with only slight modifications.

Two other forms of an expansion in partially renormalized vertices will be discussed, one based on the renormalized harmonic approximation, the other suited at least for some types of singular interactions.

3.1. Conventional anharmonic theory

At sufficiently low temperatures the mean square deviations of the particles around their lattice sites become small for most crystals. This means that the two-point functions, eq. (2.14), and also the higher order Green's functions will become small. It will then be a good starting point to consider only the one-point functions in eq. (2.27) for the pair distribution function,

$$\begin{aligned} g_0(l\kappa\, l'\kappa'; \boldsymbol{r}t) &= (2\pi)^{-3} \int \mathrm{d}^3k \exp\left[\mathrm{i}\boldsymbol{k}\cdot\{\boldsymbol{r} - \boldsymbol{d}(l\kappa t) + \boldsymbol{d}(l'\kappa' t)\}\right] \\ &= \delta\left(\boldsymbol{r} - \boldsymbol{d}(l\kappa t) + \boldsymbol{d}(l'\kappa' t)\right). \end{aligned} \tag{3.1}$$

According to eq. (2.26) $\mathscr{K}$ is now the first derivative of the potential taken at the equilibrium positions. Since g_0 is independent of $d^{(2)}$ we can easily integrate eq. (2.48) and find as the lowest order contribution to Ψ just the static lattice energy

$$\begin{aligned} \Psi = \phi_0 &= -(1/2\mathrm{i}\beta) \sum_{l\kappa} \sum_{l'\kappa'}{}' \int_0^{-\mathrm{i}\beta} \mathrm{d}\tau\, V(\kappa\kappa'; |\boldsymbol{d}(l\kappa t) - \boldsymbol{d}(l'\kappa' t)|) \\ &= \tfrac{1}{2} \sum_{l\kappa} \sum_{l'\kappa'}{}' V(\kappa\kappa'; |X(l\kappa) - X(l'\kappa')|), \end{aligned} \tag{3.2}$$

where the second line holds in equilibrium.

Differentiating ϕ_0 the conventional anharmonic coupling parameters are obtained

$$\phi_0(1 \ldots \nu) = -\mathrm{i}\beta\, \delta^\nu \phi_0/\delta d(1) \ldots \delta d(\nu)$$

$$= \tfrac{1}{2} \sum_{l\kappa} \sum_{l'\kappa'} \int_0^{-\mathrm{i}\beta} \mathrm{d}t\, (\hat{\boldsymbol{\delta}}(1)\cdot\nabla) \ldots (\hat{\boldsymbol{\delta}}(\nu)\cdot\nabla)\, V(\kappa\kappa'; |\boldsymbol{X}(l\kappa) - \boldsymbol{X}(l'\kappa')|), \tag{3.3}$$

where $\hat{\boldsymbol{\delta}}(i)$ is the symbol introduced following eq. (2.27). With this form of Ψ

$$\mathscr{K}(1) = \phi_0(1), \quad \mathscr{M}(12) = \phi_0(12) \tag{3.4, 5}$$

is obtained in lowest order from eqs. (2.48) and (2.50), respectively. This is the well-known harmonic approximation.

The explicit form of the phonon selfenergy in this approximation is with eq. (2.34)

$$\mathscr{M}_{\alpha\beta}(\kappa\kappa'; \boldsymbol{k}z) = \{m(\kappa)\, m(\kappa')\}^{-1/2} \sum_l \{1 - \mathrm{e}^{\mathrm{i}\boldsymbol{k}\cdot\boldsymbol{X}(l)}\}$$
$$\times \nabla_\alpha \nabla_\beta V(\kappa\kappa'; |\boldsymbol{X}(l) + \boldsymbol{X}(\kappa) - \boldsymbol{X}(\kappa')|)$$
$$= \sum_\lambda \varepsilon^*_\alpha(\kappa; \boldsymbol{k}\lambda)\, \omega_0^2(\boldsymbol{k}\lambda)\, \varepsilon_\beta(\kappa'; \boldsymbol{k}\lambda), \tag{3.6}$$

where the right-hand side does not depend on z, there is only the instantaneous part of the self energy in this approximation; $\omega_0^2(\boldsymbol{k}\lambda)$ and $\boldsymbol{\varepsilon}(\kappa; \boldsymbol{k}\lambda)$ are the eigenvalues and eigenvectors of the $3\nu \times 3\nu$ matrix $\mathscr{M}(\boldsymbol{k}z)$.

The phonon propagator is easily obtained from eq. (2.36) if the diagonal form of $\mathscr{M}$ is used

$$d_{0_{\alpha\beta}}(\kappa\kappa'; \boldsymbol{k}z) = \sum_\lambda \varepsilon^*_\alpha(\kappa; \boldsymbol{k}\lambda)\, \varepsilon_\beta(\kappa'; \boldsymbol{k}\lambda)/\{z^2 - \omega_0^2(\boldsymbol{k}\lambda)\} \tag{3.7}$$

and the spectral function defined in eq. (2.30) is

$$a_{0_{\alpha\beta}}(\kappa\kappa'; \boldsymbol{k}\omega) = (\pi/\omega) \sum_\lambda \varepsilon^*_\alpha(\kappa; \boldsymbol{k}\lambda)\, \varepsilon_\beta(\kappa'; \boldsymbol{k}\lambda)$$
$$\times \{\delta(\omega - \omega_0(\boldsymbol{k}\lambda)) + \delta(\omega + \omega_0(\boldsymbol{k}\lambda))\} \tag{3.8}$$

the subscripts 0 indicate that those are the lowest order results.

Obviously eq. (2.49) is violated. This can, however, be fixed by an extension of Ψ

$$\Psi = \phi_0 + (-1/2\mathrm{i}\beta)\, \phi_0(\overline{12})\, d(\overline{21}). \tag{3.9}$$

This leads to the first anharmonic corrections using eq. (2.48)

$$\mathscr{K}(1) = \phi_0(1) + \tfrac{1}{2}\phi_0(1\overline{12})\, d(\overline{21}) \tag{3.10}$$

and retaining just the first two terms of an iterative solution of eq. (2.50)

$$\mathcal{M}(12) = \phi_0(12) + \tfrac{1}{2}\phi_0(12\bar{1}\bar{2})\, d(\bar{2}\bar{1}) - \tfrac{1}{2}\mathrm{i}\, \phi_0(1\bar{1}\bar{2})\, d(\bar{1}\bar{3})\, d(\bar{2}\bar{4})\, \phi_0(\bar{3}\bar{4}2).$$

Retaining only those terms anticipates what will be said about the expansion parameter in the next section.

Again eq. (2.49) can be used to determine the next contribution to Ψ

$$\Psi = \phi_0 + (-1/2\mathrm{i}\beta)\, \phi_0(\bar{1}\bar{2})\, d(\bar{2}\bar{1}) + (-1/8\mathrm{i}\beta)\, \phi_0(\bar{1}\bar{2}\bar{3}\bar{4})\, d(\bar{1}\bar{2})\, d(\bar{3}\bar{4}) + (1/12\beta)\, \phi_0(\bar{1}\bar{2}\bar{3})\, d(\bar{1}\bar{4})\, d(\bar{2}\bar{5})\, d(\bar{3}\bar{6})\, \phi_0(\bar{4}\bar{5}\bar{6}) \tag{3.12}$$

and the next order contributions to $\mathcal{K}$ and $\mathcal{M}$ could be evaluated from eq. (3.12). It is obvious that arbitrary orders of this expansion can be generated in this rather dull fashion.

The equation of motion of the phonon propagator (2.36) can be transformed into an integral equation using the harmonic result, eq. (3.7)

$$d(12) = d_0(12) - \mathrm{i} d_0(1\bar{1})\, \{\mathcal{M}(\bar{1}\bar{2}) - \phi_0(\bar{1}\bar{2})\}\, d(\bar{2}2). \tag{3.13}$$

As long as we are interested only in the lowest order anharmonic corrections it is sufficient to approximate $d^{(2)}$ by $d_0^{(2)}$ in the second and third term in eq. (3.12) and to iterate eq. (3.13) once for the remaining terms.

In the calculation of the free energy from eq. (2.47) some cancellations occur and including the lowest order anharmonic corrections only, we obtain

$$\begin{aligned} \mathcal{F} &= \mathcal{F}_{\mathrm{h}} + \mathcal{F}_4 + \mathcal{F}_{33} \\ &= \phi_0 - (1/2\beta)\, (\ln d_0^{(2)})\, (\bar{1}\bar{1}) + (-1/8\mathrm{i}\beta)\, \phi_0(\bar{1}\bar{2}\bar{3}\bar{4})\, d_0(\bar{1}\bar{2})\, d_0(\bar{3}\bar{4}) \\ &\quad + (1/12\beta)\, \phi_0(\bar{1}\bar{2}\bar{3})\, d_0(\bar{1}\bar{4})\, d_0(\bar{2}\bar{5})\, d_0(\bar{3}\bar{6})\, \phi_0(\bar{4}\bar{5}\bar{6}). \end{aligned} \tag{3.14}$$

This is a well-known result. Written out in detail rather lengthy formulae appear. Since similar expressions will be obtained later they should be displayed once

$$\begin{aligned} -(1/2\beta)\, (\ln d_0^{(2)})\, (\bar{1}\bar{1}) &= \tfrac{1}{2} \sum_{\boldsymbol{k}\lambda} (1/2\pi\mathrm{i}) \oint \mathrm{d}z\, \frac{\ln\{z^2 - \omega_0^2(\boldsymbol{k}\lambda)\}}{\mathrm{e}^{\beta z} - 1} \\ &= \sum_{\boldsymbol{k}\lambda} \{\tfrac{1}{2}\omega_0(\boldsymbol{k}\lambda) + (1/\beta) \ln(1 - \mathrm{e}^{-\beta\omega_0(\boldsymbol{k}\lambda)})\}. \end{aligned} \tag{3.15}$$

Here the trace of $\ln d^{(2)}$ was evaluated in Fourier space and the sum over the z_ν converted into a contour integral, eq. (2.31). The second line is found after partial integration and deforming the integration path such that the poles at $z=-\omega_0(\boldsymbol{k}\lambda)$ are enclosed. Together with the static lattice energy ϕ_0, eq. (3.15) represents the free energy of a harmonic crystal.

For the anharmonic corrections it is convenient to introduce the

$$\{l\kappa\kappa';\boldsymbol{k}\lambda\}=\{m^{-1/2}(\kappa)\,\boldsymbol{\varepsilon}(\kappa;\boldsymbol{k}\lambda)-m^{-1/2}(\kappa')\,\boldsymbol{\varepsilon}(\kappa';\boldsymbol{k}\lambda)\,\mathrm{e}^{-i\boldsymbol{k}\cdot\boldsymbol{X}(l)}\}. \quad (3.16)$$

Inserting eqs. (2.32) and (3.8) for the phonon propagators and eq. (3.3) for the vertex

$$\mathscr{F}_4=\tfrac{1}{16}(1/N)\sum_{\boldsymbol{k}\lambda}\sum_{\boldsymbol{k}'\lambda'}\frac{n+\frac{1}{2}}{\omega_0}\frac{n'+\frac{1}{2}}{\omega_0'}\sum_{l\kappa\kappa'}(\{l\kappa\kappa';\boldsymbol{k}\lambda\}^*\cdot\nabla)(\{l\kappa\kappa';\boldsymbol{k}\lambda\}\cdot\nabla)$$
$$\times(\{l\kappa\kappa';\boldsymbol{k}'\lambda'\}^*\cdot\nabla)(\{l\kappa\kappa';\boldsymbol{k}'\lambda'\}\cdot\nabla)\,V(\kappa\kappa';|\boldsymbol{X}(\kappa)-\boldsymbol{X}(\kappa')-\boldsymbol{X}(l)|), \quad (3.17)$$

where $\omega_0=\omega_0(\boldsymbol{k}\lambda)$, $\omega_0'=\omega_0(\boldsymbol{k}'\lambda')$ and $n=n(\omega_0)$, $n'=n(\omega_0')$. The last term in eq. (3.14) becomes

$$\mathscr{F}_{33}=-\tfrac{1}{192}(1/N)\sum_{\boldsymbol{k}\lambda}\sum_{\boldsymbol{k}'\lambda'}\sum_{\boldsymbol{k}''\lambda''}\sum_{\boldsymbol{\tau}}\delta_{\boldsymbol{k}+\boldsymbol{k}'+\boldsymbol{k}'',\boldsymbol{\tau}}\frac{(n+1)(n'+1)(n''+1)}{\omega_0\omega_0'\omega_0''}$$
$$\times\left\{\frac{1-\mathrm{e}^{-\beta(\omega_0+\omega'_0+\omega''_0)}}{\omega_0+\omega_0'+\omega_0''}+3\,\frac{\mathrm{e}^{-\beta(\omega'_0+\omega''_0)}-\mathrm{e}^{-\beta\omega_0}}{\omega_0-\omega_0'-\omega_0''}\right\}$$
$$\times\sum_{l\kappa\kappa'}(\{l\kappa\kappa';\boldsymbol{k}\lambda\}^*\cdot\nabla)(\{l\kappa\kappa';\boldsymbol{k}'\lambda'\}^*\cdot\nabla)(\{l\kappa\kappa';\boldsymbol{k}''\lambda''\}^*\cdot\nabla)$$
$$\times V(\kappa\kappa';|\boldsymbol{X}(\kappa)-\boldsymbol{X}(\kappa')-\boldsymbol{X}(l)|)$$
$$\times\sum_{\bar{l}\bar{\kappa}\bar{\kappa}'}(\{\bar{l}\bar{\kappa}\bar{\kappa}';\boldsymbol{k}\lambda\}\cdot\nabla)(\{\bar{l}\bar{\kappa}\bar{\kappa}';\boldsymbol{k}'\lambda'\}\cdot\nabla)(\{\bar{l}\bar{\kappa}\bar{\kappa}';\boldsymbol{k}''\lambda''\}\cdot\nabla)$$
$$\times V(\bar{\kappa}\bar{\kappa}';|\boldsymbol{X}(\bar{\kappa})-\boldsymbol{X}(\bar{\kappa}')-\boldsymbol{X}(\bar{l})|), \quad (3.18)$$

where $\boldsymbol{\tau}=\tau_1\boldsymbol{b}_1+\tau_2\boldsymbol{b}_2+\tau_3\boldsymbol{b}_3$ is a reciprocal lattice vector.

Expressions of similar length result for the phonon self energy. The first two term of eq. (3.11) yield the instantaneous contribution

$$\mathscr{M}^0_{\alpha\beta}(\kappa\kappa';\boldsymbol{k})=\{m(\kappa)\,m(\kappa')\}^{-1/2}\sum_{l}\{1-\mathrm{e}^{-i\boldsymbol{k}\cdot\boldsymbol{X}(l)}\}$$
$$\times\left[1+(1/N)\sum_{\boldsymbol{k}'\lambda'}\frac{n'+\frac{1}{2}}{\omega_0'}(\{l\kappa\kappa';\boldsymbol{k}'\lambda'\}^*\cdot\nabla)(\{l\kappa\kappa';\boldsymbol{k}'\lambda'\}\cdot\nabla)\right]$$
$$\times\nabla_\alpha\nabla_\beta V(\kappa\kappa';|\boldsymbol{X}(\kappa)-\boldsymbol{X}(\kappa')-\boldsymbol{X}(l)|). \quad (3.19)$$

The third term of eq. (3.11) is responsible for phonon damping and a spectral representation can be found in accordance with eq. (2.35). The spectral function is

$$\Gamma_{\alpha\beta}(\kappa\kappa'; \boldsymbol{k}\omega) = \{m(\kappa)\, m(\kappa')\}^{-1/2} (\pi/4N)$$
$$\times \sum_{\boldsymbol{k}'\lambda'} \sum_{\boldsymbol{k}''\lambda''} \sum_{\boldsymbol{\tau}} \delta_{\boldsymbol{k}+\boldsymbol{k}'+\boldsymbol{k}'',\boldsymbol{\tau}} \frac{(n'+1)(n''+1)}{\omega_0'\omega_0''} [\{1-\mathrm{e}^{-\beta(\omega'_0+\omega''_0)}\} \{\delta(\omega-\omega_0'-\omega_0'')$$
$$- \delta(\omega+\omega_0'+\omega_0'')\} + 2\{\mathrm{e}^{-\beta\omega''_0} - \mathrm{e}^{-\beta\omega'_0}\}\, \delta(\omega-\omega_0'+\omega_0'')]$$
$$\times \sum_{l\bar{\kappa}} (\{l\kappa\bar{\kappa}; \boldsymbol{k}'\lambda'\}^* \cdot \boldsymbol{\nabla}) (\{l\kappa\bar{\kappa}; \boldsymbol{k}''\lambda''\}^* \cdot \boldsymbol{\nabla}) \nabla_\alpha V(\kappa\bar{\kappa}; |\boldsymbol{X}(\kappa)-\boldsymbol{X}(\bar{\kappa})-\boldsymbol{X}(l)|)$$
$$\times \sum_{l'\bar{\kappa}'} (\{l'\kappa'\bar{\kappa}'; \boldsymbol{k}'\lambda'\} \cdot \boldsymbol{\nabla}) (\{l'\kappa'\bar{\kappa}'; \boldsymbol{k}''\lambda''\} \cdot \boldsymbol{\nabla}) \nabla_\beta V(\kappa'\bar{\kappa}'; |\boldsymbol{X}(\kappa')-\boldsymbol{X}(\bar{\kappa}')-\boldsymbol{X}(l')|). \tag{3.20}$$

The general structure of Ψ, $\mathscr{K}$ or $\mathscr{M}$ can be represented by diagrams, that is collections of dots, called vertices, and lines, called propagators, connecting the vertices. Each line represents a phonon propagator and each vertex an anharmonic coupling parameter, eq. (3.3). The order of the coupling parameter agrees with the number of lines terminating at the corresponding vertex, where possibly external lines, representing the variables in $\mathscr{K}$ and $\mathscr{M}$, have to be included. The diagrams of Ψ, $\mathscr{K}$ and $\mathscr{M}$ up to the next correction to eqs. (3.10)–(3.12) are shown in fig. 1.

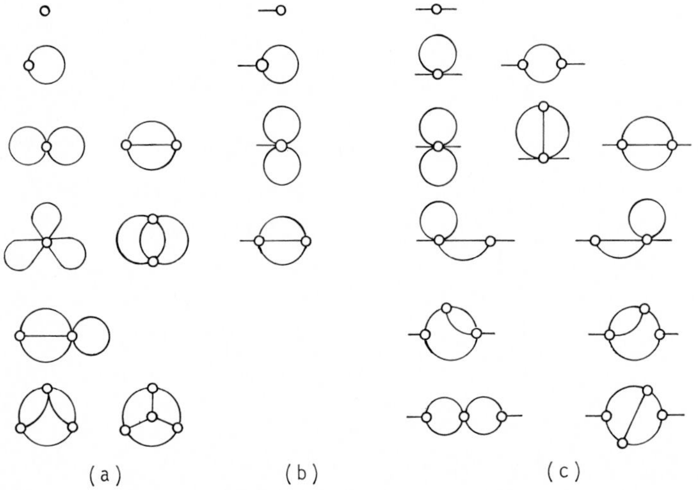

Fig. 1. The first diagrams of Ψ (a), $\mathscr{K}$ (b) and $\mathscr{M}$ (c).

3.2. Expansion parameter and convergence

It is quite obvious that we should find some scheme to order the diagrams according to their importance. This means we have to find an expansion parameter which hopefully will be small. As suggested before this quantity is connected with the mean square fluctuations of the particles around their lattice sites.

From eq. (2.32) inserting eq. (3.8) we estimate the mean square fluctuations δ to be of order

$$\delta^2 \sim \frac{n(\omega_D)+\frac{1}{2}}{m\omega_D} \sim \begin{cases} \dfrac{1}{m\omega_D}, & T \ll \theta, \\ \dfrac{T}{m\omega_D^2}, & T \gg \theta, \end{cases} \tag{3.21}$$

where m is some averaged mass if more than one kind of particles is present and ω_D is some averaged frequency, say the Debye frequency and θ the Debye temperature.

To find a dimensionless expansion parameter we need some other length. We assume that the νth derivative of the potential taken at the equilibrium position is of order

$$\mathrm{d}^\nu V(r)/\mathrm{d}r^\nu\big|_{r=a} = V_\nu \sim V_0\,\sigma^{-\nu}, \tag{3.22}$$

where again some average value is meant.

Eq. (3.6) gives an estimate for the Debye frequency

$$\omega_D^2 \sim V_0/m\sigma^2 \tag{3.23}$$

and the ratio of thermal plus zero point energy divided by the static lattice energy is of order

$$\omega_D\{n(\omega_D)+\tfrac{1}{2}\}/V_0 \sim \delta^2/\sigma^2 = \lambda, \tag{3.24}$$

where $\lambda = \delta^2/\sigma^2$ will turn out to be the expansion parameter.

Estimating $\mathscr{F}_4$, eq. (3.17), we have to recall that a factor $m^{-1/2}$ is implied in the curly bracket symbol. This gives with the $(n+\frac{1}{2})/\omega_0$ factors a δ^4 and we find its contribution relative to the thermal plus zero point energy, which is already of order λ,

$$\mathscr{F}_4/\omega_D(n_D+\tfrac{1}{2}) \sim V_4\delta^4/\omega_D(n_D+\tfrac{1}{2}) \sim \lambda. \tag{3.25}$$

The same result is found for $\mathscr{F}_{33}$

$$\mathscr{F}_{33}/\omega_D(n_D+\tfrac{1}{2}) \sim V_3^2\delta^6\{\omega_D(n_D+\tfrac{1}{2})\}^2 \sim \lambda, \tag{3.26}$$

where the second factor $\{\omega_D(n_D+\tfrac{1}{2})\}^{-1}$ comes from the exponentials and energy denominators in the curly bracket of eq. (3.18).

In general we can show that the relative contribution of a diagram of $\mathscr{F}$ containing l propagators and m vertices is of order

$$\mathscr{F}(l, m)/\omega_D(n_D+\tfrac{1}{2}) \sim \lambda^{l-m}. \tag{3.27}$$

The same arguments can be used for the phonon self energy. The order of a diagram containing l internal lines and m vertices is

$$\mathscr{M}(l, m)/m\omega_D^2 \sim \lambda^{l-m+1}. \tag{3.28}$$

To investigate the convergence of the anharmonic expansion we will make a more specific choice of the potential

$$V(r) = V_0(\alpha/r)^n. \tag{3.29}$$

The Lennard–Jones potential, commonly used for rare-gas crystals, is a sum of two such potentials where the most singular part with $n=12$ dominates the higher order derivatives. The order of magnitude of the νth derivative is

$$V_\nu/V_0 = \{(n+\nu-1)!/(n-1)!\, n^\nu\}\,\sigma^{-\nu}, \qquad \sigma = a/n, \tag{3.30}$$

where σ has been choosen such that the numerical factor is of order unity, at least for $\nu \lesssim n$.

For a Lennard–Jones potential σ is only one twelfth of the lattice constant a. This means the expansion parameter is of order unity if the mean square fluctuations δ reach this value. It is interesting to note that this value agrees pretty well with the limit given by the Lindemann melting criterion.

We will now examine several classes of diagrams with respect to their convergence properties. Let us start with diagrams of $\mathscr{M}$ of the form shown in fig. 2. This class of diagrams is generated integrating eq. (2.49) and using the first term of eq. (2.50) only to determine the next order diagram. If the numerical factor in front of the diagram with l^{-1} lines is n_{l-1}, the factor for the

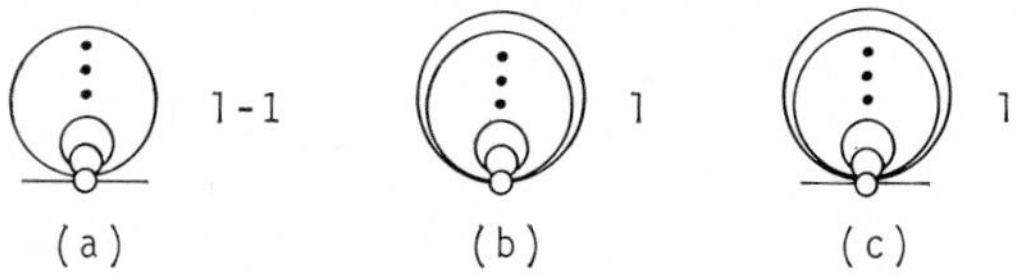

Fig. 2. Diagrams contributing to $\mathscr{M}$ (a, c) and Ψ (b).

diagram with l lines is, assuming $n_1 = \frac{1}{2}$,

$$n_l = n_{l-1}/2l = 1/2^l l! . \qquad (3.31)$$

The contribution of such a diagram with l lines is of order

$$\mathscr{M}_l(l, 1)/m\omega_D^2 \sim \{(n + 2l + 1)!/n!n^{2l+1}2^l l!\} \lambda^l \xrightarrow[l\to\infty]{} (l\lambda/n^2)^l . \qquad (3.32)$$

The numerical factor is of order unity for $l \lesssim n$ and for $\lambda < 1$ the contributions of consecuting diagrams decrease with increasing l. For $l > n$, however, the numerical factor increases and from some l on the contributions will increase again, resulting finally in a divergent series for any $\lambda \neq 0$. This means the class of diagrams shown in fig. 2 is at best semiconvergent.

Similar arguments can be applied to the class of diagrams shown in fig. 3. They are again generated integrating eq. (2.49) and using the first term of

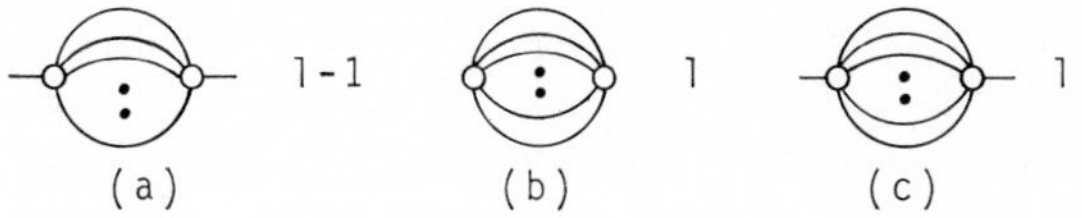

Fig. 3. Diagrams contributing to $\mathscr{M}$ (a, c) and Ψ (b).

eq. (2.50) to determine the next order, where the two derivatives with respect to $d^{(1)}$ have to be executed one at each vertex. The order of magnitude of such a diagram with $l+1$ lines is

$$\mathscr{M}_l(l + 1, 2)/m\omega_D^2 \sim \{(n + l + 1)!^2/n!^2 \, n^{2l+2} \, l!\} \lambda^l \xrightarrow[l\to\infty]{} (l\lambda/2n^2)^l . \qquad (3.33)$$

This means this class of diagrams is also diverging, but giving rise to a slightly weaker singularity.

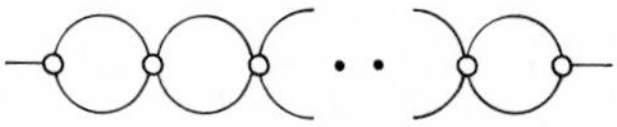

Fig. 4. Diagram contributing to $\mathscr{M}$.

A third class of diagrams which shall be investigated is shown in fig. 4 and is generated from eqs. (2.50) and (2.51) iterating (2.51) with $\delta\mathscr{M}(12)/\delta d(\overline{1}\overline{2}) = \phi(12\overline{1}\overline{2})$. The order of magnitude of such a diagram with l loops is

$$\mathscr{M}_l(2l + 1, l + 1)/m\omega_D^2$$
$$\sim \{(n + 2)!^2 \, (n + 3)!^{l-1}/2^l n!^{l+1} \, n^{3l+4}\} \lambda^l \xrightarrow[l\to\infty]{} (\tfrac{1}{2}\lambda)^l . \qquad (3.34)$$

This means this class of diagrams converges for $\lambda < 2$.

It should be mentioned that this class of diagrams shows another type of singularity for small $\boldsymbol{k}$ and ω which is connected with transport properties. In general it can be said that in a particular order l, for $l \to \infty$, the diagrams with the smallest number of vertices will diverge most. Furthermore any class of diagrams will at best lead to a semiconvergent or asymptotic expansion unless the number of vertices in each order grows proportional to the order. The diagrams of fig. 4 are of this latter kind.

On the other hand, at least for small enough λ, one might have to go to rather high orders in a particular class to see the diverging character of this class of diagrams. This makes the question of convergency an academic one for small λ.

We are, however, interested in strongly anharmonic crystals, this means $\lambda \sim 1$. Here our considerations might give us some hint which diagrams are most dangerous. Our goal therefore will be to introduce partially renormalized vertices summing up certain classes of diagrams and to find an anharmonic expansion in terms of these new effective coupling constants.

Since these vertices will be found by some averaging procedure we can also hope that the characteristic length will be larger than the one for the bare vertices, eq. (3.3). This will give a better convergence of the residual anharmonic expansion for non-singular interactions also.

3.3. Renormalized harmonic theory

The starting point for the conventional anharmonic theory was a pair correlation function with δ-function character. The next step is to include zero-point and thermal vibrations in $g(\boldsymbol{r})$ at least in a harmonic approximation. This is done formally by including the two-point functions also in determining the pair correlation function, eq. (2.27),

$$g_{\mathrm{h}}(l\kappa\, l'\kappa'; \boldsymbol{r}t) = (2\pi)^{-3} \int \mathrm{d}^3 k \exp[\mathrm{i}\boldsymbol{k}\cdot\{\boldsymbol{r} - \boldsymbol{d}(l\kappa t) + \boldsymbol{d}(l'\kappa' t)\}]$$
$$\times \exp[-\tfrac{1}{2}\boldsymbol{k}\cdot\{\boldsymbol{d}(l\kappa t, l\kappa t) + \boldsymbol{d}(l'\kappa' t, l'\kappa' t) - 2\boldsymbol{d}(l\kappa t, l'\kappa' t)\}\cdot\boldsymbol{k}]. \quad (3.35)$$

Since the integrand is a gaussian its Fourier transform is also a gaussian. In equilibrium

$$g_{\mathrm{h}}(l\kappa\, l'\kappa'; \boldsymbol{r}) = \pi^{-3} |\det \boldsymbol{\tau}(l\kappa\, l'\kappa')|^{1/2}$$
$$\times \exp[-\{\boldsymbol{r} - \boldsymbol{X}(l\kappa) + \boldsymbol{X}(l'\kappa')\}\cdot\boldsymbol{\tau}(l\kappa\, l'\kappa')\cdot\{\boldsymbol{r} - \boldsymbol{X}(l\kappa) + \boldsymbol{X}(l'\kappa')\}], \quad (3.36)$$

where

$$\boldsymbol{\tau}(l\kappa\, l'\kappa') = \tfrac{1}{2}\{\boldsymbol{d}(l\kappa t, l\kappa t) - \boldsymbol{d}(l\kappa t, l'\kappa' t)$$
$$- \boldsymbol{d}(l'\kappa' t, l\kappa t) + \boldsymbol{d}(l'\kappa' t, l'\kappa' t)\}^{-1}. \quad (3.37)$$

Inserting this form in eq. (2.26) the lowest order of $\mathscr{K}$ is found. A formal integration of eq. (2.48) yields

$$\Psi = \phi_h = (-1/2i\beta) \sum_{l\kappa} \sum_{l'\kappa'}' \int_0^{-i\beta} dt \int d^3r\, g_h(l\kappa\, l'\kappa'; rt)\, V(\kappa\kappa'; r) \tag{3.38}$$

which is the potential energy of the crystal under the assumption that the pair correlation function is harmonic.

We can introduce new coupling parameters analogous to eq. (3.3)

$$\begin{aligned}\phi_h(1\cdot\cdot\nu) &= -i\beta\delta^\nu \phi_h/\delta d(1)\cdot\cdot\delta d(\nu)|_{d(2)} \\ &= \tfrac{1}{2} \sum_{l\kappa} \sum_{l'\kappa'} \int_0^{-i\beta} dt \int d^3r\, g_h(l\kappa\, l'\kappa'; rt)\, (\hat{\boldsymbol{\delta}}(1)\cdot\nabla)\cdot\cdot(\hat{\boldsymbol{\delta}}(\nu)\cdot\nabla)\, V(\kappa\kappa'; r).\end{aligned} \tag{3.39}$$

where we have integrated by parts to obtain the second line and used again $\hat{\boldsymbol{\delta}}$ introduced following eq. (2.27). Since g_h now depends on the two-point functions as well, we have the identity

$$-2i\beta\delta\phi_h/\delta d(12) = -i\beta\delta^2\phi_h/\delta d(1)\,\delta d(2). \tag{3.40}$$

Turning the same crank as in the case of the conventional anharmonic expansion we obtain residual anharmonic corrections

$$\Psi = \phi_h + (1/12\beta)\, \phi_h(\overline{123})\, d(\overline{14})\, d(\overline{25})\, d(\overline{36})\, \phi_h(\overline{456}). \tag{3.41}$$

They have exactly the same form as the ones found in the conventional theory. Some of the diagrams, for instance $\mathscr{F}_4$, are, however contained in the definition of the renormalized vertices, eqs. (3.37) and (3.39), and do not show up explicitly any more.

The first residual anharmonic correction to the phonon self energy, responsible for damping, is

$$\mathscr{M}(12) = \phi_h(12) - \tfrac{1}{2}i\phi_h(1\overline{12})\, d(\overline{13})\, d(\overline{24})\, \phi_h(\overline{34}2). \tag{3.42}$$

Again the second term of eq. (3.11) is missing, this means it is contained in $\phi_h(12)$.

To calculate the first residual anharmonic corrections it is again sufficient to use the first term of the phonon self energy, eq. (3.42), only in determining the phonon propagators entering the anharmonic coupling constants and the anharmonic correction $\mathscr{F}_{33}$. Renormalized harmonic frequencies $\omega_h(\boldsymbol{k}\lambda)$ are introduced in exactly the same way as the harmonic frequencies $\omega_0(\boldsymbol{k}\lambda)$ given by eq. (3.6). The only difference is now that the second derivative of the potential is averaged with the gaussian, eq. (3.36).

The absence of the second and third term in Ψ, eq. (3.12), is reflected in the free energy

$$\mathscr{F} = \phi_{\mathrm{h}} + \sum_{\boldsymbol{k}\lambda} \left[\tfrac{1}{2}\omega_{\mathrm{h}}(\boldsymbol{k}\lambda)\left\{\tfrac{1}{2} - n(\omega_{\mathrm{h}}(\boldsymbol{k}\lambda))\right\} + (1/\beta)\ln\left(1 - \mathrm{e}^{-\beta\omega_{\mathrm{h}}(\boldsymbol{k}\lambda)}\right)\right] + \mathscr{F}_{\mathrm{h}33}, \quad (3.43)$$

where $\mathscr{F}_{\mathrm{h}33}$ has the same form as $\mathscr{F}_{33}$, eq. (3.18), with the derivatives of the potential replaced by their averages over the gaussian, eq. (3.36), and the harmonic frequencies $\omega_0(\boldsymbol{k}\lambda)$ replaced by the renormalized harmonic frequencies $\omega_{\mathrm{h}}(\boldsymbol{k}\lambda)$.

The next order corrections are given in diagrammatic form in fig. 5. A comparison with fig. 1 shows that the diagrams giving rise to the harmonic renormalization are now absent. The renormalized vertices are represented by open dots.

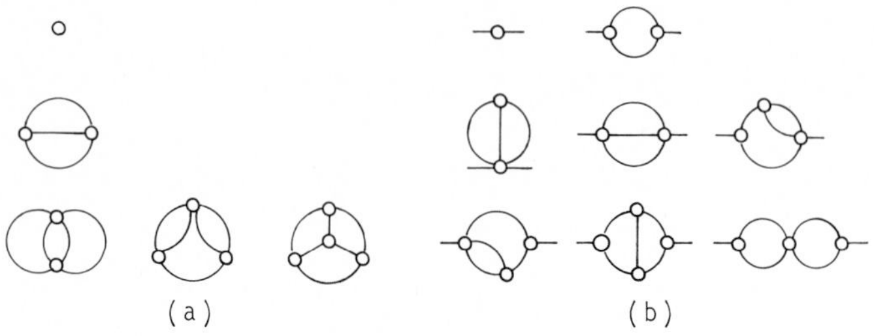

Fig. 5. The first diagrams of Ψ (a) and $\mathscr{M}$ (b).

The classification of the diagrams can again be done following the scheme discussed in the previous section. The length σ, characteristic for the potential will, however, changes since the bare vertices are replaced by averaged quantities. At least for some types of interactions σ will increase due to this average resulting in a smaller expansion coefficient.

However, it might also be that the convergency is worsened. Especially for hard core interactions this method is completely inadequate since the gaussian average diverges. In practice this difficulty is often circumvented by effective non-singular interactions in one form or another.

In situations as in solid helium conventional perturbation theory is completely inapplicable since already its starting point, the harmonic approximation, gives imaginary frequencies. This is because the second derivative of the potential is negative at the position of the next neighbours and of all others, resulting in a negative phonon self energy, eq. (3.6). At distances slightly shorter than the next neighbour distance, however, the second derivative becomes positive and the gaussian average can actually change the sign of the harmonic coupling constant resulting in real renormalized harmonic frequencies.

3.4. Expansion in instantaneous renormalized vertices

Searching for a method which is capable to handle hard core interactions, it is tempting to use renormalized vertices which are now averaged over the actual pair correlation function, as discussed by Horner (1966), and Beck and Meier (1971). Disregarding for a moment the difficulty to find this function we use as the lowest order for Ψ the potential energy

$$\Psi = \phi = (-1/2\mathrm{i}\beta) \sum_{l\kappa} \sum_{l'\kappa'}' \int_0^{-\mathrm{i}\beta} \mathrm{d}t \int \mathrm{d}^3 r\, g(l\kappa\, l'\kappa'; \boldsymbol{r}t)\, V(\kappa\kappa'; r). \tag{3.44}$$

Since $g(\boldsymbol{r})$ is now the true pair correlation function, ϕ is perfectly finite even for hard core interactions. According to eq. (2.27) the pair correlation, and with it ϕ, depends on all n-point functions. Renormalized vertices are introduced in the same way as before, eq. (3.39)

$$\phi(1 \cdots \nu) = -\mathrm{i}\beta\delta^{\nu}\phi/\delta d(1) \cdots \delta d(\nu)\big|_{d(2)d(3)\ldots}$$
$$= \tfrac{1}{2} \sum_{l\kappa} \sum_{l'\kappa'}' \int_0^{-\mathrm{i}\beta} \mathrm{d}t \int \mathrm{d}^3 r\, g(l\kappa\, l'\kappa'; \boldsymbol{r}t)\, \hat{\delta}(1)\cdot\nabla \cdots \hat{\delta}(\nu)\cdot\nabla V(\kappa\kappa'; r). \tag{3.45}$$

Since g is the true pair correlation function we have the exact results

$$\mathscr{K}(1) = \phi(1) \tag{3.46}$$

and for the instantaneous contribution to the phonon self-energy, eqs. (2.41) and (2.42),

$$\mathscr{M}^0(12) = \phi(12). \tag{3.47}$$

Differentiating with respect to higher n-point functions the same vertices can be obtained

$$\left.\frac{-2\mathrm{i}\beta\delta\phi}{\delta d(12)}\right|_{d(1)d(3)\ldots} = \phi(12), \qquad \left.\frac{-3!\,\mathrm{i}\beta\delta\phi}{\delta d(123)}\right|_{d(1)d(2)d(4)\ldots} = \phi(123). \tag{3.48}$$

The method to generate higher order corrections is now slightly different. Differentiating ϕ with respect to $d^{(1)}$ but keeping only $d^{(2)}$ fixed, this means taking into account that $d^{(3)}, \cdots$ are functionals of $d^{(1)}$, we obtain

$$\left.\frac{-\,\mathrm{i}\beta\delta\phi}{\delta d(1)}\right|_{d^{(2)}} = \phi(1) + (1/3!)\,\phi(\overline{1}\overline{2}\overline{3})\left.\frac{\delta d(\overline{1}\overline{2}\overline{3})}{\delta d(1)}\right|_{d^{(2)}} + \cdots. \tag{3.49}$$

On the other hand the first term is already the exact result for $\mathscr{K}(1)$, eq. (3.46). This means there has to be a higher order contribution to Ψ cancelling the second and higher terms in eq. (3.49).

The lowest order to the three-point function is calculated from eq. (2.15) analogous to eq. (2.50)

$$d(123) = d(1\overline{1})\,d(2\overline{2})\left.\frac{\delta\mathscr{M}(\overline{1}\overline{2})}{\delta f^{(1)}(3)}\right|_{f^{(2)}} = -\,\mathrm{i}d(1\overline{1})\,d(2\overline{2})\,d(3\overline{3})\,\phi(\overline{1}\overline{2}\overline{3}) + \cdots. \tag{3.50}$$

Including the first residual anharmonic correction, Ψ has to be

$$\Psi = \phi - (1/12\beta)\,\phi(\overline{1}\overline{2}\overline{3})\,d(\overline{1}\overline{4})\,d(\overline{2}\overline{5})\,d(\overline{3}\overline{6})\,\phi(\overline{4}\overline{5}\overline{6}) \tag{3.51}$$

such that the exact $\mathscr{K}(1)$ is reproduced, at least in this order, from eq. (2.48). A comparison with the result of the renormalized harmonic theory, eq. (3.41), shows the opposite sign for the second term. This means such a correction is contained in ϕ already twice.

The first order residual anharmonic correction to the phonon self-energy is now of the same form as before

$$\mathscr{M}(12) = \phi(12) - \tfrac{1}{2}\mathrm{i}\phi(1\overline{1}\overline{2})\,d(\overline{1}\overline{3})\,d(\overline{2}\overline{4})\,\phi(\overline{3}\overline{4}2), \tag{3.52}$$

but with the new vertices, eq. (3.45). The diagrams up to second order are shown in fig. 6, where the vertices are again represented by open dots.

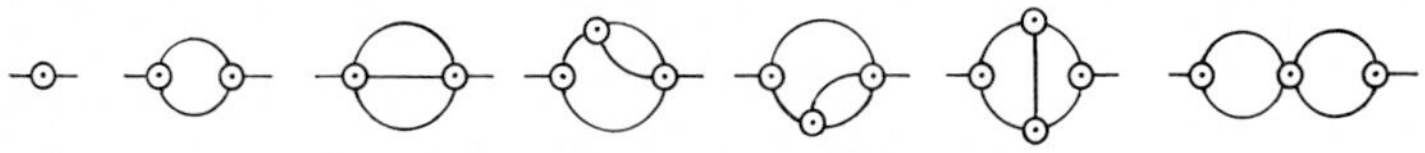

Fig. 6. The first diagrams of $\mathscr{M}$.

The usefulness of this scheme in the context of singular interactions will now turn out to be a rather delicate question. Let us start our investigations again with an inverse power potential

$$V(r) = V_0(\sigma/r)^n \tag{3.53}$$

and let us consider zero temperature for a moment. At short distances $g(\boldsymbol{r})$

will be of the form

$$g(r) \xrightarrow[r\to 0]{} \varphi_0^2(r), \tag{3.54}$$

where φ_0 is the scattering solution of an isolated pair of particles

$$\left\{\frac{\partial^2}{\partial r^2} + \frac{2}{r}\frac{\partial}{\partial r} - 2\hat{m}V(r)\right\}\varphi_0(r) = 0 \tag{3.55}$$

and $\hat{m}$ its reduced mass. For the potential, eq. (3.53), the asymptotic form of $\varphi_0(r)$ is

$$\varphi_0(r) \xrightarrow[r\to 0]{} \exp\{-(2\hat{m}V_0\sigma^n)^{1/2}\, r^{1-n/2}\}. \tag{3.56}$$

Since this quantity approaches zero for $r \to 0$ more rapidly than any power of r, all vertices, eq. (3.45) exist.

A rigorous hard sphere potential can be considered as the limit $V_0 \to \infty$ of a potential

$$V(r) = \begin{cases} V_0, & r < \sigma \\ 0, & r \geqslant \sigma. \end{cases} \tag{3.57}$$

Inside the hard core radius σ, $\varphi_0(r)$ will be

$$\varphi_0(r) = (2mV_0)^{-1/2} \exp\{-(2mV_0)^{1/2}(\sigma - r)\}, \qquad r < \sigma, \tag{3.58}$$

and

$$g(r) \sim (2mV_0)^{-1} \exp\{-2(2mV_0)^{1/2}(\sigma - r)\}, \qquad r < \sigma. \tag{3.59}$$

Integrating eq. (3.45) by parts the order of magnitude of a vertex of order ν is found to be

$$\phi^{(\nu)} \sim \int_0^\sigma r^2\, \mathrm{d}r\, (V_0/2mV_0)\, (2mV_0)^{\nu/2} \exp\{-2(2mV_0)^{\frac{1}{2}}(\sigma - r)\}$$
$$\sim V_0^{(\nu-1)/2}. \tag{3.65}$$

This means for a rigorous hard sphere potential only $\phi(1) = \mathscr{K}(1)$ is finite and all the higher order vertices diverge. Especially the instantaneous contribution to the phonon self energy, eq. (3.47) and (2.41) diverges and with it the third moment sum rule, eq. (2.39). This was observed by Kleban (1971).

Of course a hard sphere potential might be considered as a rather pathological interaction. Nevertheless the divergency of the second and higher order vertices can indicate a poor convergency in the case of a less pathological hard core interaction, for instance a Lennard–Jones potential. In this context we have to have in mind that a hard sphere potential is also the limit $n \to \infty$ of the inverse power potential, eq. (3.53).

4. Hard core interactions

Up to this point we have paid attention primarily to the interaction of collective excitations. Essentially nothing was said about the pair correlation function, especially at small distances, and how to determine it. It is quite obvious that the correct asymptotic behaviour at short distances, for example eqs. (3.56 and 3.59), can not be achieved including n-point functions of any finite order only in determining $g(\boldsymbol{r})$, eq. (2.27).

The distribution function of a given pair of particles will be ruled at short distances by the direct interaction between these two particles and the remaining particles will contribute only some kind of a potential well in which the pair moves. The idea is to construct some effective pair hamiltonian

$$\hat{h}(l\kappa\, l'\kappa') = \frac{\hat{\boldsymbol{p}}^2(l\kappa\, l'\kappa')}{2\hat{m}(\kappa\kappa')} + V(\kappa\kappa'; |\hat{\boldsymbol{x}}(l\kappa\, l'\kappa')|) + \hat{W}(l\kappa\, l'\kappa') \tag{4.1}$$

and to identify the pair correlation function with the one calculated from $\hat{h}$. Since $g(\boldsymbol{r})$ depends only on the relative coordinate we have writen $\hat{h}$ only for the corresponding operator $\hat{\boldsymbol{x}}$ and the relative momentum $\hat{\boldsymbol{p}}$; $\hat{m}$ is the reduced mass and $\hat{W}$ describes the residual interaction produced by the remaining particles. The problem is, of course, to find $\hat{W}$.

At first sight this approach seems intimately connected with one of the various forms of a scattering matrix approximation which have been derived for quantum crystals by Brueckner and Frohberg (1965), Iwamoto and Namaizawa (1966, 1971), Guyer (1969), Horner (1970), Ebner and Sung (1971), Brandow (1971) and Glyde and Khanna (1971). The differences among those papers the approach presented in the following is, however, hidden in details, for instance the determination of $\hat{W}$ and whether $\hat{h}$ is used to determine a scattering matrix or to find an approximative form of the pair correlation function, as in our case. Unfortunately both questions are connected and what appears to be correct in one case is not necessarily so for the other.

We will not discuss the scattering matrix approach further since no completely satisfactory and tractable way has been found so far to incorporate collective excitations, although this should be possible in principle.

4.1. Effective pair hamiltonian

We will concentrate now on a particular pair of particles at lattice site $\{l\kappa\}$ and $\{l'\kappa'\}$, respectively. We introduce its relative coordinate

$$\hat{\boldsymbol{x}}(l\kappa\, l'\kappa'; t) = \hat{\boldsymbol{x}}(t) = \boldsymbol{x}(l\kappa t) - \boldsymbol{x}(l'\kappa' t), \tag{4.2}$$

its relative momentum

$$\hat{\boldsymbol{p}}(l\kappa\, l'\kappa'; t) = \hat{\boldsymbol{p}}(t) = \frac{m(\kappa')\, \boldsymbol{p}(l\kappa t) - m(\kappa)\, \boldsymbol{p}(l'\kappa' t)}{m(\kappa) + m(\kappa')} \tag{4.3}$$

and its reduced mass

$$\hat{m}(\kappa\kappa') = \frac{m(\kappa)\, m(\kappa')}{m(\kappa) + m(\kappa')} = \hat{m}\,. \tag{4.4}$$

In the absence of all the other particles the relative motion would be described by

$$\hat{h}_0(l\kappa\, l'\kappa') = \frac{\hat{\boldsymbol{p}}^2(l\kappa\, l'\kappa')}{2\hat{m}(\kappa\kappa')} + V(\kappa\kappa'; |\hat{\boldsymbol{x}}(l\kappa\, l'\kappa')|), \tag{4.5}$$

whereas some residual interaction has to be added in the presence of the other particles.

To get some idea about this residual interaction let us investigate the pair correlation function, eq. (2.25), or any other expectation value of an operator depending on the relative coordinate of the given pair only

$$g_f(l\kappa\, l'\kappa'; \boldsymbol{r}t) = \hat{g}(\boldsymbol{r}t) = \operatorname{tr} T\, \delta(\boldsymbol{r} - \hat{\boldsymbol{x}}(t)) \\ \times \frac{\exp[-\mathrm{i}\,\{\int_0^{-\mathrm{i}\beta} \mathrm{d}\tau\, H(\tau) + f(\bar{1})\, \hat{x}(\bar{1}) + \frac{1}{2}x(\bar{1})\, f(\bar{1}\bar{2})\, x(\bar{2})\}]}{\operatorname{tr} T \exp[\ldots]}. \tag{4.6}$$

In principle we can evaluate the trace with respect to all particles, except the relative motion of the particular pair under consideration. This leads to

$$\hat{g}(\boldsymbol{r}t) = \hat{\mathrm{tr}}\, T\, \delta(\boldsymbol{r} - \hat{\boldsymbol{x}}(t))$$
$$\times \exp\Big[-\mathrm{i} \int_0^{-\mathrm{i}\beta} \mathrm{d}\tau \Big\{\hat{h}_0(\tau) + \hat{\boldsymbol{f}}^{(1)}(\tau)\cdot\hat{\boldsymbol{x}}(\tau)$$
$$+ \tfrac{1}{2} \int_0^{-\mathrm{i}\beta} \mathrm{d}\tau'\, \hat{\boldsymbol{x}}(\tau)\cdot\hat{\boldsymbol{f}}^{(2)}(\tau\tau')\cdot\hat{\boldsymbol{x}}(\tau') + \cdots\Big\}\Big] \Big/ \hat{\mathrm{tr}} \cdots, \tag{4.7}$$

where $\hat{\mathrm{tr}}$ is the trace over the relative coordinate. The residual interaction with the surrounding particles has been expanded and combined with the external forces. Here and in the following we suppress the indices $l\kappa\ l'\kappa'$.

In the same way we can calculate the one-point function

$$\hat{\boldsymbol{\delta}}^{(1)}(t) = \boldsymbol{d}(l\kappa t) - \boldsymbol{d}(l'\kappa' t) = \int \mathrm{d}^3 r\, \boldsymbol{r}\hat{g}(\boldsymbol{r}t), \tag{4.8}$$

and the equal time two-point function

$$\hat{d}^{(2)}_{\alpha\beta}(t)$$
$$= d_{\alpha\beta}(l\kappa t, l\kappa t) - d_{\alpha\beta}(l\kappa t, l'\kappa' t) - d_{\alpha\beta}(l'\kappa' t, l\kappa t) + d_{\alpha\beta}(l'\kappa' t, l'\kappa' t)$$
$$= \int \mathrm{d}^3 r\, \{r_\alpha - \hat{d}^{(1)}_\alpha(t)\}\, \{r_\beta - \hat{d}^{(1)}_\beta(t)\}\, \hat{g}(\boldsymbol{r}t), \tag{4.9}$$

but also the corresponding higher order n-point functions for arbitrary times.

These functions will depend on the force constants $\hat{f}^{(1)}, \hat{f}^{(2)}, \cdots$. On the other hand they can be expressed by the ordinary n-point functions, eq. (2.15), and we can use just this identity to determine the residual force constants $\hat{f}^{(n)}$. It is obvious that for instance the second order $\hat{f}^{(2)}(tt')$ has to depend explicitly on t and t' to reproduce the full time dependent behaviour of $\hat{\boldsymbol{d}}^{(2)}(tt')$. This means the full residual interaction has to contain non-instantaneous parts.

We had the physical picture of the pair of particles moving in a well produced by the remaining particles. This well is, however, not rigid. The moving pair might excite phonons in the surrounding medium at one time and reabsorbe them at some other time. This is the physical picture of the non-instantaneous residual interaction.

As long as we are using the effective pair hamiltonian only to determine the pair correlation function it appears to be sufficient to consider an instantaneous residual interaction. As an additional approximation we expand it and retain only linear and quadratic terms in $\hat{x}$. With

$$\hat{\boldsymbol{f}}^{(2)}(tt') = \delta(t-t')\,\hat{\boldsymbol{f}}^{(2)}(t) \tag{4.10}$$

we introduce a functional analogous to the free enthalpy, eq. (2.10)

$$\hat{\mathscr{G}} = -(1/\beta) \times \ln \hat{\mathrm{tr}}\, T \exp\left[-\mathrm{i}\int_0^{-\mathrm{i}\beta} \mathrm{d}\tau\,\{\hat{h}_0(\tau) + \hat{\boldsymbol{f}}^{(1)}(\tau)\cdot\hat{\boldsymbol{x}}(\tau) + \tfrac{1}{2}\hat{\boldsymbol{x}}(\tau)\cdot\hat{\boldsymbol{f}}^{(2)}(\tau)\cdot\hat{\boldsymbol{x}}(\tau)\right]. \tag{4.11}$$

Since this is now a single particle problem we can hope to actually calculate $\hat{\mathscr{G}}$, say by numerical methods.

The derivatives of $\hat{\mathscr{G}}$ are, again, the n-point functions

$$\begin{aligned} \hat{\boldsymbol{d}}^{(1)}(t) &= -\,\mathrm{i}\beta\,\delta\hat{\mathscr{G}}/\delta\hat{\boldsymbol{f}}^{(1)}(t) \\ \hat{d}^{(2)}_{\alpha\beta}(t) + \hat{d}^{(1)}_{\alpha}(t)\,\hat{d}^{(1)}_{\beta}(t) &= -\,2\mathrm{i}\beta\,\delta/\hat{\mathscr{G}}\delta\hat{f}^{(2)}_{\alpha\beta}(t). \end{aligned} \tag{4.12}$$

Equations of motion are derived in the same way as before, eqs. (2.18) and (2.19),

$$\begin{aligned} -\,\hat{m}\,\partial^2\hat{\boldsymbol{d}}^{(1)}(t)/\partial t^2 &= \hat{\boldsymbol{f}}^{(1)}(t) + \hat{\boldsymbol{f}}^{(2)}(t)\cdot\hat{\boldsymbol{d}}^{(1)}(t) + \hat{\mathscr{K}}(t), \\ -\,\hat{m}\,\partial^2\hat{d}^{(2)}_{\alpha\beta}(t)/\partial t^2 &= \sum_{\gamma}[\{\hat{f}^{(2)}_{\alpha\gamma}(t) + \hat{\mathscr{L}}_{\alpha\gamma}(t)\}\,\hat{d}^{(2)}_{\gamma\beta}(t) \\ &\qquad + \{\hat{f}^{(2)}_{\beta\gamma}(t) + \hat{\mathscr{L}}_{\beta\gamma}(t)\}\,\hat{d}^{(2)}_{\gamma\alpha}(t)], \end{aligned} \tag{4.13}$$

where the second equation holds for the equal time two-point function. We have introduced

$$\hat{\mathscr{K}}(t) = \int \mathrm{d}^3 r\,\hat{g}(\boldsymbol{r}t)\,\boldsymbol{\nabla} V(\kappa\kappa';r), \tag{4.14}$$

and

$$\begin{aligned} \sum_{\gamma}\{\hat{\mathscr{L}}_{\alpha\gamma}(t)\,\hat{d}^{(2)}_{\gamma\beta}(t) + \hat{\mathscr{L}}_{\beta\gamma}(t)\,\hat{d}^{(2)}_{\gamma\alpha}(t)\} &= -\,(2/\hat{m})\,\{\langle\hat{p}_\alpha(t)\,\hat{p}_\beta(t)\rangle_{\hat{f}} - \langle\hat{p}_\alpha(t)\rangle_{\hat{f}}\,\langle\hat{p}_\beta(t)\rangle_{\hat{f}}\} \\ &+ \int \mathrm{d}^3 r\,\hat{g}(\boldsymbol{r}t)\,[\{r_\alpha - \hat{d}^{(1)}_\alpha(t)\}\,\nabla_\beta + \{r_\beta - \hat{d}^{(1)}_\beta(t)\}\,\nabla_\alpha]\,V(\kappa\kappa';r). \end{aligned} \tag{4.15}$$

Obviously the equations of motion can also be regarded as implicit equations for the force constants $\hat{\boldsymbol{f}}^{(1)}$ and $\hat{\boldsymbol{f}}^{(2)}$ at a given $\hat{\boldsymbol{d}}^{(1)}$ and $\hat{\boldsymbol{d}}^{(2)}$. These latter quantities are determined, of course, by the ordinary one- and two-point functions according to eqs. (4.8) and (4.9).

In equilibrium $\hat{\boldsymbol{d}}^{(1)}$ and $\hat{\boldsymbol{d}}^{(2)}$ are time-independent and with it $\hat{\boldsymbol{f}}^{(1)}(t)=\hat{\boldsymbol{f}}_0^{(1)}$ and $\hat{\boldsymbol{f}}^{(2)}(t)=\hat{\boldsymbol{f}}_0^{(2)}$. The effective pair hamiltonian, eq. (4.1), becomes

$$\hat{h} = (1/2\hat{m})\, \hat{\boldsymbol{p}}^2 + V(\kappa\kappa'; |\hat{\boldsymbol{x}}|) + \hat{\boldsymbol{f}}_0^{(1)}\cdot\hat{\boldsymbol{x}} + \tfrac{1}{2}\hat{\boldsymbol{x}}\cdot\hat{\boldsymbol{f}}_0^{(2)}\cdot\hat{\boldsymbol{x}}. \tag{4.16}$$

To actually calculate the equilibrium value of the pair correlation function we use the eigenfunctions of $\hat{h}$

$$\hat{h}\hat{\psi}_\lambda(r) = \hat{\varepsilon}_\lambda\hat{\psi}_\lambda(r) \tag{4.17}$$

and with it

$$\hat{g}(r) = \sum_\lambda \exp(-\beta\hat{\varepsilon}_\lambda)\, |\hat{\psi}_\lambda(r)|^2 / \sum_\lambda \exp(-\beta\hat{\varepsilon}_\lambda). \tag{4.18}$$

From the eigenfunctions we can also calculate

$$\begin{aligned}\langle\hat{p}_\alpha\hat{p}_\beta\rangle_{f_0} &= -\sum_\lambda \exp(-\beta\hat{\varepsilon}_\lambda) \int \mathrm{d}^3 r\, \hat{\psi}^*_\lambda(r)\, \nabla_\alpha\nabla_\beta\hat{\psi}_\lambda(r) / \sum_\lambda \exp(-\beta\hat{\varepsilon}_\lambda),\\ \langle\hat{p}_\alpha\rangle_{f_0} &= 0,\end{aligned} \tag{4.19}$$

and with it $\mathscr{L}$, and of course $\hat{\mathscr{K}}$. To determine the force constants for some given $\hat{\boldsymbol{d}}^{(1)}$ and $\hat{\boldsymbol{d}}^{(2)}$ a selfconsistent solution of the equations of motion, eq. (4.13) has to be found, having in mind that the left-hand sides vanish in equilibrium.

The pair correlation function obtained here has several attractive features. By construction the mean interparticle distance and the mean square displacements agree with the values calculated from the ordinary n-point functions. Furthermore $\hat{g}(\boldsymbol{r})$ has the correct asymptotic behaviour at short distances. Generalizations of this method are possible in two directions, at least in principle. Considering only an instantaneous residual interaction higher order expansions, this means higher order $\hat{f}^{(\nu)}$ can be included. They have to be determined such that consistency with higher order equal time n-point functions is achieved. The limitation is in the rather tedious calculation of those functions. On the other hand non-instantaneous contributions could be included and determined such that consistency with the time dependent Green's functions is obtained. The limitation here is that the problem in this case can not be reduced to an effective pair hamiltonian and the corresponding Schrödinger equation, (4.17).

We would like to remind that the indices $l\kappa\, l'\kappa'$ labeling a given pair of particles have been dropped throughout this paragraph. This means that for each non-equivalent pair different force constants $\hat{\boldsymbol{f}}_0^{(\nu)}(l\kappa\, l'\kappa')$ have to be determined and with it the solutions to the pair Schrödinger equation. In practice, however, it will be sufficient to do this only for the first or perhaps the second shell of neighbours.

4.2. Phonon self-energy

Having found the pair correlation function, at least in equilibrium, we could use the renormalization scheme discussed in § 3.4, determine $\mathscr{K}$ and $\mathscr{M}$ up to any desired order and determine $d^{(1)}$ and $d^{(2)}$ selfconsistently.

On the other hand we have argued that this scheme fails for a rigorous hard sphere interaction and might still, lead to a poorly convergent series in case of a less pathological hard core interaction.

In the following we discuss the first steps in a new renormalization scheme, which, already in lowest order, contains contributions from all diverging classes of diagrams, for instance the ones shown in figs. 2 and 3. The resulting renormalized vertices will turn out to be finite even for a rigorous hard sphere interaction. They will, however, be energy dependent or, in other words, contain non-instantaneous contributions. This is actually what has to be expected since the expansion in rigorous instantaneous vertices, discussed in § 3.4, had led to divergencies.

The pair correlation function is, in the approximation of the previous paragraph, a functional of the one point function $\hat{\boldsymbol{d}}^{(1)}(t)$ and of the equal time two-point function $\hat{\boldsymbol{d}}^{(2)}(t)$. For the phonon self-energy, eq. (2.50) we have to know the derivatives $\delta\hat{g}(\boldsymbol{r}t)/\delta\hat{\boldsymbol{d}}(t)$, where $\hat{\boldsymbol{d}}(t)$ is the one- or two-point function. We introduce its Fourier transform assuming again periodicity in time

$$\frac{\delta\hat{g}(\boldsymbol{r}z_\nu)}{\delta\hat{\boldsymbol{d}}(z_\nu)} = \int_0^{-\mathrm{i}\beta} \mathrm{d}t\, \mathrm{e}^{\mathrm{i}z_\nu t}\, \delta\hat{g}(\boldsymbol{r}t)/\delta\hat{d}(0). \tag{4.20}$$

Actually $\hat{g}(\boldsymbol{r}t)$ is a functional of the forces $\hat{f}(t)$ which themselves depend on the one- and two-point functions $\hat{\boldsymbol{d}}(t)$. This can easily be taken into account

$$\delta\hat{g}(\boldsymbol{r}z)/\delta\hat{d}^{(1)}_\alpha(z)\big|_{\hat{d}^{(2)}}$$
$$= \sum_\beta \frac{\delta\hat{g}(\boldsymbol{r}z)}{\delta\hat{f}^{(1)}_\beta(z)}\bigg|_{\hat{f}^{(2)}} \frac{\delta\hat{f}^{(1)}_\beta(z)}{\delta\hat{d}^{(1)}_\alpha(z)}\bigg|_{\hat{d}^{(2)}} + \sum_{\beta\gamma} \frac{\delta\hat{g}(\boldsymbol{r}z)}{\delta\hat{f}^{(2)}_{\beta\gamma}(z)}\bigg|_{\hat{f}^{(1)}} \frac{\delta\hat{f}^{(2)}_{\beta\gamma}(z)}{\delta\hat{d}^{(1)}_\alpha(z)}\bigg|_{\hat{d}^{(2)}}. \tag{4.21}$$

A corresponding expression exists for the derivative with respect to $\hat{d}^{(2)}$. The derivatives of the forces with respect to $\hat{d}^{(1)}$ and $\hat{d}^{(2)}$ are easily calculated from $\delta\hat{g}/\delta\hat{\boldsymbol{f}}$ using the identity

$$[\delta\hat{\boldsymbol{f}}(z)/\delta\hat{\boldsymbol{d}}(z)] = [\delta\hat{\boldsymbol{d}}(z)/\delta\hat{\boldsymbol{f}}(z)]^{-1}, \tag{4.22}$$

where $(\delta\hat{\boldsymbol{f}}(z)/\delta\hat{\boldsymbol{d}}(z))$ is a matrix made up of the derivatives of the components of $\hat{\boldsymbol{f}}^{(1)}(z)$ and $\hat{\boldsymbol{f}}^{(2)}(z)$ with respect to the components of $\hat{\boldsymbol{d}}^{(1)}(z)$ and $\hat{\boldsymbol{d}}^{(2)}(z)$. The right-hand side is the matrix inverse of the corresponding matrix $(\delta\hat{\boldsymbol{d}}(z)/\delta\hat{\boldsymbol{f}}(z))$. Its elements are easily calculated from $\delta\hat{g}(\boldsymbol{r}z)/\delta\hat{\boldsymbol{f}}(z)$. This latter quantity has now to be calculated. We evaluate the trace in eq. (4.7) in the basis given by the $\hat{\psi}_\lambda$

$$\begin{aligned}\hat{g}(\boldsymbol{r}t) = \sum_\lambda \Big\langle \hat{\psi}_\lambda \Big| \Big[T \exp\Big\{ -\mathrm{i} \int_t^{-\mathrm{i}\beta} \mathrm{d}\tau \big(\hat{h}(\tau) + \delta\hat{\boldsymbol{f}}^{(1)}(\tau)\cdot\hat{\boldsymbol{x}}(\tau) \\ + \tfrac{1}{2}\hat{\boldsymbol{x}}(\tau)\cdot\delta\hat{\boldsymbol{f}}^{(2)}(\tau)\cdot\hat{\boldsymbol{x}}(\tau)\big)\Big\}\Big]\, \delta(\boldsymbol{r}-\hat{\boldsymbol{x}}) \Big[T\exp\Big\{-\mathrm{i}\int_0^t \mathrm{d}\tau \cdots\Big\}\Big]\Big| \hat{\psi}_\lambda \Big\rangle \\ \Big/ \sum_\lambda \Big\langle \hat{\psi}_\lambda \Big| T\exp\Big\{-\mathrm{i}\int_0^{-\mathrm{i}\beta} \mathrm{d}\tau \cdots\Big\}\Big| \hat{\psi}_\lambda \Big\rangle \\ = \sum_\lambda \tilde{\psi}^*_\lambda(\boldsymbol{r}, t+\mathrm{i}\beta)\, \tilde{\psi}_\lambda(\boldsymbol{r}, t) \Big/ \sum_\lambda \langle \tilde{\psi}_\lambda(0) | \tilde{\psi}_\lambda(-\mathrm{i}\beta)\rangle,\end{aligned} \tag{4.23}$$

where $\hat{f}(t) = \hat{f}_0 + \delta\hat{f}(t)$ is assumed. The time dependent wave functions are

$$|\tilde{\psi}_\lambda(t)\rangle = T\exp\Big\{-\mathrm{i}\int_0^t \mathrm{d}\tau\big(\hat{h}(\tau) + \cdots\big)\Big\} |\hat{\psi}_\lambda\rangle, \tag{4.24}$$

and obey the equation of motion

$$\mathrm{i}\partial\tilde{\psi}_\lambda(\boldsymbol{r}t)/\partial t = \{\hat{h} + \delta\hat{\boldsymbol{f}}^{(1)}\cdot\boldsymbol{r} + \tfrac{1}{2}\boldsymbol{r}\cdot\delta\hat{\boldsymbol{f}}^{(2)}\cdot\boldsymbol{r}\}\, \tilde{\psi}_\lambda(\boldsymbol{r}t). \tag{4.25}$$

For small $\delta\hat{f}(t)$ we can linearize, introducing

$$\tilde{\psi}_\lambda(\boldsymbol{r}t) = \exp(-\mathrm{i}\hat{\varepsilon}_\lambda t)\, \{\hat{\psi}_\lambda(\boldsymbol{r}) + \delta\chi_\lambda(\boldsymbol{r}t)\}, \tag{4.26}$$

and find the inhomogeneous differential equation

$$\{\mathrm{i}\partial/\partial t + \hat{\varepsilon}_\lambda - \hat{h}\}\, \delta\chi_\lambda(\boldsymbol{r}t) = \{\delta\hat{\boldsymbol{f}}^{(1)}(t)\cdot\boldsymbol{r} + \tfrac{1}{2}\boldsymbol{r}\cdot\delta\hat{\boldsymbol{f}}^{(2)}(t)\cdot\boldsymbol{r}\}\, \hat{\psi}_\lambda(\boldsymbol{r}). \tag{4.27}$$

For $\delta\hat{f}(t)$ periodic in time we introduce again the Fourier coefficients

$$\chi_{\lambda\alpha}^{(1)}(\boldsymbol{r}z_\nu) = \int_0^{-\mathrm{i}\beta} \mathrm{d}\tau \exp(\mathrm{i}z_\nu\tau)\, \delta\chi_\lambda(\boldsymbol{r}\tau)/\delta\hat{f}_\alpha^{(1)}(0)\big|_{\hat{f}^{(2)}},$$
$$\chi_{\lambda\alpha\beta}^{(2)}(\boldsymbol{r}z_\nu) = \int_0^{-\mathrm{i}\beta} \mathrm{d}\tau \exp(\mathrm{i}z_\nu\tau)\, \delta\chi_\lambda(\boldsymbol{r}\tau)/\delta\hat{f}_{\alpha\beta}^{(2)}(0)\big|_{\hat{f}^{(1)}}, \tag{4.28}$$

which are solutions to

$$\{z + \hat{\varepsilon}_\lambda - \hat{h}\}\, \boldsymbol{\chi}_\lambda^{(1)}(\boldsymbol{r}z) = \boldsymbol{r}\hat{\psi}_\lambda(\boldsymbol{r}),$$
$$\{z + \hat{\varepsilon}_\lambda - \hat{h}\}\, \boldsymbol{\chi}_\lambda^{(2)}(\boldsymbol{r}z) = \boldsymbol{r}\boldsymbol{r}\hat{\psi}_\lambda(\boldsymbol{r}). \tag{4.29}$$

or, expanding χ in eigenfunctions to $\hat{h}$

$$\boldsymbol{\chi}_\lambda^{(1)}(\boldsymbol{r}z) = \sum_{\lambda'} \hat{\psi}_{\lambda'}(\boldsymbol{r})\, \langle\hat{\psi}_{\lambda'}|\, \boldsymbol{r}\, |\hat{\psi}_\lambda\rangle/(z - \hat{\varepsilon}_{\lambda'} + \hat{\varepsilon}_\lambda),$$
$$\boldsymbol{\chi}_\lambda^{(2)}(\boldsymbol{r}z) = \sum_{\lambda'} \hat{\psi}_{\lambda'}(\boldsymbol{r})\, \langle\hat{\psi}_{\lambda'}|\, \boldsymbol{r}\boldsymbol{r}\, |\hat{\psi}_\lambda\rangle/(z - \hat{\varepsilon}_{\lambda'} + \hat{\varepsilon}_\lambda). \tag{4.30}$$

Inserting these results in eq. (4.23) we find

$$\left.\frac{\delta\hat{g}(\boldsymbol{r}z)}{\delta\hat{\boldsymbol{f}}^{(1)}(z)}\right|_{\hat{f}^{(2)}} = \frac{\sum_\lambda \{\hat{\psi}_\lambda^*(\boldsymbol{r})\, \boldsymbol{\chi}_\lambda^{(1)}(\boldsymbol{r}z) + \boldsymbol{\chi}_\lambda^{*(1)}(\boldsymbol{r} - z)\, \hat{\psi}_\lambda(\boldsymbol{r})\} \exp(-\beta\hat{\varepsilon}_\lambda)}{\sum_\lambda \exp(-\beta\hat{\varepsilon}_\lambda)}$$
$$= \sum_{\lambda\lambda'} \hat{\psi}_\lambda^*(\boldsymbol{r})\, \hat{\psi}_{\lambda'}(\boldsymbol{r})\, \langle\hat{\psi}_{\lambda'}|\, \hat{\boldsymbol{x}}\, |\hat{\psi}_\lambda\rangle\, \mathscr{R}_{\lambda\lambda'}(z), \tag{4.31}$$

with

$$\mathscr{R}_{\lambda\lambda'}(z) = \frac{\exp(-\beta\hat{\varepsilon}_\lambda) - \exp(-\beta\hat{\varepsilon}_{\lambda'})}{z - \hat{\varepsilon}_{\lambda'} + \hat{\varepsilon}_\lambda} \cdot \frac{1}{\sum_{\lambda''} \exp(-\beta\hat{\varepsilon}_{\lambda''})} \tag{4.32}$$

and a corresponding result for the derivative with respect to $\hat{f}^{(2)}$.

The derivatives of $\hat{\mathscr{K}}$ with respect to the forces have the structure

$$\delta\hat{\mathscr{K}}(z)/\delta\hat{\boldsymbol{f}}^{(1,2)}(z)\big|_{\hat{f}^{(2,1)}}$$
$$= \sum_{\lambda\lambda'} \langle\hat{\psi}_\lambda|\nabla V(\kappa\kappa'; |\hat{\boldsymbol{x}}|)\, |\hat{\psi}_{\lambda'}\rangle\, \langle\hat{\psi}_{\lambda'}|\, \boldsymbol{y}^{(1,2)}\, |\hat{\psi}_\lambda\rangle\, \mathscr{R}_{\lambda\lambda'}(z), \tag{4.33}$$

where $\boldsymbol{y}^{(1)} = \hat{\boldsymbol{x}}$ and $\boldsymbol{y}^{(2)} = \hat{\boldsymbol{x}}\hat{\boldsymbol{x}}$, and corresponding

$$\delta\hat{d}_\alpha^{(1)}(z)/\delta\hat{\boldsymbol{f}}^{(1,2)}(z)\big|_{\hat{f}^{(2,1)}} = \sum_{\lambda\lambda'} \langle\hat{\psi}_\lambda|\hat{x}_\alpha|\, \hat{\psi}_{\lambda'}\rangle\, \langle\hat{\psi}_{\lambda'}|\boldsymbol{y}^{(1,2)}|\, \hat{\psi}_\lambda\rangle\, \mathscr{R}_{\lambda\lambda'}(z),$$
$$\delta\hat{d}_{\alpha\beta}^{(2)}(z)/\delta\hat{\boldsymbol{f}}^{(1,2)}(z)\big|_{\hat{f}^{(2,1)}} = \sum_{\lambda\lambda'} \langle\hat{\psi}_\lambda|\{\hat{x}_\alpha - \hat{d}_\alpha^{(1)}\}\, \{\hat{x}_\beta - \hat{d}_\beta^{(1)}\}\, |\hat{\psi}_{\lambda'}\rangle$$
$$\times \langle\hat{\psi}_{\lambda'}|\boldsymbol{y}^{(1,2)}\, |\hat{\psi}_\lambda\rangle\, \mathscr{R}_{\lambda\lambda'}(z). \tag{4.34}$$

This enables us to calculate $\delta\hat{\mathscr{K}}(t)/\delta\hat{\boldsymbol{d}}^{(1)}(t')|_{\hat{d}^{(2)}}$ according to eq. (4.21) and with it the first term of the phonon self energy, eq. (2.50).

Since the first matrix element in eq. (4.33) contains only the first derivative of the potential, its contribution will be finite even in the case of a rigorous hard sphere potential. This means the leading contribution to the phonon self-energy will be finite, at least for small z where the factor $\mathscr{R}_{\lambda\lambda'}(z)$ reduces the effect of highly excited pair states $\hat{\psi}_\lambda$ and $\hat{\psi}_{\lambda'}$ in eq. (4.33). This is, however, the interesting regime.

As a function of z eqs. (4.33) and (4.34) have poles at the real axis whenever $z=\hat{\varepsilon}_\lambda-\hat{\varepsilon}_{\lambda'}$. The inverse of eq. (4.34) has zeros at the same positions cancelling the poles of eq. (4.33) if for instance $\delta\hat{\mathscr{K}}/\delta\hat{\boldsymbol{d}}$ is calculated from eq. (4.21). This means this quantity is regular at $z=\hat{\varepsilon}_\lambda-\hat{\varepsilon}_{\lambda'}$. There are, however, zeros in eq. (4.34) which show up as poles in its inverse and also in $\delta\hat{\mathscr{K}}/\delta\hat{\boldsymbol{d}}$. They are unphysical and a consequence of the fact that non-instantaneous contributions to the residual interaction were omitted. In other words we had assumed a rigid well produced by the surrounding particles. If non-instantaneous residual forces were included, this means if the rigidity of the well would be relaxed, excited pair states could decay emitting phonons into the medium. This would shift the poles and zeros away from the real axis into the unphysical sheet of the complex z plane leaving a branch cut along the real axis.

In practice these poles are rather unimportant since the first one appears at approximately twice the Debye frequency, this means above the one-phonon spectrum. Furthermore its residue is small. The qualitative behaviour of the real part of $\hat{\mathscr{M}}(z)=\delta\hat{\mathscr{K}}(z)/\delta\hat{\boldsymbol{d}}(z)$ is sketched for real $z=\omega$ in fig. 7, dashed curve. The solid line is expected if non-instantaneous residual forces were included.

We will now briefly discuss the behaviour in the limit $z\to\infty$ to see whether the correct instantaneous contribution to the phonon self energy is obtained

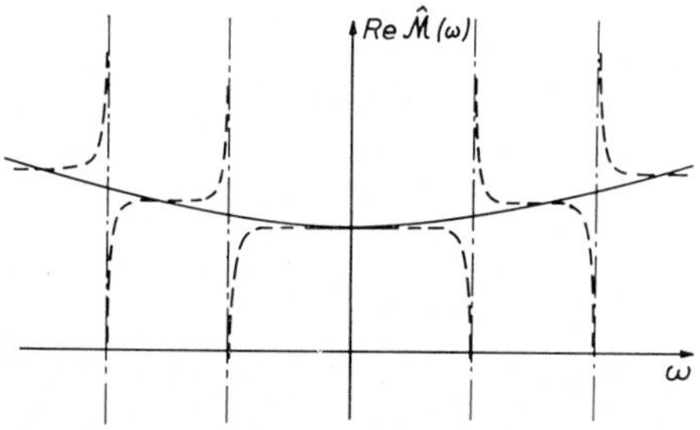

Fig. 7. Qualitative behaviour of Re $\hat{\mathscr{M}}(\omega)$ as a function of ω.

from the present approximation. Starting with eq. (4.31) we expand $\mathscr{R}_{\lambda\lambda'}(z)$, eq. (4.32), in powers of z^{-1}. Due to symmetry with respect to λ and λ' the first non-vanishing contribution is

$$\begin{aligned} z^2\,\delta\hat{g}(\boldsymbol{r}z)/\delta\hat{\boldsymbol{f}}^{(1)}(z)\big|_{\hat{f}^{(2)}} &\to \langle[\delta(\boldsymbol{r}-\boldsymbol{x}),[\hat{h},\hat{\boldsymbol{x}}]]\rangle = -(1/\hat{m})\,\boldsymbol{\nabla}\cdot\hat{g}(\boldsymbol{r}),\\ z^2\,\delta\hat{g}(\boldsymbol{r}z)/\delta\hat{f}^{(2)}_{\alpha\beta}(z)\big|_{\hat{f}^{(1)}} &\to -(1/2\hat{m})\,\{r_\alpha\nabla_\beta + r_\beta\nabla_\alpha\}\,\hat{g}(\boldsymbol{r}), \end{aligned} \tag{4.35}$$

and correspondingly for eq. (4.34)

$$\begin{aligned} z^2\,\delta\hat{d}^{(1)}_\alpha(z)/\delta\hat{f}^{(1)}_\beta(z)\big|_{\hat{f}^{(2)}} &\to (1/\hat{m})\,\delta_{\alpha\beta},\\ z^2\,\delta\hat{d}^{(2)}_{\alpha\beta}(z)/\delta\hat{f}^{(1)}_\gamma(z)\big|_{\hat{f}^{(2)}} &\to 0, \end{aligned} \tag{4.36}$$

and similar expressions are found for the remaining derivatives in the limit $z\to\infty$. Because of the vanishing derivative in eq. (4.36) the inverse of $\delta\hat{\boldsymbol{d}}/\delta\hat{\boldsymbol{f}}$ is easy to calculate and we find from eq. (4.21)

$$\delta\hat{g}(\boldsymbol{r}z)/\delta\hat{\boldsymbol{d}}^{(1)}(z)\big|_{\hat{d}^{(2)}} \to -\boldsymbol{\nabla}\hat{g}(\boldsymbol{r}). \tag{4.37}$$

This result reproduces exactly eq. (2.41). This means the correct instantaneous self energy is obtained, except for using an approximate pair correlation function.

In order to calculate the first residual anharmonic corrections, the second term in eq. (2.50), we introduce a functional $\hat{\mathscr{F}}$ depending on $\hat{\boldsymbol{d}}^{(1)}$ and $\hat{\boldsymbol{d}}^{(2)}$. Analogous to eq. (2.43) we find from eq. (4.11)

$$\begin{aligned} \hat{\mathscr{F}} = \hat{\mathscr{G}} - (\mathrm{i}/\beta)\int_0^{-\mathrm{i}\beta} \mathrm{d}\tau\,[\hat{\boldsymbol{f}}^{(1)}(\tau)\,\hat{\boldsymbol{d}}^{(1)}(\tau)&\\ + \tfrac{1}{2}\hat{\boldsymbol{f}}^{(2)}(\tau)\,\{\hat{\boldsymbol{d}}^{(2)}(\tau) + \hat{\boldsymbol{d}}^{(1)}(\tau)\,\hat{\boldsymbol{d}}^{(1)}(\tau)\}]& \end{aligned} \tag{4.38}$$

and for the first derivatives

$$\begin{aligned} -\mathrm{i}\beta\,\delta\hat{\mathscr{F}}/\delta\hat{\boldsymbol{d}}^{(1)}(t)\big|_{\hat{d}^{(2)}} &= -\hat{\boldsymbol{f}}^{(1)}(t) - \hat{\boldsymbol{f}}^{(2)}(t)\,\hat{\boldsymbol{d}}^{(1)}(t)\\ &= \hat{\mathscr{K}}(t) + \hat{m}\,\partial^2\hat{\boldsymbol{d}}^{(1)}(t)/\partial t^2,\\ -2\mathrm{i}\beta\,\delta\hat{\mathscr{F}}/\delta\hat{d}^{(2)}_{\alpha\beta}(t)\big|_{\hat{d}^{(1)}} &= -\hat{f}^{(2)}_{\alpha\beta}(t) = \hat{\mathscr{L}}_{\alpha\beta}(t) + \tfrac{1}{2}\hat{m}\,\partial^2\delta_{\alpha\beta}/\partial t^2. \end{aligned} \tag{4.39}$$

Our goal is to find a $\hat{\Psi}$ corresponding to eqs. (2.47)–(2.49). It should be noted that Ψ vanishes for vanishing interaction $V(r)$ and the same has to be postulated for $\hat{\Psi}$. This means if $\hat{\mathscr{F}}_0$ is the functional corresponding to $\hat{\mathscr{F}}$ in the absence of $\hat{V}$, then $\hat{\Psi} = \hat{\mathscr{F}} - \hat{\mathscr{F}}_0$, $\hat{\mathscr{F}}_0$ can in principle be calculated in exactly the same way as $\hat{\mathscr{F}}$. For our purposes it is, however, only necessary to know that such a $\hat{\Psi}$ exists.

We know, however, the derivatives of $\hat{\Psi}$

$$\begin{aligned} &- \mathrm{i}\beta\, \delta\hat{\Psi}/\delta\hat{d}^{(1)}(t)\big|_{\hat{d}^{(2)}} = \hat{\mathscr{K}}(t), \\ &- 2\mathrm{i}\beta\, \delta\hat{\Psi}/\delta\hat{d}^{(2)}(t)\big|_{\hat{d}^{(1)}} = \hat{\mathscr{L}}(t) - \hat{\mathscr{L}}_0(t) = - \hat{f}^{(2)}(t) + \hat{f}_0^{(2)}(t) \end{aligned} \tag{4.40}$$

and also the second derivatives from eqs. (4.33), (4.34) and (4.21). Higher order derivatives can be calculated in exactly the same way. In the second line of eq. (4.40) $\hat{\mathscr{L}}_0(t)$ has been substracted since $\hat{\mathscr{L}}(t)$, eq. (4.15) does not vanish for vanishing potential because of the $\langle \hat{p}_\alpha(t)\, \hat{p}_\beta(t)\rangle_{\hat{f}}$ term, in contrast to $\hat{\mathscr{K}}$. Instead of calculating $\mathscr{L} - \mathscr{L}_0$ it is much easier to calculate $\hat{f}^{(2)} - \hat{f}_0^{(2)}$. Especially in equilibrium it is almost trivial to determine $\hat{f}_0^{(2)}$ since the problem is just that of a simple harmonic oscillator.

Having in mind that the indices $l\kappa\ l'\kappa'$ labeling a given pair of particles were suppressed, we introduce as the lowest order Ψ

$$\tilde{\phi} = \tfrac{1}{2} \sum_{l\kappa} \sum_{l'\kappa'}{}' \hat{\Psi}(l\kappa\ l'\kappa') \tag{4.41}$$

and renormalized anharmonic coupling constants

$$\begin{aligned} \tilde{\phi}(1) &= - \mathrm{i}\beta\delta\tilde{\phi}/\delta d(1) = \textstyle\sum'_{l'\kappa'} \hat{\mathscr{K}}(l\kappa\ l'\kappa'; t), \\ \tilde{\phi}(12) &= - 2\mathrm{i}\beta\delta\tilde{\phi}/\delta d(12), \\ \tilde{\phi}(1;2) &= - \mathrm{i}\beta\delta^2\tilde{\phi}/\delta d(1)\, \delta d(2), \\ \tilde{\phi}(1;23) &= - 2\mathrm{i}\beta\delta^2\tilde{\phi}/\delta d(1)\, \delta d(23), \\ \tilde{\phi}(12;34) &= - 4\mathrm{i}\beta\delta^2\tilde{\phi}/\delta d(12)\, \delta d(34). \end{aligned} \tag{4.42}$$

It should be noted that $\tilde{\phi}(12) \neq \tilde{\phi}(1;2)$. It is, however, reasonable to assume that this difference is of higher order. Since $\hat{\Psi}$ depends by construction on the equal time two-point function only, $\tilde{\phi}(12)$ contains a factor $\delta(t_1 - t_2)$. The same is true for $\tilde{\phi}(1;23)$ with respect to t_2 and t_3 and for $\tilde{\phi}(12;34)$ with respect to t_1 and t_2, and separately t_3 and t_4; $\tilde{\phi}(1;2)$, on the other hand, depends explicitly on $t_1 - t_2$ or its Fourier transform on the energy, as discussed before. The same is true for the other vertices with respect to the variables separated by semicolons.

Including the first order residual anharmonic interaction to the phonon self energy we find again the same structure as earlier

$$\mathscr{M}(12) = \tilde{\phi}(1;2) - \tfrac{1}{2}\mathrm{i}\tilde{\phi}(1;\overline{12})\, d(\overline{13})\, d(\overline{24})\, \tilde{\phi}(\overline{34};2), \tag{4.43}$$

where we have again assumed that the difference between $\tilde{\phi}(1;23)$ and $\tilde{\phi}(1;2;3)$ is of higher order; $\tilde{\phi}(1;2;3)$ is the third derivative with respect to $d^{(1)}$.

We will assume in general that the order of a vertex corresponds only to its number of variables, disregarding the appearance of semicolons, and that the difference between two vertices differing only by the number of semicolons is of higher order. We can then generate higher order approximations in essentially the same way as discussed before. The advantage of the present scheme is, however, that no divergences due to the hard core occur.

As mentioned earlier divergences associated with hydrodynamic phenomena arise from the class of diagrams having the structure shown in fig. 4. To handle these phenomena the integral equation (2.51) has to be solved. In lowest order we find

$$\mathscr{M}(12) = \tilde{\phi}(1;2) - \tfrac{1}{2}\tilde{\phi}(1;\overline{12})\, d(\overline{13})\, d(\overline{24})\, Q(\overline{34};2), \tag{4.44}$$

and

$$Q(12;3) = \mathrm{i}\phi(12;3) - \tfrac{1}{2}\phi(12;\overline{12})\, d(\overline{13})\, d(\overline{24})\, Q(\overline{34};2). \tag{4.45}$$

We will, however, not discuss this equation any further since this would be outside the scope of this article.

If we are interested in the equilibrium free energy we have to calculate $\hat{\Psi}$ as discussed earlier. On the other hand it is much easier to calculate the energy expectation value

$$E = (-1/2\mathrm{i}\beta)\, \Delta(\overline{12})\, d(\overline{21}) + \phi, \tag{4.46}$$

where the first term is the kinetic energy and the second the potential energy given by eq. (3.44). To calculate ϕ we should, of course, use the approximate pair correlation function.

It should be pointed out that quantities like the specific heat or the compressibility might be different if derived from $\mathscr{F}$ or from E. The differences will, however, be of higher order in λ and could, in principle, be used as a test on the convergence.

4.3. Adiabatic approximation

To actually carry through the scheme just outlined is a rather ambitious task, nevertheless feasible. The difficulties lie mainly in the self-consistent determination of the residual force constants, and in calculating the derivatives, eqs. (4.33), (4.34). We will now discuss a simplified version of this approximation scheme which still contains essentially all the physics, but leads to equations which are somewhat easier to handle.

The equilibrium pair correlation function determined previously had the following features: it had the correct asymptotic behaviour at small distances, it was normalized to unity, its centre-of-mass was given by $\hat{\boldsymbol{d}}^{(1)}$, eq. (4.8), and its width by $\hat{\boldsymbol{d}}^{(2)}$, eq. (4.9). Within these limitations its shape was determined by the fact that the residual interaction, (i.e., the potential well created by the surrounding particles) was expanded up to quadratic contributions.

A different form of the well would, of course, change the form of the pair correlation function, but only within the limitations given above. On the other hand we do not know much about this well anyway, except that it has to produce the correct centre of mass and the correct width. It is, therefore equally well justified to guess the form of the pair correlation function such that it shows the correct asymptotic behaviour at small distances, the correct centre of mass, the correct width and that it is normalized to unity. These restrictions do not leave much freedom any more. We know furthermore that $g(\boldsymbol{r})$ is a gaussian, eq. (3.36), for a harmonic crystal. All of those features are in corporated into the form

$$g(l\kappa\, l'\kappa';\boldsymbol{r}) = \hat{\gamma}_0(r)\,\{\hat{a}_0 + \hat{a}_1(r-\hat{R}) + \hat{a}_2(r-\hat{R})^2\}\,g_{\mathrm{h}}(l\kappa\, l'\kappa';\boldsymbol{r}). \tag{4.47}$$

The short range correlation function $\hat{\gamma}_0(r)$ installs the correct asymptotic form and we have to choose $\hat{\gamma}_0(r)$ such that

$$\hat{\gamma}_0(r) \to \begin{cases} \exp(-\beta V(\kappa\kappa';r)), & T\to\infty, \\ \hat{\psi}_0^2(r), & T\to 0, \end{cases} \tag{4.48}$$

where $\hat{\psi}_0$ is a solution to the free pair scattering equation $\hat{h}_0\hat{\psi}_0=0$.

In principle $\hat{a}_1$ and $\hat{a}_2$ should be a vector or a tensor, respectively. We have, however, choosen scalars and $r=|\boldsymbol{r}|$, $\hat{R}=|\boldsymbol{X}(l\kappa)-\boldsymbol{X}(l'\kappa')|$. This choice is the simplest way to ensure the integrability conditions eq. (4.42), this means the requirement $\delta\mathscr{K}(1)/\delta d(2)=\delta\mathscr{K}(2)/\delta d(1)$. In contrast to the previously discussed approach this is not automatically fulfilled in this simplified version. Since there are now only three constants left to be determined selfconsistently, the consistency conditions, eqs. (4.8) and (4.9) can not be fulfilled exactly. They are, of course, valid for g_{h}. The remaining factor in eq. (4.47) affects mainly the longitudinal components of the consistency condition, this means the components parallel to $\hat{\boldsymbol{R}}$. The transverse are changed only very little, or in some cases not at all due to symmetry. We will therefore determine the parameters a_i such that the normalization and the longitudinal components of the consistency condition are fulfilled.

To calculate the parameters a_i we introduce the moments

$$\hat{\mu}_{ij} = \int \mathrm{d}^3 r \{r - \hat{R}\}^i \{(\boldsymbol{r} - \hat{\boldsymbol{X}})\cdot\hat{\boldsymbol{e}}\}^j \,\hat{\gamma}_0(r)\, g_\mathrm{h}(l\kappa\, l'\kappa'; \boldsymbol{r}), \tag{4.49}$$

where $\hat{\boldsymbol{e}} = \hat{\boldsymbol{X}}/\hat{R}$ is a unit vector pointing in the longitudinal direction. The normalization and consistency conditions can be written as

$$\sum_{j=0}^{2} \hat{a}_j \hat{\mu}_{ji} = \hat{I}_i, \tag{4.50}$$

where $\hat{I}_0 = 1$, $\hat{I}_1 = 0$, and $\hat{I}_2 = \frac{1}{2}\hat{\tau}_\ell^{-1}$ and $\hat{\tau}_\ell = \hat{\boldsymbol{e}}\cdot\boldsymbol{\tau}(l\kappa\, l'\kappa')\cdot\hat{\boldsymbol{e}}$ is the longitudinal component of the width tensor, eq. (3.37). The determination of a consistent pair distribution function requires now only integrations, eq. (4.49) and the solution of the three linear equations (4.50).

In the preceding paragraph the energy dependence of $\delta\hat{g}(\boldsymbol{r}, z)/\delta\hat{\boldsymbol{d}}^{(1)}(z)$ was discussed and a weak dependence for energies smaller and of the order of the Debye frequency was expected. It will therefore be a good approximation for a phonon calculation to use the value for $z = 0$. There are now two contributions to $\delta\hat{g}(\boldsymbol{r}, 0)$, the one arising from the harmonic part, corresponding to the renormalized harmonic approximation. In addition changes in the constants a_i have to be included. There are easily calculated from eq. (4.50)

$$\sum_j \delta\hat{a}_j\, \hat{\mu}_{ji} = \delta\hat{I}_i - \sum_j \hat{a}_j\, \delta\hat{\mu}_{ji}, \tag{4.51}$$

where $\delta\hat{I}_0 = 0$, $\delta\hat{I}_1 = 0$, $\delta\hat{I}_2 = \frac{1}{2}\delta\hat{\tau}_\ell^{-1}$ and

$$\delta\hat{\mu}_{ij} = \hat{\mu}_{i\,j-1}\,\delta\hat{R} + \{\hat{\tau}_\ell^2 \hat{\mu}_{i\,j+2} - \tfrac{1}{2}\hat{\tau}_\ell \hat{\mu}_{ij}\}\,\delta\hat{\tau}_\ell^{-1}. \tag{4.52}$$

The calculation of $\delta\hat{g}$ and with it that of the renormalized higher order coupling constants, eq. (4.42), has again been reduced to integrations and coupled linear equations.

It is convenient to introduce the functions $\hat{W}_i(r)$ integrating

$$\mathrm{d}\hat{W}_i(r)/\mathrm{d}r = \hat{\gamma}_0(r)\,(r - \hat{R})^i\, \mathrm{d}V(\kappa\kappa'; r)/\mathrm{d}r. \tag{4.53}$$

with the boundary condition $\hat{W}_i(r) \to 0$ for $r \to \infty$. With it

$$\begin{aligned}\tilde{\phi}(1;2) = \tfrac{1}{2} \sum_{l\kappa} \sum_{l'\kappa'}{}' \int_0^{-i\beta} \mathrm{d}t \int \mathrm{d}^3 r \sum_{i=0}^{2} \hat{W}_i(r)\, \{\hat{a}_i (\hat{\boldsymbol{\delta}}(1)\cdot\boldsymbol{\nabla})(\hat{\boldsymbol{\delta}}(2)\cdot\boldsymbol{\nabla}) \\ + (\delta\hat{a}_i/\delta\hat{R})(\hat{\boldsymbol{\delta}}(1)\cdot\hat{\boldsymbol{e}})(\hat{\boldsymbol{\delta}}(2)\cdot\hat{\boldsymbol{e}})(\hat{\boldsymbol{e}}\cdot\boldsymbol{\nabla})\}\, g_\mathrm{h}(l\kappa\, l'\kappa'; \boldsymbol{r}),\end{aligned} \tag{4.54}$$

and

$$\tilde{\phi}(1;23) = -\tfrac{1}{2}\sum_{l\kappa}\sum_{l'\kappa'}{}' \int_0^{-i\beta} \mathrm{d}t \int \mathrm{d}^3r \sum_{i=0}^{2} \hat{W}_i(r)\{\hat{a}_i(\hat{\delta}(1)\cdot\nabla)(\hat{\delta}(2)\cdot\nabla)(\hat{\delta}(3)\cdot\nabla)$$

$$+4(\delta\hat{a}_i/\delta\hat{\tau}_\ell^{-1})(\hat{\delta}(1)\cdot\hat{e})(\hat{\delta}(2)\cdot\hat{e})(\hat{\delta}(3)\cdot\hat{e})(\hat{e}\cdot\nabla)\}\, g_{\mathrm{h}}(l\kappa\, l'\kappa';\, \boldsymbol{r}). \quad (4.55)$$

This enables us to calculate the phonon self-energy up to the first residual anharmonic correction according to eq. (4.43). We would like to remind that $\hat{\delta}(1)$ was defined following eq. (2.27) and $\hat{W}_i$ and $\hat{a}_i$ and its derivatives are different for each shell of neighbours.

We come back once again to the energy dependence of the renormalized vertices, eq. (4.42), determined by $\delta\hat{g}(\boldsymbol{r}z)/\delta\hat{d}(z)$. This has now been replaced by its value at $z=0$. Fig. 8 shows $g(r)$ as a function of $r=\hat{\boldsymbol{e}}\cdot\boldsymbol{r}$ for three adjacent values of $\hat{R}$, indicated by arrows. We see that $\hat{g}(\boldsymbol{r})$ changes its form such that the steep rise at short distances stays essentially at the hard core radius, whereas the centre of mass moves. If the frequency is increased the pair correlation function can not follow to adjust its form, until in the limit $z\to\infty$ a rigid displacement takes place, as discussed in eq. (4.37). This means

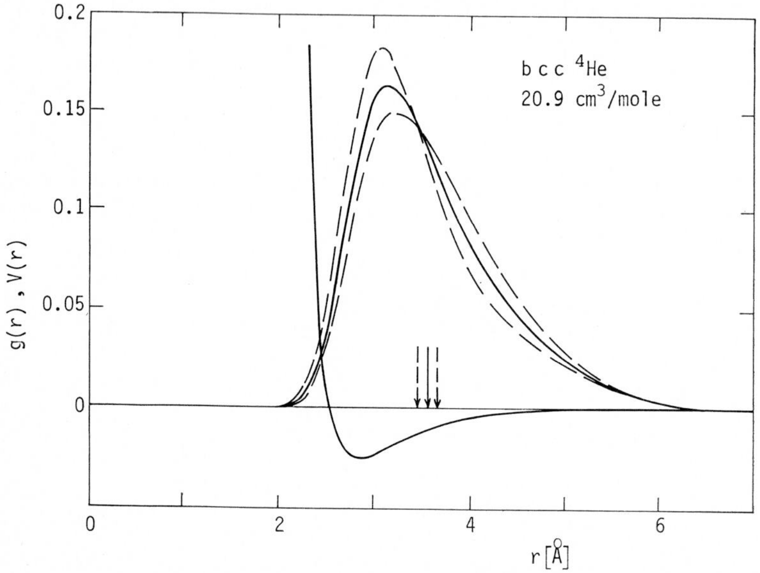

Fig. 8. Pair correlation function for three adjacent mean interparticle distances, indicated by arrows.

there will be some characteristic relaxation time for the pair correlation function to readjust itself according to fig. 8. Since this process takes place at short distances, this means in the hard core region, the corresponding relaxation will be short, say compared to a typical phonon period. This means the short range correlations are expected to follow the lattice vibrations adiabatically.

4.4. Discussion

The different anharmonic expansions which have been discussed, were distinct primarily by the form of the harmonic and anharmonic coupling constants. The differences vanish in the limit of vanishing thermal or zero-point motions and are expected to become more and more significant with increasing fluctuations of the lattice particles around their sites. This will now be demonstrated on hand of results of numerical calculations on different rare-gas crystals using a Lennard–Jones interaction. The effect of increasing fluctuations can be studied either as a function of temperature, being most pronounced near melting, or as a function of density, being most pronounced at low densities or pressures. This latter way is especially appropriate for the quantum crystals ^{3}He and ^{4}He which exist in a limited regime in temperature only, but can rather easily be obtained at various densities.

We will compare several expressions for the 'harmonic' coupling constants.

1. The true harmonic coupling constant $\phi_0 = \Delta V(r)|_{R_{ij}}$, where we are actually interested in the trace $\sum_\alpha \phi^0_{\alpha\alpha}$. The value which will be displaid is for next neighbours.
2. The zero-frequency limit of $\tilde{\phi}(1;2)$ calculated from eq. (4.54), denoted by $\tilde{\phi}_0$.
3. The high-frequency limit $\tilde{\phi}_\infty = \mathscr{M}^0(1,2)$ calculated from eqs. (3.45) and (3.47) using the pair correlation function, eq. (4.47).
4. The selfconsistent harmonic coupling constant ϕ_{h} given by eq. (3.39). Since the integral would diverge at short distances, a cut-off radius has been introduced. The justification for this procedure lies in the fact that the integrand $g_{\text{h}}(r)\,V(r)$ has a pronounced minimum at some distance smaller than the zero of the potential, at least for a relative width $\delta/a \lesssim 0.2$, where δ is given by eq. (3.21) and a is the lattice constant. The cut-off radius was choosen to coincide with this minimum but could be varied for $\delta/a \lesssim 0.15$ considerably without giving rise to a significant change in ϕ_{h}. Such a form has actually been used for neon and for helium at high pressures by Goldmann et al. (1970) and by others.

Fig. 9 shows the different resulting 'harmonic' coupling constants relative to $\tilde{\phi}_0$ as a function of the relative mean square fluctuations. The bars at the bottom of the figure give the range of existence for argon and neon at zero pressure and temperatures between absolute zero and melting. For ^{4}He the range of existence for the hcp and fcc phase at zero temperature for varying density is given. Compared to $\tilde{\phi}_0$ the harmonic values are always lower and

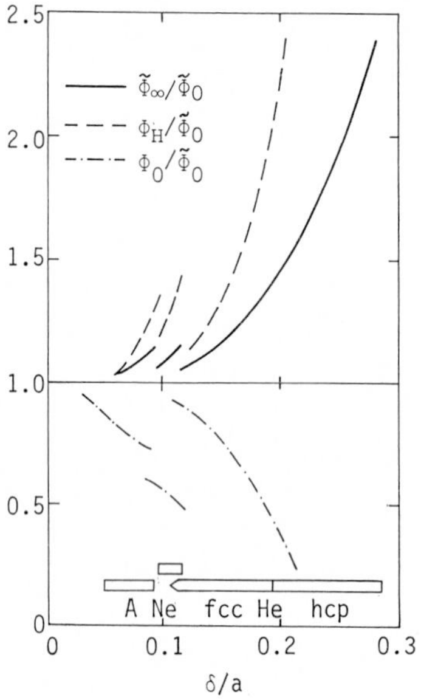

Fig. 9. Comparison of second order coupling constants used in different expansions.

might reach negative values in helium below approximately 1000 atm. As expected the difference between $\tilde{\phi}_0$ and ϕ_0 vanishes with increasing density or pressure and above approximately 10 000 atm helium behaves like a classical crystal at low temperatures. In a similar fashion argon changes its character from a weakly anharmonic crystal at zero temperature, where $\tilde{\phi}_0 \simeq \phi_0$, into a strongly anharmonic crystal near melting where ϕ_0 differs considerably from $\tilde{\phi}_0$. Neon stands in between a classical and a quantum crystal with $\phi_0 \simeq \frac{1}{2}\tilde{\phi}_0$.

The differences among the three renormalized vertices are less dramatic, at least for neon and argon. The differences between the zero and infinite frequency limit are still 15% at melting. The cut-off procedure leads to renormalized harmonic vertices 30% or 40% above $\tilde{\phi}_0$ for argon and neon, respectively.

The situation is quite different for helium where drastic differences even between $\tilde{\Phi}_\infty$ and $\tilde{\Phi}_0$ are found. This demonstrates the limitations of the expansion in terms of instantaneous renormalized vertices, discussed in §3.4. It is also interesting to note that the differences between $\tilde{\Phi}_\infty$ and $\tilde{\Phi}_0$ are of the same order of magnitude as the next order anharmonic correction, the second term in eq. (4.43), or even larger.

Similar investigations of the corresponding third order coupling constants show still more pronounced differences among the different renormalization procedures. Such a behaviour is expected since the influence of the hard core is enhanced considering higher order derivatives.

References

Beck, H. and Meier, P. (1971), Z. Physik **247**, 189.

Boccara, N. and Samara, G. (1965), Physics **1**, 219.

Born, M. and Von Kármán, Th. (1912), Phys. Z. **13**, 297.

Born, M. (1951), Fests. der Akad. der Wissensch. Göttingen, I. Mathem.-Physik. Klasse (Springer, Berlin 1951).

Brandow, B.H. (1971), Phys. Rev. **A4**, 422.

Brenig, W. (1963), Z. Physik **171**, 60.

Brueckner, K.A. and Frohberg, J. (1965), Prog. Theor. Phys. Suppl. Extra Number, 363.

Choquard, P. (1967), *The anharmonic crystal* (Benjamin, New York).

Debye, P. (1912), Ann. d. Phys. **39**, 789.

De Dominicis, C. and Martin, P.C. (1964), J. Math. Phys. **5**, 31.

Ebner, C. and Sung, C.C. (1971), Phys. Rev. **A4**, 269.

Feenberg, E. (1969), *Theory of quantum fluids* (Academic, New York).

Feyman, R.P. (1954), Phys. Rev. **94**, 262.

Fredkin, D.R. and Werthamer, N.R. (1965), Phys. Rev. **138A**, 1527.

Gillessen, P. and Biem, W. (1971), Z. Physik **242**, 250.

Glyde, H.R. and Khanna, F.C. (1971), Can. J. Phys. **49**, 2997.

Goldman, V.V., Horton, G.K. and Klein, M.L. (1970), Phys. Rev. Lett. **24**, 1424.

Götze, W. (1967), Phys. Rev. **156**, 951.

Götze, W. and Michel, K.H. (1969), Z. Physik **223**, 199.

Guyer, R.A. (1969), Solid State Physics **23**, 413.

Hooton, D.J. (1955), Z. Physik **142**, 42.

Horner, H. (1966), Thesis (Techn. Hochschule München).

Horner, H. (1967), Z. Physik **205**, 72.

Horner, H. (1970), Phys. Rev. **A1**, 1712, 1722.

Horner, H. (1971a), Solid State Commun. **9**, 79.

Horner, H. (1971b), Z. Physik **242**, 432.

Horner, H. (1972), J. Low. Temp. Phys. **8**, 511.

Iwamoto, F. and Namaizawa, H. (1966), Prog. Theor. Phys. Suppl. **37**, 234.

Iwamoto, F. (1971), Prog. Theor. Phys. **45**, 682.

Kadanoff, L.P. and Baym, G. (1962), *Quantum statistical mechanics* (Benjamin, New York).

Kerr, W.C. and Sjölander, A. (1970), Phys. Rev. **B1**, 2723.
Kleban, P. (1971), Phys. Rev. Lett. **27**, 657.
Klein, M.L. and Horton, G.K. (1968), Proc. L. T. 11, St. Andrews, Scotland, **1**, 553.
Koehler, T.R. (1966), Phys. Rev. Lett. **17**, 89.
Koehler, T.R. (1968), Phys. Rev. **165**, 942.
Koehler, T.R. and Werthamer, N.R. (1971), Phys. Rev. **A3**, 2074.
Leibfried, G. and Ludwig, W. (1961), Solid State Physics **12**, 275.
Lindemann, F. (1910), Phys. Z. **11**, 609.
Meissner, G. (1968), Phys. Letters **27A**, 261.
Nosanow, L.H. (1966), Phys. Rev. **146**, 120.
Plakida, N.M. and Siklos, T. (1969), Phys. Stat. Sol. **33**, 103.
Werthamer, N.R. (1969), Am. J. Phys. **37**, 763.

CHAPTER 9

Self-Consistent Phonons

W. GÖTZE

Physik-Department der Technischen Universität and Max-Planck-Institut für Physik und Astrophysik, München, Germany

K. H. MICHEL

Institut für Festkörperforschung, Jülich, Germany

Dynamical Properties of Solids, edited by G. K. Horton and A. A. Maradudin

Contents

Introduction

Originally the phonon concept has been introduced for the simplest excitations of a harmonic crystal lattice. These elementary excitations are characterized by the pseudo-momentum $\boldsymbol{p}$, by the polarisation index α, and by the excitation energy $\hbar\omega\binom{\alpha}{\boldsymbol{p}}$. All modes of an harmonic crystal can be represented as superpositions of one-phonon excitations. In many respects the system behaves like a gas of non-interacting particles. If anharmonicities are taken into account, one-phonon and multiple-phonon excitations are not eigenstates of the system any more. A phonon can decay into two phonons, a phonon can be scattered by another phonon and so on. The crystal behaves like a system of interacting particles. Such nontrivial many-body systems have been studied in great detail during the past two decades, and in this chapter we want to apply some of the techniques developed to analyze excitations of anharmonic crystal lattices.

Correlation functions are the appropriate mathematical tool to describe many-particle systems. Therefore we briefly review in §1 the relevant formulae for these quantities which will be used throughout the chapter. Since correlation functions are built up of matrix elements of the hamiltonian resolvent we start in §1.1 by listing some identities for the resolvent. In particular the representation of resolvent matrix elements as continued fractions is formulated. Approximations in this paper will be constructed by taking into account a finite number of terms of this representation. In §1.2 response functions are defined conventionally as Fourier transforms of retarded commutators. These functions are of direct physical relevance since they determine the dynamical susceptibilities of the system and expectation values of operator products. Then the Kubo–Mori theory is applied in §1.3 to find exact representations for the correlation functions in terms of self-energy kernels. The equations obtained are useful, since they explicitly express all the symmetries of the susceptibilities and ensure the correct static limits. Furthermore the equations provide a method for separating the secular motion from the non-secular one.

In §2 the hamiltonian for the ideal anharmonic crystal is specified and phonons are defined as resonances of the dynamical displacement–displacement susceptibility.

The phonon self-energy is singular in the low-frequency and small wave-number limit, and § 3 is devoted to a correct treatment of this singularity. In § 3.1 exact equations for the coupled secular displacement and energy density fluctuations are derived. Then in § 3.2 the generalized self-energies which enter those equations of motion are expressed in terms of memory kernels, which we propose to evaluate by standard perturbation theory. In § 3.3 it is shown that the long-wavelength limits of the static wave-number dependent susceptibilities, which enter the equations of § 3.1 also, are given by the isothermal elastic constants, by the specific heat and by the tension tensor respectively. Then it is shown in § 3.4 that there are two types of low-frequency phonons: acoustic phonons whose velocities are given by the adiabatic elastic constants and diffusion phonons, which are centered at zero frequency and have a lifetime proportional to the square of the wavelength. The results of § 3.3 are used to identify the acoustic phonons with first sound propagation, to show that the diffusion phonons are due to heat conduction, and to identify the self-energy constants with the phenomenological heat conduction and viscosity transport coefficients.

Usually, direct perturbation theory can not be applied to evaluate dynamical susceptibilities, since these functions have resonances. Therefore one introduces for instance the phonon self-energy, which is a better candidate for approximations. In the low-frequency limit, however, the self-energy has resonances too, and therefore the generalized self-energies have been introduced in § 3.1. The latter quantities are regular as far as the frequency behaviour is concerned, but they diverge for small anharmonicities. Therefore the memory functions have been introduced in § 3.2, which at least in finite order approximations do not show divergencies. It is the aim of sections two and three to demonstrate how to approach successively from the physical quantity to quantities being regular enough to allow an approximative treatment. In this way one can assure, that approximations do not influence the qualitative features of the exact results, like conservation laws, sum-rules, and symmetries.

The last section is devoted to demonstrating, that the formalism used is flexible enough to produce approximations most easily. Phonon operators are introduced in § 4.1 on the basis of the static restoring forces and in § 4.2 it is shown for some examples, how to get self-consistent or non-self-consistent approximations for these restoring forces. In § 4.3 the remaining static susceptibilities are derived in leading approximation and in § 4.4 the standard second-order result for the phonon self-energy is obtained. Finally, in § 4.5

the leading approximation for the memory kernels are given. In this way closed formulae for the transport coefficients are found. These results agree with variational solutions of the phenomenological Boltzmann-type equation for the phonon gas, but here the formulae are obtained without making the long detour of a derivation of master equations.

1. Correlation functions

1.1. The resolvent formalism

Let us first remember some results of the resolvent theory (Dunford and Schwartz 1967). With $\mathfrak{H}$ we denote a Hilbert space of vectors $A, B, \cdots$. The scalar product of two vectors is abbreviated by (A, B); it is linear with respect to the second variable. Operators in $\mathfrak{H}$ will be denoted by script letters. In $\mathfrak{H}$ the time evolution is given by the hermitian operator $\mathscr{H}$ according to

$$A(t) = \exp[\mathrm{i}\mathscr{H}t]\, A. \tag{1.1}$$

The resolvent of $\mathscr{H}$ will be denoted by $\mathscr{R}(z)$

$$\mathscr{R}(z) = [z - \mathscr{H}]^{-1}. \tag{1.2}$$

It is a holomorphic function for all non-real z and decreases for large z like

$$\mathscr{R}(z) = 1/z + \mathscr{H}/z^2 + \cdots. \tag{1.3}$$

Let further $A_\alpha (\alpha = 1, 2, \cdots, s)$ denote a set of s linear independent vectors in $\mathfrak{H}$. Then

$$(A_\alpha, A_\beta) = \chi^0_{\alpha\beta} \tag{1.4}$$

is a non-singular $s \times s$ matrix. Matrices of rank s will be denoted by a tilde, e.g. $\tilde{\chi}^0$. We introduce a z-dependent matrix $\tilde{\Phi}(z)$ by

$$(A_\alpha, \mathscr{R}(z)\, A_\beta) = \Phi_{\alpha\beta}(z). \tag{1.5}$$

$\tilde{\Phi}(z)$ is holomorphic for non-real z and because of eq. (1.3), (1.4) it decreases for large z like

$$\Phi_{\alpha\beta}(z) = \chi^0_{\alpha\beta}/z + (A_\alpha, \mathscr{H} A_\beta)/z^2 + \cdots. \tag{1.6}$$

We also remember that every function $F(z)$ which is holomorphic for

$\operatorname{Im} z \neq 0$ and decreases like $1/z$ for large z can be written as a spectral integral

$$F(z) = \int d\omega\, F''(\omega)/(\omega - z)\,\pi . \tag{1.7a}$$

Here F'' is the discontinuity of $F(z)$ across the real axis

$$F(\omega \pm i0) = F'(\omega) \pm iF''(\omega). \tag{1.7b}$$

In particular $\tilde{\Phi}$ can be represented as a spectral integral with

$$\Phi''_{\alpha\beta}(\omega) = -\pi\left(A_\alpha, \delta(\omega - \mathscr{H})\, A_\beta\right). \tag{1.8}$$

Hence $\tilde{\Phi}''$ is a negative hermitian matrix

$$\tilde{\Phi}''(\omega) = \tilde{\Phi}''^{\dagger}(\omega) \leqslant 0 . \tag{1.9}$$

From eq. (1.7a) one then finds for $\operatorname{Im} z \neq 0$

$$\det \Phi_{\alpha\beta}(z) \neq 0 , \tag{1.10}$$

and, consequently $\tilde{\Phi}^{-1}(z)$ is also holomorphic for non-real z.

Because of eq. (1.6) one can write

$$\tilde{\Phi}(z) = [z - \tilde{\Omega} + \tilde{M}(z)]^{-1}\, \tilde{\chi}^0 . \tag{1.11}$$

Here $\tilde{\Omega}$ is a frequency independent $s \times s$ matrix

$$\tilde{\Omega} = \tilde{\omega}\tilde{\chi}^{0-1}, \qquad \omega_{\alpha\beta} = (A_\alpha, \mathscr{H} A_\beta). \tag{1.12a, b}$$

$\tilde{M}(z)$ is a matrix which is holomorphic for $\operatorname{Im} z \neq 0$ and which decreases like $1/z$ for large z. We write it in terms of another matrix $\tilde{m}$

$$\tilde{M}(z) = \tilde{m}(z)\, \tilde{\chi}^{0-1} . \tag{1.13}$$

The matrix $\tilde{\omega}$ is hermitian. To show a similar property for $\tilde{m}$ we write eq. (1.11) in the more symmetrical form

$$\tilde{\Phi}(z) = \tilde{\chi}^0\, [z\tilde{\chi}^0 - \tilde{\omega} + \tilde{m}(z)]^{-1}\, \tilde{\chi}^0 . \tag{1.14}$$

Since $\tilde{\chi}^0$ is hermitian and $\tilde{\Phi}^{\dagger}(z) = \tilde{\Phi}(z^*)$, we see that also $\tilde{m}^{\dagger}(z) = \tilde{m}(z^*)$, i.e. $\tilde{m}''(\omega)$ is hermitian

$$m''^{*}_{\alpha\beta}(\omega) = m''_{\beta\alpha}(\omega). \tag{1.15}$$

Because

$$\tilde{\Phi}''(\omega) = -\tilde{\chi}^0 [\omega\tilde{\chi}^0 - \tilde{\omega} + \tilde{m}(\omega + \mathrm{i}0)]^{-1} \tilde{m}''(\omega) \times [\omega\tilde{\chi}^0 - \tilde{\omega} + \tilde{m}(\omega - \mathrm{i}0)]^{-1} \tilde{\chi}^0, \quad (1.16)$$

where $\tilde{m}''$ is a positive matrix

$$\tilde{m}''(\omega) \geqslant 0. \quad (1.17)$$

Let us consider a symmetry operation $\mathscr{U}$

$$\mathscr{U}^{\dagger}\mathscr{H}\mathscr{U} = \mathscr{H}. \quad (1.18)$$

If $\mathscr{U}$ is unitary one obtains from definition (1.5)

$$(A_\alpha, \mathscr{R}(z) A_\beta) = (\mathscr{U}A_\alpha, \mathscr{R}(z) \mathscr{U}A_\beta) \quad (1.19)$$

and if $\mathscr{U}$ is anti-unitary one gets

$$(A_\alpha, \mathscr{R}(z) A_\beta) = (\mathscr{U}A_\alpha, \mathscr{R}(z^*) \mathscr{U}A_\beta)^*. \quad (1.20)$$

From eq. (1.14) one can find similar symmetry relations for $\tilde{\omega}$ and $\tilde{m}(z)$.

The functions $\Phi_{\alpha\beta}(z)$ are introduced as a convenient tool to characterize the spectrum of $\mathscr{H}$. Since the resonances of $\Phi_{\alpha\beta}(z)$ are of greatest interest approximations must not be discussed for $\tilde{\Phi}$ but for the inverse. For this reason it is fruitful to introduce $\tilde{\Omega}$ and $\tilde{M}$. To be prepared for the following approximate calculations we remember the perturbation theory for nearly degenerate spectra. Let us define a linear operator $\mathscr{P}$ in $\mathfrak{H}$ by

$$\mathscr{P}A = \sum_{\alpha\beta} A_\alpha [\tilde{\chi}^{0-1}]_{\alpha\beta} (A_\beta, A). \quad (1.21)$$

Obviously, $\mathscr{P}$ is the projector on the s-dimensional subspace $\mathfrak{H}_{\mathscr{P}} = \mathscr{P}\mathfrak{H}$ spanned by the vectors A_α. Let $\mathscr{Q}$ denote the projector on the orthogonal complement $\mathfrak{H}_{\mathscr{Q}} = \mathscr{Q}\mathfrak{H}$

$$\mathscr{P} = \mathscr{P}^2 = \mathscr{P}^{\dagger}, \qquad \mathscr{Q} = \mathscr{Q}^2 = \mathscr{Q}^{\dagger}, \quad (1.22\text{a, b})$$

$$\mathscr{P}\mathscr{Q} = \mathscr{Q}\mathscr{P} = 0, \qquad \mathscr{P} + \mathscr{Q} = 1. \quad (1.23\text{a, b})$$

Then one obtains from eq. (1.2)

$$[z\mathscr{P} - \mathscr{P}\mathscr{H}\mathscr{P}]\, \mathscr{P}\mathscr{R}(z)\, \mathscr{P} - \mathscr{P}\mathscr{H}\mathscr{Q}\mathscr{Q}\mathscr{R}(z)\, \mathscr{P} = \mathscr{P}, \quad (1.24\text{a})$$

and

$$[z\mathscr{Q} - \mathscr{Q}\mathscr{H}\mathscr{Q}]\, \mathscr{Q}\mathscr{R}(z)\, \mathscr{P} = \mathscr{Q}\mathscr{H}\mathscr{P}\mathscr{R}(z)\, \mathscr{P}. \quad (1.24\text{b})$$

Introducing the reduction of $\mathcal{H}$ on subspace $\mathfrak{H}_{\mathcal{Q}}$

$$\mathcal{H}_{\mathcal{Q}} = \mathcal{Q}\mathcal{H}\mathcal{Q} \tag{1.25}$$

and the corresponding resolvent in $\mathfrak{H}_{\mathcal{Q}}$

$$\mathcal{R}_{\mathcal{Q}}(z) = [z - \mathcal{H}_{\mathcal{Q}}]^{-1}, \tag{1.26}$$

eq. (1.24b) can be solved formally. Substituting the result for $\mathcal{Q}\mathcal{R}(z)\mathcal{P}$ into eq. (1.24a) one obtains

$$[z\mathcal{P} - \mathcal{P}\mathcal{H}\mathcal{P} - \mathcal{P}\mathcal{H}\mathcal{Q}\mathcal{R}_{\mathcal{Q}}(z)\,\mathcal{Q}\mathcal{H}\mathcal{P}]\,\mathcal{P}\mathcal{R}(z)\,\mathcal{P} = \mathcal{P}. \tag{1.27}$$

This is an equation for operators acting in the s-dimensional space $\mathfrak{H}_{\mathcal{P}}$. Taking the α, β matrix element and using eqs. (1.4), (1.5), (1.22) one reobtains relation (1.11) with the identity (1.12) for $\tilde{\Omega}$ as well as the representation for $\tilde{m}(z)$

$$m_{\alpha\beta}(z) = -\,(\mathcal{Q}\mathcal{H}A_{\alpha}, \mathcal{R}_{\mathcal{Q}}(z)\,\mathcal{Q}\mathcal{H}A_{\beta}). \tag{1.28}$$

In other words, $\tilde{m}$ again is a function like $\tilde{\Phi}$ but defined in subspace $\mathfrak{H}_{\mathcal{Q}}$.

Since $\tilde{m}$ is given by the resolvent in $\mathfrak{H}_{\mathcal{Q}}$ one can continue representing it in the form (1.11) etc., obtaining a continued fraction representation for $\tilde{\Phi}$. In elementary applications eq. (1.12b) gives the first order secular matrix of perturbation theory; $\tilde{m}$ gives the second order corrections. In nuclear physics $\tilde{m}$ plays the role of the optical potential, hiding all non-considered scattering channels. In this chapter $\tilde{m}$ will be the phonon dynamical matrix. As second step of the continued fraction representation $\tilde{m}$ will represent the general non-local transport coefficients. As third step $\tilde{m}$ will be the memory kernels determining the transport coefficients. Stopping at this stage by replacing $\mathcal{H}$ by a zeroth order approximation the evaluation of $\tilde{\Phi}$ will be reduced to the inversion of $s \times s$ matrices and evaluation of z-independent matrix elements.

1.2. Response functions

To connect the resolvent theory with questions of direct physical relevance we use concepts described e.g. in the work of Zubarev (1960) (Kadanoff and Martin 1963, Martin 1965). If H denotes the hamiltonian of the system Heisenberg's equation of motion for operators A, B reads

$$A(t) = \exp(\mathrm{i}Ht)\,A\,\exp(-\,\mathrm{i}Ht) \tag{1.29}$$

and the expectation value of operators is given by

$$\langle A\rangle = \mathrm{tr}[\exp(-\,H/T)\,A]/\mathrm{tr}[\exp(-\,H/T)]. \tag{1.30}$$

Here T is the temperature. Units are chosen such that Planck's constant $\hbar$ and Boltzmann's constant k_B are unity. The correlation function of two operators A and B is given as Fourier transform of the retarded commutator

$$\chi_{AB}(z) = -\langle\langle A; B\rangle\rangle_z = \mathrm{i}\int \mathrm{d}t\,\theta(t)\exp(\mathrm{i}zt)\langle[A(t), B(0)]\rangle \tag{1.31}$$

for $\mathrm{Im}z>0$. A corresponding definition holds for $\mathrm{Im}z<0$. $\theta(t)$ denotes the step function; it is zero for $t<0$ and one for $t\geqslant 0$. From eq. (1.29) one obtains the equations of motion

$$z\langle\langle A; B\rangle\rangle_z = \langle[A, B]\rangle + \langle\langle[A, H]; B\rangle\rangle_z = \langle[A, B]\rangle - \langle\langle A; [B, H]\rangle\rangle_z . \qquad (1.32\mathrm{a, b})$$

The correlation functions are holomorphic for non-real z and decrease like $1/z$ for large z. Hence a spectral representation according to eq. (1.7) can be given. From eq. (1.31) one finds for the spectral function

$$\chi''_{AB}(\omega) = \tfrac{1}{2}\int \mathrm{d}t\exp(\mathrm{i}\omega t)\langle[A(t), B(0)]\rangle . \tag{1.33}$$

From eq. (1.32) one finds for the large-z asymptotic behaviour

$$\chi_{AB}(z) = -\langle[A, B]\rangle/z + \cdots . \tag{1.34}$$

Identity (1.33) yields the symmetry relations

$$\chi''_{AB}(\omega) = -\chi''_{A^\dagger B^\dagger}(-\omega), \qquad \chi''_{AB}(\omega) = -\chi''_{BA}(-\omega) \qquad (1.35\mathrm{a}, 36\mathrm{a})$$

or equivalently with eq. (1.7a)

$$\overset{*}{\chi}_{AB}(z) = \chi_{A^\dagger B^\dagger}(-z^*), \qquad \chi_{AB}(z) = \chi_{BA}(-z). \qquad (1.35\mathrm{b}, 36\mathrm{b})$$

If U is a unitary symmetry operation, i.e. if $U^\dagger HU=H$, one gets

$$\chi''_{AB}(\omega) = \chi''_{U^\dagger AU,\, U^\dagger BU}(\omega), \tag{1.37}$$

and a similar equation for $\chi(z)$. If $\bar{\chi}$ denotes the correlation function formed with the time reflected hamiltonian and $\bar{A}$, $\bar{B}$ denote the time reflected operators A, B one obtains

$$\chi''_{AB}(\omega) = \bar{\chi}''^{*}_{\bar{A}\bar{B}}(\omega), \qquad \chi_{AB}(z) = \overset{*}{\bar{\chi}}_{\bar{A}\bar{B}}(z^*). \qquad (1.38\mathrm{a, b})$$

Furthermore one finds

$$\chi''_{A^\dagger A}(\omega)/\omega \geqslant 0, \tag{1.39}$$

and thus

$$\chi_{A^\dagger A}(z=0) \geqslant 0. \tag{1.40}$$

The function χ'' is of interest because it gives thermal averages by the fluctuation dissipation theorem

$$\langle AB\rangle = \int \mathrm{d}\omega\,[1+n(\omega)]\,\chi''_{AB}(\omega)/\pi\,. \tag{1.41a}$$

Here $n(\omega)$ abbreviates the Bose function

$$n(\omega) = [\exp(\omega/T)-1]^{-1}\,. \tag{1.41b}$$

It is even more interesting that χ describes the linear response of the system under the influence of a time-dependent perturbation

$$\delta H = -\,Bb(t) \tag{1.42}$$

which is switched on at $t\to -\infty$. Here $b(t)$ is the force which induces a time-dependent change of operator A, say

$$\delta\langle A\rangle(t) = \langle A(t)\rangle - \langle A(t=-\infty)\rangle\,. \tag{1.43}$$

Introducing Fourier transforms of time-dependent functions by

$$f(\omega) = \int \mathrm{d}t\,\exp(\mathrm{i}\omega t)\,f(t)\,, \tag{1.44}$$

first order Dirac perturbation expansion with respect to δH yields

$$\delta\langle A\rangle(\omega) = \chi_{AB}(\omega+\mathrm{i}0)\,b(\omega)\,. \tag{1.45}$$

In particular one finds for the response due to a perturbation switched on arbitrary slowly

$$b(t) = b\mathrm{e}^{\varepsilon t}\theta(-t)\,,\quad \varepsilon\to +0\,,\quad \delta\langle A\rangle(t=0) = \chi_{AB}(z=0)\,b\,. \tag{1.46a, b}$$

Thus $\chi_{AB}(z=0)$ is the static and $\chi_{AB}(z)$ is the dynamic A–B susceptibility of our system. These susceptibilities can be measured directly. In §2 we will characterize phonons as resonances of certain susceptibilities. Often one measures resonances by determining the energy absorption. Even though this is a non-linear response function it can be expressed in terms of susceptibilities:

$$\delta\langle H\rangle(t=+\infty) = \int \mathrm{d}\omega\,\omega\chi''_{B^\dagger B}(\omega)\,b(\omega)\,b^*(\omega)/\pi\,. \tag{1.47}$$

1.3. Generalized Bloch–Langevin equations

Let us follow now the original work of Kubo (1957) and Mori (1965) to connect the susceptibilities with function Φ of the resolvent theory. As linear space $\mathfrak{H}$ used in §1.1 we choose the space of operators used in §1.2. Because of eq. (1.40) a scalar product can be defined by

$$(A, B) = \chi_{A^\dagger B}(z=0), \tag{1.48}$$

and hence $\mathfrak{H}$ is a Hilbert space. One can check easily that eq. (1.29) defines a unitary mapping $\mathscr{U}(t)$ in $\mathfrak{H}$ with $\mathscr{U}(t_1)\,\mathscr{U}(t_2)=\mathscr{U}(t_1+t_2)$. Thus there exists a representation like eq. (1.1) and one obtains

$$\mathscr{H}A = [H, A]. \tag{1.49}$$

From the definitions and from eq. (1.32) one finds two useful formulae

$$(\mathscr{H}A)^\dagger = -\mathscr{H}A^\dagger, \quad (A, \mathscr{H}B) = \langle [A^\dagger, B] \rangle. \tag{1.50, 51}$$

Symmetry operations U are related with operations $\mathscr{U}$ in $\mathfrak{H}$ by

$$\mathscr{U}A = U^\dagger A U. \tag{1.52}$$

We associate with the set of s vectors A_α an $s \times s$ dynamical susceptibility matrix in the following way

$$\chi_{\alpha\beta}(z) = \chi_{A^\dagger{}_\alpha A_\beta}(z). \tag{1.53}$$

The right-hand side of eq. (1.4) then is the static $A_\alpha^\dagger - A_\beta$ susceptibility. Combining eq. (1.5) with (1.48) and (1.31) one finds the connection between $\tilde{\chi}(z)$ and $\tilde{\Phi}(z)$

$$\tilde{\Phi}(z) = [\tilde{\chi}^0 - \tilde{\chi}(z)]/z. \tag{1.54}$$

Hence the susceptibilities can be obtained from $\tilde{\Phi}$. In particular

$$\tilde{\Phi}''(\omega) = -\tilde{\chi}''(\omega)/\omega. \tag{1.55}$$

The functions $\Phi_{\alpha\beta}$ describe the relaxation of the system toward equilibrium if it has been perturbed by an adiabatic perturbation (1.46a). Denoting the Laplace transform of non-equilibrium values by

$$\delta\langle A_\alpha^\dagger\rangle(z) = -\mathrm{i}\int_0^\infty \exp(\mathrm{i}zt)\,\delta\langle A_\alpha^\dagger\rangle(t)\,\mathrm{d}t, \tag{1.56a}$$

one finds from eq. (1.45)

$$\delta\langle A_\alpha^\dagger\rangle(z) = \sum_{\beta\gamma} \Phi_{\alpha\beta}(z)\,\chi^{0\,-1}_{\beta\gamma}\,\delta\langle A_\gamma^\dagger\rangle(t=0). \tag{1.56b}$$

Studying the linear response or studying the relaxation toward equilibrium is equivalent.

Representation (1.11) implies the following representation of $\tilde{\chi}$:

$$\tilde{\chi}(z) = [z - \tilde{\Omega} + \tilde{M}(z)]^{-1} [\tilde{M}(z) - \tilde{\Omega}] \tilde{\chi}^0 . \tag{1.57}$$

The physical interpretation of this equation becomes more transparent if one writes it in time space using eqs. (1.43), (1.44), (1.45)

$$\partial_t \langle A_\alpha \rangle^\dagger(t) = -\mathrm{i} \sum_\beta \Omega_{\alpha\beta} [\langle A_\beta^\dagger \rangle (t) - \langle A_\beta^\dagger \rangle^\ell (t)] + \mathrm{i} \sum_\beta \int_{-\infty}^{t} \mathrm{d}t' \, M_{\alpha\beta}(t-t') [\langle A_\beta^\dagger \rangle (t') - \langle A_\beta^\dagger \rangle^\ell (t')] . \tag{1.58}$$

Here $\langle A \rangle^\ell (t)$ denotes the local equilibrium value of operator A under perturbation (1.42)

$$\langle A \rangle^\ell (t) = \langle A \rangle (t = -\infty) + \chi_{AB}(z=0)\, b(t) . \tag{1.59}$$

Result (1.58) is a generalized Bloch–Langevin equation. $\Omega_{\alpha\beta}$ are the restoring forces and M expresses the memory effects of the system. Only if approximately $M \propto \delta(t)$ the relaxation at time t is given by the dynamical variables at the same time. In other words, the Bloch–Langevin equations in the strict sense are obtained only, if one is allowed approximately to replace $\tilde{M}(z)$ by z independent constants $\tilde{M}(+\mathrm{i}0)$; $M'(0)$ then gives corrections to the restoring forces while $M''(0)$ expresses the friction coefficients. Eqs. (1.15) are Onsager's symmetry relations.

It is now also evident that the formalism of § 1.1 is especially useful if one wants to separate low lying secular excitations (like density fluctuations, energy density fluctuation, one-phonon states) from higher lying non-secular excitations (like many-phonon scattering states). One has to start with operators A_α which represent the low lying modes. The influence of the other modes on the low lying ones is given by $\tilde{\Omega}$ and $\tilde{M}$. The motion of the non-secular modes occurs in space $\mathfrak{H}_2$ with time evolution operator $\mathcal{Q}\mathcal{H}\mathcal{Q}$. Since this motion does not have secular frequencies it can be treated by perturbation theory. $\mathfrak{H}_2$ can also be interpreted as noise reservoir for the secular motion.

2. The ideal anharmonic crystal

2.1. The model

For the sake of simplicity we will restrict the discussion to Bravais lattices. We assume the atoms to be distinguishable and label them in the usual way (Born and Huang 1956, Maradudin et al. 1963) by integer vectors $\boldsymbol{n}=(n_1, n_2, n_3)$; $n_i=0, \pm 1, \pm 2, \cdots$. By means of subscripts i, j, k, l, m, n we will denote the three coordinate directions $(1=x, 2=y, 3=z)$; summation convention will be used. The equilibrium position of the $\boldsymbol{n}$th atom, which depends on the temperature T and the external pressure p, will be denoted by $\boldsymbol{X}(\boldsymbol{n})$. Units are chosen such that the mass of the particles and the volume of the elementary cell are unity. The crystal may consist of N unit cells and we will always be interested in the limit $N\to\infty$.

As dynamical variables of the system we choose as usual the deviations of the $\boldsymbol{n}$th atom in the ith direction from its equilibrium point $\varphi_i(\boldsymbol{n})$. The corresponding momentum operator will be denoted by $\pi_i(\boldsymbol{n})$. Hence

$$[\varphi_i(\boldsymbol{n}), \pi_j(\boldsymbol{m})] = \mathrm{i}\delta_{\boldsymbol{n},\boldsymbol{m}}\delta_{i,j}\,. \tag{2.1}$$

According to our definition one has

$$\langle\varphi_i(\boldsymbol{n})\rangle = 0 \tag{2.2a}$$

and because of time reversal symmetry

$$\langle\pi_i(\boldsymbol{n})\rangle = 0\,. \tag{2.2b}$$

The hamiltonian is written in the form (Leibfried and Ludwig 1961)

$$H = \tfrac{1}{2}\sum_{\boldsymbol{n}} \pi_i(\boldsymbol{n})\,\pi_i(\boldsymbol{n}) + \sum_{\nu=0}^{\infty} (1/\nu!)\, V(\boldsymbol{n}_1 i_1, \cdots, \boldsymbol{n}_\nu i_\nu)\, \varphi_{i_1}(\boldsymbol{n}_1)\cdots\varphi_{i_\nu}(\boldsymbol{n}_\nu)\,. \tag{2.3}$$

The coupling coefficients V are considered to be given. They are symmetric functions of their ν arguments. Because of the invariance of the system under infinitesimal translations one finds (Leibfried and Ludwig 1961) for $\nu\geqslant 2$

$$\sum_{\boldsymbol{n}} V(\boldsymbol{n}i, \cdots) = 0\,. \tag{2.4}$$

The $\nu=0$ coupling coefficient is the static lattice energy. This quantity is irrelevant for the dynamics. It depends on T and p, since the equilibrium positions depend on temperature and pressure. The $\nu=1$ term is the sum of one term due to static external surface forces $F_i^{\mathrm{ex}}(\boldsymbol{n})$ and another term due to internal forces; the latter contribution obeys eq. (2.4). With notation (1.49) one finds the equations of motion

$$\mathscr{H}\varphi_i(\boldsymbol{n}) = -\,\mathrm{i}\pi_i(\boldsymbol{n})\,, \tag{2.5a}$$

$$\mathscr{H}\pi_i(\boldsymbol{n}) = \mathrm{i}\sum_{\nu=0}^{\infty} (1/\nu!)\, V(\boldsymbol{n}i, \boldsymbol{n}_1 i_1, \cdots, \boldsymbol{n}_\nu i_\nu)\, \varphi_{i_1}(\boldsymbol{n}_1)\cdots\varphi_{i_\nu}(\boldsymbol{n}_\nu)\,. \tag{2.5b}$$

To express the spatial periodicity of the equilibrium state Fourier transforms will be used for quantities $A(\boldsymbol{n})$ defined on the lattice

$$A(\boldsymbol{k}) = N^{-1/2} \sum_{\boldsymbol{n}} \exp[-\mathrm{i}\boldsymbol{k}\cdot\boldsymbol{X}(\boldsymbol{n})]\, A(\boldsymbol{n}). \tag{2.6a}$$

Here and in the following $\boldsymbol{k}$, $\boldsymbol{q}, \cdots$ denote vectors of the first Brillouin zone. The inverse transformation reads

$$A(\boldsymbol{n}) = N^{-1/2} \sum_{\boldsymbol{k}} \exp[\mathrm{i}\boldsymbol{k}\cdot\boldsymbol{X}(\boldsymbol{n})]\, A(\boldsymbol{k}). \tag{2.6b}$$

If there is a quantity $A(\boldsymbol{n}_1, \cdots, \boldsymbol{n}_\nu)$ which is translational invariant, i.e. $A(\boldsymbol{n}_1, \cdots, \boldsymbol{n}_\nu) = A(\boldsymbol{n}_1 + \boldsymbol{n}, \cdots, \boldsymbol{n}_\nu + \boldsymbol{n})$, the Fourier transform $A(\boldsymbol{k}_1, \cdots, \boldsymbol{k}_\nu)$ is proportional to $\Delta(\boldsymbol{k}_1 + \cdots + \boldsymbol{k}_\nu)$. Here $\Delta(\boldsymbol{k})$ is equal to one or to zero depending on whether $\boldsymbol{k}$ is a vector of the reciprocal lattice or not. In particular we have for two-point functions

$$A(-\boldsymbol{k}_1, \boldsymbol{k}_2) = \begin{cases} 0, & \boldsymbol{k}_1 \neq \boldsymbol{k}_2, \\ NA(\boldsymbol{k}), & \boldsymbol{k}_1 = \boldsymbol{k}_2, \end{cases} \tag{2.7a}$$

where

$$A(\boldsymbol{k}) = \sum_{\boldsymbol{n}} \exp[\mathrm{i}\boldsymbol{k}\cdot\boldsymbol{X}(\boldsymbol{n})]\, A(\boldsymbol{n}, \boldsymbol{0}). \tag{2.7b}$$

In Fourier space we have the commutation relations (2.1) and the equations of motion (2.5)

$$[\varphi_i^\dagger(\boldsymbol{k}), \pi_j(\boldsymbol{q})] = \mathrm{i}\delta_{ij}\delta_{\boldsymbol{qk}}, \quad \mathscr{H}\varphi_i(\boldsymbol{k}) = -\mathrm{i}\pi_i(\boldsymbol{k}), \tag{2.8a, b}$$

$$\mathscr{H}\pi_i(\boldsymbol{k}) = \mathrm{i} \sum_{\nu=0}^{\infty} (1/\nu!)\, V(\boldsymbol{k}i, -\boldsymbol{k}_1 i_1, \cdots, -\boldsymbol{k}_\nu i_\nu)\, \varphi_{i_1}(\boldsymbol{k}_1) \cdots \varphi_{i_\nu}(\boldsymbol{k}_\nu). \tag{2.8c}$$

Time reflexion and space inversion are the general symmetry operations of our system. Obviously one has for space inversion

$$\varphi_i(\boldsymbol{k}) \to -\varphi_i(-\boldsymbol{k}), \quad \pi_i(\boldsymbol{k}) \to -\pi_i(-\boldsymbol{k}), \tag{2.9a, b}$$

and for time reflexion

$$\varphi_i(\boldsymbol{k}) \to \varphi_i(-\boldsymbol{k}), \quad \pi_i(k) \to -\pi_i(-\boldsymbol{k}). \tag{2.10a, b}$$

Because φ and π are hermitian one gets

$$\varphi_i^\dagger(\boldsymbol{k}) = \varphi_i(-\boldsymbol{k}), \quad \pi_i^\dagger(\boldsymbol{k}) = \pi_i(-\boldsymbol{k}). \tag{2.11a, b}$$

Later we will need the energy density operator $E(\boldsymbol{n})$. Its definition is unique only up to modification within the spatial range of the coupling coefficients. We shall need that E is hermitian

$$E^{\dagger}(\boldsymbol{k}) = E(-\boldsymbol{k}), \tag{2.12}$$

that it is invariant under space inversion

$$E(\boldsymbol{k}) \to E(-\boldsymbol{k}), \tag{2.13}$$

as well as under time reflexion

$$E(\boldsymbol{k}) \to E(-\boldsymbol{k}). \tag{2.14}$$

Furthermore it should be regular in $\boldsymbol{k}$ and

$$\lim_{\boldsymbol{k}\to 0} E(\boldsymbol{k}) = HN^{-1/2}. \tag{2.15}$$

A possible definition is

$$E(\boldsymbol{n}) = \tfrac{1}{2}\pi_i(\boldsymbol{n})\,\pi_i(\boldsymbol{n}) + \sum_{\nu=0}^{\infty} (1/\nu!) \sum_{\boldsymbol{n}_2,\cdots,\boldsymbol{n}_\nu} V(\boldsymbol{n}i, \boldsymbol{n}_2 i_2, \cdots, \boldsymbol{n}_\nu i_\nu) \times \varphi_i(\boldsymbol{n})\,\varphi_{i_2}(\boldsymbol{n}_2)\cdots\varphi_{i_\nu}(\boldsymbol{n}_\nu). \tag{2.16}$$

Finally we notice that A and $\mathscr{H}A$ have the same symmetries.

2.2. Phonon resonances

We follow the convention and define phonons as resonances of the displacement–displacement correlation function $\langle\langle \varphi_i^{\dagger}(\boldsymbol{q}); \varphi_j(\boldsymbol{q})\rangle\rangle_z$. Only the $\boldsymbol{q}\to 0$ limit of this function is directly related with experimental quantities; for other experiments like neutron scattering the displacement correlation function is only a necessary and useful piece of information but it is not sufficient for the analysis. We do not want to discuss this problem further in this chapter. Since φ is closely connected with π we will also consider $\langle\langle \varphi_i^{\dagger}(\boldsymbol{q}); \pi_j(\boldsymbol{q})\rangle\rangle_z$ and $\langle\langle \pi_i^{\dagger}(\boldsymbol{q}); \pi_j(\boldsymbol{q})\rangle\rangle_z$. The set of operators A_α thus is chosen as

$$A_\alpha = \{\varphi_i(\boldsymbol{q}), \pi_i(\boldsymbol{q});\, i = 1, 2, 3\}. \tag{2.17}$$

The 6-dimensional space $\mathfrak{H}_{\mathscr{P}}$ is the sum of the 3-dimensional space spanned by $\varphi_i(\boldsymbol{q})$ and the 3-dimensional space spanned by $\pi_i(\boldsymbol{q})$. Correspondingly we will write 6×6 matrices like $\tilde{\chi}$ as 2×2 matrices whose elements are 3×3 matrices.

Because of eqs. (2.5a), (1.51) and (2.1) one obtains

$$(\pi_i(\boldsymbol{n}), \pi_j(\boldsymbol{m})) = \delta_{ij}\delta_{\boldsymbol{nm}} \quad \text{and} \quad (\pi_i(\boldsymbol{n}), \varphi_j(\boldsymbol{m})) = 0.$$

The only non-trivial static susceptibility is $(\varphi_i(\boldsymbol{n}), \varphi_j(\boldsymbol{m}))$ which we abbreviate by D^{-1}

$$D_{ij}^{-1}(\boldsymbol{q}) = (\varphi_i(\boldsymbol{q}), \varphi_j(\boldsymbol{q})), \tag{2.18a}$$

hence

$$\tilde{\chi}^0(\boldsymbol{q}) = \begin{pmatrix} D_{ij}^{-1}(\boldsymbol{q}) & 0 \\ 0 & \delta_{ij} \end{pmatrix}. \tag{2.18b}$$

Because of eqs. (1.35b), (1.36b) and reflexion symmetry $D_{ij}(\boldsymbol{q}) = D_{ij}^*(\boldsymbol{q})$, i.e. D is a real symmetric matrix depending on $\boldsymbol{q}^2$. Because of eq. (1.40) D_{ij} is positive definite.

From eqs. (2.17), (1.51) one obtains for the matrix $\tilde{\omega}$ in eq. (1.12b)

$$\tilde{\omega} = \begin{pmatrix} 0 & \mathrm{i} \\ -\mathrm{i} & 0 \end{pmatrix}, \tag{2.19a}$$

and hence for the restoring-force matrix (1.12a)

$$\tilde{\Omega}(\boldsymbol{q}) = \begin{pmatrix} 0 & \mathrm{i} \\ -\mathrm{i}D(\boldsymbol{q}) & 0 \end{pmatrix}. \tag{2.19b}$$

Projector $\mathscr{P}$ in eq. (1.21) has the form

$$\mathscr{P}A = \pi_i(\boldsymbol{q})(\pi_i(\boldsymbol{q}), A) + \varphi_i(\boldsymbol{q})\, D_{ij}(\boldsymbol{q})(\varphi_j(\boldsymbol{q}), A). \tag{2.20}$$

Because of eq. (2.8a) $\mathscr{Q}\mathscr{H}\varphi_i(\boldsymbol{q}) = 0$ and consequently the matrix $\tilde{m}$ in eq. (1.28) is given by a 3×3 matrix $P_{ij}(\boldsymbol{q}, z)$ in the form

$$\tilde{m}(\boldsymbol{q}, z) = \begin{pmatrix} 0 & 0 \\ 0 & P_{ij}(\boldsymbol{q}, z) \end{pmatrix} = \tilde{M}(\boldsymbol{q}, z). \tag{2.21}$$

Here we have

$$P_{ij}(\boldsymbol{q}, z) = -(\mathscr{Q}\mathscr{H}\pi_i(\boldsymbol{q}), \mathscr{R}_{\mathscr{Q}}(z)\, \mathscr{Q}\mathscr{H}\pi_j(\boldsymbol{q})). \tag{2.22}$$

Substituting the previous results into eq. (1.57) one obtains with definition (1.31) the equations of motion for the relevant correlation functions

$$\begin{pmatrix} z\delta_{ij} & -\mathrm{i}\delta_{ij} \\ \mathrm{i}D_{ij}(\boldsymbol{q}) & z\delta_{ij} + P_{ij}(\boldsymbol{q}, z) \end{pmatrix} \begin{pmatrix} \langle\langle \varphi_j^\dagger(\boldsymbol{q}); \varphi_k(\boldsymbol{q}) \rangle\rangle_z & \langle\langle \varphi_j^\dagger(\boldsymbol{q}); \pi_k(\boldsymbol{q}) \rangle\rangle_z \\ \langle\langle \pi_j^\dagger(\boldsymbol{q}); \varphi_k(\boldsymbol{q}) \rangle\rangle_z & \langle\langle \pi_j^\dagger(\boldsymbol{q}); \pi_k(\boldsymbol{q}) \rangle\rangle_z \end{pmatrix} = \begin{pmatrix} 0 & \mathrm{i}\delta_{ik} \\ -\mathrm{i}\delta_{ik} & -P_{ik}(\boldsymbol{q}, z) \end{pmatrix}. \tag{2.23}$$

In particular one finds

$$[z^2\delta_{ik} - D_{ik}(\boldsymbol{q}) + zP_{ik}(\boldsymbol{q}, z)]\, \langle\langle \varphi_k^\dagger(\boldsymbol{q}), \varphi_n(\boldsymbol{q}) \rangle\rangle_z = \delta_{in}. \tag{2.24}$$

Let us assume that zP can be neglected. Then eq. (2.24) is formally identical with the equation of motion of the familiar harmonic approximation (Born and Huang 1956, Maradudin 1963) with D denoting the dynamical matrix. One has three branches of phonons without damping in this case. The phonon frequencies are given by the static susceptibility χ^0. In particular a divergence of χ^0 for instance at a phase transition point implies the existence of a soft mode. One should be aware that D defined by eq. (2.18a) contains all anharmonic interaction effects. The matrix $zP_{ij}(\boldsymbol{q}, z)$, which vanishes in the static limit, reflects the existence of phonon scattering states. In particular zP determines the damping of phonons due to decay processes. The matrix zP determines the broadening of the phonon resonances.

The concept of a phonon will be useful only, if the resonances of $\langle\langle\varphi_i, \varphi_j\rangle\rangle$ are not too ill defined, i.e. if it makes sense to neglect zP in a zeroth approximation compared to D. Accepting this point of view we will derive some exact formulae, which will be used in §4 in order to obtain better approximations.

From eqs. (2.5), (2.22) one realizes that the hamiltonian

$$H_0 = \tfrac{1}{2}\sum_{\boldsymbol{n}} \pi_i(\boldsymbol{n})\, \pi_i(\boldsymbol{n}) + \tfrac{1}{2}\sum_{\boldsymbol{n},\, \boldsymbol{m}} \varphi_i(\boldsymbol{n})\, D_{ij}(\boldsymbol{n}, \boldsymbol{m})\, \varphi_j(\boldsymbol{m}) \tag{2.25}$$

implies eqs. (2.23), (2.24) with $P=0$. Let us write then

$$H = H_0 + H'. \tag{2.26}$$

Correspondingly we split $\mathscr{H} = \mathscr{H}_0 + \mathscr{H}'$ and obtain

$$\mathscr{H}_0 \varphi_i(\boldsymbol{k}) = -\,\mathrm{i}\pi_i(\boldsymbol{k}), \qquad \mathscr{H}_0 \pi_i(\boldsymbol{k}) = \mathrm{i} D_{ij}(\boldsymbol{k})\, \varphi_j(\boldsymbol{k}), \tag{2.27a, b}$$

$$\mathscr{H}' \varphi_i(\boldsymbol{k}) = 0, \qquad \mathscr{H}' \pi(1) = \mathrm{i}\rho(1), \tag{2.28a, b}$$

$$\rho(1) = \sum_{\nu=0}^{\infty} (1/\nu!)\, V'(1, \bar{1}, \cdots, \bar{\nu})\, \varphi^\dagger(\bar{1}) \cdots \varphi^\dagger(\bar{\nu}). \tag{2.28c}$$

Here and in the following we will abbreviate $1 = \boldsymbol{k}_1, i_1$ etc., $-1 = -\boldsymbol{k}_1, i_1$ and imply summation convention for variables with a bar. We have

$$\begin{aligned} V'(1, \bar{1}, \cdots, \bar{\nu}) &= V(1, \bar{1}, \cdots, \bar{\nu}), \quad \text{if } \nu \neq 1, \\ V'(1, \bar{1}) &= V(1, \bar{1}) - D(1, \bar{1}). \end{aligned} \tag{2.29}$$

The operator ρ obeys $\rho^\dagger(1) = \rho(-1)$. Operator $\mathscr{H}_0$ describes the motion of non-interacting phonons, $\mathscr{H}'$ describes the interactions.

To evaluate scalar products of vectors A with φ one proceeds by getting on one hand from eqs. (1.51), (2.1)

$$(A, \mathscr{H}\pi(2)) = \langle [A^\dagger, \pi(2)] \rangle$$

and on the other hand from eqs. (2.27), (2.28)

$$(A, \mathscr{H}\pi(2)) = \mathrm{i}(A, \varphi(\bar{2}))\, D(\bar{2}, 2) + \mathrm{i}(A, \rho(2)).$$

Hence

$$(A, \varphi(2)) = \{-\mathrm{i}\langle [A^\dagger, \pi(\bar{2})] \rangle - (A, \rho(\bar{2}))\}\, D^{-1}(\bar{2}, 2). \tag{2.30}$$

In particular one finds for $A = \varphi(1)$ with eqs. (2.18), (2.1)

$$(\varphi(1), \rho(2)) = 0, \tag{2.31a}$$

or equivalently

$$D_{ij}(\boldsymbol{q}) = V(\boldsymbol{q}i, -\boldsymbol{q}j) + \sum_{\nu=2}^{\infty} (1/\nu!)\, V(\boldsymbol{q}i, -\boldsymbol{k}_1 i_1, \cdots, -\boldsymbol{k}_\nu i_\nu)$$
$$\times (\varphi_{i_1}(\boldsymbol{k}_1) \cdots \varphi_{i_\nu}(\boldsymbol{k}_\nu), \varphi_k(\boldsymbol{q}))\, D_{kj}(\boldsymbol{q}). \tag{2.31b}$$

Expressing the correlation functions in these equations in terms of H' and D we will obtain approximate non-linear equations for D. The solution then expresses the one-phonon restoring forces, taking into account self-consistently the many-phonon correlations.

From eq. (2.20) one obtains

$$\mathscr{Q}\mathscr{H}\pi(1) = \mathrm{i}\rho(1) \tag{2.32}$$

and furthermore with eqs. (2.27), (2.28)

$$\mathscr{P}\mathscr{H}A = -\mathrm{i}\{\pi(\bar{1})\, D(\bar{1}, \bar{2})\, (\varphi(\bar{2}), A) + \pi(\bar{1})\, (\rho(\bar{1}), A)$$
$$- \varphi(\bar{1})\, D(\bar{1}, \bar{2})\, (\pi(\bar{2}), A)\}. \tag{2.33}$$

3. *Low-frequency phonons*

3.1. Equations for the secular motion

Translational invariance (2.4) implies that all coupling coefficients $V(\boldsymbol{k}_1 i_1, \cdots, \boldsymbol{k}_\nu i_\nu)$ vanish, whenever one of the arguments $\boldsymbol{k}$ tends to zero. Because of eq. (2.31b) the same holds for the restoring forces D, i.e. one can write the formula

$$D_{ik}(\boldsymbol{q}) = Z_{ik,\, jl}(\boldsymbol{q})\, q_j q_l, \tag{3.1a}$$

with $Z(\boldsymbol{q})$ denoting a continuous function for small wave numbers

$$\lim_{\boldsymbol{q}\to 0} Z_{ik,\,jl}(\boldsymbol{q}) = Z_{ik,\,jl}\,. \tag{3.1b}$$

Because of space inversion symmetry $Z_{ik,\,jl}(\boldsymbol{q})$ is even in $\boldsymbol{q}$ and by construction it is invariant under permutations of i with k or of j with l. Because of time reversal symmetry it is real. Equivalently one can write

$$\sum_{\boldsymbol{n}} D_{ij}(\boldsymbol{n}, \boldsymbol{m}) = \sum_{\boldsymbol{m}} D_{ij}(\boldsymbol{n}, \boldsymbol{m}) = 0\,. \tag{3.1c}$$

The restoring forces vanish for $\boldsymbol{q}=0$, i.e. $\varphi_i(\boldsymbol{q})$ and $\pi_i(\boldsymbol{q})$ represent zero frequency modes for $\boldsymbol{q}\to 0$. This is evident, since a translation of the crystal as a whole as well as an acceleration to a fixed momentum ($N\to\infty$!) does not require energy. For $\boldsymbol{q}\neq 0$ but small, $\varphi_i(\boldsymbol{q})$ and $\pi_i(\boldsymbol{q})$ represent low lying modes.

To discuss the low-frequency phonons one has to know something about the selfenergy $P(\boldsymbol{q}, z)$ entering eqs. (2.23), (2.24). Because of eqs. (2.32), (2.28c), (2.4) one can write

$$\mathscr{Q}\mathscr{H}\pi_i(\boldsymbol{q}) = -\, J'_{ij}(\boldsymbol{q})\, q_j\,, \tag{3.2a}$$

with $J'_{ij}(\boldsymbol{q})$ denoting the momentum current operator which is continuous for small $\boldsymbol{q}$

$$\lim_{\boldsymbol{q}\to 0} J_{ij}(\boldsymbol{q}) = J'_{ij}\,. \tag{3.2b}$$

From eq. (2.22) one obtains

$$P_{ik}(\boldsymbol{q}, z) = \mathrm{i}\alpha_{ik,\,jl}(\boldsymbol{q}, z)\, q_j q_l\,, \tag{3.3a}$$

with

$$\alpha_{ij,\,kl}(\boldsymbol{q}, z) = \mathrm{i}\big(J'_{ij}(\boldsymbol{q}), \mathscr{R}_{\mathscr{Q}}(z)\, J'_{kl}(\boldsymbol{q})\big)\,. \tag{3.3b}$$

If zP can be neglected in eq. (2.24) the resonance frequencies are proportional to $|\boldsymbol{q}|$. Then the correction zP would be explicitly proportional to $|\boldsymbol{q}|^3$. Consequently, if and only if α remains finite for z and $\boldsymbol{q}$ approaching zero zP can be neglected compared to D in the long-wavelength limit. In the next approximation α would give us some small corrections including damping phenomena. In order to analyze the behaviour of α one has to evaluate it approximately. One finds already in lowest order (see §4.4) that α diverges unless the temperature is zero

$$\lim_{\boldsymbol{q},\, z\to 0} \alpha(\boldsymbol{q}, z) = \infty \quad \text{if} \quad T\neq 0\,. \tag{3.4}$$

Hence, the low lying modes at non-zero temperature are not given by $D_{ij}(\boldsymbol{q})$.

The reason for the divergence of α is the existence of low lying modes which have not been extracted at the very beginning. These modes are energy density fluctuations given by $E(\boldsymbol{q})$. Because of eq. (2.15) $E(\boldsymbol{q}=0)$ is a zero frequency mode and therefore $E(\boldsymbol{q})$ for small $\boldsymbol{q}$ should be low lying. These modes are coupled to $\varphi_i(\boldsymbol{q})$ by thermal expansion. To treat all low lying modes on the same footing let us include $E(\boldsymbol{q})$ in the set of A_α. Actually, instead of using $E(\boldsymbol{q})$ we want to work with

$$\varepsilon(\boldsymbol{q}) = E(\boldsymbol{q}) - \varphi_i(\boldsymbol{q})\, D_{ij}(\boldsymbol{q})\, (\varphi_j(\boldsymbol{q}), E(\boldsymbol{q})), \tag{3.5}$$

i.e. $\varepsilon(\boldsymbol{q})$ is orthogonal to φ, π. As set of operators to start with we choose

$$A_\alpha = \{\varphi_i(\boldsymbol{q}), \pi_j(\boldsymbol{q}), \varepsilon(\boldsymbol{q})\}. \tag{3.6}$$

The 7-dimensional space $\mathfrak{H}_{\mathscr{P}}$ is the orthogonal sum of the 3-dimensional space spanned by $\varphi_i(\boldsymbol{q})$, of the 3-dimensional space spanned by $\pi_i(\boldsymbol{q})$, and of the 1-dimensional space spanned by $\varepsilon(\boldsymbol{q})$. Correspondingly we will write 7×7 matrices as 3×3 block matrices.

Abbreviating the susceptibility

$$(\varepsilon(\boldsymbol{q}), \varepsilon(\boldsymbol{q})) = C(\boldsymbol{q})\, T, \qquad \lim_{q \to 0} C(\boldsymbol{q}) = C, \tag{3.7a, b}$$

we obtain from (2.18)

$$\tilde{\chi}^0(\boldsymbol{q}) = \begin{pmatrix} D_{ij}^{-1}(\boldsymbol{q}) & & \\ & \delta_{ij} & \\ & & C(\boldsymbol{q})\, T \end{pmatrix}. \tag{3.8}$$

Because of reflexion symmetry and eq. (1.35b) $C(\boldsymbol{q})$ is a real even function. In addition to the commutators expressed in eq. (2.19a) we have $(\varphi, \mathscr{H}\varepsilon)=0$, $(\varepsilon, \mathscr{H}\varepsilon)=0$ because of time reversal symmetry. Furthermore one gets from eqs. (2.27b), (2.28c)

$$\begin{aligned}(\pi_i(q), \mathscr{H}\varepsilon(q)) &= -\,\mathrm{i}(\rho_i(\boldsymbol{q}), \varepsilon(\boldsymbol{q})) \\ &= -\,\mathrm{i} \sum_{\nu=2}^{\infty} (1/\nu!)\, V^*(\boldsymbol{q}i, -\boldsymbol{k}_1 i_1, \cdots, -\boldsymbol{k}_\nu i_\nu)\, (\varphi_{i_1}(k_1) \cdots \varphi_{i_\nu}(k_\nu), \varepsilon(\boldsymbol{q})).\end{aligned} \tag{3.9}$$

Note, that the sum starts at $\nu=2$ since ε is perpendicular on φ. The right-hand side vanishes for $\boldsymbol{q}$ approaching zero and therefore one can write

$$(\pi_i(\boldsymbol{q}), \mathscr{H}\varepsilon(\boldsymbol{q})) = -\,T\beta_{ij}(\boldsymbol{q})\, q_j, \qquad \lim_{q \to 0} \beta_{ij}(\boldsymbol{q}) = \beta_{ij}. \tag{3.10a, b}$$

Because of space inversion symmetry $\beta_{ij}(q)=\beta_{ij}(-q)$ and because of eq. (1.35b) $\beta_{ij}(\boldsymbol{q})$ is real. Hence

$$\tilde{\omega} = \begin{pmatrix} 0 & \mathrm{i} & 0 \\ -\mathrm{i} & 0 & -T\boldsymbol{\beta}(\boldsymbol{q})\,\boldsymbol{q} \\ 0 & -T\boldsymbol{\beta}(\boldsymbol{q})\,\boldsymbol{q} & 0 \end{pmatrix}, \tag{3.11}$$

and the restoring forces (1.12a) are given by

$$\tilde{\Omega} = \begin{pmatrix} 0 & \mathrm{i} & 0 \\ -\mathrm{i}D & 0 & -\boldsymbol{\beta}(\boldsymbol{q})\,\boldsymbol{q}/C(\boldsymbol{q}) \\ 0 & -T\boldsymbol{\beta}(\boldsymbol{q})\,\boldsymbol{q} & 0 \end{pmatrix}. \tag{3.12}$$

The projector $\mathscr{P}$ in eq. (1.21) has the form

$$\begin{aligned} \mathscr{P}A = \varphi_i(\boldsymbol{q})\, D_{ij}(\boldsymbol{q})\,(\varphi_j(\boldsymbol{q}), A) \\ + \pi_i(\boldsymbol{q})\,(\pi_i(\boldsymbol{q}), A) + \varepsilon(\boldsymbol{q})\,[C(\boldsymbol{q})\,T]^{-1}(\varepsilon(\boldsymbol{q}), A). \end{aligned} \tag{3.13}$$

Notice that the operator $\mathscr{Q}=1-\mathscr{P}$ differs from the one used in §2 and in eqs. (3.2a), (3.3b). As before we have $\mathscr{Q}\mathscr{H}\varphi=0$ and therefore the matrix $\tilde{m}$ in eq. (1.28) has the form

$$\tilde{m}(\boldsymbol{q}, z) = \begin{pmatrix} 0 & 0 & 0 \\ 0 & P^{\pi\pi} & P^{\pi\varepsilon} \\ 0 & P^{\varepsilon\pi} & P^{\varepsilon\varepsilon} \end{pmatrix}. \tag{3.14}$$

Introducing current operators by

$$\mathscr{Q}\mathscr{H}\pi_i(\boldsymbol{q}) = -J_{ij}(\boldsymbol{q})\,q_j, \qquad \lim_{q\to 0} J_{ij}(\boldsymbol{q}) = J_{ij}, \tag{3.15a, b}$$

$$\mathscr{Q}\mathscr{H}\varepsilon(\boldsymbol{q}) = -J_i(\boldsymbol{q})\,q_j, \qquad \lim_{q\to 0} J_i(\boldsymbol{q}) = J_i, \tag{3.16a, b}$$

one can write explicitly

$$P^{\pi\pi}_{ik}(\boldsymbol{q}, z) = \mathrm{i}\eta_{ij,kl}(\boldsymbol{q}, z)\, q_j q_l, \tag{3.17a}$$

$$\eta_{ij,kl}(\boldsymbol{q}, z) = i(J_{ij}(\boldsymbol{q}), [z-\mathscr{H}_{\mathscr{Q}}]^{-1}\, J_{kl}(\boldsymbol{q})), \tag{3.17b}$$

$$P^{\varepsilon\varepsilon}(\boldsymbol{q}, z) = \mathrm{i}\lambda_{nm}(\boldsymbol{q}, z)\, q_n q_m, \tag{3.18a}$$

$$\lambda_{nm}(\boldsymbol{q}, z) = \mathrm{i}(J_n(\boldsymbol{q}), [z-\mathscr{H}_{\mathscr{Q}}]^{-1}\, J_m(\boldsymbol{q})), \tag{3.18b}$$

$$P^{\pi\varepsilon}_i(\boldsymbol{q}, z) = P^{\varepsilon\pi *}_i(-\boldsymbol{q}, z^*) = \mathrm{i}\xi_{i,jl}(\boldsymbol{q}, z)\, q_j q_l, \tag{3.19a}$$

$$\xi_{i,jl}(\boldsymbol{q}, z) = \mathrm{i}(J_{ij}(\boldsymbol{q}), [z-\mathscr{H}_{\mathscr{Q}}]^{-1}\, J_l(\boldsymbol{q})). \tag{3.19b}$$

Since $\mathscr{Q}$ in eq. (3.2a) differs from $\mathscr{Q}$ in eq. (3.15a) by the last term on the right-hand side of eq. (3.13) one finds from eq. (3.10a)

$$J_{ij}(\boldsymbol{q}) = J'_{ij}(\boldsymbol{q}) - \varepsilon(\boldsymbol{q})\,\beta_{ij}(\boldsymbol{q})/C(\boldsymbol{q}). \tag{3.20}$$

By introducing $\varepsilon(\boldsymbol{q})$ we have subtracted a slow mode contribution from the current J'. From eq. (1.50) one finds that the currents are hermitian

$$J^{\dagger}_{ij}(\boldsymbol{q}) = J_{ij}(-\boldsymbol{q}), \qquad J^{\dagger}_{i}(\boldsymbol{q}) = J_{i}(-\boldsymbol{q}), \tag{3.21a, b}$$

and from the symmetries discussed in §2.1 one finds that for spatial as well as for time reflexions

$$J_{ij}(\boldsymbol{q}) \to J_{ij}(-\boldsymbol{q}), \qquad J_{i}(\boldsymbol{q}) \to -J_{i}(-\boldsymbol{q}). \tag{3.22a, b}$$

The hermiticity (3.21) implies with eq. (1.35b), (1.36b)

$$\eta^{*}_{ij,kl}(\boldsymbol{q}, z) = -\eta_{kl,ij}(-\boldsymbol{q}, z^{*}) = +\eta_{ij,kl}(\boldsymbol{q}, z^{*}), \tag{3.23a}$$
$$\lambda^{*}_{nm}(\boldsymbol{q}, z) = -\lambda_{m,n}(-\boldsymbol{q}, z^{*}) = +\lambda_{n,m}(\boldsymbol{q}, z^{*}). \tag{3.23b}$$

Reflexion and time reflexion symmetry implies

$$\eta_{ij,kl}(\boldsymbol{q}, z) = \eta_{ij,kl}(-\boldsymbol{q}, z) = -\eta^{*}_{ij,kl}(-\boldsymbol{q}, z^{*}), \tag{3.24a}$$
$$\lambda_{nm}(\boldsymbol{q}, z) = \lambda_{nm}(-\boldsymbol{q}, z) = -\lambda^{*}_{nm}(-\boldsymbol{q}, z^{*}), \tag{3.24b}$$
$$\xi_{i,jl}(\boldsymbol{q}, z) = -\xi_{i,jl}(-\boldsymbol{q}, z) = +\xi^{*}_{i,jl}(-\boldsymbol{q}, z^{*}). \tag{3.24c}$$

The Bloch–Langevin equation (1.57) now contains all low lying secular modes due to the conservation laws. The non-secular motion is given by η, λ, ξ. These functions we can assume to behave regularly for $\boldsymbol{q}$ and z tending to zero [except for the discontinuity expressed in eq. (1.7b)]. Using the symmetry relations derived above one obtains

$$\lim_{z\to +i0}\lim_{\boldsymbol{q}\to 0} \xi_{i,jl}(\boldsymbol{q}, z) = 0, \qquad \lim_{z\to +i0}\lim_{\boldsymbol{q}\to 0} \lambda_{nm}(\boldsymbol{q}, z) = \lambda_{nm} \tag{3.25a, b}$$
$$\lim_{z\to +i0}\lim_{\boldsymbol{q}\to 0} \eta_{ij,kl}(\boldsymbol{q}, z) = \eta_{ij,kl}, \tag{3.25c}$$

where λ and η are real quantities and $\lambda_{nm} = \lambda_{mn}$, $\eta_{ij,kl} = \eta_{kl,ij}$. They are given by the spectral function on the right-hand side of eqs. (3.17b), (3.18b), and because of eq. (1.9) they are positive definite matrices.

Before resuming the discussion of the low lying modes in §3.4 we want to examine the various parameters in more detail.

3.2. Memory functions

For an examination of the self-energy functions η, λ, ξ eqs. (3.17) to (3.19) are not very useful. Actual perturbation theory for these quantities will use $\mathscr{H}_0$ as a starting point. For $\boldsymbol{q} \to 0$, however, $J(\boldsymbol{q})$ is an eigenfunction of $\mathscr{H}_0$ with an eigenfrequency zero. Hence η, λ, ξ will diverge for vanishing phonon interactions. To get hands on this problem the resolvent formalism is exploited again with

$$A_\alpha = \{J_{ij}(\boldsymbol{q}), J_i(\boldsymbol{q})\} \tag{3.26}$$

representing the basis in $\mathfrak{H}_{\mathscr{Q}}$. The projector on the 12-dimensional subspace spanned by A_α will be denoted by $\hat{\mathscr{P}}$; $\hat{\mathscr{Q}} = 1 - \hat{\mathscr{P}}$. Because of time reflexion symmetry one obtains for the susceptibilities

$$(J_{ij}(\boldsymbol{q}), J_k(\boldsymbol{q})) = 0 \tag{3.27}$$

and for the restoring forces

$$(J_{ij}(\boldsymbol{q}), \mathscr{H}_{\mathscr{Q}} J_{kl}(\boldsymbol{q})) = 0\,, \qquad (J_i(\boldsymbol{q}), \mathscr{H}_{\mathscr{Q}} J_l(\boldsymbol{q})) = 0\,. \tag{3.28a, b}$$

For the memory functions

$$\hat{m}_{\alpha\beta}(\boldsymbol{q}, z) = -\left(\hat{\mathscr{Q}} \mathscr{H}_{\mathscr{Q}} A_\alpha, \left[z - \mathscr{H}_{\mathscr{Q}\hat{\mathscr{Q}}}\right]^{-1} \hat{\mathscr{Q}} \mathscr{H}_{\mathscr{Q}} A_\beta\right) \tag{3.29}$$

no obvious simplifications are possible. A divergence of η, λ and ξ for vanishing interactions can be produced by a vanishing of $\hat{m}$. Hence $\hat{m}_{\alpha\beta}$ are the appropriate quantities for which a perturbation expansion can be tried.

The formulae obtained can be simplified considerably in the limit $\boldsymbol{q} \to 0$. From eq. (3.13) one obtains in general

$$\begin{aligned} \mathscr{P}\mathscr{H} A = {} & \mathrm{i}\varphi_i(\boldsymbol{q})\, D_{ij}(\boldsymbol{q})\, (\pi_j(\boldsymbol{q}), A) \\ & + \pi_i(\boldsymbol{q})\, (\mathscr{H}\pi_i(\boldsymbol{q}), A) + \varepsilon(\boldsymbol{q})\, [C(\boldsymbol{q})\, T]^{-1}\, (\mathscr{H}\varepsilon(\boldsymbol{q}), A)\,. \end{aligned} \tag{3.30}$$

The first term on the right-hand side vanishes for $\boldsymbol{q} \to 0$ because of eq. (3.1a), and the other two vanish since $\pi(\boldsymbol{q}=0)$ and $\varepsilon(\boldsymbol{q}=0)$ are constants of motion. Hence

$$\lim_{\boldsymbol{q} \to 0} \mathscr{Q}\mathscr{H} A = \mathscr{H} A\,. \tag{3.31}$$

In eqs. (3.15)–(3.19) $\mathscr{Q}$ is always multiplied with $\mathscr{H}$ as in the previous equation. Hence one can drop $\mathscr{Q}$ completely and write in particular for the quantities (3.25)

$$\eta_{ij,kl} = \lim_{z\to i0} i(J_{ij}, [z - \mathscr{H}]^{-1} J_{kl}), \tag{3.32a}$$

$$\lambda_{n,m} = \lim_{z\to i0} i(J_n, [z - \mathscr{H}]^{-1} J_m). \tag{3.32b}$$

Because of eqs. (1.5) and (1.53) the right-hand side of eqs. (3.32) can be represented by current–current response functions. The formulae obtained in this way are Kubo's formulae for the transport coefficients η and λ (Kubo 1957, Mori 1965).

For $\boldsymbol{q}\to 0$ the matrix elements $(J_i, \mathscr{H} J_{ij})$ vanish because of space reflexion symmetry. Similarly, there is no coupling between ε and π currents in eq. (3.29). Hence one can perform the analysis (3.26) to (3.29) for either set $A_\alpha = \{J_{ij}\}$ and $A_\alpha = \{J_i\}$ separately. With

$$\hat{\mathscr{Q}}A = A - J_{ij}\, \chi^{0\ -1}_{ij,kl} (J_{kl}, A) \tag{3.33a}$$

one obtains $\hat{\mathscr{Q}}\mathscr{H} J_{ij} = \mathscr{H} J_{ij}$ because of eq. (1.51) and thus

$$\hat{m}_{ij,kl} = -\lim_{z\to i0} (\mathscr{H} J_{ij}, [z - \mathscr{H}_{\hat{\mathscr{Q}}}]^{-1} \mathscr{H} J_{kl}). \tag{3.33b}$$

There is no restoring force matrix $\tilde{\omega}$. Similarly one finds

$$\hat{\mathscr{Q}}A = A - J_i \chi^{0\ -1}_{ij} (J_j, A), \qquad \hat{m}_{ij} = -\lim_{z\to i0} (\mathscr{H} J_i, [z - \mathscr{H} \hat{\mathscr{Q}}]^{-1} \mathscr{H} J_j). \tag{3.34a, b}$$

Equations (3.33), (3.34) are the appropriate starting point for perturbation expansions.

3.3. Long-wavelength theorems

In this section we want to discuss the long-wavelength limits Z, C and β defined in eqs. (3.1), (3.7) and (3.10) respectively. These quantities can be related to thermodynamical derivatives. To find these relations one has to be careful in performing the limit $N\to\infty$, since the equilibrium of the crystal under hydrostatic pressure p is defined by external surface forces.

Let us consider the perturbation operator

$$\delta H = -\sum_{\boldsymbol{n}} \{\varphi_i(\boldsymbol{n})\, F_i(\boldsymbol{n}) + E(\boldsymbol{n})\, \theta(\boldsymbol{n})/T\}. \tag{3.35}$$

The generalized forces $F_i(\boldsymbol{n})$, $\theta(\boldsymbol{n})/T$ are switched on arbitrary slowly according to eqs. (1.42), (1.46a). From eqs. (1.46b) and (1.48) one obtains for the change of an operator $A^\dagger$ in linear approximation

$$\delta\langle A^\dagger\rangle = \sum_{n} \{(A, \varphi_i(\boldsymbol{n}))\, F_i(\boldsymbol{n}) + (A, E(\boldsymbol{n}))\, \theta(\boldsymbol{n})/T\}. \tag{3.36}$$

In particular

$$\delta\langle\varphi_j(\boldsymbol{m})\rangle = \sum_{n} \{(\varphi_j(\boldsymbol{m})\, \varphi_i(\boldsymbol{n}))\, F_i(\boldsymbol{n}) + (\varphi_j(\boldsymbol{m}), E(\boldsymbol{n}))\, \theta(\boldsymbol{n})/T\}, \tag{3.37a}$$

or with eq. (2.18)

$$F_i(\boldsymbol{n}) = \sum_{m} D_{ik}(\boldsymbol{n}, \boldsymbol{m})\, \{\delta\langle\varphi_k(\boldsymbol{m})\rangle - \sum_{l} (\varphi_k(\boldsymbol{m}), E(\boldsymbol{l}))\, \theta(\boldsymbol{l})/T\}. \tag{3.37b}$$

Eliminating F one finds with definition (3.5)

$$\delta\langle A^\dagger\rangle = \sum_{n,m} (A, \varphi_i(\boldsymbol{n}))\, D_{ik}(\boldsymbol{n}, \boldsymbol{m})\, \delta\langle\varphi_k(\boldsymbol{m})\rangle + \sum_{n} (A, \varepsilon(\boldsymbol{n}))\, \theta(\boldsymbol{n})/T. \tag{3.38}$$

With the aid of the previous formula one can get an expression for the derivative of an expectation value with respect to temperature changes for fixed strains. One has to put $\theta(\boldsymbol{n}) = \delta T$ in eq. (3.35) and $\delta\langle\varphi\rangle = 0$ in eq. (3.38):

$$\partial\langle A^\dagger\rangle/\partial T\big|_{\text{fixed strains}} = \sum_{n} (A, \varepsilon(\boldsymbol{n}))/T. \tag{3.39}$$

Similarly, one finds the isothermal change of expectation values under homogeneous deformations (Born and Huang 1956, Maradudin et al. 1963) by putting $\theta = 0$ and

$$\delta\langle\varphi_k(\boldsymbol{m})\rangle = u_{kl} X_l(\boldsymbol{m}). \tag{3.40}$$

Hence

$$\partial\langle A^\dagger\rangle/\partial u_{kl}\big|_{\text{fixed temperature}} = \sum_{nm} (A, \varphi_i\ \boldsymbol{n}))\, D_{ik}(\boldsymbol{n}, \boldsymbol{m})\, X_l(\boldsymbol{m}). \tag{3.41}$$

The simplest example is obtained by using the total hamiltonian in eq. (3.39). With eqs. (2.15), (2.7) one gets

$$\begin{aligned}(1/N)\, \partial\langle H\rangle/\partial T &= \sum_{n} (E(\boldsymbol{n}), \varepsilon(0))/T \\ &= \lim_{\boldsymbol{q}\to 0} (E(\boldsymbol{q}), \varepsilon(\boldsymbol{q}))/T.\end{aligned}$$

With eq. (3.5) one obtains for the constant C in eq. (3.7)

$$C = (1/N)\, \partial\langle H\rangle/\partial T \quad \text{(fixed strains)}. \tag{3.42}$$

The constant C thus is identified with the specific heat at constant strains.

The other examples are related to the stress tensor σ_{ij} defined conventionally by

$$\sigma_{ij} = \sum_{n} F_i^{\text{ex}}(\boldsymbol{m})\, X_j(\boldsymbol{m})/N\,. \tag{3.43a}$$

This equation is easily shown to be equivalent to the derivative of the free energy F with respect to homogeneous deformations

$$\sigma_{ij} = (1/N)\, \partial F/\partial u_{ij} \quad \text{(temperature fixed)}. \tag{3.43b}$$

In actual calculations one uses eq. (3.43b) since surface effects do not enter this formula. For general discussions eq. (3.43a) is more convenient. Let us split the total hamiltonian into an internal part H^{int} and an external part due to the surface forces

$$H = H^{\text{int}} - \sum_{m} F_i^{\text{ex}}(\boldsymbol{m})\, \varphi_i(\boldsymbol{m}), \qquad \mathscr{H} = \mathscr{H}^{\text{int}} + \mathscr{H}^{\text{ex}}. \tag{3.44a, b}$$

One gets in particular

$$\mathscr{H}\pi_i(\boldsymbol{m}) = \mathscr{H}^{\text{int}}\pi_i(\boldsymbol{m}) - \mathrm{i}F_i^{\text{ex}}(\boldsymbol{m}). \tag{3.44c}$$

For all operators A one has the equilibrium condition

$$\langle \mathscr{H} A \rangle = \langle [H, A] \rangle = 0\,. \tag{3.45}$$

Application to $\pi_i(\boldsymbol{m})$ gives with eq. (3.44c) an expression for the stress tensor in terms of expectation values

$$\sigma_{ij} = -\,\mathrm{i} \sum_{m} \langle \mathscr{H}^{\text{int}}\pi_i(\boldsymbol{m})\rangle\, X_j(\boldsymbol{m})/N\,, \tag{3.46a}$$

an equation one could have obtained also directly from eq. (3.43b). Since $\mathscr{H}^{\text{int}}\pi$ and $\mathscr{H}\pi$ differ by a C-number only, one arrives with eqs. (1.46b), (1.50) at

$$\delta\sigma_{ij} = \mathrm{i} \sum_{m} \delta \langle (\mathscr{H}\pi_i(\boldsymbol{m}))^{\dagger} \rangle\, X_j(\boldsymbol{m})/N\,. \tag{3.46b}$$

Let us apply eq. (3.39) to work out the right-hand side to

$$\partial\sigma_{ij}/\partial T = \mathrm{i} \sum_{mn} (\mathscr{H}\pi_i(\boldsymbol{m}), \varepsilon(\boldsymbol{n}))\, X_j(\boldsymbol{m})/NT\,.$$

Because of eqs. (2.4), (2.5b) one can replace $X(\boldsymbol{m})$ under the sum by

$X(\boldsymbol{m}) - X(\boldsymbol{n})$. After this replacement the limit $N \to \infty$ can be performed and translational invariance can be used to obtain

$$\begin{aligned}\partial\sigma_{ij}/\partial T &= -\,\mathrm{i}\sum_{\boldsymbol{n}} (\mathscr{H}\pi_i(0), \varepsilon(\boldsymbol{n}))\, X_j(\boldsymbol{n})/T \\ &= \lim_{\boldsymbol{q}\to 0} (\partial/\partial q_j) \sum_{\boldsymbol{n}} \exp[-\,\mathrm{i}\boldsymbol{q}\cdot \boldsymbol{X}(\boldsymbol{n})]\,(\mathscr{H}\pi_i(0), \varepsilon(\boldsymbol{n}))/T\,.\end{aligned}$$

From eq. (2.7b) one obtains for the constants β_{ij} defined in eq. (3.10) the formula

$$\beta_{ij} = -\,\partial\sigma_{ij}/\partial T \quad \text{(strains fixed)}. \tag{3.47}$$

Hence β_{ij} have been identified as the tension tensor. The symmetry of σ_{ij} implies the same for β_{ij}.

The third example is found by analysing

$$S_{ij,kl} = \partial\sigma_{ij}/\partial u_{kl} \quad \text{(temperature fixed)}. \tag{3.48}$$

These coefficients are connected with the isothermal elastic constants of the system under pressure p by (Born and Huang 1956, Maradudin et al. 1963)

$$C_{ij,kl} = S_{ij,kl} + p(\delta_{ij}\delta_{kl} - \delta_{il}\delta_{jk}), \tag{3.49}$$

and the elastic constants have the usual symmetries

$$C_{ij,kl} = C_{ji,kl} = C_{ij,lk} = C_{kl,ij}\,. \tag{3.50}$$

For the sake of later reference we notice that the adiabatic elastic constants $C'_{ij,kl}$ have the same symmetry relations (3.50) as the isothermal ones and are given by

$$C'_{ij,kl} = C_{ij,kl} + \beta_{ij}\beta_{kl}T/C\,. \tag{3.51}$$

The coefficients S follow from eqs. (3.46b), (3.41) with the aid of $(\mathscr{H}\pi_i(\boldsymbol{n}), \varphi_j(\boldsymbol{m})) = -\mathrm{i}\delta_{ij}\delta_{\boldsymbol{nm}}$

$$S_{ij,kl} = \sum_{\boldsymbol{nm}} D_{ik}(\boldsymbol{n}, \boldsymbol{m})\, X_j(\boldsymbol{m})\, X_l(\boldsymbol{n})/N\,.$$

The $N \to \infty$ limit can not be carried out. But if one considers

$$S_{ij,kl} + S_{il,kj} = \sum_{\boldsymbol{nm}} D_{ik}(\boldsymbol{n}, \boldsymbol{m})\,[X_j(\boldsymbol{m})\, X_l(\boldsymbol{n}) + X_l(\boldsymbol{m})\, X_j(\boldsymbol{n})]/N$$

one can add under the sum $-X_j(\boldsymbol{n})\, X_l(\boldsymbol{n}) - X_j(\boldsymbol{m})\, X_l(\boldsymbol{m})$ because of eq. (3.1c). Thus

$$S_{ij,kl} + S_{il,kj} = -\sum_{\boldsymbol{nm}} D_{ik}(\boldsymbol{n}, \boldsymbol{m})\,[X_j(\boldsymbol{n}) - X_j(\boldsymbol{m})]\,[X_l(\boldsymbol{n}) - X_l(\boldsymbol{m})]/N\,.$$

Now translational invariance and eqs. (3.1a), (3.1b), (2.7b) yield

$$S_{ij,kl} + S_{il,kj} = 2Z_{ik,jl}, \tag{3.52a}$$

or with eq. (3.49) one obtains the desired formula, which connects the long-wavelength limit of the restoring forces with the isothermal elastic constants

$$2Z_{ik,jl} = C_{ij,kl} + C_{il,kj}. \tag{3.52b}$$

The symmetries of $C_{ij,kl}$ allow to derive

$$C_{ij,kl} = Z_{ik,jl} + Z_{jk,il} - Z_{ji,kl}. \tag{3.52c}$$

Finally one obtains for eq. (3.1a)

$$D_{ik}(\boldsymbol{q}) = C_{ij,kl} q_j q_l + \mathrm{O}(q^4). \tag{3.53}$$

The coefficients Z, C and β have been introduced in eqs. (3.1), (3.7), (3.10) as static susceptibilities. With the aid of eq. (1.7a), (1.31) and (1.48) they can be expressed as ω^{-1}–sums of the absorptive parts of the corresponding response functions. Thus one obtains three types of sum rules

$$-\lim_{\boldsymbol{q}\to 0} \int \mathrm{d}\omega \,\langle\!\langle \varepsilon(-\boldsymbol{q}), \varepsilon(\boldsymbol{q})\rangle\!\rangle''/\pi\omega = CT, \tag{3.54a}$$

$$+\lim_{\boldsymbol{q}\to 0} (\partial/\partial q_j) \int \mathrm{d}\omega \,\langle\!\langle \pi_i(-\boldsymbol{q}), \mathscr{H}\varepsilon(\boldsymbol{q})\rangle\!\rangle''/\pi\omega = T\beta_{ij}, \tag{3.54b}$$

$$-\lim_{\boldsymbol{q}\to 0} q_j q_l\, C_{ij,kl} \int \mathrm{d}\omega \,\langle\!\langle \varphi_k(-\boldsymbol{q}), \varphi_n(\boldsymbol{q})\rangle\!\rangle''/\pi\omega = \delta_{in}. \tag{3.54c}$$

These sum rules are not too helpful. But static susceptibilities can be approximated by straightforward perturbation theory (see §4). Therefore it is very helpful to have related the thermodynamical quantities C, β_{ij}, $C_{ij,kl}$ to static susceptibilities.

3.4. First sound and diffusion phonons

Let us write down now the equation of motion (1.57) for the response functions (1.57). After elimination of the π-functions one obtains in the $(\boldsymbol{q}, z)\to 0$ limit

$$\begin{pmatrix} z^2\delta_{ik} - [C_{ij,kl} - \mathrm{i}z\eta_{ij,kl}]\, q_j q_l & \mathrm{i}\beta_{ij} q_j/C \\ -\mathrm{i}zq_j\beta_{jk}T & z + \mathrm{i}\lambda_{jl} q_j q_l \end{pmatrix}$$
$$\times \begin{pmatrix} \langle\!\langle \varphi_k(-\boldsymbol{q}); \varphi_n(\boldsymbol{q})\rangle\!\rangle & \langle\!\langle \varphi_k(-\boldsymbol{q}); \varepsilon(\boldsymbol{q})\rangle\!\rangle \\ \langle\!\langle \varepsilon(-\boldsymbol{q}); \varphi_n(\boldsymbol{q})\rangle\!\rangle & \langle\!\langle \varepsilon(-\boldsymbol{q}); \varepsilon(\boldsymbol{q})\rangle\!\rangle \end{pmatrix} = \begin{pmatrix} \delta_{in} & -\mathrm{i}T\beta_{ij} q_j \\ 0 & -\mathrm{i}TC\lambda_{jl} q_j q_l \end{pmatrix}. \tag{3.55}$$

These are the exact equations of motion for the displacements and energy density. The equations are coupled by the tension tensor $\beta_{ij} = -\partial\sigma_{ij}/\partial T$ which characterizes thermal expansion. The direct restoring forces for the displacements are the isothermal elastic constants $C_{ij,kl}$. There are no static restoring forces for the energy density. The mode damping is given by $\eta_{ij,kl}$ and λ_{jl}. This damping is due to the decay of one secular mode into non-secular modes. The complicated non-linear motion problems are hidden in an actual evaluation of $C_{ij,kl}$, β_{ij}, C, $\eta_{ij,kl}$ and λ_{jl}.

Equation (3.55) is valid for such small frequencies z and such small wave-numbers $\boldsymbol{q}$ for which the functions $Z(\boldsymbol{q})$, $C(\boldsymbol{q})$, $\beta_{ij}(\boldsymbol{q})$ defined in eqs. (3.1), (3.7), (3.10) as well as the functions $\eta(\boldsymbol{q}, z)$, $\lambda(\boldsymbol{q}, z)$, $\xi(\boldsymbol{q}, z)$ can be approximated by their zeroth Taylor coefficients. It does not offer difficulties to make this statement quantitative for the three z-independent quantities. A thorough going analysis of the three z-dependent quantities is rather difficult and has not been tried yet. The range of validity may be very small if there are other low lying modes. Such modes show up as small z-resonances in $\eta(\boldsymbol{q}, z)$ (e.g. near a Martensitic phase transition) or in $\lambda(\boldsymbol{q}, z)$ (e.g. in the second sound regime). The most convenient way to obtain a large enough range of validity of the equations of motion is to include the slow modes at the very beginning. This procedure is the complete analogue of the inclusion of $\varepsilon(\boldsymbol{q})$ in the set A_α, eq. (3.5), to handle the resonance in $\alpha(\boldsymbol{q}, z)$.

From eq. (3.55) one derives the closed equation of motion (2.24), (3.3) for the displacement correlation function

$$[z^2\delta_{ik} - C_{ij,kl}q_jq_l + z\alpha_{ij,kl}(\boldsymbol{q}, z)\, q_jq_l] \langle\langle \varphi_z(-\boldsymbol{q}), \varphi_n(\boldsymbol{q})\rangle\rangle_z = \delta_{in}, \tag{3.56}$$

where one has

$$\alpha_{ij,kl} = \mathrm{i}\eta_{ij,kl} - \frac{\beta_{ij}\beta_{kl}T/C}{z + \mathrm{i}\lambda_{nm}q_nq_m}. \tag{3.57}$$

The discussion of eq. (3.4) is evident now. The function $\alpha(\boldsymbol{q}, z)$ has a diffusion pole of strength β^2T/C; the strength vanishes for zero temperature. Quantity $z\alpha(\boldsymbol{q}, z)$ is finite but discontinuous.

It is straightforward to determine the phonon resonances from eq. (3.57). There is one type of resonances having a linear dispersion law

$$\omega(\boldsymbol{q}) = qv(\boldsymbol{q}/q) + \mathrm{O}(q^2). \tag{3.58}$$

For $z = \omega(\boldsymbol{q})$ the $\boldsymbol{q} \to 0$ limit of $z\alpha(\boldsymbol{q})$ is non-zero and one gets as characteristic equation for $v(\boldsymbol{q}/q)$

$$\det[v(\boldsymbol{q}/q)\,\delta_{ik} - C'_{ij,kl}q_jq_l/q^2] = 0, \tag{3.59}$$

where $C'_{ij,kl}$ is given by eq. (3.51). These modes are first sound, i.e. displacement waves whose velocity depends on the direction but is independent of the wavelength and whose damping vanishes proportional to the square of the frequency. The velocity is given by the adiabatic elastic constants. These resonances do not exhaust the sum rule (3.54c). There is another phonon located at $\omega=0$ whose width is proportional to the square of the wave number. It is produced by the pole on the second Riemann sheet at

$$\omega(\boldsymbol{q}) = -\,\mathrm{i}\lambda_{nm}q_nq_m + \mathrm{O}(q^3). \tag{3.60}$$

The two phonon resonances can be determined experimentally by inelastic light scattering.

In the long-wavelength, low-frequency regime one expects the modes of the system to be describable in phenomenological terms. To see this let us introduce

$$\delta\langle\varphi_i(\boldsymbol{q})\rangle(t) = s_i(\boldsymbol{q}, t), \qquad \delta\langle\varepsilon(\boldsymbol{q})\rangle(t)/C = T(\boldsymbol{q}, t). \tag{3.61a, b}$$

After redoing the spacial Fourier transform one obtains for the Bloch–Langevin equations (3.55) and (1.58) in the absence of forces

$$\partial_t^2 s_i = [C_{ij,kl}\partial_j\partial_l + \eta_{ij,kl}\partial_j\partial_l\partial_t]\, s_k - \beta_{ij}\partial_j T\,, \tag{3.62a}$$

$$\partial_t T = \lambda_{ij}\partial_i\partial_j T - \beta_{jk}\partial_j\partial_t s_k\,. \tag{3.62b}$$

These are the well-known equations of elasto-thermodynamics. Since β_{ij} has been identified as the change of the stress with temperature the quantity $T(\boldsymbol{r}, t)$ has the phenomenological meaning of the local temperature change. Since C has been identified as the specific heat at constants strains $\varepsilon(\boldsymbol{q})$ has the meaning of a heat density operator. The coefficients λ and η are the thermal conductivity and the viscosity, respectively.

Thus the work based on the analysis of the eqs. (3.62), in particular the one by Landau and Placzek (1934), is incorporated in the microscopic lattice dynamics. Especially, microscopic expressions for the various parameters entering eqs. (3.62) have been derived in subsections 3.2, 3.3.

4. *Approximations*

4.1. Undamped phonons

As starting point for approximations one can use the hamiltonian H_0 defined in eq. (2.25) with the aid of the static restoring forces. Operators φ and

π are not eigenfunctions of $\mathscr{H}_0$. The eigenfunctions are given by appropriate linear combinations. To find these functions we remember that $D_{ik}(\boldsymbol{q})$ is a hermitian positive matrix. Thus it can be written as

$$D_{ij}(\boldsymbol{q}) = \sum_{\alpha=1}^{3} e_i\begin{pmatrix}\alpha\\ \boldsymbol{q}\end{pmatrix} \omega^2\begin{pmatrix}\alpha\\ \boldsymbol{q}\end{pmatrix} e_j^*\begin{pmatrix}\alpha\\ \boldsymbol{q}\end{pmatrix}. \tag{4.1a}$$

Here the $\omega^2\binom{\alpha}{\boldsymbol{q}}$ denote the positive eigenvalues of D_{ik}. The frequencies $\omega\binom{\boldsymbol{q}}{\alpha}$ we choose positive. Because of time reversal symmetry $\omega\binom{\alpha}{\boldsymbol{q}} = \omega\binom{\alpha}{-\boldsymbol{q}}$. The $e_i\binom{\alpha}{\boldsymbol{q}}$ denote the eigenvectors of D_{ik} obeying

$$\sum_{\alpha} e_i\begin{pmatrix}\alpha\\ \boldsymbol{q}\end{pmatrix} e_j^*\begin{pmatrix}\alpha\\ \boldsymbol{q}\end{pmatrix} = \delta_{ij}, \qquad \sum_{i} e_i\begin{pmatrix}\alpha\\ \boldsymbol{q}\end{pmatrix} e_i^*\begin{pmatrix}\beta\\ \boldsymbol{q}\end{pmatrix} = \delta^{\alpha\beta}. \tag{4.1b, c}$$

Because of time reversal symmetry one can fulfill the convention $e_j^*\binom{\alpha}{\boldsymbol{q}} = e_j\binom{\alpha}{-\boldsymbol{q}}$. Because of reflexion symmetry of Bravais lattices D_{ij} has been shown to be real, i.e. we can also choose the $e_j\binom{\alpha}{\boldsymbol{q}}$ to be real. To simplify the notations we will abbreviate

$$\begin{pmatrix}\alpha\\ \boldsymbol{q}\end{pmatrix} = (q), \qquad \begin{pmatrix}\alpha\\ -\boldsymbol{q}\end{pmatrix} = (-q) \tag{4.2}$$

and use the summation convention with respect to q whenever possible. Now it is easy to check from eqs. (2.27) that $\mathscr{H}_0$ has the eigenvector

$$b_k = \tfrac{1}{2}e_j(k)\left[(2\omega_k)^{1/2}\,\varphi_j(\boldsymbol{k}) + \mathrm{i}(2/\omega_k)^{1/2}\,\pi_j(\boldsymbol{k})\right]) \tag{4.3}$$

for eigenvalue $-\omega_k$, and $b_k^\dagger$ as eigenvector with eigenvalue $+\omega_k$

$$\mathscr{H}_0 b_k = -\,\omega_k b_k, \qquad \mathscr{H}_0 b_k^\dagger = \omega_k b_k^\dagger. \tag{4.4}$$

The commutation relations (2.8a) imply the Bose commutation relations for the b's

$$[b_k, b_p^\dagger] = \delta_{kp}, \qquad [b_k, b_p] = [b_k^\dagger, b_p^\dagger] = 0. \tag{4.5a, b}$$

The inverse transformation is given by

$$\varphi_i(\boldsymbol{k}) = \sum_{\alpha} e_i(k)\,(2\omega_k)^{-1/2}\;\; b_k + b_{-k}^\dagger), \tag{4.6a}$$

$$\pi_i(\boldsymbol{k}) = -\,\mathrm{i}\sum_{\alpha} e_i(k)\,(\tfrac{1}{2}\omega_k)^{1/2}\,(b_k - b_{-k}^\dagger). \tag{4.6b}$$

The operators b_k, $b_k^\dagger$ are the annihilation and creation operators respectively for phonons of energy ω_k and polarisation $e_i(k)$. Each product of these operators is an eigenvector of $\mathscr{H}_0$ also, e.g.

$$\mathscr{H}_0 b_{k_1} b_{k_2} = (-\omega_{k_1} - \omega_{k_2})\, b_{k_1} b_{k_2}, \tag{4.7a}$$

$$\mathscr{H}_0 b^\dagger_{k_1} b_{k_2} = (\omega_{k_1} - \omega_{k_2})\, b^\dagger_{k_1} b_{k_2}, \tag{4.7b}$$

$$\mathscr{H}_0 b^\dagger_{k_1} b^\dagger_{k_2} = (\omega_{k1} + \omega_{k_2})\, b^\dagger_{k_1} b_{k_2}. \tag{4.7c}$$

The ground state of H_0 is the phonon vacuum, $b^\dagger_{k_1}$ creates one-phonon states, $b^\dagger_{k_1} b^\dagger_{k_2}$ two-phonon states etc. Since

$$H_0 = \sum \omega_k (b^\dagger_k b_k + \tfrac{1}{2}) \tag{4.8}$$

the phonon number $N = \sum b^\dagger_k b_k$ is a conserved quantity for H_0. One should be aware that the phonon parameters ω_k, $e_i(k)$ and hence the phonon operators depend on the temperature and on the pressure, since the dynamical matrix $D_{ik}(\boldsymbol{q})$ depends on those quantities.

The averages and correlation functions formed with H_0 also will be indicated by a subscript zero. It is a trivial task to evaluate these quantities. At first all expectation values and correlation functions are zero unless the number of creation operators equals the number of annihilation operators. In particular all functions built up of an odd number of phonon operators vanish. The simplest non-zero function can be calculated with eqs. (1.32a), (4.4), (4.5)

$$(z - \omega_k) \langle\langle b_k;\, b^\dagger_p \rangle\rangle_0 = \delta_{kp}. \tag{4.9a}$$

Hence the spectral function (1.7b) reads

$$\langle\langle b_k;\, b^\dagger_p \rangle\rangle''_0 = -\pi \delta(\omega - \omega_k)\, \delta_{kp}. \tag{4.9b}$$

From eqs. (1.41a), (4.5a) one can calculate the expectation values

$$\langle b^\dagger_k b_p \rangle_0 = \delta_{kp} n_k, \qquad \langle b_p b^\dagger_k \rangle_0 = \delta_{kp}(1 + n_k), \tag{4.9c, d}$$

where n_k denotes the Bose function (1.41b) for energy ω_k. A little more complicated are functions of the type $\langle\langle A;\, b^\dagger_k \rangle\rangle_0$ where A denotes some operator. The equation of motion (1.32b) yields

$$(z - \omega_k) \langle\langle A;\, b^\dagger_k \rangle\rangle_0 = \langle [A,\, b^\dagger_k] \rangle. \tag{4.10a}$$

With eq. (4.9a) one finds the solution

$$\langle\langle A;\, b^\dagger_k \rangle\rangle_0 = \langle [A,\, b^\dagger_p] \rangle \langle\langle b_p;\, b^\dagger_k \rangle\rangle_0. \tag{4.10b}$$

Similarly

$$(z + \omega_k) \langle\!\langle A; b_k \rangle\!\rangle_0 = \langle [A, b_k] \rangle , \tag{4.11a}$$

$$\langle\!\langle A; b_k \rangle\!\rangle_0 = - \langle [A, b_p] \rangle \langle\!\langle b_p^\dagger; b_k \rangle\!\rangle . \tag{4.11b}$$

With eq. (4.6a) one obtains then by induction for odd ν

$$\langle\!\langle \varphi_{i_1}(\boldsymbol{k}) \cdots \varphi_{i_\nu}(k_\nu); \varphi_i(\boldsymbol{k}) \rangle\!\rangle_0 = \sum_{k=1}^{\nu} \{\textstyle\sum \text{all products of } \langle \varphi_{i_\alpha}(\boldsymbol{k}_\alpha)\, \varphi_{i_\beta}(\boldsymbol{k}_\beta) \rangle_0 ;\, \alpha \neq k\} \times \langle\!\langle \varphi_{i_k}(\boldsymbol{k}_k); \varphi_i(\boldsymbol{k}) \rangle\!\rangle_0 . \tag{4.12}$$

For the expectation values one obtains with eqs. (4.6a), (4.9) the formula

$$\langle \varphi_i^\dagger(\boldsymbol{k})\, \varphi_j(\boldsymbol{p}) \rangle_0 = \delta_{\boldsymbol{k}\boldsymbol{p}} \sum_\alpha e_i \begin{pmatrix} \alpha \\ \boldsymbol{k} \end{pmatrix} \left[1 + 2n \begin{pmatrix} \alpha \\ \boldsymbol{k} \end{pmatrix} \right] \left[2\omega \begin{pmatrix} \alpha \\ \boldsymbol{k} \end{pmatrix} \right]^{-1} e_j \begin{pmatrix} \alpha \\ \boldsymbol{k} \end{pmatrix} . \tag{4.13}$$

As last example let us consider two-phonon functions. The equation of motion (1.32a) leads to

$$[z + \omega_{k_1} - \omega_{k_2}] \langle\!\langle b_{k_1}^\dagger b_{k_2}; b_{p_2}^\dagger b_{p_1} \rangle\!\rangle_0 = \delta_{k_2 p_2} \langle b_{k_1}^\dagger b_{p_1} \rangle - \delta_{k_1 p_1} \langle b_{p_2}^\dagger b_{k_2} \rangle ,$$

and hence

$$\langle\!\langle b_{k_1}^\dagger b_{k_2}; b_{p_2}^\dagger b_{p_1} \rangle\!\rangle_0 = \delta_{k_1 p_1} \delta_{k_2 p_2} [n_{k_1} - n_{k_2}] / [z - \omega_{k_2} + \omega_{k_1}] . \tag{4.14a}$$

Similarly one finds

$$\langle\!\langle b_{k_1}^\dagger b_{k_2}^\dagger; b_{p_2} b_{p_1} \rangle\!\rangle_0 = - \{\delta_{k_1 p_1} \delta_{k_2 p_2} [1 + n_{k_1} + n_{k_2}] / [z + \omega_{k_1} + \omega_{k_2}]\} + \{k_1 \leftrightarrow k_2\} , \tag{4.14b}$$

$$\langle\!\langle b_{k_1} b_{k_2}; b_{p_2}^\dagger b_{p_1}^\dagger \rangle\!\rangle_0 = + \{\delta_{k_1 p_1} \delta_{k_2 p_2} [1 + n_{k_1} + n_{k_2}] / [z - \omega_{k_1} - \omega_{k_2}]\} + \{k_1 \leftrightarrow k_2\} . \tag{4.14c}$$

The equations of § 1.2 thus provide a most efficient apparatus to evaluate the relevant correlation functions and expectation values for the undamped phonon approximation. By definition the one-phonon functions are simple δ-resonances. The many-phonon functions, which enter for instance the light absorption or neutron scattering functions, have resonances obtained by superposition of one-phonon energies.

4.2. Restoring forces and elastic constants

The most important static correlation functions entering the formulae of §§ 2 and 3 are the static displacement–displacement susceptibilities (2.18). To derive approximations for these quantities let us introduce cumulant products of displacement operators by defining

$$\varphi(1)\cdots\varphi(\nu)=\sum_{\mu_1}\varphi(\mu_1)\langle\varphi(1)\cdots\varphi(\nu)\rangle+\sum_{\mu_1\mu_2}\tfrac{1}{2}(\varphi(\mu_1)\,\varphi(\mu_2))_c \times\langle\varphi(1)\cdots\varphi\ \nu)\rangle+\cdots+(\varphi(1)\cdots\varphi(\nu))_c. \quad (4.15)$$

One verifies

$$\langle[(\varphi(1)\cdots\varphi(\nu))_c,\pi]\rangle=0. \quad (4.16)$$

Furthermore one introduces renormalized vertices

$$V^{R}(1\cdots\nu)=\sum_{\mu=0}^{\infty}(1/\mu!)\,V(1\cdots\nu,\bar{1}\cdots\bar{\mu})\,\langle\varphi(\bar{1})\cdots\varphi(\bar{\mu})\rangle. \quad (4.17)$$

Equation (2.3b) yields

$$D_{ij}(\boldsymbol{q})=V^{R}(\boldsymbol{q}i,-\boldsymbol{q}j)+(A_i(\boldsymbol{q}),\varphi_k(\boldsymbol{q}))\,D_{kj}(\boldsymbol{q}), \quad (4.18)$$

where

$$A_i(\boldsymbol{q})=\sum_{\nu=2}^{\infty}(1/\nu!)\,V^{R}(\boldsymbol{q}i,\bar{1}\cdots\bar{\nu})\,(\varphi^{\dagger}(\bar{1})\cdots\varphi^{\dagger}(\bar{\nu}))_c. \quad (4.19)$$

The last term in eq. (4.18) can be reformulated with eqs. (2.28)–(2.30) and (4.16) to

$$(A_i(\boldsymbol{q}),\varphi_k(\boldsymbol{q}))\,V^{R}(\boldsymbol{q}k,-\boldsymbol{q}j)=-(A_i(\boldsymbol{q}),A_j(-\boldsymbol{q})). \quad (4.20)$$

The first term on the right-hand side of eq. (4.18) is linear in H', the second is quadratic. One could proceed by expanding the right-hand side of (4.20) but we want to stop at this stage.

If one wants to evaluate D only up to linear terms one can drop the second term on the right-hand side of eq. (4.18) and use eq. (4.12) to evaluate eq. (4.17). Thus one finds

$$D_{ij}^{(1)}(\boldsymbol{q})=\sum_{\nu=0}^{\infty}(1/\nu!\,2^{\nu})\,V(\boldsymbol{q}i,-\boldsymbol{q}j,\boldsymbol{k}_1i_1,-\boldsymbol{k}_1j_1,\cdots,\boldsymbol{k}_\nu i_\nu,-\boldsymbol{k}_\nu j_\nu) \times\langle\varphi_{i_1}^{\dagger}(\boldsymbol{k}_1)\,\varphi_{j_1}(\boldsymbol{k}_1)\rangle\cdots\langle\varphi_{i_\nu}^{\dagger}(\boldsymbol{k}_\nu)\,\varphi_{j_\nu}(\boldsymbol{k}_\nu)\rangle. \quad (4.21a)$$

Because of eqs. (4.1a), (4.13) this is a non-linear equation to determine the phonon parameters. Since the temperature enters the Bose function in eq. (4.13) the solution will depend on the temperature also. The solution of eq. (4.21a) has been invented originally (Born 1951, Hooton 1955a, b, 1958) by variational techniques and is called self-consistent or renormalized harmonic approximation. This approximation is equivalent to what is called molecular field of Hartree approximation in other fields of many-body physics; and it suffers from all the well-known deficiencies of this primitive approximation.

If the series of fluctuation products on the right-hand side of eq. (4.21a) converges rapidly one can approximate it by the first few terms. In zeroth order one finds the harmonic approximation

$$D_{ij}^{(1)}(\boldsymbol{q}) = V(\boldsymbol{q}i, -\boldsymbol{q}j). \tag{4.21b}$$

Here the restoring forces depend on the temperature only implicitly through the equilibrium positions $\boldsymbol{X}(\boldsymbol{n})$ of the particles. The first correction is given by

$$D_{ij}^{(1)}(\boldsymbol{q}) = V(\boldsymbol{q}i, -\boldsymbol{q}j) + \tfrac{1}{4}\sum_{\boldsymbol{p}\alpha} V(\boldsymbol{q}i, -\boldsymbol{q}j, \boldsymbol{p}k, -\boldsymbol{p}l)$$
$$\times\, e_k\begin{pmatrix}\alpha\\ \boldsymbol{p}\end{pmatrix} e_l\begin{pmatrix}\alpha\\ \boldsymbol{p}\end{pmatrix}\left[1 + 2n\begin{pmatrix}\alpha\\ \boldsymbol{p}\end{pmatrix}\right] \Big/ \omega\begin{pmatrix}\alpha\\ \boldsymbol{p}\end{pmatrix}. \tag{4.21c}$$

where the phonon parameters on the right-hand side are taken from eq. (4.1a) or from eq. (4.21b) depending on whether or not one wants to treat the phonons self-consistently.

The first improvement of approximation (4.21) is given by

$$D_{ij}^{(2)}(\boldsymbol{q}) = D_{ij}^{(1)}(\boldsymbol{q}) - F_{ij}(\boldsymbol{q}), \tag{4.22a}$$

with

$$F_{ij}(\boldsymbol{q}) = (A_i(\boldsymbol{q}), A_j(\boldsymbol{q})). \tag{4.22b}$$

The susceptibility F can be evaluated with H_0. Taking into account cubic anharmonicities only one derives from eqs. (4.6a), (4.14) and (4.19)

$$F_{ij}(\boldsymbol{q}) = \sum_{\boldsymbol{k}_1\boldsymbol{k}_2} V^{\mathrm{R}}(\boldsymbol{q}i, -\boldsymbol{k}_1 i_1, -\boldsymbol{k}_2 i_2)\, e_{i_1}(k_1)\, e_{i_2}(k_2)\, V^{\mathrm{R}}(-\boldsymbol{q}j, \boldsymbol{k}_1 j_1, \boldsymbol{k}_2 j_2)$$
$$\times\, e_{j_1}(k_1)\, e_{j_2}(k_2)\left(\frac{1 + n_{k_1} + n_{k_2}}{\omega_{k_1} + \omega_{k_2}} + \frac{n_{k_1} - n_{k_2}}{\omega_{k_2} - \omega_{k_1}}\right)\Big/ 16\omega_{k_1}\omega_{k_2}. \tag{4.22c}$$

Again eqs. (4.22) are non-linear relations to determine the phonon parameters. The function $F_{ij}(\boldsymbol{q})$ describes the influence of two-phonon states on the one-phonon restoring forces. Because of the pseudo delta function contained in V^{R} there is actually only one summation over the first Brillouin zone on the right-hand side of eq. (4.22c), and hence the numerical work for a discussion of eq. (4.22c) is of the same order as the one for a discussion of eq. (4.21c).

Taking the long-wavelength limit of D one obtains approximations for the isothermal elastic constants from eqs. (3.1) and (3.52c). In the simplest approximation the formulae derived from eq. (4.22) reduce to the ones originally (Feldman 1964) obtained by performing the derivative of the harmonic lattice energy with respect to homogeneous deformations. Thus we suggest to extend these results to the complete Brillouin zone and, if necessary, to make the equations self-consistent. As a result one would obtain phonons being closer to physical resonances than the harmonic ones.

4.3. Specific heat and β-tensor

Since it is indeed a straightforward matter to perform the perturbation expansion for static quantities in the manner demonstrated in §4.2, we want to confine ourselves in the following to determine the leading contributions of the relevant quantities. Using definition (4.17) one obtains for the energy density up to the static lattice energy

$$E(\boldsymbol{n}) = V^{\mathrm{R}}(\boldsymbol{n}i)\,\varphi_i(\boldsymbol{n}) + \tfrac{1}{2}\pi(\boldsymbol{n})\,\pi(\boldsymbol{n}) + \tfrac{1}{2}\sum_{\boldsymbol{m}} \varphi_i(\boldsymbol{n})\,V^{\mathrm{R}}(\boldsymbol{n}i, \boldsymbol{m}j)\,\varphi_j(\boldsymbol{m})$$

$$+ \frac{1}{3!}\sum_{\boldsymbol{n}_1\boldsymbol{n}_2} V^{\mathrm{R}}(\boldsymbol{n}i, \boldsymbol{n}_1 i_1, \boldsymbol{n}_2 i_2)\,(\varphi_i(\boldsymbol{n})\,\varphi_{i_1}(\boldsymbol{n}_1)\,\varphi_{i_2}(\boldsymbol{n}_2))_{\mathrm{c}} + \cdots. \tag{4.23a}$$

To calculate the projection of E on φ one applies eq. (2.30) and obtains

$$V^{\mathrm{R}}(1, \bar{1})\,(\varphi(\bar{1}), X) = -\,(A(1), X)$$

for each operator X having the property $\langle[X, \pi]\rangle = 0$. Here the operator A is defined by eq. (4.19). Hence one finds for the heat density (3.5)

$$\varepsilon(\boldsymbol{n}) = \varepsilon_0(\boldsymbol{n}) + \varepsilon'(\boldsymbol{n}) + \varepsilon''(\boldsymbol{n}), \tag{4.23b}$$

where

$$\varepsilon_0(\boldsymbol{n}) = \tfrac{1}{2}\left[\pi_i(\boldsymbol{n})\,\pi_i(\boldsymbol{n}) + \sum_{\boldsymbol{m}} \varphi_i(\boldsymbol{n})\,D_{ij}(\boldsymbol{n}, \boldsymbol{m})\,\varphi_j(\boldsymbol{m})\right], \tag{4.23c}$$

$$\varepsilon'(\boldsymbol{n}) = \tfrac{1}{2}\sum_{\boldsymbol{l}} \varphi_j(\boldsymbol{l})\,(A_j(\boldsymbol{l}), [\pi_i(\boldsymbol{n})\,\pi_i(\boldsymbol{n}) + \sum_{\boldsymbol{m}} \varphi_k(\boldsymbol{n})\,D_{ki}(\boldsymbol{n}, \boldsymbol{m})\,\varphi_i(\boldsymbol{m})])$$

$$+ \tfrac{1}{6}\sum_{\boldsymbol{n}_1\boldsymbol{n}_2} V^{\mathrm{R}}(\boldsymbol{n}i, \boldsymbol{n}_1 i_1, \boldsymbol{n}_2 i_2)\,(\varphi_i(\boldsymbol{n})\,\varphi_{i_1}(\boldsymbol{n}_1)\,\varphi_{i_2}(\boldsymbol{n}_2))_{\mathrm{c}} + \cdots. \tag{4.23d}$$

$$\varepsilon''(\boldsymbol{n}) = +\,\tfrac{1}{2}\sum_{\boldsymbol{m}} \varphi_i(\boldsymbol{n})\,F_{ij}(\boldsymbol{n}\boldsymbol{m})\,\varphi_j(\boldsymbol{m}). \tag{4.23e}$$

Here F is given by eq. (4.22c). In the preceding equations ε has been evaluated up to and including quadratic terms in H'.

In leading order one can work with ε_0 and obtains in Fourier space with eqs. (2.6), (2.7)

$$\varepsilon_0(\boldsymbol{q}) = \tfrac{1}{2}N^{-1/2} \sum_{k_1k_2} \Delta(\boldsymbol{q} - \boldsymbol{k}_1 - \boldsymbol{k}_2)\,[\pi_i(\boldsymbol{k}_1)\,\pi_i(\boldsymbol{k}_2) + \varphi_i(\boldsymbol{k}_1)\,D_{ij}(\boldsymbol{k}_2)\,\varphi_j(\boldsymbol{k}_2)]\,. \tag{4.24}$$

This expression differs from the conventional one

$$\varepsilon^0(\boldsymbol{q}) = N^{-1/2} \sum_{\alpha k} \omega \begin{pmatrix} \alpha \\ \boldsymbol{k} \end{pmatrix} b^\dagger \begin{pmatrix} \alpha \\ \boldsymbol{k} - \frac{1}{2}\boldsymbol{q} \end{pmatrix} b \begin{pmatrix} \alpha \\ \boldsymbol{k} + \frac{1}{2}\boldsymbol{q} \end{pmatrix}. \tag{4.25}$$

However, using the results of §4.1 one verifies

$$(A, \varepsilon_0(\boldsymbol{q}) - \varepsilon^0(\boldsymbol{q}))_0 = \mathrm{O}(q^2) \tag{4.26}$$

for all vectors (of finite length). Trivially, the left-hand side vanishes for all vectors, which are not bilinear in the phonon operators; and for the bilinear vectors eqs. (4.14) yield the statement. Now we are allowed to replace ε_0 by every operator, which converges towards ε_0 for small $\boldsymbol{q}$. This is because the introduction of $\varepsilon(\boldsymbol{q})$ was necessary and relevant for small $\boldsymbol{q}$'s only. For the sake of simplicity we will use $\varepsilon^0(\boldsymbol{q})$ in the following.

Then the static heat–heat susceptibility (3.7) reads

$$C(\boldsymbol{q}) = (1/TN) \sum_{k} \omega(k)\, m_{\boldsymbol{q}}(k)\, \omega(k), \tag{4.27a}$$

where

$$m_{\boldsymbol{q}}(k) = [n(\boldsymbol{k}^\alpha + \tfrac{1}{2}\boldsymbol{q}) - n(\boldsymbol{k}^\alpha - \tfrac{1}{2}\boldsymbol{q})]/[\omega(\boldsymbol{k}^\alpha - \tfrac{1}{2}\boldsymbol{q}) - \omega(\boldsymbol{k}^\alpha + \tfrac{1}{2}\boldsymbol{q})]\,. \tag{4.27b}$$

In particular one finds for the specific heat

$$C = (1/TN) \sum_{k} \omega^2(k)\, m(k), \tag{4.28a}$$

$$m(k) = \lim_{\boldsymbol{q}\to 0} m_{\boldsymbol{q}}(k) = -\,\partial n(k)/\partial\omega(k)\,. \tag{4.28b}$$

Equation (4.28) has the well-known form from the harmonic theory, except that the frequencies $\omega(k)$ here are defined with the correct static restoring forces (4.1a). In particular one obtains from eqs. (4.28) for low temperatures the Debye law with the correct sound velocities involved.

For the static $\mathscr{H}\pi - \varepsilon$ susceptibility one derives from eqs. (3.9), (3.10) in leading order

$$T\beta_{ij}(\boldsymbol{q})\, q_j = \tfrac{1}{2}\mathrm{i}V^{\mathrm{R}}(-\,\boldsymbol{q}i, \boldsymbol{k}_1 i_1, \boldsymbol{k}_2 i_2)\,(\varphi_{i_1}(\boldsymbol{k}_1)\,\varphi_{i_2}(\boldsymbol{k}_2), \varepsilon(\boldsymbol{q}))\,.$$

From eqs. (4.6a), (4.14), (4.25) and (4.27b) one finds then

$$\beta_{ij}(\boldsymbol{q})\, q_j = (1/\tfrac{1}{2}T\sqrt{N})\, \mathrm{i} \sum_{\boldsymbol{k}\alpha} V^{\mathrm{R}}(-\boldsymbol{q}\,\mathrm{i}, \boldsymbol{k}+\tfrac{1}{2}\boldsymbol{q}\; i_1, -\boldsymbol{k}+\tfrac{1}{2}\boldsymbol{q}\; i_2)$$
$$\times\, m_{\boldsymbol{q}}\begin{pmatrix}\alpha\\ \boldsymbol{k}\end{pmatrix} e_{i_1}\begin{pmatrix}\alpha\\ \boldsymbol{k}+\frac{1}{2}\boldsymbol{q}\end{pmatrix} e_{i_2}\begin{pmatrix}\alpha\\ \boldsymbol{k}-\frac{1}{2}\boldsymbol{q}\end{pmatrix} \omega\begin{pmatrix}\alpha\\ \boldsymbol{k}\end{pmatrix}$$
$$\times\left[\omega\begin{pmatrix}\alpha\\ \boldsymbol{k}+\frac{1}{2}\boldsymbol{q}\end{pmatrix}\omega\begin{pmatrix}\alpha\\ \boldsymbol{k}-\frac{1}{2}\boldsymbol{q}\end{pmatrix}\right]^{-1/2}. \tag{4.29}$$

In particular for the tension tensor

$$\beta_{ij} = (1/TN)\sum_{k} \omega(k)\, K_{ij}(k)\, m(k), \tag{4.30a}$$

$$K_{ij}(k) = \mathrm{i}\sqrt{N}\,[\partial V(-\boldsymbol{q}i, \boldsymbol{k}+\tfrac{1}{2}\boldsymbol{q}\; i_1, -\boldsymbol{k}+\tfrac{1}{2}\boldsymbol{q}\; i_2/\partial q_j]$$
$$\times\, e_{i_1}(k)\, e_{i_2}(k)/(\omega(k)\, 2). \tag{4.30b}$$

In lowest approximation the preceding formula agrees with that one, originally (Leibfried and Ludwig 1961) derived by evaluating the change of the harmonic entropy under homogeneous deformations.

4.4. High-frequency phonon self-energy

According to the discussions of § 3 one expects eq. (2.22) to yield reasonable approximations for the phonon self-energy matrix $P_{ik}(\boldsymbol{q}, z)$ unless the frequency z and the wave number $\boldsymbol{q}$ tend to zero. In particular one can derive phonon damping from the absorptive part P''. From eq. (2.32) one obtains

$$P_{ik}(\boldsymbol{q}, z) = -(\rho_i(\boldsymbol{q}), \mathscr{R}_{\mathscr{Q}}(z)\, \rho_k(\boldsymbol{q})), \tag{4.31a}$$

where one obtains with the aid of eqs. (2.28c), (2.29), (4.19) and (4.22) in linear approximation with respect to anharmonicities

$$\rho_i(\boldsymbol{q}) = A_i(\boldsymbol{q}). \tag{4.31b}$$

Here P is quadratic in A and in leading order one can work out the correlation function for the hamiltonian $\mathscr{H}_0$. In particular one finds from eq. (2.33) $\mathscr{P}\mathscr{H}_0 A = 0$ and therefore $\mathscr{Q} = 1$ in eq. (4.31). As a result one gets in leading order

$$P_{ik}(\boldsymbol{q}, z) = -(A_i(\boldsymbol{q}), \mathscr{R}(z)\, A_k(\boldsymbol{q}))_0. \tag{4.31c}$$

Introducing the response function

$$F_{ik}(\boldsymbol{q}, z) = -\langle\!\langle A_i^{\dagger}(\boldsymbol{q}); A_k(\boldsymbol{q})\rangle\!\rangle_z, \tag{4.32a}$$

whose static value is the function $F_{ij}(\boldsymbol{q})$ of eq. (4.22b), one derives from eq. (1.54)

$$P_{ik}(\boldsymbol{q}, z) = [F_{ik}(\boldsymbol{q}, z) - F_{ik}(\boldsymbol{q}, 0)]/z. \tag{4.32b}$$

Restricting ourselves to cubic anharmonicities we obtain from eqs. (4.14) the result:

$$P_{ik}(\boldsymbol{q}, z) = P^{(1)}_{ik}(\boldsymbol{q}, z) + P^{(2)}_{ik}(\boldsymbol{q}, z), \tag{4.33a}$$

where

$$P^{(\alpha)}_{ik}(\boldsymbol{q}, z) = \sum_{k_1 k_2} V^{\mathrm{R}}(\boldsymbol{q}i, -\boldsymbol{k}_1 i_1, -\boldsymbol{k}_1 i_2)\, e_{i_1}(k_1)\, e_{i_2}(k_2) \times V^{\mathrm{R}}(-\boldsymbol{q}k, \boldsymbol{k}_1 j_1, \boldsymbol{k}_2 j_2)\, e_{j_1}(k_1)\, e_{j_2}(k_2)\, (8\omega_{k_1}\omega_{k_2})^{-1}\, N^{(\alpha)}_{(k_1, k_2, z)}, \tag{4.33b}$$

$$N^{(1)} = \frac{1 + n_{k_1} + n_{k_2}}{\omega_{k_1} + \omega_{k_2}} \left(\frac{1}{\omega_{k_1} + \omega_{k_2} - z} - \frac{1}{\omega_{k_1} + \omega_{k_2} + z} \right), \tag{4.33c}$$

$$N^{(2)} = +\, 2(n_{k_1} - n_{k_2})/(z + \omega_{k_1} - \omega_{k_2})\, (\omega_{k_1} - \omega_{k_2}). \tag{4.33d}$$

Using bare vertices and harmonic phonon parameters these formulae reduce to the ones originally obtained by diagram techniques (Kokkedee 1962).

Let us reconsider the discussion of $\alpha(\boldsymbol{q}, z)$ given in §3.1. For small $\boldsymbol{q}$ one can write

$$V^{\mathrm{R}}(\boldsymbol{q}i, -\boldsymbol{k}_1 i_1, -\boldsymbol{k}_2 i_2) = q_j (\partial/\partial q_j)\, V(\boldsymbol{q}i, -k_1 i_1, -k_2 i_2)\, \delta_{\boldsymbol{q}-\boldsymbol{k}_1-\boldsymbol{k}_2}. \tag{4.34}$$

Splitting α into two contributions corresponding to eqs. (4.33c) and (4.33d) one finds $\alpha^{(1)}(\boldsymbol{q}, z)$ to be continuous for small $\boldsymbol{q}, z$ while for small $\boldsymbol{q}$ with definitions (4.28b), (4.30b)

$$\mathrm{i}\alpha^{(2)}_{ik, jl}(\boldsymbol{q}, z) = (-1/N) \sum_k K_{ij}(k)\, K_{kl}(k)\, m(k)/[z - \boldsymbol{v}(k)\, \boldsymbol{q}], \tag{4.35}$$

where

$$v_i \begin{pmatrix} \alpha \\ \boldsymbol{k} \end{pmatrix} = \partial\omega \begin{pmatrix} \alpha \\ \boldsymbol{k} \end{pmatrix} / \partial k_i. \tag{4.36}$$

For zero temperature $m(k)$ vanishes. For non-zero temperature $m(k)$ is positive and $\alpha^{(2)}$ diverges for $\boldsymbol{q}, z \to 0$.

4.5. Transport coefficients

The last quantities we have to derive are approximations for the transport coefficients or memory kernels defined in §3.2. From eqs. (3.16) and (4.25) one obtains in leading approximation for the heat current

$$J_\alpha = \lim_{q\to 0} \sum_{k} \gamma_\alpha(\boldsymbol{k})\, b^\dagger_{\boldsymbol{k}-\frac{1}{2}\boldsymbol{q}} b_{\boldsymbol{k}+\frac{1}{2}\boldsymbol{q}}/\sqrt{N}, \tag{4.37}$$

where

$$\gamma_\alpha\ k) = v_\alpha(k)\,\omega(k), \quad \alpha = 1, 2, 3, \tag{4.38}$$

and v denotes the phonon group velocity. To find the corresponding expression for the momentum current in eq. (3.15) let us remember eqs. (2.32), (3.2a) and (4.31b) to find

$$J'_{ij}q_j = \tfrac{1}{2}V^{\mathrm{R}}(\boldsymbol{q}i, -\boldsymbol{k}_1 i_1, -\boldsymbol{k}_2 i_2)\,\varphi_{i_1}(\boldsymbol{k}_1)\,\varphi_{i_2}(\boldsymbol{k}_2).$$

On the right-hand side those contributions which are due to terms $b_{k_1}b_{k_2}$ and $b^\dagger_{-k_1}b^\dagger_{-k_2}$ can be dropped. These contributions can be treated by perturbation theory and yield the term $P^{(1)}_{ij}$ in eq. (4.33); in particular this term does not contribute in the interesting $z=0$ limit. Using eqs. (3.20) and (4.30) one obtains eq. (4.37) with

$$\gamma_\alpha(k) = K_{ij}(k) - \beta_{ij}\omega(k)/C, \quad \alpha = (i, j), \quad i, j = 1, 2, 3. \tag{4.39}$$

With eq. (4.28b) the current–current susceptibility reads

$$\chi^0_{\alpha\beta} = (J_\alpha, J_\beta) = (1/N) \sum_{\alpha} \gamma_\alpha(k)\, m(k)\, \gamma_\beta(k). \tag{4.40}$$

From eqs. (4.33), (4.34) and the underlying definitions one then arrives at the formula for the transport coefficients

$$\lambda_{\alpha\beta}, \eta_{\alpha\beta} = \chi^0_{\alpha\gamma}\hat{m}^{-1}_{\gamma\delta}(\mathrm{i}0)\,\chi^0_{\delta\beta}. \tag{4.41}$$

We mention, that in Grüneisen's approximation the right-hand side of eq. (4.39) vanishes and hence there is no viscosity then.

The determination of $\hat{m}$ now proceeds in complete analogy to the one outlined in §4.4. In leading order the projector $\hat{\mathcal{Q}}$ in eqs. (3.33b) and (3.34b) can be replaced by unity and then eq. (1.54) yields

$$\hat{m}_{\alpha\beta}(z) = (\chi_{\alpha\beta}(z) - \chi_{\alpha\beta}(0))/z, \tag{4.42a}$$

where

$$\chi_{\alpha\beta}(z) = -\langle\!\langle \mathcal{H}J_\alpha; \mathcal{H}J_\beta\rangle\!\rangle_z. \tag{4.42b}$$

Here one finds in leading approximation

$$\mathscr{H}J_\alpha = \tfrac{1}{2}N^{-1/2} \sum_{k_1k_2k_3} \gamma_\alpha(k_1)\,[V^*(k_1k_2k_3)\, b_{k_1}(b_{k_2} + b^\dagger_{-k_2})\,(b_{k_3} + b^\dagger_{-k_3}) - V(k_1k_2k_3)\, b^\dagger_{k_1}(b_{-k_2} + b^\dagger_{k_2})\,(b_{-k_3} + b^\dagger_{k_3})], \qquad (4.43a)$$

where

$$V(k_1k_2k_3) = V^{\mathrm{R}}(\mathbf{k}_1 i_1, \mathbf{k}_2 i_2, \mathbf{k}_3 i_3)\, e_{i_1}(k_1)\, e_{i_2}(k_2)\, e_{i_3}(k_3)\,(8\omega_{k_1}\omega_{k_2}\omega_{k_3})^{-1/2}. \qquad (4.43b)$$

The correlation function on the right-hand side of eq. (4.42b) can be worked out for the hamiltonian H_0. Substituting eqs. (4.43) into (4.42b) the remaining work is the evaluation of a number of three-phonon functions such as

$$g_{k_1k_2k_3,\, p_1p_2p_3}(z) = \langle\langle b^\dagger_{k_1} b^\dagger_{k_2} b_{-k_3};\, b_{p_1} b_{p_2} b^\dagger_{-p_3}\rangle\rangle\,. \qquad (4.44a)$$

These functions are determined by the same technique, which led to eqs. (4.14) for the two-phonon functions, and one finds for instance for the right-hand side of the preceding equation

$$g_{k_1k_2k_3,\, p_1p_2p_3} = \{\delta_{k_1p_1}\delta_{k_2p_2}\delta_{k_3p_3}[n_{k_1}n_{k_2}(1 + n_{k_3}) - (1 + n_{k_1})(1 + n_{k_2})\, n_{k_3}] \times [z + \omega_{k_1} + \omega_{k_2} - \omega_{k_3}]^{-1}\} + \{p_1 \leftrightarrow p_2\}. \qquad (4.44b)$$

Collecting all terms and performing the $z \to \mathrm{i}0$ limit in eq. (4.42a) one arrives at the final result for the memory kernels entering eq. (4.41)

$$\hat{m}_{\alpha\beta}(\mathrm{i}0) = \sum_{k_1k_2k_3} W(k_1; k_2k_3)\,[\gamma_\alpha(k_1) - \gamma_\alpha(k_2) - \gamma_\alpha(k_3)] \times [\gamma_\beta(k_1) - \gamma_\beta(k_2) - \gamma_\beta(k_3)], \qquad (4.45a)$$

where

$$W(k_1; k_2k_3) = |V(k_1k_2k_3)|^2\, 2\pi\, \delta(\omega_{k_1} - \omega_{k_2} - \omega_{k_3})\,[Tm_{k_1}m_{k_2}m_{k_3}]^{1/2}. \qquad (4.45b)$$

Here the V's are given by the modified vertices (4.43b), the weight functions $m(k)$ are defined in eq. (4.28b) and the γ's are defined in eq. (4.38) or (4.39) depending on whether one wants to discuss the heat conductivity or the viscosity. A formula like (4.45) for the heat conductivity has been discussed originally (Leibfried and Schlömann 1954) starting from the Peierls equation for the interacting phonon gas and solving this equation approximately with a variational Ansatz.

References

BORN, M. (1951), in: Festschrift d. Akad. d. Wiss. Göttingen, Germ.

BORN, M. and HUANG, K. (1956), *Dynamical theory of crystal lattices*, Clarendon Press, Oxford, England.

DUNFORD, N. and SCHWARTZ, J. T. (1967), *Linear operators*, Interscience Publ. Inc., New York.

FELDMAN, J.L. (1964), Proc. Phys. Soc. (London) **84**, 361.

HOOTON, D.J. (1955a), Phil. Mag. **46**, 422.

HOOTON, D.J. (1955b), Z. Phys. **142**, 42.

HOOTON, D.J. (1958), Phil. Mag. **3**, 49.

KADANOFF, L.P. and MARTIN, P.C. (1963), Ann. Phys. (N.Y.) **24**, 419.

KUBO, R. (1957), J. Phys. Soc. Japan **12**, 570.

MORI, H. (1965), Progress in Theoretical Physics **33**, 423.

KOKKEDEE, J.J.J. (1962), Physica **28**, 374.

LANDAU, L.D. and PLACZEK, G. (1934), Phys. Z. Sowjetunion **5**, 21.

LEIBFRIED, G. and LUDWIG, W. (1961), in: *Solid State Physics*, F. Seitz and D. Turnbull ed., Acad. Press Inc., New York, **12**.

LEIBFRIED, G. and SCHLÖMANN, E. (1954), Nachrichten der Akad. d. Wiss. Göttingen, Math. Phys. Klasse, 71.

MARADUDIN, A.A., MONTROLL, E.W. and WEISS, G.H. (1963), in: *Solid State Physics*, F. Seitz and D. Turnbull ed., Acad. Press Inc., New York, Supl. 3.

MARTIN, P.C. (1965), in: *Statistical mechanics of equilibrium and non-equilibrium*, J. Meixner ed., North-Holland.

ZUBAREV, D.N. (1960), Soviet Physics Usp. **3**, 320.

CHAPTER 10

Neutron Spectroscopy and Lattice Dynamics

G. DOLLING

"Atomic Energy of Canada Limited"
Chalk River Nuclear Laboratories,
Chalk River, Ontario, Canada

Dynamical of Properties Solids, edited by
G. K. Horton and A. A. Maradudin

Contents

1. Introduction

Many properties of solids are describable in terms of the behaviour of certain basic excitations such as phonons, excitons, magnons, etc. In order to understand these properties, it is most desirable to study the appropriate basic excitations in as much detail as possible over a wide range of conditions (of temperature, pressure, etc.). The most powerful techniques for such studies involve the observation of the scattering of radiation from the solid: in general, one attempts to measure the changes in energy and momentum suffered by the radiation as it passes through the solid and interacts in various ways with the basic excitations. In this chapter we shall be concerned mainly with the use of beams of thermal neutrons as a radiation probe to study in particular the phonons in a solid, which are of course just the quanta associated with the vibrations of the atoms in a crystal lattice. Some brief remarks on the application of X-ray thermal diffuse scattering measurements to the study of lattice vibrations will be given in §2.10. Much of the discussion of this chapter applies equally well to the study of excitations ther than phonons, (magnons, or spin waves in magnetic materials, have also been very widely studied by neutron scattering methods) but these topics are outside the scope of the present book.

1.1. Properties of phonons

We have seen in chapter 1 that the vibrational properties of crystalline solids are quite well described in terms of a whole spectrum of normal modes, each characterized by a frequency, ν, and a wave vector $\boldsymbol{q}$. The normal mode frequencies, or phonon frequencies, range from zero to $\approx 10^{14}$, and are typically of order 10^{12} Hz (or 1 THz). The wave vector $\boldsymbol{q}$, whose magnitude is $2\pi/\lambda$ where λ is the wavelength of the normal mode, ranges from zero to values of the order of the reciprocal of the interatomic spacings in the crystal, and hence is typically of order 10^8 cm^{-1}. For any given wave vector, there will usually be several different modes, often having distinct frequencies, and we denote these different modes by a subscript j. In any crystalline solid, there is a more or less well-defined "dispersion" relation, $\nu = \nu_j(\boldsymbol{q})$, between the frequency and wave vector of the normal modes. The frequency ν is precisely defined only in a perfect crystal in which the interatomic forces are purely harmonic. In any real crystal, there are imperfections of various types, and also anharmonic contributions to the interatomic forces, and these effects introduce a spread Δ in ν, or an energy width for the phonon. This width arises because the lifetimes of the phonons in a real crystal are limited by scattering from imperfections or from other phonons. The presence of anharmonic effects also means that the dispersion relation is temperature and pressure dependent. In magnetic crystals, there may be interactions between the spin wave excitations and the phonons which cause changes in the phonon frequency and frequency width; similarly, in materials containing conduction electrons, there may be interactions between the phonons and the plasmons, or plasma oscillations in the electron gas.

In general, therefore, if we wish to study the phonons, or lattice vibrations of a solid, we will be interested in the frequencies ν_j, the widths Δ_j, and the temperature and/or pressure dependence of these quantities, as a function of the wave vector $\boldsymbol{q}$. We may also be concerned with the frequency distribution function $g(\nu)\,\mathrm{d}\nu$ which tells us how many normal modes have frequencies in the range ν to $\nu + \mathrm{d}\nu$. In the next sub-section, we discuss in general terms why thermal neutrons are extremely valuable as a radiation probe to determine all these phonon properties, what are the problems involved in making measurements of thermal neutron scattering processes, and how these methods compare with other techniques such as light scattering (or absorption) and X-ray diffuse scattering.

1.2. Why neutron scattering?

The chief reason for the importance of thermal neutron beams in the study of the solid state is that the energy of a neutron, as obtained for example from the moderator of a nuclear reactor, is typically of the same order as the energy of a phonon in a solid, and also that the de Broglie wavelength λ of that neutron is of the order of interatomic distances. Electromagnetic radiation, perhaps the most important alternative probe in the study of lattice vibrations, may be matched in this way with a solid either in respect of its energy or in respect of its wavelength, but not both at the same time. Thus the energy of infrared radiation is in the correct range, but its wavelength is $\sim 10^4$ longer than typical interatomic distances, while an X-ray of wavelength

3 Å has an energy corresponding to a 'temperature' 5×10^7 K! Proponents of light scattering and neutron scattering techniques are fond of displaying their relative merits by means of energy–wave-vector plots (the wave vector of the radiation, k, is 2π/wavelength), showing the regions of this space which may be investigated by various experimental techniques. Two of these are shown superimposed in fig. 1; the areas enclosed by dashed lines represent the judgement of Raman scattering specialists (e.g. Fleury 1971), while the dotted lines indicate the views of at least one prominent neutron scattering expert (Egelstaff 1966). The three solid lines show the relationship between energy E and wave vector $|\boldsymbol{k}|$ for electromagnetic radiation, thermal neutrons, and typical sound waves, respectively. The '99% ranges' in this figure represent the energy and wave vector ranges required by the probe in order to study 99% of the phonons in a typical crystal. The essential feature of the thermal neutron scattering method is that it lies precisely at the region of overlap between these two 99% ranges. There is also, one may add, remarkable unanimity of viewpoints concerning the location of this sphere of influence for the neutron scattering method. It may be used to study directly

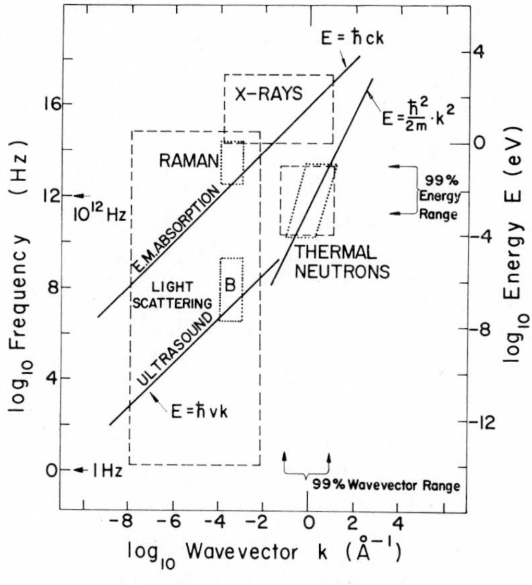

Fig. 1. Comparison of various radiation probes used in studies of the dynamical properties of solids. The areas outlined by dotted and dashed lines represent the appropriate ranges of usefulness of each probe, sketched from two different viewpoints (see text). The location of the thermal neutron areas at the intersection of the two 99% ranges is the *raison d'être* of thermal neutron scattering methods.

the properties of phonons of any wave vector $\boldsymbol{q}$ throughout the entire Brillouin zone, whereas light scattering techniques are restricted to $\boldsymbol{q}$ values which are extremely small on an atomic scale, at least so far as first order (or one-phonon) scattering is concerned. Perhaps the main disadvantage of neutron scattering is its relatively poor resolution, of order 1% in energy or wave vector, as compared with that ordinarily obtainable in light scattering experiments. It is for this reason that the neutron scattering areas in fig. 1, do not extend to very small wave vectors, even though such neutron scattering is clearly possible in practice: the neutron can of course be scattered from phonons of very small $\boldsymbol{q}$, but the observation is obscured by scattering involving many more phonons of larger wave vector which is allowed by the resolution of the spectrometer, so that any fine structure at low $\boldsymbol{q}$ is lost. The figure does have the virtue, however, of illustrating the complementary nature of the various probes which may be utilized in the study of phonon spectra.

1.3. Interactions of thermal neutrons with solids

When a thermal neutron impinges on a solid material, it may either be absorbed or scattered in various ways, or, more usually, it may pass through the solid without change. The cross-section for neutron absorption varies very considerably from one element to another, from 2.4×10^5 barn for ^{157}Gd to less than 2×10^{-4} barn for ^{16}O (1 barn $= 10^{-24}$ cm^2; these cross-sections are appropriate for neutrons of energy 0.025 eV, or de Broglie wavelength 1.8 Å). Elements with high absorption cross-sections are more difficult, perhaps impossible in some cases, to study by neutron scattering techniques, but this is an experimental restriction for only a few isotopes of relatively few elements. From the present viewpoint, of course, the scattering processes are of prime importance, and we shall now consider these a little more closely. Detailed theoretical calculations of the scattering cross-sections have previously appeared in the literature, for example by Van Hove (1954), Glauber (1955), Sjolander (1964), Lomer and Low (1965). The last named reference is one chapter of a comprehensive description of the development of thermal neutron scattering up to 1965.

The essential features of the calculation of the cross-section are as follows:

(a) Since the de Broglie wavelength of a thermal neutron is much greater ($\sim 10^5 \times$) than the size of the nucleus, only s-wave scattering from the nucleus is important, and this is isotropic and independent of neutron energy.

(b) The interaction between the neutron and the ith nucleus is represented by the Fermi pseudopotential, which is a δ-function:

$$v_i(r) = (2\pi\hbar^2 b_i/m)\,\delta(\boldsymbol{r} - \boldsymbol{r}_i),$$

where m is the neutron mass an b_i is the so-called bound atom scattering length. The possibility of expressing the potential in this simple form depends upon the assumption that the scattering by a single nucleus is very weak (first order Born approximation).

(c) The scattering from the entire assembly of nuclei in the solid is then obtained by summing over the scattering from individual nuclei with due regard to the relative phases of these scattered waves. In general, this will clearly depend on a complicated correlation function describing the relative positions of all nuclei as a function of time. The most important of these functions is the well-known time-dependent pair correlation function defined by Van Hove (1954).

(d) The scattering lengths b_i may not be the same for all nuclei of the same element, since different isotopes will scatter differently, and also, if the nuclear spin is non-zero, the scattering amplitude will depend on whether the neutron and nuclear spins are parallel or antiparallel. Normally, these nuclei having different scattering lengths will be distributed randomly throughout the crystal, and in this case it is convenient to split up the total scattering cross-section σ_t into two parts, a *coherent* (σ_{coh}) and an *incoherent* (σ_{inc}) part. The precise definitions of these cross-sections are given in detail in the aforementioned references, but the essential points may be understood from the following simple discussion. Let us refer to the very complicated motions of the nuclei in the crystal by a symbolic wave function Ψ. Then the total scattering cross-section may be written

$$\sigma_t = \Psi \langle b_i b_j \rangle, \tag{1.1}$$

where $\langle \cdots \rangle$ denotes an average over all pairs of nuclei i, j. If we denote those terms in which $i = j$ by the subscript s (self, or single nucleus) and terms $i \neq j$ by subscript d (interference, or distinct nuclei), then

$$\begin{aligned}\sigma_t &= \Psi_s \langle b_i^2 \rangle + \Psi_d \langle b_i \rangle^2 = \Psi_s \{\langle b_i^2 \rangle - \langle b_i \rangle^2\} + \{\Psi_s + \Psi_d\} \langle b_i \rangle^2 \\ &= \sigma_{inc} + \sigma_{coh}\,.\end{aligned} \tag{1.2}$$

We note that the coherent cross-section depends on the square of the mean scattering length, and contains 'interference' and 'self' components of our symbolic wave function. The incoherent cross-section, on the other hand, depends only on the scattering from individual nuclei (no interference effects), and is zero if all the b_i are equal. The importance of this division of σ_t lies in the fact that Ψ contains two delta-functions.

$$\delta\{E_0 - E_1 \mp \sum_l h\nu_j(\boldsymbol{q}_l)\}\,\delta\{\boldsymbol{k}_0 - \boldsymbol{k}_1 - \boldsymbol{Q}\}, \tag{1.3}$$

where

$$\boldsymbol{Q} = \sum_l \boldsymbol{q}_l + 2\pi\boldsymbol{\tau}.$$

The summation over l indicates that the scattering process may involve the creation and/or annihilation of l phonons of wave vectors $\boldsymbol{q}_l$. $\boldsymbol{\tau}$ is any vector of the reciprocal lattice of the crystal, and $\boldsymbol{Q}$ is called the momentum transfer vector, since $\hbar\boldsymbol{Q}$ is in fact the momentum change suffered by the neutron during the scattering process. $E_0\,(E_1)$ and $\boldsymbol{k}_0\,(\boldsymbol{k}_1)$ are the incident (scattered) neutron energies and wave vectors respectively ($E_0 = \hbar^2|\boldsymbol{k}_0|^2/2m$).

The first delta-function, which expresses conservation of energy, appears in both Ψ_s and Ψ_d, but the second one, conservation of pseudo- or crystal-momentum, appears only in Ψ_d. Thus the incoherent scattering cross-section contains no information about the relative positions of different nuclei in the crystal: measurement of σ_{inc} can only give information on the energies or energy distributions of phonons and other excitations in the crystal. Measurements of the coherent scattering, however, can be used to obtain information about the crystal structure and about the phonon dispersion relation $\nu = \nu_j(\boldsymbol{q})$. If $l = 0$ in eq. (1.3), we have elastic coherent, or Bragg, scattering, for which $E_0 = E_1$ and the scattering is confined in wave vector space to a set of reciprocal lattice points $\boldsymbol{\tau}$, from which the crystal structure in real space may be deduced. If $l = 1$, we have *one-phonon coherent inelastic* scattering, which is the scattering process of most interest to us in the present context. Multiphonon processes ($l \geqslant 2$) are usually to be regarded as a nuisance, contributing unwanted background scattering which makes the observation of the coherent one-phonon scattering more difficult. Of similar nuisance value are all incoherent scattering processes, except in a certain class of experiments, mainly concerned with hydrogenous materials, in which one deliberately measures the incoherent one-phonon scattering. In these experiments, which are possible because the scattering cross-section of hydrogen is mainly incoherent, one is interested in measurements of energy levels, or energy distributions; efforts are made to minimize any coherent scattering effects in such cases.

1.4. One-phonon coherent scattering

We shall now specialize to the case of coherent scattering of a monoenergetic beam of neutrons from a single crystal, in which one phonon of frequency $\nu_j(\boldsymbol{q})$ is involved, and give the detailed form of the symbolic wave function for this case, following Waller and Fröman (1952). The crystal is deemed to be made up of a very large number N of identical unit cells occupying a total volume V, each cell containing s distinct atoms of mass m_s. (The adjective distinct implies a distinguishable crystallographic location within the unit cell). The result is

$$\sigma_1(\boldsymbol{k}_0 \to \boldsymbol{k}_1)_{\mathrm{coh}} = [\pi h/M\nu_j(\boldsymbol{q})]\,(N/V)\,(k_1/k_0) \times \{n_j(\boldsymbol{q}) + \tfrac{1}{2} \pm \tfrac{1}{2}\}\,|G_j(\boldsymbol{Q})|^2\,\Delta_1\Delta_2\,, \quad (1.4)$$

where $M = \sum_s m_s$, the total mass of one unit cell (cell index L),

$$n_j(\boldsymbol{q}) = \{\exp[h\nu_j(\boldsymbol{q})/k_{\mathrm{B}}T] - 1\}^{-1}, \quad \text{the population factor}, \quad (1.5)$$

$$\Delta_1 = \delta\{E_0 - E_1 \mp h\nu_j(\boldsymbol{q})\}, \quad (1.6)$$

$$\Delta_2 = \delta\{\boldsymbol{k}_0 - \boldsymbol{k}_1 - \boldsymbol{q} - 2\pi\boldsymbol{\tau}\}, \quad (1.7)$$

$$G_j(\boldsymbol{Q}) = \boldsymbol{Q}\sum_s b_s \boldsymbol{U}_{sj}(\boldsymbol{q})\exp[-(2\pi\mathrm{i}\boldsymbol{\tau}\cdot\boldsymbol{r}_s)]\exp(-W_s). \quad (1.8)$$

W_s is the Debye–Waller factor and $\boldsymbol{r}_s$ is the position within the cell of the sth nucleus, whose scattering length is b_s. The upper (lower) signs in (1.4), (1.6) refer to pnonon creation (annihilation) respectively. $\boldsymbol{U}_{sj}(\boldsymbol{q})$ is the eigenvector of the sth nucleus in the jth normal mode of propagation vector $\boldsymbol{q}$. It is obtained by diagonalizing the dynamical matrix [see chapter 1, eq. (3.5)] in the form

$$D_{\alpha\beta}(\boldsymbol{q}, ss') = (m_s m_{s'})^{-1/2} \sum_{L'} \phi_{\alpha\beta}(Ls, L's')\,\mathrm{e}^{\mathrm{i}\boldsymbol{q}\cdot[\boldsymbol{r}(L's') - \boldsymbol{r}(Ls)]}, \quad (1.9)$$

where $\phi_{\alpha\beta}(Ls, L's')$ is a force constant defining the interaction between two nuclei at $\boldsymbol{r}(Ls)$, $\boldsymbol{r}(L's')$. Eq. (1.4) is the cross-section for a single phonon mode. To obtain the coherent one-phonon cross-section actually measured in an experiment, we must integrate over the range of phonon modes 'observed' by the spectrometer during an experimental scan. This is in general not completely trivial since E_0, $\boldsymbol{k}_0$ and E_1, $\boldsymbol{k}_1$ are related. A very common situation in certain time-of-flight spectrometers (§2.6) is one in which E_0, $\boldsymbol{k}_0$ and the direction of $\boldsymbol{k}_1 = \hat{\boldsymbol{k}}_1$ are fixed, and only E_1 and $|\boldsymbol{k}_1|$ vary over the experimental scan. As $|\boldsymbol{k}_1|$ varies, the point at which Δ_2 (conservation of crystal momentum) is satisfied moves through reciprocal space. The frequency $\nu_j(\boldsymbol{q})$ corresponding to this point will also vary; to first order, it will change by an amount $\boldsymbol{k}_1 \cdot \nabla_{\boldsymbol{q}} \nu_j(\boldsymbol{q})$. This change will match the change in $E_0 - E_1$, to a greater or lesser extent, and hence Δ_1 (conservation of energy) may be satisfied over a greater or lesser range within the experimental scan. Mathematically, one eveluates eq. (1.4) as follows. To integrate over Δ_2, multiply by the density of points in reciprocal space, $NV/(2\pi)^3$, and divide by the number of unit cells to obtain the cross-section per unit cell. Then take account of the integral over Δ_1, which varies according to the experimental conditions as mentioned above, by introducing the jacobian J_j. The cross-section then becomes

$$\sigma_{1\,\mathrm{coh}} = [N\hbar/4\pi M \nu_j(\boldsymbol{q})]\,(k_1/k_0)\,\{n_j(\boldsymbol{q}) + \tfrac{1}{2} \pm \tfrac{1}{2}\}\,|G_j(\boldsymbol{Q})|^2\,|J_j|^{-1}. \quad (1.10)$$

As demonstrated first by Waller and Fröman (1952), for the type of experimental scan described above, the jacobian takes on the simple form

$$J_j = 1 \mp (h/2E_1)\,\boldsymbol{k}_1 \cdot \nabla_{\boldsymbol{q}} \nu_j(\boldsymbol{q}). \quad (1.11)$$

The $-(+)$ signs here refer to phonon creation (annihilation) processes. Another even more common situation, encountered in experiments with crystal spectrometers is one in which $|\boldsymbol{k}_1|$ and $\boldsymbol{Q}$ (and hence $\boldsymbol{q}$) are held fixed as E_0 and the directions of $\boldsymbol{k}_1$ and $\boldsymbol{k}_0$ are varied during the scan. In this case, there is no functional dependence of $\nu_j(\boldsymbol{q})$ on $E_0 - E_1$ in eq. (1.6), and so the integration is trivial and, at least to first order, $J_j = 1$. This is one of the many excellent reasons for the popularity of the so-called 'constant-$\boldsymbol{Q}$' scans. Many other types of experimental scan can be carried out, and the form of J_j must be evaluated separately for each type. The results for a few popular types of linear scan are summarized in §2.5.

2. *Methods of neutron spectrometry*

2.1. Basic principles

The energy resolution of a typical neutron inelastic scattering measurement is, as noted in §1.2, of order 1%. There are at present only two ways of defining thermal neutron energies to this level of precision, (*i*) by utilizing the phenomenon of coherent elastic (Bragg) scattering of neutrons from selected planes of atoms in a crystal of known lattice spacings, and (*ii*) by 'chopping' the neutron beam into pulses and then measuring the time of flight of these pulses over a known distance. A wide variety of neutron spectrometers has been constructed over the past decade or so, utilizing methods (*i*) and (*ii*) or combinations of these. Before discussing these spectrometers in detail, we briefly enumerate some relevant properties both of Bragg scattering from crystals and of pulsed neutron beams, in order to provide some degree of experimental perspective to those unfamiliar with this subject.

Firstly, let us consider Bragg scattering from a typical crystal, which is governed by the well-known law $\lambda = 2d \sin \theta$. λ is the de Broglie wavelength of the neutron ($\lambda = 2\pi/k$, where k is the wave vector, related to the neutron energy by $E = \hbar^2 k^2/2m$), d is the spacing or separation between the reflecting planes of atoms, and 2θ is the angle through which the neutron beam is scattered or 'reflected'. Values of d for typical crystal planes range from 0.8 to 3.5×10^{-8} cm, so that a range of angles 2θ from 20° to 160°, can be employed to provide neutron wavelengths from about 0.5 to 6 Å. If $2\theta = 60°$, and the angular divergence of the beam (defined by collimation and crystal mosaic spread, see §2.2) is 0.3°, then the wavelength λ will be defined with 0.55% resolution (i.e. 1.1% energy resolution).

Secondly, we consider what characteristics of pulsed neutron beams we would need to achieve the same resolution. Thermal neutrons have a range of velocity $v \, (v = h/m\lambda)$ between about 500 and 5000 m/sec, with a typical velocity being 2000 m/sec. In principle, it is possible to obtain arbitrarily high resolution by having very long flight paths, but practical considerations usually place a limit of about 4 m on these path lengths. The typical neutron flight time is thus 2000 μsec, and so the neutron pulse length must be no more than 10 μsec to achieve 1% energy resolution. There are also limits (2 cm in the above example) on the sample size and detector thickness imposed by the resolution requirements. The presently available methods of producing thermal neutron pulses (see §§2.6, 2.11) can readily provide pulses in the range 5 to 10 μsec, but it is extremely difficult to reduce the pulse width significantly below 5 μsec. Very high resolution must then be obtained by very long flight paths.

High resolution in crystal spectrometers, on the other hand, is obtained by means of very fine collimation of the neutron beams and by using reflecting crystals of low mosaic spread. In either type of spectrometer, of course, the ultimate limit of resolution is imposed by the necessity to achieve a reasonable count-rate in the detector. In a given experiment, the count-rate varies inversely as a fairly high power (4 or 5) of the overall experimental resolution; this limit, of order 1% energy resolution, is thus set by the neutron fluxes obtainable from present-day neutron sources. More detailed remarks about the resolution function for various types of spectrometer will be made in the appropriate sections (§§2.5–2.8).

All inelastic neutron scattering spectrometers so far constructed, operate within a fixed plane, usually horizontal, although a few vertical plane instruments are also in use. By the plane of the spectrometer we mean the plane containing the neutron beams incident upon and scattered from the specimen. Let us define an orthogonal set of axes xyz with x and y defining the plane of the spectrometer. The neutron wave vectors are thus $\boldsymbol{k}_0 = (k_{0x}, k_{0y}, k_{0z} = 0)$ and $\boldsymbol{k}_1 = (k_{1x}, k_{1y}, k_{1z} = 0)$, and the conservation equations (1.6) and (1.7) can be written

$$(\hbar^2/2m)\,(k_{0x}^2 + k_{0y}^2 - k_{1x}^2 - k_{1y}^2) = \pm\, h\nu_j(\boldsymbol{q}), \tag{2.1}$$

$$k_{0x} - k_{1x} = Q_x = 2\pi\tau_x + q_x, \qquad k_{0y} - k_{1y} = Q_y = 2\pi\tau_y + q_y, \qquad (2.2, 3)$$

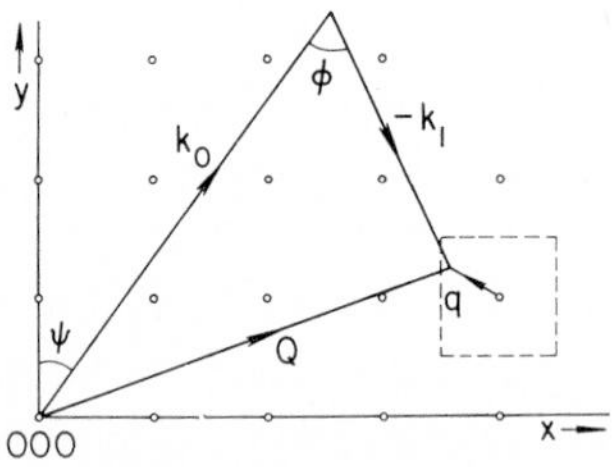

Fig. 2. Reciprocal lattice diagram for a typical crystal. The small circles are reciprocal lattice points in the (xy) plane which contains the incident and scattered neutron wave vectors $\boldsymbol{k}_0$ and $\boldsymbol{k}_1$.

The experimental conditions can best be visualized with the help of a reciprocal lattice diagram, fig. 2, showing the relationship between the neutron wave vectors and the orientation of the crystal specimen. [The simpler situation of a liquid or gas specimen is a special case where only $|\boldsymbol{Q}|$ is important, see §2.4, eq. (2.13)]. The crystal orientation ψ may be defined by the angle between a selected crystal axis, say, y, and the incident neutron beam $\boldsymbol{k}_0$. The sign convention followed at Chalk River, where the x–y plane is horizontal for all spectrometers, is that $+\psi$ denotes a clockwise rotation of y with respect to $\boldsymbol{k}_0$, and $+\phi$ implies a clockwise deflection of $\boldsymbol{k}_1$ with respect to $\boldsymbol{k}_0$ (the observer is assumed to be looking down on the spectrometer). The arrangement in fig. 2 therefore corresponds to negative values for both ψ and ϕ. With this convention, eqs. (2.2) and (2.3) can be expressed in terms of the spectrometer angles:

$$Q_x = -\,|\boldsymbol{k}_0| \sin\psi - |\boldsymbol{k}_1| \sin(\phi - \psi), \tag{2.4}$$

$$Q_y = |\boldsymbol{k}_0| \cos\psi - |\boldsymbol{k}_1| \cos(\phi - \psi). \tag{2.5}$$

The way in which the magnitudes $|\boldsymbol{k}_0|$ and $|\boldsymbol{k}_1|$ are determined depends on the type of spectrometer, but for the moment we shall assume that they are known. It is clear that we have 3 relations, eqs. (2.1), (2.4) and (2.5), between 4 experimental variables, $|\boldsymbol{k}_0|$, $|\boldsymbol{k}_1|$, ϕ and ψ, so that an additional condition of some sort is required to completely specify any experimental point. In crystal spectrometers, §2.2, a very common additional condition is to select a fixed value for $|\boldsymbol{k}_1|$, although any of the other 3 variables may be treated in this way if desired. The almost universal practice in time-of-flight spectrometers, §2.6, is to fix $|\boldsymbol{k}_0|$, since the incident neutron energy cannot readily be changed during the course of an experimental scan.

2.2. Crystal spectrometers

The development of crystal spectrometers up to 1965 has been reviewed by Iyengar (1965). In the present section, therefore, we begin with a brief résumé of early spectrometer designs, and then discuss some more recent developments. Emphasis will be placed on various practical problems which are peculiar to crystal spectrometers, and on how these problems can be solved. We shall see that even the most advanced designs are in essence the same as that originally conceived by Brockhouse (1961); most of the improvements are either in the direction of greater efficiency (e.g. more efficient reflecting crystals, multiple detectors, etc.) or of greater convenience to the user (e.g. on-line computer control). The latter is actually a very important point, and one not always fully appreciated: that if the experimenter is able to work with a very convenient and reliable instrument, he will have more time and opportunity to think about the physics of the material being studied.

A schematic diagram of the triple axis crystal spectrometer developed by Brockhouse is shown in fig. 3. The source of thermal neutrons is a section of the heavy water moderator of the NRU reactor, Chalk River. These neutrons, having an approximately maxwellian spectrum of energies, escape through a hole cut in the reactor shielding, and enter a large rotatable shielding drum. A single crystal monochromator, X_1, at the center of this drum, is used to Bragg reflect neutrons of a particular wavelength and energy through the angle $2\theta_m$, so that they pass through the collimator C_2 and fall upon the sample S. A low sensitivity monitor detector M_2 measures the flux of neutrons incident on the sample, and its counting rate is normally used to control the signal counting times during an experiment. A typical monitor detector consists of a thin layer of natural uranium inside a box with thin aluminium windows. Neutron detection is by means of the ^{235}U fission

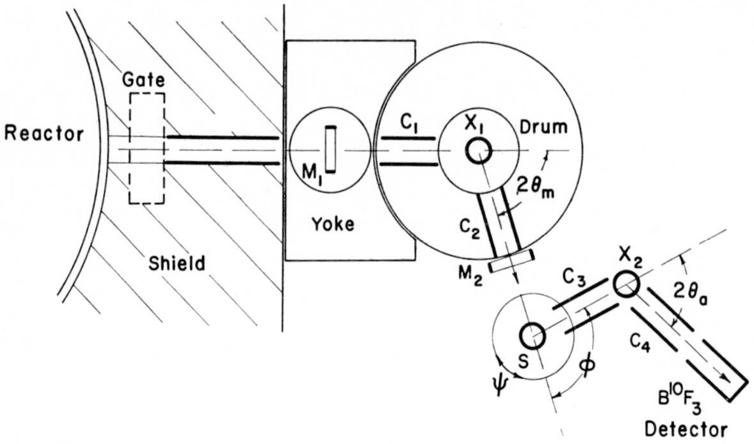

Fig. 3. Schematic diagram of the triple axis crystal spectrometer at the C-5 facility, NRU reactor, Chalk River. C_1–C_4 are collimators for defining the direction of the neutron beam as it is scattered in turn by the monochromator crystal X_1, specimen S and analyser crystal X_2. M_1 and M_2 are monitor detectors for the white radiation and the monoenergetic neutron beam respectively.

reaction, and the efficiency is typically $\sim 10^{-4}$, and inversely proportional to the incident neutron wave vector $|\boldsymbol{k}_0|$. The time taken to count a given number of neutrons in the beam is thus directly proportional to $|\boldsymbol{k}_0|$. The sample sits on a rotatable table whose orientation is denoted by ψ. After scattering from the sample, the neutrons pass through collimator C_3, and those with the appropriate energy may be Bragg reflected from the analyser crystal X_2 into the signal detector. This detector, together with the analyser crystal, is surrounded by hydrogenous, boron-loaded shielding material of about 6″ thickness, to reduce as far as possible the detection of neutrons other than those travelling along the collimated path prescribed above. Hydrogenous shielding material is used, because of the very high scattering cross-section of hydrogen, to moderate any fast and epi-thermal neutrons down to thermal energies, whereupon they may be efficiently absorbed by the ^{10}B isotope of natural boron. ^{6}Li and cadmium are also excellent neutron absorbers, the latter being very widely used as a shielding material in neutron spectroscopy.

The collimators consist of cadmium-plated steel tubes of square cross-section (2″ × 2″ inside dimensions), in which a number of cadmium-plated thin steel plates may be mounted, parallel to each other and spaced at regular intervals ('Soller slits'). In this particular spectrometer, the collimator C_1 usually has no Soller slits, since the angular spread or divergence of the incident neutron beam arising simply from the distance (21′) between the neutron source and the crystal X_1 is already sufficient for most experiments. The source is an ellipse approximately 4″ high by 3″ wide, so that the angular divergence as seen from a point on X_1 is roughly 1° vertically and 0.7° horizontally. While this horizontal divergence is adequate for many purposes, the 1° vertical divergence is often unnecessarily restrictive, since experiments are frequently performed with a mirror plane of symmetry of the specimen parallel to the (horizontal) plane containing the neutron beams. The properties of the crystal (e.g. phonon frequencies) often change only slowly along a line perpendicular to a mirror plane, so that the vertical divergence may well be relaxed in order to increase the neutron count rates without significant loss of resolution. A vertical divergence of 2° or 3° is often quite acceptable. Reactor neutron sources should therefore be designed with this in mind: elliptical holes and sources with a major-to-minor-axis ratio of 2 or 3 would be much more valuable than the circular holes provided at most of today's research reactors. Additional Soller slit collimators may always be inserted if higher resolution is required for particular experiments. That such additional collimation may sometimes be necessary has recently been elegantly demonstrated by Cowley and Pant (1970). If, for example, two branches of the dispersion relation are degenerate along a symmetry direction, and if the splitting for any adjacent wave vector is proportional to the distance from that symmetry direction, then a measurement of the degenerate mode may give rise to a double peak in the scattered neutron energy distribution, instead of the expected single peak. This kind of spurious double peak may be observed with any type of spectrometer, if the vertical divergence is too large. If this problem is suspected, therefore, the experiment should be repeated with suitable additional collimation.

The distances between X_1 and S and between S and X_2 are only a few feet, so it is normally necessary to introduce vertical Soller slits in the C_2 and C_3 collimators in order to restrict the horizontal divergence of the neutrons incident on and scattered from the specimen. Collimators in use at all 4 Chalk River spectrometers are between 8″ and 20″ in length, and the spacing of the Soller slits is variable from 0.043″ upwards. The final collimator C_4 is usually a fairly coarse one (3° divergence), designed to restrict the entry of unwanted 'background' neutrons rather than to control the scattered neutron energy resolution. The latter is governed by a combination of the collimator C_3 and the mosaic spread of the analyser crystal X_2.

In the original Brockhouse instrument, the signal detector is, as shown in fig. 3, a $^{10}BF_3$ gas detector. The ^{10}B isotope has a large cross-section for the (n, α) nuclear reaction, 3800 barns for 1.8 Å neutrons, and these α-particles produce considerable ionization in the gas through which they pass. The ionization cloud is readily detected by means of the electrical pulse it produces on contact with a suitable high voltage electrode inside the $2\frac{1}{2}''$ diameter detector tube. The electrical characteristics of these detectors are excellent, providing the BF_3 gas pressure is about 1 atm or less. The detection efficiency is approximately given by $[1-\exp(n\sigma_a]l)]$ where n is the number of ^{10}B atoms/cc, σ_a is the neutron absorption cross section, and l the active length of the detector (in cm). For typical thermal neutrons, an efficiency of 80 to 90% can readily be achieved with $l=40$ cm and a gas pressure of 0.8 atm.

In recent years, the $^{10}BF_3$ detector has been largely superseded by the more compact ^3He gas detector; this makes use of the (n, p) nuclear reaction, which has a cross-section of 5400 barns for 1.8 Å neutrons. Good electrical characteristics can be achieved with up to 10 atm total gas pressure (some krypton is normally mixed with the helium to improve the characteristics). This means that very high efficiency ^3He detectors can have much smaller physical dimensions than comparable BF_3 detectors, so that much less heavy shielding must be carried by the detector arm which pivots about the analyser crystal X_2. On the other hand, it seems that currently available ^3He detectors require more careful attention than the standard BF_3 type, since rather small changes in conditions (e.g. bias voltage) may make the ^3He detector sensitive to γ-rays as well as to thermal neutrons. The γ-ray flux normally present in the vicinity of the reactor can then contribute to the background count-rate in the detector. The advantage of small size – a typical ^3He detector for a crystal spectrometer is about the size and shape of a package of 20 cigarettes – is probably decisive, however, and a gradual replacement of BF_3 detectors is to be expected. Further technical details on these and other neutron detectors have been described by Cocking and Webb (1965).

The monochromator and analyser crystals act as mirrors for specific neutron energies, and as such the reflecting planes must obey Snell's law at all times. As the C_2 collimator rotates through $2\theta_m$, the crystal X_1 must rotate by θ_m in order to maintain the correct reflecting conditions. The 'half-angling' mechanism utilized in the Chalk River spectrometers operate on the principle that the axis of a wheel rolling on a fixed plate moves at half the rate of the topmost point on its rim. Full mechanical details are given in a comprehensive report by McAlpin (1963). Another popular method of achieving this half-angling effect is to provide a separate 'θ_m-motor' to drive the monochromator crystal itself at half the rate of rotation of C_2. This method is used, for example, in triple-axis spectrometers at the Oak Ridge National Laboratory (Wilkinson et al. 1968).

In order to exploit the full versatility of this type of spectrometer, it is most desirable to be able to drive all 4 angles $2\theta_m$, $2\theta_a$, ψ and ϕ independently, with a precision of the order of 0.01°. In the Brockhouse instrument, each angle is driven by an alternating current synchronous motor which also drives a cam wheel. A microswitch actuated by the cam gives a pulse for every $\frac{1}{8}$° rotation of the angle, and the motor is switched off when the required number of $\frac{1}{8}$° increments has been completed. The cam position is adjusted to allow for the 'coast' of the axis, due to its inertia, beyond the point at which the motor is switched off. When the motor reverses direction, there is significant 'backlash' in the transmission, which must be allowed for. In the case of the ψ motor of the Brockhouse spectrometer, for example, this backlash can be adjusted so as to amount to precisely $\frac{1}{8}$°. An extra incremental pulse is then introduced by the control mechanism whenever the ψ angle changes direction. The actual numbers of $\frac{1}{8}$° increments to be given to each motor are read from a reel of punched paper tape produced by an external off-line computer. Many crystal spectrometers are controlled by means of punched paper tape or punched cards, and it is usually quite convenient to operate in this manner, in spite of the fact that some degree of advance planning is necessary to ensure an adequate supply of suitable control tapes or cards. One of the advantages of an on-line computer is that it removes this inconvenience, since all the motor increments for any desired experimental scan can be generated in situ with essentially no delay.

The necessity of large amounts of shielding materials has already been mentioned. Whatever type of thermal neutron source is employed, substantial fluxes of fast neutrons and γ-rays are produced along with the thermal neutrons, and these must be prevented as far as possible from escaping into the working space around the spectrometer. The monochromator shielding drum in particular contains considerable quantities of lead and/or tungsten to absorb γ-rays, hydrogenous material to moderate fast neutrons, and boron compounds to absorb the resulting thermal neutrons. Cadmium is not so useful as boron in very high flux areas since each absorbed neutron releases an equally unpleasant γ-ray. As the shielding drum rotates, it is of course necessary to permit the unobstructed entry of neutrons through C_1 and exit through C_2. In the Brockhouse spectrometer, this is achieved by leaving an open sector of some 30° on the reactor side of the drum. A

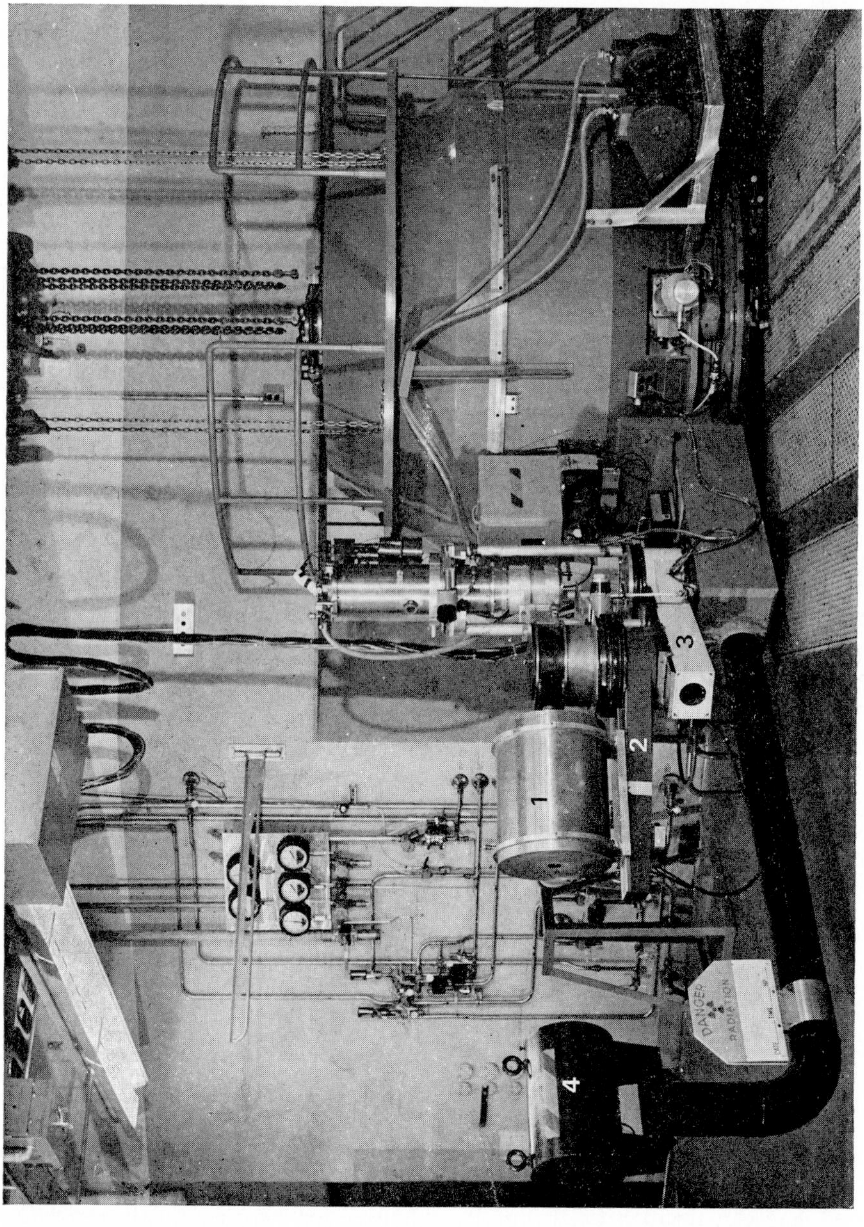
1
2
3
4
DANGER
RADIATION

limited range of $2\theta_m$ angles is thereby allowed, and the unshielded 30° sector is protected by the sides of the yoke (fig. 3). The range of allowed $2\theta_m$ angles may be changed by manually repositioning appropriate shielding sectors. Spectrometers of more recent construction, such as those at Brookhaven, Oak Ridge and also at Chalk River, have employed a system of shielding wedges which can be lifted individually by a few inches so as to ride over the incoming neutron beam passing through C_1. Some details of the Oak Ridge design are shown in fig. 4. A photograph of this instrument, with a specimen crystal mounted in a cryostat for low temperature experiments, is shown facing this page. The size of the residual unshielded sector on the reactor side of the drum is much reduced by this wedge arrangement, with consequent reduction in background radiation levels. At the same time, the range of $2\theta_m$ angles available under automatic control is much increased.

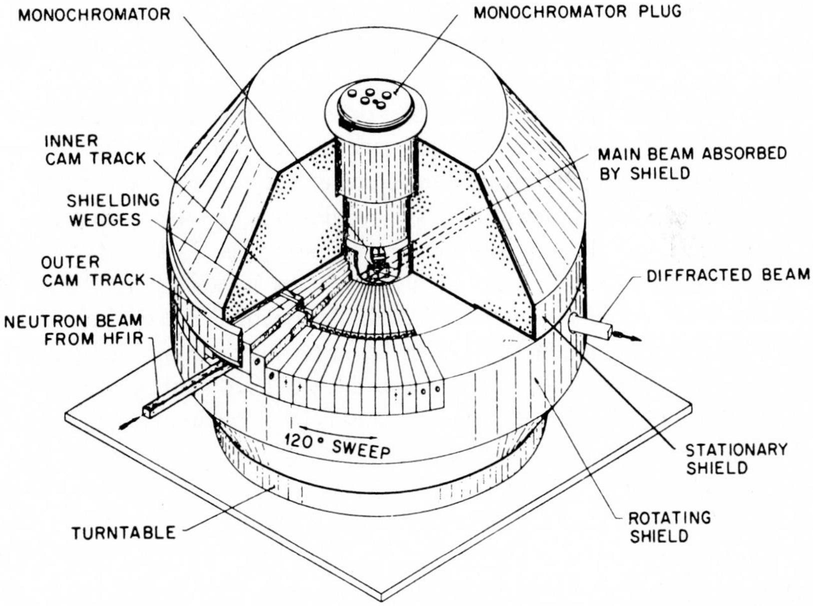

Fig. 4. Cut-away drawing of the monochromator shielding drum of the Oak Ridge triple axis crystal spectrometer, showing the system of shielding wedges riding over the incoming beam from the High Flux Isotope Reactor (HFIR). A photograph of this instrument is shown opposite to this page. The sample is mounted near the bottom of the tall metal cryostat, and the detector is inside the cylindrical shield (1). The analyser crystal is hidden from view by a black (boron carbide-resin) shield above the junction of arms (2) and (3). The cylinder (4) prevents the escape of those monoenergetic neutrons which pass straight through the specimen.

2.3. Crystal reflectivity and order contamination

An extremely important factor in the use of crystal spectrometers is of course the reflectivity of the monochromator and analyser crystals. The ideal monochromator should be able to reflect with 100% efficiency neutrons within a preselected small range of energies and incident upon it within an appropriate small angular range. There is a considerable literature of the subject of crystal reflectivity (see, for example, Bacon 1962), and many methods of improving reflectivities and other characteristics of crystals. Many of these methods involve mechanical distortion, either at room temperature (for metals, e.g. copper, see Brockhouse et al. 1968), or at high temperatures (e.g. germanium, see Barrett et al. (1963), Dolling and Nieman (1967), and pyrolitic graphite, see Riste (1970). The reflectivity of piezo-electric crystals such as quartz can be vastly improved by subjecting them to radio frequency oscillations [see Galociova et al. (1970) and earlier references cited therein]. Undistorted single crystals of silicon have been cut into parallel slices less than 1 mm thick and the slices stacked together (Frey 1971) so that each is held at a slightly different angle. The stack can also be bent slightly to produce a curved reflecting crystal which displays desirable focusing characteristics. Increased reflectivity has also been produced in crystals of CaF_2 (Alefeld 1969) by maintaining a steep temperature gradient, up to 230 K/cm, across the reflecting planes. This gradient gives rise to a distribution of plane spacings d_{hkl}, thus increasing the spread of neutron energies which may be reflected. This method is technically awkward, however, and the Debye–Waller factor for the Bragg-reflecting planes is decreased by the high temperatures involved. A simpler method of introducing a distribution of plane spacings is by changing the composition of a suitable alloy single crystal. Thin sheets of pure copper and copper with various amounts of aluminum (4–8%) may be stacked together to form a composite monochromator. The production of alloy crystals with the alloy composition being continuously varied during the growing process has been suggested by Rustichelli (1970, 1972).

The reflectivities of crystals always decrease as the neutron energy approaches the epi-thermal range, although the point at which it falls below, say, 50% of its peak value, varies from one material to another. The reflectivity usually displays somewhat irregular dips arising from the occasional depletion of the incident beam by other unwanted Bragg reflections. (This effect is virtually absent in pyrolitic graphite since this has so few well-defined Bragg reflections.) Experiments may have widely varying requirements as regards resolution, neutron energies, and so on. In view of all these factors, it is highly desirable to have many monochromator/analyser crystals, with a range of mosaic spreads, in order to optimize reflectivity and resolution for any particular experiment.

Many neutron scattering experiments are facilitated by the use of polarized neutron beams. A common method of producing a monochromatic beam of polarized neutrons is to employ a ferro- or ferri-magnetic crystal as the monochromator. The polarization of the scattered neutrons may likewise be determined by means of a similar magnetic analyser crystal, such as cobalt–8% iron. A highly versatile polarized-beam crystal spectrometer has been described by Wilkinson et al. (1968). The usefulness of this type of spectrometer, when used in its polarized beam mode, is confined almost entirely to the study of magnetic excitations (spin waves) and magnetic structure, so that a detailed discussion of it is outside the scope of this book.

One of the more important problems of the crystal spectrometer is that of order contamination: if a given plane (hkl) of the monochromator crystal is in the correct orientation to reflect neutrons of wavelength λ_0 (energy E_0) through the angle $2\theta_{\mathrm{m}}$, then all planes $(h'k'l')$ where $h'=nh$, $k'=nk$, $l'=nl$, n any integer, will simultaneously be in a position to reflect λ_0/n wavelength neutrons (energy n^2E_0) in the same direction. Similarly, the analyser may reflect neutrons of energy m^2E_1, m any integer, where E_1 is the energy of those scattered neutrons we actually wish to detect. Thus the neutrons can be regarded as undergoing scattering processes governed by conservation conditions, eqs. (1.6), (1.7),

$$n^2E_0 - m^2E_1 = \pm\, h\nu_{nm}(\boldsymbol{q}_{nm}), \qquad n\boldsymbol{k}_0 - m\boldsymbol{k}_1 = 2\pi\boldsymbol{\tau} + \boldsymbol{q}_{nm}. \tag{2.6, 7}$$

At first sight, it may seem that since n and m can be any integers it would be impossible to derive unambiguous values for ν_{nm} and $\boldsymbol{q}_{nm}$. There are, however, several methods of dealing with this problem, the more important of which are (*i*) careful planning of the experiment, (*ii*) use of crystals whose structure is such that the scattering power (or structure factor) of certain higher order planes is zero, (*iii*) use of polycrystalline filters such as Be, (*iv*) use of pyrolitic graphite filters, (*v*) use of mechanical velocity selectors. We shall now comment briefly on each of these methods.

By careful planning we mean the utilization of all our available knowledge of the spectrum of neutrons from the source, and of the dispersion relation $\nu=\nu_j(\boldsymbol{q})$ for the excitations in the sample crystal. The flux of neutrons obtainable from a typical reactor falls off quite rapidly as the energy increases beyond the maxwellian peak (see §2.11). For example, the ratio of the fluxes of 0.2 eV to 0.05 eV neutrons is about 40, so that if $2\theta_m$ is chosen to set $E_0 = 0.05$ eV, we may well be able to ignore the possibility of observing scattering processes involving $n^2 E_0$ for all $n \geqslant 2$. We may also be able to set upper limits on the sample excitation energies $h\nu_j(\boldsymbol{q})$. Let this upper limit be $h\nu_{\max}$, and let us observe a scattering process involving an excitation energy $h\nu < h\nu_{\max}$:

$$E_0 - E_1 = h\nu\,, \qquad E_0 - m^2 E_1 \leqslant \pm\, h\nu_{\max}\,,$$
$$\therefore (m^2 - 1)\, E_1 \geqslant h(\nu \pm \nu_{\max})\,. \tag{2.8}$$

If we chose E_1 high enough, then eq. (2.8) will be satisfied for all $m > 1$, so that none of these scattering processes involving $4E'$, $9E'$, etc., will be energetically possible. The initial study of a new specimen may therefore be safely carried out, albeit with rather poor resolution, simply by performing neutron energy experiments with E_1, and hence E_0, suitably large. Subsequently, high resolution measurments may be performed with E_1 and E_0 small enough for processes governed by eq. (2.6) to be allowed. But coherent scattering is also governed by eq. (2.7), so that we may calculate all the appropriate v_{nm} and $\boldsymbol{q}_{nm}$ values and check whether any are likely to obey the dispersion relation determined by the earlier experiments. For simple materials, with few branches to the dispersion relation, it is usually possible, by careful choice of E_1 and $\boldsymbol{Q} = 2\pi\boldsymbol{\tau} + \boldsymbol{q}$, to avoid all potential higher order scattering processes.

One of the most troublesome of these spurious processes, as is evident from eq. (2.8), is for $n=1$, $m=2$. This process may be effectively eliminated by use of an analyser crystal plane having zero structure factor for the second order reflection, Ge(111) and Ge(113) are popular candidates for this purpose, and their use allows a substantial increase in flexibility of experimental conditions. Theoretically, the (222) reflection of Ge is completely absent, but in practice, high reflectivity distorted Ge crystals show a small (222) reflectivity, of order 0.1% of the (111) reflectivity. This arises because of certain double Bragg scattering (Renninger 1937) processes

$$\boldsymbol{k}_0 - \boldsymbol{k}_2 = 2\pi\boldsymbol{\tau}_2\,, \qquad \boldsymbol{k}_2 - \boldsymbol{k}_1 = 2\pi\boldsymbol{\tau}_3\,,$$
$$\therefore \boldsymbol{k}_0 - \boldsymbol{k}_1 = 2\pi(\boldsymbol{\tau}_2 + \boldsymbol{\tau}_3) = 2\pi\boldsymbol{\tau}_1\,, \tag{2.9}$$

where $\boldsymbol{\tau}_2$ and $\boldsymbol{\tau}_3$ have finite structure factors even though $\boldsymbol{\tau}_1$ is theoretically absent. This effect can be minimized by rotating the reflecting crystal about the vector $\boldsymbol{\tau}_1$. The multiple-slice silicon type of reflecting crystal may well prove to be even better than distorted Ge for avoiding second order reflections. In its favor, silicon has very low absorption and incoherent scattering cross-sections, and its scattering cross-section for unwanted fast neutrons is also much lower than that of Ge.

The possibility of using polycrystalline materials such as Be for order elimination arises from the fact that coherent elastic scattering cannot occur if the neutron wavelength exceeds twice the largest *d*-spacing between reflecting planes in the material. This 'cut-off' wavelength λ_c for Be is 3.92 Å. The average neutron scattering cross-section is about 6 barns for $\lambda < \lambda_c$, and falls by more than an order of magnitude for $\lambda > \lambda_c$. The residual coherent scattering at long wavelength is inelastic and may be further reduced (another factor of 10) by cooling the Be filter to liquid nitrogen temperatures. It is then easy to see that the insertion of a moderate length (say 10 cm) of polycrystalline Be into the collimator C_4 (fig. 3) will discriminate very strongly against short wavelength neutrons. If the analyser is set to reflect 4 Å neutrons into the detector, then any 2 Å or higher order contaminant neutrons will be attenuated by a factor of 1500. The value of this filtering technique is limited because the wavelength of the desired neutrons (incident or scattered, depending on the location of the filter) must be kept greater than 3.92 Å. This severely restricts the regions of $(\boldsymbol{Q}, \nu)$ space which can be studied.

This rather striking filtering property of Be has also been used in the past to eliminate the analyser crystal entirely for certain kinds of experiment where the Q-space resolution is not critical. The Be filter allows transmission of neutrons of energies between 0 and 0.005 eV (i.e. 4 Å), so that a detector shielded by Be behaves as an efficient analyser for scattered neutron energies within this narrow range. Further refinements of this technique, involving a differential Be–BeO filter with somewhat better resolution, have also been used to advantage (Iyengar et al. 1965).

Pyrolitic graphite may also be used as a selective neutron filter in certain narrow energy ranges (Brockhouse et al. 1964), Loopstra 1966, Shirane and Minkiewicz 1970). The filter consists of several slabs of pyrolitic graphite placed in the neutron beam so that the unique c-axis of each slab is aligned parallel to the beam. Neutrons of wavelength $\lambda = 2d \sin(90 - \beta)$, where d is the spacing of any set of reflecting planes (hkl) and β is the angle between the c-axis and the normal to the (hkl) planes, are very efficiently reflected away by the graphite. It turns out that the neutron transmission curve for a typical pyrolitic graphite filter displays two deep minima near energies of 0.055 and 0.059 eV, while retaining very high transmission for neutrons of energies about $\frac{1}{4}$ of these. Discrimination of factors of a few thousand can be achieved in favor of neutrons of energies 13.7 and 14.8 meV (Shirane and Minkiewicz 1970). Neutrons of these energies are of much wider utility than the 5 meV neutrons available with Be filter methods, but the limitations imposed by all these energy restrictions are often inconvenient.

Discrimination against faster neutrons may also be achieved by means of large perfect (low mosaic spread) single crystals such as quartz (Brockhouse 1961), magnesium oxide or bismuth. The scattering of fast neutrons is predominantly inelastic (collisions with individual nuclei) and interference phenomena such as Bragg scattering only become important in the thermal energy range. However, in a highly perfect single crystal, only a few crystal planes will be in the correct orientation to Bragg-reflect neutrons of the appropriate energies, so that the strong elastic scattering characteristic of polycrystalline materials is much reduced. Thus a single crystal filter may transmit thermal neutrons quite well while providing good discrimination against faster neutrons. The filtering action is, however, less complete and less efficient than that obtainable with polycrystalline filters. Single crystal filters are perhaps most valuable when placed in the neutron beam inside the reactor shielding, before the monochromator crystal. A very useful arrangement is that installed at the L3 facility, NRU reactor, Chalk River: this consists of an in-pile liquid nitrogen cooled cryostat, in which a drum rotatable about a horizontal axis parallel to but displaced a few inches from the neutron beam from the reactor. The drum has 3 orientations, in each of which the neutron beam is interrupted by a different amount of single crystal quartz, namely 12″, 6″ and 0″ in length. The transmission of longer wavelength neutrons through the quartz is much improved by cooling to 77 K. The two benefits derived from insertion of a length of quartz crystal into the beam are (*i*) substantial reduction (a factor of about 4 for 6″ quartz) in the background count rate and (*ii*) a reduction in the number of higher order and other faster neutrons detected by the monitor detector. Since the signal counting time is normally governed by the monitor count rate, it is important to ensure as far as possible that the monitor counts only those neutrons of the desired energy E_0, especially if accurate intensity measurements are required. Single crystal bismuth is most useful in situations where there is a high flux of unwanted γ-rays in the beam from the reactor, since the γ-ray scattering cross-section of bismuth is much higher than that of quartz.

Finally, we should mention the use of mechanical velocity selectors for elimination of higher order neutrons. These devices resemble turbines in that they consist of a rotor, having a large number of cadmium-plated helical blades, which rotates at high speed about an axis parallel to and laterally displaced from the neutron beam. The neutrons travel down the helical channels in between the blades, near the periphery. Only those neutrons with a velocity matched to the rotor speed will avoid striking the blades and hence be transmitted. Relatively poor resolution is sufficient to achieve discrimination against higher order neutrons, and so the blades may be thin and the channels rather wide, to permit quite high transmission (60% or more) of the desired first order neutrons. In practice, however, such velocity selectors have not so far been very widely used in neutron scattering work with crystal spectrometers: they are quite heavy and bulky, and would be awkward to mount between the specimen and analyser crystals in order to remove order contamination from the scattered neutron beam. It would also be desirable to have an automatic rotor speed control to permit continuous variation of neutron energy during an experiment, particularly if the selector is mounted before the monochromator. Furthermore, the other methods mentioned above for dealing with order continuation seem to be simpler (and cheaper!) and probably more reliable.

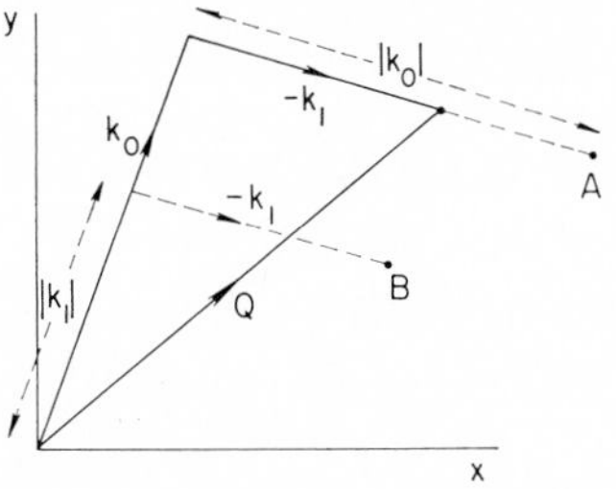

Fig. 5. Reciprocal lattice diagram illustrating two types of scattering process which may give rise to spurious peaks in the scattered neutron energy distributions observed with crystal spectrometers.

Before leaving the subject of order contamination, we should mention a somewhat different phenomenon which can also give rise to spurious peaks in the scattered neutron distributions. The reciprocal lattice diagram, fig. 5, shows two possibilities for observing such peaks. If the neutron beam incident on the specimen can be Bragg-reflected *in the direction of the analyser crystal*, then even though the analyser is not set to Bragg-reflect this beam (since $|\boldsymbol{k}_1| \neq |\boldsymbol{k}_0|$), some diffuse scattering into the detector will occur. This corresponds to the situation where point A (fig. 5) coincides with a reciprocal lattice vector of the specimen crystal. Conversely, neutrons of wave vector $\boldsymbol{k}_1$, having been diffusely scatterd from the monochromator crystal, may be Bragg-reflected from the specimen and then from the analyser into the detector; this will occur if point B coincides with a reciprocal lattice vector. In either case, the intensity of this scattering process (2 Bragg reflections plus

1 diffuse scattering) may well be comparable with that expected for the coherent one-phonon scattering of primary interest. Spurious peaks arising from these processes are highly specific, however, and for this reason are frequently very sharp compared to typical phonon lines. A slight change of experimental conditions is sufficient to displace points A or B to a safe distance from any reciprocal lattice vector.

2.4. Double monochromators and multiple detector systems

One of the most expensive components of the modern triple axis crystal spectrometer is the heavy shielding drum for the monochromator crystal, with its rotatable segments and arrangement of shielding wedges. Much of this expense may be avoided by means of the double monochromator system (Brockhouse et al. 1968, Almqvist et al. 1968) shown schematically in fig. 6.

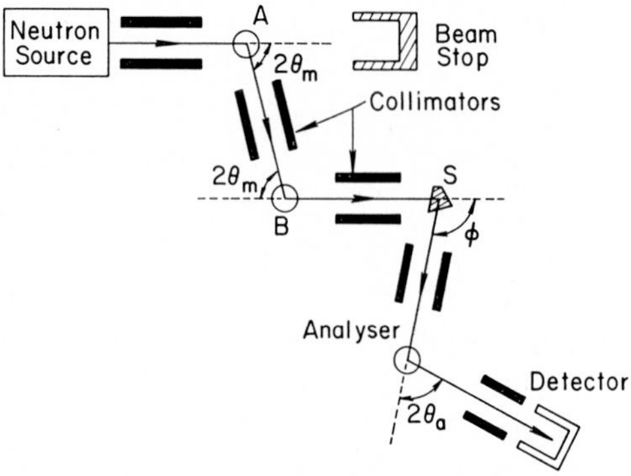

Fig. 6. Schematic diagram of a triple axis crystal spectrometer with a double monochromator arrangement to produce the monoenergetic neutron beam incident upon the fixed sample, S.

The monochromatic beam from the first crystal A is reflected by crystal B along a path parallel to the initial beam from the source. The neutron energy is varied by rotating both crystals and, if necessary, translating the crystals along the lines shown dotted in fig. 6 so that crystal B always interrupts the beam reflected from crystal A. The sample S is then set in a fixed position for all incident neutron energies, and most of the heavy shielding around the double monochromator remains fixed and may be relatively inexpensive. Another advantage of this arrangement is that the thermal neutron beam falling on the specimen is likely to be 'cleaner', i.e. accompanied by fewer unwanted fast neutrons, than that from a single monochromator. On the other hand, the double monochromator is presumably less efficient than a single crystal (unless the second crystal reflects with 100% efficiency), and there are some additional problems involved in setting up the two crystals in the correct orientations and in ensuring that they remain properly oriented while $2\theta_m$ is varied. It is not a trivial matter to change from one pair of monochromators to another, so that the spectrometer is rather less flexible in practice than a single monochromator spectrometer.

Another development in crystal spectrometers has been the introduction of multiple analyser/detector systems for observing scattering at several different angles simultaneously. As we shall see in §2.6, multiple detectors are standard in conventional time-of-flight machines, but their use in crystal spectrometers has so far been rather limited (Iyengar 1966, Glaser et al. 1969). The main reason for this is connected with the fact that the crystal spectrometer is usually operated so as to obtain highly specific information about the scattering function $S(\boldsymbol{Q}, \nu)$. In a typical experimental scan, S may be measured over a range of ν for a preselected fixed value of $\boldsymbol{Q}$ (method of constant-$\boldsymbol{Q}$, Brockhouse 1961). Other possible modes of operation are described in §2.5. One of the most important features of the crystal spectrometer is this capability of such specific types of scan, and it is highly desirable to retain this feature for multiple detector systems. Consider an experiment in which f independent analyser/detector systems are set up to observe neutrons scattered through angles ϕ_f with wave vectors $\boldsymbol{k}_f$ from a given specimen crystal. Each of the f detectors is arranged so that $\boldsymbol{Q}_f = \boldsymbol{k}_0 - \boldsymbol{k}_f$ is kept constant. We may rewrite eqs. (2.1), (2.4) and (2.5):

$$(\hbar^2/2m)(k_{0x}^2 + k_{0y}^2 - k_{fx}^2 - k_{fy}^2) = \pm h\nu_j(\boldsymbol{q}_f), \tag{2.10}$$

$$Q_{fx} = -|\boldsymbol{k}_0| \sin\psi - |\boldsymbol{k}_f| \sin(\phi_f - \psi), \tag{2.11}$$

$$Q_{fy} = |\boldsymbol{k}_0| \cos\psi - |\boldsymbol{k}_f| \cos(\phi_f - \psi). \tag{2.12}$$

As mentioned in §2.1, for $f = 1$ only, we have 3 equations and 4 variables ($|\boldsymbol{k}_0|$, $|\boldsymbol{k}_1|$, ϕ_1, ψ) so that an additional condition, such as a particular value for $|\boldsymbol{k}_0|$ or $|\boldsymbol{k}_1|$ is required to specify any point on the scan. When the second detector $f = 2$ is added, 3 more equations are introduced but only 2 additional variables ($|\boldsymbol{k}_2|$ and ϕ_2). Thus all 6 variables are fixed by the act of specifying the desired $\boldsymbol{Q}_f$ and $\nu_j(\boldsymbol{q}_f)$ values, and so two independent scans having any desired sequence of $\boldsymbol{Q}_f$ and $\nu_j(\boldsymbol{q}_f)$ values can be performed simultaneously, provided of course that solutions to the equations exist having physically acceptable ϕ_f and ψ values. When a third detector is added, we can no longer perform any scan we like, because $|\boldsymbol{k}_0|$ and ψ have already been fixed by the first two detectors. There are a number of possibilities for partial specification of these additional scans, for example, we may choose $\boldsymbol{Q}_3$ to fall on some specified line in reciprocal space. We must also take into account the physical or real space occupied by each analyser/detector combination, which begins to impose a serious restriction on available angles when several detectors are installed. For efficient utilization of 3 analyser/detector systems (which are in operation at each of two multi-axis spectrometers at Chalk River), it is necessary to employ computer programs to select scans of various types which may be carried out simultaneously without collisions between the several moving parts of the spectrometer. It is also necessary to have the shielding for each analyser/detector which will automatically allow for movements of the analyser angles $2\theta_a$ during the scans. Without going into further details, it is clear that the characteristic flexibility of the 'multi-axis' crystal spectrometer is severely impaired by the use of more than 3 or 4 detectors. A schematic diagram of the multi-axis crystal spectrometers mounted at the L3 facility, NRU reactor, Chalk River, is given in fig. 7. The neutron beam from the reactor passes through the rotatable, liquid nitrogen-cooled quartz filter described in §2.3, and strikes the first monochromator crystal. The reflected beam passes through a monitor detector and is then scattered by the sample. Three independent analyser/detector systems can be used to measure the energy distributions of neutrons at three variable scattering angles. Most of the neutron beam, however, passes through the first monochromator and falls upon the second monochromator crystal, which provides monoenergetic neutrons for studying a second specimen. (It should be noted that there is no advantage in placing two monochromators on the same beam line if separate beam ports are available for each at the reactor: the second specimen in fig. 7 receives only about $\frac{1}{3}$ of the neutron flux seen by the first specimen simply because of its increased distance from the neutron source.)

We should mention in passing that the limitation on the number of detectors applies only to spectrometers designed for single crystal studies. Multi-axis crystal spectrometers for studying liquid, polycrystalline or amorphous specimens may readily be designed with a large number of independent detectors (10 to 20). There is no orientation angle ψ associated with these specimens, and only the magnitude of the momentum transfer vector $\boldsymbol{Q}$ is of importance. Eqs. (2.11) and (2.12) reduce to the single equation

$$|\boldsymbol{Q}_f|^2 = |\boldsymbol{k}_0|^2 + |\boldsymbol{k}_f|^2 - 2\,|\boldsymbol{k}_0|\,|\boldsymbol{k}_f|\cos\phi_f\,. \qquad (2.13)$$

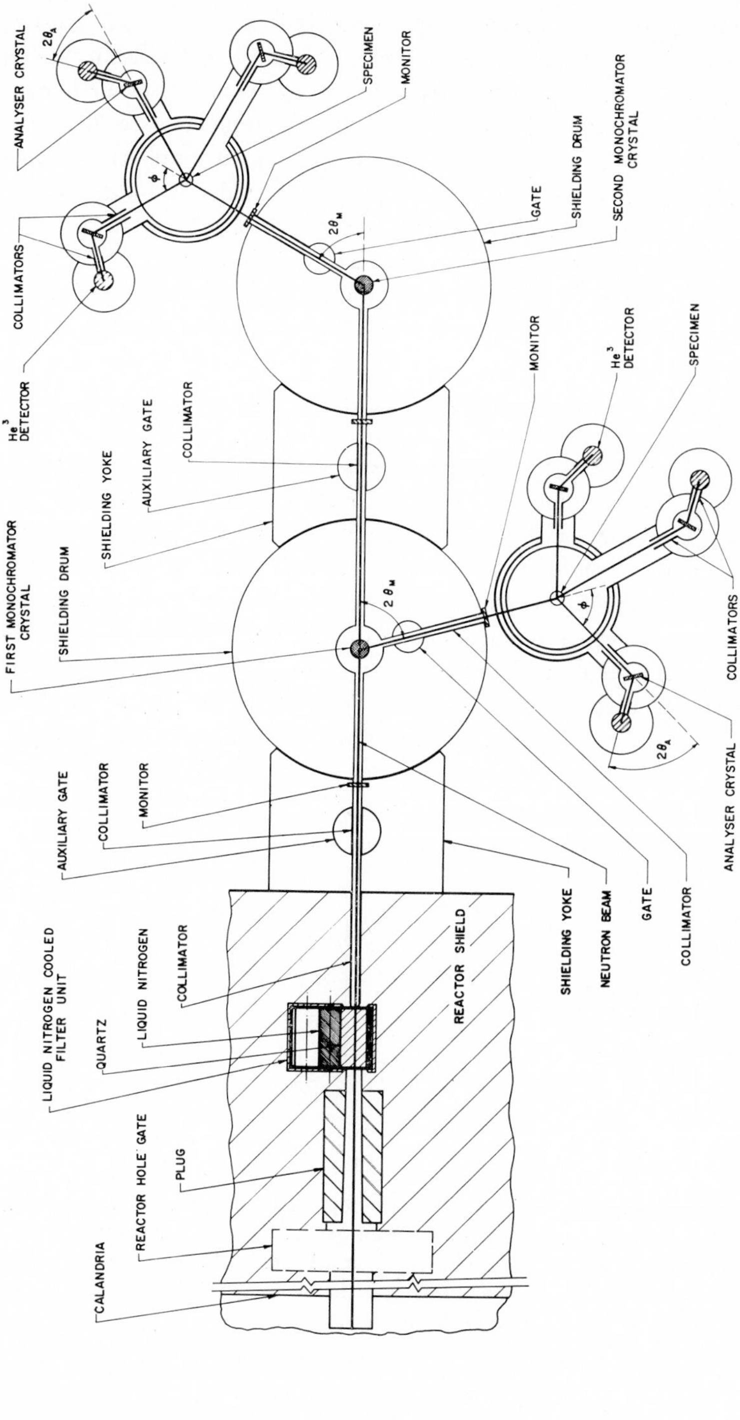

Fig. 7. Schematic diagram of the multi-axis crystal spectrometer at the L3 facility, NRU reactor, Chalk River. It consists of two independent spectrometers (which could be mounted at different reactor facilities if desired), each of which is equipped with three independent analyser/detector systems for performing simultaneous experimental scans.

It is therefore always possible to specify both $|Q_f|$ and the energy transfer $h\nu_f$ for every point on the scan for any number of independent detectors operating simultaneously. The only operating restrictions are associated with choosing reasonably spaced ϕ_f values so that adjacent analyser/detector systems do not collide. This difficulty can be minimised by placing all the (unshielded) analysers and detectors inside a communal shield constructed in a wide arc about the specimen position. Such a multi-detector system would be very heavy and bulky, so that it would be especially appropriate to use it in conjunction with a double monochromator arrangement which permits a fixed position of the sample and hence also of the communal detector shield.

2.5. Modes of operation and focusing properties of crystal spectrometers

In §2.1 we listed the basic equations governing the energy and momentum changes in a coherent inelastic neutron scattering experiment. Since all 4 quantities $|\boldsymbol{k}_0|$, $|\boldsymbol{k}_1|$, ϕ and ψ are independently variable in a typical crystal spectrometer, and since there are only 3 equations to satisfy (provided we consider wave vectors in one plane only), there are obviously a large number of possible ways in which to conduct an experimental scan consisting of intensity measurements at a sequence of points in $(\boldsymbol{Q}, \nu)$ space. Perhaps the most commonly used types of scan are those in which $|\boldsymbol{k}_0|$ or $|\boldsymbol{k}_1|$ are kept constant during the scan. Furthermore, it is convenient to select a sequence of points separated by fixed 'step lengths', $\Delta\boldsymbol{Q}$ and $\Delta\nu$, where, most usually, either $\Delta\boldsymbol{Q}$ or $\Delta\nu$ is set to zero. If $\Delta\boldsymbol{Q}=0$, we have the constant-$\boldsymbol{Q}$ scan (Brockhouse 1961) and if $\Delta\nu=0$, we have the constant energy scan

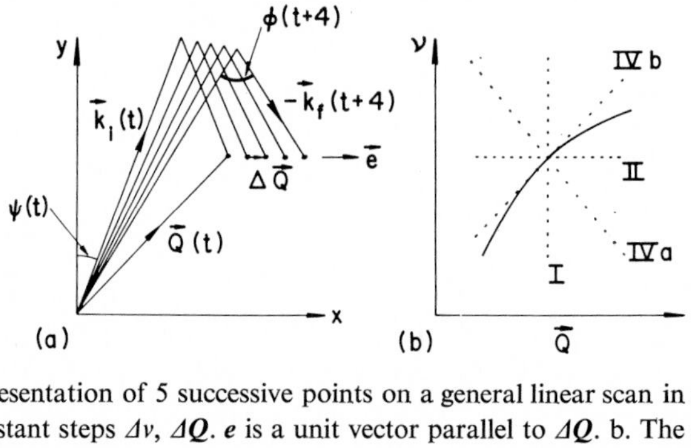

Fig. 8.a. Representation of 5 successive points on a general linear scan in which ν and $\boldsymbol{Q}$ change by constant steps $\Delta\nu$, $\Delta\boldsymbol{Q}$. $\boldsymbol{e}$ is a unit vector parallel to $\Delta\boldsymbol{Q}$. b. The dotted straight lines represent various possibilities for the linear scan in fig. 8a. I and II are constant-$\boldsymbol{Q}$ and constant energy scans respectively. The solid line is a typical dispersion curve for excitations in a crystal.

(Stedman 1961). A rather general type of linear scan is a combination of these two, in which $\Delta \boldsymbol{Q}$ has a fixed direction, $\boldsymbol{e}$, and a magnitude given by $a\,\Delta\nu$ where a is a constant. Fig. 8a is a reciprocal lattice diagram showing 5 successive points (t to $t+4$) on such a general linear scan, while fig. 8b illustrates the locus in $(\boldsymbol{Q}, \nu)$ space of successive points on various types of scan with respect to a typical dispersion curve. We have already mentioned in § 1.4 a very common type of scan for time-of-flight spectrometers, in which $|\boldsymbol{k}_0|$ and ϕ are kept fixed. The locus of successive points in this scan would be an arbitrary parabola in fig. 8b. We have also quoted the jacobian, eq. (1.11), of the transformation required to obtain the integrated intensity α of a one-phonon peak from the theoretical cross-section. For completeness, we list the analogous expressions appropriate to the crystal spectrometer scans described above.

(*i*) Constant-$\boldsymbol{Q}$ scan: $\alpha = \int I(\nu)\,\mathrm{d}\nu = A(\boldsymbol{Q})$,

where $A(\boldsymbol{Q})$ is given by eq. (1.10) with $|J_j| = 1$; (2.14)

(*ii*) Constant energy scan:

$$\alpha = \int I(\boldsymbol{Q})\,\mathrm{d}\boldsymbol{Q} = A(\boldsymbol{Q})/|\boldsymbol{e}\cdot\nabla_{\boldsymbol{Q}}\nu_j(\boldsymbol{Q})|\,; \tag{2.15}$$

(*iii*) General linear scan:

$$\alpha = \int I(\omega, \boldsymbol{Q})\,\mathrm{d}\omega = A(\boldsymbol{Q})/|1 - a\boldsymbol{e}\cdot\nabla_{\boldsymbol{Q}}\nu(\boldsymbol{Q})|\,. \tag{2.16}$$

In the last two equations, $\boldsymbol{e}$ is a unit vector in the direction of $\Delta\boldsymbol{Q}$, $|\Delta\boldsymbol{Q}| = a\,\Delta\nu$, and $\nabla_{\boldsymbol{Q}}\nu(\boldsymbol{Q})$ is the gradient of the dispersion curve being studied. It should be emphasized that all these expressions are derived on the assumptions that the experimental resolution is extremely good and that the second derivative of the dispersion curve is negligible over the spectrometer resolution function. Further details of these matters have been given by Dolling and Sears (1973).

No discussion of crystal spectrometers would be complete without some mention of its focusing properties, and we shall conclude this section with a qualitative description of why these properties arise, and how they may be calculated and used to good advantage in actual experiments. The resolution of spectrometers or of various components of spectrometers has already been briefly mentioned. For a triple axis crystal spectrometer, fig. 3, there are contributions to the resolution from each of the collimators and from the mosaic spread of the monochromator and analyser crystals. The distribution in neutron wave vector produced by the crystal mosaic spread, β, and a Soller slit collimator, divergence α, is illustrated in fig. 9. The collimation produces a wave vector spread $\Delta \boldsymbol{k}_c = \alpha|\boldsymbol{k}| \operatorname{cosec} \theta$ in a direction perpendicular to the vector $\boldsymbol{\tau}$ of the reciprocal lattice, where θ is the Bragg angle. The mosaic spread, on the other hand, gives rise to a wave vector spread $\Delta \boldsymbol{k}_m = \beta \boldsymbol{k} \cot \theta$, for a fixed direction of the reflected beam. The convolution of $\Delta \boldsymbol{k}_c$ and $\Delta \boldsymbol{k}_m$ is a distribution whose halfvalue contour is an ellipse. As

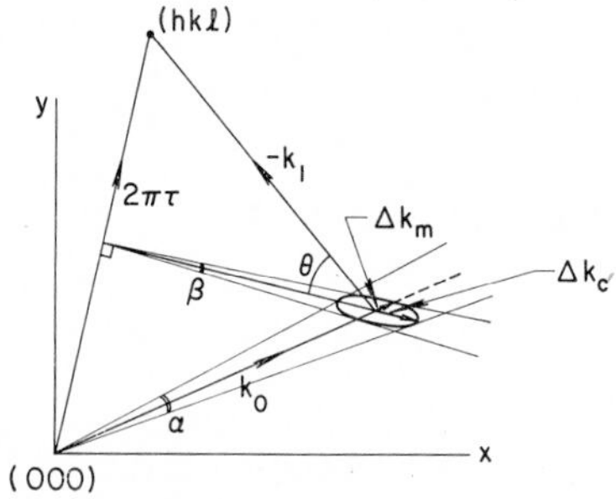

Fig. 9. Contributions to the wave vector resolution of a neutron beam reflected from a crystal with mosaic spread β and passing through a collimator of angular divergence α. $|\boldsymbol{k}_1| = |\boldsymbol{k}_0|$. The ellipse represents the half-value contour of the resulting resolution function in the (xy) plane.

suggested in fig. 9, this ellipse, for both monochromator and analyser crystals, is usually rather elongated in practice, with a major to minor axis ratio of about 4. The resolution of the whole spectrometer is the convolution of ellipsoidal contributions from each component. This total resolution function, $R(\boldsymbol{Q}-\boldsymbol{Q}_m, \nu-\nu_m)$, expresses the probability of detecting a scattered neutron whose wave vector transfer $\boldsymbol{Q}$ and energy change ν differ from the mean values $\boldsymbol{Q}_m$ and ν_m of these quantities. Although R is a 4-dimensional function, the component of $\boldsymbol{Q}-\boldsymbol{Q}_m$ normal to the plane of the spectrometer (§2.1) is uncorrelated with the in-plane components and with $\nu-\nu_m$, so that all the important features can be seen in the corresponding 3-dimensional function. The half-value contour surface of this function is an ellipsoid, often referred to as the resolution ellipsoid. The course of any coherent neutron scattering experiment to determine a phonon dispersion relation can be thought of as a stepwise motion of this ellipsoid through the dispersion surface $\nu_j(\boldsymbol{q})$. The elongated nature of the ellipse may lead to focusing effects, since the width of the observed neutron group will depend strongly on the relative orientation of the resolution ellipsoid and the tangent plane of the dispersion surface at the point of crossing. A simple 2-dimensional illustration of the effect is sketched in fig. 10 for an acoustic mode determination on either side of a reciprocal lattice point. The experiment on the left yields a broad group since

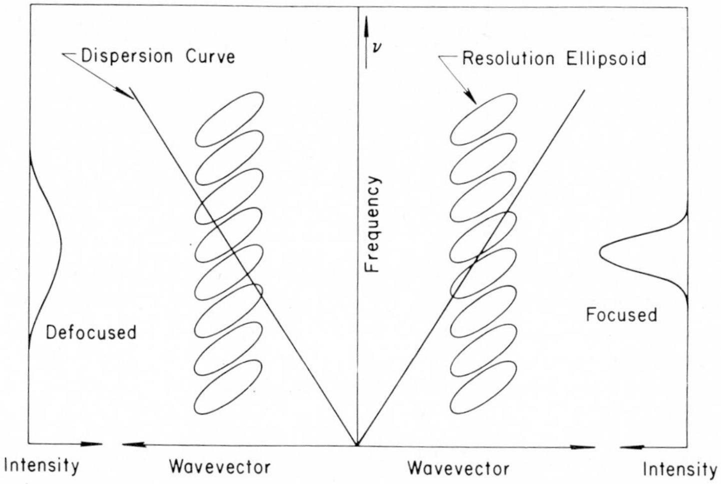

Fig. 10. Simplified illustration of focusing effects arising from the elongated shape of the resolution ellipsoid.

the resolution ellipse has some intersection with the dispersion curve, and hence neutron scattering strength, for many successive points on the scan.

To a first approximation, we can consider separately the contribution to the resolution of each component. It is convenient to consider a new energy transfer coordinate $\nu' = \nu - (\hbar/m)\,\Delta\boldsymbol{Q}\cdot\nabla_{\boldsymbol{q}}\nu_j(\boldsymbol{q})$, where $h\nu = E_0 - E_1$, $\Delta\boldsymbol{Q}$ is the appropriate component of the total wave vector resolution and $\nabla_{\boldsymbol{q}}\nu_j(\boldsymbol{q})$ is the gradient of the dispersion curve, assumed constant over a region at least as large as the resolution function. The resolution, expressed in terms of this new coordinate is thus of the form

$$\Delta\nu' = (\hbar/m)\,\Delta\boldsymbol{Q}\cdot[\boldsymbol{k}/2\pi - \nabla_{\boldsymbol{q}}\nu_j(\boldsymbol{q})]. \tag{2.17}$$

We evaluate all the contributions to $\Delta\nu'$ as $\Delta\boldsymbol{Q}$ is set equal to $\Delta\boldsymbol{k}_c$, $\Delta\boldsymbol{k}_m$ for both monochromator and analyser crystals and collimators in turn, and compute the square root of the sum of squares of each contribution. (All quantities are assumed to have gaussian distributions.) It is impossible to arrange matters so that all contributions are negligible, but it is usually fairly easy, assuming we have a good estimate of $\nabla_{\boldsymbol{q}}\nu_j(\boldsymbol{q})$, to make one or two of the larger contributions very small or zero. For example, Stedman (1968) has described a simple geometrical construction, fig. 11, which shows how to make the $\Delta\boldsymbol{k}_c$ contributions zero simultaneously for both monochromator and analyser. This type of construction is quite adequate for deciding on the appropriate experimental arrangement for optimum focusing.

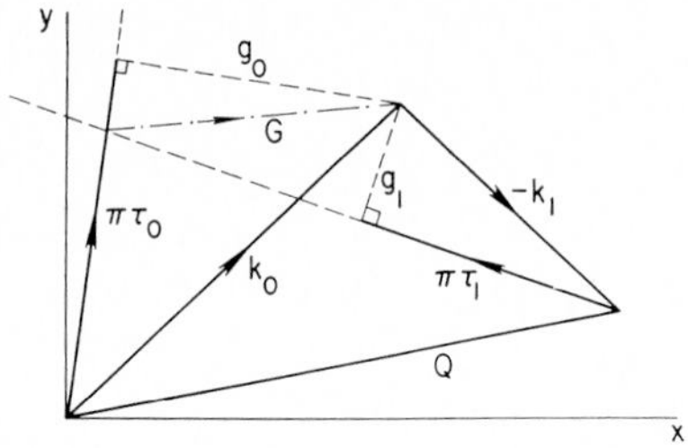

Fig. 11. Graphical illustration of focusing applied to both monochromator and analyser crystals. G is proportional to the gradient $\nabla_q \nu_j(\boldsymbol{q})$ and the vectors $\boldsymbol{g}_0$, $\boldsymbol{g}_1$ are parallel to the $\Delta \boldsymbol{k}_c$ contributions arising from these two crystals. They are seen to be perpendicular to the vectors $(\boldsymbol{k}_0 - \boldsymbol{G})$ and $(\boldsymbol{k}_1 - \boldsymbol{G})$ respectively, thus giving zero contributions to $\Delta\nu'$ according to eq. (2.17).

It may sometimes be desirable, however, to make very precise calculations of the instrumental resolution. For example, the natural line width of a phonon in a crystal at temperatures far below the melting point may be very small compared with the resolution, so that a very accurate calculation of the latter is essential if a significant line width is to be derived by unfolding it from the observed neutron group. Rather complicated analytical expressions for R have been derived by Collins (1963) and by Cooper and Nathans (1967). Although these expressions are straightforward to evaluate by means of a computer program, they are extremely lengthy and require a profuse notation, not particularly conducive to an understanding of the basic ideas involved. For further details, the interested reader is referred to the papers cited or to an admirable review by Bjerrum Møller and Nielsen (1970). A Monte Carlo method of obtaining R, by following the paths in real space of neutrons traveling through spectrometer, has also been described by Dietrich (1968). This method has the advantage that the actual physical dimensions of the spectrometer components and the specimen are taken into account in the calculation of the scattered neutron group intensity.

Finally, mention should be made of a method of measuring the spectrometer resolution function for the case that $\nu_m \approx 0$ and $\boldsymbol{Q}_m$ is close to a vector $\boldsymbol{\tau}$ of the reciprocal lattice (Nielsen and Bjerrum Møller 1969). The scattered neutron intensity $I(\boldsymbol{Q}_m, \nu)$ given by the integral of the cross-section $\sigma(\boldsymbol{Q}, \nu)$ over the resolution function:

$$I(\boldsymbol{Q}_m, \nu) = \int\int R(\boldsymbol{Q} - \boldsymbol{Q}_m, \nu - \nu_m)\, \sigma(\boldsymbol{Q}, \nu)\, \mathrm{d}\boldsymbol{Q}\, \mathrm{d}\nu \,. \tag{2.18}$$

For a Bragg peak represented by the vector $\boldsymbol{\tau}$, $\sigma(\boldsymbol{Q}, \nu) \simeq \delta(\boldsymbol{Q} - \boldsymbol{\tau})\, \delta(\nu)$, so that the Bragg peak intensity effectively maps out the function R. The elongation of the resolution ellipse may be easily seen in such a mapping. Since R can be expected to be a slowly varying function, the experimental values obtained in this way are quite useful for a small range of ν about zero.

2.6. Time-of-flight spectrometers

The development of time-of-flight spectrometers up to 1965 has been reviewed by Brugger (1965). The basic idea behind this type of instrument is that a pulse of monoenergetic neutrons is incident on the specimen, which is surrounded by a battery of detectors. The output signal from each detector is electronically sorted by a multichannel analyser according to the arrival time of the scattered neutrons with respect to some defined start time, say, the arrival time of the incident neutron pulse at the specimen position. After a suitable time interval, another neutron pulse arrives at the specimen, and the scattered neutrons are time-analysed in the same way. Typically, the pulse width is between 5 and 50 μsec, and the interval between successive pulses is between 10^{-3} and 10^{-2} sec. This interval is normally sufficient to avoid 'frame overlap', i.e. ambiguity as to whether a given detected neutron originated from the immediately previous incident pulse or from an earlier pulse in the train. Assuming this ambiguity can be avoided, it is clear that the scattered neutron velocity and energy can be deduced from the time of flight of the neutrons over the known distance from sample to detector. The attraction of this basic concept arises from the possibility of detecting a large proportion of all the scattered neutrons, by having a large number of detectors, and by simultaneous energy analysis instead of the point by point analysis characteristic of crystal spectrometers. However, the duty cycle of the instrument (the ratio of the pulse width to the interval between pulses) is very low, usually less than 1%, so that almost all the neutrons from a continuous source such as a nuclear reactor are rejected by the device which produces the incident neutron pulses. Time-of-flight spectrometers of this conventional type are clearly better suited for use with pulsed neutron sources (see also §§2.9, 2.11).

A very common way of producing a train of neutron pulses is by means of a mechanical chopper, and a wide variety of such choppers has been used in neutron spectroscopy. The axis of rotation of the chopper may be parallel to the neutron beam, as in the mechanical velocity selectors mentioned in §2.3, or perpendicular to the beam, as in the simple Fermi chopper (Fermi et al. 1947) and the more sophisticated curved slot rotors designed by Pickles and

Hazlewood (1960) for use in the four-phased-rotor spectrometer built at Chalk River (Egelstaff et al. 1961). The path of a neutron of velocity v in the rotating system of coordinates of a chopper rotating with angular velocity ω is an archimedean spiral $r = v\theta/\omega$ (r is the spiral radius at a turn angle θ). Thus if a narrow slot of this spiral shape is cut in an otherwise solid disc of neutron absorbing material, and if the disc is then rotated at an angular speed ω about an axis perpendicular to a collimated neutron beam, then only those neutrons of the velocity $v = \omega r/\theta$ will be able to pass through the disc without touching the sides of the slot. Practical rotors depart from this idealized situation in several ways. Normally, only a small segment of the spiral is required, and it is quite adequate to approximate the spiral shape by a circular arc, which greatly simplifies machining problems. Several parallel circular slots are often used in order to increase the effective area of the neutron beam, and of course the slots have a finite width which means that neutrons having a finite spread in velocity (magnitude and direction) may be transmitted through the device. A detailed calculation of the transmission function of a system of parallel circular slots is straightforward though fairly complicated (see for example Marseguerra and Pauli (1959), Komura and Cooper (1970): the following simple treatment will serve to demonstrate several important features, and it is also good enough for the purpose of designing rotors.

We consider the rotor shown in fig. 12, which has one slot of width a and mean radius of curvature R cut so that its centre line (dashed) passes through the rotor centre O. A perfectly collimated neutron beam directed along A′OB′... is incident on the rotor. The approximation we make is to replace the

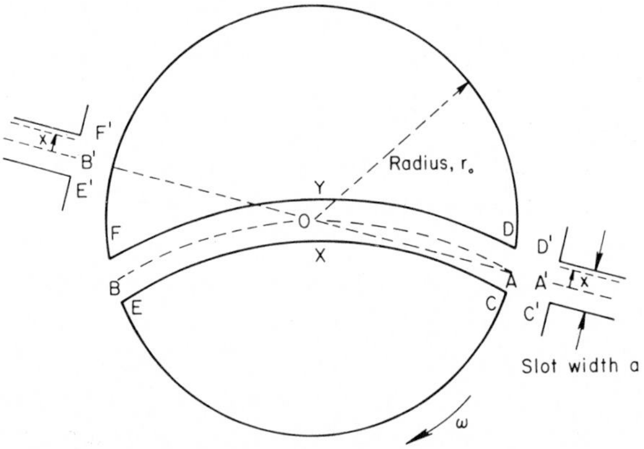

Fig. 12. Plan view of a neutron chopper or rotor with one curved slot.

solid rotor by the three apertures CD, XY and EF. Let a neutron arrive at the edge of the rotor at a time when the aperture CD is open. If its velocity is such that by the time it has traversed the rotor diameter ($2r_0$), the aperture EF has rotated to its 'open' position, then the neutron will be transmitted. We neglect edge effects, in which a neutron may be capable of passing through the apertures but would in practice touch a side of the slot en route and be absorbed or scattered. We are also neglecting the fact that a real neutron beam is not perfectly collimated, but it is easy to see how to allow for this. A transmission function can be calculated in this way which is quite adequate for most purposes.

Consider a neutron of velocity v_x traveling parallel to A′OB′ but displaced a distance x from this line. The time of flight $F(v_x)$ of the neutron across the rotor diameter is

$$F(v_x) = 2r_0/v_x. \tag{2.17}$$

We define a time scale such that at time $t=0$, the point C is just opposite D′ (i.e. the first aperture CD is just about to open). At time $t=t_{x_i}$, C is opposite the neutron path at x, and at time $t=t_{x_f}$, D has reached this point. Thus t_{x_i} and t_{x_f} are the earliest and latest times at which a neutron at x may enter the first aperture. Similarly, we define T_{x_f} and T_{x_i} as the earliest and latest times at which that neutron may escape through aperture EF. If ϕ is the angle BOB′ in fig. 12, then

$$t_{x_i} = \frac{1}{\omega r_0}\left(\tfrac{1}{2}a - x\right), \qquad t_{x_f} = \frac{1}{\omega r_0}\left(\tfrac{3}{2}a - x\right),$$

$$T_{x_i} = \frac{1}{\omega r_0}\left(\tfrac{1}{2}a + x\right) + \phi/\omega, \qquad T_{x_f} = \frac{1}{\omega r_0}\left(\tfrac{3}{2}a + x\right) + \phi/\omega. \tag{2.18}$$

The transmitted intensity of neutrons of velocity v_x during one rotor cycle is proportional to the length of time during which they may be transmitted. This length of time $I(v_x)$ is given, for neutrons of slower (faster) than average velocity $\bar{v}$ by

$$I(v_x < \bar{v}) = T_{x_f} - t_{x_i} - 2r_0/v_x, \quad I(v_x > \bar{v}) = T_{x_i} - t_{x_f} + 2r_0/v_x. \tag{2.19}$$

The transmission function at distance x is therefore a triangular function of reciprocal velocity. It is easy to see that the maximum, minimum and mean reciprocal velocities transmitted by the entire slot are given by

$$\frac{1}{v_{\min}} = \frac{\phi + 2a/r_0}{2r_0\omega}, \quad \frac{1}{v_{\max}} = \frac{\phi - 2a/r_0}{2r_0\omega}, \quad \frac{1}{v_{\text{mean}}} = \frac{\phi}{2r_0\omega} = \frac{m}{h}\lambda_{\text{mean}}, \tag{2.20}$$

where λ_{mean} is the mean de Broglie wavelength, m the neutron mass and h is Planck's constant. The total transmission function is a superposition of triangles each corresponding to neutrons transmitted at distances x between $\pm\frac{1}{2}a$. The result of this superposition is the curve, sketched in fig. 13, made up of 4 parabolic sections. A similar curve describes the transmitted intensity

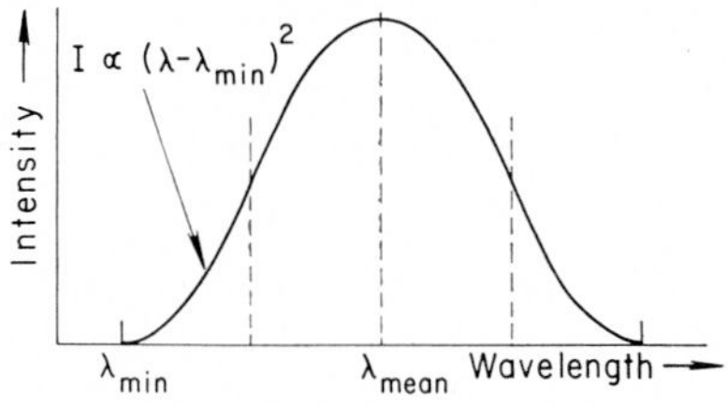

Fig. 13. Sketch of the transmitted intensity of a perfectly collimated neutron beam through a curved slot rotor, as a function of wavelength λ.

of neutrons of all wavelengths as a function of time. For any particular neutron wavelength, the transmitted intensity is a triangular function of time. The mean wavelength λ_{mean}, eq. (2.20), is determined by the rotor speed and slot radius of curvature $R = r_0/\phi$. The wavelength resolution is proportional to $a/\omega r^2$, the time resolution or burst time to $a/\omega r_0$, and the duty cycle is $a/2\pi r_0$. It is clear that for a given duty cycle, it is best to have a large rotor spinning at very high speed for optimum overall resolution. The strength of materials places upper limits on these quantities, which, with present technology, are of order 50 cm diameter and 1000 cycles/sec respectively. Two curved slot rotors (Pickles and Hazlewood 1960) are illustrated in fig. 14. Typical dimensions (in cm) are $r_0 = 12.5$, $a = 0.6$, $R = 50$. When

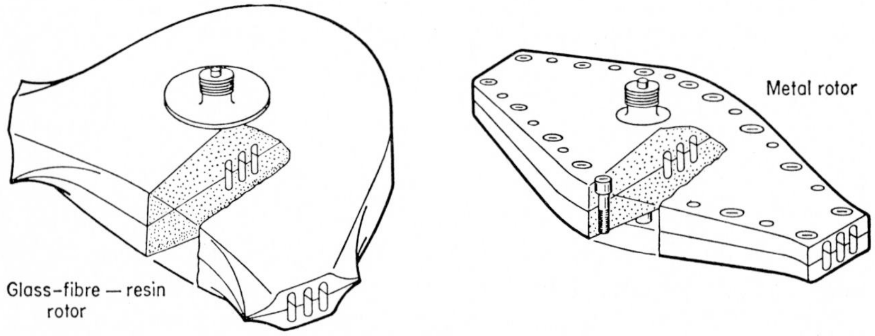

Fig. 14. Two types of high-speed curved slot rotors designed for time-of-flight spectrometers at Harwell and Chalk River.

spun at 600 cycles/sec, $\lambda_{mean}=1.05$ Å while $\Delta\lambda=\Delta\lambda_{max}-\lambda_{min}=0.82$ Å. While this wavelength resolution is much too poor for most purposes, the duty cycle is just under 1% and the total spread of the neutron pulse in time is quite acceptable, about 14 μsec. The wavelength resolution can readily be improved to the desired level by inserting a second rotor of similar design into the pulsed beam transmitted by the first rotor. The second rotor is driven at the same speed and its phase with respect to the first rotor is carefully controlled so that its slots are 'open' when neutrons of the desired velocity arrive. If the distance between the 2 rotors is D, the improvement factor in resolution is easily seen to be D/r_0, which is commonly a factor of 10 to 20. In the four-phased-rotor spectrometer (Egelstaff et al. 1961) which remained in operation at Chalk River until 1965, two of the rotors were used to define the monoenergetic thermal neutron beam, and the other two were of crude resolution, designed to reduce the flux of unwanted fast neutrons which would otherwise fall directly on the specimen and produce unacceptably high background count rates in the detectors. The two crude resolution rotors are dispensed with in certain other conventional time-of-flight spectrometers (e.g. Dyer and Low 1961, Krebs 1968). There is a substantial literature on the subject of the resolution (in energy and time), transmitted intensity and pulse shapes obtained by various systems of phased rotors. These questions are fully reviewed by Brugger (1965), to which the reader is referred for further details.

Having produced a pulsed beam of monoenergetic neutron incident upon our specimen, we now set up an array of many detectors at well-defined distances from the specimen. A typical detector system consists of 20 to 30 detectors at fixed angles of scattering, mounted on an arc of radius 1 to 5 m, and housed inside a communal shield designed so that each detector 'sees' only the specimen: neutrons arriving from other directions are scattered away or absorbed by the shield. Since the detector–specimen distance must be well-defined, within the overall spectrometer resolution, it is normally necessary to use detectors less than a few cm thick. Although BF_3 detectors (see section 2.2) have been used for this purpose, their efficiencies at this thickness are generally rather low; ^{3}He detectors are more widely used, and some spectrometers have employed scintillation-type detectors which can be made only a millimetre thick. In this detector, a neutron absorbing element such as ^{6}Li or ^{10}B is combined with a scintillating phosphor, usually ZnS, so that each absorbed neutron produces a flash of light which can be detected by a photomultiplier tube. Perhaps the chief disadvantage of these detectors in comparison with the other types mentioned is their increased sensitivity to

γ-rays. Complete technical details (for making the phosphor-absorber mixture, constructing the detector, typical electrical characteristics and neutron efficiencies) may be found in the article by Cocking and Webb (1965). These authors also provide a useful comparative digest of detector characteristics, and conclude that ^{3}He detectors are probably best for all types of neutron spectrometer.

2.7. Hybrid spectrometers

Many variations in spectrometer design are possible if the two techniques of neutron diffraction and neutron chopping are combined. One of the most successful of these is the rotating crystal spectrometer developed by Brockhouse (1961). Some improvements have been made to this basic instrument (Woods et al. 1968) and we shall now briefly describe this more modern version, a schematic diagram of which is shown in fig. 15.

Every time a particular set of atomic planes, eg. (111), rotates through the Bragg reflection position, a pulse of neutrons of the appropriate wavelength is diffracted through the angle $2\theta_m$ in the direction of the specimen. Depending on the crystal rotation axis, there may be several positions within one rev-

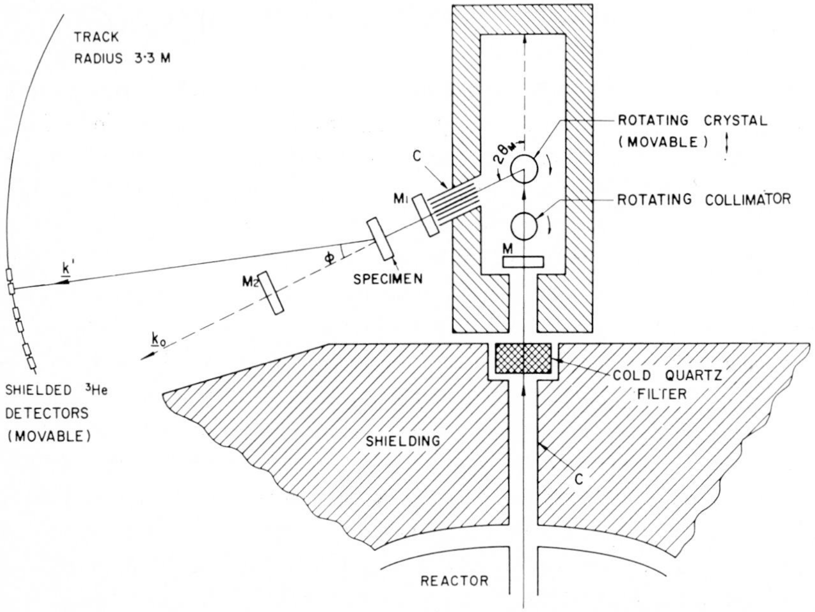

Fig. 15. Schematic diagram of the Chalk River rotating crystal spectrometer.

olution at which various reflecting planes come into play in addition to the desired (111) planes. In addition, reflection by higher order planes such as (222) and/or (333) will occur at the same times as the (111) reflections. All these unwanted reflections are virtually eliminated by the rotating collimator situated at a preselected distance from the monochromator. This collimator spins at the same rate as the monochromator and the phase between the two devices is adjusted so that only those neutrons of the desired wavelength can

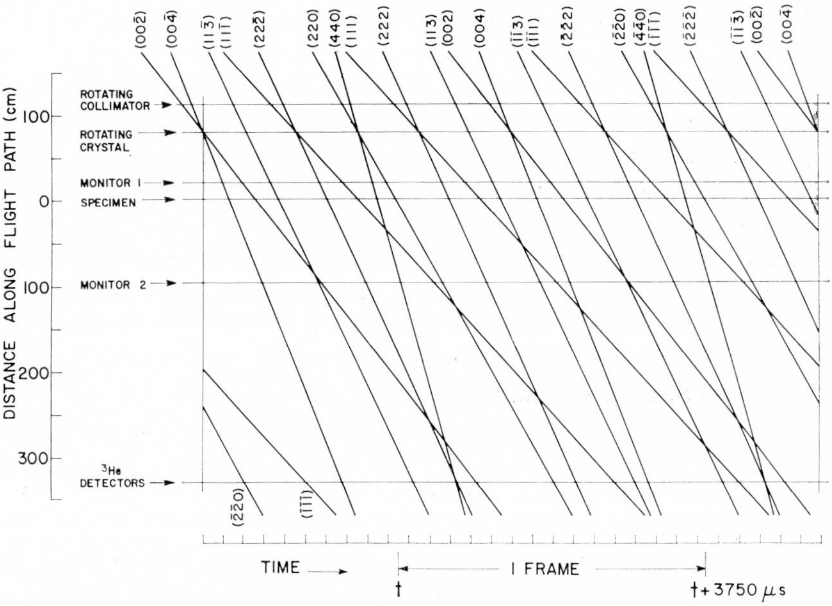

Fig. 16. Rotating crystal-rotating collimator phasing diagram for a fcc crystal (in this case aluminum) with the $(1\bar{1}0)$ plane horizontal and $2\theta_m = 105°$.

be transmitted and then Bragg reflected towards the specimen. Fig. 16 is a plot of position along the entire flight path for neutrons reflected from various reflecting planes as a function of time in an aluminium monochromator crystal with a [110] axis of rotation. This kind of diagram is used to determine the optimum spacing between the rotating collimator and rotating crystal and other relevant experimental parameters. Another important advantage of the rotating collimator is that is substantially reduces the intensity of neutrons of any energy which would otherwise be diffusely scattered by the monochromator and give rise to a time-independent background count rate.

A mirror attached to the drive shaft for the rotating crystal reflects a light beam onto a photocell twice per revolution, and the resultant pulses trigger the electronic timing circuits which measure the time of flight of the neutrons scattered from the specimen, across a 3.3 m flight path into a shielded bank of ^{3}He detectors, each of 40 cm active length and 1.5 cm thick. As each neutron is detected, the number of time channels elapsed since the start pulse and also a detector identification code number are written onto magnetic tape. Normally, the data for one 24-hour run are accumulated in this way and then read off into a large off-line computer for subsequent sorting and analysis. The angle of scattering ϕ may be varied over a 95° range since the detector shield runs on a circular track centered on the (fixed) specimen position. The monochromator angle $2\theta_m$ can be varied between 150° and 100° by moving the rotating crystal back and forth as shown in fig. 15. $2\theta_m$ and ϕ are kept constant during individual runs which may last for several hours or several days.

The resolution function for the rotating crystal spectrometer displays some interesting features in addition to those discussed previously in connection with static crystal spectrometers and mechanical choppers. These arise from the Doppler effect on the incident neutrons of the moving reflecting planes of the monochromator crystal, and from the various possible neutron path lengths through the instrument, leading to modifications of the pulse width (in time) and reflected intensities. Full details are given in the paper by Brockhouse (1961). A more recent analysis of the resolution function of a rotating crystal spectrometer has been given by Furrer (1971).

Other rotating crystal spectrometers, such as that constructed by Harling (1966, 1968) differ in detail but are in principle very similar to the Chalk River instrument, and will not be described further.

Another interesting variation of the hybrid spectrometer has been described by Buras (1966) and by Maliszewski et al. (1968). A schematic diagram is shown in fig. 17a. Polychromatic neutrons from a pulsed source (or from a single mechanical chopper operating in conjunction with a continuous source) are incident upon the specimen S. Scattered neutrons are observed by several analyser–detector systems similar to those described in §2.4, except that here the output from each detector is time-analysed so that the flight times of the neutrons from the pulsed source (or a monitor detector close to it) to the detector can be determined. The energy and velocity of the scattered neutrons is of course known from the preset value of the analyser angle $2\theta_a$, so that the arrival time of the pulse at S, and hence also the incident neutron velocity, can be calculated. The number of independent detectors in limited to about

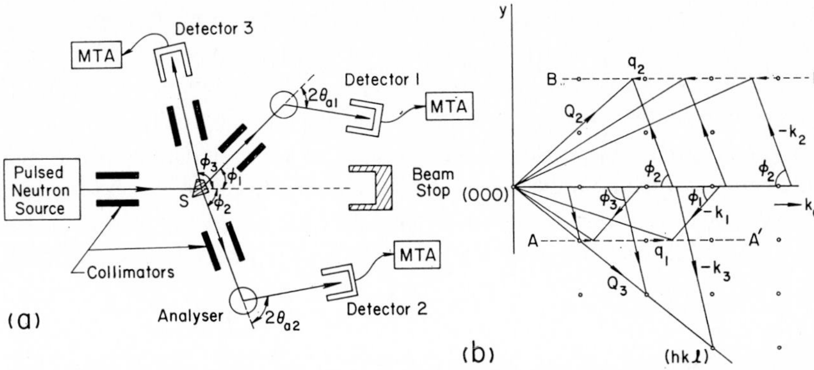

Fig. 17.a. Schematic diagram of an 'inverted geometry' time-of-flight spectrometer. The output from each detector is fed into a multi-channel time analyser (MTA) which is triggered by the incident neutron pulses. Detectors 1 and 2 may be used for inelastic scattering measurements at the same time as neutron diffraction studies are being carried out with detector 3. b. Reciprocal lattice diagram appropriate to the 3 detectors arranged according to fig. 17a. The direction of $\boldsymbol{k}_0$, the vectors $\boldsymbol{k}_1$, $\boldsymbol{k}_2$, and the angles ϕ_1 and ϕ_2 have been selected so that the observed peaks will correspond to coherent one-phonon scattering processes associated with reduced phonon wave vectors $\boldsymbol{q}_1$, $\boldsymbol{q}_2$ along lines AA′, BB′, joining adjacent reciprocal lattice points. (Such lines are often directions of high symmetry in the sample crystal.) $|\boldsymbol{k}_3| = |\boldsymbol{k}_0|$ for the intense (Bragg reflection) peaks observed by detector 3.

3 or 4 by space requirements. Since the specimen is in the direct line from the neutron source, it must be surrounded by a massive shield similar to the monochromator shielding drum of a triple axis crystal spectrometer. Expeimental scans are performed with the angles ϕ and $2\theta_a$ fixed for each detector. Referring to the appropriate reciprocal lattice diagram, fig. 17b, we see that any peak in the time-of-flight spectrum corresponds to some point along one of the dotted lines parallel to $\boldsymbol{k}_0$. By suitable choice of ϕ, $2\theta_a$, and the direction of $\boldsymbol{k}_0$ with respect to the crystal axes (x, y), dispersion curve measurements may therefore be made for phonon wave vectors along selected high symmetry directions.

If a detector is set up to observe the scattered neutrons without any intervening analyser crystal (see detector 3 in fig. 17a), then it will detect primarily those neutrons which are Bragg-reflected from the specimen. (Coherent elastic scattering is many orders of magnitude more intense than inelastic scattering provided the specimen is not too hot). Time-of-flight analysis of the output from this detector will therefore yield a series of intense peaks corresponding to Bragg reflection of neutrons of different wavelengths in the incident pulse. These wavelengths can readily be obtained from the measured total flight times on the assumption that all the scattering is elastic, as indicated in fig. 17b. The end points of the vectors $-\boldsymbol{k}_3$ corresponding to any time-of-flight peaks in detector 3 are reciprocal lattice points of the crystal specimen. Conditions must of course be chosen correctly so that the dotted line $\boldsymbol{Q}_3$ does indeed pass through the desired reciprocal lattice points. In this way, information about the crystal structure of the specimen may be obtained at the same time as measurements of the dynamical properties. The relevance of this possibility to the study of phase transitions has been stressed by Buras (1966) (see also §3.3).

2.8. Correlation methods

In the previous two sections we have described several instruments which make use of pulsed neutron beams. When these are deployed at a conventional reactor, itself a continuous source of neutrons, then more than 99% of the available neutrons are rejected at the outset. It is however possible to make much greater use of these neutrons by applying correlation methods to time-of-flight spectrometers, and there have been considerable developments in this direction during the past few years. We first discuss the basic principles behind these methods, and then describe three of the most promising types of practical spectrometers based on these principles.

Let $I(t)$ denote the intensity of a monoenergetic neutron beam incident on the specimen as a function of time. A single delta-function pulse arriving at time $t=0$ would then be represented by $I(t)=\delta(t)$. The time-of-flight spectrum of neutrons scattered from the specimen depends upon a function $S(t)$ of the specimen alone. In the case of a delta-function input pulse, the time-of-flight spectrum actually observed will be

$$Z(t) = \int_{-\infty}^{\infty} S(t')\,\delta(t-t')\,\mathrm{d}t' = K\,S(t), \tag{2.21}$$

where K is a constant. In random noise theory, $S(t)$ is referred to as the impulse response function of the system. If $S(t)$ is non-zero only in a finite range of t from 0 to T, say, then the integration need only be from 0 to T, and a sequence of delta-function neutron pulses separated by at least time T could be used to determine $S(t)$. This is of course the basis of the conventional time-of-flight spectrometers described in previous sections: the time T_0 between successive pulses is usually chosen so that $T_0 \geqslant T$ for the specimen concerned, in order to avoid the problem of frame overlap. If I (t) is a more complex function, then the observed time-of-flight spectrum can be written in the form

$$Z(t) = (1/T) \int_0^T S(t')\, I(t - t')\, \mathrm{d}t' + B(t), \tag{2.22}$$

where $B(t)$ is the background count rate. This equation assumes the validity of the principle of linear superposition. What we wish to do, of course, is to extract the scattering function $S(t)$ from $Z(t)$ under conditions in which the neutron beam is switched on for a large fraction of all time instead of the very low utilization, less than 1%, of the conventional method.

It is well-known (see for example Lee 1961, Uhrig 1970) that the cross-correlation between the input and the output of a dynamic system is equal to the convolution of the impulse response function and the autocorrelation function of the input. In our case, the input is the train of neutron pulses incident on the specimen, $I(t)$, the output is the observed time-of-flight spectrum $Z(t)$, and the specimen itself is the dynamic system, whose impulse response function is $S(t)$. Let us denote a correlation function of two functions x and y by ϕ_{xy}, and for the moment, let us neglect the background term $B(t)$:

$$\begin{aligned}
\phi_{IZ}(\tau) &= T^{-1} \int_0^T I(t)\, Z(t + \tau)\, \mathrm{d}t \\
&= T^{-1} \int_0^T \mathrm{d}t\, I(t) \cdot T^{-1} \int_0^T \mathrm{d}t'\, S(t')\, I(t + \tau - t') \\
&= T^{-1} \int_0^T \mathrm{d}t'\, S(t') \cdot T^{-1} \int_0^T \mathrm{d}t\, I(t)\, I(t + \tau - t') \\
&= T^{-1} \int_0^T \mathrm{d}t'\, S(t')\, \phi_{II}(\tau - t') \\
&= T^{-1} \int_0^T \mathrm{d}t\, S(\tau - t)\, \phi_{II}(t).
\end{aligned} \tag{2.23}$$

In the special case of a perfectly random input signal, the autocorrelation function $\phi_{II}(t)$ becomes a delta function so that the impulse response function $S(\tau)$ is directly proportional to the cross-correlation $\phi_{IZ}(\tau)$. This result is true even if the term $B(t)$ had been included, since this is uncorrelated with the random input signal (whose mean value is zero). A train of neutron pulses with these characteristics cannot be realised in practice, however, since negative pulses do not exist, and the background count rate therefore cannot be entirely eliminated, although it will be substantially reduced. Other practical problems are that the neutron pulses cannot be switched on and off with infinite frequency and sharpness and that the pulse on- or off-time must be a certain 'pseudo-random' number of finite-sized time intervals Δt. The adjective pseudo-random implies that the train of pulses is random within a certain interval (one 'frame'), after which the pulse train is repeated. The autocorrelation function of a pseudo-random train of pulses is thus a periodic sequence of peaks of finite width and the cross-correlation function $\phi_{IZ}(\tau)$, eq. (2.23) is the desired scattering function of the specimen, folded with this periodic sequence.

The smallest practicable value for Δt is about 5 μsec at the present time. A pseudo-random sequence $+1$ and -1 signals may be generated with a feedback shift-register [see Uhrig (1970) for details and further references]. The output of a 4-stage register is shown at the top of fig. 18. A signal $+1$ (-1) means that the neutron beam is switched on (off), and after a time period $T=(2^4-1)\,\Delta t=15\Delta t$, the whole cycle is repeated. The autocorrelation function, at the bottom of fig. 18, shows the periodic sharp peaks of finite width Δt, with an intervening small negative background. For any point in this background region, the autocorrelation function comprises (2^3-1) values of $+1$ and 2^3 values of -1, the net result being -1. This is reduced to $-\frac{1}{15}$ when the main peaks are normalized to 1. The contribution of any uncorrelated background $B(t)$ to the cross-correlation function would likewise be reduced by a factor $(2^4-1)=15$. The end result of this cross-correlation analysis is of course the time-of-flight spectrum of the neutrons scattered from the specimen. The neutron energy and momentum transfers corresponding to any peaks in the spectrum are then derived in the same way as in the conventional time-of-flight spectrometers.

As mentioned earlier, it is advisable to choose T large enough that the impulse response function or scattering function has fallen essentially to zero within one cycle or frame. Typically T might be 2500 μsec, and if $\Delta t=5$ μsec, then a 9-stage shift register would be suitable for generating the pseudo-random sequence. If the frame length T is chosen too small, then the phenomenon of frame overlap will appear just as in conventional instruments.

Perhaps the most direct way of producing the desired pseudo-random neutron pulses is by means of a mechanical chopper of the type constructed by Gompf et al. (1968). A sequence of absorbing blocks made from a gadoli-

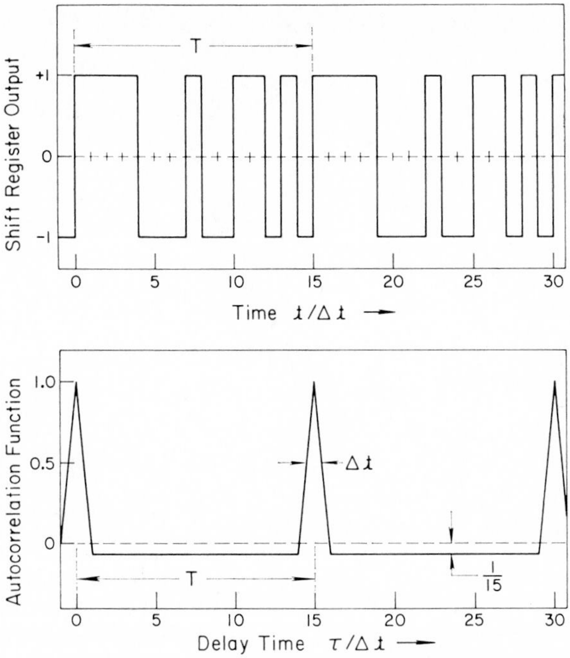

Fig. 18. The output of a 4-stage shift register as a function of time, and the autocorrelation function of an idealised pseudo-random train of neutron pulses based on that output.

nium oxide (Gd_2O_3)–epoxy mixture are glued onto an aluminum alloy rotor of 51 cm diameter, in the pseudo-random pattern (in fact, two identical sequences of 127 units each) sketched in fig. 19a. The basic unit of absorber width is 0.63 cm at the outside edge. The layout of the spectrometer and electronics is shown in fig. 19b. A continuous beam of neutrons from a reactor falls on a Be single crystal monochromator. The monochromatic beam passes through the edge of the rotating disc and is thereby chopped into pseudo-random pulses having a basic width $\Delta t = 32$ μsec (at 7382 rev/min). Neutrons are scattered along a flight tube to a detector whose output is time-analysed and cross-correlated with the input signal. The resolution of this instrument is only moderate on account of the rather large Δt value and the 7-stage sequence. Increasing the number of pulses in the sequence to 511 (9 stages) would involve either a reduction of the basic absorber width by a factor 4 or a corresponding increase in the disc diameter. Neither of these changes would be easy to make. A more fundamental problem with the mechanical chopper, however, is that its pseudo-random sequence is fixed

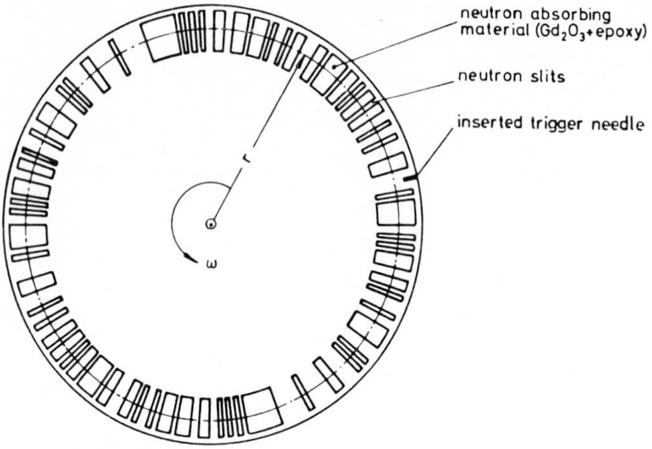

(a)

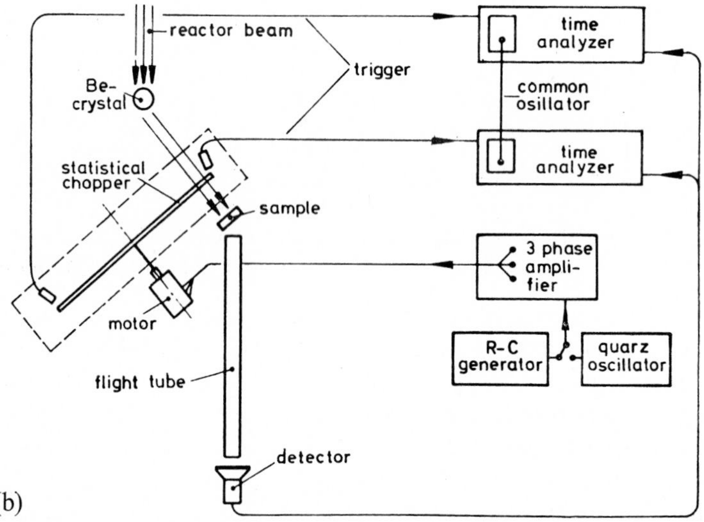

(b)

Fig. 19.a. Schematic diagram of a mechanical correlation chopper. Two pseudo-random sequences of (2^7-1) units each are produced by appropriate neutron absorbing blocks glued onto the perimeter of an aluminum alloy rotor which is itself almost transparent to thermal neutrons. b. Layout of the spectrometer and associated electronic equipment. The continuous beam from the reactor is monochromated by the Be crystal and then chopped into pseudo-random pulses before falling on the specimen.

and not readily changed to suit different experimental conditions. (This problem is of course common to all mechanical chopper systems.) Indeed, it is not at all necessary that the duty cycle of the chopper should be 50%, as in the examples discussed so far. Much lower duty cycles, even down to a few

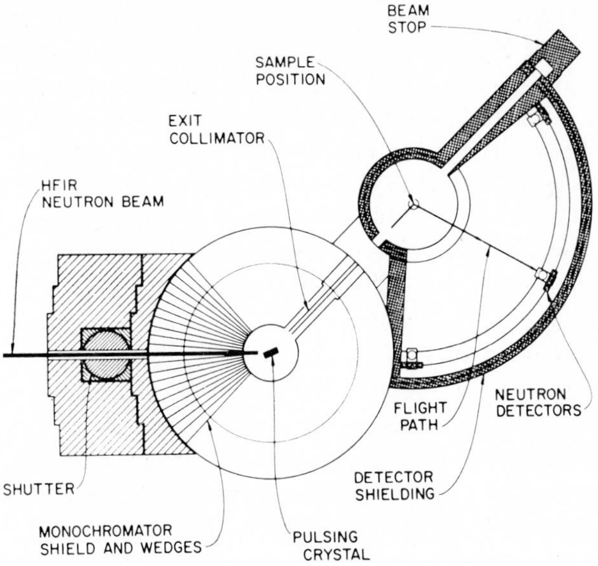

Fig. 20. Schematic diagram of the magnetically-pulsed time-of-flight spectrometer at the High Flux Isotope Reactor, Oak Ridge.

percent, may be advantageous for certain types of experiment. This degree of versatility can hardly be achieved by mechanical means, but is quite possible in a different type of correlation spectrometer which has been developed principally by Mook at the Oak Ridge National Laboratory (Mook and Wilkinson 1970). A schematic diagram of the spectrometer is shown in fig. 20. The monochromator shielding drum arrangement is the same as that used for the Oak Ridge triple axis spectrometers, and fifteen ^{3}He-type detectors are housed in a communal shield and may be driven independently to any desired position on an arc centred on the specimen position. A flight path of 1.5 m is chosen as a compromise between the need for adequate time-of-flight resolution and the engineering difficulties involved in manipulating the rather heavy detection system with the required precision. (It is supported by a system of air bearings.) The incident neutron beam is pulsed by changing the direction of the atomic magnetic moments in a ferrite monochromator crystal with an applied magnetic field. The (111) Bragg reflection of the ferrite $^7Li_{0.5}Fe_{2.5}O_4$ is almost entirely due to magnetic scattering, since the nuclear scattering lengths cancel out for this composition. Thus the intensity of the monochromatic beam can be varied from essentially zero (actually, a few percent of peak intensity), when the magnetic field is applied along the scattering vector, to a maximum when the field is applied perpendicular to the scattering vector. Peak reflectivities comparable to those obtained with other commonly used monochromators can be obtained, and since the magnetic anisotropy is small, the magnetic spin system can be changed rapidly: the beam can be switched on or off in about 2 μsec. The neutrons are reflected from a variety of locations within the monochromator crystal, and this introduces a broadening of any neutron pulse by several microseconds. The minimum usable value of the basic pulse width Δt is thus about 5 μsec. Any desired pattern of neutron pulses can be produced by appropriate pulsing of the external magnetic field at the crystal, with an electronic pulse train stored on magnetic tape. A PDP 15-30 computer is employed to operate the magnetic pulser, using the optimum pulse train for any given experiment, to record the time-of-flight spectra for each detector, to set all the detector angles, specimen orientation and monochromator angle, and finally to compute the cross-correlation functions necessary to obtain the scattering function of the specimen.

The two spectrometers described above make use of pseudorandomly modulated neutron beams as input to the scattering system. A slightly different technique, using sinusoidally modulated neutron beams, has been employed by Colwell et al. (1968) as the basis for the so-called Fourier chopper spectrometer. A neutron absorbing disc with equal slots or transparent sections uniformly spaced around its perimeter is used to produce a roughly sinusoidal modulation of the monochromatic neutron beam reflected from a crystal in much the same kind of arrangement as that shown in fig. 19, except that the crystal is placed after the disc. The scattered neutron time-of-flight spectrum is measured for a succession of different rotation speeds of the disc, corresponding to different frequencies of the sinusoidal modulation. The time analyser has 4 suitably phased time channels. The scattering function is obtained as a Fourier synthesis of these observed spectra, a technique well known in electrical network theory. One annoying difference with neutron pulses (as compared with electrical signals) is that the modulation is at best of the form $(1+\cos \omega t)$, since negative pulses do not exist. Also, special filtering techniques are needed to damp out spurious 'side-lobes' arising from incomplete Fourier synthesis. Nevertheless, both practical tests and computer simulation of this method, admittedly with comparatively simple scattering functions, have demonstrated its potential application in this field. Perhaps the main disadvantage of the method is the fact that a whole series of experimental runs with different modulation frequencies must be carried out, and this data analysed by computer, before a single intelligible result (e.g. phonon frequency) is available to the experimenter.

In this rather brief survey of correlation methods, we have not mentioned the problem of statistical fluctuations and how these affect the cross-correlated spectra. The mathematical details of this problem are quite complicated (see for example Reichardt et al. 1970; it is desirable to have some information about the structure of these spectra in order to optimise the duty cycle and other experimental variables. An important drawback to the method is that the statistical errors tend to be determined by the height of the large peaks in the spectrum, so that the observation of nearby small peaks is made that much more difficult.

2.9. Intercomparison of spectrometers

This has been a subject of considerable controversy for many years, since the builders and proponents of each type of spectrometer have naturally tended to emphasize its advantages at the expense of the other types. It now seems, however, to be generally agreed that different classes of experiment require different spectrometers for optimum performance. It is not sufficient simply to calculate the total number of scattered neutrons detected per unit time by the spectrometer for a given incident neutron source strength. This quantity, which we might call the neutron efficiency of the spectrometer, is certainly important: but it is equally important to consider the quality of the information obtained, to answer questions like 'What precisely do we want to know about our specimen, and in what form do we really wish to have this information?'

We saw in §2.5 that triple axis spectrometers have the capability to perform highly specific scans along pre-selected lines in $(\boldsymbol{Q}, \nu)$ space. Only a small number of such scans may be carried out simultaneously, and so the rate of accumulation of results is relatively low. These spectrometers are therefore ideally suited for coherent neutron scattering experiments to determine a relatively small quantity of specific information about phonon dispersion curves in single crystals. The scattering consists of a number of deltafunction peaks; theoretical analysis of the results is vastly facilitated by maximum use of group theoretical methods, which inevitably favors high symmetry points and lines in $\boldsymbol{Q}$ space; any prior information about the heat capacity of the specimen, its elastic and dielectric constants, and so on, may be effectively used to narrow down the ranges of $\boldsymbol{Q}$ and ν of interest in the neutron experiments; and finally the result of each scan is extremely valuable in the planning of future scans. All these factors emphasize the need for a spectrometer which scans ($\boldsymbol{Q}$, ν) space in a controlled and selective manner, and which provides immediately intelligible results from each scan. Easy and rapid adjustability of instrumental resolution and of neutron energy are also most valuable in this class of experiments. The triple axis, or more generally, the multi-axis crystal spectrometer, fulfils all these requirements to a much greater degree than is possible with present-day time-of-flight spectrometers. The conventional time-of-flight design in particular, with many detectors at fixed scattering angles, with the incident neutron energy not readily changed (certainly not during a scan), and with many components of the instrumental

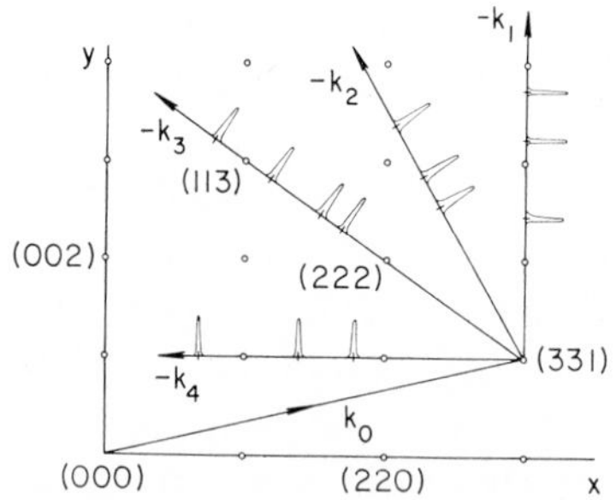

Fig. 21. Illustration of a possible arrangement for a time-of-flight spectrometer, enabling the observation of phonons propagating along high symmetry directions in a cubic crystal specimen. Peaks in detectors 1, 3 and 4 are observed along the [001], [111] and [110] directions respectively, while phonons observed by detector 2 will in general have off-symmetry wave vectors. Note that the values of $\boldsymbol{k}_0$ and the various angles of scattering must be precisely chosen for such 'high-symmetry' scans.

resolution quite difficult to adjust in any way, is rather poorly suited to dispersion curve measurements. Some of these difficulties have been avoided or minimised in more recent time-of-flight spectrometers, such as the Mook spectrometer described in §2.8 (Mook and Wilkinson 1970). The detectors are independently and automatically moveable under computer control, and the incident neutron energy is also readily adjustable, so that it is quite possible to ensure that many of the phonons measured in each scan will have wavevectors along selected high symmetry directions in the crystal, as illustrated schematically in fig. 21. Measurements at specific $\boldsymbol{Q}$ values (zone boundary points, reciprocal lattice points, etc.) will still be rather awkward to arrange, however. Similar remarks apply to the hybrid spectrometers of Buras (1966) and Maliszewski et al. (1968) (§2.7). Two additional factors may need to be considered in connection with phonon dispersion curve measurements. Firstly, if the available neutron source is repetitively pulsed, as in a pulsed reactor or accelerator, then the conventional (though not correlation) time-of-flight spectrometer becomes much more attractive: its much more efficient use of the available neutrons will probably outweigh its disadvantages in other respects. Secondly, if it is required to study the behavior of the phonons or other excitations under conditions of very high magnetic field, or in time-varying states of the crystal arising from pulses of electric or magnetic fields, heat pulses, or similar transient phenomena, then the possibility of pulsing the specimen in phase with the incident neutron pulse will also merit close attention. Experiments of this kind have been suggested by Buras (1966), but none have been attempted to date.

Some experiments, however, involve the measurement of large numbers of phonon frequencies for any and all wave vectors in a plane of the specimen. Experiments on liquids often involve measurement of $S(|\boldsymbol{Q}|, \nu)$ for wide ranges of $|\boldsymbol{Q}|$ and ν. Experiments on complex organic compounds, usually hydrogenous, involve the observation of neutron incoherent scattering over wide ranges of energy, without regard to wave vector of course. Indeed, if the primitive unit cell is very large for a complex crystal, the Brillouin zone is correspondingly very small, and the wave vector dependence of coherent scattering becomes much less important than the energy levels of the system. In these cases, highly specific information about a selection of points in $(\boldsymbol{Q}, \nu)$ space may well be less useful than a large quantity of less specific information. Here, the high duty cycle and large number of detectors of the correlation chopper would be extremely valuable in conjunction with continuous sources of neutrons, while the conventional chopper has evident advantages for use with a pulsed neutron source.

Further discussion of this subject may be found in the articles by Brugger (1965) and Iyengar (1965), and in more recent papers by Woods et al. (1970), Dorner and Stiller (1970) and Stedman (1970).

2.10. X-ray diffuse scattering

When an X-ray beam falls on a crystalline solid, it may be scattered in various ways by reason of its interaction with the electrons. As is well known, the X-ray diffraction pattern obtained from a single crystal is the Fourier transform of the total electronic distribution, and almost all our knowledge of the structure of crystals has been derived from suitable applications of this fact. In the same way that thermal neutrons may be scattered inelastically from a crystal with the creation or annihilation of one or more phonons, there are also one-phonon and multi-phonon contributions to X-ray scattering. The X-ray energy is however very much higher than that of typical phonons, so that these inelastic contributions cannot be resolved (in energy) as they can be in the case of neutron scattering. There is in addition another mechanism for the inelastic scattering of X-rays, the Compton effect, in which individual electrons recoil from the incident X-ray, thereby changing the energy and momentum of the latter. The differential cross-section for the one-phonon scattering of X-rays is essentially the same as that for thermal neutrons, eq. (1.4), with the following two changes: (*i*) the structure factor $G_j(\boldsymbol{Q})$, eq. (1.8), contains an additional form factor $f_s(\boldsymbol{Q})$ which expresses the Fourier transform of the electronic distribution around the sth nucleus ($f=1$ for the nuclear scattering of neutrons), and (*ii*) the cross-section for the wave vector transfer $\boldsymbol{Q}$ must be integrated over all modes of that wave vector (i.e. integration over energy).

If we observe X-ray scattering corresponding to a particular $\boldsymbol{Q}$ not equal to a reciprocal lattice vector, therefore, we will observe a diffuse intensity arising from one-phonon, multiphonon and Compton scattering. On the assumption that accurate corrections can be made for the last two contributions, then the resulting one-phonon component may be analysed to derive information about the lattice vibrations corresponding to that $\boldsymbol{Q}$, since it is proportional to a sum over all modes $\nu_j(\boldsymbol{Q})$, weighted by population factors and phonon eigenvectors $U_{s_j}(\boldsymbol{Q})$. In practice, this procedure is extremely difficult if not impossible except for highly symmetric crystals with one or two atoms per cell, in which the eigenvectors are fixed (or at least tightly controlled!) by symmetry. Even in such cases, the difficulty of making adequate corrections for multiphonon and Compton scattering has given rise to many quite unreliable results for phonon dispersion relations. It would seem that reasonably successful results can be obtained only if substantial guidance from theoretically calculated dispersion curves is available, as was the case for the experiments of Buyers and Smith (1966) on NaCl, for example. Later inelastic neutron scattering experiments by Raunio et al. (1969) showed good agreement with the X-ray results for the TA [100] branch; the LO [111] and LA [111] branches showed discrepancies of about 5% and 10–15% respectively. This level of accuracy compares well with that achieved in some earlier X-ray diffuse scattering experiments (carried out without assistance from theoretical models) in which measured phonon frequencies were in error by factors of 2. X-ray measurements of one phonon frequency relative to another one on the same branch can often be made with good accuracy, however, since systematic errors tend to cancel out, so that this technique has found some application (Paskin and Weiss 1962, Costello and Weymouth 1969) in the study of small anomalies in dispersion curves, such as those arising from the Kohn effect (Kohn 1959). Another obviously useful application of the method is to the measurement of phonon dispersion curves in materials which, for one reason or another, cannot be studied by the more powerful neutron coherent scattering techniques. Cadmium, which its high absorption, and vanadium, with its very low coherent scattering length, are examples of such materials. An X-ray study of vanadium has indeed been made recently by Colella and Batterman (1970). In general, however, the information obtained from X-ray diffuse scattering experiments is of value mainly as an independent check on interatomic or intermolecular force models derived from phonon frequencies measured by neutron scattering and/or optical techniques. The force model is used to generate phonon frequencies and eigenvectors, from which the X-ray diffuse scattering (one phonon and multiphonon) at various $\boldsymbol{Q}$ values may be computed for comparison with experiment.

2.11. Thermal neutron sources and neutron guide tubes

This section is a brief survey of various means of producing intense beams of thermal neutrons and of directing these beams towards the neutron spectrometer. At the present time, high neutron fluxes can be produced either in a nuclear fission reactor or by allowing a beam of energetic charged particles from an accelerator to fall on a suitable target. The fast neutrons (several MeV) obtained by such means must then be moderated or slowed down by successive collisions with the nuclei in the moderator. If sufficient moderation time is allowed, and if neutron losses are negligible, then the neutrons achieve a maxwellian equilibrium distribution of energies

$$\eta(E)\,\mathrm{d}E = N_0\pi^{-1/2}E^{1/2}(k_\mathrm{B}T)^{-3/2}\exp(-E/k_\mathrm{B}T)\,\mathrm{d}E, \tag{2.26}$$

where N_0 is the total number of neutrons/cc. In practice, T, the 'neutron temperature', is approximately equal to the moderator temperature except at very low temperatures where a lack of suitable energy levels in the moderator may effectively prevent neutron energy losses beyond a certain point. The neutron flux, that is, the number of neutrons crossing unit area per unit time, is obtained by multiplying eq. (2.26) by the neutron velocity $(2E/m)^{1/2}$. The peak of this flux distribution as a function of energy occurs at $E_\mathrm{m} = k_\mathrm{B}T$. In addition to this maxwellian distribution for the thermalized neutrons, there will be a high energy '$1/E$ tail' of neutrons still in the slowing down process. The conventional method of extracting a beam from the moderator is simply to allow the neutrons to escape down a straight hole, typically several inches in diameter, fitted with a shielding plug having a tapered hole to narrow down the beam to a size comparable to that of the monochromator crystal or mechanical chopper slots. In certain circumstances (see below), it may be advantageous to conduct the beam away from the moderator by means of evacuated guide tube, in which the neutrons are totally reflected from the walls of the tube.

The great majority of all neutron inelastic scattering experiments to date have been performed with neutron beams obtained fiom steady-state nuclear reactors. The peak thermal neutron flux in reactors such as the High Flux Beam Reactor at Brookhaven National Laboratory (Palevsky 1965) is about $10^{15}/\mathrm{cm}^2/\mathrm{sec}$. It seems unlikely that future reactors will achieve continuous fluxes more than a factor of 10 higher than this. In principle it might be possible to produce fluxes in excess of $10^{16}/\mathrm{cm}^2/\mathrm{sec}$ by allowing an intense proton beam from a high energy accelerator to fall on a heavy metal target (Bartholomew 1966). Each proton generates many high energy neutrons by spallation, and these are subsequently moderated in a tank of heavy water surrounding the target. One of the major problems of sustaining high neutron fluxes is that of removing the heat generated per neutron produced. The idea of suitably pulsing the source, be it a reactor or an accelerator, derives its attraction from the possibility of having brief pulses of extremely high intensity while keeping the average heat generation down to acceptable levels. So far, however, this idea has not been exploited for inelastic neutron scattering to any great extent–the only pulsed reactor which has been used for this purpose is the IBR-1 at Dubna (Blokhin et al. 1961, Ananiev et al. 1969). The same is true for accelerator-based pulsed sources; a small number of inelastic neutron scattering experiments have been performed with an electron linear accelerator (e.g. McReynolds and Whittemore 1961), but it is fair to say that no existing accelerator can compete with present day reactors as an intense source of neutrons.

The large number and wide variety of nuclear reactor sources now in existence are such that any detailed description of them is well outside the scope of this chapter. The subject has been reviewed by Cocking and Webb (1965), who tabulate the characteristics of several typical sources and describe the facilities for extracting neutron beams from them.

The temperature dependence of the peak energy E_m noted above has led to the development of both hot and cold moderators as a means of enhancing the flux of high and low energy neutrons respectively as compared with the

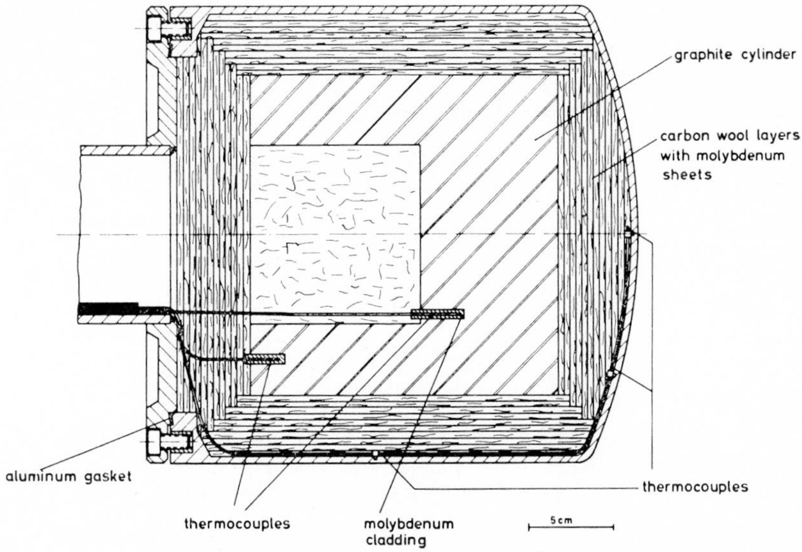

Fig. 22. The Karlsruhe hot source: the graphite source block has a re-entrant hole to simulate black-body radiation conditions. Low-density carbon wool between molybdenum sheets provides excellent thermal isolation of the graphite from the magnesium aluminum alloy case, so that nuclear radiation heating in the graphite is sufficient to produce source temperatures up to 1650 K.

flux obtained with the moderator near room temperature. We now comment briefly on the advantages and disadvantages of these special moderators, referring the reader again to the article by Cocking and Webb for details of the many designs which have been tried. A recent discussion† of hot and cold sources also contains much interesting and useful information.

Beryllium oxide and graphite are two of the most suitable materials from which hot moderators may be made: they may be operated safely at high temperatures, they are efficient moderators and also convenient structural materials. When installed in a high flux region of a nuclear reactor, surrounded by several heat radiation shields, the γ- and fast neutron radiation heating in the moderator block raises its temperature by ≈ 1000 K, so that no additional electrical heating is required. BeO has been used successfully in the DIDO hot source (Egelstaff et al. 1968), while graphite is the material used in the FR2 source (Abeln et al. 1968). The latter, illustrated in fig. 22, has a 10 cm

† *Instrumentation for Neutron Inelastic Scattering Research*, International Atomic Energy Agency, Vienna (1970), pp. 249–274.

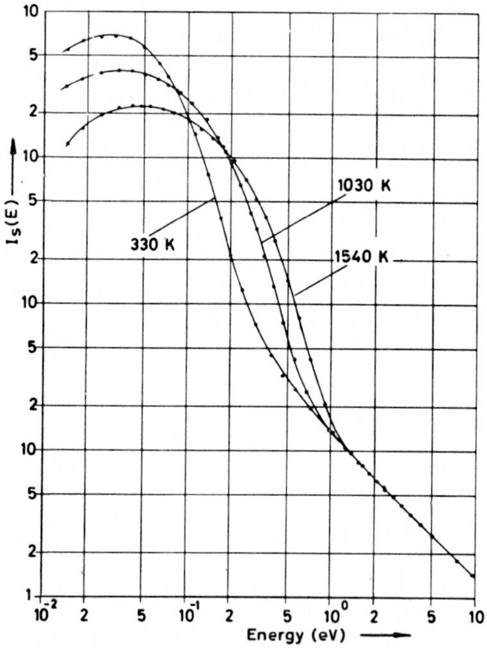

Fig. 23. Neutron flux distributions, as functions of energy, obtained from the Karlsruhe hot source. (The 330 K curve represents the distribution obtained with the source removed.)

diameter re-entrant hole in order to approach more nearly to black-body radiation conditions. The neutron flux distribution as a function of energy obtained from this source is shown in fig. 23, for source temperatures 330 K, 1030 K and 1540 K. We notice that all 3 distributions give nearly the same flux at 0.1 eV, below which the 330 K distribution is clearly superior. Above 1 eV, all the distributions merge into the same '$1/E$' tail mentioned above. Between 0.2 and 0.5 eV, however, the 1540 K moderator provides about 5 times higher fluxes than at 330 K. This neutron energy range is extremely useful for the study of high energy phonons, such as the internal modes of molecular solids, and it is here that we may expect considerable advances from the future use of hot sources.

By comparison with the simplicity of hot sources, a typical cold source is a rather complex device, involving significant safety hazards and expensive refrigeration equipment (the estimated installed cost of the liquid deuterium source at the Grenoble High Flux Reactor exceeds 10^6 dollars†). The chief

† See p. 272 of reference quoted in footnote on p. 597.

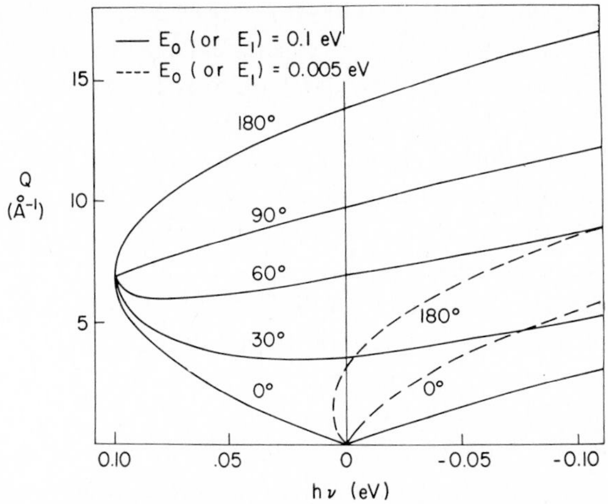

Fig.. 24 The wave vector transfer $\boldsymbol{Q}$ as a function of the energy transfer $h\nu$ for two incident energies E_0 and several angles of scattering ϕ. The curves are the same for scattered neutron energies E_1 except that the sign of $h\nu$ is reversed.

value of cold sources is for enhancing the flux of neutrons of wavelength longer than 4 Å (energy less than 0.005 eV), and very substantial gain factors ($\sim$50 for 0.001 eV neutrons) can be achieved with a source designed to be an integral part of a new reactor. While some experiments may well be carried out with these low energy neutrons, and certain experiments specifically require such neutrons, it is generally the case that the use of cold neutrons considerably restricts the flexibility of the neutron scattering method. This fact is well illustrated in fig. 24, taken from Brockhouse (1961), which shows the ranges of wave vector and energy transfers theoretically attainable when the incident neutron energy E_0 is 0.1 or 0.005 eV, for various angles of scattering. Two important points should be noted as regards the use of 0.005 eV incident neutrons:

i) With few exceptions, it restricts the experimenter to the observation of *energy gain* processes in the sample. Eq. (1.5) shows that the population factor is

$$n_j(\boldsymbol{q}) = [\exp(h\nu_j(\boldsymbol{q})/k_B T) - 1]^{-1}$$

for such processes. If the sample temperature T is low compared to $h\nu_j(\boldsymbol{q})/k_B$, then

$$n_j(\boldsymbol{q}) \sim \exp(-h\nu_j(\boldsymbol{q})/k_B T),$$

leading to exponentially small scattering cross-sections. This presents a fatal restriction for a very wide range of experiments on temperature-dependent effects in phonon spectra, particularly those relating to soft-mode phase transitions (see §3.3).

ii) Only a narrow range of $\boldsymbol{Q}$ may be studied for a given energy transfer $h\nu$, even when the experimental conditions allow neutron energy gain processes to be observed. This restriction is particularly severe when the one-phonon structure factor, eq. (1.8), (or the magnetic electron form factor in spin wave measurements) varies considerably with $\boldsymbol{Q}$ so that the experimenter's freedom of choice is already curtailed. Also, there are usually practical limits on the available scattering angles, so that the accessible area of $(\boldsymbol{Q}, \nu)$ space is even less than that shown in fig. (24).

Certain types of experiment, such as measurements of quasi-elastic scattering and of very low energy transitions at low momentum transfers, may nevertheless be greatly facilitated by the use of long-wavelength neutrons from cold sources. Many more such experiments will presumably be performed during the next few years, with the help of the large number (about 15) of cold sources presently installed or under construction in many parts of the world.

The use of guide tubes for conducting thermal neutron beams from source to spectrometer has received increasing attention in the past few years. The reflectivity, in the optical sense of the word, of a material of refractive index μ is given by (Goldberger and Seitz 1947)

$$R = \frac{(\mu^2 - \cos^2\gamma)^{1/2} - \cos\gamma}{(\mu^2 - \cos^2\gamma)^{1/2} + \cos\gamma}, \tag{2.27}$$

where γ is the angle of incidence (and reflection) and

$$\mu^2 = 1 - \lambda^2 (N\bar{b}/\pi). \tag{2.28}$$

N is the number of atoms/cm^3, $\bar{b}$ is the coherent scattering length of the nuclei and λ is the neutron wavelength. Since $\bar{b}$ is positive for most nuclei, $\mu<1$ and $R=1$ for angles of incidence $\gamma<\gamma_c$ where $\cos\gamma_c=\mu$. The critical angle γ_c is proportional to λ and is 0.1° per Å for nickel, for example. It has been shown theoretically, and confirmed by experiment, that a neutron may suffer many such total reflections in the course of traveling along a guide tube, with relatively small total attenuation. For example, a straight nickel plated guide tube 10 m long with a cross-section 2 × 5 cm can be made with a transmission of 95% for 4 Å and 78% for 16 Å neutrons. Perhaps the two

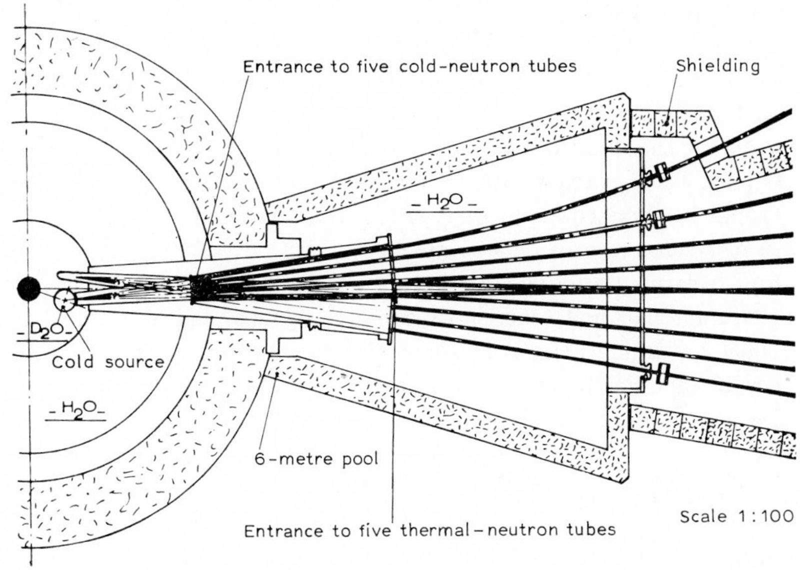

Fig. 25. Layout of the two sets of neutron guide tubes installed in the High-Flux Reactor at Grenoble. One set of tubes conducts very slow neutrons from the liquid deuterium cold source to experimental areas far removed from the reactor core.

most important uses of guide tubes are for reduction of unwanted fast neutron background and for more efficient utilization of neutron beam facilities. Both these objectives are achieved by removing the neutron spectrometers a large distance from the neutron source. The guide tube arrangements at the High Flux Reactor at the Max von Laue–Paul Langevin Institute at Grenoble (Jacrot 1970) are sketched in fig. 25. Two series of long curved guide tubes serve to conduct neutron beams from two sources (one of which is the liquid deuterium cold source mentioned above) to several spectrometers at remote stations, not shown in fig. 25, where there is sufficient space for all necessary shielding, etc. The fast neutron background at the spectroueters is much reduced since only long wave length neutrons are conducted down the tubes. Faster neutrons are not totally reflected and therefore pass straight out of the guide tubes into suitable shielding.

Guide tubes are obviously most suited for transmitting beams of long wave length ($\lambda > 4$ Å) neutrons, although they may also be useful in the range 1 to 4 Å, for experiments in which fairly tight incident beam collimation is acceptable. Suitable guide tubes for the latter range from 30 to 100 m in length.

3. *Experimental results*

In this section we describe a few arbitrarily chosen examples of the results which have been obtained by application of neutron inelastic scattering techniques to the study of phonons in general, and also to the study of phase transitions. These examples are given simply to illustrate the kind of results which may be obtained for a variety of materials. An attempt has been made, in the Appendix, to provide a comprehensive list of useful references to all neutron inelastic scattering experiments on elemental solids, simple compounds, molecular and other more complex crystals, and also alloys and materials containing defects, in which the phonon dispersion curves, frequency distribution function, and/or phase transitions related to normal modes, were the primary objects of study.

3.1. Elements and simple compounds

The phonon dispersion relation of bismuth has been measured by Yarnell et al. (1964), by Sosnowski et al. (1968) and most recently by MacFarlane (1971), whose results are shown in fig. 26. A triple axis crystal spectrometer was used to measure the dispersion curves at 75 K for modes propagating along 5 directions of high symmetry in the crystal. The sum of the squares of the six normal mode frequencies shows a very pronounced variation as a function of phonon wave vector $\boldsymbol{q}$, with substantial dips near the Γ and X points. Bismuth has a rhombohedral (and almost cubic) structure resembling that of the low-temperature phase of GeTe and some GeTe–SnTe alloys (which have the cubic NaCl structure above their transition temperatures). While there are similar effects present in the dispersion curves of Bi and of SnTe (Pawley et al. 1966, Cowley et al. 1969a) it seems likely that a satisfactory interpretation of the normal modes of Bi will require a more complex (or else an entirely new) model of the interatomic forces and electronic screening effects.

Very considerable and successful efforts have recently been made to grow single crystals of solid helium suitable for neutron inelastic scattering studies, stimulated of course by the intense theoretical interest in this very special quantum solid. The dispersion curves have been obtained for the hcp phase of ^{4}He by Minkiewicz et al. (1968) at a molar volume of 21.1 cm^3 and by Reese et al. (1971) at a molar volume of 16.0 cm^3. A selection of these results is shown in figs. 27 and 28. Many of the normal modes are reasonably well-defined excitations although those of the higher frequency tend to be highly

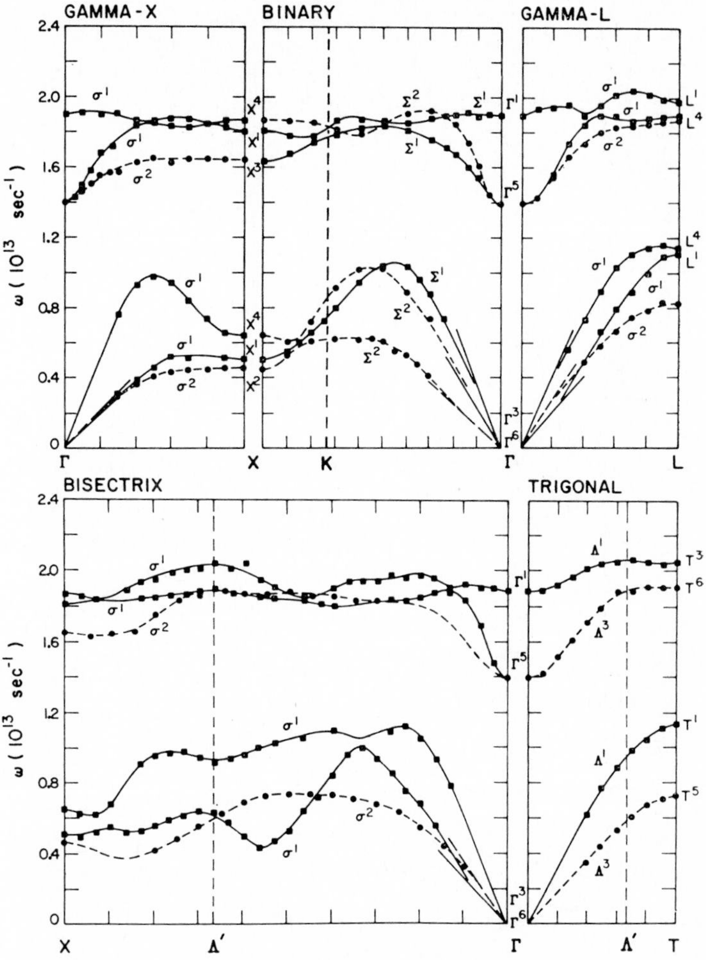

Fig. 26. Phonon dispersion curves for bismuth at 75 K (Macfarlane 1971). The smooth curves through the experimental points are merely guides to the eye. $\omega = 2\pi\nu$.

damped, and some unexplained neutron groups have also been observed (fig. 28). As is well-known, a purely harmonic force model for solid ^{4}He, based on a Lennard–Jones potential, predicts imaginary phonon frequencies for all wave vectors. However, the root mean square displacement of the ^{4}He atoms is a large fraction, $\sim\frac{1}{3}$, of the nearest-neighbor distance, so that it is not too surprising that a model with atomic potentials defined with respect to fixed equilibrium positions should exhibit such unrealistic properties.

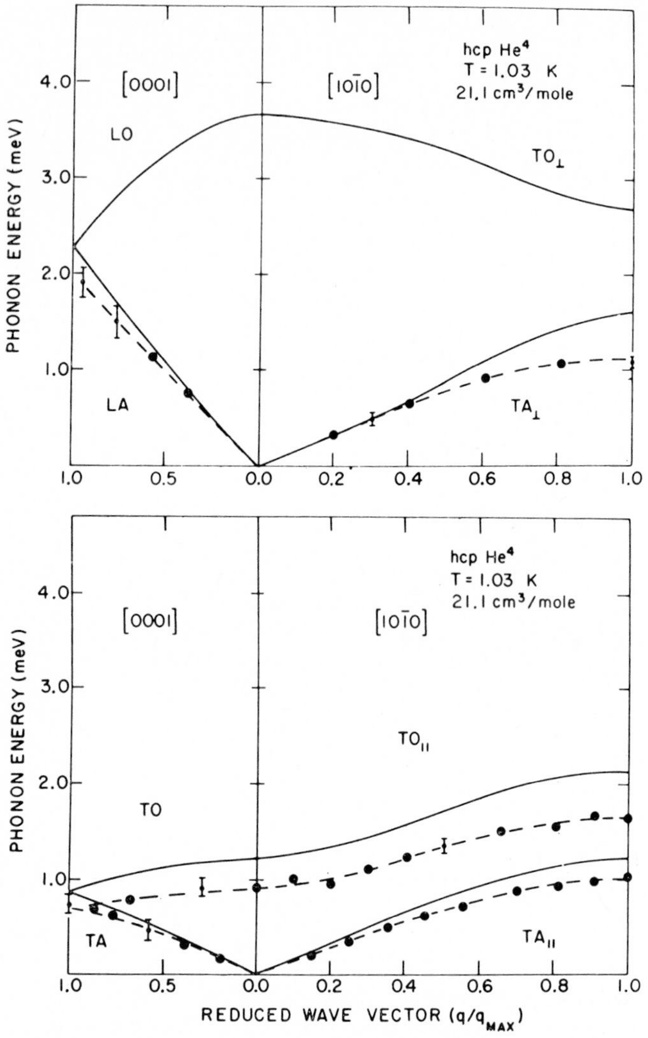

Fig. 27. Phonon dispersion curves for the hcp phase of solid helium at 1.03 K and a molar volume of 21.1 cm^3 (Minkiewicz et al. 1968). 1 meV ≡ 0.242 THz ≡ 8.06 cm^{-1}. The solid lines represent theoretical calculations of Gillis et al. (1968).

Much progress has been made in the understanding of these results by means of the self-consistent phonon theory of Koehler and co-workers (Koehler 1968, Gillis et al. 1968), although there are still many unsettled questions to occupy both theorists and experimentalists in this field. A complete account

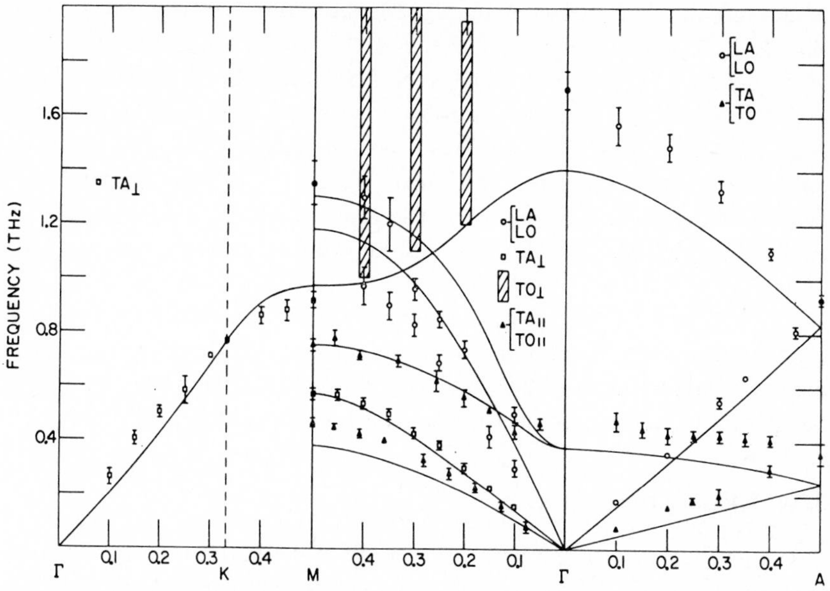

Fig. 28. Phonon dispersion curves for the hcp phase of solid helium at 4.2 K and a molar volume of 16.0 cm³ (Reese et al. 1971). The shaded areas indicate regions of scattered neutron intensity of unknown origin. The solid lines represent theoretical calculations of Gillis et al. (1968).

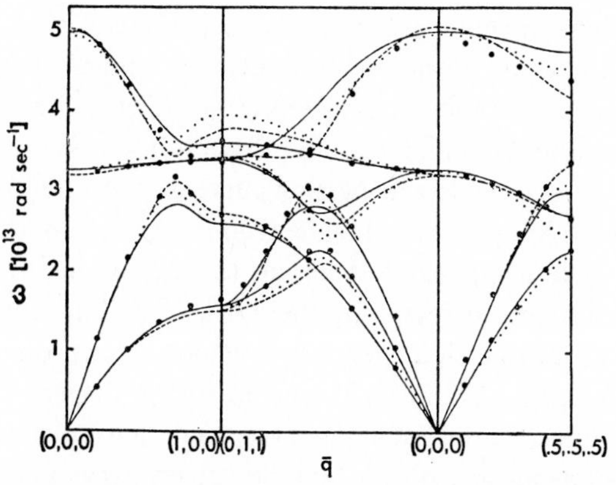

Fig. 29. Phonon frequencies for NaCl at 80 K, compared with calculated curves based on three variations of the shell model for the interatomic forces (Raunio et al. 1969).

of our present knowledge of the dynamics of solid helium is given in the chapter by T. R. Koehler in Volume 2 of this work, while the subject of self-consistent phonon theories in general is discussed in chapter 9.

Our final example in this subsection is the phonon dispersion relation of NaCl, which was one of the earliest to be studied theoretically but which has only recently been measured by neutron inelastic scattering (Raunio et al. 1969, Schmunk and Winder 1970). The results of Raunio et al. (1969) are compared with three variants of the well-known shell model for alkali halides in fig. 29.

All of these examples are of measurements made by means of triple axis crystal spectrometers. The vast majority of dispersion curves for simple materials have in fact been measured in this way, although a few examples of comparable time-of-flight measurements can be found (see Appendix).

3.2. Molecular compounds

The first reasonably comprehensive study of the lattice modes of a molecular crystal was made for the highly symmetric globular molecule DHMT-deuterated hexamethylene tetramine (Dolling and Powell 1970). Lattice modes, or external, or intermolecular modes, are those involving translational and/or librational motions of the essentially rigid molecules. An excellent review of the subject of intermolecular modes has been given by Venkataraman and Sahni (1970). The frequencies of these modes in propagating in various directions in DHMT at 100 K are plotted in fig. 30. The word 'molecular' is often used to describe compounds containing one or more groups of atoms, relatively tightly bound to each other within each group, but weakly coupled to other atoms or 'molecular groupings'. A good example is ammonium chloride, whose external modes have been studied by Teh et al. (1969), Smith et al. (1969) and Teh and Brockhouse (1971). The third reference contains rather complete dispersion curve data for the deuterated form, ND_4Cl, as shown in fig. 31. As may be seen in the Appendix and in chapter 17, more and more complicated materials (having more atoms per cell) are being studied by neutron scattering methods. Coherent scattering observations, to obtain the dispersion curves directly, are most profitable when there are relatively few, say 20 or less, branches of the dispersion relation, and when the Brillouin zone is reasonably large, leading to substantial and highly informative $\boldsymbol{q}$-dependence. As the number of branches per unit energy interval increases, and as the Brillouin zone shrinks, the situation changes and average properties such as the density of states (phonon frequency distribu-

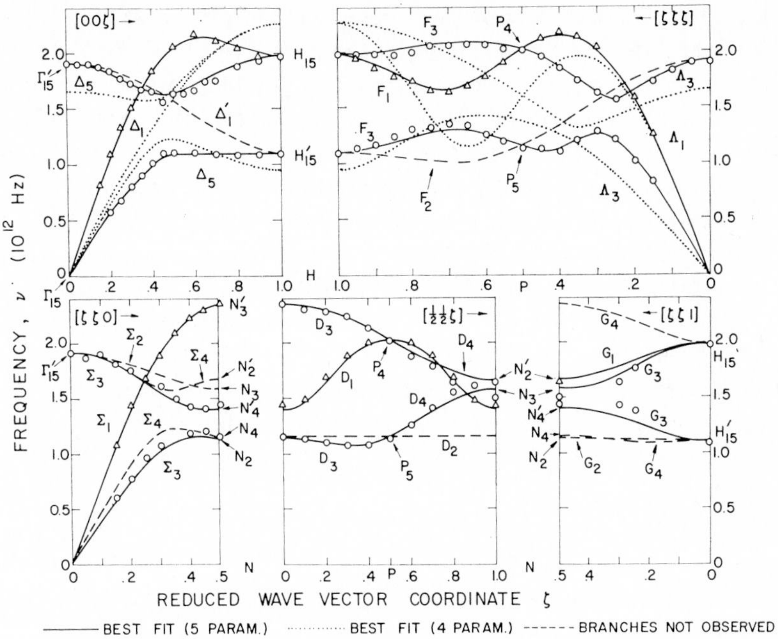

Fig. 30. Frequencies of external modes of vibration of deuterated hexamethylenetetramine (DHMT) at 100 K, compared with empirical intermolecular force models (Dolling and Powell 1970).

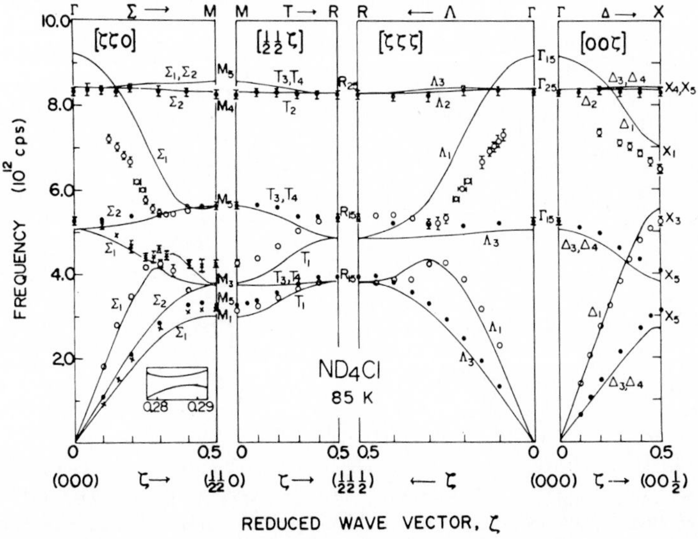

Fig. 31. Frequencies of external modes in ND_4Cl at 85 K, compared with theoretical calculations based on a rigid-ion model (Teh and Brockhouse 1971).

tion) become more useful and more easily measurable. These may be measured by neutron incoherent scattering experiments, or by coherent scattering measurements at sufficiently large wave vector $\boldsymbol{Q}$ that an incoherent approximation is valid (Placzek and Van Hove 1955, Lomer and Low 1965). The power of various multi-detector time-or-flight spectrometers can often be fully exploited in this kind of measurement, since the information required is not so specifically $\boldsymbol{Q}$-dependent as it is in the experiments described in §§3.1 and 3.3.

We conclude this subsection with an example of an incoherent scattering measurement, on hexamethyl benzene (HMB), by Rush and Taylor (1966). The dynamical behaviour of this rather interesting material, of composition $C_6(CH_3)_6$, has been studied by a wide variety of techniques, e.g. nuclear magnetic resonance, Raman scattering, infra-red and ultra-violet absorption, and its structure has been determined by X-ray and by thermal neutron diffraction experiments [see Hamilton et al. (1969) for detailed references].

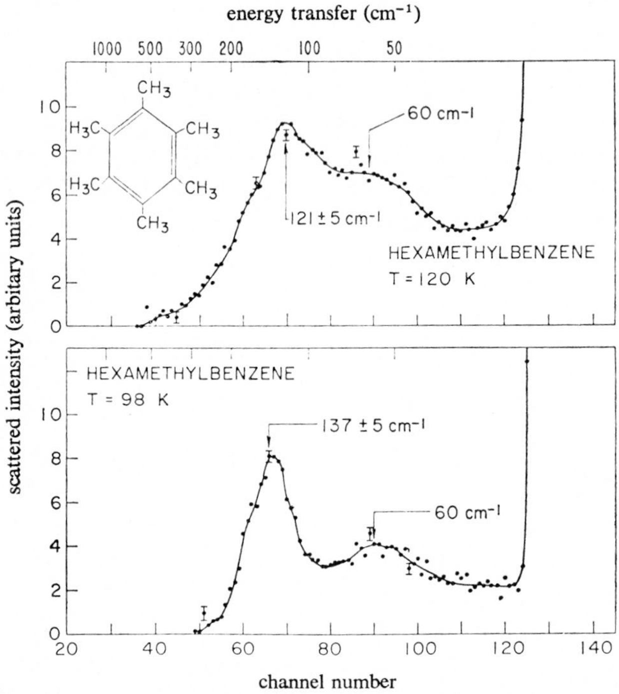

Fig. 32. Inelastic neutron scattering spectra from powdered samples of hexamethylbenzene. The peaks with maxima at 121 and 137 cm^{-1} have been assigned to methyl group rotations, while the broad peak at 60 cm^{-1} arises from external modes of vibration (Rush and Taylor 1966). 100 $cm^{-1} \equiv 3.0$ THz.

HMB is triclinic with 1 molecule per unit cell at 293 K, and exhibits a λ-transition at 116 K whose mechanism is still rather obscure in spite of all the above-mentioned investigations. The inelastic neutron scattering spectra obtained from powdered HMB, above and below the 116 K transition are shown in fig. 32. The peaks with maxima at 121 and 137 cm^{-1}) (3.63 and 4.11 THz) are assigned to rotational motions (internal modes) of the methyl groups, while the broad peak at 60 cm^{-1}) arises from lattice modes. The measurements were made with a cold-neutron, single chopper spectrometer with neutron energy gain. Perhaps the most important point to emphasize here is the need to correlate the results for these complex materials obtained by many different techniques; an individual technique, such as inelastic neutron scattering, can provide valuable data which may be difficult to interpret correctly without complementary information obtained by other methods.

3.3. Phase transitions

An extraordinary stimulus to the theoretical and experimental study of several types of solid phase transitions was provided some 10 years ago by Cochran (1959) and Anderson (1960), who suggested that certain kinds of phase transition might be triggered by normal mode instabilities. If, for example, the frequency of a long-wavelength transverse optic mode decreases with temperature, and reaches zero at a finite temperature, then the crystal lattice will become unstable against this mode and a structural phase transition will ensue. This 'soft-mode' behavior was convincingly demonstrated by Cowley (1962) for the case of a zone-centre transverse optic mode in $SrTiO_3$. Later, the 110 K transition in $SrTiO_3$ was attributed by Fleury et al. (1968) to the instability of a mode at the [111] zone boundary (R point). This was quickly confirmed by appropriate neutron scattering measurements both at Brookhaven (Yamada and Shirane 1969) and at Chalk River (Cowley et al. 1969b). The frequency of this Γ_{25} mode, as measured by the former authors, is plotted as a function of temperature above the transition in fig. 33. There are now many examples in the literature (see Appendix) of neutron scattering investigations of solid phase transitions. In some cases, such as the ferroelectric phase transition in KD_2PO_4 (Paul et al. 1970, Skalyo et al. 1970) no soft mode behavior is observed as such. All the normal modes which are seen show only small temperature dependences and do not change markedly at the transition. However, intense and highly temperature-dependent critical scattering (i.e. neutron scattering from critical fluctuations of crystalline order) is observed, the analysis of which has led to a greater

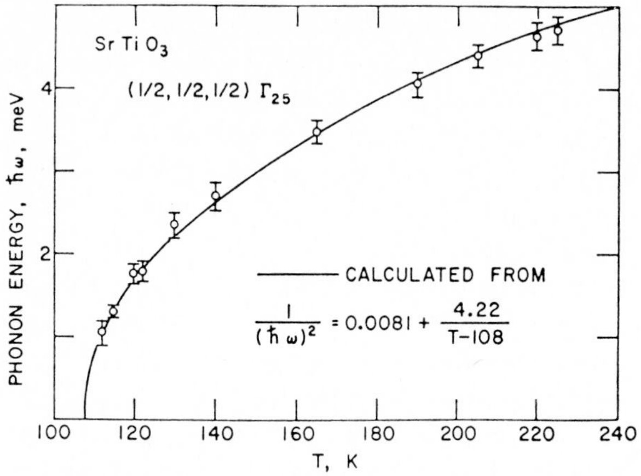

Fig. 33. Temperature dependence of the Γ_{25} mode in $SrTiO_3$ above the 110 K phase transition (Yamada and Shirane 1969). The solid line represents a modified Curie-Weiss law.

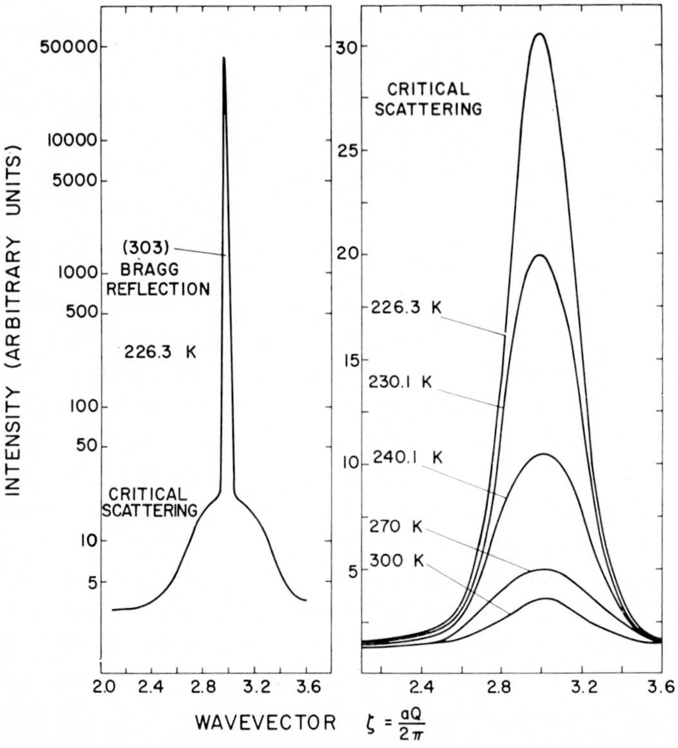

Fig. 34. Intensity of the quasi-elastic scattering along the line (ζ, 0, 3) (Paul et al. 1970). The left hand diagram shows the ferroelectric scattering and the (3, 0, 3) Bragg reflection. The right hand diagram shows the temperature dependence of the ferroelectric scattering above the 223 K phase transition.

understanding of the mechanism of this transition. The temperature-dependence of the critical scattering in the neighborhood of the (303) Bragg reflection, according to Paul et al. (1970), is shown in fig. 34.

In addition to these extreme examples of $SrTiO_3$ (virtually undamped soft mode) and KD_2PO_4 (completely overdamped mode giving rise to critical scattering), there are several intermediate cases of partially-damped soft modes. It would be inappropriate in this chapter to enter into a detailed description of all these phenomena, since a full account may be found in the chapter by H. S. Gillis in Volume 2 of this work. The examples serve, however, to illustrate a whole class of neutron scattering experiments in which the behavior of a few special modes is of primary physical interest. The major part of the total scattering function $S(\boldsymbol{Q}, \nu)$ in these cases is not required for an understanding of the phase transitions. It is not surprising, therefore, to discover that triple axis crystal spectrometers have almost invariably been employed in these experiments.

4. Concluding remarks

4.1. Links between theory and experiment

The primary purpose of theories of lattice dynamics is to obtain a complete description and understanding of the force field which keeps the atoms bound together in any solid. In order to compare theory with experiment, we need experimental information on the basic dispersion relation between the frequency and wave vector of the normal modes of vibration, on the line-widths or line-shapes of the modes and their temperature and/or pressure dependence, and on the behavior of the modes in the presence of defects or other departures from perfect crystalline regularity. The first experimental problem (after a suitable specimen has been acquired) is to determine as much of the dispersion relation $\nu_j(\boldsymbol{q})$ as is required. For relatively simple, highly symmetric crystals, both the measurement of normal frequencies and the identification of the model label j is quite straightforward, and one may quickly proceed to attack the more difficult problems of measuring line shapes, temperature dependence, effects of impurities, and so on. As the crystals being studied become more complex, however, both the measurement and the identification of normal modes become rapidly much more difficult. The measurements may be difficult because of the resolution problems when there are many branches close together, and even when these are resolved, it may not be a trivial matter to identify the polarization vectors for each mode. It is then almost essential to make the maximum use of the crystal symmetry and of any relevant information which may be available from other experimental techniques (e.g. elastic constants, infra-red and Raman frequencies). It may well be necessary to make use of a theoretical force model, based on sound physical ideas as far as possible, and fitted to whatever experimental data are definitely known, in order to calculate normal mode frequencies and eigenvectors, and hence the inelastic structure factor, eq. (1.8), for comparison with the new and hitherto unidentified results. If a satisfactory description of the new results is not provided by the model, then its parameters are adjusted, or a different model set up, until satisfactory agreement is finally achieved. This tedious and often hazardous procedure was necessary in the study of (external) normal modes in orthorhombic sodium nitrite, $NaNO_2$ (Sakurai et al. 1970). It is clear that the crystal structure and chemical composition of a material does not have to be unduly complex before severe experimental difficulties are encountered by the technique of one-phonon coherent scattering of neutrons. And these problems are in addition to that of obtaining suitable single crystal specimens in the first place. Optimum sizes of crystals are typically in the range 1 to 50 cm^3, although it may sometimes be possible under favorable conditions to work with smaller specimens, of order 0.1 cm^3. Hydrogeneous materials also pose considerable (usually insurmountable) problems for the coherent scattering method. Deuteration may sometimes be an acceptable way to deal with this problem (see §3.2 for example), but on the other hand the properties of the material are often profoundly altered by substituting deuterium for hydrogen, so that investigation of the deuterated compound may not throw much light on the physics of the hydrogenous material.

All these factors conspire to place limits on the applicability of coherent one-phonon scattering, and indicate the increasing utility of incoherent (or at least wave vector-averaged) scattering experiments for the more complex and especially hydrogenous materials. In these experiments, it will usually be impossible to identify unambiguously the peaks observed in the scattered neutron energy distribution, without considerable guidance from results of other techniques and from the basic chemistry and stereochemistry of the material.

4.2. Future prospects

The development of experimental equipment in this field has been continuous for the past 15 years or so, and at the present time the rate of introduction of ingenious new techniques shows no signs of slackening off–it may indeed be accelerating. We can expect that the fluxes of thermal neutrons available for beam experiments will increase with the completion of new steady-state reactors such as that at Grenoble, and of high flux pulsed reactors such as the IBR-2 at Dubna. It is also to be hoped that the enormous potential of high-current particle accelerators for obtaining high thermal neutron fluxes may soon be realised. We can expect further increases in the utilization of any given source flux. Many monochromator crystals now in use have reflectivities in the 20 to 60% range, so there is obviously some room for improvement here. A few of the likely improvements are in the development of low mosaic spread pyrolitic graphite ($\leqslant 0.3°$), of multiple slices of silicon (Frey 1971), or variable composition alloys to produce a distribution of plane-spacings (Rustichelli 1970, 1972), and in the more widespread use of curved monochromator crystals to achieve spatial focusing of the reflected beam. All of these possibilities have yet to be fully exploited. The correlation techniques described in subsection 2.8 seem capable of substantial further development. It is theoretically possible (Reichardt et al. 1970) to construct a statistical double chopper spectrometer which would make use of a range of incident neutron energies rather than the monoenergetic beams employed to date. Neutrons of all energies are incident successively on two mechanical choppers with pseudorandom transmission patterns, spinning at known speeds and relative phase. After being chopped into pseudorandom sequences twice, the neutrons are scattered along known flight paths into an array of detectors. The counting rate in any detector is given by a double integration over the product of the desired transfer function (i.e. scattering cross-section) and the transmission functions of the two choppers. The cross-section is finally obtained from a double cross-correlation calculation. The complexity of this scheme is perhaps rather intimidating to the experimentalist whose main purpose is to obtain information about the lattice dynamics of the specimen rather than about the dynamics of the spectrometer. It is clear, however, that there are many avenues of exploration in the field of correlation techniques, some of which will no doubt prove very fruitful. Another development whose potential has only recently been successfully demonstrated is concerned with position-sensitive detectors. In the analyser system of a conventional triple axis spectrometer, scattered neutrons are reflected by the analyser into the detector one energy at a time. If the analyser is large, however, it can accept scattered neutrons over a range of scattering angles ϕ and reflect them simultaneously through a range of angles $2\theta_a$ into a suitable array of detectors. Individual detectors would however be too bulky and unnecessarily complicated for this application. A single long detector with the capability of defining the position at which any detected neutron arrived has many advantages. In effect, such an analyser system could record many different scattered neutron energies simultaneously in much the same way as is done in the conventional time-of-flight spectrometer. Indeed, the performance of the latter, per detector, appears to be very similar to that of a triple axis spectrometer equipped with this new type of analyser (Kjems and Reynolds 1972), except of course that the low duty cycle of the conventional time-of-flight spectrometer is eliminated. Two-dimensional position-sensitive detectors may also have a significant impact on future spectrometer designs. Mention should be made of the technique developed by Alefeld et al. (1968) to obtain very high energy resolution in a crystal spectrometer, about 2×10^{-7} eV, by means of back-reflection, $2\theta_m \approx 180°$. Application of this method in special circumstances may well be of value in the future.

We may expect that the neutron scattering methods described in this chapter will continue to be employed for various lattice dynamical studies as well as for investigating other excitations such as magnons. As is evident from the Appendix, the emphasis up to now has been on the measurement of phonon dispersion curves for relatively simple crystalline solids and of the frequency distributions or mean phonon energies in more complex and mainly hydrogenous compounds. This work will be extended to more and more complicated materials as suitable specimens, high enough resolution and adequate neutron intensities permit. At the present time, we are still some distance from being able to study the normal modes of deoxyribonucleic acid by means of neutron inelastic scattering, but the time may not be too far off when significant experiments along these lines will be performed. In addition, there is considerable scope for measurements in less complicated solids of phonon line shapes and frequency shifts as functions of temperature, pressure, electric and/or magnetic fields, in relation to the study of anharmonic effects, interactions between phonons and other excitations, and effects of impurities and alloying.

Appendix

REFERENCES TO LATTICE DYNAMICS STUDIES BY NEUTRON INELASTIC SCATTERING

Materials are divided into 5 categories, namely elements, diatomic compounds, other inorganic compounds (mostly non-hydrogenous), alloys and mixed crystals, and finally organic and/or hydrogenous compounds. In the first 4 categories, an attempt has been made to provide the latest reference for every material which has been studied, although a few important earlier references have also been included, particularly where these contain significant additional information. In most cases, however, the earlier work can be found by consulting the latest references given. A few materials (marked with an asterisk) in the fifth category have been studied by coherent scattering techniques, while the majority refer to incoherent scattering measurements. A rather arbitrary selection from the very large number of such experiments is listed here. This type of experiment has been reviewed by Janik and Kowalska (1965) and by Boutin and Yip (1968).

A few of the references cited are either unpublished (as yet) or abstracts only. These are provided so that the interested reader may contact the authors for more detailed information.

i. Elements

Ag	Kamitakahara and Brockhouse (1969)
Al	Stedman and Nilsson (1966)
Ar	Dorner and Egger (1971), Batchelder et al. (1971)
Au	Reichardt et al. (1969a)
Be	Schmunk (1966)
Bi	Macfarlane (1971)
C_{diam}	Warren et al. (1967)
C_{graph}	Page (1968), Nicklow et al. (1970)
Co	Scherm et al. (1972)
Cr	Bjerrum Møller and Mackintosh (1965b), Shaw and Muhlestein (1971)
Cu	Svensson et al. (1967), Nicklow et al. (1967)
D_2	Nielsen and Bjerrum Møller (1971)
Fe	Bergsma et al. (1967), Minkiewicz et al. (1967), Brockhouse et al. (1967), Van Dijk and Bergsma (1968)
Ga	Waeber (1969), Reichardt et al. (1969b)
Ge	Brockhouse and Dasannacharya (1963), Nilsson and Nelin (1971)
H_2	Nielsen and Carneiro (1972)
He_{hcp}	Minkiewicz et al. (1968), Reese et al. (1971)
He_{fcc}	Traylor et al. (1972)
He_{bcc}	Osgood et al. (1972)
Ho	Leake et al. (1969b), Nicklow et al. (1971)

In	Smith and Reichardt (1969)
K	Cowley et al. (1966), Buyers and Cowley (1969)
Kr	Daniels et al. (1967)
Li	Smith et al. (1968)
Mg	Iyengar et al. (1965), Pynn and Squires (1968)
Mo	Woods and Chen (1964), Walker and Egelstaff (1969)
Na	Woods et al. (1962), Millington and Squires (1971)
Nb	Nakagawa and Woods (1965), Sharp (1969)
Ne	Leake et al. (1969a)
Ni	Birgeneau et al (1964), Dewit and Brockhouse (1968)
Pb	Brockhouse et al. (1962), Stedman et al. (1967)
Pd	Miiller and Brockhouse (1971)
Pt	Ohrlich and Drexel (1968), Dutton and Brockhouse (1970)
Rb	Copley et al. (1968)
S	Pawley et al. (1971)
Sb	Sosnowski et al. (1971), Sharp and Warming (1971)
Sc	Wakabayashi et al. (1971b)
Se	Gissler et al. (1968), Hamilton et al. (1971)
Si	Dolling (1962)
Sn_{white}	Price (1967), Rowe (1967)
Sn_{grey}	Price et al. (1971)
Ta	Woods (1964)
Tb	Gylden Houmann and Nicklow (1970)
Te	Gissler et al. (1968), Powell and Martel (1970)
Th	Reese et al. (1972)
Ti	Mozer et al. (1965), Wakabayashi (1972)
Tl	Worlton and Schmunk (1971)
V	Page (1967)
W	Chen and Brockhouse (1964)
Y	Sinha et al. (1970)
Zn	Borgonovi et al. (1963), Iyengar et al. (1968), Almqvist and Stedman (1971)
Zr	Bezdek et al. (1970)

ii. Diatomic compounds

AgCl	Vijayaraghavan et al. (1970)
BeO	Ostheller et al. (1968)
CaO	Saunderson and Peckham (1971), Vijayaraghavan et al. (1972)

CoO	Sakurai et al. (1968)
CsBr	Daubert (1970), Rolandson and Raunio (1971a)
CsCl	Ahmad et al. (1971)
CuCl	Carabatos et al. (1971)
CuZn	Gilat and Dolling (1965)
GaAs	Dolling and Waugh (1965)
GaP	Yarnell et al. (1968)
GaSe	Powell et al. (1972b)
InSb	Price et al. (1971)
KBr	Woods et al. (1963)
KCl	Raunio and Almqvist (1969), Copley et al. (1969)
KI	Dolling et al. (1966)
LiF	Dolling et al. (1968)
LiH	Verble et al. (1968)
MC*	Smith and Glaser (1970), Smith (1972)
MgO	Peckham (1967)
MnO	Haywood and Collins (1969)
NaBr	Reid et al. (1970)
NaCl	Raunio et al. (1969), Schmunk and Winder (1970)
NaF	Buyers (1967)
NaI	Woods et al. (1963)
NiS	Briggs et al. (1972)
PbS	Elcombe (1967b)
PbTe	Cochran et al. (1966)
RbBr	Rolandson and Raunio (1971b)
RbCl	Raunio and Rolandson (1970)
RbF	Raunio and Rolandson (1970)
RbI	Saunderson (1966)
SnTe	Pawley et al. (1966), Cowley et al. (1969a)
TlBr	Cowley and Okazaki (1967)
ZnS	Feldkamp et al. (1969), Bergsma (1970)
ZnSe	Hennion et al. (1971)

iii. Other inorganic compounds (mostly non-hydrogenous)

BaF_2	Hurrell and Minkiewicz (1970)
$BaTiO_3$	Shirane et al. (1970a), Harada et al. (1971)

* MC denotes carbides of Hf, Nb, Ta, V, U or Zr.

$CaCO_3$	Cowley and Pant (1970)
CaF_2	Elcombe and Pryor (1970)
$CaSO_4 \cdot H_2O$	Stedman et al. (1972)
$CaWO_4$	Steinman et al. (1972)
CO_2	Powell et al (1972a)
CoF_2	Martel et al. (1968)
Cu_3Zn	Hallman and Brockhouse (1969)
CsSH	De Graaf et al.(1972)
Fe_3Al	Van Dijk and Bergsma (1968)
$KCoF_3$	Holden et al. (1971)
KD_2PO_4	Paul et al. (1970), Skalyo et al. (1970)
$KMnF_3$	Gesi et al. (1972)
KN_3	Rao et al. (1971)
$KTaO_3$	Shirane et al. (1967)
$LaAlO_3$	Axe et al. (1969)
MgF_2	Kahn et al. (1968)
Mg_2Pb	Wakabayashi et al. (1972a)
Mg_2Sn	Kearney et al. (1970)
$MgZn_2$	Eschrig et al. (1972)
MnF_2	Rotter et al. (1972)
MoS_2	Wakabayashi et al. (1972b)
$NaNO_2$	Sakurai et al. (1970)
$NaNO_3$	Powell and Martel (1971)
NaSH	De Graaf et al. (1972)
$NbSe_2$	Wakabayashi et al. (1972b)
Nb_3Sn	Shirane and Axe (1971)
ND_4Cl	Teh and Brockhouse (1971)
$ND_4D_2PO_4$	Meister et al. (1969)
NH_4Cl	Smith et al. (1969)
$PbTiO_3$	Shirane et al (1970b)
SiO_2	Elcombe (1967a), Axe and Shirane (1970)
$SrTiO_3$	Cowley (1964), Yamada and Shirane (1969), Cowley et al. (1969b)
TiO_2	Traylor et al. (1971)
UO_2	Dolling et al. (1965)

iv. Alloys and mixed crystals

Be–Cu	Natkaniec et al. (1967)

Bi–Pb–Tl	Ng and Brockhouse (1967)
Co–Fe	Powell et al. (1971)
Cr–W	Bjerrum Møller and Mackintosh (1965a), Cunningham et al. (1970)
Cu–Al	Nicklow et al. (1968)
Cu–Au	Svensson and Kamitakahara (1971)
Cu–Ni	Sakamoto and Hamaguchi (1968)
Ge–As, Ga	Dolling (1965)
Ge–Si	Wakabayashi et al. (1971a)
KBr–RbBr	Buyers and Cowley (1968)
KCl–NH_4Cl	Smith et al. (1972)
Li–Mg	Natkaniec et al. (1967)
Mg–Pb	Chernoplekov and Zemlyanov (1966)
Nb–H	Verdan et al. (1968)
Nb–Mo	Powell et al. (1968)
Ni–Fe	Hallman and Brockhouse (1969)
Ni–Pd	Kamitakahara and Brockhouse (1972)
Ni–V	Mozer et al. (1966)
PbTe–SnTe	Dolling and Buyers (1973)
Pd–Fe	Maliszewski et al. (1971), Stirling et al. (1972)
Pt–V	Mozer et al. (1966)
Si–P	Dolling (1965)
SnTe–GeTe	Lefkowitz et al. (1970)
Ta–Nb	Als-Nielsen (1968)
Ti–U	Chernoplekov et al. (1967)
Ti–Zr	Mozer et al. (1965), Chernoplekov et al. (1963)
V–H	Verdan et al. (1968)
Zr–H	Gouch et al. (1971)

v. Organic and/or hydrogenous compounds

NH_3, NH_4 salts, NH_4 complexes	Bajorek et al. (1965), Janik (1965)
H_2O, hydroxides, hydrated salts	Safford et al. (1963), Bajorek et al. (1965), Burgman et al. (1968)
D_2O	Renker (1969)*
Hydrides of Ce, Th, U	Karimov et al. (1967)
HF, HCl, HBr, fluorides	Janik (1965), Boutin and Safford (1965), Axmann et al. (1969)

CH_4	Janik (1965), Dorner and Stiller (1966), Janik et al. (1969)
n-paraffins	Boutin et al. (1965)
Carboxylic acids	Collins and Haywood (1970)
Neopentane	De Graaf and Sciesinski (1970)
Polyethylene	Feldkamp et al. (1968)*
Teflon (PTFE)	Lagarde et al. (1969)*, Piseri et al. (1973)*
Adamantane	Stockmeyer and Stiller (1967), Dolling (1970)*
Hexamethylene tetramine	Dolling and Powell (1970)*
Hexamethyl benzene	Rush and Taylor (1966)
$C_6H_4Cl_2$, $C_6H_2Cl_4$	Reynolds and White (1969)
$C_6D_4Cl_2$	Kjems et al. (1972)*
Naphthalene	Pawley and Yeats (1969)*
Fluorine derivatives of cyclohexane	Leadbetter et al. (1972)

* Coherent scattering measurements

References

ABELN, O., W. DREXEL, W. GLASSER, F. GOMPF, W. REICHARDT and H. RIPFEL (1968), in *Neutron inelastic scattering* (Intern. Atomic Energy Agency, Vienna) **2**, 331.

AHMAD, A.A.Z., H.G. SMITH and M.K. WILKINSON (1971), Oak Ridge Nat. Lab. Rep. ORNL-4669, 41.

ALEFELD, B. (1969), Z. f. Physik **228**, 454.

ALEFELD, B., M. BIRR and A. HEIDEMANN (1968), in *Neutron inelastic scattering* (Intern. Atomic Energy Agency, Vienna), **2**, 381.

ALMQVIST, L., G. RAUNIO and R. STEDMAN (1968), in *Neutron inelastic scattering* (Intern. Atomic Energy Agency, Vienna), **1**, 295.

ALMQVIST, L. and R. STEDMAN (1971), J. Phys. F. (Metal Phys.) **1**, 785.

ALS-NIELSEN, J. (1968), in *Neutron inelastic scattering*, (Intern. Atomic Energy Agency, Vienna), **1**, 35.

ANANIEV, V.D., et al. (1969), Joint Inst. for Nuclear Research Report, JINR 13-4395 (in Russian).

ANDERSON, P.W. (1960), in *Fizika dielektrikov*, ed. G. I. Skanavi, (Akademia Nauk SSSR, Fizicheskii Inst. in P.N. Lebedeva, Moscow), 290.

AXE, J.D. and G. SHIRANE (1970), Phys. Rev. **B1**, 342.

AXE, J.D., G. SHIRANE and K.A. MULLER (1969), Phys. Rev **183**, 820.

AXMANN, A., W. BIEM, P. BORSCH, F. HOSSFELD and H. STILLER (1969), Disc. Farad. Soc., No. 48, p. 69.

BACON, G.E. (1962), *Neutron diffraction*, 2nd ed., (Clarendon Press, Oxford).

BAJOREK, A., T.A. MACHEKHINA and K. PARLINKSI (1965), in *Inelastic scattering of neutrons* (IAEA, Vienna), **2**, 355.

BARRETT, C.S., M.H. MUELLER and L. HEATON (1963), Rev. Sci. Instr. **34**, 847.

BARTHOLEMEW, G.A. (1966), in *Intense neutron sources*, Proc. of U.S.A.E.C./E.N.E.A. Seminar, CONF-660925 (TID-4500), (Nat. Bureau of Standards, Springfield, Virginia), 637.

BATCHELDER, D.N., B.C.G. HAYWOOD and D.H. SAUNDERSON (1971), J. Phys. C (Solid St. Phys.) **4**, 910.

BERGSMA, J. (1970), Phys. Letters **32A**, 324.

BERGSMA, J., C. VAN DIJK and D. TOCCHETTI (1967), Phys. Letters **24A**, 270.

BEZDEK, H.F., R.E. SCHMUNK and L. FINEGOLD (1970), Phys. Stat. Solidi **42**, 275.

BIRGENEAU, R.J., J. CORDES, G. DOLLING and A.D.B. WOODS (1964), Phys. Rev. **136**, A1359.

BJERRUM MØLLER, H. and A.R. MACKINTOSH (1965a), Phys. Rev. Letters **15**, 623.

BJERRUM MØLLER, H. and A.R. MACKINTOSH (1965b), in *Inelastic scattering of neutrons* (Intern. Atomic Energy Agency, Vienna), **1**, 1195.

BJERRUM MØLLER, H. and M. NIELSEN (1970), in *Instrumentation for neutron inelastic scattering research*, (Intern. Atomic Energy Agency, Vienna), 49.

BLOKHIN, G.E., et al. (1961), Atomnaya Energiya **10**, 437 (in Russian).

BORGONOVI, G., G. CAGLIOTI and J.J. ANJAL (1963), Phys. Rev. **132**, 683.

BOUTIN, H., H. PRASK, S.F. TREVINO and H. DANNER (1965), in *Inelastic scattering of neutrons* (IAEA, Vienna), **2**, 407.

BOUTIN, H. and G.J. SAFFORD (1965), in *Inelastic scattering of neutrons* (IAEA, Vienna), **2**, 393.

BOUTIN, H. and S. YIP (1968), *Molecular spectroscopy with neutrons* (M.I.T. Press, Cambridge, Mass., U.S.A.).

BRIGGS, G.A., C. DUFFILL, M.T. HUTCHINGS, R.D. LOWDE, N.S. SATYA MURTHY, D.H. SAUNDERSON, M.W. STRINGFELLOW, W.B. WAEBER and C.G. WINDSOR (1972), Proc., Symp. on Neutron Inelastic Scattering, Grenoble, France, March 6–10, paper E-15, (IAEA, Vienna).

BROCKHOUSE, B.N. (1961), in *Inelastic scattering of neutrons in solids and liquids*, (Intern. Atomic Energy Agency, Vienna) 113.

BROCKHOUSE, B.N. and B.A. DASANNACHARYA (1963), Solid State Commun. **1**, 205.

BROCKHOUSE, B.N., T. ARASE, G. CAGLIOTI, K.R. RAO and A.D.B.W. WOODS (1962), Phys. Rev. **128**, 1099.

BROCKHOUSE, B.N., S. HAUTECLER and H. STILLER (1964), in *The interaction of radiation with solids*, eds. R. Strumane et al., (North-Holland Publ. Co. Amsterdam), 580.

BROCKHOUSE, B.N., H.E. ABOU-HELAL and E.D. HALLMAN (1967), Solid State Commun. **5**, 211.

BROCKHOUSE, B.N., G.A. DE WIT, E.D. HALLMAN and J.M. ROWE, (1968), in *Neutron in inelastic scattering* (Intern. Atomic Energy Agency, Vienna), **2**, 259.

BRUGGER, R.M. (1965), in *Thermal neutron scattering*, ed. P.A. Egelstaff, (Academic Press, New York), 54.

BURAS, B. (1966), in *Intense neutron sources*, Proc. of U.S.A.E.C./E.N.E.A. Seminar, CONF-660925 (TID-4500), (Nat. Bureau of Standards, Springfield, Virginia), 677.

BURGMAN, J.O., J. SCIESINSKI and K. SKOLD (1968), Phys. Rev. **170**, 808.

BUYERS, W.J.L., (1967), Phys. Rev. **153**, 923.

BUYERS, W.J.L. and R.A. COWLEY (1968), in *Neutron inelastic scattering* (Intern. Atomic Energy Agency, Vienna), **1**, 43.

BUYERS, W.J.L. and R.A. COWLEY (1969), Phys. Rev. **180**, 755.

Buyers, W.J.L. and T. Smith (1966), Phys. Rev. **150**, 758.

Carabatos, C., B. Hennion, K. Kunc, F. Moussa and C. Schwab (1971), Phys. Rev. Letters **26**, 770.

Chen, S.H. and B.N. Brockhouse (1964), Solid State Commun. **2**, 73.

Chernoplekov, N.A. and M.G. Zemlyanov (1966), Sov. Phys. JETP **22**, 315.

Chernoplekov, N.A., M.G. Zemlyanov, E.G. Brovman and A.G. Chicherin (1963), in *Inelastic scattering of neutrons in solids and liquids*, **2**, 173.

Chernoplekov, N.A., G.K. Panova, M.G. Zemlyanov, B.N. Samoilov and V.I. Kutaitsev (1967), Phys. Stat. Solidi **20**, 767.

Cochran, W. (1959), Phys. Rev. Letters **3**, 412; see also Cochran, W. (1960), Advan. Phys. **9**, 387.

Cochran, W., R.A. Cowley, G. Dolling and M.M. Elcombe (1966), Proc. Roy. Soc. (Lond.) **A293**, 433.

Cocking, S.J. and F.J. Webb (1965), in *Thermal neutron scattering*, ed. P.A. Egelstaff (Academic Press, New York), 142.

Colella, R. and B.W. Batterman (1970), Phys. Rev. **B1**, 3913.

Collins, M.F. (1963), Brit. J. Appl. Phys. **14**, 805.

Collins, M.F. and B.C.G. Haywood (1970), J. Chem. Phys. **52**, 5740.

Colwell, J.F., P.H. Miller and W.L. Whittemore (1968), in *Neutron inelastic scattering*, (Intern. Atomic Energy Agency, Vienna), **2**, 429.

Cooper, M.J. and R. Nathans (1967), Acta Cryst. **23**, 357.

Copley, J.R.D., B.N. Brockhouse and S.H. Chen (1968), in *Neutron inelastic scattering*, (Intern. Atomic Energy Agency, Vienna), **1**, 209.

Copley, J.R.D., R.W. MacPherson and T. Timusk (1969), Phys. Rev. **182**, 965.

Costello, J. and J.W. Weymouth (1969), Phys. Rev. **184**, 694.

Cowley, R.A. (1962), Phys. Rev. Letters. **9**, 159.

Cowley, R.A. (1964), Phys. Rev. **134**, A981.

Cowley, E.R. and A. Okazaki (1967), Proc. Roy. Soc. (Long.) **A300**, 45.

Cowley, E.R. and A.K. Pant (1970), Acta Cryst. **A26**, 439.

Cowley, R.A., A.D.B. Woods and G. Dolling (1966), Phys. Rev. **150**, 487.

Cowley, E.R., J.K. Darby and G. Pawley (1969a), J. Phys. C (Solid St. Phys.) **2**, 1916.

Cowley, R.A., W.J.L. Buyers and G. Dolling (1969b), Solid State Commun. **7**, 181.

Cunningham, R.M., L.D. Muhlestein, W.H. Shaw and C.W. Tompson (1970), Phys. Rev. **B2**, 4864.

Daniels, W.B., G. Shirane, B.C. Frazer, H. Umebayashi and J.A. Leake (1967), Phys. Rev. Letters **18**, 548.

Daubert, J. (1970), Phys. Letters **32A**, 437.

De Graaf, L.A. and J. Sciesinski (1970), Physica **48**, 79.

De Graaf, L.A., J.J. Rush and R.L. Livingston (1972), Proc. Symp. on Neutron Inelastic Scattering, Grenoble, France, March 6–10, paper B-6 (IAEA, Vienna).

DeWit, G.A. and B.N. Brockhouse (1968), J. Appl. Phys. **39**, 451.

Dietrich, O.W. (1968), Nucl. Instr. and Methods, **61**, 296.

Dolling, G. (1962), in *Inelastic scattering of neutrons in solids and liquids* (Intern. Atomic Energy Agency, Vienna), **2**, 37.

Dolling, G. (1965), in *Inelastic scattering of neutrons* (Intern. Atomic Energy Agency, Vienna), **1**, 249.

Dolling, G. (1970), Trans. Amer. Cryst. Assoc. **6**, 73.

DOLLING, G. and J.L.T. WAUGH (1965), in *Lattice dynamics*, ed. R.F. Wallis (Pergamon Press, New York), 19.

DOLLING, G. and H. Nieman (1967), Nucl. Instr. and Methods **49**, 117.

DOLLING, G. and B.M. POWELL (1970), Proc. Roy. Soc. Lond. **A319**, 209.

DOLLING, G. and W.J.L. BUYERS (1973), J. Nonmetals **1**, 159.

DOLLING, G. and V.F. SEARS (1973), Nucl. Instr. and Methods **106**, 419.

DOLLING, G., R.A. COWLEY and A.D.B. WOODS (1965), Can. J. Phys. **43**, 1397.

DOLLING, G., R.A. COWLEY, C. SCHITTENHELM and I.M. THORSON (1966), Phys. Rev. **147**, 577.

DOLLING, G. H.G. SMITH, R.M. NICKLOW, P.R. VIJAYARAGHAVAN and M.K. WILKINSON (1968), Phys. Rev. **168**, 970.

DORNER, B. and H. EGGER (1971), Phys. Stat. Solidi **43**, 611.

DORNER B. and H.H. STILLER (1966), Phys. Stat. Solidi **18**, 795.

DORNER, B. and H.H. STILLER (1970), in *Instrumentation for neutron inelastic scattering Research* (Intern. Atomic Energy Agency, Vienna), 19.

DUTTON, D.H. and B.N. BROCKHOUSE (1970), Bull. Am. Phys. Soc. **15**, 810.

DYER, R.F. and G.G. LOW (1961), in *Inelastic scattering of neutrons in solids and liquids* (Intern. Atomic Energy Agency, Vienna), 179.

EGELSTAFF, P.A. (1966), in *Research applications of repetitively pulsed boosters and reactors*, (Intern. Atomic Energy Agency, Vienna).

EGELSTAFF, P.A., S.J. COCKING and T.K. ALEXANDER (1961), in *Inelastic scattering of neutrons in solids and liquids* (Intern. Atomic Energy Agency, Vienna), 165.

EGELSTAFF, P.A., R.D. MOFFITT and D.H. SAUNDERSON (1968), Nucl. Instr. and Methods **59**, 245.

ELCOMBE, M.M. (1967a), Proc. Phys. Soc. **91**, 947.

ELCOMBE, M.M. (1967b), Proc. Roy. Soc. (Lond.) **A300**, 210.

ELCOMBE, M.M. and A.W. PRYOR (1970), J. Phys. C (Solid St. Phys.) **3**, 492.

ESCHRIG, H., K. FELDMANN, K. HENNIG and L. WEISS (1972), Proc. Symp. on Neutron Inelastic Scattering, Grenoble, France, March 6–10, paper A–15 (I.A.E.A., Vienna).

FELDKAMP, L.A., G. VENKATARAMAN and J.S. KING (1968), in *Neutron inelastic scattering* (Intern. Atomic Energy Agency, Vienna), **2**, 159.

FELDKAMP, L.A., G. VENKATARAMAN and J.S. KING (1969), Solid State Commun. **7**, 1571.

FERMI, E., J. MARSHALL and L. MARSHALL (1947), Phys. Rev. **72**, 193.

FLEURY, P.A. (1971), private communication.

FLEURY, P.A., J.F. SCOTT and J.M. WORLOCK (1968), Phys. Rev. Letters **21**, 16.

FREY, F. (1971), Nucl. Instr. and Methods, **96**, 471.

FURRER, A. (1971), Acta Cryst. **A27**, 461.

GALOCIOVA, D., J. TICHY, J. ZELENKA, R. MICHALEC and B. CHALUPA (1970), Phys. Stat. Solidi (a)**2**, 211.

GESI, K., J.D. AXE, G. SHIRANE and A. LINZ (1972), Phys. Rev. **B5**, 1933.

GILAT, G. and G. DOLLING (1965), Phys. Rev. **138**, A1053.

GILLIS, N.S., T.R. KOEHLER and N.R. WERTHAMER (1968), Phys. Rev. **175**, 1110.

GISSLER, W., A. AXMAN and T. SPRINGER (1968), in *Neutron inelastic scattering* (Intern. Atomic Energy Agency, Vienna), **1**, 245.

GLASER, E.A., H. NIEMAN, M. POTTER, G. DOLLING, A.D.B. WOODS, R.A. COWLEY and E.C. SVENSSON (1969), AECL report, AECL-3512 (Atomic Energy of Canada Ltd., Chalk River, Ontario), 47.

GLAUBER, R.J. (1955), Phys. Rev. **98**, 1692.

GOLDBERGER, M.L. and F. SEITZ (1947), Phys. Rev. **71**, 294.

GOMPF, F., W. REICHARDT, W. GLASER and K.H. BECKURTS (1968), in *Neutron inelastic scattering* (Intern. Atomic Energy Agency, Vienna), **2**, 417.

GOUCH, J.G., O.K. HARLING and L.C. CLUNE (1971), Phys. Rev. **B4**, 2558.

GYLDEN HOUMANN, J.C. and R.M. NICKLOW (1970), Phys. Rev. **B1**, 3943.

HALLMAN, E.D. and B.N. BROCKHOUSE (1969), Can. J. Phys. **47**, 1117.

HAMILTON, W.C., J.W. EDMONDS, A. TIPPE and J.J. RUSH (1969), Disc. Farad. Soc., No. 48, p. 192.

HAMILTON, W.C., M. KAY and B. LASSIER (1971), Amer. Cryst. Assoc. meeting at Ames, Iowa, 27.

HARADA, J., J.D. AXE and G. SHIRANE (1971), Phys. Rev. **B4**, 155.

HARLING, O.K. (1966), Rev. Sci. Instr. **37**, 697.

HARLING, O.K. (1968), in *Neutron inelastic scattering* (Intern. Atomic Energy Agency, Vienna), **2**, 271.

HAYWOOD, B.C.G. and M.F. COLLINS (1969), J. Phys. C (Solid St. Phys.) **2**, 46.

HENNION, B., F. MOUSSA, G. PEPY and K. KUNC (1971), Phys. Letters **36A**, 376.

HOLDEN, T.M., W.J.L. BUYERS, E.C. SVENSSON, R.A. COWLEY, M.T. HUTCHINGS, D. HUKIN and R.W.H. STEVENSON (1971), J. Phys. C (Solid St. Phys.) **4**, 2127.

HURRELL, J.P. and V.J. MINKEIWICZ (1970), Solid State Commun. **8**, 463.

IYENGAR, P.K. (1965), in *Thermal neutron scattering*, ed. P.A. Egelstaff (Academic Press, New York), 98

IYENGAR, P.K. (1966), in Proc. Symp. on *Inelastic scattering of neutrons by condensed systems*, Brookhaven National Lab. Rep. BNL–940, p. 179.

IYENGAR, P.K., G. VENKATARAMAN, P.R. VIJAYARAGAHVAN and A.P. ROY (1965), in *Inelastic scattering of neutrons* (Intern. Atomic Energy Agency, Vienna), **1**, 153.

IYENGAR, P.K., G. VENKATARAMAN, Y.H. GAMEEL and K.R. RAO (1968), in *Neutron inelastic scattering* (Inter. Atomic Energy Agency, Vienna), **1**, 195.

JACROT, B., (1970), in *Instrumentation for neutron inelastic scattering research* (Intern. Atomic Energy Agency, Vienna), 225.

JANIK, J.A. (1965), in *Inelastic scattering of neutrons* (Intern. Atomic Energy Agency, Vienna), **2**, 243.

JANIK, J.A. and A. KOWALSKA (1965), in *Thermal neutron scattering*, ed. P.A. Egelstaff (Academic Press, New York), 453.

JANIK, J.A., K. OTNES, G. SOLT and G. KOSALY (1969), Disc. Farad. Soc., No. 48, p. 87.

KAHN, R., J.P. TROTIN, D. CRIBIER and C. BENOIT (1968), in *Neutron inelastic scattering* (Intern. Atomic Energy Agency, Vienna), **1**, 289.

KAMITAKAHARA, W.A. and B.N. BROCKHOUSE (1969), Phys. Letters **29A**, 639.

KAMITAKAHARA, W.A. and B.N. BROCKHOUSE (1972), Proc. Symp. on Neutron Inelastic Scattering, Grenoble, France, March 6–10, paper A-6, (Intern. Atomic Energy Agency, Vienna).

KARIMOV, I., M.G. ZEMLYANOV, M.E. KOST, V.A. SOMENKOV and N.A. CHERNOPLEKOV (1967), Sov. Phys. Sol. State **9**, 1366.

KEARNEY, R.J., T.G. WORLTON and R.E. SCHMUNK (1970), J. Phys. Chem. Solids **31**, 1085.

KJEMS, J.K. and P.A. REYNOLDS (1972), Proc. 5th IAEA Symp. on Neutron Inelastic Scattering, Grenoble (March, 1972), paper F-4.

KJEMS, J.K., P.A. REYNOLDS and J.W. WHITE (1972), Proc. 5th IAEA Symp. on Neutron Inelastic Scattering, Grenoble (March, 1972), paper B-2.

KOEHLER, T.R. (1968), Phys. Rev. **165**, 942.

KOHN, W. (1959), Phys. Rev. Letters **2**, 393.

KOMURA, A. and M.J. COOPER (1970), Jap. J. of Appl. Phys. **9**, 866.

KREBS, K. (1968), in *Neutron inelastic scattering* (Intern. Atomic Energy Agency, Vienna), **2**, 298.

LAGARDE, V., H. PRASK and S. TREVINO (1969), Disc. Farad. Soc., No. 48 p. 15.

LEADBETTER, A.J., D. LITCHINSKY and A. TURNBULL (1972), Proc. Symp. on Neutron Inelastic Scattering, Grenoble, France, March 6–10, paper B–5 (I.A.E.A. Vienna).

LEAKE, J.A., W.B. DANIELS, J. SKALYO, B.C. FRAZER and G. SHIRANE (1969a), Phys. Rev. **181**, 1251.

LEAKE, J.A., V.J. MINKIEWICZ and G. SHIRANE (1969b), Solid State Commun. **7**, 535.

LEE, Y.W. (1961), *Statistical theory of communication* (John Wiley and Sons, Inc., New York), 341.

LEFKOWITZ, I., M. SHIELDS, G. DOLLING, W.J.L. BUYERS and R.A. COWLEY (1970), J. Phys. Soc. Japan **28S**, 249.

LOMER, W.M. and G.G. LOW (1965), in *Thermal neutron scattering*, ed. P.A. Egelstaff (Academic Press, New York), 1.

LOOPSTRA, B.O. (1966), Nucl. Instr. and Methods **44**, 181.

MACFARLANE, R.E. (1971), in *The physics of semimetals and narrow-gap semiconductors*, eds. D.L. Carter and R.T. Bate (Pergamon Press, New York), 289.

MALISZEWSKI, E., V.V. NITC, I. SOSNOWSKA and J. SOSNOWSKI (1968), in *Neutron inelastic scattering* (Intern. Atomic Energy Agency, Vienna), **2**, 313.

MALISZEWSKI, E.F., J. SOSNOWSKI and A. CZACHOR (1971), J. Phys. F. (Metal Phys.) **1**, 339.

MARSAGUERRA, M. and G. PAULI (1959), Nucl. Instr. and Methods **4**, 140.

MARSHALL, W. and R. STUART (1961), in *Inelastic scattering of neutrons in solids and liquids* (Intern. Atomic Energy Agency, Vienna), 75.

MARTEL, P., R.A. COWLEY and R.W.H. STEVENSON (1968), Can. J. Phys. **46**, 1355.

MCALPIN, W. (1963), AECL Report, CGRP-956, (Atomic Energy of Canada, Chalk River, Ontario, Canada).

MCREYNOLDS, A.W. and W.L. WHITTEMORE (1961), in *Inelastic scattering of neutrons in solids and liquids* (Intern. Atomic Energy Agency, Vienna), 421.

MEISTER, H., J. SKALYO, B.C. FRAZER and G. SHIRANE (1969), Phys. Rev. **184**, 550.

MIILLER, A.P. and B.N. BROCKHOUSE (1971), Can. J. Phys. **49**, 704.

MILLINGTON, A.J. and G.L. SQUIRES (1971), J. Phys. F. (Metal Phys.) **1**, 244.

MINKIEWICZ, V.J., G. SHIRANE and R. NATHANS (1967), Phys. Rev. **162**, 528.

MINKIEWICZ, V.J., T.A. KITCHENS, F.P. LIPSCHULTZ, R. NATHANS and G. SHIRANE (1968), Phys. Rev. **174**, 267.

MOOK, H.A. and M.K. WILKINSON (1970), in *Instrumentation for neutron inelastic scattering research* (Intern. Atomic Energy Agency, Vienna), 173.

MOZER, B., K. OTNES and H. PALEVSKY (1965), in *Lattice Dynamics*, ed. R.F. Wallis (Pergamon Press, New York), 63.

MOZER, B., K. OTNES and C. THAPER (1966), Phys. Rev. **152**, 535.

NAKAGAWA, Y. and A.D.B. WOODS (1965), in *Lattice Dynamics*, ed. R.F. Wallis (Pergamon Press, New York), 39.

NATKANIEC, I., K. PARLINSKI, A. BAJOREK and M. SUDNIK-HRYNKIEWICZ (1967), Phys. Letters **24A**, 517.

NG, S.C. and B.N. BROCKHOUSE (1967), Solid State Commun. **5**, 79.

NICKLOW, R.M., G. GILAT, H.G. SMITH, L.J. RAUBENHEIMER and M.K. WILKINSON (1967), Phys. Rev. **164**, 922.

NICKLOW, R.M., P.R. VIJAYARAGHAVAN, H.G. SMITH, G. DOLLING and M.K. WILKINSON (1968), in *Neutron inelastic scattering* (Intern. Atomic Energy Agency, Vienna), **1**, 47.

NICKLOW, R.M., N. WAKABAYASHI and H.G. SMITH (1970), Bull. Am. Phys. Soc. **15**, 383.

NICKLOW, R.M., N. WAKABAYASHI and P.R. VIJAYARAGHAVAN (1971), Phys. Rev. **B3**, 1229.

NIELSEN, M. and H. BJERRUM MØLLER (1969), Acta Cryst. **A25**, 547.

NIELSEN, M. and H. BJERRUM MØLLER (1971), Phys. Rev. **B3**, 4383.

NIELSEN, M. and K. CARNEIRO (1972), Proc. Symp. on Neutron Inelastic Scattering, Grenoble, France, March 6–10, paper A-10 (I.A.E.A. Vienna).

NILSSON, G. and G. NELIN (1971), Phys. Rev. **B3**, 364.

OHRLICH, R. and W. DREXEL (1968), in *Neutron inelastic scattering*, (Intern. Atomic Energy Agency, Vienna), **1**, 203.

OSGOOD, E.B., V.J. MINKIEWICZ, T.A. KITCHENS and G. SHIRANE (1972), Phys. Rev., **A5**, 1537.

OSTHELLER, G.L., R.E. SCHMUNK, R.M. BRUGGER and R.J. KEARNEY (1968), in *Neutron inelastic scattering* (Intern. Atomic Energy Agency, Vienna), **1**, 315.

PAGE, D.I. (1967), Proc. Phys. Soc. **91**, 76.

PAGE, D.I. (1968), in *Neutron inelastic scattering* (Intern. Atomic Energy Agency, Vienna), **1**, 325.

PALEVSKY, H. (1965), in *Inelastic scattering of neutrons* (Intern. Atomic Energy Agency, Vienna), **2**, 455.

PASKIN, A, and R.J. WEISS (1962), Phys. Rev. Letters **9**, 199.

PAUL, G.L., W. COCHRAN, W.J.L. BUYERS and R.A. COWLEY (1970), Phys. Rev. **B2**, 4603.

PAWLEY, G.S. and E.A. YEATS (1969), Solid State Commun. **7**, 385.

PAWLEY, G.S., W. COCHRAN, R.A. COWLEY and G. DOLLING (1966), Phys. Rev. Letters **17**, 753.

PAWLEY, G.S., R.P. RINALDI and C.G. WINDSOR (1971), in *Phonons*, ed. M.A. Nusimovici (Flammarion Sciences, Paris), 223.

PECKHAM, G. (1967), Proc. Phys. Soc. (Lond.) **90**, 657.

PICKLES, J.R. and R. HAZLEWOOD (1960), A.E.R.E. report, AERE X/PR/2357 (United Kingdom Atomic Energy Authority, Harwell, England).

PISERI, L., B.M. POWELL and G. DOLLING (1973), J. Chem. Phys. **58**, 158.

PLACZEK, G. and L. VAN HOVE (1955), Nuovo Cimento **1**, 233.

POWELL, B.M. and P. MARTEL (1970), Proc. 10th Int. Conf. on Physics of Semiconductors, ed. S.P. Keller et al. (USAEC Springfield, Va.) 851.

POWELL, B.M. and P. MARTEL (1971), Bull. Am. Phys. Soc. **16**, 311.

POWELL, B.M., P. MARTEL and A.D.B. WOODS (1968), Phys. Rev. **171**, 727.

POWELL, B.M., E.C. SVENSSON and A.D.B. WOODS (1971), Atomic Energy of Canada Ltd. Report AECL-3966, p. 55.

POWELL, B.M., G. DOLLING, L. PISERI and P. MARTEL (1972a), Proc. Symp. on Neutron Inelastic Scattering, Grenoble, France, March 6–10, paper B-3 (IAEA, Vienna).

POWELL, B.M., S. JANDL and J.L. BREBNER (1972b), to be published.

PRICE, D.L. (1967), Proc. Roy. Soc. (Lond.) **A300**, 25.

PRICE, D.L., J.M. ROWE and R.M. NICKLOW (1971), Phys. Rev. **B3**, 1268.
PYNN, R. and G.L. SQUIRES (1968), in *Neutron inelastic scattering*, (Intern. Atomic Energy Agency, Vienna), **1**, 215.
RAO, K.R., S.F. TREVINO, H. PRASK and R.D. MICAL (1971), Phys. Rev. **B4**, 4551.
RAUNIO, G. and L. ALMQVIST (1969), Phys. Stat. Solidi **33**, 209.
RAUNIO, G. and S. ROLANDSON (1970), Phys. Rev. **B2**, 2098.
RAUNIO, G., L. ALMQVIST and R. STEDMAN (1969), Phys. Rev. **178**, 1496.
REESE, R.A., S.K. SINHA, T.O. BRUN and C.R. TILFORD (1971), Phys. Rev. **A3**, 1688.
REESE, R.A., S.K. SINHA and D.T. PETERSON (1973), Phys. Rev. **B8**, 1332.
REICHARDT, W., W. DREXEL, R. ORLICH and W. GLASER (1969a), Physikertag, Vorabdrücke Kurzfassungen Fachber. 34th, p. 52.
REICHARDT, W., R.M. NICKLOW, G. DOLLING and H.G. SMITH (1969b), Bull. Am. Phys. Soc. **14**, 378.
REICHARDT, W., F. GOMPF, K.H. BECKURTS, W. GLASER, G. EHRET and G. WILHELMI (1970), in *Instrumentation for neutron inelastic scattering research* (Intern. Atomic Energy Agency, Vienna), 147.
REID, J.S., T. SMITH and W.J.L. BUYERS (1970), Phys. Rev. **B1**, 1833.
RENKER, B. (1969), Phys. Letters **30A**, 493.
RENNINGER, M. (1937), Z.f. Physik **106**, 141.
REYNOLDS, P.A. and J.W. WHITE (1969), Disc. Farad. Soc., No. 48, p. 131.
RISTE, T. (1970), in *Instrumentation for neutron inelastic scattering research* (Intern. Atomic Energy Agency, Vienna), 91.
ROLANDSON, S. and G. RAUNIO (1971a), Phys. Rev. **B4**, 4617.
ROLANDSON, S. and G. RAUNIO (1971b), J. Phys. C (Solid St. Phys.) **4**, 958.
ROTTER, C.A., J.G. TRAYLOR, R.M. NICKLOW and H.G. SMITH (1972), to be published.
ROWE, J.M. (1967), Phys. Rev. **163**, 547.
RUSH, J.J. and T.I. TAYLOR (1966), J. Chem. Phys. **44**, 2749.
RUSTICHELLI, F. (1970), Nucl. Instr. and Meth. **83**, 124.
RUSTICHELLI, F. (1972), Proc. Fifth IAEA Symp. on Neutron Inelastic Scattering, Grenoble (March 1972), paper F-2.
SAFFORD, G., V. BRAJOVIC and H. BOUTIN (1963), J. Phys. Chem. Solids **24**, 771.
SAKAMOTO, M. and Y. HAMAGUCHI (1968), in *Neutron inelastic scattering* (Intern. Atomic Energy Agency, Vienna), **1**, 181.
SAKURAI, J., W.J.L. BUYERS, R.A. COWLEY and G. DOLLING (1968), Phys. Rev. **167**, 510.
SAKURAI, J., R.A. COWLEY and G. DOLLING (1970), J. Phys. Soc. Japan **28**, 1426.
SAUNDERSON, D. (1966), Phys. Rev. Letters **17**, 530.
SAUNDERSON, D.H. and G. PECKHAM (1971), J. Phys. C (Solid St.Phys.) **4**, 2009.
SCHERM, R.H., N. WAKABAYASHI, H.A. MOOK and M.K. WILKINSON (1972), to be published.
SCHMUNK, R.E. (1966), Phys. Rev. **149**, 450.
SCHMUNK, R.E. and D.R. WINDER (1970), J. Phys. Chem. Solids **31**, 131.
SHARP, R.I. (1969), J. Phys. C. (Solid St. Phys.) **2**, 421.
SHARP, R.I. and E. WARMING (1971), J. Phys. F (Metal Phys.) **1**, 570.
SHAW, W.M. and L.D. MUHLESTEIN (1971), Phys. Rev. **B4**, 969.
SHIRANE, G. and J.D. AXE (1971), Phys. Rev. **B4**, 2957.
SHIRANE, G. and V.J. MINKIEWICZ (1970), Nucl. Instr. and Methods **89**, 109.
SHIRANE, G., R. NATHANS and V.J. MINKIEWICZ (1967), Phys. Rev. **157**, 396.

SHIRANE, G., J.D. AXE, J. HARADA and A. LINZ (1970a), Phys. Rev. **B2**, 3651.
SHIRANE, G., J.D. AXE, J. HARADA and J.P. REMEIKA (1970b), Phys. Rev. **B2**, 155.
SINHA, S.K., T.O. BRUN, L.D. MUHLESTEIN and J. SAKURAI (1970), Phys. Rev. **B1**, 2430.
SJOLANDER, A. (1964) in *Phonons and phonon interactions*, ed. T.A. Bak (W.A. Benjamin, Inc., New York), 76.
SKALYO, J., B.C. FRAZER and G. SHIRANE (1970), Phys. Rev. **B1**, 278.
SMITH, H.G. (1972), Proc. Conf. on Superconductivity of d- and f-band metals, Rochester, N.Y., October 1971 (American Institute of Physics), Conf. Proc. No. 4.
SMITH, H.G. and W. GLASER (1970), Phys. Rev. Letters **25**, 1611.
SMITH, H.G. and W. REICHARDT (1969), Bull. Am. Phys. Soc. **14**, 378.
SMITH, H.G., G. DOLLING, R.M. NICKLOW, P.R. VIJAYARAGHAVAN and M.K. WILKINSON (1968), in *Neutron inelastic scattering* (Intern. Atomic Energy Agency, Vienna), **1**, 149.
SMITH, H.G., J.G. TAYLOR and W. REICHARDT (1969), Phys. Rev. **181**, 1218.
SMITH, H.G., N. WAKABAYASHI and R.M. NICKLOW (1972), Proc. Symp. on Neutron Inelastic Scattering, Grenoble, France, March 6–10, paper A-9 (IAEA, Vienna).
SOSNOWSKI, J., S. BEDNARSKI and A. CZACHOR (1968), in *Neutron inelastic scattering* (Intern. Atomic Energy Agency, Vienna) **1**, 157.
SOSNOWSKI, J., E.F. MALISZEWSKI, S. BEDNARSKI and A. CZACHOR (1971), Phys. Stat. Solidi (b) **44**, K65.
STEDMAN, R. (1961), Private communication quoted by BROCKHOUSE (1961).
STEDMAN, R. (1968), Rev. Sci. Instr. **39**, 878.
STEDMAN, R. (1970), in *Instrumentation for neutron inelastic scattering research* (Intern. Atomic Energy Agency, Vienna), 37.
STEDMAN, R. and G. NILSSON (1966), Phys. Rev. **145**, 492.
STEDMAN, R., L. ALMQVIST, G. NILSSON and G. RAUNIO (1967), Phys. Rev. **162**, 545.
STEDMAN, R., L. ALMQVIST, G. RAUNIO and G. NILSSON (1969), Rev. Sci. Instr. **40**, 249.
STEDMAN, R., L. ALMQVIST and S. ROLANDSON (1972), Proc. Symp. on Neutron Inelastic Scattering, Grenoble, France, March 6–10, paper B-8 (IAEA, Vienna).
STEINMAN, D.K., J.S. KING and H.G. SMITH (1972), Proc. Symp. on Neutron Inelastic Scattering, Grenoble, France, March 6–10, paper B-4 (IAEA, Vienna).
STIRLING, W.G., R.A. COWLEY and M.W. STRINGFELLOW (1972), J. Phys. F (Metal Phys.) **2**, 421.
STOCKMEYER, R. and H. STILLER (1967), Phys. Stat. Solidi **19**, 781.
SVENSSON, E.C., B.N. BROCKHOUSE and J.M. ROWE (1967), Phys. Rev. **155**, 619.
SVENSSON, E.C. and W.A. KAMITAKAHARA (1971), Can. J. Phys. **49**, 2291.
TEH, H.C. and B.N. BROCKHOUSE (1971), Phys. Rev. **B3**, 2733.
TEH, H.C., B.N. BROCKHOUSE and G.A. DE WIT (1969), Phys. Letters **29A**, 694.
TRAYLOR, J.G., H.G. SMITH, R.M. NICKLOW and M.K. WILKINSON (1971), Phys. Rev. **B3**, 3457.
TRAYLOR, J.G., C. STRASSIS, R.A. REESE and S.K. SINHA (1972), Proc. Symp. on Neutron Inelastic Scattering, Grenoble, France, March 6–10, paper A-12 (IAEA, Vienna).
UHRIG, R.E. (1970), *Random noise techniques in nuclear reactor systems* (Ronald Press Co., New York).
VAN DIJK, C. and J. BERGSMA (1968), in *Neutron inelastic scattering* (Intern. Atomic Energy Agency, Vienna) **1**, 233.
VAN HOVE, L. (1954), Phys. Rev. **95**, 249.
VENKATARAMAN, G. and V.C. SAHNI (1970), Rev. Mod. Phys. **42**, 409.

VERBLE, J.L., J.L. WARREN and J.L. YARNELL (1968), Phys. Rev. **168**, 980.
VERDAN, G., R. RUBIN and W. KLEY (1968), in *Neutron inelastic scattering* (IAEA, Vienna), **1**, 223.
VIJAYARAGHAVAN, P.R., R.M. NICKLOW, H.G. SMITH and M.K. WILKINSON (1970), Phys. Rev. **B1**, 4819.
VIJAYARAGHAVAN, P.R., MARSONGKOHADI and P.K. IYENGAR (1972), Proc. Symp. on Neutron Inelastic Scattering, Grenoble, France, March 6–10, paper A-8 (Intern. Atomic Energy Agency, Vienna).
WAEBER, W.B. (1969), J. Phys. C (Solid St. Phys.) **2**, 903.
WAKABAYASHI, N. (1972), to be published.
WAKABAYASHI, N., R.M. NICKLOW, and H.G. SMITH (1971a), Phys. Rev. **B4**, 2558.
WAKABAYASHI, N., S.K. SINHA, and F.H. SPEDDING (1971b), Phys. Rev. **B4**, 2398.
WAKABAYASHI, N., A.A.Z. AHMAD, H.R. SHANKS and G.C. DANIELSON (1972a), Phys. Rev. **B5**, 2103.
WAKABAYASHI, N., H.G. SMITH and R.M. NICKLOW (1972b), to be published.
WALKER, C.B. and P.A. EGELSTAFF (1969), Phys. Rev. **177**, 1111.
WALLER, I. and P.O. FRÖMAN (1952), Ark. Fys. **4**, 183.
WARREN, J.L., J.L. YARNELL, G. DOLLING and R.A. COWLEY (1957), Phys. Rev. **158**, 805,
WILKINSON, M.K., H.G. SMITH, W.C. KOEHLER, R.M. NICKLOW and R.M. MOON (1968). in *Neutron inelastic scattering* (Intern. Atomic Energy Agency, Vienna), 253.
WOODS, A.D.B. (1964), Phys. Rev. **136**, A781.
WOODS, A.D.B. and S.H. CHEN (1964), Solid State Commun. **2**, 233.
WOODS, A.D.B., B.N. BROCKHOUSE, R.H. MARCH and A.T. STEWART (1962), Phys. Rev. **128**, 1112.
WOODS, A.D.B., B.N. BROCKHOUSE, R.A. COWLEY and W. COCHRAN (1963), Phys. Rev. **131**, 1025.
WOODS, A.D.B., E.A. GLASER and R.A. COWLEY (1968), in *Neutron inelastic scattering* (Intern. Atomic Energy Agency, Vienna) **2**, 281.
WOODS, A.D.B., G. DOLLING and R.A. COWLEY (1970), in *Instrumentation for neutron inelastic scattering research* (Intern. Atomic Energy Agency, Vienna), 1.
WORLTON, T.G. and R.E. SCHMUNK (1971), Phys. Rev. **B3**, 4115.
YAMADA, Y. and G. SHIRANE (1969), Phys. Rev. **177**, 858.
YARNELL, J.L., J.L. WARREN, R.G. WENZEL and S.H. KOENIG (1964), I.B.M. J. Res. Develop. **8**, 234.
YARNELL, J.L., J.L. WARREN, R.G. WENZEL and P.J. DEAN (1968), in *Neutron inelastic scattering* (Intern. Atomic Energy Agency, Vienna) **1**, 301.

Subject Index

Author Index